CHILD PSYCHIATRY
Modern Approaches

CHILD PSYCHIATRY
Modern Approaches

edited by

MICHAEL RUTTER
MD FRCP FRCPsych DPM

Professor of Child Psychiatry,
Institute of Psychiatry
Hon. Consultant Psychiatrist,
The Bethlem Royal Hospital and
The Maudsley Hospital, London

LIONEL HERSOV
MD FRCP FRCPsych DPM

Consultant Psychiatrist,
The Bethlem Royal Hospital and
The Maudsley Hospital
Senior Lecturer,
Hon. Consultant in Psychological Medicine,
The Royal Postgraduate Medical School and
Hammersmith Hospital, London

BLACKWELL SCIENTIFIC PUBLICATIONS
OXFORD LONDON EDINBURGH MELBOURNE

© 1977 by
Blackwell Scientific Publications
Editorial offices:
Osney Mead, Oxford OX2 OEL
8 John Street, London WCIN 2ES
9 Forrest Road, Edinburgh EHI 2QH
214 Berkeley Street, Carlton
    Victoria 3053, Australia

First published 1976
Reprinted 1979

Set in Monophoto Plantin
Printed and bound in Great Britain by
Butler and Tanner Ltd,
Frome and London

DISTRIBUTORS

USA
    Blackwell Mosby Book Distributors
    11830 Westline Industrial Drive
    St Louis, Missouri 63141

Canada
    Blackwell Mosby Book Distributors
    86 Northline Road, Toronto
    Ontario M4B 3E5

Australia
    Blackwell Scientific Book
    Distributors
    214 Berkeley Street, Carlton
    Victoria 3053

British Library
Cataloguing in Publication Data

Child psychiatry: modern approaches
Bibl.-Index
I. Rutter, Michael 2. Hersov,
Lionel Abraham
618.9′28′9   RJ 499
Child psychiatry

ISBN 0-632-00151-8

Contents

Contributors   ix

Preface   xiii

Acknowledgements   xv

I. INFLUENCES ON DEVELOPMENT

1. Individual differences   3
   M. Rutter

2. Polygenic influences   22
   J. Shields

3. Separation, loss and family relationships   47
   M. Rutter

4. Other family influences   74
   M. Rutter

5. Sociocultural influences   109
   M. Rutter

6. Adoption   136
   L. Hersov

7. Chromosome anomalies   163
   V. Cowie

8. Brain injury   185
   D. Shaffer

II. SOME DEVELOPMENTAL THEORIES

9. Learning theories   219
   M. Berger

10. Piaget: causes and alternatives   239
    P. Bryant

11. Psychoanalytic theories   255
    C. Dare

III. CLINICAL ASSESSMENT

12. Diagnostic appraisal and interviewing   271
    A. Cox & M. Rutter

13. Psychological testing   306
    M. Berger

14. The EEG   334
    R. Harris

15. Classification   359
    M. Rutter

IV. CLINICAL SYNDROMES

16. Disorders in preschool children   387
    N. Richman

17. Adolescent disorders   407
    P. Graham & M. Rutter

18. Emotional disorders   428
    L. Hersov

19. School refusal   455
    L. Hersov

20. Nondelinquent disturbances of conduct   487
    S. Wolff

21. Delinquency 510
    D. West

22. Hyperkinetic syndrome 524
    D. Cantwell

23. Reading difficulties 556
    M. Rutter & W. Yule

24. Enuresis 581
    D. Shaffer

25. Faecal soiling 613
    L. Hersov

26. Drug taking 628
    H. Blumberg

27. Clinical aspects of drug misuse 646
    P. H. Connell

28. Tics and Tourette's syndrome 674
    J. Corbett

29. Speech delay 688
    M. Rutter

30. Infantile autism and other child psychoses 717
    M. Rutter

31. Psychotic disorders in adolescence 748
    D. Steinberg

32. Psychosomatic relationships 771
    P. Graham

33. Atypical psychosexual development 788
    R. Green

34. Mental retardation—medical aspects 807
    B. Kirman

35. Mental retardation—psychiatric aspects   829
     J. Corbett

V. APPROACHES TO TREATMENT

36. Treatment of delinquents   859
     T. Gibbens

37. Inpatient units and day-hospitals   880
     L. Hersov & A. Bentovim

38. Drug treatment   901
     D. Shaffer

39. Behavioural approaches   923
     W. Yule

40. Dynamic treatments   949
     C. Dare

41. Psychiatric social work   967
     F. Sussenwein

     Index   992

Contributors

Arnon Bentovim   MB BS FRCPsych DPM
Consultant Psychiatrist, The Hospital for Sick Children, Great Ormond Street and the Tavistock Clinic, London

Michael Berger   BA(Hons) Dip.Psych PhD
Senior Lecturer in Child Development, Institute of Education, London

Herbert H. Blumberg   BA MA PhD
Lecturer, Department of Psychiatry, Institute of Psychiatry, London

P. E. Bryant   MA(Cantab) PhD(London)
Lecturer, Department of Experimental Psychology, Oxford University, and Fellow, St. John's College

Dennis P. Cantwell   MD
Associate Professor, Department of Psychiatry, University of California at Los Angeles School of Medicine; Director of Residency in Training in Child Psychiatry, UCLA School of Medicine; and Coordinator of Professional Education, University Affiliated Facility, Division of Mental Retardation and Child Mental Health

P. H. Connell   MD FRCP FRCPsych DPM
Consultant Psychiatrist, The Bethlem Royal Hospital and The Maudsley Hospital, London

John Corbett   MB MRCP MRCPsych DPM DCH
Consultant Psychiatrist, The Bethlem Royal Hospital and The Maudsley Hospital, London

Valerie Cowie   MD PhD FRCPsych DPM
Consultant Psychiatrist, Queen Mary's Hospital for Children, Carshalton

Antony D. Cox   MA MPhil MB BCh MRCP MRCPsych
Consultant Psychiatrist, The Bethlem Royal Hospital and The Maudsley Hospital; formerly Lecturer, Department of Child and Adolescent Psychiatry, Institute of Psychiatry, London

Christopher Dare   BA MB MRCP MRCPsych DPM
Consultant Psychiatrist, The Bethlem Royal Hospital and The Maudsley Hospital, London

Trevor C. N. Gibbens   MD FRCP FRCPsych
Professor of Forensic Psychiatry, Institute of Psychiatry, London

P. J. Graham   FRCP FRCPsych
The Walker Professor of Child Psychiatry, Institute of Child Health, The Hospital for Sick Children, Great Ormond Street, London

Richard Green   MD
Professor, Departments of Psychiatry and Behavioral Science, and Psychology, State University of New York at Stony Brook

Ruth Harris   MD DCH
Consultant Clinical Neurophysiologist, The Bethlem Royal Hospital and The Maudsley Hospital, London and Queen Mary's Hospital for Children, Carshalton

Brian Kirman   MD FRCPsych
Consultant Psychiatrist, Fountain and Carshalton Group of Hospitals, and Honorary Associate Physician, St. George's Hospital and The Maudsley Hospital, London

Naomi Richman   MA MRCPsych MSc
Senior Lecturer, Institute of Child Health, London

James Shields   BA(Oxon) Hon.MD(Zurich)
Reader in Psychiatric Genetics, Institute of Psychiatry, London

David Shaffer   MB BS MRCP MRCPsych DPM
Senior Lecturer, Department of Child and Adolescent Psychiatry, Institute of Psychiatry, London

Derek Steinberg   MB BS(Lond) MPhil MRCPsych DPM
Consultant Psychiatrist, The Bethlem Royal Hospital and The Maudsley Hospital, London

Fraida Sussenwein   BA(Soc.Sci.) Cert. in Mental Health
Lecturer, Department of Sociological Studies, University of Sheffield

D. J. West   MD PhD
Reader in Clinical Criminology, Institute of Criminology, University of Cambridge

Sula Wolff   BM BCh MA FRCP FRCPsych DPM DCH
Consultant Child Psychiatrist, Royal Hospital for Sick Children, Edinburgh and Part-time Senior Lecturer, Department of Psychiatry, University of Edinburgh

William Yule   MA Dip.Psychol.
Senior Lecturer in Psychology, and in Child and Adolescent Psychiatry, Institute of Psychiatry, and Principal Psychologist, The Bethlem Royal Hospital and The Maudsley Hospital, London

Preface

These are exciting times for anyone working in the field of child psychiatry. A wider understanding of child development now throws a clearer light on deviations from the normal pattern; knowledge of the nature and causes of psychiatric disorders in childhood is steadily increasing; new and effective methods of treatment are evolving; and clinical and education services for children with mental disorders are growing in scope and sophistication. The first academic departments of child psychiatry in the United Kingdom are now established to meet the needs for teaching and research and to add to the existing body of knowledge. A serious concern to raise training standards in the specialty has led to recommendations on the range and content of training and a national exercise to visit and appraise all training schemes is under way.

For these reasons the time seemed ripe for a new and different textbook of child psychiatry. Our aim has been to provide an accurate and comprehensive account of the current state of knowledge through the integration of research approaches and findings with the understanding which comes from clinical experience and practice. Each chapter scrutinises existing information and emphasises areas of growth and fresh ideas on a particular topic in a rigorous and critical fashion but also in practical vein to help clinicians meet the needs of individual children and their families.

In planning the book we had to decide how to choose authors of individual chapters. Obviously we wanted colleagues who had made important contributions in their fields of interest and who could write with authority and knowledge. We were fortunate in our choice and we are deeply indebted to all of them. We also decided that it would be appropriate to invite contributions from those who had worked at The Bethlem Royal and The Maudsley Hospital or its closely associated postgraduate medical school, The Institute of Psychiatry. Over the years 'The Maudsley' has played a major role in training psychiatrists from all parts of the world and members of its staff have been among the leaders in both research and clinical practice. The fact that we have all worked at the same institution has produced some similarities: a firm acceptance of the value of interdisciplinary collaboration; an intense interest in new ideas and creative thinking; a commitment to the integration of academic and clinical approaches; a concern for empirical findings; and a belief in the benefits that follow from open discussion between people who hold differing views. As all of us work with children we have a common concern with developmental theories and with the process of development. However, as will also be apparent, we do not share any single theoretical viewpoint. A variety of theoretical approaches are represented in the chapters which also reflect a differing emphasis on biological, sociocultural, behavioural and psychodynamic aetiologies and formulations.

It is also fitting that this book should be based on The Joint Hospital as it has played such an important part in the development of child psychiatry. Children with psychiatric disorders were first seen at The Bethlem Royal Hospital as long ago as 1800 and Henry Maudsley was unusual among the psychiatrists of his day in appreciating the importance of psychiatric disorders arising in childhood. In his *Physiology and Pathology of Mind*, published in 1867, he included a 34-page chapter on 'Insanity of early life'. The Maudsley Hospital first opened its doors just over half a century ago, children have always been included among its patients and the Children's Department became firmly established during those early years. Since then, and especially with the first British academic appointment in child psychiatry at the Institute of Psychiatry in the 1950s, it has trained many child psychiatrists who now practice in all parts of the globe.

The book is organised into five sections. The first eight chapters review different influences on psychological development in childhood and are followed by three which discuss the foremost developmental theories. A third section describes some of the crucial issues in clinical assessment and the fourth deals systematically with the various clinical syndromes and their treatment. The final section comprises six chapters which bring together knowledge on some of the main therapeutic approaches. We have sought to include most of the topics and issues which are central to modern child psychiatry but there has been no attempt to cover all known syndromes and symptoms. Instead the focus has been on concepts and methods with special emphasis on those areas where development of new ideas or knowledge has been greatest.

We hope that the book's contents will be of interest and use to all those professionally concerned with the care, study and treatment of children with psychiatric disorders. We will be satisfied if, in the words of Sir Aubrey Lewis, it also helps the psychiatrist in training to acquire 'reasoning and understanding' and fits him 'to combine the scientific and humane temper in his studies as the psychiatrist needs to'.

       M. Rutter   *London, 1976*
       L. Hersov

Acknowledgements

We would like to thank the following for permission to use material in this book which has been published elsewhere: Spastics International Medical Publications, *The Child with Delayed Speech*; Heinemann Educational Books Ltd., *Cycles of Disadvantage: A Review of Research*; Penguin Books Ltd., *Helping Troubled Children*; Crosby Lockwood Staples, *Residential Psychiatric Treatment of Children*; and The Editor, *Child Adoption*.

We are also deeply indebted to Joy Maxwell who undertook much of the typing, helped in the correcting of proofs and was primarily responsible for the onerous task of checking references. Without her stamina, patience and good humour our task in preparing this book would have been even more daunting than it was. We would also like to thank Doreen Blake for compiling the index.

PART I

Influences on development

CHAPTER 1

Individual differences

M. RUTTER

Until relatively recently most people have tended to assume all babies are basically pretty much alike and that later differences in behaviour are largely a result of environmental experiences, brain damage or mental disease. Recent research has shown these assumptions to be false. Even in infancy, babies differ markedly in their temperamental attributes and these differences carry important implications for later development. This chapter will review the evidence on these individual differences in terms of their relevance for psychiatric practice.

DIFFERENCES IN EARLY INFANCY

Gesell (1937) was one of the first workers to investigate temperamental differences in young children. Using film records and direct observations, he noted fifteen behavioural traits which were evident in the first year of life and which appeared to show reasonable continuity up to five years. Thomas and his colleagues (1963) developed the approach, using systematic interviews with parents regarding their children's day-to-day behaviour. Nine categories of behavioural style (that is *how* the child behaved, rather than *what* he did) were derived from an inductive analysis of the initial interview protocols. These categories were activity level or energy output, rhythmicity of biological functions (sleep/wake cycle, hunger/satiety, etc.), approach or withdrawal to new situations, intensity of emotional reaction (e.g. whether the child roared with laughter or smiled quietly), threshold of sensory responsiveness, adaptability (that is how easily his behaviour changed in response to altered circumstances), quality of mood, distractability and attention span/persistence. Children in the first few months of life were found to differ markedly in these features, a conclusion supported by Carey's later work (1970, 1972) using a questionnaire modification of the same approach.

These studies all used some kind of rating of overt behaviour. In addition, there are numerous investigations which have shown individual differences

3

with respect to experimental or laboratory measures (see review by Berger 1973). For example, Korner *et al* (1968) showed interindividual variation in various oral behaviours such as frequency of finger-sucking; Bridger and Birns (1968) found that babies differed in their responses to stress and pacification; McGrade (1968) demonstrated the same in responses to nipple withdrawal; several groups of workers have demonstrated early differences in autonomic reactivity (Steinschneider 1967); and others have shown variations in muscle tension and irritability (Bench & Parker 1970). Although there is still a lot to learn about the patterning and meaning of these differences, there is no doubt that very young babies already show marked individual variations in behaviour. The beginnings of personality are evident very early in life.

Sex differences

Some behavioural differences are sex-related (see reviews by Garai & Scheinfeld 1968; Gray & Buffery 1971; Hutt 1972; Korner 1973; and Maccoby & Jacklin 1975). For example, it is fairly well established that, from as early as social play begins (i.e. age 2–2½ years), males are more aggressive than females, both verbally and physically. This increased male aggressiveness persists right through childhood into adult life. In addition, from adolescence onwards (but not in early childhood) boys exceed girls in visuospatial and mathematical skills. On the other hand, especially after early adolescence (but to some extent in earlier childhood) girls have a greater verbal ability. The evidence is less clear-cut but it is probable that, in infancy, girls are more sensitive and responsive than boys to a variety of sensory stimuli, especially those concerning the mouth and skin. In social settings, boys also tend to be more active, competitive and dominant—although these differences depend somewhat upon the type of situation and setting.

Of course many influences—both psychosocial and biological—help shape these sex differences in behaviour but the difference between boys and girls in aggressiveness seems to have its main roots in biological factors. The main evidence in favour of a biological explanation comes from five sources. First, increased aggressiveness in boys is found in all cultures. Second, the sex difference is found in a wide range of animal species—not just in man. Third, the differences are present from very early in life. Fourth, levels of aggression are responsive to sex hormones. Thus, Goy (1968) found that female monkeys masculinised during pregnancy showed greater rough and tumble and chasing play than did normal females. A study in humans (where the excess male hormone in pregnancy came from glandular disease or hormone treatment) also found an apparently increased tendency to tomboyish behaviour in girls (Money & Ehrhardt 1968). Finally, an additional Y chromosome seems to be associated with a somewhat increased tendency to aggressive behaviour (Nielson & Christenson 1974). Although the greater maturity of female infants has to be taken into account, this cannot explain those sex differences which persist throughout development into maturity. The exact mechanisms remain uncertain, but there seems little doubt that there are some biologically determined sex differences in behavioural style which are present from early infancy.

However, while this conclusion probably holds for assertiveness and aggression there are many other behaviours (such as dependency, conformity and fearfulness) on which the sexes sometimes differ but for which biological explanations seem not to apply. These attributes appear later in childhood, are not consistent across animal species and do not seem to be influenced by hormones or chromosomes. Altogether, it seems very likely that social and cultural influences play an important role in determining these other sex differences.

Quite apart from temperamental differences, it should be added that boys are biologically more vulnerable than girls to almost every kind of physical hazard (see Rutter 1970a).

Origins of individual differences in temperament

The few twin studies that have been carried out indicate the importance of hereditary factors in temperamental differences. Thus, Freedman and Keller (1963) and Vandenberg (1969) found that monozygotic twins were significantly more alike than dizygotic twins on a variety of measures of social and motor behaviour. Rutter, Korn and Birch (1963) found evidence for both genetic and non-genetic determinants of temperamental attributes in a small sample of twins from the New York longitudinal study (Thomas *et al* 1963; 1968). Torgersen and Kringlen (1976) made a systematic investigation of a much larger sample of 53 same-sexed twin pairs on the same set of temperamental features. At 9 months of age the MZ pairs were significantly more alike than the DZ pairs on all nine behavioural measures. In an investigation of 52 pairs of twin girls aged 6 to 10 years, Scarr (1969) showed substantial heritability for social introversion–extraversion. Although the studies are few in number it may be safely concluded that genetic factors play an important part in the determination of individual differences in temperament. However, as Dobzhansky (1967) suggested, it is likely that those aspects of behaviour which are polygenetically inherited are not specific traits but rather patterns of growth and ways of responding to the environment.

There is also some evidence that minor congenital physical anomalies may be associated with differences in behaviour, especially impulsiveness and hyperactivity in boys (Quinn & Rapoport 1974; Waldrop *et al* 1968). The mechanisms involved in the association remain unknown.

Organic damage or injury to the brain is associated with marked effects on behavioural development (see Chapter 8) which may be mediated in part by alterations in temperamental characteristics, although this possibility has been little studied to date. Sleep difficulties in the infancy period have been found to be associated with asphyxia at birth (Moore & Ucko 1957; Ucko 1965) and it seems likely that perinatal difficulties may influence behavioural development even when overt neurological disorder is absent. However, again, the matter has been little investigated. Temperamental features may be normal in many mentally retarded children (Chess & Korn 1970; Baron 1972) but, overall, behavioural problems are much increased in this group (Rutter 1971). Clearly, physical factors can influence temperament but little is known about their importance or mode of action.

Animal studies, which have shown that maternal emotional stress during pregnancy can affect offspring behaviour, make it quite likely that a human mother's affective state during pregnancy might have at least temporary effects on postnatal behaviour, but the evidence is so far quite inconclusive (Joffe 1969).

There is, however, extensive evidence that family and other environmental influences during childhood can affect behavioural development (see Chapters 3, 4 and 5). Unfortunately, the data are not such as to enable any determination of how far the effects are on temperament.

In summary, the knowledge on the origins of temperamental differences is extremely fragmentary. It is possible only to come to the unexciting conclusion that the differences are certainly due in part to genetic factors, but that to an important but uncertain degree, physical and psychosocial factors are also influential.

Persistence of temperamental differences

Several longitudinal studies have examined continuities and discontinuities in children's behaviour as they grow older (see Bloom 1964; Rutter 1970a; Berger 1973). For example, the Berkeley Growth study (Schaefer & Bayley 1963) used observations during cognitive testing; the Fels study (Kagan & Moss 1962) employed a variety of ratings of observed behaviour; the Guidance study (Bronson 1966; 1969) used interview data; the Topeka project (Escalona & Heider 1959; Murphy *et al* 1962) included a variety of approaches; and the New York study (Thomas *et al* 1963; 1968) developed the interview measures of temperament already described. From these various studies it may be concluded that there is considerable temperamental consistency from year to year, especially during later childhood, but that the changes over longer periods are considerable. Within the normal range of personality variation, no predictions to maturity can be made from ratings in infancy, although by 3 years of age characteristic patterns of responsiveness are becoming more stable and are beginning to show some (although still slight) meaningful relationships . ith later patterns of behaviour (Rutter 1970a). The prediction to *abnormality* of behaviour, however, is slightly stronger (see below).

It should be appreciated that predictions from early infancy are poor for all measures. Physical measures in early childhood predict the adult state better than do psychological measures but even so the correlations from infancy are low. Thus, Tanner *et al* (1956) found that an infant's length at birth correlated only 0·25 with adult height (although by one year the correlation has risen to 0·65). Lipton *et al* (1966) found little correlation between autonomic measures in the neonatal period and the same measures at 5 months, but greater stability between $2\frac{1}{2}$ and 5 months.

The possible reasons for the rather low consistencies in temperament between infancy and adulthood include (a) the neonatal measures are to some extent a function of the intrauterine environment; (b) the variations in part reflect differing rates of maturation; (c) the functions tested in infancy are not directly comparable with those assessed in later childhood; (d) temperament continues to mature and develop throughout childhood and adolescence; and temperamental development is modified by environmental circumstances (Rutter 1870a).

The findings are entirely compatible with a patterned and meaningful course of development, but they do *not* support a 'trajectory' or 'fixed potential' view which supposes that a child's innate disposition thrusts him forth on a developmental course which may be distorted or deflected by environmental hazards but in which the constitution remains fundamentally unaltered (Rutter 1975). Rather the evidence suggests that there is continuity throughout development, but a fluid continuity in which the personality is shaped by ongoing interactions and transactions between the environment and the individual. The role of temperament in this process has now to be considered.

Associations between temperament and disorder

Before considering *how* temperament might be important in relation to disorder, it is necessary to consider the evidence that it has an effect. This has now been demonstrated in several rather different prospective studies.

The New York group (Thomas *et al* 1968) studied temperamental attributes in a longitudinal study of children from predominantly professional middle-class families. Comparisons were made between the characteristics of the third of the children who developed some kind of (mostly mild) behavioural disturbance leading to the parents obtaining a psychiatric opinion and the remainder of the children for whom the parents did not seek psychiatric help. It was found that even as early as the second year of life, and before symptoms of disorder were evident, the children who were later to develop behavioural difficulties showed different temperamental characteristics (Rutter *et al* 1964). Children with markedly irregular patterns of functioning (as shown for example by the fact that they woke and went to sleep at unpredictable times), who were slow to adapt to novel circumstances, whose emotional responses were usually of high intensity and whose predominant mood was negative (miserable or irritable rather than contented or placid) were those most likely to come to notice later because of behavioural difficulties. Over two-thirds of the children with all four of these 'difficult' attributes developed problems and it was clear that there was an important association between children's styles of behaviour in early childhood and the risk of developing behavioural problems when older. However, a limitation of the study was that there was no assessment of the children's disorder which was independent of psychiatric referral (that is, there was no systematic psychiatric assessment in those not referred).

This defect was remedied in a more recent study by Graham *et al* (1973) using rather similar measures of temperament in a group of children of predominantly working-class London families in which one parent was under psychiatric care. It is striking that in this very different group of families much the same characteristics were associated with a high risk of the children developing psychiatric disorder in middle childhood (the disorders in this sample were more severe than in the New York study). The children most likely to show disorder a year later were those with markedly irregular sleeping, eating and bowel habits; whose behaviour lacked malleability, in that it was difficult to change; and who were less fastidious, being more tolerant of mess and dirt than most children (a variable not examined in the New York study). There was also some indication that, as in the New York investigation, the children with disorder at home showed more negative mood and greater intensity of emotional expression.

The attributes of negative mood, low regularity, low malleability and low fastidiousness were combined to form a temperamental adversity index (Rutter, Quinton & Yule 1977). It was found that children with high temperamental adversity scores at the start of the study were three times as likely as those with low scores to show psychiatric disorder one year later (as assessed from an interview with the mother). There was an even greater increase (eight-fold) in terms of behavioural deviance at school a year after the initial temperamental assessment. It could be argued that the t.a. index was only measuring the early signs of disorder. However, this is unlikely to be the explanation as the t.a. index provided a stronger prediction of deviance at school than did a measure of disorder at home (the measures of t.a. and disorder both coming from the same source, i.e. the mother).

Particular attention was also paid to sleep problems in Bernal's detailed longitudinal study of some 100 children from birth to school age (Bernal 1973; Richards & Bernal 1974). The group of children with sleep difficulties at 14 months differed from birth in being slower to begin crying and regular breathing, and being more fussy and irritable in the first week of life and in sleeping for shorter periods from the time they were born. Although quite differently measured, these characteristics are similar to those found important in the New York and London studies described above.

All three investigations demonstrated that a child's own temperamental characteristics have an important association with the later development of emotional behavioural disorders. The fact that the studies involve such different groups of families and children and yet produce such similar findings indicates that the effects found are likely to be of general importance. It seems that emotionally intense children, slow to adapt to new situations, whose behaviour is difficult to change, with irregular sleeping, eating and bowel habits, who tend to be irritable and negative in mood and who are unusually tolerant of messiness and disorder have an increased risk of psychiatric problems during childhood. Conversely the easy, adaptable, regular child of positive mood is much less likely to develop behavioural problems.

Of course, although some characteristics may always put the child at risk, many characteristics may be adaptive or maladaptive according to circumstances. For example in the studies discussed so far the child's activity level was not a particularly important variable. But, in a study of institutional infants under 5 months of age, Schaffer (1966) found that the most active infants were the ones who were least likely to show developmental retardation. In these circumstances a high activity level proved to be a protective factor in an environment which provided little stimulation. Similarly, Carey (1974) found that babies with a low sensory threshold (which is not a generally 'difficult' temperamental feature) were the ones most likely to wake up at night between 6 and 12 months of age. In a similar study using the questionnaire he developed to measure temperamental attributes (1970), Carey showed that babies with the generally 'difficult' features of irregularity, low adaptability, initial withdrawal, emotional intensity and negative mood were significantly more likely to sustain lacerations needing sutures during the first 2 years of life than babies who did not have these characteristics. Both these studies are based on the systematic use of the questionnaire in private paediatric practice.

The New York study showed the importance of temperamental differences in a group of children who are not subject to any unusual stresses; the London study did so in a group experiencing the chronic stresses associated with parental illness and sometimes marital discord. Stacey and her colleagues (1970) have also produced findings which suggest the importance of individual differences in relation to the acute stress of admission to hospital. They report that children said by their mothers (in retrospect) to make poor relationships with adults or with other children and to be socially inhibited, uncommunicative and aggressive were the ones most likely to be disturbed by admission.

Temperamental characteristics have also been shown to be important with respect to both reading difficulties and delinquency. Several studies have indicated that children who show restlessness, poor concentration and impulsiveness are more likely than other children to have difficulty in learning to read (see Rutter & Yule 1973; also Chapter 23). The same characteristics, especially impulsiveness, together with aggressiveness and insensitivity to the feelings of others (as measured rather later in childhood), have been linked with delinquency (see Rutter & Madge 1976).

Quite apart from temperamental attributes other personal features have also been shown to be linked with the development of psychiatric disorder. For example it has been found that children with peculiar names are more likely than other children to develop psychiatric problems (Bagley & Evan-Wong 1970). There is also evidence from sociometric studies (Gronlund 1959) and from children's responses to pictures (Richardson *et al* 1961; Goodman *et al* 1963; Richardson & Royce 1968; Salvia *et al* 1975) that an unpleasant facial or physical appearance is associated with social rejection. Likewise it appears that delinquents tend to be less physically attractive than other people (Cavior & Howard 1973) and there is some slight suggestive evidence (Lewison 1965; Ogden 1959) that the surgical treatment of minor deformities and disfigurements in delinquents may lead to an improvement in behaviour.

In summary, there is good evidence that individual differences in temperamental attributes play an important role in the development of psychological problems of various kinds. The next issue is *how* temperamental adversity puts the child at an increased psychiatric risk.

How temperamental differences influence development

Effect on others

Although most studies of parent–child interaction have assumed that it is parents who influence children, a number of writers in recent years (see Bell 1968; 1971; 1974) have argued that the interaction is a two-way affair in which children also help shape parental behaviour. The validity of this notion has now been shown in a variety of rather different studies. For example, Levy (1958) found in a study of nursing mothers that each mother's behaviour towards her infant was considerably influenced by what state the baby was in when brought for feeding—whether awake or asleep, placid or irritable. Yarrow (1963) found that the maternal behaviour of a foster mother was altered by the attributes of the infant placed in her home. Different infants elicited different maternal behaviour so that the amount of stimulation and comfort she provided varied with the infant's temperamental characteristics. Recently Campbell (1974) has also shown that active infants in a neonatal nursery get more attention from the nurse than do the inactive infants (an observation which helps to explain Schaffer's finding that the more active infants were less affected by depriving environment—it was likely that because they elicited stimulation they were in fact less deprived).

Physical or developmental handicaps in the child may also influence parental behaviour. Chavez *et al* (1974) found that malnourished children in Mexico received less parental attention than did better nourished youngsters. It was thought that the weak non-specific cries of the malnourished children were often ineffective in gaining parental attention. Similarly, it appears that children with congenital handicaps receive patterns of parenting which are somewhat different to those experienced by normal children (Cummings *et al* 1966). In addition, there is some evidence that a child's level of language skills influences the nature and extent of parental communication (Siegel 1963; Siegel & Harkins 1963; Spradlin & Rosenberg 1964).

There is also very limited experimental evidence that children's characteristics help shape parental behaviour. Osofsky and O'Connell (1972) manipulated the extent to which children exhibited dependent behaviour by varying the level of difficulty of the laboratory tasks they had to perform. They found that when the children were being dependent their mothers interacted more with them, both verbally and physically, and displayed more controlling behaviour. In short, there is a growing body of evidence that children's characteristics serve to *elicit* different behaviours from other people. So far this effect has been studied only to a very limited extent and the specificities in the effects of different temperamental attributes are not known.

Nevertheless it is not difficult to see how the attributes associated with later disorder might have effects on parents. The highly irregular child who never settles to a steady sleeping or eating routine poses particular problems for his mother who will find it difficult to arrange her life just because her child is so unpredictable. The malleable child who easily adapts to changes and new situations is likely to be very much easier to bring up than his non-adaptable brother whose behaviour is so tiresomely difficult to alter. Because children with these attributes are so difficult to rear, they may well arouse more irritation and the parents may come to expect problems because they have occurred before. Such expectations may become self-fulfilling in their effect on the child, and so a vicious circle is created.

The London study to which reference has already been made (Graham *et al* 1973; Rutter, Quinton & Yule 1977) provides some evidence that this does in fact occur. Children with high scores on the temperamental adversity index were only slightly more likely than other children to come from homes with marital discord. However, within such homes they were *much* more likely than other children to be the subject of parental hostility and criticism. Whereas the great majority of children with high scores on the t.a. index were the subject of much parental criticism, this was true for only a minority of those with low scores on the t.a. index. It seemed that children with adverse temperamental features were more likely to be scapegoated at times of family difficulty. Parental criticism and hostility were strongly associated with the development of behavioural deviance and psychiatric disorder in children. Often parents were highly critical because of their own difficulties (many were chronically depressed), but *which* children were the subject of criticism was determined in large part by the children's characteristics.

Some children are much easier to love than others because they are lively, responsive and interesting. More of an effort may be required to love a passive, inert and unresponsive infant who seems to 'give nothing back'. Parental behaviour is not merely instinctive. Parents need the child to look at them, to cuddle, to smile and to respond to their overtures and if, for any reason the child does not do that, being a parent may be more of an effort. This is illustrated for example by the Klaus and Leiderman studies (Klaus *et al* 1972; Leiderman *et al* 1973; Leifer *et al* 1972) which showed that mothers of small premature babies who were separated from them in the first few weeks of life (because they were in an incubator or an intensive care nursery) tended to be less confident and less attentive to their babies. This effect probably arose in part from the fragile rather unresponsive nature of very premature babies, and partly from the lack of contact with the baby during the early period when mothering skills should be developing. Other studies, too, have shown that in any one family it is the children who were born after difficulties in pregnancy or delivery and who were separated from their mothers in the neonatal period who are the ones most likely to be battered (Lynch 1975).

It is not, of course, a simple matter of some children being difficult and some easy. It is also a question of interaction with parental attributes. Although there are some children whom nearly all parents would find rewarding and easy, and some who would pose problems to practically anyone, there are many whose characteristics lead to less consistent responses. Some parents like a lively active, mischievous child but others may find him wearing and prefer a quieter, passive, inactive youngster. Accordingly, in assessing parent child interaction it is necessary to determine how each responds to the other and which attributes *they* find rewarding and which aggravating. These will not necessarily be the same in all families.

These concerns have led to efforts to develop ways of measuring sequences of parent–child interaction (see several chapters in Lewis & Rosenblum 1974). It is not enough to measure, for example, how much the mother talks to her child it is also necessary to determine the extent to which she does so in response to cues from her infant. The characteristic of being able to 'read' babies' behaviour and interpret their communications is an important part of parenting (Bell & Ainsworth 1972). Of course responsiveness is in part a function of parental characteristics but also it is likely to be influenced by the clarity and consistency of the signals provided by the child. So far very little is known about these qualities of parent–child interaction and even less about the child's contribution to the process. Much has still to be learned about the ways in which children's characteristics shape other people's responses to them. However, it is already clear that this is one of the important ways in which temperamental differences influence development.

Range of experiences

Another way in which temperamental attributes may operate is in shaping other types of life experiences (Rutter 1975). What children do is determined in part by what they are like. For example, an active, exploratory child is likely to have many more adventures and more social experiences than his inactive and passive brother. The first child will learn by trying out new things and will encounter new situations not experienced by the second child. His behaviour in later childhood will have been shaped not only by what sort of child he is, but also by what sort of things he has done and the latter depends to some extent on the former. The friendly, approaching child will meet more people and make more friends than a timid withdrawing child. Because of this he may adapt more easily to a separation experience which places him in the care of a strange adult. The experience may be less stressful to him because he generally has a positive approach to new people, because he thereby gets more attention, but also because he has met more people before, is more used to meeting people and therefore the situation is less strange to him. This is probably one of the explanations why the children studied by Stacey and her colleagues (1970) were less likely to show disturbance following admission to hospital if they had previously experienced brief separations in happy circumstances.

The Isle of Wight study (Rutter, Tizard & Whitmore 1970) showed that children with chronic physical illnesses or handicaps were somewhat more likely than other children to exhibit reading difficulties or psychiatric problems. Within this group reading difficulties were associated with the frequency of school absence. It appears that the chronic handicap was of importance in the children's development in part because of its effect on their experiences. They were more likely to have frequent absences from school and of course some of them were also more likely to have experienced the stresses of hospital admission.

Effective environment

A third mode of operation of temperamental attributes is their influence on what is an *effective* environment for the child. The distinction between an *objective* and *effective* environment is most easily appreciated by considering some gross handicap such as deafness. The home filled with lively conversational interchange objectively constitutes a richly stimulating linguistic environment but, to the deaf child, effectively it is a barren environment because he cannot hear what is said. The reality of this distinction is shown by Meadow's comparison of deaf children reared by hearing parents and deaf children reared by deaf parents (1968). In almost all respects the deaf children brought up by deaf parents were better adjusted in terms of sociability, popularity, emotional responses, willingness to communicate with strangers and lack of communicative frustration, they wrote better English compositions and their achievements in school work were greater. Only in speech and lip reading ability were there no differences. Why it was better for the deaf children to have deaf parents is not known with certainty but probably the important reasons were (a) that deaf parents were more accepting of a deaf child; and (b) that they communicated better and earlier with the child by means of signs and gestures. Because of this the deaf parents probably provided an effectively more stimulating environment although objectively, at least to a hearing child, it would be lacking in linguistic stimulation. The finding emphasises that the best environment for one child is not necessarily the best for another. The same sort of effect, in lesser degree, may be seen with the variation in temperamental attributes. For example, children vary greatly in their distractability by extraneous stimuli. In a school classroom situated next the railway, some children will not notice the noise of passing trains, whereas others will be constantly startled and interrupted in whatever they are doing whenever an engine goes by. To some extent this will be a function of how engrossed they are in their work, also to some extent it will be a reflection of a more pervasive temperamental attribute. An indication of this is provided by Carey's finding (1974) that babies with a low threshold to sensory stimulation were more likely to wake up at night. Children vary in their sensitivity and this variation will result in their experiencing the environment in rather different ways—the world will not be the same for them.

Competence

What children are capable of and what they achieve will also have a major influence on their lives. Both intellectual competence and adaptability are likely to help determine how children respond to various sorts of stressful experiences. The importance of poor adaptability as one of the adverse temperamental features has already been noted in connection with the New York and London studies. Adaptability is important because changed circumstances may be less stressful for a child who can accommodate himself to the new situations he encounters. Just as many old people find changes very stressful because they have become rigid and routine in their habits and because they no longer have the skills to cope with a novel environment, so the child who lacks malleability and competence will also find changes stressful (Rutter 1975). The child who can cope during times of stress or limited resources will be less likely to succumb to the difficulties he faces.

In the school situation the child who is good at his work is in a favoured position because the work is less of a struggle, because life consists of a series of successes instead of failures and because the teachers will probably view him more positively. The child who falls behind in his school work is at a serious disadvantage for the obverse of the same reason. Many studies have shown that behavioural problems are very much more common in children who are behind in their reading (Rutter, Tizard & Whitmore 1970; Varlaam 1974) and in children who are less intelligent (Rutter 1971). There are probably several reasons for this association, but one of them is that educational failure leads to such opprobrium that the child becomes disenchanted with school, finds the whole thing a negative experience and reacts adversely to this painful situation.

Athletic prowess is important because of the pleasure given by success in any field of activity and because of its relevance to popularity with other children, as already noted above.

Social skills are probably the most crucial of all, in view of the importance of interaction with other people as a source of learning and of pleasure. In part these skills are based on temperamental attributes—some children are 'naturally' outgoing whereas others are not—and in part they rely on appropriate learning experiences (Argyle 1967). Social competence involves not only the possession of social skills but also the ability to interpret social situations. Odom *et al* (1973) found that deaf children had difficulty analysing and interpreting emotion-producing situations. This may be one factor which causes some deaf children to have difficulties in social situations.

Vulnerability

Finally in this connection there is the rather imprecise concept of 'vulnerability'. Vulnerability to physical hazards has already been discussed in connection with sex differences. Presumably there is a comparable vulnerability to psychological stresses. Certainly boys seem to be more often adversely affected by family discord and stressful separation experiences (Rutter 1970b). In adult life, too, men appear to succumb more easily to the stresses associated with bereavement and natural disaster. However, there are exceptions (girls seem just as likely to be harmed by poor quality institutional upbringing, Wolkind & Rutter 1973), and there is no evidence on whether any vulnerability that does exist is inborn or acquired. The matter requires further study.

It is noteworthy that children with organic brain damage are more likely than other children to develop psychiatric problems even in the absence of psychosocial stress or disturbance (see Chapter 8). This suggests the possibility that they may have an increased biological susceptibility. It is of course a common observation that there are large individual differences in children's responses to privation and stress. We still know relatively little about what these differences are due to and how they operate but it is an issue which requires much greater understanding.

CONCLUSIONS

There is good evidence that from infancy onwards children vary greatly in their temperamental attributes, that these differences are partly a result of polygenic influences and are partly determined by other biological factors and by life experiences. The existence of temperamental differences is of profound significance for children's later development and temperamental adversity has been shown to be related to the later development of psychiatric disorder in several independent investigations. It is not a matter of personality features predestining a child to developmental disorder; rather it is a matter of temperamental attributes having an effect on the way other people behave to the child and the range of activities and situations he experiences, on his perception of the environment, of his competence in coping with the world and with changing life circumstances, and on his vulnerability to a variety of psychosocial hazards. The nature of these interactions and the manner in which they are influenced by temperament has important implications for the planning of psychiatric treatment as well as for diagnostic assessment (see examples given in Rutter 1975). Individual differences have played but a small part in child psychiatric research up to now. The findings from research undertaken during the last 10 years make it clear that they will have to receive more attention in the future.

REFERENCES

ARGYLE M. (1967) *The Psychology of Interpersonal Behaviour*. Harmondsworth: Penguin Books

BAGLEY C. & EVAN-WONG L. (1970) Psychiatric disorder and adult and peer group rejection of the child's name. *J. Child Psychol. Psychiat.* **11**, 19–27

BARON J. (1972) Temperament profile of children with Down's syndrome. *Dev. Med. Child Neurol.* **14**, 640–643

BELL R. Q. (1968) A reinterpretation of the direction of effects in studies of socialisation. *Psychol. Rev.* **75**, 81–95

BELL R.Q. (1971) Stimulus control of parent or caretaker behaviour by offspring. *Dev. Psychol.* **4**, 63–72

BELL R.Q. (1974) Contributions of human infants to care giving and social interaction. In Lewis M. & Rosenblum L.A. (eds.) *The Effect of the Infant on its Caregiver.* London: Wiley

BELL S.M. & AINSWORTH M.D.S. (1972) Infant crying and maternal responsiveness. *Child Dev.* **43**, 1171–1190

BENCH J. & PARKER A. (1970) On the reliability of the Graham/Rosenblith behaviour test for neonates. *J. Child Psychol. Psychiat.* **11**, 121–131

BERGER M. (1973) Early experience and other environmental factors: an overview. 1. Studies with humans. *In:* Eysenck H.J. (ed.) *Handbook of Abnormal Psychology*, 2nd edn. London: Pitman Medical

BERNAL J.F. (1973) Night waking in infants during the first 14 months. *Dev. Med. Child Neurol.* **15**, 760–769

BLOOM B.S. (1964) *Stability and Change in Human Characteristics.* London: Wiley

BRIDGER W.H. & BIRNS B. (1968) Experience and temperament in human neonates. In Newton R. & Levine S. (eds.) *Early Experience and Behavior*, Springfield, Illinois: Charles C Thomas

BRONSON W.C. (1966) Early antecedents of emotional expressiveness and reactivity control. *Child Dev.* **37,** 793–810

BRONSON W.C. (1969) Stable patterns of behavior; the significance of enduring orientations for personality development. *In* Hill J.P. (ed.) *Minnesota Symposia on Child Psychology,* vol. 2. Minneapolis: University of Minnesota Press

CAMPBELL D. (1974) Personal communication

CAREY W.B. (1970) A simplified method for measuring infant temperament. *J. Pediatr.* **77,** 188–194

CAREY W.B. (1972) Clinical applications of infant temperament measurements. *J. Pediatr.* **81,** 823–828

CAREY W.B. (1974) Night waking and temperament in infancy. *J. Pediatr.* **84,** 756–758

CAVIOR N. & HOWARD R. (1973) Facial attractiveness and juvenile delinquency among black and white offenders. *J. Abnorm. Child Psychol.* **1,** 202–213

CHAVEZ A., MARTINEZ C. & YASCHINE T. (1974) The importance of nutrition and stimuli on child mental and social development. *In* Cravioto J., Hambraeus L. & Vahlquist B. (eds.) *Early Malnutrition and Mental Development.* Symposia of the Swedish Nutrition Foundation. Stockholm: Almquist & Wilksell

CHESS S. & KORN S. (1970) Temperament and behavior disorders in mentally retarded children. *Arch. gen. psychiat.* **23,** 122–130

CUMMINGS S.T., BAYLEY M.C. & RIE H.E. (1966) Effects of the child's deficiency on the mother: A study of mothers of mentally retarded, chronically ill and neurotic children. *Amer. J. Orthopsychiat.* **36,** 595–608

DOBZHANSKY T. (1967) On types, genotypes and the genetic diversity in populations. *In* Spuhler J.N. (ed.) *Genetic Diversity and Human Behavior.* Chicago: Aldine

ESCALONA S. & HEIDER G. (1959) *Prediction and Outcome: A Study in Child Development.* New York: Basic Books

FREEDMAN D.G. & KELLER B. (1963) Inheritance of behaviour in infants. *Science* **140,** 196–198

GARAI J.E. & SCHEINFELD A. (1968) Sex differences in mental and behavioral traits. *Genet. Psychol. Monogr.* **77,** 169–299

GESELL A. (1937) Early evidences of individuality in human infant. *Scientific Monthly* **45,** 217–225

GOODMAN N., RICHARDSON S.A., DORNBUSCH S.M. & HASTORF A.H. (1963) Variant reactions to physical disabilities. *Amer. sociol. Rev.* **28,** 429–435

GOY R.W. (1968) Organising effects of androgen on the behaviour of rhesus monkeys. *In* Michael R.P. (ed.) *Endocrinology and Human Behaviour.* London: Oxford University Press

GRAHAM P., RUTTER M. & GEORGE S. (1973) Temperamental characteristics as predictors of behavior disorders in children. *Amer. J. Orthopsychiat.* **43,** 328–339

GRAY J.A. & BUFFERY A.W.H. (1971) Sex differences in emotional and cognitive behaviour in mammals including man: adaptive and neural bases. *Acta Psychol.* **35,** 89–111

GRONLUND N.E. (1959) *Sociometry in the Classroom.* New York: Harper

HUTT C. (1972) *Males and Females.* Harmondsworth: Penguin

JOFFE J.N. (1969) *Pre-natal determinants of behaviour.* Oxford: Pergamon

KAGAN J. & MOSS H.A. (1962) *Birth to Maturity: a Study in Psychological Development.* New York: Wiley

KLAUS M.H., JERAULD R., KREGER N.C., McALPINE W., STEFFA M. & KENNELL J.H. (1972) Maternal attachment: importance of the first postpartum days. *N. Engl. J. Med.* **286**, 460–463

KORNER A.F. (1973) Sex differences in newborns with special references to differences in the organisation of oral behaviour. *J. Child Psychol. Psychiat.* **14**, 19–29

KORNER A.F., CHUCK B. & DONTCHOS S. (1968) Organismic determinants of spontaneous oral behaviour in neonates. *Child Dev.* **39**, 1145–1157

LEIDERMAN P.H., LEIFER A.D., SEASHORE M.J., BARNETT C.R. & GROBSTEIN R. (1973) Mother–infant interaction: effects of early deprivation, prior experience and sex of infant. *Res. Publ. Assoc. Res. Nerv. Ment. Dis.* **51**, 154–175

LEIFER A.D., LEIDERMAN P.H., BARNETT C.R. & WILLIAMS J.A. (1972) Effects of mother–infant separation on maternal attachment behavior. *Child Dev.* **43**, 1203–1218

LEVY D.M. (1958) *Behavioral Analysis: Analysis of Clinical Observations of Behavior as Applied to Mother–Newborn Relationships.* Springfield, Illinois: Charles C Thomas

LEWIS M. & ROSENBLUM L.A. (eds.) (1974) *The Effect of the Infant on its Caregiver.* London: Wiley

LEWISON E. (1965) An experiment in facial reconstructive surgery in a prison population. *Canad. med. Assoc. J.* **92**, 251–254

LIPTON E.L., STEINSCHNEIDER A. & RICHMOND J.B. (1966) Autonomic functions in the neonate. VII maturational changes in cardiac control. *Child Dev.* **37**, 1–16

LYNCH M.A. (1975) Ill-health and child abuse. *Lancet* **ii**, 317–319

MACCOBY E.E. & JACKLIN C.N. (1975) *The Psychology of Sex Differences.* London: Oxford University Press

MEADOW K.P. (1968) Toward a developmental understanding of deafness. *J. rehab. Deaf.* **2**, 1–18

McGRADE B.J. (1968) Newborn activity and emotional response at 8 months. *Child Dev.* **39**, 1247–1252

MONEY J. & EHRHARDT A.A. (1968) Pre-natal hormonal exposure: possible effects on behaviour in man. *In* Michael R.P. (ed.) *Endocrinology and Human Behaviour.* London: Oxford University Press

MOORE T. & UCKO L.E. (1957) Night waking in early infancy. *Arch. Dis. Child.* **32**, 333–342

MURPHY L.B. and collaborators (1962) *The Widening World of Childhood: Paths towards Mastery.* New York: Basic Books

NIELSON J. & CHRISTENSEN A.L. (1974) Thirty-five males with double Y chromosome. *Psychol. Med.* **4**, 28–37

ODOM P.B., BLANTON R.L. & LAUKUF, C. (1973) Facial expressions and interpretation of emotion arousing situations in deaf and hearing children. *J. Abnorm. Child Psychol.* **1**, 139–151

OGDEN D.A. (1959) Use of surgical rehabilitation in young delinquents. *Brit. med. J.* **i**, 432–434

OSOFSKY J.D. & O'CONNELL E.J. (1972) Parent–child interaction: daughters' effects upon mothers' and fathers' behaviors. *Dev. Psychol.* **7**, 157–168

QUINN P.O. & RAPOPORT J.L. (1974) Minor physical anomalies and neurological status in hyperactive boys. *Pediatrics* **53**, 742–747

RICHARDS M. & BERNAL J. (1974) Why some babies don't sleep. *New Society* **27**, 509–511

RICHARDSON S.A., GOODMAN N., HASTORF A.H. & DORNBUSCH S. (1961) Cultural uniformity in reaction to physical disabilities. *Amer. sociol. Rev.* **26**, 241–247

RICHARDSON S.A. & ROYCE J.C. (1968) Race and physical handicap in children's preference for other children. *Child Dev.* **39**, 467–480

RUTTER M. (1970a) Psychological development—predictions from infancy. *J. Child Psychol. Psychiat.* **11**, 49–62

RUTTER M. (1970b) Sex differences in children's responses to family stress. *In* Anthony E.J. & Koupernik, C. (eds.) *The Child in His Family.* London: Wiley

RUTTER M. (1971) Psychiatry. *In* Wortis J. (ed.) *Mental Retardation: An Annual Review*, vol. 3. New York: Grune & Stratton

RUTTER M. (1975) *Helping Troubled Children.* Harmondsworth: Penguin

RUTTER M., QUINTON, D. & YULE, B. (1977) *Family Pathology and Disorder in Children* (in preparation). London: Wiley

RUTTER M. & MADGE N. (1976) *Cycles of Disadvantage: a Review of Research.* London: Heinemann

RUTTER M. & YULE W. (1973) Specific reading retardation. *In* Mann L. & Sabatino D. (eds.) *The First Review of Special Education.* Philadelphia: Buttonwood Farms

RUTTER M., KORN S. & BIRCH H. (1963) Genetic and environmental factors in the development of primary reaction patterns. *Brit. J. Soc. Clin. Psychol.* **2**, 161–173

RUTTER M., TIZARD J. & WHITMORE K. (eds.) (1970) *Education, Health and Behaviour.* London: Longman

RUTTER M., BIRCH H., THOMAS A. & CHESS S. (1964) Temperamental characteristics in infancy and the later development of behavioural disorders. *Brit. J. Psychiat.* **110**, 651–661

SALVIA J., SHEARE J.B. & ALGOZZINE B. (1975) Facial attractiveness and personal-social development. *J. Abnorm. Child Psychol.* **3**, 171–178

SCARR S. (1969) Social introversion-extraversion as a heritable response. *Child Dev.* **40**, 823–832

SCHAEFER E. & BAYLEY N. (1963) Maternal behavior, child behavior, and their intercorrelations from infancy through adolescence. *Mon. Soc. Res. Child Dev.* **28**, 1–127

SCHAFFER E.R. (1966) Activity level as a constitutional determinant of infantile reaction to deprivation. *Child Dev.* **37**, 595–602

SIEGEL G.M. (1963) Adult verbal behavior with retarded children labeled as 'high' or 'low' in verbal ability. *Amer. J. Ment. Def.* **3**, 417–424

SIEGEL G.M. & HARKINS J.P. (1963) Verbal behavior of adults in two conditions with institutionalized retarded children. *J. Speech Hearing Dis.* Monograph Supplement **10**, 39–47

SPRADLIN J.E. & ROSENBERG S. (1964) Complexity of adult verbal behavior in a dyadic situation with retarded children. *J. Abnorm. Soc. Psychol.* **68**, 694–698

STACEY M., DEARDEN R., PILL R. & ROBINSON D. (1970) *Hospitals, Children and their Families: The Report of a Pilot Study.* London: Routledge & Kegan Paul

STEINSCHNEIDER A. (1967) Developmental psychophysiology. *In* Brackbill Y. (ed.) *Infancy and Early Childhood.* New York: Free Press

TANNER J.M., HEALY M.J., LOCKHART R.D., MacKENZIE J.D. & WHITEHOUSE R.H. (1956) Aberdeen growth study: 1. The prediction of adult body measurements from measurements taken each year from birth to 5 years. *Arch. Dis. Child.* **31,** 372–381

THOMAS A., CHESS S. & BIRCH H.G. (1968) *Temperament and Behavior Disorders in Children.* New York: University Press

THOMAS A., BIRCH H.G., CHESS S., HERTZIG M.E. & KORN S. (1963) *Behavioral Individuality in Early Childhood.* New York: University Press

TORGERSEN A.M. & KRINGLEN E. (1976) The origin of temperamental differences in infants. A study of new-born twins. (Submitted for publication)

UCKO L.E. (1965) A comparative study of asphyxiated and non-asphyxiated boys from birth to 5 years. *Dev. Med. Child Neurol.* **7,** 643–657

VANDENBERG S.G. (1969) Contributions of twin research to psychology. *In* Manosevitz M., Lindzey G. & Thiessen D.D. (eds.) *Behavioral Genetics.* Century Psychology series. New York: Appleton-Century-Crofts

VARLAAM A. (1974) Educational attainment and behaviour at school. *Greater London Intelligence Quarterly,* No. 29, December 1974, 29–37

WALDROP M., PEDERSON F.A. & BELL R.Q. (1968) Minor physical anomalies and behaviour in pre-school children. *Child Dev.* **39,** 391–400

WOLKIND S. & RUTTER M. (1973) Children who have been 'In Care'—an epidemiological study. *J. Child Psychol. Psychiat.* **14,** 97–105

YARROW L.J. (1963) Research in dimensions of early maternal care. *Merrill–Palmer Quart.* **9,** 101–114

CHAPTER 2

Polygenic influences

J. SHIELDS

GENES AND BEHAVIOUR

Although major chromosome abnormalities, in particular Down's syndrome, account for some 25 per cent of admissions to hospitals for the severely subnormal, and monogenic inborn errors of metabolism, of which phenylketonuria is much the commonest, account for a further 2 per cent or so, genetic influences in childhood psychiatric disorders, in so far as they are relevant, will be largely polygenic in nature, i.e. the effect of the products of many genes combining with environmental influences of many kinds. It is with the role of polygenic inheritance in child psychiatry that this chapter is concerned.

When we say that a disease or a syndrome or a behavioural trait is inherited, we speak loosely. To be accurate, it is only the genes which are inherited, or the DNA with its encoded sequence of aminoacids. Everything else is acquired in the course of development. Genetically, man is a very varied creature. In the last resort every individual, with the exception of monozygotic twins, will be found to have a unique enzymatic constitution, which will be reflected in a great number of ways in an individual's physical, neurochemical and physiological characteristics, and hence in some of his personality traits and his liability to disease (Harris 1970). While one of the aims of psychogenetics is to throw light on part of the complex chain of events between genes and behaviour, the more usual concern is to discover how much difference genetic variation makes for a particular trait or disorder.

Twin and adoption studies

Since familial may not mean genetic, focus is turned to twin and adoption studies. The classical twin study compares resemblance in genetically identical (monozygotic) pairs brought up together with that in genetically dissimilar (dizygotic) pairs brought up together in order to estimate the influence of genetic differences under similar environments. The study of adopted or fostered children endeavours to assess the effect of different environments on groups that are similar genetically, and in particular to separate the effects of the environment and the genes usually provided by the same parents.

Twin and adoption studies have difficulties of their own. We can refer to some of them briefly. The environments of monozygotic (MZ) twins are in some respects more similar than those of dizygotic (DZ) twins, and it is possible that for some traits this might make MZ pairs more alike than DZ and so lead to an overestimation of the role of heredity. However, the study of twins brought up apart, not sharing the same microenvironment (Shields 1962), and of MZ twins wrongly believed by their parents to be DZ (Freedman 1965; Scarr 1968) and of resemblance in MZ twins with very close and not so close relationships (Shields 1954; Parker 1964) all argue against the importance of this source of bias. Of course, the question cannot be answered in general terms. Particularly in childhood the influence of one twin on the other may account for some similarities and for some differences in behaviour. Other potential biases in twin studies lead to an underestimation of heredity and an overestimation of the social environment. These are prenatal factors of various kinds, such as the unequal sharing of the placenta which sometimes makes MZ twins less alike than they would otherwise be. The importance of unbiassed sampling in twin studies is well recognised. It is also true that the mean intelligence of twins is some five IQ points lower than that of single-tons.

Like twins, adopted children are in some respects unrepresentative of the general population, as are their biological and adoptive parents. Selective placement of higher risk children in poorer homes is a potential source of uncertainty in the interpretation of results. Problems of confidentiality rule out the possibility of adoption studies in many countries. However, the uncertainties and the inevitably small samples in both twin and adoption studies dealing with a particular syndrome do not detract from their importance; and it is with these studies that we shall be principally concerned.

For a general discussion of twin studies the reader is referred to Mittler (1971), and for further details about the genetic aspects of mental abnormality to the textbooks of Rosenthal (1970) and Slater and Cowie (1971) and to a review by the present author (Shields 1973).

NORMAL INTELLIGENCE AND PERSONALITY

Many psychiatric disorders in childhood may be the reaction of individuals towards the tail of the population distributions of intelligence and personality.

Intelligence and 'heritability'

The range of intellectual differences within sibships, predicted by genetic theory, argues against any attempts to account for differences in normal intelligence purely on a cultural or social class basis. The important contribution of genetic factors is best illustrated by the contrast between the correlation coefficient of 0·23 between the IQ's of unrelated individuals reared together (median of four studies) and that of 0·75 between those of MZ twins reared apart (four studies). Studies in different countries at different times and using different tests are in quite good agreement (Erlenmeyer-Kimling & Jarvik 1963).

To answer the question '*how much* heredity?', attempts have been made to estimate the heritability (h^2) of a trait, i.e. the proportion of its total variance due to genetic variation. For IQ h^2 has frequently been estimated as about 0·80 or a little less (Jensen 1972). Heritability is not a property of the genes but concerns variance within a population. It applies to a trait measured in a particular way within a particular group. The magnitude of h^2 will depend on the degree of trait-relevant variation in the population studied. If environmental factors are uniformly good (or bad), h^2 will be higher than if there are important environmental differences within the population. Similarly, if genetic factors are uniform, heritability will be zero, even if the environment has almost no effect on the trait. h^2 for hair colour will be high in NW Europe, zero in China. Heritability does not apply to individuals: one cannot say that every individual's IQ is determined 80 per cent by his genes and 20 per cent by his environment—one person may score IQ 70 almost entirely on account of his genes and another almost entirely on account of his environment. Nor can an estimate of heritability within a population be assumed to apply to the mean difference between groups such as races. Training and practice can influence h^2 estimates. h^2 for maze running in the mouse increased with practice, while in the rat h^2 for defaecation in the open field test (a measure of emotionality) decreased on successive tests (Broadhurst 1968).

However, the fact that one cannot expect a global statement of the importance of heredity for any general class of behaviour does not mean that nothing can be learned from heritability estimates. The comparison of h^2 for different traits, under different circumstances, and obtained from different classes of relative, can be of value. Of further interest are attempts to apportion the variance due to such factors as gene dominance, assortative mating, the interaction of specific genotypes and environments, the correlation between genotype and environment, specific and general environmental factors, and error (Jinks & Fulker 1970). The simpler analyses count the effects of genetic–environmental correlation (such as attempts to treat different genotypes according to their supposed needs) as due to heredity, while measurement error is counted with environment.

Attempts have been made to distinguish genetically between general intelligence and the specific abilities (verbal, spatial, etc.) and between associative and cognitive learning abilities. It seems that intelligence is not a uniform trait genetically but findings are inconsistent as to which special abilities have the highest heritability (Vandenberg 1968). Since 1962 there have been three new studies of twins reared apart (Shields 1962; Juel-Nielsen 1965; Burt 1966) the results of which are in fairly good agreement with one another (Jensen 1972) and with the earlier study by Newman and his colleagues (1937). The environmental causes of difference are multifactorial, but these studies attempted to identify some of them. Despite its limitations, tested IQ was found to have a higher heritability than educational achievement which is much more dependent on the environment. MZ twins brought up apart were no more alike on tests of attainment than DZ twins brought up together.

Personality variation

Temperamental and personality traits are more difficult to assess than intelligence, and findings are more dependent on mental state. It is therefore not surprising that the results from studies of normal twins employing personality scales of one kind or another are not so consistent as they are in the cognitive field. Correlations and heritability estimates vary quite widely according to sex, sample and test. According to Lindzey *et al* (1971) a representative intrapair correlation on personality tests is 0·46 for MZ pairs and 0·28 for DZ pairs which is about half the respective correlations on IQ tests. Work using questionnaires (e.g. Gottesman 1966), mostly with American high school twins, was reviewed by Vandenberg (1967). Similar results were generally found in subsequent work, such as that of Scarr (1969) using rating scales and other methods with 6 to 10-year-old girl twins, by Owen and Sines (1970) using the WISC and the Missouri Children's Picture Series with 6 to 14-year-old twins, and by Claridge *et al* (1973) using a variety of cognitive tests, inventories and physiological measures with adult volunteer twins from Glasgow. Genetic factors are most often evident in traits such as degree of sociability and energy, and they are frequently identifiable in tests of emotionality and anxiety. Slater and Shields (1969) argued that evidence from a variety of sources, including animal breeding, physiological studies and clinical work, pointed to the existence of genetic variability in anxiety proneness, the anxiety state being best understood on a model according to which the genetic diathesis interacts with environmental stressors.

Genetic factors need not be manifest early on and infantile characteristics do not necessarily predict behaviour in later childhood. Nevertheless, two studies based on observations of young twins may be mentioned which suggest that genetic factors influence smiling response and fear reactions in infancy (Freedman 1965) and also influence primary reaction patterns such as withdrawal and activity (Rutter *et al* 1963), traits found to be relatively stable and established in early childhood. Developmental patterns and temperament are relevant in child psychiatry and are areas in which genetic variation is likely to be of some importance.

TWIN AND ADOPTION STUDIES OF ABNORMAL BEHAVIOUR

Behaviour disorders in unselected twin schoolchildren

Personality questionnaire and other test results from children bear a somewhat uncertain relationship to the social, educational and medical disorders that are the concern of child psychiatry. Of more direct relevance to the genetic aspects of psychiatric problems in childhood is an attempt by Shields (1954) to investigate neurotic traits and behaviour disorders in a sample of 62 same-sex pairs of 12 to 15-year-old twins from LCC schools in four south London boroughs. The sample was unselected for psychiatric symptomatology.

Assessments were based mainly on a history of the twins and descriptions of their behaviour obtained from the parents on the lines of a semi-structured psychiatric social history. Observations of the twins' behaviour and school reports were also taken into account. In the light of all the data, the author attempted to rate the family background, the degree of behavioural psychopathology, the resemblance in personality and the closeness of the twin relationship. Modern standards would of course require procedures for securing reliability and independence of the assessments.

Taking a liberal interpretation of neurotic traits and behaviour disorders, 63 per cent of the male and 47 per cent of the female twins had at some time in their lives been disturbed in their behaviour in such a way as might have warranted referral to a social agency (Grade 1, moderately severe) or had suffered from a milder or more transient disturbance of a similar kind (Grade 2, mild). Such disorders were regarded as part of normal variation and the cutting point between Grade 2 and the 'normal' Grades 3 and 4 as arbitrary.

The study showed the influence of both genetic and environmental factors. Presence of a Grade 1 or 2 disorder was significantly correlated with home environment, tending to occur in families assessed as poor from the psychological point of view. This was interpreted as evidence of environmental effects. A comparison of MZ and DZ pairs as to whether one, both or neither of the twins was 'disordered' suggested some degree of polygenic influence. For the present chapter we shall restrict ourselves to the 41 pairs in which one or both twins was rated as disordered (Table 2.1). It was concluded that polygenic influences had a relatively greater effect on the kind of childhood disorder manifested than on its presence or severity. The findings could not easily be accounted for by differences in the way parents treated DZ as compared with MZ twins or by the closeness of the twin relationship in MZ pairs. The latter was not associated with degree of personality resemblance; however, it was related to family environment, the twins from psychologically poor environments tending to have the poorer mutual relationships. MZ twins were far from being replicas of one another. Quite as impressive as their degree of similarity were the differences in behaviour between DZ

Table 2.1 Concordance for behaviour disorder in twin schoolchildren (data of Shields 1954)

	2 twins disordered			1 twin disordered	Total pairs
	Very similar disorders	*Essentially similar disorders*	*Essentially different disorders*		
MZ	6 26%	8 35%	3 13%	6 26%	23
DZ	0 0%	1 6%	8 44%	9 50%	18

twins brought up in the same home. In one DZ pair the twins were nicknamed 'the terror' and 'the professor'. This is not the sort of difference one would expect in an MZ pair.

Genetic factors were thought to play a part through their influence on maturity, intelligence and temperamental characteristics such as anxiety and impulsiveness. They seemed to play little part in juvenile delinquency as such. While no specific symptom was invariably concordant in MZ pairs, enuresis gave some indication of genetic influence: of 6 MZ pairs, 4 were concordant, while this was so in none of 10 DZ pairs. Tics were usually discordant in MZ pairs. A subsequent study of MZ twins reared apart (Shields 1962) supported these findings. Bakwin (1970) studied sleepwalking in pairs of twins obtained through New York mothers of twins clubs. In 9 out of 19 MZ pairs both twins were affected, compared with only one out of 14 same-sex DZ pairs. He suggested that sleepwalking was a manifestation of immaturity occurring on a genetic basis. Further reports on his sample of 542 pairs, not selected specifically on account of abnormality, indicated a genetic contribution to the aetiology of reading disability (see p. 40), enuresis, constipation, carsickness and nailbiting (Bakwin 1971a, b, c, d 1973; Bakwin & Davidson 1971). In a series of papers (references in Shields 1973) Abe used grandparents as informants about sleep and other disturbances in their children and grandchildren at the same early age.

In MZ twins brought up apart (Shields 1962) reunion during childhood resulting in disruption of home life generally brought with it difficulties in adjustment which proved temporary. The study of foster-home-reared children by Heston *et al* (1966) showed that even severe childhood disturbances resulting from emotionally traumatic institutional care can be spontaneously reversed by the time of adulthood. In their study based on the children of schizophrenic mothers and controls, psychopathology in adult life depended on genetic factors rather than on the type of early environment.

Maudsley Children's Department twins, 1949–58

In view of the lack of systematic twin studies in general child psychiatry, a summary is now given of an unpublished study by the present author of all twins from same-sex pairs who were admitted under the age of 16 as in- or outpatients to the Maudsley Hospital between the years 1949 and 1958 inclusive and, with few exceptions, investigated and followed up along with their cotwins to 1961 or later. There were 54 such twin probands from 41 pairs; in 13 pairs both twins were referred to the hospital in their own right on the same or different occasions. The proportion of patients who were twins and the relative proportions of MZ and DZ pairs were about what would be expected, and the proportion of inpatients was similar to that of singletons, but the twins differed from other Maudsley patients in a number of ways. More cases, both MZ and DZ, were referred from other hospitals than was so with Maudsley children as a whole. The excess of males is even greater than usual, especially in MZ pairs. There were 22 male and 4 female MZ probands, 18 male and 10 female DZ probands. There may be a relative excess of cases presenting problems of low intelligence and possible organic features, though this is difficult to judge, since the official diagnosis of most cases in the department at that time was 'primary behaviour disorder'.

Concordance can be expressed in different ways. One can count each pair once only (n=41) or the affected cotwins of probands (n=54). One can include or exclude the 4 cotwins who presented a significant problem but without any referral to a psychiatrist or a juvenile court. Whichever method was used, MZ pairs were significantly more alike than DZ pairs. Table 2.2 shows the results of two different methods. In each case the MZ pairs are nearly twice as often concordant as the DZ, suggesting that genetic factors do play some role in child psychiatry. Male pairs were rather more often concordant than female pairs, but female pairs showed more MZ : DZ difference.

Genetic factors seem to be of greater importance for one kind of disorder than another. Seven probands had received an official diagnosis of mental deficiency and 10 an 'organic' diagnosis (mostly epilepsy). Of the remaining probands, 19 had aggressive behaviour disorders (all diagnosed 'primary behaviour disorder' and referred on account of delinquency or because they

Table 2.2   Maudsley children's department twins: sample concordance rates

	No. of pairs	Proportion concordant MZ	DZ
(a) Pairwise rate. Both twins referred to psychiatrist or juvenile court	41	11/17 65%	8/24 33%
(b) Proband method. Partially concordant pairs included as concordant	54	23/26 88%	13/28 46%

Table 2.3   Maudsley children's department twins: concordance by diagnostic group

Diagnostic group	Proportion concordant* MZ	DZ
Defective	4/4 100%	0/3 0%
Organic	6/6 100%	1/4 25%
Delinquent, aggressive	4/5 80%	9/14 64%
Other	9/11 82%	3/7 43%
Total	23/26 88%	13/28 46%
Concordant: same group	20/23 87%	8/13 62%

*Criteria of Table 2.2(b)

were unmanageable at school), and the remainder was a mixed group of 18 cases with anxiety symptoms, speech disturbances, reading disability, enuresis or other disorders. As will be seen from Table 2.3 the first two groups showed the highest MZ concordance and the biggest MZ : DZ contrast. Concordant MZ pairs included a pair of high-grade defectives with sexual problems; a pair of low-grade defectives with suspected psychosis; two pairs of epileptics, in one of which both twins were aggressive, destructive and of low intelligence and in the other both had petit mal; two pairs with reading disability, in one of which both twins had screaming attacks as well; and a pair of enuretic girls. Night terrors and an obsessive compulsive licking habit were among the discordant pairs. In a pair of overactive MZ boys it may have been a poorer relationship with the father that resulted in only one of the twins stealing persistently and later adopting an alias, though it is hard to distinguish cause and effect in such interactions.

The aggressive/delinquent group showed less MZ:DZ difference than the others. Indeed, when the boys in this group are considered, concordance was practically the same in DZ pairs (7 out of 9) as MZ pairs (4 out of 5). Concordant MZ pairs were more alike than concordant DZ pairs. Table 2.3 shows that they more often fell into the same diagnostic group. An example of a concordant DZ pair may be given:

Cases 11/12   Both seen at age 8, A for blackouts and headaches (diagnosis: idiopathic epilepsy, good prognosis): B for stealing, lying and temper (diagnosis: delinquent behaviour disorder, bad prognosis, mother can't cope). Both prognoses proved correct. At 16 A was doing well in the RAF, B not so well at an approved school.

By way of contrast we may mention an MZ pair from a relatively normal family setting.

Case 25   Both twins were asthenic, shortsighted boys with IQs in the upper 70s, lower than the rest of the family. They were enuretic till 7, at which age both were seen in a child guidance clinic for pilfering. The more robust twin, A, truanted more. His first conviction was at 12 for stealing, after which he was seen 60 times in the Maudsley Children's Department. Though he responded at first, prognosis was doubtful. By age 24 he had 15 convictions which included arson and false pretences; he has been in Borstal and prison. B had 7 convictions between ages 15 and 22 when he disappeared but had not been in prison. Both twins are given to pseudologia; they are hypochondriacal; they have received much hospital treatment for injuries which have proved selfinflicted; they have deserted their wives for shorter or longer periods. Both have been in psychiatric care: A simulated schizophrenia, B epilepsy. They are generally diagnosed as abnormal personalities of an asocial, inadequate, hysterical or psychopathic kind. Since attending different secondary schools and leaving home separately in adolescence, their careers developed independently. (For further description see Slater (1961), Proband MZ 12, and Gottesman & Shields (1972), Pair MZ 10.)

Rosanoff *et al* and delinquency in twins

Though the study by Rosanoff *et al* (1941) is old and open to criticism on methodological grounds, it comprises 197 same-sex pairs where one or both twins were juvenile delinquents or had other childhood behaviour difficulties.

Adult criminality and opposite-sex pairs were also studied. Table 2.4 shows the main findings which in some respects resemble those of the Maudsley series. MZ twins described as 'both affected' had more similar disorders than concordant DZ pairs. The group of childhood behaviour difficulties showed the possible influence of genetic factors and included problems based on excessive shyness, excessive impulsiveness and dull intelligence. There was

Table 2.4 Concordance for child behaviour difficulties, juvenile delinquency and adult criminality in monozygotic and same-sex dizygotic twins (data of Rosanoff *et al* 1941)

	MZ		DZ	
Child behaviour difficulties				
Preneurotic and prepsychotic types				
Male pairs	14/19	74%	10/19	53%
Female pairs	8/10	80%	11/32	34%
Total	22/29	76%	21/51	41%
Predelinquent types				
Male pairs	8/8	100%	5/9	56%
Female pairs	14/14	100%	8/19	42%
Total	22/22	100%	13/28	46%
Juvenile delinquency				
Male pairs	29/29	100%	12/17	71%
Female pairs	11/12	92%	9/9	100%
Total	40/41	98%	21/26	88%
Total childhood disorders				
Male pairs	51/56	91%	27/45	60%
Female pairs	33/36	92%	28/60	47%
Total	84/92	91%	55/105	52%
Adult criminality				
Male pairs	29/38	76%	5/23	22%
Female pairs	6/7	86%	1/4	25%
Total	35/45	78%	6/27	22%

however no MZ:DZ difference in respect of juvenile delinquency. Indeed concordance was 100 per cent in DZ female pairs. The case histories contained many phrases such as 'Father, in penitentiary, had encouraged the twins to steal'.

As already mentioned, the Maudsley Twin Study found concordance for delinquency or aggressive behaviour disorder in boys to be 80 per cent in MZ and 78 per cent in DZ pairs. In another small study, from Japan (Hayashi 1967), concordance for juvenile delinquency was 73 per cent in 15 MZ pairs and 75 per cent in 4 DZ pairs. In a mixed group of neurotic and psychopathic twins Slater (1953) noted 3 DZ pairs in which, despite marked differences in personality, both twins developed very similar behaviour disorders in childhood; psychogenic precipitation appeared to be highly important. According to these findings it would seem that in some social settings if one twin gets into trouble the other twin is very likely to do so too and it makes little difference whether the twins are genetically identical or not. The influence of one twin on the other is perhaps more likely in juvenile delinquency than in other disorders to influence the concordance rate.

Returning to the Rosanoff study we find a greater MZ:DZ concordance ratio in adult criminality than juvenile delinquency which might suggest that it is in the persistent adult criminal rather than in the average juvenile offender that the effects of any hereditary influence on crime are to be seen.

The early twin studies on adult crime suggested that it is among the psychopathic recidivists that an indirect genetic influence on criminality is most evident. The well-known study by Lange (1929) was largely based on this type of criminal. A more recent population-based twin study from Denmark (Christiansen 1970) reports lower rates than previous studies but confirms a higher concordance for serious crime than for minor offences. Since most persistent criminals start early, juvenile delinquency may therefore be a mixed group. A larger part may be situationally determined and be relatively uninfluenced by constitutional factors: many such cases will cease to be problems after adolescence. A smaller core group would go on to contribute to persistent crime and do so partly on account of various kinds of polygenic influences on personality, such as those on impulsiveness and low intelligence.

Robins (1966) found that sociopathic boys seen in a child guidance clinic tended to become sociopathic adults and tended to have sociopathic fathers, but was understandably reluctant to invoke a definite genetic component in the transmission. Although the sociopathy rate remained high when the boys had had no contact with their sociopathic fathers, they may have been reared by their mothers in homes that were very inadequate in other respects.

Of particular importance in this area, therefore, are adoption studies in which a subject does not receive his environment from the same parents who give him his genes. Two recent studies on criminality and psychopathy based on archive material from Denmark deserve special attention here. Although they deal with disorder in the adult, they merit consideration in a volume on child psychiatry, since there are grounds for supposing that similar characteristics were evident in childhood.

Adoption study of criminality

Hutchings (1972; Hutchings & Mednick 1974) had access to the names of all 1145 male nonfamilial adoptees from the Copenhagen area, born 1924–47, and those of their biological and adoptive parents except for some missing fathers. He also had access to the files of the Danish Police Record Office on all persons known to the police. The adoptees were transferred to their adoptive homes at a mean age of 12 months, and their mean age when the police files were searched was 35 years. The 1145 adoptees were compared with the same number of nonadopted controls, whose fathers were matched for occupational status with the adoptive fathers. The incidence of criminality is fairly high in this population and higher in the adoptees (16·2 per cent) than the controls (8·8 per cent). Criminal offences in Denmark are similar

Table 2.5 Criminality of known fathers related to criminal record of adoptees and controls (data of Hutchings 1972)

Offence of offspring	Biological fathers of adoptees		Adoptive fathers of adoptees		Biological fathers of nonadopted controls	
	No. of fathers	Percent criminal	No. of fathers	Percent criminal	No. of fathers	Percent criminal
None	473	31·1%	554	9·2%	706	9·5%
Minor only	334	37·7%	385	14·0%	314	12·4%
Criminal	164	48·8%	180	21·7%	100	21·0%

to indictable offences in Great Britain. There was evidence of selective placement of the adoptees in that the social class of the biological and adoptive fathers was significantly associated, but the biological children of criminal fathers were not more often placed with criminal adoptive fathers than would be expected by chance.

Table 2.5 shows that the presence or absence of offences among the adoptees was related to the criminal record of the father in all three groups. The association between criminal offspring and criminal adoptive father points to the influence of environmental factors and that between criminal biological father and criminal adoptee to hereditary factors. A remarkably large number of children placed for adoption had criminal fathers. It is also surprising that so many adoptive fathers had a criminal record. The rule which was generally applied by the adoption agencies at that time was that persons adopting children should have been free from a criminal record for 5 years. The sample was large enough to apply a cross-fostering design, as in the two middle rows of Table 2.6. This suggests that the hereditary effect may be more important than the environmental effect in this study. The highest rate of criminality was observed when both adoptive and biological fathers had a criminal record.

Hutchings went on to make a more detailed study of the 143 criminal adoptees with identifiable biological fathers born 1890 onwards, comparing them with the same number of control adoptees not known to the police. They were matched for age and for adoptive father's occupation. Median age of transfer to the adoptive home (6–7 months) did not differ between the groups, indicating that age at placement was not of vital importance in relation to subsequent criminality among adoptees. Once again the findings

Table 2.6   Criminality of adoptees, including results of a crossfostering experiment (data of Hutchings 1972)

	No. of adoptees	Percent criminal
Neither father known to police	333	10·4%
Adoptive father criminal, biological father not known to police	52	11·2%
Biological father criminal, adoptive father not known to police	219	21·0%
Adoptive and biological fathers both criminal	58	36·2%

Table 2.7   Fathers of criminal and noncriminal adoptees (data of Hutchings 1972)

	No. of criminal fathers			
	Biological		Adoptive	
143 criminal adoptees	70	49%	33	23%
143 control adoptees	40	28%	14	10%

demonstrated the influence of both genetic and environmental effects (Table 2.7).

Very little of the genetic effect could be explained by associations with mental illness in the families. Nor was there a correlation between pregnancy or birth complications of the probands and their subsequent criminality. Hutchings considers that genetically transmitted characteristics of the autonomic nervous system could to a certain extent explain the inheritance of criminal behaviour, placing certain individuals at greater risk of succumbing to crime.

Crowe (1972; 1974) studied the children of female offenders from Iowa who had given up their babies for adoption. By the age of 25 there were significantly more arrests and criminal convictions among these offspring than in a control group. Personal follow-up investigation showed that 6 of the index group of 46 offspring (13 per cent) had 'definite antisocial personality', compared with none of the control adoptees; diagnosis was made blind. In 5 of the 6 antisocial cases the biological father as well as the biological mother had a criminal record. Environmental circumstances such as age at adoption, broken home and psychiatric abnormality in the adoptive parents did not differ significantly between the index and control groups. However, it was interesting that the antisocial index adoptees differed from those index adoptees who were not antisocial in certain unfavourable conditions. Notable among these was the length of time spent in temporary care such as orphanages before final adoption. Although the control group had been equally exposed to the same conditions, they did not develop a high rate of disorder. The findings seemed to point to the importance of interaction between genetic endowment and environmental factors in the development of antisocial personality.

Adoption study of psychopathy

Also employing the register of Copenhagen nonfamilial adoptions, Schulsinger (1972) made a genetic-environmental investigation of psychopathy—or at least of the kind of psychopathy to come to psychiatric attention. As in Kety and Rosenthal's (1968) study of schizophrenia in which Schulsinger took part, the Danish register of psychiatric admissions was used to locate cases of abnormality. Psychopathy was defined as inappropriate, nonpsychotic, impulse-ridden or acting-out behaviour, persisting after the age of 19. Diagnostic agreement between three raters was 82 per cent. 57 index cases of psychopathic adoptees were found, 40 of them males, mean age 36. These were matched with 57 adoptees, similar in sex, age at first placement, number of early environmental shifts and social class of adopting family. Then the incidence of mental disorder in the adoptive and biological relatives of each group was examined blindly. The relatives included were parents, full sibs and half-sibs. Cases of doubtful psychopathy, criminality, alcoholism and hysterical character, along with psychopathy proper, were termed psychopathic spectrum disorders.

If the family environment is of major importance for this kind of psychopathy when it occurs in the usual family setting, there should be more psychopathy and other disorders among the adoptive relatives of psychopaths than in any other group, but this was not found, as can be seen by comparing the second column of Table 2.8 with the others. If the genes play a part in the transmission there should be an excess of psychopathy among the biological relatives of the index cases, and this is in fact the most heavily loaded

of the four groups. The contrast shows up most when the diagnosis is specified. The clearest comparison for psychopathy is that which considers the
fathers only. Of the biological fathers 9 per cent were psychopathic, a much
higher rate than in any of the other groups. The influence of environmental
factors was not so readily seen in Schulsinger's study of psychopaths as in
Hutchings' study of criminals or in the twin study by Slater and Shields
(1969) of personality disorder in adults. The latter study from the Maudsley
Hospital found that in only 55 per cent of 33 MZ pairs in this group did
both twins merit a psychiatric diagnosis.

Table 2.8 An adoption study of psychopathy (data of Schulsinger 1972)

Mental disorder in relatives	57 Psychopathic adoptees				57 Control adoptees			
	Biological relatives (n = 305)		Adoptive relatives (n = 131)		Biological relatives (n = 285)		Adoptive relatives (n = 133)	
Any mental disorder	58	19·0%	18	13·7%	37	13·0%	16	12·0%
Psychopathic spectrum disorder	44	14·4%	10	7·6%	19	6·7%	7	5·3%
Psychopathy, strict	12	3·9%	1	0·8%	4	1·4%	2	1·5%
Psychopathy, fathers only	5/54	9·3%	1/54	1·9%	1/56	1·8%	0/57	0·0%

Other adoption studies

By way of contrast a recent study by Bohman (1970; 1972) failed to show
any clearcut effects of heredity or environment. This was a study of all 168
children adopted early through a Stockholm adoption society and followed
up to the age of 10–11 only. The adoptees had more conflict with their peers
than did a group of control children. 38 biological fathers were registered
as abusers of alcohol and 40 were on the Swedish criminal register, both rates
being higher than would be expected. However, the children of these abusers
of alcohol and criminals did not contribute more than their share to the adoptees with school adjustment problems. Of course, the children are not yet
in the risk period of alcoholism or criminality and it is also possible that the
carefully selected adoptive homes may have protected them from manifesting
behaviour disorders to which they might be predisposed.* Turning to the
adoptive homes, the education of the adoptive parents was not correlated with
the children's school performance, nor did adoptive mothers treated for
mental illness have more than their share of maladjusted children. In other

---

* At the older median age of 17 Cunningham *et al* (1975) found more psychiatrically
disturbed children (particularly hyperkinetic males) in the adopted-away offspring of
59 psychiatrically disturbed biological parents than in 54 control adoptees.

words adjustment of the children was relatively independent of the biological and environmental variables investigated. Bohman considered that some of the behavioural disturbances of the children may have been connected with the adoptive situation itself, a topic which is discussed by Hersov in Chapter 6.

In his studies of children offered for adoption at birth, Bohman (1971) went on to investigate those who had been fostered, not adopted—a less favourably selected group than the adoptees. He now found an association between poor adjustment of the foster child and registration of the biological father as criminal or alcoholic, but this applied to girls only and not to boys. He did not consider his findings could be explained by negative expectations of foster parents knowing the history of the biological father, since this should have affected the boys. Nor were they accounted for by those children who were later returned to their own fathers. Rutter (1970) has also discussed the apparently more 'genetic' causes of resemblance between children and their mentally ill parents in the case of girls than boys. If we accept the view that boys are more susceptible than girls to psychological as well as biological stresses, it follows that it will take more to cause disorder in a girl than a boy. Cowie *et al* (1968) found this applied to the environments of delinquent girls. The same reasoning should apply to possible genetic factors and so might explain why Bohman was able to detect an association between disorders in the biological fathers and adjustment of the girl foster children but not the boys.

An earlier adoption study on alcoholism (Roe 1944; Roe *et al* 1945) was of interest because it suggested that a favourable foster home environment could have a protective effect. None of the 36 children of alcoholic parentage was known to be alcoholic at a mean age of 31, and only 3 used alcohol regularly; unfortunately there was no information about drinking habits in 7 cases. On the other hand, 10 of the children of alcoholics had been in 'serious trouble' during adolescence, compared with only 2 in the control group of 25 children of normal parentage; but the findings are difficult to interpret, since the mean age of placement of the children in the alcoholic group ($5\frac{1}{2}$ years) was significantly later than that of the control group.

A recent study of alcoholism by Goodwin *et al* (1973; 1974) indicated the influence of genetic factors. Using the Danish registers once again they studied the sons of alcoholics placed early for nonfamilial adoption and found a higher prevalence of alcohol problems and divorces than in a control group of adoptees. The incidence of alcoholism (about 20 per cent) in the adopted sons was no less than that found in the sons of the same alcoholic parents who had not been adopted.

Summary of conclusions of twin and adoption studies

What can be concluded from the twin and adoption studies of child behaviour disorder, adult criminality and psychopathy which we have described? Twin studies gave evidence of genetic influences on intelligence, personality and the kind of disorder an individual is likely to develop in response to stress. However, in the case of most juvenile delinquency the genes seem to make little difference. Only in the case of some antisocial behaviour developing on the basis of a personality disorder did the genetic constitution appear to play a major if indirect part. Classical twin studies have been criticised on the grounds that MZ pairs have a more similar environment than DZ pairs and this might account for the MZ : DZ differences. However, studies of MZ twins reared apart and not sharing a similar microenvironment show that this criticism is without force.

Robins' follow-up study of St. Louis child-guidance patients of the 1920s was consistent with the involvement of genetic factors in what she called 'sociopathic personality' in males, but it could not provide a critical test of the hypothesis. However, the nonfamilial adoption studies of Schulsinger on psychopathy and Hutchings on criminality support the hypothesis, as does the work of Goodwin *et al* on alcoholism, and Crowe on the children of female offenders. The fact that criminals and alcoholics are not necessarily sociopaths or psychopaths or genetic deviants makes the findings all the more remarkable.

Bohman's adopted or fostered subjects are too young to be of much relevance to the sociopathy issue. Only in the case of fostered girls was there a positive association between criminal or alcoholic biological fathers and maladjustment in the child. Bohman's study, like that of Seglow *et al* (1972), suggests that children adopted into homes which are above average socioeconomically or otherwise favourable can be protected from behaviour disturbances to which they might otherwise have been liable, had they been brought up by criminal fathers or unmarried mothers. Since some children in Copenhagen between the wars were adopted by fathers with a criminal record, Hutchings was able to show the influence of such a history on the police record of the child.

Clearly the hypothesis of genetic influences on sociopathy cannot be dismissed, even though it needs to be refined. Tasks ahead are to try to identify the constitutional bases on which it may develop; to find means of distinguishing the situational juvenile delinquent or child guidance patient from those at risk of developing a chronic personality disorder; and to discover the best means of protecting them from such a development.

FAMILY STUDIES OF SPECIFIC DISORDERS

Studies of the parents of disturbed children (e.g. Wolff & Acton 1968) characteristically report a raised prevalence of psychiatric illness and personality disorder in mothers and of sociopathic personalities in fathers. The fact that an environmental contribution can be shown (e.g. Rutter 1966) does not rule out the possibility of a genetic contribution as well, though as already noted this is difficult to prove from family studies alone, especially when symptoms consist mainly of social deviance.

Studies of the parents and sibs of patients with more specific disorders may be more suggestive of genetic influences beyond those that affect temperament and general intelligence. Genetic studies can make a contribution to psychiatric nosology. For instance, Kolvin *et al* (1971) confirmed from family data that infantile autism and other childhood psychoses with onset before age 3 are aetiologically distinct from those with later onset. Schizophrenic-like childhood psychosis with onset after age 5, though rare, seemed to be closely related to adult schizophrenia. As in other studies no excess of schizophrenia was found among the parents of infantile psychotics, whereas 9·4 per cent of the parents of the later onset children were schizophrenic. There are reasons for believing that genetic factors, possibly polygenic, make an important, specific contribution to the aetiology of schizophrenia (Gottesman & Shields 1972).

The most thorough genetic family studies of specific childhood syndromes are those of dyslexia and enuresis by Hallgren and of stammering by Kay, and from these it would appear that there is some evidence for genetic factors in several cases of these aetiologically complex disorders.

Dyslexia

Hallgren (1950) carried out a systematic study of specific dyslexia involving extensive personal investigation of 116 probands and their parents and sibs. The dyslexic probands came from the Stockholm Child Guidance Clinic and from a secondary school where the mean IQ was above average. As many as 10 per cent of consecutive admissions to the school were regarded as dyslexic. Of the probands 80 per cent were found to have a dyslexic parent and within this group about half the probands' sibs were also similarly affected. Hallgren considered that a dominant gene was involved in this group and that the remaining 20 per cent was heterogeneous. There was less dyslexia in the relatives of the school probands than in those of the clinic probands, but the rate was still considerably raised. Irrespective of whether a parent was dyslexic, prevalence in sibs was 46·6 per cent in the clinic group and

31·7 per cent in the school group. Dyslexics more often had other problems than nondyslexics, but there was not thought to be any excess of mental disorders among their parents.

As summarised by Hermann (1956), all 11 MZ twin pairs studied so far were concordant for dyslexia, while 9 out of 27 DZ pairs were concordant. Recently Bakwin (1973) reported a 14 per cent prevalence of reading disability, as defined by him, in his middle-class New York twin sample. 52 of the 57 backward readers in the MZ pairs had an affected cotwin (91 per cent) compared with 18 of the 40 DZ cases (45 per cent). The MZ concordance rate was 6·5 times the prevalence, the DZ rate 3·1 times (Shields 1975). One cannot generalise about the extent of genetic influence in behaviour disorder from Bakwin's restricted sample, but his reading retardation findings suggest that in some families a specific gene may be a major contributing factor in this multifactorially determined disorder. Further studies in other settings, using recent methods of assessment, would be worthwhile.

Enuresis

In 1957 Hallgren reported his equally thorough investigation of the relatives of 229 enuretic probands from the psychiatric departments of two Swedish children's hospitals. Nocturnal enuresis occurred in about 30 per cent of fathers and brothers as against an expected 12 per cent and in about 18 per cent of mothers and sisters as against an expected 8 per cent. Unfavourable background factors such as broken homes and maternal psychiatric illness were significantly high in children with diurnal enuresis. While some cases were nongenetic, Hallgren thought there was a large nuclear genetic group of primary nocturnal enuresis. He could claim nothing certain about mode of inheritance. There was less to be said in favour of a single gene than in the case of his dyslexia study and more in favour of polygenic inheritance.

A familial basis of enuresis was confirmed in a recent survey of an unselected (nonhospital) sample from Newcastle (Kolvin *et al* 1972). 132 enuretics were found among 2472 children aged 8–10. In over 60 per cent of the 94 cases studied in detail there was a positive family history and 44 had one or more affected sibs. There was no association with personality. This was interpreted as supporting the developmental delay theory, according to which enuresis is related to a structural or neurophysiological immaturity subserving bladder control, which can be exaggerated by errors of learning and emotional factors.

Stuttering

In another population survey of Newcastle children (Andrews & Harris 1964) 78 stutterers were found. Stuttering had occurred in approximately 4 per cent of the boys and 2 per cent of the girls. Kay (1964) made a genetic analysis of this material and a further 132 clinic cases. In the combined data about 20 per cent of the parents and sibs had stuttered—rather more in the case of the presumably more severe clinic material than in the survey material. Only 4·7 per cent of second degree relatives were affected. Most stutterers had not been in contact with another stutterer, and it was difficult to account for the findings by nongenetic factors alone.

Table 2.9   Stuttering according to sex of proband and relative (after Kay 1964)

	Stutterers (percent and standard error)	*Ratio to risk in same sex in general population*
Female relatives of 175 male probands	6·3 ± 1·4	3·2
Male relatives of 175 male probands	18·2 ± 2·2	4·6
Female relatives of 38 female probands	12·9 ± 4·3	6·5
Male relatives of 38 female probands	27·5 ± 5·7	6·9

The risk of stuttering in sibs of probands was related to the type of parental mating: about 67 per cent when both parents had stuttered, 40 per cent with one parent affected, and 10 per cent with neither parent affected. The sex difference in the population was thought to be due to the relative physiological immaturity of the male child. It was of interest not only that male relatives were more often affected than female as one would expect from the sex incidence, but also that the relatives of female cases were more often affected than the relatives of male cases (Table 2.9). This is what one would expect according to a polygenic model of inheritance. As the less predisposed sex, affected females will in general require more of the relevant genes than affected males, and hence their relatives will have more such genes. Stuttering meets the criteria of polygenic inheritance (Carter 1969). However, as is often the case, the theory of a dominant gene plus polygenes and environment could also fit the data.

CONCLUSIONS

Our discussion of some of the relevant twin, adoption and family studies has shown that genetic factors contribute to the aetiology of childhood psychiatric disorders. The extent and nature of the genetic contribution require confirmation and elucidation in further studies. It is clear that it is not the disorders as such that are inherited but a predisposition to some of them. Problems of particular interest are the degree of generality or specificity of the genetic factors, the aetiological heterogeneity of syndromes and the stage in development at which genetic influences exert their most distinctive effect. The more successfully high risk subjects can be identified, the better the chances of understanding the pathogenesis of a disorder and of developing appropriate environmental measures to prevent or ameliorate it. One man's meat may be another man's poison, as is quite literally the case in phenylketonuria.

It would be rash to predict at what stages in the pathway from genes to behaviour new developments will be most promising for elucidating genetic-environmental interactions. The extent of the influence on behaviour of variation in chromosome morphology remains uncertain. In some conditions identifiable genetic enzyme polymorphisms may eventually be found to play a minor role—or a major one if some monogenic theories are correct. Advances in the fields of psychopharmacology and pharmacogenetics may prove promising, as may developments in clinical and genetic EEG studies (Young *et al* 1972) and in psychophysiology. However, for the bulk of childhood behaviour disorder we may have to be satisfied for some time with such deductions as can be made from well-designed family and epidemiological studies with improved clinical and psychometric measures of personality dimensions and disorders.

It is a misconception to think that an interest in genetics implies a racialist, reactionary or fatalistic attitude or denies the importance of environment. The influences of genetics and environment are complementary, not contradictory. Continued scientific attention to behaviour genetics in a developmental context focusses attention on the individual and 'offers our best hope of eliminating misunderstandings about the nature of human differences' (Behaviour Genetics Association 1973).

REFERENCES

ANDREWS G. & HARRIS M. (eds.) (1964) *The Syndrome of Stuttering*, Clinics in Developmental Medicine, No. 17. London: Heinemann

BAKWIN H. (1970) Sleep-walking in twins. *Lancet* ii, 446–447

BAKWIN H. (1971a) Enuresis in twins. *Amer. J. Dis. Child.* 121, 222–225

BAKWIN H. (1971b) Nail-biting in twins. *Dev. Med. Child Neurol.* 13, 304–307

BAKWIN H. (1971c) Persistent finger-sucking in twins. *Dev. Med. Child Neurol.* 13, 308–309

BAKWIN H. (1971d) Car-sickness in twins. *Dev. Med. Child Neurol.* **13,** 310–312

BAKWIN H. (1973) Reading disability in twins. *Dev. Med. Child Neurol.* **15,** 184–187

BAKWIN H. & DAVIDSON M. (1971) Constipation in twins. *Amer. J. Dis. Child.* **121,** 179–181

BEHAVIOR GENETICS ASSOCIATION (1973) Statement by Executive Committee.

BOHMAN M. (1970) *Adopted Children and their Families.* Stockholm: Proprius

BOHMAN M. (1971) A comparative study of adopted children, foster children and children in their biological environment born after undesired pregnancies. *Acta Paediatr. Scand.* Supplement 221

BOHMAN M. (1972) A study of adopted children, their background, environment and adjustment. *Acta Paediatr. Scand.* **61,** 90–97

BROADHURST P.L. (1968) Experimental approaches to the evolution of behaviour. *In* Thoday J.M. & Parkes A.S. (eds.) *Genetic and Environmental Influences on Behaviour,* Edinburgh: Oliver & Boyd

BURT C. (1966) The genetic determination of differences in intelligence: a study of monozygotic twins reared together and apart. *Brit. J. Psychol.* **57,** 137–153

CARTER C.O. (1969) Genetics of common disorders. *Brit. Med. Bull.* **25,** 52–57

CHRISTIANSEN K.O. (1970) Crime in a Danish twin population. *Acta Genet. Med. Gemellol.* **19,** 323–326

CLARIDGE G., CANTER S. & HUME W.I. (1973) *Personality Differences and Biological Variations: a Study of Twins.* Oxford: Pergamon

COWIE J., COWIE V. & SLATER E. (1968) *Delinquency in Girls.* London: Heinemann

CROWE R.R. (1972) The adopted offspring of women criminal offenders. *Arch. Gen. Psychiat.* **27,** 600–603

CROWE R.R. (1974) An adoption study of antisocial personality. *Arch Gen. Psychiat.* **31,** 785–791

CUNNINGHAM L., CADORET R.J., LOFTUS R. & EDWARDS J.E. (1975) Studies of adoptees from psychiatrically disturbed biological parents: psychiatric conditions in childhood and adolescence. *Brit. J. Psychiat.* **126,** 534–549

ERLENMEYER-KIMLING L. & JARVIK L.F. (1963) Genetics and intelligence: a review. *Science* **142,** 1477–1479

FREEDMAN D.G. (1965) An ethological approach to the genetical study of human behavior, *In* Vandenberg S.G. (ed.) *Methods and Goals in Human Behavior Genetics.* New York: Academic Press

GOODWIN D.W., SCHULSINGER F., HERMANSEN L., GUZE S.B. & WINOKUR G. (1973) Alcohol problems in adoptees raised apart from alcoholic biological parents. *Arch. Gen. Psychiat.* **28,** 238–243

GOODWIN D.W., SCHULSINGER F., MØLLER N., HERMANSEN L., WINOKUR G. & GUZE S.B. (1974) Drinking problems in adopted and nonadopted sons of alcoholics. *Arch. Gen. Psychiat.* **31,** 164–169

GOTTESMAN I.I. (1966) Genetic variance in adaptive personality traits. *J. Child Psychol. Psychiat.* **7,** 199–208

GOTTESMAN I.I. & SHIELDS J. (1972) *Schizophrenia and Genetics: a Twin Study Vantage Point.* New York: Academic Press

HALLGREN B. (1950) Specific dyslexia ('congenital word-blindness'): a clinical and genetic study. *Acta Psychiat. Neurol. Scand.* Supplement 65

HALLGREN B. (1957) Enuresis, a clinical and genetic study. *Acta Psychiat. Neurol. Scand.* Supplement 114

HARRIS H. (1970) *The Principles of Human Biochemical Genetics*. Amsterdam: North-Holland

HAYASHI S. (1967) A study of juvenile delinquency in twins. *In* Mitsuda H. (ed.) *Clinical Genetics in Psychiatry*, Tokyo: Igaku Shoin

HERMANN K. (1956) Congenital word-blindness. *Acta Psychiat. Neurol. Scand.* Supplement **108**, 177–184

HESTON L.L., DENNEY D.D. & PAULY I.B. (1966) The adult adjustment of persons institutionalized as children. *Brit. J. Psychiat.* **112**, 1103–1110

HUTCHINGS B. (1972) Environmental and genetic factors in psychopathology and criminality. Unpublished MPhil Thesis, University of London

HUTCHINGS B. & MEDNICK S.A. (1974) Registered criminality in the adoptive and biological parents of registered male adoptees. *In* Mednick S.A. *et al* (eds.) *Genetics, Environment and Psychopathology*, Amsterdam: North-Holland

JENSEN A.R. (1972) *Genetics and Education*. London: Methuen

JINKS J.L. & FULKER D.W. (1970) A comparison of the biometrical genetical, MAVA and classical approaches to the analysis of human behavior. *Psychol. Bull.* **73**, 311–349

JUEL-NIELSEN N. (1965) Individual and environment. A psychiatric–psychological investigation of monozygotic twins reared apart. *Acta Psychiat. Scand.* Supplement 183

KAY D.W.K. (1964) The genetics of stuttering, *In* Andrews G. & Harris M. (eds.) *The Syndrome of Stuttering*, Clinics in Developmental Medicine, No. 17. London: Heinemann

KETY S.S., ROSENTHAL D., WENDER P.H. & SCHULSINGER F. (1968) The types and prevalence of mental illness in the biological and adoptive families of adopted schizophrenics, *In* Rosenthal D. & Kety S.S. (eds.) *The Transmission of Schizophrenia*. Oxford: Pergamon

KOLVIN I., OUNSTED C., RICHARDSON L.M. & GARSIDE R.F. (1971) Studies in the childhood psychoses: III. The family and social background in childhood psychoses. *Brit. J. Psychiat.* **118**, 396–402

KOLVIN I., TAUNCH J., CURRAH J., GARSIDE R.F., NOLAN J. & SHAW W.B. (1972) Enuresis: a descriptive analysis and a controlled trial. *Dev. Med. Child Neurol.* **14**, 715–726

LANGE J. (1929) *Verbrechen als Schicksal, Studien an kriminellen Zwillingen*. Leipzig: Thieme

LINDZEY G., LOEHLIN J., MANOSEVITZ M. & THIESSEN D. (1971) Behavioral genetics, *In* Mussen P.H. & Rosenzweig M.R. (eds.) *Annual Review of Psychology*, Vol. 22, California, Annual Reviews Inc.

MITTLER P. (1971) *The Study of Twins*. Penguin Science of Behaviour. London: Penguin

NEWMAN H.H., FREEMAN F.N. & HOLZINGER K.J. (1937) *Twins: a Study of Heredity and Environment*. Chicago: University of Chicago Press

OWEN D.R. & SINES J.O. (1970) Heritability of personality in children. *Behav. Genet.* **1**, 235–247

PARKER N. (1964) Close identification in twins discordant for obsessional neurosis. *Brit. J. Psychiat.* **110**, 496–504

ROBINS L.N. (1966) *Deviant Children Grown Up*. Baltimore: Williams & Wilkins

ROE A. (1944) The adult adjustment of children of alcoholic parents raised in foster-homes. *Quart. J. Studies Alcohol* **5**, 378–393

ROE A., BURKS B. & MITTELMANN B. (1945) Adult adjustment of foster-children of alcoholic and psychotic parentage and the influence of the foster-home. Memoirs of the Section of Alcohol Studies, Yale University, No. 3, *Quart. J. Studies Alcohol*, New Haven

ROSANOFF A.J., HANDY L.M. & PLESSET I.R. (1941) The etiology of child behavior difficulties, juvenile delinquency and adult criminality with special reference to their occurrence in twins. *Psychiat. Monogr. (California)* No. 1, Sacramento, Department of Institutions

ROSENTHAL D. (1970) *Genetic Theory and Abnormal Behavior*. New York: McGraw-Hill

RUTTER M. (1966) *Children of Sick Parents: An Environmental and Psychiatric Study*. Institute of Psychiatry, Maudsley Monographs No. 16. London: Oxford University Press

RUTTER M. (1970) Sex differences in children's responses to family stress, *In* Anthony E.J. & Koupernik C. (eds.) *The Child in his Family*, New York: Wiley-Interscience

RUTTER M., KORN S. & BIRCH H.G. (1963) Genetic and environmental factors in the development of 'primary reaction patterns'. *Brit. J. Soc. Clin. Psychol.* **2**, 161–173

SCARR S. (1968) Environmental bias in twin studies. *In* Vandenberg S.G. (ed.) *Progress in Human Behavior Genetics*. Baltimore: Johns Hopkins Press

SCARR S. (1969) Social introversion–extraversion as a heritable response. *Child Devel.* **40**, 823–832

SCHULSINGER F. (1972) Psychopathy: heredity and environment. *Internat. J. Ment. Health* **1**, Nos. 1–2, 190–206

SEGLOW J., PRINGLE M.L. KELLMER & WEDGE P. (1972) *Growing up Adopted*. Windsor: NFER

SHIELDS J. (1954) Personality differences and neurotic traits in normal twin school-children. *Eugenics Rev.* **45**, 213–246

SHIELDS J. (1962) *Monozygotic Twins Brought up Apart and Brought up Together*. London: Oxford University Press

SHIELDS J. (1973) Heredity and psychological abnormality. *In* Eysenck H.J. (ed.) *Handbook of Abnormal Psychology*, 2nd edn., London: Pitman Medical

SHIELDS J. (1975) Some recent developments in psychiatric genetics. *Arch. Psychiat. Nerv.* **220**, 347–360

SLATER E. (1953) (with the assistance of Shields J.) *Psychotic and Neurotic Illnesses in Twins*. Medical Research Council special Report Series, No. 278, London

SLATER E. (1961) The thirty-fifth Maudsley lecture: 'Hysteria 311'. *J. Ment. Sci.* **107**, 359–381

SLATER E. & COWIE V.A. (1971) *The Genetics of Mental Disorders*. London: Oxford University Press

SLATER E. & SHIELDS J. (1969) Genetical aspects of anxiety. *In* Lader M.H. (ed.) *Studies of Anxiety*, British Journal of Psychiatry Special Publication No. 3, Ashford, Kent, Headley

VANDENBERG S.G. (1967) Hereditary factors in normal personality traits (as measured by inventories). *In* Wortis J. (ed.) *Recent Advances in Biological Psychiatry*, vol. 9, New York: Plenum Press

VANDENBERG S.G. (1968) Primary mental abilities or general intelligence? Evidence from twin studies. *In* Thoday J.M. & Parkes A.S. (eds.) *Genetic and Environmental Influences on Behaviour*, Edinburgh: Oliver & Boyd

WOLFF S. & ACTON W.P. (1968) Characteristics of parents of disturbed children. *Brit. J. Psychiat.* **114**, 593–601

YOUNG J.P.R., LADER M.H. & FENTON G.W. (1972) A twin study of the genetic influences on the electroencephalogram. *J. Med. Genet.* **9**, 13–16

CHAPTER 3

Separation, loss and family relationships

M. RUTTER

Bowlby (1975) and others have argued that separation experiences play a crucial role in the genesis of anxiety and hence in the development of a broad range of psychiatric disorders occurring in childhood. Indeed, it was once claimed that prolonged separation experiences were the foremost cause of delinquency (Bowlby 1951), and even short separations were regarded with such alarm that in 1951 the WHO advised that the use of day nurseries and crèches inevitably caused permanent psychological damage. Subsequent research has shown that these early views were exaggerated and unnecessarily pessimistic (Rutter 1971; 1972). Nevertheless it has been found that certain sorts of separation experiences constitute important causes of short-term distress, and that in some circumstances, they also play a part in the development of more prolonged psychiatric disorders in later childhood and adolescence (see below). Accordingly, it is important to know what is special about the separations which cause distress and disorder and what differentiates them from those which do not cause harm and which may indeed even be happy and positive experiences. To answer these questions it is first necessary to consider some of the relevant evidence on children's early social and emotional development.

EARLY SOCIAL AND EMOTIONAL DEVELOPMENT

During the early months of life infants do not usually show any fear of strange persons or strange situations (Bronson 1968; 1972; Schaffer 1971a; Schaffer & Parry 1969; 1970), although they are distressed by rapidly approaching objects that loom on them (Bower et al 1970). About 6 to 8 months of age most infants are beginning to show a consistent fear of strangers (Bronson 1972; Morgan & Ricciuti 1969; Scarr & Salapatek 1970; Schaffer & Parry 1969; 1970) and towards the end of the first year they tend to turn to their parents when confronted by strange persons or objects (Schaffer 1971a). It is also only about the time of their first birthday that infants show anticipatory

47

fear (Levy 1951). Strangeness, together with sudden noise and movement, continue to arouse fear up to age 2 or 3 years but thereafter these fears decline (Jersild & Holmes 1935). Experimental studies have also shown that 1 to 3 years is the age period when infants are most likely to show distress when their mother walks out leaving them in a strange room (Ainsworth & Wittig 1969; Bowlby 1975; Maccoby & Feldman 1972; Rheingold 1969). Older children are less likely to show distress and are comforted more rapidly when the mother returns.

Fear of the dark and of animals are at a peak about 2 to 5 years and are then gradually replaced by fears of imaginary dangers (ghosts and the like), with nightmares being most frequent at 4 to 6 years of age (Jersild 1954; Jersild & Holmes 1935). During the school years, children show much less fear of actual objects or experiences but fears of imaginary things or of possible events in the future remain important. During middle childhood they gradually become more aware of death and what it means and fears of illness and of dying rise in frequency (Jersild & Holmes 1935; Anthony 1940; Nagy 1948; Childers & Wimmer 1971). Social anxieties also increase during middle and later childhood. A fear of open or of closed spaces does not usually occur in marked degree until about the time of puberty (Marks 1969).

Somewhat parallel developments occur in social attachments (Bowlby 1969; Schaffer 1971b). During the first year of life an infant's smiling goes through four main phases (Ambrose 1961; Gewirtz 1965; Wolff 1963). First, spontaneous reflex smiling without social meaning is present in the first few weeks of life. About 5 to 6 weeks this is replaced by unselective social smiling which occurs in response to faces of any kind. Thirdly, about 3 or 4 months the social smiling becomes somewhat selective so that it is more easily elicited by familiar persons. Finally, from about 6 or 7 months there is differential social responsiveness so that whether the child smiles and how he smiles is very dependent on who he is with.

In the first few months after birth, infants tend to respond in much the same way to both familiar adults and strangers. However, some time about the age of 7 months the infant usually develops an attachment to a specific person. There is much individual variation in when this happens and the range extends from $3\frac{1}{2}$ to 15 months (Schaffer & Emerson 1964; Ainsworth 1967). The attachment is shown in many different ways such as a greeting response to the person concerned, distress when they go away, differential following of the person, use of the person as a haven of safety and reduction of fear in a strange environment when the person is present (Ainsworth 1967; Stayton *et al* 1973). These attachments or bonds develop in children reared in institutions as well as in ordinary families (Stevens 1975), although like social smiling (Ambrose 1961) they may be somewhat delayed in their appearance, particularly if the institution has provided meagre social interaction (Schaffer 1963). Moreover, if a toddler is separated from his parents and is looked after by someone else even for a period of 1 to 2 weeks, he tends to develop fresh attachments to the new caretaker (Robertson & Robertson 1971).

Much has still to be learned about the factors which influence this development of attachments, but it is clear that neither feeding nor caretaking are essential features. Moreover, attachments do not necessarily develop to the person who spends most time with the child. The intensity of interaction probably has more effect than the duration. Attachment tends to be strongest when someone plays with the child and gives him a lot of attention, especially if this is associated with responsiveness and sensitivity to the baby's signals (Ainsworth 1967; Ainsworth *et al* 1971; Schaffer & Emerson 1964; Stayton & Ainsworth 1973). Probably, sensitive responsiveness is the quality in any interaction most likely to foster attachment. A baby's tendency to seek attachments is increased by anxiety and fear as well as by illness and fatigue (Bowlby 1969; Maccoby & Masters 1970), and attachments are particularly likely to develop to the person who brings comfort at such times. The development of attachments also tends to be inhibited by a generally unstimulating environment (Schaffer 1963). Of course, the degree of attachment is likely to be influenced by characteristics of the child as well as of his environment (e.g. Freedman 1965). Children differ in this respect as in many others.

All studies have shown that most children develop multiple attachments. However, there is continuing controversy on whether these attachments all have the same meaning. Bowlby (1969) has suggested that there is an innate bias for a child to attach himself especially to *one* figure and that this main attachment differs in kind from attachments to other subsidiary figures. However, this statement involves two rather different propositions, one of which is supported by the evidence and one of which is not. The first proposition is that the several attachments are not of equal strength and are not freely interchangeable. This is supported by the findings from several studies which show there is a persisting hierarchy among attachments with some continuing to be stronger than others (Schaffer & Emerson 1964; Ainsworth 1967). Even in institutions children tend to have their 'favourite' adults to whom they will go in preference to others (Stevens 1975). The second proposition is that the first or main attachment differs in kind from all other subsidiary attachments. Most research findings suggest that this is *not* the case. The proposition may be tested in two rather different ways. First, it may be determined whether the function or effects of all attachments are similar in quality even though they differ in intensity. The evidence indicates that they are. Thus, young children protest or are distressed if the person to whom they are attached leaves them. This has been shown to be so for fathers as well as for mothers (Spelke *et al* 1973). Similarly, attachment is demonstrated by the reduction of anxiety in a strange situation when the person to whom attachment is shown is present. This has been demonstrated for sibs (Heinicke & Westheimer 1965) for peers (Kissel 1965; Schwarz 1972) and for adult caretakers in a nursery (Arsenian 1943) as well as for mothers. However, this does not occur with strangers. In addition, infants follow and seek closeness with fathers as well as with mothers, whereas they do not with strangers (Cohen & Campos 1974). Second, the proposition may be tested by determining if the difference in intensity of attachment between the person top of the hierarchy and the person second in the hierarchy is greater than that between the second and third persons. Stevens (1975) found that in most cases it was not, although in some children it was. Although the evidence is not decisive it may be concluded that multiple attachments tend to have rather similar functions but that there is a persisting hierarchy among attachments which differ markedly in intensity.

In the earlier studies of attachment there was an implicit assumption that attachment was a unitary concept. Subsequent work has confirmed that there are positive (but quite low) intercorrelations between most of the behaviours said to indicate attachment (Coates *et al* 1972a, and b; Maccoby & Feldman 1972; Masters & Wellman 1974). However, it has also become evident that not all attachment behaviours function in the same way (Rosenthal 1973; Stayton & Ainsworth 1973). Probably, at least two distinctions need to be made. First, there is the difference between attachment behaviour and persisting bonds. Infants show a general tendency to seek attachments and if familiar figures are absent they soon seek new attachments to other people (Robertson & Robertson 1971). However, the concept of bonding implies a *selective* attachment (Cohen 1974) which persists over time even during a period of no contact with the person with whom bonds exist (although of course the child's ability to maintain bonds during an absence is far less in infancy than it is in later childhood). The importance of this distinction was shown in the Harlow experiments with rhesus monkeys. Infants reared in social isolation clung to inanimate models (so-called 'cloth mothers') and rushed back to them when threatened or frightened, as by a blast of air (Harlow 1958; Harlow & Zimmermann 1959). The behaviour clearly indicates attachment. However, follow-up studies have indicated that these early attachments did *not* lead to normal social relationships in adult life, as peer or parent attachments usually do (Harlow & Harlow 1969). The difference between human attachment behaviour and bonding is shown by Tizard and Rees (1975) findings regarding institutional children. Four-year-old children reared in institutions showed *more* clinging and following behaviour than family-reared children but also they were *less* likely to show selective bonding or deep relationships.

The second distinction is between secure and insecure bonding (Stayton & Ainsworth 1973). One of the characteristics of bonding is that it enables children to feel secure and to explore in strange situations. The apparent 'purpose' of bonding is to give the child security of relationships in order to stop clinging and following, and in that sense to become detached. Thus, Stayton and Ainsworth (1973) found that the children of sensitive responsive mothers showed more positive greeting on reunion and more following behaviour (suggesting 'stronger' attachments than those showed by the children of insensitive unresponsive mothers), but *less* crying on separations (suggesting more 'secure' attachments). Similarly, Spelke *et al* (1973) found that infants who were *least* fearful with strangers (and hence most secure) had had the most interaction with their fathers. It is also relevant that Hinde and Spencer-Booth (1970) showed that infant rhesus monkeys who exhibited most distress after separation were those who had experienced most rejection from their mothers and for whom there was the most tension in the infant–mother relationship.

Further research is necessary to sort out the various dimensions of attachment and bonding. However, it may be that bonding is best differentiated from attachment behaviour by the presence of *selectivity* in relationships which persist over time and place. The strength of bonding may be best determined by the degree of *reduction* of distress in a frightening situation when the bonded person is present. The security of bonding, on the other hand, may perhaps be assessed by the relative *lack* of distress following separation or the extent of moving away from the bonded person in a strange situation (obviously this measurement would have to control for strength for bonding as assessed above). If this formulation is correct, the implication is that attachment behaviour is strongest in toddlers but that bonding is most secure in older children. Furthermore, it implies that an institutional environment with a very large number of caretakers but an ample range of stimulating experiences will foster attachment behaviour but not bonding.

Acute distress reactions following separation experiences

Acute reactions to separation have been most studied with respect to children admitted to hospital or to a residential nursery (Vernon *et al* 1965; Yarrow 1964). There is good evidence that many (but not all) young children show an immediate reaction of acute distress and crying (the period of 'protest'), followed by misery and apathy (the phase of 'despair') and finally there may be a stage when the child becomes apparently contented and seems to lose interest in his parents ('detachment' in Robertson and Bowlby's terms). When the child returns to his parents he may ignore them at first or turn away and seem to reject them. Then for several weeks or even months he is 'difficult', bad-tempered and clinging. He follows his mother everywhere around the house, holding onto her skirts and appearing very reluctant to leave her even for a moment. At the same time he often seems angry and demanding and may hit out at his parents. In this situation the mother and father may become cross and fed-up with the child's tiresome behaviour and push him away or reprimand him. This usually results in a further increase in the child's clinging and demanding (see Rutter 1972 and Bowlby 1975 for references to research).

Although studies of children in hospital or a residential nursery are nearly always considered as examples of separations from mother, in fact of course they involve separations from mother *and* father *and* sibs *and* the home environment. A consideration of the factors which modify the distress shown in these circumstances helps clarify the mechanisms involved and also indicates ways of preventing acute distress reactions.

Systematic observations of children admitted to hospital have shown that emotional distress is most marked in children aged 6 months to 4 years, but even in this age group it is present in only some children. Distress does occur in some older children admitted to hospital but it tends to be less severe, less prolonged and it is present in a lower proportion of children. Under the age of about 6 months there is usually *no* distress associated with admissions to hospital. The observation that distress does not occur below the age when attachments first develop and that distress becomes less frequent at the age when attachment behaviour is waning suggests that the distress may be the result of an interference with attachment. This suggestion is supported by the evidence that the distress is much less if children are admitted to hospital with a parent (Fagin 1966; Vernon *et al* 1967). Distress following admission to hospital may also be reduced by daily visiting (Faust *et al* 1952; Illingworth & Holt 1955; Prugh *et al* 1953; Woodward & Jackson 1961). Unfortunately, it is not possible from these studies to determine how much reduction in distress was due to the visiting *per se* as the experimental programmes included many other improvements in hospital regime. It should be noted that daily visiting is often associated with tearfulness and distress immediately after the visiting but the benefits are shown in the reduced disturbance on return home. It seems that while in early childhood the presence of familiar family members may be most important in preventing distress following hospitalisation, in older children counselling and other ways of helping children cope with their worries about illness and hospital may also be important (see Wolff 1973).

The evidence that the distress is associated with some kind of interference with attachment behaviour leaves open the question whether the distress arises because separation disrupts an existing bond or because conditions during the separation fail to facilitate attachment behaviour. This has been examined by Robertson and Robertson (1971) who compared the results of short-term fostering (1–2 weeks) in a family setting and a residential nursery. In both settings the children showed some unhappiness and alteration in behaviour, suggesting that separation as such constitutes a stress. On the other hand, marked distress reactions were *only* found in the residential nursery children, suggesting that separation was *not* the most important variable. Unlike the residential nursery the family fostering provided a continuing intense personal interaction with the *same* individual over time which is likely to have fostered attachment. Also, however, the family took special steps to maintain the children's bonds with their parents (by keeping to familiar routines, retaining familiar toys and by talking about their parents) and it may be that in these circumstances the separation was less likely to disrupt bonds.

Animal studies have shown that infant monkeys show acute distress when their mothers are taken away, even if the infants remain in their usual environment (see Hinde & Davies 1972). Accordingly, distress may follow separation even if there is no change of place. On the other hand, the hospital studies have shown that frightening experiences and lack of play opportunities aggravate children's distress. Short-term experimental studies indicate that toddlers fuss and fret more if there is nothing to play with (Rheingold & Samuels 1969). However, one study (Gershaw & Schwarz 1971) showed that, on their own, toys do little to ameliorate distress following separation and a familiar toy is no better in this respect than a novel toy.

Young children with secure bonds and strong attachments react adversely to removal from their homes and families particularly if this involves impaired parental care. Such separations should therefore be regarded as stressful for normal children in the preschool age period. However, there is evidence which suggests that the effects are worse for children with *insecure* bonds or with poor family relationships. Mention has already been made of the finding that infant rhesus monkeys showed much more disturbance following separation if there had been maternal rejection and a tense mother–infant relationship before the separation (Hinde & Spencer-Booth 1970). A detailed analysis of the findings suggests that much of the postseparation distress is a direct consequence of interference with harmonious parent–infant relationships (Hinde & Davies 1972). The same studies also indicated that the mother's behaviour towards the clinging infant *after* reunion played an important role in the emotional disturbance. Human evidence is meagre but both short-term (Fagin 1966; Vernon *et al* 1965) and long-term (Quinton & Rutter

1976) studies suggest that emotional disturbance following hospital admission is more likely if the child has a poor relationship with his parents or comes from an unhappy unstable home. Of course, security is also likely to stem from previous happy separations which have taught the child that separations need not be equated with either stressful experiences or disrupted relationships. Thus, Stacey *et al* (1970) found that children who were undisturbed by hospital admission were more likely than distressed children to have had *more* brief 'normal' separation experiences such as staying overnight with friends or relatives, having baby-sitters, attending nursery school and being left all day with a familiar person.

Several lessons may be drawn from these findings although the evidence is still incomplete and often circumstantial. First, children's needs and susceptibilities differ according to their stage of development. Hospital admission is likely to be particularly stressful in children aged 6 months to 4 years and therefore, whenever possible, admissions should be avoided during that age period. Second, the quality of care during a separation will markedly influence children's reactions to it. Good care should include not only adequate toys and play opportunities, good physical facilities and warm responsive handling but also individualised personal interaction with a *small* number of familiar people who have a special responsibility for the child (see Wolff 1973 and Rutter 1975 for a fuller discussion of these points). The last is especially important with preschool children. With older children counselling and other attempts to help them understand their experiences may also be beneficial in preventing disturbance after hospital admission. Third, the stresses associated with separation or with a strange environment may be much reduced by maintaining contact with familiar family figures with whom the child has already developed bonds. In this connection the mother has a special importance with most young children, but relationships with other family members serve 'much the same role in varying degrees. Fourth, the child's ability to cope well with acute stressful separations is much influenced by the quality of his long-term family relationships and by the security of his emotional bonds. Insecure children from unhappy homes are probably specially at risk of suffering from stressful separations. Fifth, the reaction of the parents to the child's clinging and demanding behaviour on return home is probably an important influence in the continuation of the distress reaction. Parents need to be helped to understand the meaning of children's difficult behaviour after a stressful separation. Sixth, children need to learn to be physically detached from their families even though emotional bonds remain (Schaffer 1971b). It appears that at least two main features aid this detachment process; a secure relationship with a sensitive responsive parent and the experience of *graded* separations in happy circumstances. Infants are able to tolerate only brief separations whereas older children can maintain bonds over much longer periods. Parents need to *gradually* introduce their children to happy separations in which the child remains with a familiar adult during the time the parent is away. The length of the separation needs to be gauged both by the maturity of the child, the security of his relationships and the familiarity of the setting during the separation.

Long-term disorders following separation experiences

As already discussed, transient parent–child separation can lead to acute short-term distress. Can it also lead to long-term psychiatric problems? Certainly, many children remain anxious about separation for some months, and occasionally even years, after a single stressful separation experience. Furthermore, most studies have shown that children subjected to separation experiences in early childhood do have a slightly increased risk of later psychological disturbance (Ainsworth 1962). On the other hand, several independent investigations have shown that children can be separated from their parents for quite long periods in early childhood with surprisingly little in the way of long-term effects (Bowlby *et al* 1956; Naess 1959, 1962; Andry 1960; Douglas *et al* 1968). The question, then, is why do most separation experiences *not* lead to long-term problems and what is different about the minority that do? Rutter (1971) examined the latter point in a detailed study of the families of psychiatric patients with children of school age or younger. It was found that children separated from both parents came from more disturbed homes than did children who had never experienced separation. Many of the children were separated because they had been taken into care following some family crisis and often this occurs against a background of more long-standing family difficulties (Schaffer & Schaffer 1968; Wolkind & Rutter 1973).

Further analysis showed that a separation from both parents which had lasted at least 4 weeks was associated with antisocial disorder in boys. However, this association applied *only* in homes where there was a very poor marriage relationship between the parents. The finding suggested that the disorder might have arisen less from the separation as such and more from the discord and disturbance which surrounded the separation. This suggestion was supported by the further observation that whereas separations due to some kind of family disorder/or deviance were associated with antisocial disorder, those due to a physical illness or a holiday were not.

Studies of 10-year-old boys in the general population have shown that short-term admissions to a foster home or an institution are followed by a much increased risk of antisocial disorder (Wolkind & Rutter 1973). However, these short periods tend to be brief episodes in a long history of deleterious influences acting on the child. Children from unhappy homes are particularly prone to be damaged by stressful separations and the short experience of being 'in care' probably increases their risk of developing antisocial problems. However, the long exposure to family discord and to other disadvantageous living conditions is usually more important.

Douglas (1975) and Quinton and Rutter (1976) have made similar studies of the long-term effects of hospital admission. Both investigations showed *no* association between single admissions of less than a week and any kind of disorder in later childhood or adolescence. However, *multiple* admissions when the first admission had taken place during the preschool years, was associated with an increased risk of both psychiatric disorder and delinquency. Quinton and Rutter (1976) noted that children with multiple hospital admissions were much more likely than other children to come from disadvantaged homes. When this was taken into account repeated admissions to hospital were still associated with later psychiatric disorder but the association was most marked in children from deviant, discordant or disadvantaged families.

In summary, the findings show that *single* separation experiences at any age rarely have long-term sequelae. This observation is in keeping with the wider literature which shows that acute stresses usually have long-term consequences only if they are also associated with chronic stresses (Rutter 1972). On the other hand, *recurrent* hospital admission (and probably also other kinds of stressful separation) is associated with an increased risk of psychiatric disorder. The increased risk is sufficiently great to warrant the avoidance of admitting children to hospital unless really necessary, but multiple admissions account for only a small minority of disorders in childhood and adolescence. Of course, two admissions to hospital lasting in total only a few weeks amount to a negligible proportion of the child's life and it is necessary to consider how they might lead to long-term psychiatric problems. The crucial data are lacking but the answer may lie in the effects of short-term stress on long-term parent–child interaction. This is suggested by the observation that disorders are more likely to arise when the children come from unhappy or troubled homes (Quinton & Rutter 1976) and by the animal evidence that the distress following acute separations is in large part a function of disturbances in mother–infant interaction (Hinde & Spencer-Booth 1970; Hinde & Davies 1972). Hospital admission in early childhood often leads to clinging and 'difficult' behaviour which interferes with family relationships and it may also sensitise children in such a way that they may be more likely to react adversely next time they go to hospital, which in turn puts a further strain on the family when the child returns home. In this way, although the admissions last only a very short time the disturbed parent–child interaction may last much longer.

Other acute stresses

Much less is known about the effects of other acute stresses in childhood, although there is some slight evidence suggesting that they play a part in the genesis of emotional disturbance. Douglas (1973) found that a high number of stress events in the first 4 years were associated with an increased likelihood of later enuresis. Some of the stress events studied involved separations but stresses such as the birth of a younger sib and a move of home did not. Unfortunately, these other stresses were not looked at separately. Heisel *et al* (1973) also found that a high number of stresses were more common in children with psychiatric disorders and with certain physical disorders than in children from the general population. They, too, made no differentiation according to the type of event.

A small scale longitudinal study of London children (Moore 1975) showed that the birth of a younger sib led to difficulties in some 15 per cent of children. These were expressed in terms of 'problem' behaviour and a disturbed mother–child relationship at least as often as in hostility to the baby. Difficulties were most likely to follow the birth of a sib in children under the age of 3 years who had not experienced previous separations. It appears that loss of parental attention due to the competing needs of the new baby may be the crucial variable. If this proves to be so, and research into the mechanisms involved is much needed, the difficulties might be reduced by the mother and father taking steps to ensure that the new arrival did not result in a reduction of interest and interaction with the older child. It is possible, too, that giving the older child a role of responsibility with the baby may aid this process by enhancing the child's self-esteem and by reducing the sense of competition with the baby.

The same study showed that moving house led to disturbance in about a fifth of children. The relevant factors seemed to be change of routine (especially in children under 2 years), loss of familiar figures (friends and relatives) and familiar surroundings, and problems in the parents' adaptation to the move. Disturbances were observed to be most frequent in anxious children from families with insecure relationships and a generally unstable pattern of life. Again it seems that acute stresses are most likely to affect children who lack stable relationships and who already experience chronic stresses.

In adults there is good evidence that acute life stresses are associated with the onset of depression (Paykel *et al* 1969; Brown *et al* 1973a, b, 1975; Cooper & Sylph 1973; Jacobs *et al* 1974). The timing of these stresses, the much higher rate of stresses among depressed people than among well-matched control populations, the fact that the stresses studied were not brought about by the individual himself, and the confirmation of patient findings within general population samples all indicate that the stresses are of considerable causal importance. A variety of events may serve as stresses but those most strongly associated with depression seem to involve the experience of a threatened or actual loss (such as separation from spouse, life-threatening illness in someone close, migration of children or notice to quit), or an actual or perceived life failure/rejection for a job, rebuff by a loved one, or failure to obtain promotion. To date, these factors have not been studied in childhood but clinical experience suggests that they may well be important in the genesis of emotional disturbances during adolescence, and possibly also in earlier childhood. The matter requires study.

Bereavement

In adults, the death of a loved person is commonly followed by prolonged grief (Marris 1958). Bereavement is an important precipitant of depressive disorder and suicide, and the death of a spouse markedly increases the likelihood of death from natural causes in the surviving marriage partner (see Rutter & Madge 1976). It seems that mental disorder following bereavement is most likely when the bereaved person lacks support from his family group. Nevertheless, Rutter (1966) showed that there was a connection between bereavement and psychiatric disorder in children. Although only a small proportion of children attending psychiatric clinics have lost a parent by death, he found that the proportion was significantly greater than that in the general population. The association with psychiatric disorder is not as strong as when the child has lost a parent by divorce or separation (see below) but bereavement is followed by a significant, if small, increase in the risk of psychiatric disturbance. This risk appears to be greatest when the parent dies during the child's third or fourth year of life, and there is some suggestion that the risk is increased if the death involves the parent of the same sex as the child. This may be because the same-sexed parent has a special importance in the processes of indentification or because of a need for a model for appropriate sex-role behaviour in later childhood or adolescence. In this connection, it is relevant that most of the disorders in Rutter's study did not arise until well after the parent's death.

In young children, personal grief is generally not as marked and not as prolonged as it is in adults. Rutter found that some adolescents developed depression, or sometimes antisocial behaviour, as part of a grief reaction, but for most children the acute grief following bereavement was probably less important than the many adverse consequences for the family which stemmed from bereavement. Frequently the surviving parent became depressed or emotionally withdrawn, the family sometimes broke-up (with the child going into care or staying with relatives), often there was social and economic privations if the death involved loss of the main bread-winner in the family, and problems also stemmed from later parental remarriage and tensions with the arrival into the family of a step-parent. All these circumstances are likely to have secondary ill-effects on the children.

Broken homes and marital discord

Numerous studies have shown an association between a 'broken home' and an increased risk of delinquency and antisocial behaviour (Rutter 1971 and 1972). Interestingly, this association does not seem to apply to neurosis and emotional disorders to the same extent. In the past there has been the assumption that the main damage stemmed from the stress of family separation. However, a variety of research findings have now shown that this is not the case. Three separate investigations (Douglas *et al* 1968; Gibson 1969; Gregory 1965) have demonstrated that the risk of delinquency is *much* increased if the parents divorce or separate, but that the risk is only *slightly* raised if a parent dies. This suggests that it may be the family discord and disharmony rather than the break-up of the family as such, which leads to antisocial behaviour. To test that hypothesis, it is necessary to determine whether parental discord is associated with antisocial disorder in the children even when the home is *un*broken. This has been shown in several independent studies. For example, in the follow-up of the Cambridge–Somerville study, McCord and McCord (1959) found that boys from homes rated (from contemporaneous records) as quarrelsome and neglecting (but unbroken) were more likely to become delinquent than boys from cohesive unbroken homes or from broken homes. This finding has been confirmed by several recent studies with rather better and more systematic measures of family discord. Thus, West and Farrington (1973) found that delinquency was twice as common when there was marital disharmony or serious parental conflict as when family relationships were smoother. In a study of adult patients' families, Rutter (1971) showed a strong relationship between marital discord and antisocial behaviour in the children. Over the course of 5 years (during a prospective longitudinal study), 36 per cent of the children from discordant marriages showed persisting behavioural deviance at school compared with 7 per cent of those from nondiscordant marriages at the start of the study (Quinton, Rutter & Rowlands 1976). Similarly in general population studies of 10-year-old children in inner London and on the Isle of Wight (Rutter *et al* 1975) those from families with severe marital discord had both an increased rate of behavioural deviance at school and of psychiatric disorder as assessed from detailed parental interviews. Among Isle of Wight adolescents with a persistent psychiatric disorder, 30 per cent came from homes where the parents had a poor marriage relationship, compared with $6\frac{1}{2}$ per cent of control children without psychiatric disorder (Rutter *et al* 1976). Furthermore, Power *et al* (1974) found that among boys who had already made a Court appearance for delinquency, those from intact homes with severe and persistent family problems were more likely to become recidivist than those from either intact homes without serious problems or broken homes. In multiple problem families it seems that family discord is associated with an increased risk of child psychiatric disorder (Tonge *et al* 1975) but not of delinquency (Tonge *et al* 1975; Wilson 1974).

In short, antisocial disorders and delinquency tend to be commoner in unhappy unbroken homes than in harmonious but broken ones. It may be concluded that it is the ongoing disturbance in family relationships, rather than the family break-up as such, which does most of the damage. Of course it could be argued that family discord does not have a true environmental effect, but rather that the impaired relationships reflect genetically determined personality attributes. However, there is considerable circumstantial evidence against this suggestion (Rutter 1971; Rutter, Quinton & Yule 1977). First, genetic factors play only a small part in the pathogenesis of delinquency (see Chapter 2). Second, even within a group of parents with personality disorder there is still an association between marital discord and antisocial disorder in the children. Third, the association is strongest when the discord directly involves or impinges on the children. Fourth, children who experience severe family discord in early childhood are less likely to show later psychiatric disorder if they subsequently experience harmonious family relationships. It may be concluded that, although genetic factors doubtless play some part, marital discord also has an adverse environmental influence leading to antisocial disorder in the children.

Marital disharmony creates an important psychiatric and delinquent risk for the children in the family, but many children develop normally in spite of poor family relationships. Accordingly, it is necessary to determine which factors in a bad marital situation help protect the children (Rutter 1975). There have been only a few investigations which have tried to disentangle the threads in these circumstances, but the available evidence suggests some useful leads (Rutter 1971; Rutter, Quinton & Yule 1977; Rutter 1977). First, children may be harmed by either open hostility in the home or by a lack of warmth and positive affection. However, it seems that on the whole it is overt quarrelling and discord which are the most serious. Therefore, there is something to be gained by the parents trying to avoid their differences leading to arguments, fights and an atmosphere in the home, even if their relationship remains cool and strained. Second, the effect on the child is worse if he becomes embroiled in the parental disputes. If the marriage becomes very difficult or if the parents separate or divorce, it is very important to help both parents realise that whatever their differences, they remain mother and father to the child. Disputes over custody and access (Jonsson 1967) are likely to harm the child and denigration of the other parent will do the same. It is sometimes hard for parents to realise that the child will probably go on loving *both* of them even though the marriage has broken down irretrievably.

Third, the child is more likely to be damaged if the discord is prolonged over many years. Whereas this may seem self-evident, it means that the sooner marital disputes can be resolved, the better it will be for the child. Fourth, the ill-effects are not necessarily irreversible. Rutter and his colleagues (Rutter 1971; Rutter, Quinton & Yule 1977) found that if there was a change for the better in the family relationships, the outlook for the child's psychological development correspondingly improved. However, it remains uncertain how readily, how completely and how often the adverse effects of disturbed relationships in early childhood may be reversed. Fifth, the child is at a specially high risk if in addition to the marital discord one or both parents have a personality disorder of such severity as to cause a chronic handicap. This means, in effect, that where the parents have shown disordered behaviour and relationships throughout their adult life, as well as not making a successful marriage, the outlook for the child is particularly poor. Sixth, the effects of hostility and negative behaviour toward the child seem to be worse if these are also associated with parental anxiety, depression and other forms of emotional disturbance which impinges on the child. Finally, Rutter (1971) found that, to a considerable extent; a good relationship with one parent could make up for a bad relationship with the other or for gross marital discord. Whether or not this also means that a good relationship with someone outside the home (another relative, a teacher or a friend) may also exert some protective effect remains uncertain, but it certainly seems worthwhile striving to make sure that the child has at least one sound, lasting relationship he can rely on.

It is not known exactly which mechanisms are involved in the process by which family discord leads to child psychiatric disorder, but there is circumstantial evidence suggesting the probable operation of three main mechanisms. First, it seems that children need stable, warm, intimate family relationships, upon which to build their own social behaviour and relationships outside the home. Discord and quarrelling interfere with the development of such family relationships and insofar as they do, the child is likely to be harmed. The evidence in favour of the hypothesised mechanism is the finding (Rutter 1971) that a good relationship provides a protective effect in an otherwise hostile environment, and the variety of findings that children with insecure relationships are more vulnerable to stress (see above). Second, quarrelling provides a deviant model of interpersonal behaviour and insofar as the child follows this model his own behaviour may become disturbed. There is no direct evidence that this occurs but numerous studies have shown that children do tend to imitate aggressive models (Bandura 1969). Third, it might be supposed that where there is severe marital discord the child is likely to find it more difficult to learn how he is expected to behave. That is, that parents who are engaged in marital disputes are more likely than other parents to provide inconsistent discipline and child-rearing. Again, there is some evidence in support of this view (McCord & McCord 1959; West & Farrington 1973) but the critical comparisons which could determine the relative importance of these mechanisms have yet to be undertaken. Finally, when parents are in dispute, the child may have conflicting loyalties which give rise to strain and anxiety. Insofar as this is the case it would appear that part of the problem lies in the child's response to and perception of the family conflict as well as in the direct effects of the discord.

One-parent families

Children who are brought up in homes with one parent are more likely than other children to show psychiatric problems or be delinquent. However, it is much less certain how far the children's problems stem from the lack of a father or mother and how far from the many adverse factors that happen to be associated with the situation of only having one parent. These adverse factors concern both the circumstances which lead to being a solitary parent and also the circumstances which follow such a situation. The three main reasons for a child being reared in a one-parent home are illegitimacy, parental divorce or separation and parental death.

West and Farrington (1973) found that delinquency was twice as common in illegitimate boys as in the population as a whole. However, nearly half the illegitimate boys were living with two parents. The National Child Development Study (Crellin *et al* 1971) showed that 7-year-old illegitimate children were twice as likely as legitimate children to be maladjusted. But, interestingly, the illegitimate children living with two parents were, if anything, *more* likely than those with one parent to show problems. It seems clear that, while illegitimacy puts the child at risk, the additional factor of being reared in a one-parent family made little difference.

As already discussed, with homes broken by divorce or separation it is the discord and disharmony preceding the break which constitute the main stress factor. It remains uncertain how far parental remarriage helps or hinders the child's psychological development. Children may find the arrival of a step-parent stressful (Heilpern 1943; Podolsky 1955) and this can increase the risk of psychiatric problems (Langner & Michael 1963). Probably it is the quality of the step-parent–child relationship which is important rather than the number of parents in the home.

The circumstances following the loss of one parent are also very important. Thus, it has been found that single-parent households tend to have a much lower income than do two-parent homes (Hunt *et al* 1973). Furthermore, single parents tend to be less well educated and their homes are more likely to be overcrowded and to lack basic household amenities. This social privation may well be at least as important for the child's development as the lack of a parent.

Of course, there are specific issues associated with having only one parent (Rutter 1975). First, there is the effect on the remaining parent who will lack the emotional, social and material support usually provided by the spouse. When things go wrong, the single parent will have to look outside the immediate family for advice and help. Society too puts special pressures and stresses on the unmarried mother and on the separated parent. Second, the child is himself subject to the social discriminations associated with the lack of a parent. Third, the child lacks the opportunity of seeing how two adults live together in a close and harmonious relationship—a lack which may make marital relationships more difficult for him later. Fourth, if the same-sexed parent is missing from the home, the child will lack an important model of sex-appropriate behaviour and the opportunity parents provide for same-sexed identification.

For all these reasons it has usually been supposed that boys brought up in a home without a father will tend to be more effeminate and will lack masculine identity (see Biller 1974). The converse has been thought to apply to girls reared without a mother. In fact, although the evidence is shaky and unsatisfactory, it seems that this usually does not occur (Herzog & Sudia 1973). Most boys reared only by mothers are as masculine as any other boys. However, that does not mean that fathers are unimportant. To the contrary, there is good evidence that they have a substantial influence on children's development (Biller 1974; Lamb 1975). Obviously, too, there are many advantages to being brought up by two parents. However, the findings suggest that parents are not the only available source of masculine or feminine identity and that the absence of a father from the home does not necessarily impair a boy's masculine identity.

In summary, although there are ill-effects stemming from being brought up in a one-parent family, the effects are probably less uniform and less severe than is widely assumed. In general the number of parents in the home is probably less crucial to the child's development than the relationships and behaviour provided by whoever is present. Furthermore, family life is determined not only by the particular characteristics of the individual family members but also by the social circumstances and environment within which the family live.

Working mothers

Although frequently blamed for their children's troubles, it is now apparent that working mothers have children with no more problems than the children of women who remain at home (Yudkin & Holme 1963; Etaugh 1974; Wallston 1973). This has been shown in a wide range of studies using different measures of children's behaviour (e.g. Davie *et al* 1972; West & Farrington 1973; Douglas *et al* 1968) and it may be concluded that provided good alternative arrangements with stable relationships and high-quality care are used no harm should come to children when their mothers go out to work. This is a very important proviso but one which applies equally to mothers who are not working. Attendance at a day nursery need not interfere with normal mother–child attachment (Caldwell *et al* 1970) and there is no evidence that the use of day nurseries as such has any long-term ill-effects (Yudkin & Holme 1963). Of course, day nurseries vary greatly in quality and some are quite poor and may well have a deleterious influence. Improvements are certainly needed in the day-care provision which is available but it is attention to the quality of child care which is required rather than the prevention of mothers going out to work.

One of the relevant issues is that the period of looking after young children seems to be a particularly stressful one for many women. Richman (see Chapter 16) found depression to be very common in the mothers of preschool children and Brown *et al* (1975) showed that depression was more frequent in women under stress who were not working and who had three or more children under 14 years of age at home. It seems that a job outside the home may sometimes enable mothers to be more content and have an increased range of interests, so having more to give their family. Whether going out to work is beneficial or not will depend to a considerable extent on the effect it has on the mother's mental health and on the relationships she has with her children. It is important that the pattern of day-care be one that facilitates parent–child interaction, increases parental responsibility and enables both mothers and fathers to have time for talk and play with their children. This is possible, as shown by the Israeli kibbutzim (Irvine 1966; Miller 1969) but unfortunately it is far from the rule in this country. If mothers are to have the energy to cope with both a job and their children, it is also desirable for them to be able to work part-time (as most with children under 3 years are likely to wish to do).

Lack of bonding

Thirty years ago Bowlby (1946) noted that affectionless psychopathy was particularly associated with frequent changes of mother-figure during the first 2 years of life. He suggested that the children had been damaged by separation experiences, but subsequent research has indicated that the damage may stem from a failure to form bonds or attachments rather than from any breaking of bonds. This is most likely to arise in long-stay institutions where there is a very large number of adults looking after each child and where the turnover of staff prevents the child developing a lasting relationship with any one person.

Moore (1963), in a study of working mothers, found that the small number of children who had gone from 'pillar to post' in a succession of unsatisfactory and unstable child-minding arrangements (often with periods in institutions or residential nurseries) were the one group to suffer. Their behaviour in early childhood was characteristically clinging, dependent and attention-seeking.

Tizard and Rees (1975) studied 26 $4\frac{1}{2}$-year-old children who had been reared since early infancy in institutions which were of high quality in many respects. The children's behaviour and relationships were compared with those of a group of adopted children and of another group of ordinary working class children reared by their biological parents. Emotional and behaviour problems were no more frequent in the institution-reared children, but their affectional relationships with adults tended to be of a different quality. A third of the institution children seemed emotionally detached from adults and paid little attention to them. Another third also had no specific bonds with particular adults but were generally clinging, attention-seeking and overfriendly to strangers. About a third of the adopted children were also said to be overfriendly to strangers. Neither pattern was found in the children reared with their biological parents.

Data are not yet available on how far these patterns of relationships persist into later childhood and adult life. However, there is some evidence that if the same pattern of upbringing continues the children may go on showing a deviant pattern of social relationships. Goldfarb (1955) noted that children who remained in institutions until after the age of 3 years were especially characterised by an inability to keep rules, a lack of guilt, a craving for affection and an inability to make lasting relationships. The study is open to criticism in terms of both the measures used and the uncertainty regarding the factors which influenced when the child left the institution. However, his findings are in keeping with Pringle and Bossio's (1958; 1960) observations that children admitted to institutions in infancy often were unable to make relationships with adults or children, and with Wolkind's (1974a, b) better-controlled investigation. Wolkind made a systematic study of children in long-term institutional care and found that, although there was a wide range of disturbances, a particular pattern of social disinhibition and superficial overfriendliness was almost confined to children first admitted to care before their second birthday.

While no firm conclusions are yet possible, the evidence strongly suggests that a failure to form bonds in early childhood is particularly likely to lead to attention-seeking uninhibited indiscriminate friendliness and sometimes finally to a personality characterised by a lack of guilt and an inability to form lasting relationships (Rutter 1972). How often this occurs is not known and not all individuals with affectionless psychopathy have this background (Rutter 1972). Also it remains uncertain how far a child's ability to form bonds is limited to the early years of life. Certainly, once a child has developed bonds he can transfer these to other people when he is older—the ability to form bonds is not lost (this seems also to be so with monkeys, Mason & Kenney 1974). However, how far he can develop bonds *for the first time* in later childhood if he did not have the opportunity to form selective attachments in infancy remains uncertain. The evidence suggests that children may find it more difficult to develop stable selective attachments for the first time after the age of 3 or 4 years, but more data are required to determine the nature and limits of this 'sensitive' period for initial bonding (if its existence can be confirmed).

Institutional rearing

Several studies of children in children's homes or other institutions have shown them to have a high rate of psychiatric problems—particularly of conduct disorders (Mapstone 1969; Yule & Raynes 1972; Wolkind 1974a, b). However, this is as true of children admitted for only a week or so as of those in institutions for many years (Wolkind & Rutter 1973). Children admitted into care frequently come from and return to homes with considerable difficulties in family relationships and with various types of psychosocial disadvantage (Mapstone 1969; Schaffer & Schaffer 1968; Wolkind & Rutter 1973). The evidence strongly suggests that with these children (unlike those with the particular pattern of detachment or indiscriminate friendliness) the main causes lie in the long-term family disturbance and discord rather than in institutional rearing *per se*. However, the admission into care adds additional stresses on children already vulnerable as a result of chronic family problems.

CONCLUSIONS

There is ample evidence that several forms of separation, loss and disturbed family relationships play an important part in the genesis of different kinds of child psychiatric disorder. In the past these adverse family experiences have often been included under the general term of 'maternal deprivation'. The concept was undoubtedly useful in focussing attention on the sometimes grave consequences of deficient or disturbed care in early life (Rutter 1972). However, 'maternal deprivation' has not been discussed as such in this chapter because the experiences it includes are too heterogeneous and the effects too varied for the concept to have any further usefulness (Rutter 1972). Furthermore, the term is misleading in that in most cases the deleterious influences are *not* specifically tied to the mother and are not due to deprivation in the sense of loss. On the other hand, there can be no doubt that a child's relationships with his parents and with other family members do have an important influence on his psychosocial development. Some of the possible processes and mechanisms have been outlined in this chapter. Much has still to be learned about these, but already enough is known to constitute a basis for a discriminating therapeutic intervention with children suffering from separation, loss and disturbed family relationships.

REFERENCES

AINSWORTH M.D. (1962) The effects of maternal deprivation: a review of findings and controversy in the context of research strategy. In *Deprivation of Maternal Care: A Reassessment of its Effects*. Public Health Papers No. 14. Geneva: World Health Organization

AINSWORTH M.D. (1967) *Infancy in Uganda: Infant Care and the Growth of Love*. Baltimore: Johns Hopkins Press

AINSWORTH M.D., BELL S.M. & STAYTON D.J. (1971) Individual differences in strange-situation behaviour of one-year-olds. *In* Schaffer H.A. (ed.) *The Origins of Human Social Relations*. London: Academic Press

AINSWORTH M.D. & WITTIG B.A. (1969) Attachment and exploratory behaviour of one year olds in a strange situation. *In* Foss B.M. (ed.) *Determinants of Infant Behaviour*, vol. 4, London: Methuen

AMBROSE J.A. (1961) The development of the smiling response in early infancy. *In* Foss B.M. (ed.) *Determinants of Infant Behaviour*, vol. 1. London: Methuen

ANDRY R.G. (1960) *Delinquency and Parental Pathology*. London: Methuen

ANTHONY S. (1940) *The Child's Discovery of Death*. London: Kegan & Paul

ARSENIAN J.M. (1943) Young Children in an insecure situation. *J. Abnorm. soc. Psychol.* **38**, 225–249

BANDURA A. (1969) Social-learning theory of identificatory processes, *In* Goslin D.A. (ed.) *Handbook of Socialisation Theory and Research*. Chicago: Rand McNally

BILLER H.B. (1974) *Paternal Deprivations: Family, School, Sexuality and Society*. London: Lexington Books

BOWER T.G.R., BROUGHTON J.M. & MOORE M.K. (1970) Infant responses to approaching objects: an indicator of responses to distal variables. *Percept. Psychophysics.* **9**, 193–196

BOWLBY J. (1946) *Forty-four Juvenile Thieves: Their Characters and Home-life*. London: Ballière, Tindall & Cox

BOWLBY J. (1951) *Maternal Care and Mental Health*. Geneva: World Health Organization

BOWLBY J., AINSWORTH M., BOSTON M. & ROSENBLUTH D. (1956) The effects of mother-child separation: a follow-up study. *Brit. J. Med. Psychol.* **29**, 211–247

BOWLBY J. (1969) *Attachment and Loss*, vol. I: *Attachment*. London: Hogarth Press

BOWLBY J. (1975) *Attachment and Loss*, vol. 2: *Separation: Anxiety and Anger*. Harmondsworth: Penguin

BRONSON G.W. (1968) The development of fear in man and other animals. *Child Dev.* **39**, 409–431

BRONSON G.W. (1972) Infants' reactions to unfamiliar persons and novel objects. *Monogr. Soc. Res. Child Dev.* **37**, Serial No. 148

BROWN G.W., SKLAIR F., HARRIS T.O. & BIRLEY J.L.T. (1973a) Life events and psychiatric disorder. 1. Some methodological issues. *Psychol. Med.* **3**, 74–87

BROWN G.W., HARRIS T.O. & PETO J. (1973b) Life events and psychiatric disorder. 2. Nature of causal link. *Psychol. Med.* **3**, 159–176

BROWN G.W., BHROLCHAIN M.N. & HARRIS T. (1975) Social class and psychiatric disturbance among women in an urban population. *Sociology* **9**, 225–254

CALDWELL B.M., WRIGHT C.M., HONIG A.C. & TANNENBAUM J. (1970) Infant day care and attachment. *Amer. J. Orthopsychiat.* **40**, 397–412

CHILDERS P. & WIMMER M. (1971) The concept of death in early childhood. *Child Dev.* **42**, 1299–1301

COATES B., ANDERSON E.P. & HARTUP W.W. (1972a) Interactions in the attachment behaviour of human infants. *Develop. Psychol.* **6**, 218–230

COATES B., ANDERSON E.P. & HARTUP W.W. (1972b) The stability of attachment behaviours in the human infant. *Develop. Psychol.* **6**, 231–237

COHEN L.J. (1974) The operational definition of human attachment. *Psychol. Bull.* **81**, 107–217

COHEN L.J. & CAMPOS J.J. (1974) Father, mother, and stranger as elicitors of attachment behaviours in infancy. *Develop. Psychol.* **10**, 146–154

COOPER B. & SYLPH J. (1973) Life events and the onset of neurotic illness: an investigation in general practice. *Psychol. Med.* **3**, 421–435

CRELLIN E., PRINGLE M.L. KELLMER & WEST P. (1971) *Born Illegitimate: Social and Educational implications*. Windsor: NFER

DAVIE R., BUTLER N. & GOLDSTEIN H. (1972) *From Birth to Seven: A report of the National Child Development Study*. London: Longman

DOUGLAS J.W.B., ROSS J.M. & SIMPSON H.R. (1968) *All Our Future*. London: Peter Davies

DOUGLAS J.W.B. (1973) Early disturbing events and later enuresis. *In* Kolvin I., Mac Keith R.C. & Meadow S.R. (eds.) *Bladder Control and Enuresis*. Clinics in Develop. Med. Nos. 48/49. London: SIMP/Heinemann

DOUGLAS J.W.B. (1975) Early hospital admissions and later disturbances of behaviour and learning. *Dev. Med. Child Neurol.* **17,** 456–480

ETAUGH C. (1974) Effects of maternal employment on children: a review of recent research. *Merrill–Palmer Quart.* **20,** 71–98

FAGIN C.M.R.N. (1966) *The Effects of Maternal Attendance during Hospitalization on the Post-Hospital Behavior of Young Children: A Comparative Study*. Philadelphia: F.A. Davis

FAUST O.A., JACKSON K., CERMAK E.G., BURTT M.M. & WINKLEY R. (1952) *Reducing Emotional Trauma in Hospitalized Children*. Albany Research Project, Albany, New York (cited Yarrow, L.J., 1964)

FREEDMAN D.G. (1965) Hereditary control of early social behaviour, *In* Foss B.M. (ed.) *Determinants of Infant Behaviour*, vol. 3. London: Methuen

GERSHAW N.J. & SCHWARZ J.C. (1971) The effects of a familiar toy and mother's presence on exploratory and attachment behaviors in young children. *Child Dev.* **42,** 1662–1666

GEWIRTZ J.L. (1965) The course of infant smiling in four child rearing environments in Israel. *In* Foss, B.M. (ed.) *Determinants of Infant Behaviour*, vol. 3. London: Methuen

GIBSON H.B. (1969) Early delinquency in relation to broken homes. *J. Child Psychol. Psychiat.* **10,** 195–204

GOLDFARB W. (1955) Emotional and intellectual consequences of psychologic deprivation in infancy: a revaluation. *In* Hoch P.H. & Zubin J. (eds.) *Psychopathology of Childhood*. New York: Grune & Stratton

GREGORY I. (1965) Anterospective data following childhood loss of a parent. *Arch. gen. Psychiat.* **13,** 110–120

HARLOW H.F. (1958) The nature of love. *Amer. Psychol.* **13,** 673–685

HARLOW H.F. & HARLOW M.K. (1969) Effects of various mother–infant relationships on rhesus monkey behaviours. *In* Foss B.M. (ed.) *Determinants of Infant Behaviour*, vol. 4. London: Methuen

HARLOW H.F. & ZIMMERMANN R.R. (1959) Affectional responses in the infant monkey. *Science* **130,** 421–432

HEILPERN E.P. (1943) Psychological probems of stepchildren, *Psychoanalyt. Rev.* **30,** 163–176

HEINICKE C.M. & WESTHEIMER I.J. (1965) *Brief Separations*. London: Longman

HEISEL J.S., REAM S., RAITZ R., RAPPAPORT M. & CODDINGTON R.D. (1973) The significance of life events as contributing factors in the diseases of children. III. A study of pediatric patients. *J. Pediat.* **83,** 119–123

HERZOG E. & SUDIA C.E. (1973) Children in fatherless families. *In* Caldwell B.M. & Ricciuti H.N. (eds.), *Review of Child Development Research*, vol. 3. Chicago: University of Chicago Press

HINDE R.A. & DAVIES L. (1972) Removing infant rhesus from mother for 13 days compared with removing mother from infant. *J. Child Psychol. Psychiat.* **13,** 227–237

HINDE R.A. & SPENCER-BOOTH, Y. (1970) Individual differences in the responses of rhesus monkeys to a period of separation from their mothers. *J. Child Psychol. Psychiat.* **11**, 159–176

HUNT A., FOX J. & MORGAN M. (1973) *Families and Their Needs.* London: HMSO

ILLINGWORTH R.S. & HOLT K.S. (1955) Children in hospital: some observations on their reactions with special reference to daily visiting. *Lancet* **ii**, 1257-1262

IRVINE E.E. (1966) Children in kibbutzim: thirteen years after. *J. Child Psychol. Psychiat.* **7**, 167–178

JACOBS S.C., PRUSOFF B.A. & PAYKEL E.S. (1974) Recent life events in schizophrenia and depression. *Psychol. Med.* **4**, 444–453

JERSILD A.T. & HOLMES F.B. (1935) *Children's Fears.* Child Develop. Monogr. No. 20. New York: Teachers College, Columbia University

JERSILD A.T. (1954) Emotional development. *In* Carmichael L. (ed.) *Manual of Child Psychology*, 2nd edn. London: Chapman & Hall

JONSSON G. (1967) Delinquent boys, their parents and grandparents. *Acta Psychiat. Scand.* Suppl., **43**, 195

KISSEL S. (1965) Stress-reducing properties of social stimuli. *J. Pers. soc. Psychol.* **2**, 378–384

LAMB M.E. (1975) Fathers: forgotten contributors to child development. *Human Dev.* **18**, 245–266

LANGNER T.S. & MICHAEL S.T. (1963) *Life Stress and Mental Health.* New York: Free Press

LEVY D. (1951) Observations of attitudes and behavior in the child health center. *Amer. J. publ. Hlth.* **41**, 182–190

MACCOBY E. & FELDMAN S.S. (1972) *Mother-attachment and stranger reactions in the third year of life.* Monogr. Soc. Res. Child Dev. 37, Serial No. 146

MACCOBY E. & MASTERS J.C. (1970) Attachment and dependency. *In* Mussen P.H. (ed.) *Carmichael's Manual of Child Psychology*, 3rd edn. New York: Wiley

McCORD W. & McCORD J. (1959) *Origins of Crime: a New Evaluation of the Cambridge-Somerville Youth Study.* New York: Columbia University Press

MAPSTONE E. (1969) Children in care. *Concern* **3**, 23–28

MARKS I. (1969) *Fears and Phobias.* London: Heinemann

MARRIS P. (1958) *Widows and their Families.* London: Routledge & Kegan Paul

MASON W.A. & KENNEY M.D. (1974) Redirection of filial attachments in rhesus monkeys: dogs as mother surrogates. *Science* **183**, 1209–1211

MASTERS J.C. & WELLMAN, H.M. (1974) The study of human infant attachment: a procedural critique. *Psychol. Bull.* **81**, 218–237

MILLER L. (1969) Child rearing in the kibbutz. *In* Howells J.H. (ed.) *Modern Perspectives in International Child Psychiatry.* Edinburgh: Oliver & Boyd

MOORE T. (1963) Effects on the children, *In* Yudkin S. & Holme A. (eds.) *Working Mothers and Their Children.* London: Michael Joseph

MOORE T. (1975) Stress in normal childhood. *In* Levi L. (ed.) *Society: Stress and Disease*, vol. 2: *Childhood and Adolescence.* London: Oxford University Press

MORGAN G.A. & RICCIUTI H.N. (1969) Infants' responses to strangers during the first year. *In* Foss B.M. (ed.) *Determinants of Infant Behaviour*, vol. 4. London: Methuen

NAESS S. (1959) Mother–child separation and delinquency. *Brit. J. Delinq.* **10**, 22–35

NAESS S. (1962) Mother–child separation and delinquency: further evidence. *Brit. J. Criminol.* **2**, 361–374

NAGY M. (1948) The child's theories concerning death *J. genet. Psychol.* **73**, 3–27

PAYKEL E.S., MYERS J.K., DIENELT M.N., KLERMAN C.L., LINDENTHAL L.J. & PEPPER M.P. (1969) Life events and depression: a controlled study. *Arch. gen. Psychiat.* **21**, 753–760

PODOLSKY E. (1955) The emotional problems of the step-child. *Mental Hygiene* **39**, 49–53

POWER M., ASH P., SHOENBERG E. & SIREY C. (1974) Delinquency and the family. *Brit. J. Social Work* **4**, 13–38

PRINGLE M.L. KELLMER & BOSSIO V. (1958) Intellectual, emotional and social development of deprived children. *Vita Humana* **1**, 66–92

PRINGLE M.L. KELLMER & BOSSIO V. (1960) Early prolonged separations and emotional maladjustment. *J. Child Psychol. Psychiat.* **1**, 142–170

PRUGH D.G., STAUB E.M., SANDS H.H., KIRSCHBAUM R.M. & LENIHAN E.A. (1953) A study of the emotional reactions of children and families to hospitalization and illness. *Amer. J. Orthopsychiat.* **23**, 70–106

QUINTON D., RUTTER M. & ROWLANDS O. (1976) An evaluation of an interview assessment of marriage. *Psychol. Med.* (in press)

QUINTON D. & RUTTER M. (1976) Early hospital admissions and later disturbances of behaviour: an attempted replication of Douglas' findings. (Develop. Med. Child Neurol. **18**, 447–459)

RHEINGOLD H.L. (1969) The effect of strange environment on the behaviour of infants. *In* Foss B.M. (ed.) *Determinants of Infant Behaviour*, vol. 4. London: Methuen

RHEINGOLD H.L. & SAMUELS H.R. (1969) Maintaining the positive behaviour of infants by increased stimulation. *Devel. Psychol.* **1**, 520–527

ROBERTSON J. & ROBERTSON J. (1971) Young children in brief separations: a fresh look. *Psychoanal. Study of the Child* **26**, 264–315

ROSENTHAL M.K. (1973) Attachment and mother–infant interaction: some research impasses and a suggested change in orientation. *J. Child Psychol. Psychiat.* **14**, 201–208

RUTTER M. (1966) *Children of Sick Parents: An Environmental and Psychiatric Study.* Institute of Psychiatry Maudsley Monographs No. 16. London: Oxford University Press

RUTTER M. (1971) Parent–child separation: Psychological effects on the children. *J. Child Psychol. Psychiat.* **12**, 233–260

RUTTER M. (1972) *Maternal Deprivation Reassessed.* Harmondsworth: Penguin

RUTTER M. (1975) *Helping Troubled Children.* Harmondsworth: Penguin

RUTTER M. (ed.) (1977) *The Child, His Family and the Community.* (In preparation.) London: Wiley

RUTTER M., GRAHAM P., CHADWICK O. & YULE W. (1976) 'Adolescent turmoil—fact or fiction?'. *J. Child Psychol. Psychiat.*, **17**, 35–56

RUTTER M. & MADGE N. (1976) *Cycles of Disadvantage: a Review of Research* (in press). London: Heinemann

RUTTER M., QUINTON D. & YULE B. (1977) *Family Pathology and Disorder in Children.* (In preparation.) London: Wiley

RUTTER M., YULE B., QUINTON D., ROWLANDS O., YULE W. & BERGER M. (1975) Attainment and adjustment in two geographical areas: III. Some factors accounting for area differences. *Brit. J. Psychiat.* **126**, 520–533

SCARR S. & SALAPATEK P. (1970) Patterns of fear development during infancy. *Merrill–Palmer Quart.* **16,** 53–90

SCHAFFER H.R. (1963) Some issues for research in the study of attachment behaviour. *In* Foss B.M. (ed.) *Determinants of Infant Behaviour,* vol. 2. London: Methuen

SCHAFFER H.R. (1971a) Cognitive structure and early social behaviour. *In* Schaffer H.R. (ed.) *The Origins of Human Social Relations.* London and New York: Academic Press

SCHAFFER H.R. (1971b) *The Growth of Sociability.* Harmondsworth: Penguin

SCHAFFER H.R. & EMERSON P.E. (1964) The development of social attachments in infancy. *Monogr. Soc. Res. Child Devel.* **29,** 1–77

SCHAFFER H.R. & PARRY M.H. (1969) Perceptual and motor behaviour in infancy as a function of age and stimulus familiarity. *Brit. J. Psychol.* **60,** 1–9

SCHAFFER H.R. & PARRY M.H. (1970) The effects of short-term familiarisation on infants' perceptual-motor coordination in a simultaneous discrimination situation. *Brit. J. Psychol.* **61,** 559–569

SCHAFFER H.R. & SCHAFFER E.B. (1968) *Child Care and the Family.* Occ. Papers on Social Admin. No. 25. London: Bell

SCHWARZ J. (1972) Effects of peer familiarity on the behaviour of preschoolers in a novel situation. *J. Pers. Soc. Psychol.* **24,** 276–284

SPELKE E., ZELAZO P., KAGAN J. & KOTELCHUCK M. (1973) Father interaction and separation protest. *Develop. Psychol.* **9,** 83–90

STACEY M., DEARDEN R., PILL R. & ROBINSON D. (1970) *Hospitals, Children and their families: The Report of a Pilot Study.* London: Routledge & Kegan Paul

STAYTON D.J. & AINSWORTH M.D. (1973) Individual differences in infant responses to brief, everyday separations as related to other infant and maternal behaviours. *Develop. Psychol.* **9,** 226–235

STAYTON D.J., AINSWORTH M.D. & MAIN D.B. (1973) The development of separation behaviour in the first year of life: protest, following and greeting. *Develop. Psychol.* **9,** 213–225

STEVENS A. (1975) Attachment and polymatric rearing. Thesis for DM, University of Oxford

TIZARD B. & REES J. (1975) The effect of early institutional rearing on the behaviour problems and affectional relationships of four-year-old children. *J. Child Psychol. Psychiat.* **16,** 61–74

TONGE W.L., JAMES D.S. & HILLAM S.M. (1975) Families without hope: A controlled study of 33 problem families. *Brit. J. Psychiat.* Spec. Publ. No. 11

VERNON D.T.A., FOLEY J.M., SIPOWICZ R.R. & SCHULMAN J.L. (1965) *The Psychological Responses of Children to Hospitalization and Illness.* Springfield, Illinois: Charles C Thomas

VERNON D.T.A., FOLEY J.M. & SCHULMAN J.L. (1967) Effect of mother–child separation and birth order on young children's responses to two potentially stressful experiences. *J. Pers. Soc. Psychol.* **5,** 162–174

WALLSTON B. (1973) The effects of maternal employment on children. *J. Child Psychol. Psychiat.* **14,** 81–96

WEST D.J. & FARRINGTON D.P. (1973) *Who Becomes Delinquent?* London: Heinemann

WILSON H. (1974) Parenting in poverty. *Brit. J. Social Work* **4,** 241–254

WOLFF P.H. (1963) Observations on the early development of smiling. *In* Foss B.M. (ed.) *Determinants of Infant Behaviour* vol. 2. London: Methuen

WOLFF S. (1973) *Children Under Stress*. Harmondsworth: Penguin

WOLKIND S.N. (1974a) The components of 'affectionless psychopathy' in institutionalized children. *J. Child Psychol. Psychiat.* **15,** 215–220

WOLKIND S.N. (1974b) Sex differences in the aetiology of antisocial disorders in children in long-term residential care. *Brit. J. Psychiat.* **125,** 125–130

WOLKIND S. & RUTTER, M. (1973) Children who have been 'In Care'—an epidemiological study. *J. Child Psychol. Psychiat.* **14,** 97–105

WOODWARD J. & JACKSON D. (1961) Emotional reactions in burned children and their mothers. *Brit. J. Plastic Surgery* **13,** 316–324

WHO EXPERT COMMITTEE ON MENTAL HEALTH (1951) *Report on the Second Session 1951*, Geneva: World Health Organization

YARROW L.J. (1964) Separation from parents during early childhood. *In* Hoffman M.L. & Hoffman L.W. (eds.) *Review of Child Development Research*, vol. 1. New York: Russell Sage Foundation

YUDKIN S. & HOLME A. (1963) *Working Mothers and Their Children*. London: Michael Joseph

YULE W. & RAYNES N.V. (1972) Behavioural characteristics of children in residential care. *J. Child Psychol. Psychiat.* **13,** 249–258

CHAPTER 4

Other family influences

M. RUTTER

Quite apart from the effects of separation, loss and disturbed relationships (see Chapter 3), there are a host of ways in which children's experiences of family life influence their development. This has given rise to a vast literature which has been critically assessed in a variety of both selective and comprehensive reviews (Becker 1964; Caldwell 1964; Granville-Grossman 1968; Hetherington & Martin 1972; Rutter 1972; 1975; Rutter & Madge 1976; Walters & Stinnett 1971; Wolff 1970; 1973). No attempt will be made to reassess the legion of family factors sometimes thought to be associated with one or other type of psychiatric disorder. Rather, attention will be focussed on key aspects of patterns of child-rearing, of parental deviance and of intergenerational cycles. Whenever possible, conclusions will be drawn in ways which carry implications for clinical practice.

PATTERNS OF CHILD REARING

Psychosexual development

In the past, psychologists and psychiatrists have been much concerned to advise parents on when to wean and toilet train, and on what methods to use. Much of the concern stemmed from adherence to the early psychoanalytic view of psychosexual development in terms of oral, anal and latency stages. However, research findings have shown that, although psychoanalytic insights have added depth to our understanding of child development, the concept of psychosexual stages is misleadingly over-simplified (Rutter 1971b; 1975; White 1960).

The first year of life was termed the oral phase because mouthing and sucking constitute such prominent aspects of a baby's behaviour and because the mouth seemed to be the main source of sensual satisfaction (see Buxbaum 1959). Certainly the oral area is a particularly sensitive one in infants (Lustman 1956) and undoubtedly infants not only gain pleasure from sucking but also tend to suck objects as a form of exploration and satisfaction. On the other hand, young infants spend much time in exploratory play activities of a non-oral kind (Piaget 1951; Gesell 1940; Millar 1968; White 1959) and even at this tender age some infants appear to be getting pleasure from genital stimulation (Halverson 1940; Kinsey *et al* 1948; Newson & Newson 1963). Moreover, mother–child attachment does not primarily depend on sucking and feeding (Bowlby 1969); yet the development of selective attachments is one of the most crucial tasks in the first year to eighteen months (see Chapter 3). For these and other reasons, psychoanalysts have come to question some of the notions implicit in the concept of 'orality' (Sandler & Dare 1970).

The second and third years of life were originally thought of as the anal stage in which libidinal energies were primarily centred on eliminatory functions. Again, it is obviously true that this is the age when the child begins to gain control of his bowels and bladder and his attempts to do so constitute sources of both interest and exploration for him. But toilet training probably involves less parental investment of energies than was the case at the time Freud made his observations (Caldwell 1964) and there are many other developments of greater importance in the second and third years (White 1960; Elkind 1968). Genital play is quite common in preschool children (Levy 1928; Sears, Maccoby & Levin 1957) and games involving undressing or sexual exploration are also prevalent (Isaacs 1933; Newson & Newson 1968). Furthermore, several studies using a variety of methods (Bernstein 1955; Beloff 1957; Hetherington & Brackbill 1963) have failed to find significant associations between the timing or severity of toilet training and so-called 'anal' personality traits.

Freud's views on the phallic stage (Freud 1905), in which libidinal attention shifts to the genital area at about 4 to 6 years, are probably more valid. As already noted, there is an obvious genital component in many of children's games at this time. However, castration anxiety and the Oedipus complex are also essential components of this stage according to psychoanalytic views. Because of the supposed unconscious nature of many of the child's sexual feelings, these hypotheses have proved difficult to test. Conn (Conn 1940; Conn & Kanner 1947) used doll-play techniques to study children's reactions to the discovery of genital differences. Many of the children could not recall how they felt when they first saw the genitals of the opposite sex but a third (boys more than girls) reported castration thoughts. Castration anxiety undoubtedly occurs but it seems doubtful whether it is universal and its importance for development is even more dubious.

The Oedipus complex, that is the child's attachment to the opposite-sexed parent and hostility to the same-sexed parent, has been even more difficult to test. Direct questions to children as to which parent they love have usually failed to demonstrate the supposed sex difference. On the other hand, projective techniques have produced age-specific findings which tend to support the Oedipus complex although there is great individual variation in whether children show the Oedipal pattern of relationships at age 5 years or so (Friedman 1952). Cross-cultural studies (Honigmann 1954) also suggest that the development of hostility to the same-sexed parent depends very much on the family pattern of relationships characteristic of particular societies. The evidence regarding the Oedipus complex is too contradictory and unsatisfactory to give rise to any firm conclusions but it seems that many children do go through a phase in which there is some antipathy to the same-sexed parent. Whether this is based on feelings of sexual rivalry is quite unknown, and what significance, if any, it has for later development is equally uncertain. It should also be said that the Oedipus complex seems to be far from universal and is probably dependent on family circumstances rather than innate predisposition.

Freud (1922) claimed that the emergence of castration anxiety led to a period of more or less complete sexual latency. Anna Freud (1947) similarly argued that sexual development came to a standstill during the middle years of childhood and that this phase of latency differentiated humans from other animals. However, research findings have shown these views to be mistaken. Although children do come to play almost exclusively with those of their own sex (Campbell 1939), and although there may be greater concealment of sex interests during middle childhood, nevertheless overt sex activities and interests are common and widespread (Bernick 1965; Reese 1966). Masturbation gradually increases in frequency (Ramsey 1943; Kinsey *et al* 1948) and heterosexual interests show a systematic progression (Broderick & Fowler 1961; Broderick & Rowe 1968).

The psychoanalytic view of adolescence as a period of revival of Oedipal conflicts remains largely untested. The view that this is a period of greatly increased and more specific sex interests is of course, well supported by evidence (Schofield 1965) but that view is shared by all developmental theories.

It should be added that the early psychoanalytic view of libido as a drive with an energy component of a quantitative nature, giving rise to a hydraulic system of energies flowing in certain directions or becoming dammed up and then released, has also failed to be supported by the evidence (see Hinde 1960; Hunt 1960; Rutter 1971b).

Although the psychoanalytic concept of sexuality beginning in infancy or early childhood has been well established, the notion of fixed libidinal energies has proved mistaken and Freud's description of psychosexual stages has been found to be misleading in certain important respects.

Infant care

As much of the research on infant care practices had its origins in predictions based on the psychoanalytic theory of psychosexual stages, it is not surprising that most of the findings have been negative or inconclusive. Caldwell (1964) reviewed the literature in 1964 and concluded that the timing of various aspects of infant care was of very little significance and that questions such as whether the child was breast fed or bottle fed and what method of toilet training was used were of little psychological importance. Studies undertaken since 1964 have done nothing to alter this conclusion.

On the other hand, it would be untrue to say that the pattern of infant care is unimportant. Feeding and toileting are vital parts of the child's day and the way the parents undertake these activities is important (Ainsworth 1973). Thus, feeding (whether by bottle or breast) provides a good opportunity to hold, talk to, and respond to the infant. This interaction provides experiences which influence the child's development. The act of feeding the child does more than just provide nutriment and the effect is not the same if the infant is merely left with a propped-up bottle to feed himself. *How* the baby is looked after is probably of considerable significance, but it is the social and psychological context of the care which matters rather than its chronology and mechanics (Rutter 1975). The little that is known on these matters was discussed in Chapter 3.

Parental constraint and overprotection

Thirty years ago, Hewitt and Jenkins (1949) in a study of clinic patients found that, compared with antisocial youngsters, overinhibited neurotic children were particularly likely to have been constrained and restricted in their activities. In particular, the mothers of anxious children tended to be described (in case notes) as having an infantilising, overprotective attitude (Jenkins 1968). The findings have been broadly confirmed in a variety of more recent studies (Lewis 1954; Rosenthal *et al* 1959; 1962; Bennett 1960). However, there are two main problems in the interpretation of these findings. First, the methods of measuring parental behaviour were rather crude and open to a variety of biasses. Second, the results show that the mothers of neurotic children are more restrictive than the mothers of aggressive children but they do not show whether there is any difference between the mothers of neurotic children and the mothers of normal children. In short, is it that the mothers of neurotic children are *over*controlling or is it that the mothers of aggressive children are *under*controlling?

Although the data do not exist to provide a firm answer to that question, recent research has provided some clarification. Baumrind (1967) made a well planned study of small groups of nursery school children, using a combination of observational and interview techniques. The best adjusted children had parents who were warm, nurturant, supportive and controlling with high expectations. The parents of insecure, apprehensive children were also controlling (although *not* more so) but differed in being less nurturant and more inclined to frighten their children. The families also showed more discord and poorer relationships. In contrast, the parents of impulsive aggressive children were *less* controlling, *less* demanding and *less* well organised than both the other groups. The results apply to behavioural differences within a fairly normal group of children and cannot necessarily be extended to children with psychiatric disorder. However, the findings do suggest that it is not so much that the parents of insecure and apprehensive children are overcontrolling, but rather that they exert their control in a manner which generates anxiety and fails to provide emotional support. On the other hand, the parents of impulsive aggressive children seem to be *under*controlling in relation to the parents of both normal and neurotic children.

However, there may also be differences in parental functioning within groups of emotionally disturbed children. Thus, Rutter, Quinton and Yule (1977) found that both the degree of parental control of children's leisure activities and also the level of parental expectations of children's autonomy bore no relationship to emotional disorder in the children. Similarly, Berg (Berg 1974; Berg & McGuire 1974), using a specially developed parental questionnaire, found that the parents of neurotic children were no more overprotective than the parents of normal children. On the other hand, the mothers of school-phobic youngsters did show an increased tendency to foster dependency (more so in terms of affectionate contact than in household tasks or leisure). The results are in keeping with Eisenberg's (1958) direct observations of mother–child interaction in preschool children with separation problems. The children were overprotected but the essential feature was anxious oversolicitude related to the mother's apprehension over separation. It may be tentatively concluded that the harm probably comes from the parent's uncertainty, anxiety and lack of support together with a restriction of social autonomy rather than from the degree of control as such.

Levy's (1943) classical study of maternal overprotection offers insights into how this behaviour may arise. He took a group of children attending a psychiatric clinic and from within this group identified those children who had been subjected to marked maternal overprotection, as defined in terms of excessive contact with the child, prolongation of infantile care and prevention of independence. These mothers and children were compared with a control group of clinic children who had not been overprotected. The excessive contact in the overprotected group might be either physical or social. There was undue fondling and mothering, nearly a third of the children (all aged 8 years plus) were still sleeping with their mothers, and the mother–child contact was so extensive as to exclude other relationships. The prolongation of infantile care was shown by dressing, bathing and feeding the child long after this was necessary and by excessive servicing of the child, being at his beck and call to get whatever he wanted. The prevention of independence was demonstrated by the child not being allowed to help in the house with washing-up, repairs and other chores; by restriction of his social contacts through determining whom he played with and through not allowing him out to play without permission; and by excessive guarding of the child, fighting his battles and encouraging him to come immediately for help if teased or frustrated.

By comparing the overprotective mothers with the control mothers, Levy was able to show the various ways in which excessive overprotection could arise. First, there were factors in the child. Compared with the control group, the overprotected children were more likely to have been born after various experiences which had threatened the possibility of a successful pregnancy. A quarter of the children had been born after long periods of sterility; in other cases there was a history of miscarriages, the death of the other children or serious complications during the pregnancy. In short, there were reasons why the overprotected child should have been more valued than other children as a result of difficulties in conception or birth. Also, after the children had been born, the overprotected youngsters had an excess of chronic or life-threatening illnesses and three times as many operations as the controls. In these cases the illness had been a cause of reasonable overprotection at the time, the problem lay only in its continuation. These findings emphasise the child's role in shaping parental behaviour.

Second, there were factors in the mother's own childhood. Although the mothers were generally stable and active people, many of them had been brought up in homes which lacked warmth and love. They were determined to give their children what they themselves had lacked but rather 'overdid' it in developing an excessively solicitous and protective approach to the child.

Third, there were factors in the marriage. The fathers were generally submissive men who took little part in the family life. In three-quarters of the cases there was little social life shared between the husband and wife and in the same proportion there was sexual maladjustment. In these cases it seemed that the mother's marital relationship had to some extent been displaced on to the child. She was seeking in an overly close relationship with the child some compensation for what she missed in her husband.

Fourth, Levy noted that although deliberately excluded from the sample, overprotection may arise as a response to feelings of hostility and rejection towards the child which the mother only half recognises and is unable to accept. This is particularly likely to arise when feelings of love and hate coexist in an uneasy ambivalence. Fifth, although also not included in Levy's series, overprotection may arise directly from some forms of emotional disturbance in the parent which give rise, as it were, to an abnormal 'need' for the child's dependency. The parents of emotionally disturbed youngsters include a disproportionately large number with neurotic disorders (see below) and the children appear particularly at risk when they become involved in the parental fears, obsessions or other symptoms (Rutter 1966).

Discipline

There is a large literature on parental attitudes to child-rearing and on disciplinary techniques but much of the research is open to such serious methodological objections that few conclusions can be drawn with any confidence. Questionnaires which aim to assess general attitudes to child-rearing have proved ineffectual in that they measure social mores rather than the parent's behaviour towards any particular child (Becker & Krug 1965). They do not reflect the fact that parents respond rather differently towards each of their children and they fail to distinguish between attitudes and behaviour (which are far from synonymous). Interview techniques are rather more discriminating but even so the methodological problems are considerable and many of the findings in much-quoted studies have proved difficult to replicate (Yarrow *et al* 1968).

With the necessary reservations which stem from these limitations, it may be concluded that the particular method of discipline used is of very little consequence (Becker 1964). Properly used, love-oriented techniques, reasoning, and chastisement have all been found to be effective. Within quite broad limits, the degree of discipline also seems not to be crucial. However, the evidence does suggest that these elements are particularly important; the affectional context within which discipline takes place, the efficiency of the techniques used, and the specific behaviours subjected to discipline.

Many studies have indicated that extreme parental criticism, rejection and hostility is associated with a high rate of aggression, delinquency and disorders of conduct in the children (Andry 1960; Bandura & Walters 1959; Glueck & Glueck 1950; McCord & McCord 1959; West & Farrington 1973; Rutter, Quinton & Yule 1977). In practice, these negative parental feelings and behaviours are often associated with high frequency of punishment and with marital disharmony and family tension or conflict. The evidence is clear enough that the children have a much increased risk of conduct disorders when they experience a strongly negative or rejecting relationship with their parents. Probably the ill-effects stem both from the stresses associated with disturbed family relationships and also from the fact that parental approval and disapproval (i.e. disciplinary techniques) are likely to have less impact when the parents are neither loved nor respected.

It is only quite recently that specific attention has been given to the efficiency of disciplinary techniques. However, the few pilot studies which have been conducted do suggest that the timing and character of parental responses can be very influential in shaping children's behaviour for better or worse (Johnson *et al* 1971; Patterson 1973; Patterson & Cobb 1971). The parents of problem children seem to differ from other parents in being less good at recognising when and how to intervene, in giving less encouragement and praise for good behaviour, in responding erratically and inconsistently to bad behaviour, and in giving a lot of attention (both positive and negative) when the child is misbehaving. There is a failure to encourage the child when he is doing what he should be doing and an undue preoccupation with his misdeeds. It should be emphasised that it is not primarily a question of being generally firm or generally permissive but rather of knowing when to be each. Thus, the giving of attention and comfort when babies cry is usually effective in making them more secure and contented because in most instances the crying is a sign of distress or discomfort (Bell & Ainsworth 1972). In contrast, the giving of attention when children are disruptive in the classroom is likely to make things worse because such behaviour often has an attention-seeking component (Becker *et al* 1967). Efficient discipline requires a discriminating and understanding response. Parental skill lies in knowing how to vary the response to different behaviours and to different children with appropriate recognition of the ways in which their needs vary according to temperament, developmental level and circumstances.

Laboratory, family and classroom studies considered together suggest four other elements which make for efficient discipline. First, as noted above, there is the quality of the parent–child relationship. Children are more likely to follow the guidance of parents whom they love and with whom they identify. Second, the timing of responses is important. Both rewards and punishments tend to be more effective when given early and in immediate response to what the child has done (see Hoffman 1970; Walters *et al* 1965). Thirdly, although rules are not effective in themselves, the consistency and principles of disciplinary demands are very relevant. It is better to have a few rules firmly applied than a mass of regulations haphazardly enforced. Children are likely to respond better when they understand what the rules are and can see that they are reasonable and for a purpose. A large number of studies have shown that markedly inconsistent discipline is associated with an increased likelihood of conduct disorders and delinquency (e.g. Bandura & Walters 1959; McCord & McCord 1959; Glueck & Glueck 1950; West & Farrington 1973). This is probably partly because inconsistent discipline is likely to be ineffective discipline but also partly because inconsistency tends to be associated with parental tension and conflict (see above studies and also Baruch & Wilcox 1944).

Fourthly, the balance of rewards and punishments is influential. Results tend to be better when there is a premium on praise and a minimum of prohibitions. Thus, classroom studies show that ignoring deviant behaviour tends to be ineffective unless it is combined with approval for appropriate behaviour (Becker *et al* 1967; Madsen *et al* 1968).

Lastly, *which* behaviours are the subject of discipline is likely to be important. Thus, many studies have shown that delinquents tend to be poorly supervised by their parents who neither know where they go nor attempt to regulate their activities (Glueck & Glueck 1950; Craig & Glick 1964; West & Farrington 1973). Poor supervision tends to be closely associated with family disadvantage and disorganisation and West and Farrington (1973) found that parental supervision was of little significance once parental criminality and low income had been taken into account. On the other hand, Wilson (1974) found that poor supervision was the factor most strongly associated with delinquency in a group of multiple-problem families.

Sometimes discipline tends to be thought of largely in terms of punishment, as if the main objective was the suppression of 'bad behaviour'. Of course, it is not. In the first place the enhancement of 'good' behaviour is at least as important as the reduction of 'wrongdoing', so that encouragement and praise are central. But even more crucial is the fact that the real objective is to enable the child to develop his own internal controls. It is necessary for him to gain his own set of values (which will not necessarily be the same as those of his parents) in order for him to regulate his behaviour without remaining dependent on other people's rewards and punishments. There is a large body of both theoretical writings and research on the factors that facilitate the development of a conscience and a set of moral values (see Hoffman 1970). It has proved difficult to develop adequate measures of internalisation and the research findings do not lead to very clear-cut conclusions. However, it appears that it is probably helpful for the child to participate in family decisions about behaviour in the home and to understand and be able to discuss rules and principles. On the other hand, it is also clear that many factors other than discipline are important. These include the nature of parental models and the process of identification (see below).

Family communication and patterns of dominance

There is a widespread belief that impaired communication within the family and unsatisfactory patterns of dominance play a major role in the genesis of psychiatric disorder (Bell 1961; 1962; Ferreira 1963; Skynner 1969). To a considerable extent this belief has been a force behind the increasing use of conjoint family therapy. However, the research findings remain rather contradictory and inconclusive concerning the extent to which abnormal patterns of communication or dominance in the family are actually associated with psychiatric disorder. Undoubtedly, much of the uncertainty stems from the difficulty in studying these aspects of family life. Many of the concepts about communication lack clarity (Mishler & Waxler 1965; Olson 1972) and many of the studies suffer from major methodological limitations (Waxler & Mishler 1970; Haley 1972; Hetherington & Martin 1972; Riskin & Faunce 1972; Jacob 1975).

Because, for obvious reasons, most people are unable to provide accurate reports of how family members communicate and interact with one another, most investigators have relied on some means of observing families talking together. Although there have been some observational studies in the families' own homes (Lytton 1971), there has been a greater use of structured interactions in the laboratory. Strodtbeck (1951) first devised a revealed differences technique in which family members answer standardised questions individually and are then brought together to reconcile their views. Since then a variety of modifications have been introduced (Farina 1960; Ferreira & Winter 1968) and many studies have used a procedure in which families are asked to talk together in order to come to agreed decisions on a series of hypothetical situations involving either supposedly neutral topics such as choice of a meal at a restaurant or problem oriented topics such as what to do when a son has been found truanting. Dominance has been assessed in terms of measures which include amount and order of speaking, together with proportion of successful interruptions; conflict by number of interruptions and of disagreements; and efficiency of communication by failures to agree and time taken to reach decisions. There are obvious problems in whether these measures reflect what they are purported to assess (low and variable intercorrelations have usually been reported between variables supposed to be measuring the same thing, Becker & Iwakami 1969; Hetherington *et al* 1971) and in whether structured interactions in the laboratory reflect the usual patterns of interaction in the home. In addition, possible biasses stem from studying cases and controls in different settings or with different expectations, from the diagnostic heterogeneity of patients studied, and from the ways in which controls are chosen. Also high refusal rates among controls (only 20 per cent agreed to participate in the study by Becker & Iwakami 1969) and cases (Mead & Campbell 1972 approached 61 families before obtaining a sample of 20 with a drug-abusing child) have frequently introduced serious possibilities of unrepresentative findings (Cox *et al* 1976).

For all these reasons, considerable caution is needed in the interpretation of findings and in the comparison of different studies. Nevertheless, a few conclusions may be drawn. First, there do not appear to be any clear connections between patterns of dominance and either psychiatric disorder or delinquency.

Studies of the normal population have given rise to varied findings but most have shown that the commonest pattern is for a balance of power in the home with husbands taking some decisions on their own, wives doing likewise and some decisions being taken jointly (Centers *et al* 1971). Family interaction of normal families studies have shown both mother dominance (Murrell & Stachowiak 1967) and father dominance (Schuham 1970) but the more usual pattern has been some kind of balance between the two (Hetherington *et al* 1971). Similar variability has been found in families of disturbed children and many studies report no differences from controls (Jacob 1975). Where differences have been found, disturbed families have tended to show less differentiated patterns of dominance (i.e. they are less hierarchical) and to have fathers who are less dominant. However, there are too many exceptions for much to be made of these occasional differences.

The findings on communication conflict, as measured by interruptions, are equally contradictory (Jacob 1975). Some studies find more interruptions in normal families (Becker & Iwakami 1969; O'Connor & Stachowiak 1971) while others find more in families with a disturbed child (Leighton *et al* 1971). However, it seems likely that this is a poor measure of conflict and it should be noted that most investigators have confined study to families in which the child has lived continuously with both biological parents (so excluding the high proportion in which marriages have broken down). On the other hand, although the findings are not entirely consistent, many studies have shown more negative feelings and fewer positive feelings in the interactions of families with a disturbed child. Thus, Schulman *et al* (1962) observed more hostile and rejecting behaviour by the parents of boys with conduct disorders; Alexander (1973) showed more defensive communications in the families of runaways; Bugental *et al* (1971) found that mothers (but not fathers) of disturbed children gave more messages in which there was a conflict between the emotions expressed in the verbal content and those indicated by the tone of voice or facial expression; and several studies have shown more disagreements in the families of disturbed children (Gassner & Murray 1969; Mead & Campbell 1972; Byassee & Murrell 1975).

The findings on clarity and accuracy of family communications are inconclusive if ratings of clarity are used (Jacob 1975). Nevertheless, there is some highly suggestive evidence that families with a deviant or disturbed child have less efficient patterns of communication. O'Connor and Stachowiak (1971) noted that the parents of poorly adjusted 10–12-year-old children tended to make long speeches directed at no one in particular and although they interrupted less often than control parents they did so less successfully. Moreover, several studies have found that families with disturbed children take longer to come to decisions or to resolve disagreements (Haley 1967; Ferreira & Winter 1968; Gassner & Murray 1969; Schuham 1970; Murrell 1971) or are less productive in joint tasks such as making up stories (Murrell & Stachowiak 1967).

Conclusions can only be tentative but the balance of findings indicate that discussions in families with problem children tend to give rise to more tension and disagreement than they do in families of normal children. There is nothing very distinctive about the sequence or patterns of communication but families with a disturbed child often show more negative feelings when talking together and may give more conflicting messages. But, perhaps the most striking characteristic of many families with a problem child is their inefficient communication, both in the sense that discussion tends to be associated with fruitless disputes and in the sense that it often fails to give rise to an agreed solution. Very few studies have made distinctions between diagnostic groups and it is not known whether communication difficulties are associated with particular types of psychiatric disorder.

Of course, the situations studied have been rather artificial and it remains uncertain how far discussions in the laboratory can be taken as a valid measure of the family's usual mode of communication. Certainly, there is evidence that patterns of interaction in the house and in the laboratory are sometimes rather different (Lytton 1971). Nevertheless, interview data confirm that parental disagreements are more frequent in families with a problem child (e.g. Baruch & Wilcox 1944). It could be that these are simply a measure of discord and lack of affection but it seems that in addition some families suffer from poor communication and ineffective decision making processes. How far these difficulties contribute to the causation of the child's disorder cannot be determined from the interactional studies. The most satisfactory test would be whether improvements in the child's behaviour can systematically be related to improvements in family communication. However, there are few satisfactory studies of family therapy or of improvements in family functioning as a result of therapy (Wells *et al* 1972; Gurman 1973); and the only two studies which attempted to look at the way changes in family interaction were associated with therapeutic benefit produced contradictory findings (Epstein *et al* 1972; Alexander & Parsons 1973).

Family size

Numerous studies have shown that individuals from large families tend to have a lower level of intelligence and of reading attainment than those from small families (see review by Rutter & Madge 1976). Various hypotheses have been put forward to account for the finding. A purely genetic explanation seems improbable (Rutter & Mittler 1972). On the other hand, the observation that the association is less marked (although still present) in upper social groups and may be less strong among Catholic families (Clausen 1966) does suggest that part of the explanation may lie in differences between the sort of people who have large families and those who do not (Oldman *et al* 1971; Askham 1975). There is some evidence that children from large families receive less adequate infant care and less encouragement in schooling than do other children (Douglas 1964) and financial and material resources are considerably less in large families (Land 1969; Ministry of Social Security 1967). The fact that the association between family size and attainment is strongest with verbal skills and the fact that it is already maximal during the early years of schooling has led to the suggestion that at least part of the explanation lies in the child's linguistic environment at home during the pre-school years (Nisbet 1953; Douglas *et al* 1968; Rutter & Mittler 1972). There is probably less intensive interaction and less communication between parents in large families (although this has not been systematically measured) and the greater frequency of cross-talk is likely to make the linguistic environment less clear in large families.

Several investigations have shown that children from large families (at least 4 or 5 children) are twice as likely to develop conduct disorders, just as they are more liable to become delinquent (see Rutter & Madge 1976). In contrast, youngsters with emotional disturbance are, if anything, more likely to come from small families.

The mechanisms involved remain ill-understood. One factor may be the educational retardation which is commoner in large families (see above) and which predisposes to conduct disorder (see Chapter 23). Another may be the overcrowding and social disadvantage which is so often associated with large family size. Discord and conflict may be more frequent in large families, although this has not been systematically studied. Also parental discipline and supervision may be more difficult when there are a lot of children to look after. The presence of many young children seems to make mothers more vulnerable to stress and hence to depression (Brown *et al* 1975). Furthermore, some children may be unwanted. In this connection, it is pertinent to note that Forssman and Thuwe (1966) found a high rate of problems in children born after an application for therapeutic abortion had been refused. A similar trend was also evident in the better controlled study by Dytrych *et al* (1975) but the differences from the matched control group were quite small. It was interesting that many women who had not wanted their children later came to love them. There is a great need to know more about the ways in which family interaction and relationships are influenced by the number of children.

Ordinal position

There is good evidence that first-born children tend to have a higher level of scholastic and work achievement than later-born children (see Rutter & Madge 1976). On the other hand, there is also a slight but consistent tendency for the eldest child to have a greater likelihood of developing an emotional disorder (Rutter, Tizard & Whitmore 1970). The reasons for this are not fully understood but two factors are probably the most important. First, it has been found that parents tend to interact differently with their first child (Lasko 1954; Clausen 1966; Hilton 1967). Parents talk and play more with their first born but also they are more anxious, restrictive, punitive, inconsistent and interfering. With the second child they tend to be more relaxed, more confident and more consistent in their handling. Second, the eldest child has the problem of adjusting to the arrival of brothers or sisters, a stress not experienced by the youngest child in the family.

PARENTAL DEVIANCE

Parental criminality

A host of studies have shown that parental criminality tends to be associated with delinquency in the children (see Rutter & Madge 1976). Thus, investigations in Scandinavia (Otterstrom 1946; Jonsson 1967), Britain (Ferguson 1952; West & Farrington 1973) and the USA (Robins & Lewis 1966; Robins *et al* 1975) have all demonstrated that the rate of delinquency in the children increases two or three fold when a parent is criminal, and even more so if both parents are criminal. The presence of delinquent sibs in the family yet further increases the risk of delinquency (Ferguson 1952; West & Farrington 1973; Robins *et al* 1975) and it appears that part of the association between large family size and delinquency may be a result of the children's exposure to delinquent brothers and sisters.

To some extent, the association between parental criminality and delinquency in the children seems to be a function of selective prosecution of persons from families in which someone has a criminal record (West & Farrington 1973; Farrington *et al* 1975). On the other hand, this is far from the whole explanation as parental criminality is also associated with increased delinquent acts as reported by the boys themselves and with troublesome behaviour as assessed from teacher ratings (West & Farrington 1973; Farrington *et al* 1975). Furthermore, general population studies in London and the Isle of Wight have found that paternal criminality is associated with a two-fold increase in psychiatric disorder in the children, as assessed from parental interview as well as with behavioural deviance as shown at school (Rutter *et al* 1975).

A variety of mechanisms are likely to be involved in these associations. Genetic factors probably play some part, although hereditary influences are not very powerful in juvenile delinquency (see Chapter 2). Poor care of the children and disturbed family relationships may be more important. McCord and McCord (1959) found that the risk of delinquency was greatest in the case of cruel and neglecting criminal fathers and that the risk was only slightly elevated if the criminal parent was loving (although the number in the latter category was too small for the finding to be reliable). Similarly, West and Farrington (1973) found that criminal parents tended to exercise poor supervision over their children and when this was taken into account the link between parental criminality and delinquency in the sons was much reduced. The same study indicated that parental criminality was closely linked to low income and large family size, but even after matching the groups on these variables the delinquents still had more criminal parents. That low social status and poverty are *not* the explanation is also shown by Robins *et al*'s (1975) finding that even within a disadvantaged black inner city population parental criminality was still associated with delinquency in the children.

Modelling of deviant behaviour may be another mechanism. This is suggested by the association with delinquency in older sibs and by the finding that this association is especially marked when neither parent is criminal (West & Farrington 1973). A modelling explanation is consistent with Robins' finding (Robins *et al* 1975) that delinquency in the children was more strongly associated with parental criminality in adult life than with parental delinquency as juveniles. On the other hand, direct modelling of criminal behaviour is unlikely in view of West and Farrington's (1973) observation that most of the parents had ceased to be active criminals by the time their children became delinquent. Identification with the same-sexed parent is also an insufficient explanation as the links for both boys and girls are equally strong with criminality in mothers and fathers. In this connection it is noteworthy that the majority of criminal mothers are married to criminal fathers, although the converse is not true (West & Farrington 1973; Robins *et al* 1975).

Parental mental disorder

A variety of early studies, reviewed in Rutter (1966), suggested that chronic neuroses, depression and personality disorders was quite common in the parents of children attending psychiatric clinics. This observation has since been confirmed by more recent systematic investigations. Rutter (1966) found that one in five children attending a psychiatric clinic had a parent who had also been under psychiatric care, a rate three times that in a matched control group of children attending dental clinics. The link with child psychiatric disorder was strongest when the parent exhibited long-standing abnormalities of personality and when the parental symptoms directly impinged on the child. Similarly, Wolff and Acton (1968) found that personality disorders were over twice as common in parents of children attending a psychiatric clinic compared with the parents of nonpatients attending the same school classes. Emotional disorders were also more frequent in the mothers of psychiatric clinic children. This association is not an artefact of referral practices because in a general population study, Rutter *et al* (1975) found that neurotic disorders were much commoner in the mothers of 10-year-old children with psychiatric disorder than in the mothers of similarly aged normal children. Richman (1975) found the same in a general population study of preschool children. Intergenerational continuities can also be examined by studying the offspring of adults with psychiatric disorder. Early studies (see Rutter 1966) indicated that the children of patients with neurotic, depressive or personality disorders showed an increased rate of psychiatric problems and that the risk seemed to be especially great if the parental illness adversely affected the parent–child relationship. On the whole, the children of psychotic parents suffered less. However, Rice *et al* (1971) in an American study, noted that the children of parents with severe mental illness could suffer from the disruption, turmoil and tensions associated with the illness.

The matter has been investigated further by Rutter, Quinton and Yule (1977) by means of a 4-year prospective study of the families of adult patients with children of school age or younger. Nearly twice as many of the patients' children showed persisting emotional or behavioural difficulties compared with school classroom controls. Psychiatric problems in the children were especially likely if the parents had a personality disorder or if there was persisting marital discord. The clinical type or severity of the parental illness did not seem particularly important but the risk to the child was greater in families where the parental disorder had a marked social impact or where it was associated with gross irritability towards the child.

Several total population epidemiological studies in Canada (Buck & Laughton 1959) and in Britain (Kellner 1963; Hare & Shaw 1965) have also shown that mental ill-health in parents (and especially in mothers) is associated with an increased rate of emotional and behaviour disorders in the children. Intergenerational continuities in child psychiatric disorder were investigated most directly by Robins (1966) in her systematic and thorough follow-up into middle age of 525 child-guidance clinic patients and a matched group of 100 nonpatient schoolchildren. At follow-up the offspring of the adults who had been patients as children showed more behavioural disturbance than did the offspring of nonpatients. However, the groups did not differ in terms of 'nervousness' and the difference with respect to conduct disorders mainly applied to the small proportion of expatients who had gone on to show sociopathy in adult life with concomitant family discord and marital strife.

Again, it is likely that several different mechanisms are involved in the links between parental mental disorder and psychiatric problems in the children. Doubtless, genetic factors play some part. However, several findings point to the additional influence of environmental factors (Rutter, Quinton & Yule 1977). First, the associations with child disorder are greater in the case of symptoms measured in terms of social context and impact than of symptoms assessed by clinical type or severity. Second, within a patient sample, disorder in the children is more strongly linked with marital discord and disturbed family relationships than it is with any clinical variable. Third, neurosis in men is associated with an increased risk of their wives developing neurosis—a consequence which stems from pathological interaction more than heredity (see below).

It appears that parental mental illness leads to psychiatric disorder in the children in large part as a result of the family disturbances with which it tends to be associated. It has been found that family discord and marital disharmony are considerably more common when one parent has a psychiatric condition (Rutter, Quinton & Yule 1977; Rutter 1977), and that *within* a group of families in all of which one parent is a psychiatric patient marital disharmony is strongly associated with conduct disorder in the sons (Rutter 1971a). When a parent is ill, the children are more likely to be placed in care or removed from home and this, too, has been found to be associated with the development of psychiatric problems (Wolkind & Rutter 1973). At least so far as boys are concerned, parental mental disorder seems to lead to psychiatric problems partly because of the accompanying family discord and marital harmony.

However, discord does not seem to be a major factor in the genesis of psychiatric disorder in girls and even in boys discord does not constitute a sufficient explanation. Accordingly, other mechanisms must be invoked. The longitudinal study of patients' families undertaken by Rutter, Quinton and Yule (1977) showed that problems in the children were more likely when mood disturbance in the patients directly impinged on the child, a finding in keeping with Rutter's (1966) earlier observation based on a case notes study. Weissman *et al* (1972) have shown that depressed women are impaired in their mothering in terms of diminished emotional involvement, impaired communication, disaffection, increased hostility and resentment. These effects are all likely to increase the psychiatric risk for the children.

Other investigations have also shown that in patients' marriages there tends to be more conflict over child-rearing, more segregation in decision-making, less affection by husbands and greater dominance by one marriage partner over the other (Kreitman *et al* 1971). Another study, using an experimental interaction, noted that psychiatric patients and their spouses differed in their patterns of communication from surgical patients and their spouses (Hinchliffe *et al* 1975). In view of the evidence linking inefficient communication patterns with child psychiatric disorder (see above) these abnormal patterns of family interaction may help explain why parental mental disorder is associated with psychiatric problems in the children.

The pathogenic interactions may also be responsible for the well-demonstrated finding that the wives of men with psychiatric disorder show a marked tendency to develop depressive or neurotic disorders themselves (Buck & Ladd 1965; Hare & Shaw 1965; Hagnell & Kreitman 1974; Kreitman 1964; Kreitman *et al* 1970; Ovenstone 1973; Rutter, Quinton & Yule 1977). At one time the finding was taken as an indication of assortative mating but the evidence that the effect is more evident in the wives of ill husbands than in the husbands of ill wives, and that patient–spouse concordance in neurotic manifestations is low soon after marriage but increase with duration of marriage is more in keeping with a 'contagion' of disorder. This spread of disorder is likely to be a function of the increased contact between husbands and wives and the greater social isolation of patient couples compared with the general population (Nelson *et al* 1970), as well as the maladaptive features of the marital interaction.

In summary, the children of parents with a chronic or recurrent mental disorder have a substantially increased risk of psychiatric disorder. The risk, however, is not an inevitable consequence of the parental illness but rather is a result of the involvement of the children in abnormal parental behaviour and of the associations between parental illness on the one hand and family discord, maladaptive communication and impaired parent–child interaction on the other.

CHILDHOOD EXPERIENCES AND PARENTING BEHAVIOUR

In both this chapter and the previous one various comments have been made about the origins of parental behaviour. It has been apparent that the way parents treat their children is a function of many factors including personality characteristics, current mood state, marital relationship, social circumstances and also the temperamental characteristics of the children (see Chapter 1). Patterns of family life and of child-rearing are also influenced by changing social mores and public attitudes, as well as by more personal influences. This tendency is reflected in the marked changes in family life which have taken place during recent years in both Britain and the United States (see Rutter & Madge 1976). During the last few decades there have been marked shifts towards earlier marriage and earlier child-bearing, a higher proportion of illegitimate children, more frequent divorce and smaller families. In addition, however, research findings show that an individual's personal experiences of child-rearing influence the way in which he brings up his own children a generation later.

Thus, Illsley and Thompson (1961) in a systematic study of Aberdeen primiparae found that women whose childhood homes had been broken by divorce or separation were more likely to conceive outside marriage and more likely to become pregnant as a teenager. Crellin *et al* (1971) also found that women from broken homes were more likely to have illegitimate children. Wolkind *et al* (1976) showed that childhood separations which had occurred in the context of family discord or disruption were associated with a greatly increased risk of both teenage pregnancy and unmarried motherhood. The associations did not apply when the separations had taken place in stable families. Several studies have indicated that people from unhappy or broken homes are more likely themselves to make unsatisfactory marriages and to divorce or separate (Waller & Hill 1951; Langner & Michael 1963; Gurin, Veroff & Feld 1960). It should be noted that this link with marital discord and marital breakdown does *not* occur in the case of people whose childhood homes were broken by parental death. Frommer and O'Shea (1973a, b) found that women who had been separated from their parents in childhood because of family discord had more difficulties in infant care and were more likely to have infants with problems than nonseparated women.

Not much is known about intergenerational continuities in methods of child-rearing, but there is extensive evidence that grossly abnormal parenting, as reflected in child-battering, is strongly associated with seriously adverse childhood experiences (see Rutter & Madge 1976). Systematic studies (Oliver *et al* 1974; Smith *et al* 1973; 1974; 1975) have shown that a quarter to a third of battering parents were illegitimate, and most had been subject to serious abuse or neglect in their own childhoods. The same investigations indicated that battering parents tended to have personality disorders and to make unhappy marriages. Most were punitive and many were overinvolved with their children, but also most provided poor supervision.

In summary, there is good evidence linking the experience of an unhappy and disrupted family life in childhood with teenage pregnancy, extramarital conception, marriage breakdown and, possibly, less satisfactory neonatal care. However, in spite of important and statistically significant associations, most individuals from unhappy homes do *not* show these characteristics in adulthood. Intergenerational continuities are probably greater in the case of seriously abnormal parenting such as child-battering.

Little is known regarding the mechanisms which link childhood experiences with parenting behaviour when adult (see Rutter & Madge 1976 for a discussion of this matter). Animal studies clearly demonstrate that abnormal experiences in early life can cause grossly abnormal parenting behaviour at maturity and it seems highly probable that although heredity plays a part in humans, environmental mediation also occurs. It should be noted that the animal findings show that, when abnormal mothering is due to adverse experiences in early life, the effects may still be reversible to a substantial extent (Harlow & Suomi 1971; Suomi & Harlow 1972; Novak & Harlow 1975). How far this applies in humans is not known but parental behaviour is likely to prove to be modifiable to some degree. What circumstances or what interventions are needed to facilitate improvements in parenting when parents have been damaged by childhood experiences remains to be determined.

SOME PSYCHOLOGICAL MECHANISMS IN MORAL DEVELOPMENT

There has been very extensive research into the process of moral development (see review by Hoffman 1970) and into the variables influencing aggressive behaviour (see reviews by Feshbach 1970 and Berkowitz 1973). A detailed consideration of these topics would extend well beyond the scope of this chapter, and most of the studies have not been concerned in any way with psychiatric disorder. However, some discussion of these issues is necessary in order to understand the various ways in which family influences may effect children's development and behaviour.

Frustration

In 1939, Dollard and his colleagues published an influential monograph in which they suggested that aggression was always a consequence of frustration.

This hypothesis has not been easy to test if only because of the difficulties involved in assessing 'frustration'. Nevertheless subsequent research has clearly shown that the notion was a misleading oversimplification (Feshbach 1970; Berkowitz 1973). Not all frustration leads to aggression and not all aggression is due to frustration. Nevertheless, numerous studies have shown that frustration is a potent source of emotional arousal and that often this affective state leads to aggressive behaviour. However, it may lead to other behaviours and whether or not aggression is shown will depend on the behavioural options available, previous learning experiences, age and sex (in general, girls are less likely to respond to frustration with aggression). Davitz (1952), for example, showed that children could be trained to respond constructively rather than aggressively to frustration. In short, frustration tends to produce a feeling state which provides a motive to inflict injury, but children may learn to cope with this feeling in a variety of ways which do not involve aggressive behaviour.

If this interpretation of the evidence is correct, it would be expected that parental behaviour which increases frustrations *and* which fails to facilitate unaggressive coping mechanisms would be particularly likely to increase aggression in the children. Parents who provide little warmth or support, who are critical and rejecting, and who are inconsistent in their behaviour might be thought to fall into just that category. As discussed in this and the previous chapter, this is indeed the kind of parental behaviour which is associated with disorders of conduct (which often include aggressive behaviour).

Catharsis

The concept of catharsis—meaning the process by which anger or other emotions is discharged—is closely related to the frustration hypothesis. The idea is that once anger has been aroused it creates an energy state which can only be dealt with by discharging the aggression or hostility in some way. The whole idea of reservoirs of energy which have to be released is out of keeping with the available evidence (see Hinde 1960) which throw doubt on the catharsis hypothesis. However, the hypothesis has also been subjected to a variety of specific experimental investigations, usually with results that run counter to the catharsis idea. Thus, Feshbach (1956) showed that children told a story with aggressive themes and then provided with toys which lent themselves to aggressive play showed *more* aggression than children told a neutral story and given nonaggressive toys. These children were not frustrated and it could be argued that prior frustration is necessary for catharsis to occur. Two subsequent studies by Feshbach (Feshbach 1961; Feshbach & Singer 1971) have produced findings consistent with the catharsis hypothesis. He found that watching aggressive films or TV programmes decreased aggression in angered subjects. However, a replication by Wells (cited Surgeon-General 1972) of the Feshbach and Singer study showed an increase in *physical* aggression following the watching of violent TV programmes in parallel with the decrease in *verbal* aggression. A variety of other studies (see Berkowitz 1973) have all shown that angry subjects who watch aggressive films tend to become more aggressive. Moreover, Mallik and McCandless (1966) in a well controlled study found that aggressive play increased subsequent aggression in previously frustrated schoolchildren. There is no satisfactory evidence on the extent to which competitive sport increases or decreases aggression (Berkowitz 1962), but strong competition generally increases conflict and may lead to violence (Sherif *et al* 1961).

In summary, the weight of evidence suggests that frustrated individuals who watch aggressive films or who participate in aggressive play usually become *more*, rather than less, aggressive. An apparently cathartic effect has been shown in some circumstances but it is not the usual result.

Interpretations and perceptions

This rather negative conclusion might seem to run counter to the widespread experience that 'getting it off your chest' can help. However, the reduction of tension which can occur following a discussion of aggressive feelings may have nothing to do with catharsis. Thus, in the already mentioned study by Mallik and McCandless (1966) it was found that discussion of the factors that led to frustration decreased aggression, although aggressive play had increased it. A variety of other studies (see Berkowitz 1973) have also suggested that aggressive responses to frustration may be reduced by helping people to alter their perceptions about the frustrating incident or about the individuals who caused the frustration. It is not just a question of gaining 'insight' but rather of achieving a perception which puts the happening in more positive or sympathetic terms. If the understanding involves a perception of the frustration as having an aggressive intent this may increase the aggressive response (Epstein & Taylor 1967).

Sherif's famous 'Robbers' Cave' experiment (Sherif *et al* 1961) in which adolescent boys at a holiday camp were divided into competing groups, indicated that participation in cooperative activities can also reduce conflict and hostility. When the boys had to work together in order to reach a common goal, hostile feelings between the groups markedly reduced. Other studies (see Hartup 1970) have also shown that cooperative activities tend to increase positive social interaction whereas competition tends to have less consistent effects but often increases negative feelings especially if the competition is unequal. External threat, on the other hand, may increase solidarity within a group at the same time as it leads to hostility to the outsider. The classical studies of White and Lippitt (1960) on the effects of various types of adult leadership on schoolboys showed that the most harmonious atmosphere was created by democratic leadership which allowed the boys to participate in decision-making. Authoritarian leadership was quite effective in getting tasks completed but tended to lead to either an aggressive or apathetic social climate.

None of these experimental findings are readily translatable into a family context. However, the family constitutes a social group and social influences will apply there as in any other group. The evidence suggests that little is likely to be gained by a laissez-faire atmosphere in which aggression and negative feelings are freely allowed. On the other hand, a family setting which facilitates cooperative activities and which encourages discussion of difficulties in ways which enhance appreciation of other people ought to diminish aggression and other disruptive activities. The limited findings which indicate that benefits of family harmony and effective communication with efficient problem-solving are in keeping with this suggestion.

Response to aggression

A variety of both naturalistic and experimental studies have shown that aggression is related as much to the effects it provides as to the frustrating or other circumstances which precede it (Feshbach 1970). Thus, Patterson *et al* (1967), in a study of aggressive events among nursery schoolchildren, observed that the majority of aggressive acts resulted in some kind of positive reinforcement. Similarly, Brown and Elliot (1965) showed that when nursery schoolteachers ignored aggressive acts and paid increased attention to cooperative behaviour, the children's aggressive acts declined in frequency. In short, aggressive behaviour persists in part because it succeeds in gaining attention or in provoking a response which encourages further aggression.

It would seem to follow from this that punishment of aggression or disruptive behaviour should stop it. Under carefully controlled conditions punishment may indeed have this beneficial effect (Gardner 1969). However, often it does not and, as already noted, parents who punish frequently or severely tend to have children who are *more* aggressive or disruptive (Becker 1964; Feshbach 1970). There are several reasons why this happens (Feshbach 1970; Rutter 1975). First, high frequency of punishment is often associated with great inconsistency, and so with very inefficient reinforcement. Second, highly punitive parents are often also cold and rejecting and the adverse parent–child relationship is likely to increase aggression. Third, experimental studies indicate that punishment is really successful only when the child has other more acceptable ways of coping or responding. But parents who punish frequently often fail to provide adequate alternatives for the child and fail to reward nonaggressive responses. Fourth, what seems like punishment may actually be rewarding. Thus, the child whose father bellows and shouts at him may be reinforced by the satisfaction of getting his father angry and making him lose control. Fifth, punishment may be disruptive in its effects by causing panic or resentment. Sixth, corporal punishment or angry shouting not only serves as a response to the child's aggression but also as a model of how to behave. The model of aggression provided by the parent may make it more likely that the child will behave similarly (see below).

The findings, taken together, suggest that parents who consistently encourage cooperative behaviour and nonaggressive acts are likely to be most successful in promoting positive social interaction in their children. However, for this pattern of parental response to work well it is also necessary that the discipline should take place within the context of a warm relationship and that the punishment should *not* be of a kind which provides a model of aggression or loss of control. This conclusion is broadly in line with the research findings on parental discipline (see above).

Imitation

As discussed, children's behaviour may be altered by both the conditions which precede and by those which follow their behaviour. However, in addition, vicarious learning also takes place in which children's behaviour is modified by their observations of the behaviour of other people. There is an extensive body of evidence from experimental studies which supports this conclusion (Bandura 1969; Flanders 1968). Typically, children's play in the laboratory is observed before and after a period in which they watch films or real life situations in which the actors behave in particular ways, displaying aggression, altruism or self-denial). The usual findings have been that the children's post-test behaviour is influenced by the activities they observed. However, various factors influence the extent of imitation. First, children are more likely to imitate behaviour which is merely an exaggeration of their usual style of response. Thus, aggressive children are more likely to increase in aggression after watching films of fighting and violence than are children who were nonaggressive to begin with. Second, on the whole, children are more likely to imitate someone of high status or someone admired by them. Third, there is some tendency (although results are not entirely consistent) for imitation to be more likely in the context of a warm or nurturant relationship. Fourth, children are somewhat more likely to imitate someone who is dominant or who controls resources.

Of course, it must be recognised that most of the studies took place under somewhat artificial conditions so that the results cannot necessarily be generalised to real life. On the other hand, findings in relation to aggressive behaviour after watching actual behaviour programmes are generally (but not always) similar (Surgeon General 1972). Furthermore, modelling has been shown to be an effective means of reducing fears (Bandura & Menlove 1968; White & Davis 1974) or social withdrawal (O'Connor 1969; Evers & Schwarz 1973). It may be concluded that children do learn by imitation.

From these findings it may be assumed that children are likely to be influenced by the models of behaviour provided by their parents. Moreover, imitation will possibly be greater in harmonious homes than in discordant families, and possibly greater, too, when the parents are dominant and controlling, than when they are passive and ineffectual. This may explain why in 'problem families' where adult delinquency is very common, psychiatric problems in the children are related to marital disharmony and parental mental disorder whereas delinquency is not (Wilson 1974; Tonge *et al* 1975). The tentative suggestion could be made that in these circumstances delinquency was in considerable part a modelled behaviour in basically normal children whereas psychiatric disorder was a sign of psychopathology which had arisen by quite different mechanisms.

Identification and conscience

Children, as they grow older, become better able to conceptualise right and wrong. In the preschool period, behaviour control is largely dependent on immediate consequences. However, gradually the child learns sets of rules laid down by parents or teachers. Finally, notions of right or wrong based on adult authority are replaced by principles of conscience—a higher order morality based on the child's own ideas. Following Freud's teaching, it is widely thought that this adoption of internalised personal standards is based in large part on a process of identification. This process means that the child comes to think, feel and behave as though someone else's characteristics belonged to him—not only does he emulate them but he feels *with* them and thereby learns to share their values.

There is little doubt that something on these general lines does occur. However, the concepts have proved difficult to define (see Kagan 1958; Bronfenbrenner 1960) and even more difficult to test (Hoffman 1970). It has become clear that moral development is not an entirely unitary process (Hoffman 1970), that when faced with authority people readily violate internalised standards (Milgram 1974), and that identification is often selective rather than total (Hoffman 1970). Undoubtedly, imitation forms much of the basis of identification (Bandura 1969) although whether the two processes are synony-mous is more doubtful. In spite of mountains of research, only very limited and tentative statements are possible regarding the process of moral develop-ment. Hoffman (1970) concluded that (a) the early development of morality was largely based on social learning; (b) that later developments were facili-tated by an interaction with authority figures who behaved rationally and by the individuals own experience in taking the role of authority; (c) that the disciplinary process involved a linking of rule violation with anxiety (or guilt); and (d) that the further process of moral development was built upon the child's capacity for empathy.

CONCLUSION

There are both dangers and difficulties in deriving principles of child-rearing from laboratory experiments. The fact that broadly similar conclusions stem from interview and observation studies in the home and from experimental investigations does not make the conclusions correct. Nevertheless, if we are to help families function better and if we are to adapt to changing sociocul-tural conditions it is essential that we understand the mechanisms and prin-ciples involved. Knowing a rather heterogeneous list of disparate research findings is not enough, any more than is a reliance on clinical experience. Both in this chapter and the previous one, an attempt has been made to outline the possible processes of psychological development which lie behind the re-search findings. It should be appreciated, however, that many of the con-clusions are necessarily tentative and most have the status of hypotheses rather than firm knowledge.

REFERENCES

AINSWORTH M.D. (1973) The development of infant–mother attachment. *In* Caldwell B.M. & Ricciuti H.N. (eds.) *Review of Child Development Research*. Chicago: Uni-versity of Chicago Press

ALEXANDER J.F. (1973) Defensive and supportive communications in normal and devi-ant families. *J. Cons. Clin. Psychol.* **40**, 223–231

ALEXANDER J.F. & PARSONS B.V. (1973) Short-term behavioural intervention with delin-quent families: impact on family process and recidivism. *J. Abnorm. Psychol.* **81**, 219–225

ANDRY R.G. (1960) *Delinquency and Parental Pathology*. London: Methuen

ASKHAM J. (1975) *Fertility and Deprivation*. London: Cambridge University Press

BANDURA A. (1969) Social-learning theory of identificatory processes. *In* Goslin D.A. (ed.) *Handbook of Socialization Theory and Research*. Chicago: Rand McNally

BANDURA A. & MENLOVE F.L. (1968) Factors determining vicarious extinction of avoidance behavior through symbolic modelling. *J. Pers. Soc. Psychol.* **8,** 99–108

BANDURA A. & WALTERS R.H. (1959) *Adolescent aggression.* New York: Ronald

BARUCH D.W. & WILCOX J.A. (1944) A study of sex differences in pre-school children's adjustment coexistent with interparental tensions. *J. Genet. Psychol.* **64,** 281–303

BAUMRIND D. (1967) Childcare practices anteceding three patterns of pre-school behaviour. *Genet. Psychol. Monogr.* **75,** 43–88

BECKER J. & IWAKAMI E. (1969) Conflict and dominance within families of disturbed children. *J. Abnorm. Psychol.* **74,** 330–335

BECKER W.C. (1964) Consequences of different kinds of parental discipline. *In* Hoffman M.L. & Hoffman L.W. (eds.) *Review of Child Development Research,* vol. 1. New York: Russell Sage Foundation

BECKER W.C. & KRUG R.S. (1965) The parent attitude research instrument—a research review. *Child Dev.* **36,** 329–365

BECKER W.C., MADSEN C.H., ARNOLD C.R. & THOMAS D.R. (1967) The contingent use of teacher attention and praise in reducing classroom behaviour problems. *J. Spec. Educ.* **1,** 287–307

BELL J.E. (1961) *Family group therapy.* Publ. Hlth. Monogr. No. 64. Washington, DC: U.S. Publ. Hlth. Serv.

BELL J.E. (1962) Recent advances in family group therapy. *J. Child Psychol. Psychiat.* **3,** 1–15

BELL S.M. & AINSWORTH M.D.S. (1972) Infant crying and maternal responsiveness. *Child Dev.* **43,** 1171–1190

BELOFF H. (1957) The structure and origin of the anal character. *Genet. Psychol. Monogr.* **55,** 141–172

BENNETT I. (1960) *Delinquent and Neurotic Children: A Comparative Study.* New York: Basic Books

BERG I. (1974) Self-administered dependency questionnaire for use with mothers of schoolchildren. *Brit. J. Psychiat.* **124,** 101–109

BERG I. & McGUIRE R. (1974) Are mothers of school-phobic adolescents overprotective? *Brit. J. Psychiat.* **124,** 10–13

BERKOWITZ L. (1962) *Aggression: A Social and Psychological Analysis.* New York: McGraw-Hill

BERKOWITZ L. (1973) Control of aggression. *In* Caldwell B.M. & Ricciuti H.N. (eds.) *Review of Child Development Research Vol. 3.* University of Chicago Press

BERNICK N. (1965) The development of children's sexual attitudes as determined by the pupil-dilation response. Unpublished doctoral dissertation, University of Chicago, cited Kohlberg (1967)

BERNSTEIN A. (1955) Some relations between techniques of feeding and training during infancy and certain behaviour in childhood. *Genet. Psychol. Monogr.* **51,** 3–44

BOWLBY J. (1969) *Attachment and Loss.* vol. 1: *Attachment.* London: Hogarth Press

BRODERICK C.B. & FOWLER S.E. (1961) New patterns of relationships between the sexes among preadolescents. *Marriage and Family Living* **23,** 27–30

BRODERICK C.B. & ROWE G.P. (1968) A scale of preadolescent heterosexual development. *J. Marriage and the Family* **30,** 97–101

BRONFENBRENNER U. (1960) Freudian theories of identification and their derivatives. *Child Dev.* **31,** 15–40

BROWN P. & ELLIOTT R. (1965) Control of aggression in a nursery school class. *J. Exp. Child Psychol.* **2,** 103–107

BROWN G.W., BHROLCHAIN M.N. and HARRIS T. (1975) Social class and psychiatric disturbance among women in an urban population. *Sociology,* **9,** 225–254

BUCK C. & LADD K. (1965) Psychoneurosis in marital partners. *Brit. J. Psychiat.* **111,** 587–590

BUCK C. & LAUGHTON K. (1959) Family patterns of illness: the effect of psychoneurosis in the parent upon illness in the child. *Acta Psychiat.* **34,** 165–175

BUGENTAL D.E., LOVE L.R., KASWAN J.W. & APRIL C. (1971) Verbal-non-verbal conflict in parental messages to normal and disturbed children. *J. Abnorm. Psychol.* **77,** 6–10

BUXBAUM E. (1959) Psychosexual development: the oral, anal and phallic phases. *In* Levitt D. (ed.) *Readings in Psychoanalytic Psychology.* New York: Appleton

BYASSEE J.E. & MURRELL S.A. (1975) Interaction patterns in families of autistic, disturbed and normal children. *Amer. J. Orthopsychiat.* **45,** 473–478

CALDWELL B.M. (1964) The effects of infant care. *In* Hoffman M.L. & Hoffman L.W. (eds.) *Review of Child Development Research,* vol. 1. New York: Russell Sage Foundation

CAMPBELL E.H. (1939) The social-sex development of children. *Genet. Psychol. Monogr.* **21,** 461–552

CENTERS R., RAVEN B.H. & RODRIGUEZ A. (1971) Conjugal power structure: a re-examination. *Amer. Social. Rev.* **36,** 264–278

CLAUSEN J.A. (1966) Family structure, socialization and personality. *In* Hoffman L.W. & Hoffman M. (eds.) *Review of Child Development Research,* vol. 2. New York: Russell Sage Foundation

CONN J.H. (1940) Children's reactions to the discovery of genital differences. *Amer. J. Orthopsychiat.* **10,** 747–754

CONN J.H. & KANNER L. (1947) Children's awareness of sex differences. *J. Child Psychiat.* **1,** 3–57

COX A., RUTTER M., YULE B. & QUINTON D. (1976) Bias resulting from missing information: Some epidemiological findings. (Submitted for publication)

CRAIG M.M. & GLICK S.J. (1964) *A manual of procedures for application of the Glueck prediction table.* New York: City Youth Board

CRELLIN E., PRINGLE M.L. KELLMER & WEST P. (1971) *Born illegitimate: social and educational implications.* Windsor: NFER

DAVITZ J.R. (1952) The effects of previous training on post frustration behaviour. *J. Abnorm. Soc. Psychol.* **47,** 309–315

DOLLARD J., DOOB L., MILLER N., MOWRER O. & SEARS R. (1939) *Frustration and Aggression.* New Haven, Connecticut: Yale University Press

DOUGLAS J.W.B. (1964) *The Home and the School.* London: MacGibbon & Kee

DOUGLAS J.W.B., ROSS J.M. & SIMPSON H.R. (1968) *All Our Future: A Longitudinal Study of Secondary Education.* London: Peter Davies

DYTRYCH Z., MATEJCEK Ü., SCHÜLLER V., DAVID H.P. & FRIEDMAN H.L. (1975) Children born to women denied abortion. *Family Planning Perspectives* **7,** 165–171

EISENBERG L. (1958) School phobia: a study in the communication of anxiety. *Amer. J. Psychiat.* **114,** 712–718

ELKIND D. (1968) Cognition in infancy and early childhood. *In* Brackbill Y. (ed.) *Infancy and Early Childhood.* New York: Free Press

EPSTEIN S. & TAYLOR S.P. (1967) Instigation to aggression as a function of degree of defeat and perceived aggression intent of the opponent. *J. Pers.* **35,** 265–289

EPSTEIN N.B., SIGAL J.J. & RAKOFF V. (1972) Methodological problems in family interaction research. *In* Framo J.L. (ed.) *Family Interaction: a Dialogue Between Family Researchers and Family Therapists.* New York: Springer

EVERS W.L. & SCHWARZ J.C. (1973) Modifying social withdrawal in preschoolers: The effect of filmed modeling and teacher praise. *J. Abnorm. Child Psychol.* **1,** 248–256

FARINA A. (1960) Patterns of role dominance and conflict in parents of schizophrenic patients. *J. Abnorm. Soc. Psychol.* **61,** 31–38

FARRINGTON D.P., GUNDRY G. & WEST D.J. (1975) The familial transmission of criminality. *Medicine, Science and The Law* **15,** 177–186

FERGUSON T. (1952) *The Young Delinquent in his Social Setting.* London: Oxford University Press

FERREIRA A. (1963) Family myth and homeostasis. *Arch. Gen. Psychiat.* **9,** 457–463

FERREIRA A. & WINTER W. (1968) Information exchange and silence in normal and abnormal families. *Family Process* **7,** 251–276

FESHBACH S. (1956) The catharsis hypothesis and some consequences of interaction with aggressive and neutral play objects. *J. Pers.* **24,** 449–462

FESHBACH S. (1961) The stimulating versus cathartic effects of vicarious aggressive activity. *J. Abnorm. Soc. Psychol.* **63,** 381–385

FESHBACH S. (1970) Aggression. *In* Mussen P.H. (ed.) *Carmichael's Manual of Child Psychology,* 3rd edn., vol. 2. London: Wiley

FESHBACH S. & SINGER R. (1971) *Television and Aggression.* San Francisco: Jossey-Bass

FLANDERS J.P. (1968) A review of research on imitative behaviour. *Psychol. Bull.* **69,** 316–337

FORSSMAN H. & THUWE I. (1966) One hundred and twenty children born after application for therapeutic abortion refused. *Acta Psychiat. Scand.* **42,** 71–88

FREUD A. (1947) Emotional and instinctual development. *In Indications for Child Analysis and Other Papers* (1945–1956, 1969). London: Hogarth Press

FREUD S. (1905) Three essays on the theory of sexuality *In* Strachey J. (ed.) *The Standard Edition of the Complete Psychological Works of Sigmund Freud,* vol. VII. London: Hogarth Press

FREUD S. (1922) Two encyclopaedia articles. *In* Strachey J. (ed.) *The Standard Edition of the Complete Psychological Works of Sigmund Freud,* vol. XVIII. London: Hogarth Press

FRIEDMAN S.M. (1952) An empirical study of the castration and Oedipus complexes. *Genet. Psychol. Monogr.* **46,** 61–130

FROMMER E.A. & O'SHEA G. (1973a) Antenatal identification of women liable to have problems in managing their infants. *Brit. J. Psychiat.* **123,** 149–156

FROMMER E.A. & O'SHEA G. (1973b) The importance of childhood experience in relation to problems of marriage and family-building. *Brit. J. Psychiat.* **123,** 157–160

GARDNER W.I. (1969) Use of punishment procedures with the severely retarded: a review. *Amer. J. Ment. Defic.* **74,** 86–103

GASSNER S. & MURRAY E.J. (1969) Dominance of conflict in the interactions between parents of normal and neurotic children. *J. Abnorm. Psychol.* **74,** 33–41

GESELL A. (1940) *The First Five Years of Life.* London: Methuen

GLUECK S. & GLUECK E.T. (1950) *Unraveling Juvenile Delinquency.* New York: Commonwealth Fund

GRANVILLE–GROSSMAN K.L. (1968) The early environment in affective disorder. *In* Coppen A. & Walk A. (eds.) *Recent Developments in the Affective Disorders. Brit. J. Psychiat.* Special Publication No. 2. Ashford, Kent: Headley Bros

GURIN G., VEROFF J. & FELD S. (1960) *Americans View Their Mental Health.* New York: Basic Books

GURMAN A.S. (1973) The effects and effectiveness of marital therapy: a review of outcome research. *Family Process* **12**, 145–170

HAGNELL O. & KREITMAN N. (1974) Mental illness in married pairs in a total population. *Brit. J. Psychiat.* **125**, 293–302

HALEY J. (1967) Experiment with abnormal families: testing done in a restricted communication setting. *Arch. Gen. Psychiat.* **17**, 53–63

HALEY J. (1972) Critical overview of present status of family interaction research. *In* Framo J. (ed.) *Family Interaction: a Dialogue Between Family Researchers and Family Therapists.* New York: Springer

HALVERSON H.M. (1940) Genital and sphincter behaviour of the male infant. *J. Genet. Psychol.* **56**, 95–136

HARE E.H. & SHAW G.K. (1965) *Mental Health on a New Housing Estate*, Institute of Psychiatry Maudsley Monograph No. 12. London: Oxford University Press

HARLOW H.F. & SUOMI S.J. (1971) Social recovery by isolation-reared monkeys. *Proc. Nat. Acad. Sci. U.S.A.* **68**, 1534–1538

HARTUP W.W. (1970) Peer interaction and social organization. *In* Mussen P.H. (ed.) *Carmichael's Manual of Child Psychology*, 3rd edn., vol. 2. London: Wiley

HETHERINGTON E.M. & BRACKBILL Y. (1963) Etiology and covariation of obstinacy, orderliness and parsimony in young children. *Child Dev.* **34**, 919–943

HETHERINGTON E.M. & MARTIN B. (1972) Family interaction and psychopathology in children. *In* Quay H.C. and Werry J.S. (eds.) *Psychopathological Disorders of Childhood.* New York: Wiley

HETHERINGTON E.M., STOUWIE R.J. & RIDBERG E.H. (1971) Patterns of family interaction and child-rearing attitudes related to three dimensions of juvenile delinquency. *J. Abnorm. Psychol.* **78**, 160–176

HEWITT L.E. & JENKINS R.L. (1949) *Fundamental Patterns of Maladjustment: The Dynamics of Their Origin.* Springfield, State of Illinois

HILTON I. (1967) Differences in the behaviour of mothers toward first and later-born children. *J. Pers. Soc. Psychol.* **7**, 282–290

HINCHLIFFE M., HOOPER D., ROBERTS F.J. & VAUGHAN P.W. (1975) A study of the interaction between depressed patients and their spouses. *Brit. J. Psychiat.* **126**, 164–172

HINDE R.A. (1960) Energy models of motivation. *Symp. Soc. exp. Biol.* **14**, 199–213

HOFFMAN M.L. (1970) Moral development. *In* Mussen P.H. (ed.) *Carmichael's Manual of Child Psychology*, 3rd edn., vol. 2. London: Wiley

HONIGMANN J.J. (1954) *Culture and Personality.* New York: Harper

HUNT J.McV. (1960) Experience and the development of motivation: some reinterpretations. *Child Dev.* **31**, 489–504

ILLSLEY R. & THOMPSON B. (1961) Women from broken homes. *Social. Rev.* **9**, 27–53

ISAACS S. (1933) *Social Development in Young Children.* London: Routledge & Kegan Paul

JACOB T. (1975) Family interaction in disturbed and normal families: a methodological and substantive review. *Psychol. Bull.* **82**, 33–65

JENKINS R.L. (1968) The varieties of children's behavioural problems and family dynamics. *Amer. J. Psychiat.* **124**, 1440–1445

JOHNSON S.M., WAHL G., MARTIN S. & JOHANSSON S. (1971) How deviant is the normal child: a behavioural analysis of the preschool child and his family. Unpublished paper, Assoc. Advancement of Behaviour Therapy, Washington, DC

JONSSON G. (1967) Delinquent boys, their parents and grandparents. *Acta Psychiat. Scand.* Suppl., 195

KAGAN J. (1958) The concept of identification. *Psychol. Rev.* **65**, 296–305

KELLNER R. (1963) *Family Ill Health: an investigation in general practice.* London: Tavistock

KINSEY A.C., POMEROY W.B. & MARTIN C.E. (1948) *Sexual Behavior in the Human Male.* Philadelphia: W.B. Saunders

KREITMAN N. (1964) The patient's spouse. *Brit. J. Psychiat.* **110**, 159–173

KREITMAN N., COLLINS J., NELSON B. & TROOP J. (1970) Neurosis and marital interaction: I. Personality and symptoms. *Brit. J. Psychiat.* **117**, 33–46

KREITMAN N., COLLINS C., NELSON B. & TROOP J. (1971) Neurosis and marital interaction. IV. Manifest psychological interaction. *Brit. J. Psychiat.* **119**, 243–252

LAND H. (1969) *Large Families in London.* Occasional Papers on Social Administration No. 32. London: Bell

LANGNER T.S. & MICHAEL S.T. (1963) *Life Stress and Mental Health.* London: Collier–Macmillan

LASKO J.K. (1954) Parent behavior toward first and second children. *Genet. Psychol. Monogr.*, **49**, 96–137

LEIGHTON L., STOLLAK G. & FERGUSON L. (1971) Patterns of communication in normal and clinic families. *J. Cons. Clin. Psychol.* **36**, 252–256

LEVY D.M. (1928) Fingersucking and accessory movements in early infancy: an etiologic study. *Amer. J. Psychiat.* **7**, 881–918

LEVY D.M. (1943) *Maternal Overprotection.* New York: Columbia University Press

LEWIS H. (1954) *Deprived Children.* London: Oxford University Press

LUSTMAN S.L. (1956) Rudiments of the ego. *Psychoanal. Study Child* **11**, 89–98

LYTTON H. (1971) Observation studies of parent–child interaction: a methodological review. *Child Dev.* **42**, 651–684

McCORD W. & McCORD J. (1959) *Origins of Crime.* New York: Columbia University Press

MADSEN C.H., BECKER W.C. & THOMAS D.R. (1968) Rules, praise and ignoring: elements of elementary classroom control. *J. Appl. Behav. Anal.* **1**, 139–150

MALLICK S.K. & McCANDLESS B.R. (1966) A study of catharsis of aggression. *J. Pers. Soc. Psychol.* **4**, 591–596

MEAD D.E. & CAMPBELL S.S. (1972) Decision-making and interaction in families with and without a drug-abusing child. *Family Process* **11**, 487–498

MILGRAM S. (1974) *Obedience to Authority.* London: Tavistock

MILLAR S. (1968) *The Psychology of Play.* London: Penguin

MINISTRY OF SOCIAL SECURITY (1967) *Circumstances of Families.* London: HMSO

MISHLER E. & WAXLER N. (1965) Family interaction processes and schizophrenia: a review of current theories. *Merrill–Palmer Quart.* **11**, 269–316

MURRELL S.A. (1971) Family interaction variables and adjustment of non clinic boys. *Child Dev.* **42**, 1485–1494

MURRELL S.A. & STACHOWIAK J. (1967) Consistency, rigidity and power in the interaction patterns of clinic and non clinic families. *J. Abnorm. Psychol.* **72**, 265–272

NELSON B., COLLINS J., KREITMAN N. & TROOP J. (1970) Neurosis and marital interaction, II. Time sharing and social activity. *Brit. J. Psychiat.* **117**, 47–58

NEWSON J. & NEWSON E. (1963) *Patterns of Infant Care in an Urban Community.* London: Allen & Unwin

NEWSON J. & NEWSON E. (1968) *Four Years Old in an Urban Community.* London: Allen & Unwin

NISBET J.D. (1953) *Family Environment: a Direct Effect of Family Size on Intelligence.* Occasional papers on Eugenics, No. 8. The Eugenics Society

NOVAK M.A. & HARLOW H.F. (1975) Social recovery of monkeys isolated for the first year of life. 1. Rehabilitation and therapy. *Develop. Psychol.* **11**, 453–465

O'CONNOR R.D. (1969) Modification of social withdrawal through symbolic modelling. *J. Appl. Behav. Anal.* **2**, 15–22

O'CONNOR W.A. & STACHOWIAK J. (1971) Patterns of interaction in families with low adjusted, high adjusted and mentally retarded members. *Family Process* **10**, 224–241

OLDMAN D., BYTHEWAY B. & HOROBIN G. (1971) Family structure and educational achievement. *J. Biosoc. Sci. Suppl.* **3**, 81–91

OLIVER J.E., COX J., TAYLOR A. & Baldwin J.A. (1974) *Severely Ill-treated Young Children in North-East Wiltshire.* Oxford University Unit of Clinical Epidemiology Research Report No. 4

OLSON D.H. (1972) Empirically unbonding the double bond: review of research and conceptual reformulations. *Family Process* **11**, 69–94

OTTERSTROM E. (1946) Delinquency and children from bad homes. *Acta Paediat.* **33**, Suppl. 5

OVENSTONE I.M.K. (1973) The development of neurosis in the wives of neurotic men I. Symptomatology and personality. *Brit. J. Psychiat.* **122**, 35–45

PATTERSON G. (1973) Reprogramming the families of aggressive boys. *In* Thoresen C. (ed.) *Behavior Modification in Education,* Part I. Chicago: University of Chicago Press

PATTERSON G. & COBB J.A. (1971) A dyadic analysis of 'aggressive' behaviours. *In* Hill J.P. (ed.) *Minnesota Symposia on Child Psychology,* vol. 5. Minneapolis: University of Minnesota Press

PATTERSON G., LITTMAN R.A. & BRICKER W. (1967) Assertive behaviour in children: A step toward a theory of aggression. *Monogr. Soc. Res. Child Develop.* **32**, Serial No. 113

PIAGET J. (1951) *Plays, Dreams and Imitation in Childhood.* New York: Norton

RAMSEY G.V. (1943) The sexual development of boys. *Amer. J. Psychol.* **56**, 217–233

REESE H.W. (1966) Attitudes toward the opposite sex in late childhood. *Merrill–Palmer Quart.* **12**, 157–163

RICE E.P., EKDAHL M.C. & MILLER L. (1971) *Children of Mentally Ill Parents: Problems in Child Care.* New York: Behavioral Publications

RICHMAN N. (1975) Prevalence of Behaviour Problems in 3-year-old children: An epidemiological study in a London borough. *J. Child Psychol. Psychiat.* **16**, 272–287

RISKIN J.E. & FAUNCE E.E. (1972) An evaluative review of family interaction research. *Family Process* **11**, 365–455

ROBINS L.N. (1966) *Deviant Children Grown Up.* Baltimore: Williams & Wilkins

ROBINS L.N. & LEWIS R.G. (1966) The role of the antisocial family in school completion and delinquency: a three-generation study. *Sociol. Quart.* **7**, 500–514

ROBINS L.N., WEST P.A. & HERJANIC B.L. (1975) Arrests and delinquency in two generations: a study of black urban families and their children. *J. Child Psychol. Psychiat.* **16**, 125–140

ROSENTHAL M.J., FINKELSTEIN M., NI E. & ROBERTSON R.E. (1959) A study of mother–child relationships in the emotional disorders of children. *Genet. Psychol. Monogr.* **60**, 65–116

ROSENTHAL M.L., NI E., FINKELSTEIN M. & BERKWITS G.K. (1962) Father–child relationships and children's problems. *Arch. Gen. Psychiat.* **7**, 360–373

RUTTER M. (1966) *Children of Sick Parents: an Environmental and Psychiatric Study.* Institute of Psychiatry Maudsley Monograph No. 16. London: Oxford University Press

RUTTER M. (1971a) Parent–child separation: Psychological effects on the children. *J. Child Psychol. Psychiat.* **12**, 233–260

RUTTER M. (1971b) Normal psychosexual development. *J. Child Psychol. Psychiat.* **11**, 259–283

RUTTER M. (1972) *Maternal Deprivation Reassessed.* Harmondsworth: Penguin

RUTTER M. (1975) *Helping Troubled Children.* Harmondsworth: Penguin

RUTTER M. (1977) (ed.) *The Child, His Family and the Community.* (In preparation.) London: Wiley

RUTTER M. & MADGE N. (1976) *Cycles of Disadvantage: a Review of Research.* London: Heinemann

RUTTER M. & MITTLER P. (1972) Environmental influences in language development. *In* Rutter M. & Martin J.A.M. (eds.) *The Child with Delayed Speech.* Clinics in Devel. Med. No. 43. London: SIMP/Heinemann

RUTTER M., QUINTON D. & YULE W. (1977) *Family Pathology and Disorder in Children.* (In preparation.) London: Wiley

RUTTER M., TIZARD J. & WHITMORE K. (eds.) (1970) *Education, Health and Behaviour.* London: Longman

RUTTER M., YULE B., QUINTON D., ROWLANDS O., YULE W. & BERGER M. (1975) Attainment and adjustment in two geographical areas. III: Some factors accounting for area differences. *Brit. J. Psychiat.* **126**, 520–533

SANDLER J. & DARE C. (1970) The psychoanalytic concept of orality. *J. Psychosom. Res.* **14**, 211–222

SCHOFIELD M. (1965) *The Sexual Behaviour of Young People.* London: Longman

SCHUHAM A.I. (1970) Power relations in emotionally disturbed and normal family triads. *J. Abnorm. Psychol.* **75**, 30–37

SCHULMAN R.E., SHOEMAKER D.J. & MOELIS I. (1962) Laboratory measurement of parental behaviour. *J. Cons. Psychol.* **26**, 109–114

SEARS R.R., MACCOBY E.E. & LEVIN H. (1957) *Patterns of Child Rearing.* Evanston, Illinois: Row, Petersen

SHERIF M., HARVEY O.J., WHITE B.J., HOOD W.R. & SHERIF C.W. (1961) *Intergroup Conflict and Cooperation: The Robbers' Cave Experiment.* Norman, Oklahoma: University of Oklahoma Press

SKYNNER A.C.R. (1969) A group-analytic approach to conjoint family therapy. *J. Child Psychol. Psychiat.* **10**, 81–106

SMITH S.M. & HANSON R. (1975) Interpersonal relationships and child-rearing practices in 214 parents of battered children. *Brit. J. Psychiat.* **127**, 513–525.

SMITH S.M., HANSON R. & NOBLE S. (1973) Parents of battered babies: a controlled study. *Brit. Med. J.* **iv**, 388–391

SMITH S.M., HANSON R. & NOBLE S. (1974) Social aspects of the battered baby syndrome. *Brit. J. Psychiat.* **125**, 568–582

STRODTBECK F. (1951) Husband and wife interaction over revealed differences. *Amer. Soc. Rev.* **16**, 468–473

SUOMI S.J. & HARLOW H.F. (1972) Social rehabilitation of isolate-reared monkeys. *Develop. Psychol.* **6**, 487–496

SURGEON GENERAL (1972) *Television and Growing Up: the Impact of Televised Violence.* Washington DC: US Govt. Printing Office

TONGE W.L., JAMES D.S. & HILLAM S.M. (1975) Families without hope: a controlled study of 33 problem families. *Brit. J. Psychiat.* Special Publication No. 11.

WALLER W.W. & HILL R. (1951) *The Family: a Dynamic Interpretation.* New York: Dryden

WALTERS J. & STINNETT N. (1971) Parent–child relationships: a decade review of research. *J. Marriage and the Family* **33**, 70–111

WALTERS R.H., PARKE R.D. & CANE V.A. (1965) Timing of punishment and the observation of consequences to others as determinants of response inhibition. *J. Exp. Child Psychol.* **2**, 10–30

WAXLER N. & MISHLER E.G. (1970) Experimental studies of families. *In* Berkowitz, L. (ed.) *Advances in Experimental Social Psychology*, vol. 5. London: Academic Press

WEISSMAN M.M., PAYKEL E.S. & KLERMAN G.L. (1972) The depressed woman as a mother. *Soc. Psychiat.* **7**, 98–108

WELLS R.A., DILKES T.C. & TRIVELLI N. (1972) The results of family therapy: a critical review of the literature. *Family Process* **11**, 189–207

WEST D.J. & FARRINGTON D.P. (1973) *Who Becomes Delinquent?* London: Heinemann

WHITE R.W. (1959) Motivation reconsidered—the concept of competence. *Psychol. Rev.* **66**, 297–333

WHITE R.W. (1960) *Competence and the psychosexual stage of development. In* JONES M.R. (ed.) Nebraska Symposium on Motivation, vol. 8, Lincoln, Nebraska: University of Nebraska Press

WHITE W.C. & DAVIS N.T. (1974) Vicarious extinction of phobic behaviour in early childhood. *J. Abnorm. Child Psychol.* **2**, 25–32

WHITE R.K. & LIPPITT R. (1960) *Autocracy and Democracy: an Experimental Enquiry.* New York: Harper & Row

WILSON H. (1974) Parenting in poverty. *Brit. J. Soc. Work* **4**, 241–254

WOLFF S. (1970) Behaviour of pathology of parents of disturbed children. *In* Anthony E.J. & Koupernik C. (eds.) *The Child in his Family*, vol. 1, New York: Wiley

WOLFF S. (1973) *Children Under Stress.* Harmondsworth: Penguin

WOLFF S. & ACTON W.P. (1968) Characteristics of parents of disturbed children. *Brit. J. Psychiat.* **114**, 593–601

WOLKIND S. & RUTTER M. (1973) Children who have been 'in Care'; an epidemiological study. *J. Child Psychol. Psychiat.* **14**, 95–105

WOLKIND S., KRUK S. & CHAVES L.P. (1976) Childhood separation experiences and psycho-social status in primiparous women: Preliminary findings. *Brit. J. Psychiat.* **128,** 391–396

YARROW M.R., CAMPBELL J.D. & BURTON R.V. (1968) *Child Rearing: An Inquiry into Research and Methods.* San Francisco: Jossey-Bass

CHAPTER 5

Sociocultural influences

M. RUTTER

In previous chapters children's development, both normal and abnormal, has been considered in relation to a variety of influences within the family. However, as children grow older an increasingly large part of their life is spent at school and in neighbourhood activities outside the home. Also, too, families themselves are but one part of a wider social network and so the subject of forces stemming from the community in which they live, the people with whom they mix, prevailing cultural attitudes and the sociopolitical framework provided by local and central government and its institutions. These influences need to be assessed if there is to be a proper understanding of why people behave in the way that they do, as well as an understanding of the host of opportunities, pressures and stresses which impinge on children from factors outside the immediate family.

Geographical areas and delinquency

Since the pioneer Chicago studies of Shaw and McKay (1942) it has been evident that crime and delinquency are often concentrated in particular geographical areas. These may be city slums (Lander 1954; Mays 1963) or new housing estates (Mannheim 1948; Morris 1957; Jones 1958; Spencer 1954). Furthermore, differences in delinquency rates have been found between boroughs (Wallis & Maliphant 1967), between wards within a borough (Power et al 1972; Edwards 1973), between enumeration districts within a ward (Gath et al 1976) and even between streets in a small neighbourhood (Jephcott & Carter 1954). Areas with high rates of juvenile delinquency tend to have high rates of adult crime as well and, in general, rates are higher in industrial cities than in nonindustrial towns and higher in both of these than in rural areas (Grunhut 1956; McClintock & Avison 1968). High delinquency areas are usually poor, overcrowded neighbourhoods of low social status but they are not necessarily the most physically dilapidated. Offenders do not always live in the areas in which they commit their crimes, but marked variations between areas have been noted regardless of whether these are examined by place of crime or by home address.

The limited available evidence suggests that these delinquency areas remain fairly stable over time. Wallis and Maliphant (1967) showed that the distribution of offenders between London areas was much the same as it had been 40 years earlier (Burt 1925). Castle and Gittus (1957) showed much the same over a 20-year time span in Liverpool.

Although marked differences in crime rates between areas has been amply demonstrated there continues to be uncertainty about the explanation for the findings. Varying police practices could account for some of the findings (McClintock & Avison 1968) but it seems unlikely that these are a sufficient explanation. In the first place detection rates tend to be lowest in the major cities where the proportion of offenders is especially high. Secondly, the areas with high delinquency rates tend to be the same areas which have high rates of child psychiatric referral (Gath *et al* 1976). An alternative explanation is that families with a predisposition towards crime drift or are attracted into inner city areas. This may well occur to some extent but the area differences, at least for child psychiatric disorder, remain even when comparisons are restricted to individuals born and bred in the area (Rutter *et al* 1975a). Altogether it seems that there is likely to be something about living in certain areas which predisposes to crime but whether these influences reside in social mores, in neighbourhood pressures or in personal living conditions remains uncertain. This matter is discussed further below.

Social status and delinquency

Many sociological theories are based on the assumption that delinquency is predominantly a working-class phenomenon and in the past both local (Mannheim *et al* 1957; Morris 1957; Little & Ntsekhe 1959) and national (Douglas *et al* 1966) studies have shown that delinquency is more frequent in British boys who are sons of manual workers than in those from professional or other middle class homes. Nevertheless, other recent investigations have shown little or no association between delinquency and occupation or status assessed on the Registrar-General's classification (Palmai *et al* 1967; West & Farrington 1973).

There are several possible explanations for these contradictory findings. First, studies have varied in their measurement of social class. Thus, West and Farrington (1973) found no association between fathers' occupation and delinquency in the children, but delinquency was associated with low family income, poor housing and neglected accommodation. Furthermore, low income was itself associated with several measures of family adversity or conflict.

It seems that low income usually stood for a constellation of unfavourable home features. Probably poverty itself did not cause delinquency but it made delinquency more likely because low income predisposed to a variety of family difficulties and troubles which were more directly associated with delinquency.

A further consideration is whether the higher proportion of delinquents from poor homes may stem in part from differences in the way police deal with people from varying social backgrounds. The evidence suggests that this is indeed the case (West & Farrington 1973). Thus, Belson (1968) found little social class difference in the amount of stealing among London boys when stealing was based on the boy's own report rather than official records. However, boys in the top social group who admitted to a lot of stealing were much less likely to have been caught by the police. Also, Reiss and Rhodes (1961) found that delinquent acts were more common among working class boys living in a working class area but not in those with homes in a middle class neighbourhood.

On the other hand, the studies have all shown that there are social class differences in the *type* of offences committed. For example Belson (1968) found that stealing from a stall or from a barrow, and stealing from a goods yard or docks, were much more common among working class boys. McDonald (1969) found no social class difference for serious theft, but truancy and the carrying of weapons were more frequent in lower working class boys. On the other hand, traffic offences, embezzlement, tax frauds and other illegal financial practices are more typically middle class, for the obvious reason of greater opportunity (Wootton 1959; Cicourel 1968).

In short there is some tendency for an association between social class and delinquency but to some extent this is probably an artefact of differences in the way police deal with people according to their social background. However, there are also true differences in both the extent and type of offences according to social background.

SOME SOCIOCULTURAL THEORIES OF DELINQUENCY

A large variety of sociocultural theories have been put forward to explain the social class and area differences in rates of delinquency and crime. Unfortunately many of the theories overlap considerably with one another and there is a paucity of evidence upon which to assess the merits and demerits of competing hypotheses (Walker 1965; West 1967). However, the few available findings may be used to provide some evaluation of the main theoretical approaches (Rutter & Madge 1976).

Delinquency as part of a normal subcultural pattern of behaviour

Mays (1954) observed a high rate of delinquency among adolescent boys attending a youth club in an underprivileged part of Liverpool. He argued that, in this area, delinquency was part of an identifiable lower working class pattern of behaviour to which the majority of normal healthy but underdisciplined youngsters conformed. In his view (Mays 1954; 1972) delinquency was not usually a matter of individual maladjustment nor did it constitute a positive rejection of middle class culture. It was just normal behaviour acceptable to the subculture in which the boys lived. Downes (1966) and Willmott (1969) studying adolescents in London came to broadly similar conclusions.

The evidence that delinquent acts are very common (Belson 1968) and the findings that in most cases delinquency is a passing phase (Glueck & Glueck 1944; McCord & McCord 1959; West & Farrington 1973) are in keeping with the view that stealing may constitute a normal pattern of behaviour. On the other hand the same studies suggest that this is as much so for middle class as for working class boys. It may be concluded that for youngsters in all social groups there are types of petty theft which are so common and so lightly regarded that they may be considered 'normal'. This phenomenon is found in all strata of society but it applies to isolated delinquent acts rather than to persisting delinquency.

Recidivist delinquents frequently show evidence of a more general maladjustment (Stott 1960; 1966; Conger & Miller 1966) or a disturbance of emotions and behaviour (see Rutter & Madge 1976). Also, even in high delinquency areas, delinquents tend to be unpopular with their peers (West & Farrington 1973; Roff *et al* 1972).

The evidence indicates that recidivist delinquency is frequently associated with other evidence of disturbance and with social rejection. For these reasons it can rarely be regarded as 'normal' in any meaningful sense. On the other hand delinquent behaviour is certainly subject to social influences (see below).

Differential association

It is clear that the peer group exercises an important influence on children's behaviour and attitudes. This is easily seen in the way children conform to fads and fashions in dress, hair styles, pop music, styles of speech and the like. It has also been shown experimentally. For example, when asked to judge the length of a set of black lines in a group situation, children tend to follow the majority of other children (Berenda 1950). This is so even when the other children are stooges who have been taught to make deliberately wrong estimates of length. On the whole, young children are more likely to conform, girls are more suggestible than boys, low status children follow group norms more than high status children and temperamental differences also influence conformity. Sutherland (1939) was the first to systematically apply these influences to delinquency. He argued that delinquency was a behaviour learned through interaction with other people and that the likelihood of people becoming delinquent was directly related to the frequency and consistency of their contacts with delinquent individuals. In his later writings he included the notion that the nature of the interactions with delinquents as well as their frequency was important. However, there is considerable difficulty in defining what sort of associations might favour violations of the law (Cressey 1964).

Several observations suggest that differential association may play some part in the spread of delinquency in crime (see Rutter & Madge 1976). First, most delinquent acts are committed together with other children (West & Farrington 1973). Second, delinquency is as strongly associated with delinquency in a person's brothers and sisters as with crime in his parents. Third, youngsters living in a high delinquency area or attending a high delinquency school are more likely to become delinquent than similar children living in other areas and attending other schools. Fourth, boys who claim delinquents as friends are more likely to admit to delinquent behaviour than boys who say their friends are not delinquent (Voss 1964). Fifth, in an American study Reiss and Rhodes (1964) showed that the probability of a boy committing a specific delinquent act was statistically dependent upon the commission of similar acts by other members of his friendship group. Sixth, West and Farrington (1973) found that the number of delinquent acts committed by a boy's friends and acquaintances was predictive of his own future convictions.

All these findings are in keeping with the suggestion that mixing with delinquents makes it more likely that you yourself will become delinquent. However, it is difficult to rule out the possibility that at least some of the effect is due to youngsters prone to delinquency for other reasons seeking out delinquent friends (Robins & Hill 1966) or to the group of friends all being subject to some other criminogenic influences.

The difficulties are illustrated by the interpretation of the associations with crime in parents. West and Farrington (1973) found that most criminal parents had ceased to commit criminal acts by the time their children were growing up and furthermore that parental crime predisposed to delinquency of late rather than early onset. This suggested that direct modelling of criminal behaviour was unlikely to be important. Furthermore, social work reports suggested that even parents who had been delinquent themselves were censorious toward delinquent behaviour in their sons. Paternal crime was linked with poor supervision and when this was taken into account there was only a slight association between parental criminality and subsequent delinquency. It may be that the link reflects parenting standards rather than direct social learning, or it may be that the parents transmit attitudes towards crime to their children (Cabral 1969) rather than teaching them specific criminal acts.

Labelling

It has been suggested that once a person is labelled as a criminal or delinquent his subsequent course of behaviour is shaped by public recognition of him as such (Wilkins 1964; Lemert 1967; Cicourel 1968). Labelling may increase both the visibility of delinquent behaviour and also the likelihood of its recurrence. This may come about in a variety of ways. Thus the possession of a delinquent record will make it more likely that a person will come under police surveillance so that his offences come more readily to official notice. Secondly, when delinquent activities are met with severe sanctions, rejection and social exclusion the boy may turn back to a delinquent group for the status and satisfaction otherwise denied him. In contrast a tolerant response to deviance may make further deviance less likely (Wilkins 1964). Thirdly, the experience of conviction may modify a person's self-image and attitudes in such a way that he comes to feel more aggressive and antiauthority, as suggested by the evidence on attitude changes following conviction in West and Farrington's study (1973).

How far these processes in fact lead to the perpetuation of delinquent or criminal activities is not known. There is some evidence that the experience of conviction may sometimes serve to perpetuate delinquent activities (Robins 1966; Gold & Williams 1969; Gold 1970; West 1967) but size of the effect has still to be demonstrated.

Delinquent contracultures

Several American writers have emphasised the development of delinquent 'contracultures'. Thus, Merton (1957) argued that if the social structure effectively blocks access to the goals desired by lower class members, the group becomes frustrated in its aspirations and some individuals contract out and reject both the traditional goals and means. Cloward and Ohlin (1961) similarly suggested that in a society which denies opportunities to some social groups, those who fail to achieve their goals may blame the inadequacy of the existing institutional organisation and find a collective solution in delinquent gangs. Cohen (1955) too, hypothesised that working class boys develop a delinquent contraculture as a means of dealing with status frustration. Certainly there is evidence that many adolescents are frustrated in education and employment (Fyvel 1961). Scholastic failure is frequently associated with delinquency (see Chapter 23) and it may be that this leads some youngsters to opt out and develop a contrary set of values (Rutter, Tizard & Whitmore 1970). On the other hand it is doubtful if many delinquents actually hold overtly oppositional views (Matza 1964) and organised delinquent gangs are not common in Britain (Scott 1956), although they do occur (Patrick 1973). So far there has been no systematic test of the validity of this type of delinquent contraculture as an explanation for delinquency in Britain. However, the very different social situations in this country and in the USA mean that American findings cannot automatically be applied here.

Conclusion

There can be little doubt that sociocultural influences stemming from the structure of Society, from prevailing attitudes, from differing opportunities and from status hierarchies do have an influence on delinquent behaviour. Delinquent acts are a form of social behaviour and like other social behaviours they are to some extent shaped and modified by community influences and social forces. However, the psychiatrist is largely concerned with those varieties of delinquency which are linked with disturbances of emotions and relationships and persistently impaired personal functioning. These conditions have a generally poor prognosis and often lead to personality disorders in adult life (Robins 1966).

AREA DIFFERENCES IN PSYCHIATRIC DISORDER

Psychiatric conditions also vary in rate according to area and social conditions, but the explanation of these differences may not be the same as for delinquency. Many studies have shown that rates of adult mental disorder vary greatly between different geographical areas. Thus, Sainsbury (1955) showed marked differences between London boroughs and suicide rates. He found that suicide was most frequent in areas characterised by social isolation, population mobility and social disorganisation. He argued that an environment which lacked cohesion and failed to provide stable social contacts might predispose a person to suicide. Sainsbury's data referred to the 1936–38 period but a quarter of a century later Whitlock (1973a, b) found much the same pattern. Similar differences were found in areas outside London. In men high suicide rates were found mainly in the textile towns with a falling population and were associated with isolation and loneliness. Similar area differences in rates of treated psychiatric disorder have been found for both adults and children (Faris & Dunham 1939; Hare & Shaw 1965; Sundby & Nyhus 1963; Häfner & Reimann 1970; Bagley *et al* 1973; Bain 1974; Gath *et al* 1976; Ødegaard 1975).

In general, psychiatric referral rates have tended to be higher if a person is living in high density city areas of low social status. The early studies showed that the highest rates were often in the decaying areas in the middle of the cities but this has not always been found in more recent studies. The pattern has been found to vary with the type of mental illness and differences are due in part to variations in service utilisation rather than to rates of disorder. Furthermore, much of the association found is explicable in terms of the 'drift' of patients into poor areas rather than the effect of the area on the individual (Levy & Rowitz 1970; 1971). Furthermore, the variation is not simply a function of inner city areas. In an epidemiological study of small towns Leighton *et al* (1963) found that mental disorder was much commoner in rural slum areas than in socially cohesive and prosperous communities. They suggested that the lack of social integration and the lack of affectionate ties were more important as causes of psychological problems than low social status or poor physical conditions.

Area differences in child psychiatric disorder have been most systematically examined by Rutter and his colleagues (Rutter *et al* 1975a, c; Rutter & Quinton 1976; Rutter 1976). A series of epidemiological studies was undertaken to compare the rates of disorder in an inner London borough and the Isle of Wight. Ten-year-old children and their parents constituted the sample and the same standardised measures were systematically applied in the same way by the same team of researchers in both areas. First, the total population was screened using questionnaires and tests of proven reliability and validity. Then, in the second stage, large representative samples were studied intensively by means of detailed personal interviews with the parents, by interviews with schoolteachers and by psychological testing of the children. The findings showed that child psychiatric disorder (both emotional disturbance and conduct disorder) was twice as common in inner London as on the Isle of Wight. The same applied to neurosis and depression in the mothers and to crime in the fathers. A variety of checks confirmed that the child psychiatric diagnosis had equal reliability and validity in the two areas and it seemed clear that disorder was truly twice as common in inner London as on the Isle of Wight. Furthermore, the data indicated that the difference still applied to children born and bred in London to parents born and bred in London, so that a 'drift' factor could not be invoked. Also, selective *out* migration had not occurred.

Detailed measures of family interaction, relationships and style of life were obtained in both areas in order to determine why psychiatric disorder was so much more frequent in London. Both in the metropolis and on the island child psychiatric disorder was associated with family discord and disruption, parental illness and criminality and social disadvantage (as indicated by large family size, overcrowding and lack of home ownership). An index of 'family adversity' was constructed from these variables and used to compare the two areas. It was found that family adversity was three times as frequent in London as on the Isle of Wight. Furthermore, if the two populations were standardised for frequency of family adversity, the difference in rate of child psychiatric disorder almost disappeared. In short, London children showed more psychiatric disorder because they were more likely to come from overcrowded, unhappy homes with ill or deviant parents. The difference between the two areas was explicable simply in terms of the higher rate of family adversity in London and when the two areas were compared in terms of children from *similar* family circumstances no difference in rate of psychiatric disorder was found. It appeared that city life had little *direct* adverse affect on children but rather the effects were mediated through the family, and to a lesser extent the school (see below).

However, these findings only pushed the question back one stage further. It was necessary also to determine why London families were more likely to be disadvantaged, why women in London showed higher rates of psychiatric disorder and why marital discord was also so much more frequent in the capital. The answers to these questions are as yet incomplete but the findings available so far suggest a rather different set of mechanisms to those operating in the case of child psychiatric disorder. Thus, on the Isle of Wight, depression in the mothers of 10-year-old children was strongly associated with disturbed interpersonal relationships, but not with low social status. On the other hand, in London, although depression showed some association with relationship difficulties, it also showed a strong association with low social status as measured by their husbands' occupations. The association was a result of *current* social circumstances as the same association did not apply to the women's social class of origin. The evidence therefore suggested that depression in London women was more common, *not* because they experienced more of the same kind of troubles which lead to depression on the Isle of Wight, but rather because they experienced *different* troubles. The findings suggested that inner city stresses applied particularly to working class women. Other studies suggest a further narrowing down to women who do not go out to work and who have young children at home (Brown *et al* 1975).

STRESSES OF INNER CITY LIFE

The next question is what it is about inner city life which leads to stress and disorder. Animal studies have shown that overcrowding, and especially the process of becoming overcrowded (Cassel 1972), can lead to social dis-organisation (Calhoun 1962) and heightened aggression (Hamburg 1971). It has often been suggested on the basis of these animal findings that overcrowd-ing will have similar ill effects in humans (Carlestam 1971). However, the parallel between animal studies and the human situation is not particularly close and population density *per se* may not be the crucial factor (Gillis 1974). In the first place, most of the animal studies have involved competition for limited resources and this factor may be at least as important as the crowding together of people. City slums may or may not be overcrowded but almost always they do involve a serious lack of community facilities. It may be that it is the inadequate provision of play space, sports facilities, social clubs, coffee bars and the like which is more important than the high population density. Secondly, there is a good deal of confusion in the literature between popula-tion density in terms of persons per square mile and overcrowding in the sense of number of persons per room in the house. High densities in the cities are not always associated with high rates of disorder (Jacobs 1961; Schmitt 1963) and a study by Galle *et al* (1972) indicated that crime and mental dis-order were more strongly associated with overcrowded households than with high population density. Furthermore, Gillis (1974) found that delinquency was more strongly correlated with multiple occupancy dwelling than with either type of overcrowding. A Ministry of Housing and Local Government Report (1970) on families living at high density also failed to find adverse effects on family life of high density housing. Although a point may be reached when overall population density has serious consequences, it seems that per-sonal overcrowding in the home is usually more important than the number of people living in a particular geographical area and, furthermore, that the quality and type of housing is probably still more important than overcrowd-ing of any kind.

People need both privacy (Westin 1967) and social contacts (Alexander 1972) and stress may arise when the right balance between the two is not attained. Mitchell (1971) in a study in Hong Kong, found that high density housing was associated with emotional disorder mainly when the crowding meant enforced contact with nonfamily members. Strains arose from lack of control over living space. Proshanky *et al* (1970) has suggested that the adverse effect of the lack of privacy stems from low control over personal territory and from the restrictions imposed on free choice of movement and behaviour. Newman (1973) has emphasised the importance of 'defensible space', by which he means personal territory with a clearly identifiable status and layout which enables people to know their neighbours and so easily spot strangers. Newman produced some data which indicated that estates which lacked defensible space had higher rates of vandalism and delinquency. It seems highly plausible that patterns of life are indeed influenced by the structure of housing estates, but Newman's data have been questioned (Hillier 1973) and it is uncertain whether the main influence is on rates of crime or, rather, on the places where crimes are committed.

High-rise flats   In recent years much concern has been expressed about the effects of living in multistorey tower blocks (Jephcott 1971; Richman 1974; Department of the Environment 1972). Mothers of preschool children face particular difficulties if they live in high-rise flats. Probably, they are more likely to express dissatisfaction and are more likely to become depressed than women living in ground floor flats or in houses. However, the findings on the psychiatric consequences of living in blocks of flats are somewhat contradictory (Fanning 1967; Richman 1974; Moore 1974). It remains uncertain how far the stresses stem from living in a tower block or rather derive from the patterns of life created by particular kinds of housing estates.

Anonymity   Another factor which may be important in relation to the high rates of social disorder in inner city areas is the anonymity and lack of mutual obligation compared with small town life (Hamburg 1971). Several studies have shown that people living in major cities are less likely than small town inhabitants to give aid to strangers and are less likely to respect other people's property (Zimbardo 1969; Milgram 1970). The anonymity in metropolitan areas means that a person's activities are much less likely to be observed by someone who knows him. This may lead to a diminution in social controls, although evidence on this point is lacking.

Community   Neighbourhood or community ties may also be important (Lee 1968; Suttles 1972; Proshansky *et al* 1970; Kasarda & Janowitz 1974). However, 'community' is a confusing concept as it refers both to a geographical area and to a set of social relationships which may or may not coincide. Our knowledge of the factors that lead people to make most of their social contacts locally, and to become involved in neighbourhood activities and organisations, is very limited. Also the psychiatric benefits of community involvement have been little investigated. However, it seems that people identify with a quite small area (a radius of about half a mile) and that community involvement is greatest when people work in the same area as that in which they live, when there is social heterogeneity, and when people have lived in the area for at least several years. It may also be that clear demarcation of areas increases social involvement. However, the evidence suggests that length of residence in an area is the variable most strongly associated with feelings of community attachment and sentiment (Kasarda & Janowitz 1974). In contrast, increasing population size and density do not appear to weaken the bonds of kinship or friendship. The findings imply that inner city areas may be less cohesive and less neighbourly because of the high population turnover and the high proportion of people coming to live there from other parts of the country or from abroad, rather than because of the concentration of people packed into a small area.

Rehousing   Satisfaction with housing and identification with an area also tend to go together (Hartman 1963). However, satisfaction with housing and good quality of housing are by no means synonymous. It is not uncommon to find that slum dwellers do not want to leave the area where they live although they would like improved housing facilities (Vereker *et al* 1961 ; Ministry of Housing and Local Government 1963). Rehousing may be disruptive through the breaking up of neighbourhood friendships and altered patterns of social interaction (Fried 1963), lessened contact with kin, increased travelling time to work and longer working hours to pay for higher rents may all contribute to the isolation of housewives on new housing estates. On the other hand, if rehousing is undertaken with proper attention to these factors, it may have benefits in terms of mental health (Wilner *et al* 1962). Moving house is not associated with any consistent pattern of improvement or deterioration in children's mental health (Kantor 1965). Whether the move has beneficial or adverse effects will depend not only on the effect on housing conditions but also on the effects on patterns of social interaction and family and friendship ties.

Homelessness   The psychiatric consequences of homelessness have been little studied. However, it is likely that the unsettled conditions of life in temporary accommodation and the apparent discrimination against the homeless bring stresses for the children (Cox 1971). In this connection, it should be noted that the majority of persons admitted to housing for the homeless are parents with young children and many are families without a father (Greve *et al* 1971 ; Glastonbury 1971). One parent families tend to be particularly seriously disadvantaged in terms of both poverty and living conditions (Hunt *et al* 1973; DHSS 1974).

    It is very difficult to disentangle which of the many stresses associated with life in inner city areas and in poor housing conditions are most important as factors contributing to the genesis of psychiatric disorder in children and their parents. However, as already noted, for the children (but possibly not for the parents) the stresses seem to be largely mediated through the family rather than through influences outside the home. Also, recent findings have shown that it is the *combination* of stresses which is most important (Rutter 1976). The presence of one family stress is not associated with any appreciable increase in the risk for child psychiatric disorder. However, the rate of disorder goes up markedly when there are multiple family stresses. It appears that there is an interaction between stresses so that their combined effect is greater than the sum of their individual parts.

SCHOOL VARIATIONS

Quite apart from differences according to the area in which people live, several studies have shown marked differences in delinquency rates between schools (Power et al 1967; 1972; Gath et al 1972; 1976; Cannan 1970; Clegg & Megson 1968; Yule & Rutter 1976). Clear differences in rates of absconding have also been found between schools for delinquent boys (Clarke & Martin 1971).

Power found that secondary schools differed markedly in their rates of delinquency, and that these differences persisted over a 10-year period. Closely similar findings for an outer London borough were reported by Gath et al (1972), who went on to show that the same variability between schools applied to child guidance referral rates. The interschool differences in these studies could reflect either variations in service utilisation or police practice, or variations in the prevalence of disorder. However, other studies have indicated that there are marked differences between schools in how children behave—differences which are not a function of referral policy or police practice. Thus both Galloway (1976) and Reynolds and Murgatroyd (1974) found large variations between schools in rates of absenteeism. Yule and Rutter (1976) found the same but also showed that schools varied markedly in rates of behavioural deviance (as assessed by teacher questionnaire) as well as by absenteeism and delinquency. This was so for primary schools (Rutter et al 1975c) and also for secondary schools (Yule & Rutter 1976).

Undoubtedly part of the explanation for these school differences lies in selective intake. Farrington (1972) found that high delinquency secondary schools had a much higher intake of children who were troublesome at primary school than did low delinquency secondary schools. Yule and Rutter (1976) found the same but went on to show by standardisation techniques that selective intake was not sufficient to explain the differences in either delinquency rate or behavioural deviance between schools. Primary schools varied markedly in the proportions of behaviourally deviant children even after taking into account where the children lived and whether or not they came from disturbed or disadvantaged homes. Secondary schools varied similarly after taking into account both these factors and also the children's behaviour as assessed in primary school.

Because Yule and Rutter's (1976) findings showed that there were *changes* in children's behaviour according to which secondary school they attended, there is the strong implication that school life has an influence on pupils' behaviour. Much earlier studies have produced findings which suggest that schools could have a persisting influence on attitudes as well as behaviour. Newcomb (1963) showed that students attending a particular American college became progressively less conservative in their attitudes during their time at college, in spite of coming from conservative families. This change to a more liberal viewpoint did not occur among students at other colleges. The findings were explicable in terms of the fact that liberal views were associated with popularity and prestige among students and also with involvement in college affairs. The college had a liberal ethos which had developed over the years and which seemed to influence each new lot of students in a predictable way. Twenty years later a follow-up study showed that the ex-students had tended to select like-minded, nonconservative people to marry but for the most part their liberal views persisted.

It seems that experiences at school help shape children's development and behaviour. Unfortunately, relatively little is known about which factors make for differences in the school environment and even less about how these operate. Neither the size and type of school, nor the age and structure of the buildings makes much difference, apart from the fact that delinquency rates tend to be lower in schools where the children are selected on the basis of high academic attainment (Power *et al* 1972; Gath *et al* 1976). Rather the differences seem to lie in the atmosphere, ethos and pattern of school life. Schools constitute miniature societies which influence children by the values they set as much as by the personal interactions between individual staff and pupils (Shipman 1968). Schools tend to have a distinctive climate which sets the tone for what is expected of staff and pupils (McDill & Rigsby 1973). There are many suggestions concerning the factors which determine which sort of institution a school becomes and how organisational features may impinge on pupils, but so far there has been little systematic research into these matters (Biddle 1970).

Rutter *et al* (1975c) showed that behaviour difficulties were commoner in children attending primary schools with high rates of teacher and pupil turnover. Schools which lacked stability in staffing and which had a high proportion of children coming and going were those with the most problems. The teacher–child ratio made little difference. The problems were also greater in schools with a large proportion of poor children or of children from immigrant families.

In an interesting participant observer study of social relations in the secondary school, Hargreaves (1967) noted some of the ill effects of rigid streaming. There was considerable antagonism between the upper and lower streams and very little social mixing between them, in spite of some cooperation in joint activities such as sport. In the upper streams there tended to be quite good teacher–pupil relationships and the youngsters were generally committed to both the school and the educational process. On the other hand, less experienced staff took the lower streams, the teachers had negative expectations of the boys and there were fewer educational rewards. Essentially, the lowest streams formed an antischool subculture in which there was a high delinquency rate. Children in these streams were exposed to middle class academic values but were constantly frustrated by their being denied any status in that system.

It is probable that several different factors play a part in this process. First, there is the varying extent to which children of different abilities can get rewards from the school system. Resentment is likely to be felt by children who consistently fail to get rewards and yet see these received by other children. Secondly, there is the extent to which children are given autonomy and responsibility in the school system. Studies with adults show that people who are given responsibility in a social structure, such as in a factory, tend to shift their attitudes towards the values of the system in which they hold responsibility (see Kelvin 1970). Thirdly, there is the effect of negative labels. Children, like adults, tend to live up or down to what is expected of them.

Another aspect of schooling concerns the potential clash between the values and mores in schools and the youth culture outside it. Sugarman (1967), in a study of four London secondary schools, observed that high commitment to teenage culture tended to involve a repudiation of the values and norms of the school. He suggests that this clash might be reduced if the school included more of the teenage social system both by extending the range of extra curricular activities and by giving the adolescents responsibility in organising these activities. For many children, a similar clash exists between the culture of the school and the culture of the home.

The style of teaching may also have an impact on personal relationships in the school. For example, White and Lippitt (1960) compared authoritarian, democratic and laissez-faire approaches in getting 10 and 11-year-old children to make masks at school. Relationships were best in the democratic approach in which children were led and guided but also were involved in decision-making. They worked better when their leader was out of the room and they got on best with him. An authoritarian approach was efficient in getting the children to work but tended to be associated with feelings of aggression to the leader. The laissez-faire group, who were neither ordered nor guided, did worst on all criteria. The organisation of groups and determination of goals also has important effects on interpersonal relationships. Sherif *et al* (1961) in the Robbers' Cave experiment showed that friendly and co-operative group interaction was most likely when adolescents were working towards a common goal. Competition produced strong and productive in-group loyalties but had the disadvantage of hostile intergroup interaction.

The model of behaviour provided by the teachers both in their interaction with the children and with each other is also important. Extensive use of violence in discipline, as by corporal punishment, may set an example of dealing with problems by aggression. This may partly explain why Clegg and Megson (1968) found in a survey of Yorkshire schools that behaviour was best and delinquency least in schools where corporal punishment was used sparingly or not at all. They also reported the situation in a severely disruptive school where one of the serious problems was the general slackness of staff, who were poor time-keepers and showed little interest in the school. The staff set a model of idleness and noninvolvement to the children and when a new head set about transforming the school into a harmonious and well-respected place, one of his first tasks was to increase the standards, motivation and involvement of the teachers.

In addition to these broader social influences in the school, the details of how teachers interact with children in the classroom are also very important (O'Leary & O'Leary 1972). Observational studies have shown that disruptive behaviours in the classroom tend to diminish if they are ignored by the teacher and if the teacher gives systematic approval and attention when the children behave well (Becker *et al* 1967; Hall *et al* 1968). Firm, quiet reprimands are more effective than angry punitive responses (O'Leary *et al* 1969; Kounin 1970). Discipline tends to be best with teachers who can cope with more than one issue at a time, who are in touch with the group situation in class, who are active, and who maintain the children's interest and involvement in the task (Kounin 1970). While these various studies give useful leads on what may be crucial features in school life, knowledge is still lacking on the key requirements of a good school. Further research in this important area is much needed.

CHILDREN IN IMMIGRANT FAMILIES

Several surveys using teacher questionnaires have indicated that children of West Indian parents have rates of behavioural deviance above those found in indigenous children (Schools Council 1970; Bagley 1972; Rutter *et al*

1974). This higher rate of behavioural difficulties applied to restlessness and poor concentration and socially disapproved conduct of various kinds. However, there was no appreciable excess in emotional difficulties. Less is known about the behaviour of children in other immigrant groups but one study (Kallarackal & Herbert 1976) found that behavioural problems measured in the same way were actually less common in children with Indian parents than in white English children. The findings indicate that teachers perceive more problems in children of West Indian background but these problems are not necessarily equivalent to psychiatric disorder. Accurate estimates of psychiatric prevalence can only be obtained from epidemiological studies of the general population using personal interview methods.

Only one such study has been published (Rutter *et al* 1974) and that refers to 10-year-old children of West Indian parents. Both parents and teachers of the children were interviewed. The teacher interview assessment supported the questionnaire findings in showing that the West Indian children's behaviour at school presented more problems than did that of children from indigenous families, but the difference between groups was less than on the questionnaire. The West Indian children showed more socially disapproved conduct but no more emotional disorder and no more difficulties getting along with other children. In contrast, the parental interview findings showed no differences in psychiatric disorder between the West Indian and nonimmigrant children. The results suggested that this was not a methodological artefact but rather a true reflection of the fact that West Indian children showed more problems at school than they did at home. This tendency for so many disorders in West Indian children to be present only at school was particularly marked but it is a phenomenon found in several previous studies of nonimmigrant children (Rutter, Tizard & Whitmore 1970; Mitchell & Shepherd 1966).

There are several possible reasons for the relatively high rate of disorders in school in this group. First, there is the matter of migration itself. This did not seem to be an important factor in that disorders were just as common in children of West Indian parentage born in this country. However, there were very few recent migrants in the group studied by Rutter *et al.* The stresses of moving from one country to another may well be more important in the period immediately after migration. Also they may well be more critical for adolescents who leave the West Indies to join their parents in this country; a group so far not systematically studied. Second, a high proportion of West Indian children are considerably retarded in their educational attainments (Yule *et al* 1975) and it is known that reading retardation and disorders of conduct are strongly associated (Rutter, Tizard & Whitmore 1970). Third, children from immigrant families tend to go to schools with characteristics such as high pupil turnover (Rutter *et al* 1975b) which are known to be associated with high rates of problem behaviour (Rutter *et al* 1975c). Fourth, there is strong evidence of racial discrimination in this country (Daniel 1968; Mackintosh & Smith 1974). It is likely that children's awareness of this discrimination will be greater at school and consequently more likely to lead to problems there. Other factors shown to be related to behavioural difficulties in West Indian children are a 'broken home', being admitted into care and disturbed parent–child relationships (Rutter *et al* 1975b). Poor housing conditions and separation from parents as such, however, did not seem to be important in this connection (Bhatnagar 1970; Bagley 1972; Rutter *et al* 1974).

Apart from differences between children from West Indian and from indigenous families in the level of psychiatric disorder as shown at school, there are differences in the *pattern* of disorders. Unlike the native English, children of West Indian parentage with conduct disorders do not show much emotional disturbance and have few major difficulties in peer relationships (Rutter *et al* 1974). This together with the situation specificity of much behaviour suggests that disorders may be more immediately reactive than is usually the case with conduct problems. On the other hand, Nicol (1971) found that the prognosis for West Indian children attending psychiatric clinics was no different from that of white children. The most striking difference between West Indian and indigenous children concerns the pattern of diagnosis. In indigenous girls emotional disorders are much commoner than conduct disorders. However, both general population and clinic studies have shown that this is not the case in West Indian girls as in boys; conduct disorders predominate. The reason for this difference remains uncertain.

Little is known concerning psychiatric disorder in preschool and adolescent children of immigrant parents. One clinic study (Prince 1967) suggested that language disorders and social withdrawal might be particularly common in preschool West Indian children. The suggestion needs to be tested by means of general population studies.

Unlike the situation in the USA, the children of black migrants to Britain have a delinquency rate which is about the same as (or slightly below that of) nonimmigrants (Lambert 1970). There is some suggestion that with the rising level of unemployment (Community Relations Commission 1974) delinquency in West Indian teenagers is becoming more frequent (Pearce 1974) but reliable data are lacking. In the docklands where black settlements have been established for several generations, rates of juvenile and adult crime have not been particularly high amongst second generation migrants (e.g. Richmond 1954).

Studies are in general agreement that children of immigrant parents, although showing a wide range in abilities and performance, tend to have mean scores on vocabulary and reading well below those of native white children (Yule *et al* 1975). However, children of foreign parentage who are born in this country have considerably better educational attainments and considerably higher scores on tests of intellectual performance than do children born abroad who migrate to Britain during middle childhood or adolescence (Yule *et al* 1975). This pattern is most marked with respect to children from West Indian families, other immigrants are also disadvantaged educationally but not usually to the same degree or in quite the same way. The reasons for the sometimes low scholastic attainment of children from immigrant families are many and various and considerable uncertainty remains about their relative importance (Rutter & Madge 1976). However, the possible reasons include factors such as multiple social disadvantage (Community Relations Commission 1973), less satisfactory schooling and family circumstances (see below). With children born abroad, malnutrition may also have played a part.

In some respects the housing problems of black immigrants are similar to those of all newcomers to cities who arrive with very limited means at a time when many local authority housing lists are overfull or even closed and in conditions where they obtain a very low priority in housing allocation. However, for black immigrants these difficulties are multiplied many times by racial discrimination. Frequently, the results have been overcrowding, multiple occupancy and high rents. The study of West Indian families in London (Rutter *et al* 1975b) showed that they were living in less satisfactory housing conditions than the rest of the population. Overcrowding was twice as frequent and a higher proportion lacked the basic household amenities. On the other hand, nearly half the West Indian families owned their own house compared with less than one in five of the indigenous families. In spite of discrimination in housing and other adverse circumstances, they had done a great deal to improve their situation, but a price had been paid in terms of wives working long hours (much more so than in the indigenous families) and the property was often old, poor quality and bought under disadvantageous financial arrangements.

A further difference between the West Indian and nonimmigrant families concerned family size. Three-fifths of the West Indian mothers had at least five children, a rate over double that in the indigenous group. This was frequently associated with overcrowding. In view of the known association between large family size and low reading attainment, this large number of children may have serious educational consequences.

Many more children in West Indian families had been looked after by non-relatives—other studies have shown the often poor quality of these arrangements (Yudkin 1967; Jackson 1973)—and more had been taken into the care of the local authority (Fitzherbert 1967; Rutter *et al* 1975c). The West Indian parents were deeply concerned for their children and usually had good relationships with them. However, Pollak (1973) found that they provided fewer toys and interacted less with their children in the preschool period, probably a reflection of a lesser emphasis in West Indian families on the importance of play in children's development.

The quality of family relationships in the West Indian families was found to be just as good as in the indigenous families and there were no differences in the rates of parental mental disorder or criminality. Also contrary to popular belief, in most respects the family pattern in the two groups was mostly similar. In both the 'nuclear family' consisting of stable marriages was the norm and the fathers were quite involved in the family—although possibly single-parent families were a little more common than in the indigenous population.

In one respect, the pattern of discipline differed. West Indian children were expected to help more at home and they were generally more self-reliant. On the other hand, they were rather more restricted in their social activities. West Indian parents sometimes complain that discipline in the schools is lax and deficient. Conversely, teachers sometimes feel that West Indian parents are unduly harsh. This arises through a cultural difference in attitudes to discipline. The children may sometimes find the disparity between what is expected at home and what is expected at school confusing and troublesome.

Other immigrant groups

The child-rearing findings discussed so far all apply to families of West Indian origin. Fewer data are available on other immigrant groups. However, it is known that Hindu and Moslem religious views and attitudes to women influence child-rearing patterns in a way that may mark the Asian household as different from those of white neighbours (Ferron 1973). James (1974) described the strong family ties of Sikh families in Britain and the constraints on children which stem from religious or cultural duties and rituals. Arranged marriages are still common, there are restrictions on the social life of teenagers (especially girls), and the home upbringing for girls tends to be seen as largely a preparation for marriage and motherhood. Children's questioning and exploration are actively encouraged but many children have to be bilingual because Punjabi continues to be spoken at home. Families of African origin also differ in patterns of child-rearing. Holman (1973) found that West African students were much more likely than indigenous or other immigrant groups to make use of private fostering arrangements for preschool children.

Although some of these arrangements provide good quality care, private foster parents were often found to be unsuitable in Holman's study.

CONCLUSIONS

The available data on sociocultural influences on children's behaviour and development are inadequate in many respects. However, sufficient evidence is available to indicate that patterns of family life are shaped and modifed by sociocultural mores and by social circumstances. Furthermore, children are influenced by the relationships they make outside the home, and experiences at school and in the community, as well as by the more intense interactions of personal family life. Child psychiatrists need to be aware of these wider sociocultural influences and to understand the various ways in which they may operate if they are to appreciate the nature of their patients' difficulties and if they are to make the most appropriate treatment plans.

REFERENCES

ALEXANDER C. (1972) The city as a mechanism for sustaining human contact. *In* Gutman R. (ed.) *People and Buildings.* New York: Basic Books

BAGLEY C. (1972) Deviant behaviour in English and West Indian schoolchildren. *Res. in Educ.* **8,** 47–55

BAGLEY C., JACOBSON S. & PALMER C. (1973) Social structure and the ecological distribution of mental illness, suicide and delinquency. *Psychol. Med.* **3,** 177–187

BAIN S.M. (1974) A geographer's approach in the epidemiology of psychiatric disorder. *J. biosoc. Sci.* **6,** 195–220

BECKER W.C., MADSEN C.H., ARNOLD C.R. & THOMAS B.A. (1967) The contingent use of teacher attention and praise in reducing classroom behaviour problems. *J. Spec. Educ.* **1,** 287–307

BELSON W.A. (1968) The extent of stealing by London boys. *Advancement of Science* **25,** 171–184

BERENDA R. (1950) *The Influence of the Group on the Judgements of Children.* New York: King's Crown Press

BHATNAGAR J. (1970) *Immigrants at School.* London: Cornmarket Press

BIDDLE B.J. (1970) The institutional context. *In* Campbell W.J. (ed.) *Scholars in Context. The Effects of Environments on Learning.* New York: Wiley

BROWN G.W., BHROLCHAIN M.N. & HARRIS T. (1975) Social class and psychiatric disturbance among women in an urban population. *Sociology* **9,** 225–254

BURT C. (1925) *The Young Delinquent.* London: University of London Press

CABRAL R.M. (1969) Intergenerational differences in making moral judgements. Abstract of PhD dissertation in Dissertation Abstracts International, No. 105–181

CALHOUN J.B. (1962) Population density and social pathology. *Scientific American* **206,** 139–148

CANNAN C. (1970) Schools for delinquency. *New Society* **16,** 1004

CARLESTAM G. (1971) The individual, the city and stress. *In* Levi L. (ed.) *Society, Stress and Disease*, vol. 1: *The Psychosocial Environment and Psychosomatic Diseases*. London: Oxford University Press

CASSEL J. (1972) Health consequences of population density and crowding. *In* Gutman R. (ed.) *People and Buildings*. New York: Basic Books

CASTLE I.M. & GITTUS E. (1957) The distribution of social defects in Liverpool. *Sociol. Rev.* **5**, 43–64

CICOUREL A.V. (1968) *The Social Organization of Juvenile Justice*. New York: Wiley

CLARKE R.V. & MARTIN D.N. (1971) *Absconding from Approved Schools*. London: HMSO

CLEGG A. & MEGSON B. (1968) *Children in Distress*. Harmondsworth: Penguin

CLOWARD R.A. & OHLIN L.E. (1961) *Delinquency and Opportunity*. London: Routledge & Kegan Paul

COHEN A.K. (1955) *Delinquent Boys: The Culture of the Gang*. London: Routledge & Kegan Paul

COMMUNITY RELATIONS COMMISSION (1973) Multiple Deprivation and Minority Groups. CRC/73/113. Mimeographed Report

COMMUNITY RELATIONS COMMISSION (1974) *Unemployment and Homelessness: A Report*. London: HMSO

CONGER J.J. & MILLER W.C. (1966) *Personality, Social Class, and Delinquency*. New York: Wiley

COX G.M. (1971) *Circle of Despair*. London: Shelter

CRESSEY D.R. (1964) *Delinquency, Crime and Differential Association*. Amsterdam: Martinus Nijhoff

DANIEL W.W. (1968) *Racial Discrimination in England*. Harmondsworth: Penguin

DEPARTMENT OF HEALTH AND SOCIAL SECURITY (1974) *Report of the Committee on One-Parent Families (Finer Report)*. London: HMSO

DEPARTMENT OF THE ENVIRONMENT (1972) *The Estate Outside the Dwelling: Reactions of residents to aspects of housing layout*. London: HMSO

DOUGLAS J.W.B., ROSS J.M., HAMMOND W.A. & MULLIGAN D.G. (1966) Delinquency and social class. *Brit. J. Criminol.* **6**, 294–302

DOWNES D.M. (1966) *The Delinquent Solution: a Study in Subcultural Theory*. London: Routledge & Kegan Paul

EDWARDS A. (1973) Sex and area variations in delinquency rates in an English city. *Brit. J. Criminol.* **13**, 121–137

FANNING D.M. (1967) Families in flats. *Brit. Med. J.* iv, 382–386

FARIS R.E. & DUNHAM H.W. (1939) *Mental Disorders in Urban Areas*. Chicago: University of Chicago Press

FARRINGTON D. (1972) Delinquency begins at home. *New Society* **21**, 495–497

FERRON O. (1973) Family, marital and child-rearing patterns in different ethnic groups. *In* Watson P. (ed.) *Psychology and Race*. Harmondsworth: Penguin

FRIED M. (1963) Grieving for a lost home. *In* Duhl L.J. (ed.) *The Urban Condition*. New York: Basic Books

FITZHERBERT K. (1967) *West Indian Children in London*. Occasional Papers on Social Administration No. 19. London: Bell

FYVEL T.R. (1961) *The Insecure Offenders*. London: Chatto & Windus

GALLE O.R., GOVE W.R. & McPHERSON J.M. (1972) Population density and pathology: what are the relations for man? *Science* **176**, 23–30

GALLOWAY D. (1976) Size of school, socio-economic hardship, suspension rates and persistent unjustified absence from school. *Brit. J. educ. Psychol.* **46**, 40–47

GATH D., COOPER B. & GATTONI F. (1972) Preliminary communication: Child guidance and delinquency in a London Borough. *Psychol. Med.* **2**, 185–191

GATH D., COOPER B., GATTONI F. & ROCKETT D. (1976) *Child Guidance and Delinquency in a London Borough.* London: Oxford University Press

GILLIS A.A. (1974) Population density and social pathology: the case of building type, social allowances and juvenile delinquency. *Social Forces* **53**, 306–314

GLASTONBURY B. (1971) *Homeless Near a Thousand Homes.* National Institute for Social Work Training Series No. 21. London: Allen and Unwin

GLUECK S. & GLUECK E.T. (1944) *After-Conduct of Discharged Offenders.* London: Macmillan

GOLD M. (1970) *Delinquent Behavior in an American City.* Monterey, California: Brooks/Cole

GOLD M. & WILLIAMS J.R. (1969) National study of the aftermath of apprehension. *Prospectus* **3**, 3–12

GREVE J., PAGE D. & GREVE S. (1971) *Homelessness in London.* Edinburgh: Scottish Academic Press

GRUNHUT M. (1956) *Juvenile Offenders Before the Courts.* London: Clarendon Press

HÄFNER H. & REIMANN H. (1970) Spatial distribution of mental disorders in Mannheim, 1965. *In* Hare E. & Wing J. (eds.) *Psychiatric Epidemiology.* London: Oxford University Press

HALL R.V., LUND D. & JACKSON D. (1968) Effects of teacher attention on study behavior. *J. Appl. Behav. Anal.* **1**, 1–12

HAMBURG D.A. (1971) Crowding, stranger contact, and aggressive behaviour. *In* Levi L. (ed.) *Society, Stress and Disease*, vol. 1. *The Psychosocial Environment and Psychosomatic Diseases.* London: Oxford University Press

HARE E. & SHAW G.K. (1965) The patients' spouse and concordance on neuroticism. *Brit. J. Psychiat.* **111**, 102–103

HARGREAVES D.H. (1967) *Social Relations in a Secondary School.* London: Routledge & Kegan Paul

HARTMAN C.W. (1963) Social values and housing orientations. *J. Soc. Issues*, **19**, 113–131

HILLIER W. (1973) In defence of space. *J. Roy. Instit. Brit. Architects* **80**, 539–544

HOLMAN R. (1973) *Trading in Children: a study of private fostering.* London: Routledge & Kegan Paul

HUNT A., FOX J. & MORGAN M. (1973) *Families and their Needs.* London: HMSO

JACOBS J. (1961) *The Death and Life of Great American Cities.* New York: Random House

JACKSON B. (1973) The childminders. *New Society*, **26**, 521–524

JAMES A.G. (1974) *Sikh Children in Britain.* London: Institute of Race Relations/ Oxford University Press

JEPHCOTT P. (1971) *Homes in High Flats: Some of the Human Problems Involved in Multistorey Housing.* Edinburgh: Oliver & Boyd

JEPHCOTT A.P. & CARTER M.P. (1954) *The Social Background of Delinquency.* Nottingham: University of Nottingham

JONES H. (1958) Approaches to an ecological study. *Brit. J. Delinq.* **8**, 277–293

KALLARACKAL A.M. & HERBERT M. (1976) The happiness of Indian immigrant children. *New Society* **35,** 422–424

KANTOR M.B. (1965) Some consequences of residential and social mobility for the adjustment of children. *In* Kantor M.B. (ed.) *Mobility and Mental Health.* Springfield, Illinois: Charles C Thomas

KASARDA J.D. & JANOWITZ M. (1974) Community attachment in mass society. *Amer. Sociol. Rev.* **39,** 328–339

KELVIN P. (1970) *The Bases of Social Behaviour.* New York: Holt, Rinehart and Winston

KOUNIN J.S. (1970) *Discipline and Group Management in Classrooms.* New York: Holt, Rinehart & Winston

LAMBERT J. (1970) *Crime, Police and Race Relations.* London: Oxford University Press

LANDER B. (1954) *Towards an Understanding of Juvenile Delinquency.* New York: Columbia University Press

LEE T. (1968) Urban neighbourhood as a socio-spatial schema. *Human Relations,* **21,** 241–267

LEIGHTON D.C., HARDING J.S., MACKLIN D.B., MACMILLIN A.M. & LEIGHTON A.H. (1963) *The Character of Danger.* New York: Basic Books

LEMERT E.M. (1967) *Human Deviance, Social Problems and Social Control.* New York: Prentice Hall

LEVY L. & ROWITZ L. (1970) The spatial distribution of treated mental disorders in Chicago. *Social Psychiat.* **5,** 1–11

LEVY L. & ROWITZ L. (1971) Ecological attributes of high and low rate mental hospital utilization areas in Chicago. *Social Psychiat.* **6,** 20–28

LITTLE W.R. & NTSEKHE V.R. (1959) Social class background of young offenders from London. *Brit. J. Delinq.* **10,** 130–135

MACINTOSH N. & SMITH D.J. (1974) *The Extent of Racial Discrimination.* London: PEP Broadsheet No. 547

McCLINTOCK F.H. & AVISON N.H. (1968) *Crime in England and Wales.* London: Heinemann

McCORD W. & McCORD J. (1959) *Origins of Crime: a new evaluation of the Cambridge–Somerville Youth study.* New York: Columbia University Press

McDILL E.L. & RIGBY L.C. (1973) *Structure and Process in Secondary Schools: the academic impact of educational climates.* Baltimore: Johns Hopkins University Press

McDONALD L. (1969) *Social Class and Delinquency.* London: Faber & Faber

MANNHEIM H. (1948) *Juvenile Delinquency in an English Middletown.* London: Kegan Paul, Trench, Trubner

MANNHEIM H., SPENCER J. & LYNCH G. (1957) Magisterial policy in the London Juvenile courts. *Brit. J. Delinq.* **8,** 13–33; 119–138

MATZA D. (1964) *Delinquency and Drift.* New York: Wiley

MAYS J.B. (1954) *Growing Up in the City.* Liverpool: University Press

MAYS J.B. (1963) Delinquency areas—a re-assessment. *Brit. J. Criminol.* **3,** 216–230

MAYS J.B. (ed.) (1972) *Juvenile Delinquency, The Family and The Social Group, A Reader.* London: Longman

MERTON R.K. (1957) *Social Theory and Social Structure.* New York: Free Press

MILGRAM S. (1970) The experience of living in cities. *Science* **167,** 1461–1468

MINISTRY OF HOUSING AND LOCAL GOVERNMENT (1963) *Living in a Slum: a Study of People in a Central Slum Clearance Area in Oldham.* London: HMSO

MINISTRY OF HOUSING AND LOCAL GOVERNMENT (1970) *Families living at High Density: a Study of Estates in Leeds, Liverpool and London.* London: HMSO

MITCHELL R.E. (1971) Some social implications of high density housing. *Amer. Soc. Rev.* **36**, 18–29

MITCHELL S. & SHEPHERD M. (1966) A comparative study of children's behaviour at home and at school. *Brit. J. Educ. Psychol.* **36**. 248–254

MOORE N.C. (1974) Psychiatric illness and living in flats. *Brit. J. Psychiat.* **125**, 500–507

MORRIS T.P. (1957) *The Criminal Area.* London: Routledge & Kegan Paul

NEWCOMB T.M. (1963) The persistence and regression of changed attitudes: long range studies. *J. social Issues*, **19**, 3–14

NEWMAN O. (1973) *Defensible Space.* London: Architectural Press

NICOL A.R. (1971) Psychiatric disorder in the children of Caribbean immigrants. *J. Child Psychol. Psychiat.* **12**, 273–287

ØDEGAARD O. (1975) *Social and Ecological Factors in the Etiology, Outcome, Treatment and Prevention of Mental Disorders* (Psychiatrie der Gegenwart, Band III). Berlin: Springer–Verlag

O'LEARY K.D., BECKER W.C., EVANS M.B. & SAUDARGAS R.A. (1969) A token reinforcement program in a public school: a replication and systematic analysis. *J. Appl. Behav. Anal.* **2**, 3–13

O'LEARY K.D. & O'LEARY S.F. (1972) *Classroom Management: the Successful Use of Behaviour Modification.* Oxford: Pergamon

PALMAI G., STOREY P.B. & BRISCOE O. (1967) Social class and the young offender. *Brit. J. Psychiat.* **113**, 1073–1082

PATRICK J. (1973) *A Glasgow Gang Observed.* London: Eyre Methuen

PEARCE K.S. (1974) West Indian boys in community home schools. *Community Schools Gazette* **68**, 317–339; 376–407

POLLAK M. (1973) *Today's Three Year Olds in London.* London: Heinemann

POWER M.J., ALDERSON M.R., PHILLIPSON C.M., SCHOENBERG E. & MORRIS J.N. (1967) Delinquent Schools? *New Society* **10**, 542–543

POWER M.J., BENN R.T. & MORRIS J.N. (1972) Neighbourhood, school and juveniles before the courts. *Brit. J. Criminol.* **12**, 111–132

PRINCE G. (1967) Mental health problems in pre-school West Indian children. *Matern. Child Care* **3**, 483–486

PROSHANSKY H.M., ITTELSON W.H. & RIVLIN L.G. (1970) The influence of the physical environment on behavior: some basic assumptions. *In* Proshansky H.M., Ittelson W.H. & Rivlin, L.G. (eds.) *Environmental Psychology: Man and his Physical Setting.* New York: Holt, Rinehart & Winston

REISS A.J. Jnr. & RHODES A.L. (1961) The distribution of juvenile delinquency in the social class structure. *Amer. Sociol. Rev.* **26**, 720–732

REISS A.J. & RHODES A.L. (1964) An empirical test of differential association theory. *J. Res. Crime Delinq.* **1**, 5–18

REYNOLDS D. & MURGATROYD S. (1974) Being absent from school. *Brit. J. Law and Society* **1**, 78–81

RICHMAN N. (1974) The effects of housing on pre-school children and their mothers. *Dev. Med. Child Neurol.* **16**, 53–58

RICHMOND A.H. (1954) *Colour Prejudice in Britain: a Study of West Indian Workers in Liverpool, 1942–1951.* London: Routledge & Kegan Paul

ROBINS L.N. (1966) *Deviant Children Grown Up*. Baltimore: Williams & Wilkins

ROBINS L.N. & HILL S.Y. (1966) Assessing the contribution of family structure, class and peer groups to juvenile delinquency. *J. Crim. Law Criminol. & Pol. Sci.* **57**, 325–334

ROFF M., SELLS S.B. & GOLDEN M.M. (1972) *Social Adjustment and Personality Development in Children*. Minneapolis: University of Minnesota Press

RUTTER M. (1976) (ed.) *The Child, His Family and The Community* (In preparation). London: Wiley

RUTTER M., COX A., TUPLING C., BERGER M. & YULE W. (1975a) Attainment and adjustment in two geographical areas: I. The prevalence of psychiatric disorder. *Brit. J. Psychiat.*, **126**, 493–509

RUTTER M. & MADGE N. (1976) *Cycles of Disadvantage: a Review of Research* (in press). London: Heinemann Educational

RUTTER M. & QUINTON D. (1976) Psychiatric disorder—ecological factors and concepts of causation. *In* McGurk H. (ed.) *Ecological Factors in Human Development* (in press). Amsterdam: North-Holland

RUTTER M., TIZARD J. & WHITMORE K. (eds.) (1970) *Education Health and Behaviour*. London: Longman

RUTTER M., YULE W., BERGER M., YULE B., MORTON J. & BAGLEY C. (1974) Children of West Indian immigrants—I. Rates of behavioural deviance and of psychiatric disorder. *J. Child Psychol. Psychiat.* **15**, 241–262

RUTTER M., YULE B., MORTON J. & BAGLEY C. (1975b) Children of West Indian immigrants—III. Home circumstances and family patterns. *J. Child Psychol. Psychiat.* **16**, 105–123

RUTTER M., YULE B., QUINTON D., ROWLANDS O., YULE W. & BERGER M. (1975c) Attainment and adjustment in two geographical areas: III. Some factors accounting for area differences. *Brit. J. Psychiat.* **126**, 520–533

SAINSBURY P. (1955) *Suicide in London: an Ecological Study*. Institute of Psychiatry Maudsley Monographs No. 1. London: Oxford University Press

SCHMITT R.C. (1963) Implications of density in Hong Kong. *J. Amer. Instit. Planners* **29**, 210–217

SCHOOLS COUNCIL (1970) *Teaching English to West Indian Children*. Working Paper No. 29. London: Evans/Methuen Educational

SCOTT P.D. (1956) Gangs and delinquent groups in London. *Brit. J. Delinq.* **7**, 4–26

SHAW C.R. & McKAY H.D. (1942) *Juvenile Delinquency and Urban Areas*. Chicago: University of Chicago Press

SHERIF M., HARVEY O.J., WHITE B.J., HOOD W.R. & SHERIF C.W. (1961) *Intergroup Conflict and Cooperation: The Robbers' Cave Experiment*. Norman, Oklahoma: University of Oklahoma Press

SHIPMAN M.D. (1968) *Sociology of the School*. London: Longman

SPENCER J.C. (1954) *Crime and the Services*. London: Routledge & Kegan Paul

STOTT D.H. (1960) The prediction of delinquency from non-delinquent behaviour. *Brit. J. Delinq.* **10**, 195–210

STOTT D.H. (1966) *Studies of Troublesome Children*. London: Tavistock

SUGARMAN B. (1967) Involvement in youth culture. *Brit. J. Sociol.* **18**, 151–164

SUNDBY P. & NYHUS P. (1963) Major and minor psychiatric disorders in males in Oslo: an epidemiological study. *Acta psychiat. Scand.* **39**, 519–547

SUTHERLAND E.H. (1939) *Principles of Criminology.* Philadelphia: Lippincott

SUTTLES G.D. (1972) *The Social Construction of Communities.* Chicago: University of Chicago Press

VEREKER C., MAYS J.B., GITTUS E. & BROADY M. (1961) *Urban Redevelopment and Social Change: A study of social conditions in Central Liverpool, 1955–56.* Liverpool: University Press

VOSS H.L. (1964) Differential association and reported delinquent behavior: a replication. *Social Problems* **12,** 78–85

WALKER N. (1965) *Crime and Punishment in Britain.* Edinburgh: University Press

WALLIS C.P. & MALIPHANT R. (1967) Delinquent areas in the county of London: ecological factors, *Brit. J. Criminol.* **7,** 250–284

WEST D.J. (1967) *The Young Offender.* Harmondsworth: Penguin

WEST D.J. & FARRINGTON D.P. (1973) *Who Becomes Delinquent?* London: Heinemann

WESTIN A.F. (1967) *Privacy and Freedom.* New York: Atheneum

WHITE R.K. & LIPPITT R. (1960) *Autocracy and Democracy: an Experimental Enquiry.* New York: Harper & Row

WHITLOCK F.A. (1973a) Suicide in England and Wales 1959–63. Part 1: The County Boroughs. *Psychol. Med.* **3,** 350–365

WHITLOCK F.A. (1973b) Suicide in England and Wales 1959–63. Part 2: London. *Psychol. Med.* **3,** 411–420

WILKINS L.T. (1964) *Social Deviance.* London: Tavistock

WILLMOTT P. (1969) *Adolescent Boys of East London.* Harmondsworth: Penguin

WILNER D.M., WALKLEY R.P., PINKERTON T.C. & TAYBACK M. (1962) *The Housing Environment and Family Life: a Longitudinal Study of the Effects of Housing on Morbidity and Mental Health.* Baltimore: Johns Hopkins Press

WOOTTON B. (1959) *Social Science and Social Pathology.* London: Allen and Unwin

YUDKIN S. (1967) *0–5: a Report on the Care of Pre-school Children.* National Soc. Children's Nurseries

YULE B. & RUTTER M. (1976) Unpublished data

YULE W., BERGER M., RUTTER M. & YULE B. (1975) Children of West Indian immigrants. II. Intellectual performance and reading attainment. *J. Child Psychol. Psychiat.* **16,** 1–17

ZIMBARDO P.G. (1969) The human choice: individuation, reason and order versus deindividuation, impulse and chaos. *In* Arnold W.J. & Levine D. (eds.) *Nebraska Symposium on Motivation,* vol. 17. Lincoln: University of Nebraska Press

CHAPTER 6
Adoption

L. HERSOV

Adoption practice is increasing in its scope and complexity and requires the skills of several disciplines. A child psychiatrist may be asked to help with the assessment of deviant emotional and intellectual development in infants and toddlers, including those with various physical handicaps (Lewis 1965); to give a prediction about the likelihood of later mental disorder in a child where there is a history of functional psychosis or personality disorder in the natural parents (Shields 1975); or to assess the long-term prognosis for emotional development and psychiatric disorder in children who have been 'In Care' in institutions for the early part of their life and who are now being offered for adoption. With the changing pattern of adoption it is likely that physically handicapped children formerly not considered suitable, and who have a somewhat increased risk for psychiatric disorder (Rutter *et al* 1970) will now be considered for adoption more often.

For the psychiatrist, the legal implications of adoption are important and he may be called to Court to give evidence for one or other side in litigation over refusal by a mother to part with her child or in issues over applications by foster parents to adopt (Maclay 1969). In addition the human, personal, social and psychological elements in adoption are encountered in day-to-day work in psychiatric practice with adults and children. A psychiatrist can also be a medical member of an adoption case committee which deals with problems of consent and the suitability of prospective adopters, as well as the follow-up of children successfully placed for adoption.

ADOPTION STATISTICS AND TRENDS

The number of legal adoptions in Great Britain rose steadily over the 10 years from 14 668 in 1958 to reach a peak of 26 986 in 1968 (Cmnd 5107 HMSO 1972). The figures then declined and have continued to do so, so that the number of orders registered in 1975 was 21 299 (Office of Population Censuses and Surveys, HMSO 1976). Between 2 and 3 per cent of all live-born infants in Great Britain are adopted (Forfar 1969a) and until recently

136

the majority were extrafamilial adoptions, i.e. to a family other than that of origin. The number of adoptions by natural parents either alone, or much more commonly by a step-parent, has risen considerably in recent years, probably reflecting higher rates of divorce and remarriage. In 1962 there were 4630 such adoptions (Cmnd 5107 HMSO 1972) and 14 567 in 1975 which is nearly 70 per cent of the total (Office of Population Censuses and Surveys, HMSO 1976).

More use of contraception and the increasing number of legal abortions contributes to a falling birth rate. A changing attitude to illegitimacy, supplementary benefits, day-care provision and more reasonable chances of employment have led to many more unmarried mothers keeping their babies as they are now more able to bring up their children over the years. All these factors have contributed to a situation where fewer babies are being offered for adoption. There is, however, evidence that illegitimate children brought up by their mothers make less progress on average than legitimate children or illegitimate children given up for adoption (Crellin *et al* 1971).

Attitudes towards adoption placements of coloured children of mixed race and older children are also changing. The need for homes for such children has only recently been estimated by the British Adoption Project. They found that 445 coloured children were adopted through agencies, comprising 3 per cent of adoption orders made for agency-placed children in 1966, while 415 were known to agencies who might have been placed but for their race. At the end of 1966 there were still 846 coloured children on agencies' files needing homes (Raynor 1970). The situation is improving so that some agencies are able to place coloured children without much difficulty and efforts are now being made by the Adoption Resource Exchange to include older coloured children within their scope of work.

There is a general principle that adoption placements are best made at an early age, indeed as young as possible, but recent studies have shown that older children can be successfully adopted (Jaffe & Fanshel 1970). Kadushin (1970) studied 91 children in the USA who were adopted between the ages of 5 and 12 years following termination of natural parents rights because of abuse and neglect. 'Successful' adoption was assessed in terms of the adoptive parents' satisfactions and dissatisfactions rather than child's development or adjustment. Over four-fifths of these later adoptions were rated 'successful', but an unfavourable outcome was more likely if the child showed more behavioural disturbance, had experienced more than the average number of changes of foster care prior to placement and still retained a strong emotional attachment to his natural mother.

There is a trend for adoption agencies in Great Britain to extend their range and services to include children with 'special needs'. Particular interest has focussed on those children in the care of the Social Services who could possibly be placed with families and thus meet the constant demand from prospective adopters. A study was set up (Rowe & Lambert 1973) to enquire into the present situation in child placement agencies and to provide data on those children whose social workers wanted to find homes for them. The findings were that 626 children (22 per cent of the whole group) of 2812 children covered by the study were thought to need a substitute family. In national terms this amounts to about 7000 children. Two out of three in the sample were boys of school age, and one in four was coloured, most often full or part West Indian. The most serious bar to placement was thought to be below average intelligence although behaviour problems were noted more frequently than any other difficulty (one-third of the sample). Management problems and aggressive or destructive behaviour were most common; stealing and lying were less frequent. A quarter of the children showed difficulty in relating to adults or other children and 30 per cent had a shallow emotional response. A fifth wet the bed. It was considered that aggressive/destructive behaviour was a greater obstacle to family placement than social withdrawal or poor relationships.

Several recent studies of children in residential care have shown that emotional and behaviour disorder is significantly more common than among children in the general population (Yule & Raynes 1972; Wolkind & Rutter 1973; Wolkind 1974; Mapstone 1969). Boys were affected more than girls (Yule & Raynes 1972; Wolkind & Rutter 1973), Wolkind (1974) also found that enuresis was a common finding as part of a psychiatric disorder in the group studied and that those with antisocial disorder were rated more frequently as severely handicapped. He suggests on the basis of the present and other evidence (Wolkind & Rutter 1973) that both the disorder and the prolonged stay in care are secondary to the family situation; many of the children appeared to be severely damaged in terms of difficulties with relationships and behaviour by their experiences prior to admission to residential care. Tizard and Rees (1975) compared a group of children aged $4\frac{1}{2}$ years who had been continuously reared since early infancy in institutions of generally high quality, with a group living at home and a group either adopted or restored to their natural mothers after spending their first 2–4 years in a residential nursery. There were 24 adopted children in the one comparison group. Their behavioural problems and affectional relationships were assessed and compared and the findings showed significantly fewer problems and more satisfactory development than among the institutional children. The adopted children easily formed attachments to their adoptive parents, but in a third, the parents were concerned by their overfriendliness to strangers. The authors conclude that given 'good' nurseries with a high staff–child ratio adoption of the children at a later stage than is usual does not necessarily mean behavioural problems or difficulties in relationships but further study of development during school-age is needed to determine whether the observed modes of response remain permanent or break down. The findings in all these studies have relevance to decisions about whether a child in care should be reunited with his family or whether alternative placements such as fostering or adoption should be sought.

CHARACTERISTICS OF ADOPTIVE PARENTS

Extrafamilial adoptive parents are mainly drawn from the middle class as shown by studies from the USA (Leahy 1933), Sweden (Bohman 1970) and the UK (Lewis 1960; Humphrey & Ounsted 1964; Kornitzer 1968; Humphrey 1969; Grey & Blunden 1971; Seglow *et al* 1972). Kornitzer's (1968) findings suggest that this is in part due to factors in the selection process by adoption agencies which tend to favour the more well-to-do applicants of higher social status. However, there is now an increasing acceptance of working class applicants for children (Humphrey 1969). This and other changes in adoption practice mean that we need to look again at those qualities in a home and family which will support the development of children as what is needed for a handicapped child or an older child from an institutional background may well be very different from that appropriate for a younger infant. As applicants for adoption must be at least 21 years of age (if nonrelatives one of them must be at least 25 years), it is not surprising that adoptive mothers and fathers tend to be older than natural parents in the general population. Grey and Blunden (1971) found that 53 per cent of all male and 38 per cent of female nonparental applicants were 35 years or older. The figures were 61 per cent and 42 per cent respectively in the National Child Development Study (Seglow *et al* 1972), but this included a quarter of their sample in which the child was not the first to be adopted. A further reason for the increased age of the applicants is the time between marriage and acceptance of childlessness as well as the time taken to reach a decision to adopt and then for the application to be accepted and a baby found. Bohman (1970) has pointed out that even though good physical health is a basic requirement for selection as an adoptive parent, the greater age of adopting parents may involve a higher risk of disease and death than in a younger population with children of the same age. He commented on the relatively high morbidity among his sample of adopters. Seglow *et al* (1972) did not find more ill-health among older than younger adopters, but found a generally high incidence of poor health among adoptive mothers of whom 42 per cent were believed to be infertile, a significantly high proportion.

It appears that couples who wish to adopt infants are different from those who adopt older children. Older children are more often adopted by couples of lower social status (Maas 1960) and, in the USA, are more often placed with farm families (Leahy 1933). Maas (1960) suggested that working class couples may be more able to accept children with psychological and physical disorders and so adopt these children more frequently than middle class families who may be more successful in adopting infants. Kadushin (1962) also found that couples who are marginally eligible for adoptive status because of age, health and other related factors are more likely to accept children with special needs.

Humphrey (1969) looked at the reason for deciding to adopt a child in a detailed interview study of 40 children and adopting couples selected via a postal questionnaire (with an 80 per cent return rate) sent to women who had attended a hospital infertility clinic over a 10-year period. The sample had a normal social class distribution but was limited by the exclusion of childless couples who had not sought medical advice.

Compared with the adoptive mothers, the childless wives tended to be slower in their psychosexual development, taking longer to acquire a knowledge of conception, having few serious attachments before marriage and marrying later. Humphrey suggested that these factors implied slower maturation, but social and psychological factors are probably more important. A happy childhood appeared less important than the concept of happy family life derived from the couple's own parents. Where this was so, adoption was most likely to be acceptable, but a couple were likely to be discouraged from adopting where their recollection of both parental marriages was of difficulties. The implication for adoption practice is the value of enquiry into the family background of both applicants, particularly on the issue of parental harmony. Uneasiness derived from such a background could well be reflected in the adopters' response to their own family problems.

ASSESSMENT OF CHILDREN FOR ADOPTION

The regulations of the Adoption Act of 1958 (HMSO) provide that a 'report on the health of the infant signed by a fully registered medical practitioner must be obtained by the society' i.e. the adoption agencies which carry out the majority of legalised adoptions. No indication is given in the regulations of the appropriate type of examination, but the report has to be detailed and comprehensive, even though there is no requirement as to training or experience in the assessment of infants. There is now increasing pressure for raised standards in terms of the use of comprehensive medical report forms, as well as training in developmental assessment for those doctors who carry out adoption examinations. A proper assessment of an infant or child requires an adequate background medical history of the biological mother and if possible the father, a history of the pregnancy and delivery and any disorder in the perinatal period, as well as data on the infant's subsequent progress.

It is still possible that a significant number of infants are unhappily rejected for adoption because an inexperienced examiner has found minor or trivial defects which are narrowly or rigidly interpreted. No infant should be rejected unless the opinion of a consultant paediatrician has been sought about him (Forfar 1969b). On the other hand, an inadequate examination may miss gross defects such as severe mental subnormality, cerebral palsy, or visual and auditory defects with far-reaching consequences if these infants are then placed for adoption. Forfar (1969b) discussing the medical criteria for adoptibility stresses that considerable knowledge is needed to recognise actual and potential defects. He estimates that between 10 and 20 per cent of preplacement medical assessments cause problems about adoptibility. These are such instances as Huntington's chorea in a grandparent, epilepsy or mental subnormality in a biological parent or a history of functional psychosis. Genetic or psychiatric consultation and advice may be necessary to predict the risks when there is schizophrenia, manic depressive disorder, epilepsy or a degenerative disease of the central nervous system in one or both biological parents. The medical findings and predictions should be discussed with the adoption society so that they can be related to the other judgements, social and psychological, which will be made in the decision about adoption (Forfar 1969b). Above all, the prospective adopters must be active participants in this process and be fully informed about the nature of the prognosis and developmental implications of any medical problem in the infant.

There are difficulties in assessment and prediction in instances where an infant displays early slow development, or certain abnormal neurological signs which may disappear in time, or has a history of emotional privation or deprivation (Illingworth 1968). However, improved methods of developmental assessment by paediatricians or community physicians trained in these methods may in future ensure more accurate measurement of an infant's present level of intellectual development and future development, and lead to more accurate prediction even though there will always be a margin for error in a number of instances.

Until about 30 years ago most adoption agencies considered children with more serious mental defects as not adoptable, and the emphasis was on placing the mentally and physically normal (usually white) infant. Then, as today, the majority of prospective adopters particularly those younger couples preferred an infant who has been assessed as healthy and potentially normal in development and with a good hereditary background. There is now a trend towards a broader definition of an adoptable child which includes those with medical conditions provided a family can be found which will accept the 'imperfect' child with his particular physical and mental capacities. The desirable goal of placement in early infancy is often difficult to reach in children with medical conditions, for these infants are often held in foster care or a children's home until a preplacement medical evaluation can be completed. Illingworth (1968) stated that an experienced paediatrician should be able to diagnose a definitely abnormal infant at the age of 6 months, but that in some cases it is fair to the prospective adopters to postpone the decision until 10 months of age if there are still doubts about the infant's health and future development.

Massarik and Franklin (1967) carried out a retrospective study of California agency placements of 449 children with medical conditions which required special casework and medical consideration in planning placement. 135 children were excluded because of insufficient information or because the medical condition was fully corrected before placement. This left 314 children with 59 rated as 'severe', 71 as 'moderate', and 184 as 'minor' in the degree of severity and correctability of the medical condition. The range of diagnoses included blindness, congenital heart defects, achondroplasia and cerebral palsy among those rated as 'severe'; cataracts, undescended testicle and cleft palate among the 'moderate'; and hernia, strabismus and hypospadias in the group rated as 'minor'. A control group of 105 children with no medical condition were randomly selected from among agency placements during the same time period. The final comparison involved 169 study families and 70 control families. Data were collected by means of a joint interview with the parent and an unstructured period of observation of the child.

It was found that children with severe medical conditions could be successfully placed, thrive physically and emotionally, and become integrated into their families. Successful placement appeared to be enhanced by the presence of other children in the family. The experience of development and behaviour in a presumably normal child may have enabled these parents to adapt more easily to meeting the special needs of the handicapped child. Maladaptive stressful family relationships occurred more often in middle class families than in upper or lower class families. The finding that upper class families showed a sensitive awareness of the handicapped child's special problems runs counter to commonly held beliefs. Most parents coped successfully with problems arising during their child's development. The persistent problems were more often behavioural than medical but occurred most frequently in children with severe medical conditions. Placement of children with medical problems is certainly possible, but requires rather special qualities in adopters. The outcome in terms of parental experience and coping ability is likely to vary according to the severity of the medical condition and this in itself may lengthen the time scale of placement. Special care is needed to explain to prospective applicants the size, extent and nature of the medical, social and psychological problems that may confront them. The combined help of a paediatrician and experienced medical social worker may be necessary to explain the range and limits of the child's developmental potential and to allay anxiety. In this way misconceptions arising out of ignorance can be avoided and the confidence gained can be reinforced by later paediatric consultation if necessary. Although the severely handicapped child makes great demands upon the parents' time and the family's stability, it is more often the concomitant emotional disturbance which poses the greater problems of management (Knight 1970; 1971).

Children with physical disorders face difficulties in terms of limitations of normal activity, lack of important formative experiences and negative self-image, as well as the reactions that the handicap calls out in the children's parents. The rate of psychiatric disorder in children with physical disorder is somewhat greater than in the general population, and for children with neuroepileptic conditions, the rate is three or four times that in the general population (Rutter *et al* 1970; see also Chapter 8). In discussion with prospective adopters of handicapped children, particular emphasis must be given to the possibility of transient emotional disturbance and frank psychiatric disorder at different stages of development. In this way, and by offering help later if needed, there is the possibility of early prevention of problems.

Knight (1971) has also written on the difficult problem of placement of children for adoption in families with an already seriously handicapped child. She argues that each application should be treated on its individual merits, but that in almost all instances the decision will be taken against placement.

Adoption is in any case a complex process with emotional reactions and the prior existence in the family of a handicapped child adds to the complications of accepting a normal child for adoption. It may be harder to meet the adopted child's need for acceptance, affection, security and new experience, in the face of the demands and anxieties already imposed by the handicapped child. There is an absence of hard evidence as to the outcome in such circumstances, but Gath (1974) in a study of sibling reactions to a mongol child in a family, found that boys and girls younger than the mongol child are not likely to be adversely affected, although older children, especially girls, are more at risk for developing psychiatric disorder. She concludes that when the risk of a second mongol child is unacceptable in a family, adoption agencies could feel more confident about placing a child in such a family than hitherto.

The situation where one prospective adopter suffers from a physical disability or has a history of psychiatric disorder poses equal problems in selection. The research of Rutter (1966), Wolff and Acton (1968) and Anthony (1969) has shown that there is a strong association between chronic parental illness especially mental illness and psychiatric disorder in children, but not all parental illnesses affect children's development, and the sex and ordinal position of a child in a family influences the differential effect of parental illness. The 'seriousness' of the parental psychiatric disorder does not seem as important as the involvement of the child in the symptoms of parental disorder. Rutter (1970) has shown that when parents have a long-standing disorder of personality there is likely to be family disharmony involving the children and associated with behaviour disorder in the children. Hersov (1973) has discussed the implications for adoption practice of knowledge about the self-limiting nature of particular psychiatric disorders in adults and their response to treatment. A history of such illnesses should not necessarily debar a parent or parents from being considered as prospective adopters.

THE ADOLESCENT GIRL AND ADOPTION

The unmarried pregnant adolescent girl presents an increasing problem with medical, social, legal and psychological implications. Opinions vary as to the factors associated with pregnancy in such circumstances. Anderson *et al* (1960) concluded that 'in 76% of cases studied the pregnancy followed naturally enough from the pursuit of adolescent practices normal to the whole society' while Lewis (1971) regards illegitimate pregnancy as a manifestation of adolescent upset in which unconscious wishes, depression, impulsive acting-out and other psychological factors interact with social permissiveness and self-fulfilling prophecies by parents. However, there are many contradictions in the research findings which often reflect sampling bias (Pauker 1969).

No one explanation covers the entire spectrum of out-of-wedlock pregnancies and a large share of the 'cause' must be ascribed to chance, especially among adolescents pregnant for the first time.

The social and psychological circumstances in which such pregnancies occur are extremely important in deciding what to advise. The main alternatives are therapeutic abortion, carrying to term and delivery (during which time marriage may occur, often to another adolescent), placement for adoption after delivery and finally the setting up of a one-parent family (the 'lone' parent). Another possibility is that the child is taken over by the girl's parents and reared as their own, although difficulties may then arise in family relationships when the child grows older. Obviously, each case must be considered individually but some guidelines are available.

The absolute number of children born out of wedlock in England and Wales has declined since the peak level in 1967, but the proportion has slightly increased relative to the number of legitimate births. In 1972, 8·6 per cent of all live births were illegitimate compared with 4·6 per cent in 1955 and 9·3 per cent in 1945. For girls under 16 years of age the number of illegitimate live births has risen from 871 in 1961 to 1513 in 1971, and this trend is similar for illegitimate births to mothers under the age of 20 years.

In 1970 there were 1791 legal abortions carried out on adolescents under the age of 16 years in England and Wales and 1403 illegitimate live births were registered. In 1971 2 per cent of the total notified abortions in England and Wales were carried out on girls under 16 years of age and of the total of all recorded pregnancies on girls under 16 years 40 per cent ended in live births whereas 60 per cent ended in notified abortions (Report of the Committee on the Working of the Abortion Act HMSO 1974). The last comparison suggests that at least since the introduction of the Abortion Act, therapeutic abortion has been used as a means of dealing with the distressing problem of pregnancy in adolescents in more than half the instances that came to medical notice in that year. Although the procedure may appear to be an obvious and practical answer to the problem in the individual case, doubts have been expressed about therapeutic abortion on the grounds of possible physical and psychological sequelae. Gordon (1970) writes that 'when contemplating termination of pregnancy in the young unmarried teenage patient, consideration must be given to the potential reproductive performance of the patient if the pregnancy is allowed to continue, and this should be weighed against any long-term undesirable sequelae associated with abortion in this group of patients'.

Some writers (Osofsky & Osofsky 1970) maintain that pregnant teenagers are a high risk group from the medical, social and educational viewpoint, that complications of pregnancy occur more frequently than in the general population with a higher incidence of prematurity, fetal and neonatal mortality. A critical look at these pessimistic studies usually from the USA, shows that the higher incidence of complications is associated with unmarried mothers, low income and low educational status, and too late and too inadequate use of antenatal care. When adequate care was provided to married teenage pregnant girls in relatively middle class conditions, the incidence of complications was much lower (La Barre 1969). Obeng (1969) studying a group of 91 pregnant girls aged 13–16 years in London, found a slightly increased incidence of toxaemia, excessive weight gain and anaemia with three times as many congenital anomalies among the infants born, compared with a control group. However, labour proved to be easier and quicker than in older primigravida and Gordon (1970) concludes that the evidence from this and other studies (Lewis & Nash 1967; Utian 1967) suggests, that if the pregnancy continues the physical problems are in fact not significant, so that childbirth is actually safer in primipara aged 16 years or under. Gordon (1973) points out that there are potential long-term hazards of termination of pregnancy even where termination occurs during the first trimester. These include effects on later fertility, pregnancy complications and abnormalities in labour and premature birth in subsequent pregnancies.

The information on the psychosocial aspects of teenage pregnancy where termination is requested and carried out, hardly compares with the above. Most studies and reviews deal with adult women and in only a few is particular concern given to pregnancy in adolescent girls. Sloane (1969) after reviewing studies in the USA, Great Britain and the Continent on adult women, concludes that there are no clear-cut psychiatric indications for therapeutic abortion for the risk of precipitation and exacerbation of an existing psychosis is small and unpredictable, and suicide is rare. Little new psychiatric illness appears after therapeutic abortion that can be related to the procedure and Patt *et al* (1969) conclude that with rare exceptions abortions were genuinely therapeutic in relieving emotional disturbance. Sloane (1969) observed that the psychological effects of a continued pregnancy resulting from rape or incest have been little studied although most people would agree that such circumstances are psychologically undesirable especially in juveniles. Tredgold (1964) includes rape as grounds for termination provided that the evidence for this having occurred was convincing.

Hausknecht (1972) in New York City reports that 10 per cent of therapeutic abortions were carried out in women 17 years or younger and these tended to have pregnancies of longer gestation (i.e. 13 weeks or more) than the group of women as a whole. This was also found in England and Wales (Lane Committee Report 1974) where 34 per cent of pregnancies in girls under 16 years were terminated at a gestation of 13 weeks or more compared with 22 per cent for those over 16 years. The obvious reasons are denial of pregnancy or attempts to conceal for as long as possible, but there are implications in terms of lack of antenatal care and difficulty of operation. There are varying and complex reasons for 'having a baby' and no one particular set of circumstances. Major emotional disturbance was rare following the operation and there was usually a sense of relief associated with euphoria. The risks of termination were no greater, with good medical care, than in termination in older women. Perez-Reyes and Falk (1973) studied a socially mixed sample of 71 girls 16 years and younger who applied for termination in North Carolina, USA. The psychiatric criterion followed in recommending abortion was the patient's wish to have a termination having considered and discussed the possibilities. When in doubt, patients were encouraged to think it over, to discuss it further with parents, boyfriends and others and to come to a decision. Hausknecht (1972) and others (Lane Committee 1974) stresses the need for discussion and counselling for those about to have an abortion, so that they are clear in their own minds that they desire the operation and understand its significance and consequences. Gough (1966) considers that greater access to legal termination could be one of the most helpful things to provide in schoolage pregnancies, but warns against the dangers of forcing this upon a schoolgirl who may then become pregnant again and conceal this until it is too dangerous to intervene. The Lane Committee (1974) was strongly of the opinion that a pregnancy should not be terminated without a girl's consent and that the assessment of the situation should be careful and extensive and always include some discussion with the girl.

Perez-Rayes and Falk (1973) found that generally the parents had suggested or supported therapeutic abortion, but sometimes feelings among mothers were very mixed. The commonest reason for wanting a termination was for the girl to be able to continue her education, the second was the girl's immaturity as perceived by parents. The girls themselves gave a variety of reasons for wanting termination including unreadiness to rear a child, a wish to continue their education, financial insecurity, fear of social consequences of illegitimate pregnancy, parental unwillingness to accept responsibility for the child, lack of support from putative father and the anticipated pain of bearing a child and then giving it up for adoption.

Immediate postoperative feelings among the girls were of depression, guilt, anger and worry mainly among the black girls who felt criticised by relatives for not carrying to term. Follow-up 6 months after the operation in only 41 girls showed no marked change in general health or emotional state and psychological testing on the MMPI (Hathaway & McKinley 1951) showed a decrease in depression and a profile more approaching the normal as compared with preoperative testing.

Perez-Reyes and Falk (1973) also emphasise the importance of help by parents and medical personnel in allowing the girl to come to her own decision about termination. A positive relationship between the girl and her parents, especially her mother, makes for freer discussion and a better outcome, so that the girls are able to overcome their painful emotional feelings and continue their schooling. Gough (1966) stresses the amount of help a young girl needs with her feelings about a terminated pregnancy.

However, it is difficult to draw firm conclusions about the later emotional and psychological effects of termination of pregnancy and how often these effects occur particularly in adolescent girls. What little evidence exists is based on studies of psychiatric populations of older women and the results are often contradictory. Kaye and Schapira (1967) after reviewing the literature reported a very good outcome after abortion in 85 per cent of cases, 10–15 per cent experiencing severe self-reproach or regrets for a time and

1–2 per cent suffering definite psychiatric illness not necessarily connected with the abortion. Long-term follow-up studies of psychiatrically normal women whose pregnancies were terminated for social reasons are lacking. In general, few women escape some degree of physical or emotional trauma however short-lived as the result of termination of pregnancy (RCOG 1972). The conclusion of the Lane Committee (Cmnd 5579 HMSO 1974) was that in the majority of pregnancies in girls under 16 years, whether there is temperamental instability or not, therapeutic abortion can be justified on account of the girl's immaturity and the attendant risks to her health.

If the teenage unmarried mother decides to carry her child to term the course of the pregnancy may be uneventful if family and social support is available, but suicidal attempts and other manifestations of psychiatric disorder may occur (Gabrielson *et al* 1970). This may represent a response to the stresses of pregnancy per se but is more likely to be an outcome of a high rate of psychiatric disorder prior to pregnancy.

A teenager may carry to term in the expectation of marriage to the putative father during pregnancy or later. This socially acceptable solution is not without its problems for teenage marriages run a considerably higher risk of breaking down especially where there has been a premarital pregnancy (Dominian 1968).

It is the experience of those concerned in providing social work help to pregnant girls that the majority will seek termination and, of the remainder, relatively few will be prepared to carry the child to term with the intention of relinquishing the child for adoption. The reasons are manifold including the possibility that it is the emotionally disturbed or unstable girl who decides to have her baby and then has doubts about the decision to relinquish for adoption even though these ideas had been entertained and possibly discussed.

PREDICTABILITY OF DEVELOPMENT FROM ASSESSMENT IN INFANCY

The assessment of infants for adoption includes not only the detection of severe subnormality, neurological defects, congenital anomalies and other features which may impede physical and psychological development, but also some attempt at predicting whether the infant has a normal potential for later development. Illingworth (1968) claimed that only a very small number (3·4 per cent) of 156 infants he had originally assessed at 6–10 months were misclassified in terms of broad grouping on later intellectual assessment at age 6–7 years. Rutter (1970) argued that, in spite of consistencies and meanings in psychological development, the level of prediction that can be made at

6 months is very poor, and that no useful predictions of psychological characteristics within the normal range can be made. Some crude differentiation in terms of levels of intelligence (normal, mildly subnormal or severely subnormal) is possible in the first year of life, but an appreciable number will be seriously misclassified. Important aspects of cognitive and emotional growth only develop in the second year of life and are strongly influenced by the sort of environment experienced by the infant and young child. There is little connection between the tangible criteria of age, religion and socioeconomic circumstances so often used by adoption agencies and the later outcome in terms of the children's emotional stability. There has been little research evaluation of different methods of selection, and so there is no way of telling which is the most effective for the purpose. Although the better agencies use trained case-workers to carry out a series of careful interviews designed to assess motivation to adopt, marital stability, love of children etc, these qualities are not defined nor is any special attention given to the assessment of personality disorder or psychiatric illness, although there is now a large body of data on the factors in family life and the qualities in parents which give rise to psychiatric disorder in childhood or later life (Rutter 1966, Wolff & Acton 1968).

Triseliotis (1970) has discussed the belief among many adoption caseworkers that a reasonable matching up of adoptive parents and child is more likely to ensure the success of the adoption placement. This practice of 'matching' parents and child appears to include the search for similarities in physical appearance, intellectual capacity, race, religion and cultural background, and even the imponderables of personality and temperament. This practice, now fortunately receding, was based on unproven assumptions about child development and social class prejudice, rather than fact. It is not possible, nor is it desirable, to match child and adoptive parents for either intellectual or other qualities of personality except in the crudest fashion. There are dangers in raising adoptive parents' expectations which are then not fulfilled and even if matching were attempted it would be better to match on the basis of the child's natural parents rather than on any prediction from an examination in infancy (Rutter 1970). Carter (1968) points out that the mechanisms of inheritance are such that any couple can naturally have a variety of children although it would be unlikely for an extreme difference of hair or eye colour to occur within a natural family.

At present 'matching' seems much less of an issue in adoption practice than it was and the emphasis has shifted from stressing similarities to helping adopters accept potential inherent differences (Triseliotis 1970), Kirk (1964) has argued that acknowledgement by adopters of their minority status and of the differences between their families and natural families is necessary for good social adjustment, communication and emotional stability within adoptive families, and his views have influenced modern adoption practice to some extent.

PREVALENCE, AETIOLOGY AND PSYCHOPATHOLOGY OF PSYCHIATRIC DISORDERS IN ADOPTED CHILDREN

Any psychiatric unit dealing with children and adolescents whether in a hospital or a community service is bound to see families with an adopted child. Questions often arise whether adopted children are overrepresented in clinical populations, whether there are social and psychological factors which differentiate adopted children and their families from natural families, and whether psychiatric disorder in adopted children is different in terms of sex distribution, severity, pattern of symptoms and diagnostic category at different ages.

It is often stated that the parents of adopted children seek psychiatric help for their children more often than nonadopted children and that adopted children are more often referred to psychiatric clinics on the assumption that being an adopted child increases the likelihood of disorder. The impression that this was so originally came from clinical case studies often of very small numbers of cases, usually emphasising an aspect of the child's individual psychopathology and deviant family relationships (Eiduson & Livermore 1953; Glatzer 1955). Two reports of clinical populations in the USA, one from the Menninger Clinic, the other from a private psychiatric clinic in Southern California, gave rise to much discussion and concern among adoption workers. The first (Toussieng 1962) reported an incidence of 10·9 per cent of adopted children attending a clinic over a 5-year period compared with nonadopted attenders. The second reported a 100-fold increase of adopted children in private psychiatric practice (13 per cent) compared with the supposed number of adopted children in the general population (Schechter 1960). This last figure was a wrong interpretation of a published adoption rate (Kirk *et al* 1966) and the author amended it later (Schechter *et al* 1964) but still held to the opinion based on his enquiries that there was a higher percentage of adopted children with emotional disturbance in child guidance clinics, state hospitals, private residential treatment centres and private psychiatric practice. The most recent study of requests for psychiatric treatment for adopted children at the Children's Service of UCLA Department of Psychiatry (Work & Anderson 1971) showed a frequency of between 2·1 per cent and 3·1 per cent but there was no comparison with the base-rate for adoption in the state population nor are social and economic factors taken into account and there is no control group.

In all these reports little or no account was taken of referral bias, income levels and social class distribution of the families at the different clinics. Adoptive families are generally among the higher socioeconomic groups in the population which in the USA at least (Kirk *et al* 1966) tend to make more use of private counselling and psychiatric services, thus leading to overrepresentation in these particular clinical case loads which cannot be generalised to the population as a whole (Lawton & Gross 1964). It is also possible that the numbers of adopted children in the population may differ in different States in the USA so that general population figures might not hold for a particular State. A careful study from New York State bore out these criticisms (Goodman *et al* 1963). Here, the annual base-rate for adopted children in a community served by a mental health centre was calculated and found to be relatively higher than for the country as a whole. When the adopted children were divided into those adopted by a relative (intrafamilial), and those adopted extrafamilially, further differences were found. The conclusions were that extrafamilially adopted children were brought to a clinic 1·4 times as frequently as would be expected from their existence in the community and the rate at which they were brought to a low income community clinic (2·4 per cent) was much lower than rates reported at higher income clinics or in private psychiatric practice. A further study from St. Louis, USA (Simon & Senturia 1966), found a higher incidence (2·6 per cent) of extrafamilial adoptions in a clinical sample attending a hospital psychiatric department. This is about 2·5 times greater than the figure for extrafamilial adoptions in the St. Louis area as a whole (1 per cent). The clinical sample included adults as well as children and adolescents and when the total was broken down further, higher rates of attendance were found for children and adolescents than for adult patients. Why this was so is difficult to understand, indeed relatively little is as yet known of the long-term mental health aspects of adoption. A study from Norway of 250 persons who had grown up in adoptive homes and who were examined with regard to the incidence of crime and mental disorder (Bratfos *et al* 1968) showed that the incidence of these conditions did not differ in any special way from the rest of the population. One possible explanation of the differing incidence in childhood and adult life is that family tensions lead to psychiatric referral in childhood and adolescence and these are reduced when the person moves away from home. It seems therefore that studies from the USA using the methods described show that there are more psychiatrically disturbed adopted children and adolescents attending various psychiatric services in certain areas than would be expected from their actual numbers in the population.

In the UK no such excess was found in a survey of adopted children seen at Child Guidance Clinics reported by the NAMH in 1954 (Addis *et al* 1954), but Pringle (1961) reported a much higher incidence of (8·9 per cent) adopted children in a population of 2593 maladjusted children in special schools than in the general population (2 per cent). One possible explanation is that a recommendation for special school placement might be influenced by an adoptive family situation as was the case with broken homes and approved school placement, thus leading to an excess of children from this background. However, Humphrey and Ounsted (1963–64) reported a hospital sample of 45 adopted children seen in Oxford referred with psychiatric disorder over a 4-year period. This represented a frequency of 2·9 per cent. They then calculated the proportion of adopted children at large by comparing the average number of live births with the average number of adoption orders over the last decade, arriving at a national figure of adoption of 2 per cent of live births or 1·3 per cent excluding children adopted by their own mothers. They found that adopted children had been referred with more than twice the expected frequency, a significant difference.

The potential sampling bias in clinical populations and other factors mentioned earlier mean that the only accurate way of investigating the differential prevalence and incidence of disturbance in adopted children is the epidemiological method. In this country the National Child Development Study (1958) Cohort, a longitudinal follow-up study of 17 000 births in 1958 has provided the chance of studying a random sample. By the time the children were 7 years old some 182 of 640 surviving illegitimate children had been adopted by people other than their own mothers. Comparisons can therefore be made on a number of factors between illegitimate, adopted and legitimate children. A detailed account of the adopted group has been published (Seglow *et al* 1972). The information about 'maladjustment' is derived from the Bristol Social Adjustment Guides (Stott 1966) which are completed by a teacher rather than by clinical assessments and the use of combined parent and teacher questionnaires as has been done in other large-scale surveys (Rutter *et al* 1970). Overall, there was no difference between the adopted and all the other children in the whole cohort, but the illegitimate children who remained with their own mothers showed a markedly higher degree of 'maladjusted' behaviour as assessed by scores on the guides. A higher proportion (23 per cent) of adopted boys are maladjusted than boys in the cohort as a whole (17 per cent) and more adopted boys than girls were also scored as maladjusted. This is partly accounted for by the fact that there was a higher proportion of boys among the adopted than in the cohort as a whole. On the findings of these and educational attainment tests the adopted resembled the legitimate rather than the illegitimate. Both the illegitimate and the adopted showed patterns of syndromes of scores indicating hostility to adults and children. Anxiety for acceptance by other children was a specific characteristic of the group of adopted children. On other tests adopted children did better at reading and had parents who were more interested in their school performance. Social class factors do play a part in this finding for adopted children grew up more often in smaller middle class families and were slightly worse in reading when compared with nonadopted children from similar social backgrounds. The figures for attendance at Child Guidance Clinics showed that within the whole cohort the percentage attendance was highest amongst the illegitimate (3 per cent) followed by adopted (2 per cent) and then legitimate (1 per cent). However, the number of cases in each group was far too small for any firm conclusions to be drawn. Above all, no data are given about differences between the illegitimate children relinquished for adoption and those who were kept by their mothers. There is some evidence (Vincent 1961; Yelloly 1965) that mothers who keep their illegitimate children are more emotionally unstable and immature and it is possible that these factors will militate against favourable development in infancy and childhood in children who have already been exposed to hazards during pregnancy and delivery. It may be that the more intelligent and stable mothers chose adoption so that these children had the advantage of a better genetic endowment from the outset.

In a study from Sweden, 168 adopted children (93 boys and 75 girls) representing all children born within 2 years and placed by one agency were compared with a control group of classmates of the same sex (Bohman 1970). Their ages ranged from 10 to 11 years at follow-up and information was gathered from the children's teachers and by interviewing the adoptive parents. The adopted boys showed a significantly higher amount of maladjustment in school, in the form of multiple symptoms of emotional disturbance compared with controls of the same sex and with the adopted girls in the sample. There was no significant difference between adopted girls and their controls. The symptoms took the form of psychomotor unrest, poor concentration and conflicts with peers. There were only two cases of severe psychiatric disorder with resultant social maladjustment. However, antisocial behaviour was relatively seldom reported by adoptive parents.

The earlier reports from the USA are clinical studies of small numbers of patients without control groups giving the impression that adopted children attending clinics were more often severely disturbed boys, presenting most often with aggressive and antisocial behaviour in older children and adolescents, i.e. over the age of 11 years, whereas those seen in private practice were diagnosed more often as having psychoneurotic disorders (Eiduson & Livermore 1953; Schechter 1960; Toussieng 1962; Schechter *et al* 1964). In this country Jackson (1968) reported on 40 'unsuccessful adoptions' meaning that the children were referred to two London Child Guidance Clinics on account of seriously disturbed interpersonal relationships and other symptoms of emotional disturbance. She concluded that neither early age of the child at adoption, nor the time and manner of telling the child can ensure success in adoption. Nearly half the sample were below 10 years at referral, there was an equal number of boys and girls and an excess of violent aggressive behaviour and sexual acting-out was found. Factors influencing referral and selection of cases for inclusion in the study as well as the absence of a control group make these findings difficult to evaluate.

The much smaller number of controlled studies differ in their diagnostic classification and methods of selection and matching but do provide a sounder basis for generalisation. Humphrey and Ounsted (1963; 1964) in a controlled study of 80 adopted children referred in the Oxford region found that the rate of psychiatric referral increased with the approach and onset of puberty and that adopted children did not differ from others in their symptoms except where they were placed after the age of 6 months when their symptoms were more often those of stealing and destructiveness. There were twice as many boys as girls in the latter group, which included a number of children adopted after 2 or more years of adverse circumstances of upbringing and care. Two studies from the USA found that adopted children were not more seriously disturbed than other attenders at psychiatric clinics, but were referred significantly more often with antisocial behaviour or personality disorders (Offord *et al* 1969; Menlove 1965). However, one study showed the later the age of adoption the greater the frequency and severity of antisocial behaviour (Offord *et al* 1969) whereas the other found that aggressive symptomatology was not more characteristic of those adopted after 6 months compared with those adopted before this age (Menlove 1965).

The evidence so far suggests that adopted children are overrepresented in clinical populations and that the diagnosis of *antisocial* or *conduct disorder* is often made. The reasons for this are as complex and multifactorial, including factors present in the biological parents (Cunningham *et al* 1975), as would be expected in any case of *conduct disorder* but recent research has picked out certain factors which are said to be particularly related to adopted children and their families. These can be discussed under several broad headings.

Biological and social factors related to pregnancy

It has been asserted that adopted children are more vulnerable for several reasons. As the majority are illegitimate (89 per cent—Seglow *et al* 1972) they are potentially at risk in terms of inadequate antenatal care (Crellin *et al* 1971) subsequent birth hazards such as low birth-weight, and adopted boys show a higher incidence of clumsiness, poor physical coordination and fidgety restless behaviour in later life (Seglow *et al* 1972). It has also been suggested that their often single mothers are exposed to much personal and social stress during pregnancy, moreover the time of decision about giving up a child is one of tension and uncertainty, so that both these sets of factors may impinge on the child to its detriment (Crellin *et al* 1971).

Experience prior to placement

Many experienced adoption workers have emphasised the importance of the breaks in the continuity of care of the infant prior to placement as a potential source of stress and have argued for placement as early as possible (certainly before 6 months) and for limiting the number of moves to the absolute minimum. Studies show that immediate disturbance is reduced in infants placed for adoption who were moved prior to the time of developing focussed attachments, round about 5 to 6 months and that after this time disturbance is greater (Yarrow 1965). The long-term effects of separation are probably not as severe and long-lasting as had been formerly believed (Rutter 1972), and there is still a need to disentangle the factors which produce immediate and temporary effects from those which are long-lasting. Yarrow *et al* (1971) studied 53 children, 29 girls and 24 boys of whom were placed in fairly high socioeconomic level adoptive homes by 6 months of age. The environment in infancy was assessed by direct observation and interviews with foster and adoptive mothers and at 10 years the adopted children were tested and interviewed. The children varied greatly in their development; long-term effects of infantile traumata could not be discounted, but also constitutional factors played a part and there were sex differences in children's responses to various experiences. Eldred *et al* (1976) found age of placement unrelated to psychopathology in adulthood.

Social status, personality, attitudes, behaviour and expectations of adoptive parents

Little is known about the relationship between the personality, attitudes and expectations of adoptive parents and psychiatric disorder in their adopted children. Adoptive families vary greatly in parental personality and family structure and there is not a 'standard' adoptive family. However, although the adoptive family resembles an ordinary family, in many respects it is set apart in certain ways, partly because of the attitude in our society to illegitimacy and blood ties, and partly because adoptive parents are a minority or deviant group, i.e. they have to come to terms with their infertility (Humphrey 1969), miss the experience of pregnancy, childbirth and usually the

first few months with the infant. All these factors are assumed to favour difficulties in upbringing. Kirk (1964) holds that adopters are usually unprepared
for their roles as parents and need much more help in this than is usually
given them. He feels it is important for them to acknowledge rather than
deny their differences from natural parents, to build an identity on this in
company with other adoptive parents and to maintain communication over
this and other issues with their children.

The controlled study from Sweden by Bohman (1970) of 168 adopted
children placed by the Stockholm Adoption Agency and followed up at
the age of 10–11 years, showed no correlation between adoptive parents' age,
socioeconomic circumstances and own up-bringing and the behavioural
and educational adjustment of the children. This supports the findings of
other studies that there is little connection between the adjustment of adoptive children and the external characteristics of the adopters such as age, social
class, income and educational standard (Seglow *et al* 1972). It has been said
that the development and quality of adjustment of adopted children is influenced by the emotional climate of the adoptive home and the parental relationship, but systematic data are lacking. The personal qualities of the
adopters are obviously important. These include not only attitudes to the
particular child itself but to having to adopt because of infertility, and the
implications of illegitimacy for the future development of a child. This particularly applies to adopted girls, with the notion of the 'bad seed' sometimes
becoming a self-fulfilling prophecy. Attitudes of the adopters' own parents
and own siblings, the wider family and friends may play a much larger part
than is realised, particularly where 'hard to place' or 'coloured' babies are
concerned. Implicit criticism by grandparents and explicit denial of the support to a family with small children which is usually given to a couple with
a natural child, can make matters very difficult for some adoptive parents.
Many if not all of these factors singly or in combination have been invoked
as potential 'causes' of psychiatric disorder in adopted children.

There is still no agreement as to the method and timing of telling a child
about their adoption (Schwartz 1975). Some have maintained that early and
repeated telling is incompatible with psychoanalytic knowledge of young
childrens' needs and stages of development, others that the young child
should be told by his parents (Schechter 1967). While many of these issues
are specific to adoption and families with adopted children, there are others
which are shared with natural families. Much more research is needed before
it will be possible to say what combination of factors is significantly related
to emotional disturbance (Eldred *et al* 1976).

There is much disagreement in the literature on adoption as to whether
there is a specific psychopathology in the psychiatric disorders of adopted

children. Those who see the fact of adoption as of primary importance emphasise the effect on the child of experiences such as the substitution at or around
the time of birth of the natural by a surrogate mother which they maintain
leads to specific difficulties in establishing healthy object relations different
to those encountered by the ordinary infant in his own family (Reeves 1971).
Others stress the importance of late discovery of the fact of adoption by the
child and the confusing effect on identity formation, identifications and self-
image of having two sets of parents, the unknown natural parents who are
figures of fantasy and the adoptive parents as representatives of reality. This
leads to splitting into 'good' and 'bad' parents, opportunities for playing off,
manipulation, and hurtful comment from both parents and child and the
mutual projection of negative feelings (Schechter 1960).

Other authorities emphasise the damage of repeated early telling of how
the child was 'chosen' implying that the natural parents cruelly rejected or
deserted the child and that this leads to feelings of mistrust, of being unloved
and unwanted, which may persist into adult life (Peller 1961), even though
most adoption experts consider it important for the adoptive child to learn
about this from an early age, certainly before starting school (Schechter 1967).
They maintain that the risks of attempted secrecy and denial of information
to the child are much greater because the shock of later 'finding out' from
others can have serious effects on the child and adolescent leading to a critical
and resentful attitude because of their adoptive parents' lack of trust in them.
This may so shake their faith that they build up an idealised picture of their
natural parents and even try to find them (Schechter 1960).

A recent study from Scotland where an adopted person can obtain information about his biological parents from official records (Triseliotis 1973)
showed how many adolescents felt deprived and confused when they were
earlier denied the knowledge which they later sought out themselves and were
resentful and critical of parents who were reluctant to tell. The great majority
in the sample of 70 adoptees learned of their adoptive status well after the
age usually recommended by adoption experts and with the exception of two
were adamant that it was their right to know and their parents' duty to tell.
The author of the study is careful to point out that his findings refer only
to those adoptees who felt the need to enquire into their origins. Distress,
unhappiness and dissatisfaction were characteristic of many adoptees studied
but not of adopted people in general. A more recent study (Eldred *et al* 1976)
suggests that negative reactions to disclosure can be reduced if children are
told early in life.

On the other hand, Chess (1969), an experienced child psychiatrist, takes
the line that the problems that occur between parents and adopted children
are the same that would occur given the same personalities and circumstances

if the children were not adopted. She does agree that the adoption situation may intensify problems of overprotection and overindulgence but holds no brief for the notion that the biological tie has any magical preventive effect on psychiatric disorder. She attributes many of the problems to the fact that adults tend to assume that what bothers them also bothers their children, so that adopting parents project their own uncertainties on to the children. She would not regard adoption in itself a potential source of difficulty, but agrees it can be of great significance to some parents and children as a secondary and complicating factor but almost never as the nucleus of the difficulty. It may become a source of stress in adolescence, particularly when doubts about identity and security boil up into intense conflicts with parents and compensatory fantasy about natural parents.

SUMMARY

The opinion and advice of psychiatrists can be of help in decisions about the suitability of couples to adopt particularly where there is a history of psychiatric illness in one or both partners. Findings from psychiatric research are clarifying the associations between parental psychiatric disorder and emotional disturbance in children so that predictions about possible future disturbance can be made in some instances. Child psychiatrists can be of use in the assessment of deviant emotional development in infants and toddlers considered for adoption. As 'hard-to-place' including physically handicapped children are increasingly likely to be offered for adoption, child psychiatrists could be of help in assessing and predicting the possibility of psychiatric disorder in this 'at risk' group.

Adopted children appear to be overrepresented in clinical populations attending child psychiatric clinics with more boys than girls presenting with conduct disorders. The true incidence of psychiatric disorder among adopted children and adolescents within the general population still requires clarification by epidemiological studies. Opinions vary about the reasons for psychiatric disorder, some emphasising the primary fact of adoption, and its effects on parental attitudes, expectations and child-rearing practices. Others stress its implications for the adopted child and adolescent's perception of his natural and adoptive parents as well as the difficulties in terms of identity and self-image. Some regard the adopted child as potentially more vulnerable because of biological and social factors whereas others do not consider adoption in itself as a potential source of difficulty regarding psychiatric disorder as having the same origins as in biological or natural families.

A quotation from address by White Franklin (1954) provides an apposite conclusion. 'Adoption is a technical method which helps to solve such serious problems as illegitimacy, childlessness, absolute and relative, and the nurture of the unwanted or unattached child. It is also a human enterprise where sin or wickedness or foolishness are met by pity and love, where biology jostles passion and the intruder—reason—has little place and less power.' This was said over 20 years ago. One hopes with more facts and better research that reason will increasingly have more place and power.

REFERENCES

ADDIS R.S., SALZBERGER F. & RABL E. (1954) *A Survey Based on Adoption Case Records.* London: National Association for Mental Health

ADOPTION ACT (1958) London: HMSO

ANDERSON E.W., KENNA G.C. & HAMILTON M.W. (1960) A study of extramarital conception in adolescence. *Psychiat. Neurol.* **139**, 313–362

ANTHONY E.J. (1969) A clinical evaluation of children with psychotic parents. *Amer. J. Psychiat.* **126**, 177–184

BOHMAN M. (1970) *Adopted Children and their Families.* Stockholm: Proprius

BRATFOS O., EITINGER L. & TAU T. (1968) Mental illness and crime in adopted children and adoptive parents. *Acta Psychiat. Scand.* **44**, 376–384

CARTER C. (1968) Genetic considerations in adoption. *In Genetic and Psychological Aspects of Adoption.* The Association of British Adoption Agencies. Aberdeen: The University Press

CHESS S. (1969) *An Introduction to Child Psychiatry*, 2nd edn. New York: Grune & Stratton

CRELLIN E., PRINGLE M.L. KELLMER & WEST P. (1971) *Born Illegitimate, Social and Educational Implications.* Windsor: NFER

CUNNINGHAM L., CADORET R.J., LOFTUS R. & EDWARDS J. (1975) Studies of adoptees from psychiatrically disturbed biological parents: psychiatric conditions in childhood and adolescence. *Brit. J. Psychiat.* **126**, 534–549

DOMINIAN J. (1968) *Marital Breakdown.* Harmondsworth: Penguin

EIDUSON B.T. & LIVERMORE J.B. (1953) Complications in therapy with adopted children. *Amer. J. Orthopsychiat.* **23**, 795–802

ELDRED C., ROSENTHAL D., WENDER P., KETY S., SCHULSINGER F., WELNER J. & JACOBSEN B. (1976) Some aspects of adoption in selected samples of adult adoptees. *Amer. J. Orthopsychiat.* **46**, 279–290

FORFAR J. (1969a) The role of the paediatrician in adoption medical practice. *Lancet* **i**, 1201–1203

FORFAR J. (1969b) Worth and need in medico-social assessment: the adoption situation. *Child Adoption* **57**, 25–33

GABRIELSON I.W., KLERMAN L.V., CURRIE J.B., TYLER N.C. & JEKEL J.F. (1970) Suicide attempts in a population pregnant as teenagers. *Amer. J. Publ. Health* **60**, 2289–2301

GATH A. (1974) Sibling reactions to mental handicap: a comparison of the brothers and sisters of mongol children. *J. Child Psychol. Psychiat.* **15**, 187–198

GLATZER H.T. (1955) Adoption and delinquency. *Nerv. Child* **11**, 52–56

GOODMAN J.D., SILBERSTEIN R.M. & MANDELL W. (1963) Adopted children brought to child psychiatric clinic. *Arch. Gen. Psychiat.* **9**, 451–456

GORDON H. (1970) Problems of teenage pregnancy. *In* Bodley Scott R. & Milnes Walker R. (eds.) *The Medical Annual.* Bristol: John Wright

GORDON H. (1973) Abortion as a method of population regulation: the problems. *Brit. J. Hosp. Med.* **9,** 303–306

GOUGH D. (1966) The very young mother. *In Pregnancy in Adolescence.* London: National Council for the Unmarried Mother and her Child

GREY E. & BLUNDEN R.M. (1971) *A Survey of Adoption in Great Britain.* Home Office Research Studies. London: HMSO

HATHAWAY S.R. & McKINLEY J.C. (1951) *The Minnesota multiphasic Personality Inventory* (Revised) New York: The Psychological Corporation

HAUSKNECHT R.O. (1972) The termination of pregnancy in adolescent women. *In* Altched A. (ed.) *The Paediatric Clinics of North America* **19.** Philadelphia: W.B. Saunders

HERSOV L.A. (1973) The psychiatrist and modern adoption practice. *Child Adoption* **71,** 17–31

HUMPHREY M.E. & OUNSTED C. (1963) Adoptive families referred for psychiatric advice. I: The children. *Brit. J. Psychiat.* **109,** 599–608

HUMPHREY M.E. & OUNSTED C. (1964) Adoptive families referred for psychiatric advice. II: The parents. *Brit. J. Psychiat.* **110,** 549–555

HUMPHREY M. (1969) *The Hostage Seekers.* The National Bureau for Co-operation in Child Care. London: Longman

ILLINGWORTH R. (1968) Assessment for adoption. *In Genetic and Psychological Aspects of Adoption.* The Association of British Adoption Agencies. Aberdeen: The University Press

JACKSON L. (1968) Unsuccessful adoptions: a study of 40 cases who attended a child guidance clinic. *Brit. J. Med. Psychol.* **41,** 389–398

JAFFE B. & FANSHEL D. (1970) *How They Fared in Adoption: a Follow-up Study.* New York: Columbia University Press

KADUSHIN A. (1970) *Adopting Older Children.* New York: Columbia University Press

KAYE D.K.W. & SCHAPIRA K. (1967) Psychiatric sequelae of termination of pregnancy. *Brit. Med. J.* **1,** 299, 252–253

KIRK H.D. (1964) *Shared Fate: a Theory of Adoption and Mental Health.* London: Collier–Macmillan

KIRK H.D., JONASSON K. & FISH A.D. (1966) Are adopted children especially vulnerable to stress? *Arch. Gen. Psychiat.* **14,** 291–298

KNIGHT I. (1970) Placing the handicapped child. *Child Adoption* **62,** 27–35

KNIGHT I. (1971) Placement of children into families with a seriously handicapped child. *Child Adoption* **63,** 56–59

KORNITZER M. (1968) *Adoption and Family Life.* London: Putnam

LA BARRE M. (1969) Motherhood. *In The Double Jeopardy The Triple Crisis: Illegitimacy Today.* New York: The National Council on Illegitimacy

LAWTON J.J. & GROSS S.Z. (1964) Review of psychiatric literature on adopted children. *Arch. Gen. Psychiat.* **11,** 635–644

LEAHY A.M. (1933) Some characteristics of adoptive parents. *Amer. J. Sociol.* **30,** 548–563

LEWIS H. (1960) Medical responsibility in adoption. *Brit. Med. J.* **1,** 1197–1200

LEWIS H. (1965) The psychiatric aspects of adoption. *In* Howells J.G. (ed.) *Modern Perspectives in Child Psychiatry.* Edinburgh: Oliver & Boyd

Lewis M. (1971) *Clinical Aspects of Child Development.* Philadelphia: Lea & Febiger

Lewis Y.B. & Nash P.J. (1967) Pregnancy in patients under 16 years. *Brit. Med. J.* ii, 733–736

Maas H.S. (1960) The successful adoptive parent applicant. *Social Work* 5, 14–20

Maclay D.T. (1969) The children's psychiatrist in court cases concerning adoption. *Child Adoption* 57, 35–38

Mapstone E. (1969) Children in care. *Concern* 3, 23–28

Massarik F. & Franklin D.S. (1967) *Adoption of Children with Medical Conditions.* Research Department Report No. 1. Los Angeles: Children's Home Society of California

Menlove F.L. (1965) Aggressive symptoms in emotionally disturbed adopted children. *Child Develop.* 36, 519–532

Obeng B.B. (1969) Pregnancy in girls under 16 years. *J. Obstet. Gynaec. Br. Commonwealth.* 76, 640–644

Office of Population Censuses and Surveys Monitor (1976) FM3 76/3. London: HMSO

Offord D.R., Aponte J.F. & Cross L.A. (1969) Presenting symptomatology of adopted children. *Arch. Gen. Psychiat.* 20, 110–116

Osofsky H.J. & Osofsky J.D. (1970) Adolescents as mothers. *Amer. J. Orthopsychiat.* 40, 825–834

Patt S.L., Rappoport R.G. & Barglow P. (1969) Follow-up of therapeutic abortion. *Arch. Gen. Psychiat.* 20, 408–414

Pauker J.D. (1969) Girls pregnant out of wedlock. *In The Double Jeopardy The Triple Crisis: Illegitimacy Today.* New York: National Council on Illegitimacy

Peller L.E. (1961) About 'telling the child' about his adoption. *Bull. Philadelph. Assoc. Psychoanal.* 11, 145–154

Perez-Reyes M.E. & Falk R. (1973) Follow-up after therapeutic abortion in early adolescence. *Arch. Gen. Psychiat.* 28, 120–125

Pringle M.L. Kellmer (1961) The incidence of some supposedly adverse family conditions and of left-handedness in schools for maladjusted children. *Brit. J. Educ. Psychol.* 31, 183–193

Raynor, L. (1970) *Adoption of Non-White Children.* London: Allen & Unwin

Reeves A.C. (1971) Children with surrogate parents: cases seen in analytic therapy and an aetiological hypothesis. *Brit. J. Med. Psychol.* 44, 155–171

Report of the Departmental Committee on the Adoption of Children (1972) Cmnd. 5107. London: HMSO

Report of the Committee on the Working of the Abortion Act (1974) Cmnd. 5579. London: HMSO

Rowe J. & Lambert L. (1973) *Children Who Wait.* London: Association of British Adoption Agencies

Rutter M. (1966) *Children of Sick Parents.* Institute of Psychiatry, Maudsley Monograph No. 16. London: Oxford University Press

Rutter M. (1970) Psychological development: predictions from infancy. *J. Child Psychol. Psychiat.* 11, 49–62

Rutter M. (1972) *Maternal Deprivation Reassessed.* Harmondsworth: Penguin

Rutter M., Tizard J. & Whitmore K. (eds.) (1970) *Education, Health and Behaviour.* London: Longman

Schechter M.D. (1960) Observations of adopted children. *Arch. Gen. Psychiat.* 3, 21–32

SCHECHTER M.D., CARLSON P.V., SIMMONS J.Q. & WORK H.H. (1964) Emotional problems in the adoptee. *Arch. Gen. Psychiat.* **10**, 109–118

SCHECHTER M.D. (1967) Psychoanalytic theory as it relates to adoption. *J. Amer. Psychoanal. Assoc.* **15**, 695–708

SCHWARTZ E.M. (1975) Problems after adoption: some guidelines for paediatric involvement. *J. Pediatr.* **87**, 991–994

SEGLOW J., PRINGLE M.L. KELLMER & WEDGE P. (1972) *Growing up Adopted.* Windsor. NFER

SHIELDS J. (1975) Schizophrenia, genetics and adoption. *Child Adoption* **2**, 19–24

SIMON M.M. & SENTURIA A.G. (1966) Adoption and psychiatric illness. *Amer. J. Psychiat.* **122**, 858–867

SLOANE R.B. (1969) The unwanted pregnancy. *New Engl. J. Med.* **280**, 1206–1213

STOTT D.H. (1966) *The Social Adjustment of Children.* Manual to Bristol Social Adjustment Guides, 3rd edn. London: University of London Press

TIZARD B. & REES J. (1975) The effect of early institutional rearing on the behaviour problems and affectional relationships of four-year-old children. *J. Child Psychol. Psychiat.* **16**, 61–73

TOUSSIENG P.W. (1962) Thoughts regarding the aetiology of psychological difficulties in adopted children. *Child Welfare* **41**, 59–65

TREDGOLD R.F. (1964) Psychiatric indications for termination of pregnancy. *Lancet* **ii**, 1251–1254

TRISELIOTIS J. (1970) *Evaluation of Adoption Policy and Practice.* Edinburgh: University of Edinburgh

TRISELIOTIS J. (1973) *In Search of Origins: the Experiences of Adopted People.* London: Routledge & Kegan Paul

UNPLANNED PREGNANCY (1972) *Report of the Working Party of the Royal College of Obstetricians and Gynaecologists.* London: RCOG

UTIAN W.H. (1967) Obstetrical implications of pregnancy in primigravidae aged 16 years or less. *Brit. Med. J.* **ii**, 734–736

VINCENT C.E. (1961) *Unmarried Mothers.* New York: Free Press of Glencoe

WHITE FRANKLIN A. (1954) Discussion on adoption. *Proc. Roy. Soc. Med.* **47**, 1045–49

WOLFF S. & ACTON W.P. (1968) Characteristics of parents of disturbed children. *Brit. J. Psychiat.* **114**, 593–601

WOLKIND S. & RUTTER M. (1973) Children who have been 'in care': an epidemiological study. *J. Child Psychol. Psychiat.* **14**, 97–105

WOLKIND S. (1974) The components of 'affectionless psychopathy' in institutionalised children. *J. Child Psychol. Psychiat.* **15**, 215–220

WORK H.H. & ANDERSON H. (1971) Studies in adoption. Requests for psychiatric treatment. *Amer. J. Psychiat.* **127**, 948–950

YARROW L.J. (1965) Theoretical implications of adoption research. *In Perspectives in Adoption Research.* New York: Child Welfare League of America

YARROW L.J., GOODWIN M.S., MANNHEIMER H. & MILOWE I.D. (1971) Infancy experiences and cognitive and personality development at ten years. Presented at American Orthopsychiatric Association Meeting, March 22nd

YELLOLY M.A. (1965) Factors relating to an adoption decision by the mothers of illegitimate infants. *Sociol. Rev.* **13**, 5–13

YULE W. & RAYNES M. (1972) Behavioural characteristics of children in residential care in relation to indices of separation. *J. Child Psychol. Psychiat.* **13**, 249–258

CHAPTER 7

Chromosome anomalies

V. COWIE

In very precise terms, all genetically determined disorders are associated with chromosome anomalies, inasmuch as the chromosomes are the vehicles of the genetic code. The majority of chromosomal changes are too small to be seen. For example, mutant genes which are held responsible for conditions such as phenylketonuria, probably consist of infinitesimal changes in the DNA molecule at particular loci on the chromosomes. But according to general usage, only those changes in structure and number of the chromosomes which are large enough to be seen by our present microscopic techniques are designated as chromosome abnormalities.

AUTOSOMAL AND SEX CHROMOSOME ANOMALIES

In man, the normal somatic cell nucleus contains 46 chromosomes. Of these, 44 (22 pairs of matching chromosomes) are apparently common to both sexes. These are the autosomal chromosomes. The remaining pair, making up the full diploid cell complement of 46 pairs, consists of the two sex chromosomes. In the female these are matching, being two X chromosomes. In the male the pair consists of one X and a much smaller Y chromosome.

A variety of chromosome abnormalities are detectable by present microscopic techniques. The commonest of these is *aneuploidy*, or the presence of too many or too few chromosomes in the cell nucleus. The presence of an extra chromosome, so that there are three instead of the usual two chromosomes normally paired is known as *trisomy*. More rarely, trisomy may be exceeded, and multiple extra chromosomes may appear; this is seen more frequently with sex chromosomes, particularly the X chromosome, than with the autosomes. For example, a number of males have been reported with three or four X chromosomes in each cell. Although the majority of affected individuals show equal aneuploidy in all of the cells examined, occasionally *mosaicism* is seen. This is a mixture of more than one strain of cell in an individual. Thus both normal and aneuploid cells may be seen, or a mixture of two or even more kinds of aneuploidy with or without normal cells. Again mosaicism is seen more frequently involving the sex chromosomes than the autosomal chromosomes. About one-third of all sex-chromatin-positive males (males with more than one X chromosome) are XY/XXY mosaics, and about one-third, or even more of all females with additional X chromosomes are mosaics (Forssman 1970).

Translocation occurs when two chromosomes break and there is reciprocal exchange and fusion of the fragments. This may lead to an excess of chromosomal material in the cell complement, amounting to equivalent trisomy, when an abnormally large chromosome compounded of the major parts of two chromosomes are present, though the overall chromosome number is normal. *Deletion* of part of a chromosome may sometimes be seen. This anomaly is associated with the 'cri-du-chat' syndrome. A variety of rarer anomalies exist involving structural changes in the chromosomes, such as ring formation. A standard international notation for the various chromosome abnormalities has been drawn up and has been revised from time to time (Hamerton *et al* 1972).

Very generally speaking, autosomal anomalies are associated with marked anatomical changes, widespread throughout the body, and with mental subnormality which is often severe or profound. On the other hand, sex chromosome anomalies are less closely associated with physical malformations, though the burden of the defect seems to lie in the genital tract (Court Brown 1962) and often the gonad shows a characteristic pathology. Sex chromosome anomalies are often associated with some degree of mental retardation, though this association is not as close as in the case of autosomal chromosome defects. Usually the intellectual deficit is much milder than with autosomal chromosomal defects and there is evidence that many individuals with sex chromosome anomalies are within the normal range of intelligence. For example, Israelsohn and Taylor (1961) report that Ferguson-Smith has observed a number of adult chromatin-positive males who were above average intelligence. It seems that a proportion of triple-X females are of normal or even superior intelligence, though many are subnormal (Kidd, Knox & Mantle 1963). A wide distribution of IQ scores have been obtained from patients with Turner's syndrome, extending well into the normal range (Money 1963). Although the XYY chromosome complement formerly was believed to be closely associated with mental subnormality often of profound degree, later observations have shown the correlation to be much less constant than it was first thought to be, and some males of normal intelligence have been found to have the XYY constitution (Griffiths *et al* 1969). It seems that the more extra sex chromosomes there are, the greater is the intellectual impairment (Polani 1969). Thus clinical observations of males with an XXXXY sex chromosome complement have shown them all to be severely mentally subnormal (Jancar 1964).

SEX CHROMOSOME ABNORMALITIES AND MENTAL AND BEHAVIOURAL DISORDERS

Besides their association with intellectual impairment, sex chromosome anomalies may show an association with a variety of psychiatric disorders, especially deviations of personality and behaviour. This has been reviewed comprehensively by Forssman (1970).

It might be expected that of all kinds of psychiatric abnormality, sexual deviations would be the most likely to be connected with sex chromosome anomalies. The main body of evidence from studies of the nuclear sex of individuals with deviant sexual behaviour and from observations of the sexual behaviour and attitudes of those with sex chromosome abnormalities confirms the view that there is no specific connexion between anomalies of chromosomal sex and sexual behaviour. In an early study, Pare (1956) found normal male chromosome patterns in the cells of 50 homosexuals and this finding has been confirmed by many later investigations. From time to time, occasional cases have been described of males with Klinefelter's syndrome (who possessed an extra X chromosome) who showed transsexualism and/or transvestitism (Money 1963; Money & Pollitt 1964). It would seem that such sporadic and exceptional coincidences are fortuitous random occurrences. One of these rare examples, of transsexualism in an individual with a sex chromosome abnormality (a woman with XO/XX mosaicism) reported by James, Orwin and Davies (1972), is of special interest as regards child psychiatry, in that from the age of 8 this patient proclaimed her wish to be male and insisted on dressing as a boy.

Although a diminished sexual urge is a not infrequent finding in patients with chromosomal abnormalities, especially in males with Klinefelter's syndrome, this is usually associated with a general lack of drive. The personality and behavioural characteristics that have been observed in the main syndromes associated with sex chromosome disorders are summarised in the following paragraphs. Apart from studies of cognitive ability, the bulk of other kinds of psychiatric observation have been made on adults, and much work remains to be done investigating the behavioural traits of children known to have sex chromosome abnormalities.

Mechanisms remain obscure by which sex chromosome anomalies may be associated with behavioural problems in the absence of gross organic defect, as for example in the XYY syndrome. A number of pointers suggest organic brain changes as a basis for the psychiatric effects seen in association with sex chromosome abnormalities (Cowie 1972a). They include EEG changes observed in series of patients with various chromosome anomalies (Hambert and Frey 1964; Mellbin 1966; Poole 1969) and psychometric studies showing cognitive changes in patients with Turner's syndrome similar to those seen in patients with brain damage. Attention has been drawn to the possibility that neurological disorders, other than EEG abnormalities, may be connected with Klinefelter's syndrome (Nielsen 1965).

The nature of a causal connection between a sex chromosome abnormality and possible organic changes in the brain remains open to conjecture. Hambert (1964) suggested a possible connexion between Klinefelter's syndrome and epilepsy which might be extended to other sex chromosome syndromes with psychiatric concomitants. He put forward the hypothesis that the chromosome aberration may lead to abnormality in the tissue of the central nervous system to make it more vulnerable than otherwise to damage. Other possibilities are a hormonal imbalance (e.g. of testosterone in the case of Klinefelter's syndrome) which may damage the developing brain. Also, aneuploidy like other forms of embryopathy may lead to premature birth, predisposing to brain damage. Polani (1969) suggests possible cytogenetical mechanisms in sex chromosome anomalies which may lead to structural malformation or to more subtle changes of a functional rather than a structural type. He considers that we may be dealing with quantitative effects modulated by the sex chromosomal material, and quotes Pauling (1968) who propounded an orthomolecular hypothesis that 'a physiological abnormality such as decreased permeability of the blood-brain barrier for the vital substance or increased rate of metabolism of the substance in the brain may lead to a cerebral deficiency and to mental disease'.

A practical consideration for the clinician is the indications that call for an investigation of the chromosomes apart from the well-known stigmata which are usually seen in association with abnormalities of the autosomal chromosomes. Marked somatic signs are far less frequent in association with the sex chromosome anomalies. Perhaps the best general advice which should be taken judiciously, is that the possibility of a sex chromosome anomaly could be entertained in the presence of behaviour disturbances in patients with abnormal stature. It must be borne in mind, of course, that there are very many causes of abnormality in stature. Males with Klinefelter's syndrome and the XYY syndrome, however, may tend to be unusually tall. The prepubertal boy described by Cowie and Kahn (1968) was abnormally large from birth onwards, which is consistent with the manifestation of increased height from a young age. Females with Turner's syndrome are dwarfed in stature and rather doll-like in appearance. These are only general leads, and exceptions to the rule of tallness have been emphasised recently in connexion with the XYY syndrome.

Klinefelter's syndrome

The first psychiatric observations of patients with Klinefelter's syndrome were made by Züblin (1953). His six patients were below average intelligence, showed signs of emotional immaturity and childishness, had difficulty in establishing relationships with others, tended to be withdrawn and solitary, and were apathetic, querulous and lacked drive, including libido. They were sensitive about the physical manifestations of their condition, which included gynaecomastia, small testes and sparse hair. This general picture fits in with later observations of Pasqualini, Vidal and Bur (1957) who studied 31 Klinefelter subjects. These patients tended to be idle, lacked vital interests, were shy and restrained, and had few friends. A mean IQ of 81 was estimated for the group. It is of interest that they were said to have been hypokinetic and timid from an early age, which suggests that the personality traits which appear to be characteristic of Klinefelter's syndrome may become manifest in childhood. Abnormal encephalograms have been reported in adults with Klinefelter's syndrome (Forssman & Hambert 1963) but there is evidence suggesting that EEG abnormalities may be seen in childhood, this observation having been made by Dumermuth (1961) who studied 14 boys with sex-chromatin-positive Klinefelter's syndrome.

Amongst adults with Klinefelter's syndrome there is evidence of a raised incidence of a wide variety of frank psychiatric disorders. Early observations of importance in this connexion were those of Court Brown (1962), Forssman and Hambert (1963) and Nielsen (1964), and their findings have been supported by a considerable body of subsequent evidence, much of which has been the result of work carried out in Denmark and Sweden, and which has been well summarised and discussed by Forssman (1970). Less is known, however, about the frequency and type of mental disturbances amongst children with Klinefelter's syndrome (Nielsen *et al* 1970). More observations made currently are needed on the psychiatric manifestations of Klinefelter's syndrome in childhood. Most of our present knowledge about this comes from retrospective reports, in which the observations tend to be scanty, probably because the psychological features in childhood have not given rise to particular difficulties. Thus, for example, in the excellent case histories of patients with Klinefelter's syndrome from a sample taken from a psychiatric hospital and a neurological ward and five medical wards by Neilsen (1969), many of the subjects are reported to have developed normally as children; in some cases it is said that little is known about childhood development; but in others there are hints of neurotic or personality difficulties. For example: 'at about the age of 12 he began to withdraw from his previous schoolfriends, becoming very quiet, inactive and sensitive to their teasing him for being a fat boy' (Case no. 22). 'He was more sensitive than his siblings, and thinks he suffered more than they did from the poverty of his home' (Case no. 24). 'He has always been very dependent, somewhat childish and different from his siblings' (Case no. 19). 'The patient was considered different from his siblings, and he was to some extent disliked by his mother as well as his siblings' (Case no. 15). 'As a boy, he was easy-going and good-natured, but he later became rather supercilious and querulous, although he was much more childish and immature than his siblings. He always played with children younger than himself, a fact that, to some extent, may have been caused by his handicap (club foot)' (Case no. 4).

In an investigation of 50 severely hypogonadal male patients a comparison was made with regard to nervous symptoms in childhood (again from retrospective information) between 34 patients with a sex chromosome complement 47,XXY and 16 patients with the normal male karyotype, 46,XY. No statistical differences were found with respect to nervous symptoms in childhood, nocturnal enuresis or nailbiting, neither was the frequency of nocturnal enuresis or nailbiting in both patient groups significantly higher than that in an unselected sample of Danish boys. Three of the 34 patients with 47,XXY had been admitted to a child psychiatric ward; it was thought that the aetiology of their mental illness was most probably a combination of the immature personality due to their sex chromosome abnormality and the stressful, disharmonious environment in which they grew up (Nielsen *et al* 1969).

The paucity of psychiatric information about children with Klinefelter's syndrome arises no doubt because the condition is not very frequently diagnosed before adult years, many cases being ascertained through clinics dealing with infertility. As Frøland (1969) points out (with reference apparently confined to physical manifestations), if Klinefelter's syndrome is defined according to the clinical picture, the syndrome is not apparent before the age of puberty. However, systematic cytogenetic screening surveys are being carried out, especially among the newborn, which should give the opportunity for individuals with Klinefelter's syndrome and other conditions associated with chromosomal abnormalities to be followed from infancy onwards, so that full psychiatric information may be obtained.

The XYY syndrome

An early report of the XYY syndrome concerned a 44-year-old man, 6 ft tall (Hauschka *et al* 1962). His chromosomes had been investigated on account of abnormalities in his progeny from two marriages including one mongol child with autosomal trisomy G. No psychiatric abnormalities were noted in his case, and his only failing recorded was his inability to keep employers satisfied with his performance as a manual worker.

Three years later the first series of patients with the XYY sex chromosome complement were reported (Jacobs *et al* 1965). These were discovered in an investigation of males in the Scottish state hospital of Carstairs. Out of 197 patients with criminal records detained there, seven were found to have the XYY sex chromosome constitution, and later two more were discovered in the investigation of a further series of patients at the same hospital (Price *et al* 1966). All nine of these XYY patients were reported to suffer from a severe degree of personality disorder (Price & Whatmore 1967). Seven were mentally subnormal with IQs ranging between 60 and 80. Their personalities showed extreme instability and irresponsibility. In their criminal behaviour they did not appear to have considered any but the most immediate consequences of their actions, and their attitude towards the future was unrealistic and lacked constructive aims. Their emotional responses were shallow, and their greatest difficulty appeared to be in social adjustment, arising from emotional instability, combined with an incapacity to tolerate the mildest frustration. It may be of special relevance in child and adolescent psychiatry to note that compared with a control group of patients in the same hospital, the XYY group had become involved with the law on account of criminal behaviour at an earlier age. Three of the nine XYY patients had been convicted before the age of 10 years; the mean age at first conviction for the group was 13·1 years. None of the eighteen controls had been convicted before the age of 10 years, and the mean age of first conviction for the control group was 18 years. The difference between the means was statistically significant at a 5 per cent level. At least five of the nine XYY patients had been in trouble with police or education authorities before their first conviction on account of minor offences or persistent truancy.

Severe early behaviour problems that, at least in some cases, may be concomitant with the XYY sex chromosome constitution, are shown in a report by Cowie and Kahn (1968). This was the first recorded observation of a prepubertal boy within the normal intelligence range with an XYY chromosome complement. He had begun wandering from home at 2 years. At $4\frac{1}{2}$ years he was referred to a child-guidance clinic because he was unmanageable at home, destructive, mischievous and defiant. He would smash toys, rip the curtains, set fire to the room in his mother's absence and kick the cat and his infant brother. He seemed to lack fear and would climb high ladders in buildings, climb out on to window sills several storeys up and walk into the sea regardless of depth. He had sudden periods of overactivity, lasting from several hours to a few days. Between these, he would play happily and constructively and his mother described two personalities—one considerate and happy, the other disgruntled and unstable. At 5 years he started school and his behaviour became intolerable at times. He was suspended from school on several occasions because of dangerous and aggressive use of sharp instruments. However, school reports indicated periods of stability, cooperation and politeness. Eventually, his aggressive behaviour necessitated his transfer to a residential school for maladjusted boys. This boy was found to have intelligence within the normal range: at 5 years 2 months he scored IQ of 95 on the Revised Stanford–Binet test.

Shortly after this report, an account was published of a prepubertal boy (aged 10) with XY/XYY mosaicism (Kajii *et al* 1968). Although this boy had learning difficulties and a full-scale WISC IQ of 85, it was reported that he showed no unusual or antisocial behaviour, though he was hyperkinetic. More emphasis in this case report was laid on his tall stature (5 ft 2 in.) prognathism, gross malformations of the hands and abnormal dermatoglyphics. Field and Faed (1974) have reported a further case.

Although at first tall stature and personality defects leading to outbursts of violence and antisocial behaviour were thought to be cardinal and constant features of the XYY syndrome, subsequent observations have indicated that these signs are by no means always present, and there seems to be considerable variability in the phenotype. From the first reports, it seemed likely that the XYY constitution was accompanied also by intellectual impairment, but this is not so in all cases. Individuals of normal and even superior intelligence have been found to have an XYY sex chromosome constitution. Pitcher (1971) points out that the findings have been biassed towards subnormality: of 83 institutionalised subjects whose intelligence levels had been reported at the time of his review, 41 were below the normal range, 3 had IQs above 110, but no fewer than 39 were of average intelligence. If these figures were a reliable reflection of the overall distribution of intelligence among XYY males, it would seem that while their mean level is lower than that of the general population, at least 50 per cent are of average intelligence. An example of an XYY patient of superior intelligence reported by Scott and Kahn (1968) scored IQ 118 on the Matrices test, and on the WAIS test, full scale IQ 118, verbal IQ 130 and performance 101. Scott and Kahn felt that it might be premature to impute anything more to the XYY syndrome than tallness and a tendency to an, as yet ill-defined, immaturity of personality. It has been shown, however, that tallness is not a constant feature of the XYY syndrome. For example, an XYY individual of average height was reported by Kahn *et al* (1971) who was diagnosed in a cytogenetic survey of 175 factory apprentices. At the age of 16 years 8 months this boy was 5 ft $7\frac{3}{4}$ in. tall. It was felt that this case illustrated that in order to obtain a better estimate of the frequency of XYY individuals it is necessary to study a cross-section of all heights of any given population. Pitcher (1971) summarises pooled data available and notes that in populations studied where height was not a factor in selection, 19 XYY males were identified in a total population of 4558, a frequency of 0·42 per cent; whereas in the populations selected by height, 83 XYY males were identified in a total population of 2722, a frequency of 3·05 per cent. Taking, however, only the criminal populations, the figures are 17 males in 2412 (0·7 per cent) in the group with no selection by height, and 76 in 1847 (4·1 per cent) when height was a selection factor. On the basis of Pitcher's calculations these figures appeared to be statistically significant: at barely the 5 per cent level for males unselected by height, but highly so for the tall groups, especially the American ones.

The variability of the phenotype in the XYY syndrome could be clarified by prospective studies of XYY males identified in newborn surveys. This would also give the opportunity for special observation of the manifestations of the syndrome in childhood and adolescence, which is called for by existing reports of early behaviour disturbances and antisocial acts. It would also show the extent to which this chromosome anomaly is compatible with physical and psychological normality. Maclachlan (1969) asked the pertinent question: 'if the incidence of XYYs in the population is 1·5/1000 and only about 70 XYYs have been found in the United Kingdom—one expects 1500 among every million males—where are these other XYYs?' It is not unlikely that ascertainment has rested too heavily on the correlates of the syndrome that at first became apparent, and a longitudinal follow-up of XYY infants from neonatal surveys, together with larger surveys of randomly selected groups of clinically normal males than those hitherto studied, may throw light on this question.

Turner's syndrome

In females with Turner's syndrome the somatic cell complement of chromosomes is only 45, with only one X chromosome as the sole representative of the sex pair. This sex chromosome complement is known conventionally as XO. Turner's syndrome may be taken as representing the extreme end of the spectrum of ovarian dysgenesis. Bartalos and Baramki (1967) define gonadal dysgenesis as a condition characterised by the absence of germ cells from the gonads and the development of female genital ducts and external genitalia. They divide gonadal dysgenesis into three clinical entities: first, pure gonadal dysgenesis, where there is normal stature and no somatic anomalies; secondly, gonadal dysgenesis with short stature as the only somatic anomaly; and thirdly, Turner's syndrome, where short stature is accompanied by other somatic anomalies. These anomalies include webbing of the neck, a low growth of hair over forehead and nape of neck, a wide carrying-angle of the arms, a broad, flat shield-shaped chest with widely spaced nipples, absence of secondary sexual development and primary amenorrhoea. These last two features are directly related to the ovarian dysgenesis which is basic to the syndrome, and the ovary is nonfunctioning and may be represented only by a sliver of fibrous tissue (the 'ovarian streak') with a few non-functioning graafian follicles.

It is not unlikely that many of the psychological features that have come to be associated with Turner's syndrome are secondary, resulting from sensitivity due to marked shortness of stature or oddness of appearance or of physiological function. Thus it was found by Sabbath *et al* (1961) that of seven adolescent girls with ovarian dysgenesis, the degree of dwarfing of stature appeared to influence their attitudes and behaviour. Four had the appearance of midgets, being under 4 ft 7 in. tall. They had high, thin voices, and doll-like features. Their demeanour was described as ranging from tomboyishness to exaggerated prissiness. In interview they were shy, and spoke with an air of detachment and vagueness. The taller girls (4 ft 11 in. to 5 ft 5 in. tall) looked younger than their ages but looked more like early adolescents than the others in the group. They also showed a broader range of interests and spoke more freely and spontaneously. A matter of major concern common to the whole group, however, was their shortness of stature. Some were concerned about their lack of feminine shape and the fact that they did not menstruate, others denied that they felt different in these respects, or pretended not to care. Sabbath *et al* (1961) considered that the vague attitude and relative blandness in the group resulted from a powerful sweeping denial used to handle the many conflicts arising out of their congenital abnormality.

In a psychological study of 19 girls and women with Turner's syndrome by Hampson, Hampson and Money (1955) similar observations were made of lack of involvement, vagueness and passivity of personality. Although none of the subjects were considered neurotic or psychotic, their personality make-up was in general characterised by lack of mastery, absence of aggressiveness and poor initiative. In a later study by Money and his colleagues at Johns Hopkins University School of Medicine, it was again found that girls with Turner's syndrome were more passive than their controls with respect to outdoor activities and childhood fights (Ehrhardt, Greenberg & Money 1970). They were highly interested in weddings and marriage, in all forms of maternalism from doll play to baby care, and in their feminine appearance. The data agreed with former studies from the same research unit (Hampson,

Hampson & Money 1955, quoted above; and Shaffer 1963) in showing that girls and women with Turner's syndrome are unequivocally feminine in their gender role and gender identity.

Ehrhardt, Greenberg and Money (1970) make the point that psychosexual differentiation depends on more than one factor alone, and that any attempt to attribute gender identity simply to either genetic, hormonal or social–environmental factors must result in oversimplification and misconception. This open-minded approach encourages examination of all facets of the problem as they present themselves. One such facet is the possibility that various psychological features observed in Turner's syndrome may be related to some extent with organic cerebral changes. At least two different approaches in research into the condition have given reasonable expectations that this may be so. First, abnormalities in the EEG records of patients with Turner's syndrome have been reported. Mellbin (1966) reported a small selected group of four women with an XO sex chromosome constitution, all of whom were psychiatric patients, but with widely differing symptomatology. One had a long-standing psychosis; another who was epileptic had a history of an acute psychotic episode; the third suffered from a personality defect with manifestations of extreme immaturity and dependence; the fourth had anorexia nervosa. All had abnormal EEG records, though these also were varied: one showed a mild nonspecific abnormality in both temporal regions; the others showed more lateralised focal or paroxysmal abnormalities. A second type of approach which led to findings suggestive of an organic basis for psychological changes in Turner's syndrome was the work of Shaffer (1962). He carried out psychometric tests in a group of patients aged 5–30 years, using the WISC or WAIS and the Benton Visual Retention Test. He found a pattern of cognitive strengths and weaknesses consistent with those found in cases of brain damage. He made the suggestion that the cognitive defect observed was characteristic of Turner's syndrome, and that it might stem from an organic defect associated with the chromosomal anomaly. This work was pursued further by Money (1963) who investigated the IQ distribution of 16 of the patients already studied by Shaffer together with 21 other patients with Turner's syndrome. A statistically significant difference was found between verbal IQ (mean 103 $\pm$ SD 19) and performance IQ (mean 86 $\pm$ SD 15), and this discrepancy, which had also been found by Shaffer, was attributed to a specific disability in space-form appreciation.

The triple-X sex chromosome constitution

The incidence of triple-X babies in surveys of the newborn indicates that this is a rare sex chromosome anomaly. Maclean *et al* (1962) pooled the findings from newborn surveys in Edinburgh and Berne, and the results showed 4 triple-X females out of 4838 births. Polani (1969) reviewing the prevalence of triple-X women in samples of patients with mental disorders, observed that their frequency among women diagnosed as 'schizophrenic' is about five times the newborn incidence and of the same order among females in hospitals for the mentally subnormal. Indeed, the proportion (15 out of 3329) of triple-X females in the combined findings from three surveys of mentally subnormal females (Fraser *et al* 1960; Maclean *et al* 1962; Johnston *et al* 1961) is significantly higher ($p < 0.001$) than the proportion from newborn surveys, but this comparison leaves out of account the consideration as to whether there is any difference in mortality at any age between triple-X females and those with a normal sex chromosome complement (Slater & Cowie 1971). Findings in smaller surveys than those considered above however have supported an increased proportion of triple-X females among the mentally subnormal. Thus Ridler *et al* (1963) found 2 triple-X females in a survey of 735 mentally subnormal female patients, and Hamerton *et al* (1962) found 1 in a survey of 196 patients, this patient being grossly dysplastic and with severe spastic quandriplegia.

It should be noted, however, as Polani (1969) points out that, as a group, triple-X females are not phenotypically distinctive. From the point of view of intelligence alone, mental subnormality is not found in all cases, and a proportion of triple-X females are of normal or even superior intelligence. With respect to mental disorders other than mental subnormality, in a psychiatric study of 22 triple-X females receiving hospital care, a wide range of psychiatric diagnostic categories were met with, and it was considered that the diagnoses of those patients not mentally subnormal were broadly typical of the mental hospital populations from which they were drawn (Kidd, Knox & Mantle 1963). When matched against controls, the triple-X patients differed significantly in showing a greater intensity of impairment of interpersonal relationships and a greater degree of social withdrawal. Also, a higher proportion of triple-X patients than controls showed retardation of speech and action, ideas of reference and persecutory ideas. Overall, marked psychosocial inadequacy was the most pronounced psychological feature.

There are at least hints that an organic basis may underlie psychiatric phenomena in triple-X patients. In the study by Kidd *et al* (1963), of 11 mentally subnormal patients 1 had epilepsy, another epilepsy with psychosis and no fewer than 3 had the diagnosis of postencephalitic state. This poses the question in these cases whether or not the brain was particularly vulnerable constitutionally, and was hit especially hard by encephalitis with severe sequelae. Of the patients in the normal IQ range in the same study, one was diagnosed as having organic brain disease with psychosis. Asaka *et al* (1967) reported 2 triple-X women with schizophrenic symptoms. Asaka and his colleagues discuss the possibility as to whether the organic brain lesion indicated by minor organic signs in the EEG in both cases and in the air-encephalogram in one might have some aetiological significance for schizophrenic psychosis in triple-X females.

Just as with XYY males, very little is known about the psychiatric manifestations of the triple-X syndrome in females in childhood and adolescence. Long-term follow-up studies of triple-X females found in newborn surveys are called for. Also large-scale cytogenetical surveys of 'normal' subjects randomly selected at later ages would be a starting point for research in this area.

Autosomal chromosome anomalies

Apart from mental subnormality, the autosomal chromosome anomalies are without concomitants likely to be of interest in the general field of child psychiatry. Therefore they will be dealt with very briefly here. An immense body of literature has been built up over the years with respect to autosomal chromosome anomalies in man, since the first finding of Lejeune *et al* (1959) that an abnormal condition in man, mongolism, was associated with the presence of an extra chromosome in the somatic cell nucleus. Many of the autosomal chromosome anomalies reported appear to be sporadic, but some are seen time and again and are accompanied by the same signs with a frequency that merits their being classified as syndromes. Only three syndromes will be mentioned here, these being the ones most often seen.

Mongolism (Down's Syndrome; Autosomal Trisomy G)

This is the commonest of the syndromes associated with abnormalities involving an autosomal chromosome. Its incidence has been estimated as about 1 in 666 live births (Carter & MacCarthy 1951), though this may be an underestimate because it was based on diagnosis in the neonatal period, and some cases may fail to be noticed until later. Allowing for this, Zappella and Cowie (1962) calculated that the incidence among live births may be closer to 1 in about 557. One of the features that has been recognised for many years, is the relationship of mongolism to late maternal age. This fact has now taken on a new importance, in connexion with prenatal diagnosis by amniocentesis.

In about 94 per cent of mongols the chromosome abnormality is trisomy of one of the smallest autosomal chromosomes, a chromosome of the G group. For accuracy the trisomy associated with mongolism is referred to as *autosomal* trisomy G, because the Y chromosome, which is a sex chromosome and not an autosomal chromosome, also belongs to the G group, but is not implicated in mongolism. A small proportion of mongols show variations from this pattern. In about 3 per cent, the major part of the extra chromosome may be fused on to either the major part of another chromosome in the G group, or on to one of the D group (G/G or D/G translocation). In just over 2 per cent of mongols, mosaicism may be seen, in which some cells are trisomic and others have the normal complement of chromosomes. Thus the following proportions were found by Richards *et al* (1965) from the pooled data from eleven unselected surveys:

	Per cent of mongol subjects
Autosomal trisomy G	94
D/G translocation	1·5
G/G translocation	1·8
Mongol mosaicism	2·4

It has been suggested that the admixture of normal cells with cells with an abnormal chromosome complement in mosaicism may have a tendency to bring the phenotypic manifestations closer to normal. Penrose and Smith (1966) for example, put forward evidence to suggest that the intelligence levels of mosaic mongols is greater than that of nonmosaic mongols. This was based on unpublished observations by Penrose that in 17 mosaic mongols the intelligence range was roughly from the imbecile level to above normal average, with a mean at about IQ 70. The females were noticeably higher than the males and the highest score was obtained by a female with IQ 122. Penrose and Smith in 1966 remarked that little is known about the level of intelligence in relation to the degree of mosaicism that is present, and this still remains an open question. Sachs (1971) in a study of trisomy G/normal mosaicism draws attention to the conclusions of Chaudhuri and Chaudhuri (1965) that it is impossible to establish a definite relationship between the proportions of various cell lines and physical features or level of intellectual attainment, which seems to be confirmed by the contradictory statements of other authors.

The physical features of mongolism add up to make a distinctive clinical picture, and yet every individual case is a little different from the others. All the features recognised as characteristic of the condition may not be present. For example, the readily seen single palmar crease is absent in many cases, but finer examination of the dermatoglyphics will almost certainly show abnormalities. The most obvious physical features, which enable the condition to be recognised even at birth, include a rather small round head, somewhat wider than normal in the biparietal diameter; palpebral fissures which slant upwards and outwards; epicanthic folds at the inner corners of the eyes; a broad, flat nasal bridge; forward-facing nostrils; small ears; short neck with loose neck skin in the neonatal period, and occasionally with webbing later; single palmar creases (certainly not always present, and often unilateral); a short incurved little finger with sometimes a single interphalangeal crease; wide spacing between the first and second toe, with sometimes a deep furrow on the sole running back from this space. The baby is usually extremely floppy, and hypotonia and laxity of the joints is a persisting feature. The peripheral circulation is usually poor, and the skin may show a purplish mottling. In some cases a congenital heart defect may be present. Less frequently developmental defects of the alimentary tract are seen, including pyloric stenosis or rectal atresia.

A question that most parents ask as soon as they know of their child's condition, is the degree to which he is likely to be mentally handicapped. It is recognised by most authorities that a maximum IQ of 70 on standard tests is usually all that can be expected, even from those patients relatively gifted, and children with mongolism achieve on average only about one-third of the usual level of intellectual development (Kirman 1976). In an aim to estimate the upper limit of the range of intelligence in mongolism, Dunsdon *et al* (1960) selected 52 mongols from a group of 390; the selected children were all those who had attended primary schools, private schools and schools for the educationally subnormal, and a few others who had seemed relatively bright at interview. Of these, 44 came for interview and test. The highest IQ (Terman Merrill) was 68 for a youth aged 17 years 7 months. The proportion of those with IQ scores of 45 and over in the original sample of 390 was estimated to be 6–7 per cent, and of those with IQs of 55 and over, 1–2 per cent.

Brinkworth and Collins (1969) stress the importance of early contact and stimulation, and have written a practical guide for parents, teachers and others handling infants with mongolism as to how this can be best achieved. In his foreword to this manual, Penrose points out that to guard against disappointment it should be remembered that not all mongol children are equally capable, and, moreover, it has been frequently observed that mongol children develop in an encouraging way up till about the age of 5 years but thereafter proceed much more slowly. The manual has, however, been of help and encouragement to many parents, and has been a valuable instrument in overcoming the nihilistic outlook that tended to prevail in the past regarding the training of mongol children.

Edwards' syndrome (trisomy E)

Edwards *et al* (1960) first reported a baby with multiple congenital anomalies and trisomy of a chromosome of the E group. Since then, a number of such cases have been reported. As in mongolism, there is some variation of the clinical and pathological features from case to case, but an overall clinical picture of the condition includes many of the features present in the patient first described. This child, a girl, had a peculiarly shaped head, the cranium being long in its anteroposterior diameter, wide in the occipitoparietal diameter and narrow in the frontal diameter. The infant had a broad, flat nasal bridge, a small triangular mouth, micrognathia and a receding chin. The ears were pixie-like, and were low-set and malformed, being abnormally wide between the crus antehelicis and the helix margin. The neck was webbed, and the shoulders so mobile they could be made nearly to meet. The chest was shield-shaped; the nipples were widely spaced. The fingers and toes were short and stubby with misshapen flat nails. There was webbing between the second and third toes. By the time she was examined at 9 weeks it was clear that she was mentally retarded. She suffered from jaundice from the first week of life. The hepatic ducts and common bile duct were very small. Her liver became enlarged and despite a cholecystojejunostomy, the jaundice deepened and she died. Congenital heart defects were found on postmortem examination.

Additional physical defects in cases reported subsequently include clawing of the fingers with an overriding index finger, renal anomalies, limited abduction of the hips and rocker-bottom feet. Often the dorsum of the feet are puffy and swollen. Most of these infants seem to die in the first few months of life; of 43 cases reported by Taylor and Polani (1964) most died under 6 months and the mean age of death was approximately 90 days.

The severe mental subnormality associated with this syndrome is not surprising in view of the structural abnormalities found in the brain. A considerable range of cerebral defects have been found, from a mere shortening of the corpus callosum and defective falx cerebri, to complete fusion of the lateral ventricles and total absence of the corpus callosum (Norman, personal communication, 1965). Ectopic anomalies near the lateral ventricles and in some cases in the cerebellum have been reported by Terplan *et al* (1970).

Cri-du-Chat syndrome

This condition was first discovered by Lejeune *et al* (1963) who reported distinctive clinical features and a chromosome abnormality (partial deletion of a B group chromosome) in three children. The clinical features included a round, moon-shaped face, hypertelorism, palpebral fissures that slanted downwards and outwards (in contrast to the upward and outward slope of the eyes in mongolism); epicanthic folds; a well-developed prominent nasal bridge; micrognathia; low-set ears; marked generalised hypotonia. A single palmar crease may be present. Part of a B group chromosome was found to be missing. A number of cases have been reported since, and the chromosome anomaly is believed to be a partial deletion of the short arms of a No. 5 chromosome. The syndrome is associated with low birth weight, slow growth and the unusual feature of a cat-like cry in infancy.

Later, a child with a somewhat different pattern of congenital abnormalities was found with a partial deletion of another chromosome of the B group: No. 4 (Wolf *et al* 1965). The cat-like cry was absent, and the clinical features included hare-lip, coloboma, preauricular dimple, epicanthic folds, underdeveloped dermal ridges, severe mental deficiency and epileptic seizures. Other cases have been reported since and it is accepted that this is a syndrome distinct from the cri-du-chat syndrome although it involves the same kind of chromosome anomaly (a partial deletion) of a chromosome of the same group.

PRE-NATAL DIAGNOSIS OF CHROMOSOME ABNORMALITIES

The development of techniques for the prenatal diagnosis of chromosome abnormalities represents a major breakthrough in clinical genetics, with very practical implications as regards mental subnormality associated with cytogenetical defects. A number of inborn errors of metabolism, also associated with mental subnormality, can also be detected by this method of amniocentesis.

A sample of amniotic fluid for the analysis of fetal cells can be made as early as the eighth week of pregnancy by transvaginal puncture, but for various reasons this is rarely done and the optimal time for obtaining a sample is usually considered to be from the twelfth to fourteenth week after conception. By then the amniotic fluid can be tapped by transabdominal puncture. The procedure is not without an element of risk, which should always be explained to the expectant mother and her husband before it is undertaken. In experienced hands, and under the proper conditions of complete surgical asepsis, however, the risks are regarded as very slight; they include haemorrhage, infection, premature labour and possibly trauma to the fetus. In practice these are so rare that it is considered more hazardous to neglect to carry out amniocentesis when this procedure is indicated than to run the small risk of complications associated with it (Gordon 1969). Primitive undifferentiated cells, possibly from the genitourinary tract or nasopharynx of the fetus, can be extracted from the fluid and cultured for chromosome or biochemical investigations.

For obvious reasons, including the risk involved (even though small) and the limited resources as yet for this highly expert investigation, the selection of candidates calls for much discretion. The investigation can be regarded as appropriate for expectant mothers of several categories (Cowie 1972b). Amongst these are women who have previously borne a child with mongolism or another condition associated with a chromosomal defect; mothers who are known to be, or whose husbands are known to be, carriers of balanced chromosomal translocations; and mothers who have become pregnant late in the reproductive period and therefore stand at an increased risk for bearing a child with mongolism or possibly another condition associated with a chromosome abnormality.

Although the investigation would be pointless unless abortion were acceptable if the findings indicated abnormality in the fetus, it should be emphasised that abortion is by no means an inevitable sequel to prenatal diagnosis by amniocentesis. More often it is a means of reassurance that all is well. This point is well brought out by Ferguson-Smith *et al* (1971) who investigated the chromosomes in amniotic cell cultures from 29 out of 30 consecutive patients referred for genetic counselling in pregnancy. All of these women were extremely anxious regarding the outcome of the pregnancy, but in every case this was alleviated by prenatal diagnosis. Several of the patients had asked for termination initially, therefore the overall effect of amniocentesis was to save pregnancies, and the only abortion performed was in the carrier of a fatal X-linked granulomatous disease where the fetus was found to be male and, thus, at risk.

Although there is an increasing demand for amniocentesis as its existence is becoming more widely known, a number of women find it unacceptable for religious, emotional and other reasons. Therefore, in cases in which it is indicated, the suggestion that this investigation could be of help should be made with tact and feeling. Used with discretion, prenatal diagnosis by amniocentesis is one of the most valuable and practical developments of recent years, considering the damaging effects that often accompany chromosome abnormalities.

REFERENCES

ASAKA A., TSUBOI T., INOUYE E., NAGUMO Y., HAMADA S. & OKADA K. (1967) Schizophrenic psychosis in triple-X females. *Folia Psychiat. Neurol. Japon.* **21,** 271–281

BARTALOS M. & BARAMKI T.A. (1967) *Medical Cytogenetics.* Baltimore: Williams & Wilkins

BRINKWORTH R. & COLLINS J. (1969) *Improving Mongol Babies and Introducing Them to School.* N.I. Region, Belfast: National Society for Mentally Handicapped Children

CARTER C. & MACCARTHY D. (1951) Incidence of mongolism and its diagnosis in the newborn. *Brit. J. soc. Med.* **5,** 83–90

CHAUDHURI A. & CHAUDHURI K.C. (1965) Chromosome mosaicism in an Indian child with Down's syndrome. *J. med. Genet.* **2,** 131–135

COURT BROWN W.M. (1962) Sex chromosomes and the law. *Lancet* **ii,** 508–509

COWIE J. & KAHN J. (1968) XYY constitution in prepubertal child. *Brit. med. J.* **1,** 748–749

COWIE V. (1972a) Chromosomal abnormalities and mental disorders. *Postgrad. med. J.* **48,** 212–215

COWIE V. (1972b) Prenatal diagnosis of genetic disease by amniocentesis. *Ob/Gyn Digest,* October 1972, 37–42

DUMERMUTH G. (1961) EEG-Untersuchungen beim jugendlichen Klinefelter-Syndrom. *Helv. paediat. Acta* **16,** 702–710

DUNSDON M.I., CARTER C.O. & HUNTLEY R.M.C. (1960) Upper end of range of intelligence in mongolism. *Lancet* **i,** 565–568

EDWARDS J.H., HARNDEN D.G., CAMERON A.H., CROSSE V.M. & WOLFF O.H. (1960) A new trisomic syndrome. *Lancet* **i,** 787–789

EHRHARDT A.A., GREENBERG N. & MONEY J. (1970) Female gender identity and absence of fetal gonadal hormones: Turner's syndrome. *The Johns Hopkins Medical J.* **126,** 237–248

FERGUSON-SMITH M.E., FERGUSON-SMITH M.A., NEVIN N.C. & STONE M. (1971) Chromosome analysis before birth and its value in genetic counselling. *Brit. med. J.* **4,** 69–74

FIELD M. & FAED M. (1974) 47XYY chromosome constitution, physical growth and psychological disturbance—a case study. *J. Child Psychol. Psychiat* **15,** 323–327

FORSSMAN H. & HAMBERT G. (1963) Incidence of Klinefelter's syndrome among mental patients. *Lancet* **i,** 1327

FORSSMAN H. (1970) The mental implications of sex chromosome aberrations. *Brit. J. Psychiat.* **117,** 353–363

FRASER J.H., CAMPBELL J., MACGILLIVRAY R.C., BOYD E. & LENNOX B. (1960) The XXX syndrome frequency among mental defectives and fertility. *Lancet* **ii,** 626–627

FRØLAND A. (1969) *Klinefelter's syndrome. Clinical, endocrinological and cytogenetical studies.* Copenhagen: Costers Bogtrykeri

GORDON H. (1969) Amniocentesis. *Brit. J. Hosp. Med.* **2,** 2000–2005

GRIFFITHS A.W., RICHARDS B.W., ZAREMBA J., ABRAMOWICZ T. & STEWART A. (1969) An investigation of a group of XYY prisoners. *In* West D.J. (ed.) *Criminological Implications of Chromosome Abnormalities.* Cambridge: University of Cambridge/ Institute of Criminology

HAMBERT G. (1964) Positive sex chromatin in men with epilepsy. *Acta med. Scand.* **175,** 663–665

HAMBERT G. & FREY T.S. (1964) The electroencephalogram in the Klinefelter syndrome. *Acta psychiat. Scand.* **40,** 28–36

HAMERTON J.L., JACOBS P.A. & KLINGER H.P. (1972) Standardization in human cytogenetics. *Cytogenetics* **11,** 313–362

HAMERTON J.L., JAGIELLO G.M. & KIRMAN B.H. (1962) Sex-chromosome abnormalities in a population of mentally defective children. *Brit. med. J.* **1,** 220–223

HAMPSON J.L., HAMPSON J.G. & MONEY J. (1955) The syndrome of gonadal agenesis (ovarian agenesis) and male chromosomal pattern in girls and women: psychologic studies. *Bull. Johns Hopkins Hosp.* **97**, 207–226

HAUSCHKA T.S., HASSON J.E., GOLDSTEIN M.N., KOEPF G.F. & SANDBERG A.A. (1962) An XYY man with progeny indicating familial tendency to non-disjunction. *Amer. J. hum. Genet.* **14**, 22–30

ISRAELSOHN W.J. & TAYLOR A.I. (1961) Chromatin-positive presumed Klinefelter's syndrome. *Brit. med. J.* **i**, 633–635

JACOBS P.A., BRUNTON M., MELVILLE M.E., BRITTAIN R.P. & McCLEMONT W.F. (1965) Aggressive behaviour, mental subnormality and the XYY male. *Nature* (Lond.) **208**, 1351–1352

JAMES S., ORWIN A. & DAVIES D.W. (1972) Sex chromosome abnormality in a patient with transsexualism. *Brit. med. J.* **3**, 29

JANCAR J. (1964) Mentally defective males with XXXXY chromosomes. *In* Oster J. & Sletved H.V. (eds.) *Scientific Study of Mental Retardation.* International Copenhagen Congress on the Scientific Study of Mental Retardation, Copenhagen

JOHNSTON A.W., FERGUSON-SMITH M.A., HANDMAKER S.D., JONES H.W. & JONES G.S. (1961) The triple-X syndrome; clinical, pathological, and chromosomal studies in three mentally retarded cases. *Brit. med. J.* **2**, 1047–1052

KAHN J., COATES T., MAXWELL J.M., MUTTON D.E. & REED F.S. (1971) An XYY individual of average height. *Brit. med. J.* **3**, 521

KAJII T., NEW R.L. & GARDNER L.I. (1968) XY/XYY mosaicism in a prepubertal boy with tall stature, prognathism, and malformations of the hands. *Pediatrics* **41**, 984–988

KIDD C.B., KNOX R.S. & MANTLE D.J. (1963) A psychiatric investigation of triple-X chromosome females. *Brit. J. Psychiat.* **109**, 90–94

KIRMAN B.H. (1976) *The Mentally Handicapped Child.* Amsterdam: Elsevier

LEJEUNE J., GAUTIER M. & TURPIN R. (1959) Études des chromosomes somatiques de neuf enfants mongoliens. *C.R. Acad. Sci.* **248**, 1721–1722

LEJEUNE J., LAFOURCADE J., BERGER R., VIALATTE J., BOESWILLWALD M., SERINGE P. & TURPIN R. (1963) Trois cas de deletion partielle du bras court d'un chromosome 5. *C. R. Acad. Sci. (Paris)* **257**, 3098–3102

MACLACHLAN T.K. (1969) Criminological implications of sex chromosome abnormalities: a review. *In* West D.J. (ed.) *Criminological Implications of Chromosome Abnormalities.* Cambridge: University of Cambridge/Institute of Criminology

MACLEAN N., MITCHELL J.M., HARNDEN D.G., WILLIAMS J., JACOBS P.A., BUCKTON K.A., BAIKIE A.G., COURT BROWN W.M., McBRIDE J.A., STRONG J.A., CLOSE H.G. & JONES D.C. (1962) A survey of sex-chromosome abnormalities among 4514 mental defectives. *Lancet* **i**, 293–296

MELLBIN G. (1966) Neuropsychiatric disorders in sex chromatin negative women. *Brit. J. Psychiat.* **112**, 145–148

MONEY J. (1963) Cytogenetic and psychosexual incongruities with a note on space-form blindness. *Amer. J. Psychiat.* **119**, 820–827

MONEY J. & POLLITT E. (1964) Cytogenetic and psychosexual ambiguity: Klinefelter's syndrome and transvestism compared. *Arch. Gen. Psychiat.* **11**, 589–595

NIELSEN J. (1964) Klinefelter's syndrome and behaviour. *Lancet* **ii**, 587–588

NIELSEN J. (1965) Klinefelter's syndrome in a neurological ward. *Acta neurol. Scand.* **41,** 197–214

NIELSEN J. (1969) *Klinefelter's Syndrome and the XYY Syndrome.* A genetical, endocrinological and psychiatric-psychological study of 33 severely hypogonadal male patients and two patients with karyotype 47, XYY. Copenhagen: Munksgaard

NIELSEN J., SØRENSEN A., THEILGAARD A., FRØLAND A. & JOHNSEN S.G. (1969) *A Psychiatric–Psychological Study of 50 Severely Hypogonadal Male Patients including 34 with Klinefelter's Syndrome, 47, XXY.* Universitetsforlaget I Aarhus. Copenhagen: Munksgaard

NIELSEN J., BJARNASON S., FRIEDRICH U., FRØLAND A., HANSEN V. & SØRENSEN A. (1970) Klinefelten's syndrome in children. *J. Child. Psychol. Psychiat.* **11,** 109–119

NORMAN R.M. (1965) Personal communication

PARE C.M.B. (1956) Homosexuality and chromosomal sex. *J. psychosom. Res.* **1,** 247–251

PASQUALINI R.Q., VIDAL G. & BUR G.E. (1957) Psychopathology of Klinefelter's syndrome: review of 31 cases. *Lancet* **ii,** 164–167

PAULING L. (1968) Orthomolecular psychiatry: carrying the concentrations of substances normally present in the human body may control mental disease. *Science* **160,** 265–271

PENROSE L.S. & SMITH G.F. (1966) *Down's Anomaly.* London: Churchill

PITCHER D.R. (1971) The XYY syndrome. *Brit. J. hosp. Med.* **5,** 379–393

POLANI P.E. (1969) Abnormal sex chromosomes and mental disorder. *Nature* **223,** 680–686

POOLE E.W. (1969) EEG findings in male patients with sex chromosome abnormalities in a security prison. *In* West D.J. (ed.) *Criminological Implications of Chromosome Abnormalities.* Cambridge: University of Cambridge/Institute of Criminology

PRICE W.H., STRONG J.A., WHATMORE P.B. & McCLEMONT W.F. (1966) Criminal patients with XYY sex-chromosome complement. *Lancet* **i,** 565–566

PRICE W.H. & WHATMORE P.B. (1967) Behaviour disorders and pattern of crime among XYY males identified at a maximum security hospital. *Brit. med. J.* **1,** 533–536

RICHARDS B.W., STEWART A., SYLVESTER P.E. & JASIEWICZ V. (1965) Cytogenetic survey of 225 patients diagnosed clinically as mongols. *J. ment. Def. Res.* **9,** 245–259

RIDLER M.A.C., SHAPIRO A. & McKIBBEN W.R. (1963) Sex chromatin abnormalities in female subnormal patients. *Brit. J. Psychiat.* **109,** 390–394

SABBATH J.C., MORRIS T.A., MENZER-BENARON D. & STURGIS S.H. (1961) Psychiatric observations in adolescent girls lacking ovarian function. *Psychosom. Med.* **23,** 224–231

SACHS E.S. (1971) *Trisomy G/normal mosaicism. A cytological and clinical investigation.* Leiden: H.E. Stenfert Kroese NV

SCOTT P.D. & KAHN J. (1968) An XYY patient of above average intelligence as a basis for review of the psychopathology, medico-legal implications of the syndrome, and possibilities for prevention. *In* West D.J. (ed.) *Psychopathic Offenders.* Cambridge: University of Cambridge/Institute of Criminology

SHAFFER J.W. (1962) A specific cognitive deficit observed in gonadal aplasia (Turner's syndrome). *J. clin. Psychol.* **18,** 403–406

SHAFFER J.W. (1963) Masculinity–feminity and other personality traits in gonadal aplasia (Turner's syndrome). *In* Beigel H.G. (ed.) *Advances in Sex Research.* New York: Hoeber

SLATER E. & COWIE V. (1971) *The Genetics of Mental Disorders*. London: Oxford University Press

TAYLOR A.I. & POLANI P.E. (1964) Autosomal trisomy syndromes, excluding Down's. *Guy's Hosp. Rep.* **113,** 231–249

TERPLAN K.L., LOPEZ E.C. & ROBINSON H.B. (1970) Hisologic structural anomalies in the brain in trisomy 18 syndrome. *Amer. J. Dis. Child.* **119,** 228–235

WOLF U., REINWEIN H., PORSCH R., SCHROTER R. & BAITSCH H. (1965) Defizienz an den kursen Armen eines Chromosoms Nr. 4. *Hum. Genet* **1,** 397–413

ZAPPELLA M. & COWIE V. (1962) A note on time of diagnosis in mongolism. *J. ment. Def. Res.* **6,** 82–85

ZUBLIN W. (1953) Zur Psychologie des Klinefelter-syndroms. *Acta endocr. (Kbh.)* **14,** 137–144

CHAPTER 8

Brain injury

D. SHAFFER

In 1838 Guislain attributed disturbed behaviour in some children to brain injury, and descriptions of the epileptic constitution and the equation of epilepsy with insanity can be traced to a very much earlier period. These relationships have come under closer scientific scrutiny over the past decade and much of this chapter will be devoted to summarising recent research. In addition, there has recently developed a school of child psychiatry that attributes a very wide spectrum of abnormal behaviour in childhood to 'minimal brain damage' (or 'dysfunction'). This chapter will endeavour to examine the evidence for and against such claims.

LIKELIHOOD OF PSYCHIATRIC DISORDER

'Does brain damage increase the likelihood of psychiatric disorder?' In answering the fundamental question, it is important to bear in mind the biassing effect of conditions which are known to be associated with psychiatric disorder and which occur more frequently in brain damaged children. For example, a brain damaged population will include more children with low IQ, educational difficulties and physical handicap. Some forms of brain damage—for example, those resulting from obstetric and neonatal complications, head injury and lead poisioning—occur more often in children from socially and otherwise disadvantaged families. Studies which do not take these factors into account may misleadingly attribute effects to brain injury rather than to sequelae or associations which do not affect all brain damaged children.

The single most useful study in this regard is the total population study undertaken by Rutter et al (1970a) on all children known to have epilepsy or unequivocal brain damage living on the Isle of Wight. The rate of disorder was compared with that amongst children in the general population and with other children suffering from chronic physical illness and/or handicap not involving the CNS (see Table 8.1). It will be seen that the rate of disorder

Table 8.1   Prevalence of psychiatric disorder in neuroepileptic children aged 5–14 years attending school

Group	Percent with psychiatric disorder
General population (10 and 11-year-old children)	6·6
Physical disorders, not involving the brain	11·6
Brain disorders	34·3
Uncomplicated epilepsy	28·6
Lesion about brain stem, no fits	37·5
Lesion above brain stem, with fits	58.3

From Rutter, Graham & Yule (1970) *A Neuropsychiatric Study in Childhood*, London, Heinemann.

was significantly greater in the neuroepileptic children than in children from other groups.

In this study, the high rate of disorder can not be explained as an artefact of the generally lower intelligence of the brain damaged children for it remained evident after the groups had been standardised for IQ. Nor can the association be explained as being due to the nonspecific effects of chronic illness, for the brain damaged children had a much higher rate of disorder than children with other forms of chronic disease. The specific effects of physical handicap have been further investigated in a study (Seidel *et al* 1975) in which the prevalence of disorder in crippled children handicapped as a result of cerebral palsy or other CNS pathology was compared with that amongst children with muscular, peripheral nervous or orthopaedic disease. The groups had comparable degrees of physical handicap, yet disorder was almost twice as common in the cerebral palsied group.

Nor can the high rate of psychiatric disorder be explained by social and family factors. In the Isle of Wight survey this was shown by comparing indices of social deprivation and family disharmony in the brain damaged and a control group. Despite their much higher rate of disorder, the background of the brain injured group did not differ significantly from the controls. This relationship was also examined in a study of children who had suffered traumatic brain damage (Shaffer *et al* 1975). In this group there was both a high rate of psychiatric disorder and a high rate of family and social disadvantage. Yet when the study population was standardised for adverse social and family circumstance, the rate of disorder in the brain injured group was still greater than would have been expected in uninjured children with a comparable degree of disadvantage.

Other, uncontrolled, studies in representative groups of brain damaged or epileptic children (Gudmundsson 1966; 1967; Pond & Bidwell 1960) have also revealed rates of disorder greater than those that would be expected in the general population. Although these studies are in many respects methodologically less satisfactory than the Isle of Wight survey, they are broadly consistent and strengthen the conclusion that brain injury significantly increases the likelihood of psychiatric disorder. What factors increase or decrease the likelihood of psychiatric complications in brain damaged children?

FACTORS MODIFYING APPEARANCE OF PSYCHIATRIC COMPLICATIONS

Age

Experiments with animals suggest that the CNS is most vulnerable to injury during periods of rapid growth (Dobbing 1974). Dobbing and Sands (1973) have studied a series of fetal and infant brains and have shown that in humans the CNS growth spurt begins at 12 weeks after conception and continues until the third or fourth year of life, although not all tissues grow most rapidly at the same time. Thus rapid neuronal multiplication takes place between 12 and 18 weeks, during which time the fetus is relatively invulnerable to deficiencies in placental functions, but is of course open to injury by irradiation, infection and the effect of drugs. Glial calls proliferate rapidly between 20 weeks and 1 year and from then until the end of the fourth year myelinisation is the dominant process. During this latter period the organism is vulnerable to the effect of malnutrition, through either placental dysfunction or medical or environmental causes. The growth spurt also varies in different areas of the brain. The cerebellar growth spurt is of particular interest for it starts relatively late, at a stage when the fetus has become vulnerable to nutritional variation, and is at a peak at the time of delivery. This growth pattern suggests a pathological basis for the frequent finding of complex, though minor, motor disturbances in children who have a history of perinatal abnormality.

There is supporting clinical evidence that is consistent with the notion that the young developing brain is more vulnerable to *generalised damage*. For example, lasting *neurological* and *intellectual* handicap after encephalitis or meningitis is most likely after infection during the first 2 years of life (Finley *et al* 1967). There is evidence of later intellectual deficit among children who have suffered from episodes of severe metabolic upset or chronic starvation during early life (Klein *et al* 1975; Cravioto & Delicardie 1972; Steinhausen 1974), and localised head injury before the age of 4 has a worse prognosis with respect to intellectual function than comparable injuries in older children (Shaffer *et al* 1975).

The effects of age at injury on other aspects of later behaviour have not received much study. However, Shaffer *et al* (1975) failed to find an association between age at injury and psychiatric outcome in a group of children who had incurred cortical injuries at times varying between 6 months and 12 years of age.

On the other hand, psychiatric abnormalities are more common in adults with temporal lobe epilepsy who had their first attacks during childhood (Taylor & Falconer 1968; Gudmundsson 1966). However, it is not clear whether this is due to a biological effect on the developing brain, to differences in the pathology of early and late onset epilepsy, or to the social effects resulting from epilepsy during a formative and vulnerable time of life.

By contrast, the effects of *localised injury* on more *specific* cortical functions may be more benign when the injury occurs at an early age. Thus Basser (1962) and Lenneburg (1967) noted that recovery of speech function after unilateral brain damage is greater in children damaged before the age of 4 and is less good thereafter. This suggests a degree of plasticity in the immature brain which may facilitate recovery of locally represented functions.

Sex

Psychiatric disorder in the general population is more common amongst boys than in girls. This does not appear to be the case amongst brain damaged children. Thus Rutter *et al* (1970a) found equal rates of disturbance amongst boys and girls in the epidemiological study on the Isle of Wight. Shaffer *et al* (1975) also found equal rates of psychiatric disorder amongst boys and girls who had had a penetrating head injury. It is not clear why the protection that girls appear to enjoy against the development of psychiatric disorder should be overcome by head injury. However, it may be that amongst intact children, girls' invulnerability is a function of temperament or cognitive advantage and that it is these factors which are especially likely to be affected by brain damage.

Locus

Lishman (1968) in his study of penetrating head wounds in *adults* found that psychiatric disorder occurred more often after left hemisphere or frontal injury. In the only comparable study in childhood (Shaffer *et al* 1975) no locus effect on behaviour could be demonstrated. This discrepancy could be due to differences in method or sampling, to age related differences in vulnerability (see above), or to the different mechanisms which predispose to adult and child disorder.

Although apparently unrelated to the locus of gross structural damage, psychiatric disorder does appear to be associated with the locus of origin of focal epilepsy. Thus on the Isle of Wight study, psychiatric disorder was especially common in children with psychomotor epilepsy, and other un-controlled studies have similarly shown a high rate of disorder in children with this condition (Aird & Yamamoto 1966; Ounsted *et al* 1966).

In contrast to the effects on behaviour, locus has an important effect on cognitive function. For example, Kershner & King (1974), comparing hemi-plegic children matched for full scale IQ found that those with right-sided lesions did less well on visuo-motor function tests and those with left-sided lesions did less well on tests of verbal intelligence. These findings are in general consistent with other less adequately controlled investigations (Annett 1974; McFie 1961).

Type of brain damage

The Isle of Wight survey suggested that the *prevalence* of psychiatric disorder varies with the type of brain damage. Thus, whilst children suffering from idiopathic epilepsy without associated disorders were about 4 times as likely to have a psychiatric disorder and children with structural abnormality about 5 times as likely, when a child had both structural damage and epilepsy the rate was increased even further.

It is often held that the type of neurological disorder is related to the *form* of psychiatric disturbance. There was no evidence of this being the case in the Isle of Wight survey, although numbers with different conditions were small. Amongst the many studies which have suggested that diagnosis is in some way related to type of disorder, few have been controlled, or, at best, controls have been inappropriate. Thus Hackney *et al* (1968) and Komrower and Lee (1970) reported that children with phenylketonuria and children with galactosaemia were characteristically apathetic and withdrawn. Spain (1974) tested hydrocephalic survivors at the age of 6 and found them to have certain language characteristics described as 'hyperverbal' and Chess *et al* (1971) noted that a high proportion of rubella embryopathy survivors showed aut-istic features, although suggested that this was due to the pattern of their disabilities rather than to any specific viral effects. However, none of these investigations used comparably retarded children as controls, so that it is not possible to say that the findings are characteristic of the condition or whether similar behaviour patterns are found as often in similarly retarded or handi-capped children without that particular type of brain damage.

It has also been held that there is a relationship between EEG character-istics of certain epileptic children and the form of the psychiatric disorder. Thus Nuffield (1961), comparing children with generalised (3 cps spike and wave) and focal (predominantly temporal lobe) epilepsy found significant differences, more of the former showing neurotic and more of the latter conduct disorders. However, this interesting finding has not been replicated (Ritvo *et al* 1970) and in Nuffield's study no mention is made of electrographic consistency across time, nor were the groups of children adequately standardised with respect to various nonorganic factors which might selectively lead to a predominance of a given type of disorder.

Severity of brain damage

Very little is known about how psychiatric outcome is affected by the severity of brain damage, and in particular whether minor degrees of damage increase the prevalence of psychiatric disorder. This is an item of crucial importance in the controversial issue of minimal brain damage and will be discussed in greater detail below.

One of the few studies in which it has been possible to quantify severity has been that carried out by Shaffer *et al* (1975) on just under 100 children who had suffered a penetrating head injury of the skull. These children incurred varying degrees of localised and general damage. Thus only a half lost consciousness at any time, whilst a further third of the group were in coma for more than 24 hours. In this study, no association was found between psychiatric outcome and severity of injury as indicated by length of coma. A possible interpretation of this finding is that there is a very low threshold of severity for psychiatric disorder which may follow on from only mild injuries.

MINIMAL BRAIN DAMAGE

The concept of a characteristic psychiatric syndrome attributable to 'minimal' brain damage was first advanced by Strauss and Lehtinen in 1947. Strauss, a paediatric neurologist, described a constellation of clinical features including overactivity, inattention and conduct disorder, along with perceptual and learning problems not otherwise explicable by intellectual deficit. This association of behavioural and cognitive abnormalities appears to have led Strauss and others to assume that the psychiatric disorder resulted from underlying brain dysfunction and that brain injury could be inferred from the presence of given behaviour, even in the absence of corroborating neurological evidence. This, it was claimed, might not be available because of the 'minimal' nature of the underlying damage or dysfunction. The concept gained widespread support buttressed by reports of the so-called 'characteristic' behaviours in groups of manifestly brain damaged children (e.g. Ingram

1956; Ounsted 1955), and by studies which noted that children attending psychiatric clinics had often had illnesses or perinatal complications of a sort known to be associated with neurological damage (Knobloch and Pasamanick 1966). Others observed that minor or 'soft' neurological signs and nonspecific EEG changes were found more often in children with learning and behaviour problems than in controls (Kennard 1960; Stevens *et al* 1968) and this too increased the plausibility of a common psychiatric syndrome of organic origin.

Although the use of the concept has become widespread, it has engendered a reaction and a great deal of criticism. In part this has been a result of the use of imprecise terminology such as 'minimal' or 'dysfunction' which appears to cloak simplistic notions of the extremely complex nature of both brain function and the determinants of behaviour (Bax & McKeith 1963; Herbert 1964), in part because empirical studies showed that allegedly pathognomonic behaviours were largely independent of neurological dysfunction (Schulman *et al* 1965; Shaffer *et al* 1974), and in part because of politico-philosophical anxieties about 'labelling' (Schrag & Divoky 1975). This has led to a limited retreat so that the more persistent supporters of the syndrome (Wender 1972) have now elaborated detailed, but largely unsupported, hypotheses about probable mechanisms. Similarly, ideas of syndrome specificity have given way to notions that almost all disturbed behaviour in childhood is likely to reflect underlying brain dysfunction. The attractions of the concept may rest in the way—by contrast with environmentalist theory—it lifts the responsibility for disturbance or maladjustment from family or school. However, the diagnosis carries with it implications for treatment and treatability which are not entirely benign (Werry 1974), in particular increasing the likelihood that psychoactive stimulants—with their attendant risks—will be prescribed and that other forms of treatment will be withheld.

In order to examine the validity of the concept of minimal brain damage a crucial question is whether or not apparently transient or mild brain disorder i.e. one which *appears* only temporarily to disturb brain function, may nevertheless lead to more permanent effects on behaviour and/or cognition. It will be the purpose of the remainder of this section to examine the evidence for this.

Complications of pregnancy and delivery and perinatal illness

A history of abnormal pregnancy or delivery, prematurity, asphyxia etc. is common in children attending psychiatric clinics (Knobloch & Pasamanick 1966). It has been concluded from observations of this sort that mild forms of brain damage suffered during the perinatal period lead to the later development of psychiatric and learning problems. Before reaching this conclusion two important methodological considerations need to be kept in mind. The first is that illness or pathology during the first week of life is common and is almost certainly an imperfect index of brain injury. Thus Chamberlain *et al* (1976) in their survey of all births taking place throughout the UK during one week in April 1970 found that approximately 5 per cent of all infants born took longer than 3 minutes to establish respiration and as many as 11 per cent spent some time during the first week of life in a special-care unit. Indicators of this sort are commonly used to examine the effects of perinatal factors on later IQ or behaviour—yet by no means all such children will be brain injured and meaningful effects may be obscured because of this. In examining this problem it is therefore important to arrive at a more direct measure of neurological disturbance. A measure which might prove useful in this regard is the neonatal neurological examination, and Prechtl (1965) has reported that a large number of neonates born after a complicated pregnancy or delivery show neurological abnormalities when examined during the first week of life.

The second consideration is the relationship between perinatal morbidity and social and family disadvantage. In Chamberlain's survey the perinatal mortality rate in the UK in 1970 correlates closely with maternal height which in turn is bound up with social class. Perinatal mortality for illegitimate births is approximately twice the national average and is similarly increased in births to widowed, divorced and separated mothers. Mortality is also higher in late born children of large families (Butler & Alberman 1969). Birth weight too is directly correlated with social class and so indirectly are neonatal convulsions which, in Chamberlain's survey occurred significantly more often in children being fed on cow's milk, a practice which occurs less often amongst middle class mothers.

Given these difficulties, what evidence is there that perinatal illness increases the likelihood of later psychiatric disorder or reduced IQ? In one of the few studies which have directly investigated the effect of abnormal neonatal neurological state on later behaviour. Kalverboer *et al* (1973) reexamined at the age of five, 33 children without gross brain damage who had shown nonlocalising neurological abnormalities when examined during the neonatal period. No relationship was noted between initial and later neurological state and there was only a weak relationship with behaviour measured in an experimental situation. Children who had shown the neonatal 'apathy syndrome' (Prechtl 1965) showed more distress when separated from mother, and children with the neonatal 'hyperexcitability syndrome' played *more* constructively under difficult conditions. Social and family factors were uncontrolled, numbers were small, behaviour in an experimental situation may not be representative of behaviour in more complex real life situations, and it may be that behaviour disturbance in a child with slight brain injury would more likely be manifest during times of scholastic stress, i.e. after the age of 5 when these children were studied. Nevertheless, further research using measures of this sort may offer the best opportunities for our understanding of these relationships.

The evidence from adequately controlled studies which have used less direct indicators of brain injury varies according to whether behaviour, intelligence or educational achievement is examined.

Behaviour Davie *et al* (1972) reporting on the National Child Development Study, which included all children born in the UK during one week in 1958, found only trivial differences in social adjustment between children of normal and low birth weight at age 7, after social class had been taken into account. Graham *et al* (1962) could find no differences in behaviour, at the age of 3, between 350 children who had suffered from clearly documented neonatal asphyxia and a group of carefully matched controls. Ucko (1965), using less satisfactory indicators of asphyxia but more detailed measures of behaviour and temperament obtained longitudinally during the preschool period, noted that previously asphyxiated children were more irregular in sleeping and other behaviours, and were generally more difficult to manage than non-asphyxiated children. None of these outcome measures is ideal, but it seems likely that persisting effects, if any, lie predominantly in style or temperament.

Intelligence Gottfried (1973) has reviewed the large number of studies which have examined the relationship between neonatal asphyxia and later intellectual deficit and found that studies showing an effect are almost equally balanced by studies which do not. However, in those studies which do show a relationship, differences are of a minor order, and in no prospective study did mean IQ fall into the subnormal range.

Educational difficulties Davie *et al* (1972) analysing reading attainment at the age of 7 of children included in the National Child Development Study found a slight but significant relationship between birth weight and later reading attainment after allowing for social class. In summary, despite the extensive literature, this is an inadequately researched area in which appropriately controlled studies using valid measures of initial neurological dysfunction and meaningful behaviour outcome measures are lacking. The apparent absence of any major effect of perinatal factors may be an indication of their generally benign nature or it may be that actual effects are being obscured by the 'noise' in the systems under study.

Infection of the CNS

There is no convincing evidence that children who recover from viral or pyogenic meningitis are any more likely than noninfected children to develop significant *behaviour* disturbances, although it must be emphasised that outcome measures and controls in most studies are deficient (Muller *et al* 1958; Gibbs *et al* 1964). The effects on intelligence are less clear cut—thus Dodge and Swartz (1965), examining mainly older children, found that a history of pyogenic meningitis had no effect on IQ. By contrast, Sells *et al* (1975) found impairment of IQ and language skills of children who had had an enteroviral infection of the CNS before the age of one.

Psychiatric morbidity following rheumatic disease is however well documented. Studies by Freeman *et al* (1965) and Keeler and Bender (1952) suggest that a large proportion of children who require hospital treatment for Sydenham's chorea will have later or persistent psychiatric symptoms. Susceptibility to later disorder would appear to be increased even in subjects in whom CNS involvement is less obvious. Thus Wertheimer (1963) followed up groups of children who had had rheumatic fever, Sydenham's chorea, and both random controls and controls who had suffered from other forms of chronic illness. Children who had had rheumatic syndromes at puberty were 4 times more likely to require subsequent psychiatric admission than either control group. Rheumatic symptoms at other ages did not appear to increase the risk of later psychiatric morbidity in this study. The reason for this age dependent vulnerability is not known. Rheumatic disease is also associated with social deprivation (McClaren *et al* 1975) and it may be that simple effects of CNS damage or social deprivation become linked in a more complex fashion at puberty.

Head injury

Head injury is common in childhood. Craft *et al* (1972) found that in Newcastle-upon-Tyne nearly one-sixth of all paediatric hospital admissions were for observation and treatment of head injury, and in that area this constituted the single most common reason for admission to hospital during childhood. Most injuries appear trivial, and admission is undertaken to ensure prompt observation of any complications. The development of later behaviour or emotional problems in this group, in whom it might reasonably be assumed that some brain damage has taken place is of especial interest. If it could be shown that these children ran an increased risk for later psychiatric disorder, support would be given to the notion that slight brain damage could become manifest in cognitive and behavioural disorder in the absence of persistent motor or sensory abnormality.

However, as with perinatal disorder, the study of head injury is complicated by selection factors, both with respect to the personality of children involved in accidents and their home background. For example, Manheimer and Mellinger (1967) in a study of children who had been involved in more than one accident found them to be more extravert and more daring than nonaccident controls. Craft *et al* (1972) compared classroom behaviour scores based on observations made before their accident on a consecutive series of children admitted to hospital following a head injury. Of the head injured children 22 per cent had deviant scores, compared with 13 per cent of the controls, and both Klonoff and Paris (1974) and Rune (1970) in less satisfactory retrospective studies estimated that about one-third of children admitted for treatment of head injuries had shown abnormal or difficult behaviour before their injury.

Most head injuries in childhood, at least in the UK, involve injuries to children under the age of 5 who are injured as pedestrians or cyclists (Field 1975). It would not be surprising, therefore, to find that as a group, such children are more likely to come from homes in which the parents themselves are under stress and for this or other reasons are deficient in the way in which they care for or supervise their children. This contention is supported by a comparison of the family characteristics of children who had previously received a head injury (Shaffer *et al* 1975) and a randomly selected control group of inner city children (Rutter *et al* 1975). Using similar measures of marital adjustment, unhappy marriages were noted more than 3 times as often amongst the families of head injured children, whose mothers also scored significantly higher than the control group on a Malaise Inventory.

Specific studies on the sequelae of *mild* head injury are lacking but it is clear that psychiatric disorder may follow injury in the absence of persisting motor or sensory signs. An example is Shaffer *et al*'s (1975) study in which it was found that almost two-thirds of the group were disturbed, but that fewer than 10 per cent had any residual neurological impairment. Other studies (Black *et al* 1969; Hjern & Nylander 1964; Klonoff & Paris 1974) similarly suggest that psychiatric problems may result from head injury without other clinical evidence of persistent brain damage.

Metabolic upset

The most common form of metabolic upset affecting children is that of chronic or acute malnutrition in association with poverty. Attempts to study the effects of this condition (Hertzig *et al* 1972; Cravioto & Delicardie 1972) are complicated by the compounding of malnutrition with social and other forms of deprivation which themselves have an effect on cognitive and social development. Attempts have been made to circumvent this problem by examining the social and cognitive development of children from otherwise normal backgrounds who had suffered from malnutrition or acute metabolic upset as a result of some medical condition. Ellis and Hill (1975) contrasting the development of children with cystic fibrosis who had experienced early episodes of malnutrition with other children with the same condition without early malnutrition, failed to find an effect of malnutrition on either intelligence or educational attainment. Another model is offered by pyloric stenosis in which the episode of malnutrition is localised in time and complete recovery follows successful treatment. Klein *et al* (1975) examined IQ, educational attainment and classroom behaviour in schoolage children who had suffered from pyloric stenosis with varying degrees of weight loss. They used sibling and nonsibling controls and found that where weight loss had exceeded 10 per cent of body weight there was later impairment of learning ability and, in particular, impairment of short-term memory. Classroom behaviour and social maturity were unaffected. It is not clear whether these changes were a result of malnutrition or other aspects of the acute metabolic upset which may accompany severe pyloric stenosis.

Another common form of metabolic disturbance which may affect the central nervous system is that associated with high serum lead levels. However, high lead levels are found especially often in children with a history of pica and in children who live in old and dilapidated accommodation. There are therefore major methodological difficulties in sorting out the effects of pre-existing disorder and social disadvantage. Even such studies as those of de la Burde and Choate (1972; 1975), which found significant psychiatric and cognitive effects after very careful and extensive matching of social and family factors, cannot be accepted without question as the high lead children still differed with respect to earlier pica and quality of housing. Lansdown *et al*'s (1974) investigation within a whole community that had been exposed to lead pollution in the air suggests a strategy for overcoming these difficulties.

Behaviour ratings and psychological test results were obtained in a total population of 6–17-year-olds living near a lead smelter. The children living nearest the smelter were found to have the highest serum lead levels, but no relationship was found between lead and either IQ or behaviour ratings.

However, the study may have been confounded by social factors, for the families living closest to the smelter were also more settled, and this may have lead to a paradoxical weighting of favourable social factors in favour of the lead exposed group.

These areas are difficult to research. Nevertheless, evidence from a number of sources suggest that undoubted brain damage may result not only in transient motor or sensory abnormalities but in more lasting effects on behaviour and cognitive and intellectual performance. To that extent the concept of behavioural disorder reflecting underlying but occult brain damage, seems reasonable. Is there, however, a basis for diagnosing brain damage solely on the basis of behaviour?

SYNDROMES CHARACTERISTIC OR PATHOGNOMONIC OF BRAIN INJURY

Strauss and Lehtinen (1947), Clements and Peters (1962) and other exponents of the minimal brain dysfunction syndrome at one time held that brain injury could be inferred by characteristic behaviour disturbance, and in particular by the hyperkinetic syndrome, even in the absence of other evidence of neurological disorder. To some extent psychiatrists such as Wender (1972) have moved away from this position, suggesting that almost all forms of disturbance in childhood may be a manifestation of underlying brain dysfunction. Although there is little to support Wender's suggestions that brain dysfunction underlies most psychiatric disturbance in childhood, the change from beliefs in pathognomonic syndromes is welcome as being more in accordance with available fact.

Brain injured children may develop any type of psychiatric disorder. However, there is little evidence that they are especially likely to develop any particular type of disorder. This was shown on the Isle of Wight survey (Rutter *et al* 1970a) where the range of diagnoses amongst brain damaged and epileptic children with a disturbance was broadly similar to that found amongst non-brain-injured children. However, surveys of this sort may fail to show relationships between some uncommon psychiatric conditions occurring predominantly or uniquely amongst children with brain pathology. An example of this sort is the hyperkinetic syndrome. Very few children were diagnosed as hyperactive in the Isle of Wight survey, but the syndrome did appear to be slightly but not significantly more common amongst children with brain damage. In the USA, the diagnosis is used very much more frequently and is commonly held to be diagnostic of underlying brain damage or dysfunction. Although the syndrome is dealt with in greater detail in

Chapter 22 it is worthwhile examining its alleged relationship to brain damage in the present context.

The diagnosis 'hyperactivity syndrome' is an unsatisfactory one, both imprecise and unreliable. One reason for this is that in practice it appears to rely heavily on parents' or teachers' reports of overactivity or poor concentration. Yet these descriptions are used so frequently that their discriminating value must be very slight. For example, Lapouse and Monk (1958) noted that more than 50 per cent of parents in an unselected population considered their son to be overactive. Similarly, in the Isle of Wight Survey (Rutter *et al* 1970b), it was found that approximately one-third of 10–11-year-old boys who were ultimately judged *not* to have a psychiatric disorder were described as overactive or inattentive by both parents and teachers.

Given that reports of overactivity are inherently unreliable, is there evidence that activity level, when measured objectively, relates in any way to brain damage? Schulman *et al* (1965) compared the whole day motor activities of brain damaged children with controls using an actometer device and found no difference. Werry *et al* (1972) refers to a number of factor analytic studies which show little tendency for hyperactivity, inattention, emotional lability or inconsistency to relate, either to each other or to indices of brain damage. However, it might be that brain damaged children are more active or less attentive than others only in certain situations, as for example in a classroom with its social distractions, or conversely at a time when cognitive or attentional demands are being made. Shaffer *et al* (1974) examined this possibility by comparing neurologically normal and abnormal groups with and without a conduct disorder in two different settings. In one children were invited to play with a number of different toys ranged out over a testing room, and motor activity and attention shifts were recorded. In the other the children performed a vigilance task and were instructed to sit still (on a chair which recorded wriggling movements). It was found that neurological state did not influence attention or activity in either situation. The children with a conduct disorder, regardless of associated neurological disease, were more active and less attentive in both situations. In other words, inattention and overactivity appeared as nonspecific correlates of a conduct disorder rather than as a specific indicator of brain damage.

In summary, the hyperactivity syndrome, although described in the literature with seeming clarity and little ambiguity, is in reality a difficult clinical diagnosis to make in a reliable way. In an experimental situation where such problems can be overcome there is little evidence to support a specific association between its clinical features and neurological dysfunction.

Another syndrome often held to be associated with brain damage is *infantile autism*. Electroencephalogram abnormalities, epileptic fits, poor motor coordination and abnormalities of pregnancy and delivery have been reported in a large proportion of children showing autistic patterns of behaviour (Rutter & Lockyer 1967; Kolvin 1971). Autistic behaviour is allegedly disproportionately common in phenylketonuria (Hackney *et al* 1968), and in survivors of rubella embroyopathy (Chess *et al* 1971) and has been reported in association with toxoplasmosis, galactosaemia and congenital syphilis. Rutter (1974) has postulated a neurodysfunctional model to explain the behavioural abnormalities associated with the condition. However, despite these findings, surveys of autistic children consistently reveal a sizeable proportion of cases in which there is no evidence of CNS pathology.

The 'catastrophic rage syndrome' was first described by Goldstein (1948). Ounsted *et al* (1966) reported that a large number of children seen in the Oxford clinics with temporal lobe epilepsy showed pathological rage reactions. However, the data were obtained retrospectively from case notes in which behaviours had not been systematically noted. It is not possible in the Ounsted study to differentiate the so-called 'rage syndrome' from other forms of antisocial or aggressive conduct disorder and at present there is no reason to believe that there exists any specific syndrome of aggression and poor impulse control which differs materially from similar behaviours seen in children without brain damage.

In summary, there is no evidence that any one behavioural syndrome is in itself diagnostic of brain injury and no neurological diagnosis can be inferred solely on the basis of behaviour. Conversely, one cannot be certain that specific types of brain damage do not predispose to specific types of behaviour disorder. The evidence for this is for the moment lacking because of the tendency to lump brain injured children into relatively large and undiscriminating categories. What is needed are further studies employing more precise definitions of brain damage and type of psychiatric disorder.

POSSIBLE MECHANISMS

Having established that brain injured children are very much more likely to be psychiatrically disturbed, it is important to examine some of the mechanisms through which disturbance is brought about for this may lead to a rational and useful approach to treatment.

Social and family disadvantage

The same family and social factors may influence the development of psychiatric disorder in both brain injured and normal children. Harrington and Letemendia (1958) showed that children with a past history of a head injury referred for psychiatric treatment were more likely to come from a broken or unhappy home than those who did not. Gruenberg and Pond (1957) found the same amongst epileptic children, and in the Isle of Wight study (Rutter *et al* 1970a), broken homes, emotional upset in the mother and social disadvantage were all significantly more common in disturbed brain injured children than in brain injured children without psychiatric problems.

It seems reasonable to investigate whether brain injury acts to increase the vulnerability of a child to family and social stress i.e. whether there is an interaction between disadvantage and damage, and that in combination their effect is greater than would be expected from either alone? If this were so, one would expect to find that the rate of disorder increases more steeply with increases in disadvantage in injured than in noninjured children. It is possible to study this hypothesis by examining the relationship between disorder and disadvantage in the 96 head injured children described by Shaffer *et al* (1975) and the inner city control population described by Rutter *et al* (1975). In this example, both head injured children and controls have been standardised for family and social disadvantage, using indices which include broken or unhappy home, psychiatric disorder or delinquency in either parent, overcrowding and a previous history of being in care. Each of these factors can be expected to be independent of any organic factor in the patient and have been shown empirically to discriminate between the children in each group with and without a disturbance; furthermore, there is a linear

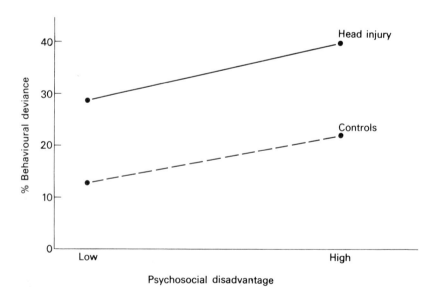

Figure 8.1 Behavioural deviance and psychosocial disadvantage—head injury study.

relationship between the score on this index and rate of psychiatric disturbance. Were brain damage and social and family disadvantage to interact, one would expect that the rate of disorder would increase more steeply with disadvantage in the brain damaged subjects, and yet Figure 8.1 shows that this is not the case. Rather, this particular investigation suggests that both brain and environmental factors are important but that they act independently of each other.

Social stigma and handicap

In 1971 the Office of Health Economics published an opinion survey on public attitudes to epilepsy. Of those surveyed 32 per cent stated that they would not knowingly allow their child to play with an epileptic child. The impact that such attitudes may have in practice is difficult to assess for many children have only infrequent or nocturnal fits and their epilepsy may not be known to others outside their family. In the Isle of Wight study (Rutter *et al* 1970a), parents and teachers were questioned about the child's popularity amongst its peers. As a group, children with CNS disorders were not viewed as significantly less popular by either parents or teachers than other children with chronic physical handicap. However, disturbed children regardless of neurological state, were seen as less popular, suggesting that lack of friends was secondary to disturbance rather than a cause of it.

Stigma or handicap attached to any associated physical crippling cannot in itself be held to account for the high rate of disorder in brain damaged children. This was shown in Seidel *et al*'s (1975) study referred to above and is a conclusion that can also be drawn from studies on hemispherectomy (Wilson 1970) which is reported to result in improvements in psychiatric disorder, although leaving the child with the pre-existing hemiplegia. Nevertheless, it seems likely that these factors do in some measure lead to social isolation and to depression of self-esteem and may well influence the way in which parents or close family view their children.

Intellectual and educational handicap

Psychiatric disturbance in childhood is associated both with low IQ and with learning difficulties (Rutter *et al* 1970b). Both of these factors are common amongst children with brain injury. For example, various surveys of children with cerebral palsy suggest that only about one-quarter have an IQ in the average range (e.g. Ingram 1955). In the Isle of Wight group (Rutter *et al* 1970a) 42 per cent of the brain-damaged children had a full scale IQ of less than 86. Yet although low IQ almost certainly contributes to the high rate of disorder it cannot account for the whole difference which, as mentioned above, persists even when only children of average IQ or above are considered (Rutter *et al* 1970a).

Learning difficulties are also common amongst brain injured children. Thus on the Isle of Wight 18 per cent of the epileptic children and 40 per cent of the children with structural lesions were more than 2 years behind on expected reading attainment. In Shaffer *et al*'s (1975) study of children who had had localised head injury, approximately 30 per cent showed a similar degree of specific reading retardation.

It is not yet clear why this should be. Specific cognitive deficits which might make reading more difficult have not been identified. For example, brain injured nonreaders do not appear to differ from nonreaders without brain injury when assessed on a large number of language and psychometric tests (Mattis *et al* 1975). Nor do attentional deficits identified in the laboratory seem to relate to actual educational attainment (Stores & Hart 1976). However, unwanted effects of anticonvulsant drugs may be a factor in some epileptic children. Laboratory studies on volunteers suggest that both phenytoin (Idestrom *et al* 1972) and phenobarbitone (Hutt *et al* 1968) have an adverse effect on psychomotor function and learning abilities. It also seems that adverse effects on learning may take place in the absence of other evidence of neurotoxicity (Logan & Freeman 1969). Other nonspecific factors such as repeated absences from school, and in some cases lowered expectations on the part of teachers and parents (Hartlage & Green 1972) might also play a part in causing the high rate of educational backwardness.

Educational failure may lead to stigma at school and in turn lowered self-esteem in the child with consequent maladaptive behaviour responses. Rutter (1976) has pointed out how such problems may be more acute when educationally handicapped children are placed in an ordinary rather than in a special school. It seems that when allowance is made for educational difficulty secondary behaviour problems are less likely to develop. This was suggested by Griffiths' (1969) finding that children with severe language disorders develop behaviour problems *after* transfer to ordinary school, and by Seidel *et al*'s (1975) study which showed that the relationship between psychiatric disorder and low IQ or reading backwardness was *less* marked amongst crippled children attending special schools than had been noted amongst the general child population attending ordinary schools.

Temperament

Brain damaged children have often been thought to differ with respect to their *style* of behaviour. There have, however, been very few studies which have set out to examine the relationship between temperament or style and brain injury. Thomas and Chess (1975) have described three brain injured children who had been included in their New York longitudinal study. Two of the three children had favourable temperamental characteristics but it is clearly difficult to generalise from such a small sample. Ucko's study (1965) referred to above found that children with a clinical record suggestive of neonatal asphyxia differed significantly on a number of temperamental variables from those without neonatal symptoms. In particular, they were more irregular in their sleep patterns, resistant to change, sensitive to noise, anxious when they came to start school and generally more troublesome than the non-asphyxiated comparison group. These differences held after careful control for socioeconomic characteristics. It is interesting, however, that the children in both this study and in the comparable St Louis study (Ernhart *et al* 1963) did not differ with respect to overactivity or inattentiveness from nonasphyxiated controls.

Transactional effects

Rutter (1976) has stressed the importance of considering transactional effects in the genesis of disturbance amongst brain injured children; that is, as a result of brain injury the child influences its environment in such a way as to further increase the disadvantage that it endures. An example of this can be drawn from Dorner's (1975) findings that mothers of adolescents with spina bifida have on average more depressive symptoms than has been found amongst the mothers of children without handicap. Unfortunately, this investigation did not examine whether depression in the child was in turn related to depression in the mothers although this seems a reasonable possibility. The fact that mothers do behave differently towards their brain damaged children has been illustrated by Shere's (1957) study of mothers' interaction with twin children, one of whom was cerebral palsied. Mothers were more directive to the cerebral palsied child who, in turn, participated less in family decisions. Similarly, Hartlage and Green (1972) examined dependent behaviour in epileptic and other children, and found that the parents of the epileptics had lower expectations than the parents of other groups of chronically ill or disabled children. It is easy to see how differences of this sort could interfere with the development of coping abilities in the handicapped child and in turn the effect that this might have on self-esteem and social behaviour generally.

Another example of the effect of parental attitudes on child's behaviour is illustrated by Hjern and Nylander (1964) in their study on head injured children. A group of parents who had received positive and encouraging counselling and prognosis at the time of their discharge from hospital were compared with a group whose parents had received no specific predictions or guidance. They found a lower rate of maladjustment in the former group, although a possible source of bias was that the experimenters who made the assessments were also aware of the type of management given to the child. Unrealistically low parental expectations might arise from an appraisal of the child's physical or mental handicap influenced by current social attitudes, or they might arise from the temperamental qualities of the child itself. Thus Gallagher (1957) contrasting groups of retarded children (without physical handicap) with and without brain injury, noted that the brain injured group were more demanding, less able to defer gratification needs and appeared more anxious in a social situation. Furthermore, the brain injured children engendered more hostile and negative responses from their attendants which in turn seemed to increase their anxiety and deviant behaviour.

DETECTION OF BRAIN DAMAGE: INVESTIGATIONS

There are frequently occasions in clinical psychiatric practice when support is sought for a presumptive diagnosis of brain damage. A case may present with a vague or equivocal history of birth difficulties but little else to suggest organic abnormality. In such instances recourse may be made to investigations such as a physical examination for 'soft signs' or EEG or psychometric investigations. Such investigations may also be used in screening programmes designed to identify children at risk for the development of learning or behaviour problems. How helpful are these in establishing a diagnosis of neurological abnormality or in predicting behaviour or learning difficulties?

Neurological examination for 'soft signs'

A number of neurological signs have been described as occurring more frequently in groups of children with behaviour or learning problems than in 'normal' children (Adams *et al* 1974; Kennard 1960; Hertzig *et al* 1969; Rutter *et al* 1966; 1970a; Myklebust 1973; Stine *et al* 1975; Wolff & Hurwitz 1973). Such signs include involuntary movements of a choreic or athetoid type, motor abnormalities such as synkinesis (mirror movements), dysdiadochokinesis (difficulty in performing rapid alternating movements) and general clumsiness, as well as sensory abnormalities, in particular dysgraphaesthesia (inability to identify or reproduce shapes outlined by the examiner on the palmar surface of the child's outstretched hand).

Such signs are often referred to as being 'soft'. Rutter *et al* (1970a) have pointed out that the term 'soft' is used to describe different groups of signs for quite different reasons. Some are labelled 'soft' because they run a developmental course and do not have any clear locus of origin. Such signs are not pointers to disease in the traditional sense and their pathological roots are obscure. Most of the signs mentioned above, all of which are age-related (Peters *et al* 1975), would come into this category. Most, however, can be elicited readily and reliably (Rutter *et al* 1970a). A different group of signs are considered 'soft' because they are minor in degree and because they are difficult to detect in a reliable fashion. Such signs would include reflex or tone asymmetries.

Almost all studies have shown a relationship between the presence of these signs and age and IQ. They are also sex related, and for a given age and IQ occur more frequently in boys. When such factors are taken into account most signs fail to discriminate between problem and nonproblem children, although both dysdiadochokinesis and dysgraphaesthesia are found more often amongst such children after taking account of age, sex and IQ (Adams *et al* 1974; Myklebust 1973; Peters *et al* 1975).

Nevertheless, in our present state of knowledge, the extent to which these signs can be used for screening or diagnosis is very limited. For one reason they are imperfectly related to other measures of neurological dysfunction. Thus Capute *et al* (1968) found that of 106 children with 'soft' signs only 8 per cent had marked EEG abnormalities and 49 per cent had normal EEGs. Rutter *et al* (1970a) found up to 5 abnormal neurological signs in 16 per cent of children who had no other evidence of neurological disorder. Taken alone, therefore, the presence of a 'soft' sign cannot be equated with brain damage.

A second reason is that soft signs also occur in many otherwise normal children. Thus Adams *et al* (1974) found that 10 per cent of 9–11-year-olds without behaviour or learning problems had dysgraphaesthesia and 8 per cent dysdiadochokinesis. Rutter *et al* (1970a) found that 14 per cent of normal 10–11-year-olds showed mirror movements and Wolff and Hurwitz (1966) found that choreatiform movements could be elicited in 11 per cent of normal children. High base rates of this sort greatly reduce the predictive and hence screening value of a test. To illustrate this point, let us say that the prevalence of severe learning disorders in a school population of 8–10-year-olds is 10 per cent and that a screening programme was set up to use a sign such as dysdiadochokinesis to predict learning difficulties at the time of school entry. We do not know predictive value of these signs but using Adam's figures (in which the rate of dysdiadochokinesis in boys with severe learning disorders was 34 per cent and in normal boys 8 per cent), for every 1000 children studied, 110 children would have the abnormal neurological sign, but of these only 1 in 5 would go on to have learning difficulties. These figures err on the side of usefulness for if used on younger children it is likely that the number of false positives would be still further increased. It may be that the predictive value of the neurological examination could be increased by using weighted combinations of signs and this would seem a worthwhile area for further study.

EEG   Whatever other value the EEG might have in our dealings with disturbed or brain damaged children, it is clearly of marginal help in diagnosis. The reasons for this have been dealt with in this volume (see Chapter 14) and elsewhere (Burnett & Struve 1974) and include the high proportion of manifestly brain damaged or disturbed children with normal EEGs and conversely the large number of children without apparent neurological, behavioural or learning abnormality with 'abnormal' EEGs (Eeg-Olofsson *et al* 1971; Hughes 1971).

A more useful application may prove to lie in the relationship between EEG abnormality and response to treatment. Thus Satterfield (1973) noted that within a group of children with 'hyperactive' disorders there was a good response to methylphenidate in 25 per cent of children without EEG or 'soft' signs on neurological examination, but that the improvement rate was twice that in children with both EEG and neurological abnormalities. Children with abnormalities on neurological examination but with normal EEGs did not differ significantly from those with neither EEG nor neurological abnormality. This is clearly an important finding which requires replication.

Psychometry   Psychometric tests are often used to 'diagnose' brain damage. In a sense this is an illogical procedure for the term brain damage encompasses a heterogenous group of conditions affecting different cognitive, motor and perceptual functions in different ways. The tests that are utilised tap one or other or all of these functions and resultant deficits will be reflected in test performance. This suggests that a more useful way of using psychometry is in defining and quantifying specific areas of dysfunction or deficit. Such problems have been critically reviewed by Herbert (1964) and Webster (1970).

Nevertheless, tests are used widely to give weight or otherwise to a putative diagnosis of brain damage. It is therefore worthwhile examining the value of two of the tests most frequently used for this purpose (a) discrepancy and scatter on the Wechsler Intelligence Scale for Children (WISC) (Wechsler 1949), and (b) the Koppitz scoring of the Bender Gestalt Test (Koppitz 1964).

WISC Verbal/Performance discrepancies, with Performance decrements, do occur more frequently in brain damaged children than in normals. For example, in the Isle of Wight survey $P < V$ discrepancies of more than 25 points were 3 times as common in brain injured as in normal children. However, discrepancies of this magnitude occur in about 5 per cent of the normal population (Field 1960). The base rate problem illustrated above with respect to soft signs, holds with even greater force in this case. Assuming a prevalence rate of brain injury of 1·5 per cent, for every 10 children with a 25-point discrepancy, on average only 1 will prove to have brain damage. Dispersion, or scatter of WISC subtest scores, has also been used as an indicator of brain injury but this has not been validated and is further complicated by findings (Maxwell 1961; Rowley 1961) that children with behaviour disorders have more subtest scatter and show greater verbal–performance discrepancy than normal children. Subtest decrements alleged to be pathognomonic of brain injury, e.g. a low score on Block Design, are also sensitive to psychopathology (Caputo *et al* 1962).

The Bender–Gestalt test is a test of perceptual motor function. Although there are significant differences between the scores of groups of brain injured children and normal controls, the level of misclassification is too high to be clinically useful. Thus in Koppitz's original validation study (1969), 10 per cent of brain damaged children had better than average scores and 31 per cent of normals had below average scores. This study was done on children with clear evidence of brain damage. In practice, the test should be most useful where diagnosis is in doubt. Friedman *et al* (1967) have used the test under conditions which approximate a clinical situation. A group of children referred to a clinic with suspected brain damage were tested before any other investigation or enquiry had been made. When all information had been collated it was found that 60 per cent of the children who had lower than expected scores on the Bender had no other evidence of neurological disorder, whereas 64 per cent of the children with better than expected scores were ultimately found to have other evidence of CNS abnormality.

In summary, therefore, psychometric tests should not be relied upon to give a diagnosis but can be more usefully used to quantify motor coordination, memory or learning ability and possibly also establish indications for drug therapy.

TREATMENT

There is always the risk that the disturbed, brain damaged child will be seen to have problems which are fixed and untreatable. This may lead to such children being denied treatment that would have been offered to a child with a similar disorder who was not brain damaged. Yet, as Rutter (1976) has pointed out, most of the effects of brain injury on behaviour appear to be indirect, and this in itself offers hope for treatment.

There is in all cases a need to help the family and child deal with specific handicaps. Counselling and case-work may be helpful in allowing both patient and family to come to terms with the child's limitations whilst at the same time searching out and recognising positive abilities and attributes. Therapy of this sort is also important in helping the family to avoid or over-come problems such as overprotection and the encouragement of depen-dency, and also the situation in which the handicaps are being overlooked or denied whilst the child is scapegoated or made subject to unwarranted criticism.

The child and its family may lack basic knowledge about the nature of the illness or disability. Dorner (1975) noted that adolescents with spina bifida were often ignorant of the reason for their disability and in certain cases believed that their condition might lead to imminent death. The most com-mon form of brain injury is that which follows trauma. Specialist and general practitioner follow-up of even quite severe head injury is often limited and inappropriate. Thus Shaffer *et al* (1975) found that the mean number of fol-low-up attendances of children who had had compound depressed fractures of the skull was less than 3, a large number of children were not being followed up at all and follow-up enquiries seemed to centre on neurological recovery rather than on the development of behaviour or educational difficulties. Many of the parents seemed unaware of the limits that were permissible after head injury and as a consequence tended to overprotect and restrict their child unduly. The therapist may therefore be able to provide important help to the child and family by offering a more leisurely and sensitive opportunity for enquiries of a largely medical nature than is possible in the hurried atmos-phere of a neurological or neurosurgical clinic.

Specific educational and cognitive handicaps or difficulties need to be identified and, where indicated, remedial teaching tailored to the child's needs may be required (Rutter & Yule 1975). Direct contact with the child's school may alleviate teachers' anxieties and may also serve to acquaint the school with suspected difficulties. Paradoxically, the need for this type of help may be especially important in children with mild disability in whom the need for assistance or special attention is not clearly apparent.

Where a brain injured child is receiving anticonvulsant drugs, regular psychometric testing undertaken at the same time as measurement of anti-convulsant serum levels may be helpful. Children may tolerate relatively high concentrations of drug without showing motor signs of toxicity, although learning ability and thought may be adversely affected (see Chapter 38).

The value of stimulants or other psychotropic drugs in the management of children with *unequivocal* brain damage is unclear. Satterfield (1973) has suggested that children with 'minimal brain dysfunction' may actually be *more* responsive to stimulant treatment than other children. But this was based on a study of children with soft signs and nonspecific EEG changes and there is by contrast anecdotal evidence that children with clear cut neurological disorders may be *more* prone to unwanted effects (Ounsted 1955).

Some problems affecting brain damaged children will be amenable to behaviour therapy. Specific applications have been described by Zlutnick *et al* (1975), and Daniels (1975) who have suggested ways in which behaviour therapy can reduce the frequency of convulsions, especially when it is possible to identify a characteristic behaviour preceding seizures.

Finally, although the place of surgery remains inadequately documented, there are anecdotal reports of improvement in psychiatric state in children with temporal lobe epilepsy after temporal lobectomy (Falconer & Davidson 1974) and after hemispherectomy (Wilson 1970; White 1961) in children with severe epilepsy and infantile hemiplegia.

PROGNOSIS

How do brain damaged children fare as they grow up? Do they have more or less difficulty in adjusting to adult life than other disturbed children? Do they experience more problems during childhood, when coping mechanisms are poorly developed and when attentional and cognitive demands are especially great, or do their difficulties continue into adult life?

There have as yet been no systematic controlled follow-up studies which have set out to examine these questions. Taylor and Falconer (1968) and Gudmundsson's (1966) findings that psychiatric problems occur more commonly in adults whose epilepsy had begun in childhood suggest a poor prognosis as do Dorner's (1975) findings of a high rate of depression in adolescents with spina bifida. However, no information is available on earlier psychiatric state in any of these studies. The study on spina bifida children is uncontrolled and a high proportion of undamanged adolescents of the same age are known to suffer from similar thoughts and feelings. In the epilepsy studies, it is not possible to determine whether difficulties are due to differences in underlying pathology or to an earlier onset of disturbance. Some information is available from Robins' (1966) study in which a large group of children who had presented with psychiatric problems were traced and interviewed in adult life. The group included a number of children who had had epilepsy, head injuries and encephalitis. Of the children 19 per cent without any form of chronic physical illness in childhood, 17 per cent of those who had had epilepsy and 33 per cent of those who had had head injuries were later diagnosed as sociopaths. These differences not being statistically significant. The analysis with respect to these factors was a rudimentary one, not standardising or controlling for other factors which predisposed towards or protected from sociopathy and excluded children of low IQ. Nevertheless the results are interesting and do not give reason to take an unduly pessimistic view of the later social development of disturbed children with brain damage.

REFERENCES

ADAMS R.M., KOCSIS J.J. & ESTES R.E. (1974) Soft neurological signs in learning-disabled children and controls. *Amer. J. Dis. Child.* **128,** 614–618

AIRD R.B. & YAMAMOTO T. (1966) Behavior disorders of childhood. *Electroenceph. clin. Neurophysiol.* **21,** 148–156

ANNETT M. (1974) Laterality of childhood hemiplegia and the growth of speech and intelligence. *Cortex* **9,** 4–39

BASSER L.S. (1962) Hemiplegia of early onset and the faculty of speech with special reference to the effects of hemispherectomy. *Brain* **85,** 427–460

BAX M. & MACKEITH R. (1963) *Minimal Cerebral Dysfunction.* Clinics in Dev. Med. No. 10. London: SIMP/Heinemann

BLACK P., JEFFRIES J.J., BLUMER D., WELLNER A. & WALKER A. (1969) The post-traumatic syndrome in children. *In* Walker A.E., Caveness W.F. & Critchley M. (eds.) *The Late Effects of Head Injury.* Springfield, Illinois: Charles C Thomas

BURNETT L.L. & STRUVE F.A. (1974) The value of EEG study in minimal brain dysfunction. *J. Clin. Psychol.* **30,** 489–495

BUTLER N.R. & ALBERMAN E.D. (eds.) (1969) *Perinatal Problems.* Edinburgh: E. & S. Livingstone

CAPUTE A.J., NIEDERMEYER E.F. & RICHARDSON F. (1968) The electroencephalogram in children with minimal cerebral dysfunction. *Pediatrics* **41,** 1104–1114

CAPUTO D.V., EDMONSTON W.E., L'ABATE L. & RONDBERG S.R. (1962) Extended Report: Type of Brain Damage and Intellectual Functioning in Children. Paper read at Midwestern Psychol. Assoc. Mtg. Chicago. Washington University School of Medicine publication

CHAMBERLAIN R., CHAMBERLAIN C., HOWLETT B. & CLAIREAUX A. (1976) *British Births 1970, Vol. 1. The First Week of Life.* London: Heinemann

CHESS S., KORN S.J. & FERNANDEZ B. (1971) *Psychiatric Disorders of Children with Rubella.* London: Butterworth

CLEMENTS S.D. & PETERS J.E. (1962) Minimal brain dysfunction in the school age child. *Arch. gen. Psychiat.* **6,** 185–197

CRAFT A.W., SHAW D.A. & CARTLIDGE N.E. (1972) Head injuries in children. *Brit. Med. J.* **iv,** 200–203

CRAVIOTO J. & DELICARDIE E.R. (1972) Environmental correlates of severe clinical malnutrition and language development in survivors from Kwashiorkor or marasmus. *Nutrition, the Nervous System and Behaviour.* Proceedings of the seminar on malnutrition in early life and subsequent mental development, Mona, Jamaica., 10–14 Jan. 1972

DANIELS L.K. (1975) The treatment of grand-mal epilepsy by covert and operant conditioning techniques. *Psychosomatics* **16,** 65–67

DAVIE R., BUTLER N. & GOLDSTEIN H. (1972) *From Birth to Seven: a Report of the National Child Developmental Study.* London: Longman

DE LA BURDE B. & CHOATE M.S. (1972) Does asymptomatic lead exposure in children have latent sequelae? *J. Pediat.* **81**, 1088–1091

DE LA BURDE B. & CHOATE M.S. (1975) Early asymptomatic lead exposure and development at school age. *J. Pediat.* **87**, 638–642

DOBBING J. (1974) The later development of the brain and its vulnerability. *In* Davis J.A. & Dobbing J. (eds.) *Scientific Foundations of Paediatrics*. London: Heinemann

DOBBING J. & SANDS J. (1973) The quantitative growth and development of the human brain. *Arch. Dis. Child.* **48**, 757–767

DODGE P.R. & SWARTZ M.N. (1965) Bacterial meningitis: a review of selected aspects. II: Special neurological problems, post-meningitis complications and clinico-pathological correlations. *New Engl. J. Med.* **272**, 954–96c

DORNER S. (1975) The relationship of physical handicap to stress in families with an adolescent with spina bifida. *Dev. Med. Child. Neurol.* **17**, 765–777

EEG-OLOFSSON O., PETERSEN I. & SELLDEN U. (1971) The development of the electroencephalogram in normal children from the age of 1 through 5—paroxysmal activity. *Neuropaediat.* **2**, 375–404

ELLIS C.E. & HILL D.E. (1975) Growth, intelligence and school performance in children with cystic fibrosis who have had an episode of malnutrition during infancy. *J. Pediat.* **87**, 565–568

ERNHART C.B., GRAHAM F.K., EICHMAN P.L., MARSHALL J.M. & THURSTON D. (1963) Brain injury in the pre-school child: some developmental considerations. II Comparison of brain injured and normal children. *Psychol. Monog.* **77**, 17–33

FALCONER M.A. & DAVIDSON S. (1974) The rationale of surgical treatment of temporal lobe epilepsy with particular reference to childhood and adolescence. *In* Harris P. & Mawdsley C. (eds.) *Epilepsy: Proceedings of the Hans Berger Centenary Symposium*. Edinburgh: Churchill-Livingstone

FIELD J.G. (1960) Two types of table for use with Wechsler's intelligence scales. *J. Clin. Psychol.* **16**, 3–8

FIELD J.H. (1975) *A study of the epidemiology of head injury in England and Wales, with particular application to rehabilitation*. Dept. of Health and Social Security. London: HMSO

FINLEY K.H., FITZGERALD L.H., RICHTER R.W., RIGGS N. & SHELTON J.T. (1967) Western encephalitis and cerebral ontogenesis. *Arch. Neurol.* **16**, 140–164

FREEMAN J.M., ARON A.M., COLLARD J.E. & MACKAY M.C. (1965) The emotional correlates of Sydenham's chorea. *Pediatrics* **35**, 42–49

FRIEDMAN J., STROCHAK R.D., GITLIN S. & GOTTSAGEN M.L. (1967) Koppitz Bender scoring system and brain injury in children. *J. Clin. Psychol.* **23**, 179–182

GALLAGHER J.J. (1957) A comparison of brain injured and non brain injured mentally retarded children on several psychological variables. *Mon. Soc. Res. Child. Dev.* no. 22 (2)

GIBBS F., GIBBS E., SPIES H. & CARPENTER P. (1964) Common types of childhood encephalitis. *Arch. Neurol.* **10**, 1–11

GOLDSTEIN K. (1948) *Language and Language Disturbances*. New York: Grune & Stratton

GOTTFRIED A.W. (1973) Intellectual consequences of perinatal anoxia. *Psychol. Bull.* **80**, 231–242

GRAHAM F.K., ERNHART C.B., THURSTON C.B. & CRAFT M. (1962) Development three years after perinatal anoxia and other potentially damaging newborn experiences. *Psychol. Monog.* **76,** 1–53

GRIFFITHS C.P. (1969) A follow-up study of children with disorders of speech. *Brit. J. Dis. Communic.* **4,** 46–56

GRUENBERG F. & POND D.A. (1957) Conduct disorders in epileptic children. *J. Neurol. Neurosurg. Psychiat.* **20,** 65–68

GUDMUNDSSON G. (1966) Epilepsy in Iccland; a clinical and epidemiological investigation. *Acta Neurol. Scand.* Suppl. 25

GUDMUNDSSON K.R. (1967) Cerebral palsy in Iceland. *Acta Neurol. Scand.* Suppl. 34

GUISLAIN J. (1838) *Abhandlung über die Phrenopathien.* Stuttgart: Rieger

HACKNEY I.M., HANLEY W.B., DAVIDSON W. & LINDSAY L. (1968) Phenylketonuria, mental development, behaviour and termination of low phenyaline diet. *J. Pediat.* **72,** 646–655

HARRINGTON J.A. & LETEMENDIA F.J. (1958) Persistent psychiatric disorders after head injuries in children. *J. Ment. Sci.* **104,** 1205–1218

HARTLAGE L.C. & GREEN J.B. (1972) The relation of parental attitudes to academic and social achievement in epileptic children. *Epilepsia* **13,** 21–26

HERBERT M. (1964) The concept and testing of brain damage in children: a review. *J. Child Psychol. Psychiat.* **5,** 197–216

HERTZIG M.E., BIRCH H.G., RICHARDSON S.A. & TIZARD J. (1972) Intellectual levels of school children severely malnourished during the first two years of life. *Pediatrics* **49,** 814–824

HERTZIG M.E., BORTNER M. & BIRCH H.G. (1969) Neurologic findings in children educationally designated as brain damaged. *Amer. J. Orthopsychiat.* **39,** 437–446

HJERN B. & NYLANDER I. (1963) Acute head injuries in children: traumatology, therapy and prognosis. *Acta Paediat. Scand.* Suppl. 152

HUGHES J.R. (1971) Electroencephalography and learning disabilities. *In* Myklebust H.R. (ed.) *Progress in Learning Disabilities,* Vol. II. New York: Grune & Stratton

HUTT S.J., JACKSON P.M., BELSHAM A. & HIGGINS G. (1968) Perceptual motor behaviour in relation to blood phenobarbitone level: a preliminary report. *Dev. Med. Child Neurol.* **10,** 626–632

IDESTROM C.M., SCHALLING D., CARLQUIST U. & SJOQUIST F. (1972) Acute effects of diphenylhydantoin in relation to plasma levels. Behavioural and psychophysiological studies. *Psychol. Med.* **2,** 111–120

INGRAM T.T. (1955) A study of cerebral palsy in the childhood population of Edinburgh. *Arch. Dis. Child.* **30,** 85–98

INGRAM T.T. (1956) A characteristic form of overactive behaviour in brain damaged children. *J. Ment. Sci.* **102,** 550–558

KALVERBOER A.F., TOUWEN B.C. & PRECHTL H.F. (1973) Follow-up of infants at risk of minor brain dysfunction. *Ann. New York Acad. Sciences* **205,** 173–187

KEELER W.R. & BENDER L. (1952) A follow-up study of children with behaviour disorder and Sydenham's chorea. *Amer. J. Psychiat.* **109,** 421–428

KENNARD M.A. (1960) Value of equivocal signs in neurologic diagnosis. *Neurology (Minneap.)* **10,** 753–764

KERSHNER J.R. & KING A.J. (1974) Laterality of cognitive functions in achieving hemiplegic children. *Percept. Mot. Skills* **39,** 1283–1289

KLEIN P.S., FORBES G.B. & NADER P.R. (1975) Effects of starvation in infancy (pyloric stenosis) on subsequent learning abilities. *J. Pediat.* **87,** 8–15

KLONOFF H. & PARIS R. (1974) Immediate, short term and residual effects of acute head injuries in children: neuropsychological and neurological correlates. *In* Reitan R.M. & Davison L.A. (eds.) *Clinical Neuropsychology: Current Status and Applications.* Washington DC: Winston

KNOBLOCH H. & PASAMANICK B. (1966) Prospective studies on the epidemiology of reproductive casualty: methods, findings and some implications. *Merrill–Palmer Quart.* **12,** 27–43

KOLVIN I. (1971) Psychoses in childhood—a comparative study. *In* Rutter M. (ed.) *Infantile Autism: Concepts, Characteristics and Treatment.* Edinburgh: Churchill–Livingstone

KOMROWER G.M. & LEE D.H. (1970) Long-term follow up of galactosemia. *Arch. Dis. Child.* **45,** 367–373

KOPPITZ E.M. (1964) *The Bender Gestalt Test for Young Children.* New York: Grune & Stratton

LANSDOWN R.G., SHEPHERD J., CLAYTON B.E., DELVES H.T., GRAHAM P.J. & TURNER W.C. (1974) Blood lead levels: behaviour and intelligence: a population study. *Lancet* **i,** 538–541

LAPOUSE R. & MONK M.A. (1958) An epidemiologic study of behavioural characteristics in children. *Amer. J. Pub. Hlth.* **48,** 1134–1144

LENNEBERG E.H. (1967) *Biological Foundations of Language.* New York: Wiley

LISHMAN W.A. (1968) Brain damage in relation to psychiatric disability after head injury. *Brit. J. Psychiat.* **114,** 373–410

LOGAN W.J. & FREEMAN J.M. (1969) Pseudodegeneration disease due to Diphenylhydantoin intoxication. *Arch. Neurol.* **21,** 631–637

MANHEIMER D.I. & MELLINGER G.D. (1967) Personality characteristics of the child accident repeater. *Child Dev.* **38,** 491–513

MATTIS S., FRENCH J.H. & RAPIN J. (1975) Dyslexia in children and young adults. Three independent neuropsychological syndromes. *Dev. Med. Child. Neurol.* **17,** 150–163

MAXWELL A.E. (1961) Discrepancies between the pattern of abilities for normal and neurotic children. *J. Ment. Sci.* **107,** 300–307

McCLAREN M.J., HAWKINS D.M., KOORNHOF H.J., BLOOM K.R., BRAMWELL-JONES D.M., COHEN E., GALE G.E., KANAREK K., LACHMAN A.S., LAKIER J.B., POCOCK W.A. & BARLOW J.B. (1975) Epidemiology of rheumatic heart disease in black schoolchildren of Soweto, Johannesburg. *Brit. Med. J.* **3,** 474–478

McFIE J. (1961) Intellectual impairment in children with localised post-infantile cerebral lesions. *J. Neurol. Neurosurg. Psychiat.* **24,** 361–365

MULLER R., NYLANDER I., LARRSON L.E., WIDEN L. & FRANKENHAEUSER M. (1958) Sequelae of primary aseptic meningoencephalitis: a clinical sociomedical electroencephalographic and psychological study. *Acta Psychiat. Neurol. Scand.* Suppl. **126,** 1–115

MYKLEBUST H.R. (1973) Identification and diagnosis of children with learning disabilities: an interdisciplinary study of criteria. *Semin. Psychiat.* **5,** 55–77

NUFFIELD E.J. (1961) Neurophysiology and behaviour disorders in epileptic children. *J. Ment. Sci.* **107,** 438–458

OFFICE OF HEALTH ECONOMICS (1971) *Epilepsy in Society.* London: OHE

OUNSTED C. (1955) The hyperkinetic syndrome in epileptic children. *Lancet* **ii,** 303–11

OUNSTED C., LINDSAY J. & NORMAN R. (1966) *Biological Factors in Temporal Lobe Epilepsy.* Clinics in Dev. Med. No. 22. London: SIMP/Heinemann

PETERS J.E., ROMING J.S. & DYKMAN R.A. (1975) A special neurological examination of children with learning disabilities. *Dev. Med. Child Neurol.* **17**, 63–78

POND D.A. & BIDWELL B.H. (1960) A survey of epilepsy in 14 general practices. II: Social and psychological aspects. *Epilepsia* **1**, 285–299

PRECHTL H.F. (1965) Prognostic value of neurological signs in the newborn infant. *Proc. Roy. Soc. Med.* **58**, 3–4

RITVO E.R., ORNITZ E.M., WALTER R.D. & HANLEY J. (1970) Correlation of psychiatric diagnosis and EEG findings: a double blind study of 184 hospitalized children. *Amer. J. Psychiat.* **126**, 988–996

ROBINS L.N. (1966) *Deviant Children Grown Up.* Baltimore: Williams & Wilkins

ROWLEY V.T. (1961) Analysis of the WISC performance of brain damaged and emotionally disturbed children. *J. Consult. Psychiat.* **25**, 553

RUNE V. (1970) Acute head injuries in children. *Acta Paediat. Scand.* Suppl. 209

RUTTER M. (1974) The development of infantile autism. *Psychol. Med.* **4**, 147–163

RUTTER M. (1976) Brain damage syndromes in childhood: concepts and findings. *J. Child Psychol. Psychiat.* (in press)

RUTTER M., GRAHAM P. & BIRCH H.G. (1966) Interrelations between the choreiform syndrome, reading disability and psychiatric disorder in children of 8–11 years. *Dev. Med. Child Neurol.* **8**, 149–159

RUTTER M., GRAHAM P. & YULE W. (1970a) *A Neuropsychiatric Study in Childhood.* Clinics in Dev. Med. No. 35/36. London: SIMP/Heinemann

RUTTER M. & LOCKYER L. (1967) A five to fifteen year follow-up study of infantile psychosis. I: Description of sample. *Brit. J. Psychiat.* **113**, 1169–1182

RUTTER M., TIZARD J. & WHITMORE K. (eds.) (1970b) *Education, Health and Behaviour.* London: Longman

RUTTER M., YULE B., QUINTON D., ROWLANDS O., YULE W. & BERGER M. (1975) Attainment and adjustment in two geographical areas. III Some factors accounting for area differences. *Brit. J. Psychiat.* **125**, 520–533

RUTTER M. & YULE W. (1975) The concept of specific reading retardation. *J. Child Psychol. Psychiat.* **16**, 181–197

SATTERFIELD J.H. (1973) EEG issues in children with minimal brain dysfunction. *Semin. Psychiat.* **5**, 35–47

SCHRAG P. & DIVOKY D. (1975) *The Myth of the Hyperactive Child.* New York: Pantheon Books

SCHULMAN J.L., KASPAR J.C. & THRONE F.M. (1965) *Brain Damage and Behaviour: A Clinical-Experimental Study.* Springfield, Illinois: Charles C Thomas

SEIDEL U.P., CHADWICK O. & RUTTER M. (1975) Psychological disorders in crippled children: a comparative study of children with and without brain damage. *Dev. Med. Child Neurol.* **17**, 563–573

SELLS C.J., CARPENTER R.L. & RAY C.G. (1975) Sequelae of central nervous system enterovirus infections. *New Eng. J. Med.* **293**, 1–4

SHAFFER D., CHADWICK O. & RUTTER M. (1975) Psychiatric outcome of localised head injury in children. *In* Porter R. & FitzSimons D.W. (eds.) *Outcome of Severe Damage to the Central Nervous System.* CIBA Foundation Symposium No. 34. Amsterdam: Elsevier-Excerpta Medica-North-Holland

SHAFFER D., McNAMARA N. & PINCUS J.H. (1974) Controlled observations on patterns of activity, attention and impulsivity in brain damaged and psychiatrically disturbed boys. *Psychol. Med.* **4**, 4–18

SHERE M.O. (1957) The socio-emotional development of the twin who has Cerebral Palsy. *Cerebral Palsy Review* **18**, 16–18

SPAIN B. (1974) Verbal and performance ability in pre-school children with spina bifida. *Dev. Med. Child Neurol.* **16**, 773–780

STEINHAUSEN H.C. (1974) Psychological evaluation of treatment in phenylketonuria intellectual, motor and social development. *Neuropaediat.* **5**, 146–156

STEVENS J.R., SACHDEV K. & MILSTEIN V. (1968) Behaviour disorders of childhood and the electroencephalogram. *Arch. Neurol.* **18**, 160–177

STINE O.C., SARATSIOTIS J.M. & MOSSER R.S. (1975) Relationships between neurological findings and classroom behavior. *Amer. J. Dis. Child.* **129**, 1036–1040

STORES G. & HART J. (1976) Reading skills of children with generalised and focal epilepsy attending ordinary schools. *Dev. Med. Child Neurol.* (in press)

STRAUSS A.A. & LEHTINEN L.E. (1947) *Psychopathology and Education of the Brain Injured Child*, vol. 1. New York: Grune & Stratton

TAYLOR D.C. & FALCONER M.A. (1968) Clinical, socio-economic and psychological changes after temporal lobectomy for epilepsy. *Brit. J. Psychiat.* **114**, 1247–1261

THOMAS A. & CHESS S. (1975) A longitudinal study of 3 brain damaged children. *Arch. gen. Psychiat.* **32**, 457–462

UCKO L.E. (1965) A comparative study of asphyxiated and non-asphyxiated boys from birth to 5 years. *Dev. Med. Child Neurol.* **7**, 643–657

WEBSTER E.C. (1970) The Bender–Gestalt Test with young children: a critique. MSc (Psychology) dissertation. University of London

WECHSLER D. (1949) *Wechsler Intelligence Scale for Children* (Manual). New York: The Psychological Corporation

WENDER P. (1972) The minimal brain dysfunction syndrome in children. *J. Nerv. Ment. Dis.* **155**, 55–71

WERRY J.S. (1974) Minimal brain dysfunction (neurological impairment) in children. *N.Z. Med. J.* **80**, 94–100

WERRY J.S., MINDE K., GUZMAN A., WEISS G., DOGAN K. & HOY E. (1972) Neurological status compared with neurotic and normal children. *Amer. J. Orthopsychiat.* **42**, 441–451

WERTHEIMER N.M. (1963) A psychiatric follow-up of children with rheumatic fever and other chronic diseases. *J. Chron. Dis.* **16**, 223–237

WHITE H.H. (1961) Cerebral hemispherectomy in the treatment of infantile hemiplegia. *Confinia Neurologica* **21**, 1–50

WILSON P.J. (1970) Cerebral hemispherectomy for infantile hemiplegia. *Brain* **93**, 147–180

WOLFF P.H. & HURWITZ I. (1966) The choreiform syndrome. *Dev. Med. Child Neurol.* **8**, 160–165

WOLFF P.H. & HURWITZ I. (1973) Functional implications of the minimal brain damaged syndrome. *Semin. Psychiat.* **5**, 105–115

ZLUTNICK S., MAYVILLE W.J. & MOFFAT S. (1975) Modification of seizure disorders: the interruption of behavioural chains. *J. Appl. Behav. Anal.* **8**, 1–12

PART II
Some developmental theories

CHAPTER 9

Learning theories

M. BERGER

Learning plays an immense role in the emergence of psychological disorders, as well as in individual development. The processes of learning have been studied by psychologists for many decades and the findings need to be understood, together with their limitations. Theories of learning, and scientific psychology more generally, continue to make important contributions to psychiatry. This chapter discusses these matters with special reference to the issues which need to be understood in assessing the contributions of theory and research in learning.

PSYCHOLOGY AND CHILD PSYCHOLOGY

The study of children has always been a part of psychology, but it is only in recent years that a widespread interest in child psychology has emerged. Because, up to a couple of decades ago, psychology was essentially adult orientated, child psychology today reflects many of the characteristics of general psychology. Many theories of child behaviour and development, and many methods used to study them, are theories and methods derived from adult psychology. The study of temperament in children had its immediate origins in the research on adult personality. Similarly, the study of children's learning has been profoundly influenced by theories and research on adult and on animal learning. The work of Piaget is an important exception to this general pattern.

The recent recognition that psychological development encompasses the life span and that many of the issues relevant to childhood are common to all ages (Goulet & Baltes 1970; Nesselroade & Reese 1973; see also *Developmental Psychology*) is a significant conceptual advance. It serves to link areas of psychology previously treated independently.

Recent important critical analyses of contemporary psychology (Harré & Secord 1972; Levine 1974; Cronbach 1975) raise issues of direct relevance to child psychology and ultimately to clinical practice. According to Harré and Secord (1972), 'three fundamental ideas' have been 'taken for granted as providing a sound methodological and theoretical foundation for a behavioural science'. These ideas are the mechanistic model of man, a conception of causality which emphasises external or environmental stimuli as the source of behaviour, and the acceptance of a methodology firmly based in the philosophies of logical positivism. The 'more a behavioural science has fitted itself to these conceptions, the more scientific status it has believed itself to deserve' (Harré & Secord 1972). Along with these views there goes the great emphasis which much of contemporary psychology places on laboratory experiments as the primary (if not sole) source of its data.

This viewpoint has been criticised on the grounds that the methodological and theoretical basis of contemporary psychology is inappropriate; that it has produced a psychology which is so narrow in scope and value that a major reorientation is required (Cronbach 1975; Levine 1974; Harré & Secord 1972). In particular, the emphasis on the 'laboratory' experiment is regarded as excessive and often misplaced.

While much of general psychology today still adheres to the traditional narrow form of scientific method, the more youthful child psychology is less constricted. Nevertheless, the imprint of its parent remains. Thus, Reese and Lipsitt (1970) distinguish several features of what they call experimental child psychology which reflect preferences rather than absolute choices. They state that experimental child psychologists prefer to study basic processes as opposed to the 'whole' child; prefer basic to socially relevant research; and use experimental as opposed to naturalistic and other nonexperimental methods. There is ample evidence that the narrow experimental tradition of psychology still exerts an important influence on child psychology but it is not as widespread as in general psychology. Much greater use is being made of nonmanipulative, naturalistic observation, as for example in the many studies of mother–child interaction which takes place outside the research 'laboratory'. Even in such studies, however, the legacy of the narrower tradition remains in the form of attempts to minimise the effects of bias and subjectivity. This at least is a desirable legacy. Indeed, it would be fair to say that contemporary child psychology is more 'scientific', given our present understanding of science (Harré 1972), than is general psychology.

MODELS OF MAN AND BEHAVIOUR

The diversity and controversies of contemporary psychology can only be understood with a knowledge of a fundamental polarity which exists in the underlying psychological models of man. These models, the mechanistic and the organismic, are logically independent and cannot be assimilated (Reese

& Overton 1970). Most learning theories reflect the mechanistic view; the work of Piaget rests upon an underlying organismic model. Mechanistic and organismic models were not invented by psychologists. They were borrowed, knowingly or inadvertently, from pre-existing schools of philosophy and science (Harré 1972; Harré & Secord 1972; Reese & Overton 1970).

The mechanistic model views man as a machine constructed of elementary parts into which the more complex phenomena can be reduced. The application of forces to the machine causes a chainlike sequence of reactions in its parts. In behaviourist learning theories, stimuli (the equivalent of forces) produce responses which in turn act as stimuli for further responses. Complex behaviour is thus seen in terms of stimuli (S) and responses (R), the elementary components of behaviour. From this basis there arises the family of S-R theories which attempt to account for a great variety of behavioural phenomena.

The mechanistic model further views human and animal organisms as reactive, rather than as active. Reactions are elicited mainly by external events, the equivalent of externally applied forces. A particularly important characteristic of this model is its treatment of 'development' which is not seen in terms of changes in the structure of the organism, but rather as 'epiphenomenal or as reducible to quantitative change ...' (Reese & Overton 1970). To account for developmental changes, the model introduces the possibility of operations which are qualitatively different. As Reese and Overton state '... the organism, like the elementary particles of classical physics, does not exhibit basic qualitative changes'. A final characteristic of the model is its adoption of the view that, at some point in its history, the organism is 'empty': it begins as a *tabula rasa* which is filled by exposure to environmental experiences.

In contrast, the organismic model views man as a living organised system which is inherently active and undergoing continual change, both qualitative and quantitative. The organism is seen as a whole which is more than a simple sum of its parts. According to this view, man is the *source* of acts, rather than a product of acts instigated by external or peripheral forces. In the course of development, the individual is regarded as undergoing qualitative changes in organisation which cannot be simply reduced to previously existing properties. Psychological theories which emerge from the organismic view (Piaget, Erikson and others) are identified with the biological sciences rather than with the sciences of physics and chemistry as these were expressed towards the end of the last century.

There are a number of important controversies within both the organismic and mechanistic traditions. The nativistic view, for instance, maintains that psychological structures are present from birth as complete structures, whereas an interactionist view proposes that such structures (while partly present) emerge out of the interaction between existing organisation and the activity of the individual. The views of Chomsky on language development are identified with the former, those of Piaget with the latter. Both however represent a basic organismic orientation. An equally fundamental divergence of views is found within the mechanistic tradition. Bandura (1969, 1974) has consistently rejected a purely S-R model which fails to take account of central mechanisms. His conception of observational learning explicitly sees the human learner as someone who actively processes information, reorganises it and then uses the restructured information to guide future behaviour. This activity is located centrally (in the brain). The introduction of this central mechanism as part of the theory is one of the characteristics of 'social learning theory' which serves to distinguish it from the general class of S-R theories of learning. It is a S-O-R theory where O stands for organism. Theories of the S-O-R- type are referred to as cognitive theories. However, as Reese and Overton (1970) emphasise, the introduction of central mediating systems '... in no way changes the basic ideal model', man as a mechanical system.

While the views of Piaget and Chomsky are seen as reconcilable, as are the differences between say Bandura and Skinner, the differences between organismic and mechanistic theories are not (Reese & Overton 1970).

The controversies both between the basic models and within each may seem somewhat removed from the daily realities of psychiatry and applied psychology. Yet they are intimately related to the ways in which behaviour and its disorders are understood and treated, and the models dictate the type of research which is undertaken. The many differences between psycho-dynamic and behavioural approaches to treatment have their roots in the mechanistic–organismic polarisation. Evidence that these issues are of current concern is provided by Bandura's (1974) paper on behaviour theory and models of man. Bandura attempts to show that social learning views, unlike those of the 'radical' behaviourists (e.g. Skinner), are compatible with all aspects of the oganismic orientation, even though his basic stance is still mechanistic in the final analysis.

These issues pervade all psychology and are not restricted to either age-based divisions (child and adult psychology) or topic-based divisions (learning, perception, personality etc.). However, no scientific theory attains respectability simply because it is cast within a mechanistic or an organismic framework. What sets scientific theories apart is that they are tested 'under the discipline of the experimental method' (Harré 1972, p. 24). This discipline is severe. Provided that the experiment itself is methodologically sound, a 'theory whose consequences are not borne out by experiment and observation must be modified ...' (Harré 1972, p. 24). Theories emanating from the organismic and mechanistic frameworks are ultimately acceptable only insofar as they survive the tests of science.

THEORIES OF LEARNING

Learning is difficult to define in a generally acceptable manner. However, there is some consensus as to which phenomena should be recognised as instances of learning. Prejudices, food preferences, reading, reciting the alphabet, some forms of deviant behaviour, driving a motor car and other patterns of behaviour are generally recognised as learned. One of the tasks of psychology is to explain how these patterns come about. The proposed answers are included in a *number* of theories of greater or lesser compass. The fact that there is no solution as yet to the problem of learning indicates immediately that there is no such thing as 'learning theory'. Psychologists who propose that their explanations are based on 'learning theory', or that a therapeutic approach is based on 'learning theory', use the term in its general sense. What is usually meant is that the explanation employs the principles and concepts associated with a particular theory learning, or that the therapeutic procedure is modelled on certain learning experiments.

Historically, learning theories tended to be comprehensive in scope. It was assumed that the theory would be able to account for all the major learning phenomena. Contemporary psychology is much less ambitious; research and theory aim at the understanding of just one or two of the major learning phenomena. While it is still possible to detect the historical antecedents in much of present-day learning research and theory, the demarcations between earlier theoretical positions are much less pronounced (Hilgard & Bower 1975). Even so, controversies remain (see below).

Learning theories, experimental psychology and child development

A detailed analysis and discussion of the learning theory tradition in child psychology has been provided by White (1970). Attention is drawn here to a limited number of salient points.

The traditional learning theories never attempted to develop a comprehensive theory solely on the basis of information derived from the study of children. The subjects were animals and adults. As White puts it, for 'child psychologists at least, the tradition offers no articulated learning theory or even a theory of child development'. This is not meant to imply that the tradition had no impact on child psychology. It had, and still has, an important if waning influence. One of the important influences was the provision of an interpretative system of concepts and mechanisms which are applied in an attempt to understand the phenomena of child development (Baldwin 1967; Gewirtz 1969; Staats 1971). These systems have a high degree of generality in the sense that they can 'explain' most phenomena, a characteristic they share with their psychoanalytic counterparts.

A second important effect of the learning theory tradition was the impact it had on research. For reasons which are not particularly clear, before this impact child psychology was largely preoccupied with normative studies. Through the influence of the learning tradition it moved in the direction of experimental research. Contemporary child psychology displays this influence in the form of laboratory experiments and mechanistic models, although it would be incorrect to assume that they are the only methods and orientations that are influential. They are counterbalanced by a broadly based scientific approach and by organismic theories. Child psychology has been influenced by the learning theory tradition, but it has not totally identified with it.

Thus, the major theories of child development include some which are quite explicitly organismic (see Baldwin 1967), and which use a terminology and approach which are substantially different from those generally found in the learning theory framework. The differences between the basic orientations give rise to controversy. For example, there are substantially different accounts of 'identification' and of its emergence in development (Gewirtz 1969; Kohlberg 1969). Similarly, the concept of 'attachment' is the subject of varied theoretical interpretations (see Gewirtz 1972). No attempt will be made here to list and explore the many differences, although some will be mentioned in order to highlight important differences between learning and other approaches in child psychology.

Characteristics of the learning theory approach

Learning theories have a number of important generally accepted assumptions. The most basic is that behaviour is learned. Theories are concerned with *how* behaviour is learned. The emphasis on learning is not intended to deny genetic factors in behaviour, and indeed few if any writers would reject their importance. However, given their preoccupations with the acquisition of behaviour through learning, genetic factors have been neglected or only minimally considered.

Two forms of learning, classical (respondent) and instrumental (operant) conditioning play an important role in all theories of learning. However, theorists vary in the extent to which their attempts to 'explain' behaviour use the two forms of conditioning. (It should be noted here that conditioning is not an explanation. It is 'simply a descriptive term for learning through paired experiences' (Bandura 1974).) Skinner, for example, has developed an approach to learning which depends totally on respondent and operant conditioning and the patterning of reinforcements to which the individual has been exposed. Other theorists concede that the two types of conditioned response are important but insufficient to cope with complex behaviour.

Bandura (1969) utilises three distinct regulatory systems to account for behaviour. The first is the pairing of external stimuli with autonomic or instrumental events, the second is the system of behavioural control which emerges through feedback from responses, predominantly in the form of reinforcing consequences. The third system, considered by Bandura to be the most influential, is a central 'cognitive' mechanism which codes and organises stimulus inputs, formulates hypotheses which are modified as a consequence of experienced rewards and punishments, and eventually become established as a system of rules and strategies to guide behaviour in specific situations. The single or joint action of these systems give rise to the many variations seen in normal as well as abnormal behaviour.

The use of this third mechanism in Bandura's system constitutes a major departure from the operant or radical psychology of Skinner. As he has commented recently, 'Over the years, proponents of the more radical forms of behaviourism have not only disclaimed interest in mentation but also marshaled [sic] numerous reasons why cognitive events are inadmissible in causal analyses' (Bandura 1974).

Almost without exception learning theorists are committed to empirical, usually laboratory, investigation. Apart from methodological inadequacies which may cloud the outcome of research (and hence require that the research be repeated) empirical findings are rarely questioned. The findings are treated as 'facts'. Differences among theorists arise in the interpretation that is to be given to these 'facts'.

A further common feature is the adoption of the underlying assumption that learning occurs through the contiguous association of events, an assumption that is present in the work of Pavlov, Hull and Skinner, among others. Among the proponents of associationism, there are differences between those who see contiguous association as necessary and sufficient, and those who regard temporal contiguity as necessary but not sufficient.

At a general level, there is a fairly clear distinction between the stimulus-response theories and the cognitive theories (Hilgard & Bower 1975). Stimulus-response theorists generally cast their interpretations to terms of the operation of 'peripheral' intermediaries, talk in terms of the acquisition of 'habits' and propose that in learning to solve problems, the learner, in a trial and error fashion, employs previous habits which have been acquired. Cognitive psychologists invoke 'central' or ideational mechanisms which mediate between stimulus and response or input and output. They believe that the learner acquires cognitive 'structures' and that problem solving is accomplished by 'insight', that is, the internal reorganisation of what has been learned.

It would be inappropriate to consider theories within the stimulus-response framework and those within the cognitive framework as free from differences among themselves. Two issues illustrate this point. Some stimulus-response theorists believe that reinforcement, something equivalent to reward or punishment, is essential if the stimulus-response link is to be accomplished. Others hold that contiguity in time is sufficient. A second source of difference concerns the form of increment that characterises learning. Is it an all-or-none process, or does it take place through small increments? Cognitive psychologists differ in the answer they choose, as do stimulus-response theorists. A detailed discussion of these and other points of difference can be found in Hilgard and Bower (1975).

Social-learning theory

It is important at this point to distinguish two uses of the phrase 'social-learning theory'. In its primary sense, 'social-learning theory' has been used to refer to an extensive body of theory and research which was built upon conditioning and learning principles and general S-R theory. Social-learning theory, in this instance, was an attempt by a number of psychologists to construct a theory of child development within the framework of S-R psychology. Its other special characteristics was the attempt to use S-R theory to explain important developmental notions originally elaborated by Freud (Baldwin 1967). Thus, certain concepts served to focus social-learning research on the development of dependency, the socialisation of aggression, and the development of conscience and self control. For the theorists working in the S-R framework, social-learning (or more appropriately, the learning of social behaviour) tended to be looked upon as a special class of learning. Also, consistent with S-R theory, it was assumed that it was the environment external to the child which was immediately and totally responsible for the social behaviour patterns of the child. In a sense, the child was excluded from the theories as a source of influence in its socialisation. As will be noted later, this one-sided orientation has been finally cast out of psychological theorising (Bell 1968).

It is not possible to examine here the massive research literature and accompanying theory which has been a direct product of the attempt to apply learning theories to child development. Baldwin (1967) provides a succinct account of both the theory and some of the important studies which have been carried out within the social-learning framework. A variety of approaches to social-learning, ranging from the radical behaviourist approach of Gewirtz (1969) to the cognitive developmental analyses of Kohlberg (1969) will be found in Goslin (1969).

In its current sense, social-learning theory refers to what Hilgard and Bower (1975) call a 'balanced synthesis of cognitive psychology with the principles of behaviour modification' (p. 599). It is essentially an approach to learning which attempts to combine the principles of operant psychology with an approach which accepts internal events and processes as important in regulating behaviour. The work of Bandura (1969) and Mischel (1968) exemplifies the social-learning theory orientation as this is understood today (Thoresen 1973). An instructive and historically pertinent example of the differences between operant psychology and social-learning theory is found in the different ways in which they attempt to explain the fact that children show a strong inclination to imitate the behaviour of adults. According to the radical position of Gewirtz (1969), the child initially imitates because those of his actions (presumably randomly generated at first) which matched those of the adults about him were selectively reinforced by the adults. This tendency to imitate becomes established through reinforcement and once established it is maintained as a consequence of intermittent reinforcement from the socialising adults. For social-learning theorists, imitation skill is not a consequence of each of the component actions having been reinforced. Rather, an observational learning mechanism is proposed; the individual attends to the model whose behaviour will be imitated. What he observes is then encoded in memory, so that, once attended to, it is learned. Reinforcement simply acts to motivate the performance. The only other intervening process is that which translates the cognitively encoded action into a motor action.

The propensity of individuals to learn through observation is a theme which was present in the older social-learning approaches as well as in the more recent expositions. It was used, for example, as a mechanism to account for the learning of aggressive responses (Bandura & Walters 1959; 1963) as well as in attempts to account for 'identification'. One aspect of the notion of identification is the internalisation of social rules (Baldwin, 1967) and one of the ways in which this is thought to be accomplished is through imitation.

Theories of learning and abnormal behaviour

The assumptions which underlie the conceptualisation and treatment of psychological disorders have sometimes been referred to as 'models' of disorders. A distinction has also been made between generic 'medical' or 'disease' models and 'learning' or 'psychological' models (Buss 1966; Maher

1970; Garfield 1974). It is generally appreciated that within both medicine and psychology, disorders are viewed in a variety of ways and that in both fields heterogeneous models are used. There are however certain assumptions concerning causality which differ in the two sets of models. An important assumption in medicine is that 'outer' symptoms are caused by 'inner' dysfunction. Treatment principles are geared to removing the underlying cause. Failure to do so leads to a recurrence of the disorder. Some of the assumptions and treatment principles have been readily transferred to 'psychopathology' and are obvious, for example, in psychodynamic psychology.

Learning models, in their extreme form, have among their assumptions, the view that the symptom is the disease. The disorder has been learned in much the same way that other learning occurs, that it arises because of insufficient learning, overlearning or inappropriate learning (Buss 1966). Some proponents of learning models introduce biological predispositions. Others pay less attention to, or ignore, biological factors *per se*, arguing that these will affect how the learning takes place, and may affect what is learned, but will not affect the fact that the symptoms have been learned.

The work of Dollard and Miller (1950) represents an important attempt to utilise a Hullian learning theory approach (see Hilgard & Bower 1975), as a basis for a theory of personality and psychopathology. Their approach accepted many of the assumptions and mechanisms proposed by Freud and then attempted to recast these in terms more consistent with an experimental psychological approach and the concepts of Hull. For example, fear was treated as a learned drive and experimental studies of conflict were used as illustrations of, or models for, the types of conflict considered to be important in Freudian theory.

The existence of individual differences in 'conditionability', and other predispositions, is a major concept in Eysenck's (1967) theory of the development of abnormal behaviour. He proposes that individuals will differ in the rate at which they form conditioned responses as a function of their degree of extraversion. It is proposed that introverts learn more readily than extraverts and are therefore predisposed to disorders in which there are learning excesses. Extraverts, being less efficient in their learning, tend to have disorders characterised by insufficient learning. Within Eysenck's theory, conditionability (learning) has the status of a coherent characteristic. This conception has given rise to some dispute as a consequence of experimental attempts to validate the theory. It is now recognised that '. . . such differences as may exist in responsiveness to conditioning are less general than was originally supposed; it seems likely that the conditioning schedule adopted, . . . the nature and intensity of the unconditioned stimulus, . . . and possibly the type of response to be conditioned, . . . govern the circumstances in which such differences can be expected' (Trasler 1973). It is therefore unlikely that conditionability is as homogeneous or as simple as is proposed in the theory.

Arising from these views, it is generally accepted that the basic approach to therapy must consist of relearning, unlearning or new learning, and not the removal of underlying causes. It would be naïve to assume that all proponents of learning models believe that removing symptoms removes the disorder in every case, although doubtless some extremists have made such proposals. Learning therapists do not believe that behaviour therapy with Down's syndrome children will cure them. What they do emphasise is that by helping the child to learn a different or new skill, they can improve the way in which such a child adjusts to his surroundings and to the demands which it places on him. For other forms of disorder, such as simple phobias, it would seem that symptomatic treatment is curative (see Chapter 39).

The central theme of the learning orientation, that '. . . virtually all behaviour is learned . . .' (Sherman 1973) is thus extended so that there is no discontinuity between normal and abnormal behaviour. The latter simply represents exaggerated forms of the former. The categorisation of disorders becomes an exercise in delineating and differentiating among the ways in which behaviour patterns are distorted. Reese and Lipsitt (1970) for example, present a two-fold scheme of 'desirable responses too low in strength' and 'undesirable responses too high in strength'. Ross (1974) puts forward a similar scheme, expressed in terms of 'excess' and 'deficient' behaviour, but goes on to distinguish a variety of subcategories within each. Thus, he suggests that excess behaviour can take two forms, excessive 'approach responses' and excessive 'avoidance responses'.

While it is recognised that biological factors (genetic-constitutional) are important in normal and abnormal behaviour (Eysenck 1967; Bandura 1969; Ross 1974), and that present behaviour is a function of previous learning, most proponents of a learning approach give only token recognition to them. It is argued in defence of this position that biological factors cannot be 'subject to manipulation by a therapist wishing to induce behaviour change' (Ross 1974, p. 248; Gelfand & Hartmann 1975). Treatment can only focus on the individual's current physiological state and on his current environmental conditions. However, on the grounds that physiological state is 'changeable only by changing environmental conditions' (Ross 1974), treatment focusses entirely on present patterns of behaviour and their environmental context. Functional analysis, the major approach to assessment for learning based therapies (described in Chapter 39), is based on this concept of disorders. Given this approach, it is readily seen why classification takes the simple forms illustrated earlier.

Most treatment techniques used by learning (or behaviour) therapists are direct by-products of research inspired by theories of learning. Laboratory experiments provided a set of principles and the principles were used to generate specific techniques for behaviour change which have important clinical applications.

This presentation of the learning approach to aetiology, classification and treatment is not atypical, even though there are minor variations from one writer to the next. Cognitive theorists within the learning tradition (e.g. Bandura 1974), do at least give the individual some credit as an agent in modifying his own behaviour. But the learning approach to the concept and treatment of behaviour disorders emerges directly out of the more fundamental mechanistic orientation and an emphasis on laboratory experiment.

Although behaviour therapy techniques have their roots in theories and research on learning, their use in clinical practice does not require a belief in the underlying theories or a commitment to laboratory based research. Whether or not they work is a complex, but empirical, question. Further, the fact that certain patterns of behaviour can be modified through the application of such principles and techniques does not necessarily imply that the original learning followed the same principles. The efficacy of behavioural approaches to treatment is not a direct function of the adequacy of the associated theory. If this were to be the sole criterion by which all treatment procedures are to be accepted, most psychiatrists and psychologists would be out of work.

Experimental psychology, learning theories and personality development

Experimental psychology and learning theories are not synonymous. The former refers to a style of work which has the goal of providing explanations for psychological phenomena based on scientific methods. The latter refer to one content area which has often employed a narrow concept of the scientific method. Some topics in child psychology are discussed here within the experimental psychology framework.

It is widely accepted that 'individuals will differ on almost any characteristic which a psychologist chooses to investigate' (Brody 1972, p. 4). Some forms of individual differences are considered to fall within the realm of personality and temperament. The concept of personality includes intelligence but intelligence will not be discussed here, although most of the issues apply equally to cognitive development.

Researchers have attempted to uncover (or, more properly, impose) a systematic organisation among the diversity of individual differences. Systematic individual differences are conceptualised in terms of temperamental attributes or traits (sociability, activity, aggressiveness, etc.) or in terms of types such as extraversion (Eysenck 1967) which are essentially traits which cluster together. Extraversion, for example, is made up of sociability and impulsiveness. These traits and types are further regarded as dispositions to react in certain ways both across situations and over time. That is, personality traits are said to influence behaviour. Psychological theories of personality development may emphasise the genetic-constitutional basis of personality (e.g. Eysenck 1967) in which the biological genotype emerges as a phenotype through learning experiences. Alternatively, theories may choose to minimise biological factors (Staats 1971). In the latter case, for all practical purposes, personality characteristics are regarded as learned. For example, Staats (1971) asserts '... personality characteristics, although general and enduring, are themselves learned'.

Personality theories thus choose to emphasise 'biology plus learning' or learning alone and the resolution of their differences has important implications for the way in which personality development will be understood. For this reason, it is necessary to consider some recent assessments of these competing explanations of personality.

The position adopted by Staats represents one approach to the evidence presented by trait and type theories; an acceptance of the 'facts' but recasting them in terms more acceptable to their own theoretical orientation, in this case that of S-R learning theory. An alternative tactic is to attempt to destroy, methodologically or otherwise, any evidence for the 'existence' of traits as general and enduring predispositions which influence behaviour. This latter tactic was adopted by Mischel (1968). The essence of Mischel's arguments is that the evidence for personality traits tends to be artefactual, and that, in any case, behaviour is determined by the individuals learning history and factors operating in the situation. Behaviour in any situation, according to Mischel, shows little if any relationship to what individuals say when filling in personality questionnaires. Mischel's orientation has been called 'situationism' (Bowers 1973), a position which emphasises situational or environmental determinants in behaviour. It is a position which stems directly from an underlying mechanistic model and attempts via social learning theory, to account for individual differences. Mischel has recently revised his views (Mischel 1973) but the implications of his original position need nevertheless to be considered.

Situationism has been the subject of a wide-ranging critical analysis (Bowers 1973). On the basis of his examination of the limited evidence, Bowers concludes that both situationists and trait theorists have tended to overstate their case. If total variation of behaviour is 100 per cent, then, according to Bowers' analysis of published studies, an average of about 13 per cent of this variation is due to the person (personality traits), 10 per cent due to the situation and 21 per cent to the interaction between persons and situations. What is important in this analysis is not the precise numerical values (they are based on a limited, but not a specially selected, number of studies), but the relative smallness of the variation attributable to traits and situations, the larger value for the interaction, and the substantial proportion of variation not accounted for (even allowing that errors of measurement will account for some unknown but small proportion of the variation). Bowers concludes that traits have a larger effect than was credited by the situationists, but that situations have a stronger effect than that allowed by trait theorists. But perhaps the most striking feature of his analysis is that influential contemporary psychological theories have not been able as yet to account for the major component of variation.

The recognition that traits, situations and their interaction contribute to behavioural variation does not necessarily carry implications for the origins of traits. It is possible to argue, assuming the validity of Bowers' analysis, that perhaps psychology should not be concerned with such a minor source of variation. However, given that traits (on their own and in interaction) do appear to contribute a nontrivial amount of variation, their origins and development merit further study if a full understanding of behaviour is to be achieved. Two types of theory (the 'biology plus learning' and 'learning types) have been advanced to account for the 'existence' of personality traits.

The evidence in favour of the biological basis of personality differences derives from various sources. None on their own provides conclusive proof, but in combination they lead to the strong (rather than definite) conclusion that some personality dispositions are genetic-constitutional in origin.

The study of neonatal behaviour is one recent and important source of such evidence. It is now generally recognised that from birth, the infant is a complex and organised being, and that it is more competent than was originally believed (Berger 1972; Schaffer 1974). It is also apparent that irrespective of which characteristic one chooses to observe, individual differences are present (Berger 1972). Although conceivable, it is highly unlikely that such differences in organisation and competence can be attributed to learning, at least insofar as learning is conventionally understood. In making this assertion, it is not being claimed that environmental factors do not affect the behaviour of the newborn baby. There is evidence that before, during and after birth, babies are responsive to a host of external (to them) influences which affect their behaviour (Joffe 1969; Berger 1972; Herbert 1974 (see Chap. 2); Korner 1973; Sander 1969), and that at least some of the phenomena of conditioning can be demonstrated (Reese & Lipsitt 1970). However, any attempts to explain the complexity, organisation and competence of the neonate in terms of any of the current learning theories simply lacks credibility.

Studies of early behaviour have led to a profound shift in the orientation of child psychologists which is consistent with this argument. Until fairly recently, most psychologists concerned with socialisation were influenced in their theories and research by that aspect of the mechanistic model which emphasised external causality operating on the empty organism. The personal and social characteristics of children were understood only in terms of what had happened to them. The empty child was shaped into a person by the actions of his family and the rest of his social environment. The child himself had nothing to do with this.

By 1968, psychologists, as it were, had rediscovered the child. Accumulating evidence highlighted the inadequacy of the earlier views. It is now accepted that the child must be seen as an active agent in its socialisation, and that personal and social change have to be regarded in terms of the interaction between the child and external influences (Bell 1968; 1971; 1974; Harper 1971; Lewis & Rosenblum 1974). The influence exerted by the infant on its care-givers is evident almost from the time of its birth. This is manifest in individually different patterns of crying, sleep-waking, the ways in which it succumbs or fails to respond to varied attempts at pacification and the intensity of its reactions to forms of stress (see Berger 1972; 1975; Lewis & Rosenblum 1974). It is difficult to see how learning theories are to account for neonatal individuality.

Evidence of early individuality does not on its own refute the learning theory interpretation of personality. Evidence is also needed on the stability of these patterns of individuality, but this involves major methodological and interpretative problems. On the methodological side, it is necessary to obtain repeated observations over very long periods of time with, ideally, very short intervals between observations. The evidence available to date either fails to satisfy the duration criterion, or it fails to satisfy the frequency criterion (Bloom 1964; Kagan & Moss 1962). The interpretative problem arises in inferring continuity from forms of behaviour which may change over time. For example, are the motor activity of the newborn child moving about in its crib, the active play of the 3-year-old child, the activeness of the 10-year-old in school and of the dynamic business executive all manifestations of a common underlying biological predisposition towards being active? Behaviour changes its forms over time and the inference of continuity has to be derived out of increasing variety.

The task of identifying continuities is further complicated by the tendency of different writers to use different labels for the same pattern of behaviour. Even with these difficulties however, there is sufficient evidence of both short and long term stabilities in certain individual characteristics. This is not to imply that such characteristics, when identified, are fixed and rigid.

Variability is also found but the evidence of stability is not overridden (Berger 1972; Clarke & Clarke 1972; Buss & Plomin 1975; Freeman 1974).

Another source of evidence derives from twin studies of personality differences. Such research is not without its own special limitations, but despite these, the general trend of the data is such that it would be very difficult to recast them solely in terms of learning (Berger 1972; Buss & Plomin 1975; Freeman 1974).

Within the social-learning framework, there have been various attempts to link personality characteristics in children to the child-rearing practices of their parents. The one-sided nature of this orientation (parents affect children) has already been noted. Empirical studies which have attempted to support this view are at best, equivocal (Yarrow *et al* 1968). Theories which ignore the evidence of biological factors in personality and its development can only be incomplete at best, and at worst trivial. Rather than try to account for all behaviour, it would seem more appropriate for learning theorists to discover the ways in which the principles and mechanisms which they postulate interact with genetic-constitutional factors to generate complex patterns of behaviour.

The clinician who wishes to apply the information gleaned from psychological theories of learning and personality is, unfortunately, confronted by a set of competing theories whose differences at this point in time are yet to be resolved.

Apart from Eysenck's (1967) theory, there are few approaches which have systematically attempted to link a biologically based personality theory with learning. As was noted earlier, the concept of conditionability which is central to Eysenck's formulations still lacks a sound empirical basis. It might be more appropriate, as Brody (1972) suggests, to link the Eysenck personality dimensions with the principles and mechanisms derived from social learning theories. Given Bowers' (1973) observations, a theory which relies solely on personality traits in an attempt to explain behaviour is unlikely to arrive at an understanding of complex behaviour. Similarly, a 'pure' learning orientation is likely to be unsuccessful.

Within an applied setting, there appears to be little doubt that to date, the most useful applications of learning theories have emerged from the operant approach of Skinner and the social learning orientation of Bandura and others. The choice of a personality framework is somewhat more problematical, especially in work with children. There is no doubt that the system proposed by Thomas *et al* (1968) appears to be clinically relevant. However, it is as yet incompletely developed, both conceptually and methodologically. The modification of this approach to temperament proposed by Graham *et al* (1973), while also clinically useful, requires further development. An alternative scheme proposed by Buss and Plomin (1975) reduces the number of temperamental characteristics to four, and they report that, so far, only three of these (emotionality, activity, sociability) have a strong empirical basis. The fourth, impulsivity, is still somewhat dubious (Buss & Plomin 1975). The major advantage of these systems is their explicit concern with the development and expression of personality in children, although Buss and Plomin have not linked their approach to clinical problems. Eysenck's (1967) theory of personality has always been concerned with abnormal behaviour and two of the major dimensions (extraversion and emotionality or neuroticism) appear to be among the most well validated dimensions in psychological theories of personality (Brody 1972). They appear similar to the temperamental characteristics identified by Buss and Plomin (1975) and there is other evidence that the extraversion-neuroticism pattern is consistent with the findings from independent personality studies of children (Bronson 1969; Scarr 1969). The two major difficulties with the Eysenckian dimensions are firstly, that as a typological system, it is too general to be of immediate practical value, and, secondly, that the theory has never been explicitly concerned with personality development.

While it is important to recognise the differences between these theories, the similarities are equally striking and it is not unlikely that many of the differences will be eventually resolved. In the interim, clinicians will probably use the framework most suited to their particular problems.

CONCLUSIONS

Psychological theories and methods, particularly in child psychology, are characterised by pockets of homogeneity overlaid by diversity and controversy. This state is inevitably frustrating for clinicians who require coherence. Where coherence is absent, it tends to be imposed, usually in somewhat oversimplified terms. Once this is done, the next step is readily taken, that is, full identification with an approach or total rejection. Stereotypes certainly abound—psychodynamics, behaviourism, psychotherapy, behaviour therapy, science and nonscience—as does full commitment to them.

The underlying theme of this chapter is that any orientation has to be seen at several levels ranging from its models of science and of man to specific therapeutic techniques. At each level there is homogeneity, diversity and complexity so that total rejection or uncritical acceptance are usually the reflection of an oversimplified assessment.

REFERENCES

BALDWIN A.L. (1967) *Theories of Child Development.* New York: Wiley

BANDURA A. (1969) *Principles of Behavior Modification.* New York: Holt, Rinehart & Winston

BANDURA A. (1974) Behavior theory and the models of man. *Amer. Psychol.* **29,** 859–869

BANDURA A. & WALTERS R.H. (1959) *Adolescent Aggression.* New York: Ronald Press

BANDURA A. & WALTERS R.H. (1963) *Social Learning and Personality Development.* New York: Holt, Rinehart & Winston

BELL R.Q. (1968) A reinterpretation of the direction of effects in studies of socialization. *Psychol. Rev.* **75,** 81–95

BELL R.Q. (1971) Stimulus control of parent or caretaker behaviour by offspring. *Dev. Psychol.* **4,** 63–72

BELL R.Q. (1974) Contributions of human infants to caregiving and social interaction. *In* Lewis M. & Rosenblum L.A. (eds.) *The Effect of the Infant on its Caregiver.* New York: Wiley

BERGER M. (1972) Early experience and other environmental factors: an overview. *In* Eysenck H.J. (ed.) *Handbook of Abnormal Psychology,* 2nd edn. London: Pitman Medical

BERGER M. (1975) Clinical psychology services for children. *Bull. Br. Psychol. Soc.* **28,** 102–107

BLOOM B. (1964) *Stability and Change in Human Characteristics.* New York: Wiley

BOWERS K.S. (1973) Situationism in psychology: an analysis and a critique. *Psychol. Rev.* **80,** 307–336

BRODY N. (1972) *Personality: Research and Theory.* New York: Academic Press

BRONSON W.C. (1969) Stable patterns of behavior: the significance of enduring orientations for personality development. *In* Hill J.P. (ed.) *Minnesota Symposia on Child Psychology.* Minneapolis: University of Minnesota Press

BUSS A.H. (1966) *Psychopathology.* New York: Wiley

BUSS A.H. & PLOMIN B. (1975) *A Temperament Theory of Personality Development.* New York: Wiley

CLARKE A.D.B. & CLARKE A.M. (1972) Consistency and variability in the growth of human characteristics. *In* Wall W.D. & Varma B.P. (eds.) *Advances in Educational Psychology. I.* London: University of London Press

CRONBACH L.J. (1975) Beyond the two disciplines of scientific psychology. *Amer. Psychol.* **30,** 116–127

DOLLARD J. & MILLER N.E. (1950) *Personality and Psychotherapy.* New York: McGraw-Hill

EYSENCK H.J. (1967) *The Biological Basis of Personality.* Springfield, Illinois: Charles C Thomas

FREEMAN D.G. (1974) *Human Infancy: An Evolutionary Perspective.* New Jersey: LEA

GARFIELD S.L. (1974) *Clinical Psychology.* Chicago: Aldine

GELFAND D.M. & HARTMANN D.P. (1975) *Child Behavior Analysis and Therapy.* New York: Pergamon

GEWIRTZ J.L. (1969) Mechanisms of social learning: some roles of stimulation and behavior in early human development. *In* Goslin D.A. (ed.) *Handbook of Socialization Theory and Research.* Chicago: Rand McNally

GEWIRTZ J. (1972) (ed.) *Attachment and Dependency*. Washington, DC: Winston

GOSLIN D.A. (1969) (ed.) *Handbook of Socialization Theory and Research*. Chicago: Rand McNally

GOULET L.R. & BALTES P.B. (1970) (eds.) *Life-Span Developmental Psychology*. New York: Academic Press

GRAHAM P., RUTTER M. & GEORGE S. (1973) Temperamental characteristics as predictors of behavior disorders in children. *Amer. J. Orthopsychiat.* **43**, 328–339

HARPER L.V. (1971) The young as a source of stimuli controlling caretaker behavior. *Dev. Psychol.* **4**, 73–88

HARRÉ R. (1972) *The Philosophies of Science*. London: Oxford University Press

HARRÉ R. & SECORD P.F. (1972) *The Explanation of Social Behaviour*. Oxford: Blackwell

HERBERT M. (1974) *Emotional Problems of Development in Children*. London: Academic Press

HILGARD E.R. & BOWER G.H. (1975) *Theories of Learning*, 4th ed. New Jersey: Prentice-Hall

JOFFE J.M. (1969) *Prenatal Determinants of Behaviour*. Oxford: Pergamon

KAGAN J. & MOSS H.A. (1962) *Birth to Maturity: a Study in Psychological Development*. New York: Wiley

KOHLBERG L. (1969) Stage and sequence: the cognitive-developmental approach to socialization. *In* Goslin D.A. (ed.) *Handbook of Socialization Theory and Research*. Chicago: Rand McNally

KORNER A. (1973) Individual differences at birth: implications for early experience and later development. *In* Westman J.C. (ed.) *Individual Differences in Children*. New York: Wiley

LEVINE M. (1974) Scientific method and the adversary model. *Amer. Psychol.* **29**, 661–677

LEWIS M. & ROSENBLUM L.A. (1974) (eds.) *The Effect of the Infant on its Caregiver*. New York: Wiley

MAHER B. (1970) *Introduction to Research in Psychopathology*. New York: McGraw-Hill

MISCHEL W. (1968) *Personality and Assessment*. New York: Wiley

MISCHEL W. (1973) Toward a cognitive social learning reconceptualization of personality. *Psych. Rev.* **86**, 252–283

NESSELROADE J.R. & REESE H.W. (1973) (eds.) *Life-Span Developmental Psychology*. New York: Academic Press

REESE H.W. & LIPSITT L.P. (1970) (eds.) *Experimental Child Psychology*. New York: Academic Press

REESE H.W. & OVERTON W.F. (1970) Models of development and theories of development. *In* Goulet L.R. & Baltes P.B. (eds.) *Life-Span Developmental Psychology*. New York: Academic Press

ROSS A.O. (1974) *Psychological Disorders of Children*. New York: McGraw-Hill

SANDER L.W. (1969) Regulation and organization in the early infant-caretaker system. *In* ROBINSON R.J. (ed.) *Brain and Early Behaviour*. London: Academic Press

SCARR S. (1969) Social introversion–extraversion as a heritable response. *Child. Dev.* **40**, 823–832

SCHAFFER H.R. (1974) Early social behaviour and the study of reciprocity. *Bull. Br. Psychol. Soc.* **27**, 209–216

SHERMAN A.R. (1973) *Behavior Modification: Theory and Practice.* Monterey: Brooks/ Cole

STAATS A.W. (1971) *Child Learning, Intelligence and Personality.* New York: Harper & Row

THOMAS A., CHESS S. & BIRCH H.G. (1968) *Temperament and Behavior Disorders in Children.* New York: University Press

THORESEN C.E. (1973) Behavioral Humanism. *In* Thoresen C.E. (ed.) *Behavior Modification in Education.* Chicago: University of Chicago Press

TRASLER G. (1973) Criminal behaviour. *In* Eysenck H.J. (ed.) *Handbook of Abnormal Psychology*, 2nd edn. London: Pitman Medical

WHITE S. (1970) The learning theory approach. *In* Mussen P.H. (ed.) *Carmichael's Manual of Child Psychology*, Vol. 1. New York: Wiley

YARROW M.R., CAMPBELL J.D. & BURTON R.V. (1968) An enquiry into research and methods. *Child Rearing.* San Francisco: Jossey-Bass

CHAPTER 10

Piaget: causes and alternatives

P. BRYANT

Any theory about the way children develop sooner or later has to face two sorts of problem. The first is what the developmental changes are, that is, how children's behaviour and abilities change as they grow older. The second question is what causes these changes. These are separable questions, since one could quite plausibly produce a lot of evidence about the first without throwing any light on the second.

Indeed this seems to be roughly the case with most theories about perceptual and cognitive development. The theories usually cover both questions, since they suggest not only what the differences are between older and younger children but also what leads to these differences. However, the actual evidence is usually not directly relevant to the causal question.

Nor is the reason for this discrepancy hard to find. Cognitive and perceptual experiments discover what children can do at different points in time. They are excellent for demonstrating what a child does when he is 5 and when he is 7 and thus show how the 7-year-old differs from the 5-year-old—a developmental difference. But the actual changes take place gradually and usually unseen. They do not on the whole happen in the psychologist's laboratory, and without being able to witness the changes directly it is very difficult to see how the psychologist can experiment directly on the variables which lead to the change.

There are recognised ways of trying to get around this problem. One common tack is to try to produce the developmental change in the laboratory and to examine which conditions lead to the change and which do not. Undoubtedly experiments like these can tell us what caused the change in the laboratory. But the trouble is that these factors are not necessarily the same as those which produced the change in real life. This danger is illustrated by the fact that there are several instances in the literature where the same developmental change has, in different experiments, been produced by quite different conditions which apparently have nothing whatsoever to do with each other.

239

Another approach is to do nothing experimentally about the causal question, but simply to infer from the nature of the developmental changes what their causes must be. The obvious difficulty here is that any conclusion must be indirect and thus speculative. So either way the problem remains a difficult one which ought to be recognised, even if no ready solutions are at hand. Yet, it is hardly ever discussed.

Nothing illustrates the discrepancy just described more clearly than the theories of Jean Piaget. Here is by far the most coherent, comprehensive and influential account of perceptual and conceptual development that we have ever had. His work deals with children from birth through to late adolescence. It covers an immense amount of ground, dealing with such diverse topics as the baby's original reaching for an object, the school child's grasp of concepts of number, the acquisition of moral rules, and the strength of the visual illusions at different stages in childhood. These, and many other areas of behaviour, are incorporated by Piaget in one comprehensive scheme, which hangs together in an extremely impressive manner.

Piaget's theories concern both the changes which take place during childhood and their causes. The changes themselves are primarily logical ones. Piaget's idea is that the child originally has no effective logical machinery to cope with things which happen to him. He cannot make simple logical manœuvres, such as incorporating two separate experiences into a deductive inference. He does not understand and cannot use certain logical principles, such as the principle that a quantity always stays the same unless something is added to it or subtracted from it. These and other logical abilities only come to him gradually during childhood. The evidence for these changes largely rests on a number of experiments whose aim it is to show that younger children do not have these abilities and cannot solve certain problems, while older children do apparently make the correct logical moves in the same tasks. The experiments then demonstrate in one way and another that the older child differs from the younger. They set out what the developmental changes are.

Discovering such changes obviously leads one on to the causal question. If Piaget is right in saying that the child only discovers how to make deductive inferences around the age of 7 years or so, what, we may ask, led him to this discovery? Piaget has an answer which centres around his notion of equilibrium.

Development, as he sees it, consists in a series of qualitative changes following one from the other in a step-like fashion and in a set order which is the same for every child. The child proceeds in steps from one plateau to another, and it is the move to the next plateau which constitutes the developmental change. Most of the time that the child remains on a particular plateau he is said to be in some sort of conceptual 'equilibrium'. By this Piaget means that he can account for his experiences in his environment satisfactorily. However, inevitably, he will begin to have other experiences which simply do not fit into his conceptual framework. He cannot explain them to himself, and the consequent puzzlement is said to lead him into a state of 'disequilibrium', an unpleasant state which the child does his best to resolve. In fact, he resolves it by altering his conceptual framework, and in doing so he reaches a new plateau, on which he is in equilibrium once more. However the very fact that his logical mechanisms are no longer the same will lead him into new sets of experiences, some of which will put him into disequilibrium again, and so the whole process will repeat itself.

This causal theory covers the whole of development. It deals as much with the 12-month-old's discovery that objects which are hidden from view still go on existing as it does with the adolescent's learning how to design the sort of experiment which would isolate the factors controlling the swing of a pendulum. Precisely because of its generality the notions involved are abstract, and it is rather hard to see how they could be put in a concrete and testable form. However the most striking thing about the theory is the lack of any systematic attempt to verify it or to disprove it.

This need not surprise us. It is difficult enough, as has already been pointed out, to test causal theories in development. It is even more difficult when the ideas involved are very abstract. The point must be made, because it affects the whole debate on the importance of Piaget's massive experimental work. For it means that the different aspects of Piaget's theories have to be evaluated in different ways.

When we consider whether Piaget is correct in saying that logical development takes place as it does, we have the experiments to look at, and we can ask ourselves whether the experiments really do test what they are meant to test. But looking at the causal notions is a much less satisfying task, and it brings us face to face with the question whether it ever will be possible to gather good evidence either for or against them—a question, one might add, which is not just an academic one, since Piaget himself makes it clear that it is the causal side of his theory which is most relevant to educational methods (1969).

DISCOVERING THE DEVELOPMENTAL CHANGES

Piaget's account of human development divides it into three main periods. First comes the sensori-motor period, which starts at birth and is complete by the end of the child's second year. During this the child learns about some basic properties of his environment, and of his relations to this environment.

He realises, for example, that the objects around him exist independently of him, and later that these objects go on existing when he no longer perceives them. He begins to be able to grasp simple cause effect relationships. He builds up an effective understanding of spatial relationships, and at a primitive level he even begins to understand that one thing can symbolise another. All these things however are said to be understood on the plane of action. That is to say, what the child understands is tied up in what he does and is not conceptualised or expressed in any explicit way.

The next major step is called the concrete operations period, and the major changes which characterise this period take place between roughly 5 and 11 years. These changes involve the acquisition of a set of basic rules capable of being expressed explicitly and used with a wide variety of material and in a large number of situations. The possession of these rules frees him from the domination of his immediate perception. They enable the child to make deductive inferences and thus to measure, and also to grasp the principle of invariance of quantity and thus to understand the basic rules of number, mass, weight and volume. Moreover his social behaviour changes fundamentally. He is able to understand that in many ways other people's views and knowledge will differ from his, and he learns the basis and significance of rules in formalised social situations such as playing competitive games.

Finally there is the formal operations period, which covers roughly the time of adolescence. At this time the child's thinking frees itself still further from environmental constraints. When he is younger the child is limited to explaining to himself what has happened or what is happening, whereas during adolescence he can manipulate propositions about what is possible. Among other things this ability to form and combine propositions enables him to carry out experiments in a hypothetico-deductive manner. He can work out what possible factors could control a particular phenomenon, and can also decide how to discover which are the important factors and how they interact.

The immense volume of evidence which Piaget and his colleagues have produced to support the notion of these three very different periods cannot be described in one short chapter. Luckily they are summarised very clearly in at least two authoritative books about the theory by Flavell (1963) and by Furth (1969). Instead this chapter concentrates on a few specific examples of some of the developmental changes which Piaget discovered and the ways in which he explained them. The question is how well, in these examples, Piaget's data tend to support his hypotheses about what children do and do not understand at different ages.

One of the three examples will be taken from the work on the sensori-motor period and two from the concrete operations period.

The permanence of objects and the sensori-motor period

During its first few months the baby, according to Piaget, lives in an impermanent world. At first the neonate has no clear idea of the difference between himself and his environment. By 4 months or so, however, he has made this distinction, but his understanding of what goes on in his environment is severely limited by his complete inability to grasp what happens or might happen to things which he can no longer perceive. Indeed according to Piaget he does not think that these things go on existing once they disappear from sight or hearing. Not only is he unable to work out what his mother is doing when she goes out to the kitchen. He also does not even realise that she still exists. Moreover this state lasts in one form or another for some time. He only really begins to grasp the permanence of objects by the age of roughly 12 months.

This obviously is a startling suggestion, for if it is true it means that the baby lives in an extremely bizarre and unpredictable environment, in which objects and people constantly disintegrate and reappear in an entirely inexplicable manner. It is interesting to note that the suggestion is typical of a very important side of Piaget's contribution. One of the most striking things about his ideas is the remarkable leaps of imagination which enable him to wonder whether children at different ages understand things which seem glaringly obvious to any adult, and to work out what would be the consequence if the child did not understand the principle in question.

Piaget uses two observations about the behaviour of 6–12-month-old babies, both of which are described in his two books on infancy, *The Origins of Intelligence in the Child* (1953) and *The Child's Construction of Reality* (1954), to support his hypothesis about these children's failure to understand the permanence of objects. These both concern babies' reactions to objects which have been hidden, and they can be described very easily.

The first observation was that children between the ages of about 6 to 9 months would not reach for some attractive object such as a toy, once they saw it being hidden under a cover. Though it was well within their reach and though they clearly had the requisite motor abilities they appeared to lose interest as soon as the object disappeared. Piaget argues from this that they thought that its existence had ceased.

The second observation concerns older children between 9 and 12 months, and here the situation is more complex. By this age they can solve the simple problem of retrieving a hidden object, but according to Piaget they cannot cope with a change in its position. His interesting observation was that if there are now two hiding places, say a cover and a cushion, and first he hides it for a few times in one hiding place (A) the baby will reach for it perfectly well. But when he then hides it, with the child watching all the while, in the second place (B) the baby begins to make mistakes and, in fact, typically reaches to A. Whatever it means, this observation certainly raises an intriguing paradox. For the child has shown himself perfectly capable of using visual information about the position at which the object was hidden in order to retrieve it, when he did reach for the object correctly at A. Yet when he has the same information about B he does not use it.

Piaget's interpretation of the error is somewhat complex. Again he links it to the child's understanding of the permanence of objects. His suggestion is that at this stage the baby still does not grasp this idea properly. When he reaches successfully for the hidden object after it is hidden at A he understands what then happens only in terms of the success of his actions. The baby thinks that it was his action of reaching to A which recreated the object, and that this object still did not exist when it was hidden. And this, Piaget suggests, is demonstrated by the way the baby persists in reaching at A when he has seen the object disappear at B. The baby now thinks that all he has to do to recreate it is to reach back to A.

This then is the basis for Piaget's case about what children think of objects which they no longer perceive. Interestingly the points which can be made about this evidence and its relationship to his conclusions are much the same as the points which can be made about most other aspects of his theory. The first is that the phenomena have proved surprisingly reliable. These particular results were based on observations of only three babies, Piaget's own. Yet quite large scale studies have confirmed that babies around the age of 6–9 months do not reach for hidden objects (Decarie 1962; Miller, Cohen & Hill 1970) and also that older children faced with the A then B hiding situation do tend to reach correctly in A hiding trials but to make errors in the following B trials (Gratch & Landers 1971; Landers 1971). There can be little doubt that these characteristic errors do exist.

Secondly, the observations themselves are remarkably ingenious. It seems obvious now that the error of reaching to A after seeing something hidden at B (now commonly called the A–B error) poses an important problem. But it also seems likely that if Piaget had not pointed this out, any experimenter stumbling across this curious pattern of behaviour probably would have dismissed it as an experimental nuisance.

Thirdly, there is considerable leeway between the data and Piaget's explanation of it. His explanation, it is true, is a possible one, but there are alternative explanations, and there is no sign that Piaget either considers these or in any way attempts to rule them out. There is now some further evidence that some of these alternatives might be as plausible as Piaget's own.

If we take the first pattern of behaviour in which the younger babies did not reach at all, we can see that this might have nothing to do with concepts of permanence. One possibility is that the child knows that the object is still there, but still does not know what to do about it. Just because the child can make the movements which are needed one cannot be sure that he knows what are the appropriate movements to make. Indeed there is one experiment by Bower (1971) which seems to support this idea strongly.

He looked at 6-week-old babies' reactions to objects being hidden behind a screen, but he examined not their reaching but their heart rate. He did this because he argued that heart rate is a good index of surprise. He also suggested that a baby who thought that an object existed when it was hidden behind a screen would be surprised if the screen was then removed and the object was not there. So Bower hid the object behind his screen which he then removed; for half the babies the object was still there, while for the other half it was not. Bower found that if the screen was removed straightaway it was the babies for whom the object was no longer there whose heart rate changed. The babies who saw the object still there when the screen was removed showed no such change, and therefore were not, according to Bower, surprised. This experiment suggests that the children knew that the object went on existing when it disappeared, and it also implies that the error which Piaget found had nothing to do with any failure to comprehend the object's permanence, but rather was caused by difficulties in putting this knowledge into effect.

When we turn to the A–B error we can see that this also can be explained in at least one other way. The error involves a repetition of a specific movement which has been successful in the past, and there is one good reason, which has nothing much to do with hiding, why one might expect such repetition in a 9-month-old baby. Typically he has been static all his life. He has lain, or sat, wherever he was put, sometimes for long periods of time, until someone picked him up and put him somewhere else. If someone is static the relation of the spatial position of things to his position is also static. A baby lying on his back with a rattle suspended above him is stationary and so is the rattle. This means that the baby can grasp the rattle again and again simply by repeating the same movement. He may initially locate the position of the rattle by seeing where it is, but this visual information can in a real sense be regarded as being redundant from then on, if the baby is capable of remembering the movement he made to get him to the rattle before. Because he has not moved in space all that he has to do is to repeat his previous arm movement.

Of course this strategy for remembering the position of objects in space would become hopelessly inadequate once the child began to move about under his own steam, as he does increasingly towards the end of his first year. It is no good remembering where something is in terms of the movement you made to it if you have changed your own position in space since making that movement. Thus it could be suggested that the child commits the A–B error not because he does not understand the permanence but because he has got into the habit of not bothering too much about the visual information about space. Instead he remembers the positions of things in terms of the movements he made to them. It would also follow that the baby gets out of this habit when his experiences in crawling and walking show him what an inadequate strategy this is for recording information about positions in space.

One prediction of this alternative hypothesis is that it should not matter too much whether the object was hidden or not, since if the baby is not using visual information he should still make the error even if the object is in full view. Piaget's hypothesis on the other hand since it concerns permanence, firmly links the error to situations in which the object disappears. Practically all the experiments on the A–B error have involved hiding the object behind some opaque cover. However recently Butterworth (unpublished) has shown very clearly that the error occurs also when the objects are in full view both at A and at B. He also showed that in this situation the error was very nearly as great as when the covers completely hid the object.

This evidence is probably more consistent with the alternative hypothesis than with Piaget's, although it is by no means conclusive. Obviously a great deal remains to be done to sort out this interesting pattern of errors. However, these data do perhaps show that Piaget's interpretation is only one of a possible set of alternatives, which still need to be sorted out.

Concrete operations and transitive inferences

Perhaps the clearest instance of a logical ability which Piaget thinks that younger children do not have and which is acquired as they grow older is the ability to make transitive inferences. A transitive inference involves combining two judgments about quantity to produce a third and entirely new judgment. Thus the information that $A > B$ and $B > C$ leads to the inference that $A > C$. Piaget's claim was that children up to the age of 7 or 8 years cannot make this inference (Piaget 1970). Up till that age they treat the two separate pieces of information ($A > B$ and $B > C$) as separate and cannot put them together.

Here then is a suggestion of logical deficiency which could prove extremely serious. For if a child cannot make or understand such an inference he cannot measure. All measurements must involve some understanding of the use of a common measure (such as B in the example) to connect two quantities. Nor, as Piaget is at pains to point out, can a child understand much about the ordinal nature of number, if he does not realise that because 2 is more than 1 and 3 more than 2, 3 is also more than 1.

The usual way Piaget tested transitive inference and the way adopted by most of his followers was simply to show children three quantities in two pairs and to ask them to combine them in an inference. Piaget (1970) describes this approach in the following way. 'We present two sticks to a child, stick A being smaller than stick B. Then we hide stick A and show him stick B together with a larger stick C. Then we ask him how A and C compare. Pre-operational children will say that they do not know because they have not seen them together—they have not been able to compare them.' From results like these Piaget concludes that the ability to make this kind of deductive inference about quantity does not emerge until the age of 7 or 8 years.

Again this claim is startling, again the experimental situation is an interesting one and again there are alternative explanations for the way children behave in this situation. If we take the children who fail we can see that they may indeed be unable to combine separate judgments as Piaget suggests, but that there is also another possible explanation. They may simply have forgotten one or both of the judgments which they have been asked combine. There is really no particular reason why a 6-year-old should bother to remember that stick A was smaller than stick B. So the interesting question arises whether children combine two separate judgments both of which they knew thoroughly and could remember well. Piaget's theory would predict that they could not, whereas anyone holding to the alternative explanation would have to suggest that they could solve the problem in that form.

There is also a difficulty about the children who succeed in Piaget's version of the task. It is just possible that they might not actually be making a transitive inference. They might, instead, be simply repeating a verbal label they remembered from the initial comparisons. The trouble is that the correct answer to A in the initial AB comparisons is 'larger', and to C in the initial BC comparisons, 'smaller'. Yet 'larger' is also the correct answer to A and 'smaller' to C in the inferential AC comparison. Therefore, the successful children might not be working out how A and C compare through their relationship to the common measure B. Instead they may simply be regurgitating an association in a totally noninferential manner.

How then does one ensure a genuine inference? One way is to increase the number of quantities involved from three to five $(A > B > C > D > E)$. This would make four initial comparisons $A > B$, $B > C$, $C > D$, and $D > E$. There are three quantities which occur twice in these initial comparisons. These are B, C and D, and each of these is the larger in one comparison and the smaller in the other. Thus any inference made out of these could not be solved simply by repeating a verbal label, larger or smaller. Such an inferential comparison would be between B and D.

Some time ago Bryant and Trabasso (1971) combined these two pre-cautions—about memory and about repeating verbal labels—in one experi-ment in which five sticks of different colours and lengths were used and in which the children had to learn the four initial comparisons $A > B$, $B > C$, $C > D$ and $D > E$ rather thoroughly. It was also checked whether they remembered these initial comparisons at the same time as they were asked the inferential questions in the second stage of the experiments.

This task was given to 4, 5 and 6-year-olds and it was found that all these groups were able to make the crucial inferential comparison between B and D, and that they could do so even when they never saw the actual lengths of the coloured rods. This result has recently been replicated with 4-year-olds (de Boysson-Bardies & O'Regan 1973). It was concluded that young children are perfectly well able to combine separate judgments about quantity always provided that they can remember them.

However even this conclusion can be criticised. In the paper just mentioned, de Boysson-Bardies and O'Regan (1973) suggest an alternative explanation for the discovery that children can reach the conclusion that $B > D$ on the basis of the four comparisons $A > B$, $B > C$, $C > D$ and $D > E$. They suggest that the child quickly realises that A and E are end-points, A being the largest of the five sticks and E the smallest. Then they remember that the end-point with which B was associated in the initial comparisons was A—the largest $(A > E)$, while the end-point with which D was associated was E—the smallest $(D > E)$. By associating B with the large end-point and D with the small end-point, or by making just one of these associations they conclude that B is greater than D. This, of course, would not be a logical inference, because there is no logical reason why an object which has always been compared with the largest of a set of lengths should be larger than a quantity which has always been compared with the smallest.

The objection seems valid, and one is left with the question of how to sort it out. One obvious way is to increase the number of quantities involved from five to seven, making six initial comparisons in all. But this is well beyond the child's capacity. He simply cannot remember all these initial com-parisons. Another approach is to design a task in which it is impossible to make a logical inference, but in which each of two quantities is compared to a different end-point of a series. We did this with 4 and 5-year-old children. We showed them the ends of four coloured sticks, whose absolute lengths they never saw, and we taught them that A was the longest and D the smallest. At the same time they learned that $A > B$, that $C > D$ and also that $A > D$. Then we tested their memory for these comparisons, at the same time asking them how B and C compare. If the counterargument to ours is correct then the children should have judged B to be greater than C since B was associated with the larger end-point and C with the smaller. This did not happen.

In fact most of the time the children actually said that B was smaller than C, or C larger than B, which seems to suggest that in this illogical situation they are repeating the verbal labels attached to these quantities in the initial comparisons—a result which confirms the need for the initial precaution of having five rather than three quantities.

On balance the evidence seems to suggest that Piaget might be wrong about this issue. It looks as though these children do have a basic ability to reach logical inferences. Yet is this all that has to be said about the issue? At least, one ought to add that this conclusion itself raises an interesting question. If the children can make inferences when they are given all the information which they have to combine, how do they put this inferential ability into effect in real life, where they will often have to know what evidence to gather in order to be able to make an inference? Certainly it is doubtful that they make all the inferences available to them, just as it is doubtful whether any adult manages to do this in his normal life.

There may, then, be a distinction between the logical abilities a child has and the extent to which he uses them effectively. This is a distinction which would have educational as well as theoretical significance, since if it is true that children have logical abilities, which they cannot put into effect fully, it would be the teacher's job to draw these abilities out and to show the child how to profit by them. Even if Piaget's original hypothesis about transitive inferences proves not to be right, he has done a useful job by drawing our attention to the importance of this particular logical ability.

Concrete operations and the conservation experiment

Almost certainly Piaget's best-known suggestion is that children do not begin to understand the principle of the invariance of quantity until they are 7 years old or so. Quantities stay the same when their perceptual appearance changes. A row of counters spread out still has the same number of counters and liquid tipped from a fat glass to a thin one still retains its old volume as it acquires its new shape. The quantity only changes when something is added to it or taken away from it. This is obvious to us, but not, Piaget claims, to the 6-year-old. He will think that a change in perceptual appearance is often tantamount to a change in quantity. He will judge, for example, that spreading out a row of counters actually increases the number of counters in the row.

The evidence for this striking suggestion comes from the familiar conservation experiment. Although the experiment was carried out with many different types of material its basic form never varies. It involves comparisons between two quantities. At first the quantities look exactly alike and the child usually judges them to be equal. Then one of the two quantities is changed and the child once more has to compare them. Very often at this stage the child says that the two quantities are no longer equal. Piaget argues that this means that he does not understand that the quantity whose perceptual appearance has changed still stays the same.

An example is the number task. Here the child is shown two rows of counters equal in number and lined up alongside each other in a one-to-one correspondence like two ranks of soldiers. He has to compare them and almost invariably says that they are equal. At this stage the experimenter spreads out one row (or bunches it up). Then he asks the child to compare the two rows again. Let us call the two rows in the original state A and B and the transformed row B_1. Then the whole process can be described as $A = B$, B to B_1, $A?B_1$. The results, which have always been amply confirmed in other studies, are that up to the age of 7 children usually say that there are more counters in B_1 if it has been spread out or less if it has been bunched up. They say this even though before the transformation they judged that $A = B$. Older children, on the other hand, maintain after, as well as before, the B to B_1 transformation that the two quantities are equal.

From these results Piaget draws two conclusions. The first is that the children who fail do not understand the principle of invariance. They must think, he suggests, that spreading out a row of counters increases its number. His second argument is that the children who answer correctly do grasp this principle, at any rate as far as number is concerned.

We can take these conclusions separately. The conclusion about the children who succeed is probably right, and it is interesting to note how they must solve the problem. Assuming for the moment that they do not actually count the counters, they must solve the problem by means of a transitive inference. They must combine their knowledge that $A - B$ with their realisation that the transformed B retains the same quantity as always $(B = B_1)$ to produce the inference that $A = B_1$. Thus, as Elkind (1967) originally pointed out, solving the conservation problem involves making a transitive inference as well as understanding the principle of invariance.

This analysis bears directly on the interpretation of the younger children's failures, for it means that the failures themselves are more ambiguous than Piaget suggests. They may indeed be due to a failure to understand invariance, which is Piaget's idea, or, on the other hand, they may be due to an inability to make transitive inferences. There is a certain irony in putting forward this alternative explanation since, as we have seen, Piaget himself maintains that children at this age cannot make transitive inferences. In this way, he provides the strongest suggestion for one explanation of the conservation failures which constitutes a powerful alternative to his own.

However it has already been shown that the evidence that young children cannot make such inferences is rather weak, and so it follows that this particular alternative is not an attractive one. However, there is another alternative explanation for the conservation failures which in many ways is more of a challenge. This is the suggestion that the failure is the result of an irreconcilable conflict between two conflicting judgments which the young child has no rational means of resolving.

We have known for many years that children wrongly use length as a cue when they have to compare the number of objects in two groups. As early as 1890 Binet was able to show that 4-year-old children consistently judged the longer of two rows to be the more numerous, even when it was not. They seem to use this irrelevant cue as consistently as they do the one-to-one correspondence cue which characterises the first display in the number conservation task. This must mean that they cannot know that length is a totally unreliable cue for judging number, and it strongly implies that they think it as good a cue as the one-to-one correspondence cue.

We can now consider the conservation task again. Here the child is shown first a display in one-to-one correspondence, and then this is transformed into a display in which one row is longer than the other. The first display makes him think that the two rows are equal, while the second must lead him to the conclusion that they are unequal. These are conflicting judgments, and precisely because the child thinks that length is a reliable cue, here is a conflict which he has no rational way of resolving. So it may be the case that the child understands perfectly well that $B = B_1$ but simply cannot work out whether it is the judgment about the first or the second display which is right. Unable to make a reasoned decision he simply adopts the judgment characteristic of the more recent display.

How can the two alternatives be distinguished? One way is to try to remove the conflict, by teaching the child that length is the wrong cue for number. According to the conflict theory the child who is given this sort of training effectively should then be able to solve the conservation problem because the conflict will be removed. He should know that judgments based on one-to-one correspondence are more reliable than those based on length, and so should maintain his first judgment over the transformation.

There are two experiments which appear to show something like this, one by Gelman (1969) the other by Bryant (1974). Both teach the child that length is wrong, and neither apparently teach anything about the principle of invariance. Yet in both, the experimental training procedures lead to an improvement in the number of solutions in conservation tasks, while appropriate control tasks do not. Thus there is some evidence which on balance supports the alternative interpretation couched in conflict. However, it is not conclusive evidence, because it could still be argued that in these last two experiments the training that length was wrong could itself somehow prompt the acquisition of the principle of invariance which Piaget claims ordinarily leads to success in conservation tasks.

Thus once more we are faced with a set of experiments which tackle a problem of great importance, and once again Piaget has been able to suggest that children might not understand something which is immediately obvious to any adult, a suggestion which for that very reason is extremely original. Finally once more there are plausible alternatives to Piaget's own explanation.

The fact that there is usually more than one explanation for any set of results is a commonplace in experimental psychology. It is usually accepted without comment and people will nearly always agree quite readily that it is the job of further experiments to try to sort these alternatives out. Sometimes it seems however that this concensus does not extend to Piaget's theories. This is a pity because the immense value of the theory probably lies as much in the further work which it will provoke as in the data which have already been produced.

The causal question

We are left with Piaget's ideas about causes which have been immensely influential, but which have been the target of very little direct research. Piaget argues that there are two basic mechanisms which determine the process of equilibrium and disequilibrium which were described earlier. These are assimilation and accommodation. Assimilation means the child's attempts to understand and to interpret whatever happens to him in terms of his existing conceptual framework. To quote Piaget's characteristic prose, assimilation is 'the incorporation of objects into the schemas of behaviour; those schemas are nothing other than the catcher of the actions capable of being actively repeated' (Piaget 1950).

Accommodation, on the other hand, involves restructuring the conceptual framework at the time of disequilibrium when experiences which the child has had can no longer be assimilated within this framework. It is accommodation which is most closely associated with the actual occurrence of developmental changes.

These are very broad terms, covering as they do the whole of development, and we may ask what grounds there are for believing in them. These turn out to be quite meagre. The actual evidence offered by Piaget and his colleagues tends to be negative. Its aim is to show that alternative causal notions are not valid. For example, there is the work of Sinclair (1967) a colleague of Piaget's which attempts to show that the acquisition of language cannot on its own be regarded as an important cause of logical development. Piaget's department has also tried to show in a long series of experiments that formal training is not really effective in producing the logical abilities in which Piaget is interested. These experiments are also neatly summarised by Sinclair (1974). The conclusions from these experiments can themselves be questioned on a number of grounds, but it is perhaps more important to realise that negative results such as these should not convince us that assimilation and accommodation do exist.

It really is very hard to see what evidence would be convincing. The difficulty is not only the usual one in establishing causes in development. There is also a problem of thinking of specific instances of assimilation and accommodation. Precisely what are the experiences with quantity which a young child cannot assimilate and which lead him to make the accommodation which itself is the cause of the child's acquiring the principle of invariance? We are given no idea, and we are left with the suspicion that the terms equilibrium, disequilibrium, assimilation and accommodation are really just a grand way of saying that the child must develop through informal experience— an assertion for which there is, it must be faced, very little evidence.

I conclude that Piaget's contribution lies much more in determining what developmental changes there are rather than what causes them. His description and explanation of these developmental changes is provocative and imaginative. That there are alternative explanations to his is something which in no way detracts from the value of his contribution. The experiments which his theory provoke are as much an achievement for this theory both when they do not support it as when they do.

REFERENCES

BOWER T.R.G. (1971) The object in the world of the infant. *Scientific American* **225,** 31–38

DE BOYSSON–BARDIES B. & O'REGAN K. (1973) What children do in spite of adults' hypotheses. *Nature* **246,** 531–534

BRYANT P.E. (1974) *Perception and Understanding in Young Children.* London: Methuen

BRYANT P.E. & TRABASSO T. (1971) Transitive inferences and memory in young children. *Nature* **232,** 456–458

DECARIE T.G. (1962) *Intelligence and Affectivity.* New York: International Universities Press

ELKIND D. (1967) Piaget's conservation problems. *Child Dev.* **38,** 15–27

FLAVELL J.H. (1963) *The Developmental Psychology of Jean Piaget.* Princeton: van Nostrand

FURTH H.G. (1969) *Piaget and Knowledge, Theoretical Foundations.* New York: Prentice-Hall

GELMAN R. (1969) Conservation acquisition: a problem of learning to attend to relevant attributes. *J. exp. Child Psychol.* **7,** 167–187

GRATCH G. & LANDERS W.F. (1971) Stage IV of Piaget's theory of infant's object concept, a longitudinal study. *Child Dev.* **42,** 359–372

LANDERS W.F. (1971) Effects of differential experience on infants' performance in a Piagetian Stage IV object–concept task. *Dev. Psychol.* **5,** 48–54

MILLER D., COHEN L. & HILL K. (1970) A methodological investigation of Piaget's theory of object concept development in the sensori-motor period. *J. exp. Child Psychol.* **9,** 59–85

PIAGET J. (1950) *The Psychology of Intelligence.* London: Routledge & Kegan Paul

PIAGET J. (1953) *The Origin of Intelligence in the Child.* London: Routledge & Kegan Paul

PIAGET J. (1955) *The Child's Construction of Reality.* London: Routledge & Kegan Paul

PIAGET J. (1969) *Science of Education and the Psychology of the Child.* London: Longman

PIAGET J. (1970) *Genetic Epistemology.* New York: Columbia University Press

SINCLAIR H. (1967) *Acquisition du langage et développement de la pensée.* Paris: Dunod

SINCLAIR H. (1974) Recent Piagetian research in learning studies. *In* Schwebel M. & Raph J. (eds.) *Piaget in the Classroom.* London: Routledge & Kegan Paul

CHAPTER 11

Psychoanalytic theories

C. DARE

Psychoanalysis began as a treatment devised by Freud for the hysterical conditions that came to him as a neurologist in private practice. However, psychoanalysis was also used to refer to the system of psychology developed to describe (and to explain) the phenomena that he observed in his patients (Jones 1953). There was no a priori reason why this system should include a view of development. Psychoanalysis came to include a type of developmental psychology, not because psychoanalysts wished to understand child development as such, but rather because their adult patients' free associations in psychoanalytic treatment continually brought childhood reminiscences to their attention. Freud found himself attempting to understand his patients' current experiences, especially their neurotic conflicts, as an outcome of earlier mental and life processes. From time to time Freud supplemented these retrospective reconstructions by direct observations of infants and children; he also 'treated' one child through the medium of the child's father (Freud 1909). However, Freud clearly considered such observations as of secondary importance to psychoanalytic treatment which he viewed as the only proper source of data for theory construction. His views on development were principally derived through an attempt to make sense of the present in terms of the past. '... the work of analysis aims at inducing the patient to give up the repressions (using the word in its widest sense) belonging to his earlier development and to replace them by reactions of a sort that would correspond to a psychically mature condition ... His [the psychoanalysts's] task is to make out what has been forgotten from the traces which it has left behind or more correctly, to construct it' (Freud 1937a, pp. 258–259). Essentially, psychoanalytic views on development are generalisations about·developmental course as perceived by looking back on the past, within a treatment in which a therapist attempts to help a patient make sense out of his present life, in terms of past experiences. Like all psychoanalytic theories, they constitute a postdictive system (Rapaport 1959).

Contemporary psychoanalytic theories of development are all structured by their derivation in the context of and for the purposes of psychoanalytic therapeutic treatments. When psychoanalysts use techniques other than those of reconstruction to understand child development, their work has a very different quality from mainstream psychoanalysis and is difficult to reintegrate within general psychoanalytic theory. The work of Escalona (1969) and of Bowlby (1969; 1973) are two different examples of this situation.

Psychoanalytic propositions continue to be modified, added to and amended in the light of changing analytic experience. Despite a lack of commitment to direct observation, there is no doubt that contemporary psychoanalysis has been enriched by data which have extended 'pure' analytic material. Firstly, contemporary psychoanalysts are often engaged in direct clinical work with children. Secondly, during training, many psychoanalysts are required to make regular observations and reports on an infant or young child over a period of a year. The observations are brought to seminar discussions involving several subjects, often of differing ages. Thirdly, a number of hypotheses derived from psychoanalytic proposition have been subject to formal, empirical scientific investigation.

It is uncertain what effect these three sources of childhood material have had upon the development and application of psychoanalysis. On the one hand, psychoanalysts have more experience and information about the actual nature of children than Freud had. But, on the other hand, psychoanalysts tend to use such material only in the manner of Freud, namely to confirm notions already derived from observations made in the course of psychoanalytic treatments. Data that are contrary to psychoanalytic propositions tend to be explained away. Of course this tendency applies also to many clinicians who are not psychoanalysts. Facts or observations that contradict a course of action that is normally effective or useful are not kept in focus. Such tendencies are not compatible with the development of a wholly scientific empirical deductive theory. But that is not the purpose of much psychoanalytic theorising. Bowlby (1969; 1973) has attempted to integrate direct observationally derived theories of attachment behaviour into a theory of development which is directed towards psychoanalysts as much as towards behavioural scientists. However, it is not yet apparent that psychoanalysts have made a clinical response to these concepts. On the other hand, Mahler's work (Mahler *et al* 1975), which is both clinical and observational, has been more directly used by clinicians. Boston (1975) has argued that contemporary discoveries in academic child psychology are relevant to psychoanalysis by showing that academic child psychology is producing experimental evidence to justify beliefs already held by psychoanalysts (namely those concerning the perceptual abilities and object discrimination capacities of infants and the complex subtlety of infant–mother interactions).

It is worthwhile to consider why psychoanalysis has been relatively un-responsive to empirical observations of children's development. Part of the answer lies in the nature of psychoanalysis which concentrates on the ontogeny of the subjective experiences of the self. Because of this, objective observa-tions will always tend to miss the point. The situation has been summed up in the following quotation: 'The elegance [of psychoanalysis as a theory] lies in Freud's discovery that a few simple principles can account for the most varied and seemingly meaningless behaviours; dreams, mistakes, jokes, hyp-nosis and symptoms. Psychoanalytic therapy occupies itself with finding meanings in such apparently meaningless behaviour; yet when psychoanalysts attempt to formulate their ideas systematically, they abandon this enterprise and assume the airs and graces of scientists, talk about energies, forces, cath-exes, layers: mechanical and physical analogues rather than meanings' (Loev-inger 1966, p. 432).

Experimental child psychologists in their attitude to psychoanalysis vary from hostile dismissiveness to patient or impatient respect. One tendency is to see psychoanalytic ideas as sources of hypotheses or stimuli for research, rather than as scientific hypotheses or theories in their own right. For example: '... Psychoanalytic theory has contributed significantly to progress in child psychology. It is the source of many hypotheses about personality develop-ment, and it delineated critical areas for scientific investigation' (Mussen *et al* 1969, p. 17). A similar point of view has been taken by Medinnus (1967): 'A tremendous increase in the parent–child research literature has taken place in the past decades. Several factors contributing to this trend can be dis-cerned. First, Freudian emphasis on the importance of the early years—and especially the effect on later personality and behaviour and of the child's rela-tionship with his parents during these years—led to a large body of research investigations. Although ... most of the Freudian inspired research has yielded negative or inconclusive results ... his early research set the pattern for a great many of the parent–child concerns to follow' (p. v.). However, the more hypotheses derived from psychoanalysis are put into a testable form the less they tend to be recognisably psychoanalytic. In a general form the hypotheses are not usually disprovable. Baldwin has said of psychoanalytic theory of development (1967): '[it is] incomparably rich in detail ... attempt-ing to encompass all of human behaviour within a general set of postulates, assumptions and derivations ... [but] it poses great difficulties for empirical testing' (pp. 374–376).

A social psychologist (Jahoda 1970) commented that the social anthropo-logist: '... assumes that the psychologist has access to universally valid generalizations relating to complex aspects of personality and behaviour which are not available to himself. Unfortunately, this faith is unjustified.

The only all-embracing theory of this kind is psychoanalysis. Because this meets the need of anthropologists . . . it has already been seized upon by them; in fact, a good deal of it has become so much part of their intellectual stock-in-trade that they are apt to forget its origins' (p. 38). The same could be said of the *weltanschauung*, at least in North America, that psychoanalytic notions are 'part of the stock-in-trade' of psychologists who study development. For example, the experimental investigation of children's identification with a parent derived in large part from psychoanalytic views.

Utilising this background, this chapter has a two-fold purpose. First, contemporary psychoanalytic approaches to development are summarised, mainly in a schematic tabular form. Second, note is taken of some empirical studies that are relevant to the psychoanalytic ideas.

Psychoanalytic theories of development

This subject is commonly referred to in the singular as though there was just one psychoanalytic theory of development. In fact, there are many, each with distinctive and separate features. For example, it is commonly assumed that Freud's theories of development are entirely concerned with psychosexual development (Freud 1905). However, this is by no means the case for he concerned himself with the development of object relationships and self-esteem (1914); with the development of the conscience and of ideals (1923); with the development of anxiety (1926); and with the development of defence mechanisms and self-object discrimination (1920).

The accompanying tables are an extended summary of the developmental views of Sigmund Freud (1905; 1914; 1920; 1923; 1926), of Anna Freud (1966); of Klein (1932; 1948); of Erikson (1950; 1959b); of Mahler (1968; 1975) and of Winnicott (1957; 1965).

Table 11.1   Sigmund Freud's views (1905; 1914; 1920; 1923; 1926)

Data source

1   Reconstructions in the course of adult treatments.
2   'Live' observations of children.

General characteristics of theory of development

1   Predominately phasic and psychosexual ('Development of the Libido').
2   'Cognitive' theory: development from primary to secondary process thinking occurs throughout childhood.
3   Ego development occurs from birth (1937b); superego formation occurs with the 'resolution' of the Oedipus complex.

Infant state

1 Very sensitive to stimuli and hence in need of stimulus barrier (1920).
2 Mental apparatus functions solely in accord with pleasure–pain principle.
3 Thinking totally primary process with ready resource to hallucinatory gratification.
4 Mental apparatus conceived of as akin to the adult id.
5 Absence of capacity to differentiate self and other (State of 'primary narcissism', Freud 1914).

1st year

1 Dominated by oral part-instinctual drive.
2 Use of projection and retreat into fantasy as main defence mechanism.
3 Sexuality largely 'autoerotic' (e.g. nonnutritive sucking).

2nd year

1 Dominated by anal part-instinctual drive. Sadism and wish to control object occurs.
2 Thinking largely primary process with much use of omniscience and omnipotence in fantasy.

3rd–5th year

1 Increasingly dominated by genital sexuality with increasing allo-sexuality organising object longings, culminating in the Oedipus complex.
2 Differentiation of sexes by penis envy of girls and castration anxiety of boys.
3 Ability to delay gratification increases and responsiveness to demands of reality show ego development.
4 Ability to identify with adults increased by object longings and disappointments.

5 yrs—puberty

1 Sexuality largely latent.
2 Turning towards peers and extrafamilial figures in response to Oedipal disappointments.
3 Superego development develops increasingly in the direction of accepting adult ideals and demands.

Adolescence

1 Resurgence of all part-instinctual drive longings moving towards an adult capacity for 'genital sexuality' (altruistic love).
2 Adult balance of ego, superego and id.

Table 11.2 Anna Freud's views (1966)

Data source

1 Adult and child analysis.
2 Infant observation in residential and day nurseries.
3 Long-term follow-up of children from above settings.

General characteristics of theory of development

1 Phasic theory of psychosexual development integrated with a theory of an aggressive drive.
2 Complex view of ego development especially of defences (A. Freud 1937), frustration tolerance, sublimation capacity etc.: Full acknowledgment of cognitive development.
3 Extensive reference to normality and use of notion of developmental lines of normal development (A. Freud 1963).

Infant state

1 Accepts much of Sigmund Freud's view.
2 Biological unity of mother–child parallelled by a view of the child experiencing the mother as part of himself.
3 Instinctual drive seen as oral libido.

1st year

1 Part objects perceived and given fluctuating but increasing importance.
2 Objects, although recognised towards the end of the first year, only given importance as being 'need-satisfying'.
3 Mouth used for exploration as well as libidinal satisfaction (cf. Hoffer 1949; 1950).

2nd year

1 Object-constancy established.
2 Highly ambivalent object relationships characteristic of anal-sadism with ego-attitudes of clinging, controlling and torturing.
3 Bodily independence developing.

3rd–5th year

1 Increasing object centredness of libidinal strivings replaces need-satisfying use of objects.
2 Admiration, sexual exhibitionism, sexual identity develop.
3 Child increasingly takes over from the mother for body care. Takes on adult attitudes to dirt, regularity etc.

5 yrs—puberty

1 Oedipal phase terminates with the superego becoming structured and longings for exclusive and 'sexual' relationship with parent as object wanes.
2 Sublimation capacity increases rapidly.
3 Increasing internalisation of conflicts previously enacted with parents.
4 Increasing capacity to cooperate with children and to function at school in accordance with the demands of a teacher. Can work as well as play.

Adolescence

1 Preadolescence differentiated from adolescence as a state of psychological preparation for the physically induced changes of adolescence.
2 Repressed preoedipal and oedipal longings return with part-object, need-fulfilling and ambivalent types of object-relations discernible.

Table 11.3   Klein's views (Klein 1932; 1948; Segal 1973)

Data source

Adult and child analysis.

General characteristics of theory of development

1 Stresses role of unconscious fantasies ('phantasies') created in infancy as affecting the whole of subsequent mental life.

2 Telescoped view of early childhood as the time when defences are laid down against the crucial early anxieties. These defensive techniques (above all 'projection', 'projective identification' and 'splitting') form the bases for 'psychotic' mechanisms in everyone.

3 Death instinct used extensively as an explanatory concept with a notion of envy as a primary motivation operative in early infancy and having an 'innate' quality.

Infant state

1 From the beginning of life there is a mental life dominated by fantasies of bits of the parents ('part-objects') treated as though they were comparable to the older persons fantasy enactments with whole persons, i.e. mother's breasts experienced as possessing personal characteristics and responsiveness.

2 Images of the fantasy life are largely produced from within the baby under the impact of the drives and of envy having object demanding qualities. Although internally produced these fantasy images will tend to be projected on to the outside world if they have frightening aspects.

1st year

1 First year seen as time when crucial orientation towards the major developmental tasks structure the whole of the future trends of the personality and the tendency to mental health or illness.

2 *Paranoid-schizoid position* dominates the first few weeks and months of life, i.e. the world becomes populated with fearsome, attacking, retaliatory part-objects, the origin of their frightfulness being the projected murderous destructive rage of the untamed death instincts of the baby put outside of the infant.

3 This slowly gives way to the depressive position in which the baby becomes aware that he is himself the origin of the death instincts with their oral biting and cruel qualities. Furthermore, the child being aware of his need and dependence on his mother knows that he is attacking her (all in fantasies), the baby therefore becomes filled with remorse and despair: hence *depressive position*.

4 Primary envy of the parental couple (thought as likely, in the first instance, to be represented by a part-object, e.g. as an interacting 'breast-penis' rather than as copulating adults) results in the first evidence of the Oedipus complex being perceived in the first months of life. Fears of parental retaliation for such envy are thought to contribute to the infant's mental life.

2nd year

Continued attempts to balance depressive and paranoid-schizoid positions and to manage the anxieties produced by the accompanying fantasies.

3rd–5th years

No essential additional conceptualisations.

5 years–puberty

No essential additional conceptualisations.

Adolescence

No essential additional conceptualisations.

Table 11.4   Erikson's views (1950; 1959)

Data source

1   Child and adult analysis.
2   Cross-cultural and historical studies (1959a; 1970).
3   Direct observational studies (1937).

General characteristics of theory of development

1   Epigenetic theory with each stage seen as a developmental crisis imposing tasks on the developing organism.
2   Acceptance of concepts of aggressive and sexual drives.
3   Attempts to integrate social and cultural factors.

Infant state

1   Baby considered to live and love through mouth contact with mother.

1st year

1   Stage of crisis of BASIC TRUST.
2   Beginnings of early forms of autonomy.
3   Emphasis on the 'first oral' phase being a general 'mode' of incorporative tendencies.
4   'Second oral' phase seen as one in which activity on, through and off things is emphasised.

2nd year

1   Stage of AUTONOMY VERSUS SHAME AND DOUBT.
2   Anality emphasised as an eliminatory/expulsive mode of engaging the world rather than being seen as a sensual gratification.
3   Gradual control and pleasure in control of general masculature as well as of sphincter muscles.

3rd–5th years

1   Stage of INITIATIVE VERSUS GUILT.
2   Play seen as having a role in enabling identifications to be tried out before being taken on more permanently as established identities.

5 years–puberty

1 Stage of INDUSTRY VERSUS INFERIORITY.
2 Importance given to school or comparable social institution as a source of ego characteristics themselves structuring the attitude of the person to his own instinctual drives.
3 Capacity to work as well as play emphasised.
4 Violent drives normally dormant.

Adolescence

1 Summarised as a crisis of identity or of IDENTITY VERSUS IDENTITY DIFFUSION.
2 Possibility of seeing self as existing in historical time.
3 Certainty of the self opposes consciousness of identity.
4 Experimentation in sexual role and in ideological and leadership identities takes place.

Table 11.5 Mahler's views (Mahler 1948; Mahler *et al* 1975)

Data source

1 Clinical work with severely disturbed 'psychotic' children.
2 Systematic observations.

General characteristics of theory of development

1 Accepts many contemporary 'classical' psychoanalytic views, but contributes to the understanding of the separation and individuation of the infant.
2 Emphasises the role of a complicated interaction between the mother and the developing infant.

Infant state

1 Initially mother and infant seen as being in a state of psychological 'symbiosis'.
2 The first week of life seen as being spent in a state of disorientation and hallucination described as 'autistic'.

1st year

1 0–4 months: Increased capacity to distinguish pain and pleasure and to be aware of need satisfying object.
2 4–9 months: Separation individuation beginning but *symbiosis* with a mother perceived as separate begins to be established.

2nd year

1 10–16 months: The *practising subphase*, in which the physical ability of the infant to move away from mother is seen as enabling active mastery of separation to occur; A 'love affair with the world' occurs.
2 16–25 months: The *subphase of rapprochement*. Gradual internalisation through ego identification occurs. Pleasure in physical automomy and ability to speak are mitigated by awareness of vulnerability and the limitation of power.

3rd–5th year

No characteristic additions.

5 years–puberty

No characteristic additions.

Adolescence

No characteristic additions.

Table 11.6   Winnicott's view (1957; 1958; 1965)

Data source

1   Consultant paediatric practice.
2   Psychoanalytic work with children and adults.

General characteristics of theory of development

1   Poetic evocation of child development and maternal experience in an individual language difficult to link with other approaches.
2   Accepts much of Klein.
3   Especially concerned with the development of the self and distinguishes 'true' and 'false' self-development. Also especially concerned with the capacity to be alone and to play.
4   Utilises the notion of transitional objects and transitional phenomena in order to understand the separation of the child from the mother.
5   Complex views on mother–infant interaction.

Infant state

1   Accepts much of Klein.
2   Emphasises the 'holding' role of the mother whereby the baby learns that his intense terror and anxiety will not destroy him.
3   Emphasises the need for the baby to have the illusion that his mother's care is his own creation.

1st year

1   As the mother lets the baby know that her care comes from her and not from him the child develops an ego. 'The good enough' mother meets the smallest baby's needs as soon as he feels them whereas the older baby is allowed to wait but not too long. A baby that is not allowed to feel in charge of his own need satisfaction will have to develop a premature self-help ego—a 'false self'. A baby whose needs are met too promptly for too long will not develop an ego or a self.
2   Capacity to care and feel compunction ('ruth', the opposite of ruthless) begins in the first year out of being looked after 'well enough'.

2nd year

1   Emphasise growth of love and caring capacity.
2   Rage continues to be a problem and requires good 'holding' but not usually too much patience.

3rd–5th year

Much interest in the development of the use of objects that represent mother's caring and enable the development of an internal image of a mother who is caring although absent.

5 years–puberty (1958b)

1 The child needs to be alone in the company of others whilst forming intense relationships without sexuality.

2 Uses other people for imitation and some identification but does not use love relationships.

Adolescence

The period of the 'doldrums' when the person has to await finding out who they are.

These tables (Tables 11.1–11.6) outline psychoanalytic theories of development as if they were constructed to describe development as it occurred and not, as is the usual case, on looking back. The result shows that Freud and Klein, who worked almost entirely with analytic material, tend to be represented by an account of the development of hypothetical entities. (Freud with the superego or the libido, for example, and Klein with the development of the depressive position or the paranoid–schizoid position.) Those psychoanalysts, such as Anna Freud and Margaret Mahler, who have made more direct observations of development, produce developmental notions that are more directly descriptive and apparently more open to empirical validation, although actually this is not the case. This is especially the case with Anna Freud's concept of developmental lines (1963).

The examples of psychoanalytic views included in the tables serve only to illustrate influential but differing approaches. The work of Spitz (1957; 1965), might have replaced that of Mahler, in that he too has used a mixture of psychoanalytic clinical observation work with a specific group of damaged children (1945; 1946) and direct observations of children.

Robert White (1963) might also have replaced Mahler, in that he also has added further developmental concepts to classical psychoanalysis. His additional emphasis on the role of competence in ego development provides a necessary complement to the other aspects already outlined.

The views of Michael Balint (1968) concerning the role of the mother in establishing the nature of the personality of the infant as he emerges from the first year of life, could have supplemented or replaced the account of Winnicott's views. Like Winnicott his ideas were formed as a result of a mixture of direct work with children and subsequent extensive psychoanalytic treatment of adults.

Few analysts would contradict Freud's general outline of psychosexual development, although many would not retain an idea of the libido as implying amounts of psychic energy (Holt 1967; Applegarth 1971). Most analysts accept the importance of aggression in terms of people's subjective experience of their need for self-control and their occasional wishes to hurt and damage, but this does not imply universal psychoanalytic acceptance of the concept of a death instinct (Gillespie 1971). Similarly, few analysts would deny the importance of envy as a human motivation, but Klein's view that it is a primary innate given in human development is not always accepted (Joffe 1969).

There is a general agreement amongst psychoanalysts that the first year of life must have some importance for subsequent development but there is a wide range of concepts concerning that general proposition, and certainly there is little empirical evidence to support either the general or any of the specific propositions. Thus, Bernstein concludes a review of his own and others' work on the subject of infantile influences upon adult personality by saying: 'The findings also offer evidence that a priori assumptions about the specific consequences of infantile experiences are to be received with considerable caution. In principle, the assertion that infantile experiences have demonstrable effects in later life has been verified' (Bernstein 1955, p. 43). The caution has been repeated by many experimental investigators. Nevertheless, Kline, in a thorough and extensive review of attempts to validate psychoanalytic propositions, concludes that: '... any blanket rejection of Freudian theory as a whole simply flies in the face of the evidence' (Kline 1972, p. 346). However, his conclusions mainly refer to Freudian theory about mental mechanism and not about psychoanalytic theories of development.

Psychoanalysts have become increasingly interested in the development of the relationship and interaction of the infant with the significant figures in his world, rather than with the vicissitudes of a hypothetical libidinal drive. As a consequence, the whole interest in oral and anal influences on character development, which were such a feature of postwar research, has become less. Hence, the work of Newson (1974) or of Schaffer (1974) on the interactional aspects of development become more interesting. There is a common and clearly understandable tendency for psychoanalysts to be behindhand with their knowledge of techniques and findings in experimental child psychology whilst child psychologists certainly seem rather out of date in what they take to be psychoanalytic approaches to development.

REFERENCES

APPLEGARTH A. (1971) Comments on aspects of the theory of psychic energy. *J. Amer. psychoanal. Assoc.*, **19**, 379–416

BALDWIN A.L. (1967) *Theories of Child Development.* New York: Wiley

BALINT M. (1968) *The Basic Fault.* London: Tavistock Publications

BERNSTEIN A. (1955) Some relations between techniques of feeding and training during infancy and certain behavior in childhood. *Genetic Psychol. Monogr.* **51**, 3–44

BOSTON M. (1975) Recent research in developmental psychology. *J. Child Psychother.* **4**, 15–34

BOWLBY J. (1969) *Attachment and Loss,* vol. I: *Attachment.* London: Hogarth Press

BOWLBY J. (1973) *Attachment and Loss,* vol. I: *Separation Anxiety and Anger.* London: Hogarth Press

ERIKSON E.H. (1937) Configurations in play-clinical notes. *Psychoanal. Q.* **6**, 139–214

ERIKSON E.H. (1950) *Childhood and Society.* New York: Norton

ERIKSON E.H. (1959a) *Young Man Luther.* London: Faber & Faber

ERIKSON E.H. (1959b) *Identity and the Life Cycle.* New York: International Universities Press

ERIKSON E.H. (1970) *Gandhi's Truth.* London: Faber & Faber

ESCALONA S. (1969) *The Roots of Individuality.* London: Tavistock Publications

FREUD A. (1937) *The Ego and the Mechanisms of Defence.* London: Hogarth Press

FREUD A. (1963) The concept of developmental lines. *Psychoanal. Study Child* **18**, 245–266

FREUD A. (1966) *Normality and Pathology in Childhood.* London: Hogarth Press

FREUD S. (1905) Three Essays on the Theory of Sexuality. *Standard Edition,* **7**. London: Hogarth Press

FREUD S. (1909) Analysis of a phobia in a five-year-old boy. *Standard Edition,* **10**, London: Hogarth Press

FREUD S. (1914) On narcissism: an introduction. *Standard Edition,* **14**. London: Hogarth Press

FREUD S. (1920) Beyond the Pleasure Principle. *Standard Edition,* **18**. London: Hogarth Press

FREUD S. (1923) The Ego and the Id. *Standard Edition,* **19**. London: Hogarth Press

FREUD S. (1926) Inhibitions, Symptoms and Anxiety. *Standard Edition,* **20**. London: Hogarth Press

FREUD S. (1937a) Constructions in analysis. *Standard Edition,* **23**. London: Hogarth Press

FREUD S. (1937b) Analysis terminable and interminable. *Standard Edition,* **23**. London: Hogarth Press

GILLESPIE W.H. (1971) Aggression and instinct theory. *Int. J. Psycho-Anal.* **52**, 155–160

HOFFER W. (1949) Mouth, hand and ego-integration. *Psychoanal. Study Child* **3/4**, 49–56

HOFFER W. (1950) Oral aggressiveness and ego development. *Int. J. Psycho-Anal.* **31**, 156–160

HOLT R.R. (1967) Beyond vitalism and machanism: Freud's concept of psychic energy. *In* Masserman J.H. (ed.) *The Ego. Science and Psychoanalysis,* vol. 11. New York: Grune & Stratton

JOFFE W. (1969) A critical review of the status of the envy concept. *Int. J. Psycho-Anal.* **50**, 533–545

JAHODA G. (1970) A psychologist's perspective. *In* Mayer P. (ed.) *Socialization: Approach from Social Anthropology.* London: Tavistock Publications

JONES E. (1953) *Sigmund Freud: Life and Work*. London: Hogarth Press

KLEIN M. (1932) *The Psycho-Analysis of Children*. London: Hogarth Press

KLEIN M. (1948) *Contributions to Psycho-Analysis, 1921–1945*. London: Hogarth Press

KLINE P. (1972) *Fact and Fantasy in Freudian Theory*. London: Methuen

LOEVINGER J. (1966) Three principles for a psychoanalytic psychology. *J. Abnorm. Psychol.* **71**, 432–443

MAHLER M.S. (1968) *On Human Symbiosis and the Vicissitudes of Individuation*. New York: International Universities Press

MAHLER M.S., PINE S. & BERGMAN A. (1975) *The Psychological Birth of the Infant*. London: Hutchinson

MEDINNUS G.R. (1967) Editor's preface, *In* Medinnus G.R. (ed.) *Readings in the Psychology of Parent–Child Relations*. New York: Wiley

MUSSEN P.H., CONGER J.J. & KAGAN J. (1969) *Child Development and Personality*. New York: Harper & Row

NEWSON J. (1974) Towards a theory of infant understanding. *Bull. Br. psychol. Soc.* **27**, 251–257

RAPAPORT D. (1959) The structure of psychoanalytic theory: a systemizing attempt. *In* Koch S. (ed.) *Psychology: A Study of a Science*. vol. 3. *Formulations of the Person and the Social Context*. New York: McGraw-Hill

SCHAFFER H.R. (1974) Early social behaviour and the study of reciprocity. *Bull. Br. psychol. Soc.* **27**, 209–216

SEGAL H. (1973) *Introduction to the Work of Melanie Klein*. London: Hogarth Press

SPITZ R. (1945) Hospitalism: an inquiry into the genesis of psychiatric conditions in early childhood. *Psychoanal. Study Child.* **1**, 53–74

SPITZ R. (1946) Hospitalism: a follow-up report. *Psychoanal. Study Child.* **2**, 113–117

SPITZ R. (1957) *No and Yes*. New York: International Universities Press

SPITZ R. (1965) *The First Year of Life*. New York: International Universities Press

WHITE R.W. (1963) *Ego and Reality in Psychoanalytic Theory*. New York: International Universities Press

WINNICOTT D.W. (1957) *The Child and the Family*. London: Tavistock Publications

WINNICOTT D.W. (1958) *Collected Papers: Through Paediatrics to Psycho-Analysis*. London: Tavistock Publications

WINNICOTT D.W. (1965) *The Maturational Processes and the Facilitating Environment*. London: Hogarth Press

PART III
Clinical assessment

CHAPTER 12

Diagnostic appraisal and interviewing

A. COX AND M. RUTTER

This chapter is concerned with the concepts and skills which are involved in the process of diagnostic appraisal. This is the first task which faces the clinician with any new referral and it is a most important one because it constitutes the basis of all treatment plans. Many questions have to be considered in this process: Why has this child or this family been referred and what are the factors which led to referral? Is there a psychiatric disorder, and if there is what is its nature? What are the functions and meaning of the behaviours giving rise to concern? All these and other issues need to be included in the initial diagnostic formulation if it is to be of value in planning treatment. Of course, the process of diagnostic appraisal does not come to an end with the beginning of treatment. Rather, diagnosis enables the clinician to develop a set of working hypotheses about how best to intervene. Treatment must then be monitored to enable him to know if the hypotheses were right. The therapeutic process may well lead to a clearer understanding of the problems, and the response to treatment may force a re-evaluation of the therapeutic plan. For all these reasons diagnosis and treatment necessarily merge one into the other and the process of initial assessment must be undertaken in a way which facilitates the family's engagement in and cooperation with therapy. This chapter is largely concerned with what is involved in the first interviews at the time of initial clinic attendance.

DIAGNOSTIC CONSIDERATIONS

Referral to the clinic

There are many reasons why children get referred to psychiatric clinics and many factors play a part in the referral process. While the great majority of children who are referred have some form of psychiatric disorder, the presence of disorder is rarely a *sufficient* reason for referral. If it were, all children with disorder would get to attend a clinic and numerous studies have shown that this is far from the case (Rutter, Tizard & Whitmore 1970). In fact only a small minority of children with psychiatric disorder ever see a psychiatrist and many receive no form of professional help. In part it is a question of people being aware or unaware that there is a problem. Thus, it is quite common for adolescents to experience marked feelings of misery and distress without adults realising it (Rutter *et al* 1976). In part, too, it is a matter of recognising that particular symptoms mean that there is a problem. There are many parents of children with obvious psychiatric disorder who do not recognise their children's difficulties (Rutter, Tizard & Whitmore 1970). They may feel that the child is merely 'naughty' or 'not trying' or that the child will 'grow out of it' if left alone. These views and attitudes tend to vary from week to week (Graham & Rutter 1968) and often they are influenced by particular events or crises. No notice may be taken of a desperately unhappy child until he runs away from home or swallows his mother's pills.

An aggressive child may be tolerated at school until he hits or threatens the teacher, and then what was a minor discipline problem becomes a 'real' disorder warranting psychiatric referral.

Also, to some extent the reasons for referral may lie in the parents or in the family rather than in the child himself. Thus, Shepherd *et al* (1971) compared children attending clinics and those not attending clinics, the children in both cases having roughly comparable disorders. It was found that, compared with the mothers of children with psychiatric disorder who were *not* attending clinics, the clinic mothers were more likely to have suffered nervous complaints themselves and to be worried about their children. In addition, more of the clinic mothers came from broken homes.

In the same way, a marked increase in referrals from a particular school may reflect rising tensions and insecurity among the staff (Rutter 1975). Although all the children may have psychiatric problems, the fact that they have all been referred to the clinic at the same time may have as much to do with the school circumstances as with the individual children's problems.

For all these reasons the diagnostic appraisal must focus on the social context and manner of referral as well as on the child. With children, the initial complaints do not usually come from the child himself—instead they come from a parent, teacher or some other adult who is worried about the child's behaviour. This means that it is necessary to understand the dynamics of the process of referral. Who is concerned about the child? *Why* is he concerned *now*, rather than at some other time?

Kanner (1957) has described how symptoms serve several rather different functions. First, they are an 'admission ticket' to the clinic, indicating that there is a problem to be studied. Second, they may be a signal that something is wrong within the child. Third, they may act as a safety valve, as when rebellion and defiance are used as a response to an intolerable situation. Fourth, they may be a means of solving problems as when a child copes with his anxiety about school by complaining of a belly-ache and going to bed. Fifth, the symptom may be a nuisance, as when fighting and aggressive behaviour at school cause annoyance to teachers. The diagnostic evaluation must include an appraisal of what the symptoms mean in each child referred; not only in psychiatric terms but also in terms of their meaning to the child himself, to his family and to the referral agent.

Developmental process

Children are developing organisms and any diagnostic assessment needs to be made in the context of a developmental framework: a developmental approach is necessary for several rather different reasons. First, children behave differently at different ages and it is necessary for the clinician to know the range of behaviours to be expected at each age if he is to judge what is normal and what is abnormal. Secondly, in order to assess the severity of psychiatric disturbance it is useful to consider how far there has been interference with the normal course of psychological development (Rutter 1975). Just as the milestones of sitting, standing and walking provide a guide to motor development, so there are comparable indices of social and psychological development. Thus, children develop emotional bonds and attachments which initiate the process of socialisation; they move from solitary to parallel to cooperative play and then develop friendships which deepen and persist to an increasing extent with maturity (Bowlby 1971; Schaffer 1971). Psychosexual development similarly goes through predictable stages (Rutter 1971). Thirdly, different phases of development are associated with different stresses and different susceptibilities and these must also be taken into account. For example, the toddler age period is the time when children are most likely to be adversely affected by hospital admission or separation experiences (Prugh *et al* 1953; Schaffer & Callender 1959), and adolescence is the time when depressive mood swings are most common (Rutter *et al* 1976). Fourthly, if the clinician is to understand how problems have arisen he must understand the processes which underlie both normal and abnormal development (Rutter 1975). Accordingly, diagnostic appraisal must involve an assessment of the course of the child's development as well as the current situation and current problems. It must also take into account epidemiological findings on the nature and prevalence of psychiatric disorder.

Epidemiology and follow-up

Epidemiological studies indicate that over the course of 1 year some 5 to 15 per cent of children suffer from emotional or conduct disorders of sufficient severity to handicap them in their everyday life (Rutter, Tizard & Whitmore 1970; Rutter *et al* 1975). The figures for preschool children (see Chapter 16) and for adolescents (see Chapter 17) are of roughly the same order. This means that psychiatric disorders in childhood are very common, although no more so than in adult life (Rutter *et al* 1976).

Isolated 'problems' such as fears, tantrums or nightmares are very much commoner still. Thus, Lapouse and Monk (1958; 1959) found that a third of 6- to 12-year-old children experience nightmares and a half have multiple fears. Numerous other epidemiological studies of the general population have shown the same thing (see reviews by Rutter, Tizard & Whitmore 1970; Shepherd, Oppenheim & Mitchell 1971; Tuddenham *et al* 1974). It is clear therefore that a large proportion of normal children exhibit symptoms or behaviour of a type which might well be judged 'pathological' in a clinic setting. Such isolated problems rarely merit a diagnosis of psychiatric disorder. However, even in the case of clear disorders with multiple symptoms, the same epidemiological investigations show that usually no sharp line can be drawn between normality and psychiatric disorder. Many normal children have transient minor problems of a type which, appropriately, might be regarded as psychiatric disorder if the disturbance was more severe and more persistent. In short, psychiatric conditions differ *quantitatively* from normal in terms of severity, persistence and social impairment but minor variations of the same behaviour can be found in many essentially normal children. Only a very few psychiatric conditions in childhood constitute diseases or illnesses which differ *qualitatively* from normality.

These findings have led some investigators to conclude that many psychiatric disorders are no more than temporary exaggerations of widely distributed reaction patterns (Lapouse & Monk 1958; Shepherd *et al* 1966), and hence of little importance and with a low priority for services. Certainly, this follows with respect to the large numbers of children with transient isolated difficulties but it does *not* apply to the 5 to 15 per cent of the general population with psychiatric disorders associated with functional impairment. In the first place, the disorders are associated with appreciable personal suffering and are often accompanied by serious difficulties of other kinds, such as poor scholastic attainment (Rutter, Tizard & Whitmore 1970). Secondly, there is a strong tendency for the disorders to persist over at least several years of childhood and adolescence (Graham & Rutter 1973; Rutter 1976; Stennett 1966; Zax *et al* 1968; Cowen *et al* 1973). This is particularly so with conduct disorders but it is also true for emotional disorders. Thus, in the Isle of Wight study three-quarters of the youngsters with conduct disorders at age 10 years still showed handicapping conditions 4 years later. Nearly half (46 per cent) of those with emotional disorders at 10 years still had handicapping problems in adolescence, a rate over twice that in the general population (Graham & Rutter 1973). The findings for London children over a comparable age period were closely similar (Rutter 1976). Follow-up into adult life (Robins 1966; 1972) confirms the poor prognosis on a wide range of indices (crime, employment, marriage, psychiatric state, etc) for individuals showing a conduct disorder in childhood. The adult outcome for those with emotional disorders is very much better. Early studies of shy, withdrawn or 'nervous' children indicated that very few had neurotic disorders in adult life. However, recent studies suggest that the prognosis may not be quite so good for children with severe emotional disorders, such as may be reflected in persisting school refusal (Tyrer & Tyrer 1974) or obsessional conditions (Warren 1965). With these more handicapping disorders the link with adult neurosis may be stronger, although still many children with emotional disorders develop into normal well-functioning adults.

It is clear that many psychiatric disorders in childhood are *not* unimportant problems which will soon clear up if left alone. The issue then arises how to differentiate these more severe and persistent disorders from the host of minor difficulties which affect normal children. Epidemiological and longitudinal study data provide useful guidelines on what elements need to be included in the diagnostic appraisal. First, the number of different emotional and behavioural difficulties is relevant. The greater the number of 'symptoms', the more likely the child is to have a clinically significant psychiatric disorder (Glidewell 1957; Rutter, Tizard & Whitmore 1970; Rutter *et al* 1975). Second, for each 'symptom' the more severe it is and the more frequently it occurs the greater is the likelihood of psychiatric disorder (Glidewell *et al* 1957; Shepherd *et al* 1971; Rutter *et al* 1976). Third, some behaviours are much better indicators of disorder than are others. Thus, so-called 'neurotic traits of childhood' such as nailbiting and thumb-sucking are very poor psychiatric indicators (Rutter, Tizard & Whitmore 1970), whereas poor peer relations is not only a good indicator of current disorder (Rutter, Tizard & Whitmore 1970) but also it is a strong predictor of *persisting* disorder (Roff *et al* 1972; Cowen *et al* 1973; Sundby & Kreyberg 1968). Fourth, the age and sex appropriateness of the behaviour needs to be taken into account. For example, school refusal in young children (where it is nearer to the normal period of separation anxiety) has a better prognosis than school refusal in later childhood or adolescence (Rodriguez *et al* 1959).

Shepherd *et al* (1971) have summarised the information needed to make a judgement regarding the presence of psychiatric disorder in childhood under six headings: (a) the frequency or intensity of the problem; (b) the abnormality of the behaviour in relation to age and sex norms; (c) the number of other abnormal behaviours; (d) the duration and type of disturbance; (e) attitudes to the problem; and (f) the circumstances in which the behaviour occurs. Rutter (1975) has added four criteria by which to assess the severity of functional impairment: (i) the amount of personal suffering; (ii) the extent of restriction of social activities; (iii) the degree of interference with normal psychological development; and (iv) the effects of the child's behaviour on others.

These considerations mean that the initial diagnostic appraisal must include quite detailed and systematic information about the child's behaviour over time. Another epidemiological finding which is relevant in this connection is the observation that there is only moderate agreement between different informants when reporting on the same behaviour (Lapouse & Monk 1958; Peterson *et al* 1959; Becker 1960; Sherwin *et al* 1965; Rutter, Tizard & Whitmore 1970; Shepherd, Oppenheim & Mitchell 1971; Wolff 1967; Rutter *et al* 1976). There are several reasons why these discrepancies occur. First, people vary in their access to information. This most obviously arises in relation to children's anxiety, fears and depression when parents have to rely to a considerable extent on the child's communications about his inner feeling states. It also arises with the child's peer relationships because many peer interactions take place away from the family. There is no adequate substitute for an interview with the child to obtain data on these items (Rutter & Graham 1968). Secondly, people vary in their perceptions of behaviour. What appears pathological overactivity to one person may seem only natural exuberance to another. This emphasises the need to obtain accurate descriptions of what the child actually did on particular occasions. Generalisations and value judgements are a poor, and misleading, substitute. Thirdly, it is quite common for disorders to be partially, or even entirely, specific to certain situations (Mitchell & Shepherd 1966; Rutter, Tizard & Whitmore 1970). Children may be aggressive and disruptive at home but not at all so at school; or fearful and anxious when away from the family but never with their parents. This is not just an artefact of differences between observers because single observers often report that children behave in strikingly different ways in different situations.

The finding that disorders often show relative situation-specificity has two important implications. First, it means that information must always be sought from several sources; in practice usually the child, his parents and the school as a minimum. Secondly, it implies that disorders must be regarded in *interactional* terms. That is to say the problem lies in the interaction between a child and his environment and not just within the child himself. This conclusion has important consequences for both diagnostic formulations and treatment plans. For the most part disorders cannot be viewed simply as either disease states or an intrapsychic conflict. The essence of psychiatric disorders in childhood lies in the importance of interpersonal interactions and of the social context. Therapeutic interventions must be planned accordingly.

Of course it does not mean that factors within the child are unimportant, for that is far from the case (see Chapters 1 and 2). Nor does it necessarily mean that disorders are best classified in interactional terms. Whereas there is good evidence that diagnoses based on phenomenology have good validity and convey clinically useful information (see Chapter 15), such evidence is so far lacking in the case of family or interactional systems of classification. However, epidemiological studies do indicate the strong associations between child psychiatric disorder and both family relationships and interactions (see Chapter 4) and also school and community influences (see Chapter 5). Furthermore, family variables have been shown to relate to the course of delinquency (Power *et al* 1974; Knight & West 1975) and may well do so similarly with psychiatric conditions. As a result, the initial diagnostic appraisal needs to include an adequate assessment of family life and relationships and of environmental influences outside the home.

Diagnostic formulation

Diagnosis involves picking out the key features of the psychiatric disorder, and classification means a grouping and labelling of the disorder according to the denominators which it has *in common* with other similar conditions (Rutter 1975). It is a useful thing to do both because it narrows down the field in terms of causes, treatment and prognosis and because it provides a shorthand language of communication with other professionals (see Chapter 15). However, by definition it necessarily provides a crude grouping which disregards all that is unique about the child. A further process of diagnostic formulation is required to bring out the qualities which are different and distinctive about the individual child and his family. The formulation puts forward ideas and suggestions about the biological or psychological mechanisms which might be operating, about the underlying causes and precipitants of the disorder in *this* child, about the factors leading to a continuation of the disorder and of the potential strengths and ameliorating factors which could be utilised in formulating a treatment plan.

If this process is to occur during the initial diagnostic appraisal it is essential that a *problem-solving* approach be followed in taking a history and in making observations. It is quite inadequate merely to collect a lot of facts in the hope that some sense will come of them when they are all put together. Rather the clinician must be formulating hypotheses to be tested from the very first moment he meets the family. These hypotheses may concern family interactions or the nature of the child's problems.

For example, school refusal may arise amongst other things as a result of fear of school, separation anxiety, a general social withdrawal or a combination of these (see Chapter 19). If these possible mechanisms are to be differentiated it will be necessary to ask appropriate questions (Rutter 1975). Questions on what the child is like when he is *not* at school will help to determine whether there is general social withdrawal (such as with a depressive disorder). If he is cheerful and lively then this would make withdrawal unlikely, whereas if he is withdrawn, miserable, and lacking in interest that would support such a hypothesis. Questions on whether the school refusal varies with the school situation or school curriculum will help to determine whether the refusal is associated with anxiety about happenings at school. Similarly, questions on whether the school refusal varies with what is happening at home (i.e. is worse when father is out of work or mother ill or an onset associated with mother starting a job outside the home) will point to the importance or otherwise of anxieties about the home or family. The possibility of separation anxiety can be assessed by asking about separations unconnected with school (such as when the parents go out at night or when the child stays with friends or relatives). In short, the interviewing and observations need to be specifically tailored to the issues relevant to each child's problems as well as systematically covering a range of possible difficulties and situations.

Much the same points arise with respect to individual items of behaviour (Rutter 1975). The therapist must understand the meaning and function of each behaviour and this requires an analysis of the various factors in the child and in the environment which either increase or decrease the likelihood of the behaviour occurring. As Anna Freud (1965) has pointed out, apparently similar behaviours may have quite different meanings and serve different functions and these must be taken into account when planning treatments. She gives the example of temper tantrums which may be no more than a normal motor outlet for ill-controlled emotions in a young child, an aggressive-destructive outburst, or an anxiety attack which builds up to panic. These may be differentiated by examining the associated behaviours and by a functional analysis of the prior circumstances, precipitants and contingencies of each key behaviour. By prior circumstances is meant the more long-lasting conditions which play a part in determining behaviour (e.g. the lack of communication skills which increase the likelihood of frustration tantrums in the child with a language handicap; or mother's depression which increases the child's insecurity and which initiates maladaptive patterns of mother–child interaction). By precipitants is meant the happenings which immediately precede the problem behaviours and which seem to trigger them off (e.g. the unexpected contact with a dog which leads to panic and a tantrum in the child with a severe dog phobia). By contingencies is meant what immediately *follows* the behaviour, in circumstances where the behaviour seems to bring about a predictable response (such as the parental attention which regularly comes to the child whose tantrums have an attention-seeking component). Again the process of diagnostic appraisal must be focussed and purposeful so that sufficient information is obtained on the key problems in order for their meaning and function to be determined.

The chapter so far has outlined some of the main concepts and principles which underlie the process of diagnostic appraisal. It is evident that systematic and detailed factual information is required on various aspects of the child's behaviour and on patterns of family life and relationships. In addition, the initial interviews must be designed to assess feelings, attitudes and emotions which have to be observed as well as reported. Finally, as the diagnostic appraisal will usually lead on to some form of treatment, the process must establish relationships with the child and his family and provide a modus operandi for subsequent therapeutic interventions. This means that the therapist must establish trust and give confidence but must also provide feedback so that the family are helped to look at the problem areas and to appreciate the roles expected of them in therapy. The remainder of the chapter will be concerned with what is known on the skills, strategies and tactics which are relevant to this process.

INTERVIEWING PARENTS

There is a very extensive research literature on the skills involved in interviewing (see Richardson *et al* 1965; Cannell & Kahn 1968, for good reviews). Although most of the research has been concerned with interviews in settings and with purposes very different from those in clinical psychiatry, many of the findings are relevant. Interviewing, both diagnostic and therapeutic, is the chief tool-in-trade of the psychiatrist and above all it is the skill which every psychiatrist must possess. There are serious problems to be overcome if interviews are to provide accurate unbiassed information (Yarrow 1963; Yarrow *et al* 1968), but several studies have shown that skilled interviewing can give rise to reliable and valid measures of child psychiatric disorder (Graham & Rutter 1968; Rutter *et al* 1975), of the marriage (Quinton *et al* 1976), and of many aspects of family life and relationships (Brown & Rutter 1966; Rutter & Brown 1966). The relevant skills and techniques are most conveniently described under the different purposes of the interview.

Eliciting information about behaviour, events and situations

Widely differing recommendations have been made about the best way to obtain accurate and meaningful information. Some writers have suggested a nondirective technique which may encourage the informant to talk on the issues which he thinks are important (Deutsch 1939; Gill *et al* 1954; Lisansky 1969). The assumption is that the informant's thought processes and mental associations will naturally lead to the most clinically significant material. Others have advocated a series of standard questions followed by nonspecific probes but no cross-examination (Spitzer *et al* 1964; 1970). Yet others have argued that there must be both systematic coverage of all relevant areas and flexible probing and specific cross-questioning to get an accurate picture of actual behaviour (Wing *et al* 1967). In any assessment of the relative merits and demerits of these contrasting approaches attention must be paid to the range of information obtained, its accuracy and its clinical pertinence.

These issues have been examined experimentally by Marquis and his colleagues (1972a) in terms of people's reports of what they had just seen in a short film. It was found that the interview atmosphere (supporting or challenging) made no difference to either the accuracy or completeness of information obtained (at least in the experimental situation studied in which the informants had not themselves been involved in the events). However, specific detailed structured questions produced very much fuller information than did free reporting. The effects of interview style on accuracy were very much less, but for difficult-to-remember items specific questions tended to produce slightly more misleading answers.

Clinical studies have produced broadly comparable findings. Saghir (1971) compared a highly structured interview with a more traditional free-style (but not undirected) interview in terms of their efficiency in assessing the present mental state of adult psychiatric patients. The structured interview produced much more extensive information. Graham and Rutter (1968) compared parents' spontaneous reports of their child's behaviour with the results of systematic questioning. The latter gave rise to fuller information which showed superior reliability (as indicated by the correlation between interviews by different people one month apart in time).

Cox, Hopkinson and Rutter (Cox *et al* 1976; Hopkinson *et al* 1976) are the only investigators to have systematically studied interview techniques in the clinical setting of a child psychiatric setting. They made video-tape recordings of the first interviews with the parents of children newly referred to the clinic. Interviewer behaviour and informant responses were assessed in several different ways, all shown to have satisfactory interrater reliability. Frequency counts were made of different types of interviewer statement or question and also of specified interviewer nonverbal behaviours. In addition, systematic assessments were made of both verbal and nonverbal sequences of interaction between psychiatrist and the parent. These interview variables were then related to measures of the range and depth of factual information obtained and to the range and extent of emotional feelings expressed by the parent. In terms of the child's behaviour and development and of family life and relationships, systematic questioning produced much more detailed information on a wider range of items. Unless the parents were specifically asked they tended not to give information about family relationships or the child's development. It may be concluded that what the parents think important is not necessarily the same as what the psychiatrist regards as relevant. Cox and his colleagues also found that there was no relationship between the quality of factual information obtained and the degree of emotional expression by the parents. That is, interview techniques which were superior in obtaining factual data had no necessary disadvantage in tapping people's feelings. It is evident that systematic questioning is definitely superior to free reporting when it comes to obtaining full and detailed factual information.

It should be added that supposedly nondirective techniques to encourage free reporting are considerably more biassing than usually supposed. For example, Truax (1966) found that Rogers, a major proponent of nondirective techniques, actually used warmth and empathy quite differentially in a way which influenced the patient's reporting. Other therapists have also been found to respond differentially (Truax 1968) and it is clear that apparently nondirective techniques can have an important influence on what the informant says, even though the interviewer is unaware that he is having such an effect. It has been shown that interviewers in a variety of settings can exert a considerable influence on what informants talk about simply by the timing of social encouragements such as smiles and nods, of expressions of interest ('yes', 'good', 'mm-mm' and the like) and of when they write notes (Gelder 1968; Krasner 1958; Matarazzo & Wiens 1972; McGinnies 1970). In this way interviewers have been shown to influence how much their informants talk about different topics (Kanfer & McBrearty 1962; Quay 1959; Salzinger & Pisoni 1961; Weiss *et al* 1960) and also the feelings and attitudes they express (Hildrum & Brown 1956; Insko & Butzine 1967). In social survey and research interviews, informants' responses have been readily biassed in the direction of the interviewer's expectations (Cosper 1969; Feldman *et al* 1951; Hyman *et al* 1954; Wyatt & Campbell 1950) and it is likely that the same occurs in psychiatric interviewing. An effect of this kind was reported by Newson and Newson (1963) who found that the mothers of young children gave rather different reports of child-rearing to Health Visitors than to University interviewers. It must be concluded that, whether they are aware of it or not, psychiatrists will influence what their patients say simply by virtue of when they show interest or encouragement. It is wise to use this influence knowingly in a way which minimises bias rather than to run unknowingly the risk of unconscious selective distortion.

Thus, by the way he listens, by the model he sets and by what he says, the psychiatrist can make clear to his patients the kind of information he wants (Cannell & Axelrod 1956; Goldstein 1971; Heilbron 1971; Marlatt 1972). However, in the initial interview with the parents, the task should not be entirely defined by the psychiatrist. Litwak (1956) has pointed out that the interviewer's use of words may be different from that of his informant. This consideration has implications for the order in which various techniques are used. If the interviewer leads straight into systematic specific questioning without learning the language and viewpoint of the parent, he may get misleading answers. It is likely, too, that if the parents cannot start by putting the problem in their own terms they may not feel understood. This is likely to affect both their preparedness to give certain information and their desire to cooperate in therapy.

When going on to systematic questioning, flexible supplementary probing will often be required to clarify the meaning of initial answers (Guest 1947; Shapiro & Eberhart 1947; Wyatt & Campbell 1950). However, the way this is done needs to be modified to suit different informants and different situations. It has been found that short simple questions lead to more accurate reporting of recent health events by poorly educated informants than do long complex questions (Marquis *et al* 1972b). Social reinforcement of answers (saying things such as 'Mm-mm, we're interested in that') also improved accuracy of reporting by less educated informants. But, in both cases the *reverse* applied to more educated informants.

Multiple choice, leading and 'yes–no' questions all carry the danger of reducing accuracy (Cahalan *et al* 1947; Marquis *et al* 1972a). Multiple choice questions (e.g. 'does he have tantrums once a week or twice a week?') may present alternatives which are not applicable or which do not cover the appropriate area. 'Yes–no' questions also limit the range of answers and present the additional problem that some people have a general tendency to answer 'yes' or 'no' to most questions (Couch & Kemiston 1960). Leading questions carry the danger of suggesting wrong answers. Although the biassing effect of certain kinds of leading questions may have been exaggerated (Dohrenwend & Richardson 1964), a negatively phrased leading question about an unexplored item (e.g. 'he doesn't wet the bed, does he?') is clearly unsatisfactory. Impersonal leading questions (e.g. 'was there a ... ?') are also more likely to lead to inaccurate answers than are personal questions (e.g. 'did you see a ...?'), presumably because the former requests an opinion whereas the latter emphasises the informant's role as an observer (Burtt & Gaskill 1932). Leading questions are really only desirable as a means of providing feedback that the interviewer has understood, as checks on information just given, or as a means of enquiring into areas where there may be underreporting because of embarrassment (Richardson *et al* 1965; Brandt 1972). Thus, it may be preferable to ask 'how often do you and your husband disagree about what time Johnny comes in at night?' rather than 'do you and your husband ever disagree . . . ?' in order to indicate acceptance of the fact that married couples often do disagree.

A further issue in obtaining accurate factual information is the need to differentiate between what in fact happened and what the informant felt about what happened. General questions such as 'how much does your husband help at home?' are unsatisfactory because there is an ambiguity as to whether opinions, attitudes or descriptions are being asked for (Brown & Rutter 1966; Rutter & Brown 1966). Hoffman (1957; 1960) has suggested that the request for specific details of particular recent events leads to more dispassionate reporting. It seems that a focus on the cognitive task of remembering what actually happened helps to divest the event of much of its emotional meaning. The interviewing methods of Brown and Rutter (Brown & Rutter 1966; Rutter & Brown 1966) which utilise this approach confirm that the technique enables a good differentiation between events and attitudes about the events.

Retrospective recall

Numerous studies have shown that reports about events or happenings in the past, even as recently as a year previously, are very subject to inaccuracy and systematic distortion (Brown & Rutter 1966; Chess *et al* 1966; Haggard *et al* 1960; Robbins 1963; Rutter & Brown 1966; Wenar 1963; Yarrow *et al* 1970). Considerable caution is needed before accepting as accurate a parental account of things in the past. However, not all things are recalled equally badly. Certain well-defined items such as period of gestation, birth weight, age when the child walked and serious illnesses are recalled fairly accurately. *Whether* something occurred is better remembered than *when* it occurred. Also major events are more likely to be recalled than are minor happenings; thus, prolonged hospital admissions or those involving surgery are more likely to be remembered than overnight or very brief stops in hospital (Cannell *et al* 1961). On the other hand, threatening events, unpleasant experiences or situations giving rise to anxiety tend to be underreported or less easily remembered (Goddard *et al* 1961; Janis 1958; Cannell *et al* 1961; Lishman 1974). Retrospective recall of interpersonal relationships, child-rearing practices, more subtle aspects of behaviour and sequences of events are particularly subject to systematic bias. On the whole, there is a tendency to distort accounts of the past to coincide more with current feelings and attitudes, with stereotypes of behaviour or with prevailing views on child-rearing (Robbins 1963; Chess *et al* 1966; Yarrow *et al* 1970). One study found a tendency for mothers to overestimate their husbands' periods away from home and to underestimate their children's emotional and behavioural diffi- culties during their preschool years (Yarrow *et al* 1970). These tendencies must be borne in mind when interpreting retrospective information.

Eliciting emotions and feelings

Almost all writers on interviewing have emphasised the need to establish rap- port. Rapport is a confused term but includes the notion that the informant trusts the interviewer so that there is mutual understanding and cooperation (Brown 1972; Vontress 1971). Sometimes it has been assumed that this means maximum informality but this is probably wrong (Hyman *et al* 1954). Undue informality orients the informant to a 'social' rather than a 'task' orientation. This may inhibit emotional expression because individuals do not usually reveal intimate details at a first social meeting (Miller 1952). Also there is a possibility of distortion in that informants may only express attitudes conso- nant with the interviewer's expectations so as not to disturb the friendly inter- change (Hyman *et al* 1954; Ulrich & Trumbo 1965). In addition, parents may perceive very informal behaviour as dissonant with the professional role, and so be disconcerted (Argyle 1969). How far these biasses actually occur is not known but it is evident that maximum informality does not necessarily aid rapport and the expression of emotion.

Empathy means a sensitivity to people's feelings together with an ability to communicate understanding in a language well attuned to the feelings. It tends to be associated with warmth (Shapiro 1969), and a warm tone of voice and responsive facial expression are probably important in leading an informant to feel understood (English & Jelenevsky 1971; Shapiro 1968; 1969). Both empathy and warmth contribute to the development of rapport and have been shown to increase self-exploration in psychotherapy (Truax & Carkhuff 1967). However, although at least *some* warmth is necessary in interviewing, a variety of findings suggest that *very high* levels of warmth or of behaviours associated with warmth may be disadvantageous.

Warmth may be conveyed by tone of voice, smiling, nodding and brief expressions of interest or approval (Breed 1972; Heller 1968; Reece & Whit- man 1961; Strong *et al* 1971). These behaviours, together with eye contact and physical proximity, tend to indicate a positive evaluation (Mehrabian 1971) and may encourage emotional expression (Argyle 1969; Flanders 1968;

Heller *et al* 1966; Matarazzo & Wiens 1972). On the other hand, high rates of indiscriminate smiling and nodding tend to cause informants to stop talking, perhaps because they suggest that the interviewer has heard enough or understood all (Heller 1968). Also, very warm behaviour is sometimes interpreted as a need for approval (Heller 1968; Rosenfeld 1966a, b) which may lead some informants to withdraw. Furthermore, people vary in the intimacy or social distance which they like to maintain (Argyle 1969). When two people interact it seems that they tend to adjust their behaviour to achieve an emotional equilibrium at a level of intimacy which suits them both. Accordingly, it is probably best for the interviewer to maintain an intermediate level of warmth at first and then modify it according to the individual informant's responses. This means not sitting too close (Boucher 1972; Dinges & Oetting 1972; Patterson 1968) or too far away—say about 5 feet. Sitting diagonally probably avoids the competitive ethos of direct facing and also the undue intimacy of being side by side (Cook 1970). It also allows sensitive adjustment of eye to eye gaze. Sitting behind a desk is not conducive to patient relaxation (White 1953) and an emphasis on authority probably produces too much social distance and so discourages free emotional expression.

The evidence is circumstantial and incomplete but, apart from avoiding extremes, it seems that the degree of warmth or closeness is probably not a crucial variable in eliciting emotions. Empathy may be more important. The findings from the naturalistic clinical interviewing study by Cox and his colleagues (Cox *et al* 1976; Hopkinson *et al* 1976), to which reference has already been made, indicate that interviewing styles are strongly associated with differences in the amount and range of emotions expressed by informants. First, interviewers who listened and who talked less elicited more parental emotions than those who frequently spoke and asked a lot of questions. This was particularly the case with negative feelings which were more inhibited by excessive talking by the interviewer. Second, a proportionately greater use of open questions (i.e. those requiring a descriptive answer such as 'what happened if you tried to stop her?' or 'can you tell me more about that?') elicited more emotions than a greater use of closed questions (i.e. those answerable by 'yes' or 'no' or a number, time, date or person—such as 'who looked after her?' or 'did it happen in the morning?').

Quite apart from these general styles, sequential analysis of the interviews showed that three specific techniques—open enquiries about feelings, expressions of sympathy, and reflective interpretations—were particularly effective in eliciting emotions. Open enquiries involved questions such as 'how did that make you feel?' or 'what does it feel like taking over children in midstream?'. Expressions of sympathy were mainly apparent in the tone of voice used. Reflective interpretations included statements such as 'you must have both felt kind of angry about that' or 'it frightens you'. By the nature of things reflections frequently involve warmth and sympathy and may therefore be reinforcing (Adams *et al* 1962a, b; Noblin *et al* 1963). On the other hand, this is often not the case with challenging interpretations or confrontations which proved to be less effective in eliciting emotions in the study by Cox *et al* (1976). This is in keeping with evidence from psychotherapy which suggests that interpretations which are too dissonant or which provoke too strong an emotional response can inhibit the expression of feelings (Bierman 1969; Kanfer *et al* 1960; Pope & Siegman 1965). Anderson (1968) found that confrontations given by warm empathic interviewers increased adult patients' self-exploration but those given by less warm and less empathic interviewers did not do so.

Establishing a therapeutic relationship

Less is known about the value of different interview styles and techniques in preparing families for therapy. Cox *et al* (1976) found that informants who expressed a lot of feelings in the initial interview perceived the psychiatrist as more understanding than did the informants who showed little emotion. The therapeutic studies of Truax and Carkhuff (1967) suggest that warmth, empathy and understanding facilitate therapy and presumably for this reason are also valuable in the initial diagnostic interview. Contrary to some teaching, the balance of evidence suggests that most patients prefer their therapists to be active and directive rather than passive (Bierman 1969; Heller 1968; Lennard & Bernstein 1960; Matarazzo & Wiens 1972; Shapiro & Budman 1973). This is particularly so with unsophisticated clients (Heilbron 1971). One study of admission interviews with psychiatric inpatients showed them to be less anxious when the interviewer used structured questioning rather than just open encouragements to talk (Dibner 1958). Heller (1968) has suggested that active directive interviewers are better liked because they give their respondents more clues on how to behave. Verbally active techniques also promote better subsequent attendance for treatment (Heilbron 1971; Lennard & Bernstein 1960; Shapiro & Budman 1973).

The initiation of treatment involves some kind of agreement or contract between the therapist and patient. This needs to take account of the patient's attitudes and view of the problem as well as the clinician's evaluation.

Various methods have been advocated as a means of induction into different types of treatment (e.g. Bessell 1971; Feusterheim 1972). Little is known about their effectiveness but there is some suggestion that preparation for psychotherapy may increase its effectiveness (Bierman 1969; Goldstein 1971; Heilbron 1971). It seems desirable that clients should be given some guidance on what is expected of them in therapy but there is little systematic data on how much difference this makes.

Combining techniques

It is sometimes feared that the techniques most suitable for eliciting facts make it very difficult to elicit feelings, and vice-versa. Fortunately, the evidence shows that this is not the case, although rather different approaches are needed for the two. The available evidence suggests that the overall needs of the diagnostic appraisal are likely to be best met by an approach in which open questions with minimal cross-examination are used at the start of the interview, in order to obtain the informant's perception of the problem and to gauge his style of language and interaction. This needs to be followed by a systematic coverage of a broader range of topics and by detailed questioning on all key areas. Specific examples of actual recent behaviour are to be preferred to generalisations and on the whole negative leading, multiple-choice and yes–no questions should be avoided. Although some closed questions are helpful, there should be a preponderance of open enquiries. The interviewer should be sympathetic, reflective, understanding and encouraging; also empathic and warm but not overintimate or intrusive. A moderate degree of activity and directiveness is desirable but the interviewer should not interrupt or talk excessively; neither should he be very passive. The structure of the interview needs to be sufficiently flexible for the interviewer to respond to the cues given by informants and to meet their emotional needs, while at the same time ensuring a systematic coverage of important topics.

The interview has been described as a 'conversation with a purpose' (Bingham & Moore 1924), a definition that emphasises the need for the interviewer to have his objectives clearly in mind and to 'manage' the interview in order to reach those objectives. This requires specific skills (Menninger 1962) and somewhat different approaches may be needed for different people. However, while retaining flexibility and individuality, there is a need for the diagnostic interview to present comparable stimuli to all informants otherwise their responses cannot be compared (Balint & Balint 1961). The interview serves as a standard stimulus for eliciting emotions and attitudes (Balint & Balint 1961; Chapple 1953; Rutter & Brown 1966), as well as a means of enquiring for information.

Assessing family life and relationships

Rutter and Brown (Brown & Rutter 1966; Rutter & Brown 1966) have shown that, with the use of these interviewing techniques, sensitive, reliable and valid measures of quite subtle aspects of family life and relationships can be obtained from a single interview with one parent. A methodological study was undertaken with 30 families in all of which there were children of school age or younger. For each family there were separate interviews by different interviewers with the father, the mother and the two parents together. There was good interrater reliability (r = 0·85–0·95) and reasonable agreement (r = 0·60–0·70) between husband and wife for most measures of family activities (participation in household tasks, leisure activities, parent–child interaction, etc). However, care and skill were needed in questioning if attitudinal biasses in reporting were to be avoided. Also, it was necessary to enquire specifically into each aspect of family interaction if information on an adequate range of family behaviours is to be obtained.

High interrater reliability (r = 0·80–0·85) was achieved on measures of feelings such as warmth, criticism, dissatisfaction and hostility. Furthermore, the feelings expressed by a mother when talking about her husband when interviewed on her own agreed well with the feelings shown towards him when he was present in a separate and independent conjoint interview. However, training in the recognition of emotions as well as in interviewing was needed. By the use of tape recordings and group discussions, interviewers were taught to recognise differences in tone of voice as shown in the speed, pitch and intensity of speech. Emotional meaning and the nature of social relationships (Argyle 1969) are conveyed in vocal as well as verbal aspects of speech (Alpert *et al* 1963; Kramer 1963; Starkweather 1956), in facial expression (Ekman *et al* 1972) and in gesture (Reece & Whitman 1961). Clinicians need to acquire skills in observing these phenomena and to apply these observational skills during diagnostic interviews. Noting the emotional reactions of informants is as crucial an aspect of interviewing as listening to what they say.

Quinton, Rutter and Rowlands (1976) have also shown that an interview with one marriage partner can be used to make reliable and valid judgements of the marriage relationship which predict well to later marital discord, divorce or separation. Evaluations of the marriage are very important in the diagnostic appraisal because of the relatively strong associations between marital disharmony and psychiatric disorder in the children. Of the marriages rated as showing marked discord, 28 per cent had ended in divorce or lasting separation 4 years later compared with $3\frac{1}{2}$ per cent in those without marked discord. In order to assess the marriage it is not enough to ask people how they get on together or whether they are satisfied with the marriage. Rather, attention needs to be paid to items such as the frequency and severity of quarrelling and bickering, the amount of expressed affection and concern and the presence or absence of overt tension in the relationship. Lengthy interviewing is not required (Vaughn & Leff 1976), but it is necessary to ask about irritability, quarrelling and separations and to obtain enough discussion about family activities and about the behaviour of both husband and wife to elicit feelings and attitudes about the marriage (Quinton, Rutter & Rowlands 1976).

A great deal of information about family life and relationships can be obtained from a simple interview with one parent and, indeed, this is possibly the best and most efficient means of assessing many aspects of the family. However, it is important to note those aspects which cannot adequately be assessed in this way. First, reports by one parent about the emotions and feelings of the other have only weak validity (Becker 1960; Brown & Rutter 1966; Rutter & Brown 1966). This finding alone is enough to indicate the need to interview *both* parents of children referred to psychiatric clinics. Secondly, people have great difficulty in reporting accurately even quite crude aspects of communication and decision-making (Kenkel 1957; Kenkel & Hoffman 1956; Brown & Rutter 1966). If these features of family interaction are to be evaluated (and they show some association with child psychiatric disorder—see Chapter 4), some type of conjoint family interview is required (see below). Thirdly, although parents can give accurate reports of the duration and types of parent–child interaction, they are much less accurate about the timing and sequences of interaction (Douglas *et al* 1968). If knowledge on sequences is required, as it may well be if there is to be understanding of what is going wrong in parent–child interactions, there is no substitute for some form of observation either in the home or the clinic (see below).

Conjoint interviews and observations of family interaction

The waiting room provides an important opportunity for observing family interaction which should not be missed. How far people sit apart provides information about their social relationships (Engebretson 1973) and it is worth noting if any of the family members are sitting away from or with their back to the others (making sure, of course, that this is not a function of the available chairs). The way in which the family part (if they are not all to be seen together), and the way in which they greet each other on return may also be informative. However, much can be learned from interviewing the whole family together (Ackerman 1966; Howells 1968; Skynner 1969). It provides the opportunity for immediate observation of live interactions as they occur so allowing accurate appraisal of detailed sequences in context together with the associated feelings and emotions (Cox 1975). It is claimed that the presence of young children by their spontaneity, will provide 'natural' sequences of parent–child interaction. By getting the family to discuss their problems together, it may be possible to observe patterns of communication and dominance. Only by observing the family together will it be possible to determine how the parents respond to the child's communications (sympathetically, critically, mockingly or simply by ignoring them), to note how one member tends to be isolated by the others, or to see how children and parents exert control over each other by assertiveness, sarcasm or patterns of reinforcement. For all these reasons it is usually desirable to interview the family as a group at some point during the diagnostic appraisal. However, the development of measures of family interactions is still in its infancy (Watzlawick 1966; Wells 1973) and it remains uncertain how far the observed interactions are distorted by the clinic setting and the observing (and participating) interviewer. Mildly negative feelings may be more readily elicited in a single interview (Rutter & Brown 1966) and because of its complexity the family interview is less efficient as a means of gathering a wide range of historical data. Also, some people (perhaps especially fathers and those with an authoritarian personality, Slipp *et al* 1974) find conjoint interviews stressful and one study found that the subsequent nonattendance rate was greater when interviews were conjoint rather than individual (Shapiro & Budman 1973). As a result, in most diagnostic appraisals it will be desirable to see the family both together and separately.

Various forms of structured tasks have been used as research devices to assess interaction. Thus, patterns of family decision-making have been examined by first obtaining the individual opinions of family members and then asking the family group to reach a joint opinion, either with or without knowledge of the previous individual opinions (see Chapter 4). The technique has the problem of artificiality and the drawback that the same task may have different meanings to different families. In an attempt to overcome these difficulties, more personally meaningful material may be used as the basis for family discussion (Goldstein *et al* 1968). Eventually, observations of such structured interactions may be worth including in clinical assessments of the family, but at present they remain research tools.

Because parents tend to behave differently with their children in different settings (Hatfield *et al* 1967), a home visit is often valuable. Not only may this be very rewarding in what it reveals about patterns of family life, but also it is likely to provide useful information about home circumstances and the characteristics of the neighbourhood. As a means of studying family interactions it has all the richness of conjoint family interviews but obviously the presence of the observer may alter other people's behaviour (Patterson 1972). Moreover there are the same difficulties in developing appropriate and sensitive measures of parental behaviour. Research measures are being developed (Hemsley *et al* in preparation) but are not yet at a stage when they can be applied clinically.

Assessing child psychiatric disorder

The reliability and validity of psychiatric assessments based on parental interviews have been examined in three studies by Rutter and his colleagues (Graham & Rutter 1968; Rutter, Tizard & Whitmore 1970; Rutter *et al* 1975). The interrater agreement on severity of psychiatric disorder has been high in all cases ($r = 0.81-0.85$). Furthermore, it has been found that psychiatrists and nonmedical social scientists show a high measure of agreement on these psychiatric ratings (Rutter *et al* 1975). The consistency of parental reporting was assessed by having 36 mothers interviewed on two occasions several weeks apart by different interviewers. The correlation between psychiatric ratings on the two occasions was 0.64, with 76 per cent agreement on the presence of definite disorder (Graham & Rutter 1968). The agreement between the two interviews on individual symptoms was more variable, being high for most items (e.g. stealing, worrying, tantrums, enuresis and specific fears) but rather lower for misery, unhappiness, disobedience and relationship difficulties. In preschool children, the assessments of overactivity, concentration and worrying seem to pose special difficulties (Richman & Graham 1971).

The validity of psychiatric assessments cannot be assessed directly in view of the absence of any objective criterion. However, circumstantial evidence of validity is provided by the high measure of agreement between parental interview measures and independent assessments based on information from teachers or an interview with the child (Rutter, Tizard & Whitmore 1970; Rutter *et al* 1975). It may be concluded that a systematic parental interview with a parent provides a good assessment of child psychiatric disorder.

INTERVIEWS WITH CHILDREN AND ADOLESCENTS

Most of the principles and techniques described in connection with parental interviewing apply equally to interviews with children and adolescents. However, there are differences and special considerations (Hall 1947; Goodman & Sours 1967; Rich 1968; Rutter & Graham 1968). First, the referral is likely to have been initiated by adults and the child himself may not choose to be involved in the diagnostic or therapeutic process. Often parents will have given him a somwhat misleading impression of the purposes of the consultation and the child's misconceptions are liable to block or distort communication. As a result, it is particularly important for the clinician to describe what is going to happen and what are the obligations and intentions. This applies particularly to confidentiality as the child's assumption (with good basis) is likely to be that anything he says to an adult may be discussed with his parents or teachers. With an older child or adolescent it is usually advisable to obtain their account first before seeing the parents on their own in order to emphasise that respect and attention will be paid to his point of view.

A second consideration is that young children are less able than adults to communicate their thoughts and feelings in words. This means that play and toys have to be introduced as an additional medium of communication (Werkman 1965). Useful techniques have been developed in which free play with dolls and family figures can be utilised to discover the child's feelings about other members of the family (Conn 1939; Levy 1933). This approach has also been structured to constitute more formal projective tests (Anthony & Bene 1957; Howells & Lickorish 1963), which some clinicians have found useful although their validity remains uncertain. The toys which are the most useful interview aids are those which allow creativity in terms of either artistic productions (painting, drawing, Plasticine, etc) or sequential play (Beiser 1955; Despert 1937). In order to assess young children's ability to use objects meaningfully and to engage in make-believe play it is important to have a selection of miniatures such as family figures, dolls' houses, toy soldiers, toy cars, tea sets, toy brushes or other domestic equipment (Sheridan 1969; Lowe 1975). However, elaborate toys are not necessary and it is very important not to have the room cluttered with toys and playthings (Despert 1937; Reisman 1973). The interview constitutes a standardised setting for observing specific aspects of behaviour (Yarrow 1960) so that it is important to regulate not only the form of the interview but also the physical setting of the room and the play equipment which is available. If these are not reasonably comparable from interview to interview, there is no means by which the behaviour and responses of one child can be contrasted with those of others. The use of toys, of course, does not mean that verbal communication plays no part. On the contrary, provided the language is appropriate, direct and indirect questioning is possible with even quite young children. Indeed, at least with school age children it is usually appropriate to have some form of systematic discussion about possible fears, worries, unhappiness, tempers and peer relationships (Rutter & Graham 1968). This does not mean standardised questions as the style of asking must be adapted to the child's developmental level, sociocultural background and personal circumstances. The interviewer has to convey to the child his interest in him and in his ideas, feelings and activities, but also he has to maintain enough neutrality and objectivity to observe the child effectively (Yarrow 1960).

In order to assess children's attention span, persistence and distractability, it is also useful to give the children some tasks to perform. These may range from the very informal such as drawing or making something to the more formal such as serial numbers or mental arithmetic. While these features should also be assessed as part of psychological testing, it is desirable to make the observations in more than one type of setting. For example, hyperactive children are usually much better controlled and better functioning in a structured environment. The diagnostic appraisal needs to evaluate children's strengths, as well as their weaknesses, and particularly to note how behaviour varies according to circumstances.

Some mutually agreed basis for further contact or therapy also needs to be established at the first interview. The child's perspective of his difficulties may well differ from that of his parents and any contract with him should be based on what he sees as his problems (Reisman 1973).

Reliability and validity of the diagnostic interview with the child

There have been very few attempts to assess the reliability and validity of diagnostic psychiatric interviews with children. Sherwin *et al* (1965) reported preliminary findings on a 20 minute psychiatric examination of the child. The examination evaluation correlated only moderately (0·31–0·45) with the score on a parental questionnaire, suggesting that to some extent the interview and questionnaire produced overlapping measures of psychopathology. Fuller data are available from Rutter and Graham's (1968) study of psychiatric interviews with 10- to 11-year-old children. They showed that a half-hour interview with a child who is being seen for the first time without any background information can elicit a wide enough range of emotions and behaviour for a psychiatrist to make a provisional judgement on whether the child exhibits any psychiatric disorder. Eighty-nine children were interviewed twice by different psychiatrists and the correlation between their ratings of psychiatric state was 0·89 indicating a high degree of reliability. The validity of the findings based on an interview with the child was shown by the good agreement with ratings based on information from parents and teachers. Of the children with psychiatric disorder on parents' and teachers' reports, the great majority (74–81 per cent) showed abnormalities on a personal interview compared with only a minority of youngsters (22–33 per cent) in the general population. The validity findings for psychiatric interviews with 14–15-year-olds were similar (Rutter *et al* 1976).

The reliability of psychiatric judgements on individual items of behaviour was generally good (at least 80 per cent agreement between observers) but it was noticeable that to some extent children behaved differently in different interviews. The reliability of judgements on emotional responsiveness, relationship with interviewer, poor concentration, annd overactivity was good and these items were also good indicators of psychiatric abnormality. The same was true of an anxious facial expression and a preoccupation with anxious topics but it was noteworthy that psychiatrists also (misleadingly) tended to interpret fidgetiness and mannerisms as evidence of anxiety. In fact, so-called 'tension habits' were found to have little psychiatric importance. Depressive mood proved to be difficult to assess (particularly in shy, withdrawn or unresponsive children who spoke little) but in spite of only moderate reliability it was a good sign of psychiatric disorder. Interestingly, many of the children with conduct or delinquency problems also showed mood disturbance. The psychiatric interview with the child was found to be especially important for the detection of depression in adolescents (Rutter *et al* 1976). Often parents and teachers were unaware of teenagers' marked feelings of misery and self-depreciation.

Play

Clinically a great deal can be learned about a child's development by asking about and observing his play. Particularly with young children, play warrants special attention in both the parental interview and the interview with the child, and it is the aspect most often overlooked by the novice. Many errors in the diagnosis of mental retardation could be avoided by proper attention to play (Rutter & Martin 1972). Both parents and doctors tend to place a disproportionate emphasis on speech and motor milestones which constitute a most uncertain guide to intellectual level. On the other hand, although a child's play is inevitably influenced by the toys and opportunities available to him, a lot can be learned by careful questioning and observation. In observing the child himself, particular attention should be paid to the way he approaches a new toy or task; to the extent to which he is curious and interested in objects; to his skill in understanding how things work; to his constructional abilities and most of all to the degree of system and logic he uses in finding out how to use or manipulate objects, toys or implements. Similarly, it is informative to ask parents about how the child usually spends his time and about his use of toys and pattern of play. Does he investigate what toys will do and does he understand how they should be used? Does he push a toy car along the floor or does he put it in his mouth? Does he use toys only in a stereotyped way or does he develop their uses to make a game? Does he investigate and explore things and find out how they work?

Children's games involving meaningful use of objects and make-believe play also reflect a child's knowledge of verbal concepts or 'inner language' (Sheridan 1969; Rutter 1972), an important point in the assessment of children delayed in speech. By the age of 18 months or so children should be able to use real objects such as a hair brush, spoon or cup in a way which indicates that they have understood their use, and by their second birthday they should be able to do the same thing with miniature toys. The parent may be asked whether the child 'talks' into a toy telephone or just takes it apart. In the clinic the same functions may be assessed by handing the child objects such as a baby's brush and comb, a doll or a toy car and observing what he does with them. Imaginative play should be progressing during the third and fourth years and by enquiry and observation the clinician should find out whether the child puts dolls to bed, plays tea-parties, has battles with toy soldiers or has other make-believe games.

Quite apart from reflecting language development and intellectual skills, play is a rich source of data on the child's feelings and thoughts and on his social relationships (Millar 1968). Particularly during the preschool years, a child's fantasy play may closely reflect his current concerns and anxieties. It is not that what occurs in his play actually happened but rather that his wishes, fears and attitudes are often reflected in the imaginary situations he portrays in his play. Interpretation of these requires some knowledge of the child and the clinician should not leap to conclusions too quickly on the basis of his own fantasies rather than those of the child. Even so, much can be learned by observation of fantasy play, and with an adult he trusts a child may come to express his feelings fairly overtly using the conventions of putting his thoughts into the characters in the game.

Neurological screening

Because of the important associations between organic brain dysfunction and psychiatric disorder in children (see Chapter 8), a neurological screening examination should always form part of the psychiatric diagnostic appraisal. With younger children this can be largely done within the context of play without any loss of rigour (Goodman & Sours 1967). Also no undressing other than baring the arms and removing shoes and socks is necessary. The important thing is to decide which elements of the neurological examination are useful in *screening* for the presence of abnormality, as distinct from diagnosing the condition once a neurological disorder has been shown to be present (Rutter, Graham & Yule 1970; Touwen & Prechtl 1970). In terms of an adult-style examination, the main items which should be retained are inspection of the movements of eyes, tongue and face; testing of hearing and vision; distal-limb power, tone and coordination; posture, gait and balance; deep tendon reflexes; plantar responses; and fundal examination.

The last two items are best left to the end as the ones least likely to be accepted easily by the child. The testing of sensation to touch, pain, vibration and temperature is usually unrewarding and time consuming and can safely be omitted from a screening procedure. The same applies to some of the cranial nerve examinations, to abdominal reflexes and to proximal muscle power and tone. Of course if the screening examination shows abnormalities, a full neurological examination should be undertaken but not all elements are equally important in screening.

In addition, however, there are a number of other tests which should be included in screening. These all refer to neuro-developmental features in which function has to be assessed quantitatively in relation to the child's chronological and mental age. Among the most important are assessment of speech and language (Rutter 1972; Rutter, Graham & Yule 1970), of clumsiness (Walton *et al* 1962; Gubbay *et al* 1965), visuo-motor disabilities (Brenner *et al* 1967; Walker 1965), associated or mirror movements (Fog & Fog 1963) and involuntary movements (Touwen & Prechtl 1970). Some people have also included tests of response to multiple or complex sensory input (Ozer 1968). Although many of these are included in the groups of so-called 'soft signs', they can be observed reliably (Rutter, Graham & Yule 1970). The 'softness' of the signs lies in the difficulties of interpretation and the uncertain association with structural brain damage.

If any clinical abnormalities are found in these neuro-developmental features, it may well be important to quantify the abnormality more exactly by the variety of neuropsychological tests devised for this purpose (see Rutter, Graham & Yule 1970).

OTHER DATA

Because children often behave differently in different situations (see above), it will almost always be necessary to obtain an account of the child's behaviour, attainments, attitudes and relationships at school. In the first instance, this may be gathered by asking the school for a report. Usually the information will be more focussed and relevant if the school knows the particular questions and issues on which data are required. In addition to free comment by teachers it is sometimes useful to have more standardised (but necessarily less individualised) information in the form of a behavioural questionnaire. In Britain, Rutter (Rutter 1967; 1976; Rutter, Tizard & Whitmore 1970; Rutter *et al* 1975) has developed a short scale which has been shown to have satisfactory reliability and validity as a screening instrument (although not for individual diagnosis). A longer scale with more complicated scoring has been produced by Stott (1963) and others have been developed in the USA (e.g. Conners 1969).

If the child shows problems at school, fuller information will usually be required and this is best obtained through personal contact (by telephone or interview) with the teachers who know the child best. The object is not just to gather data on the child's behaviour but to understand the school's point of view and perception of the situation, to discover teachers' attitudes and responses to the child, to appreciate the nature of the school environment, to assess the qualities of the child's interactions with staff and pupils, and to establish the basis for the school's involvement in therapy if this seems appropriate. The principles and issues are closely similar to those already discussed in relation to parents and families and, as with the home, observations are sometimes needed in addition to interviews.

Depending on circumstances, other sources of data may also need to be tapped. The family doctor may have useful information on the process of referral, on family circumstances, on past treatment and on current medication which have not been included in the referral letter. Similarly, social services may already have had contact with the family. The same applies to health visitors, education welfare workers, and a variety of voluntary agencies. Again, contacts need to be used to gain their perception of the problem and to establish a basis for treatment as well as to obtain information on the referral problem.

CONCLUSIONS

No attempt has been made in this chapter to provide a 'cook-book' description of how to carry out a diagnostic appraisal. Many useful suggestions on what to do in practice are available in the papers and books to which reference has been made. It will be appreciated that art as well as science are needed if the initial interviews are to serve their purpose optimally. However, as indicated by the research reviewed in this chapter, epidemiological and other investigations have produced useful pointers on the nature of child psychiatric disorder which have implications for the strategies to be employed in making a diagnostic appraisal. Furthermore, studies of interviewing styles and techniques have already provided important leads as to how to set about interviewing children and their families.

Knowledge is most deficient on the ways in which the initial contact can facilitate engagement in therapy.

REFERENCES

ACKERMAN N.W. (1966) *Treating the Troubled Family*. New York: Basic Books
ADAMS H.E., BUTLER J. & NOBLIN C.D. (1962a) Effects of psychoanalytically derived interpretations: a verbal conditioning paradigm. *Psychol. Rep.* **10,** 691–694
ADAMS H.E., NOBLIN C.D., BUTLER J.R. & TIMMONS E.O. (1962b) The differential

effect of psychoanalytically derived interpretations and verbal conditioning in schizophrenics. *Psychol. Rep.* **11**, 195–198

ALPERT M., KURTZBERG R.L. & FRIEDHOFF A.J. (1963) Transient voice changes associated with emotional stimuli. *Arch. gen. Psychiat.* **8**, 362–365

ANDERSON S.C. (1968) Effects of confrontation by high-and-low functioning therapists. *J. Counsel. Psychol.* **15**, 411–416

ANTHONY E.J. & BENE E. (1957) A technique for the objective assessment of the child's family relationships. *J. ment. Sci.* **103**, 541–555

ARGYLE M. (1969) *Social Interaction*. London: Methuen

BALINT M. & BALINT E. (1961) *Psychotherapeutic Techniques in Medicine*. London: Tavistock Publications

BECKER W.C. (1960) The relationships of factors in parental ratings of self and each other to the behavior of kindergarten children as rated by mothers, fathers, and teachers. *J. Consult. Psychol.* **24**, 507–527

BEISER H.R. (1955) Play equipment for diagnosis and therapy in therapeutic play techniques. *Amer. J. Orthopsychiat.* **25**, 761–770

BESSELL R. (1971) *Interviewing and Counselling*. London: Batsford

BIERMAN R. (1969) Dimensions of interpersonal facilitation in psychotherapy and child development. *Psychol. Bull.* **72**, 338–352

BINGHAM W.V. & MOORE B.V. (1924) *How to Interview*. New York: Harper

BOUCHER M.L. (1972) Effect of seating distance on interpersonal attraction in an interview situation. *J. Cons. Clin. Psychol.* **38**, 15–19

BOWLBY J. (1971) *Attachment and Loss*, vol. 1: *Attachment*. Harmondsworth: Penguin

BRANDT R.M. (1972) *Studying Behaviour in Natural Settings*. New York: Holt, Rinehart & Winston

BREED G. (1972) The effect of intimacy: reciprocity or reatreat? *Br. J. Soc. cllin. Psychol.* **11**, 135–142

BRENNER M.W., GILLMAN S., ZANGWILL O.L. & FARRELL M. (1967) Visuo-motor disability in school children. *Brit. med. J.* **4**, 259–262

BROWN B.M. (1972) The multiple techniques of broad spectrum psychotherapy. *In* Lazarus A.A. (ed.) *Clinical Behavior Therapy*. New York: Brunner/Mazel

BROWN G.W. & RUTTER M. (1966) The measurement of family activities and relationships: a methodological study. *Hum. Rel.* **19**, 241–263

BURTT H.E. & GASKILL H.V. (1932) Suggestibility and the form of the question. *J. Appl. Psychol.* **16**, 358–373

CAHALAN D., TAMULONIS V. & VERNER H. (1947) Interviewer bias involved in certain types of opinion survey questions. *Int. J. Opin. Att. Res.* **1**, 63–77

CANNELL C.F. & AXELROD M. (1956) The respondent reports on the interview. *Am. J. Sociol.* **62**, 177–181

CANNELL C.F., FISHER G. & BAKKER T. (1961) Reporting of hospitalization in the health interview survey. *Health Statistics, Series D*, No. 4 (reprinted in *Vital and Health Statistics 1965*, Series 2, No. 6). US Dept. Health, Educ. and Welfare, Public Health Service

CANNELL C.F. & KAHN R.L. (1968) Interviewing. *In* Lindzey G. & Aronson F. (eds.) *Handbook of Social Psychology*, vol. 2. 2nd edn. Cambridge, Massachusetts: Addison-Wesley

CHAPPLE E.D. (1953) The standard experimental (stress) interview as used in interaction chronograph investigations. *Hum. Org.* **12**, 23–32

CHESS S., THOMAS A. & BIRCH H.G. (1966) Distortions in developmental reporting made by parents of behaviorally disturbed children. *J. Amer. Acad. Child Psychiat.* **5,** 226–234

CONN J.H. (1939) The play interview: a method of studying children's attitudes. *Amer. J. Dis. Child.* **58,** 1199–1214

CONNERS C.K. (1969) A teacher rating scale for use in drug studies with children. *Amer. J. Psychiat.* **126,** 884–888

COOK M. (1970) Experiments on orientation and proxemics. *Hum. Rel.* **23,** 66–76

COSPER R. (1969) Interviewer bias in a study of drinking practices. *Quart. J. Stud. Alc.* **30,** 152–157

COUCH A. & KEMISTON K. (1960) Yeasayers and Naysayers. *J. Abnorm. Soc. Psychol.* **60,** 151–174

COWEN E.L., PEDERSON A., BABIGIAN H., IZZO L.D. & TROST M.A. (1973) Long-term follow-up of early detected vulnerable children. *J. Cons. Clin. Psychol.* **41,** 438–446

COX A. (1975) The assessment of parental behaviour. *J. Child Psychol. Psychiat.* **16,** 255–259

COX A., HOPKINSON K.F. & RUTTER M. (1976) Psychiatric interview techniques. Part 1. (In preparation)

DESPERT J.L. (1937) Technical approaches used in the study and treatment of emotional problems in children. 5. The playroom. *Psychiat. Quart.* **11,** 677–693

DEUTSCH F. (1939) The associative anamnesis. *Psychoanalytic Quart.* **8,** 354–381

DIBNER A.S. (1958) Ambiguity and anxiety. *J. Abnorm. Soc. Psychol.* **56,** 165–174

DINGES N.G. & OETTING E.R. (1972) Interaction distance and anxiety in the counselling dyad. *J. Counsel. Psychol.* **19,** 146–149

DOHRENWEND B.S. & RICHARDSON S.A. (1964) A use for leading questions in research interviewing. *Hum. Org.* **23,** 76–77

DOUGLAS J.W.B., LAWSON A., COOPER, J.E. and COOPER E. (1968) Family interaction and the activities of young children. *J. Child Psychol. Psychiat.* **9,** 157–171

EKMAN P., FRIESEN W.V. & ELLSWORTH P. (1972) *Emotion in the Human Face: Guidelines for research and an integration of findings.* New York: Pergamon

ENGEBRETSON D.E. (1973) Human territorial behaviour: the role of interaction distance in therapeutic interventions. *Amer. J. Orthopsychiat.* **43,** 108–116

ENGLISH R.W. & JELENEVSKY S. (1971) Counselor behavior as judged under audio, visual and audiovisual communication conditions. *J. Counsel. Psychol.* **18,** 509–513

FELDMAN J.S., HYMAN H.H. & HART C.W. (1951) A field study of interviewer effects on the quality of survey data. *Pub. Opin. Quart.* **15,** 734–761

FEUSTERHEIM H. (1972) The initial interview. *In* Lazarus A.A. (ed.) *Clinical Behaviour Therapy.* London: Butterworths

FLANDERS J.P. (1968) A Review of research on imitative behaviour. *Psychol. Bull.* **69,** 316–337

FOG E. & FOG M. (1963) Cerebral inhibition examined by associated movements. *In* Bax M. & MacKeith R. (eds.) *Minimal Cerebral Dysfunction.* Clinics in Develop. Med. No. 10. London: SIMP/Heinemann

FREUD A. (1966) *Normality and pathology in childhood.* London: Hogarth Press

GELDER M.G. (1968) Verbal conditioning, as a measure of interpersonal influence in psychiatric interviews. *Brit. J. Soc. Clin. Psychol.* **7,** 194–209

GILL M., NEWMAN R. & REDLICH F.C. (1954) *The Initial Interview in Psychiatric Practice.* New York: International Universities Press

GLIDEWELL J.C., MENSH I.N. & GILDEA M. C.-L. (1957) Behavior symptoms in children and degree of sickness. *Amer. J. Psychiat.* **114**, 47–53

GODDARD K.E., BRODER A. & WENAR C. (1961) Reliability of pediatric histories: a preliminary report. *Pediatrics*, **28**, 1011–1018

GOLDSTEIN A.P. (1971) *Psychotherapeutic Attraction.* Oxford: Pergamon

GOLDSTEIN M.J., JODD L.L., RODNICK G.H., ALKINE A. & GOULD E.A. (1968) A method of studying social influence and coping patterns within families of disturbed adolescents. *J. nerv. ment. Dis.* **147**, 233–251

GOODMAN J.D. & SOURS J.A. (1967) *The Child Mental Status Examination.* New York: Basic Books

GRAHAM P. & RUTTER M. (1968) The reliability and validity of the psychiatric assessment of the child. II: Interview with the parent. *Brit. J. Psychiat.* **114**, 581–592

GRAHAM P. & RUTTER M. (1973) Psychiatric disorder in the young adolescent: A follow-up study. *Proc. Roy. Soc. Med.* **66**, 1226–1229

GUBBAY S.S., ELLIS E., WALTON J.N. & COURT S.D.M. (1965) Clumsy children: a study of apraxic and agnosic defects in 21 children. *Brain* **88**, 295–312

GUEST L. (1947) A study of interviewer competence. *Int. J. Opin. Att. Res.* **1**, 17–30

HAGGARD E.H., BREKSTAD A. & SKARD A.G. (1960) On the reliability of the anamnestic interview. *J. Abnorm. Soc. Psychol.* **61**, 311–318

HALL M.B. (1947) *Psychiatric Examination of the School Child.* London: Arnold

HATFIELD J.S., FERGUSON L.R. & ALPERT R. (1967) Mother–child interaction and the socialisation process. *Child Develop.* **38**, 365–414

HEILBRON A.B. (1971) Female preference for therapist initial interview style as a function of 'client' and therapist social role variables. *J. Counsel. Psychol.* **18**, 285–291

HELLER K. (1968) Ambiguity in the interview interaction. *In* J.M. Schlien (ed.) *Research in Psychotherapy III.* Washington, DC: American Psychological Association

HELLER K, DAVIS J.D. & MYERS R.A. (1966) The effect of interviewer style in a standardised interview. *J. Consult. Psychol.* **30**, 501–508

HEMSLEY R., CANTWELL D., HOWLIN P. & RUTTER M. (1976) Paper in preparation

HILDRUM D.C. & BROWN R.W. (1956) Verbal reinforcement and interview bias. *J. Abnorm. Soc. Psychol.* **53**, 108–111

HOFFMAN M.L. (1957) An interview method for obtaining descriptions of parent–child interaction. *Merrill–Palmer Quart.* **4**, 76–83

HOFFMAN M. (1960) Power assertion by the parent and its impact on the child. *Child Develop.* **31**, 129–143

HOPKINSON K.F., COX A. & RUTTER M. (1976) Psychiatric interviewing techniques. Part 2. (In preparation)

HOWELLS J.G. & LICKORISH J.R. (1963) The family relations indicator: a projective technique for investigating intra-family relations designed for use with emotionally disturbed children. *Brit. J. educ. Psychol.* **33**, 286–296

HOWELLS J.G. (1968) *Theory and Practice of Family Psychiatry.* Edinburgh: Oliver & Boyd

HYMAN H.H., COBB W.J., FELDMAN J.J., HART C.W. & STEINBER C.H. (1954) *Interviewing in Social Research.* Chicago: University of Chicago Press

INSKO C.A. & BUTZINE, K.W. (1967) Rapport, awareness and verbal reinforcement of attitude. *J. Pers. Soc. Psychol.* **6**, 225–228

JANIS I.L. (1958) *Psychological Stress.* New York: Wiley

KANFER F.H. & MCBREARTY J.F. (1962) Minimal social reinforcement and interview content. *J. Clin. Psychol.* **18**, 210–215

KANFER F.H., PHILIPS J.S., MATARAZZO J.D. & SASLOW G. (1960) Experimental modification of interviewer content in standardised interviews. *J. Consult. Psychol.* **24**, 528–536

KANNER L. (1957) *Child Psychiatry*, 3rd edn. Springfield, Illinois: Charles C Thomas

KENKEL W.F. (1957) Influence differentiation in family decision making. *Sociol. soc. Res.* **42**, 18–25

KENKEL W.F. & HOFFMAN D.K. (1956) Real and conceived roles in family decision making. *Marr. Fam. Living* **18**, 311–316

KNIGHT B.J. & WEST D.J. (1975) Temporary and continuing delinquency. *Brit. J. Criminol.* **15**, 43–50

KRAMER E. (1963) Judgement of personal characteristics and emotions from non-verbal properties of speech. *Psychol. Bull.* **60**, 408–420

KRASNER L. (1958) Studies of the conditioning of verbal behaviour. *Psychol. Bull.* **55**, 148–170

LAPOUSE R. & MONK M. (1958) An epidemiological study of behavior characteristics in children. *Amer. J. Publ. Health* **48**, 1134–1144

LAPOUSE R. & MONK M. (1959) Fears and worries in a representative sample of children. *Amer. J. Orthopsychiat.* **29**, 803–818

LENNARD H.L. & BERNSTEIN A. (1960) *The Anatomy of Psychotherapy.* New York: Columbia University Press

LEVY D.M. (1933) Use of play technic as experimental procedure. *Amer. J. Orthopsychiat.* **3**, 266–277

LISANSKY E.T. (1969) History taking and interviewing. *Mod. Treatment* **6**, 656–687

LISHMAN W.A. (1974) The speed of recall of pleasant and unpleasant experiences. *Psychol. Med.* **4**, 212–218

LITWAK E. (1956) A classification of biased questions. *Amer. J. Sociol.* **62**, 182–186

LOWE M. (1975) Trends in the development of represential play in infants from one to three years—an observational study. *J. Child Psychol. Psychiat.* **16**, 33–47

MARLATT G.A. (1972) Task, structure and the experimental modification of verbal behaviour. *Psychol. Bull.* **78**, 335–350

MARQUIS K.H., MARSHALL J. & OSKAMP S. (1972a) Testimony validity as a function of question form, atmosphere, and item difficulty. *J. appl. soc. Psychol.* **2**, 167–186

MARQUIS K.H., CANNELL C.F. & LAURENT A. (1972b) Reporting health events in household interviews: effects of reinforcement, question length, and reinterviewers. *Vital and Health Statistics Series 2*, No. 45. US Dept. Health, Education and Welfare

MATARAZZO J. & WIENS A.N. (1972) *The Interview: Research on its Anatomy and Structure.* Chicago: Aldine

MCGINNIES E. (1970) *Social Behaviour: A Functional Analysis.* Boston, Massachusetts: Houghton Mifflin

MEHRABIAN A. (1971) Non-verbal communication. *In* Cole J.K. (ed.) *Nebraska Symposium on Motivation.* Vol. 19. Lincoln, Nebraska: University of Nebraska Press

MENNINGER K.A. (1962) *A Manual for Psychiatric Case Study.* New York: Grune & Stratton

MILLAR S. (1968) *The Psychology of Play.* Harmondsworth: Penguin

MILLER S.M. (1952) The participant observer and 'over-rapport'. *Amer. Sociol. Rev.* **17**, 97–99

MITCHELL S. & SHEPHERD M. (1966) A comparative study of children's behaviour at home and at school. *Brit. J. educ. Psychol.* **36**, 248–254

NEWSON J. & NEWSON E. (1963) *Patterns of Infant Care in an Urban Community.* London: Allen & Unwin

NOBLIN C.D., TIMMONS E.O. & REYNARD M.C. (1963) Psychoanalytic interpretations as verbal reinforcers: importance of interpretation content. *J. Clin. Psychol.* **19**, 479–481

OZER N.M. (1968) The neurological evaluation of school-age children. *J. Learning Disab.* **1**, 84–87

PATTERSON G.R. (1972) Changes in status of family members as controlling stimuli: a basis for describing treatment process. *Oregon Research Institute, Research Monograph* **12**, No. 4

PATTERSON M. (1968) Spatial factors in social interaction. *Hum. Rel.* **21**, 351–361

PETERSON D.R., QUAY H.C. & CAMERON G.R. (1959) Personality and background factors in juvenile delinquency as inferred from questionnaire responses. *J. Consult. Psychol.* **23**, 395–399

POPE B. & SIEGMAN A.W. (1965) Interviewer specificity and topical focus in relation to interviewer productivity. *J. Verbal Learning and Verbal Behaviour* **4**, 188–192

POWER M.J., ASH P.M., SHOENBERG E. & SIREY E.C. (1974) Delinquency and the family. *Brit. J. Social Work* **4**, 13–38

PRUGH D.G., STAUB E.M., SANDS H.H., KIRSCHBAUM R.M. & LENIHAN E.A. (1953) A study of the emotional reactions of children and families to hospitalization and illness. *Amer. J. Orthopsychiat.* **23**, 70–106

QUAY H.C. (1959) The effect of verbal reinforcement on the recall of early memories. *J. Abnorm. Soc. Psychol.* **59**, 254–257

QUINTON D., RUTTER M. & ROWLANDS O. (1976) An evaluation of an interview assessment of marriage. *Psychol. Med.* (in press)

REECE M.M. & WHITMAN R.N. (1961) Warmth and expressive movements. *Psychol. Rep.* **8**, 76

REISMAN J.M. (1973) *Principles of Psychotherapy with Children.* New York: Wiley

RICH J. (1968) *Interviewing Children and Adolescents.* London: Macmillan

RICHARDSON S.A., DOHRENWEND B. & KLEIN D. (1965) *Interviewing.* New York: Basic Books

RICHMAN N. & GRAHAM P.J. (1971) A behavioural screening questionnaire for use with three-year-old children. Preliminary findings. *J. Child Psychol. Psychiat.* **12**, 5–33

ROBBINS L. (1963) The accuracy of parental recall of aspects of child development and child rearing practice. *J. Abnorm Soc. Psychol.* **66**, 261–270

ROBINS L.N. (1966) *Deviant Children Grown Up.* Baltimore: Williams & Wilkins

ROBINS L.N. (1972) Follow-up studies of behavior disorders in children. *In* Quay H.C. & Werry J.S. (eds.) *Psychopathological Disorders of Childhood.* New York: Wiley

RODRIGUEZ A., RODRIGUEZ M. & EISENBERG L. (1959) The outcome of school phobia: a follow-up study based on 41 cases. *Amer. J. Psychiat.* **116**, 540–544

ROFF M., SELLS S.B. & GOLDEN M.M. (1972) *Social Adjustment and Personality Development in Children*. Minneapolis: University of Minnesota Press

ROSENFELD H.M. (1966a) Instrumental affiliative functions of facial and gestural expression. *J. Pers. Soc. Psychol.* **4**, 65–72

ROSENFELD H.M. (1966b) Approval seeking and approval-inducing functions of verbal and non-verbal responses in the dyad. *J. Pers. Soc. Psychol.* **4**, 597–605

RUTTER M. (1967) A children's behaviour questionnaire for completion by teachers: preliminary findings. *J. Child Psychol. Psychiat.* **8**, 1–11

RUTTER M. (1971) Normal psychosexual development. *J. Child Psychol. Psychiat.* **11**, 259–283

RUTTER M. (1972) Clinical assessment of language disorders in the young child. *In* Rutter M. & Martin J.A.M. (eds.) *The Child with Delayed Speech*. Clinics in Develop. Med. No. 43. London: SIMP/Heinemann

RUTTER M. (1975) *Helping Troubled Children*. Harmondsworth: Penguin

RUTTER M. (1976) Prospective studies to investigate behavioural change. *In* Strauss J.S., Babigian H.M. & Roff M. (eds.) *Methods of Longitudinal Research in Psychopathology*. New York: Plenum (in press)

RUTTER M. & BROWN G.W. (1966) The reliability and validity of measures of family life and relationships in families containing a psychiatric patient. *Soc. Psychiat.* **1**, 38–53

RUTTER M., COX A., TUPLING C., BERGER M. & YULE W. (1975) Attainment and adjustment in two geographical areas. I. The prevalence of psychiatric disorder. *Brit. J. Psychiat.* **126**, 493–509

RUTTER M. & GRAHAM P. (1968) The reliability and validity of the psychiatric assessment of the child. I: Interview with the child. *Brit. J. Psychiat.* **114**, 563–579

RUTTER M., GRAHAM P., CHADWICK O. & YULE W. (1976) Adolescent turmoil: fact or fiction? *J. Child Psychol. Psychiat.* **17**, 35–56

RUTTER M., GRAHAM P. & YULE W. (1970b) *A Neuropsychiatric Study in Childhood*. Clinics in Develop. Med. Nos. 35/36. London: SIMP/Heinemann

RUTTER M. & MARTIN J.A.M. (eds.) (1972) *The Child with Delayed Speech*. Clinics in Develop. Med. No. 43. London: SIMP/Heinemann

RUTTER M., TIZARD J. & WHITMORE K. (eds.) (1970a) *Education, Health and Behaviour*. London: Longman

SAGHIR M.T. (1971) A comparison of some aspects of structured and unstructured psychiatric interviews. *Amer. J. Psychiat.* **128**, 180–184

SALZINGER K. & PISONI S. (1961) Some parameters of the conditioning of verbal affect responses in schizophrenic subjects. *J. Abnorm Soc. Psychol.* **63**, 511–516

SCHAFFER H.R. (1971) *The Growth of Sociability*. Harmondsworth: Penguin

SCHAFFER H.R. & CALLENDER W.M. (1959) Psychological effects of hospitalization in infancy. *Pediatrics* **24**, 528–539

SHAPIRO D.A. (1969) Empathy, warmth and genuineness in psychotherapy. *Brit. J. Soc. Clin. Psychol.* **8**, 350–361

SHAPIRO J.G. (1968) Relationships between visual and auditory cues of therapeutic effectiveness. *J. Clin. Psychol.* **24**, 236–239

SHAPIRO R.J. & BUDMAN S.H. (1973) Defection, termination and continuation in family and individual therapy. *Family Process* **12**, 55–67

SHAPIRO S. & EBERHART J. (1947) Interviewer differences in an intensive interview survey. *Int. J. Opin. Att. Res.* **1**, 1–17

SHEPHERD M., OPPENHEIM A.N. & MITCHELL S. (1966) Childhood behaviour disorders and the child guidance clinic: an epidemiological study. *J. Child Psychol. Psychiat.* **7**, 39–52

SHEPHERD M., OPPENHEIM B. & MITCHELL S. (1971) *Childhood Behaviour and Mental Health.* London: University of London Press

SHERIDAN M. (1969) Playthings in the development of language. *Health Trends* **1**, 7–10

SHERWIN A.C., SCHOELLY M.L., KLEIN B.L., SCHWARTS M.C. & KHAN M.G. (1965) Determination of psychiatric impairment in children. *J. nerv. ment. Dis.* **141**, 333–341

SKYNNER A.C.R. (1969) Indications and contra-indications for conjoint family therapy. *Int. J. Soc. Psychiat.* **15**, 245–249

SLIPP S., ELLIS S. & KRESSEL K. (1974) Factors associated with engagement in family therapy. *Family Process* **13**, 413–428

SPITZER R.L., ENDICOTT J., FLEISS J.L. & COHEN J. (1970) The psychiatric status schedule. *Arch. Gen. Psychiat.* **23**, 41–55

SPITZER R.L., FLEISS J.L., BURDOCK E.I. & HARDESTY A.S. (1964) The mental status schedule; rationale, reliability and validity. *Compr. Psychiat.* **5**, 384–395

STARKWEATHER J.A. (1956) Content-free speech as a source of information about the speaker. *J. Abnorm Soc. Psychol.* **52**, 394–402

STENNETT R.G. (1966) Emotional handicap in the elementary years: phase or disease? *Amer. J. Orthopsychiat.* **35**, 444–449

STOTT D.H. (1963) *The Social Adjustment of Children*, 2nd edn. London: University of London Press

STRONG S.R., TAYLOR R.G., BRATTON J.C. & LOPER R.G. (1971) Non-verbal behaviour and perceived counselor characteristics. *J. Counsel. Psychol.* **18**, 554–561

SUNDBY H.S. & KREYBERG P.C. (1968) *Prognosis in Child Psychiatry.* Baltimore: Williams & Wilkins

TOUWEN B.C.L. & PRECHTL H.F.R. (1970) *The Neurological Examination of the Child with Minor Nervous Dysfunction.* Clinics in Develop. Med. No. 38. London: SIMP/Heinemann

TRUAX C.B. (1966) Reinforcement and non-reinforcement in Rogerian psychotherapy. *J. Abnorm. Psychol.* **71**, 1–9

TRUAX C.B. (1968) Therapist interpersonal reinforcement of client self-exploration and therapeutic outcome in group psychotherapy. *J. Counsel. Psychol.* **15**, 225–231

TRUAX C.B. & CARKHUFF R.R. (1967) *Towards Effective Counseling and Psychotherapy: Training and Practice.* Chicago: Aldine

TUDDENHAM R.D., BROOKS J. & MILKOVICH L. (1974) Mothers' reports of behaviour of ten-year-olds: relationships with sex, ethnicity, and mother's education. *Development. Psychol.* **10**, 959–995

TYRER P. & TYRER S. (1974) School refusal, truancy, and adult neurotic illness. *Psychol. Med.* **4**, 416–421

ULRICH L. & TRUMBO D. (1965) The selection interview since 1949. *Psychol. Bull.* **63**, 100–116

VAUGHN C. & LEFF J. (1976) The measurement of expressed emotion in families of psychiatric patients. *Brit. J. soc. clin. Psychol.* (in press)

VONTRESS C.E. (1971) Racial differences: impediments to rapport. *J. Counsel Psychol.* **18**, 7–13

WALKER M. (1965) Perceptual, coding, visuo-motor and spatial difficulties and their neurological correlates: a progress note. *Develop. Med. Child Neurol.* **7**, 543–548

WALTON J.N., ELLIS E. & COURT S.D.M. (1962) Clumsy children: developmental apraxia and agnosia. *Brain* **85**, 603–612

WARREN W. (1965) A study of adolescent psychiatric in-patients and the outcome six or more years later. II: The follow-up study. *J. Child Psychol. Psychiat.* **6**, 141–160

WATZLAWICK P. (1966) A structured family interview. *Family Process* **5**, 256–271

WEISS R.L., KRASNER L. & ULLMANN L.P. (1960) Responsivity to verbal conditioning as a function of emotional atmosphere and pattern of reinforcement. *Psychol. Rep.* **6**, 415–426

WELLS C.F. (1973) The conjoint family diagnostic interview and the family index of tensions. *Family Process* **12**, 126–144

WENAR C. (1963) The reliability of developmental histories. *Psychosom. Med.* **25**, 505–509

WERKMAN S.L. (1965) The psychiatric diagnostic interview with children. *Amer. J. Orthopsychiat.* **35**, 764–771

WHITE A.G. (1953) The patient sits down: a clinical note. *Psychosom. Med.* **15**, 256–257

WING J.K., BIRLEY J.L.T., COOPER J.E., GRAHAM P. & ISAACS A.D. (1967) Reliability of a procedure for measuring and classifying 'present psychiatric state'. *Brit. J. Psychiat.* **113**, 499–515

WOLFF S. (1967) Behavioural characteristics of primary school children referred to a psychiatric department. *Brit. J. Psychiat.* **113**, 885–893

WYATT D. & CAMPBELL D. (1950) A study of interview bias as related to interviewers' expectations and own opinions. *Int. J. Op. Att. Res.* **4**, 77–83

YARROW L.J. (1960) Interviewing children. *In* Mussen P.H. (ed.) *Handbook of Research Methods in Child Development*. New York: Wiley

YARROW M.R. (1963) Problems of methods in parent–child research. *Child Devel.* **34**, 215–226

YARROW M.R., CAMPBELL J.D. & BURTON R.V. (1968) *Child-rearing: an enquiry into research and methods.* San Franciso: Jossey-Bass

YARROW M.R., CAMPBELL J.D. & BUETON R.V. (1970) Recollections of childhood: a study of retrospective methods. *Monogr. of Soc. for Res. in Child Devel.* **35**, No. 5.

ZAX M., COWEN E.L., RAPPAPORT J., BEACH D.R. & LAIRD J.D. (1968) Follow-up study of children identified early as emotionally disturbed. *J. Cons. Clin. Psychol.* **32**, 369–374

CHAPTER 13

Psychological testing

M. BERGER

Psychological tests are a primary source of objective and clinically relevant information about psychological attributes and functions. As such, they form part of the multidisciplinary approaches required in order to provide an adequate assessment and solution of the problems children and their families bring to the clinic.

In the past, the contribution of psychologists was restricted to the administration of a limited range of tests aimed at answering a circumscribed set of questions. Testing was seen as an end in itself and psychologists tended to adopt the role of technicians whose job it was to provide one or two numbers. This role is no longer acceptable or appropriate and it is in the process of being discarded. The administration and scoring of tests are undoubtedly technical skills, but the understanding of tests, their proper interpretation, and the integration of test data into clinical practice demands much more. Testing is part of the wider process of assessment which, in turn, is linked to treatment. It is only in this context that testing becomes meaningful and valuable. This chapter describes some of the basic characteristics of psychological tests and of psychological testing in that clinical context.

ASSESSMENT AND TESTING

It is important to distinguish between 'the assessment', the process of assessment, and psychological testing. An assessment is a set of statements about an individual and his circumstances in relation to some problem. Assessment, as a *process*, is the bringing together of relevant information from a variety of sources, that is 'the systematic collection, organisation and interpretation of information about a person and his situations' (Sundberg & Tyler 1962), which may be used for 'the prediction of his behaviour in new situations' (Jones 1970). Of course, assessments are never undertaken *in vacuo*; they are instigated to solve a clinical problem which predetermines the form and goals of assessment.

The term *psychological test* is most commonly associated with procedures and instruments for measuring intelligence (the IQ test), personality, educational attainment (level and extent of skill in reading, mathematics, spelling) or, on occasion, for diagnosing 'brain damage', 'thought disorder' or disorders of language and perception. In the past, a definition of 'psychological test' which simply encompassed this narrow range of procedures would have been acceptable. This is no longer the case. A test must now be seen as any 'systematic procedure for observing a person's behaviour and describing it with the aid of a numerical scale or a category system' (Cronbach 1970). On the basis of this definition, many procedures including those traditionally used, are viewed as tests. The diagnostic interview (see Chapter 12), in so far as it is systematic, falls within the compass of this broader description. A systematic procedure for observing the interaction between mother and child, as well as procedures for measuring pulse and respiration rate in response to stress, also constitute tests in terms of Cronbach's definition.

This definition, in effect, means that any systematic measurement procedure is a test. Such a definition encourages the psychologist to broaden his conception of 'tests' so that when needs dictate he will explore the wide range of techniques which exist in psychology, rather than attempt to solve problems only by recourse to the traditional tests. Such a definition also encourages the development of new tests. This latter aspect is illustrated by the following case.

A 16-year-old boy, who was being treated for a number of difficulties, complained that he was having difficulty in writing. Specifically, he said he felt he was using excess pressure when writing and that after a few minutes of writing his forearm became very tense. On the basis of an initial discussion, it appeared that this was handicapping him and that a further investigation was needed. A simple test was devised. Ten sheets of paper were stapled together to form a booklet and carbon paper was inserted between each sheet. He was then asked to copy a short paragraph onto the top sheet, one at his own pace, and another as quickly as possible. When this was done, it was possible to count how many sheets of the booklet were marked by his writing. The same test was then carried out on a number of people using an identical procedure. It was obvious that the patient was using very much more pressure than the 'control' subjects. A period of relaxation training failed to alleviate the problem. He was then asked to use a special pressure-sensitive ballpen in his daily writing. The pen was constructed so that the tip would disappear into the housing if too much pressure was exerted. After a period using this pen, he reported that his arm was no longer tense and that he no longer felt he was using excessive pressure. A repeat of the initial test confirmed this.

This case also illustrates the distinction between assessment and testing. In this instance, the 'test' consisted of the set of pages and the writing tasks.

It provided a direct measure of pressure, indexed by the number of pages marked by the writing. The assessment incorporated the statements of the patient and the data from the test on both patient and 'control' group. It can therefore be seen that 'assessment' covers a wider range of activities than does testing. It may involve the use of tests to obtain some information, but need not do so.

NATURE OF PSYCHOLOGICAL TESTS

All psychological tests depend ultimately on observable behaviour. This means that the behaviour has to occur 'naturally' or else be deliberately elicited before testing is possible. Tantrums, speech, aggressive acts and clinging to mother in a strange situation are instances of 'naturally' occurring behaviours. Asking a child to read, solve a problem, fill in a questionnaire or imitate a particular movement are examples of specially elicited behaviours. On the basis of what is observed, inferences are then made about certain higher-level psychological attributes. If the child solves the problem we may infer that he is intelligent; if he clings to his mother, we may conclude that he has separation anxiety. Psychological tests are so devised that they will facilitate the observation of behaviour patterns that are of interest. Where they differ from other approaches is in the attempt to provide a systematic basis for the observations.

A second important feature of psychological tests is the attempt to quantify the observations, either in terms of magnitude or in terms of some category system (to which numbers can be applied). The numbers obtained in the first instance are termed raw scores. Such scores may indicate the presence, absence or difference between a set of characteristics ($0 =$ symptom absent; $1 =$ symptom present). Alternatively, they may index the *frequency*, *duration* or *intensity* of some characteristic. Tantrums can occur with a certain frequency, they may last varying periods of time, or they can be graded according to their intensity. A set of reasoning problems can produce the number of correct solutions, or the time taken to complete the set.

Raw scores, in themselves, are of little value. They gain meaning only in comparison with some criterion or what are called *norms*. Psychological tests utilise two main types of normative data, those based on the individual's own performance and those based on the performance of some comparable group in a similar situation and/or on the same set of tasks. The child who, before treatment, could only approach within 15 feet of a feared object and who after a period of treatment manages to touch the object, provides an illustration of the individual's own performance being used as the criterion. A further illustration is provided in the case of a child who on initial testing could only read ten words and who is then able to read thirty words following remedial teaching.

For some purposes, it is important to know how an individual child's performance compares with that of a group of similar children. Does a 10-year-old boy show the same facility in fine motor coordination as his peers? Can a 5-year-old girl understand sentences of a given level of complexity as well as her age mates? The answers to these questions presuppose the availability of data from comparable groups given the same tasks. If this information is available (i.e. there are group norms), it becomes possible to determine the relative status of the child. There are several ways of expressing an individual's performance relative to that of the criterion group. The average score in the group may be computed and the individual's score can then be described as below, equal to, or above the group average. Or, it is possible to determine what percentage of children in the criterion group obtained scores less than the score obtained by the given child. Describing a score as being at the 15th percentile is a simplified way of stating that the child's raw score was better than the scores of 15 per cent of children in the criterion group. If more discriminating measures are required, it is possible to derive these from the raw scores using various arithmetical transformations (Anastasi 1968). It should however be emphasised that the degree of refinement needed is essentially a function of the presenting problem. Crude measures are adequate for some purposes but not others.

Intelligence tests provide the most common examples of the use of standards based on group norms. The IQ derived from such tests is simply a number which expresses how successful the child was relative to comparable children on the same set of tasks. They are called intelligence tests mainly because it is assumed (on the basis of some evidence) that the degree of success in these tasks is a function of some hypothetical psychological function called 'intelligence'.

Occasionally, performance on a test is expressed in the form of an age-equivalent score called mental age, reading age, arithmetic age or language age. Age scores indicate that the child has achieved a level of performance (raw score) equal to that obtained by a criterion group of children of a particular chronological age. Thus, a reading age of 10 years indicates that the child obtained the same raw score as the average raw score obtained by children aged 10 years. If the child happened to be 8 years old, his reading age of 10 years indicates that he is more advanced in his reading than other 8-year-olds.

Age scores can be useful in clinical practice even though they have a number of important limitations (Anastasi 1968). A 6-year-old child with a 'language comprehension age' of 3 years is, according to the test results, only capable of understanding language at the level of a 3-year-old. If the tester is satisfied that the score is accurate, he may well recommend that parents and teachers adopt a less complex language when they talk to the child, at the same time as providing them with guidance on how to encourage the development of comprehension.

NORM- AND CRITERION-REFERENCED TESTS

Psychological tests can be classified in a number of ways. One important classification distinguishes between norm-referenced and criterion-referenced tests (Popham & Husek 1969). Norm-referenced tests are designed to enable the individual to be compared with some criterion group on a given set of tasks. As Popham and Husek state, 'the meaningfulness of the individual score emerges from the comparison'. A 'below average IQ' for example is an abbreviated description of a score which is below the average score obtained by similar individuals on the particular test. Most of the tests traditionally encountered in clinical practice (IQ and attainment tests, tests of language ability, clumsiness, 'brain damage', etc) are of the norm-referenced type.

When designed to ascertain the individual's status relative to some criterion, tests are termed criterion-referenced. The tester using such an instrument is not concerned with how the individual compares with others but rather with the extent to which he has reached some criterion or standard. Criterion-referenced tests are most commonly used for defining treatment goals and are applied as part of the on-going evaluation of treatment. Such a test would be used in the initial assessment of the severely retarded child who has not yet learned to dress himself. The criterion in this case might be 'no longer needs any help to get dressed'. Initial testing would reveal what he can and cannot do, and treatment would then aim at helping him develop the skills necessary for independence. Periodic application of the test would index progress, and the outcome of each testing would be fed back into the therapeutic programme, modifying it as necessary. Treatment would continue until the criterion as defined by the test is reached. The psychologist using such a criterion measure is not at this point concerned with how well the child dresses himself when compared with other children. If he were, a norm-referenced test would be used.

STANDARDISED AND NONSTANDARDISED TESTS

Standardised and *nonstandardised* tests must also be distinguished. Standardised tests have a standard set of materials, and the procedures for testing and scoring, and the instructions given to the testee are fully specified. In some cases the procedure is so complex that special training is required before the test can be used. Most intelligence tests are standardised but a carefully structured interview in which the questions, the order of questioning and the form of the probes are explicitly laid down is another example. The more a tester departs from the standardised procedures, the less likely is it that accurate results will be obtained and, consequently, the less useful the result.

Nonstandardised tests have procedures which are flexible, and decisions as to what to do and how to do it are left to the discretion of the tester.

This classification of tests is not absolute. Almost all standardised tests have at least some procedural components that are left to the decision of the tester and some nonstandardised tests may contain essential specified procedures. Neither type of test is intrinsically 'best'. Both have their advantages and limitations and the choice of type of test must ultimately depend on the purpose of testing. However, with standardised procedures there is less scope for subjectivity and whim, with the result that equally skilled testers are likely to produce the same result. But with this type of test there is less freedom to follow leads which arise in the course of testing and which may be clinically relevant. While this restriction would not be encountered using nonstandardised procedures other difficulties could arise: with nonstandardised procedures different testers might reach different conclusions simply because they asked different questions. This limitation might not be serious in some situations but can be hazardous in clinical practice because wrong conclusions can lead to irrelevant and inappropriate treatment. For example, simply asking an observer whether a child improved or not as a consequence of being given medication will elicit replies dependent on their understanding of what is meant by 'improved'. Replies to such a question may simply reflect individual differences in understanding and not actual clinical changes. A more systematic approach which included a wide range of specific questions (Has his sleep been affected? Is he more or less active?) is likely to yield more consistent information.

SELECTION OF TESTS

The psychologist's decision to use a particular test depends on three major factors.

A clear statement of the problem

In the first instance, the problem has to be clearly stated, either by the psychologist on the basis of his own impressions or by the colleague who requests a psychological assessment. The person making the request must be clear about what needs to be investigated and why, in order for this to be communicated to the psychologist. Clarity is especially important if the psychologist is not going to have the opportunity to discuss any ambiguities. 'What is the child's level of intelligence?'; 'Johnny is clumsy. Please confirm.', 'How has he managed to adjust to his new school?' are illustrations of inadequate problem statements that can lead to irrelevant answers. 'Adjustment', for example, is a very general concept. It can imply coping with the academic demands of the school, not coming into conflict with teachers, other children, school helpers, or making friends, taking part in games, and so on. Test procedures (for instance, direct observations) could be used to answer any or all of these questions. But what the person making the referral really wanted to know is whether the child still has tantrums when the teacher asks him to do some work, are the tantrums still as frequent and how does the teacher cope? Further, if he is still having tantrums, can the teacher be helped to reduce their occurrence and can she be given guidance on how to cope with them when they occur? With the problem stated in this way the psychologist can readily decide on what to do; speak to the teacher and, if necessary, arrange to spend time observing the child and teacher in the classroom, institute a programme for the teacher, monitor what goes on and arrange to follow up at regular intervals.

The task for the psychologist is thus to ensure that problems are stated in a way that is meaningful without distorting the intentions of those who pose the problem.

Availability of tests

Once the problem is clear, a decision can be taken as to the most appropriate method of solving it. Frequently, the problems which arise can be tackled by resort to familiar procedures. On occasion, the nature of the problem may be such as to require a search of the psychological literature to uncover specific tests such as those listed and evaluated in the Mental Measurements Yearbook (Buros 1972) or in other publications (e.g. Johnson & Bommarito 1971; Walker 1973).

For some clinical problems, the psychologist may employ a different tactic, using his knowledge of the research literature to seek out studies which provide the necessary procedures and normative data. For example, this need may arise with the child who appears to be impulsive, who answers questions without thinking, grabs at what he wants and guesses at words when reading. Several problems confront the clinician: is this child more impulsive than children of the same age and sex? Are his parents intolerant of this type of behaviour? If he is abnormally impulsive does he need to be treated and how can this be done?

A search of the literature reveals a substantial body of research on what is called reflection-impulsivity, a characteristic on which children vary (Kagan 1966; Yando & Kagan 1968). The Matching Familiar Figures Test was devised to measure the degree of impulsivity for research on cognitive behaviour. It requires the child to select one drawing which matches another, the latter being embedded in a set of similar but not identical drawings. Each set is presented to the child, and the number of incorrect choices as well as the time taken to make the choice are used as measures of impulsivity. It has been used with nonhandicapped children and also with those who have neurological disorders (Shaffer *et al* 1974). Also, there is some evidence that placing an impulsive child in a classroom with a 'reflective' teacher tends to reduce the degree of impulsivity (Yando & Kagan 1968).

If studies on impulsivity are used as a basis for clinical assessment and treatment, the studies must be suitable. Thus, the psychologist must consider whether the child being considered is similar to the subjects in the research studies. Comparability may be ascertained on the basis of the age, sex, intelligence and social class of the subjects. If it appears that these data are inadequate, arrangements will need to be made to test a comparable group of children, perhaps from the child's class at school. Account will also have to be taken of the specificity of the MFF test. Does an 'impulsive' score on the test predict impulsivity in other situations, as well as on other tests. If it does, then it is possible to use the MFF test as the sole measure. If not, additional measures using direct observations in various settings will be needed.

Data gathered from a variety of sources are then used to provide a baseline against which to assess the effects of various forms of treatment. For example, modelling and self-instruction may be used to modify impulsivity (Meichenbaum & Goodman 1971). In addition, the school might be asked to move the child to another class with a more reflective teacher or some form of medication might be tried.

Suitability of tests

A test must be relevant to the clinical problem but also it must produce measures which are accurate (i.e. *reliable*) and meaningful (i.e. *valid*).

Reliability   Any measurement entails some degree of error but it is important to select tests which are least prone to error. Several criteria are available (see Cronbach 1970; Stanley 1971) but only two will be considered here.

A test should produce consistent results when given to the same individual by two or more testers, that is it should have high interobserver agreement (*interrater reliability*). If a diagnostic interview yielded different conclusions when carried out by different interviewers, it would be difficult to decide which conclusion to use. Similarly, an observation schedule which gave different results when used by different observers after watching the same child, would be of little value. Such considerations guide the selection of all psychological tests.

The second criterion to be satisfied is that of *retest-reliability* or stability. If it can be assumed that the psychological attribute being measured is relatively stable (e.g. intelligence), then the same test given on two occasions should yield similar results. If even short-term stability of the attribute cannot be assumed, then this criterion is irrelevant.

Validity   Validity is concerned with the *statistical* and *psychological* meaning or interpretation of test scores. An IQ of 115, strictly interpreted, simply indicates that the child's score on a particular test was above the average score obtained by comparable children on that test. Similarly, a reading age of 7 years indicates that the child can read with the same facility as the average 7-year-old child.

These statistical interpretations are governed by the characteristics of the normative group. Only if normative data are derived from a large representative or random sample, are general interpretations (such as those above) possible. If the data are derived from a narrow or biassed sample (e.g. only middle class 10-year-olds who were in school on a given day), interpretations have to be similarly limited.

Psychological interpretations presuppose the availability of evidence regarding the practical implications of particular scores. If research shows that children who get an IQ of 110 or more on a particular test tend to succeed at university, then an IQ of 115 can be used as an indication of probable success at university. Similarly, if there is evidence that children with a reading age of 7 years on a particular test no longer need closely supervised reading lessons, then this interpretation can be made when a child obtains a reading age of 7 on that test.

It has been the custom to ask 'Is this test valid?' but this question is incomplete. It is necessary to ask 'If this test is given, will it be possible to make an interpretation that is relevant to the clinical problem?' This question can only be answered on the basis of suitable research data. If such data are available, testing can proceed. If not, some other procedure has to be found.

Test validation, at a general level, is concerned with the accumulation of data which will allow psychological interpretations to be made. Such data are obtained from specially designed validation studies, or they may arise as a by-product of other studies. A good illustration of the latter is provided by a series of follow-up studies of autistic children (Rutter & Lockyer 1967; Lockyer & Rutter 1969). One of the findings of these studies was that a shortened form of the Wechsler Intelligence Scale for Children could be used as an important index of prognosis. On the basis of these findings, and given that the same diagnostic and test procedures are used, it becomes possible to use test scores to make differential predictions about the future status of an autistic child.

The use of test scores in clinical practice requires all interpretations to be tied to available empirical data, as well as to the procedures used in gathering such data. This stringent approach has evolved as psychologists have come to appreciate the sensitivity of tests. Any departure from the prescribed administration procedures, or the use of tests on groups for whom there are no validity data is likely to lead to incorrect interpretations (Cronbach 1975). The skill and special contribution of the psychologist resides not in the ability to administer tests—most people can quickly master the mechanics of test administration—but in the ability to correctly interpret test findings on the basis of a knowledge of the research literature.

The topics of 'reliability' and 'validity' are of central importance in psychological testing. In the past, they have been treated separately (Stanley 1971; Cronbach 1971) although it is recognised that in practice they are complementary. In fact, both can be subsumed, at least in part, under 'generalisability', a concept which has come to assume a major role in testing (Wiggins 1973; Cronbach *et al* 1972; Levy 1974).

Because tests are used for some *purpose* (APA 1966), the question of reliability should be posed in the form 'Is this test reliable for the purpose intended?', or, as Cronbach *et al* (1972) put it, 'To what extent can an observed score be generalized?' The observed score stems from a single measurement on a particular test given on one occasion, by one tester in one physical setting, with the testee in a 'narrow' psychological and physical state. Would other testers have obtained a similar score? Would the testee obtain similar scores on different occasions on the same or different tests of the same function? How adequately would the single test score predict scores an hour later, 3 months later, or in 10 years' time? Which of these questions is asked depends very much on the purpose of testing. It is known that scores on certain IQ tests are good predictors for short- but not for long-term estimates of IQ. If the tester is interested in only the long-term predictive accuracy, then he needs to ask of a test: 'Will it allow an accurate long-term prediction of IQ?' In the older terminology, he would enquire about the *retest* reliability of the test for the period he is interested in. In Cronbach's terminology, the question would be 'Will I be able to *generalise* to test results 10 years hence if this test is used?' Cronbach (1970) prefers the term generalisability to reliability because the former 'immediately implies "generalisation to what?"' (p. 154). The same score may have different degrees of generalisability. If a test has very precise instructions for its administration, and all users of the test are trained in its use, then it would be acceptable to conclude that we can readily generalise across testers: i.e. a substantial majority of testers will obtain the same observed score. But a test score with high intertester generalisability may not be generalisable to untrained testers or to performance on the same test six months hence. As Cronbach *et al* (1972) state, the *'question of "reliability" thus resolves itself into a question of accuracy of generalization or generalizability'* (p. 15, italics in original).

In selecting a test to measure fine motor coordination, the interest is not in the score *per se*. Rather, the psychologist wants to be able to make a general statement about the adequacy of fine motor coordination. The practical problem is that any test can only sample a few of the diverse characteristics of fine coordination (or intelligence or language). Thus, it is important to know, if, after giving the test, it will be possible to comment on fine coordination generally, and not just in relation to those items sampled by the test. This, in the older terminology, is a validity problem. In terms of generalisability concepts, the question takes the form 'Will I be able to comment on (generalise about) fine coordination in all its manifestations on the basis of the single test score?' It should be noted that irrespective of the terminology, the question is an empirical one requiring appropriate research to provide an answer.

In summary, three considerations influence the decision to use a particular test. The first is a sufficiently clear statement of the problem. The second is the availability of tests and thirdly, the suitability of the test.

The questions of test suitability are problems of generalisability. They exist at two levels. At the first level we are concerned with generalisability in relation to the test score. At the second level we are concerned with generalisability as it relates to psychological interpretations of the score. These considerations determine whether or not a test will be used in clinical practice.

TESTS FOR USE WITH CHILDREN

Most psychologists have readily available a set of tests which have been found to be useful for the more common clinical problems. These will include a range of intelligence tests appropriate for children of different ages (Sattler 1974) as well as tests which can be used for children whose difficulties necessitate the use of special procedures. For example, most tests of intelligence require the child to give spoken answers to questions. Such tests would be inappropriate for testing an elective mute or a child who had a severe speech impediment. Therefore, a test has to be chosen which does not require spoken answers. The Peabody Picture Vocabulary Test (Dunn 1965) only requires the child to point to the answer (one of a set of pictures) and it would be a more appropriate test for children with such difficulties.

As a substantial number of the clinical problems of children are associated with difficulties in educational skills, psychologists usually have available a set of tests to help assess educational attainment (achievement). These will include tests of reading, number and spelling skills. Problems of language and motor coordination are encountered with sufficient frequency in some clinics for there to be available a further set of tests to aid the assessment of such difficulties.

DIAGNOSTIC TESTING

The potential value of tests as diagnostic instruments has been recognised for a long time (Garfield 1974). Diagnostic testing can be used to identify broad clinical syndromes such as 'brain damage', personality disorder, schizophrenia, and the like; or it can aim to identify specific difficulties or assets, that is, what the child can or cannot do. For the latter purpose, tests focus on specific aspects of functioning, such as visual or auditory perception, learning and memory, reading, writing and motor skills.

There has been a general, but not yet total, decline in diagnostic testing of the first type, largely because of the lack of implications for treatment and the technical difficulties in test construction for diagnosis. In the past, diagnostic testing was especially concerned with the identification of 'brain damage' in children, an area in which diagnostic testing has displayed some of its more severe limitations (Herbert 1964; 1974; Werry 1972). However, the early approaches were based on outmoded views of brain–behaviour relationships (Davison 1974) and more recent developments, using extended batteries of tests, are not necessarily misplaced. In addition to aiding diagnosis, such test batteries provide a more comprehensive specification of the clinically relevant deficits due to brain damage (Davison 1974). But, methodological problems remain (Reitan 1974), and such tests are not yet suitable for routine use. At the present time, the detection and description of functional deficits and skills involving attention, memory, motor coordination, impulsivity and the like, are more appropriate goals for diagnostic testing (Herbert 1964; 1974).

A variety of procedures can be used to identify specific assets and deficits.
a An extreme score (as on tests of motor coordination, spelling or reading) can be indicative of either a special difficulty or an outstanding ability.
b Assets or handicaps can be identified by contrasting the test scores of individuals with and without some special characteristic or diagnosis, which

must be identified on the basis of clear criteria. A cut-off score is computed which maximises the proportion of the special group identified and minimises the proportion of 'normals' included. Many of the gross diagnostic tests utilise this approach.

c Compendium tests (i.e. tests made up of a number of sub-tests) can also be used. Each sub-test produces its own score and the pattern of scores provides a profile of abilities. The possibility arises that certain profile patterns, for example high scores on three particular sub-tests accompanied by low scores on two others may be indicative of a specific disorder.

d A variant of the profile approach is provided by the pattern produced when a battery or collection of tests is given. Here again, test scores produce a pattern or profile which may have diagnostic implications.

e A change in score (increase or decrease) on repeated testing may also have diagnostic implications, as in the detection of deterioration in some aspect of functioning.

While the procedures described above appear to be dissimilar, they share common features. The most important of these is that the diagnosis is based on a *difference* between scores. That is, one score is in effect subtracted from another and the result, a *difference score*, is the basis of diagnosis. It has come to be appreciated that such scores present peculiar difficulties and that, because of these, difference scores can only be used when certain conditions are satisfied. Each score has some degree of error and when a difference between two scores is computed, the error components are added together, thereby increasing the unreliability (Angoff 1971). Although there are procedures (regression analysis, expectancy tables) for overcoming these statistical difficulties, few test procedures currently available employ them.

Regression procedures

The 'diagnosis' of specific reading retardation is one example of the appropriate use of such scores. In this procedure, the child is given a shortened version of the WISC (Wechsler 1949) and the Neale Analysis of Reading Ability (1958). Then, taking account of both the age and intelligence of the child, using a special statistical formula, it becomes possible to estimate what reading age would be expected. Given that certain assumptions have been satisfied, this estimation (or regression) procedure simply indicates the average reading age obtained by children in the general population who are of the same chronological age and IQ as the child who has been tested. The difference between the reading age obtained by the child and that expected from comparable children is then examined. If this difference is very substantial, beyond a predetermined value, the child is 'diagnosed' as being specifically retarded in reading. By ensuring that only very large differences are used to reach a diagnosis, the problems of unreliability are minimised. The clinical implications of specific reading difficulty are discussed in greater detail in Chapter 23.

Expectancy tables

An acceptable alternative to regression procedures is the use of expectancy tables.

It is very common to find that a child's score on the Verbal Scale of the WISC (or WPPSI—Wechsler 1967) differs from his score on the Performance Scale. The first question that needs to be considered is the *reliability* of the difference. That is, what is the probability of the difference being due simply to errors of measurement? Field (1960) has provided a set of expectancy tables which enables such a difference to be evaluated. For example, a difference of 12 points between Verbal and Performance IQs obtained by a $7\frac{1}{2}$-year-old child could arise by chance 10 per cent of the time simply because of error. Hence, there would seem little to be gained by pursuing this difference further. On the other hand, a difference of 25 points could arise by chance one in a thousand times. Therefore, it is very unlikely that the observed difference is due to errors of measurement and the clinician must entertain the hypothesis that the difference is a 'real' one which *may* be clinically important. Before proceeding further, however, account has to be taken of the 'abnormality' of the difference. That is, in the statistical sense, how frequently a difference of a given magnitude arises in the population of children. Field (1960) has also provided a set of expectancy tables for evaluating the abnormality of differences between Verbal and Performance IQs. It will be found that 38 per cent of children aged $7\frac{1}{2}$ years obtain discrepancies of 12 points between their Verbal and Performance IQs on the WISC, and about 8 per cent are expected to obtain a difference as large as 25 points. Thus, although it is unlikely to be due to chance errors, a difference of 25 points occurs so frequently in this age group that any attempt to attach clinical significance to it is likely to be misleading. See Sattler (1974) for detailed expectancy tables covering the commonly used children's intelligence tests.

The techniques mentioned above are equally relevant to compendium test profiles and to differences which occur when testing is repeated. Profile score differences are in fact particularly prone to the effects of unreliability. It is known that the longer the test, the more likely it is to be reliable. Profile scores (and thus differences between them) that are based on comparatively short sub-tests tend to be inherently unreliable, so that differences between them are likely to be even more suspect than are other differences. Maxwell (1959) has provided a set of expectancy tables to help evaluate sub-test differences on the WISC.

When properly applied, regression techniques and expectancy tables (see Thorndike 1963; Angoff 1971; and Cronbach 1970; 1971 for a more technical discussion) are capable of producing useful diagnostic information. However, they constitute only part of the prerequisites for diagnostic testing. Once reliable differences have been identified, further research is then needed to overcome other technical problems. For example, diagnostic procedures are usually developed on the basis of group studies. Clinical practice requires that these procedures should be appropriate for individual work. Assume that a diagnostic test has been developed which identifies children with problems of fine motor coordination. Before a clinician can use such a test, he has to know the probability of misdiagnosis when the test is used with an individual; and this information has to be related in turn to other types of information (see Gathercole 1968 for a discussion of screening efficiency; also Chapter 8).

Diagnostic testing has very marked limitations, but, with attention to appropriate statistical techniques, it can be useful as amply illustrated by the procedures used to detect specific reading retardation. It is important that such advances are not obscured because of the failure of other procedures which have been less carefully developed.

PRESCRIPTIVE TEACHING

Prescriptive teaching is a form of teaching, therapy or modification aimed at overcoming the specific deficits identified in diagnostic testing. Remedial intervention of this type is of course not aimed simply at overcoming the deficit because it is a deficit. Rather, this approach presupposes that the deficits are responsible for some more general difficulty such as a reading handicap. One illustration of such an approach is the Frostig Test (Frostig *et al* 1964) and its accompanying remedial programme.

In a somewhat simplified form, the logic employed by users of the Frostig package has as its initial and tenable assumption that reading competence is partially determined by appropriately developed perceptual capacities. If there is an imbalance, a reading handicap will arise. If this imbalance can be corrected, reading difficulties will be overcome. The test itself is structured so that its individual sub-tests will detect perceptual deficits. The remedial programme is tailored to overcome such deficits.

The use of this and other diagnostic-remedial packages requires an empirically well-supported chain of validation studies. Parts of this chain can be short-circuited for the sake of parsimony but in the final analysis, evidence is required that specific perceptual training improves an ability such as reading. For the Frostig package, such evidence is yet to be provided (Hammill & Wiederholt 1973). As it happens, there is also evidence that this test is inadequate as a diagnostic test. For example, Ward (1970) found that the individual components are not independent of each other. Hammill and Wiederholt (1973), in their review of research on the Frostig test and remedial programme, comment that although the total score may be useful, the sub-tests lack reliability and validity. They go on to note that 'the research indicates that the Frostig training program in perception has no effect on reading and has a questionable effect on school readiness and perception itself'.

The Illinois Test of Psycholinguistic Abilities (Kirk *et al* 1968) is a popular test used for diagnosing language difficulties (and is thus potentially useful as a basis for devising treatment). Unfortunately, it too lacks adequate support for its use as a diagnostic instrument. As Sedlak and Weener (1973) conclude, '. . . the extent to which it can accomplish its purpose of accurately diagnosing psycholinguistic abilities and disabilities is largely undetermined.'

Although diagnostic–prescriptive teaching is theoretically 'an enviable and desirable model, there is little empirical support for the concept' in education (Ysseldyke 1973). The approach is important in so far as it is an attempt to tailor treatment to the problems of the individual. But, its acceptance as an applied strategy must await not only better diagnostic tests but also more substantial evidence of its practical effectiveness.

TARGET ASSESSMENT

Although nearly all tests sample behaviour, a substantial proportion of them are used to make inferences about underlying psychological characteristics. A test of personality, such as the Junior Eysenck Personality Inventory (S.B.G. Eysenck 1965) requires the child to answer 'yes' or 'no' to a standard set of questions. On the basis of the answer pattern, inferences are then made about the child's personality; his degree of extraversion and emotionality (neuroticism).

In recent years, there has been an increasing dissatisfaction with this type of approach (Mischel 1968) and attempts have been made to replace such procedures with supposedly more appropriate and relevant approaches such as *target assessment* (O'Leary 1972). This is based on the direct observation of target behaviours, that is those patterns of behaviour which are thought to be 'undesirable' or inappropriate (tantrums, aggressive acts, self-mutilation, poor attention, phobic avoidance, reading failure, etc.).

O'Leary (1972) distinguishes between functional and static target assessment. A functional assessment is a deliberate attempt to discover the antecedents and consequences of the target behaviours, with a view to isolating those which control the undesirable patterns. A young child who shows tantrums in school would be observed in an attempt to find out what precipitates the tantrums and what environmental consequences appear to maintain them. Some of the antecedents might include failing at a task, being teased by another child, or not getting what he wants; and some of the consequences might include attention from the teacher, reaction from peers, and being excluded from the classroom. The observer first identifies as many as possible of the precipitating and consequential factors and then attempts to isolate those which control the behaviour. This is done by systematically manipulating each of the factors in turn and observing what happens to the target behaviours, a procedure sometimes called functional analysis (see also Chapter 39).

In the static approach, less attention is paid to the precipitants and consequences. The main focus is the target behaviour itself (for example a specific phobia) and there is no systematic attempt to isolate the full sequence of functional components. It is, as O'Leary points out, difficult to draw a clear distinction between the assessment (or diagnostic) and modification aspects of target assessment. In the course of such an assessment, a number of environmental events are isolated as potential factors controlling the particular behaviour pattern. Systematic manipulation of these factors, together with concurrent monitoring of the target behaviour, may reveal which of these factors is most potent in controlling the behaviour. In identifying such factors the 'diagnosis' has emerged and the process of manipulation is, in effect, the 'treatment'. Hence, in target assessment, the older distinction between assessment and treatment is not particularly relevant.

One of the important characteristics of this approach is the attempt to clearly specify what is observed. By an ongoing direct observation programme there is feed-back to the assessor–therapist and a direct monitoring of the treatment effects. Once the target behaviour has been identified, its frequency or duration is measured. This is the 'baseline' or naturally occurring characteristic of the behaviour. The goal of treatment is to produce changes in these pretreatment characteristics in the direction desired by the therapists.

While there is a tendency for proponents of target assessment to present it as the alternative to other test procedures, such a view is misconceived. Target assessment is an important addition to testing. By itself, it could never encompass the wide range of problems encountered in clinical practice. At the same time, its importance should not be underestimated. Many of the behaviour patterns which bring children to the attention of clinics arise and are maintained by external circumstances. Target assessment not only helps to isolate these determinants but also carries with it direct implications for treatment.

PSYCHOLOGICAL TESTING IN CLINICAL PRACTICE

The sources of variation in test performance

Psychological testing can be stressful for many individuals and other factors, such as poor lighting, external distractions and the like can also disrupt test performance. The personal and situational factors which produce inaccurate test results are among the many factors which can lead to chance variations in test score (see Stanley 1971; Cronbach 1970).

The term 'variation' is used in this context in place of the term random or chance error because errors are essentially those chance factors which are unrelated to the tester's purpose. Given that purposes can differ, what constitutes error will vary accordingly. For example, for the purpose of obtaining an accurate IQ, the fact that the test situation is stressful and could lead to a disrupted performance will mean that little confidence can be placed in the final score. However, some tests (e.g. The Nufferno Tests—Furneaux 1955) deliberately set out to examine what happens to an individual when placed in a stressful as opposed to a nonstressful situation. Thus what constitutes error in one context is meaningful variation in another.

The *test format* can be a major influence on the level of score obtained. Questions can be open-ended or multiple choice; they can be presented orally or read by the testee; in some, time limits are imposed, in others not. Each test, with its own peculiarities may be prone to certain types of errors and not others. The Schonell Graded Word Reading Test (Schonell & Schonell 1956) consists of 100 words which are used to measure reading accuracy. On this test the child is not helped by contextual cues as the words are unrelated. The Neale Analysis of Reading Ability (Neale 1958) is also designed to give a measure of reading accuracy. However, as it is made up of prose passages, the child may be able to guess correctly because of the contextual cues.

Floor and *ceiling effects* are two special problems that may arise in testing. Most tests are designed to cover a certain range of ability and if the ability of the testee is near to either extreme of the range, the resulting scores will be inaccurate. Ceiling effects occur when the ability of the individual is above the maximum score obtainable on the test, as suggested by his getting all or nearly all of the items correct. Floor effects arise when very few of the testee's abilities can be sampled by the test. These effects are indicated when the individual fails to get any of the test items correct* or when only the

---

* Should this happen, the tester has to make sure that the testee actually understands what is required of him. Occasionally, floor effects can arise because of the interaction of a handicap and the test format, e.g. the poor reader being given a test in which he has to read the questions.

first few items are correct and later ones are failed. Even when a few successes are followed by consistent failure, the tester should not consider the result a reliable one. This follows from the known general relationship between *test length* and reliability, i.e. reliability is known to increase as test length increases (Cronbach 1970).

The scores obtained by young and by handicapped children are particularly prone to the unreliability associated with test length. The young child may not be capable of the sustained concentration required for some tests and testing may have to be discontinued. The handicapped child may not be able to do parts of the tests simply because of the nature of his handicap.

The procedures involved in the *administration and scoring* can also be a major source of differences. Tests vary in the explicitness of the instructions given to the tester. Some require special training in their use if they are to be administered correctly whereas others are less controlled. Testers will vary in the way they interpret the instructions. Sometimes, the form of follow-up questions is specified and for other tests this point may not be considered. On some tests, there can be ambiguity as to what constitutes the correct answer, particularly on open-ended questions. Timing and scoring procedures, too, are prone to varied interpretations, thus adding to the potential source of errors.

The *physical setting* in which testing is carried out can have an impact on the performance of the testee. Heat, light, extraneous noises, the presence of distractions such as toys, or sitting facing a window, are other possible sources of variation which need to be taken into account.

Perhaps the most significant influences on variability in performance, especially in the handicapped individual, are the various *intrapersonal characteristics* of the testee and their *interactions* with the many factors described above. For example, the scores obtained by the distractable child tested in distracting surroundings may differ markedly from those obtained from testing in a less distracting setting. Similarly the effects of confronting the persistent child with time limited test items will differ from the results on a test where attempts at solution were not constantly interrupted. Attention must also be drawn to the interaction of the 'slow to warm up' child (Thomas *et al* 1968), a strange test setting and a short test. Again, quite a different score might be anticipated if he were given an extended opportunity to settle and a longer test to complete.

More transient individual characteristics, such as health, fatigue, motivation, response sets, proneness to guessing, test sophistication, chance information, fluctuations of memory, comprehension of instructions, reaction to the appearance, sex, race, accent of tester, are among the many possible sources which can impinge on test performance. Some may act to increase scores and others to lower them. Seligman (1975) provides an important discussion of motivation in test performance.

While it is not possible to prevent the effect of all the factors considered, the test user can, by clear observation of the testing interaction, at least be in a position to judge the effect of testing on the testee. By doing so, he will be in a better position to judge the typicality of the individual's reaction to testing. If he detects disturbing and disrupting influences, it is necessary to qualify the obtained results. The tester should also take steps to ensure that the consumers of his data do not isolate the scores from the context in which they were obtained. Some users of psychological test data are inclined to look only at the numbers and this practice should be strongly and actively discouraged.

The testing of children

Many of the points made in the preceding paragraphs apply to testing generally, but the testing of children poses some special problems.

The tester has to recognise that he is sampling behaviour at a period of rapid development in an individual who may not be able to understand what is required or communicate even if he knows. The younger the child, or the more handicapped he is, the more must such considerations be taken into account. The psychologist must have a detailed knowledge of child development, its disorders, and the role and influence of family, school and society on individual development. This knowledge guides the preparation of the setting and the selection of procedures to be used; and provides a basis for understanding the meaning of children's behaviour and hence aids the evaluation of test results.

Because of the rapid rates at which certain abilities develop, skills may emerge in a short space of time and such changes can alter the outcome on repeated testing. It is also possible for one test to sample a particular area of skill in such a way that competence cannot be demonstrated whereas an alternative approach is able to demonstrate competence. Two examples commonly found in the psychiatric setting illustrate this point. 'Comprehension' can be tested in a number of ways. One test may require the child to verbalise his response whereas another may simply require him to point at an object. Both are legitimate approaches. However, the child who is shy, or who has a speech delay or impediment may produce substantially different results when tested on these two tests. Even seemingly trivial occurrences such as having left spectacles at home or a hearing aid set at a sub-optimal volume may have a profound impact on test outcome.

In general, tests developed for use with nonhandicapped children are likely to yield inappropriate conclusions when applied to the handicapped. Special care has to be exercised to ensure that their particular disabilities do not place them at a disadvantage. Tests should be carefully chosen for each individual child taking into account his difficulties. Occasionally, standardised procedures will have to be modified but this may lead to changed reliabilities and validities. The tester then has to balance limitations on interpretations against the possibly improved validity of the modified test in the individual case.

Incomplete testing is a special form of modified testing which requires careful interpretation. Autistic children, among others, usually only complete parts of the Merrill Palmer (Stutsman 1948) test or several sub-tests of the WISC. Apart from problems of reliability, interpretations have initially to be restricted to the statistical. That is, the results can be used as indices of the level at which the child can perform a class of cognitive tasks. Scores should not be given their usual labels (MA or IQ for example) unless it is made quite explicit that the 'IQ' is based on an incomplete or nonstandard administration of the test. The reason for this sanction is that some scores have a variety of implications which may not hold if they are based on non-standard procedures or if they are used to generalise about atypical individuals.

Whilst no hard and fast rules can be put forward, clinical experience suggests that the following points should be given some weight in selecting testing procedures. Motivational factors are important in all testing, and tests constructed for use with children generally incorporate items which will arouse and maintain their interest. This is especially necessary when testing handicapped children who will often have encountered failure and may be unwilling to persist with items which they find difficult. It may therefore be necessary to depart somewhat from the standard testing procedures and to intersperse simpler items among those which are likely to tax the child. To gain the cooperation of the child who is difficult to test, it may be necessary to begin testing at a point very much below the level at which it is thought the child may be successful. A sequence of successes may encourage him to attempt more difficult items. Also, if the child appears to enjoy a particular task and is unwilling to attempt others, it may be useful to allow him to work at this on condition that he attempts others. On occasion it may be helpful to allow parents to be present during the assessment. This is particularly so in those circumstances where the parent may be able to act as a translator of instructions for the language handicapped child. Obviously very young children are also more likely to be at ease if a parent is present. It is, however, essential to ensure that parents do not directly or inadvertently help the child with the test items. Again, the more the tester departs from standardised administration, the more he must qualify the obtained results.

Certain items on cognitive tests require the child to complete the task correctly within prescribed time limits. Some tests may also give bonus points for rapid solutions. Particular care needs to be exercised when these timed items are used with handicapped children. Children with motor coordination problems, or children who are highly distractable are most likely to be penalised if timed tests are used.

There is no doubt that some children are difficult to test and that for a given tester, procedure, circumstances and number of attempts, the statement that the child is 'untestable' may hold. However, children are not tested with the purpose of getting a test score. They are tested as part of the process of assessment of which the score is but one element. Testing is a tactic in the strategy of assessment and, with the problem clearly articulated, an answer can be arrived at in different ways. If the tester cannot wait to get a test result or is unsatisfied with only partial testing, direct observation and structured interviews with parents and teachers can be used. The Vineland Social Maturity Scale (Doll 1953) is one form of interview procedure that could be combined with others to obtain the desired information. The observations made by the tester, and those recounted by others, can be related to the tester's knowledge of child development to reach an estimate of developmental level if this is what is required. Such knowledge should also be used to guide the selection of questions that will be put to informants. For example, it is possible to formulate questions on language and social development guided by the findings of current research in these areas. As this information is not as yet incorporated in standardised tests, such questions should be posed if the assessment is in any way concerned with these aspects of functioning, irrespective of whether or not full testing was accomplished.

The ideals of testing cannot always be satisfied in clinical practice. However, the tester who is aware of these is in a position to qualify his findings in such a way that the various limitations can be taken into account by those who use the information. Three steps must be taken to ensure that the results will be seen in their full context. Firstly, detailed and systematic observations of behaviour should be made and recorded in the test report so that sources of unreliability are known. Secondly, all nonstandard procedures should be reported. Finally, a concerted effort should be made to obtain independent confirmation of test results. This can be achieved partly by relating what was seen in the test situation to information given by parents and others, and partly by comparing test scores with other developmental data. An attempt should be made at the same time to confirm that the behaviour seen during testing is 'typical' of the child in other situations. All relevant discrepancies should be investigated by whatever means possible. Testing should not be regarded as complete while unresolved discrepancies remain.

Further discussion of these points insofar as they concern the testing of the young child with delayed and deviant language development can be found in Berger and Yule (1972). A full discussion of the psychological assessment of handicapped children is presented in the volume edited by Mittler (1970).

INVESTIGATION OF SINGLE CASES: A CONTEXT FOR TESTING

Clinical practice is distinguished by its focus on the individual. In psychology, as in psychiatry, the form which this practice takes varies among individuals, who in turn are influenced by some broader theoretical orientation. One approach which is gaining wider acceptance (Davidson & Costello 1969; Yates 1970; Browning & Stover 1971) is that proposed by Shapiro (1957; 1970). This orientation regards clinical psychology as an applied branch of experimental psychology which employs the methods and findings of the parent discipline in clinical work. The essence of this approach is to formulate explicit hypotheses which are relevant to the clinical needs of the individual and then to subject such hypotheses to some form of experimental evaluation. From the psychologist's point of view, these hypotheses should be based on the findings of psychological research and their testing should be guided by the same considerations of design and measurement that operate in psychological research. That is, wherever possible, clinical problems should be conceptualised as research problems.

A research strategy has a number of components. The problem needs to be defined, hypotheses have to be formulated, a design has to be set out, suitable measurement (test) procedures must be found and the resulting data have to be evaluated for their significance. At the present time, the major practical difficulty with this approach is the statistical testing of the outcome (Dukes 1965; Hartmann 1974).

Experimental psychology provides an abundant source of hypotheses and there is now an extensive literature on the design of individual investigations (Browning & Stover 1971; Leitenberg 1973). Tests are available for the measurement of a very wide range of psychological phenomena and the principles of test design and interpretation are well developed. The central problem is thus statistical. Some procedures are available for the statistical evaluation of test results obtained from individuals (Payne & Jones 1957) but the assumptions of most statistical tests cannot be satisfied when used in relation to single individuals. Further, even the Payne and Jones procedures are limited by the availability of suitable data. Their procedures can only be used when the characteristics of the individual closely match those of individuals used in the research samples.

Some features of this approach are illustrated in the following summary of an individual investigation.

R.M., a 10-year-old boy, was originally referred to the clinic because of reading, spelling and writing difficulties. Following a full psychiatric, psychological and neurological assessment, it was decided to provide him with remedial reading as part of the treatment for his difficulties. During the initial assessments, it had emerged that in addition to being specifically retarded in reading, R.M. also showed a number of motor-coordination difficulties, a finding that is not uncommon in specifically retarded readers (Rutter et al 1970).

In the course of remedial reading it was observed that while R.M. was reading one line of prose, he appeared to be 'picking up' words or parts of words from lines above and below the line he was reading. A brief unsystematic test was carried out. This consisted of using a mask to cover all of the printed page, except for a small area of print. This was accomplished by cutting out a section of the mask only large enough to expose 6 to 8 letters on a single line. The use of this mask led to an improvement in his reading accuracy.

A number of hypotheses were advanced to account for this. One of these was that R.M. had not yet learned the left-right scanning that seems necessary in the initial stages of learning to read. A related hypothesis was that a defect in his eye-movement control (related possibly to his other motor difficulties) was interfering with the acquisition of the appropriate scanning skill. In view of the implications for treatment, it was decided to investigate his eye-movements in greater detail..

A number of studies (Abercrombie 1960; Abercrombie et al 1963) have shown important differences in the eye-movements of cerebral palsied and normal children. There are also several procedures (Rashbass 1060; 1961; Shackel 1960) available for detailed recording of eye-movements (as opposed to eye fixation). Shackel's procedure (electro-oculography) was chosen in the present instance. It uses specially designed cup-electrodes placed around the eyes and linked to a polygraph. R.M. was tested using a number of the fixation and tracking tasks described by Abercrombie et al (1963). The polygraph records revealed a degree of impairment relative to comparable normal children but not of the severity encountered in cerebral palsied children.

Had the records shown no sign of impairment, treatment would have consisted only of gradually increasing the size of the slot in the mask, and then, at a later stage, getting R.M. to use his finger to guide his eyes along the printed sentence. As his skill improved, the use of pointing would be gradually faded out. However, because there were indications of some motor difficulty, the treatment regime included the procedures described above as well as practice using other visual tracking tasks, in an attempt to improve these skills.

Individual investigations of this type are not intended to provide the answers being sought in what is commonly called research, although they can obviously stimulate such studies. Also, given the demands of the clinical setting, there is a limit to the amount of time that can be devoted to intensive studies. It is possible to generate many more hypotheses than can be tested and the opportunity to follow through even one or two in any depth is restricted. For each individual some order of priority has to be set up in relation to both clinical needs and feasibility.

The seemingly 'routine' administration of psychological tests much in evidence in child guidance clinics may appear far-removed from the model described above. What is not appreciated is that the routine administration of intelligence, attainment or similar tests is actually a form of hypothesis testing. Unfortunately, too few psychologists understand this. The implicit hypothesis is 'This child's level of ability (or skill in reading) is not a major factor in his difficulties'. It is not uncommon for intelligence and educational attainment to be important sources of difficulty with children, hence the routine use of these tests.

The case of R.M. is intended to convey something of the nature or style of approach which can be adopted in clinical work. Although the problems and procedures may be somewhat unusual, the underlying approach is not. At the present time, behavioural treatment programmes are the most common examples of this approach (see the section on Target Assessment and Chapter 39).

It is perhaps too soon to designate this style of investigation as 'scientific' although there is little doubt that it is strongly influenced by the considerations which guide scientific research. A systematic approach to the investigation of individual cases, in which tests are used as a means of hypothesis testing, is an important beginning. It is only in this framework that psychological tests can demonstrate their value.

REFERENCES

ABERCROMBIE M.L.J. (1960) Perception and eye movements: some speculations on disorders in cerebral palsy. *Cerebral Palsy Bulletin* **2**, 142–148

ABERCROMBIE M.L.J., DAVIS J.R. & SHACKEL B. (1963) Pilot study of version movements of eyes in cerebral palsied and other children. *Vision Res.* **3**, 135–153

ANASTASI A. (1968) *Psychological Testing*, 3rd edn. London: Macmillan

ANGOFF W.M. (1971) Scales, norms and equivalent scores. *In* Thorndike R.L. (ed.) *Educational Measurement*, 2nd edn. Washington: American Council on Education.

APA (American Psychological Association 1966) *Standards for Educational and Psychological Tests and Manuals*. Washington DC

BERGER M. & YULE W. (1972) Cognitive assessment in young children with language delay. *In* Rutter M. & Martin J.A.M. *The Child with Delayed Speech.* Clinics in Develop. Med., No. 43. London SIMP/Heinemann

BROWNING R.M. & STOVER D.O. (1971) *Behavior Modification in Child Treatment.* Chicago: Aldine

BUROS O.K. (1972) (ed.) *The Seventh Mental Measurements Yearbook.* Highland Park NJ: Gryphon Press

CRONBACH L.J. (1970) *Essentials of Psychological Testing,* 3rd edn. New York: Harper International Edition

CRONBACH L.J. (1971) Test validation. *In* Thorndike R.L. (ed.) *Educational Measurement,* 2nd edn. Washington: American Council on Education

CRONBACH L.J. (1975) Beyond the two disciplines of scientific psychology. *Amer. Psychol.* **30,** 116–127

CRONBACH L.J., GLESER G.C., NANDA H. & RAJARATNAM N. (1972) *The Dependability of Behavioral Measurements.* New York: Wiley

DAVIDSON P.O. & COSTELLO C.G. (1969) $N=1$, *Experimental Studies of Single Cases.* New York: van Nostrand

DAVISON L.A. (1974) Introduction. *In* Reitan R.M. & Davison L.A. (eds.) *Clinical Neuropsychology: Current Status and Applications.* Washington DC: Winston

DOLL E.A. (1953) *The Measurement of Social Competence. A Manual for the Vineland Social Maturity Scale.* Minneapolis: American Guidance Service

DUKES W.F. (1965) $N=1$. *Psychol. Bull.* **64,** 74–79

DUNN L.M. (1965) *Expanded Manual for the Peabody Picture Vocabulary Test.* Minneapolis: American Guidance Service

EYSENCK S.B.G. (1965) A new scale for personality measurements in children. *Brit. J. Educ. Psychol.* **35,** 362–367

FIELD J.G. (1960) Two types of tables for use with Wechsler's intelligence scales. *J. Clin. Psychol.* **16,** 3–7

FROSTIG M., LEFEVER D.W. & WHITTLESEY J. (1964) *The Marianne Frostig Developmental Test of Visual Perception.* Palo Alto: Consulting Psychologists Press

FURNEAUX W.D. (1955) *The Nufferno Tests of Speed, Accuracy and Level.* London University of London Press

GARFIELD S.L. (1974) *Clinical Psychology.* Chicago: Aldine

GATHERCOLE C.E. (1968) *Assessment in Clinical Psychology.* Harmondsworth: Penguin

HAMMILL D.D. & WIEDERHOLT J.L. (1973) Review of the Frostig Visual Perception Test and the related training program. *In* Mann L. & Sabatino D.A. (eds.) *The First Review of Special Education,* vol. 1. Philadelphia: Buttonwood Farms

HARTMANN D.P. (1974) Forcing square pegs into round holes: some comments on 'an analysis-of-variance model for the intrasubject replication design'. *J. Appl. Behav. Anal.* **7,** 635–638

HERBERT M. (1964) The concept and testing of brain-damage in children: a review. *J. Child. Psychol. Psychiat.* **5,** 197–216

HERBERT M. (1974) *Emotional Problems of Development in Children.* London: Academic Press

JOHNSON O.G. & BOMMARITO J.W. (1971) *Tests and Measurements in Child Development.* San Francisco: Jossey-Bass

JONES H.G. (1970) Principles of Psychological Assessment. *In* Mittler P. (ed.) *The Psychological Assessment of Mental and Physical Handicaps.* London: Methuen

KAGAN J. (1966) Reflection—impulsivity: the generality and dynamics of conceptual tempo. *J. Abnorm. Psychol.* **71,** 17–24

KIRK S.A., McCARTHY J.J. & KIRK W.D. (1968) *The Illinois Test of Psycholinguistic Abilities*, rev. edn. Urbana, Ill.: University of Illinois

LEITENBERG H. (1973) The use of single-case methodology in psychotherapy research. *J. Abnorm. Psychol.* **82,** 87–101

LEVY P. (1974) Generalizability studies in clinical settings. *Brit. J. Soc. Clin. Psychol.* **13,** 161–172

LOCKYER L. & RUTTER M. (1969) A five to fifteen year follow-up study of infantile psychosis. III: Psychological aspects. *Brit. J. Psychiat.* **115,** 865–882

MAXWELL A.E. (1959) Tables to facilitate the comparison of sub-test scores on the WISC. *J. Clin. Psychol.* **15,** 293–295

MEICHENBAUM D. & GOODMAN J. (1971) Training impulsive children to talk to themselves. A means of developing self-control. *J. Abnorm. Psychol.* **77,** 115–126

MISCHEL W. (1968) *Personality and Assessment*. New York: Wiley

MITTLER P. (1970)(ed.) *The Psychological Assessment of Mental and Physical Handicaps*. London: Methuen

NEALE M.D. (1958) *Analysis of Reading Ability*. London: Macmillan

O'LEARY D.K. (1972) The assessment of psychopathology in children. *In* Quay H.C. & Werry J.S. (eds.) *Psychopathological Disorders of Childhood*. New York: Wiley

PAYNE R.W. & JONES H.G. (1957) Statistics for the investigation of individual cases. *J. Clin. Psychol.* **13,** 115–121

POPHAM W.J. & HUSEK T.R. (1969) Implications of criterion-referenced measurement. *J. Ed. Meas.* **6,** 1–9

RASHBASS C. (1960) New method for recording eye movements. *J. Optical Soc. Amer.* **50,** 642–644

RASHBASS C. (1961) The relationship between saccadic and smooth tracking eye movements. *J. Physiol.* **159,** 326–338

REITAN R.M. (1974) Methodological problems in clinical neuropsychology. *In* Reitan R.M. & Davison L.A. (eds.) *Clinical Neuropsychology: Current Status and Applications*. Washington DC: Winston

RUTTER M., GRAHAM P. & YULE W. (1970) *A Neuropsychiatric Study in Childhood*. Clinics in Develop. Med. nos. 35/36. London: SIMP/Heinemann

RUTTER M. & LOCKYER L. (1967) A five to fifteen year follow-up study of infantile psychosis 1. Description of sample. *Brit. J. Psychiat.* **113,** 1169–1182

SATTLER J.M. (1974) *Assessment of Children's Intelligence*. Philadelphia: W.B. Saunders

SCHONELL F.J. & SCHONELL F.E. (1956) *Diagnostic and Attainment Testing*. Edinburgh: Oliver & Boyd

SEDLAK R.A. & WEENER P. (1973) Review of the Illinois test of psycholinguistic abilities. *In* Mann L. & Sabatino D.A. (eds.) *The First Review of Special Education*, vol. 1. Philadelphia: Buttonwood Farms

SELIGMAN M.E.P. (1975) *Helplessness: on depression, development and death*. San Francisco: W.H. Freeman

SHACKEL B. (1960) Electro-oculography: the electrical recording of eye position. *Proc. 3rd. Int. Conf. on Medical Electronics*. London: Institute of Electrical Engineers

SHAFFER D., McNAMARA N. & PINCUS J.H. (1974) Controlled observations on patterns of activity, attention and impulsivity in brain-damaged and psychiatrically disturbed boys. *Psychol. Med.* **4,** 4–18

SHAPIRO M.B. (1957) Experimental method in the psychological description of the individual psychiatric patient. *Internat. J. Soc. Psychiat.* **3,** 89–102

SHAPIRO M.B. (1970) Intensive assessment of the single case: an inductive-deductive approach. *In* Mittler P. (ed.) *The Psychological Assessment of Mental and Physical Handicaps*. London: Methuen

STANLEY J.C. (1971) Reliability. *In* Thorndike R.L. (ed.) *Educational Measurement*, 2nd edn. Washington DC: American Council on Education

STUTSMAN R. (1948) *Guide for Administering the Merrill-Palmer Scale of Mental Tests*. New York: Harcourt Brace & World

SUNDBERG N.D. & TYLER L.E. (1962) *Clinical Psychology*. New York: Appleton-Century-Crofts

THOMAS A., CHESS S. & BIRCH H.G. (1968) *Temperament and Behavior Disorders in Children*. New York: University Press

THORNDIKE R.L. (1963) *The Concepts of Over- and Underachievement*. New York: Bureau of Publications, Teachers College, Columbia University

WALKER D.K. (1973) *Socio-emotional Measures for Pre-school and Kindergarten Children*. San Francisco: Jossey-Bass/Dent

WARD J. (1970) The factor structure of the Frostig developmental test of visual perception. *Brit. Educ. Psychol.* **40,** 65–67

WECHSLER D. (1949) *Wechsler Intelligence Scale for Children*. New York: Psychological Corporation

WECHSLER D. (1967) *Wechsler Preschool and Primary Scale of Intelligence*. New York: Psychological Corporation

WERRY J.S. (1972) Organic factors in childhood psychopathology. *In* Quay H.C. & Werry J.S. (eds.) *Psychopathological Disorders of Childhood*. New York: Wiley

WIGGINS J.S. (1973) *Personality and Prediction*. Reading, Massachusetts: Addison-Wesley

YANDO R.M. & KAGAN J. (1968) The effect of teacher tempo on the child. *Child Devel.* **39,** 27–34

YATES A.J. (1970) *Behavior Therapy*. New York: Wiley

YSSELDYKE J.E. (1973) Diagnostic-prescriptive teaching: the search for aptitude-treatment interactions. *In* Mann L. & Sabatino D.A. (eds.) *The First Review of Special Education*, vol. 1. Philadelphia: Buttonwood Farms

CHAPTER 14

The EEG

R. HARRIS

The high incidence of electroencephalographic (EEG) abnormalities in the records taken from children with psychiatric disorders described by Jasper *et al* (1938) has been confirmed in the large number of subsequent publications on the subject. The proportion of abnormal EEGs has been consistently greater than that reported in series of normal children whatever kind of psychiatric illness has been reviewed, but especially in those surveys which have included children with a history or clinical signs or symptoms consistent with organic brain disorders. EEG examinations are usually carried out to see if there is associated organic brain disease but there are often difficulties in assessing the records in a way which is helpful to the clinician in the management of a particular patient. If however there is a known additional handicap such as mental retardation or epilepsy the EEG may give useful information in the initial study of the patient and during the clinical follow-up. Various kinds of special EEG analyses are being used increasingly to investigate disorders of cerebral electrical organisation in psychiatric illnesses of childhood. An understanding of the changes in the EEG patterns during childhood and adolescence and even more importantly, an appreciation of the variations normally found in these patterns within the different age groups, is essential in the evaluation of routine clinical EEGs and in the results of sophisticated methods of EEG analysis.

Some of the problems of assessment, incidence of abnormality and clinical correlations of the EEG findings in the practice of child psychiatry will be discussed.

TECHNIQUE

The general methods of electrode application and recording are adequate for the routine EEG tests but cooperation is needed during the electrode placement and recording and there are frequently difficulties in the management of children who have severe behaviour disturbances or who are possibly frightened by the procedure. It can be exhausting to obtain a good, artefact-free, tracing in these circumstances. EEG departments need to be told if, and how, a child is likely to be difficult so that the necessary preparations can be made. Someone familiar and friendly to accompany the child, toys, books, food, drink and calm patience may all help. A few children remain unapproachable and unfortunately the usual sedative drugs, particularly the barbiturates, tend to make them even more difficult. In the last resort, if the clinician feels that an EEG is essential, some form of anaesthesia may be required and techniques have been described using methohexitone (Frank *et al* 1966; Goldie *et al* 1968) and ketamine hydrochloride (Harris & Manford 1973).

Problems of EEG assessment in normal children

Ongoing rhythms

The ongoing EEG patterns in the waking state change with age throughout infancy, childhood and adolescence. Rhythmic activity over the postcentral regions of the head with the reactive properties of the alpha rhythm to eye opening and other forms of alerting stimuli, is usually present at about one year of age but is slower than the defined alpha frequency of 8–13 c/sec and is larger in amplitude. This activity increases in frequency and decreases in amplitude until the characteristics of alpha activity for a particular individual is reached by about 15 to 16 years of age. The rate of this evolution varies very much from one individual to another and some quite young children will show a fast and stable alpha rhythm (Figure 14.1). The slower theta and delta rhythms, normally present in the EEG of babies, persist in variable amounts throughout childhood and adolescence. These activities tend to be more prominent over the posterior than anterior regions of the head and are fairly symmetrically distributed. Posteriorly these slow components are mixed with the alpha rhythm and usually show a similar type of reactivity to stimuli. Some slow activities may persist, particularly over the posterior temporal regions, into early adult life but there is normally a decrease with increasing age. Rhythmic activities over the central regions are usually more obvious in children than in adults and like the similarly located mu rhythm of the adult they can be attenuated or blocked by proprioceptive stimuli. The central rhythms are not necessarily symmetrical and have a slower frequency and different morphology to the mu rhythm, being more sinusoidal in wave form. Occipital lambda waves are much more commonly seen, and are larger in amplitude than the lambda waves found in adults. Fast or beta rhythms are not usually a prominent feature in children's records (Berti *et al* 1970).

Analyses of the proportion, amplitude and frequency of the various components of the EEG have been carried out in normal children at different ages (Eeg-Olofsson 1970) but there still remains the difficulty of assessment of the overall pattern of the electrical activities found at a particular moment of an individual child's life. It is also known that many transient disorders

Glen C. 12/70−0054
7¾ years
26.1.70.

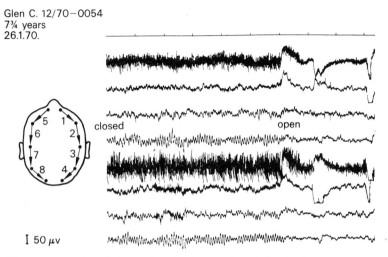

Figure 14.1   A well-formed and relatively fast alpha rhythm in a 7-year-old boy. Time marker 1 second.

such as the prodromal stage of measles (Pampiglione 1964) may cause a temporary change in the ongoing EEG pattern, usually resulting in a diffuse increase in the slower components. Mild asymmetries in the distribution of various activities over the two hemispheres may normally occur and change their lateralisation from time to time especially in young children. The electroencephalographer must therefore know the clinical state of the patient at each test and follow the trend in the EEG over a period of time before a complete evaluation of the ongoing EEG activity can be made in an individual child.

Paroxysmal abnormalities

The definitions of paroxysmal EEG abnormalities are not uniform throughout the literature and comparison of results from one paper to another is difficult. One of the largest and most carefully evaluated series of EEG examinations in normal children is that of Eeg-Olofsson (1970). Paroxysmal abnormalities are carefully defined in this monograph and include spikes, sharp waves and large amplitude slow waves occurring in focal or diffuse bursts.

There were 928 subjects in the series; 743 in the 'child' group aged 1–15 years and 185 in an 'adolescent' group of 16–21 years. The subjects had had no perinatal troubles and were without a history or clinical indication of central nervous system disease. They all showed normal physical and mental development and there was no history of mental or neurological disorder in near relatives. The EEG examinations included a period of hyperventilation in the older children, together with photic stimulation and a period of sleep in the majority. Sixteen per cent of the child group showed the 14 and 6 per sec positive spike phenomena (see below) and 15 per cent of the adolescents.

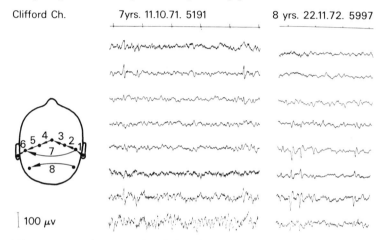

Figure 14.2   An example of the change in spike localisation. This child had infrequent seizures from $1\frac{1}{2}$ years of age. Several EEGs up to the age of 7 showed clear right sylvian or posterior temporal spike discharges. At 8 years, the right sided spikes disappeared but focal spikes were seen about the left sylvian electrode.

Excluding this feature, 15 per cent of the children and 4·9 per cent of adolescents had paroxysmal abnormalities at some time during the EEG. The records were also assessed in relation to the presence of an excess of slow frequency activity for each given year of life. Taking paroxysmal and excessive slow wave activity together, there were 68 per cent of the children and 77 per cent of the adolescents who had a totally 'normal' EEG. Below 10 years of age, paroxysmal activity tended to occur most often during drowsiness and light sleep and after puberty there was a significantly higher incidence of paroxysmal abnormality induced by photic stimulation in girls than boys. Trojaborg (1968) in a follow-up study of 242 children over 3–15 years who had spike foci in the EEG, showed that there was a change of spike localisation in 85 per cent of the children and in one half this change was from the one hemisphere to the other (Figure 14.2).

The individual varability in EEG patterns in relation to age, the incidence of abnormal wave forms in normal children, the instability of localisation of focal abnormalities and the relatively easily induced EEG disturbances during intercurrent illnesses particularly in young children, have all to be considered when making assessments of EEGs from children with psychiatric disorders.

EEG FINDINGS IN PSYCHIATRIC ILLNESSES

There are very few EEG patterns which, taken alone, are diagnostic of a particular pathological cerebral process, and none in psychiatric disorders as Ellingson (1954) found in a review of published work up to 1954. More recently, Ritvo *et al* (1970) conducted a double blind EEG study of 184 children in hospitals for psychiatric reasons and could find no significant correlations between the psychiatric diagnosis and EEG findings. A population study (Fenton *et al* 1974) of EEGs from 14-year-old schoolboys compared records of four groups: normal boys; those with psychiatric disorders; backward readers; and intellectual retardation. Global EEG abnormalities could not be related to the independently rated clinical categories. There were a few differences in the distribution of particular EEG features which did not apply however to the psychiatric group. It is not the task of the electroencephalographer to make psychiatric diagnoses but to assist the clinician as far as possible in the evaluation and management of a patient. For convenience, however, the EEG findings in some broad diagnostic groups will be considered.

Behaviour disorders

In general, the various types of behaviour disorders have been grouped together in the literature relating to the EEG, and many of the EEG studies have included children with additional clinical evidence of organic brain trouble (Kennard 1949; Secunda & Finley 1942; Stevens *et al* 1968; Stevens & Milstein 1970). This confuses the importance of the relevance of the EEG abnormalities to the various clinical problems. An asymmetric EEG in a child with behavioural difficulties and a hemiplegia would clearly relate to the brain lesion causing hemiplegia rather than to the behavioural problem. Similarly, EEG abnormalities would be expected in an epileptic child whether he or she presented behaviour difficulties or not. Where the distinction has been made between neurologically normal and abnormal children, EEG abnormalities have tended to correlate with evidence of neurological impairment (Dober 1966; Gerson *et al* 1972; Graffagnino *et al* 1968; Hansen 1970; Small

1968). Other studies have excluded children with epilepsy, known neurological defects or an overall IQ below 70 or 75. A varying incidence of EEG abnormality has been reported largely because of the different criteria of EEG assessment and type of patient included in the various series, but in general about 40 to 50 per cent of abnormal records have been found (Aird & Yamomoto 1966; Bayrakal 1965; Spilimbergo & Nissen 1971). The concept of 'minimal cerebral dysfunction' has further confused the interpretation of results in papers where no attempt has been made to distinguish children with 'soft neurological signs' (such as clumsiness, excessive restlessness, squint or other visual defect) from the neurologically intact and from children with overt neurological conditions. Paine *et al* (1968), describes the referral of the first group, mainly from the upper middle class, as 'a sign of increased concern about the less intelligent child in a competitive subculture'. The incidence of EEG abnormality in this group is about 40 per cent (Capute *et al* 1968; Paine *et al* 1968) but drops to nearly half this value if children with only affective disorders are studied (Lairy & Harrison 1968). Thus there is a 2- to 3-fold increase in the incidence of EEG abnormality in children with behaviour disorders without gross neurological or mental handicap (although possibly including minor neurological defects) in comparison with normal children. Children with specific reading difficulties show a proportion of non-specific EEG abnormalities which is similar to that found in the clinically mixed groups of children with behaviour disorders. Ayers and Torres (1967) reported an incidence of 40 per cent. Enuresis, when presenting as an isolated problem, is not associated with an increased incidence of EEG abnormality (Murphy *et al* 1970).

Hyperkinetic behaviour disorders have been considered separately by some authors as these children do present special clinical problems but from the EEG point of view the incidence and type of abnormality is similar to that found in behaviour disorders as a whole. In a total of 353 hyperkinetic children studied by Klinkerfuss *et al* (1965) definite EEG abnormalities were present in 53 per cent of patients who also had epilepsy or some neurological defect, and in 30 per cent where hyperkinesis was the only problem. An excess of slow wave activity was the most common EEG abnormality in the whole series, with focal changes predominantly in the neurologically handicapped group. A much higher overall incidence of EEG disturbance was found if minor abnormalities were included. Wikler *et al* (1970) found more abnormal EEGs in hyperkinetic children (who were among the youngest in the series) than others, in a somewhat small group of mixed behaviour disorders.

Attempts have been made by various authors to correlate the type and location of the EEG abnormality with different kinds of behavioural disorder or associated slight neurological handicap usually without any positive findings (Lucas *et al* 1965). This is a tempting exercise particularly as some focal EEG abnormalities may be marked in a single record (Figure 14.3). Lairy and Harrison (1968) for example surveyed the EEGs of 102 children aged from 6–14 years who were without encephalopathy or epilepsy but who had spike foci in their records. These children were patients at a clinic specialising in problems of psychomotor function and language. None had an IQ below 75. Systematic neurological, psychiatric and psychometric assessments were made. Motor problems occurred most often in children with unilateral spikes over the rolandic regions, visual or oculomotor difficulties correlated with

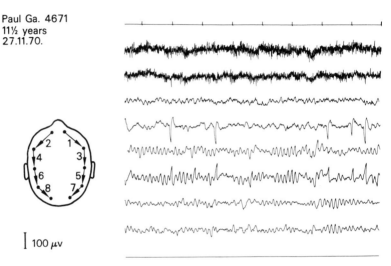

Paul Ga. 4671
11½ years
27.11.70.

100 μv

Figure 14.3   Large amplitude left sylvian spike discharges mixed with slow waves. This recording was from a child with severe behaviour problems but there were no associated neurological defects and he had never had seizures.

occipital foci and left occipital foci were predominant in children with 'perceptual motor disturbances'. Multiple symptoms were found in children with multiple spikes. These findings were compared with 100 other patients similarly assessed but who did not show spike foci in their EEGs. There was a significant difference in the motor quotient between the two groups, a poor score correlating with the incidence of spike discharges. 56 children with EEG spike foci had follow-up clinical and EEG studies, the majority showed EEG improvement parallelled by clinical improvement. Those with persistent focal EEG abnormalities tended to also have associated generalised EEG disturbances and half continued to have clinical problems, mainly of the affective type.

The significance of the spike discharges with regard to epilepsy is important. Although, as Eeg-Olofsson (1970) has shown, spikes are found in some records from a normal population of children, there is of course a close relationship with the occurrence of spikes in the EEG and the incidence of clinical epilepsy. The common findings of paroxysmal abnormalities in the EEGs of children with behaviour disorders has led some authors to prescribe and then to assess the effect of anticonvulsant treatment (Gross & Wilson 1964; Itil 1967; Jones *et al* 1955; Lindsley & Henry 1942; Waller & Kirkpatrick 1947) sometimes with assertions that the behaviour disorders were similar to those found in the 'epileptic personality' (Cutts & Jasper 1939). None of the children with spike foci followed up by Lairy and Harrison (1968) developed epilepsy and anticonvulsants were never prescribed. These authors considered the spikes to be a sign of cerebral dysfunction in the immature brain, a concept which at least spares the children from unnecessary and potentially harmful drug treatment. This view has been reinforced by Egli and Graf (1975) who followed up 76 disturbed children with spike discharges in the EEGs but who did not suffer from epilepsy. Fifty-six were treated with anticonvulsants, 26 for periods of from 3 to 17 years, but none were considered to have had their behaviour improved by drug therapy.

Another type of spike discharge, the 14 and 6/sec positive spikes first described by Gibbs (1951) and attributed to hypothalamic or thalamic epilepsy provoked a large number of publications. These wave forms were correlated with particular behaviour problems such as aggression, delinquency and intermittent somatic symptoms such as headache and abdominal pain and vomiting occurring mainly during adolescence. A review article by Henry (1963) demonstrated the fallacy of looking for a common EEG abnormality in groups of clinically similar patients where the correlations will merely reflect a particular type of clinical referral. The EEG techniques for recording this phenomenon are important, wide interelectrode spacing is required and the recording must be carried out during drowsiness and the early stages of light sleep. Using these methods Lombroso *et al* (1966) found these 14 and 6/sec positive discharges, to which they gave the name 'ctenoids', in 58 per cent of normal 13–15-year-old boys, a higher percentage than in the majority of the clinical groups studied. Paediatric encephalographers commonly see these wave forms in the EEGs of children from about 2 years of age provided the appropriate recording methods are used. The genesis is uncertain but their recognition is important as they need to be distinguished from other types of spike discharges.

Evaluation of the incidence and importance of EEG abnormality in adolescents with behaviour disorders is confused in the literature as often these children have been included with younger age groups and the 14 and 6/sec positive spike discharges, which are particularly common in adolescence, have been regarded as an abnormality. In the published series where the teenage group has been specified, and if the positive spike phenomena has been excluded from the results, the proportion of abnormal EEGs is probably only slightly more than that which might be found by chance in a normal population (Jones *et al* 1955; Low & Dawson 1961). This is in accordance with the general experience that unless there is a progressive brain disorder, or

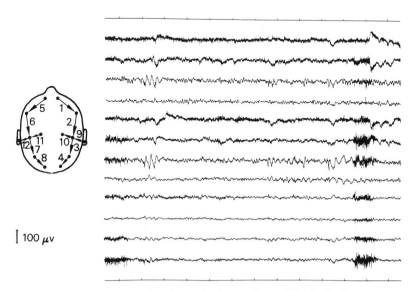

100 μv

Figure 14.4   An example of organic factors in a girl who had had behaviour problems from 15 years of age. She had been born 2 months prematurely and had had a severe convulsion at 6 months of age. Her IQ was 134 and apart from a series of 'blackouts' at 16 years there was no neurological abnormality. The EEG is abnormal and shows episodes of theta and delta activity mixed with sharp waves over both posterior temporal regions, particularly the left. These abnormalities were confirmed in a Seconal induced sleep record.

fluctuations occur in the state of a patient with epilepsy, EEG abnormalities tend to diminish or disappear during later childhood, adolescence and early adult life. This tendency has been confirmed in children with behaviour disorders in follow-up studies such as that carried out by Lairy and Harrison (1968) and was noted in Ellingson's review (1954). As in the younger age groups, there is a greater incidence of EEG abnormality in adolescents with behaviour disorders who have a history or clinical evidence of probable brain damage (Figures 14.4 and 14.5), (Jones *et al* 1955; Loomis 1965). Moreover, a group of 80 delinquent 13–18-year-old boys, all free from evidence of organic brain disease or mental retardation failed to show any great EEG difference when compared with the records from 70 normal boys in the same age group (Wiener *et al* 1966). An attempt made by Loomis *et al* (1967) to predict EEG abnormalities from clinical data in a series of 100 delinquent girls gave a 70 per cent error, a result which helps to put in perspective the reports of statistical correlations of types of adolescent behaviour disturbance such as 'overinhibition', 'unsocialised aggression', tempers, truancy, theft,

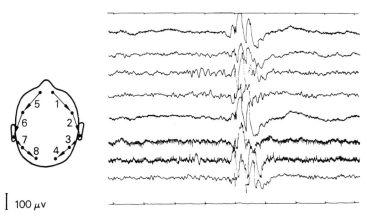

100 μv

Figure 14.5 This girl had possible organic damage complicating disturbed behaviour from 12 years of age. There had been a head injury at 13 years followed by 'delayed concussion' and a series of faints. There were no neurological abnormalities and the IQ was 105. The EEG shows an excess of theta activity over both posterior temporal regions and a burst of large amplitude delta activity mixed with sharp waves and spikes. Independent sharp waves or spikes appeared over both temporal regions during a Seconal induced sleep recording.

sex misbehaviour and retarded reading, with particular EEG abnormalities (Chen & Higgins 1966, Müller & Shamsie 1968). Unfortunately, the deviant adolescent may be involved with the law and in this situation an EEG recording is sometimes requested during the course of the medical and psychiatric examination and the result included in the report to a court. The EEG assessment can only state the current situation with regard to cerebral electrical function. This may be very valuable when epilepsy or other neurological handicaps complicate the problem but in the light of present knowledge it can hardly give information about the type of behaviour problem, its prognosis or management.

Emotional and psychosomatic disorders

There is very little work on the modification of EEG patterns in psycho-neurotic states which might occur in childhood. It is well known that in anxiety states of adults there may be a diminution in the amount and amplitude of alpha activity and an increase in the amount of fast rhythms but even so, the records would still fall within the normal range and the same is likely of such states in childhood. The EEG is unaltered by hysteria and in the rare opportunities that arise to record the EEG during 'hysterical seizures' the resting EEG patterns are unaltered although somewhat obscured by movement and muscle artefact.

Physical illness allied to psychoneurotic disturbances may alter the EEG through physiological effects. This is found, for example, in asthma where alterations in the sleep patterns have been shown (Kales *et al* 1970) and in anorexia nervosa where there are complicating metabolic abnormalities (Crisp *et al* 1968). Children suffering from the specific syndrome of recurrent abdominal pain (described in the literature variously as the periodic syndrome, cyclical vomiting, abdominal migraine and abdominal epilepsy) may be referred for psychiatric help after physical causes for their symptoms have been excluded. The literature on this syndrome has been reviewed and an additional 50 patients were described by Papatheophilou *et al* (1972). Of their cases 22 per cent had EEG abnormalities of a type associated with epilepsy but only one of these patients eventually developed undoubted epilepsy. It is of interest that there was a family history of migraine, allergy or neurosis in 68 per cent of this series.

Psychoses of childhood

This is the group with the least documentation of the routine EEG findings probably for the good reason that they are the most difficult to test. These children often require heavy sedation for the electrode placement and recording and the EEG investigations have therefore tended to be of a rather special type. In general, as in the children with various other kinds of psychiatric problems the presence of an EEG abnormality depends more upon the coexistence of other central nervous system symptomatology including epilepsy and mental retardation than upon the psychosis itself and the incidence of abnormality is similar (White *et al* 1964). Kolvin *et al* (1971) in a series of 79 patients found abnormal records in one third and low voltage EEGs were said to be a common finding. This feature had been reported earlier by Hutt *et al* (1965) and was attributed to a high state of 'physiological arousal'. Periods of low voltage activity in 4 children recorded by a telemetering system were found to coincide with stereotypies (Hutt & Hutt 1968). Creak and Pampiglione (1969) in a carefully selected group of 35 autistic and withdrawn children who were followed up from 5–19 years found no uniformity in the type of EEG abnormality nor were there many small amplitude records to support the concept of overarousal. The outlook in individual cases in this series was unpredictable and there were no EEG features that could be correlated with the clinical evolution.

There have been other investigations, based upon various EEG techniques, which have shown evidence of disordered cerebral organisation in these children but there does not appear to be any particular EEG feature to identify this group.

Organic illnesses presenting with psychiatric features

Some of the early symptoms of a cerebral tumour such as deterioration in school work and unexplained irritability, may occasionally lead initially to referral for a psychiatric opinion. The true clinical situation will soon be realised but a coincidental focal slow wave abnormality in the EEG at this stage will help in the diagnosis.

There are many encephalopathies which may present with symptoms suggestive of a psychiatric illness including those due to infections and metabolic or toxic disorders. In the majority of patients the diagnosis presents little difficulty and the EEG pattern of a diffuse and often severe slow wave abnormality will confirm the organic nature of the condition. The insidious onset of subacute sclerosing leucoencephalitis which may be first noted by a gradual intellectual deterioration and change in behaviour, can be identified by the typical, regularly recurring repetitive complex EEG discharges (Cobb 1966). Rare inborn errors of metabolism with relatively late clinical manifestations may present with psychiatric disorders (Crome & Stern 1972). Homocystinuria, porphyria and Hartnup disease are examples. There are usually associated diffuse EEG abnormalities of various types in these conditions which are not diagnostic but will give a clue to the presence of an organic illness and prompt further investigations. Other kinds of metabolic disorders due to intercurrent diseases may also present with psychiatric symptoms. An example is shown in Figures 14.6 and 14.7 of a girl who had hypoparathyroidism with an associated severe disturbance of her calcium metabolism. Her symptoms and strange attacks were initially thought to be due to hysteria but the EEG deterioration demonstrated the presence of organic disease.

Toxic conditions are not a common problem in this context, but lead, unlike the mercury portion of the old-fashioned teething powders, is still a hazard especially for children with pica or other odd oral habits such as licking old drain pipes. This kind of behavioural peculiarity is not uncommon amongst autistic and mentally retarded children in the younger age groups. As in other types of encephalopathy the EEG will show a diffuse increase in slow activity in the acute stage possibly with the later appearance of spike discharges due to brain damage. The diagnosis of lead poisoning should be considered if there is coincidental deterioration in behaviour and the EEG

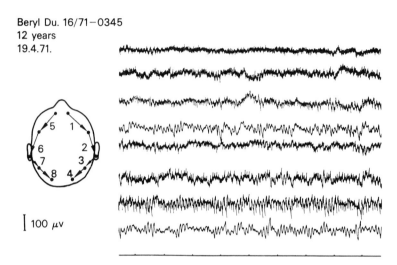

Beryl Du. 16/71−0345
12 years
19.4.71.

100 μv

Figure 14.6   This patient shows the effect of a severe metabolic disorder. For about 8 months she had had episodes of becoming 'blank', jerking legs, stiff arms and falling without loss of consciousness and also blurring of vision. She was referred for an EEG with a provisional diagnosis of hysteria. The traces are partly masked by muscle action potentials but there is a well formed, although somewhat asymmetrical alpha rhythm together with a possible excess of slow wave activity posteriorly.

in an already handicapped child living in a potentially hazardous environment. There are other rare conditions such as the onset of dementia during methotrexate therapy for acute leukaemia in childhood and once again serial EEGs will confirm the concidental drug induced toxic encephalopathy (Kay *et al* 1972).

Finally, the EEG may yield the first clue to secret drug taking in disturbed older children and adolescents. Many of the drugs used, particularly those containing barbiturates, will produce an excess of small amplitude beta activity at about 18–24 c/sec which is particularly prominent over the anterior regions of the head.

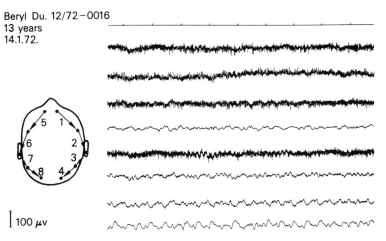

Beryl Du. 12/72—0016
13 years
14.1.72.

| 100 μv

Figure 14.7   The same patient as in Figure 14.6. The attacks
had persisted. The EEG taken 9 months later is clearly abnormal.
No alpha activity can be seen. Theta and delta activity is present
posteriorly with poorly formed slow and sharp wave complexes
over the left temporooccipital regions. This girl was found to have
hypoparathyroidism with a low blood calcium level.

Epilepsy

The diagnosis of epilepsy and the type of seizure are based essentially on
clinical observations but the presence of an EEG abnormality, particularly
spike or spike and wave discharges, can give valuable confirmation. There
is a high rate of psychiatric disorder in children with epilepsy, and the interplay of the physiological effects of epilepsy, the underlying brain damage
together with environmental factors in psychiatric problems has been discussed by Pond (1961). The survey of Graham and Rutter (1968) gave an
incidence of 34 per cent with a significantly greater number of affected children amongst those who suffered from the psychomotor type of attack. The
word 'psychomotor' has firmly replaced the outmoded term of 'epileptic equivalent' to describe the clinical automatisms and psychic behaviour of psychomotor epilepsy (Hill 1963). The combination of temporal lobe EEG abnormalities with psychomotor epilepsy is well known and the frequent association of behaviour disorders in this type of seizure has led to a number of
studies on the coincidence of temporal EEG abnormalities and psychiatric
disorder without epilepsy. These studies have been reviewed by Driver (1970)
who noted the difficulties in comparing clinical evaluations and EEG
assessments from one author to another. In children, in the light of present
knowledge, it is the substrate of the cerebral disorder which is giving rise

to the clinical combination of epilepsy and behaviour disturbance which is important rather than the location of the EEG abnormality. It is unusual to obtain repeatedly normal EEGs in children suffering from epilepsy. Abnormalities will invariably appear at some stage and may be facilitated by hyperventilation, photic stimulation or during a period of natural or drug induce sleep or drowsiness. It is rare for spike discharges to appear only at sphenoidal electrodes so that the only extra information obtained from this procedure (which involves giving a general anaesthetic), is to localise the origin of spike discharges to the mesical part of the temporal lobe. Because of

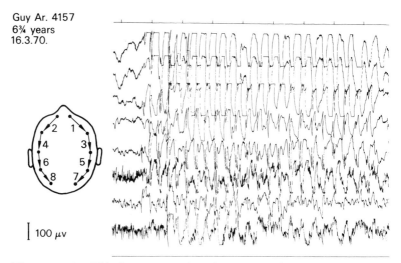

Guy Ar. 4157
6¾ years
16.3.70.

100 μv

Figure 14.8   This boy appeared to have expressive aphasia linked to an anxiety state and difficulties at school. Bursts of approximately 3 per second spike and wave discharges in the EEG accompanied by an absence attack are in keeping with some ictal disturbances being responsible for the speech difficulty.

the doubtful diagnostic value of focal spike discharges in children previously discussed, it is usually more reliable to use other EEG criteria to localise cerebral lesions such as persistent delta rhythms or a constant localised decrease in the amount and amplitude of normal EEG rhythms. Preoperative diagnosis of structural lesions in epilepsy cannot be made with certainty on EEG grounds alone in children and the EEG findings need to be supplemented by other clinical and neuroradiological assessments.

Occasionally children are referred to a psychiatrist for advice in whom the occurrence of seizures has either not been noted or the frequency underestimated. During an EEG recording there is the opportunity for prolonged combined observation of both the patient's clinical state and EEG under resting conditions and while the provocative procedures of hyperventilation and photic stimulation are carried out. Figures 14.8 and 14.9 are examples from a child whose 'absences' had previously gone unnoticed. Unrecognised episodes of minor epileptic status (Brett 1966) may also complicate the psychiatric management of a child suffering from epilepsy. These episodes are characterised by an association of almost continuous generalised spike and wave EEG discharges together with a deterioration in the child's mental state and motor performance of varying degree. The EEG and clinical abnormality

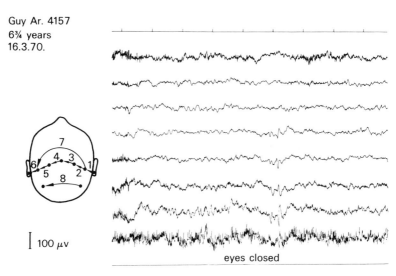

Guy Ar. 4157
6¾ years
16.3.70.

100 μv

eyes closed

Figure 14.9 The same child as in Figure 14.8. Spike discharges also appeared in his EEG, focal about the left sylvian electrode thus presenting further evidence of an organic basis for his speech behaviour.

are reversible and this can often be demonstrated during an attack by giving an intravenous injection of diazepam.

Drugs used in the treatment of epilepsy may be an added source of psychiatric illness or handicap and excessive dosage or unsuitable combinations of drugs may cause such symptoms as mental impairment, irritability or even psychoses. Patel and Crichton (1968) for example, described some severe effects of diphenylhydantoin intoxication in 13 children. Deterioration in the EEG with a diffuse excess of slow components is a valuable early indication of this particular condition. Toxic effects of other anticonvulsant drugs may produce similar EEG changes though excessive fast activity is usually also present if the barbiturate group of drugs is involved.

Retardation

Neurological deficits of all kinds and degree are commonly found in retarded children. Psychiatric disorders are also frequently present, particularly in those with severe subnormality (Rutter 1971). Epilepsy is another additional handicap with a reported incidence of 36 per cent in an unselected series (Donoghue *et al* 1970) and 32 per cent in an epidemiological survey of retarded children (Corbett *et al* 1975). The combinations of neurological handicap and seizures are very likely to be associated with EEG abnormalities in these children whether there are psychiatric disturbances present or not and as in other psychiatric problems the EEG findings will reflect the presence of these other defects rather than the behavioural abnormality. One of the most valuable contributions of the EEG in retarded children is in the evaluation of these neurological handicaps particularly in the incidence of ictal phenomena which may be confused with odd mannerisms, peculiar movements or episodic behaviour disturbances so often present in severely retarded children. Recognition of such attacks may lead to appropriate therapy and thus to an overall improvement in the child's behaviour and management (Harris 1972).

SPECIAL PROCEDURES

Apart from routine clinical recordings there have been various special EEG techniques used in the investigation of children with psychiatric disorders. Some have been relatively simple such as counting movement artefacts to quantify restlessness (Knight & Hinton 1969). The literature in this field has been reviewed by Crichton and Mackoff (1969). These authors also described the application of recording eye movements to quantify ocular hyperkinesis during tests for attention to a visual task. Other workers have looked at the reactivity i.e. attenuation or habituation of the alpha rhythm in test situations or in response to particular stimuli sometimes using telemetering systems of recording so that the subject is not restrained (Hermelin & O'Connor 1968; Martinius & Hoovey 1972; Milstein *et al* 1969; O'Connor, 1970). In general these measurements of attenuation and habituation have shown that the alpha rhythm is less responsive in the patient groups than controls with some differences in the autistic patients who showed adaptation more readily to light stimuli than other patients, but were relatively less aroused by continuous auditory stimuli. This type of measurement of alpha activity can be made from the ongoing EEG provided each stimulus or test is accurately recorded on the tracing.

Sophisticated methods of computer analysis are likely to be increasingly employed. Lairy *et al* (1969) compared the spatial and temporal configuration of the alpha rhythm in small groups of normal children with that in patients with behaviour disorders. The latter group had a greater spread of frequencies about the mean, a poorer spatial organisation and less interhemisphere co-ordination of the alpha rhythm than the normal controls. Similar findings were reported by Martinius and Hoovey (1971), thus confirming some of the observations made on the relatively less well organised ongoing rhythms from routine recordings in psychiatric patients (Berges *et al* 1966, Berges *et al* 1968).

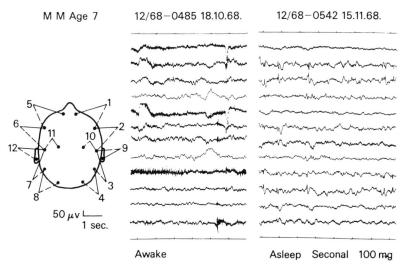

M M Age 7   12/68−0485 18.10.68.   12/68−0542 15.11.68.

50 μv
1 sec.

Awake   Asleep   Seconal   100 mg

Figure 14.10 This boy had behavioural problems and probably seizures. The record taken in the waking state shows very small and insignificant sharp waves over the right sylvian region. During Seconal-induced sleep however the spike discharges over these regions are clearly seen.

Sleep recordings have also been studied in some detail. The usual clinical application of short duration drug induced or natural sleep to facilitate the appearance of abnormal EEG phenomena is well known and in common use in most EEG departments (Figure 14.10). All night sleep recordings have also been carried out to assess the pattern of cyclical changes which normally occur. The published studies on abnormalities in the organisation of sleep cycles in children have been reviewed by Lenard (1970) and disturbances have been reported in mental retardation, phenylketonuria, hypothyroidism and some forms of epilepsy. This type of work is time consuming and requires special facilities in terms of staff and accommodation and most of the published work in psychiatry is on only small numbers of patients. Three hyperactive children given dextroamphetamine sulphate who were studied by Small *et al* (1971) showed no difference from their baseline patterns which were, in any case, similar to those of age matched controls. Caldwell *et al* (1970) found no significant differences in the overall all night power density analysis of cerebral electrical activity between normal children and those with psychotic symptoms. Onheiber *et al* (1965) compared the proportion of rapid eye movement (REM) sleep and the time to the onset of the first REM period in normal and schizophrenic children and found no differences. However Ornitz *et al* (1969) looked at the REM sleep patterns in more detail and noted that there was a reduced number of eye movements and a shorter percentage of time spent in eye movement during the REM sleep stage in young autistic children (mean age 3 years) than in normal children of similar age. The autistic children also had less slow activity but more fast rhythms in their EEGs during the REM sleep periods. These findings were confirmed in older autistic children (Ornitz 1972), although it is not known whether these findings are due to the autism alone or to associated retardation and further work is needed in this field. The classic sleep disorders of enuresis (Gabersek *et al* 1966), pavor nocturnus, nightmares and sleep walking have been shown in all night EEG recordings to occur mainly on arousal from stage IV or non-rapid eye movement periods of sleep and virtually never in REM sleep (Lenard 1970).

Averaging techniques applied to EEG waveforms have been used to study cerebral evoked potentials to various stimuli. In the waking state, visual evoked responses have been described with less hemisphere differences and smaller amplitude late components in the evoked waveform in 'dull' as opposed to 'bright' children (Rhodes *et al* 1969) and Conner (1970) noted unusual wave forms in 'poor readers'. Ornitz *et al* (1968) and Ornitz (1972) have shown a significant difference in auditory evoked potentials in autistic children when compared with control subjects. There is normally an amplitude reduction in part of the evoked waveform (N_2) to sound stimuli presented during bursts of eye movement in REM sleep. This reduction did not occur in the shorter bursts of eye movement found in autistic children. Ornitz (1972) has suggested that these findings implicate a failure of central vestibular control over sensory transmission and motor output during REM sleep in autistic children.

A waveform which can be used to test particular cerebral functions is the slow negative change seen between the cerebral evoked responses to spaced, paired stimuli of different modalities provided some action is required from the subject tested in relation to the second stimulus. This change is known as the contingent negative variation or expectancy wave and it normally does not acquire the stable adult form until about 21 years of age (Walter *et al* 1964). Examination of this wave form can obviously be applied as an objective measure in a number of test situations. Fenelon (1968) for example found that this wave was absent in dyslexic children when the second stimulus required an action related to the recognition of incorrectly spelled words. Analysis of several physiological variables have been used by Satterfield *et al* (1972) in the assessment of the state of 'arousal' in a small group of hyperkinetic children and their response to treatment with methylphenidate. Simultaneous power spectral analysis of the two EEG channels, a count of EEG movement artefact, recording cerebral evoked responses to click stimuli and skin conductance levels were carried out under controlled conditions. Low and high arousal pretreatment states were defined from these variables and a better response to therapy was found in the former. The low arousal state was said to be associated with relatively slower and larger amplitude EEG activity. Vertex to ear lobe connections were used for the EEG analysis. Although clinical EEGs were carried out, the global EEG findings with respect to the analysis were not given and this is probably a relevant factor in the evaluation of slow components in the analysis.

Computer facilities are needed to carry out the complex analysis of ongoing EEG activity and for the test programmes and evaluation of cerebral evoked wave forms. These are not yet commonly available and nor is the more important combined expertise required for both the psychiatric and EEG assessments. In child psychiatry the necessary standardisation and valid interpretation of the results cannot easily be made without paediatric experience in both these fields.

CONCLUSIONS

Abnormal EEG recordings in children with psychiatric problems depend more upon coexisting neurological defects, even if these are only slight, than upon a particular psychiatric condition. Because of the difficulties of evaluation of abnormal EEG phenomena in neurologically normal children perhaps the main indications for EEG recordings in child psychiatry, apart from some particular research interests, is to confirm the presence of an associated organic disorder. The type of EEG abnormality can rarely be used as a guide for general management (including special school placement) or drug treatment and there are few neuropathological correlates. Very little work has been done to attempt to relate the significance of particular EEG abnormalities with regard to prognosis but the frequent parallel between clinical and EEG improvement perhaps indicates the functional rather than structural implication of the EEG abnormalities in many children. In the search for an organic basis for a child's illness however, persistent or deteriorating

EEG abnormalities can obviously be of considerable clinical value. It has been suggested that an EEG is not an essential part of the evaluation of children with 'minimal cerebral dysfunction' (Dyment *et al* 1971). This may be a correct statistical view but it is a nihilistic approach for the individual child in whom the EEG findings, whether normal or abnormal, may be of help to the clinician.

The assessment of the usual routine EEG recording is only one aspect of the techniques now available. The changing EEG patterns throughout childhood of the ongoing cerebral electrical rhythms by day and night, their reactivity and variation in different circumstances and the analysis of evoked wave forms in the various clinical syndromes present a challenge to the electroencephalographer in the whole field of diagnosis and function in problems of child psychiatry.

REFERENCES

AIRD R.B. & YAMAMOTO T. (1966) Behavior disorders of childhood. *Electroenceph. Clin. Neurophysiol.* **21,** 148–156

AYERS F.W. & TORRES F. (1967) The incidence of EEG abnormalities in a dyslexic and a control group. *J. Clin. Psychol.* **23,** 334–336

BAYRAKAL S. (1965) The significance of electroencephalographic abnormality in behaviour-problem children. *Canad. Psychiat. Ass. J.* **10,** 387–392

BERGES J., HARRISON A. & LAIRY G.C. (1966) L'asynchronie des rythmes postérieurs chez l'enfant d'âge scolaire non encéphalopathe. *Rev. Neurol. (Paris)* **115,** 162–174

BERGES J., HARRISON A., LAIRY G.C. & STAMBAK M. (1968) L'EEG de l'enfant dyspraxique. *Electroenceph. Clin. Neurophysiol.* **25,** 208–220

BERTI G., BALLERINI B., MACCAGNANI F. & RICCI G.F. (1970) L'attivita rapida nell EEG dei bambini—suo significato diagnostica e clinico. *Rev. Neurol.* **40,** 230–238

BRETT E.M. (1966) Minor epileptic status. *J. Neurol. Sci.* **3,** 52–75

CALDWELL D.F., BRANE A.J. & BECKETT P.G.S. (1970) Sleep patterns in normal and psychotic children. *Arch. Gen. Psychiat. (Chicago)* **22,** 500–503

CAPUTE A.J., NEIDERMEYER E.F. & RICHARDSON F. (1968) The electroencephalogram in children with minimal cerebral dysfunction. *Pediatrics* **41,** 1104–1114

CHEN C.J. & HIGGINS C. (1966) Children's behaviour disorders and EEG patterns. *Dis. Nerv. Syst.* **27,** 52–56

COBB W. (1966) The periodic events of sub acute sclerosing leucoencephalitis. *Electroenceph. Clin. Neurophysiol.* **21,** 278–294

CONNER C.K. (1970) Cortical visual evoked response in children with learning disorders. *Psychophysiol.* **7,** 418–428

CORBETT J.A., HARRIS R. & ROBINSON R.G. (1975) Epilepsy. *In* Wortis J. (ed.) *Mental Retardation and Developmental Disabilities: An Annual Review*, vol. VII. New York: Brunner/Mazel

CREAK M. & PAMPIGLIONE G. (1969) Clinical and EEG studies on a group of 35 psychotic children. *Develop. Med. Child Neurol.* **11,** 218–227

CRICHTON J.U. & MACKOFF H.P. (1969) A clinical approach to the measurement of cerebral dysfunction. *Pediatrics* **44,** 365–374

CRISP A.H., FENTON G.W. & SCOTTON L. (1968) A controlled study of the EEG in anorexia nervosa. *Brit. J. Psychiat.* **114,** 1149–1160

CROME L. & STERN J. (1972) *Pathology of Mental Retardation,* 2nd edn. Edinburgh and London: Churchill-Livingstone

CUTTS K.K. & JASPER H. (1939) Effect of benzedrine sulfate and phenobarbital on behavior problem children with abnormal electroencephalograms. *Arch. Neurol. Psychiat. (Chicago)* **41,** 1138–1145

DOBER B. (1966) EEG—befunde bei verhaltensauffalligkeiten im kindesalter. *Psychiat. Neurol. Med. Psychol. (Leipzig)* **18,** 405–409

DONOGHUE E.C., ABBAS K.A. & GAL E. (1970) The medical assessment of mentally retarded children in hospital. *Brit. J. Psychiat.* **117,** 531–532

DRIVER M.V. (1970) Electroencephalography and the diagnosis of temporal lobe disease. *In* Price J.H. (ed.) *Modern Trends in Psychological Medicine 2.* London: Butterworths

DYMENT P.G., LATTIN J.E. & HERBERTSON L.M. (1971) The value of the electroencephalogram in evaluating children with minimal cerebral dysfunction. *J. Sch. Hlth.* **41,** 9–11

EEG-OLOFSSON O. (1970) The development of the electroencephalogram in normal children and adolescents from the age of 1 through 21 years. *Acta Paediat. Scand.* Suppl. 208

EGLI M. & GRAF I. (1975) The use of anticonvulsant treatment of behaviourally disturbed children with bio-electric epilepsy. A follow-up study of 76 cases. *Acta paedopsychiat. (Basel)* **41,** 54–69

ELLINGSON R.J. (1954) The incidence of EEG abnormality among patients with mental disorders of apparently non-organic origin. A critical view. *Amer. J. Psychiat.* **111,** 263–275

FENELON B. (1968) Expectancy waves and other complex cerebral events in dyslexic and normal subjects. *Psychonom. Sci.* **13,** 253–254

FENTON G.W., FENWICK P.B.C., DOLLIMORE J., RUTTER M. & YULE W. (1974) An introduction to the Isle of Wight EEG study. *Electroenceph. Clin. Neurophysiol.* **37,** 325

FRANK G.S., FRASER R.A. & WHITCHER C. (1966) Intramuscular methohexital for rapid induction of short duration sleep in the EEG laboratory. A study of forty-four hyperkinetic children. *Electroenceph. Clin. Neurophysiol.* **21,** 76–78

GABERSEK V., LABAR P., DUCHE D.J., SCHERRER J. & MICHAUX L. (1966) Le sommeil des enfants enuretiques. *Rev. Neurol.* **115,** 493–497

GERSON I.M., BARNES T.C., MANNINO A., FANNING J.M. & BURNS J.J. (1972) EEG of children with various learning problems. Part I—Outpatient study. *Dis. Nerv. Syst.* **33,** 170–177

GIBBS E.L. & GIBBS F.A. (1951) Electroencephalographic evidence of thalamic and hypothalamic epilepsy. *Neurology (Minneap.)* **1,** 136–144

GOLDIE L., FRIED Y., GOULD T. & PEDERSEN T.M. (1968) Electroencephalographs in the subnormal and the mentaly ill child. The use of methohexitone. *Anaesthesia* **23,** 364–371

GRAFFAGNINO P.N., BOELHOUWER C. & REZNIKOFF M. (1968) An organic factor in patients of a child psychiatric clinic. *J. Amer. Acad. Child Psychiat.* **7,** 618–638

GRAHAM P. & RUTTER M. (1968) Organic brain dysfunction and child psychiatric disorder. *Brit. Med. J.* **3**, 695–700

GROSS M.D. & WILSON W.C. (1964) Behaviour disorders of children with cerebral dysrhythmias—successful treatment of subconvulsive dysrhythmia with anticonvulsants. *Arch. Gen. Psychiat.* **11**, 610–619

HANSEN N. (1970) Cerebro-organic pathogenesis in 110 children followed-up subsequent to admission to a child psychiatric department. *Acta Psychiat. Scand.* **46**, 399–412

HARRIS R. (1972) EEG aspects of unclassified mental retardation. *In* Cavanagh J.B. (ed.) *The Brain in Unclassified Mental Retardation.* Study Group No. 3. Edinburgh and London: Churchill-Livingstone

HARRIS R. & MANFORD M.L.M. (1973) The use of ketamine hydrochloride anaesthesia for obtaining EEGs from severely disturbed patients. *Electroenceph. Clin. Neurophysiol.* **35**, 415

HENRY C.E. (1963) Positive spike discharges in the EEG and behaviour abnormality. *In* Glasser G.H. (ed.) *EEG and Behaviour.* New York: Basic Books

HERMELIN B. & O'CONNOR N. (1968) Measures of the occipital alpha rhythm in normal, subnormal and autistic children. *Brit. J. Psychiat.* **114**, 603–610

HILL D. (1963) Epilepsy: clinical aspects. *In* Hill D. & Parr G. (eds.) *Electroencephalography.* London: Macdonald

HUTT S.J. & HUTT C. (1968) Stereotype, arousal and autism. *Hum. Dev.* **11**, 277–286

HUTT S.J., HUTT C., LEE D. & OUNSTED C. (1965) A behavioural and electroencephalographic study of autistic children. *J. Psychiat. Res.* **3**, 181–197

ITIL T.M., RIZZO A.E. & SHAPIRO D.M. (1967) Study of behavior and EEG correlation during treatment of disturbed children. *Dis. Nerv. Syst.* **28**, 731–736

JASPER H.H., SOLOMON P. & BRADLEY C. (1938) Electroencephalogram analyses of behavior problem children. *Amer. J. Psychiat.* **95**, 641–658

JONES E., BAGCHI B.K. & WAGGONER R.W. (1955) Focal abnormalities of the electroencephalogram in juveniles with behavior disorder. *J. Nerv. Ment. Dis.* **122**, 28–35

KALES A., KALES J.D., SLY R.M., SCHARF M.B., TJIAUW-LING T. & PRESTON T.A. (1970) Sleep patterns of asthmatic children: all night electroencephalographic studies. *J. Allerg.* **46**, 300–308

KAY H.E.M., KNAPTON P.J., O'SULLIVAN J.P., WELLS D.G., HARRIS R.F., INNES E.M., STUART J., SCHWARTZ F.C.M. & THOMPSON E.N. (1972) Encephalopathy in acute leukaemia associated with methotrexate therapy. *Arch. Dis. Child.* **47**, 344–354

KENNARD M.A. (1949) Significance of abnormal EEGs in disorders of behavior. *Electroenceph. Clin. Neurophysiol.* **1**, 118–119

KLINKERFUSS G.H., LANGE P.H., WEINBERG W.A. & O'LEARY J.L. (1965) Electroencephalographic abnormalities of children with hyperkinetic behavior. *Neurology (Minneap.)* **15**, 883–891

KNIGHT R.M. & HINTON G.G. (1969) The effects of methylphenidate (Ritalin) on the motor skills and behaviour of children with learning problems. *J. Nerv. Ment. Dis.* **148**, 643–653

KOLVIN I., OUNSTED C. & ROTH M. (1971) Studies in the childhood psychoses: V. Cerebral dysfunction and childhood psychoses. *Brit. J. Psychiat.* **118**, 407–414

LAIRY G.C. & HARRISON A. (1968) Functional aspects of EEG foci in children. *In* Kellaway P. & Petersen O. (eds.) *Clinical electroencephalography in children.* New York: Grune & Stratton

LAIRY G.C., RÉMOND A., RIEGER H. & LESÈVRE N. (1969) The alpha average: III. Clinical application in children. *Electroenceph. Clin. Neurophysiol.* **26**, 453–467

LENARD H.G. (1970) Sleep studies in infancy. Facts, concepts and significance. *Acta Paediat. Scand.* **59**, 572–581

LINDSLEY D.B. & HENRY C.E. (1942) The effect of drugs on behavior and the electroencephalograms of children with behavior disorders. *Psychosom Med.* **4**, 140–149

LOMBROSO C.T., SCHWARTZ I.H., CLARK D.M., MUENCH H. & BARRY J. (1966) Ctenoids in healthy youths. *Neurology* **16**, 1152–1158

LOOMIS S.D. (1965) EEG abnormalities as a correlate of behavior in adolescent male delinquents. *Amer. J. Psychiat.* **121**, 1003–1006

LOOMIS S.D., BOHNERT P.J. & HUNCKE S. (1967) Prediction of EEG abnormalities in adolescent delinquents. *Arch. Gen. Psychiat.* **17**, 494–497

LOW N.L. & DAWSON S.P. (1961) Electroencephalographic findings in juvenile delinquency. *Pediatrics* **28**, 452–457

LUCAS A.R., RODIN E.A. & SIMSON C.B. (1965) Neurological assessment of children with early school problems. *Develop. Med. Child Neurol.* **7**, 145–156

MARTINIUS J.W. & HOOVEY Z.B. (1971) Automatische analyse der interokzipitalen synchronie in EEG verhaltensgestorter kinder. *Z EEG-EMG* **2**, 95–97

MARTINIUS J.W. & HOOVEY Z.B. (1972) Bilateral synchrony of occipital alpha waves, oculomotor activity and 'Attention' in children. *Electroenceph. Clin. Neurophysiol.* **32**, 349–356

MILSTEIN V., STEVENS J. & SACHDEV K. (1969) Habituation of the alpha attenuation response in children and adults with psychiatric disorders. *Electroenceph. Clin. Neurophysiol.* **26**, 12–18

MÜLLER H.F. & SHAMSIE S.J. (1968) Classification des troubles du comportement des adolescents et données eléctroencephalographiques. *Canad. Psychiat. Ass. J.* **13**, 363–370

MURPHY S., NICKOLS J. & HAMMAR S. (1970) Neurological evaluation of adolescent enuretics. *Pediatrics* **45**, 269–273

O'CONNOR N. (1970) Visual perception in autistic children. *In* Primrose D.A.A. (ed.) *Proceedings of the Second Congress of the International Association for the Scientific Study of Mental Deficiency.* Warsaw: Polish Medical Publishers

ONHEIBER P., WHITE P.T., DEMYER M.K. & OTTINGER D.R. (1965) Sleep and dream patterns of child schizophrenics. *Arch. Gen. Psychiat.* **12**, 568–571

ORNITZ E.M. (1972) Development of sleep patterns in autistic children. *In* Clemente C.D., Purpura D.D. & Mayer F.E. (eds.) *Sleep and the Maturing Nervous System.* New York: Academic Press

ORNITZ E.M., RITVO E.R., PANMAN L.M., LEE Y.H., CARR E.M. & WALTER R.D. (1968) The auditory evoked response in normal and autistic children during sleep. *Electroenceph. Clin. Neurophysiol.* **25**, 221–230

ORNITZ E.M., RITVO E.R., BROWN M.B., LA FRANCHI S., PARMELEE T. & WALTER R.D. (1969) The EEG and rapid eye movements during REM sleep in normal and autistic children. *Electroenceph. Clin. Neurophysiol.* **26**, 167–175

PAINE R.S., WERRY J.S. & QUAY H.C. (1968) A study of 'minimal cerebral dysfunction'. *Develop. Med. Child Neurol.* **10**, 505–520

PAMPIGLIONE G. (1964) Prodomal phase of measles: some neurophysiological studies. *Brit. J. Med.* **2**, 1296–1300

PAPATHEOPHILOU R., JEAVONS P.M. & DISNEY M.E. (1972) Recurrent abdominal pain: a clinical and electroencephalographic study. *Develop. Med. Child Neurol.* **14,** 31–44

PATEL H. & CRICHTON J.U. (1968) The neurologic hazards of diphenylhydantoin in childhood. *J. Pediat. St. Louis* **73,** 676–684

PINNEY E.L. Jr. (1968) Reading and arithmetic scores and EEG alpha blocking in disadvantaged children. *Dis. Nerv. Syst.* **29,** 388–390

POND D.A. (1961) Psychiatric aspects of epileptic and brain-damaged children. *Brit. Med. J.* **2,** 1372–1387; 1454–1459

RITVO E.R., ORNITZ E.M., WALTER R.D. & HANLEY J. (1970) Correlation of psychiatric diagnoses and EEG findings—a double-blind study of 184 hospitalized children. *Amer. J. Psychiat.* **126,** 988–996

RHODES L.E., DUSTMAN R.E. & BECK E.C. (1969) The visual evoked response. A comparison of bright and dull children. *Electroenceph. Clin. Neurophysiol.* **27,** 364–372

RUTTER M.L. (1971) Psychiatry. *In* Wortis J. (ed.) *Mental Retardation,* vol. III. New York: Grune & Stratton

SATTERFIELD J.H., CANTWELL D.P., LESSER L.I. & PODOSIN R.L. (1972) Physiological studies of the hyperkinetic child: I. *Amer. J. Psychiat.* **128,** 1418–1424

SECUNDA L. & FINLEY K.H. (1942) Electroencephalographic studies in children presenting behavior disorders. *J. Nerv. Ment. Dis.* **95,** 621–625

SMALL J.G. (1968) Epileptiform electroencephalographic abnormalities in mentally ill children. *J. Nerv. Ment. Dis.* **147,** 341–348

SMALL A., HIBI S. & FEINBERG I. (1971) Effects of dextroamphetamine sulfate on EEG sleep patterns of hyperactive children. *Arch. Gen. Psychiat.* **25,** 239–380

SPILIMBERGO A. & NISSEN G. (1971) Verhaltensstörungen und EEG—veranderungen bei Kindern. *Acta Paedopsychiatr. (Basel)* **38,** 59–65

STEVENS J.R. & MILSTEIN V. (1970) Severe psychiatric disorders of childhood. Electroencephalogram and clinical correlations. *Amer. J. dis. Child* **120,** 182–192

STEVENS J.R., SACHDEV K. & MILSTEIN V. (1968) Behavior disorders of childhood and the electroencephalogram. *Arch. Neurol. (Chicago)* **18,** 160–177

TROJABORG W. (1968) Changes of spike foci in children. Kellaway P. & Petersen I. (eds.) *Clinical Electroencephalography in Children.* New York: Grune & Stratton

WALKER C.F. & KIRKPATRICK B.B. (1947) Dilantin treatment for behavior problem children with abnormal electroencephalograms. *Amer. J. Psychiat.* **103,** 484–492

WALTER W.G., COOPER R., ALDRIDGE V.J., McCALLUM W.C. & WINTER A.L. (1964) Contingent negative variation, an electric sign of sensorimotor association and expectancy in the human brain. *Nature* **203,** 380–384

WHITE P.T., DeMYER W. & DeMYER M. (1964) EEG abnormalities in early childhood schizophrenia—a double blind study of psychiatrically disturbed and normal children during promazine sedation. *Amer. J. Psychiat.* **120,** 950–958

WIENER J.M., DELANO J.G. & KLASS D.W. (1966) An EEG study of delinquent and non-delinquent adolescents. *Arch. gen. Psychiat.* **15,** 144–150

WIKLER A., DIXON J.F. & PARKER J.B. Jr. (1970) Brain function in problem children and controls—psychometric neurological, and electroencephalographic comparisons. *Amer. J. Psychiat.* **127,** 634–645

CHAPTER 15

Classification

M. RUTTER

PRINCIPLES

Classification as a means of ordering information and of grouping phenomena is basic to all forms of scientific enquiry (Rutter, Shaffer & Shepherd 1975). It provides a kind of language—an agreed set of terms— by which clinicians and research workers can describe the disorders they investigate and treat. Only if there is uniformity in the usage of descriptive and diagnostic terms, can meaning be attached to clinical reports, research findings or hospital statistics. That is the purpose of classification.

The principles of classification have been clearly outlined by Hempel (1961) and the advantages and disadvantages of different approaches were well discussed by Jaspers (1962) in his classical text. The factors which could provide the structure for an ideal diagnostic scheme are undecided and are a function of the purposes for which the classification will be employed (Rutter 1965). However, it needs to be emphasised, firstly, that there is no 'natural' scheme which is there to be discovered, and secondly, that classification in no way implies the existence of disease entities (Jaspers 1962). Continua of personality characteristics or psychosocial situations may be classified just as 'illnesses' are.

It is sometimes thought that an ideal classification should be based on aetiology, but this is not necessarily so. Although aetiology is probably an indispensable part of any medical classification it is unlikely to be sufficient in itself. In the first place, most psychiatric disorders have a multifactorial causation so that a classification based on the 'main' aetiology factor would often constitute an oversimplification. Secondly, even in general medicine a single cause can often lead to very different disease states. Tertiary syphilis is a good example of this. Thirdly, treatment and prognosis may depend on the nature of the disorder rather than on the aetiology. For example, a classification of fractures must encompass the crucial distinction between injuries where there is disruption of the skin or trauma to internal organs, and those where there is not.

359

In the past many psychiatric classifications have been based on armchair theorising with the expectation that classifications should express a view about the nature of psychiatric disorders and reflect a theory about their origin. However, here, a distinction needs to be made between public and private classifications (Stengel 1959). Public classifications are intended to provide a means of communication between professionals who may have different theoretical views. Accordingly, if *mis*communication is to be avoided it is essential that classifications should *not* include theoretical concepts which are still subject to disagreement. Furthermore, such public classifications can only include those lowest common denominators in psychiatry which have been tested and accepted. As a result although these classifications are essential for clinical practice they are unlikely to be exciting. In contrast, private classifications provide a means of testing out new ideas and hence *must* include the hypothesis or notions to be investigated. Many research classifications are of this kind but they will not be discussed in this chapter.

The criteria for an adequate classification of child psychiatric disorders have been summarised by Rutter (1965), Cromwell *et al* (1975) and Rutter, Shaffer & Shepherd (1975). First, the classification must be based on facts, not concepts, and it must be defined in operational terms. This means that classification can be used satisfactorily only if there is a glossary providing meanings for its constituent terms (WHO 1974). Second, the aim is to classify disorders or problems, and *not* to classify children as persons (see below for a further discussion of this point). Children develop and change and diagnosis can only meaningfully apply to the disorder or situation at one point in time, although the diagnosis may have some prognostic value. Third, because childhood has no sharp end-point, there should not be different classifications for different age periods, although there must be provision for disorders which arise only at particular age periods (Rutter, Shaffer & Sturge 1975). The child is a developing organism and it is essential that classification takes this into account. Maturation sometimes causes the same abnormality to manifest itself in different ways at different ages (Rutter 1965). Fourth, the classification must be reliable, meaning that terms are used in the same way by different clinicians. Fifth, the classification must provide an adequate differentiation between disorders. A classification which is reliable because it fails to distinguish between conditions is of no use (Rutter, Shaffer & Shepherd 1975). Sixth, it must provide adequate coverage so that important disorders are not omitted. Stengel (1959) succinctly summarised these last two points by saying that classification terms should be jointly exhaustive and mutually exclusive. Seventh, the differentiations should have validity. For the categories to have any meaning they must be shown to differ in important respects. It is not enough for tradition or theory to separate two conditions;

it is also essential that in fact they differ in terms of aetiology, symptomatology, course, response to treatment or some other variable. Eighth, there
should be logical consistency, so that the system is based on a constant set
of principles with a clear set of precise rules (Werry 1972; Cromwell *et al*
1975). Ninth, the classification must convey information which is relevant
to the clinical situation and which aids clinical decisions. Tenth, the classification must be practicable in ordinary clinical practice. This means that it must
require only information which is likely to be routinely available; it must
be acceptable to clinicians; the instructions on its use should be clear, simple
and unambiguous; and it must be in a form which is convenient for statistical
handling. These are tall orders and no classification of child psychiatric disorders fully meets all these criteria. Nevertheless, information is available
on most of the points and data are already available to produce a classification
which is reasonably satisfactory in these terms.

MULTI-AXIAL FRAMEWORK

The first issue concerns the structure or framework for the classification.
Traditional schemes are based on a list of categories so that for each case
the clinician has to choose the term or terms which best describe the patient's
disorder. Thus, a choice has to be made between an anxiety state or depression; infantile autism or mental retardation. This works well enough in many
instances but it falls down badly in complex cases (Rutter *et al* 1969; Rutter,
Shaffer & Shepherd 1975; Tarjan *et al* 1972). The point is that psychiatric
diagnosis necessarily involves several different elements (Rutter, Shaffer &
Sturge 1975). Thus, it may be desirable to note the type of mental disorder,
whether or not there is mental retardation and also the presence or absence
of associated organic brain disease. In most cases there is no single diagnostic
term which will include these and it is necessary to use multiple codings.
Of course, multicategory schemes (such as the International Classification
of Diseases—ICD) make provision for this but there are no rules as to how
many categories to use or the order in which they should be placed. Studies
have shown that, in practice, psychiatrists vary greatly in their use of multiple
categories even when they agree on their diagnostic formulation (Rutter *et
al* 1969; Rutter, Shaffer & Shepherd 1975). This has the result that when
a condition is not coded it may mean that the condition was not present,
that it was present but not thought important, or that it was not coded in
spite of being thought important. Moreover there is no way of determining
from the coding which was the case.

The multiaxial approach was devised to remedy these deficiencies (Rutter
et al 1969; Tarjan *et al* 1972; Rutter, Shaffer & Shepherd 1975). In fact it

is no more than a logical development of the ICD multicategory scheme, in which modifications have been introduced specifically to meet the difficulties noted above. To ensure adequate coverage of data and to ensure comparability three rules are required: (1) a uniform number of codings must be made; (2) these codings must always refer to the same elements in diagnosis; and (3) they must always occur in the same order.

One version of a multiaxial system of classification was tested in a study sponsored by the World Health Organisation (Rutter, Shaffer & Shepherd 1975). It was found to have important advantages over the more usual multicategory system. Psychiatrists found that the multiaxial system made classification more uniform, was easy to apply and corresponded more closely to their usual clinical approach. Further research is necessary but the evidence to date indicates the utility of this type of scheme.

An infinite variety of elements could be included in such a multiaxial scheme, but for it to be workable in practice there must be a quite restricted number of axes. These need to be chosen on the basis of providing unambiguous information of maximum clinical usefulness in the greatest number of cases. The multiaxial scheme for child psychiatric disorders currently being tested in a further WHO study includes five axes: (1) *clinical psychiatric syndrome* (emotional disorder, conduct disorder, etc); (2) *specific delays in development* (developmental speech disorder, specific reading retardation etc); (3) *intellectual level* (normal, mildly retarded, etc); (4) *medical conditions* (cerebral palsy, asthma, etc); and (5) *abnormal psychosocial situations* (family discord, inadequate linguistic stimulation, etc).

No tested and agreed scheme for classifying psychosocial situations has been fully developed. Nevertheless, there is good evidence for the importance of psychosocial factors in the aetiology of child psychiatric disorders and for the different effects of different psychosocial situations. This issue is considered in Chapters 3, 4, and 5. The classification of medical conditions as a whole is beyond the scope of this book but the psychiatric importance of organic brain damage is discussed in Chapter 8. The remainder of this chapter will be concerned with the evidence relevant to classification on the remaining three axes.

CLINICAL PSYCHIATRIC SYNDROME AND SPECIFIC DELAYS IN DEVELOPMENT

Symptom clusters and multivariate techniques

A common approach to problems of classification in child psychiatry has been the examination of symptoms patterning by a variety of multivariate techniques (Quay 1972). There are many hazards in these statistical techniques and artefactual patterns or factors are easily produced (Maxwell 1972; Everitt 1975), so that the replication of findings in different samples is more than usually important. However, nearly all studies have demonstrated an *emotional disturbance* variable in which symptoms such as fear, anxiety, misery and somatic complaints predominate (e.g. Hewitt & Jenkins 1949; Peterson 1961; Quay 1964; Patterson 1964; Wolff 1971; Kolvin *et al* 1975, Behar & Stringfield 1974; Thompson *et al* 1976). This factor has been evident at all ages from the preschool period to adolescence. Sometimes there has been a distinction between anxious fearful behaviour and depressed inhibited behaviour (Jenkins 1966; Wolff 1971) but this has been an inconsistent finding.

There has also been general agreement on a *conduct disturbance* variable characterised by disobedience, disruptiveness, destructiveness, aggression and often by delinquent behaviour. In some investigations there has been no further differentiation within this broad variable but in others a distinction has been found between aggressive behaviour and delinquency (e.g. Collins *et al* 1962; Wolff 1971); or between unsocialised aggressive behaviour and socialised group delinquency (e.g. Hewitt & Jenkins 1949; Quay 1964, 1966). However, both these differentiations have been somewhat inconsistent and the differentiation of a socialised pattern of delinquent activities has been difficult to replicate (Field 1967).

A further *hyperkinetic grouping* of symptoms indicating overactivity, lack of concentration and poor peer relationships has also been found in many studies (e.g. Jenkins 1966; Behar & Stringfield 1974; Thompson *et al* 1976) but there has been a variable degree of overlap between this factor and that of conduct disturbance. Investigations of younger children have sometimes shown an additional factor of *enuresis/encopresis* (Wolff 1971; Kolvin *et al* 1975) and those of older children have sometimes indicated an *immaturity variable* with behaviours such as short attention span, passivity and day dreaming (e.g. Peterson *et al* 1961; Quay & Quay 1965) but neither of these has been as consistent or as well defined as the emotional disturbance and conduct disorder variables.

Factor analytic techniques necessarily produce variable or dimensions which most children possess to varying degrees. The methods are devised to group items and not to group children and for this reason they cannot be expected to give rise to distinct diagnostic syndromes. It is not unexpected, therefore, that the use of factor techniques to subdivide children according to separate diagnostic groups has usually meant that many disorders of children remain unclassified (Hewitt & Jenkins 1949; Lewis 1954). It is also in keeping with the factor analytic approach (which relies on the characteristics which children have in common) that the findings from general population samples and from clinic groups have been broadly similar.

However, clustering techniques (Everitt 1974), are available for the purpose of grouping children according to the behavioural features which they do and do not have in common. Wolkind and Everitt (1974) applied this method in a study of preschool children and, in addition to clusters indicating normal behaviour, found two which suggested emotional disturbance and a disorder of conduct. This seems a promising approach which deserves wider application but its usefulness is limited by the fact that different methods of cluster analysis often come up with different solutions to the same set of data and by the fact that there is no satisfactory means of deciding how many diagnostic clusters provide the best classification.

For obvious reasons all these techniques are entirely dependent on the measures put into the analysis and on the populations investigated. Thus, no factor of enuresis/encopresis can possibly emerge if there are no items of wetting or soiling included in the analysis. Similarly, there will not be a schizophrenia cluster if the sample studied contains no schizophrenics. While these points are self-evident they serve to explain some of the differences in findings between various investigations and also explain why some of the rarer diagnoses such as infantile autism or obsessional neurosis do not emerge as categories from these sort of studies.

On the other hand, statistical techniques to determine the validity of diagnostic distinctions between uncommon disorders are available. For example, discriminant function analyses may be used to find out the degree of overlap between two clinically defined syndromes. Bartak and Rutter (1976) used this method in a comparative study of children with infantile autism or developmental receptive dysphasia. They showed very little overlap between the groups on behavioural, language or cognitive criterion. Similarly, Kolvin *et al* (1971) showed marked differences in symptomatology between infantile psychosis (autism) and late onset psychosis (schizophrenia).

Of course, it is not enough to show that symptoms cluster together to form consistent diagnostic categories. If the categories are to be at all useful to the clinician, it is necessary to go on to ask whether the differentiations between categories have any meaning. Do the categories differ in other respects, for example: in terms of family characteristics, biological features, age of onset, sex distribution, association with scholastic problems, aetiology, response to treatment and outcome? Only if they do is the classification worthwhile.

Family characteristics

Several investigators have examined the differences in family background of groups of children defined according to their factor scores on the dimensions of behaviour discussed above. Jenkins (Hewitt & Jenkins 1949; Jenkins 1966) found that unsocialised aggressive behaviour was associated with broken homes, family hostility and maternal rejection; socialised delinquency with social disadvantage, parental neglect and delinquent associates; and emotional disturbance with physical illness, maternal anxiety and parental overcontrol. Lewis (1954), in her study of a rather different sample (children in care) broadly replicated Jenkins' findings. Hetherington *et al* (1971) investigated family interaction in delinquents and nondelinquent controls and found that socialised delinquency in boys was associated with dominance by fathers; neurotic delinquency with maternal dominance and marital conflict; and unsocialised aggression with a more variable pattern of dominance but poor participation of the boys in the decision-making process. The pattern for girls was less consistent.

Family discord (quarrelling, marital discord, hostility, etc) and family disruption have been found to be associated with disturbances of conduct and with delinquency in numerous investigations (see Rutter & Madge 1976; also Chapter 3). However, these family features have *not* been particularly associated with emotional disturbance in children (e.g. Bennett 1960; Wardle 1961; Rutter 1971b).

Mental illness in parents is associated with psychiatric disorder in the children but the associations between the form of the parental illness and the form of the child's disorder are quite weak (Rutter 1966). However, there is a slight tendency for parents with criminality or a personality disorder to have children who show hyperkinesis or disturbances of conduct, and for parents with neuroses to have offspring with emotional difficulties (Cantwell 1975; Rutter, Quinton & Yule 1977). Schizophrenia in the parents is especially linked with schizophrenia in the children and is not associated with infantile psychosis or autism (Kolvin *et al* 1971).

An institutional upbringing from infancy is particularly associated with a pattern of social disinhibition and indiscriminate friendliness (Wolkind 1974; Tizard & Rees 1975).

This syndrome is much less often seen in children admitted to institutions later in childhood. Large family size is associated with conduct disturbance but not emotional disorders, whereas being the oldest in the sibship is more characteristic of children with emotional difficulties than of delinquents (Rutter, Tizard & Whitmore 1970). Low social status has a rather inconsistent association with child psychiatric disorder but it tends to be more often linked with persistent delinquency (Knight & West 1975) than with either transient delinquency or emotional disturbance (Rutter, Tizard & Whitmore 1970). Infantile autism is the only psychiatric disorder in childhood particularly associated with a middle class background; it is not associated with any other family characteristic (see Chapter 30).

In short, although there is far from a one-to-one association between family background and the type of child psychiatric disorder, family features do differentiate significantly between emotional disturbance, hyperkinesis and conduct disorders (which are rather similar in background), infantile autism, and schizophrenia.

Biological factors

There is good evidence that brain damage increases the risk for a wide range of child psychiatric disorders (see Chapter 8). However, there are two disorders—infantile autism and disintegrative psychosis—and possibly another, the hyperkinetic syndrome, for which the association with organic brain pathology is rather stronger than is the case with other psychiatric conditions.

With respect to autism, it is noteworthy that the syndrome is particularly common in children with neurological disorders associated with 'hypsarrhythmia' (Taft & Cohen 1971) or congenital rubella (Chess *et al* 1971). But, in addition, follow-up studies have shown that, even in children without abnormalities on neurological examination, about a quarter develop epileptic fits during childhood or adolescence (Rutter 1970a). This tendency is most marked in mentally retarded autistic children (Bartak & Rutter 1976) and it is probable that the incidence of epilepsy in this subgroup is only slightly greater than in nonautistic retarded children (Rutter *et al* 1967; Corbett *et al* 1975).

There have been but few studies of children with disintegrative psychosis but the importance of brain pathology is indicated by the frequent evidence at postmortem of cortical degeneration, sometimes of a lipid type (Kanner 1957; Malamud 1959; Ross 1959; Creak 1963).

The evidence linking the hyperkinetic syndrome with brain damage is less satisfactory. Werry *et al* (1972) found minor neurological abnormalities to be more common in hyperactive children than in neurotic or normal control groups and earlier studies noted that the syndrome was particularly striking in epileptic or brain-damaged children (Ounsted 1955; Ingram 1956). There is some suggestion, too, that the hyperkinetic syndrome is more common in children with temporal lobe epilepsy than with other varieties of epilepsy (Ounsted *et al* 1966) but adequately controlled studies are lacking. Two recent studies have also demonstrated the high frequency of minor congenital anomalies (such as epicanthic folds or adherent earlobes) in hyperkinetic children (Waldrop & Halverson 1971; Quinn & Rapoport 1974). What remains uncertain, however, is how far the presence of minor physical anomalies is specific to the hyperkinetic syndrome. Quinn and Rapoport found anomalies to be just as frequent in unsocialised aggressive children though less frequent in anxious boys.

Outside these three conditions, it appears that the presence of brain damage is not associated with any particular clinical psychiatric syndrome (Rutter, Graham & Yule 1970; Shaffer *et al* 1974; 1975). Furthermore, although one study showed temporal lobe foci to be particularly associated with aggressive behaviour (Nuffield 1961) most investigations have found no consistent pattern of associations between the type of locus of EEG abnormalities or of brain injury and the type of psychiatric disorder (Aird & Yamamoto 1966; Stevens *et al* 1968; Ritvo *et al* 1970; Shaffer *et al* 1975).

Thus, it is evident that the frequent presence of brain damage differentiates disintegrative psychosis and infantile autism (possibly also the hyperkinetic syndrome) from other psychiatric conditions, but otherwise biological features are a poor guide to psychiatric classification.

Cognitive correlates

All epidemological investigations have shown that psychiatric disabilities and a wide range of deviant behaviours are commoner in children of low IQ than in those of high IQ (Rutter 1971a). This trend is to be found throughout the IQ distribution, but is possibly most marked in the lowest IQ groups. For the most part, low IQ shows no connexion with specific psychiatric syndromes. However, mental retardation is particularly common in children with infantile autism, about three-quarters of whom have an IQ below 70 (Rutter & Lockyer 1967), with disintegrative psychosis (Heller 1930), with the hyperkinetic syndrome (Rutter, Graham & Yule 1970) and with stereotyped repetitive movements (Rutter 1971a).

The pattern of cognitive functioning also differentiates between psychiatric syndromes. Thus, children with infantile autism have been shown to differ in this respect from those with other psychiatric disorders (Lockyer & Rutter 1970) and with mental retardation (Hermelin & O'Connor 1970), and with developmental language disorders (Bartak, Rutter & Cox 1975). Cognitive level also differentiates autism from schizophrenia (Kolvin, Humphrey & McNay 1971).

Reading difficulties commonly occur in children with the hyperkinetic syndrome (Cantwell 1975) or conduct disorders (Clark 1970; Rutter, Tizard & Whitmore 1970) but are less often associated with emotional disturbances. Interestingly, there is also an age factor in that conduct disorders or delinquency arising during adolescence are *not* associated with reading failure in contrast to the strong association found when similar conditions arise in earlier childhood (Robins & Hill 1966; Rutter *et al* 1975). Autistic children differ from others in usually scoring much lower on reading comprehension than on reading accuracy (Lockyer & Rutter 1969; Rutter & Bartak 1973).

Speech and language delay are frequently followed by reading retardation whereas the clumsy child syndrome is less frequently associated with reading difficulties (see Chapter 23). Enuresis also shows only a weak association with reading difficulties (Rutter, Tizard & Whitmore 1970).

In short, autism differs from all other disorders in having a characteristic cognitive pattern reflecting verbal deficits; the hyperkinetic syndrome and conduct disorder (when it arises before adolescence) are associated with specific reading difficulties; and mental retardation is most commonly a feature in children with autism, disintegrative psychosis, stereotyped repetitive movements and to a lesser extent the hyperkinetic syndrome.

Age and sex distribution

Almost all psychiatric disorders in childhood are very much commoner in boys (Rutter, Tizard & Whitmore 1970). The one group of conditions which stands out as different are the emotional disorders, which show a roughly equal sex ratio. This not only differentiates them from other children's psychiatric disorders but also from adult neuroses which are much commoner in women (Rutter 1970b). The meaning of this sex difference between emotional disturbances in childhood and adult neuroses remains uncertain.

While a strong male preponderance (4 to 1) is seen in nearly all the disorders which involve a specific delay in development (i.e. speech or language delay, specific reading retardation, and the clumsy child syndrome), this is less evident in the case of nocturnal enuresis.

Most child psychiatric disorders can arise at any age. However, infantile autism virtually only develops during the first 3 years of life and schizophrenia rarely occurs much before puberty (Rutter, 1972). The conditions involving developmental delay (e.g. developmental language disorder or clumsy child syndrome) obviously have to begin in early childhood. Depression can occur at any age but it only becomes at all common during adolescence (Rutter *et al* 1976). Nocturnal enuresis can be present from infancy or it can arise some time after acquiring bladder control. Curiously, there appear to be no consistent differences between primary and secondary enuresis in any of the features so far examined (see Kolvin *et al* 1973).

Different phobias differ in their characteristic age of onset, thus, animal phobias almost always begin in early childhood whereas agoraphobia rarely occurs before adolescence (Rutter 1972). Anorexia nervosa also typically has an onset during adolescence (see Chapter 17).

Response to treatment

There have been surprisingly few studies which have compared diagnostic groups according to their response to different forms of treatment. Cytryn *et al* (1960) showed that the short-term prognosis of children with emotional disorders was considerably better than that for those with hyperkinetic or conduct disorders, a finding in keeping with the longer-term follow-up findings (see below). However, although there are suggestions of a differential response to treatment according to diagnosis, systematic controlled comparisons are lacking. Stimulants and the major tranquillising drugs appear to be of most value with hyperactive children, antidepressants with emotionally disturbed youngsters and tricyclics with enuretic children (see Chapter 38), but there is a lack of evidence on whether the drugs are most effective for these conditions or whether it is just that these are the disorders for which they have been most often employed. Behavioural approaches to treatment are applicable in a wide range of psychiatric disorders, and there is no close connexion between diagnosis and therapeutic techniques (see Chapter 39). However, in practice, operant methods are most used with disruptive behaviours, or with developmental delay; and desensitisation, 'flooding' or modelling with emotional disturbances. Studies of psychotherapy are few and mostly inadequate. However, what little evidence there is suggests that individual psychotherapy is most suitable for children with emotional disorders (Eisenberg *et al* 1965). Within a delinquent group, insight oriented psychotherapy probably works best with anxious adolescents with feelings of guilt and inadequacy, whereas the tougher delinquents respond better to more directive therapists who focus on issues related to external controls and the setting of limits rather than on inner feelings (Warren 1969; Palmer 1971; Quay 1974).

Obviously, it would be clinically useful to have well based knowledge on the therapeutic implications of diagnostic differences. It appears highly likely that there are important implications for treatment but research findings so far provide only the most general guidance as to what they might be.

Long-term course

There are numerous studies of both children and adolescents which show that the prognosis is best for emotional disorders, is less good for conduct disorders, less good still for hyperkinetic conditions and worst for psychoses (see Robins 1972; also Chapter 12). In addition, disorders diagnosed as 'adaptation reaction' on the basis of their mildness and short duration have been found, in fact, to have the good prognosis the diagnosis implies (Rutter,

Shaffer & Shepherd 1975). However, not only do remission rates differ but also the type of long-term outcome varies by diagnosis. Most children with emotional disturbance develop into normal healthy adults (Robins 1966); however, when disorders continue into adult life they usually take the form of depression or neurosis (Pritchard & Graham 1966; Zeitlin 1972; Graham & Rutter 1973). Youngsters with disturbances of conduct, if they show problems in adult life (as a high proportion do), tend to exhibit personality disorders with accompanying social difficulties as well as psychiatric impairment (Robins 1966). Many hyperkinetic children also show abnormalities of personality in adult life but also some become psychotic (see Chapter 22). Autism follows a fairly characteristic course with continuing social, linguistic and ritualistic problems, but often also the development of fits (Rutter 1970a).

The developmental disorders also tend to run a characteristic course. Children with speech or language delay frequently show specific reading retardation when they are older and severe spelling problems often persist into adult life even when the individual has gained adequate reading skills (Rutter & Yule 1973, see also Chapter 23). Clumsiness shows some overlap with speech delay but on the whole runs a different course. Enuresis shows least overlap with the other disorders of development, but again when the problems persist they usually continue to take the form of bedwetting.

While there are important differences in outcome between the major diagnostic categories, less is known about differences *within* these broad groups. Emotional disorders in children tend to be mixed in symptomatology and follow-up into adolescence shows little consistency in the patterns of emotional disturbance. The one exception is the relatively uncommon syndrome of obsessional neurosis in which the symptoms, when they persist, tend to continue in much the same form (Warren 1965). Anorexia nervosa is accompanied by diverse psychiatric symptomatology but follow-up studies show that, when problems continue, persistent food refusal and weight loss dominate the scene (Warren 1968). It is also one of the very few psychiatric conditions of childhood in which there is an appreciable death rate. There is also some consistency in the course of tics which persist into adult life (usually in milder degree) in about half the cases (Corbett *et al* 1969). Hysterical conversion reactions are distinctive in terms of the high proportion which turn out to be organic conditions *mis*diagnosed as hysteria (Caplan 1970). However, in the cases not due to physical disease the outcome is diverse and further disorders are often not hysterical in type.

Conclusions on classification of clinical psychiatric syndromes

There is abundant evidence, briefly outlined above, for the validity of diagnostic distinctions between the certain broad categories of child psychiatric disorder, namely emotional disorder, conduct disorder, infantile autism, schizophrenia and developmental disorders. In addition, there are reasonable grounds for separating off a number of other conditions which do not readily fit into any of the above categories—disintegrative psychosis, tics and anorexia nervosa.

Several problems remain. First, there is the matter of disorders which fall outside these groupings. The numerically most important is the group of disorders in which both emotional disturbance and disorders of conduct are marked (Rutter, Tizard & Whitmore 1970). The frequency with which they occur makes it essential to include a category of 'mixed' disorders.

There is also a difficulty in the classification of the hyperkinetic syndrome. The findings on it are somewhat contradictory but it seems to include a rather separate cluster of symptoms which sometimes are associated with organic brain pathology and which carry a rather poor prognosis. For all these reasons it warrants a diagnostic category of its own. However, there is uncertainty about how far it overlaps with conduct disorders and almost certainly it does not constitute a homogeneous category. Next, there are a few symptoms or syndromes which seem worth noting as different, but which are not readily grouped with any others. These include encopresis and stereotyped repetitive movements. Then, there are a number of conditions which mainly occur in adult life but which are also found in children—such as drug dependence or manic-depressive psychosis. Clearly, these can be classified in children in the same way as in adults. However, there are also conditions similar to but yet different from adult disorders. Thus, disorders of psychosexual identity, such as femininism in boys (see Chapter 33), have features in common with sexual deviations in adult life but are dissimilar because they precede puberty.

The second problem is how far these broad diagnostic categories can be subdivided. In particular, what subcategories of emotional disorder and of conduct disorder can be shown to have validity? In general psychiatry, it is traditional to differentiate between anxiety states, depression, hysteria and obsessional disorders, for example. It is reasonable to try to do the same in child psychiatry but there is only weak evidence for the validity of these diagnostic distinctions in adult life (see for example Brown 1942; Greer & Cawley 1966), let alone in childhood. Moreover, most emotional disorders in children have a more mixed picture which does fit easily into these text-book categories. Furthermore, different sex ratio for emotional disorder in childhood and for adult neurosis, together with the fact that most emotionally disturbed children do not become adult neurotics, raises the question of whether emotional disturbance and neurosis are the same conditions.

The main distinction within the group of conduct disorders has been that between unsocialised aggression and socialised delinquency. The findings are contradictory. Some studies have shown differences between these groups whereas others have not, and all have found that there is a considerable overlap between the two varieties of conduct disorder, even if the distinction has validity (which is still in doubt).

The third problem is how to group the various psychiatric categories. Obviously, there must be a main category of *emotional disorder* with its tentative subdivisions into separate types, including depressive disorders, adult-type neurotic conditions and mixed emotional disturbance. Secondly, there are the *conduct disorders* for which no very satisfactory subclassification exists. Thirdly, there has to be a category for *mixed disorders*. The group of *psychoses specific to childhood* probably best includes infantile autism and disintegrative psychosis, although in many ways they are somewhat different. *Schizophrenia* is sufficiently different to be classified quite separately, and there is no good reason to classify it any differently in childhood to the way it is dealt with in adult life. Sixthly, the *specific delays in development* need recognition as a distinct group. These include speech and language delay, specific reading retardation and the clumsy child syndrome. However, enuresis and encopresis appear sufficiently different (if only because the disorders often come on after previously normal development) to be classified separately. Probably there needs to be a 'rag-bag' group of *special syndromes and symptoms* not classified elsewhere. This might include enuresis and encopresis as well as tics, stereotyped repetitive movements and anorexia nervosa. Eighth, a separate category for the *hyperkinetic syndrome* is probably justified although its validity as a separate neurological entity has still to be established. Ninth, although its basis is different, it could be argued that a category of *adaptation or adjustment reaction* is needed for mild disorders of short duration. Finally, there have to be available categories for adult-type conditions which can occur in childhood (e.g. *manic-depressive psychosis*, *drug dependence*, *sexual disorders*).

Specific delays in development

It is arguable whether specific delays in development should be regarded as psychiatric disorders in the same way as the other syndromes. As already noted, in the current multiaxial scheme being tested by the WHO specific delays in development are dealt with by means of a separate axis. The main reason for this is that the delays are frequently present without any other evidence of psychiatric disturbance; that is there are no social, emotional or behavioural abnormalities outside the specific area of delayed development. On the other hand, in a substantial minority of cases there is an associated psychiatric disorder. This means that, if the delays are noted on the clinical psychiatric syndrome axis, a double diagnosis (and hence double coding for statistical purposes) will often be required. Accordingly, it may be most convenient to record specific delays in development on a separate axis. Further research is needed to determine how far this is justifiable and practicable.

INTELLECTUAL LEVEL

A person's intellectual level is usually assessed by means of some form of IQ test. In this way, quite fine subdivisions in intelligence may be made. However, for clinical purposes five main groupings may be made: normal intelligence, mild retardation, moderate retardation, severe retardation and profound retardation. These are equivalent (on an IQ test with a mean of 100 and a standard deviation of 15) to IQ ranges of 70 or greater, 50–69, 35–49, 20–34 and below 20 respectively. There are no finite distinctions between these ranges, if only because a variety of situational factors may influence test scores, because different tests tend to give somewhat different scores, and because many people show quite marked shifts in IQ (both up and down) during childhood and adolescence (Rutter 1971a; Rutter & Madge 1976). Nevertheless, the differentiation into five groups on intellectual level has been shown to be valid and to have very considerable clinic value.

Organic brain damage

No very accurate figure is available for the prevalence of organic brain disorders in children of normal intelligence, but the figure for overt neurological disorder is likely to be about one per cent (Rutter, Graham & Yule 1970). If possible neurological abnormalities are included, the prevalence may be as high as 13 per cent (Rutter, Tizard & Whitmore 1970). In children with mild mental retardation the rate of organic brain damage is very much higher than this—probably about 16 per cent with definite and a further 20 per cent, with possible, abnormalities (Rutter, Tizard & Whitmore 1970; Birch *et al* 1970). However, this still leaves over half without detectable neurological abnormality. In contrast, almost all individuals with moderate or severe retardation have definite organic brain conditions as shown by either neurological examination (Rutter, Tizard & Whitmore 1970; Birch *et al* 1970), the onset of epileptic fits (Corbett *et al* 1975) or postmortem study (Crome 1960).

Fertility and mortality

The findings for organic brain damage are paralleled by those for fertility and mortality (Tizard 1966; 1974; Kushlik & Blunden 1974; Carter 1958; Collmann & Stoller 1963). Mildly retarded individuals probably have a fertility close to those for persons of normal intelligence and a life expectancy which is slightly below normal. On the other hand, people with moderate or severe retardation tend to have very few children, probably most are not biologically capable of reproduction, physical abnormalities are prevalent, physical stature is reduced and life expectancy is well below that for the general population.

Social class distribution

Individuals with moderate or severe mental retardation come from a social class background which shows a distribution similar to that for the general population, whereas most mildly retarded children come from socially disadvantaged families (Kushlik & Blunden 1974; Birch *et al* 1970).

Family history of mental retardation

Very few of the relatives of people with moderate or severe retardation are mentally regarded (Åkesson 1962; Reed & Reed 1965). But among the close relatives of the mildly retarded, the rate of retardation is about 25 per cent, well above the figures for the general population.

Psychiatric correlates

The rate of psychiatric disorder increases markedly with diminishing intellectual level (Rutter 1971a; Birch *et al* 1970). The type of disorder also varies. The mildly retarded have disorders which approximate to those found in children of normal intelligence. However, among those with an IQ below 50 there is a much increased rate of infantile autism, hyperkinetic syndrome and stereotyped repetitive movements.

Scholastic attainment

Most mildly retarded children are able to acquire the basic scholastic skills of reading, writing and arithmetic although their levels of attainment tend to be below those for children of normal intelligence (Gunzberg 1974). Youngsters with moderate retardation may acquire some meagre skills in the

'3Rs' but their understanding is usually severely limited. On the other hand, most can achieve reasonable proficiency in mechanical tasks. Severely retarded children are likely only to gain limited social skills and most of the profoundly retarded remain completely dependent on other people even for toileting, washing and dressing. These associations between intellectual level and scholastic attainment hold for children with psychosis or other psychiatric disorders (Lockyer & Rutter 1969; Rutter & Bartak 1973) in much the same way as for mentally retarded individuals without psychiatric problems.

Employment and adult adjustment

Most mildly retarded adults are capable of ordinary employment although some require work in a sheltered setting (Tizard 1974). Particularly in early adult life, they show more marital and work difficulties than people of normal intelligence, but the differences diminish over time and the mildly retarded tend to be absorbed into the general lower class population of people in unskilled jobs. Most of the moderately retarded are capable of productive work in a sheltered setting but only a few gain jobs in the open market. The severely retarded are likely only to gain simple social skills and many require institutional care as they get older (Kushlik & Blunden 1974). Most of the profoundly retarded are severely physically handicapped and require continuous nursing care.

Summary

In summary, there are very marked differences between people with normal intelligence, with mild retardation, and with more severe retardation in terms of neurological abnormality, social background, family history, psychiatric correlates, scholastic attainment, employment, fecundity and life expectancy. Moderate, severe, and profound retardation differ largely in terms of prognosis for education, employment, social competence and life expectancy.

RELIABILITY

So far there have been only a very few studies of the reliability of psychiatric diagnosis in childhood. However, there are several investigations which have shown quite high levels of reliability on the presence/absence of child psychiatric disorder and on a crude differentiation between emotional, conduct and mixed disorders (Rutter, Tizard & Whitmore 1970; Rutter *et al* 1975). Freeman (1971) showed that psychiatrists could agree fairly well (60–72 per cent) on a subdivision into four main categories—reactive disorders, psychoneurotic disorders, personality disorders and psychiatric disorders—from the GAP scheme. The WHO study (Rutter, Shaffer & Shepherd 1975) also demonstrated good reliability on most of the main psychiatric categories (emotional disorder, autism, schizophrenia, etc) but less satisfactory agreement on some complex cases. Very little is known about the reliability of subcategories within these broad divisions but the limited available evidence suggests that their reliability is less good.

LABELLING

In recent years, there has been much concern about the effects of labelling individuals (e.g. Lemert 1967; Cicourel 1968; Scheff 1966). It has been pointed out that the use of labels which imply deviance tends to alter how people view themselves and how other people act towards them. Both for these reasons and because labels are often used to justify social control procedures, the act of labelling may sometimes lead to adverse changes in behaviour, so that the labelling serves as a self-fulfilling prophecy. People labelled as delinquent may be more likely to commit delinquent acts as a result of the labelling process, and people labelled as mentally ill may be treated as ill by others even when their behaviour is normal.

There is some uncertainty about the strength of these effects but there is evidence that in some circumstances the effects exist (Hobbs 1975; Rutter & Madge 1976). However, whether the effects are good or bad will necessarily depend on how the label alters people's responses to the labelled person. It has sometimes been assumed that a label of deviance will cause people to behave in a more damaging way. However, this need not be the case. For example, studies of teachers have shown that some respond positively to children labelled as low achievers (see Brophy & Good 1974). In these cases the labelling is likely to have a beneficial effect. The use of labels may serve to increase caring or helping responses and may initiate the delivery of services. In other cases, the reverse will apply and in yet others the label will have no effect.

The concerns over the possible ill-effects of labelling have led some people to doubt the value of any diagnosis or classification. This is a counsel of despair which is likely to hamper therapeutic processes as well as to impede communication, if only because all words serve as labels and because people tend to classify each other even if overt classification is banned. Moreover, it is an error to equate classification of *disorders* with labelling of *people* (see below). Nevertheless, there are frequent misuses of diagnosis and classification and care is required if these are to be avoided.

In the first place, it is wrong to classify people (this error is perpetuated in the very title of Hobbs' recent two volume book on the subject). It is historically wrong because medical classifications were developed to note diseases and disorders and not types of person (Rutter, Shaffer & Shepherd 1975). It is scientifically wrong because it assumes a persistence of psychiatric disorders and a fixity of personality which is completely out of keeping with what is known about development and about the course of disorders (see Chapter 12). And, it is morally offensive because it is treating humans as if they were merely the vehicle of problems. It is no more reasonable to talk about a neurotic child than it is to refer to a measly child. In both cases the label (neurosis or measles) may accurately reflect the current *problems* of the child but it does not reflect the qualities of the child *himself*.

Diagnosis and classification may properly be used to describe disorders, situations or traits but they should not be used to label people as people. This may seem a minor quibble, but the distinction is important both because of the need to emphasise that individuals have many different characteristics (each of which may be classified) and to emphasise that children change and develop. Labels are useful to indicate the current situation but it should never be assumed that the same will apply some years later.

However, this qualification regarding the use of classification is not in itself enough to prevent abuses. Three other issues need to be considered. First, by its nature, a classification has to reflect what individuals have *in common* with other individuals. The diagnosis of emotional disorder, for example, conveys much information about the ways in which a particular child's problems are similar to those of other children whose disorders are given the same label. However, the classification cannot convey the equally important information about the ways in which the child's problems differ from those of others. In other words, classification provides a very convenient shorthand description, essential for communication about groups, but inadequate as a means of discussing the difficulties of an individual child. In short, diagnostic labels are a help when a clinician is writing to someone else about a patient but they are not sufficient to describe all that is important about that patient or his problems.

Second, it is a mistake to equate classification with administrative action. It is never justifiable to assume that mentally retarded children need to be in an institution for the retarded, or that delinquents require penal action, or that children with psychiatric disorder require psychiatric treatment.

The decisions regarding care or placement must take into account social impairment, persistence of problems and availability of suitable treatments as well as the diagnosis of type of disorder. Not all people with a particular disorder require the same action and individual differences must be taken into account so that services are tailored to individuaı ́eeds (rather than slot-ting individuals into pigeon holes which offer a diagnosis cum treatment pack-age).

Third, if people are to respond positively to children with problems it is necessary that they be guided as to what might be helpful. This means that when a clinician writes or talks to a teacher or family doctor about a child with a psychiatric disorder it is not enough for him to indicate that there is a conduct disorder or low IQ or family discord, he must also go on to make explicit what these terms mean with respect to what should be done to help the child *overcome* his difficulties. If this is done in terms appropriate to the situation and to the person to whom communication is made, labels can serve to benefit the child. However, whether or not this happens will be determined by how the labels are used as much as by what the labels are. Therein lies the art as well as the science of classification.

CONCLUSION

Much further work is required to develop a really satisfactory system of clas-sification for child psychiatric disorders. However, there is already ample evi-dence to indicate practical, valid and clinically useful differentiations between the dozen or so principal diagnostic categories for clinical psychiatric syn-dromes and between the main subdivisions for mental retardation. There are also indications that a multiaxial framework is likely to prove to be the most satisfactory scheme for classification.

REFERENCES

AIRD R.B. & YAMAMOTO T. (1966) Behavior disorders of childhood. *Electroenceph. clin. Neurophysical.* **21,** 148–156

ÅKESSON H.O. (1962) *Epidemiology and Genetics of Mental Deficiency in a Southern Swedish Population.* Stockholm: Almquist & Wiksell

BARTAK L., RUTTER M. & COX, A. (1976) A comparative study of infantile autism and specific developmental receptive language disorder. III: Discriminant functions analysis. (In preparation)

BARTAK L., RUTTER M. & COX A. (1975) A comparative study of infantile autism and specific developmental receptive language disorder. I: The children. *Brit. J. Psychiat.* **126,** 127–145

BEHAR L. & STRINGFIELD S. (1974) A behavior rating scale for the preschool child. *Develop. Psychol.* **10,** 601–610

BENNETT I. (1960) *Delinquent and Neurotic Children: a Comparative Study.* New York: Basic Books

BIRCH H.G., RICHARDSON S.A., BAIRD D., HOROBIN G. & ILLSLEY R. (1970) *Mental*

Subnormality in the Community: a Clinical and Epidemiologic Study. Baltimore: Williams & Wilkins

BROPHY J.E. & GOOD T.L. (1974) *Teacher-Student Relationships: Causes and Consequences.* New York: Holt, Rinehart & Winston

BROWN F.W. (1942) Heredity in the psychoneuroses. *Proc. Roy. Soc. Med.* **35**, 785–790

CANTWELL D. (ed.) (1975) *The Hyperactive Child: Diagnosis, Management, Current Research.* New York: Spectrum Publications

CAPLAN H.L. (1970) Hysterical 'conversion' symptoms in childhood. MPhil Thesis: University of London

CARTER C.O. (1958) A life-table for mongols with the causes of death. *J. ment. def. Res.* **2**, 64–74

CHESS S., KORN S.J. & FERNANDEZ P.B. (1971) *Psychiatric Disorders of Children with Congenital Rubella.* New York: Brunner/Mazel

CICOUREL A.V. (1968) *The Social Organisation of Juvenile Justice.* New York: Wiley

CLARK M. (1970) *Reading Difficulties in Schools.* Harmondsworth: Penguin

COLLINS L.F., MAXWELL A.E. & CAMERON K. (1962) A factor analysis of some child psychiatric clinic data. *J. ment. Sci.* **108**, 274–285

COLLMAN R.D. & STOLLER A. (1963a) A life table for mongols in Victoria, Australia. *J. ment. def. Res.* **7**, 53–59

COLLMAN R.D. & STOLLER A. (1963b) Data on mongolism in Victoria, Australia: Prevalence and life expectation. *J. ment. def. Res.* **7**, 60–68

CORBETT J., HARRIS R. & ROBINSON R. (1975) Epilepsy. *Disabilities: An Annual Review,* vol. VII. New York: Brunner/Mazel

CORBETT J.A., MATHEWS A.M., CONNELL P.H. & SHAPIRO D.A. (1969) Tics and Gilles de la Tourette's syndrome: a follow-up study and critical review. *Brit. J. Psychiat.* **115**, 1229–1241

CREAK E.M. (1963) Childhood psychosis: a review of 100 cases. *Brit. J. Psychiat.* **109**, 84–89

CROME L. (1960) The brain and mental retardation. *Brit. med. J.* **i**, 897–904

CROMWELL R.L., BLASHFIELD R.K. & STRAUSS J.S. (1975) Criteria for classification systems. *In* Hobbs N. (ed.) *Issues in the Classification of Children.* San Francisco: Jossey-Bass

CYTRYN L., GILBERT A. & EISENBERG L. (1960) The effectiveness of tranquillizing drugs plus supportive psychotherapy in treating behavior disorders of children: a double-blind study of eighty outpatients. *Amer. J. Orthopsychiat.* **30**, 113–129

EISENBERG L., CONNERS C. & SHARPE L. (1965) A controlled study of the differential application of out-patient psychiatric treatment for children. *Jap. J. Child Psychiat.* **6**, 125–132

EVERITT B.S. (1974) *Cluster Analysis.* London: Heinemann Educational

EVERITT B.S. (1975) Multivariate analysis: the need for data, and other problems. *Brit. J. Psychiat.* **126**, 237–240

FIELD E. (1967) *A Validation of Hewitt and Jenkins' Hypothesis.* Home Office Research Unit Report No. 10. London: HMSO

FREEMAN M. (1971) A reliability study of psychiatric diagnosis in childhood and adolescence. *J. Child Psychol. Psychiat.* **12**, 43–54

GRAHAM P. & RUTTER M. (1973) Psychiatric disorder in the young adolescent: a follow-up study. *Proc. Roy. Soc. Med.* **66**, 1226–1229

GREER H.S. & CAWLEY R.H. (1966) *Some Observations on the Natural History of Neurotic Illness.* Mervyn Archdall Medical Monograph No. 3. Sydney, NSW: Australian Medical Association

GUNZBERG H.C. (1974) Educational planning for the mentally handicapped. *In* Clarke A.M. & Clarke A.D.B. (eds.) *Mental Deficiency; the Changing Outlook.* London: Methuen

HELLER T. (1930) About dementia infantilis. Reprinted in Howells J.G. (ed.) *Modern Perspectives in International Child Psychiatry.* Edinburgh: Oliver & Boyd

HEMPEL C.G. (1961) Some problems of taxonomy. *In* Zubin J. (ed.) *Field Studies in the Mental Disorders.* London: Grune & Stratton

HERMELIN B. & O'CONNOR N. (1970) *Psychological Experiments with Autistic Children.* Oxford: Pergamon

HETHERINGTON E.M., STOUWIE R.J. & RIDBERG E.H. (1971) Patterns of family interaction and child rearing attitudes related to three dimensions of juvenile delinquency. *J. Abnorm. Psychol.* **78,** 160–176

HEWITT L.E. & JENKINS R.L. (1949) *Fundamental Patterns of Maladjustment—The Dynamics of Their Origin.* Illinois: Michigan Child Guidance Institute

HOBBS N. (ed.) (1975) *Issues in the Classification of Children.* San Francisco: Jossey-Bass

INGRAM T.T.S. (1956) A characteristic form of overactive behaviour in brain damaged children. *J. ment. Sci.* **102,** 550–558

JASPERS K. (1962) *General Psychopathology.* Trans. Hoenig J. & Hamilton M.W. Manchester: University Press

JENKINS R.L. (1966) Psychiatric syndromes in children and their relation to family background. *Amer. J. Orthopsychiat.* **36,** 450–457

KANNER L. (1957) *Child Psychiatry,* 3rd edn. Springfield, Illinois: Charles C Thomas

KNIGHT B.J. & WEST D.J. (1975) Temporary and continuing delinquency. *Brit. J. Criminol.* **15,** 43–50

KOLVIN I., HUMPHREY M. & McNAY A. (1971) Studies in the childhood psychoses. VI. Cognitive factors in childhood psychoses. *Brit. J. Psychiat.* **118,** 415–419

KOLVIN I., MACKEITH R. & MEADOW S.R. (eds.) (1973) *Bladder Control and Enuresis.* Clinics in Develop. Med. nos. 48/49. London: SIMP/Heinemann

KOLVIN I., OUNSTED C., HUMPHREY M. & McNAY A. (1971) Studies in the childhood psychoses. II: The phenomenology of childhood psychoses. *Brit. J. Psychiat.* **118,** 385–395

KOLVIN I., OUNSTED C., RICHARDSON L. & GARSIDE R.F. (1971) Studies in the childhood psychoses. III: The family and social background in childhood psychoses. *Brit. J. Psychiat.* **118,** 396–402

KOLVIN I., WOLFF S., BARBER L.M., TWEDDLE E.G., GARSIDE R., SCOTT D.M. & CHAMBERS S. (1975) Dimensions of behaviour in infant school children. *Brit. J. Psychiat.* **126,** 114–126

KUSHLICK A. & BLUNDEN R. (1974) The epidemiology of mental subnormality. *In* Clarke A.M. & Clarke A.D.B. (eds.) *Mental Deficiency: the Changing Outlook.* London: Methuen

LEMERT E.M. (1967) *Human Deviance, Social Problems and Social Control.* Englewood Cliffs, NJ: Prentice-Hall

LEWIS H. (1954) *Deprived Children.* London: Oxford University Press

LOCKYER L. & RUTTER M. (1969) A five to fifteen year follow-up study of infantile psychosis. III: Psychological aspects. *Brit. J. Psychiat.* **115,** 865–882

LOCKYER L. & RUTTER M. (1970) A five to fifteen year follow-up study of infantile psychosis. IV: Patterns of cognitive ability. *Brit. J. soc. clin. Psychol.* **9,** 152–163

MALAMUD N. (1959) Heller's disease and childhood schizophrenia. *Amer. J. Psychiat.* **116,** 215–218

MAXWELL A.E. (1972) Difficulties in a dimensional description of symptomatology. *Brit. J. Psychiat.* **121,** 19–26

NUFFIELD E.J.A. (1961) Neurophysiology and behaviour disorders in epileptic children. *J. ment. Sci.* **107,** 438–458

OUNSTED C. (1955) The hyperkinetic syndrome in epileptic children. *Lancet* **ii,** 303–311

OUNSTED C., LINDSAY J. & NORMAN R. (1966) *Biological Factors in Temporal Lobe Epilepsy.* Clinics in Develop. Med. no. 22. London: SIMP/Heinemann

PALMER T.B. (1971) California's community treatment program for delinquent adolescents. *J. Res. Crime Delinq.* **8,** 74–92

PATTERSON G.R. (1964) An empirical approach to the classification of disturbed children. *J. Clin. Psychol.* **20,** 326–337

PETERSON D.R. (1961) Behavior problems of middle childhood. *J. Consult. Psychol.* **25,** 205–209

PETERSON D.R., BECKER W.C., SHOEMAKER D.J., LURIA Z. & HELLMER L.A. (1961) Child behavior problems and parental attitudes. *Child Dev.* **32,** 151–162

PRITCHARD M. & GRAHAM P. (1966) An investigation of a group of patients who have attended both the child and adult departments of the same psychiatric hospital. *Brit. J. Psychiat.* **112,** 603–612

QUAY H.C. (1964) Dimensions of personality in delinquent boys as inferred from the factor analysis of case history data. *Child Dev.* **35,** 479–484

QUAY H.C. (1966) Personality patterns in pre-adolescent delinquent boys. *Educ. Psychol. Measurement* **26,** 99–110

QUAY H.C. (1972) Patterns of aggression, withdrawal and immaturity. *In* Quay H.C. & Werry J.S. (eds.) *Psychopathological Disorders of Childhood.* New York: Wiley

QUAY H.C. (1974) Classification in the treatment of delinquency and antisocial behavior. *In* Hobbs N. (ed.) *Issues in the Classification of Children.* San Francisco: Jossey-Bass

QUAY H.C. & QUAY L.C. (1965) Behavior problems in early adolescence. *Child Dev.* **36,** 215–220

QUINN P.O. & RAPOPORT J.L. (1974) Minor physical anomalies and neurologic status in hyperactive boys. *Pediatrics* **53,** 742–747

REED E.W. & REED S.C. (1965) *Mental Retardation: A Family Study.* Philadelphia: W.B. Saunders

RITVO E.R., ORNITZ E.M., WALTER R.D. & HANLEY J. (1970) Correlation of psychiatric diagnoses and EEG findings: a double blind study of 184 hospitalized children. *Amer. J. Psychiat.* **126,** 988–996

ROBINS L.N. (1966) *Deviant Children Grown Up.* Baltimore: Williams & Wilkins

ROBINS L.N. (1972) Follow-up studies of behavior disorders in children. *In* Quay H.C. & Werry J.S. (eds.) *Psychopathological Disorders of Childhood.* New York: Wiley

ROBINS L.N. & HILL S.Y. (1966) Assessing the contributions of family structure, class and peer groups to juvenile delinquency. *J. crim. Law Criminol. and Police Sci.* **57,** 325–334

Ross I.S. (1959) Presentation of clinical case: an autistic child. *At* Pediatric Conference, The Babies Hospital Unit, United Hospital, Newark, NJ, vol. II, no. 2

Rutter M. (1965) Classification and categorization in child psychiatry. *J. Child Psychol. Psychiat.* **6**, 71–83

Rutter M. (1966) *Children of Sick Parents: an Environmental and Psychiatric Study.* Maudsley Monograph No. 16. London: Oxford University Press

Rutter M. (1970a) Autistic children: infancy to adulthood. *Semin. Psychiat.* **2**, 435–450

Rutter M. (1970b) Sex differences in children's responses to family stress. *In* Anthony E.J. & Koupernik C. (eds.) *The Child and His Family.* New York: Wiley

Rutter M. (1971a) Psychiatry. *In* Wortis J. (ed.) *Mental Retardation: an Annual Review* Vol. 3. New York: Grune & Stratton

Rutter M. (1971b) Parent–child separation: psychological effects on the Children. *J. Child Psychol. Psychiat.* **12**, 233–260

Rutter M. (1972) Relationships between child and adult psychiatric disorder. *Acta Psychiat. Scand.* **48**, 3–21

Rutter M. & Bartak L. (1973) Special educational treatment of autistic children: a comparative study. II. Follow-up findings and implications for services. *J. Child Psychol. Psychiat.* **14**, 241–270

Rutter M. & Lockyer L. (1967) A five to fifteen year follow-up study of infantile psychosis. I: Description of sample. *Brit. J. Psychiat.* **113**, 1169–1182

Rutter M. & Madge N. (1976) *Cycles of Disadvantage: a review of research.* London: Heinemann Educational

Rutter M. & Yule W. (1973) Specific reading retardation. *In* Mann L. & Sabatino D.A. (eds.) *The First Review of Special Education.* Philadelphia: Buttonwood Farms

Rutter M., Graham P. & Yule W. (1970) *A Neuropsychiatric Study in Childhood.* Clinics in Develop. Med. nos. 35/36. London: SIMP/Heinemann

Rutter M., Greenfeld D. & Lockyer L. (1967) A five to fifteen year follow-up study of infantile psychosis. II: Social and behavioural outcome. *Brit. J. Psychiat.* **113**, 1183–1199

Rutter M., Quinton D. & Yule B. (1977) *Family Pathology and Disorder in Children* (in preparation). London: Wiley

Rutter M., Shaffer D. & Shepherd M. (1975) *A Multiaxial Classification of Child Psychiatric Disorders.* Geneva: WHO

Rutter M., Shaffer D. & Sturge C. (1975) *A Guide to a Multi-Axial Classification Scheme for Psychiatric Disorders in Childhood and Adolescence.* London: Institute of Psychiatry

Rutter M., Tizard J. & Whitmore K. (eds.) (1970) *Education, Health and Behaviour.* London: Longman

Rutter M., Graham P., Chadwick O. & Yule W. (1976) Adolescent turmoil: fact or fiction? *J. Child Psychol. Psychiat.* **17**, 35–56

Rutter M., Cox A., Tupling C., Berger M. & Yule W. (1975) Attainment and adjustment in two geographical areas. I. The prevalence of psychiatric disorder. *Brit. J. Psychiat.* **126**, 493–509

Rutter M., Lebovici S., Eisenberg L., Sneznevskij A.V., Sadoun R., Brooke E. & Lin T-Y. (1969) A tri-axial classification of mental disorders in childhood. *J. Child Psychol. Psychiat.* **10**, 41–61

SCHEFF T. (1966) *Being Mentally Ill: a Sociological Theory*. Chicago: Aldine

SHAFFER D., CHADWICK O.F.D. & RUTTER M. (1975) Psychiatric outcome of localised head injury in children. *In* Porter R. & FitzSimons D. (eds.) *Outcome of Severe Damage to the Central Nervous System*. Ciba Foundation Symposium No. 34 (new series). Amsterdam: Elsevier–Excerpta Medica–North-Holland

SHAFFER D., MCNAMARA N. & PINCUS J.H. (1974) Controlled observations on patterns of activity, attention and impulsivity in brain damaged and psychiatrically disturbed boys. *Psychol. Med* **4**, 4–18

STENGEL E. (1959) Classification of mental disorders. *Bull. Wld. Hlth. Org.* **21**, 601–663

STEVENS J.R., SACHDEV K.K. & MILSTEIN V. (1968) Behavior disorders of childhood and the electroencephalogram. *Arch. Neurol. (Chicago)* **18**, 160–177

TAFT L.T. & COHEN H.J. (1971) Hypsarrhythmia and infantile autism: a clinical report. *J. Autism Child. Schiz.* **1**, 327–336

TARJAN M.D., TIZARD J., RUTTER M., BEGAB M., BROOKE E.M., DE LA CRUZ F., LIN T-Y., MONTENEGRO H., STROTZKA H. & SARTORIUS N. (1972) Classification and mental retardation: Issues arising in the Fifth WHO Seminar on Psychiatric Diagnosis, Classification and Statistics. *Amer. J. Psychiat.* **128**, 34–45 (Suppl.)

THOMPSON J., RUTTER M., YULE W. & BERGER M. (1976) (Paper in preparation)

TIZARD B. & REES J. (1975) The effect of early institutional rearing on the behaviour problems and affectional relationships of four-year-old children. *J. Child Psychol. Psychiat* **16**, 61–73

TIZARD J. (1966) Epidemiology of mental retardation: a discussion of a paper by E.M. Gruenberg. *Int. J. Psychiat.* **2**, 131–134

TIZARD J. (1974) Longitudinal studies: problems and findings. *In* Clarke A.M. & Clarke A.D.B. (eds.) *Mental Deficiency: The Changing Outlook*. London: Methuen

WALDROP M. & HALVERSON C. (1971) Minor physical anomalies and hyperactive behavior in young children. *In* Hellmuth J. (ed.) *The Exceptional Infant*, vol. 2. New York: Brunner/Mazel

WARDLE C.J. (1961) Two generations of broken homes in the genesis of conduct and behaviour disorders in childhood. *Brit. med. J.* **2**, 349–354

WARREN M.Q. (1969) The case for differential treatment of delinquents. *Ann. Amer. Acad. Polit. Soc. Sci.* **381**, 47–59

WARREN W. (1965) A study of adolescent psychiatric in-patients and the outcome six or more years later. II. The follow-up study. *J. Child Psychol. Psychiat.* **6**, 141–160

WARREN W. (1968) A study of anorexia nervosa in young girls. *J. Child Psychol. Psychiat.* **9**, 27–40

WERRY J. (1972) Diagnosis for psychopharmacological studies in children. *Psychopharmacol. Bull.* Spec. Suppl. to vol. 9, *Pharmacotherapy of Children*, 89–96

WERRY J., MINDE K., GUZMAN A., WEISS G., DOGAN K. & HOY E. (1972) Studies on the hyperactive child. VII: Neurological status compared with neurotic and normal children. *Amer. J. Orthopsychiat.* **42**, 441–450

WOLFF S. (1971) Dimensions and clusters of symptoms in disturbed children. *Brit. J. Psychiat.* **118**, 421–427

WOLKIND S.N. (1974) The components of 'affectionless psychopathy' in institutionalized children. *J. Child Psychol. Psychiat.* **15**, 215–220

WOLKIND S.N. & EVERITT B. (1974) A cluster analysis of the behavioural items in the preschool child. *Psychol. Med.* **4**, 422–427

WORLD HEALTH ORGANIZATION (1974) *Glossary of Mental Disorders and Guide to Their Classification.* Geneva: WHO

ZEITLIN H. (1972) A study of patients who attended the children's department and later the adults' department of the same psychiatric hospital. MPhil Dissertation: University of London

PART IV
Clinical syndromes

CHAPTER 16

Disorders in preschool children

N. RICHMAN

The young child moves gradually from complete dependency to considerable independence and autonomy, developing complex language and social behaviour in an enlarging social circle which extends from parents and sibs to other adults and children. Preschool problems centre round the establishment of acceptable patterns of behaviour in these areas; in activities such as self-control, eating, sleeping, sphincter control and in the development of a balance between dependence and independence. These problems of adaptation and adjustment occur mainly within the family, unlike those of older children whose difficulties often involve experiences outside the home. The child's dependency means that any problems are likely to involve the parents. Moreover, in the young child, behaviour difficulties more often appear to be simple reactions to family management rather than entrenched patterns of response. Difficulties may vary as the child passes through different stages and so requires less care and becomes more independent.

Looking after lively young children is physically and emotionally demanding and requires a great deal of patience and adaptability. Parents with young children are often themselves young, trying to establish themselves as adults, in their marriage, at work, etc. Most parents find the resources to deal with these responsibilities and their young children. We have some understanding of why it is sometimes difficult for them to cope, but more information is needed to find ways of identifying the vulnerable families and helping them before serious problems arise.

Identifying problems

Apart from a few well-described syndromes such as infantile autism, the classification of disorders in preschool children is not clearly established (Rutter *et al* 1969; see Chapter 15). The majority of disorders may be described as 'behaviour problems', meaning behaviour which causes distress or strain in the family. The problem can vary from a single stressful 'habit' disorder such as encopresis or a sleep disturbance, to a more global disturbance affecting many aspects of the child's functioning. All behavioural disturbances are in some sense defined by the tolerance of the containing family or community; in the young child this is very apparent because the definition of a problem is based largely on the parents' perceptions and reports about their child. Although psychological testing, developmental assessment and physical growth are useful measures of current status, it may be impossible to obtain other criteria about how a child behaves, apart from the parents' description. At this age, independent assessments such as teachers' reports or schoolwork or even the child's own ideas about how it feels may not be available. The term 'behaviour problem' must be used initially to mean that in the family there is a problem which is localised in this particular child.

Further exploration will indicate what contribution the child's characteristics have made to the development of the problem, what part is played by family interactions and experiences, how disturbed the child is in his own right and how much the difficulties express other family problems.

Prevalence of individual symptoms

There have been many studies in young children of the prevalence of individual behaviours such as tempers (Goodenough 1931), fears (Jersild & Holmes 1935), sleep (Roberts & Schoellkopf 1951; Healy 1972), and enuresis (Newson & Newson 1968; Douglas & Blomfield 1958). McFarlane *et al* (1954) in a longitudinal study of a group of normal children found that there was a peak of behavioural symptoms in the preschool child including fears, tempers, and aggressive behaviour. Aggressive behaviour appeared later in the boys and lasted longer.

Richman *et al* (1975) studied the prevalence of a number of different behaviours in a random sample of 3-year-old London children. The most frequent items reported were bedwetting (44 per cent boys and 30 per cent girls) and wetting during the day (23 per cent boys and 11 per cent girls). About one in six or seven children was reported to have food fads (13 per cent), difficulty in settling at night (13 per cent) and waking during the night (14 per cent). Soiling was reported in 12 per cent (18 per cent boys and 8 per cent girls). About the same proportion showed many fears. Poor concentration (5 per cent), severe tempers (5 per cent), unhappiness (3 per cent), excessive worrying (2 per cent) were all much less common.

Prevalence of significant disorder

'Symptoms' are widespread in young children, and it is obvious that not every child who eats or sleeps poorly or who is soiling is disturbed; the significance of individual symptoms must be examined in the context of the child's total functioning. Whether clusters of symptoms form definite clinical entities requires further analysis.

A survey of a random sample of 3-year-olds living in a London borough found that about 7 per cent had behaviour problems of moderate to marked severity and another 14 per cent had mild problems (Richman *et al* 1975). The children were initially selected as being at risk by means of a behaviour screening questionnaire dealing with 12 individual behaviours (Richman & Graham 1971) and the presence of a behaviour problem was subsequently confirmed or disconfirmed by clinical assessment. The most common clinical picture was of a child who was active, attention seeking, disobedient and difficult to manage. Anxiety and depression are difficult to evaluate in young children, and it is unlikely that 'clinical' depression occurs in the very young. As the child matures cognitively, there is increased awareness of the uncertainties of life and of human relationships. Anxiety about his or her place in the family and in the world may be associated with some of the behaviours which develop in the toddler. Irrational fears of the dark or of strange objects, rituals, perfectionist behaviour, fear about being left, sleep disorders, and food fads are common at this age, and occasionally a child may be quite handicapped by such symptoms. As yet we do not know whether such 'neurotic' reactions in the young child are associated with similar behaviours in the older child. Relatively few of the children showed a 'neurotic' picture of fears, unhappiness and timidity. There were more behaviour problems amongst the boys than the girls, but the difference was not significant, and in general both sexes showed similar sorts of problems.

Most behaviour problems for which advice is sought, a small proportion of the total, are seen by the general practitioner, health visitor, or paediatrician. The psychiatrist sees a very selected population, possibly from the most disturbed families, and those working in hospital departments are likely to see a large number of children in whom physical or developmental disorders are also present. Social class also influences referral (Wolff 1961a), as middle class parents are more likely to view psychiatric treatment favourably and working class families are more likely to be offered support by social services. About 10 per cent of referrals to a child guidance clinic are of children under 5; a large proportion of these show developmental problems. The preponderance of boys (1·5 : 1) is not as marked as with older children (Wolff 1961a).

The presenting complaints of 43 children under 5 (excluding those with obvious organic abnormalities) referred to a child guidance clinic fell into the following clinical categories—bad or unmanageable (20); fearful (6); habit disorder, such as soiling, wetting, headbanging (5); speech disorder (4); miscellaneous, e.g. breathholding (8) (Wolff 1961b).

In 135 preschool children attending a day centre in a children's hospital, the following groupings were found (Bentovim 1973): (1) About 30 per cent severe management problems; (2) 10 per cent highly anxious children afraid to separate from their mothers; (3) 11 per cent with speech and language problems; (4) 13 per cent autistic children; (5) 15 per cent with primary retardation, and smaller numbers of (6) children in their first year with severe feeding problems or failure to thrive, often at risk of being battered or (7) children with 'developmental' problems such as soiling.

DEVELOPMENTAL FACTORS

The term developmental is used in different ways, referring both to constitutional factors which hinder normal development, e.g. in the acquisition of normal speech or sphincter control, and to the disorders which often occur during the course of development—such as sleeping, and eating problems, and hyperactivity. To avoid confusion, the term 'developmental' is used here only in the first sense.

Many behaviours are considered problematic merely because they persist beyond the age expected, although they are still within the normal range. This applies particularly to sphincter control, but may be applicable in cases of overdependency, poor concentration or disobedience. In the severely retarded child, general immaturity often presents problems of management, although some of these problems could be attributed to emotional tensions in the family consequent upon having a retarded child. Whether there are other, specific maturational delays or anomalies making children more susceptible to problems is not known. For instance, it could be that impaired development of attention might lead to restlessness and poor concentration and so interfere with social learning and delay the establishment of acceptable behaviour patterns. The greater number of boys who have delayed sphincter control, overactivity and poor concentration would support this suggestion as they are known to be more vulnerable to physical damage at birth. The developmental problem of delayed language is also more common amongst boys and is highly associated with the presence of behaviour difficulties. Using a simple screening device which assessed naming skills and complexity of syntax, about 3 per cent of 3-year-olds showed delayed language development (Stevenson & Richman 1976a). Half these children also had behaviour problems compared with a prevalence of 14 per cent behaviour problems in the total population (Richman & Stevenson 1976). The language ability of the children with behaviour problems was significantly below that of a control group (Stevenson & Richman 1976b).

Friedlander *et al* (1974) found that, unlike controls, a group of children with behaviour problems paid as much attention to meaningless words as they did to meaningful ones. Some of these children were autistic but the finding held good even for those who were not, although many of these showed signs of brain damage. It has been suggested that in autistic children the primary disorder is one of language and cognition and the other behavioural abnormalities are secondary (Rutter & Bartak 1971). Possibly, behaviour difficulties are sometimes a consequence of difficulties in communication; in other cases a communication difficulty may be a sign of emotional disturbance, or common developmental abnormalities may underly both phenomena. More research is needed to disentangle the subtleties of these interactions and their underlying mechanisms (Rutter 1972; Stevenson & Richman 1976b).

Foetal distress and perinatal difficulties have been postulated as important aetiological factors in the development of behaviour problems in later childhood (Pasamanick & Knobloch 1961; Prechtl 1961) and defects in attention could be the mechanism whereby these events affect later behaviour. The findings are not easy to interpret because of the difficulty of assessing the child's state at birth (Prechtl & Beintema 1964) and of controlling for other family and social factors themselves associated with both birth injury and emotional disturbance. The emotional difficulties which the mother experiences in establishing a relationship with the infant after a difficult birth must also be taken into account.

INDIVIDUAL CHARACTERISTICS

Examining a child at one point in time gives no indication of the child's contribution to the development of strain in the family. There is now a considerable amount of evidence showing that, from birth, infants have their own individual characteristics which influence how they relate to the world and how their personalities develop (Korner 1971—see also Chapter 1).

Different patterns of attention and of persistence have been demonstrated which could have important implications for how the infant processes incoming information (Lewis 1971; McCall 1971). So far, the meaning of these differences in terms of future behaviour is not clear because knowledge is lacking on their consistency and on their relevance for the child's interactions with his environment. Each infant seems to have individual needs for different types of perceptual stimulation and individual ways of responding to stimuli. For instance, in a group of 37 infants followed for 18 months half were cuddlers who enjoyed physical contact, a quarter were intermediate and a quarter were noncuddlers. The last group were active, restless and intolerant of close physical contact (Schaffer & Emerson 1964). These differences were not related to parental handling. A child who is difficult to soothe and who cries a lot will probably initiate more contact with the caretaking adults; one who is quiet and passive may be left alone. Thus the child's individual characteristics mediate both his experiences of the world and the response of others, so that patterns of interaction are set up which affect the child's subsequent experiences and development. A child who cries frequently and demands a lot of bodily contact might be an irritation to one sort of parent who would prefer an undemanding child who is easily soothed; on the other hand, the latter might appear unresponsive to some parents who would feel rejected. There are now several studies which show the importance of individual differences for later development (see Chapter 1).

An awareness of a child's personality characteristics is very important in understanding how problems arise. Knowledge on how to respond sensitively to a child's 'basic' style could help parents improve their handling of difficult children. As yet these ideas have not had much influence on clinical practice.

Factors interfering with early parent–infant relationships

Most research on early parent–infant interaction has been done with mothers and infants and more needs to be known about father–infant interaction (Schaffer 1971).

As already noted, the infant's characteristics influence parent–infant relationships. Children who are particularly irritable, difficult to feed, or who sleep poorly, may cause a lot of strain and be difficult to accept. It has been suggested that separation from the mother at the time of birth, because of prematurity or illness in the child or mother, seriously interferes with the establishment of a good relationship. Anxiety about the child's physical state or survival may also be an important factor.

Children born to women who definitely wanted an abortion but who were unable to get one are particularly likely to be rejected after they are born. In about half such cases either the children are subsequently adopted or the mother continues to wish she had had an abortion (Pare & Raven 1970; Hook 1963). Forsmann and Thuwe (1966) followed up 120 children born after requested abortion had been refused. Compared with a control group, they had a significantly greater frequency of psychiatric illness, educational difficulties, delinquency, and admission into care. More were illegitimate and more had unsatisfactory or broken homes. The abortion laws and available social support will determine how many unwanted children are born and whether they can later be accepted, but it seems likely that the factors which lead to an abortion being requested with determination, are likely to produce difficulties in child-rearing.

Psychiatric illness following parturition may also interfere with child care.

About 1 in 500–1000 births leads to the development of a puerperal psychosis (Paffenbarger 1964). Seager (1960) found that the family history and course of illness are similar to psychotic illnesses in nonpuerperal women and concluded that the pregnancy acts as a precipitating stress in a predisposed person.

Less severe disturbances are common and may be long-lasting. Using a questionnaire, Jacobson *et al* (1965) found that 1 year after the birth 25 per cent of women had more than 6 symptoms which had arisen postpartum. In a study carried out in a general practice the rate of depression in the first 3 months after pregnancy was five times that during pregnancy (Ryle 1961). It has been estimated that about 10 per cent of women develop depression following a birth, and 4 per cent are still depressed at the end of a year.

Depressive thoughts may concern the baby. Depressed mothers may feel hostile, rejecting, or overconcerned, and they may have fears of harming the child. Psychiatric symptoms involving the child are particularly likely to be damaging (Rutter 1966). There needs to be increased awareness by doctors, health visitors, and other professionals of these depressions and of their sometimes long-lasting effects on mothering (Cohler *et al* 1974).

There is little evidence on how their own early experiences affect parents' behaviour. Certain events, such as loss of the mother before 11, may predispose girls to become depressed (Brown *et al* 1975). The effects of early separation or going into care will depend on the preceding circumstances and subsequent care (see Chapter 3). For instance, Wolkind (1974a) found that prolonged early experience of residential care was particularly associated with antisocial behaviour in girls in long-term residential care. Boys with antisocial behaviour seemed to have been affected more by lack of contact with their fathers and by large sibship size. Mothers who, at the antenatal clinic reported separation experiences before the age of 11, have also been found to be more likely to have problems with their infant in the first year (Frommer & O'Shea 1973).

Parents who are physically violent to their children may themselves have received such treatment as children (Helfer & Kempe 1968) but the evidence on this point is contradictory.

It is widely suggested that 'deficient parenting' could be improved by teaching parenting skills but, apart from programmes dealing with cognitive and language stimulation, there has been little work in this area. How could parents be helped to interact more positively with their children? There are now many day centres for mothers and young children which provide various sorts of help. In some places an emphasis is placed on support and understanding for the parents, on the assumption that if the parents' needs for nurturance are met, they will be able to be more nurturant to their children.

More specific programmes using behavioural techniques could be developed. Through these, parents might find they can respond more appropriately to their children and increase their self-esteem and sense of control (Newson & Newson 1976). Videotapes can show parents how they actually behave and also provide better models of behaviour.

FAMILY FACTORS

The association between psychiatric illness in parents and in children has been well-documented in schoolchildren (Rutter 1966; Rutter *et al* 1970a) and a similar relationship seems to hold for younger children. Rutter (1966) found that, in young children attending a child psychiatric clinic, there was a higher rate of psychiatric illness in the parents than in a group of control children. Ten per cent of the 317 children whose parents had had a psychiatric illness were under 5, compared with 3·9 per cent under 5 of the 592 children attending whose parents had not had a psychiatric illness. In a group of 43 preschool children attending a psychiatric clinic (Wolff 1961a) 17·4 per cent of the parents had been treated for psychiatric illness; this affected 23 per cent of the families involved; there was no control group for comparison.

It could be that children with disturbed parents are more likely to be referred to clinics, but the relationship between problems in children and illness in the parents is also found in community surveys, at least as far as the mothers are concerned. London mothers of preschool children with behaviour problems suffered from psychiatric illnesses, mostly depressive in type, significantly more often than the mothers of a matched group of control children. Of the problem group mothers 39 per cent were depressed compared with 27 per cent of the controls (Richman 1976). No relationship was found between the psychiatric state of the father and behaviour problems. Poor physical health in mothers was associated with behaviour problems in boys.

This relationship between disturbance in the mother and in the child could arise in several ways. Since information about the child is usually obtained from the mother it may be that her perception of the child is coloured by her depressive feelings, so that the behavioural difficulties become magnified. The child might be reacting to the mother's depression or the mother to the child's difficult behaviour, or there might be a mutual interaction between them compounded by other outside stresses.

Recent work has emphasised the high rates of depression occurring in mothers of young children. Both Richman (1974) and Brown *et al* (1975) found that about 40 per cent of working class mothers with young children had depressive illnesses over the 3 months prior to interview. In Brown's study, women with children under 6 were particularly likely to be depressed.

The mothers who became depressed were more likely to have suffered a recent stressful event and to have chronic life difficulties. Increased vulnerability to stressful events was associated with four vulnerability factors—lack of a confiding relationship with a husband or boyfriend, having three or more children under 14, having lost their own mother before the age of 11, and not going out to work. Working class women had more stressful events and more chronic difficulties in their lives, but their increased rate of depression was due to their greater propensity to react with depression when a stress occurred.

The effects of dealing with the intense emotional and physical demands of young children needs further study. Lack of independence and of satisfaction apart from the role of mother and housewife, confinement to the house, and the decline of the supportive role of the extended family are other social variables which may contribute to women's increased rates of depression (Young & Willmott 1957; Willmott & Young 1960; Gavron 1966; Grove & Tudor 1973).

Poor marital relationships are significantly associated with the occurrence of behaviour problems in both clinic samples and in the community (Richman 1976). The presence of a difficult child may be a strain on a marriage which would otherwise be satisfactory, or the child may be reacting to the parents' tensions, especially if they displace their own dissatisfactions on to the child. The dependence of the young child on his parents, and his inability to provide them with an empathic, supportive relationship makes this age particularly vulnerable. Reactions of parents whose own emotional needs are not met are seen in their most extreme form in abused children (Helfer & Kempe 1968).

Although most studies concentrate on the mother's role, it is obvious that fathers are extremely important, not only because of the emotional support they provide for the mothers (Brown *et al* 1975) but also because they provide equally significant figures with whom the child relates and identifies. Fathers take an active part in child-rearing and more attention should be paid to their influence in the marriage and on the children (Newson & Newson 1963; Howells 1968; Grunebaum & Strean 1964).

There are a number of studies of children brought up by a single-parent families. Since such families often suffer serious economic hardship and there has been disruption of the family with changes in accommodation and care-taking arrangements, it is difficult to disentangle the factors responsible for the development of behaviour problems. Children who are or have been in care have a high rate of behavioural disturbance (Wolkind & Rutter 1973; Wolkind 1974b; Yule & Raynes 1972) and this could be related both to events preceding being taken into care, and to the nature of the institutions in which they are living (Tizard & Tizard 1971).

The effects of family size and ordinal position on young children's behaviour are not known. It appears that younger children from large families are significantly more likely to have delayed language development (Richman & Stevenson 1976) and are slightly more at risk of developing behaviour problems (Richman 1976).

ENVIRONMENTAL FACTORS

Although social class is such an important variable in psychiatric disturbances in adults, it has not proved so in children. Differences in clinic studies are often due to referral patterns and are not found in community surveys. There is increasing interest in specific environmental factors which might be relevant; such as housing, neighbourhood characteristics, and schools (Rutter 1973; Brown *et al* 1975; Richman 1976).

The young child needs to play in a safe place where he can keep in contact, at least visually, with a familiar adult. An urban life, with the danger of cars, lack of garden and unknown 'neighbours', makes play outside unacceptable for many preschool children. Parks, playgrounds and playgroups can substitute for the street and the back garden but often they are either not available in the areas which need them most or are inconvenient for the parents to get to (Rose 1973). It has been suggested that flats, especially high rise buildings or tower blocks, provide an environment which is most detrimental to preschool children (Jephcott 1971; Stewart 1970).

Fanning (1967) found that service families with young children living in flats consulted their doctor more frequently and had more respiratory complaints than similar families living in houses. The mothers living in flats also had more neurotic symptoms. This finding was not confirmed by Moore (1974), who found no differences between women living in flats and those living in houses with respect to Cornell Medical Index scores or to visits to the doctor for psychiatric reasons. Family size was not important but data were not given on the ages of the children.

A study of young children living in council housing (Richman 1974) found no difference in the rates of behaviour problems amongst the children, but there was an increased rate of depression in mothers living in flats (whether low or high rise).

A more recent investigation with a large sample suggests that both in the mothers and their 3-year-old children, but not in their fathers, there is a significant increase of emotional problems in those living in flats. This is especially the case for those in tower blocks (Richman 1976). Rates of behaviour difficulty were higher than average in all the children living in council estates, 21 per cent compared with an overall rate of 14 per cent; in the low rise flats, the rate was 18 per cent and in the tower blocks 30 per cent. The rate of psychiatric illness in mothers was also higher in those living in flats. It is of interest that mothers with young children living in overcrowded conditions are particularly liable to depressive illness (Brown *et al* 1975). Whether children living in confined conditions with few opportunities for leaving their mother suffer excessively from problems like fearfulness and anxiety over separation is not yet known.

It can be argued that a selective housing policy is affecting these rates and that the most difficult families or disturbed mothers move into flats or unfurnished rooms. It is possible that the low morale of some council estates and the low prestige of living in a tower block is the significant factor rather than the building itself. However it seems likely that, particularly for mothers of young children who are confined to the house for long periods, it may be stressful to live in poor housing where the children cannot get out to play.

Problems may be exacerbated by the fact that families with young children may have moved recently into their flat, and recent moves have been shown to increase susceptibility to emotional disturbance, especially in young families (Sainsbury 1971; Hooper *et al* 1972).

SOCIAL AND CULTURAL INFLUENCES

There is a large body of research on child-rearing patterns (see Chapter 4) but relatively little is known concerning their effects on preschool children. Much research has been concerned with influences leading to delinquency and there has been less emphasis on emotional disturbance or on protective factors of any kind.

Different cultures are associated with somewhat different ways of bringing up children and comparative research would be valuable. Thus, it seems that methods of upbringing in the UK and USA encourage independence and an expectation that demands will be met. In contrast, the Japanese appear to foster dependency and conformity (Caudill & Weinstein 1966; Makita & Okonogi 1969). This might produce more anxiety over separation (Levy 1943). On the other hand, an emphasis on independence might be stressful for children not yet mature enough to cope with playgroups or nights away from home. Some children find sleeping alone difficult, but in Japan it has been customary for children to sleep with their parents or another adult (Caudill & Plath 1966). Socially determined sleeping patterns, as well as physiological factors (Bernal 1973), may play a role in sleep disorders. Similar differences may apply to eating patterns (with regard to both timing and foods available) and eating disorders. In both cases there are implications for treatment. In the same way, cultural expectations concerning the role of fathers may influence the extent to which fathers can be involved in treatment.

PROGNOSIS

The significance of preschool behaviour problems for future adjustment is not known. Prevalence surveys of older age groups show rates similar to those in the preschool child, and in older children problems have often been present for many years (Rutter *et al* 1970a). Presumably at all ages there are some difficulties which are short-lived and others which are likely to become chronic. Factors which imply poor prognosis are the presence of poor family relationships (Wolff 1961b), being in care (Wolkind & Rutter 1973), and the presence of brain damage (Rutter *et al* 1970a). Follow-up studies with older children show that those with neurotic problems tend to have a good prognosis (Michael *et al* 1957), whereas the child with conduct disorder has a high risk of developing adult mental illness and personality problems (Robins 1966).

Wolff (1961b) followed a group of children under 5 referred to a psychiatric clinic. Three to 6 years after first attendance the prevalence of aggressive symptoms and phobic and habit disorders was the same in boys and girls. The decline in frequency was most marked for aggressive symptoms in boys and for phobic symptoms in girls. Outcome was poor in all the 4 children in residential care, in 3 boys with mild brain damage which had not been identified at the time of initial contact, in those children who came from broken homes or where marital relations were poor, and when a parent had received psychiatric treatment. Boys were assessed as more disturbed on all measures of outcome. Whether children who have not attended a clinic have a similar outcome is not known.

Cross-sectional studies of behaviours such as fears, tempers, aggressive behaviour, find that the prevalence of these reaches a peak at the preschool age and diminishes in the older children (McFarlane *et al* 1954; Goodenough 1931). These maturational effects are probably one reason why it is so difficult to predict future personality in the young child. Longitudinal studies of children followed from birth have in some cases found stable temperamental characteristics continuing into adulthood, but in general prediction of future personality in the child is poor (Kagan & Moss 1965). Possibly there are certain behaviour characteristics, like defects in attention or marked variability in response, which are associated with an increased likelihood of developing behaviour difficulties throughout childhood.

SERVICES FOR THE PRESCHOOL CHILD

Although there is an awareness of the problems of preschool children and their needs, so far this has not been translated into an integrated service. This is partly due to the number of separate agencies (health, developmental, educational, social) available to deal with different aspects of needs. Such fragmentation is particularly regrettable when the problems of the parents are ignored or considered without reference to the children. Thus, mothers' feelings of isolation and depression are often dealt with separately by adult psychiatric services.

Recent plans to extend the provision of nursery school places raises the question as to the relative advantages of the various forms of preschool facility at present available—day nurseries, playgroups and nursery classes. An advantage of the playgroup is the involvement of parents, who may be stimulated by contact with new ideas and by interaction with other mothers. It seems desirable to encourage this. In some areas groups of child minders, organised by the mothers themselves, might be the most appropriate form of preschool facilities.

Provision of preschool facilities is very variable in quantity and type in different parts of the country. Often those most in need are unable to make use of what is available because of lack of money or difficulties in attending. Various studies have shown that the children attending playgroups have a low prevalence of problems (Holdsworth 1969; Keeley 1968). Thus in Birmingham, only 20 per cent of the playgroups were in 'deprived' areas and over 50 per cent were in areas classed as 'privileged'. Of the children attending 8 per cent were referred for reasons of social need and only 2·3 per cent had specific handicaps (McArdle *et al* 1972). The National Children's Bureau examined the use made of playgroups set up under the Urban Aid Programme and found that they were not attracting the children most in need (apart from those living in overcrowded conditions). Only 8 per cent of the children had any reported handicap and presumably the prevalence of handicaps in the community was much higher than that. Children with minor handicaps or from the most materially deprived homes stopped attendance sooner than others. Only 7 out of 10 children in these groups attended for as long as 10 weeks (Joseph & Parfitt 1972).

The NSPCC have set up 10 therapeutic playgroups in areas of deprivation, where children can be referred by social workers, doctors or other community agencies. The children are transported by minibus to and from the playgroup for a minimum of two sessions a week. A third of the children referred had behaviour problems and/or developmental delay. A preliminary report suggests that over a period of a year there was an improvement in the children's behaviour (Rose 1973).

Interest in cognitive and developmental gains has overshadowed research into the use of playgroups, nurseries, and nursery classes in behaviour problems, and it is not known what sort of preschool facilities are advantageous for emotional development. Possibly combining aspects of all the above in one centre would have advantages. Special efforts to enable certain parents to make use of them are obviously necessary, such as providing transport, flexible hours of attendance, and free places.

Community centres where children could be taken for a few hours in times of stress or emergency and where mothers would have someone to talk to, would be a valuable provision. For the more disturbed child different facilities may be required, although it is uncertain how much separation there should be between handicapped children and 'normal' children.

Even though the prognosis for an individual behaviour problem may be good, the stress of the immediate situation requires help. In many cases attendance at a playgroup or nursery relieves the parents' stress and enables them to cope with the child's demands. Support and discussion with a sympathetic person is important. This could be provided by a health visitor, playgroup leader, nursery nurse, or another mother with similar experience. Day centres, attached to departments of child psychiatry, have been developed to help families which require more specialised and intensive help (Bentovim & Lansdown 1973; see Chapter 37).

THERAPEUTIC MEASURES

Many therapeutic procedures are used with preschool children but there has been little systematic investigation of their efficiency. Increasing awareness of the importance of family interaction has led to family-centred therapy with all or several members of the family being seen together (see Chapters 12 and 40). Even very young children may be included in family therapy sessions. Their presence completes the family group and can elicit important family interactions. Thus, parents may allow a young child to dominate them, be overcritical of normal play and activity, or be rejecting. In this way both the family and the therapists can understand better the mechanisms producing family tensions. The parents can also see other models of responding, communicating and controlling the young child which may be helpful.

Behaviour therapy with young children is still at an experimental stage and most clinical studies have been carried out with somewhat older age groups. At present it seems most useful for self-destructive behaviour in retarded children (e.g. severe headbanging), or for disruptive behaviour such as tantrums, or in language delay. The principles of behaviour therapy may also be used more widely for discussing the management of behaviour problems such as soiling, tempers, disobedience (e.g. by the reinforcement of 'good' and extinction of 'bad' behaviour). The active involvement of parents as 'change agents' acting under a therapist's guidance is a helpful development.

Apart from anticonvulsants, there are few indications for the use of drugs in young children. Almost no satisfactory controlled clinical trials have been carried out in this age group and it seems desirable to try the effects of environmental changes before using drugs. However, sedatives such as chloral, promethazine and diazepam may be used for the sleepless or anxious child; and tranquillisers (e.g. chlorpromazine, haloperidol) or stimulants (e.g. dextroamphetamine) for the overactive child.

SCREENING IN THE COMMUNITY

Those most in contact with young children in the community—health visitors, nursery nurses, general practitioners—need to know which children are at risk for behaviour problems, e.g. children living in poor housing, in care, with a chronic illness, or who have a parent with a psychiatric illness.

Screening questionnaires which can be filled in quickly are useful instruments in these situations as long as their limitations are remembered. They cannot take into account qualitative differences between similar forms of behaviour or the severity of monosymptomatic difficulties. A questionnaire can indicate in which children further exploration of the situation is necessary.

A behavioural screening scale dealing with 12 common symptoms, which can be completed by a parent or other person familiar with the child, in under 10 minutes, was able to identify 83 per cent of children with difficult behaviour problems (Richman & Graham 1976). There were 13 per cent false positives, i.e. children identified on the questionnaire as at risk for having a behaviour problem, who on clinical grounds did not appear to have one. The scale was reliable when it was completed again after an interval of 2 to 3 weeks. Such a scale could be used routinely in child health clinics, hospital outpatient departments and preschool facilities. Experimental trials would assess its utility in alerting people to an individual child's needs, and also encourage the measurement of behaviour change in a consistent manner for purposes of evaluation.

PREVENTION

The evaluation of preventive measures has proved difficult because of uncertainties about the weights to be attached to different variables and lack of knowledge about the mechanisms involved. The possibilities are being explored of identifying highly vulnerable groups, e.g. mothers who have themselves been in care or who have had a previous psychiatric illness, are very young or live in poor social conditions, as well as babies who have experienced pregnancy or perinatal complications.

Research is being carried out into the way factors associated with pregnancy and birth affect the baby's behaviour and early mother–child interaction. It seems to be particularly important to help parents when there are complications after birth or doubts about the baby's development. Isolation of the baby at this time produces great anxiety which may lead to subsequent difficulties in acceptance by parents. Immediate discussion and explanation would help them to deal with their shock and develop more positive responses to the situation. The effect of different hospital procedures and of the management of confinements on parental emotions needs examination. The use of highly technical procedures may produce anxiety and feelings of helplessness which affect subsequent responses to the baby.

A similar situation is present in the older child who has a chronic illness or handicap. This is a great strain on the family and skilled emotional support is needed as well as medical and surgical treatment. Schoolchildren with chronic handicaps have a higher prevalence of emotional disturbance (Rutter *et al* 1970b); whether this is so in the preschool child is not known but it is likely that close cooperation between child psychiatrists and paediatricians would prevent later difficulties in some cases.

Many studies have shown that the often related factors of loss of a parent (particularly the mother) in the early years and being taken into care have a poor prognosis for later emotional stability (Yule & Raynes 1972; Wolkind 1974a). Although the young child may not show overt signs of disturbance at the time, it seems that support in bereavement and the devotion of more resources to child-care facilities might help to prevent later adverse effects.

An understanding of the isolation and stress experienced by mothers of young children could lead to various measures designed to reduce the strain. If the prevalence of behaviour problems in the children and depression in their mothers is known the efficacy of these different measures can be examined. Measures could include flexible day-care facilities and emergency nursery places for times of sudden stress, and group discussions in the antenatal clinic, child health clinic, or the various preschool facilities. Emphasis on group activity rather than on individual personality problems may reduce feelings of isolation and personal inadequacy. Further work is needed as to how the neighbourhood can play a supportive role in the lives of families with young children, e.g. by stimulating involvement of parents in playgroups or other preschool provisions, and self-help schemes like babysitting. Improved housing as well as the provision of play facilities for preschool children are obviously priorities. In areas with overcrowding or poor housing or flats, special attempts such as providing transport and flexible opening times would be necessary to encourage those most in need to attend. In treating depression in women, the effect of having young children should be taken into account.

The development of day centres attached to adult clinics is a recognition of this (Radford 1974).

Training of health visitors, nursery nurses, and others involved with young children should enable them not only to perceive where problems are likely to arise or have arisen, but to understand the mechanism of their development and give them confidence to take the initiative in finding ways of helping.

REFERENCES

BENTOVIM A. (1973) Disturbed and under five. *Spec. Educ.* **62,** 31–35

BENTOVIM A. & LANSDOWN R. (1973) Day hospitals and centres for disturbed children in the London area. *Brit. med. J.* **4,** 536–538

BERNAL J.F. (1973) Night waking in infants during the first 14 months. *Develop. Med. Child. Neurol.* **15,** 760–769

BROWN G.W., BHROLCHAIN M.N. & HARRIS T. (1975) Social class and psychiatric disturbance among women in an urban population. *Sociology* **9,** 225–254

CAUDILL W. & PLATH D.W. (1966) Who sleeps by whom? *Psychiatry* **32,** 12–43

CAUDILL W. & WEINSTEIN H. (1966) Maternal care and infant behaviour in Japanese and American urban middle class families. *In* Koening R. & Hill R. (eds.) *Yearbook of the Int. Sociological Ass.*

COHLER B.J., GRUNEBAUM H.U., WEISS J.L., GALLANT D.H. & ABERNETHY V. (1974) Social relations, stress, and psychiatric hospitalisation among mothers of young children. *Soc. Psychiat.* **9,** 7–12

DOUGLAS J.W.B. & BLOOMFIELD I.M. (1958) *Children under Five.* London: Allen & Unwin

FANNING D.M. (1967) Families in flats. *Brit. med. J.* **4,** 382–386

FORSMANN H. & THUWE I. (1966) One hundred and twenty children born after application for therapeutic abortion refused. *Acta Psychiat. Scand.* **42,** 71–88

FRIEDLANDER, B.Z., WETSTONE H.S. & McPEEK D.L. (1974) Systematic assessment of selective language listening deficit in emotionally disturbed preschool children. *J. Child Psychol. Psychiat.* **15,** 1–12

FROMMER E.A. & O'SHEA G. (1973) Antenatal identification of women liable to have problems in managing their infants. *Brit. J. Psychiat.* **123,** 149–156

GAVRON M. (1966) *The Captive Wife: Conflicts of Housebound Mothers.* London: Routledge & Kegan Paul

GOODENOUGH F.L. (1931) *Anger in Young Children.* Minneapolis: University of Minnesota

GOVE W.R. & TUDOR J.F. (1973) Adult sex roles and mental illness. *In* Huber J. (ed.) *Changing Women in a Changing Society.* Chicago: University of Chicago Press

GRUNEBAUM H.U. & STREAN H.S. (1964) Some considerations on the therapeutic neglect of fathers in child guidance. *J. Child Psychol. Psychiat.* **5,** 241–249

HEALY A. (1972) The sleep patterns of preschool children. *Clin. Pediatr.* **11,** 174–177

HELFER R.E. & KEMPE C.H. (1968) *The Battered Child.* Chicago: University of Chicago Press

HOLDSWORTH R. (1969) *3000 Children*. Plymouth: Devon Preschool Playgroup Association

HOOK K. (1963) Refused abortion: a follow up study of 249 women whose applications were refused by the National Board of Health in Sweden. *Acta Psychiat. Scand.* Suppl. 168

HOOPER D., GILL R., POWESLAND P. & INEICHEN B. (1972) The health of young families in new housing. *J. Psychosom. Res.* **16,** 367–374

HOWELLS J.G. (1968) *Theory and Practice of Family Psychiatry*. Edinburgh: Oliver & Boyd

JACOBSON L., KAIJ L. & NILSSON A. (1965) Post partum mental disorders in an unselected sample: frequency of symptoms and predisposing factors. *Brit. med. J.* **1,** 1640–1643

JEPHCOTT P. (1971) *Homes in High Flats: Some of the Human Problems Involved in Multistorey Housing*. Edinburgh: Oliver & Boyd

JERSILD A.T. & HOLMES F.B. (1935) *Children's Fears. Child Dev.* Mongr. no. 20

JOSEPH A. & PARFITT J. (1972) *Playgroups in an Area of Special Need*. Windsor: NFER

KAGAN J. & MOSS H.A. (1965) The stability of passive and dependent behaviour from childhood through adulthood. *In* Mussen P.H., Conger J.J. & Kagan J. (eds.) *Readings in Child Development and Personality*. New York: Harper & Row

KEELEY B. (1968) *1020 Playgroups*. London: Preschool Playgroups Association

KORNER A.F. (1971) Individual differences at birth: implications for early experiences and later development. *Amer. J. Orthopsychiat.* **41,** 608–619

LEWIS M. (1971) Individual differences in the measurement of early cognitive growth. *In* Hellmuth J. (ed.) *The Exceptional Infant*, vol. II: *Studies in Abnormalities*. New York: Brunner/Mazel

LEVY D.M. (1943) *Maternal Overprotection*. New York: Columbia University Press

MCARDLE I., PROSSER M. & THOMAS N. (1972) *Playgroups in an Urban Area*. Birmingham: Birmingham Association of Playgroups

MCCALL R.B. (1971) Attention in the infant: avenue to the study of cognitive development. *In* Walcher D.W. & Peters D.L. (eds.) *The Development of Self-regulatory Mechanisms*. New York: Academic Press

MCFARLANE J.W., ALLEN L. & HONZIK P. (1954) *A Developmental Study of Behaviour Problems of Normal Children Between 21 Months and 14 Years*. Berkeley and Los Angeles: University of California Press

MAKITA K. & OKONOGI O. (1969) Parental attitude and family dynamics on children's problems in Japan. *In* Howells J. (ed.) *Modern Perspectives in International Child Psychiatry*. Edinburgh: Oliver & Boyd

MICHAEL C.M., MORRIS D.P. & SOROKER E. (1957) Follow up studies of shy withdrawn children. II. Relative incidence of schizophrenia. *Amer. J. Orthopsychiat.* **27,** 331–337

MOORE N.C. (1974) Psychiatric illness and living in flats. *Brit. J. Psychiat.* **125,** 500–507

NEWSON J. & NEWSON E. (1963) *Infant Care in an Urban Community*. London: Allen & Unwin

NEWSON J. & NEWSON E. (1968) *Four years old in an Urban Community*. London: Allen & Unwin

NEWSON J. & NEWSON E. (1976) Personal communication

PAFFENBARGER R.S. (1964) Epidemiological aspects of parapartum mental illness. *Brit. J. Prev. Soc. Med.* **18,** 189–195

PARE C.M.B. & RAVEN H. (1970) Follow-up of patients referred for termination of pregnancy. *Lancet* **i,** 635–638.

PASAMANICK B. & KNOBLOCH H. (1961) Epidemologic studies on the complications of pregnancy and the birth process. *In* Caplan G. (ed.) *Prevention of Mental Disorder in Children.* New York: Basic Books

PRECHTL H.F.R. (1961) The mother-child interaction in babies and minimal brain damage. *In* Foss B.M. (ed.) *Determinants of Infant Behaviour,* vol. 2. London: Methuen

PRECHTL H.F.R. & BEINTEMA D. (1964) The neurological examination of the full-term new born infant. *Clinics in Developmental Medicine,* no. 12. London: SIMP/Heinemann

RADFORD M. (1974) Personal communication

RICHMAN N. (1974) The effects of housing on preschool children and their mothers. *Dev. Med. Child Neurol.* **16,** 53–58

RICHMAN N. (1976) Family and social factors in behaviour problems of 3 year olds (in preparation).

RICHMAN N. & STEVENSON J. (1976) Family and social factors in children with language delay (in preparation)

RICHMAN N. & GRAHAM P. (1971) A behavioural screening questionnaire for use with 3 year old children: preliminary findings. *J. Child Psychol. Psychiat.* **12,** 5–33

RICHMAN N. & GRAHAM P. (1976) A behaviour check list for identifying preschool children with behaviour problems (unpublished)

RICHMAN N., STEVENSON J. & GRAHAM P. (1975) Prevalence of behaviour problems in 3 year old children: an epidemiological study in a London borough. *J. Child Psychol. Psychiat.* **16,** 272–287

ROBERTS K.E. & SCHOELLKOPF J.A. (1951) Eating, sleeping and elimination practices in a group of $2\frac{1}{2}$ year old children. *Amer. J. Dis. Child.* **82,** 121–152

ROBINS L.N. (1966) *Deviant Children Grown Up.* Baltimore: Williams & Wilkins

ROSE N.S. (1973) *Ten therapeutic Playgroups: a Preliminary Study of the Children Attending and Their Families.* London: NSPCC

RUTTER M. (1966) *Children of Sick Parents: an Environmental and Psychiatric Study.* Institute of Psychiatry: Maudsley Monographs. No. 16. London: Oxford University Press

RUTTER M. (1972) Psychiatric causes of language retardation. *In* Rutter M. & Martin J.A.M. (eds.) *The Child with Delayed Speech.* Clinics in Develop. Med. no. 43. London: SIMP/Heinemann

RUTTER M. (1973) Why are London children so disturbed? *Proc. Roy. Soc. Med.* **66,** 1221–1225

RUTTER M., LEBOVICI S., EISENBERG L., SNEZNEVSKIJ A.V., SADOUN R., BROOKE E. & LIN T-Y. (1969) A triaxial classification of mental disorders in childhood. *J. Child Psychol. Psychiat.* **10,** 41–61

RUTTER M., GRAHAM P. & YULE W. (1970a) A neuropsychiatric study in childhood. *Clinics in Developmental Medicine,* no. 35–36. London: SIMP/Heinemann.

RUTTER M., TIZARD J. & WHITMORE K. (eds.) (1970b) *Education, Health and Behaviour.* London: Longman

RUTTER M. & BARTAK L. (1971) Causes of infantile autism: some considerations from recent research. *J. Autism Child. Schiz.* **1**, 20–32

RYLE A. (1961) The psychological disturbances associated with 345 pregnancies in 137 women. *J. Ment. Sci.* **107**, 279–286

SAINSBURY P. (1971) Moving house and psychiatric morbidity. Paper presented at the Annual Conference of the Soc. for Psychosom. Res. London

SCHAFFER H.R. & EMERSON P.E. (1964) Patterns of response to physical contact in early human development. *J. Child Psychol. Psychiat.* **5**, 1–13

SCHAFFER H.R. (1971) *The Growth of Sociability.* Harmondsworth: Penguin

SEAGER C.P. (1960) A controlled study of post-partum mental illness. *J. ment. Sci.* **106**, 214–230

STEVENSON J. & RICHMAN N. (1976a) The prevalence of language delay in a population of 3 year old children and its association with general retardation. *Develop. Med. Child Neurol.* **18**, 431–441

STEVENSON J. & RICHMAN N. (1976b) Behaviour, language and development in 3 year old children (in preparation)

STEWART W.F.R. (1970) *Children in Flats: a Family Study.* London: NSPCC

TIZARD J. & TIZARD B. (1971) The social development of 2 year old children in residential nurseries. *In* Schaffer H.R. (ed.) *The Origins of Human Social Relations.* London: Academic Press

WOLFF S. (1961a) Social and family background of preschool children with behaviour disorders attending a child guidance clinic. *J. Child Psychol. Psychiat.* **2**, 260–268

WOLFF S. (1961b) Symptomatology and outcome of preschool children with behaviour disorders attending a child guidance clinic. *J. Child. Psychol. Psychiat.* **2**, 269–276

WOLKIND S.N. & RUTTER M. (1973) Children who have been in care: an epidemological study. *J. Child. Psychol. Psychiat.* **14**, 97–106

WOLKIND S.N. (1974a) Sex differences in the aetiology of antisocial disorders in children in long term residential care. *Brit. J. Psychiat.* **125**, 125–130

WOLKIND S.N. (1974b) The components of 'affectionless psychopathy' in institutionalized children. *J. Child Psychol. Psychiat.* **15**, 215–220

YULE W. & RAYNES N.V. (1972) Behavioural characteristics of children in residential care in relation to indices of separation. *J. Child Psychol. Psychiat.* **13**, 249–258

YOUNG M. & WILLMOTT P. (1957) *Family and Kinship in East London.* London: Routledge & Kegan Paul

WILLMOTT P. & YOUNG M. (1960) *Family and Class in a London Suburb.* London: Routledge & Kegan Paul

CHAPTER 17

Adolescent disorders

P. GRAHAM AND M. RUTTER

The *Shorter Oxford English Dictionary* defines adolescence as the growing up period between childhood and maturity, said to extend over a period of some 10 years. We will follow that definition in this chapter but focus primarily on the early and middle stages of the period. It will be appreciated that adolescence cannot be given any precise limits both because of the large individual variations in the timing of the maturational process (see below) and because physical and emotional aspects of development do not necessarily run in parallel.

Many of the psychiatric disorders which occur in adolescence are closely similar to those arising in childhood or adult life, but this chapter does not aim to provide a comprehensive account of the psychiatry of adolescence. Rather, our objective is to outline some of the psychiatric issues of particular importance in this phase of development. It is therefore appropriate to begin by considering the main features of normal adolescent development.

NORMAL ADOLESCENT DEVELOPMENT

Physical changes

Tanner (1962; 1970; 1971) and Young (1971) have reviewed the physical changes associated with puberty. The production of androgens increases in both sexes at about 8 to 10 years with a further much sharper rise a few years later, this latter rise being much more marked in boys. The excretion of oestrogens also gradually rises from about 7 years of age, with a second very large and rapid rise in girls at puberty. In both sexes it is the androgens which have the most effect on sexual drive and energy and adolescence is a period of greatly increased libido, especially in boys. In girls puberty begins some 2 years earlier and extends over a slightly shorter period (3 to 4 years rather than 4 to 5) than in boys. However, the timing varies widely among normal adolescents of both sexes. Thus, in girls the menarche usually occurs at some

407

point between 10 and 16 years and in boys testicular growth is generally complete at a time between 13 and 17 years.

Puberty is accompanied by a markedly accelerated increase in height and weight; an increase which shows a variation in intensity, duration and timing which is similar in degree to that found with puberty. In boys the growth spurt typically begins at about 13 years and diminishes some $2\frac{1}{2}$ years later, with a slower growth for a few years after that. However, the growth spurt may begin as early as 10 years or as late as 16. The comparable figures for girls are about 2 years earlier. During pubescence there is much muscular development and increase in bodily strength and the physique changes to an adult configuration. However, unlike most other body organs the brain shows little further growth during adolescence.

Psychological correlates of physical changes

The timing, as well as the nature, of physical maturation during adolescence has psychological significance. One of the most puzzling correlates is the fact that early maturers have, on average, a slightly higher level of intelligence than do late maturing children. The difference is not due to an intellectual 'spurt' at puberty because the advantage is evident in early maturers well before they reach puberty and persists until at least 15 years (Douglas *et al* 1968). It is not known whether it continues into adult life. However, there are reasons for supposing that the apparent advantage in intellect shown by early maturers may be an artefact due to an association between late puberty and large family size (large family size being associated with a lower average level of verbal intelligence).

Of more direct psychiatric relevance is the observation in some American studies that early maturing boys have a slight advantage in personality (McCandless 1960). They tend to be more popular, more relaxed, more good natured and generally more poised. In contrast, the later maturers were found to feel less adequate, less self-confident and more anxious (Mussen & Jones 1957; Jones & Bayley 1950; Weatherley 1964). The personality tests used in these studies were not very satisfactory but similar differences have been shown on several tests in independent studies so that there can be some confidence in the findings. It is also notable that one study showed that the differences persisted (although diminished) into the early 30s (Jones 1957; 1965). It is of interest that the picture in girls is far less consistent; the differences between early and late maturers are less marked and vary according to age, with early maturation sometimes an advantage and sometimes a disadvantage (Jones & Mussen 1958; Faust 1960).

The explanation is almost certainly social and psychological rather than biological (Rutter 1975). Early maturing boys tend to be more muscular and part of their advantage may be the social benefits in a peer group of being strong and good at sport. That strength and athletic prowess are not so important in determining a girl's popularity may explain why early puberty does not carry the same psychological advantage in girls. A child's physique plays an active part in determining how other people react to him and the mature boy of manly appearance may be better accepted by adults too than his childish-looking friend who has yet to reach puberty. In this connexion, it is relevant that in Western societies the cultural sex role prescription for males is more clear-cut than that for females (Weatherley 1964). Sexuality is very important to adolescents and much talk centres around the topic. As a consequence, the very late maturing boy may well have many anxieties about his manhood and suffer accordingly.

Clear-cut relationships between age at puberty and psychiatric disorder have not been demonstrated. However, the few studies which have been done have mainly focussed on girls and on delinquents rather than on older emotionally disturbed boys where the greatest effects would be expected on the basis of the findings from general population studies. Henderson (1969) carried out radiological skeletal surveys on 241 normal subjects, 52 boys at an approved school and 151 psychiatric patients aged from 12 to 20 years. There were no differences in skeletal maturity between the three groups, and, as far as girls were concerned the age at menarche did not differ between patients and normal subjects. However, Littlemore *et al* (1974) found that older adolescents (over 14 years) with severe psychiatric disorder did show skeletal immaturity as assessed by wrist X-ray, although this was not so with younger adolescents. Howarth (1966) studied girls attending a psychiatric hospital and found an increased proportion of anxiety states in the year before menarche. In the Isle of Wight total population survey of 14–15-year-olds (see below) age of puberty did not differ between those with and those without psychiatric disorder (Graham *et al* in preparation).

The coming of the menarche has other important consequences for girls. It is widely recognised that there is often some emotional upset and increased irritability during the few days immediately preceding and during the menstrual period. It is less appreciated that accidents, crimes and psychiatric disturbance are all commoner during this stage of the menstrual cycle and that girls taking examinations do less well (Dalton 1969). Particularly during the early years of menstruation, the menses are sometimes associated with physical discomfort and this, too, may influence girls' reactions to the onset of periods. Of course, the menarche also carries psychological implications quite apart from its physical concomitants. Some girls may feel pleased with the indication of their feminine status but for others it carries connotations of shame and fear, as reflected in some of the colloquial terms for menstruation. Increasingly teenage girls are taking oral contraceptives and these, too, may sometimes have adverse emotional consequences (Annotation 1970). Teenage pregnancies are also on the increase (see below) and there is good evidence that the puerperium is associated with a substantial increase in psychiatric disorder (Kendell *et al* 1976).

Social changes

There are various important changes in young people's social environment during adolescence and these are likely to have an important impact on psychological development. In Britain, at age 11–12 years there is usually a transfer from primary to secondary school with its quite different social structure. Children move from class to class according to subject, there is no longer the security of a cohesive form group taught by a single teacher, and out of class contacts between teachers and children often diminish. For many youngsters adolescence is the time of competitive national examinations with the stresses they bring, and for others it is the time when their exclusion from examinations provides the mark of educational failure.

At age 16 years in Britain, adolescent paths increasingly diverge. Some continue at school in order to pass higher examinations and proceed into further education, others leave to start work and yet others leave school only to experience prolonged periods of unemployment. The path followed has various important consequences for development. Thus, those who receive further education show greater continuing intellectual development than those of similar ability who leave school earlier (see review by Rutter & Madge 1976). On the other hand, higher education tends to be associated with prolonged dependence on parents at a time of increasing maturity and this may sometimes lead to stresses between adolescents and their parents. Adolescents earning their own living are likely to have greater financial independence as well as more money to spend. Teenagers who remain out of a job after leaving school may well feel discouraged and demoralised. It is important to note that unemployment in the early years after leaving school is much commoner among black people and this, combined with the racial discrimination experienced by many in relation to jobs and housing, increases the problems they feel during adolescence (see Rutter & Madge 1976). In the USA, Allen (1973) has described how the Indian adolescent needs to prepare himself for unemployment and a devalued role in a relatively prosperous society.

Psychosexual development

Although, traditionally, the middle years of childhood have been regarded as a sexually 'latent' period, this view is now known to be mistaken (Rutter 1971). In fact it is a time of gradually increasing sex interests. Sex talk and games with a sexual component are frequent, although often concealed from adults. In the years before puberty children tend to play almost exclusively with their own sex (Campbell 1939), but chasing games such as kiss-and-chase and provocative teasing make it very evident that heterosexual interests are still lively and active although they have been rechannelled.

However, although sex interests have been present for some years by the time puberty is reached there is a marked upsurge in sexuality at that time. Of course, how it is manifest is greatly dependent on the sociocultural mores and on family expectations and restrictions, which are known to vary widely (Ford & Beach 1951). In most societies masturbation is an almost universal occurrence in adolescent boys although it is less common in girls (Pomeroy 1969a, b). In Western societies intense attachments to someone of the same sex occur fairly commonly as a transient phase in both boys and girls, but overt homosexual activities are less frequent. Such activities are considerably more prevalent in single-sex boarding schools than in day schools. It is apparent that the development of homosexual behaviour is much influenced by the social setting and by the presence or absence of heterosexual opportunities. However, it is doubtful whether this transient phase of homosexual activity has any bearing on persisting adult homosexuality.

During and after adolescence heterosexual interests and activities increase greatly; this increase begins earlier in girls than boys in keeping with their earlier onset of puberty. Schofield's English study (1965) of teenagers showed that, at the time of the study in the early 1960s, dating and kissing usually began between 13 and 16 years but a quarter of boys and almost a third of girls had had their first date by age 13. Deep kissing and breast fondling began somewhat later, but by 17 years the majority of adolescents had had these experiences. By age 18 years only a third of the boys and a sixth of the girls had had sexual intercourse. Much of the premarital sexual activity is restricted to the person eventually married and little can be regarded as promiscuous or indiscriminate (see Mussen, Conger & Kagan 1974). However, there are differences between the sexes in their approach to sexual relationships. Boys tend to have more sexual partners (implying a small core of promiscuous girls) while the girls are relatively more likely to have an enduring sexual association. Girls tend to look for a romantic relationship whereas more boys are likely to seek a sexual adventure.

In both sexes only a minority receive information on sexual behaviour and reproduction from parents and less than a fifth have the school as their main source (Schofield 1965). Friends are said to be the usual source of information and this is often in the form of obscene jokes.

Many girls now become pregnant in their teens and in a small proportion this happens during early adolescence. Thus, in England and Wales in 1972 (Registrar General 1975) there were 98 therapeutic abortions in 13-year-olds, 586 in 14-year-olds, and 2113 in 15-year-olds. The implications of premarital conception with regard to both marriage and later divorce depend to a considerable extent on the cultural attitudes to sexuality (Christensen 1960). However, in Britain illegitimate children and their mothers are subject to considerable social difficulty (Crellin *et al* 1971) and the single mother is also at a great financial disadvantage (DHSS 1974).

Friendships

Friendships are particularly important during adolescence and, compared to both younger and older people, teenagers are very good at making friends (Campbell 1964). It is a time of life when unusually close friendships do develop and young people tend to share their deeper feelings in a way which is less usual at other age periods. Friendships become increasingly durable during adolescence and relationships made during the late teens can be particularly lasting, although much will depend on how interests change during the passage into adult life. To some extent the sexes differ in their pattern of friendships in that girls' relationships tend to be deeper, more dependent and more subject to jealousy than are those of boys.

Informal peer groups and cliques become more prominent during the teenage period (Campbell 1964; Willmott 1966). At first the groups tend to be all of the same sex but these then often coalesce to form larger mixed 'sets' of people who do things together. Usually the structure is informal and changing and only occasionally is there a more regular gang with a leader. In later adolescence there is increased pairing off so that the crowd comes to consist of only loosely associated groups of couples.

Emotions

It has been widely supposed that adolescence is *usually* characterised by great psychological upheaval and disturbance which often appears similar to mental illness (Freud 1958; Blos 1970; Eissler 1958). Indeed, it has been suggested that a *lack* of disturbance is a cause for psychiatric concern (Geleerd 1961; Lindemann 1964). However, surveys of the general population have shown these views to be exaggerated and misleading (Rutter *et al* 1976). Most adolescents do not show emotional disturbance.

On the other hand, it is the case that adolescents tend to feel things particularly deeply and marked mood swings are common during the teens. A large scale study of 14–15-year-olds living on the Isle of Wight showed that over two-fifths reported that at times they felt so miserable that they cried or that they wanted to get away from everybody and everything (Rutter *et al* 1976). About a quarter reported feelings of reference, a fifth had feelings of self-depreciation and one in twelve admitted to occasional suicidal ideas. Self-report questionnaires showed that feelings of misery or depression and early morning waking were much more common in adolescents than in their mothers. An American study by Masterson (1967) also found that anxiety and depression were common in ordinary adolescents.

'Inner turmoil' as represented by feelings of misery, self-depreciation and ideas of being laughed at are quite common in 14-year-olds. These feelings cause appreciable personal suffering to the adolescent at the time but usually they do not last and often they are unnoticed by adults. Nevertheless, although common it should be emphasised that half the adolescents in the Isle of Wight study did *not* report feelings of this kind.

Personality development

Cognitive development continues during adolescence and about the age of 12 years there is the important emergence of what Piaget called formal operational thinking (Elkind 1968). Children become increasingly able to generate and explore hypotheses, to make deductions and to derive higher order abstractions. These skills are of obvious importance in relation to scholastic learning but also they are most influential in terms of many aspects of personality development. Adolescents' questioning and criticism of established views and their idealism is probably as much a function of their greater cognitive capability as a response to their social situation or pattern of upbringing (Mussen, Conger & Kagan 1974). Their emerging awareness of how things might be and how this differs from what they are, becomes increasingly important in the formation of their self-concept. Clinical experience suggests that it is in adolescence that adopted children are most likely to want to seek out their biological parents and this is also the time that many crippled children become depressingly aware of their handicaps (Elkind 1968).

Erikson (1965) has described adolescence as the period in which the main psychological task is to establish a personal identity. Of course during the middle childhood years there will have been a gradual and regular progression in young people's development of both a personal conscience and a view of their own individuality and identity (Rutter 1975). However, in our society this process tends to be both highlighted and intensified during the teenage years. Adolescents become increasingly concerned with how they appear in the eyes of others and how this compares with the way they feel they actually are. While they are still very reliant on other people's views and ideals, it is often a time of questioning and doubt as they strive to determine their own positions with respect to the crises they face. Teenagers are liable to assert their independence to do as *they* think fit and parents face the dilemma of how to provide the guidance, control and support needed by their adolescent children and yet also allow sufficient autonomy for them to learn by their own mistakes and to establish their own standards.

Adolescence is often a period of intense idealism and this may well include a rejection of many of society's norms and standards. In some cases the idealism may include an element of rebellion against home, but more frequently the sociopolitical activism of youth is rather an extension and development of their parents' own idealism. Studies of American 'hippies' and student activists (Brown 1967; Flacks 1967; Keniston 1967) show that they tend to come from privileged professional families in which the parents have presented permissive, liberal or socialist views with a strong humanitarian concern for the plight of others, but with less emphasis on personal self-control. In short, it appears that activists are often implementing the values of their socially conscious parents, although they often do so in ways of which their parents would not approve. In addition to the activists, there are also socially alienated youngsters who have rejected society's values on a much more widespread scale. Although they share many of the same family background features as the activists they are probably more likely to show personal psychological disturbance.

While this idealism is a prominent feature in some adolescents, it is necessary to recognise that only a tiny minority of adolescents are activists and protesters (Rutter 1975). Like their parents, most are rather conforming. The main difference from earlier childhood is that the standards to which they conform tend to be set by their peers as well as by their parents.

Parent–adolescent relationships

It has become customary to assume that adolescents usually become increasingly estranged from their families so that their parents feel that they can no longer 'get through' to their children. It has also been claimed that adolescents cease to be influenced appreciably by their parents, become cut off from the rest of society and develop a separate subculture of their own (Coleman 1961). In fact, systematic studies of the general population do not support that stereotype. As pointed out by several workers (Jahoda & Warren 1965; Epperson 1964) the findings from Coleman's survey of several thousand adolescents do not support his conclusions. His data show that the majority of teenagers continue to be influenced in their actions by their parents' approval or disapproval. The findings from other American studies are in agreement (Epperson 1964; Douvan & Adelson 1966; Meissner 1965; Offer 1969; Offer & Offer 1975). Although most adolescents would like their parents to be less restrictive and old-fashioned; and although arguments about clothing, hair length, pop music and how late they can stay out at night are fairly frequent; nevertheless the great majority of teenagers share a common core of values with their parents, retain harmonious family relationships and respect the need for discipline.

British findings are similar. The Isle of Wight study of 14–15-year-olds (Rutter *et al* 1976) showed that only one in six parents reported any altercations with their children although twice as many disapproved of their youngster's clothing or hair styles and often prohibition in these areas was enforced. The great majority of parents approved of their children's friends and nearly all had discussed with their children what they might do when they left school. Only a quarter of parents reported difficulties getting through to their sons and only one in ten had this problem with their daughters. Even fewer parents reported that their adolescents withdrew from family activities. Moreover where these difficulties were present they had usually been already present prior to adolescence.

Only a third of the adolescents made any criticisms of their parents during an hour-long psychiatric interview and only one in 25 boys and one in 50 girls expressed rejection of their parents. In summary, minor family disagreements are fairly common (although by no means universal) during adolescence but alienation and rejection are quite rare.

Of course, it is true that peer group influences increase considerably during adolescence (Mussen, Conger & Kagan 1974) but this does not necessarily imply a reduced parental influence nor does it imply alienation from the family. The findings on the relative influence of parents and peers during adolescence appear somewhat contradictory. Brittain (1963; 1967) produced findings which suggested that peers acted more as guides in *current* situational dilemmas while parents did so more in *future* oriented situations. However, Larson's more recent study (1972) has cast some doubt on the validity of this distinction. He found that the majority of adolescents were pro-parent in their orientations but decisions were influenced more by situational context than by either parental or peer approval.

Using projective test material with a group of English adolescents of above average intelligence, Coleman (1974) found that older teenagers were more likely than younger adolescents to express negative attitudes to peers, parents and group influences. The findings suggest that during the teens adolescents become less likely to accept or be sympathetic to authority control of any kind. In short, they become increasingly independent and self-sufficient at the same time as their friendships increase and deepen. This process usually proceeds without any loss of family ties, although obviously the nature of the ties changes markedly with increasing maturity.

SECULAR TRENDS

Adolescent development must be viewed in its family and social context and it is therefore necessary to pay attention to some of the main changes which are taking place in patterns of family life and in social conditions. The trends in Britain (Rutter & Madge 1976) and in the USA (Bronfenbrenner 1975) are rather similar. Families are becoming smaller, people are marrying younger, more girls are giving birth to their first child during their teens, the illegitimacy ratio is increasing, the divorce rate and probably the rate of family breakdowns is going up and the number of single-parent families is rising. In Britain the level of prosperity has generally increased over the last half century, but many children continue to be reared in conditions of severe social disadvantage, and the extreme of economic inequality has diminished only slightly. It should be added that the age of menarche has been gradually falling throughout this century (Tanner 1962; 1970). It is clear that we are going through a period of marked social change which will have implications for adolescence as well as for other age periods. Many of these changes are likely to make development more difficult although data are lacking on exactly what effects these changes will have.

PREVALENCE OF PSYCHIATRIC DISORDER

There have been only three general population studies of the prevalence of psychiatric disorder in adolescence. Krupinski and his colleagues (Krupinski *et al* 1967; Henderson *et al* 1971) used medical students to interview all families in an Australian town of some 2000 inhabitants in order to determine the prevalence of all forms of medical disability. Diagnoses were checked by supervisors and collateral inquiries made when thought necessary. However, the criteria for disorder were not clearly specified and it is not clear how far information from the adolescents themselves was used in diagnosis. Some 10 per cent of children, 16 per cent of adolescents and 24 per cent of adults were diagnosed as showing some form of psychiatric disorder. The findings suggest a rate of disorder which increases during adolescence and still further during adult life but as direct psychiatric assessments were not employed comparisons are problematic.

Leslie (1974) surveyed some 1000 13- and 14-year-olds in Blackburn, an industrial town in northern England. Diagnoses were based on interviews with parents and children and on questionnaires from teachers; the assessments were validated by comparison with psychiatric clinic findings in a pilot sample. Disorders of a severity reckoned to warrant referral to a clinic occurred in 21 per cent of boys and 14 per cent of girls. Comparisons with other age groups were not possible.

In the Isle of Wight study (Graham & Rutter 1973; Rutter *et al* 1976) the total population of over 2000 14- to 15-year-olds were screened using parents' and teachers' questionnaires of tested reliability and validity. Those with high (i.e. deviant) scores on either questionnaire, together with a randomly selected control group, were given an individual psychiatric assessment involving interviews with parents, teachers and the adolescents themselves. All assessments were made in ignorance of either the selection group or other findings. Psychiatric assessments were also available on 10-year-old children and on the parents of the adolescents so that it was possible to examine age differences in prevalence. When like was compared with like it was found that psychiatric disorders were slightly commoner in adolescence than in middle childhood, but in all probability the rates were fairly similar in adolescence and adult life.* The precise prevalence figure for psychiatric disorder obviously depends on the severity cut-off point used but putting all the information together the 1 year period prevalence of disorder is probably about 10 to 15 per cent. However, in addition to adolescents with generally recognisable psychiatric disorders there is a further group of teenagers who report marked suffering associated with psychiatric symptomatology but whose problems are not evident to parents and teachers. When these are included the rate rises to about 21 per cent. At present there is not the evidence to determine how far their conditions are similar or different to the others. Nevertheless, it is clear that psychiatric surveys in adolescence must include information from the teenager himself as well as from parents and teachers.

Psychiatric clinic referral rates are broadly in keeping with the epidemiological findings in suggesting some rise in referrals between childhood and adolescence but a further rise in early adult life (Baldwin 1968).

PATTERN OF PSYCHIATRIC DISORDER IN ADOLESCENCE

In both the Blackburn and Isle of Wight studies individual psychiatric diagnoses were made. About two-fifths of the adolescents with psychiatric condi-

---

* The adult figures apply only to the parents of adolescent children. If single persons had been included the adult rates would probably have been somewhat higher.

tions showed emotional disorders of some kind. Most of these were anxiety states, depression or some kind of affective disorder. Obsessive–compulsive conditions, hysteria, circumscribed phobic states and tics all affected a few individuals but were much less common. Conduct disorders also were diagnosed in some two-fifths of the psychiatric group in both studies. In about half of these there was a widespread disorder of socialisation but in the remainder the adolescents appeared to have fewer problems with their own peer group. A substantial minority of teenagers (about a fifth) showed disorders involving a mixture of antisocial behaviour and emotional disturbance. Enuresis, encopresis and the hyperkinetic syndrome were only diagnosed in a handful of children and psychoses were quite rare (in fact only one child in each study).

These figures refer to psychiatric disorders in the general population of adolescents, most of whom never attend a psychiatric clinic. Obviously, hospital statistics indicate a bigger proportion of adolescents with psychoses. Even so, Warren's (1965a, b) findings from a psychiatric hospital inpatient unit showed that only 15 per cent of younger adolescents (below $14\frac{1}{2}$ years) and 25 per cent of older adolescents were psychotic. General practice (Office of Population, Censuses and Surveys 1974) and Ministry of Defence (1974) figures suggest that the 1-year prevalence of psychosis in mid-adolescence is probably less than 1 per 1000, a figure in keeping with the Blackburn and Isle of Wight survey findings.

CHANGES IN PATTERN AT ADOLESCENCE

The pattern of findings considered so far all combine disorders *continuing* into adolescence from earlier childhood and disorders *starting* for the first time during the teenage period. The Isle of Wight findings show that these two groups differ in several important respects (Rutter *et al* 1976). Because of these differences associated with age of onset it is important to consider how the pattern of psychiatric disorder changes during adolescence compared with earlier childhood.

First, there are differences in background factors. In childhood, conduct disorders are strongly associated with reading difficulties (Rutter, Tizard & Whitmore 1970; Varlaam 1974). However, this is *not* the case with either conduct disorders (Rutter *et al* 1976) or delinquency (Robins & Hill 1966) beginning in adolescence. Also, disorders beginning in early or middle childhood are strongly associated with severe family discord and disruption. This association is present but is less marked in the case of disorders with an onset during the teenage period. However, *un*like the difference with respect to reading, the diminished association with family pathology is at least partially a function of chronicity (Rutter *et al* 1976). That is to say, gross family discord is most strongly associated with chronic psychiatric disorders, and by definition these must have started before adolescence.

Second, there is an altered sex ratio as shown both by the Isle of Wight findings (Rutter *et al* 1976) and the figures from psychiatric clinics (Rosen *et al* 1965; Baldwin 1968). During childhood, disorders in boys are much commoner than those in girls. In adolescence the sex ratio becomes more nearly equal and in adult life psychiatric disorder is considerably commoner in women. Part of this change in sex ratio is due to age related referral practices. Boys with disturbances of conduct are likely to get referred to a psychiatrist whereas in adult life men with criminal behaviour or personality disorders are likely to be often dealt with in other ways. However, in part, the altered sex ratio is real and, insofar as it is, it reflects the marked increase in emotional disorders in females as they pass from childhood to adult life. Not only does depression show a female preponderance in adult life which is less evident in childhood but so does hysteria (Caplan 1970). It is not known how far the greater vulnerability of women to depression and neurotic disorder is due to biological or social factors. Certainly there are biological factors; the importance of premenstrual tension and the puerperium have already been mentioned. In addition, it is possible (although not demonstrated) that there are genetic factors associated with a female susceptibility (Rutter 1970a). However, equally certainly there are also social factors. For example, whereas marriage serves to protect men to some extent from psychiatric disorder, this is not the case with women. It may also be that the relative lack of activities outside the home and the stresses associated with rearing small children put working class women specially at risk for depression (Brown *et al* 1975).

Third, within the group of emotional disorders, depression is relatively infrequent as a main diagnosis before puberty (although unhappiness and misery are common symptoms), but much commoner during adolescence. Thus, in the Isle of Wight study of 10-year-olds (Rutter, Tizard & Whitmore 1970), there were only three children with a depressive condition, whereas at 14–15 years there were 9 plus another 26 with an affective disorder involving both depression and anxiety (Rutter *et al* 1976). This difference indicates the beginning of a shift to an adult pattern of disorders, in which affective states predominate. As shown in Shaffer's study (1974) this rise in affective disorders during adolescence is paralleled by a rise in the incidence of completed suicide.

Fourth, the Isle of Wight studies indicated 15 cases of school refusal at 14–15 years whereas there had been none at 10 years. In many cases the school refusal formed part of a more widespread anxiety state or affective disorder but in all the reluctance to go to school constituted one of the main problems. The findings are in keeping with the clinical evidence that school refusal is most prevalent in early childhood and again in adolescence. In younger children the main problem is more in keeping with normal developmental patterns and the prognosis is usually very good. In contrast, school refusal in adolescents is more often part of a widespread psychiatric disorder and the prognosis is considerably worse (Rodriguez *et al* 1959). (See Chapter 19.)

Fifth, although not reflected in the general population studies, there are important changes in the incidence of several less common conditions. Manic-depressive psychosis is decidedly rare before puberty (Anthony & Scott 1960) but gradually becomes more common during later adolescence and early adult life. Schizophrenia can occur before puberty but it does so only rarely in psychotic form (Rutter 1972). It, too, becomes more common during the teens and twenties.

When schizophrenia occurs during adolescence it tends to show much the same symptomatology as in adult life with thought disorder, hallucinations, perplexity and disorders of movement most evident (Kolvin *et al* 1971). However, atypical psychotic states occur sufficiently often that the differential diagnosis between schizophrenia and manic-depressive psychosis can be quite difficult, and sometimes only resolved by the subsequent course. Drug dependence in Britain is rare in prepubertal children but it becomes more frequent during adolescence (see Chapters 26 & 27). Anorexia nervosa occasionally develops in the year or two just before puberty (Warren 1968) but it only reaches its peak incidence during the 15 to 20 year age period (Crisp 1967; Kendell *et al* 1973; Crisp *et al* 1976).

Sixth, there are important changes in pre-existing psychiatric conditions which occur about the time of puberty. For example, this is the peak age period for the development of epileptic fits in autistic children (Rutter 1970b). Hyperkinetic children are often less overactive than they were in earlier childhood but they frequently present major social problems and abnormalities of attention usually persist (see Chapter 22). The psychiatric care of adolescents with severe chronic psychiatric disorders (often associated with brain damage) presents many problems and there is a grave shortage of long-stay inpatient units for this group.

COURSE OF ADOLESCENT PSYCHIATRIC DISORDERS

Robins (1972) and Gossett *et al* (1973) have both provided useful reviews of follow-up studies of adolescent disorders, although the former report is mainly concerned with the course of conditions arising earlier in childhood. A further follow-up study not included in either review is that by Capes *et al* (1971) who undertook a 4-year longitudinal study of adolescents being treated for psychiatric disorder at age 12 to 13 years. In addition, both Pritchard and Graham (1966) and Zeitlin (1972) have studied the records of people treated at one psychiatric hospital both as children or adolescents and as adults. The findings of all studies are in reasonably good agreement in coming to three main conclusions.

First, most psychiatric disorders in adolescence run true to type and marked symptom fluctuation is not a common feature. There is *no* reason to suppose that symptoms are substantially more variable during adolescence than at any other age. Thus Warren (1965a, b), whose study is in many ways the largest and most systematic, found that antisocial behaviour in the years after psychiatric treatment was almost entirely confined to those originally diagnosed as having a conduct disorder. Adolescents with an emotional disorder mostly continued to show similar problems if psychiatric disorder persisted or recurred. However, a few developed psychoses (4 schizophrenic and 1 manic-depressive).

Second, the prognosis varies markedly according to diagnosis. Pooling studies, about 83 per cent of adolescents with emotional or neurotic conditions improve, some 53 per cent of those with a character or conduct disorder do so, and about 45 per cent of psychotics make gains (Gossett *et al* 1973). The British studies show diagnostic differences of the same kind but a generally lower rate of improvement in the psychoses, presumably due to a more restricted diagnosis of schizophrenia (Cooper *et al* 1972) compared with that in the USA.

Third, the prognosis for adolescent psychiatric disorders does not appear to be any different (neither better nor worse) from that for similar disorders in earlier childhood or adult life. On the basis of his own and other findings on this point, Masterson (1967) has argued that psychiatric disorders during adolescence should be taken just as seriously as at other ages. Adolescence is a period of many psychological changes but psychiatric disorder is not a normal feature and most youngsters with psychiatric conditions cannot be expected to grow out of them.

The evidence on factors other than diagnosis which influence prognosis is less satisfactory. Gossett *et al* (1973) conclude that a poor prognosis is related to early academic failure, poor peer relationships, presence of a disturbed sibling, a gradual onset, abnormalities of personality and a sluggish initial response to treatment. However, many of these variables are themselves linked to diagnosis, and it is not possible from the published findings to examine their importance after controlling for type of disorder. Stanley and Barter (1970) showed that half the adolescents admitted to hospital for a suicidal attempt attempted suicide again after leaving hospital, but the prognosis otherwise for suicide-attempters was no worse than for other adolescent psychiatric patients. As with other problems, however, continuing suicidal behaviour was most likely to occur in those adolescents with poor peer relationships, academic failure, who were not living with their parents.

AETIOLOGY

In many respects, psychiatric disorders arising in adolescence show the same pattern of correlations with background factors as seen in younger children. The two exceptions, no association with reading difficulties and a weaker association with gross family discord and disruption, have already been mentioned. However, disorders with an onset in childhood and those beginning in adolescence are both associated with parent–child alienation (usually present from before adolescence) (Rutter *et al* 1976). Adverse family influences seem important in aetiology as with disorders arising at other age periods (see Chapter 3). Although new disorders in adolescence are unassociated with educational retardation they *are* modified by school factors. There is marked secondary school variation in rates of behavioural deviance which seem to reflect school influences on children's behaviour (Yule & Rutter, in preparation). Also, as with younger age groups, behavioural deviance is much commoner among adolescents living in inner city areas than in those with homes in small towns or the countryside (Rutter 1977). In the Isle of Wight study (Graham & Rutter 1973), psychiatric disorder in adolescents as in younger children (Rutter, Tizard & Whitmore 1970) showed no marked association with low social status. However, social disadvantage may well be important as an aetiological factor in teenagers living in inner city areas. In all age groups, organic brain damage or injury is an important aetiological factor in some cases of psychiatric disorder (Rutter, Graham & Yule 1970; see also Chapter 8).

CLASSIFICATION AND TREATMENT

The various suggested schemes for the classification of adolescent psychiatric disorders have been well summarised by Weiner (1970). As with other age groups, there have been discussions on the advantages and disadvantages of classifying disorders in terms of developmental level (Serrano *et al* 1962), symptom patterns (Masterson *et al* 1966), a mixture of phenomenology and aetiology (Acton & Evans 1973), or of not classifying at all (Menninger *et al* 1963). The last argument has sometimes been based on the notion that patterns of disorder in adolescence are too changeable and unstable to be diagnosed in the usual way (Edwalds & Dimitri 1959). However, there has been a special focus on the supposed need to separate off 'adolescent adjustment reactions' as different in kind from traditional psychiatric disorders (Finch 1960).

In fact, as shown by the evidence already reviewed, there is no justification for regarding psychiatric disorders occurring in adolescence as different in kind from those occurring at other age periods. In pattern, consistency, course and aetiology, they have much in common with psychiatric conditions arising in both younger children (in terms of the emotional disturbances and disorders of conduct) and young adults (in terms of the psychoses and depressive conditions). Of course, there are particular features associated with the developmental changes evident during adolescence and also the psychiatric interviewing of adolescents involves special considerations (Acton & Evans 1973). It is also true that many (especially older) adolescents prefer to attend clinics separate from those run for children or for adults. There is a need to have 'walk-in' facilities for those teenagers who seek help for themselves but who do not wish to use the traditional channels of referral, and also it is essential to have inpatient units specifically for adolescents as their social needs are rather different from those of both younger children and adults (see Chapter 37). In short, in some respects the pattern of services for adolescents needs to be rather different from those for other age groups but the principles of psychiatric practice are generally similar. Accordingly, the classification and treatment of adolescent psychiatric disorders will be considered in other chapters together with those disorders occurring in other age groups.

REFERENCES

ANNOTATION (1970) Psychological disturbance and oral contraceptives. *Lancet* i, 1378

ACTON W. & EVANS J. (1973) The psychiatric problems of adolescence. *In* Forrest A. (ed.) *Companion to Psychiatric Studies*, vol. 2. Edinburgh: Churchill-Livingstone

ALLEN J.R. (1973) The Indian adolescent: psychosocial tasks of the plains Indian of Western Oklahoma. *Amer. J. Orthopsychiat.* **43**, 368–375

ANTHONY J. & SCOTT P. (1960) Manic-depressive psychosis in childhood. *J. Child Psychol. Psychiat.* **1**, 53–72

BALDWIN J.A. (1968) Psychiatric illness from birth to maturity: an epidemiological study. *Acta Psychiat. Scand.* **44**, 313–333

BLOS P. (1970) *The Young Adolescent: Clinical Studies.* London: Collier-Macmillan

BRITTAIN C.V. (1963) Adolescent choices and parent–peer cross-pressures. *Amer. Sociol. Rev.* **28**, 385–391

BRITTAIN C.V. (1967) An exploration of the basis of peer-compliance and parent-compliance in adolescence. *Adolescence*, **2**, 445–458

BRONFENBRENNER U. (1975) The challenge of social change to public policy and developmental research. Unpublished paper given at Annual Meeting of the Society for Research into Child Development, Denver, 12 April 1975

BROWN G.W., BHROLCHAIN M.N. & HARRIS T. (1975) Social class and psychiatric disturbance among women in an urban population. *Sociology*, **9**, 225–254

BROWN J.D. (ed.) (1967) *The Hippies*. New York: Time-Life

CAMPBELL E.H. (1939) Social-sex development of children. *Cenet. Psychol. Monogr.* **21**, 463–552

CAMPBELL J.D. (1964) Peer relations in childhood. *In* Hoffman M.L. & Hoffman L.W. (eds.) *Review of Child Development Research*, vol. 1. New York: Russell Sage Foundation

CAPES M., GOULD E. & TOWNSEND M. (1971) *Stress in Youth*. London: Oxford University Press

CAPLAN H.L. (1970) Hysterical 'conversion' symptoms in childhood. MPhil Dissertation, University of London

CHRISTENSEN H.T. (1960) Cultural relativism and premarital sex norms. *Amer. Sociol. Rev.* **25**, 31–39

COLEMAN J.C. (1974) *Relationships in Adolescence*. London: Routledge & Kegan Paul

COLEMAN J.S. (1961) *The Adolescent Society*. London: Collier-Macmillan

COOPER J.E., KENDELL R.E., GURLAND B.J., SHARPE L., COPELAND J.R.M. & SIMON R. (1972) *Psychiatric Diagnosis in New York and London*. Institute of Psychiatry Maudsley Monograph No. 20. London: Oxford University Press

CRELLIN E., PRINGLE M.L. KELLMER & WEST P. (1971) *Born Illegitimate: Social and Educational Implications*. Windsor: NFER

CRISP A.H. (1967) Anorexia nervosa. *Brit. J. Hosp. Med.* **1**, 713–718

CRISP A.H., PALMER R.L. & KALUCY R.S. (1976) How common is anorexia nervosa? A prevalence study. *Brit. J. Psychiat.* **128**, 549–554

DALTON K. (1969) *The Menstrual Cycle*. Harmondsworth: Penguin

DEPARTMENT OF HEALTH AND SOCIAL SECURITY (1974) *Report of the Committee on One Parent Families (Finer Report)*. London: HMSO

DOUGLAS J.W.B., ROSS J.M. & SIMPSON H.R. (1968) *All Our Future: A Longitudinal Study of Secondary Education*. London: Peter Davies

DOUVAN E. & ADELSON J. (1966) *The Adolescent Experience*. London: Wiley

EDWALDS R. & DIMITRI K. (1959) Treatment of the adolescent patient in a state hospital. *Psychiat. Quart.* **33**, 613–622

EISSLER K.R. (1958) Notes on problems of technique in the psychoanalytic treatment of adolescents. *Psychoanalyt. Study Child.* **13**, 223–254

ELKIND D. (1968) Cognitive development in adolescence. *In* Adams J.F. (ed.) *Understanding Adolescent Psychology*. Boston: Allyn and Bacon

EPPERSON D.C. (1964) A re-assessment of indices of parental influence in 'The Adolescent Society'. *Amer. Sociol. Rev.* **29**, 93–96

ERIKSON E. (1965) *Childhood and Society*. Harmondsworth: Penguin

FAUST M.S. (1960) Developmental maturity as a determinant in prestige of adolescent girls. *Child Dev.* **31**, 173–184

FINCH S.M. (1960) *Fundamentals of Child Psychiatry*. New York: Norton

FLACKS R. (1967) The liberated generation: An exploration of the roots of student protest. *J. Social Issues* **23**, 52–75

FORD C.S. & BEACH F.A. (1951) *Patterns of Sexual Behavior*. New York: Harper and Row

FREUD A. (1958) Adolescence. *Psychoanalyt. Study Child.* **13**, 255–278

GELEERD E.R. (1961) Some aspects of ego vicissitudes in adolescence. *J. Amer. Psychoanalyt. Ass.*, **9**, 394–405

GOSSETT J.T., LEWIS S.B., LEWIS J.M. & PHILLIPS V.A. (1973) Follow-up of adolescents treated in a psychiatric hospital. I. A review of studies. *Amer. J. Orthopsychiat.* **43**, 602–610

GRAHAM P. & RUTTER M. (1973) Psychiatric disorder in the young adolescent: a follow-up study. *Proc. Roy. Soc. Med.* **66**, 1226–1229

GRAHAM P., RUTTER M., CHADWICK O. & YULE W. (1977) *Adolescence in a Small Community* (in preparation). London: Wiley

HENDERSON A.S. (1969) The physiological maturity of adolescent psychiatric patients, juvenile delinquents and normal teenagers. *Brit. J. Psychiat.* **115**, 895–905

HENDERSON A.S., KRUPINSKI J. & STOLLER A. (1971) Epidemiological aspects of adolescent psychiatry. *In* Howells J.G. (ed.) *Modern Perspectives in Adolescent Psychiatry*. Edinburgh: Oliver & Boyd

HOWARTH R. (1966) Psychiatric disorders in early and late-maturing girls. DPM Dis., University of London

JAHODA M. & WARREN N. (1965) The myths of youth. *Sociol. Educ.* **38**, 138–149

JONES M.C. (1957) The later careers of boys who were early or late maturing. *Child Dev.* **28**, 113–128

JONES M.C. (1965) Psychological correlates of somatic development. *Child Dev.* **36**, 899–911

JONES M.C. & BAYLEY N. (1950) Physical maturing among boys as related to behavior. *J. Educ. Psychol.* **41**, 129–148

JONES M.C. & MUSSEN P.H. (1958) Self-conceptions, motivations, and interpersonal attitudes of early and late maturing girls. *Child Dev.* **29**, 491–501.

KENDELL R.E., HALL D.J., HAILEY A. & BABIGIAN H.M. (1973) The epidemiology of anorexia nervosa. *Psychol. Med.* **3**, 200–203

KENDELL R.E., WAINWRIGHT S., HAILEY A. & SHANNON B. (1976) The influence of child birth on psychiatric morbidity. *Psychol. Med.* **6**, 297–302.

KENISTON K. (1967) The sources of student dissent. *J. Social Issues* **23**, 108–137

KOLVIN I., OUNSTED C., HUMPHREY M. & McNAY A. (1971) Studies in the childhood psychoses. II. The phenomenology of childhood psychoses. *Brit. J. Psychiat.* **118**, 385–395

KRUPINSKI J., BAIKIE A.G., STOLLER A., GRAVES J., O'DAY D.M. & POLKE P. (1967) A community mental health survey of Heyfield, Victoria. *Med. J. Austr.* **1**, 1204–1211

LARSON L.E. (1972) The influence of parents and peers during adolescence: the situation hypothesis revisited. *J. Marriage and the Family*, **24**, 67–74

LESLIE S.A. (1974) Psychiatric disorder in the young adolescents of an industrial town. *Brit. J. Psychiat.* **125**, 113–124

LINDEMANN E. (1964) Adolescent behavior as a community concern. *Amer. J. Psychother.* **18**, 405–417

LITTLEMORE D., METCALFE E. & JOHNSON A.L. (1974) Skeletal immaturity in psychiatrically disturbed adolescents. *J. Child Psychol. Psychiat.*, **15**, 133–138

McCANDLESS B.R. (1960) Rate of development, body build and personality. *Psychiat. Res. Reports* **13**, 42–57

MASTERSON J.F. (1967) *The Psychiatric Dilemma of Adolescence*. London: Churchill

MASTERSON J.F., TUCKER K. & BERK G. (1966) The symptomatic adolescent: delineation of psychiatric syndromes. *Comprehensive Psych.* **7**, 166–174

MEISSNER W.W. (1965) Parental interaction of the adolescent boy. *J. genet. Psychol.* **107**, 225–233

MENNINGER K., MAYMAN M. & PRUYSER P. (1963) *The Vital Balance.* New York: Viking

MINISTRY OF DEFENCE (1974) *Statistical Tables on the Health of the Army, 1972.* London: HMSO

MUSSEN P.H. & JONES M.C. (1957) Self-conception, motivations and interpersonal attitudes of late and early maturing boys. *Child Dev.* **20**, 243–256

MUSSEN P.H., CONGER J.J. & KAGAN J. (1974) *Child Development and Personality*, 4th edn. London: Harper & Row

OFFER D. (1969) *The Psychological World of the Teenager*: a study of normal adolescent boys. New York: Basic Books

OFFER D. & OFFER J. (1975) *From Teenage to Young Manhood: a Psychological Study.* New York: Basic Books

OFFICE OF POPULATION CENSUSES AND SURVEYS (1974) *Morbidity Statistics From General Practice.* Studies on Medical and Population Subjects, no. 26. London: HMSO

POMEROY W.J. (1969a) *Boys and Sex.* New York: Delacorte

POMEROY W.J. (1969b) *Girls and Sex.* New York: Delacorte

PRITCHARD M. & GRAHAM P. (1966) An investigation of a group of patients who have attended both the child and adult departments of the same psychiatric hospital. *Brit. J. Psychiat.* **112**, 603–612

REGISTRAR-GENERAL (1975) *Statistical Review of England and Wales for the year 1973,* Part II. London: HMSO

ROBINS L. (1972) Follow-up studies of behavior disorders in children. *In* Quay H.C. & Werry J.S. (eds.) *Psychopathological Disorders of Childhood.* New York: Wiley

ROBINS L. & HILL S.Y. (1966) Assessing the contributions of family structure, class and peer groups to juvenile delinquency. *J. crim. Law, Criminol. and Police Sci.* **57**, 325–334

RODRIGUEZ A., RODRIGUEZ M. & EISENBERG L. (1959) The outcome of school phobia: a follow-up study based on 41 cases. *Amer. J. Psychiat.* **116**, 540–544

ROSEN B.M., BAHN A.K., SHELLOW R. & BOWER E.M. (1965) Adolescent patients served in outpatient psychiatric clinics. *Amer. J. publ. Hlth.* **55**, 1563–1577

RUTTER, M. (1970a) Sex differences in children's responses to family stress. *In* Anthony E.J. & Koupernik C. (eds.) *The Child in His Family.* New York: Wiley

RUTTER M. (1970b) Autistic children: infancy to adulthood. *Semin. Psychiat.* **2**, 435–450

RUTTER M. (1971) Normal psychosexual development. *J. Child Psychol. Psychiat.* **11**, 259–283

RUTTER M. (1972) Childhood schizophrenia reconsidered. *J. Autism Child. Schiz.* **2**, 315–337

RUTTER M. (1975) *Helping Troubled Children.* Harmondsworth: Penguin

RUTTER M. (ed.) (1977) *The Child, His Family and the Community* (in preparation). London: Wiley

RUTTER M. & MADGE N. (1976) *Cycles of Disadvantage: a review of research* (in press). London: Heinemann Educational

RUTTER M., GRAHAM P. & YULE W. (1970) *A Neuropsychiatric Study in Childhood.* Clinics in Develop. Med. nos. 35/36. London: SIMP/Heinemann

RUTTER M., TIZARD J. & WHITMORE K. (eds.) (1970) *Education, Health and Behaviour.* London: Longman

RUTTER M., GRAHAM P., CHADWICK O. & YULE W. (1976) Adolescent turmoil: fact or fiction? *J. Child Psychol. Psychiat.* **17,** 35–56

SCHOFIELD M. (1965) *The Sexual Behaviour of Young People.* London: Longman

SERRANO A.C., McDANALD E.C., GOOLISHIAN H.A., MACGREGOR R. & RITCHIE A.M. (1962) Adolescent maladjustment and family dynamics. *Amer. J. Psychiat.* **118,** 897–901

SHAFFER D. (1974) Suicide in childhood and early adolescence. *J. Child Psychol. Psychiat.* **15,** 275–291

STANLEY E.J. & BARTER J.T. (1970) Adolescent suicidal behavior. *Amer. J. Orthopsychiat.* **40,** 87–96

TANNER J.M. (1962) *Growth at Adolescence*, 2nd edn. Oxford: Blackwells

TANNER J.M. (1970) Physical growth. *In* Mussen P.H. (ed.) *Carmichael's Manual of Child Psychology*, 3rd edn. New York: Wiley

TANNER J.M. (1971) Sequence, tempo and individual variation in the growth and development of boys and girls aged twelve to sixteen. *Daedalus*, 907–930

VARLAAM A. (1974) Educational attainment and behaviour at school. *Greater London Intelligence Quarterly* no. 29, 29–37

WARREN W. (1965a) A study of adolescent psychiatric in-patients and the outcome six or more years later. I: Clinical histories and hospital findings. *J. Child Psychol. Psychiat.* **6,** 1–17

WARREN W. (1965b) A study of adolescent psychiatric in-patients and the outcome six or more years later. II: The follow-up study. *J. Child Psychol. Psychiat.* **6,** 141–160

WARREN W. (1968) A study of anorexia nervosa in young girls. *J. Child Psychol. Psychiat.* **9,** 27–40

WEATHERLEY D. (1964) Self-perceived rate of physical maturation and personality in late adolescence. *Child Dev.* **35,** 1197–1210

WEINER I.B. (1970) *Psychological Disturbance in Adolescence.* New York: Wiley-Interscience

WILLMOTT P. (1966) *Adolescent Boys of East London.* London: Routledge & Kegan Paul

YOUNG H.B. (1971) The physiology of adolescence. *In* Howells J.G. (ed.) *Modern Perspectives in Adolescent Psychiatry.* Edinburgh: Oliver & Boyd

YULE B. & RUTTER M. (1976) (in preparation)

ZEITLIN H. (1972) A study of patients who attended the children's department and later the adults' department of the same psychiatric hospital. MPhil Dissertation, University of London

CHAPTER 18

Emotional disorders

L. HERSOV

A distinction was made over 30 years ago between psychiatric disorders which involved emotional distress or suffering for the child and those which involved socially disapproved behaviour causing disturbance for other people (Ackerson 1931; Hewitt & Jenkins 1946). Later work using more sophisticated methods of data collection and analysis has supported this distinction (Quay 1964; see also Chapter 15). Thus, these two major groups of disorders differ in terms of symptom clustering, response to treatment, long-term prognosis, family characteristics and association with scholastic difficulties.

The first of these major groupings—that of emotional disorders—involves characteristics such as feelings of inferiority, self-consciousness, social withdrawal, shyness, anxiety, crying, hypersensitivity, depression and chronic sadness (Quay 1972). Epidemiological studies show that these disorders occur in about $2\frac{1}{2}$ per cent of preadolescent children living in small town communities (Rutter, Tizard & Whitmore 1970). However, the prevalence is greater in metropolitan areas (Rutter 1973) and rises in adolescence (Rutter *et al* 1976). During the teenage period there is also a shift from the almost equal sex ratio in early and middle childhood to the adult pattern in which emotional disorders are very much more frequent in women.

Emotional disorders in childhood include conditions with a symptomatology similar to that in adult neuroses; anxiety states, depressive disorders, obsessive-compulsive conditions, phobias, 'conversion' hysteria, and hypochondriasis. However, many emotional disorders in childhood are relatively undifferentiated, cannot easily be classified within categories of neurosis and also show surprisingly little continuity with neurotic disorders in adult life (Freud 1966; Rutter 1972). Rather than try to force all disorders of childhood into the procrustean bed of adult classification it seems preferable to use a separate general category of 'emotional disorder', a term which is without aetiological connotations, for these often are milder and less well-differentiated conditions (Rutter, Shaffer & Shepherd 1975). Of course, too, some emotional disorders in childhood (and especially in adolescence) show an

428

adult-type symptom pattern and should be diagnosed according to the usual categories of neurosis. This chapter is concerned with both types of emotional disorders.

DIAGNOSTIC CONSIDERATIONS

The diagnosis of emotional disorder is based first on an assessment of whether the child shows a psychiatric disorder; as judged by the persistent presence of disturbed behaviour, emotions or relationships, which are abnormal in the context of the child's sociocultural background and stage of psychological development, and which are accompanied by an impairment in personal or social functioning and/or a distortion of the developmental process (Rutter *et al* 1970; Rutter 1975). The specific diagnosis of emotional disorder is based on the further evaluation that the particular *pattern* of symptoms mainly involves emotional disturbance. In this connexion, Anna Freud (1966; 1970) points out that the same symptom may have different meanings in different children. Thus, a temper tantrum may be no more than a direct outlet for chaotic drive derivatives in a young child; or an aggressive destructive outburst with hostile feelings; or an anxiety attack which has escalated to uncontrollable panic (Freud 1966). Accordingly, diagnosis needs to be based on the *pattern* as a whole and not on any one symptom. Epidemiological studies also indicate that so-called 'neurotic traits' of childhood, such as thumbsucking, nailbiting, food fads, stammering and bedwetting are not valid indicators of emotional disorder. Nailbiting occurs in a third of school age children and shows little association with any general measure of emotional disturbance or psychiatric disorder (Rutter *et al* 1970).

Both thumbsucking and food fads are also extremely common and neither have much diagnostic significance. Bedwetting is often associated with psychiatric problems (see Chapter 24) but the association is as much with conduct disorder as with emotional disorder. Furthermore, it frequently occurs as an isolated developmental problem which has nothing to do with other psychiatric conditions.

The clinical–descriptive approach to diagnosis differs in some important respects from the metapsychological system used by psychoanalysts. Thus, Freud (1966) considers that infantile neuroses are precipitated by conflicts within the Oedipus complex and that the symptomatology is explained by the formula of castration anxiety→regression to fixation points→emergence of reactivated pregenital impulses→defence→compromise formations. Similarly, the (American) Group for the Advancement of Psychiatry (1966) maintained that the category of 'psychoneurotic disorder' in childhood is 'reserved for those disorders based on unconscious conflicts over the handling of sexual and aggressive impulses which, though removed from awareness by the mechanism of repression, remain active and unresolved'. Such neurotic conflicts, it is suggested, usually derive from earlier conscious conflicts between the child and important people in his environment. Anthony (1967) comments that these conscious conflicts belong almost exclusively to the preschool years of childhood; in later years they become internalised, encapsulated and relatively chronic, although many of the milder reactions resolve spontaneously. This implies a level of social and intellectual maturity reached before the age of 6 or 7 years (Kessler 1972).

It is important to recognise that the psychoanalytic claim that neuroses are due to unconscious conflict may be considered either as a tautology or as an hypothesis. The tautology consists in an approach which states in effect, that the term 'neurosis' will only be used for disorders which can be shown to be due to unconscious conflict. It follows from this convention that not all emotional disturbances are neurotic (Freud 1966), although there may be disputes as to whether most are or whether this only applies to a few (Chess 1969). Also, there may be problems in agreeing on an operational definition of unconscious conflict which can be applied in the ordinary clinical situation. However, the statement that neuroses are due to unconscious conflict cannot itself be debated. It is simply a semantic convention.

Alternatively, the statement may be considered as an hypothesis—a suggestion that most or many instances of phobia or anxiety state arise on the basis of unconscious conflict. It follows, from this view, that although particular symptoms may be fairly readily removed by environmental manipulation or behaviour modification, because these symptoms reflect inner mental conflict, removal of one set of symptoms will be replaced by others which may be different in form but which will express the same latent content and be equally disabling. The validity of this notion of symptom substitution has been widely discussed and it is apparent that there is very little evidence that it occurs more than occasionally (Yates 1958; 1962; Bookbinder 1962; Spiegel 1967; Feather & Rhodes 1972). On the other hand, there are certainly instances in which removal of one symptom is followed by its recurrence or replacement by another (see e.g. Marchant *et al* 1974). This does not necessarily indicate that the symptom is due to unconscious conflict, but it does imply that the main disorder has not been treated effectively. This may mean that therapeutic attention has not been paid to continuing environmental stresses, it may mean that the phobia stems from a more general affective disturbance, or that there has not been an accurate identification of the key problem, or it may indicate that the symptom has some functional or symbolic role. As a result of these considerations, it is always necessary to go beyond the mere identification of emotional symptoms to an analysis of their function and meaning in terms of associations with other symptoms and the links with prior circumstances, environmental precipitants and contingencies (Rutter 1975).

ROLE OF FEAR AND ANXIETY

Fear is an inevitable and necessary emotion in everyday life. However, particular fears may outlive their usefulness. Then their persistence begins to interrupt the child's capacity to adapt easily and successfully to the usual life stresses. Both changes with age and also individual differences in the expression of fear and anxiety need to be taken into account. At first, fear during infancy is mainly related to actual events in the immediate environment. As the child grows older, fantasy and imagination come to play a greater role with the child's increasing ability to reflect on past events and to anticipate the future. Thus, fears may become linked to possible future dangers or there may be apprehension about the harm that could stem from inner thoughts or impulses to action.

With increasing age, there is a decrease in fears of tangible and immediate situations, specific objects, noises, falling and danger of falling, strange objects and persons. On the other hand, fears of imaginary creatures, of the dark or of being alone or abandoned increase. In middle childhood there is some tendency for fears relating to personal safety and fears of animals to decline (Jersild *et al* 1975). Fears concerning school (such as worries about place in class, teachers or speaking in public) increase from age 9 years to 12 years. There is also an increase in fears relating to social relationships, worries about money, and vague fears about their own identity and whether they had been adopted (Angelino *et al* 1956; Lapouse & Monk 1959; Maurer 1965; Croake & Knox 1973). Bauer (1976) studied fears in 4- to 12-year-old children. He found decreases with increasing age in fears with imaginary themes such as ghosts, monsters and frightening dreams and an increase in frequency of realistic fears involving bodily injury and physical danger. He suggests that the sequence reflects changes in perception of reality with age and the greater separation of fantasy from reality in older children, who have a more elaborate system of verbal symbols to cope with reality and to identify sources of fear.

Anxiety is a universal phenomenon in everyday life. Moreover, excessive states of anxiety, either alone or in combination with depression, are present in virtually all emotional disorders. The pervasiveness of anxiety has given rise to much theoretical speculation about its origin and to many studies of its correlates and consequences. Freud's (1926) first theory of anxiety, based on a now outmoded energy model of motivation (Hinde 1960), defined it as an affect arising from libidinal energy which had been dammed up, distorted or displaced as the result of repression. In Freud's second theory, repression was said to occur because of anxiety, rather than the reverse. Anxiety was thought to play an important role in the development of symptoms, which were regarded as attempts to reduce or avoid anxiety, and so to avoid over-stimulation which exceeded that with which the organism could cope. A distinction was made between 'objective' anxiety related to a specific object or situation and 'neurotic' anxiety which is out of all proportion to real danger and is frequently related to unconscious conflicts and unacceptable impulses and wishes. Bowlby (1970; 1975) has criticised this distinction on the grounds that the personal environment defines whether dangers are realistic or not. He notes that it is not only the presence of certain situations perceived as dangerous which produces fear but also the absence of certain conditions, such as those needed for attachment. A strange situation in itself may create fear. A situation of threatened separation from a familiar person, when the person lacks any immediate means of coping with the stress may also give rise to fear. Both are applicable to children.

In learning theory, anxiety is used as a hypothetical construct which mediates the escape and avoidance responses shown by children in withdrawing from normal social interactions (Ross 1974). The process gives rise to observable phenomena which allow the inference that anxiety is present. These include changes in heart and respiratory rate, alterations in skin conductance, and restlessness, tremors and jumpiness. In addition there are usually subjective feelings of apprehension, worry, fear and impending danger, although the threatening situation or event cannot be specifically described. Ross (1974) suggests that certain experiences (which vary for different children) can elicit the arousal response called 'anxiety'. This has unpleasant qualities so that other responses, such as avoidance, which reduce anxiety are strengthened. Such maladaptive responses affect behaviour and social interactions and may interfere with a child's life sufficiently to require treatment.

In contrast to these views, the existential school of psychology holds that anxiety is not primarily a learned experience derived from past experience of painful environmental events, but rather it is a naturally occurring state of the organism from the beginning of life (Mandler 1975).

Lader (1972) notes that, like other emotions, anxiety is a feature of many clinical states including depressive, phobic, obsessional and hysterical disorders. It is the major feature in some; the so-called 'free-floating' anxiety or anxiety state. Morbid anxiety is quantitatively, but not qualitatively, different from everyday 'normal' anxiety which all people experience. The difference lies in the frequency, severity and persistence of pathological anxiety, together with its prospective quality, so that the individual cannot tolerate it in his customary fashion. Anxiety is an emotional response syndrome with several dimensions, subjective, cognitive, behavioural and physiological (Lader 1972).

Questionnaires have been used to measure anxiety in children (Castaneda *et al* 1953; Sarason *et al* 1960). However, these have been criticised on the grounds that the measures are superficial and do not really elicit the personal meaning of anxiety. Moreover they are often open to falsification of response and distortions from lack of cooperation (Jersild *et al* 1975). Findings are contradictory on how far questionnaire measures of anxiety correlate with clinical ratings (Stone *et al* 1965; Spielberger 1973; Montgomery & Finch 1974). Apart from a few studies with ambiguous results (Patterson *et al* 1960; Lore 1966), there is also surprisingly little work on the psychological correlates of anxiety in children. Accordingly, inferences have to be drawn from studies on adults: these show that physiological changes occur in a wide variety of emotional states, especially when the emotions are extreme, as in rage and panic (Lader 1969). It seems that high physiological arousal and appropriate sensory input interact to produce such states of emotion as anxiety (Lader 1972).

Anxiety states

When an abnormal degree of anxiety is diffuse and free-floating, rather than attached to specific situations, a diagnosis of anxiety state may be made. However, it is not at all uncommon for pervasive anxiety to be accompanied by obsessional, phobic or hysterical symptoms and, in large part, the distinction between anxiety states and phobic disorders or obsessional conditions is one of symptom patterning or emphasis rather than anything more fundamental.

An anxiety state can develop in children who are emotionally quite resilient and stable. However, often it arises as an accentuation of a pre-existing tendency to react with undue anxiety to ordinary stresses. These 'anxiety-prone' children may have been different from their sibs since early childhood in terms of their sensitivity and overreaction to stress, and their tendency to be worried over new situations. This habitual tendency is sometimes termed 'trait' anxiety to differentiate if from the more acute and time-limited 'state' anxiety (Lader 1972). However, it is probably more usefully viewed in terms of temperamental variation (Thomas *et al* 1968). While such temperamental attributes have their roots in biological and genetic influences, they are neither fixed nor immutable and, of course, a predisposition to anxiety may sometimes be largely determined by chronic environmental stresses (Chess 1973).

Sometimes anxiety states are precipitated by an actual frightening experience, such as a hospital operation (Langford 1937), a death of a friend or relative (Beverly 1942), or an accident. In other cases, there is contagion of anxiety from chronically anxious and dependent parents (Eisenberg 1958), who may themselves have an overt psychiatric disorder (Rutter 1966). In these families it is not just that the child 'picks up' the parental fears and worries, but also that the parental problems introduce stresses into parent–child interaction and that insecure parents may prolong the child's anxieties by their uncertain, indecisive and worrying response to them. Also, too, anxiety may arise from intrapsychic conflict, either on its own or in combination with current or past stresses (Anthony 1967).

Treatment plans must take these various factors into account. The child who adapts to new situations slowly and with excessive anxiety must be allowed extra time to make his adaptations and he must be protected against too many changes and uprootings. Such children need support and reassurance to master feelings of insecurity or failure and their parents need counselling to help them understand their children's needs and temperamental styles so that expectations for progress may be realistic. Steps should also be taken to remove currently relevant stresses, to help the child develop effective coping mechanisms, and to reduce the likelihood of future stresses.

Treatment may involve a variety of approaches, often in combination. Some children will need individual psychotherapy which is aimed at the origins of the anxiety, and which often may be brief and focussed (Rosenthal & Levine 1971). Reisman (1973) has provided a useful outline of the main principles which should underlie a psychotherapeutic approach. These are: (1) therapy should be based on a careful assessment of the actual psychological mechanisms which underlie each child's problems, rather than on the basis of theoretical considerations; (2) the psychotherapy situation should be structured to facilitate communication and the therapist should allow the child ample opportunity to express his feelings and beliefs; (3) the therapist should communicate his understanding of the child and his wish to be of help; (4) the therapist and child should define the purpose or goal of their meeting; (5) the therapist must make clear what is ineffective or inappropriate in the child's behaviour; (6) when dealing with behaviour that is dependent on social interaction, the therapist may modify it by focussing directly on the interactions where they take place (this may mean conjoint family interviews, group therapy or contact with school teachers according to where the problem lies); and (7) treatment should end when the advantages of ending outweigh the advantages of continuing (this may mean finishing before the child is fully better).

Behavioural methods may be useful to teach the child how to relax, and are also valuable in dealing with situation-specific anxiety by means of reciprocal inhibition or desensitisation (Montenegro 1968; see also Chapter 39). A temporary reduction in overt anxiety can be achieved with small doses of the phenothiazines or the benzodiazapine drugs. Occasionally, children living in particularly stressful home circumstances may benefit from admission to a psychiatric daypatient or inpatient unit (see Chapter 37), which allows a break to be made in the cycle of contagious or reinforcing family anxiety.

Phobic states

Phobic states are emotional disorders in which there is an abnormally intense dread of certain objects, or specific situations which normally do not have that effect (Marks 1969). Thus, phobias are to be differentiated from the normal psychophysiological reaction of fear to a genuine threat. These healthy and adaptive fears diminish, change or disappear during the process of normal development. Both fears and phobias involve similar behavioural expressions, subjective feelings and accompanying physiological change but in phobias the responses are excessive, persistent and maladaptive (Miller, Barrett & Hampe 1974). The development of phobias has been 'explained' in terms of various different theoretical approaches (Miller *et al* 1974). Thus, (a) social learning theory assumes that the unreasonable response to benign and ill-defined stimuli is learned; (b) psychoanalytic theory assumes the externalisation and displacement of anxiety from an unconscious conflict on to a feared object or situation; (c) development theory suggests that fears, anxieties and phobias are to be understood within a developmental context of reasonableness at one age and unreasonableness to another; (d) transactional theory maintains that phobias are embedded and maintained within an interpersonal context of family and social relationships. There is good evidence that phobias can be learned and a social learning approach provides much the most effective treatment methods for isolated fears (see below). However, the other approaches appear to have validity in some cases, particularly where there is a more complex disorder.

The phobic states most commonly encountered in children involve fears of animals, death, insects, the dark, noise and school. Rutter *et al* (1970) found that specific situational phobias were the most common among 10-year-old children; these were equally frequent in boys and girls. Specific animal phobias were only half as common and they occurred only in girls. There were no cases of handicapping social anxiety or agoraphobia. The phobia was rarely the only symptom in children with emotional disorders. This is an important finding which underlines the need for full and careful clinical assessment. Rutter *et al* (1970) remark on the ready response of children's fears and phobias to sensible parental handling and suggest that this may be a possible reason for the very small proportion of monosymptomatic phobic states seen at child psychiatric clinics in the UK.

Both studies of children and of adults (Marks & Gelder 1966; Rutter *et al* 1970) show that different types of phobia differ in their usual age of onset. Animal and insect phobias stand out clearly from other types of phobia in that most start by the age of 5 years and almost none start in adult life. They are also differentiated by a particularly good response to behavioural treatments even in cases of long-standing. Agoraphobias start at any time from late childhood to middle life with peaks of onset in late adolescence and around the age of 30 years. Social anxieties, on the other hand, usually begin at or after puberty whereas specific situational phobias can begin at any age.

Many techniques have been used in the treatment of phobias; these include psychotropic drugs, abreaction, psychotherapy and various forms of behaviour therapy. Behavioural methods constitute the treatment of choice in the case of monosymptomatic phobias. However, more complex phobic disorders often require a combination of approaches which include behavioural methods, environmental manipulation and psychotherapy.

Miller *et al* (1974) suggested that the wide range of techniques developed and used over the years in the treatment of phobias can be reduced to four basic essentials: establishing a helping relationship, stimulus clarfication, desensitisation to the stimuli, and confrontation of the stimulus.

The helping relationship develops out of interviews with the child and parents and includes a firm belief on the therapist's part that he is able to help. The understanding discussion of anxieties and frustration develops a sense of trust which facilitates other aspects of treatment. Stimulus clarification is brought about by obtaining a detailed account of precipitating events in and outside the home, the context of the phobia, the stimuli which evoke the anxiety, and the situations and actions which reduce the fear. Family relationships are assessed to determine how parents reinforce avoidance behaviour and dependency and to evaluate possibilities for altering patterns of family interaction in directions which would be helpful. In this process of stimulus clarification, it is necessary to obtain independent accounts from different sources in order to decide which are the significant stimuli.

There are various ways in which desensitisation can occur, but the best known is reciprocal inhibition in which the feared object is paired with some competing anxiety-reducing stimulus (Wolpe 1958), or graded change in which the person gradually becomes accustomed to the feared class of stimuli by progressive steps up a hierarchy from the least feared to the most feared item. Techniques of 'flooding', in which there is immediate confrontation with the phobic object have been used with school phobia (Smith & Sharpe 1970; Hersen 1968) and with noise phobia (Yule, Sacks & Hersov 1974).

Modelling has also been used successfully to eliminate specific fears (Bandura & Menlove 1968; White & Davis 1974), as have operant techniques (Crowe *et al* 1972, report a study with adults). Interpretations in psychotherapy, too, may serve to desensitise the patient to a feared situation (Sperling 1961). Many questions remain on both the mechanisms involved in these heterogeneous approaches and also on the relative efficacy of different methods in different situations (Marks 1974). However, it seems that confrontation with feared object is an essential part of the treatment (Miller *et al* 1974). This should occur in a therapeutic situation which allows the patient to receive support in coming through unscathed, and which enables him, in one way or another, to learn how to master or cope with the feared situation (Rutter 1975). Success in treatment consists in helping the family as a whole to develop coping mechanisms, to resolve their ambivalence, and to accept the need to confront the situations which they fear. Often the child has learned to deal with his fear by manipulation and avoidance behaviours which become rewarding in themselves. They must be faced frankly and the child and his parents must be helped to develop alternative solutions.

Although there is a large body of research with adults (Marks 1974), there have been fewer systematic studies with children (Berecz 1968). The largest series are with school phobia (see Chapter 19). Phobias in children under 10 years of age arise and disappear rapidly and the process may or may not be hastened with treatment. There is still a great need for studies comparing different methods of treatment rather than the single case studies or reports of small numbers of cases which abound in the literature at present.

Hysteria

Anxiety includes both the feeling of fear and also the bodily symptoms which are part of the autonomic response. These may include abdominal pain, nausea, vomiting, headache, frequency of micturition and diarrhoea. All are very frequent occurrences in children with anxiety states and phobias.

However, there is a different set of somatic symptoms which are not referrable to the autonomic nervous system but which are thought to be of emotional origin in some instances. These include psychogenic paralyses, abnormalities of gait, disorders of sensation, blindness, deafness, fits and fugues. The term 'conversion hysteria' is usually used for these disorders on the basis of the original (disputable) notion that emotional conflict has been converted into a somatic complaint.

The literature on hysteria in childhood is sparse by comparison with that on adults and opinions differ on its prevalence. Although some paediatricians have been impressed by its frequency (Proctor 1958; Nelson 1964) and early age of presentation (Ford 1952), most studies of clinical populations indicate that it is a quite uncommon disorder occurring in only some 1 to 2 per cent of referrals (Robins & O'Neal 1953; Hinman 1958; Caplan 1970). No cases were found among 10– and 11-year-olds on the Isle of Wight (Rutter *et al* 1970), nor were there any new cases seen in a similar general population study of 14-year-olds (Rutter *et al* 1976). It is sometimes said that hysteria is less frequent today than it was in the last century, but Mayou (1975) has argued that hysterical reactions in medical settings are more frequent than usually recognised. However, there is ample evidence that organic disease is often *mis*diagnosed as hysteria. Slater (1965) has outlined the pitfalls in the diagnosis of hysteria in adults and Caplan (1970) and Rivinus *et al* (1975) have done the same for childhood.

Caplan (1970) reviewed the literature on childhood hysteria and studied 28 prepubertal children referred to the Maudsley Hospital over a 22-year period. These cases were compared with an equal number of matched controls with psychoneurosis or an anxiety state. The major presenting symptoms in the hysterical cases were loss of function of one or more limbs, abnormal gait and severe pain, none of which occurred in the control group. Although emotional disturbance sometimes accompanied the hysterical symptoms, it was less frequent than in the children with anxiety states. Usually, the diagnosis of hysteria had been made by a specialist physician, rather than by a family doctor.

Nevertheless, a minimum of 13 of the 28 cases (46 per cent) were found on discharge or at follow-up 4 to 11 years later, to have an organic illness related to the presenting symptoms. The commonest reasons for misdiagnosis were unusual or peculiar symptoms of insidious onset, the absence of positive physical signs and the presence of an obvious emotional precipitant. In many cases only the progress of the disease led to a correct diagnosis. The commonest presentation in those who ultimately developed organic disease was amblyopia. It is of interest that Rivinus *et al* (1975) found deteriorating school performance, visual loss, postural disturbance and variability of symptoms to be important diagnostic features in their group of 12 children with organic neurological disease presenting as psychiatric disorders.

The 'true' cases of 'conversion hysteria' differed from the misdiagnosed cases in terms of a more rapid onset of symptoms and a more frequent family history of hysterical symptoms. It did not appear that a recent physical illness in the child predisposed toward the development of hysteria any more than toward other emotional disorders. However, there was a close time relationship between the child's symptoms and a relative's illness affecting the same site in 4 out of the 15 children with 'true' hysteria, lending some support to the notion of identification or imitation in the production of symptoms. Hysteria was three times as common in adolescents as in preadolescent children and there was an age difference in sex ratio. Below puberty hysteria occurred with equal frequency in boys and girls, whereas after puberty females far exceeded males.

Psychological mechanisms in hysteria

Anthony (1967) sets out the psychoanalytic concept of 'conversion' as a mechanism for transforming anxiety into a dysfunction of bodily structure or of organs supplied by the voluntary part of the nervous system. In this way conscious anxiety is lessened while the symptoms symbolise the inner mental conflict. An uncovering of the neurotic conflict is needed to help the child 'reconvert'.

Chodoff (1974) suggested an alternative model in which the symptom is a kind of nonverbal communication in the language of illness. Because it arises in and is conditioned by the specific setting of the doctor–patient relationship, it uses the socially accepted symbols of physical illness. A lack of verbal skills is thought to promote this process, so that hysteria might be expected to occur more commonly in children (which it does not). Rather than attempt to unearth the sources of unconscious conflict, it is preferable in treatment to use the symptom communication to understand its origin and its significance in the patient's life at the time.

Another model for understanding hysteria is that of the 'sick role' or 'abnormal illness behaviour', as put forward by Mechanic (1962), Pilowsky (1969) and Kendell (1974). People perceive symptoms differently and act upon them in different ways, stoically or anxiously. This owes much to childhood upbringing, family stress and role relationships as well as to the way parents convey to the growing child ideas about health, illness and treatment. Kendell (1974) points out that much illness behaviour arises from fear of disease, for physical illnesses act as stresses and if there is uncertainty over diagnosis, the stress is accentuated. The sociologist, Parsons (1951) has described the advantages and obligations of the 'sick role', including the parts played by parents, family and medical attendants. The motivation to continue in the 'sick role' can be very strongly reinforced by the responses of people around the patient. These concepts have proved fruitful in understanding the psychological mechanisms responsible for disorders of limb function in children which arose in the course or viral illnesses. The symptoms were clearly prolonged by the uncertainties about diagnosis and the pattern of management in hospital until the decision was taken to stop investigations and medication (Dubowitz & Hersov 1976).

Management of hysteria

It is of interest that in Caplan's (1970) series more hysterical children than controls were admitted to hospital for treatment. This possibly reflects the severity of disorder and the need for skilled long-term psychiatric care, including individual psychotherapy with the patient and case-work with parents. A number of different treatment procedures involving suggestion, environmental manipulation, or a direct approach to the symptom (Gold 1965) may all be successful in hysteria, but hypnosis has its dangers in children (Anthony 1967). The concepts of 'sick role' have proved successful in the management of hysterical disorders in a paediatric setting (Dubowitz & Hersov 1976) in which a combined paediatric-psychiatric plan of treatment using techniques of behaviour modification with the patient is allied to physiotherapy and family work. Once their perception of their child as chronically ill is changed to that of a child who is potentially healthy, parents are involved in supporting the child's 'escape with honour' from the sick role. Caplan (1970) found that most of the children with substantiated hysteria in his series recovered completely from the presenting disability either rapidly (less than 9 months) or rather slowly (more than 24 months).

Epidemic hysteria

Apart from hysterical 'conversion' disorders which occur in individual children, there is the rather different variety of 'epidemic hysteria' (Knight *et al* 1965; Moss & McEvedy 1966; Benaim *et al* 1973). Unlike the individual form, which is equally common in boys and girls, epidemic hysteria is very much more frequent in girls. Typically, it occurs among adolescents in a relatively closed community of some kind such as a boarding school or hospital. What happens is that one girl develops 'hysterical' attacks of falling or convulsions, overbreathing, or some similar phenomenon; then another does, and soon the hysteria spread to involve many more girls in the community. The girls who first have hysterical attacks are often severely disturbed individuals, but this is less often the case with later affected girls who may be more dependent and show more neurotic traits than average (Moss & McEvedy 1966; McEvedy *et al* 1966) but are otherwise quite ordinary youngsters. The spread of the disorder is to be sought in the social milieu as much as in the personality features of the affected individuals. Usually the girls who start the epidemic have a dominant and influential position within their peer group, and the epidemic starts at a time when group anxieties (such as in relation to pregnancies, sexual activities, work stresses or a death of a classmate) create an emotional vulnerability. The first essential in dealing with a hysterical epidemic is the isolation of the key figures who initiated it. Attention then needs to be paid to both the group tensions and emotions, and to the personal problems of the main instigators.

OBSESSIONAL DISORDERS

The term 'obsessive–compulsive' is used for a variety of disorders of thought and behaviour which occur in adults and in children. Most definitions follow that of Schneider (1925) translated by Lewis (1936) as: 'contents of consciousness which, when they occur, are accompanied by the experience of subjective compulsion, and which cannot be got rid of, though on quiet reflection they are recognised as senseless'. The latter considered that a feeling of resistance to the obsession was an essential feature of the diagnosis. This view is now generally accepted, but resistance is sometimes difficult to assess in young children and it has yet to be demonstrated that the presence or absence of resistance is crucial.

The persistent and repetitive thoughts which obtrude into consciousness may include words, numbers, ideas, trains of thought, images, affects or impulses to carry out certain actions. These latter compulsions are repetitive, stereotyped and often trivial motor acts such as touching, smelling, tasting and feeling the texture of objects, handwashing and cleansing activities, walking or using one's body in specific ways and checking rituals (Miller 1939).

Mild rituals and obsessions are very common as part of normal development (Freud 1966) and bedtime and dressing rituals in toddlers and pre-schoolers are well described (Gesell, Ilg & Ames 1974). Children often seem impelled to touch certain objects, to walk on or to avoid the joins between paving stones, to jump over cracks in the pavement, or make certain signs. There are widespread ritual elements in the games, chants and songs of childhood, as vividly described by Opie and Opie (1959). Peller (1954) has suggested a psychoanalytic explanation for these phenomena.

Obsessions and compulsions may increase in certain conscientious, shy and self-conscious children, so taking up time and energy and causing embarrassment. Handwashing must be done a certain number of times, schoolwork must be checked and rechecked and the child is unable to inhibit this behaviour while appreciating its futility. Judd (1965) distinguishes between the compulsive behaviour that is part of normal development and pathological compulsiveness. The former is not experienced as alien or incongruous and there is no internal need to resist the behaviour. It is experienced as pleasant, is eagerly performed, short-lived and can be easily given up under mild pressure without anxiety.

Bender and Schilder (1940) described 'impulsions' in young boys; meaning unusual preoccupations with various interests, ideas and activities which last over periods of time, even years. Although the overt clinical picture of behaviour and thought is akin to obsessive–compulsive behaviour the absence of inner resistance is the distinguishing feature. However, the authors describe the progression of this behaviour to frank compulsions or obsessional personality traits at or after puberty.

In the Isle of Wight Study (Rutter *et al* 1970), a small number of children had psychiatric disorders with prominent obsessive features, but most were also moderately anxious, and there were no cases of fully developed adult-type obsessional disorder. Clinic studies also show that frank obsessional disorders are relatively uncommon in childhood (Judd 1965; Berman 1942; Regner 1959; Ross 1964), although obsessional features are more frequent as part of other psychiatric conditions (both emotional disorders and autism—see Chapter 30).

Unlike the adult, the obsessional child usually does not or cannot always keep his thoughts or compulsions to himself. Instead he may manipulate his parents into taking part in the rituals, by insisting that they answer his repetitive questions or comply with his compulsive needs. The hostile controlling element in the interaction is often very striking to the observer. A mother who is herself compulsive may at first fit in with these demands and so reinforce the behaviour, but other parents often become impatient and hostile. They try to resist the child's pressures, usually by reasoning but sometimes by punishment. Adolescents with obsessive–compulsive disorders are often inept or lacking in social skills so that they become increasingly isolated from normal peer group activities. The misery and anxiety arising from these social difficulties may accentuate the obsessive symptoms. Obsessional thoughts and behaviour may also develop as secondary features in a depressive disorder.

Despert (1955) has described the sometimes difficult differential diagnosis between obsessive–compulsive neurosis and schizophrenia. Schizophrenia in adolescents is sometimes ushered in by obsessional preoccupations, but only some 4 per cent of long-standing obsessionals become schizophrenic (Pollitt 1969). Whether or not the figures are different for children with obsessional disorders is not known.

Adams (1973) studied 49 obsessive children (39 boys and 10 girls) who constituted about 1 per cent of psychiatric clinic referrals. Obsessional symptoms began about 6 years of age on average, but referral did not normally take place until some 4 years later. There was a gradual onset in two-thirds of the children—especially in those from middle class families. A precipitating event occurred in nearly half the cases. The whole group was of average or above average intelligence. Four-fifths of the children had both obsessions and compulsions but 8 per cent had only a compulsive life style. Over half of the children also had phobias. The symptoms were disruptive to the majority of the families. In all but one, ambivalence or aggression was shown by children to their parents, while guilt feelings were prominent in the great majority. Other members of the family had shown obsessive symptoms in nearly three-quarters of the cases. It also seemed that the emotional climate in the home often involved a high premium on etiquette, cleanliness and morality. Toilet training difficulties were rare but in two-fifths of cases bowel training was said to be rigid, punitive or prolonged.

Psychological mechanisms in obsessional disorders

Obsessional phenomena are usually thought to be defensive manœuvres to reduce anxiety (Lewis 1936; Carr 1974). Thus, a failure to perform the required action results in increasing anxiety, and performance of the compulsion provides a temporary subjective lessening of tension until the next unwelcome thought or urge occurs. However, there are limitations in this formulation as a complete explanation of obsessional behaviour (Rutter 1975; Hodgson & Rachman 1972).

According to psychoanalytic theory, the major defence mechanisms are reaction formation, undoing and isolation, while repression and displacement are also involved (Kessler 1972). These emerge in touching compulsions and handwashing to avoid contamination (isolation) and the magical beliefs in the appeasing or penitential qualities of certain thoughts and actions (undoing).

Meyer and Chesser (1970) suggest that compulsive behaviour may be a learned avoidance response to the childhood conflict in which anxiety stems from drives whose reduction is difficult because of anticipated anxiety provoking punishment. The use of 'magical' or ritualistic avoidance behaviour to deal with approach-avoidance conflict is explained from magical or animistic thinking at a stage of development when such thinking is normal. Carr (1974) put forward a model to explain compulsions in terms of cognitive processes. He suggested that compulsive neurotics always make an abnormally high subjective estimate that things will turn out badly, i.e. they appraise events as threatening, so become anxious and then reduce their anxiety by compulsive behaviours which ensure that things are more likely to turn out well.

Treatment and outcome of obsessional states

Although Adams (1973) and Berman (1942) consider that the outcome is good in the untreated case with a single episode of minor obsessional symptoms, well-established obsessional and compulsive symptoms may require long-term treatment, sometimes including hospital treatment. The prognosis is better where obsessional symptoms are secondary to a depressive disorder.

Ross (1964) followed up 17 obsessive children seen at the Maudsley Hospital and found that 6 showed full and lasting recovery while 11 showed persistent symptoms. Warren (1965) described 15 obsessive patients admitted to the Adolescent Inpatient Unit of the same hospital. In 9 the disorder began before the age of 10 years and in 6 it was of later onset. At follow-up, one had been leucotomised, 2 required further hospital treatment, 2 remained seriously handicapped with obsessional symptoms and 4 were less handicapped. Four retained a tendency to mild symptoms under stress and only 2 were normal. The best outcome was in those with the shortest history on admission. This inpatient sample included particularly severe cases so that the poor outcome may not be representative of children treated as outpatients.

Until the advent of behaviour therapy, psychotherapy with the child together with counselling of the parents constituted the main treatment method. This is still a helpful approach when there is marked general anxiety. However, the results of psychotherapy in the treatment of adult obsessional disorders are equivocal to say the least (Cawley 1974), and there are no satisfactory studies of these methods in children. Recent behavioural methods (Hodgson & Rachman 1972) using modelling, response prevention and real-life exposure appear hopeful.

Weiner (1967) has described the treatment of a 15-year-old boy with a very short history of pervasive rituals involving washing and dressing in which the maladaptive rituals were replaced with positive delimited substitute rituals. These were gradually attenuated in time so as to interfere very little with normal activity. A 7-month follow-up showed a return to normal adolescent behaviour, interests and activities.

DEPRESSIVE DISORDERS

Many children experience *mood changes* with feelings of sadness, misery and unhappiness. These may be transitory states in response to the disappointments of everyday life or to fortuitous stressful events. The normal child soon adapts to these situations and reverts to his usual state of cheerful hopefulness. As a result of genetic factors and/or early experience, some children are more predisposed than others to respond to stressful events with more lasting moods of sadness. These may continue even though the child's life experience takes a turn for the better. This persistent change in affect is the central feature of the *symptom* of depression (Lewis 1934). If, in addition, the affective change is of sufficient severity to interfere with the child's relationships at home and school, the quality of his schoolwork, and the usual pattern of his everyday life, it has become a handicapping condition sufficient to warrant the term *depressive disorder*.

Although some authorities (Graham 1974; Makita 1973) question whether these constitute distinct psychiatric conditions, there is no doubt that such clinical states exist. The uncertainty is whether the disorders represent an *illness* or *disease* with a specific aetiology, a symptom pattern, prognosis and response to treatment. The findings from the study of depressive states in adults are helpful (Hill 1968) but children are not miniature adults and the criteria for depressive disorder cannot be extrapolated from adults without taking into account both developmental considerations and family circumstances. Anthony (1967) suggests that like anxiety, depression can be viewed as a basic psychobiological affective reaction. Both are appropriate under normal circumstances of loss or threat. However, both loss and threat are difficult to define, and notions such as actual or imagined or fantasied loss have been introduced which further complicate the issue. In some respects, anxiety is a prospective emotion, a response to anticipated threat. By contrast, depression is particularly concerned with past events, situations, or relationships. In clinical practice, anxiety and depression are often found together, but it is the preponderance of the one or other which determines the diagnostic grouping.

Prevalence of depressive disorder

Rutter *et al* (1970) found an overt depressive disorder in only 3 girls and no boys among some 2000 10- and 11-year-olds in the Isle of Wight study, although a larger number of children in other diagnostic subgroups were unhappy or miserable to a considerable degree. Moreover, some 10 per cent of the general population of children were reported by parents or teachers to be miserable. At 14 years (Rutter *et al* 1976), out of 2303 adolescents in the general population, there were 9 with a depressive disorder and another 26 who had an affective disorder involving both anxiety and depression. Feelings of misery and unhappiness were very much commoner still, occurring in a fifth of the adolescents. Shaffer (1974), in a study of completed suicide in childhood, found no cases below the age of 12 years. Most of the children showed psychiatric problems before their death but this took the form of both antisocial and emotional disorders. There was a high incidence of depression and suicidal behaviour in the children's parents and siblings. Shaffer raised the question whether depression in adolescence might sometimes take the form of antisocial behaviour—a possibility also raised by Rutter's study (1966) of children's reactions to bereavement.

Prevalence figures based on psychiatric clinic populations vary widely according to concept and definition. It is clear that symptoms of depression are quite common in children with psychiatric disorder, but these occur in almost all diagnostic groups. Conditions in which severe depression is the main or only feature are very much less frequent in prepubertal children (although they are more common in adolescence). However, it is not possible to give a meaningful figure for the prevalence of depressive disorders in childhood until it is clear what the diagnostic criteria should be (see below).

Characteristics of depressive disorder

Depressive mood change, together with self-deprecation and guilt, is the central characteristic of depressive disorders but other alterations in attitudes and behaviour may also reflect changes of feeling state. Weinberg *et al* (1973) noted aggressive difficult behaviour, suicidal thoughts, sleep disturbance, a fall off in school performance, a loss of enjoyment, social withdrawal, somatic complaints, loss of mental and physical energy, and an unusual change in appetite or weight (increase or decrease). Sandler and Joffe (1965) mentioned also a sense of rejection and emphasised various features of the children's response to psychotherapy. Poznanski and Zrull (1970) stressed the diagnostic importance of a negative self-image. They also noted the difficulties in recognising depression in preschool children, although Frommer (1968) maintains that it occurs quite commonly in all age groups. Rie (1966) critically reviewed the literature on 'childhood depression' and concluded that, although the ostensible symptoms have been described in great detail, there was a general lack of criteria for making the diagnosis. Some authors appear to deny the existence of depression in childhood on theoretical grounds without recourse to empirical study (Rochlin 1959).

'Masked depression'

Many of the classifications of depressive disorder have placed much weight on the notion of 'masked depression' or 'depressive equivalents' (Malmquist 1971). These terms have been used to cover somatic complaints which are thought to reflect depression—abdominal pain, anorexia, headaches, encopresis and enuresis (Sperling 1959; Frommer 1968). They have also been used for supposedly depressive disorders without depressive mood change—including hyperactivity, aggressive behaviour, hypochondriasis, delinquency and learning difficulties (Toolan 1962; Burks & Harrison 1962; Faux & Rowley 1967; Glaser 1967). Cytryn and McKnew (1972) described 'masked depression' as the most common, but often unrecognised, variety of depressive disorders in childhood. In these cases the depression was shown in terms of self-description, fantasy and drawing at interview.

The concept of 'masked depression' or 'depressive equivalent' is not necessarily an unreasonable one (Rutter 1972). In the first place, it is clear that many children with depressive symptoms also show a wide variety of other difficulties, ranging from delinquency to hypochondriasis. Secondly, the associations between antisocial behaviour and both bereavement (Rutter 1966) and suicide (Shaffer 1974) suggest that depression may reveal itself in ways other than simple mood change. Thirdly, there is evidence that the same problem may manifest itself in different ways at different ages. For example, severe *over*activity in early life often changes to *under*activity in adolescence (Rutter *et al* 1970). Accordingly, it is entirely possible that depression could occur in childhood in an apparently disguised form with symptoms different from those seen in adult life. However, at the moment, there is a lack of evidence that this *in fact* occurs. In the absence of such evidence, and hence in the absence of adequate diagnostic criteria, the use of terms such as 'masked depression' as if they were fact rather than hypothesis, is misleading and inappropriate. On the other hand, if depressive disorders to take different forms in childhood to those in adult life this would be a matter of great theoretical and practical concern to child and adult psychiatrists. Rutter (1972) has outlined some of the conceptual issues and suggested ways in which they might be tested.

Depressive syndromes

Pearce (1974) made a systematic study of 547 children aged 1 to 17 years (and without severe mental retardation, organic psychosis, autism or schizophrenia) attending the Maudsley Hospital. A quarter of the patients were rated as having the symptom of depression, defined in terms of 'morbid depression, sadness, unhappiness, tearfulness'. The 126 children with this symptom were compared with the remainder. The depressed patients differed significantly from the others in being older, more emotionally disturbed, more likely to have a disturbed relationship with family members (but not with peers) and more likely to have experienced emotional stresses. A higher proportion were referrals from another psychiatric clinic and more were treated as inpatients. Patients with the symptom of depression differed from other children in being more likely to show suicidal ideas, altered perception, ideas of reference or morbid persecutory ideas, disturbances of sleep and eating, obsessions and school refusal. On the whole, the differentiations were greater in postpubertal adolescents than in younger children.

A discriminant functions analysis added four important findings. First, a third of the children with the symptom of depression had more in common with nondepressed children than with depressed children. This indicates that by no means all children with the *symptom* of depressed mood have the *syndrome* of depression. Second, a minority (11 per cent) of those *without* the symptom of depression (as defined) were classified on the discriminant functions analysis with the depressed children. They tended to be young children with a family history of mental disorder and with the symptoms associated with depression (suicidal feelings, morbid anxiety, sleep disturbance, eating disturbance, school refusal, etc). This implies that depression can occur as a relatively undifferentiated and amorphous response, and that this is especially likely to happen in very young children. Third, many of the symptoms often classified as 'depressive equivalents' were negatively associated with depression. For example, this was so for aggression, stealing and enuresis. Pearce (1974) concluded that the notion of 'equivalents', at least in the forms usually put forward, is not very useful. Fourth, depression (however defined) was much less frequent below age 8 years than it was in later childhood, and it was most frequent in adolescence.

Pearce's (1974) study has shown that it is possible to systematically investigate and delimit the symptoms which serve to make up the depressive disorders of childhood or adolescence. Clearly, such disorders exist. However, many questions remain. Do acute stresses and losses play the crucial role in childhood depression that they seem to do in adult depressive disorders (Brown *et al* 1973a, b)? Are depressive states in childhood forerunners of depression in adult life? What is the link with the cyclical forms of manic-depressive psychoses? Are the various genetic factors which underlie different forms of adult depression the same ones which predispose to childhood depression? What is the value of antidepressant medication? Does pharmacological, or other, elevation of mood relieve the other behavioural disturbances thought to stem from depression?

Treatment

Depressive conditions, like any other form of emotional disorder, are often associated with a variety of acute and chronic stresses both within the family and outside the home. Individual or family psychotherapy should be used, as appropriate, both to help the child find successful ways of coping with stress and also to aid more adaptive family functioning. In addition, when there is a clear-cut depressive disorder leading to impaired functioning, a trial of antidepressants is indicated. Several studies (Frommer 1968; Stack 1971; Weinberg *et al* (1973) have suggested the value of such treatment, but there have been very few adequately controlled drug trials. Claims have been made for the value of monoamine oxidase inhibitors (Frommer 1968), but most clinicians prefer the tricyclics because of their greater safety and freedom from side-effects. Electroconvulsive therapy is very rarely indicated in younger children but just occasionally it is appropriate in the most severe cases in later childhood and adolescence (Campbell 1955; Frommer 1968).

RELATIONSHIP BETWEEN CHILDHOOD EMOTIONAL DISORDER AND ADULT NEUROSIS

In many respects the emotional disorders of childhood seem similar to adult neuroses. Furthermore, studies of individuals treated for psychiatric problems in both childhood and adult life show that, *if* emotional disorders persist, they usually develop into neuroses or depressive states in adulthood (Pritchard & Graham 1966; Zeitlyn 1972). On the other hand, follow-up studies show that most children with emotional disorders go on to become normal healthy adults who do not have a neurosis (Morris *et al* 1954; Michael *et al* 1957; Robins 1966; 1972). Furthermore, the sex ratio of emotional disorders in childhood differs from that in adult life (Rutter 1972), and the types of phobia which begin in childhood are not the same as those with an onset after maturity (Marks & Gelder 1966).

It appears that some emotional disorders in childhood are precursors of adult neuroses whereas others may constitute rather different types of condition which usually carry a very good prognosis. Unfortunately, we still lack adequate criteria to differentiate these groups.

REFERENCES

ACKERSON L. (1931) *Children's Behaviour Problems.* Chicago: University of Chicago Press

ADAMS P.L. (1973) *Obsessive Children: a Sociopsychiatric Study.* London: Butterworth

ANGELINO H., DOLLINS J. & MECH E. (1956) Trends in the fears and worries of schoolchildren as related to socio-economic status and age. *J. Genet. Psychol.* **89,** 263–276

ANTHONY E.J. (1967) Psychoneurotic disorders of childhood. *In* Freedman A. & Kaplan H. (eds.) *Comprehensive Textbook of Psychiatry.* Baltimore: Williams & Wilkins

BANDURA A. & MENLOVE F.L. (1968) Factors determining vicarious extinction of avoidance behaviour through symbolic modelling. *J. Pers. Soc. Psychol.* **8,** 99–108

BAUER D.H. (1976) An exploratory study of developmental changes in children's fears. *J. Child Psychol. Psychiat.* **17,** 69–74

BENAIM S., HORDER J. & ANDERSON J. (1973) Hysterical epidemic in a classroom. *Psychol. Med.* **3,** 366–373

BENDER L. & SCHILDER P. (1940) Impulsions: a specific disorder of the behaviour of children. *Arch. Neurol. Psychiat.* **44,** 990–1008

BERECZ J.M. (1968) Phobias of childhood: etiology and treatment. *Psychol. Bull.* **70,** 694–720

BERMAN L. (1942) The obsessive compulsive neurosis in children. *J. Nerv. Ment. Dis.* **95,** 26–39

BEVERLEY B.I. (1942) Anxieties of children. *Amer. J. Dev. Child* **64,** 585–593

BOOKBINDER L.J. (1962) Simple conditioning and the dynamic approach to symptoms and symptom substitution. A reply to Yates. *Psychol. Reps.* **10,** 71–77

BOWLBY J. (1970) Reasonable fear and natural fear. *Internat. J. Psychiat.* **9,** 79–88

BOWLBY J. (1975) *Attachment and Loss*, vol. II: *Separation: Anxiety and Anger.* Harmondsworth: Penguin

BROWN G.W., SKLAIR F., HARRIS T.O. & BIRLEY J.L.T. (1973a) Life events and psychiatric disorder. 1: Some methodological issues. *Psychol. Med.* **3,** 74–87

BROWN G.W., HARRIS T.O. & PETO J. (1973b) Life events and psychiatric disorder. 2: Nature of causal link *Psychol. Med.* **3,** 159–176

BURKS H. & HARRISON S. (1962) Aggressive behavior as a means of avoiding depression. *Amer. J. Orthopsychiat.* **32,** 416–421

CAMPBELL J.D. (1955) Manic-depressive disease in children. *J. Amer. Med. Assas.* **158,** 154–157

CAPLAN H.L. (1970) *Hysterical 'Conversion' Symptoms in Childhood.* M.Phil dissertation, University of London

CARR A.T. (1974) Compulsive neurosis: a review of the literature. *Psychol. Bull.* **81,** 311–318

CASTANEDA A., PALERMO D. & McCANDLESS B.R. (1956) Complex learning and performance as a function of anxiety in children and task difficulty. *Child Dev.* **27,** 327–332

CAWLEY R.H. (1974) Psychotherapy and obsessional disorders. *In* Beech H.R. (ed.) *Obsessional States.* London: Methuen

CHESS S. (1969) *An Introduction of Child Psychiatry*, 2nd edn. 143–147. New York: Grune & Stratton

CHESS S. (1973) Marked anxiety in children. *Amer. J. Psychother.* **17,** 390–395

CHODOFF P. (1974) The diagnosis of hysteria: an overview. *Amer. J. Psychiat.* **131,** 1073–1078

CROAKE J. & KNOX F. (1973) The changing nature of children's fears. *Child Study J.* 391–405

CROWE M.J., MARKS I.M., AGRAS W.S. & LEITENBERG H. (1972) Time-limited desensitisation, implosion of shaping for phobic patients: a crossover study. *Behav. Res. Ther.* **10,** 319–328

CYTRYN L. & McKNEW D. (1972) Proposed classification of childhood depression. *Amer. J. Psychiat.* **129,** 149–155

DESPERT J.L. (1955) Differential diagnosis between obsessive-compulsive neurosis and schizophrenia in children. *In* Hoch P. & Zubin, J. (eds.) *Psychopathology of Childhood.* New York: Grune & Stratton

DUBOWITZ V. & HERSOV L. (1976) Management of children with non-organic (hysterical) disorders of motor function. *Develop. Med. Child Neurol.* **18,** 358–368

EISENBERG L. (1958) School phobia: a study in the communication of anxiety. *Amer. J. Psychiat.* **114,** 712–718

FAUX E. & ROWLEY C. (1967) Detecting depressions in childhood. *Hosp. Comm. Psychiat.* **18,** 31–38

FEATHER B.W. & RHOADS J.M. (1972) Psychodynamic behaviour therapy. *Arch. Gen. Psychiat.* **26**, 496–511

FORD F. (1952) *Diseases of the Nervous System in Infancy, Childhood and Adolescence.* Springfield, Illinois: Charles C Thomas

FREUD A. (1966) *Normality and Pathology in Childhood.* London: Hogarth Press

FREUD A. (1970) The symptomatology of childhood: a preliminary attempt at classification. *Psychoanalyt. Study Child.* **25**, 19–41. London: Hogarth Press

FREUD S. (1926) *Inhibitions, Symptoms and Anxiety.* Standard Edition, vol. 20. London: Hogarth Press

FROMMER E. (1968) Depressive illness in children. *Brit. J. Psychiat.* Spec. Pub. no. 2, 117–136

GESELL A., ILG F.L. & AMES L.B. (1974) *Infant and Child in the Culture of Today,* Revised edn. New York: Harper & Row

GLASER K. (1967) Masked depression in children and adolescents. *Amer. J. Psychotherap.* **19**, 228–240

GOLD S. (1965) Diagnosis and management of hysterical contracture in children. *Brit. Med. J.* **1**, 21–23

GRAHAM P. (1974) Depression in pre-pubertal children. *Develop. Med. Child Neurol.* **16**, 340–349

GROUP FOR THE ADVANCEMENT OF PSYCHIATRY (1966) *Psychopathological Disorders in Childhood. Theoretical considerations and a proposed classification,* vol. VI. Report no. 62

HERSEN M. (1968) Treatment of a compulsive and phobic disorder through a total behaviour therapy programme. *Psychotherap. Theory Res. Prac.* **5**, 220–224

HEWITT L.E. and JENKINS R.L. (1964) *Fundamental Patterns of Maladjustment: the Dynamics of their Origin.* Springfield, Illinois: Charles C Thomas

HILL D. (1968) Depression: disease, reaction or posture. *Amer. J. Psychiat.* **125**, 37–49

HINDE R.A. (1960) Energy models of motivation. *Symp. Soc. Exper. Biol.* **14**, 199–213

HINMAN A. (1958) Conversion hysteria in childhood. *J. Dis. Child.* **95**, 42–45

HODGSON R. & RACHMAN J. (1972) The effects of contamination and masking in obsessional patients. *Behav. Res. Ther.* **10**, 111–117

JERSILD A.T., TELFORD C.W. & SAWREY J.M. (1975) *Child Psychology,* 7th edn. London: Prentice-Hall International

JUDD L. (1965) Obsessive compulsive neurosis in children. *Arch. Gen. Psychiat.* **12**, 136–143

KENDELL R. (1974) A new look at hysteria. *Medicine* **30**, 1780–1783

KESSLER J.W. (1972) Neurosis in childhood. *In* Wolman B. (ed.) *Manual of Child Psychopathology.* New York: McGraw-Hill

KNIGHT J., FRIEDMAN T. & SULIANTI J. (1965) Epidemic hysteria: a field study. *Amer. J. Pub. Hlth.* **55**, 858–863

LADER M. (1969) Psychophysiological aspects of anxiety. *In* Lader M. (ed.) *Studies of Anxiety.* British Journal of Psychiatry Special Publication No. 3. Ashford, Kent: Headley Bros.

LADER M. (1972) The nature of anxiety. *Brit. J. Psychiat.* **121**, 481–491

LANGFORD W.S. (1937) Anxiety attacks in children. *Amer. J. Orthopsychiat.* **7**, 210–218

LAPOUSE R. & MONK M. (1959) Fears and worries in a representative sample of children. *Amer. J. Orthopsychiat.* **29**, 803–818

LEWIS A.J. (1934) Melancholia: a clinical survey of depressive states. *J. Ment. Sci.* **80,** 277–378

LEWIS A.J. (1936) Problems of obsessional illness. *Proc. Roy. Soc. Med.* **29,** 325–336

LORE R.K. (1966) Palmar sweating and transitory anxieties in children. *Child Dev.* **37,** 115–123

MAKITA K. (1973) The rarity of depression in childhood. *Acta Paedopsychiat.* **40,** 37–44

MALMQUIST C.P. (1971) Depressions in childhood and adolescence. *N. Engl. J. Med.* **284,** 887–893; 955–961

MANDLER G. (1975) *Mind and Emotion.* New York: Wiley

MARCHANT R., HOWLIN P., YULE W. & RUTTER M. (1974) Graded change in the treatment of the behaviour of autistic children. *J. Child Psychol. Psychiat.* **15,** 221–227

MARKS I.M. (1969) *Fears and Phobias.* London: Heinemann

MARKS I.M. (1974) Research in neurosis: a selective review. 2: Treatment. *Psychol. Med.* **4,** 89–100

MARKS I. & GELDER M. (1966) Different ages of onset in varieties of phobia. *Amer. J. Psychiat.* **123,** 218–221

MAURER A. (1965) What children fear. *J. Genet. Psychol.* **100,** 265–277

MAYOU R. (1975) The social setting of hysteria. *Brit. J. Psychiat.* **127,** 466–469

McEVEDY C.P., GRIFFITH A. & HALL T. (1966) Two school epidemics. *Brit. Med. J.* **2,** 1300–1302

MECHANIC D. (1962) The concept of illness behaviour. *J. Chron. Dis.* **15,** 189–194

MEYER V. & CHESSER E.S. (1970) *Behaviour Therapy in Clinical Psychiatry.* Harmondsworth: Penguin

MICHAEL C., MORRIS D. & SOROKER E. (1957) Follow-up studies of shy withdrawn children, II: relative incidence of schizophrenia. *Amer. J. Orthopsychiat.* **27,** 331–337

MILLER L.C., BARRETT C.L. & HAMPE E. (1974) Phobias of childhood in a prescientific era. *In* Davids A. (ed.) *Child Persanality and Psychopathology: Current Topics.* New York: Wiley

MILLER E. (1939) Obsessional and compulsive states in childhood *In* Gordon R.G. (ed.) *A Survey of Child Psychiatry.* London: Oxford University Press

MONTENEGRO H. (1968) Severe separation anxiety in two pre-school children: successfully treated by reciprocal inhibition. *J. Child Psychol. Psychiat.* **9,** 93–103

MONTGOMERY L.E. & FINCH A.J. (1974) Validity of two measures of anxiety in children. *J. Abnorm. Child Psychol.* **2,** 293–298

MORRIS D.P., SOROKER E. & BURRUSS C. (1954) Follow-up studies of shy withdrawn children I. Evaluation of later adjustment. *Amer. J. Orthopsychiat.* **24,** 743–754

MOSS P.D. & McEVEDY C. (1966) An epidemic of overbreathing among schoolgirls. *Brit. Med. J.* **2,** 1295–1300

NELSON W.E. (1964) *Textbook of Paediatrics,* 8th edn. Philadelphia: W.B. Saunders

OPIE I. & OPIE P. (1959) *Lore and Language of School Children.* Oxford: Oxford University Press

PARSONS T. (1951) *The Social System.* New York: Free Press

PATTERSON G.R., HELPER M.E. & WILCOTT R.C. (1960) Anxiety and verbal conditioning in children. *Child. Dev.,* **31,** 101–108

PATTERSON G.R. (1964) An empirical approach to the classification of disturbed children. *J. Clin. Psychol.* **20,** 326–337

PEARCE J.B. (1974) Childhood depression. MPhil(Psychiat.) Thesis, University of London

PELLER L. (1954) Libidinal phases, ego development and play. *Psychoanalyt. Study Child.* **10**, 178–199. New York: International Universities Press

PILOWSKY I. (1969) Abnormal illness behaviour. *Brit. J. Med. Psychol.* **42**, 347–351

POLLITT J. (1969) Obsessional states. *Brit. J. Hosp. Med.* 1146–1150

POZNANSKI E. & ZRULL J. (1970) Childhood depression: clinical characteristics of overtly depressed children. *Arch. Gen. Psychiat.* **23**, 8–15

PRITCHARD M. & GRAHAM P. (1966) An investigation of a group of patients who have attended both the child and adult departments of the same psychiatric hospital. *Brit. J. Psychiat.* **112**, 603–612

PROCTOR J.T. (1958) Hysteria in childhood. *Amer. J. Orthopsychiat.* **28**, 394–407

QUAY H. (1964) Dimensions of personality in delinquent boys as inferred from the factor analysis of case history data. *Child. Dev.* **35**, 479–484

QUAY H. (1972) Patterns of aggression withdrawal and immaturity. *In* Quay H.C. & Werry J.S. (eds.) *Psychopathological Disorders of Childhood.* New York: Wiley

REGNER E.G. (1959) Obsessive compulsive neurosis in children. *Acta Psychiat. Neurolog. Scand.* **34**, 110–125

REISMAN J. (1973) *Principles of Psychotherapy with Children.* London: Wiley

RIE H.E. (1966) Depression in childhood: a survey of some pertinent contributions. *J. Amer. Acad. Child Psychiat.* **5**, 653–685

RIVINUS T.M., JAMISON D.L. & GRAHAM P.J. (1975) Childhood organic neurological disease presenting as psychiatric disorder. *Arch. Dis. Child.* **50**, 115–119

ROBINS E. & O'NEAL P. (1953) Clinical features of hysteria in children. *The Nervous Child* **10**, 246–271

ROBINS L.N. (1966) *Deviant Children Grown Up.* Baltimore: Williams & Wilkins

ROBINS L.N. (1972) Follow-up studies of behavior disorders in children. *In* Quay H.C. and Werry J.S. (eds.) *Psychopathological Disorders of Childhood.* New York: Wiley

ROCHLIN G. (1959) The loss complex. *J. Amer. Psychoanal. Assoc.* **7**, 299–316

ROSENTHAL A. & LEVINE S. (1971) Brief psychotherapy with children: process of therapy. *Amer. J. Psychiat.* **128**, 141–146

ROSS A.O. (1974) *Psychological Disorders of Children.* New York: McGraw-Hill

ROSS J. (1964) A follow-up study of obsessional illness presenting in childhood and adolescence. DPM Dissertion, University of London

RUTTER M. (1966) *Children of Sick Parents: an Environmental and Psychiatric Study.* Institute of Psychiatry, Maudsley Monograph No. 16. London: Oxford University Press

RUTTER M., LEBOVICI S., EISENBERG L., SNEZNEVSKIJ A.V., SADOUN R., BROOKE E. & LIN T-Y. (1969) A triaxial classification of mental disorders in childhood. *J. Child Psychol. Psychiat.* **10**, 41–61

RUTTER M., TIZARD J. & WHITMORE K. (eds.) (1970) *Education, Health and Behaviour.* London: Longman

RUTTER M. (1972) Relationship between child and adult psychiatric disorders. *Acta Psychiat. Scand.* **48**, 3–21

RUTTER M. (1973) Why are London children so disturbed? *Proc. Roy. Soc. Med.* **66**, 1221–1225

RUTTER M. (1975) *Helping Troubled Children.* Harmondsworth: Penguin

RUTTER M., SHAFFER D. & SHEPHERD M. (1975) *A Multiaxial Classification of Child Psychiatric Disorders.* Geneva: WHO

RUTTER M., GRAHAM P., CHADWICK O. & YULE W. (1976) Adolescent turmoil: fact or fiction. *J. Child Psychol. Psychiat.* **17**, 35–56

SANDLER J. & JOFFE W. (1965) Notes on childhood depression. *Internat. J. Psychoanal.* **46**, 88–96

SARASON S., DAVIDSON K. & ROEBUCK B. (1960) *Anxiety in Elementary School Children.* New York: Wiley

SCHNEIDER K. (1925) Schwangszustände und Schizophrenie. *Arch. Psychiat. Nervenk.*

SHAFFER D. (1974) Suicide in childhood and early adolescence. *J. Child Psychol. Psychiat.* **15**, 275–292

SLATER E. (1965) Diagnosis of hysteria. *Brit. Med. J.* **1**, 1395–1399

SMITH R.E. & SHARPE T.M. (1970) Treatment of school phobia with implosive therapy. *J. Cons. Clin. Psychol.* **35**, 239–243

SPIEGEL H. (1967) Is symptom removal dangerous? *Amer. J. Psychiat.* **10**, 1279–1282

SPERLING M. (1959) Equivalents of depression in children. *J. Hillside Hosp.* **8**, 138–148

SPERLING M. (1961) Analytic first aid in school phobias. *Psychoanal. Quart.* **30**, 504–18

SPIELBERGER C.D. (1973) *Preliminary Manual for the State-Trait Anxiety Inventory for Children ('How I Feel Questionnaire').* Palo Alto, California: Consulting Psychologists Press

STACK J. (1971) Chemotherapy in childhood depression. *Proceedings 4th UEP Congress.* Stockholm: Almquist & Wiksell

STONE F., RAWLEY V. & KELLER E. (1965) Clinical anxiety and the children's manifest anxiety scale. *J. Clin. Psychol.* **21**, 409–412

THOMAS A., CHESS S. & BIRCH H.G. (1968) *Temperament and Behavior Disorders in Children.* New York: Universities Press

TOOLAN J.M. (1962) Depression in children and adolescents. *Amer. J. Orthopsychiat.* **32**, 404–414

WARREN W. (1965) A study of adolescent psychiatric in-patients and the outcome six or more years later. II: the follow-up study. *J. Child Psychol. Psychiat.* **6**, 141–160

WEINBERG W.A., RUTMAN J., SULLIVAN L., PENICK E., DIETZ S. (1973) Depression in children referred to an educational diagnostic centre. *J. Paediat.* **83**, 1065–1072

WEINER I.B. (1967) Behaviour therapy in obsessive–compulsive neurosis: treatment of an adolescent boy. *Psychotherap. Theory Res. Prac.* **4**, 27–29

WHITE W.C. & DAVIS M.T. (1974) Vicarious extinction of phobic behaviour in early childhood. *J. Abnorm. Child. Psychol.* **2**, 25–32

WOLPE J. (1958) *Psychotherapy by Reciprocal Inhibition.* Stanford: Stanford University Press

YATES A.J. (1958) Symptoms and symptom substitution. *Psychol. Rev.* **65**, 377–384

YATES A.J. (1962) A comment on Bookbinder's critique of symptoms and symptom substitution. *Psychol. Reps.* **11**, 102–107

YULE W., SACKS B. & HERSOV L. (1974) Successful flooding treatment of a noise phobia in an eleven year old. *J. Behav. Ther. Exper. Psychiat.* **5**, 209–211

ZEITLYN H. (1972) A study of patients who attended the childrens department and later the adults department of the same psychiatric hospital. M. Phil dissertation: University of London

CHAPTER 19

School refusal

L. HERSOV

Prolonged or recurrent absence from school is a serious cause for educational concern. Illness is much the commonest reason for school absence. Some children are unlawfully withheld from school by parents to help at home, to keep an ill or lonely parent company, to do the shopping or carrying for a phobic house-bound mother. A few of these children are brought to psychiatric notice, but the majority of referrals to child psychiatric clinics for persistent nonattendance are either truants or children who refuse to go to school. The distinction is important on both theoretical and practical grounds.

Until about 33 years ago all forms of persistent absence from school were labelled as truancy. The word 'truant' derives from an old French word which means 'an assemblage of beggars'. The connotation of roguery remained throughout the 16th and 17th centuries, but the term 'truant' was only later applied to schoolboys who failed to attend school regularly. This came much more to the fore with the introduction of compulsory education in Britain in the second half of the 19th century. The 'truant' schoolboy was also dubbed lazy, idle, neglectful of his duties and prone to antisocial acts. Truancy was considered to be a precursor of delinquency and school boards appointed men to ensure regular attendance. These 'truant officers' were cordially disliked as were the correctional schools, 'truant schools' built to house and train the offending children.

ORIGIN OF THE CONCEPT OF SCHOOL REFUSAL

In 1932 Broadwin first described what he considered to be a variant of truancy, a form of persistent nonattendance at school which was later labelled 'School Phobia' by some (Johnson *et al* 1941; Suttenfield 1954; Eisenberg 1958a) and 'School Refusal' by others (Warren 1948; Hersov 1960a, b; Millar 1961; Kahn & Nursten 1962; Bowlby 1973). Broadwin (1932) from his study of a small number of cases considered the difficulties in school attendance

455

as symptoms of a personality problem occurring in children suffering from a deep-seated obsessional neurosis or displaying a neurotic character of the obsessional type. His original description has never been bettered for clarity and vividness and has been echoed in many subsequent papers in the literature.

'The child is absent from school for periods varying from several months to a year. The absence is consistent. At all times the parents know where the child is. It is with the mother or near the home. The reason for the truancy is incomprehensible to the parents and the school. The child may say that it is afraid to go to school, afraid of the teacher, or say that it does not know why it will not go to school. When at home it is happy and apparently carefree. When dragged to school it is miserable, fearful and at the first opportunity runs home despite the certainty of corporal punishment. The onset is generally sudden. The previous school work and conduct had been fair.'

Broadwin's original observation that these children feared something terrible happening to their mother, which made them run home for reassurance and relief of anxiety was repeated in many later clinical studies and is the basis for the oft repeated statement that the apparent fear of school is really a fear of leaving home.

Partridge (1939) in a study of truancy described a psychoneurotic group of ten cases which he maintained differed from the others in that their behaviour was not a means of avoiding simple environmental difficulties or a rebellion against unhappy circumstances. All the children liked school, were obedient and reasonably well-adjusted and in all cases the school was not a major factor in truancy. Warren (1948) further emphasised the distinction between these two forms of persistent nonattendance.

Johnson *et al* (1941) stressed the fairly sharp differentiation between absence from school stemming from a deep-seated psychoneurotic disorder, and the more frequent and common delinquent variety of nonattendance. These authors coined the descriptive term 'school phobia' which was taken up in subsequent papers (Goldberg 1953; Van Houten 1948; Talbot 1957; Suttenfield 1954; Coolidge *et al* 1957) and concluded that the syndrome was not a clear-cut clinical entity but consisted in fact of phobic tendencies overlapping with other hysterical or obsessional neurotic patterns. They noted that early cases left untreated might develop into a crippling neurosis in adulthood and described a chronic phobic state in a 31-year-old female who had suffered from 'school phobia' at 13 years.

Klein (1945) pointed out that the children's fear of school could be a fear of the teacher, of other pupils or of work with expectation of failure. However, he discounted the possibility of real stresses in the school situation and explained the fears in terms of fixation at the Oedipal or preOedipal level of psychosexual development.

Both Johnson *et al* (1941) and Warren (1948) found that fear of school with refusal to attend occurred in family settings where maternal anxiety, marital disharmony and parental inconsistency were often significant factors. Warren also found that the children suffered symptoms of acute anxiety and depression and showed obsessional and hysterical phenomena. These clinical observations tended to support the notion that school phobia/refusal is not a true clinical entity with a uniform aetiology, psychopathology, course, prognosis and treatment, but rather a collection of symptoms or a syndrome occurring against the background of a variety of psychiatric disorders (Hersov 1960a, b; Davidson 1960; Millar 1961; Kahn & Nursten 1962; Shapiro & Jegede 1973). The precipitating and aetiological factors vary with age, school setting, family factors and level of development and personality factors in the individual child.

DISTINCTION BETWEEN TRUANCY AND SCHOOL REFUSAL

The clinical distinction between children who truant from school and children who are unable to go to school has been clarified in further studies (Hersov 1960a, b; Cooper 1966) although Tyerman (1968) has criticised this distinction on the grounds that such efforts are rarely accurate or desirable.

Hersov (1960a) systematically compared 50 truants and 50 school refusers with an equal number of control cases; all were drawn from Maudsley Hospital patients. The findings showed that children referred for school refusal came from families with a higher incidence of neurosis, had less experience of maternal absence in infancy and childhood, were more often passive, dependent and overprotected but generally showed a high standard of work and behaviour at school. Their school refusal was most often one manifestation of a neurotic disorder in which anxiety and depressive affect were prominent. On the other hand children referred for truancy came from larger families where home discipline was inconsistent and had more often experienced paternal absence in infancy and paternal absence in later childhood. They had changed school frequently and their standard of work was poor. Their truancy was one indication of a conduct disorder which often involved other antisocial or delinquent behaviour. Tyerman (1968) enquiring into the causes of truancy found significant associations with excessive parental control (particularly by corporal punishment), dirty homes, uninterested parents, keeping the child at home in the past without good cause and homes in a working class area. There were also associations with unhappiness in the children, unsociability and failure to persevere. Cooper (1966) found children with school refusal differed from truants in that the former came from smaller families of a higher socioeconomic level where home discipline was over-anxious in quality whereas the truants came from families lacking in concern about school attendance which was reflected in the children by carelessness and defiance of school authority.

Tennent (1969) studied 65 boys detained in a Remand Home under Section 40 of the Education Act 1944 for nonattendance at school. These were only a small proportion (4 per cent) of the total number on remand and in theory had committed no offence other than not going to school. Of this group 29 were assessed as having some degree of psychiatric abnormality and 8 were diagnosed as school refusal (criteria undefined). Certain features said to be characteristic of school refusal also occurred among truants on remand. These were (a) a marked anxiety about going to school; (b) returning home when truanting from school rather than roaming alone or in company; (c) anxiety about events at home when at school; (d) psychiatric symptoms of an affective type. This suggests the coexistence of neurotic and conduct disorders in boys on remand for school nonattendance.

However, nonattenders at psychiatric clinics may differ from those in Remand Homes. Thus, Hersov (1960a, b) found that 37 of the 50 truants referred to the Children's Department of The Maudsley Hospital had appeared in a Juvenile Court for reasons other than nonattendance compared with only one case of school refusal.

Frick (1964) reviewing the literature on school refusal found that this group seen in a clinical setting were reported as less likely to lie and steal and this was also the case in the Maudsley series. The evidence from these various studies is that some truants may suffer from a psychiatric disorder (29 out of 65 in Tennent's 1969 series) and show anxiety symptoms of the same order as those nonattenders diagnosed as school refusal. However, school refusers are highly unlikely to display antisocial behaviour and the great majority show clear evidence of neurotic disorder. Their pattern of nonattendance has a distinctive form and quality different from that of truants. The family structure and pattern of relationships and parental management of the children is also very different in the two forms of nonattendance.

Clinical picture in school refusal

The problem often starts with vague complaints of school or reluctance to attend, progressing to total refusal to go to school or to remain in school in the face of persuasion, entreaty, recrimination and punishment by parents and pressure from teachers, family doctors and educational welfare officers. The behaviour may be accompanied by overt signs of anxiety or even panic when the time comes to go to school, and most children cannot even leave home to set out for school. Many who do, return home half-way there, and some children once at school rush home in a state of anxiety. Many children insist that they want to go to school and prepare to do so but cannot manage it when the time comes.

An acute onset is more often seen in younger children, whereas older children and adolescents usually show a more insidious development of school refusal. Precipitating factors can often be found at all ages; a minor accident, illness or operation, leaving home for a school holiday or camp, a move to a new house, a change of class or school, the departure or loss of a school friend, the death or illness of a relative to whom the child was closely attached. All these events appear to represent a threat to the individual child arousing anxiety which he cannot control.

In older children and adolescents there is often no abrupt or definite change in personality but a gradual withdrawal from peer group activities formerly enjoyed such as scouts or guides or youth clubs. The youngster ceases to go out, clings to and tries to control his mother and may express a general fear or dislike of the world outside home. He may also become stubborn, argumentative and critical in contrast to his earlier compliant behaviour and often this anger is directed against his mother. Very often there is no clear precipitating factor other than a change to senior school which may have occurred as long as a term ago. Closer examination may show other behaviour problems or symptoms of a depressive disorder, or more rarely evidence that the behaviour in regard to school is part of a psychotic illness (Berg *et al* 1974a). Complex long-standing family psychopathology is common and frequently the earlier personality development of the child has been deviant in regard to social relationships with other children, anxiety when entering into new situations and a lack of normal development of independence and sexual identification. Very often the school refusal is one indication of the young adolescent's general inability to cope with the increased demands for an independent existence outside the family, and entry into normal peer group relationships.

When the clinical picture is in keeping with the above description the diagnosis is hardly in doubt. When it assumes a 'somatic disguise' (Eisenberg 1958b) careful assessment by the family doctor or paediatrician will clarify the basic problems. Here complaints may take the form of loss of appetite, nausea, vomiting, syncope, headache, abdominal pain, vague malaise, diarrhoea, limb pains, tachycardia (Schmitt 1971). These complaints occur in the mornings before school or even at school without any overt expression of fear about school which is only elicited on careful enquiry. At times the somatic symptoms are not actually experienced but fearfully anticipated, so that the child may avoid school in case he might faint or vomit in situations such as school assembly or morning prayers.

Prevalence

The prevalence of school refusal has proved difficult to establish as most of the earlier estimates were based on clinical populations covering a wide age range who have been referred to child psychiatric or child guidance clinics. The reported rate in these settings varied from 1 per cent of a complete sample of attenders over 10 years (Chazan 1962) to 8 per cent (Kahn & Nursten 1962). Smith (1970) found a rate of 3·8 per cent among children with neurotic disorders attending the Maudsley Hospital Children's Department.

However, the prevalance in a total population of 10 and 11-year-old children on the Isle of Wight was less than 3 per cent of all children with psychiatric disorders (Rutter, Tizard & Whitmore 1970). Adams *et al* (1966) and Rabiner and Klein (1969) have noted the low prevalence of black children with school phobia attending clinics in the USA. Rutter *et al* (1974) have found a surprisingly low figure for nonattendance at school generally among 10-year-old West Indian children in an Inner London borough.

It is very likely that some family doctors deal effectively with early or incipient cases of school refusal which never reach a psychiatric or child guidance clinic. Shepherd *et al* (1966) found in a study of a national sample of general practitioners that four-fifths indicated that they would themselves manage a straight-forward case of persistent school nonattendance while one-fifth would refer such children to a clinic.

Rutter *et al* (1976), in a study of 14-year-old Isle of Wight children, found 15 cases of school refusal either in association with an affective disorder or with other psychiatric symptoms. This is in marked contrast to the negligible prevalence at age 10 and 11 years.

The various studies show a pattern of prevalence which appears highest at three periods of school-going age. At entry and soon after between the ages of 5 and 7 years, probably associated with separation anxiety, at 11 years associated with change of school and a variety of neurotic disorders and again at 14 years and older. It seems likely that the last group may differ substantially from the others in the type and severity of psychiatric disorder, frequency of depressive states, and in the outcome of treatment and prognosis.

Significance of school for the child and adolescent

It is clear that going to school makes many demands upon a child which alter with age and school progress. Klein (1945) has described school as the first testing ground in society which lies outside the more protecting atmosphere of home. Going to school involves the first of many continuing separations from home and submission to outside rules and standards in a situation from which there is no escape and over which little control can be exerted. Parents are unable to intervene to save the child as they may have done up till now. Anxiety about separation from mother and home can become overwhelming and affect attendance.

Going to school means a new and exacting situation imposing many pressures. New skills are learnt but there is also the chance of relative failure instead of recognition and success as previously. New experiences and demands have to be faced, often without preparation, in competition with peers and under the eye of a mainly impersonal adult authority. A child is judged at school by performance (rather than reputation and intention) and by qualities for which he is not responsible such as intellectual endowment, race or social class. He is exposed to competitive physical activity and rougher children. It can also be very stressful for a prepubertal or late matur-ing child to be in a class with mature early adolescents who are more worldly and have very different interests and aspirations.

Moore (1966) in a longitudinal study of children's development found that a number of ordinary children have difficulties in adjusting to primary school. About 80 per cent experienced difficulties in the infants' school, of which nearly a half were of moderate or marked severity. The number decreased slightly in junior school but a substantial number still showed mild disturb-ance and these were fewer in boys than girls. From 6 to 8 years significantly more problems occurred in middle class and in only children. The commonest and most persistent type of difficulty was a general reluctance to go to school which was related to overdependence. This affected the majority of children to some degree at 6 years, decreased at 7 years, rose to a secondary peak at 8 years following transfer to junior school and then dwindled steadily till 11 years, although at that time one boy in three is still showing reluctance. Moore (1966) found that a negative attitude to school is shown by more boys than girls at every age.

Mitchell and Shepherd (1967), in a study of a random sample of over 6000 Buckinghamshire children age 5 to 15 years, found that dislike of school was associated with poor attainment and signs of anxiety at home, also more frequent headaches and pains in the stomach. An interesting point was that below the age of 11 years the children who disliked going to school had an attendance record little different from those who liked school, showing perhaps that they attended school in spite of their own inclinations and probably because of firm parental pressure. This is a group which warrants further study, particularly as such children are not included in clinic studies.

Many children who never reach a doctor or psychiatric clinic have experienced some if not all of the associated somatic symptoms of incipient school refusal at some time, e.g. loss of appetite, nausea, abdominal pain, urinary frequency or diarrhoea. Some have probably suffered from varying degrees of anxiety or even panic at the beginning of a new term or when changing school. In most instances the symptoms have been transient and successfully mastered often with the firm support of a parent and teacher. But in other children the anxiety becomes overwhelming, the parents' efforts of no avail and persistent school refusal then ensues.

Differential diagnosis

Broadwin (1932) in his classic paper viewed both everyday truancy and the atypical group of nonattenders he described, not as clinical entities but as different manifestations of total personality adjustment to difficult or threatening situations at home or school. Subsequent clinical studies have confirmed the validity of his description of the second group and there is also broad agreement about parental personality behaviour and symptomatology (Johnson *et al* 1941; Waldfogel *et al* 1957; Eisenberg 1958a; Malmquist 1965) although different patterns of parent–child interaction have also been noted (Hersov 1960a, b; Bowlby 1973). Weiner (1970) considers school refusal to be a clearly definable psychological disorder and there is some evidence that it is a precursor of adult psychiatric disorder.

The differential diagnosis in the first instance is between school refusal, truancy and nonattendance due to voluntary withholding by a parent. It is then necessary to decide within the group presenting with school refusal whether the behaviour is due to separation anxiety, a phobic manifestation, an aspect of the depressive illness, a psychotic disorder or a personality disorder.

Aetiology and psychological mechanisms

Agreement on the broad clinical phenomena has not been paralleled by agreement on the diagnostic labels of 'school phobia' or 'school refusal' or on the psychological mechanisms responsible for the behaviour. However, the literature shows that this form of persistent nonattendance is most often a manifestation of neurotic symptom formation. The term 'school phobia' is used by those who explain the behaviour in terms of individual psychopathology based on the classical psychoanalytic theory of phobic symptom formation, arising from the externalisation of frightening impulses and their displacement on to a previously neutral object or situation which is then avoided, e.g. teacher or school (Suttenfield 1954; Waldfogel *et al* 1957; Sperling 1961; 1967). The explanations based on learning theory also emphasise individual psychopathology in which the learning of maladaptive responses through respondent or operant conditioning or a mixture of both, leads to avoidance behaviour maintained by fear reduction and resultant 'school phobia' (Ross 1972a, b).

Other writers offer simple explanations that such children overvalue themselves and their achievements and try to maintain an unrealistic self-image which if threatened in school leads to anxiety, avoidance of school and attempts to maintain a narcissistic picture of the self, aided by a permissive mother (Leventhal & Sills 1964; Leventhal *et al* 1967). This hypothesis was not supported using an objective test of self-evaluation on British schoolchildren (Nichols & Berg 1970) and the latter suggest that although school phobia is a recognisable syndrome it is bound to be the product of more than one set of circumstances.

The originators of the label 'school phobia' (Johnson *et al* 1941) while describing the mixture of phobic, hysterical and obsessional features in these neurotic children also stressed the importance of a variety of precipitating factors and a particular quality in the mother–child relationship. The children were described as unduly dependent and therefore likely to be caught up in maternal anxieties and preoccupations. In later papers (Estes *et al* 1956; Johnson 1957; Davidson 1960) the view was put forward that the term school phobia emphasised a symptom (Reger 1962; Radin 1967) rather than the true underlying nature of the condition which was anxiety about leaving mother rather than simply a fear of school. This anxiety develops within a pathological mother–child relationship of mutually hostile dependency with an intense need for both to be in close physical proximity. The term 'separation anxiety' was used to describe the response to attempts to alter this pathological emotional state (Estes *et al* 1956) by pressure to go to school.

Later empirical studies supported this finding. Waldfogel *et al* (1957) found that the source of anxiety about school was the child's fear of being separated from mother. Of the 53 children studied 46 were 10 years old or younger so that the disorder occurred most commonly in younger children. Coolidge *et al* (1957) also found an acute onset of anxiety with more or less persistent clinging behaviour in 27 children, mostly girls, aged 8 years or below whereas the group aged 9 years or more appeared to have a more gradual onset in which the fear of school was part of a more generalised anxiety. Eisenberg (1958a) in a systematic study of 11 preschool children and 15 elementary schoolchildren found a basic fear of leaving mother or less commonly father. Hersov (1960a, b) found fear of separation from home in 17 out of 50 cases of school refusal alongside other fears of teachers, schoolmates and academic failure. Smith (1970) found obvious separation anxiety in 12 out of 63 cases of school refusal and anxiety when away from a parent in 9 cases. This occurred more often in children under the age of 8 years. It appears that separation anxiety is not invariably found in school refusal and that it occurs more often in younger children. However, Berg (1970) using a measure of dependency in teenage school refusers admitted to hospital found that cases of long standing without acute onset, appeared more attached to their parents than those with acute onset.

The hypothesis of general separation anxiety is therefore not supported by the clinical evidence and it appears that in some children anxiety is mainly related to some aspect of the school situation and in others their main anxiety is about leaving home and separating from parents. Eysenck and Rachman (1965b) would use the term 'school phobia' for the first group and 'separation anxiety in the school situation' for the latter, while Frick (1964) stresses the need for more research into the differentiating factors. Yates (1970) puts forward an interactional theory based on learning principles. In some children anxiety may have become attached to separation situations and been reinforced and generated by maternal anxiety. When a child goes to school he may or may not develop varying degrees of intensity of fear of school depending on his experiences there and his mother's reaction to anxiety. The implications for treatment by behaviour therapy will be discussed later. Weiner (1970) also stresses the importance of age in relation to existing psychopathology and the need to distinguish between phobic nonattendance and nonattendance due to other reasons. He suggests that this can be gauged to a certain extent from the type of experience or situation which triggers off the school refusal.

DEPRESSION AND SCHOOL REFUSAL

Depressed mood in children with school refusal has been reported by many authors (Warren 1948; 1965; Harrington & Hassan 1958; Kahn & Nursten 1962; 1964; Clyne 1966). Depression has been considered an affective symptom which may occur in any of the categories of clinical psychiatric disorder presenting as school refusal (Kahn & Nursten 1962) or as the underlying disorder masked by the psychoneurotic reactions of school phobia (Glaser 1959). Campbell (1955) regards school refusal as a manifestation of manic depressive psychosis with a strong family history and Agras (1959) puts forward the thesis that school phobia is part of the natural history of the depressive disorders and is but one of the modes of presentation of such disorders in childhood occurring within a depressive family constellation. This view is based on a small number of young children (7) not all of whom showed frank school refusal, and where there appeared to be no independent psychiatric examination of the children. The duration, degree, persistence and severity of depressed mood is not stated and seems entirely based on the accounts of the mothers who were themselves depressed. Agras (1959) puts forward the notion that either parents or child mirror the others' depression and so stimulate a regressive relationship. The evidence presented is of excessively dependent behaviour by the children from an early age rather than a true regression and it seems more likely that children will model the parents' symptoms rather than the reverse.

Hersov (1960a, b) and Davidson (1960) describe depressive reactions in children with school refusal occurring in 10 out of 50 cases and 23 out of 30 cases respectively. In the latter series the children were withdrawn, unable to take part in social activities, refusing to go out to an entertainment, often sitting about unable to concentrate or occupy themselves and some complained of 'awful feelings' in the morning, were mildly retarded with a damping down of activity. Hersov (1960a, b) found that 10 per cent of mothers and 8 per cent of fathers had required treatment for depressive illness, while Davidson (1960) found that 14 out of 30 mothers in her series had showed depressive symptoms or required treatment. She also found a high incidence of deaths or threatened deaths in the form of severe illness in close relatives or friends of the family preceding the onset of school refusal. Frommer (1972) writes that school refusal is one of the commonest presentations of phobic illness in children but appears to regard the phobic symptoms as secondary to a depressive illness ((Frommer 1967) although the children 'rarely showed a frankly depressive picture or its typical mood disorder and sometimes even denied feelings of depression'. Frommer believes that once the depressive illness has responded to treatment the secondary symptoms clear up apart from a small group which present major problems of treatment and management. Gittelman-Klein and Klein (1971) take issue with this view of depressive illness on the basis of their results from a controlled trial of imipramine treatment in school phobia. They believe that signs of demoralisation in children are equated by some authors with depression. Using a definition of depression which emphasises inability to experience pleasure and a sense of incompetence as central to the diagnosis, they found that none of their 34 school phobics had lost the capacity to experience pleasure or lost all sense of competence although 12 were rated as quite depressed. They found that almost all the children held the belief, unlike depressed adults, that they would miraculously recover and return to school. They regard school phobic children as falling within a large group of separation-anxious children and that imipramine acts to modify this separation anxiety which may in turn enable the child to return to school. This in turn is related to factors independent of drug effect, in the school and family, as well as the nature of the psychotherapeutic contact.

Clear-cut depressive disorders have been reported in older children and adolescents (Warren 1965; Glaser 1967) but Weiner (1970) states that a depressed youngster may refuse school not only because he is lethargic and slowed down but also due to acute anxiety or somatic symptoms in the school setting, symptoms which carry specific dynamic or therapeutic implications in their own right. However, it is clear that the presence of depressive illness and/or psychiatric illness is an important factor in the assessment of school refusal in all children and particularly in adolescents, for Shaffer's (1974) study of successful suicide in children and young adolescents showed that 4 cases had presented with school refusal prior to the suicidal act.

LEARNING THEORY AND BEHAVIOUR THERAPY IN SCHOOL REFUSAL

Ross (1972a, b) has described the place of behaviour therapy in the treatment of psychological disorders in children. He sets out clearly the premise on which this therapy is based and the application of learning principles to both the explanation and treatment of various disorders. He writes that 'while the learning orientation logically includes the implicit acceptance of past events as contributing to the development of the child's present difficulty, the behaviour therapist considers a detailed knowledge of the child's history unnecessary for arriving at his treatment plans' (1972b p. 901). The emphasis is on detailed and intensive assessment of the current conditions in which the behaviour occurs or fails to occur.

Ross (1972b) describes school phobia as a maladaptive avoidance response maintained by fear reduction which calls for modification or elimination. There may be either fear of school or fear of leaving home and only the former is strictly speaking a school phobia. The distinction is akin to that made by Eysenck and Rachman (1965), on the grounds that separation anxiety and school phobias require different treatment plans. Eysenck and Rachman (1965a) give more attention and weight to factors in the school situation, list in some detail possible sources of anxiety at school and are critical of studies which describe or discuss parent–child relationships and personality factors. The illustrative case history focusses on traumatic experiences in the school situation and the desensitisation treatment devised to deal with this allied to a programme of graded re-entry into school with no reference to other factors in the family situation which may have played a part in the original school refusal nor to the considerable additional treatment required following a relapse in school refusal.

However, Ross (1972b) states that the complex behaviour shown in school refusal has components of both a respondent and operant nature, for while the avoidance response may have originally served a fear—reducing function, it is then likely to be maintained by the reinforcements available in the home to the child who is not going to school. Such behaviour with a long reinforcement history becomes difficult to treat. Yates (1970) argues that the term school phobia is an oversimplification pre-empting the question whether the child is refusing to attend school or refusing to leave home. He suggests a possible interaction between these two sorts of behaviour based on the developmental and family factors which influence the growing child. Parents (mainly mothers) act as strongly reinforcing stimuli in the preschool period in that they are a refuge for frightened and uncertain children. Separation experiences in these children may be associated with increased fear and return to mother which reduces fear. Mothers may also induce or generate fear in the child by their own undue anxiety about letting the child go. If intense fear at school develops it will depend on both school experiences and mothers' (parents') reaction. The average child masters anxiety and finds school rewarding because of success, amongst other things, in school work, games and peer relationships. The vulnerable child does not find sufficiently rewarding school experiences to counteract any arousal of anxiety by traumatic experiences such as a critical or unsympathetic teacher. If this child has already developed a response of separation anxiety leading to overdependence on home as a safe refuge, this will be evoked by any particularly stressful school situations and responded to by a parent (mother) in a predictable way. Hetherington and Martin (1972) describe anxiety responses to separation in overprotected children which support Yates' formulation.

Yates (1970) thus makes an attempt at finding common ground between psychodynamic and learning theory explanations of school refusal and his formulation finds some backing in clinical experience for many children with school refusal do have a history of separation difficulties in nursery and infants' school preceding the onset of frank school refusal and their mothers show a stereotyped way of dealing with these difficulties which tends to perpetuate and reinforce the school avoidance rather than help the child over it.

Miller, Barrett and Hampe (1974) review the current state of knowledge in the behavioural treatment of school phobias and conclude that the lack of well-controlled studies means reliance upon clinical judgement and experience in the absence of general principles derived from adequate research.

The earliest description (Lazarus 1960) described the use of systematic desensitisation therapy using a hierarchy centering around the theme of separation from mother. Lazarus and Abramovitz (1962) used a variant of this method called 'emotive imagery' which involved a hierarchy of situations in which a hero image dealt with problems of self-assertion in the school setting, so called 'assertive training'.

Ross (1972a, b) is critical of the untested assumptions as to how this counter-conditioning works either at a physiological or psychological level. Lazarus *et al* (1965) used both respondent and operant approaches in a planned programme to deal with a case of school refusal in a 9-year-old boy. Emotive imagery was given up in favour of in vivo desensitisation in which the boy was exposed to increasingly difficult steps along the main dimension of re-entry to school. When anxiety was less, operant methods using tokens and rewards contingent upon going to school and remaining there alone were introduced. Parents were also instructed how to deal with situations at home which afforded reinforcement for school avoidance and secondary gain. A mild tranquilliser was used but considered ineffective and an interchange of therapists did not seem to affect the course of treatment. The case report is of interest because it clearly shows the need to involve parents in treatment in difficult cases. There must be active cooperation by and with the school as well as considerable sensitivity on the part of the therapists to gauge the sources and level of the child's anxiety and gain his confidence. Ross (1972) states that the apparent simplicity of the method should not mislead others into believing it is without risk and can be carried out by untrained or poorly trained individuals.

Other methods reported are reciprocal inhibition (Chapel 1967) and an example of systematic desensitisation which appears to also use the operant approach (Garvey & Hegrenes 1966). Patterson (1965) used a method of conditioning via successive approximations and Smith and Sharpe (1970) have used implosive therapy in the consulting room. Hersen (1970a, b; 1971a) has given thought to involving parents in retraining programmes connected with the treatment of their child's school refusal. Tahmisian and McReynolds (1971) report the case study of a 13-year-old school phobic girl successfully treated by her parents with instrumental behaviour-shaping treatment methods after an unsuccessful attempt with systematic desensitisation.

The total number of cases reported in the literature is relatively small and the cases are difficult to compare. So far there are no controlled studies nor any comparison studies with more traditional psychotherapeutic approaches especially as the latter methods have proved to be effective in all but the most severe problems. Behaviour therapists (Yates 1970) have argued that by using methods ensuring early return to school the psychodynamic therapists have in fact employed SD-R technique. This may be true but it does not obviate the need for group comparisons using different techniques. Hersen (1971b) has also criticised the absence of careful follow-up study of single patients reported in the literature. Most frequently reports of school and social adjustment are omitted and only the response in terms of school attendance is reported (Lazarus 1960; Lazarus & Abramowitz 1962; Garvey & Hegrenes 1966) but these factors are included in more recent case reports (Chapel 1967; Smith & Sharp 1970).

Kennedy (1965; 1971a) has described the rapid treatment of 50 school phobics. Cases were carefully selected according to a classification into Type I School Phobia (Coolidge *et al* 1957). This would appear to be a true phobic reaction, 'a conditioned emotional response to the separation that occurs when attending school, that is being left by one's mother to one's own devices in a school setting' (Kennedy 1971b, p. 272). Type II or the 'way-of-life phobia' (Coolidge *et al* 1957) does not appear to be a true phobic reaction but one of a complex series of maladaptive behaviours over time. Kennedy (1965) claimed that a logical and empirical differential diagnosis could be made on the basis of any 7 of the 10 differentiating symptoms he listed. Using these methods of diagnosis and treatment he claimed complete remission in 50 cases. Follow-up over several years failed to show that any other problems had appeared and the children continued to attend school.

Kennedy's first paper stimulated great interest when it appeared and his methods were used by many clinicians although no-one has yet repeated his study in spite of the clarity of the account of methods and classification. Kennedy (1965) did suggest that the disorders in Type I School Phobia were of the transient variety in the first place and that treatment may only accelerate or facilitate remission. Yates (1970) remarks on the early referral within 2 to 3 days of onset of school refusal so that the spontaneous remission rate would no doubt have been high if Kennedy had used half his subjects as an untreated control group.

In a later paper Kennedy (1971b) replies to some of the criticisms of his first study. He accepts that the cases were carefully selected on the basis of a preponderance of Type I symptoms and that because of positive factors in the family background the likelihood of return to school was high whatever treatment was undertaken. The value of the intervention lies in the rapid help it gives to parents, teachers and children in what is a rather serious problem.

Kennedy (1971b) also notes that there have been problems in distinguishing between Type I and II cases both at his clinic and at others. Mixed types are found with only half Type I symptoms and success is greater the higher the percentage of Type I symptoms. The generally favourable prognosis does not hold in well-established cases of Type II school refusal where it is impossible to secure the necessary amount of cooperation from parents, so that such cases require a mixed treatment programme with heavy outside pressure to get children back to school, as well as much supportive help for parents. In such cases a strict behaviourist approach is not as effective as a programme which combines the best aspects of both behaviourist and psychotherapeutic approaches. Patience, repetition and support as well as time for catharsis are essential and the focal point of failure seemed always to be a breakdown of cooperation and rapport with parents who lost confidence and moved elsewhere for treatment. The outcome in these cases was generally poor often with no return to school at all on a formal basis.

Kennedy (1965, 1971a, b) has made a real contribution to the management of school refusal by showing how early intervention with help from school authorities, given good parental cooperation and a defined treatment programme can produce good results if the criterion of success is simply return to school. His observations on the more complex types of school refusal echo those of others and have led many to conclude that the problems of family relationships require much more attention than they have been given in the past.

FAMILY INTERACTION IN SCHOOL REFUSAL

Although many of the earlier papers on school refusal refer in passing to family involvement or family neurosis, this aspect was not considered in any detail and the focus remained on mother–child interaction (Johnson *et al* 1941; Warren 1948; Davidson 1960; Kahn & Nursten 1962). Messer (1964) described the family treatment of a school phobic child in which he saw the whole family for regular interviews over a 2-year period. He regarded the child's behaviour as the symbolic *public* expression of a breakdown in family equilibrium arising after the mother had been seriously ill in hospital. He suggests that mother unconsciously kept the boy at home to watch over her and in this way she coped with her own anxiety. She maintained a dominant position in the family by threats that, if the patient did not behave, she would die. The boy who was panic-stricken in school also entertained fantasies of saving his mother's life by remaining at home. Family treatment helped a depressed but supportive father to become active enough to take the boy to school where he was able to remain in spite of a relapse in mother's illness.

Malmquist (1965) also deals with the question of an 'interacting family neurosis' in school refusal including significant relatives as well as the nuclear family in his formulation. He mentions the 'secondary' role accorded to father in most papers but is of the opinion that fathers are often an integral part of the family and child's emotional conflicts. Bowlby (1975) believes that a large majority of cases of school refusal can be understood as the products of one or more of four main patterns of family interaction. (a) Mother or more rarely father is a sufferer from chronic anxiety regarding attachment figures and retains the child at home to be a companion. (b) The child fears that something dreadful may happen to mother or possibly father while he is at school and so remains at home to prevent it happening. (c) The child fears that something dreadful may happen to himself if he is away from home and so remains at home to prevent that happening. (d) Mother or more rarely father fears that something dreadful will happen to the child while he is at school and so keeps him at home. Pattern (a) is the commonest but may be combined with any of the others. In the majority of cases mother is the principal agent but sometimes father is (Eisenberg 1958a; Choi 1961; Clyne 1966; Sperling 1967).

Bowlby (1973) states the need for more systematic data regarding personalities and childhood histories of parents and grandparents in order to understand the dynamics and historical origins of families in which the parents invert the parent–child relationship by demanding care from the child. There is also an attempt to explain the reasons why a child fears that harm will befall his mother while he is at school, a finding reported in many papers (Broadwin 1932; Talbot 1957; Hersov 1960a, b; Lazarus 1960; Garvey & Hegrenes 1966; Kennedy 1965). Bowlby (1973) discusses the usual explanation that the child harbours unconscious hostile wishes against mother and fears they will come true but favours a more realistic explanation which attributes the child's fears wholly or at least in part to real experiences such as actual events of death or illness in a family or threats by parents that they will commit suicide or that their child's behaviour will make them ill (Klein 1945; Messer 1964; Garvey & Hegrenes 1966; Argles & Mackenzie 1970).

Unfortunately Bowlby (1973) does not present detailed evidence on different patterns of family interaction. He cites some studies (Hersov 1960a, b; Davidson 1960; Britton 1969) which found a high incidence of psychiatric disorder, especially affective disorders among the parents of school refusers, a fairly consistent finding in clinical samples where this particular area has been looked at (Millman 1961; Berg, Butler & Pritchard 1974b). But there is really no way of telling how commonly these family patterns occur and how they are related to other family variables such as size, the child's ordinal position, socioeconomic status, etc.

Bowlby (1973) also discards the evidence from certain studies (Klein 1945; Hersov 1960b; Chazan 1962) that events or situations in school could have a significant part in causing school refusal, regarding the child's account as little more than rationalisation. This may be so in some cases and in others parents may unwittingly provide a child with an explanation through their own attempts to find a reason for the behaviour in the school situation. Clinical experience over the years has convinced the author that complaints by children and parents about any aspect of the school situation should be taken seriously and investigated as carefully as possible before discarding them as important factors in aetiology and treatment. Malmquist (1965) while expounding the virtues of a family approach, warns against the tendency to invoke family dynamics as the sole explanation so ignoring individual psychopathology and social experience outside the family. It seems reasonable to explore in depth the child's own perception of the school situation if one is to fully understand the reasons for nonattendance.

Skynner (1974) has recently reviewed those studies in the literature bearing on the role of fathers in the aetiology of school refusal. He cites as typical, comments which describe a father's failure to play a strong supportive and responsible parental role, their problems in having uncertain sexual identification and in competing with their wives for the maternal role. Even where case studies (Hersov 1960b) describe fathers as firm and controlling, Skynner regards this behaviour to be more apparent than real, often no more than defensive rigidity. He suggests that the neglect of the father's crucial role in the family dynamics and failure to bring him into treatment results from the traditional mother-centred approach in child psychiatry (Coolidge & Brodie 1974). He then describes the use of a conjoint family technique to help loosen the original exclusive mutual attachment between mother and child. However he also brings in the therapists' need to accept an authoritarian role within the social network of services provided for children and families and concludes that 'Clearly school phobia is best understood as a psychosocial problem rather than as a purely medical intra-psychic or even intra-familial disorder'. The reader may wonder just what forces were really effective in returning the child to school, the interpretations within the family sessions, or other social forces.

TREATMENT AND OUTCOME IN SCHOOL REFUSAL

Although there have been different points of emphasis in treatment, methods were broadly of a psychotherapeutic kind until the advent of behaviour therapy. Johnson *et al* (1941) emphasised family factors in treatment so focussing on both mother and child while also paying attention to the child's individual problems. Estes *et al* (1956) thought that therapy of the child alone was inadequate as the neurosis originated with the mother. Talbot (1957) proposed treatment programmes involving child, parents and school personnel, with the proviso that the older the child the more direct the treatment with the child. An initial step was to relieve all pressure from school attendance thus relieving tension in parents and school personnel and anxiety in the therapist. After allowing aggression to the therapist to be expressed in a good relationship the timing and method of re-entry to school is of great importance because anxieties about school which were quiescent until then are likely to reappear. Talbot (1957) describes a method of gradually reintroducing the child into the phobic situation at first accompanied by parents, then one parent, then a friend, followed by gradually increasing periods in the schoolroom on the grounds that exposure to the feared experience will bring the conflict into the open. Eysenck and Rachman (1965) regard this as a behaviour therapy type of treatment plan reminiscent of the familiar anxiety-hierarchy used in behaviour therapy and in some ways more suitable for the treatment of separation anxiety in a school situation.

Waldfogel *et al* (1959) have described brief intervention methods in the school situation and Sperling (1961) gives indications for a psychoanalytic first-aid programme in 'acute' school phobia brought on by a traumatic event in contrast to 'induced' school phobia where the damage is more insidious and results mainly from a pathological parent–child relationship. Waldfogel *et al* (1957) shift the emphasis in treatment from the fear of school to fear of separation from mother by expression of fantasy and interpretation. Strong support and encouragement of independent activities at the time of termination of treatment are also emphasised. Most of the psychotherapeutic approaches (Davidson 1960) emphasis the simultaneous treatment of mother and child and try to deal with separation problems without actually separating parent and child.

In contrast, residential treatment (usually in a hospital inpatient unit) has been advocated (Warren 1948; Weiss & Cain 1964; Barker 1968; Berg 1970; Hersov 1974). This course is usually indicated when the child's symptoms are of such severe pathology that there is no response to other forms of treatment and where the family environment is in itself such a pathogenic factor in supporting and maintaining the disorder that it blocks effective treatment. In other instances the child's disorder is an important part of family interaction with the disturbed child's presence maintaining a balance while also gratifying the child and reinforcing his behaviour. Admission to a unit may also ensure regular treatment (Hersov 1974) in addition to the benefits of a therapeutic environment in mastering anxiety over separation experiences (Fleck 1972).

Other contrasting approaches concern the issue of timing of return to school and the amount of pressure that can and should be applied to ensure attendance. Klein (1945) was the first proponent of early return to school using pressure up to the point of harshness in an effort to get the child back into the school building. Others have argued in favour of early return (Talbot 1957; Eisenberg 1958b; Rodriguez *et al* 1959; Berryman 1959; Glaser 1959; Kennedy 1965) on the grounds that continued absence creates secondary problems due to missing schoolwork, loss of friendships, the secondary gain of being at home, the absence of a healthy environment for emotional growth (Eisenberg 1959).

Leventhal *et al* (1967) outlined a therapeutic strategy for returning the child to school. Their emphasis is on the manipulative aspect of the child's behaviour and on the element of 'refusal' rather than phobic avoidance or separation anxiety. The small number of case histories (five) may have been specially selected but convey the flavour of the struggle between child and parents which is so familiar to any therapist who has tried to deal with school refusal in the older child or adolescent. The essence of these authors' tough-minded approach is; an early a return to school as practicable; the selection of the person or persons most likely to achieve success and helping them to act most effectively; an increasing gradient of pressure to return upon the child; and attempts to crystallise attitudes and tactics around the specific issue of return to school rather than side issues of illness, change of school, home tuition, etc. The observations on the way in which parents and others collude in the school avoidance so that consistent pressure is not maintained are pertinent as is the need to recognise these rationalisations and deceptions. Leventhal *et al* (1967) believe that 'it is likely that a dramatic concrete demonstration to the child of his true position vis-à-vis society and its requirements is much more effective than any verbal explanations, symbolic play or other forms of psychotherapeutic influence'.

Greenbaum (1964) makes a spirited attack on those who advocate early return to school and criticises Klein's (1945) suggestion that regression will occur if the child is allowed to remain at home. He also argues that although rapid return may not preclude resolution of the underlying conflict it does appear to seriously reduce the chances of remaining in treatment long enough to achieve this for the phobia may spread to include the therapist if pressure is applied. Davidson (1960) takes the view that firmness and pressure are appropriate when the time is right but if not it may provoke panic and even a suicidal attempt. She favours compromise including home tuition as a valuable temporary measure in depressed children until gradual reintroduction to school can begin, but in some cases residential school placement or hospital inpatient treatment is necessary.

The outcome of treatment is good whatever the treatment. Kennedy's (1965) 100 per cent success rate is unusual but in most treatment series the success rate is usually about two-thirds or more (Hersov 1960a, b; Davidson 1960; Coolidge; Brodie & Feeney 1964) but the prognosis seems related to severity of disorder, age of the child and the time between onset of symptoms and beginning of treatment. Rodriguez *et al* (1959) found that the prognosis was poor with children over the age of 11 years, a 36 per cent success rate as against an 89 per cent success rate in return to school in children under the age of 11 years. The findings suggest that more serious pathology is found in the older children and their families (Coolidge *et al* 1960).

Cases admitted to hospital also tend to be older with symptoms of longer duration and it is also likely that these patients and families are more deeply disturbed and have not responded to outpatient treatment. Berg (1970) reporting on 27 adolescents with school phobia treated as inpatients found that 59 per cent were attending school satisfactorily on follow-up, the remainder were undoubted failures. Of those with satisfactory attendance one-third were still poorly adapted to home and social circumstances outside the school and family. Weiss and Cain (1964) reporting on the outcome of residential treatment in 16 patients of 8–16 years including 9 adolescents found that 14 were attending school after 9 months treatment while 2 still were still in hospital. Weiss and Burke (1967) reporting a 5–10-year follow-up of 14 patients found the outcome for school and work good in all but one, but half of the group still had difficulty in personal and social relationships and several were still unable to sever ties with their families.

There is considerable interest both theoretical and practical in looking at what happens to children with school refusal when they become adults. In one study in the USA (Nursten 1963) a small group (16 cases) of young women were followed up in late adolescence or early adulthood (16–29 years—median 19 years) and interviewed 7–14 years after the completion of treatment. Four had required subsequent treatment for absence from school and college but 6 were in their last year at school, 5 in college, 2 holding jobs and 3 were married. Most were able to draw away from their families but social contacts remained limited and those married were very dependent on their husbands. As a group they had done well in spite of absence from school.

Warren (1965) in a follow-up study of adolescent psychiatric inpatients followed up 6 years or more after discharge described 16 youngsters (7 male, 9 female, 12–16 years) with school phobia, 4 of whom were found later to be seriously handicapped by phobic states, 3 lived rather limited lives because of minor phobic difficulties, 3 had other neurotic difficulties and 6 were quite well. Hodgman and Braiman (1965) writing on early university drop-outs consider that typical school refusal or phobic problems are seen in an older college population, sometimes with an early history of school refusal. Pittman *et al* (1968) described 11 cases of work phobia mainly in males of whom 9 had shown in early life a significant reluctance to go to school or overt school phobia.

Tyrer and Tyrer (1974) studied the prevalence of school refusal in 240 adult psychiatric patients and 120 controls matched for age and sex, using a specially designed questionnaire. School refusal, particularly in adolescence, occurred significantly more often among psychiatric patients and the conclusion is drawn that some children who present with problems of school refusal are at risk for psychiatric disorder in adult life, but most school refusers will become normal adults. Berg *et al* (1974c) also studied the prevalence of past school phobia in an adult population of female agoraphobic patients (786) compared with 57 nonagoraphobic neurotic controls. Past school phobia predicted an earlier onset of agoraphobia but the authors conclude that school phobia leads to agoraphobia in only a small proportion of cases, and that both conditions reflect a lasting tendency to neurotic illness. In both studies the criteria for assuming the existence of earlier school refusal/school phobia were very similar and both have the weakness inherent in a retrospective study depending on memory recall of past events. However, the trend of the findings is similar.

AN ASSESSMENT AND TREATMENT PLAN IN SCHOOL REFUSAL

It is evident that school refusal is a syndrome of emotional disturbance occurring in a number of psychiatric disorders and appearing at different ages and developmental stages in a child's life during the period between school-entry and school-leaving. 'The same final state may be reached from different initial conditions and in different ways' (Young 1964). It is improbable that there will be a uniform aetiology, psychopathology and prognosis and that one method of treatment will be appropriate for every case. The common themes which are discerned in many cases should not disguise the fact that each is a unique clinical problem which requires systematic assessment and a planned treatment programme with the aim of early return to school.

Assessment

The way in which the referral to a psychiatric clinic is made can be an important factor. General practitioners may be the first to see a child with somatic symptoms of anxiety and nonattendance at school and their management of the situation can hinder or help the course of later treatment by either reinforcing the child's and family's belief that some physical illness is present or by firmly reassuring them about its absence. This information should be elicited in this history and should include the family's reaction to this welcome or unwelcome news. Referrals from paediatricians often carry the same elements and consequences. Those from schools either direct or via an educational psychologist, divisional education welfare officer or school medical officer usually mean that nonattendance has become persistent enough to draw attention to the child and that some knowledge of the child's behaviour in school and the family's handling of the problem is available. Reasons given by parents and child for absence will need further evaluation, for very often they have been advanced by others and taken over, while the real reasons remain hidden until elicited by a careful enquiry.

The presenting symptoms may be mainly psychological in the form of anxiety, fears, some general some specific, irritability and tension, mood changes or a mixture of these, but in all cases a careful search for precipitating events and time relationships is necessary. Complaints about the school situation should be investigated systematically whether about teachers, schoolmates, particular lessons, games, bullying, sexual talk, change of class or teacher, change of school, size of school, departure of a close friend etc. These may give a clue to a phobic situation at school which the child is avoiding or to other situations which lead to anxiety or panic, isolation or withdrawal.

The age of the child and the level of independence and maturity shown in dealings with peers and in activities within and without the family are important in terms of the demands made on the child at infant, junior or secondary school. Many children may falter but recover on entry to infants' school, depending on whether they have had prior nursery school experience or not, but after that one can expect increasing competence in mastering the anxiety aroused by changing school or teachers or coping with return to school after illness. All these changing situations and experiences can appear to precipitate school refusal and weight should be given to how earlier problems over school attendance have been handled, e.g. was the child teased, shamed, punished, did parents insist on attendance or the opposite.

The genetic endowment of the child, his pattern of temperamental traits and personality structure must also be taken into account. Self-evaluation and level of aspiration and the different situations which threaten self-esteem should be assessed. Qualities in the child of stubbornness and resistance to pressure and an ability to manipulate members of the family are most important. Treatment plans will soon founder if these have been underestimated.

Family factors are all-important in many cases; particularly family methods of dealing with anxiety, anger, illness, death or upheavals due to fortuitous circumstances and other stressful circumstances. Parental (usually maternal) threats to leave home or commit suicide as a means of controlling a child or expressing anger are especially important in creating anxiety in a child so that he fears to be away from home in case something happens to his mother. Similar statements that a child's particular behaviour will lead to death or illness of a parent also provoke anxiety. The enquiry should go into the parent's own relationship, the place of the father and other children in maintaining the family equilibrium and the dominance pattern in the family, in order to discover what resources exist for consideration in any treatment plan. General attitudes to school attendance include overt support for going to school hiding covert resistance which is communicated to the child. Family psychiatric disorder may render a parent or parents incapable of exerting any consistent control or may involve the child in the parents' symptom pattern, e.g. a phobic mother communicating her own anxieties to a child so making him fearful of leaving home to face the outside world.

The examination of the child should include an assessment of psychiatric state and physical development. Immaturity, both physical and sexual, and minor handicapping conditions are important and some may be treatable. Assessment of intellectual level and academic attainment and a school visit are essential, for retardation in the basic subjects can cause anxiety and undermine the child's already precarious motivation to attend, particularly if the school is unaware of the extent of backwardness and the child's sensitivity about it. In such cases remedial help is an integral part of any treatment plan.

The diagnostic formulation should be comprehensive and framed in such a way that it is a series of clinical hypotheses about the origins of the school refusal which can then be tested by further enquiry if necessary and by response to particular methods of treatment. The first step is to decide whether the persistent nonattendance at school is to be categorised as truancy, withholding at home or school refusal. If the latter, then it is necessary to decide whether it is part of a transient adaptational reaction (commonest in younger children), a true school phobia with avoidance of the schoolroom, refusal based on separation anxiety which may present (a) as a total inability to leave home or remain alone at home without parents or (b) an inability to leave home to go to school while still able to visit friends and relations away from home. The presence of a depressive disorder or schizophrenia must be assessed particularly in older children and adolescents by evidence of social withdrawal, misery, loss of interest, sleep disturbance, thought disorder, abnormal perceptual experience, falling off in school performance and the like. In some instances frank psychiatric disorder such as a depressive illness may exist in a parent and the focus of treatment will then shift often relieving the child of anxiety and responsibility and enabling him to return to school.

There is sometimes difficulty in arriving at a hypothesis about the major factor in the school refusal, whether there is phobic avoidance to be treated by systematic desensitisation therapy, separation anxiety to be treated by conjoint family interviews and systematic desensitization of the child, or a complex family pattern of separation anxiety in parents and child with mutual manipulation and reinforcement of school avoidance. The latter should be suspected if hypotheses about phobic avoidance and depressive illness are not supported by response to effective treatment. Sometimes adolescents display other social phobias and travel phobias in addition to anxieties about school attendance.

Treatment

In most cases an attempt should be made to return the child to school as soon as possible, but this will always require careful discussion and preparation with teachers and education welfare officers (Kennedy 1965; Lassers *et al* 1973). If a scheme of systematic desensitisation is used, re-entry into the classroom situation will need to be gradual and the psychologist or psychiatrist will usually have to spend time at school with the patient before handing over to a parent. Pharmacotherapy has a place, either the use of antidepressants (for depression or separation anxiety) or the use of a mild hypnotic to ensure a good night's sleep before starting school again.

In every case much time must be spent in discussing re-entry to school with the parents and advising them how to prepare the child and deal with any emotional crises. Opinions vary as to who should accompany the child to school on the first day but it is preferable to try and mobilise any strengths within the family so that either both parents or a father alone may take the child, provided they have been encouraged to resist any pleas and entreaties to remain at home and helped to understand that firmness and resolution is a support and not a hostile rejection of the child's need. Some parents may be willing and able to attempt this, but others may be too anxious and uncertain so that a member of the clinical team or representative of the school or social agency must be brought in. The aim is to start the process going but to hand responsibility back to parents in time, while continuing to advise and support through home or clinic visits and contact with school by telephone. Family therapy or social case-work may need to continue for some time, but many families drop out of treatment once regular attendance has been established.

Milieu therapy in the form of day or inpatient hospital treatment may be needed if outpatient treatment breaks down. Usually this is necessary if the child becomes increasingly anxious or depressed, or is able to manipulate and control his parents so that they are unable to exert effective control on behaviour generally and school-going in particular. One or both parents may be too psychiatrically ill to act in accord with a treatment plan or it becomes clear that mother and child are tied together in a neurotic interaction which prevents emotional growth to independence and self-assertion. In such cases inpatient treatment with the objectives of future school attendance, social and emotional growth through experience in a therapeutic milieu is provided and hopefully also the resolution of hostile dependent relationships between parent and child. The period in hospital will serve to tell whether relapse to the former state will occur if the child returns home in which case boarding school placement may be needed, but often improvement in symptoms and changed family attitudes permit a return home to ordinary school. Ideally hospital treatment should be one part of a total treatment plan including out-patient treatment before admission and after discharge.

Once back to school on the first day contact must be maintained with child and parents by means of telephone calls to or from parents to gauge their own and the child's reactions to this first school attendance. Suggestions are made on how to deal with any new anxieties or attempts to manipulate parents to avoid school. If parents can manage unaided on successive mornings they are praised and encouraged to take total responsibility for this, but support from clinic or school must be available if there are signs of faltering or loss of resolve in either child or parents. Bringing in a schoolfriend or friends can be of great help at this stage so setting up a normal regular pattern of school-going. The child should be interviewed again after one week at school to sort out any existing or potential sources of stress and anxiety in the school or home situation which can then be discussed with teachers and parents. All concerned should be warned that the times of potential danger of breakdown of school attendance are after a weekend, after an illness requiring more than a day or two at home, the beginning of a new term, family illness or bereavement, and change to a new class or school.

Conclusion

The complexity of presentation and of psychopathology means that modern practice in the treatment of school refusal must bring together the methods of psychotherapy, family therapy, behaviour therapy, milieu therapy, and pharmacotherapy, in the context of outpatient, daypatient or hospital in-patient treatment. Although some writers have discounted the importance of school factors, these are now taken into account in trying to understand the psychological mechanisms underlying each child's behaviour and also in planning treatment to re-establish regular attendance.

Further study is still needed to define the differences the mechanisms which lead to different types of school refusal e.g. those in which separation anxiety predominates in contrast to those where phobic avoidance is the main psychopathology. It may be possible to establish sub-types of school refusal based on individual differences in psychophysiological measures of anxiety, and tests of level of aspiration and neuroticism in different children at different ages. Measures of parent–child interaction and total family interaction are also needed to arrive at an accurate description of the predominant patterns. Studies of this kind could in time be related to the different methods of treatment and management. This will lead to more precision in the choice of the most effective method of treatment with for example, emphasis on family factors or factors in the school.

Short-term and long-term outcome of various treatment also merits enquiry for follow-up studies and retrospective studies of the school history of adults with neurotic disorders show that there is a significant link between refusal to go to school and disorders in adulthood. Although the main goal of treatment is usually return to school, it may be important to establish whether treatment should also aim at better psychological functioning in family and peer group relationship as well as regular attendance and academic progress at school.

School refusal continues to interest clinicians, researchers and practitioners in all disciplines concerned with children in the home, at school and in the community. The reasons for this steady interest are well set out in the following quotation from Eisenberg (1958b).

'Beyond its own intrinsic importance, school phobia serves as a paradigm of neurotic disorders in children, for it illustrates with special clarity the relation between symptoms in the child and the psychological structure of the family. The principles of its treatment highlight general considerations in the psychotherapy of emotional disorders. Only if the physician, the school authorities and participating social agencies coordinate therapeutic efforts is rehabilitation of the family unit likely to be successful.'

REFERENCES

ADAMS P.L., McDONALD N.F. & HUEY W.P. (1966) School phobia and bisexual conflict: a report of 21 cases. *Amer. J. Psychiat.* **123**, 541–547

AGRAS S. (1959) The relationship of school phobia to childhood depression. *Amer. J. Psychiat.* **116**, 533–536

ARGLES P. & MACKENZIE M. (1970) Crisis intervention with a multi-problem family— a case study. *J. Child Psychol. Psychiat.* **11**, 187–195

BARKER P. (1968) The in-patient treatment of school refusal. *Brit. J. Med. Psychol.* **41**, 381–387

BERG I. (1970) A follow-up study of school phobic adolescents admitted to an in-patient unit. *J. Child Psychol. Psychiat.* **11**, 37–47

BERG I., HULLIN R., ALLSOPP M., O'BRIEN P. & MACDONALD R. (1974a) Bipolar manic-depressive psychosis in early adolescence: a case report. *Brit. J. Psychiat.* **125**, 416–417

BERG I., BUTLER A. & PRITCHARD J. (1974b) Psychiatric illness in the mothers of school-phobic adolescents. *Brit. J. Psychiat.* **125,** 466–467

BERG I., MARKS I., McGUIRE R. & LIPSEDGE M. (1974c) School phobia and agoraphobia. *Psychol. Med.* **4,** 428–434

BERRYMAN E. (1959) School phobia: management problems in private practice. *Psychol. Reports.* **5,** 19–25

BOWLBY J. (1973) *Attachment and Loss,* vol. 2: *Separation. Anxiety and Anger.* London: Hogarth Press

BRITTON R.S. (1969) Psychiatric disorders in mothers of disturbed children. *J. Child Psychol. Psychiat.* **10,** 245–258

BROADWIN I.T. (1932) a contribution to the study of truancy. *Amer. J. Orthopsychiat.* **2,** 253–259

CAMPBELL J.D. (1955) Manic-depressive disease in children. *J. Amer. Med. Assoc.* **158,** 154–157

CHAPEL J.L. (1967) Treatment of a case of school phobia by reciprocal inhibition. *Canad. Psychiat. Assoc. J.* **12,** 25–28

CHAZAN M. (1962) School phobia. *Brit. J. Educ. Psychol.* **32,** 209–217

CHOI E.H. (1961) Father–daughter relationships in school phobia. *Smith Coll. Stud. Soc. Work.* **31,** 152–178

CLYNE M.B. (1966) *Absent: School Refusal as an Example of Disturbed Family Relationships.* London: Tavistock Publications

COOLIDGE J.C., HAHN P.B. & PECK A.L. (1957) School phobia: neurotic crisis or way of life. *Amer. J. Orthopsychiat.* **27,** 296–306

COOLIDGE J.C., WILLER M.L., TESSMAN E. & WALDFOGEL S. (1960) School phobia in adolescence, a manifestation of severe character disturbance. *Amer. J. Orthopsychiat.* **30,** 599–607

COOLIDGE J.C., BRODIE R.D. & FEENEY B. (1964) A ten-year follow-up of sixty-six school-phobic children. *Amer. J. Orthopsychiat.* **34,** 675–684

COOLIDGE J.C. & BRODIE R.D. (1974) Observations of mothers of 49 school-phobic children: evaluated in a 10-year follow-up study. *J. Amer. Acad. Child Psychiat.* **13,** 275–285

COOPER M. G. (1966) School refusal. *Educational Research* **8,** 115–127; 223–229

DAVIDSON S. (1960) School phobia as a manifestation of family disturbance. Its structure and treatment. *J. Child Psychol. Psychiat.* **1,** 270–287

EISENBERG L. (1958a) School phobia—a study in the communication of anxiety. *Amer. J. Psychiat.* **114,** 712–718

EISENBERG L. (1958b) School phobia—diagnosis, genesis and clinical management. *The Paediatric Clinics of North America,* August, 645–660

EISENBERG L. (1959) The paediatric management of school phobia. *J. Paediat.* **55,** 758–766

ESTES H.R., HAYLETT C. & JOHNSON A. (1956) Separation anxiety. *Amer. J. Psychotherap.* **10,** 682–695

EYSENCK H.J. & RACHMAN S. (1965a) *The Causes and Cure of Neurosis.* London: Routledge & Kegan Paul

EYSENCK H.J. & RACHMAN S.J. (1965b) The application of learning theory to child psychiatry. *In* Howells J.G. (ed.) *Modern Perspectives in Child Psychiatry.* Edinburgh: Oliver & Boyd

FLECK S. (1972) Some basic aspects of family pathology. *In* Wolman B. (ed.) *Manual of Child Psychopathology.* New York: McGraw-Hill

FRICK W.B. (1964) School phobia: a critical review of the literature. *Merrill–Palmer Quart.* **10,** 361–373

FROMMER E. (1967) Treatment of childhood depression with anti-depressant drugs. *Brit. Med. J.* **1,** 729–732

FROMMER E. (1972) *Diagnosis and Treatment in Clinical Child Psychiatry.* London: Heinemann

GARVEY W.P. & HEGRENES J.R. (1966) Desensitization techniques in the treatment of school phobia. *Amer. J. Orthopsychiat.* **36,** 147–152

GITTELMAN-KLEIN R. & KLEIN D.F. (1971) Controlled imipramine treatment of school phobia. *Arch. Gen. Psychiat.* **25,** 204–207

GLASER K. (1959) Problems in school attendance: school phobia and related conditions. *Paediatrics* **23,** 371–383

GLASER K. (1967) Masked depression in children and adolescents. *Amer. J. Psychother.* **21,** 565–574

GOLDBERG T.B. (1953) Factors in the development of school phobia. *Smith Coll. Stud. Soc. Work.* **23,** 227–248

GREENBAUM R.S. (1964) Treatment of school phobias: theory and practice. *Amer. J. Psychother.* **18,** 616–633.

HARRINGTON M. & HASSAN J.W.M. (1958) Depression in girls during latency. *Brit. J. Med. Psychol.* **31,** 43–50

HERSEN M. (1970a) Behaviour modification approach to a school-phobia case. *J. Clin. Psychol.* **26,** 128–132

HERSEN M. (1970b) The complementary use of behaviour therapy and psychotherapy. Some comments. *Psychol. Record* **20,** 395–402

HERSEN M. (1971a) Resistance to direction in behaviour therapy. Some comments. *J. Gen. Psychol.* **118,** 121–127

HERSEN M. (1971b) The behavioural treatment of school phobia: current techniques. *J. Nerv. Ment. Dis.* **153,** 99–107

HERSOV L.A. (1960a) Persistent non-attendance at school. *J. Child Psychol. Psychiat.* **1,** 130–136

HERSOV L.A. (1960b) Refusal to go to school. *J. Child Psychol. Psychiat.* **1,** 137–145

HERSOV L.A. (1974) Neurotic disorders with special reference to school refusal. *In* Barker P. (ed.) *The Residential Psychiatric Treatment of Children.* London: Crosby, Lockwood Staples

HETHERINGTON E.M. & MARTIN B. (1972) Family interaction and psychopathology in children. *In* Quay H.C. & Werry J. (eds.) *Psychopathological Disorders in Childhood.* New York: Wiley

HODGMAN C.H. & BRAIMAN A. (1965) 'College phobia': school refusal in university students. *Amer. J. Psychiat.* **12,** 801–805

JOHNSON A.M., FALSTEIN E.I., SZUREK S.A. & SVENDSEN M. (1941) School phobia. *Amer. J. Orthopsychiat.* **11,** 702–711

JOHNSON, A.M. (1957) School phobia: discussion. *Amer. J. Orthopsychiat.* **27,** 307–309

KAHN J.H. & NURSTEN J.P. (1962) School refusal: a comprehensive view of school phobia and other failures of school attendance. *Amer. J. Orthopsychiat.* **32,** 707–718

KAHN J.H. & NURSTEN J.P. (1964) *Unwillingly to School*. Oxford: Pergamon

KENNEDY W.A. (1965) School phobia: rapid treatment of fifty cases. *J. Abnorm. Psychol.* **70**, 285–389

KENNEDY W.A. (1971a) *Child Psychology*. Englewood Cliffs, NJ: Prentice-Hall

KENNEDY W.A. (1971b) A behaviouristic community—oriented approach to school phobia and other disorders. *In* Richard H.C. (ed.) *Behavioural Intervention in Human Problems*. Oxford: Pergamon

KLEIN E. (1945) The reluctance to go to school. *Psychoanal. Study Child.* **1**, 263–279. New York: International Universities Press

LASSERS E., NORDAN R. & BLADHOLM S. (1973) Steps in the return to school of children with school phobia. *Amer. J. Psychiat.* **130**, 265–268

LAZARUS A.A. (1960) The elimination of children's phobias by deconditioning. *In* Eysenck H.J. (ed.) *Behaviour Therapy and the Neuroses*. Oxford: Pergamon

LAZARUS A.A. & ABRAMOVITZ A. (1962) The use of 'emotive imagery' in the treatment of children's phobias. *J. Ment. Sci.* **108**, 191–195

LAZARUS A.A., DAVIDSON G.C. & POLEFKA D.A. (1965) Classical and operant factors in the treatment of a school phobia. *J. Abnorm. Psychol.* **70**, 225–229

LEVENTHAL T. & SILLS M. (1964) Self-image in school phobia. *Amer. J. Orthopsychiat.* **34**, 685–695

LEVENTHAL T., WEINBERGER G., STANDER R.J. & STEARNS R.P. (1967) Therapeutic strategies with school phobics. *Amer. J. Orthopsychiat.* **37**, 64–70

MALMQUIST C.P. (1965) School phobia. A problem in family neurosis. *J. Amer. Acad. Child Psychiat.* **4**, 293–319

MESSER A. (1964) Family treatment of a school phobic child. *Arch. Gen. Psychiat.* **11**, 548–555

MILLAR T.P. (1961) The child who refuses to attend school. *Amer. J. Psychiat.* **48**, 398–404

MILLER L.C., BARRETT C.L. & HAMPE A.A. (1974) Phobias of childhood in a prescientific era. *In* Davids A. (ed.) *Child Personality and Psychopathology: Current Topics*, vol. 1. New York: Wiley-Interscience

MILLMAN D.H. (1961) School phobia in older children and adolescents: diagnostic applications and prognosis. *Paediatrics* **28**, 462–471

MITCHELL S. & SHEPHERD M. (1967) The child who dislikes going to school. *Brit. J. Educ. Psychol.* **37**, 32–40

MOORE T. (1966) Difficulties of the ordinary child in adjusting to primary school. *J. Child Psychol. Psychiat.* **7**, 17–38

NICHOLS K.A. & BERG I. (1970) School phobia and self-evaluation. *Brit. J. Psychiat.* **11**, 133–141

NURSTEN J.P. (1963) School phobia, projection in the later adjustment of school phobic children. *Smith Coll. Studies in Social Work* **32**, 210–224

PARTRIDGE J.M. (1939) Truancy. *J. Ment. Sci.* **85**, 45–81

PATTERSON G.A. (1965) Learning theory approach to the treatment of the school phobic child. *In* Ullmann L.P. & Krasner L. (eds.) *Case Studies in Behavior Modifications*. New York: Holt, Rinehart & Winston

PITTMAN F.S., DONALD L.G. & DEYOUNG C.D. (1968) Work and school phobia: a family approach to treatment. *Amer. J. Psychiat.* **124**, 1535–1541

RABINER C.J. & KLEIN D.F. (1969) Imipramine treatment of school phobia. *Compr. Psychiatry* **10**, 387–390

RADIN S.S. (1967) Psychodynamic aspects of school phobia. *Compr. Psychiatry* **8**, 119–128

REGER R. (1962) School phobia in an obese girl. *J. Clin. Psychol.* **18**, 356–357

RODRIGUEZ A., RODRIGUEZ M. & EISENBERG L. (1959) The outcome of school phobia: a follow-up study based on 41 cases. *Amer. J. Psychiat.* **116**, 540–544

ROSS A.O. (1972a) Behaviour therapy. *In* Quay H.C. & Werry J.S. (eds.) *Psychopathological Disorders of Childhood.* New York: Wiley

ROSS A.O. (1972b) Behaviour therapy. *In* Wolman B.B. (ed.) *Manual of Child Psychopathology.* New York: McGraw-Hill

RUTTER M., TIZARD J. & WHITMORE K. (eds.) (1970) *Education Health and Behaviour.* London: Longman

RUTTER M., YULE W. & BERGER M. (1974) The children of West Indian migrants. *New Society* **27**, 630–633

RUTTER M., GRAHAM P.J., CHADWICK O. & YULE W. (1976) Adolescent turmoil: fact or fiction? *J. Child Psychol. Psychiat.* **17**, 35–56

SCHMITT B.D. (1971) School phobia—the great imitator: A paediatrician's viewpoint. *Paediatrics* **48**, 433–441

SHAFFER D. (1974) Suicide in children and early adolescence. *J. Child Psychol. Psychiat.* **15**, 275–291

SHAPIRO T. & JEGEDE R.O. (1973) School phobia—a babel of tongues. *J. Autism. Child. Schiz.* **3**, 168–186

SHEPHERD M., COOPER B., BROWN A. & KALTON A.A. (1966) *Psychiatric Illness in General Practice.* Oxford: Oxford University Press

SKYNNER R. (1974) School phobia: a reappraisal. *Brit. J. Med. Psychol.* **47**, 1–16

SMITH R.E. & SHARPE T.M. (1970) Treatment of a school phobia with implosive therapy. *J. Consult. Clin. Psychol.* **35**, 239–243

SMITH S.L. (1970) School refusal with anxiety: a review of sixty-three cases. *Can. Psychiat. Assoc. J.* **15**, 257–264

SPERLING M. (1961) Analytic first aid in school phobias. *Psychoanal. Quart.* **30**, 504–518

SPERLING M.D. (1967) School phobias: classification, dynamics and treatment. *Psychoanal. Study Child* **22**, 375–401

SUTTENFIELD V. (1954) School phobia: a study of five cases. *Amer. J. Orthopsychiat.* **24**, 308–380

TAHMISIAN J. & McREYNOLDS W. (1971) Use of parents as behavioural engineers in the treatment of a school-phobic child. *J. Counselling Psychol.* **18**, 225–228

TALBOT M. (1957) Panic in school phobia. *Amer. J. Orthopsychiat.* **27**, 286–295

TENNENT T.G. (1969) School non-attendance and delinquency. MD Thesis, University of Oxford

TYERMAN M.J. (1968) *Truancy.* London: University of London Press

TYRER P. & TYRER S. (1974) School refusal, truancy and neurotic illness. *Psychol. Med.* **4**, 416–421

VAN HOUTEN J. (1948) Mother–child relationship in twelve cases of school phobia. *Smith Coll. Stud. Soc. Work* **18**, 161–180

WALDFOGEL S., COOLIDGE J.C. & HAHN P.B. (1957) The development, meaning and management of school phobia. *Amer. J. Orthopsychiat.* **27**, 754–776

WALDFOGEL S., TESSMAN E. & HAHN P.B. (1959) A program for early intervention in school phobia. *Amer. J. Orthopsychiat.* **29**, 324–332

WARREN W. (1948) Acute neurotic breakdown in children with refusal to go to school. *Arch. Dis. Child.* **23**, 266–272

WARREN W. (1965) A study of adolescent psychiatric in-patients and the outcome six or more years later. I: Clinical histories and hospital findings. *J. Child Psychol. Psychiat.* **6**, 1–17

WARREN W. (1965) A study of adolescent psychiatric in-patients and the outcome six or more years later. II: The follow-up study. *J. Child Psychol. Psychiat.* **6**, 141–160

WEINER I.B. (1970) *Psychological Disturbance in Adolescence.* New York: Wiley-Interscience

WEISS M. & CAIN B. (1964) The residential treatment of children and adults with school phobia. *Amer. J. Orthopsychiat.* **34**, 103–114

WEISS M. & BURKE G.B. (1967) A five–ten year follow-up of hospitalised school phobic children and adolescents. *Amer. J. Orthopsychiat.* **37**, 294–295

YATES A.J. (1970) *Behaviour Therapy.* New York: Wiley

YOUNG O.R. (1964) A survey of general systems theory. *General Systems Yearbook* **9**, 61–80

CHAPTER 20

Nondelinquent disturbances of conduct

S. WOLFF

A CLINICAL SYNDROME?

The syndromes of child psychiatry have been established in a number of ways. Astute clinicians have described the antecedents and natural history of clusters of commonly associated symptoms, often but not always consisting of readily observable behaviour patterns the presence or absence of which causes little doubt. Kanner's early infantile autism (Kanner 1944), Strauss' hyperkinetic syndrome (Strauss & Lentinen 1947) and Asperger's schizoid psychopathy of childhood (Asperger 1944) are examples of such clinical discoveries.

Other childhood psychiatric disorders have been delineated on the basis of their adult equivalents. The psychoneuroses such as conversion hysteria and obsessional neurosis; the psychosomatic disorders (for example asthma and ulcerative colitis); anorexia nervosa; and adult type psychoses such as juvenile schizophrenia and manic-depressive psychoses are examples of these.

A third group of conditions invited recognition on the basis of their most conspicuous symptoms whose identification involved little observer judgement, for example enuresis, encopresis, tic, stuttering and developmental dysphasia. Yet other diagnostic categories became attached to administratively demarcated groups of children. Mental subnormality was defined by the educational system; delinquency by the judicial system; and, on the Continent, especially in Germany, child neglect (*Verwarlosung*) by the activities of the social services.

While the first two groups of disorders are rare, the third and fourth groups are common. Equally common are psychiatric disorders which cannot be defined administratively on the basis of readily identifiable core symptoms, but which consist mainly of personality trait disorders. The emotional disorders of childhood form a subgroup of these; nondelinquent conduct disorders form another. Within these subgroups commonly occurring syndromes have yet to be defined clinically.

In recent years much energy has been invested in factorial and principal component analyses of symptoms in the hope that these would help to delineate the psychiatric syndromes of children. Many intercorrelation studies of childhood behaviour disorders have been based on clinical case records (Hewitt & Jenkins 1964; Collins *et al* 1962; Patterson 1964; Quay 1964; Achenbach 1966; Field 1967). However, the emerging syndromes, for example Hewitt and Jenkins' now classical trio of Socialised Delinquency, Unsocialised Aggression and Overinhibited Behaviour may have been biassed by the preconceptions of the psychiatrists and social workers who elicited the clinical histories and recorded the data. Even a Japanese replication of Hewitt and Jenkins' investigations, which used independent, nonclinic assessments of children, was not without a built-in bias (Kobayashi *et al* 1967).

Other investigators (see Kolvin *et al* 1975) have used systematically recorded data but have done so with normal nursery or schoolchildren. In such populations the prevalence of psychiatric morbidity is of course low and it is likely that the emerging dimensions of behaviour reflect normal behavioural variations rather than overt disorders. Clinically significant symptom clusters are more likely to be found in groups of disturbed children. In an intercorrelation study of the systematically recorded behaviour of 100 primary schoolchildren with behaviour disorders (Wolff 1971), four meaningful dimensions of behaviour emerged from a principal component analysis. The first of these, accounting for 14·8 per cent of the variance had high loadings on nondelinquent conduct disorders: disobedience, being highly strung, temper tantrums, discontent, overactivity, poor concentration and attention, quarrelling and fighting, being overdominating, being overtalkative. This suggests that one dimension of disturbed behaviour in childhood consists of aggressive, acting-out, but nondelinquent behaviour.

In the same study a search for symptom clusters, derived from charting all symptoms found to intercorrelate at above 0·30, revealed five relatively discreet clusters. The largest of these consisted of items of aggressive, acting-out but nondelinquent behaviour. Key symptoms within the cluster, that is symptoms which intercorrelated at over 0·30 with a number of other symptoms within the cluster, were overactivity (8), being highly strung (8), quarrelling and fighting (6), disobedience (6), temper tantrums (6) and discontent (5).* There were only three intercorrelations of over 0·30 with other clusters: two with a cluster of anxiety symptoms and one with a cluster of depressive symptoms. There were no links at all with the cluster of delinquent disorders (lying, stealing, wandering). The nature of the symptoms in the cluster of nondelinquent conduct disorders suggests that quite apart from other aetio-

---

* The figures in brackets indicate the number of intercorrelations of over 0·30 with other symptoms in the cluster.

logical factors, temperamental traits of high reactivity, perhaps a combination of activity level, intensity of reaction and low threshold of responsiveness as described by Thomas *et al* (1968), may contribute to the genesis of these behaviour disorders. Patterson *et al* (1967) have drawn attention to the association between high activity levels and aggressive behaviour in children. Pritchard and Graham (1966) also found separate clusters for nondelinquent conduct and delinquent disorders with a negative relation between neurotic symptoms and symptoms of delinquency.

Conners (1970) factor analysed the parent symptom ratings for 316 psychiatric clinic patients and also for 365 normal children aged between 5 and 15 years. Five meaningful factors emerged from this study: (1) aggressive-conduct disorder; (2) anxious-inhibited behaviour; (3) antisocial reaction; (4) enuresis, accompanied by encopresis only in the clinic patients; and (5) psychosomatic problems. Four of these resemble Wolff's (1971) principal components which were: (1) aggressive, acting-out behaviour; (2) manifest anxiety versus antisocial behaviour; (3) inhibited and antisocial behaviour; (4) disturbances of toilet functions.

Conners' study supports the existence of a dimension of aggressive, acting-out behaviour in psychiatrically disturbed children and, to a lesser extent, in normal children throughout the school age range. The dimension is quite distinct from delinquency.

But neither a dimension of behaviour nor a symptom cluster is equivalent to a clinical syndrome. It is noteworthy that only in Hewitt and Jenkins study (1946), were symptom clusters in children found to be statistically associated with specific clusters of environmental variables. In Wolff's (1971) analysis the four meaningful principal components accounted for only 37·1 per cent of the variance, confirming the heterogeneity of behaviour disorders in childhood which Collins *et al* (1962) had also stressed. Moreover, when cluster scores were assigned to the individual subjects, only one third of the children scored in a single cluster while many children had scores of equivalent magnitude on items of behaviour belonging to up to four different clusters.

Psychiatric syndromes are both more and less than a uniform array of symptoms. For example, the syndrome of early childhood autism is defined both by a number of key symptoms but also by the age of onset and the natural history of the disease. The symptomatology of autistic children has many similarities to that shown by other disturbed children of the same sex, age and intelligence level (Rutter 1966). Apart from the key symptoms universally present, the clinical picture of autism can vary greatly from case to case. Nevertheless, once the diagnosis is made and the degree of severity assessed, one can be fairly confident about outcome and the effectiveness of treatment.

The same is true of school refusal, of the psychoneuroses in childhood and of other, recognised syndromes.

It may yet be possible to define specific psychiatric syndromes among children with nondelinquent conduct and with other personality trait disorders. Certain recurring constellations of historical and phenomenological features spring to mind. For example, the only or oldest boy, aged between 3 and 5 years, of a mother who has just parted from a violent husband and who herself has had inadequate maternal care as a child, is described as beyond his mother's control, disobedient, destructive, defiant and constantly fighting with other children. The maternal behaviour is characterised by lack of protective care and control, demands for self-control beyond the capacities of any preschool child, failure to step in before damage is done but physical punishment and threats of abandonment in response to his misdeeds. The mother fears that the child will in later life become just like his absent father, and that she herself may be driven to lose control and injure him. Other possible 'syndromes' of nondelinquent conduct will occur to other clinicians.

It seems likely, however, in view of the multiple interacting variables and the difficulty of describing them unequivocally, that in the case of nondelinquent conduct disorders we shall have to do without specific syndromes and limit ourselves instead to considerations of the general associated, antecedent and outcome factors related to children who, whatever else may be the matter with them, also display aggressive, acting-out but nondelinquent behaviour. To this extent the correlates of such behaviour are likely to be less valuable in the management of the individual case than if we were dealing with a more specific clinical syndrome.

For purposes of broad diagnostic classification, a WHO study (Rutter *et al* 1975a) has proposed that nondelinquent as well as delinquent conduct disorders should be grouped together, whether or not they are accompanied by emotional disorders also. This is because all children with conduct disorders of whatever kind share certain characteristics: they are predominantly boys, they tend to come from lower socioeconomic backgrounds, they frequently have educational difficulties and their future outlook is less good than that of children without antisocial behaviour.

PSYCHIATRICALLY DISTURBED CHILDREN WITH A PREDOMINANTLY AGGRESSIVE SYMPTOMATOLOGY

Anna Freud (1970) has noted the lack of a one-to-one correspondence between symptoms, causes and treatment. Aggressive outbursts may be the mark of insufficient fusion between libido and aggression; of lack of control over drives in an impulsive character; or of a violent defensive reaction against underlying passive-feminine leanings in boys striving overtly for masculinity. She stresses the need for a classification which takes account of both symptomatology and the underlying psychopathology. However, her scheme rests largely on psychodynamic formulations whose clinical application has never been tested for reliability, let alone validity.

Nevertheless, her point that aggressive behaviour can be a manifestation of different underlying disturbances makes much clinical sense. Such a failure in social adaptation can arise on the basis of constitutional impairments, for example due to poor impulse control in children with organic cerebral dysfunctioning, or to ego defects and abnormal defences in children with psychotic or borderline psychotic states. It can also be caused by adverse environmental circumstances such as neglect, unstable object relations, other traumata and undue parental pressure, all of which can lead to gross ego and superego defects. Failure of parental guidance and absence of adequate parent models for identification resulting in an impaired superego and ego ideal, can lead to similar failures in social adaptation.

Aggressive behaviour disorders in constitutionally normal children

Bowlby (1973) has described functional and dysfunctional expressions of hostility in young children who have experienced separation from parents. His point is that during and after brief separations young children protest and accuse their parents of leaving them, and that normally such coercive protests and expressions of anger serve to strengthen the bond between parent and child. When separation is permanent, the child's anger serves no biological function. When children are exposed to prolonged or multiple separations or to repeated threats of abandonment on the part of angry parents, children develop hatred against their parents, and also anxiety about the expression of such hatred in case the parent will actually leave. As a result, abnormal expressions of hostility occur: irrational acts of aggression against parents and also delinquency.

Confirmation for such ideas comes from clinical studies. Jenkins (1969 and 1970) describes unsocialised, aggressive behaviour in children as environmentally caused but with predisposing constitutional factors. His cluster analyses of clinical records indicate that unsocialised aggression occurs typically in muscular boys and is a reaction to experiences of frustration within the home. Less muscular boys from similar backgrounds may wander instead. The parents' marriage is frequently unstable and the child knows he is rejected; step-parents are often in the picture; the mother tends to be inconsistently shielding and punishing. Associated symptoms are solitary stealing, sexual aggression and persisting enuresis. McCord *et al* (1961) demonstrated links between overt aggression in urban, lower class, nondelinquent boys aged 9 to 15 years, and early intrafamilial experiences of parental rejection, punitiveness and threats. They also showed that aggressive children more often had inconsistent parents and parents at odds with each other (see also Gardner (1971) below).

Aggressive behaviour disorders and delinquency

While principal component analyses of the behaviour of disturbed children have defined separate dimensions of aggressive and delinquent behaviour (Wolff 1971; Conners 1970) nevertheless the two types of conduct disorders often occur together. In the Isle of Wight survey (Rutter *et al* 1970b) 56 boys and 14 girls displayed conduct (with or without neurotic) disorders. Of these children only 17 boys and 3 girls had nondelinquent conduct disorders. We do not know how many delinquent children were nonaggressive. The Isle of Wight children were 10 and 11 years of age, and it may well be that at this age aggressive behaviour and delinquency occur together more often than at earlier or later periods of life. It has been shown, for example, that among psychiatrically disturbed and nondisturbed children disobedience was commoner under than over 8 years of age. In a psychiatrically disturbed group, destructiveness and temper tantrums occurred significantly more often in children under than over 8 years, while in a nondisturbed group overactivity and overtalkativeness were more common in the younger children. Lying, stealing, and truanting (rare in the nondisturbed group) occurred significantly more often in disturbed children over than under 8 years of age (Wolff 1967).

Both aggressive and delinquent disorders are more common in boys. Preschool disturbed boys tend to display aggressive, acting-out behaviour without delinquency (Wolff 1961). There is some evidence, requiring confirmation, that children with aggressive behaviour disorders in early life become delinquent later, while this is not so for children who in early life display neurotic disorders. Mulligan *et al* (1963) showed that children assessed by their teachers as having aggressive behaviour disorders at the age of 13 years were more likely to be delinquent at 15 years. How much this is a reflection of personality development within the children themselves, and how much a reflection of social processes within the schools (i.e. that children unpopular with their teachers are predisposed to develop delinquency) is not clear (see also Power *et al* (1972) below).

Aggressive behaviour disorders and emotional disturbance

In the Isle of Wight study 27 out of 70 children with conduct disorders, delinquent and nondelinquent, had associated emotional disturbances (Rutter *et al* 1970b). The association was the same for boys and girls but was not examined for aggressive and delinquent children separately. West (1969) in a study of predelinquent boys also found an association between nervous and conduct disorders in middle childhood. It is likely, in view of the negative association between delinquent conduct and manifestations of anxiety (Wolff 1971), that children with aggressive, nondelinquent behaviour more often have associated anxiety symptoms than children who are delinquent but nonaggressive. Moreover, aggressive behaviour without delinquency occurs at a younger age group than aggression with delinquency (see above) and anxiety symptoms such as specific fears, sleep disorders and overconcern with illness also tend to occur in younger children (Wolff 1967).

In the Isle of Wight study (Rutter *et al* 1970b) even within a short time span of 2 years, parents reported significantly fewer items of worried and fearful behaviour and also of fighting, temper loss and overactivity when their children were 12 years of age than when they were 10.

Aggressive behaviour disorders and school failure

Gardner (1971) describes vividly the overwhelming threats found in the environment of aggressive children and also the association of aggressive behaviour with educational failure. He sees all personal violence as a 'death equivalent' which in children has many disastrous consequences. One effect is on the learning process in otherwise 'normal' children exposed to acts of aggression either within or, more often, outside their home. Most non-learners in America are either black children or socioeconomically deprived urban white children. They tend to have been subjected to recurring threats in their environment constituting, in Gardner's words, 'an ever-present negative interpersonal aura and a life long expectation of aggression, violence, exclusion, derogation and defect'. Fear of aggressive acts from authority figures aimed at the child and fear of inability to control his own aggressive impulses (that is, the fear of being 'killed' or of being 'a killer') result, even in constitutionally normal children, in learning failure. Gardner describes an 'anxiety overload' in young children when parents of 4- or 5-year-olds, for example, depict the world as dangerous and alert the child constantly to possible harm (e.g. from electricity, dogs, poisons, cars) when he is not yet sufficiently mature to appreciate probabilities accurately (e.g. of lions or lightning harming *him*). Anxiety becomes overwhelming when in addition there is interpersonal violence within the family, and threats of abandonment and desertion of the child by his parents. Such children, Gardner asserts, associate aggression only with interpersonal violence and do not learn to deploy their own aggressive impulses constructively and impersonally in the form of curiosity and learning.

The Isle of Wight Study (Rutter *et al* 1970b) sheds much light on the order (including aggressive and delinquent behaviour) was associated with an IQ slightly below average in boys but not in girls. (Neurotic disorder was associated with an IQ slightly below average in girls and only very slightly below average in boys.) In contrast, educational retardation, of which severe reading retardation was the index, was highly associated with antisocial and mixed antisocial and neurotic disorders in boys and girls, and only very slightly with pure neurotic disorders in girls, and not at all in boys. On the whole overactivity, fidgetiness and poor concentration, as well as aggressive and delinquent symptoms were associated with reading retardation in boys and, to a lesser extent, in girls. It was argued on the basis of the data that while constitutional aspects of temperament as well as neurological dysfunction can contribute to the genesis both of learning difficulties and acting-out behaviour, and while certain social and family factors (low social class and large family size) do so also, nevertheless severe reading retardation is itself an important cause for the development of antisocial conduct, especially in boys. One third of retarded readers were antisocial and one third of children with antisocial disorders were retarded readers. The association between conduct disorder and reading retardation was similar for children with delinquent conduct and for children with nondelinquent antisocial disorders.

A strong association between serious educational retardation and aggressive behaviour was found also in a small group of children recently studied because they had been excluded from school (York *et al* 1972). Exclusion was invariably precipitated by seriously aggressive and disruptive behaviour at school; boys outnumbered girls 5 to 1; only one-half of the children, whose mean age was 12 years, were also delinquent; two-thirds were severely backward readers. One in seven of the children was handicapped (mental subnormality, childhood psychosis, gross neurological disease). Socioeconomically the children were deprived and in one-sixth of the families a parent had been in prison.

Aggressive behaviour disorders and brain damage

The environmental antecedents of aggressive behaviour in childhood (for example, family disruption, rejection of the child, domestic violence and exposure to threats of violence or abandonment) and organic cerebral dysfunction can singly or together contribute to the development of nondelinquent and delinquent conduct disorders, to educational retardation, and to both conditions occurring together. Socially unacceptable behaviour has been described in brain injured children from the start (Strauss & Lehtinen 1947).

Investigations of the type of psychiatric disorder associated with brain damage in children have been confounded by the fact that different studies have selected children on varying criteria for neurological impairment, age, psychiatric disorder and social and family background. Investigators of hyperkinetic children have often excluded those with gross neurological abnormalities (Werry 1968; Wikler *et al* 1970—see also Chapter 22). Others have examined only children with definite organic brain disease (Rutter *et al* 1970a—see also Chapter 8) who, unlike minimally brain-damaged children, contain many with low intelligence and physical handicap. Such children in middle childhood may suffer from any type of psychiatric disorder, not only hyperkinesis and aggressive behaviour. When hyperkinesis is defined purely in behavioural terms, the accompanying symptoms most often take the form of aggressive behaviour. Many such children come from disorganised families and in only a minority is there evidence of neurological dysfunction (Conners 1970).

Chess (1972) has compared the symptomatology of children with central nervous system pathology and other children referred for psychiatric consultation, matched for sex and age. All came from middle class homes and conduct disorders appear to have been rare. Neurological cases more often presented with hyperactivity than the controls, but of the special behavioural symptoms generally associated with brain damage only perseveration was significantly more common in the neurologically impaired group.

For the moment we must conclude that only a minority of brain-damaged children are hyperkinetic and then especially in early life. When there are family and social stresses and educational handicaps of a kind known to predispose to conduct disorders, brain damaged children without gross intellectual or physical handicap are particularly prone to develop aggressive and later also delinquent disorders. When intellectual retardation and conspicuous physical handicap accompany neurological disease, the risk of all types of psychiatric disorder is greatly increased.

Aggressive behaviour in children with psychotic and borderline psychotic states

Most descriptions of the behaviour of autistic and other psychotic children include aggression and temper tantrums, especially when the child's obsessional behaviour patterns are frustrated. Rutter (1966) demonstrated that as many psychotic children as controls (psychiatrically disturbed children matched for sex, age and intelligence) displayed aggression and temper tantrums. Nevertheless, the specific psychotic symptoms are generally so striking that the question of differential diagnosis from nondelinquent conduct disorder does not arise.

The situation is different in the case of borderline psychotic states or schizoid personality disorder. Here too aggressive and negativistic behaviour is often described. Asperger (1944) for example includes 'autistic maliciousness' in his description of autistic psychopathy of childhood. He means acts and comments hurtful to other people because they are aimed with callous unconcern at their particular weaknesses. A number of children referred because of aggressive outbursts at school turn out to be schizoid solitary children, not otherwise aggressive, whose outbursts are a catastrophic reaction in a setting (usually a crowded classroom) in which the social demands were more than they could cope with. For treatment purposes it is important to distinguish the aggressive behaviour of schizoid children from that of children with conduct disorders. Further study in this area is needed.

PREVALENCE

Because prevalence studies of behaviour disorders in childhood use different methods of assessment and of categorisation, the charting of nondelinquent conduct disorders as a single and distinct category in boys and girls of different ages is incomplete. On the Isle of Wight (Rutter *et al* 1970b) among 10- and 11-year-old children conduct disorders occurred in 4·0 per cent. Nondelinquent conduct disorders accounted for 1·1 per cent. In a London borough both rates were much higher (Rutter *et al* 1975).

Most studies of disturbed schoolage children in the community reveal a preponderance of boys among the conduct disordered (Rutter *et al* 1970b).

ANTECEDENTS OF AGGRESSIVE BEHAVIOUR IN CHILDHOOD

A distinction must be drawn between the causes of childhood aggression as part of a psychiatric disorder and the antecedents of aggressive behaviour in children in general. Among the pathogenic influences, more powerful when several are present together, overwhelming anxiety due to parent loss, parental violence and threats of abandonment, loss of self-esteem due to educational failure, cerebral dysfunction, psychosis and borderline psychotic states have been mentioned.

The determinants of aggression in childhood in general are relevant because they are likely to influence symptom choice and perhaps also to determine whether a particular child exposed to relatively minor pathogenic influences will cross the threshold to morbidity.

In many respects the antecedents of aggressive behaviour in normal children have been found to be quite similar to those of aggressive behaviour in disturbed children. A complex matrix of interacting variables is associated with childhood aggression: some constitutional, some a function of the family environment and some of the social environment the child encounters outside his own home.

Sex

All studies of behaviour in children disturbed and nondisturbed show boys to be more active and more overtly aggressive and combative than girls (McFarlane *et al* 1954; Lapouse & Monk 1958; Wolff 1961; Werry & Quay 1971). Hutt and her colleagues (Hutt 1972) found that in a nursery school boys not only display more aggression; they also elicit more aggressive responses from other children than girls. Acquisitive competition occurred predominantly between boys, who were also more retaliatory. While girls displayed more caretaking and protective behaviour towards younger children (both boys and girls), boys tended to attach themselves to older boys and try to join in their activites. Activity level plays a part in these sex differences (Patterson 1967); differential reactions of parents and teachers to boys and girls, and children's imitation of such reactions are likely to contribute. For example, Halverson and Waldrop (1970) observing mothers of $2\frac{1}{2}$-year-old boys and girls interact with their own and another mother's child, found that boys rated uncontrolled, fast moving and impulsive in their nursery had mothers who were more negative and controlling to their own than other boys. There were no differences between the girls. It was found also that girls and their mothers talked more than boys and their mothers. The mothers of the more aggressive boys acted as if they were 'set for trouble' (see also Minton *et al* 1971).

Kagan and Moss (1962) found that, while the personality trait of dependency was relatively stable over age for girls, the trait of aggressiveness was more stable in boys than in girls.

Age

In the general population and and among psychiatric clinic attenders aggressive behaviour is common in preschool children, declines during the early school years, rises at adolescence and declines once more between the ages of 15 and 21 years (McFarlane *et al* 1954; Wolff 1961; Werry & Quay 1971; Masterson 1967).

Social class

Doubt has recently been cast on the previously accepted relationship between low social class and coercive child-rearing practices on the one hand, and the more aggressive and less nurturing approach of lower class mothers with more aggressive and dependent behaviour of their young children on the other (Zigler 1971). The social class differences found for example by Sears *et al* (1957) were numerically small. All estimates of maternal behaviour based on interviews with mothers (rather than on direct observations of maternal behaviour) may reflect class differences in what is thought to be acceptable behaviour rather than actual differences in maternal behaviour (Zigler 1971). Inconsistencies between different studies have been found to reflect changing trends that have occurred over the years in child-rearing practices and that cut across class membership. This does not mean that social class is unimportant in the genesis of aggressive behaviour in childhood, but its effects may not be solely and perhaps not even primarily the result of maternal child-rearing practices.

The Isle of Wight studies (Rutter *et al* 1970b) have shown that social class was associated with psychiatric disorder and especially with conduct disorder (delinquent and nondelinquent) because lower class children were more often of low IQ and therefore more disturbed, and because lower class children were also more prone to serious reading retardation and this was associated with conduct disorder.

Teachers' negative evaluation of the ability and behaviour of lower class children, especially boys, is likely to reinforce their learning difficulties and their aggressive and other antisocial behaviour. Zigler (1971) views the slower rates of cognitive development in lower class children (whether environmentally and/or genetically determined) as the mediating factor between social class and child behaviour. However, he then proceeds to cite social class differences in parents' child-rearing practices, as if unskilled working class parents were themselves operating at lower cognitive developmental levels which explain both their behaviour and their children's educational failure.

In any case, the evidence for class differences in maternal behaviour is still accumulating. Minton *et al* (1971) showed that college educated mothers were less intrusive and prohibitive towards their 2-year-old children than the noncollege educated. They were also less physically punitive and made requests rather than commands. Girls of middle class mothers were more obedient and asked their mothers to play with them more often than girls of working class mothers. Boys were most obedient when mothers used little physical punishment and explained their prohibitions. In all cases mothers were more intrusive with boys than with girls. The Newsons (1976) showed that at the age of seven, lower class children were more aggressive and destructive than middle class children (and boys more than girls). Lower class mothers more readily resorted to physical punishment than middle class mothers (and boys were physically punished more than girls).

Perhaps the truth lies in a combination of factors. Lower class parents probably *are* different to their children: more punitive, less nurturing and more restrictive with rules than middle class parents. They also differ in their fostering of cognitive, especially language, development in their children, particularly when the sibship is large. Because duller, less verbal and more aggressive in response to more aggressive role models (see below) lower class children evoke more negative and hostile responses at school, and these tend to reinforce both delinquent and non-delinquent conduct disorders.

Size of sibship

Sibship size, highly related to social class, is likely to make its own contribution to the development of aggression in childhood, quite apart from its effects via school failure. Rutter *et al* (1970b) showed that restlessness, destructiveness, fighting, disobedience, bullying and temper tantrums were commoner in boys from large than small families, but this was not so for girls.

Anna Freud (*Lancet* 1973) stressed the aggression engendered in toddlers when cared for in large numbers in the same room, and suggested that a family should bring up only one toddler at a time. The fact that nursery school boys reinforce each others' aggressive behaviour, especially in an unstructured setting when adults do not intervene, has been shown by Patterson *et al* (1967, see below).

Family composition, parental dominance and marital discord

One in 10 US children live in fatherless households (Biller 1970). In some lower class black areas half the children may lack fathers. Biller's review indicates that fatherless boys have less masculine projective sex role behaviour and are overall rated as more dependent and less aggressive if father loss occurred at under 4 years. In lower class boys, however, father absence leads to obsessive overconcern with masculinity and, as a reaction formation, to aggressive, acting-out behaviour. Fatherless 8–9-year-old boys prefer immediate gratification and also lack trust in adult males. This together with their cognitive deficits may contribute to impair their relationship with school teachers, so that these are not used as compensatory male role models. Aggressive and delinquent behaviour develops in part as a reaction to a mother-dominated household. Tuckman and Regan (1966) found children from

broken homes to be more aggressive and antisocial and to have more educational problems. When mothers were widowed, the children tended to have
neurotic problems; divorce as a cause of father loss was most likely to lead
to aggressive behaviour, especially in boys. A further contributing factor to
this association, as yet unexplored, may be the mother's negative reaction
to men leading her both to have an unsatisfactory marriage and also to have
negative expectations of her sons.

Hetherington (1965) studied the effects of mother or father dominance
in the home on the children's sex role preference and on their identification
with parental behaviour. Boys showed sex role preferences as early as 4–5
years with little increase thereafter; in girls sex role preference reached its
maximum only at 9–11 years. Children identified with the dominant parent
and the disruption of sex role identification was greater for boys in mother-
dominated households, while sex role preference in boys and girls was most
normal when fathers were dominant.

A number of studies have related psychiatric disorder, especially conduct
disorder (without differentiating aggression from delinquency) in boys to
marital discord between parents. Rutter (1970) has discussed the possible
reasons for this excessive vulnerability of boys without reaching definite conclusions. It seems likely that because marital discord, especially when it involves physical violence, consists of attacks by the father on the mother, this
arouses special anxieties in boys because of their sex role identification. The
mother's part in such domestic violence is less obvious to the children and
her role is usually less manifestly aggressive. It would be helpful to explore
in more detail the relationship between different types of marital discord and
the display of aggressive behaviour disorders in sons and daughters.

Children's social interactions with each other

In a notable study of 3- and 4-year-old middle and upper class nursery school children, Patterson *et al* (1967) explored the importance of the
peer group in the acquisition and maintenance of assertive–aggressive behaviour. They found that the amount of social interaction was a very important
variable. Passive children with high social interaction rates soon became
aggressive and very aggressive children already interacted at a very high rate.
The amount of social interaction was found to depend both on the general
activity level of a child but also on his responsiveness to peer-dispensed reinforcers. Reinforcers of assertive–aggressive behaviour differed for different
children.

Assertive behaviour is ubiquitously reinforced among normal children
because of the 'demand' quality of aggression forcing a reaction on its
recipient. The result is that the majority of low aggressive children become

aggressive and high aggressive children remain so. Only low aggressive children with low social interactions, that is with low activity levels and low responsiveness to peers, remained nonaggressive. A child with a high activity level was also likely to be more responsive to peer dispensed reinforcers of aggressive behaviour and to become more aggressive if he was unaggressive to start with. Every time he was attacked and was able to counterattack successfully, in imitation of models provided by other, more assertive children, his level of aggressive behaviour increased.

Conditions necessary to produce an aggressive child were parental permissiveness for aggressive behaviour between siblings at home, reinforced by peer relationships outside the home. The aggressive child then when more aggressive evokes punitive and authoritarian behaviour from, especially lower class, parents. This elicits a negative, frustrated emotional state in the child contributing still further to his high amplitude assertiveness.

Both aggressive role models (adults and other children) and frequent emotionally frustrating encounters with the environment are commoner in lower class children. A structured nursery school with a teacher diverting and focussing the children's attention on other matters can counteract the development of high levels of aggression among its occupants.

An ethological study of nursery school children has identified three styles of aggressive behaviour, characteristic of individual children and persisting over time (Manning 1976). These are: *games aggression*, that is aggressive behaviour engaged in during rough and tumble play predominantly by boys; *harassment*, including teasing, threatening and physical harassment, in boys, interfering notably with social acceptance by other children; and *specific hostility*, that is assertiveness and aggression in order to obtain certain goals, observed equally in boys and girls and associated with social competence among peers. The children are being followed up and assessed psychiatrically. Preliminary findings suggest that *harassing* children tend to be identified as disturbed at school, while children with *games hostility* are eager to please in the classroom but disturbed at home and on poor terms with their siblings. Children with *specific hostility* are least disturbed.

Social processes within schools

It has been demonstrated that individual schools make their own contribution to the genesis of antisocial conduct in boys, quite apart from the family and neighbourhood environment. In areas with similar delinquency rates, some schools have consistently high and some consistently low rates of convictions (Power *et al* 1972). It is likely, although as yet undemonstrated, that school influences can affect the development of both aggressive and delinquent conduct in children. Whether the important aspects of school life are the actual teaching methods of specific skills, or techniques used for maintaining class-room discipline, or broader aspects of the social interactions between teacher and children and between teacher and teacher, have not been established. A fruitful area of research of the greatest relevance for the prevention of aggressive and delinquent conduct in children has been indicated.

The mass media

There is much debate at the present time about the possibility that the wide-spread dissemination of portrayals, especially visual, of imagined and factual acts of violence and aggression, can reinforce aggressive patterns of behaviour in certain predisposed groups of children and young people. Bandura and Walters (1963) have discussed in detail the acquisition of behaviour patterns as a result of modelling, and they cite a number of experiments in which young children, already frustrated, engaged in aggressive play in a playroom with toys when they had watched a film depicting such behaviour. Kniveton & Stephenson (1975) suggest that lower class children unfamiliar with the playroom are especially vulnerable.

A US Public Health Service Report (1972) summarise the evidence on the relationship between television violence and aggression in children. Himmelweit *et al* (1958) surveyed groups of English school children before and after their families acquired a television set and found that heavy viewing rates were related to a low IQ, a restricted social life, insecurity, maladjustment, high anxiety levels and a feeling of being rejected by peers. Overall there was no evidence that children became more aggressive with the advent of television. Younger, duller children gained in knowledge; more intelligent children fell behind with their school work. This study did not exclude the possibility that some, predisposed children may become more aggressive as a result of high television violence viewing, while others may benefit. This conclusion is reached by Schramm *et al* (1961) after a massive series of surveys relating responses to unvalidated questionnaires to television viewing rates.

A well-set-up experimental study in which institutionalised boys were exposed to controlled television viewing of high and low aggressive content over a period of 6 weeks, provides some evidence for the catharsis hypothesis: that watching television violence actually reduces aggressive behaviour (Feshbach & Singer 1971). The boys studied were adolescent and pre-adolescent, as the children in the English study had been (Himmelweit *et al* 1958).

The US report (1972) indicates that the evidence linking television violence to aggressive behaviour is better for younger schoolchildren than for adolescents, and for short-term rather than long-term effects. While surveys showing correlations cannot indicate the nature of the relationship, most experimental studies on young children have shown low positive correlations between exposure to filmed violence and aggressive behaviour. The relationship is most marked in boys, in children with high initial levels of aggression and in children from low socioeconomic groups. The consequences of the filmed violence portrayed and the setting in which the child views the films influence their effect. This report points out the complete absence of studies of the anxiety inducing effects of television violence on young children, although many mothers report sleep disturbances after certain programmes. It is likely that high anxiety levels may themselves foster aggressive behaviour in young children after viewing violent television programmes.

In a recent review, Libert and Poulos (1975) defined the conditions necessary for observation learning as exposure, acquisition (including comprehension, interpretation and storage) and acceptance of what is seen and heard as a guide for future behaviour. Acceptance can take the form of direct imitation, counter-imitation and transformation of what has been observed. They summarise evidence for the amount of time children spend with what they describe as the electronic baby sitter and teacher, and for the proportion of displays of successful violence on the screen. A recent study showed significantly increased peer ratings and self reports of aggressive behaviour in nineteen-year-old boys who at nine years were reported to prefer violent television programs, compared with boys who had no such preference, even when the level of aggression displayed by these children at the earlier age had been low (Huesmann *et al* 1973).

The fact that the television influence on the childhood population as a whole is small does not make it less important. If a minority of predisposed children can be prevented from becoming pathologically aggressive through public action, that action needs to be given serious consideration.

OUTCOME AND TREATMENT

Outcome

Most follow-up studies do not distinguish between delinquent and nondelinquent conduct disorders (e.g. Morris *et al* 1956). The association between childhood conduct disorder and adult sociopathy has been established. Robins (1966) found that one-third of boys attending a child guidance clinic with antisocial behaviour were sociopathic as adults. The proportion was the same for that subgroup who presented with aggression, although numerically this group was small. However, a majority of antisocial, aggressive and delinquent, subjects had been referred by legal agencies, and a large proportion spent some time in reformatories. Childhood aggression and adult sociopathy were rare in girls and there was no association between them. Roff (1961) compared US military service records with independently assessed child guidance case histories. Poor peer adjustment in childhood correlated with both poor service record and also with psychoneurosis in adult life; overt aggression was a feature of poor early peer relations.

Pritchard and Graham (1966) investigated adult psychiatric patients who in childhood had also attended a psychiatric department. Overall the proportion of later personality disorder was very high in this group. Patients who as children had a nondelinquent conduct disorder were less sociopathic in adult life than patients with childhood delinquency, and had fewer neurotic illnesses in adult life than patients with childhood neurotic disorders.

Robins (1970) in a review of follow-up studies of childhood behaviour disorders concludes that preschool aggressive behaviour is not predictive of later delinquency, but that aggressive behaviour in the early and middle school years, especially when accompanied by school failure is associated with subsequent delinquency.

Conger and Miller (1966) studied retrospectively a group of 271 boys who became delinquent and a group of matched controls, correlating data available from school records with later delinquency and personality functioning. Even at the kindergarten and early school age period, future delinquents showed more antisocial conduct than controls and were less well liked and less accepted by their peers. Havighurst *et al* (1962) also found that aggression in the middle school years was related to later delinquency in boys. Much less information is available about the later outcome of girls with nondelinquent conduct disorders.

Sundby and Kreyberg (1968) followed up in adult life a group of child psychiatric inpatients intensively studied but given little treatment. Among children with behaviour disorders of all kinds, with psychoneuroses and psychosomatic disorders (all called 'neurotic') outcome was good in 71, fair in 30 and poor in 23. In the fair and poor outcome groups, 40 per cent of subjects had shown hostile aggression in childhood, but of children coded as hostile aggressive 44 per cent were later healthy. On the whole, however, the child's personality 'resources', for example his capacities for play and relationships were better prognostic indices than his symptoms.

In summary, there is evidence that nondelinquent conduct disorders during the early and middle school years often lead to delinquency at adolescence, especially when there is also school failure. In boys delinquency is strongly associated with adult sociopathy, both when it manifests as antisocial conduct and as aggression in childhood. Other personality variables of the children themselves are known to affect outcome, and it seems very likely that the responses elicited by the child's behaviour from parents, at school and in the community (as yet inadequately studied) play an important part. Morris *et al* (1956) for example showed that antisocial children who could return to their own families after psychiatric hospitalisation did better than those for whom other arrangements had to be made.

Treatment

There is no evidence for the successful treatment of antisocial children with psychotherapeutic or social case-work techniques, although this does not mean that such methods are not effective for some patients. The difficulties of measuring the results of psychotherapy are formidable and no progress in this area has been made.

Szurek and Berlin (1969) have recently reprinted a number of papers dealing in a clinical-descriptive way with the psychopathology and psychotherapeutic treatment of antisocial children. These papers stress the anxiety lowering and hence therapeutic effect of imposed restraints and controls within the therapeutic setting for acting-out children.

Anna Freud's point (1970) is made explicit: that antisocial children whose lack of conscience results from a parentless state require not a psychoanalytic approach but parent surrogates of a very special kind. Attachment is a prerequisite for the formation of conscience and ego-ideal. The frustrations of clinicians are described in the face of overwhelming demands and insufficient resources for treatment, and in the face of society's magical expectations of psychiatrists which accompany its rejection of the 'soft' approach.

Most advances have taken place in the study of behaviour modification techniques for childhood conduct disorders in the classroom and by parents at home. Becker *et al* (1967) have provided evidence that regular positive reinforcement of acceptable classroom behaviour by the teacher, coupled with consistent nonresponse to aggressive and disruptive conduct, leads to a dramatic fading out of this conduct and also, as a happy by-product, a more cheerful, encouraging teacher and a more congenial classroom atmosphere. In contrast, irregularly dispensed admonitions and reproofs serve only to reinforce poor conduct and lead to a noisy and unfriendly atmosphere in the class.

Two recent papers (Berkowitz & Graziano 1972; Johnson & Katz 1973) have reviewed the rapidly increasing and now voluminous literature in this area, with special reference to parents as behaviour therapists. Until 1967 most reports consisted of single case-studies of children mainly treated in hospitals. Such studies lacked adequate control and follow-up. Sadly, behavioural techniques are still often seen as rivalling psychotherapy (Berkowitz & Graziano 1972) rather than as useful additions to the therapeutic armamentarium, and at times a degree of clinical naivety enters into the discussions.

Most reports even after 1967 consist of descriptions of the training of one or two parents as behaviour therapists for their often psychotic or brain damamged young children. How the cases were selected is unclear; and the nature of the child's disorder is often of a kind not associated with the degree of parental disorder and sociocultural deprivation found in antisocial children.

Patterson *et al* (1970) described a sophisticated programme of group training for eleven families of boys with nondelinquent conduct disorders ranging in age from 6 to 13 years. Parents were trained to follow a programmed text and to use social reinforcements, 'time-out' and token systems. Families were followed up for 6 months. Maximum change occurred in the first 4 weeks of the programme and the total professional time involved was 12 hours per family. Generalisation effects to nontarget behaviour and to the behaviour of siblings and the parents' overall view of their children were established. Again, it is not clear whether, and if so how, the families were selected. Certainly severe parental personality disorder and inability to carry through a consistent programme may explain the result of Herbert and Baer (1972) that four of six deviant children deteriorated further during a programme designed to teach their mothers the use of differential attention.

Methods of training parents have involved modelling sessions in the clinic, group training, home visits and the training of new parents by parent experts. Some programmes involve the use of rewards and penalties for parents, to the extent that trips to the hairdresser and 'steak dinners' have been used as incentives. These methods suggest that, understandably, the parents of antisocial children may, as a group, be quite difficult to involve in such treatment programmes (unlike the less disturbed and often socially more competent mothers of brain damaged or autistic children).

The evidence suggests that treatment by teachers in the classroom may be more fruitful in the management of those conduct-disordered children whose parents cannot follow through a consistent plan.

REFERENCES

ACHENBACH T.M. (1966) The classification of children's psychiatric symptoms: a factor-analytic study. *Psychol. Monog.* **80,** 1–37

ASPERGER H. (1944) Die autistischen Psychopathen im Kindesalter. *Arch. Psychiatr. Nervenkrankheiten* **117,** 76–136

BANDURA A. & WALTERS R.H. (1963) *Social Learning and Personality Development.* London: Holt, Rinehart and Winston

BECKER W.C., MADSEN C.H., ARNOLD C.R. & THOMAS D.R. (1967) The contingent use of teacher attention and praise in reducing classroom problems. *J. Spec. Educ.* **1,** 287–307

BERKOWITZ B.P. & GRAZIANO A.M. (1972) Training parents as behavior therapists: a review. *Behav. Res. Therapy* **10,** 297–317

BILLER H.B. (1970) Father absence and the personality development of the male child. *Develop. Psychol.* **2**, 181–201

BOWLBY J. (1973) *Separation, Anxiety and Anger*. London: Hogarth Press and the Institute of Psycho-Analysis

CHESS S. (1972) Neurological dysfunction and childhood behavioral pathology. *J. Autism Child. Schiz.* **2**, 299–311

COLLINS L.F., MAXWELL A.E. & CAMERON K. (1962) A factor analysis of some child psychiatric clinic data. *J. Ment. Sci.* **108**, 274–285

CONGER J.J. & MILLER W.C. (1966) *Personality, Social Class and Delinquency*. New York: Wiley

CONNERS C.K. (1970) Symptom patterns in hyperkinetic, neurotic and normal children. *Child. Dev.* **41**, 667–682

FESHBACH S. & SINGER R.D. (1971) *Television and Aggression*. San Francisco: Jossey-Bass

FIELD E. (1967) *A Validation Study of Hewitt and Jenkin's Hypothesis*. Home Office Research Unit Report No. 10, London: HMSO

FREUD ANNA (1970) The symptomatology of childhood: a preliminary attempt at classification. *Psychoanalyt. Study Child.* **25**, 19–41. London: Hogarth Press

GARDNER G.E. (1971) Aggression and violence—the enemies of precision learning in children. *Amer. J. Psychiat.* **128**, 445–450

HALVERSON C.F. & WALDROP M.F. (1970) Maternal behaviour towards own and other preschool children: the problem of 'ownness'. *Child Dev.* **41**, 839–845

HAVIGHURST R.J., BOWMAN P.H., LIDDLE G.P., MATTHEWS C.V. & PIERCE J.V. (1962) *Growing up in River City*. New York: Wiley

HERBERT E. & BAER D. (1972) Training parents as behaviour modifiers: self recording of contingent attention. *J. Appl. Behav. Analy.* **5**, 139–149

HETHERINGTON E.M. (1965) A developmental study of the effects of sex of the dominant parent on sex-role preference, identification and imitation of children. *J. Pers. Soc. Psychol.* **2**, 188–194

HEWITT L.E. & JENKINS R.L. (1946) *Fundamental Patterns of Maladjustment*. Illinois: Michigan Child Guidance Institute

HIMMELWEIT H., OPPENHEIM A.N. & VINCE P. (1958) *Television and the Child*. London: Oxford University Press

HUESMANN L.R., ERON L.D., LEFKOWITZ M.M. & WALDER L.O. (1973) Television violence and aggression: the causal effect remains. *Amer. Psychologist.* **28**, 617–620

HUTT CORRINNE (1972) Sexual differentiation in human development. *In* Ounsted C. & Taylor D.C. (eds.) *Gender Differences, their Ontogeny and Significance*. London: Churchill-Livingstone

JENKINS R.L. (1969) Classification of behavior problems of children. *Amer. J. Psychiat.* **125**, 1032–1039

JENKINS R.L. (1970) Diagnostic classification in child psychiatry. *Amer. J. Psychiat.* **127**, 680–681

JOHNSON C.A. & KATZ R.C. (1973) Using parents as change agents for their children: a review. *J. Child Psychol. Psychiat.* **14**, 181–200

KAGAN J. & MOSS H.A. (1962) *Birth to Maturity*. New York: Wiley

KANNER L. (1944) Early infantile autism. *J. Pediat.* **25**, 211–217

KNIVETON B.H. & STEPHENSON G.M. (1975) The effects of an aggressive film model on social interaction in groups of middle-class and working-class boys. *J. Child Psychol. Psychiat.* **16**, 301–314

KOBAYASHI S., MIZUSHIMA K. & SHINOHARA M. (1967) Clinical groupings of problem children based on symptoms and behavior. *Int. J. Soc. Psychiat.* **13,** 206–215

KOLVIN I., WOLFF S., BARBER L., TWEDDLE E.G., GARSIDE R., SCOTT D.McI. & CHAMBERS S. (1975) Dimensions of behaviour in infant school children. *Brit. J. Psychiat.* **126,** 114–126

Lancet (1973) Childhood origins of group aggression. Report on conference of Medical Association for the Prevention of War, **2,** 165

LAPOUSE R. & MONK M.A. (1958) An epidemiological study of behavior characteristics in children. *Amer. J. Publ. Hlth.* **48,** 1134–1144

LIBERT R.M. & POULOS R.W. (1975) Television and personality development: the socialising effects of an entertainment medium. In Davids A. (ed.) *Child Personality and Psychopathology*, Vol. 2. New York: Wiley

McCORD W., McCORD J. & HOWARD A. (1961) Familial correlates of aggression in nondelinquent male children *J. Abn. Soc. Psychol.* **62,** 79–93

McFARLANE J.W., ALLEN L. & HONZIG P. (1954) *A Developmental Study of Behaviour Problems of Normal Children between 21 months and 14 years.* Berkeley and Los Angeles: University of California Press

MANNING M. (1976) Styles of hostility and social interactions at nursery, at school and at home: an extended study of children. *J. Child Psychol. Psychiat.* Supplement (to be published)

MASTERSON J.F. (1967) *The Psychiatric Dilemma of Adolescence.* London: Churchill

MINTON C., KAGAN J. & LEVINE J.A. (1971) Maternal control and obedience in the two-year-old child. *Child Dev.* **42,** 1873–1894

MORRIS H.H., ESCOLL P.J. & WEXLER R. (1956) Aggressive behavior disorders of childhood: a follow-up study. *Amer. J. Psychiat.* **112,** 991–997

MULLIGAN G., DOUGLAS, J.W.B., HAMMOND W.A. & TIZARD J. (1963) Delinquency and symptoms of maladjustment: the findings of a longitudinal study. *Proc. roy. Soc. Med.* **56,** 1083–1086

NEWSON J. & NEWSON E. (1976) *Seven Years Old in the Home Environment.* London: Allen & Unwin

PATTERSON G.R. (1964) An empirical approach to the classification of disturbed children. *J. Clin. Psychol.* **20,** 326–337

PATTERSON G.R., LITTMAN R.A. & BRICKER W. (1967) Assertive behavior in children: a step toward a theory of aggression. *Monog. Soc. Res. Child Dev.* **32,** no. 5

PATTERSON G.R., COBB J.A. & RAY R.S. (1970) A social engineering technology for retraining aggressive boys. *In* Adams H. & Unikel L. (eds.) *Georgia Symposium in Experimental Clinical Psychology*, vol. II. Oxford: Pergamon

POWER M.J., BENN R.T. & MORRIS J.N. (1972) Neighbourhood, school and juveniles before the Courts. *Brit. J. Criminol.* **12,** 111–132

PRITCHARD M. & GRAHAM P. (1966) An investigation of a group of patients who have attended both the child and adult departments of the same psychiatric hospital. *Brit. J. Psychiat.* **112,** 603–612

QUAY H.C. (1964) Dimensions of personality in delinquent boys as inferred from the factor analysis of case history data. *Child Dev.* **35,** 479–484

ROBINS L.N. (1966) *Deviant Children Grown Up.* Baltimore: Williams and Wilkins

ROBINS L.N. (1970) Follow-up studies investigating childhood disorders. *In* Hare E.H. & Wing J.K. (eds.) *Psychiatric Epidemiology.* London: Oxford University Press

ROFF M. (1961) Childhood social interactions and young adult bad conduct. *J. Abn. Soc. Psychol.* **63,** 333–337

RUTTER M. (1966) Behavioural and cognitive characteristics of a series of psychotic children. *In* Wing J.K. (ed.) *Early Childhood Autism.* Oxford: Pergamon Press

RUTTER M. (1970) Sex differences in children's responses to family stress. *In* Anthony E.J. & Koupernik C. (eds.) *The Child and His Family.* New York: Wiley

RUTTER M., SHAFFER D. & SHEPHERD M. (1975a) *A Multi-Axial Classification of Child Psychiatric Disorders.* Geneva: World Health Organization

RUTTER M., COX A., TUPLING C., BERGER M. & YULE W. (1975b) Attainment and adjustment in two geographical areas. I. The prevalence of psychiatric disorder. *Brit. J. Psychiat.* **126,** 493–509

RUTTER M., GRAHAM P. & YULE W. (1970a) *A Neuropsychiatric Study in Childhood.* Clinics in Develop. Mod. Nos. 35/36. London: SIMP/Heinemann

RUTTER M.L., TIZARD J. & WHITMORE K. (1970a) *Education, Health and Behaviour.* London: Longman

SCHRAMM W., LYLE J. & PARKER E.B. (1961) *Television in the Lives of our Children.* California: Stanford University Press

SEARS R.R., MACCOBY E.E. & LEVIN H. (1957) *Patterns of Child Rearing.* Illinois and New York: Row and Peterson

STRAUSS A.A. & LEHTINEN L. (1947) *Psychopathology and Education of the Brain-Injured Child.* New York: Grune and Stratton

SUNDBY H.S. & KREYBERG P.C. (1968) *Prognosis in Child Psychiatry,* Oslo Universitetsforlaget, Baltimore: Williams and Wilkins

SZUREK S.A. & BERLIN I.N. (eds.) (1969) *The Antisocial Child, his Family and his Community,* New York: Science and Behavior Books

THOMAS A., CHESS S. & BIRCH H.G. (1968) *Temperament and Behaviour Disorders in Children.* London: University of London Press

TUCKMAN J. & REGAN R.A. (1966) Intactness of the home and behavioural problems in children. *J. Child. Psychol. Psychiat.* **7,** 225–233

UNITED STATES PUBLIC HEALTH SERVICE REPORT TO THE SURGEON GENERAL (1972) *Television and Growing Up: the Impact of Televised Violence.* Washington, DC: US Government Printing Office

WERRY J.S. (1968) Developmental hyperactivity. *Pediatr. Clin. North Amer.* **15,** 581–599

WERRY J.S. & QUAY H.C. (1971) The prevalence of behavior symptoms in younger elementary school children. *Amer. J. Orthopsychiat.* **41,** 136–143

WEST D.J. (1969) *Present Conduct and Future Delinquency.* London: Heinemann

WIKLER A., DIXON J.F. & PARKER J.B. (1970) Brain function in problem children and controls: psychometric, neurological and electroencephalographic comparisons. *Amer. J. Psychiat.* **127,** 594–645

WOLFF S. (1961) Symptomatology and outcome of pre-school children with behaviour disorders attending a child guidance clinic. *J. Child Psychol. Psychiat.* **2,** 269–276

WOLFF S. (1967) Behavioural characteristics of primary school children referred to a psychiatric department. *Brit. J. Psychiat.* **113,** 885–893

WOLFF S. (1971) Dimensions and clusters of symptoms in disturbed children. *Brit. J. Psychiat.* **118,** 421–427

YORK R., HERON J.M. & WOLFF S. (1972) Exclusion from school. *J. Child Psychol. Psychiat.* **13,** 259–266

ZIGLER E. (1971) Social class and the socialization process. *In* Chess S. & Thomas A. (eds.) *Annual Progress in Child Psychiatry and Child Development.* London: Butterworths

CHAPTER 21

Delinquency

D. WEST

Delinquency, it is said, is a self-limiting condition. It fades away as youngsters grow up. Unfortunately this is so only up to a point. Recent English surveys, such as that of Power *et al* (1972), show that up to a quarter of all working class boys are convicted at least once as juveniles, and of these more than half acquire at least one subsequent conviction, while more than a quarter are reconvicted on two or more occasions. This last group, the persistent delinquents, present a great problem to social workers and administrators. Their numbers appear to be steadily increasing year by year.

Persistent antisocial behaviour in childhood is a more serious indicator of the likelihood of future disturbance in adult life than is the presence of neurotic symptoms. Warren (1965), in a 6-year follow-up of psychiatrically disturbed adolescents, found that three-quarters of the former neurotics were well, whereas only a third of those originally treated for 'conduct disorder' were recovered. In her famous long-term follow-up of former child guidance patients Robins (1966) found that, of children referred for such behaviour problems as thieving, incorrigibility and aggression, 28 per cent became sociopathic personalities as adults, compared with only 4 per cent of these referred for other reasons, and only 2 per cent of a control group of normal children. Whereas neurotic symptoms are associated with a good prognosis, the presence of multiple antisocial symptoms implied a distinctly gloomy prospect. Fortunately, most of the juvenile first offenders appearing before the courts for minor crimes do not display anything like so widespread a disturbance of behaviour as the psychiatric referrals studied by Warren and Robins.

Delinquency is a problem of particular prevalence in the poorer neighbourhoods of crowded, urban areas. In their survey of London, Wallis and Maliphant (1967) found that areas of high delinquency rate were characterised by many other indices of social malaise, such as high unemployment, large numbers of overcrowded houses, large numbers of manual workers and a tendency to leave school at the earliest permitted age. The associations between delinquency and other indices of social pathology, such as illegitimate births, suicide rates, debt defaulters and notifiable medical conditions like drug dependence and venereal disease, are probably as marked today as when they were first cited in the ecological studies of the Chicago school nearly half a century ago.

In modern Britain, the distribution of juvenile delinquents varies remarkably over quite small distances. One street, or even part of a street, can be conspicuously delinquent-prone, in comparison with its neighbours. In Tower Hamlets, Power *et al* (1972) found that the greatest detectable variability was between the smallest areas studied, namely the 300 census enumeration districts. The reasons for this are difficult to specify. The policy of public housing authorities in relation to the placement of difficult families has an important influence.

Older criminological literature, especially that contributed by psychiatrists, was largely preoccupied with identifying the unfavourable and often pathological characteristics which were believed to distinguish the delinquent type from his law-abiding and healthy peers (Friedlander 1947; Lombroso 1895). Partly as a result of the challenge of modern, radical sociologists, the assumption that delinquents are in any way unusual or abnormal, or in need of psychiatric attention, is no longer accepted as self-evident. Some authorities assert that nonconformity to legal norms is a natural and inevitable reaction by those members of a competitive society who find themselves unfairly handicapped by social, educational or economic adversity. On this view, psychiatric attempts to tamper with the delinquent's attitudes and personality are unwarranted, and serve only to distract attention from the real causes, which lie in the legal and social structure, and not in the individual. Furthermore, by lending medical support to the practice of labelling social rebels deviant or sick, psychiatrists may be helping to scapegoat the most valuable members of the community, namely those who are least willing to submit docilely to social inequality. As some exponents of the 'new criminology' put it (Taylor *et al* 1973): 'A criminology which is not normatively committed to the abolition of inequalities of wealth and power, and in particular of inequalities in property and life-chances, is inevitably bound to fall into correctionalism. And all correctionalism is irreducibly bound up with the identification of deviance with pathology.'

To practitioners accustomed to seeing a succession of maladjusted children referred on account of delinquent behaviour, these ideas may seem absurd. On the other hand, psychiatric clients are not necessarily typical of delinquents in general. Moreover, it cannot be denied that the definition of a delinquent varies according to community attitudes, the state of the law and the policies of law enforcement agencies. In this country, the usual definition of a delinquent is a person who has a criminal conviction registered against his name in the Criminal Record Office. Obviously the number of juveniles who acquire such a record must have been affected by the increase in the age of criminal responsibility (that is the age at which children become liable to prosecution) and by the introduction of additional police powers to deal with juveniles without formal prosecution. If these trends were to be carried far enough, 'official' juvenile delinquency could be eliminated altogether.

It is widely believed that some of the characteristics of official delinquents are determined by social policy. For instance, the overrepresentation of lower class boys among official delinquents could be a consequence of the reluctance of parents, teachers and police to resort to the courts when dealing with misbehaviour by youngsters from middle class homes. The surprising number of juvenile delinquents from broken homes, especially among those committed to penal institutions, might be due to the preferential selection of such cases for official processing, justified by their supposed need for help. Furthermore, it is inevitable, as social conditions and attitudes change, that the kind of behaviour perceived as criminal will also change. Incidents that could be looked upon as normal aggressive play might, at some other time and place, be reported to the police as assaults. With the amplification of laws against drug abuse, and their stricter implementation, a new category of better educated and higher class youngsters are drawn into the delinquent population. Many more would be included if the law against sexual activity involving girls below the 'age of consent' were to be fully enforced.

Official delinquents are thrown up by the dynamic interaction between the youthful community and the norm enforcing agencies. It is naïve to suppose that it will always be the same kind of person, or the same range of behaviour, that will attract the delinquency label. At the present time, these interactions result in about a quarter of the male population from ordinary working class districts of England acquiring a criminal record by the age of 20. Although conceivably deviating from some ideal concept of mental health, such a high proportion of the population can scarcely be held to be seriously pathological.

The suspicion that official delinquents consist of a very small and probably biassed sample of the totality of law violators has received ample confirmation in recent criminological research. In response to confidential questionnaires or interviews young people are regularly found to admit to having committed a surprisingly large range and number of offences, only a tiny minority of which lead to criminal convictions (Hood & Sparks 1970). Similarly, population surveys to identify persons who have been victims of crime regularly reveal many more incidents than ever come to the notice of police. A certain amount of law-breaking appears to be the healthy norm among young people.

Those who never do so are the statistical deviants. Breaking the law in such a way as to attract official action is another matter. On the whole, there is a remarkable overlap between the group who produce unusually high scores on self-report delinquency tests, and the group who become official delinquents. The more serious and persistent among law-breakers tend, sooner or later, to become official delinquents. Indeed high scores on self-report delinquency have been shown to be predictive of later official convictions (Farrington 1973). On the other hand, given similar self-report scores, boys are more likely to be labelled official delinquents if they happen to have certain characteristics, notably low social class (Jaakkola 1966) or other family members already convicted (Farrington *et al* 1975).

In a survey of juvenile delinquents West and Farrington (1973) investigated this issue in some detail. They found that whether delinquents were defined by the possession of a criminal record, or alternatively by an excessive number of admissions on a self-report schedule, they ended up with similar kinds of boys. Both the self-reported delinquents and the official delinquents tended to come from poor homes, to have criminal fathers or siblings, to belong to large families, to have parents considered unsatisfactory in their child-rearing methods, and to be of below average intelligence. Since over half of the self-reported delinquents were also officially convicted delinquents, the result was scarcely surprising. It showed that, by and large, the boys who were the worst behaved according to their own admissions were the boys most likely to acquire an official conviction record. The processes of prosecution were less arbitrary than might be supposed. On the other hand, they did find some evidence that delinquent boys who avoided conviction did not conform to the usual delinquent stereotype. The minority of boys with many admissions, who remained free from juvenile convictions, shared none of the five factors that were typical of the official delinquents. It seemed that good intelligence and a good home, were some protection against conviction for delinquent behaviour.

There is an analogy here between official delinquency and officially ascertained mental subnormality. In the latter case, in addition to the major criterion of intellectual handicap, adverse social circumstances and concurrent troublesome behaviour greatly increase the probability of acquiring the label subnormal. Similarly, poor social circumstances and a troublesome or rebellious attitude towards authority greatly enhance the probability that a breach of the law will lead to the offender being recorded as a delinquent. In short, being a delinquent usually reflects something more than simple law-breaking. Since juvenile delinquents, and not unreported offenders, are the persons under consideration, the prevalence of law-breaking in the community at large is of no greater relevance to the topic of delinquency than is the distribution of low IQ in the community relevant to the topic of subnormality. This point needs emphasising in the case of delinquency because, unlike the mental health authorities, who readily admit the social component in official subnormality, the criminal justice authorities maintain a rhetoric of equality before the law, and punishment proportionate to the seriousness of the crime, which tends to obscure the realities of the delinquency label.

In the last analysis, bad behaviour in general, and law-breaking in particular, though not the only elements present, are certainly essential components of delinquency. In the recently published prospective study of delinquency development by the Cambridge Institute of Criminology (West & Farrington 1973) it was found that, by the age of 8 to 10 years many of the boys who later became official delinquents were already distinguishable from their peers by their trouble-seeking conduct, which was apparent to both teachers and classmates. The kind of misbehaviour seen in predelinquents, such as disobedience, truancy, quarrelsomeness, slovenliness and inattention, is not at all the same as the kind of misbehaviour which typically results in a prosecution later on. The great majority of findings of guilt against juveniles are for thieving or breaking in, usually committed by two or more boys together, or for taking away motor vehicles. But the boys who get caught for these somewhat stereotyped activities, especially those who acquire two or more convictions, tend to be deviant in many other aspects of their attitude and behaviour. They have been deviant as children, and followed up into young adult life they remain deviant. They tend to heavy drinking, smoking and gambling, they are more than usually sexually promiscuous, they opt for unskilled jobs that in the short-term yield more pay, they are aggressive and readily get into fights, and their attitudes are typically antiauthoritarian. The criminal type is not entirely a myth.

Some of the most notable background characteristics of male juvenile delinquents, cited in many surveys, and confirmed by the Cambridge Study, include a tendency to come from poor families with a large number of children (Ferguson 1952), a tendency to have below average intelligence (Ferracuti 1966), a tendency to have a parent with a criminal record (McCord *et al* 1959), and a tendency to have experienced unsatisfactory or negligent parental love and care (Glueck & Glueck 1950). Such background factors produce a cumulative effect: the more of them present, the more likely the boy is to become delinquent. In the Cambridge Study, 15 per cent of the population had three or more of these five adverse features present. Compared with the rest of the population, boys from this disadvantaged minority had more than six times the chance of becoming a juvenile recidivist.

Various theories of the connection between family adversity and delinquency have been put forward. For instance, bad example on the part of the parent is one explanation for the tendency of the sons of criminal fathers to acquire criminal records themselves. This cannot be the sole cause. Even when the father's last conviction occurred many years previous, and the son has never been told about it, the influence of it upon the boy is still evident.

The adverse influence of large sized families has been thought to be due to overcrowding, or to older male siblings leading their younger brothers astray. In point of fact, it appears to be the actual size of the sibship more than the degree of overcrowding, or the sex and age of the siblings, which favours delinquency. This suggests that competition among many siblings for the parents' limited resources of care and attention is the main cause of damage.

The problem is that most empirical observations about delinquency are susceptible to differing theoretical interpretations. One can for instance point to social and economic conditions as a basic cause of unsatisfactory parental behaviour, family criminality, intellectual retardation and exposure to a delinquent neighbourhood. On the other hand, it might be argued that all these ills are the product of biologically deviant or inferior parents, who fail to cope with the demands of a competitive meritocracy, and who transmit their inadequacies to their offspring.

As an explanation of criminal tendency, genetic transmission of biological deviations, although forcibly argued by some well-known authorities (Eysenck 1970), is out of fashion among Western criminologists. Nevertheless, the results of twin studies, especially the survey of a total Danish population (Christiansen 1974) do strongly suggest a genetic vulnerability, indicated by the significantly greater concordance for criminality between monozygotic than between dizygotic twins. This factor is, however, much less important in relation to commonplace juvenile delinquency than in relation to the rarer and more serious forms of criminality, which in turn are more often associated with overt signs of psychiatric disturbance. Nevertheless, there is evidence that genetics may have some relevance to youthful delinquency. A recent study by Hutchings and Mednick (1973) demonstrated that the acquisition of a criminal record by adopted sons was significantly more closely related to whether their biological fathers (with whom they had no contacts) were registered criminals than whether the fathers who brought them up were criminals. Whether an adoptive father with a criminal record produced a criminal son was to a very significant extent determined by whether the biological father was a criminal. This result suggested the presence of some genetically transmitted factor which influenced vulnerability to criminogenic environmental pressures.

Genetic vulnerability is a vague concept, unless one can pin-point the physical mechanism. Gross and detectable chromosome anomalies, such as the XYY syndrome, are far too rare to have much relevance to the generality of delinquents. However, Slater *et al* (1969) who carried out chromosome studies in a remand home for juvenile delinquents, did discover a significant excess of minor translocations.

If there is a genetic component to delinquent tendency, one might expect to find delinquency associated with characteristics known to have some hereditary basis. In the field of personality, Eysenck has long argued that neurotic extraverts have a special predisposition to delinquency, but empirical surveys of juvenile deinquents have failed to confirm this prediction (Hoghughi & Forrest 1970). In regard to physical development, a number of investigators (e.g. Gibbens 1963) claim to have found evidence for Sheldon's contention that individuals of mesomorphic physique are overrepresented among male delinquents. The correlations are small, however, and might well be secondary consequences of links between physique and social class. Another line of inquiry, the examination of EEG records, although initially promising, has failed to yield clear evidence that unselected juvenile delinquents differ significantly from nondelinquents (Loomis 1965).

Perhaps the most promising research findings indicative of constitutional differences between delinquents and nondelinquents are those which relate to the autonomic nervous system. A considerable amount of evidence has accumulated suggesting that extreme delinquents at least—the so-called primary psychopaths—tend to show relatively slight autonomic response to novel or stressful stimuli. They also show a deficit in learning in fear avoidance situations, possibly because of their low physiological arousal (Trasler 1973). While the clearest results have been reported in work on extreme and possibly pathological delinquents, some recent work has indicated that unselected populations of badly behaved schoolboys may also show some autonomic deficit in the form of slow pulse and sluggish response of pulse rate to stress (Davies & Maliphant 1971).

These somewhat esoteric findings fit in rather neatly with some of the ideas of learning theorists concerning socialisation processes. According to one school of thought, the chief mechanism whereby the infant learns conformist behaviour is by avoidance conditioning. Certain situations and responses lead to punishment. In the course of time this produces generalised avoidance reactions. The child becomes so conditioned that, whenever a similar situation or temptation arises, he feels uncomfortable at the thought of wrongdoing. In subjective terms this is the development of self-restraint and conscience. Anything which interferes with this process is liable to produce a young nonconformist or delinquent. A poor capacity for avoidance conditioning, based upon autonomic deficit, could well be one such factor.

The quality of child-rearing is probably a much more important factor. Learning theorists emphasise the need to provide ample opportunity for learning situations, the need for consistency in the application of deterrents for bad behaviour and the need to avoid overharsh punishments, which are liable to overwhelm the learning mechanism and invoke paradoxical responses. The home background of the delinquent is often defective in all these respects. If a mother is overburdened with too many children, she cannot give the necessary time and attention to any one. If children are unwanted or neglected they are exposed to fewer learning situations. If parents are erratic or inconsistent or cruel in their disciplinary methods, the conditioning becomes relatively ineffectual. If the parents are themselves poorly socialised, they will be careless or uncertain about laying down standards and disapproving nonconformity.

This somewhat mechanical model of social learning is at odds with the more psychodynamically oriented school of thought, which emphasises the quality of personal relationships, especially that of the earliest interactions between mother and child. In terms of visible parental behaviour and family situations, however, both schools of thought seem to arrive at rather similar conclusions concerning the nature of the criminogenic family. Both schools depict the typical delinquent as a poorly socialised personality.

One possible consequence of styles of upbringing is the relatively low incidence of official delinquency among girls. There are about eight convictions of male juveniles for every conviction of a girl, and far fewer girls than boys become persistent delinquens. Since girls are traditionally more closely controlled by their parents, and overtly aggressive behaviour is particularly discouraged as being unfeminine, this might explain the stricter standards of conformity acquired by girls. As cultural standards change, and 'unisex' attitudes spread, these differences may diminish. Already there is some evidence of an increasing participation by girls in predatory offences. On the other hand, temperamental contrasts between the sexes, due to biological rather than cultural factors, are also likely to have an effect (Hutt 1972). Furthermore, the respective roles of men and women in society influence their opportunities for crime. Stealing from docks and lorries is a male pursuit, whereas shoplifting is one of the few crimes more commonly committed by females than by males.

Sociologists (e.g. Schuessler *et al* 1950) have justly criticised the sort of evidence on which some criminologists base their belief in the deviant personality of criminals. The results of personality testing have been inconsistent, and highly dependent upon the way the delinquent samples are recruited as well as on the situation in which they are tested. Sometimes items included in tests, such as questions about attitudes towards police or other authorities, make it inevitable that convicted delinquents, regardless of personality, should score differently from nondelinquents on account of their special experiences. Nevertheless, a fair measure of agreement has been reached that certain characteristics, notably impulsiveness, aggressivity and antiauthoritarian attitudes, are particularly prevant among delinquents. In observations of behaviour by teachers and peers (Empey & Lubeck 1971; Farrington & West 1971) in responses to projective tests such as the Hand Test (Wagner 1969) and in self-assessments (Masters & Tong 1968), delinquents are regularly found to be more aggressive than nondelinquents.

The aggressiveness of delinquents apparently precedes any experience of conviction. Although aggression may be exacerbated by the way delinquents are dealt with by penal authorities, this cannot be the basic cause of its presence in the first place. Many experts believe with Woodmansey (1971) and Eron *et al* (1963) that the aggressiveness of delinquents is the result of cruel upbringing at the hands of hostile parents or parent substitutes. Unfortunately, an aggressive attitude provokes hostile responses, so the delinquent tends to perpetuate his own unfavourable environment. This enables him to find examples of maltreatment which serve as pseudojustification for his suspicious, hostile attitude towards society. In a celebrated thesis on *Violent Men*, Toch (1972) has demonstrated the dangerous escalation of violence which occurs in confrontations between adult criminals and police due to an interaction of the paranoid attitudes of each group.

The classic delinquent personality, with all the traits of aggressiveness, egocentricity, impulsiveness, antisocial attitudes and lack of conscience, is virtually identical with the so-called psychopathic personality. Fortunately most juvenile delinquents, although displaying some of these attributes, do not attain to the complete stereotype. All the same, there is a characteristic life style associated with a heavy commitment to delinquency which could be held to reflect these personality trends. Gambling, sexual promiscuity, drug and alcohol abuse, erratic work record, lack of interest in school or organised leisure activities, quitting the parental home at an early age, spending most of the time in the streets or in cafés, are some of the well-known features of the delinquent style of life.

The fact that delinquents tend to come from unfortunate home backgrounds and to display certain personality characteristics and social attitudes is of practical as well as theoretical interest. It means that there is scope for treatment by attempts to modify individuals, either by inducing attitude changes, or by counteracting the effects of social deprivation by providing social assistance and training opportunities. Psychiatrists are naturally attracted to this approach, since they are trained to deal with maladjusted individuals. On the other hand, many delinquents are only minimally deviant from a psychological or psychiatric standpoint. Although certain personalities are more vulnerable than others to adverse social pressures, the social factors rather than the personal factors are the main causes of delinquency. Schemes for individual treatment are certainly needed, but the wider problem of prevention calls for a different perspective.

Most juvenile delinquency is group behaviour. Delinquents commit offences in the company of their friends. They may thereby gain status in the eyes of their particular cronies, if not among their peers at large. The kinds of offences committed are very much determined by opportunity and local tradition. Delinquents follow the pattern expected of them. Stealing from chain stores and supermarkets is a very common activity, but of course only among those who live in areas where these facilities exist. Epidemics of particular kinds of offences, such as breaking open telephone coin boxes, illustrate the importance of both example and opportunity in determining delinquent conduct. In areas where many unguarded vehicles are parked, especially motor scooters, which are attractive to the young and relatively easy to move, one expects a high level of 'taking and driving' offences. These immediate, circumstantial precipitants of delinquency are too often lost sight of in psychological discussions.

Even in the most casual, opportunistic type of offence, however, personality factors will come into the picture and perhaps determine which one of a group of youngsters will actually do the deed. Some are bolder than others, some may actually enjoy risk-taking, some may have a systematic bias in their subjective estimates of the probability of capture and its consequences (Cohen 1972). These more subtle personality factors, though not unhealthy or undesirable in general, could be important influences in delinquency situations.

Many sociological theories take as their starting point the observation that delinquency, and the factors associated with delinquency, are heavily concentrated in certain urban areas and in the poorer classes of the population. It is thought that selective social pressures help to bring about a shift of social values in the classes of persons affected. Subcultures formed in this way are less likely than the dominant middle class culture to condemn thieving or aggression unequivocally. Cloward and Ohlin (1961) emphasised the effect upon working class males of finding themselves in a position where legitimate opportunities for advancement in wealth or status were impossibly difficult. This leads to condemnation of middle class rules, and a glorification of the aggressive, go-getting youngster who is not afraid to take what he wants illegally.

The belief that delinquents are committed to a working class ethos opposed to conventional morality has never really been established empirically. A sense of social injustice does not feature prominently in spontaneous accounts of motives for offences. Juvenile crimes are not, on the whole, particularly utilitarian. The thrill of the delinquent escapade, the relief of boredom and the satisfaction derived from proving one's prowess in front of peers, are often more prominent than any measurable material gain. Moreover, the sociologists are by no means agreed about the true characteristics of the delinquent subculture. Some emphasise the consistently oppositional character of the subculture, and the tendency to form adolescent gangs, led by the fiercest and most antagonistic individuals and wholeheartedly committed to the pursuit of antisocial activity. In contrast, Matza (1964) believes these extreme attitudes untypical. Few boys are committed to full-time conflict with conventional society, but many drift episodically into delinquent activity. By and large they accept society's rules. When they break the rules they have to find all kinds of excuses to justify themselves. For instance, rationalisations about the need for self-protection justify the carrying of offensive weapons. It is the availability of such rationalisations, rather than a dedicated hostility to middle class norms, which, in Matza's view, is the essential feature of delinquent subcultures.

The available evidence is too scanty to decide between these various interpretations. Most of these sociological theories have been developed in America, where social contrasts are harsher and ghetto situations more obvious than in England. In America, the rise of a black movement opposed to the property rules of white, capitalist society has given a new legitimacy to criminal activity in the eyes of certain radicals. In England, where the conflicts seem for the moment more muted, surveys such as those of Wilmott (1966) and Downes (1966) have confirmed that delinquents tend to adhere to a scale of values different from those of the middle class, but not actively hostile to conventional norms. For instance, they are likely to reject the ideas of advancement by hard work and continued training, or the concept of sacrifice for the sake of challenging or interesting jobs. They are more likely to view jobs as a necessary evil, a means of obtaining cash for immediate wants, and more likely to identify with thrill-seeking peer groups than with the socially mobile aspirants to middle class status.

Schools can provide a breeding ground for the delinquent subculture. Power *et al* (1972) found striking differences between the delinquency rates of pupils attending different state schools, even though their populations were drawn from similar neighbourhoods. The Cambridge research, while confirming the existence of big differences in delinquency rates between neighbouring secondary schools, found that these were very largely accounted for by the tendency of boys with a high delinquency potential to gravitate to the worst schools. Within a given school the practice of streaming by academic ability may lead to contrasting subcultures. In one school studied by Hargreaves (1967), the A stream the pupils were academically oriented and disapproved of delinquency, but in the D stream delinquent behaviour was the norm and delinquency served to raise a boy's status among his class mates.

So far we have discussed 'delinquents' as if they comprised some sort of homogeneous group, the members of which share fairly well-defined social and personal characteristics. This holds true to the extent that certain trends are present and generalisations are possible, but the same might also be said of some quite heterogeneous groups, such as the physically unfit. It would, however, be foolish to go searching for a universal explanation of ill-health, and it would be almost as foolish to expect a single explanation of all delinquency. The kinds of behaviour which lead to a delinquency label, as has been said, depend upon the kind of society in which one lives. In other words, the shoe pinches in different spots. An overcrowded, competitive, urban culture, oriented towards ownership of affluence, is very different from a rural community in an underdeveloped country, and different again from the culture of an authoritarian communistic regime, in which personal wealth is minimal and the official ideology emphasises conformity to group requirements rather than personal advancement. Each situation generates its own varieties of deviant. In our own community delinquency is almost synonymous with thieving, somewhere else it might consist almost exclusively of personal violence.

Even within our own culture, different subgroups of delinquent are discernible. The young sex offender or drug offender, with no record of offences of any other kind, is unlikely to conform to the general delinquent stereotype. Delinquents from grammar schools and economically favoured backgrounds are more likely to be individually maladjusted and to be suffering intrapsychic conflict than those from the working class, for whom a delinquent life style comes more naturally because it is so prevalent in their subculture. Girls who become delinquent are also more likely to be maladjusted, since delinquency is less common among females of any social class. As is well known, delinquent girls are often involved in sexual misdemeanours, and this is one of the commonest causes of girls being sent to community homes. This difference between girl and boy delinquent is somewhat artificial, for there is no particular reason to believe the boys to be more chaste. However conduct of this sort among girls, with its attendant risks of unwanted pregnancy, evokes a sharper response on the part of the authorities.

It will be seen that the topic of juvenile delinquency touches upon a wide range of psychiatric and social issues. To psychiatrists the clinical problems are the most relevant, but to the criminologist, who is concerned with the totality of juvenile delinquency, the social factors clearly dominate the picture. From a public health viewpoint also the social problems are more important. For instance, attention to such matters as the housing and educational problems of racial minorities and recent immigrants would probably yield a better pay-off (in terms of a reduction in vandalism and street 'muggings' for instance) than any amount of psychiatric service.

REFERENCES

CHRISTIANSEN K.O. (1974) Seriousness of criminality and concordance among Danish twins. *In* Hood R. (ed.) *Crime, Criminology and Public Policy.* London: Heinemann
CLOWARD R.A. & OHLIN L.E. (1961) *Delinquency and Opportunity.* London: Routledge
COHEN J. (1972) *Psychological Probability.* London: Allen & Unwin
DAVIES J.C.V. & MALIPHANT R. (1971) Autonomic responses of male adolescents exhibiting refractory behaviour in school. *J. Child Psychol. Psychiat.* **12**, 115–127
DOWNES D.M. (1966) *The Delinquent Solution.* London: Routledge & Kegan Paul
EMPEY L.T. & LUBECK S.G. (1971) *Explaining Deliquency.* Lexington, Massachusetts: D.C. Heath
ERON L.D., WALDER L.O., TOIGO R. & LEFKOWITZ M.M. (1963) Social class, parental punishment for aggression, and child aggression. *Child Dev.* **34**, 849–867
EYSENCK H.J. (1970) *Crime and Personality.* London: Paladin (rev. ed.)
FARRINGTON D.P. (1973) Self-reports of deviant behavior: predictive and stable? *J. Crimin. Law Criminol.* **64**, 99–110
FARRINGTON D.P. & WEST D.J. (1971) A comparison between early delinquents and young aggressives. *Brit. J. Criminol.* **11**, 341–358
FARRINGTON D.P., GUNRY G. & WEST D.J. (1975) The Familial transmission of criminality. *Med. Science and the Law* **15**, 177–186
FERGUSON T. (1952) *The Young Delinquent in his Social Setting: A Glasgow Study.* London: Oxford University Press
FERRACUTI F. (1966) *Intelligence and Criminality: a Bibliography.* Milan: Giuffré
FRIEDLANDER K. (1947) *The Psycho-analytical Approach to Juvenile Delinquency.* London: Kegan Paul
GIBBENS T.C.N. (1963) *Psychiatric Studies of Borstal Lads.* Institute of Psychiatry Maudsley Monographs No. 11. London: Oxford University Press
GLUECK S. & GLUECK E.T. (1950) *Unraveling Juvenile Delinquency.* Cambridge, Massachusetts: Harvard University Press
HARGREAVES D.H. (1967) *Social Relations in a Secondary School.* London: Routledge & Kegan Paul
HOGHUGHI M.S. & FORREST A.R. (1970) Eysenck's theory of criminality: an examination with Approved School boys. *Brit. J. Criminol.* **10**, 240–254
HOOD R. & SPARKS R. (1970) *Key Issues in Criminology.* London: Weidenfeld & Nicolson
HUTCHINGS B. & MEDNICK S.A. (1973) Registered criminality in the adopted and biological parents of registered male criminal adoptees. *In* Fieve R.R. *et al* (eds.) *Genetic Researches in Psychiatry* (Proceedings of the 63rd annual meeting of the American Psychopathological Association). Baltimore: Johns Hopkins University Press

HUTT C. (1972) Sex differences in human development. *Hum. Devel.* **15**, 153–170

JAAKKOLA R. (1966) Social background and criminality. *In* Antilla I. & Jaakkola R. (1966) *Unrecorded Criminality in Finland.* Helsinki: Institute of Criminology

LOMBROSO C. (1895) *L'Uomo delinquente.* Turin.

LOOMIS S.D. (1965) EEG abnormalities as a correlate of behavior in adolescent male delinquents. *Amer. J. of Psych.* **212**, 1003–1006

MASTERS F.G. & TONG J.E. (1968) The semantic differential test with Borstal subjects. *Brit. J. Criminol.* **8**, 20–31

MATZA D. (1964) *Delinquency and Drift.* New York: Wiley

McCORD W., McCORD J. & ZOLA I.K. (1959) *Origins of Crime.* New York: Columbia University Press

POWER M.J., BENN R.T. & MORRIS J.N. (1972) Neighbourhood, school and juveniles before the courts. *Brit. J. Criminol.* **12**, 111–132

ROBINS L.N. (1966) *Deviant Children Grown Up.* Baltimore: Williams & Wilkins

SCHUESSLER K.F. & CRESSEY D. (1950) Personality characteristics of criminals. *Amer. J. Sociol.* **55**, 476–484

SLATER E.T.O., KAHN J., CARTER W.I. & DERNLEY N. (1969) Chromosome studies in remand home and prison populations in West D.J. (ed.) *Criminological Implications of Chromosome Abnormalities.* Cambridge: University of Cambridge Institute of Criminology

TAYLOR I., WALTON P. & YOUNG J. (1973) *The New Criminology: for a Social Theory of Deviance.* London: Routledge & Kegan Paul

TOCH H. (1972) *Violent Men.* Harmondsworth: Penguin

TRASLER G. (1973) Criminal behaviour. *In* Eysenck H.J. (ed.) *Handbook of Abnormal Psychology.* London: Pitman Medical

WAGNER E.E. (1969) *The Hand Test Manual.* Los Angeles: Western Psychological Services

WALLIS C.P. & MALIPHANT R. (1967) Delinquent areas in the County of London: ecological factors. *Brit. J. Criminol.* **7**, 250–284

WARREN W. (1965) A study of adolescent psychiatric in-patients and the outcome six or more years later. II: The follow-up study. *J. Child Psychol. Psychiat.* **6**, 141–160

WEST D.J. & FARRINGTON D.P. (1973) *Who Becomes Delinquent?* London: Heinemann Educational

WILLMOTT P. (1966) *Delinquent Subculture in East London.* London: Routledge & Kegan Paul

WOODMANSEY A.C. (1971) Understanding delinquency. *Brit. J. Criminol.* **11**, 155–166

CHAPTER 22

Hyperkinetic syndrome

D. CANTWELL

The *hyperkinetic syndrome* was first described by the German physician, Heinrich Hoffmann, over 100 years ago (Hoffmann 1854). Since then several authors have outlined a syndrome which begins early in life, is more common in boys, and is manifested by a symptom pattern of hyperactivity, impulsivity, distractibility and excitability (Anderson 1963; Bakwin 1949; Bradley 1955; Burks 1960; Laufer & Denhoff 1957; Stewart *et al* 1966; Werry 1968a). Aggressive and antisocial behaviour, specific learning problems, and emotional lability are often considered part of the syndrome (O'Malley & Eisenberg 1973).

TERMINOLOGY

Terms such as the 'brain damage syndrome' (Strauss & Lehtinen 1947), 'minimal brain damage' (Gesell & Amatruda 1949) and 'minimal brain dysfunction' (Clements 1966) are often used synonomously with the term hyperkinetic syndrome, with a number of unfortunate consequences. Since these terms have been used in widely divergent ways by different investigators, the same children have been described by different terms and different children by the same terms. Thus, research findings cannot be readily compared.

Moreover, these terms imply 'brain damage or dysfunction' is present (and presumably causal) in the hyperkinetic syndrome. However, if brain damage is used in its literal sense to mean structural abnormality of the brain, then brain damage syndrome is an inaccurate and misleading term. While *some* hyperkinetic children may suffer from frank brain damage, it is clear that the majority do not (Werry 1972). Likewise, *most* brain damaged children do *not* present with the hyperkinetic syndrome (Rutter *et al* 1970a).

'Brain dysfunction' may be a more accurate term than 'brain damage' or describe those children who present with less well-defined disorders manifested by more subtle neurological signs. These more subtle defects in coordination, perception or language may only occasionally be associated with actual damage to the brain (Rutter 1968). However, many hyperkinetic children do not demonstrate even these subtle neurologic signs. Thus 'brain dysfunction syndrome' is an inappropriate term to describe the large percentage of hyperkinetic children who present primarily with behavioural abnormalities. Finally, techniques for the reliable and accurate quantification of brain dysfunction in children are not available. Yet prefixing the word 'minimal' to 'brain dysfunction' implies just such a quantification.

Therefore in this chapter, the term 'hyperkinetic syndrome' will be used to denote a behavioural syndrome only, with *no* implications for aetiology.

CLINICAL PICTURE

The typical child with the hyperkinetic syndrome is generally brought to professional attention early in his elementary school years. However, careful questioning usually reveals symptoms present from early childhood. The clinical picture varies from the little boy who is silly, immature and not performing academically up to expected standards to the markedly active, aggressive and antisocial child who is unable to be managed in a regular classroom setting.

Hyperactivity

Parents report that from an early age the child has always seemed to have an unusual amount of energy, less need for sleep than his sibs, and he wore out shoes, clothes, bicycles, etc., faster than other children. Parents and teachers note fidgetiness, inability to sit still for any length of time, talking a great deal and inability to keep his hands to himself. A number of methods to quantify activity level have been tried; these include the use of ballistographic, mechanical, photoelectric and ultrasonic devices (Foshee 1958; Sprague & Toppe 1966; Schulman & Reisman 1959; Bell 1968; Ellis & Pryer 1959; McFarland *et al* 1966), telemetry and motion pictures (Davis *et al* 1969; Herron & Ramsden 1967; Lee & Hutt 1964), and direct observation and ratings by observers (Doubros & Daniels 1966; Hutt *et al* 1966; Ounsted 1955; Patterson *et al* 1965). Unfortunately, results have been inconclusive and there is serious question whether hyperkinetic children actually have a clearly *greater amount* of daily motor activity or a *different type* of motor activity than nonhyperkinetic children.

Distractability

Distractability and a short attention span are more noticeable in the school but are usually reported by parents also. The typical child is unable to persevere with classwork and homework, frequently daydreams, is easily distracted from projects by extraneous stimuli, and is unable to listen to a story or take part in table games for any length of time.

Impulsivity

Impulsivity is shown by such behaviours as jumping into the deep end of a swimming pool without knowing how to swim, running into the street in front of cars, climbing out on to high roof tops and ledges, and blurting out tactless statements.

Excitability

The excitability of the hyperkinetic child is manifested by temper tantrums and fights over trivial matters, low frustration tolerance and a tendency to become overexcited and more active in stimulating situations, especially in large groups of other children.

These symptoms of hyperactivity, distractibility, impulsivity and excitability have been consistently reported (Werry 1968a; Stewart *et al* 1966; O'Malley & Eisenberg 1973) and may be considered as the cardinal symptoms of the syndrome. Many investigators feel that short attention span and distractibility are the *essential* features of the syndrome, with hyperactivity being a more variable symptom. Distractibility and attention deficit has been viewed both as a lack of stimulus inhibition and as a stimulus-seeking behaviour (Klein & Gittelman-Klein 1975a).

Other symptoms that are often, but not necessarily, associated with the hyperkinetic syndrome are: aggressive and antisocial behaviour, cognitive and learning disabilities, depression and low self-esteem.

Antisocial behaviour

It was originally thought that aggressive antisocial behaviours were a necessary component of the hyperkinetic syndrome (Strauss & Lehtinen 1947; Bradley 1955; Laufer & Denhoff 1957; Stewart *et al* 1966) and it has been suggested that the hyperkinetic syndrome is not distinct from other 'conduct disorders' (Quay 1972; Werry 1972).

Careful clinical studies reveal that only a small, but significant minority of hyperkinetic children present with antisocial behaviour when initially seen (Weiss *et al* 1971; Stewart *et al* 1966; Satterfield & Cantwell 1975). Since antisocial behaviour is more frequent in older hyperkinetic children it may develop as a secondary reaction. Children who are unable to succeed in an academic setting, who are unable to develop satisfactory peer relationships, who find rejection at home and at school, are likely to become aggressive and rebel against the values of society.

However, 'antisocial hyperkinetic' children may form an aetiologically distinct subgroup of the hyperkinetic syndrome. Thus, family studies suggest a familial and probably genetic, relationship between antisocial personality in adults and the hyperkinetic syndrome (Cantwell 1972; 1975a; Morrison & Stewart 1971; 1973). Also recent research on waking autonomic functions and EEG patterns in hyperkinetic children and in antisocial adults suggests that the majority of both groups show lower levels of basal resting physiological activation than age matched normals (de la Pena 1973). Some authors have found antisocial, aggressive hyperkinetic children to be very resistant to the psychopharmacological agents so successful with non-antisocial children (Katz *et al* 1975). Finally, there is a suggestion that among hyperkinetic children antisocial, aggressive behaviours may be mediated by dopamine, in contrast to the norepinephrine mediation of hyperactivity (Arnold *et al* 1973).

Cognitive and learning disabilities

Learning difficulties are of major importance in the hyperkinetic syndrome (Chess 1960; Cruickshank *et al* 1961; Knobel 1962; Menkes *et al* 1967; Stewart *et al* 1966; Werry 1968b). However, the nature and prevalence of these difficulties remain unclear.

Overall academic achievement is usually low for hyperkinetic children (Keogh 1971), but some writers attribute this solely to low intellectual potential. Palkes and Stewart (1972) found that the mean WISC IQs were significantly lower for hyperkinetic children than for a matched group of normal children. When the group means on scholastic achievement were adjusted for WISC Full Scale IQ, the difference between the groups was no longer significant and it was concluded that hyperkinetic children learned at a rate in keeping with their IQ. The opposite conclusion was reached by Minde *et al* (1971) who found that hyperkinetic children showed a low attainment in almost all academic subjects, which was worse than expected on the basis of their IQ. Cantwell and Satterfield (in preparation) used a multiple regression equation technique (Thorndike 1963; Yule 1967) to determine whether each normal and each hyperkinetic child in their study was functioning above or below grade level in reading, spelling, and mathematics predicted on the basis of chronological age and full scale IQ. More than three-quarters of the hyperkinetic group were educationally retarded to some degree in each of the three academic subjects, a significantly greater number than the control group. Moreover, the more severe degrees of educational retardation were almost all in the hyperkinetic group. Approximately half of the hyperkinetic group were behind more than one grade level in one subject, about one-third in two subjects, and nearly 10 per cent in all three academic subjects.

Three hypothetical mechanisms, each with some empirical support, have been proposed to explain these learning problems (Keogh 1971; Douglas 1972); (a) neurological impairment causes both the behavioural syndrome and cognitive disabilities; (b) overactivity interferes with attention and the acquisition of information; and (c) hyperkinetic children make decisions too quickly.

The Montreal group found that hyperkinetic children had more WISC subtest variability than normals but the pattern was not consistent. They also had difficulties on tasks which involved visuomotor skills, fine or gross motor coordination, or attention, and especially on a continuous performance vigilance task, their reaction times were also slower than normal (Sykes *et al* 1971; Sykes *et al* 1972). Campbell (Campbell 1969; Campbell *et al* 1971) found hyperkinetic children to be more impulsive, more field dependent and more constricted in their ability to control attention than normal children (Campbell 1969; Campbell *et al* 1971). This impulsivity and field dependence seemed to persist into early adolescence. The Montreal group failed to find any evidence of impairment in language abilities, comprehension, and conceptual thinking. Somewhat surprisingly, the hyperkinetic children appeared to be less distracted by extraneous stimuli than clinical reports would suggest (Douglas 1972). This topic requires careful research if effective remedial educational approaches are to be directed to the mechanisms underlying the cognitive and learning disabilities manifested by hyperkinetic children.

Other emotional symptoms

Apart from antisocial behaviour, the most significant symptoms are depression and low self-esteem which occur in the majority of hyperkinetic children (Weiss *et al* 1971). This has been viewed as a reaction to continuing failures (Weiss *et al* 1971; Werkman 1970) and also a 'depressive equivalent' (Malmquist 1971). It could be argued that since some hyperkinetic children respond to antidepressants (Huessy 1967) that this is evidence for a 'depressive core' to the syndrome. However, antidepressants have not been shown to be specific for depression in children (Rutter 1972) and the absence of a significant increase in affective disorder among close relatives of hyperkinetic children (Morrison & Stewart 1973; Cantwell 1975a) argues against the hypothesis of a 'depressive equivalent'. If it could be shown that the hyperkinetic children who respond to antidepressants, also have an increased prevalence rate for affective disorder in their close relatives, and go on to develop affective disorder in later life, then one could make a strong argument that in this group the hyperkinetic syndrome may be a manifestation of a primary affective disturbance. To date this has not been done.

Maturational changes in symptom pattern

The clinical picture of the hyperkinetic syndrome changes with the age of the child (Wender 1971; Denhoff 1973). The diagnosis is most difficult to make in infancy and the early preschool years. Mothers often report the baby seemed to be unusually active, hyperalert, and difficult to soothe. General irregularity of physiological functions manifested by colic, sleep and eating disturbances, and frequent crying also are commonly reported. But none of these disturbances is characteristic of hyperkinetic children alone (Thomas *et al* 1968).

Once the child begins to walk, other symptoms begin to emerge. It is at this point that the activity level and attentional difficulties become more noticeable. The typical child seems to have a distinct lack of a sense of danger, moves from one activity to another very quickly, and is relatively impervious to disciplinary measures found effective with their other children.

The diagnosis is most easily made during the school years. Behaviours which were disturbing but tolerable at home are not so easily tolerated in a classroom. Academic problems increase with passage of time and antisocial behaviours become more prevalent.

In adolescence, educational retardation, antisocial behaviour, depression and low self-esteem are most common. As hyperactivity, distractibility, impulsivity and excitability have usually diminished the diagnosis is difficult unless attention is paid to the history of hyperkinesis at an earlier age. The picture in adult life remains unclear but psychiatric problems often persist (see below).

AETIOLOGY AND CLASSIFICATION

Controversy continues on the most appropriate diagnostic term and subgrouping for hyperkinetic disorders. Several issues are relevant. First, the behavioural syndrome is sometimes associated with organic brain pathology or epilepsy (Ingram 1956; Ounsted 1955) or with low IQ (Pond 1961), but often it is not. Accordingly, it seems desirable to classify the clinical psychiatric syndrome separately from the presence or absence of neurological dysfunction and from the categorisation of intellectual level. Various WHO seminars and studies have suggested that this matter is best dealt with by means of a multiaxial classification scheme (Rutter *et al* 1969; 1975; Tarjan *et al* 1972; see also Chapter 15). Second, the syndrome may occur in pure form, together with a marked developmental delay, or in association with a gross disorder of conduct. The WHO study (Rutter *et al* 1975) suggested a subdivision into: (a) simple disturbance of activity or attention; (b) hyperactivity with developmental delay; (c) hyperkinetic conduct disorder; and (d) 'other'. The American Psychiatric Association group planning the third edition of the *Diagnostic and Statistical Manual* (DSM3) have suggested a somewhat similar grouping but have argued that 'attentional deficit disorder' is a preferable overall diagnostic term, on the grounds that this is the primary problem.

Present evidence suggests that the term hyperkinetic syndrome describes a heterogeneous group of children with different aetiologies. In some cases the disorder may be due to a structural abnormality of the brain (Werry 1972); in others there may be an abnormality of physiological arousal of the nervous system (Satterfield *et al* 1974); in others there may be a genetic basis for the disorder (Cantwell 1976; Morrison 1974), while in others there may be still undiscovered important aetiological factors.

EPIDEMIOLOGY

The prevalence of the syndrome will vary greatly with the diagnostic criteria employed, methods of investigation, and population studied. Studies using rating scales tend to give higher prevalence rates than those using direct observation and those, like most British studies, requiring the child to demonstrate hyperactivity in an interview setting. Only 2 hyperkinetic children were found in a total population study of 2199 children aged 10 and 11 on the Isle of Wight (Rutter *et al* 1970b). This compares with figures of from 5 per cent to 20 per cent in school age populations in the Netherlands (Prechtl & Stemmer 1962), Vermont (Huessy 1967), St Louis, Missouri (Stewart *et al* 1966), and Montgomery County, Maryland (Wender 1971). Teachers' reports formed the data base in most of the latter studies. The boy : girl ratio varied from 4 : 1 to 9 : 1, but factors likely to affect prevalence rates such as socioeconomic status and racial ethnic composition were not mentioned (Omenn 1973). The prevalence in children referred to a psychiatric clinic is considerably higher (Wender 1971). More studies on a total population with a wider age range of children, using precise diagnostic criteria, and with attention to ethnic and socioeconomic factors are sorely needed (Omenn 1973).

PHYSICAL AND NEUROLOGICAL FINDINGS

The physical examination is usually completely normal in hyperkinetic children but there may be defects of vision or hearing (Stewart *et al* 1966) or abnormalities of speech (de Hirsch 1973). One group of investigators (Waldrop & Halverson 1971) has reported a high incidence of minor physical anomalies (such as widely spaced eyes, curved fifth finger, adherent earlobes), especially in boys. Rapoport *et al* (1974) not only confirmed the increased incidence of minor physical anomalies, but showed that the presence of these anomalies was associated with: severity of hyperactivity; a history of hyperactivity in the father; a history of early obstetrical difficulty in the mother; and higher than normal mean plasma dopamine-B hydroxylase activity. Hyperkinetic children with minor physical anomalies may form a distinct subgroup.

Several studies have shown an excess of minor neurological ('soft signs') in hyperkinetic children (Werry 1972; Bender 1956; Silver 1952). While there has been a tendency to infer brain pathology from these signs (Kennard 1960; Laufer & Denhoff 1957), the evidence for doing so is lacking (Werry 1972; Rutter *et al* 1970a). Moreover, many of the studies suffer from serious methodological deficiences (Werry *et al* 1972; Schain 1972).

Only one study has compared carefully matched hyperkinetic, neurotic and normal groups of children using a reliable standardised neurological examination (Werry *et al* 1972). Hyperkinetic children had an excess of minor neurological abnormalities indicative of sensorimotor incoordination but there was no excess of major neurological abnormalities, of EEG abnormalities, or histories suggestive of trauma to the brain. The source and significance of these minor neurological abnormalities thus remains obscure (Rutter *et al* 1970a). Their value in the diagnosis of the hyperkinetic syndrome is questionable since only about one half (Satterfield 1973a; Millichap 1973) have even 'soft' neurological signs. However, there is some evidence that children with such signs are distinguished by a greater likelihood of response to stimulant drug treatment (Satterfield 1973b; Millichap 1973) suggesting that this may be a meaningful subgroup.

LABORATORY STUDIES

Electroencephalographic and neurophysiological studies

Studies have reported 35 to 50 per cent of hyperkinetic children have abnormal EEGs (Satterfield 1973a; Werry 1972) with an increase in slow wave activity being the most common finding. However, there are no EEG abnormalities specific to the syndrome and there is even some question whether hyperkinetic children have a greater number of EEG abnormalities than carefully matched normal and nonhyperkinetic emotionally disturbed children (Werry 1972; Eeg-Olofsson 1970; Petersen *et al* 1968).

Neurophysiological studies have been limited and inconclusive. Laufer *et al* (1957) found a significantly lower mean EEG photometrazol threshold which was raised to normal level by amphetamine. Satterfield *et al* (1972) found that lower skin conductance levels, larger amplitude and slow recoveries of evoked cortical responses compared with normals. These measures, together with high amplitude EEG and high energy in the lower frequency (0–8Hz) band of the resting EEG, also distinguished hyperkinetic children who responded best to stimulant drug treatment. The authors suggested that those hyperkinetic children who respond best to stimulant drug treatment have low CNS arousal (Satterfield *et al* 1974). Other auditory-evoked studies (Calloway 1973) and studies using electronic pupillography (Knopp *et al* 1972) have also suggested low CNS arousal in hyperkinetic children who respond best to stimulant medication. However, studies of alpha rhythms (Shetty 1971) have suggested the opposite conclusion—that hyperkinetic children who respond best to stimulants have high CNS arousal. Differing patient populations and diagnostic criteria, and differing experimental stimulus conditions make the results of these studies difficult to compare.

Metabolic, biochemical and chromosomal studies

Disorders of monoamine metabolism in hyperkinetic children have been proposed by several authors but experimental evidence to support such abnormalities is sparse. Dextroamphetamine is thought to be ten times as potent as its isomer levoamphetamine, in inhibiting catecholamine uptake by norepinephrine terminals in the brain. The two isomers are of approximately equal potency in inhibiting catecholamine uptake by dopamine neurons (Snyder *et al* 1970). Thus the differential effect of the two isomers on the behaviour of hyperkinetic children (Arnold *et al* 1973) offers indirect evidence that in some hyperkinetic children, the disorder is mediated by dopaminergic systems and in others by norepinephrinergic systems.

More direct studies of a possible metabolic abnormality have been limited. Wender *et al* (1971) failed to detect any differences in the metabolites of serotonin, norepinephrine or dopamine in the urine of a very heterogeneous group of children with 'minimal brain dysfunction' compared with a group of normal children. However, three children from the same family did have very low concentrations of serotonin in the blood platelets (Wender 1969). Coleman (1971) demonstrated low platelet serotonin concentrations in 88 per cent of 25 children with the hyperkinetic syndrome. In the two most hyperactive children, who were studied in a research ward, the serotonin concentration rose and the hyperactivity lessened during the hospital stay. On return home the serotonin values dropped to prehospitalisation levels and hyperactivity increased. Urinary monoamine metabolites in both of these children remained within normal limits during their hospital stay. In contrast, Rapoport *et al* (1970) found an inverse relationship between the degree of hyperactivity and urinary norepinephrine excretion, but the mean 24-hour urinary catecholamine excretion did not differentiate the hyperkinetic group. In addition, there was an inverse relationship between response of the hyperactivity to dextroamphetamine and urinary norepinephrine levels.

The findings suggest a possible disorder of monoamine metabolism. However, urinary and platelet data reflect brain monoamine metabolism only imperfectly. Since direct measurement of central nervous system monoamine metabolism is not a possibility, the measurement of monoamine levels and turnover in cerebrospinal fluid, as done in adults with affective disorders (Goodwin & Bunney 1973) might be more fruitful. More rigorous diagnostic criteria and control of factors such as diet, stress and adrenal steroid levels is called for in future studies (Wender 1971).

It has been claimed that hyperkinetic children suffer from vitamin deficiency allergy to certain food additives, and disorders of glucose metabolism. This, in turn, has led to enthusiastic reports of results of treatment with megavitamin therapy, allergen free diets, and hypoglycemic diets (Hoffer 1971; 1972; Cott 1969; Rimland 1973; Feingold 1973). None of these claims has yet been substantiated by proper studies.

No evidence of sex chromosome aneuploidy or other chromosome abnormality was found in the one study undertaken (Warren *et al* 1971). As there may be a genetically determined subgroup of hyperkinetic children, chromosomal studies should be repeated in families with multiple cases.

Psychometric studies

As a group, hyperkinetic children have been shown to be inferior on a wide range of intellectual, conceptual, visual-spatial, academic, motor and sensory-perception functions (Conners 1967; Douglas 1972). However, no battery of tests has been adequately standardised to ensure discrimination of an individual hyperkinetic child from a child suffering from other psychiatric or learning disorders (Conners 1967), although the battery devised by Reitan and his associates (Reitan & Boll 1973) shows promise. Although psychological tests continue to play an important part in the clinical evaluation of hyperkinetic children, their exact role and utility is still debated. Knights (1974) advocates a 'profile similarity approach' using patterns of scores on a neuropsychological test battery as an aid in the diagnosis of the hyperkinetic syndrome. Conners (1973a) recommends classifying hyperkinetic subjects into homogeneous subgroups on the basis of types or patterns of psychological test response. His factor analysis of a battery of test scores by hyperkinetic children yielded five factors: (1) general IQ; (2) achievement; (3) rote learning; (4) attentiveness; and (5) impulse control. He next identified six separate patterns of factor scores or 'cluster types'. Validity of this grouping procedure was demonstrated by showing that the six groups differed significantly from each other on the Lincoln-Oseretsky test of motor development, response to drug and placebo treatment, and cortical-evoked responses (Conners 1973a). Thus the groups of children classified on the basis of psychological functioning seemed to be homogeneous groups sharing disabilities of certain underlying psychological and physiological processes and perhaps common aetiologies.

FAMILIAL–GENETIC FACTORS

Two studies of biological parents of hyperkinetic children have revealed increased prevalence rates for alcoholism, sociopathy, and hysteria, compared with the relatives of normal children (Morrison & Stewart 1971; Cantwell 1972). One also reported a high prevalence rate in the biological second-degree relatives (Cantwell 1972). Moreover, a significant number of hyperkinetic children showed alcoholism, sociopathy and hysteria when they reached adulthood. The findings suggest that the hyperkinetic syndrome may be a familial disorder, linked with alcoholism, sociopathy and hysteria, which is passed from generation to generation.

Two recent studies revealed no increased prevalence rates for psychiatric illness or the hyperkinetic syndrome in the *non-biological* relatives of *adopted* hyperkinetic children (Morrison & Stewart 1973; Cantwell 1975a); the findings strongly suggest a genetic component. Safer (1973) has reported that 50 per cent of full sibs, but only 14 per cent of half sibs, of children with 'minimal brain dysfunction' gave histories suggesting the presence of the hyperkinetic syndrome; these data also suggest a genetic influence. Lopez (1965) found a 100 per cent concordance rate for the hyperkinetic syndrome in four monozygotic (MZ) twin pairs, while only 1 of 6 dizygotic twin (DZ) pairs was concordant for the syndrome. However, sex differences between the MZ and DZ twin pairs cloud the interpretation of the data (Omenn 1973). A larger study of 93 sets of same-sexed twins has been reported by Willerman (1973) who used a parent rating scale as a measure of hyperactivity. The heritability estimate was 0·82 for the males, 0·58 for the females and 0·77 for males and females combined, suggesting a substantial genetic component to activity level. Willerman then arbitrarily defined children with scores on the parent rating in the top 20 per cent as 'hyperactive'. There were 8 MZ and 16 DZ twin pairs with activity scores in this range. The heritability estimate for this group was 0·71. These results also are consistent with the notion that genetic factors play an important role in the hyperkinetic syndrome.

A single gene autosomal transmission is unlikely due to the excess of males with the condition (Werry 1968a). Sex-linked transmission is equally unlikely due to the high degree of apparent transmission from father to son (Morrison & Stewart 1971; Cantwell 1972). The high percentage of parents manifesting the syndrome all but rules out a simple recessive trait while the skipping of generations makes simple dominant transmission unlikely unless 'reduced penetrance' is invoked. Morrison and Stewart (1974) used Slater's method of analysis of ancestral cases to attempt to differentiate between polygenic transmission and dominant transmission with reduced penetrance. His preliminary evidence favours polygenic transmission but genetic conclusions are necessarily tentative.

NATURAL HISTORY AND PROGNOSIS

Early investigators thought that the hyperkinetic syndrome was a time limited condition which disappeared as the child grew older (Laufer & Denhoff 1957; Bakwin & Bakwin 1967; Eisenberg 1966). While the *symptom* of hyperactivity may diminish with age (Rutter 1968) it now seems that the prognosis for untreated hyperkinetic children may be quite poor. Both retrospective and prospective studies indicate that antisocial behaviour, educational retardation, depression and psychosis are prevalent in 'grown-up' hyperkinetic children.

Menkes *et al* (1967) study of 14 hyperkinetic children seen 25 years earlier indicated continuing hyperactivity in only three patients, but four were institutionalised as psychotic and two were retarded and unable to support themselves. Of the eight found to be self-supporting at follow-up, one had spent some time in jail and two had been in institutions for delinquents.

Anterospective studies by Weiss *et al* (1971), Mendelson *et al* (1971) and the Montreal group (Minde *et al* 1971; 1972) show that hyperactivity per se diminishes with age, but the children are still more restless, excitable, impulsive and distractible than their peers. Attentional and concentration difficulties remain as major problems. Chronic, severe underachievement in school in almost all academic areas is a characteristic finding. Low self-esteem, poor self-image, depression and a sense of failure are common. Antisocial behaviour occurs in up to one-quarter and 10 to 15 per cent have had actual police contact or court referral. The Mendelson study (Mendelson *et al* 1971) underscored the severity of the antisocial behaviour that occurs in the adolescent hyperkinetic child. More than half had been involved in fighting, stealing and destructive behaviour and two-thirds were considered to be 'incorrigible' by their parents. More than one-third had threatened to kill their parents, 7 per cent carried weapons, 15 per cent were fire setters, and 15 per cent were already excessive drinkers by age 16.

A slightly more optimistic outcome was reported by Laufer (1971) and Denhoff (1973) in a questionnaire follow-up of 100 former private patients with the hyperkinetic syndrome. The 66 patients who replied to the questionnaire ranged in age from 15 to 26 years at the time of follow-up. Although 50 had required some type of remedial education, of the 48 patients who answered questions regarding academic status, some 47 per cent were either in or had graduated from high school and 29 per cent was either in or had graduated from college. Difficulty with the law was reported by 30 per cent but none was in jail. Drug experimentation was reported by about 5 per cent and some 8 per cent reported excess alcohol intake. Drug overdose was reported by two patients.

Some 30 per cent reported symptoms of psychopathology such as mood swings, feelings of persecution and episodes of violence, but there were no reported suicide attempts and only 5 per cent had been psychiatric inpatients. However, some psychiatric help had been required by 35 per cent and 9 per cent were in treatment at the time of follow-up. Length of time on medication appeared to correlate significantly with academic achievement, but not with later social and emotional adjustment. Unfortunately, the study suffers from several defects; questionnaires only were used in the follow-up; nothing was said about the one-third who did not respond to the questionnaire; and not every question was answered by the two-thirds who did reply.

There are no prospective studies into adulthood. However, the finding (Morrison & Stewart 1971; Cantwell 1972) that 10 per cent of the natural parents of hyperkinetic children were themselves hyperkinetic as children and that most of these parents were psychiatrically ill as adults suggests that the hyperkinetic syndrome is a precursor to the development of psychopathology in adulthood. Retrospective studies of adults with antisocial behaviour indicate that a significant percentage were described as hyperactive, impulsive, and aggressive as children (Quitkin & Klein 1969; Shelley & Riester 1972). Data from the Cambridge–Somerville Youth Study (McCord & McCord 1960) and the Oakland Growth Study (Jones *et al* 1960) indicate that alcoholic adults were described as restless, aggressive, and impulsive as children.

While none of these findings is conclusive, they strongly suggest that the adult outcome of children with the hyperkinetic syndrome is likely to be as poor as it is in adolescence.

There are no clear cut prognostic indicators. Menkes *et al* (1967) found no predictors of any type of outcome. However, both Mendelson *et al* (1971) and the Montreal group (Weiss *et al* 1971; Minde *et al* 1971; 1972) found that family disturbance and parental abnormalities were associated with an antisocial outcome. The Montreal group found that the least academically

successful differed in having lower WISC IQ scores, greater verbal-performance discrepancies and verbal and visual-spatial problems (Weiss *et al* 1971;
Minde *et al* 1971).

The only significant predictors of behavioural outcome in the Minde *et
al* (1972) study were initial aggression scores and initial scores on the psychopathic scale of the Peterson–Quay checklist. The 'poor' group had higher
initial scores on most target symptoms as well as a low initial IQ, a positive
history of neurological abnormalities, lower socioeconomic status and more
unfavourable family circumstances. The 20 children who deteriorated over
the period of follow-up could not be differentiated on the basis of their initial
characteristics.

In the St Louis study (Mendelson *et al* 1971) 40 per cent were still in
between the outcome and the amount of treatment the patient received but
no patient received drugs or any form of intensive therapy. In the Montreal
study (Weiss *et al* 1971; Minde *et al* 1971; 1972) there was no significant
correlation between psychological adjustment and length of time the patients
had been maintained on medication (either phenothiazines or stimulants),
but there was a trend for those on prolonged medication to be more poorly
adjusted at follow-up. Half the group had received some type of psychological
treatment or counselling. The more aggressive, distractible children tended
to receive more hours of psychotherapy and the treated children had higher
initial scores on the Peterson–Quay neuroticism scale. Although this high
neuroticism score dropped to normal at follow-up, the other scale scores did
not and psychotherapeutic intervention did not differentiate the good and
poor outcome groups at follow-up. Over two-thirds of the children originally
thought to have moderate to severe learning problems had received some form
of remedial educational help. None of the children so treated showed improvement on any psychological test.

In the St. Louis study (Mendelson *et al* 1971) 40 per cent were still in
treatment there at follow-up and another 14 per cent were in treatment elsewhere. Sixty per cent of the children on stimulants were reported to have
improved for at least 6 months. No attempt was made to assess the effect
of the other treatment modalities on outcome.

Quinn and Rapoport (1975) in a 1-year follow-up study of 76 hyperkinetic
boys found that those who were still on either methylphenidate or imipramine
at the time of follow-up were rated significantly better by their teachers than
those groups receiving no treatment. However, no differences were found on
parental ratings. Twice as many children on imipramine as those on methylphenidate discontinued the medication during the course of the year.

The most disappointing results of long-term drug treatment of hyperkinetic children were obtained by Weiss *et al* (1975). They compared three

groups of children 5 years after initial evaluation: (a) 22 on chlorpromazine for 18 months to 5 years; (b) 24 children on methylphenidate from 3–5 years; and (c) 20 children who had received no drug treatment. Although the hyperactivity scores decreased significantly in all three groups, there were no significant differences between the three groups of children on any of the (rather gross) behavioural or cognitive measures. Clinical observations at follow-up indicated that methylphenidate was of benefit but apparently it had no significant effect on long-term outcome, at least on the measures used. So far there is no evidence that treatment of any type significantly alters the long-term prognosis of hyperactive children.

TREATMENT

The child with the hyperkinetic syndrome is best considered as a multihandicapped child requiring a multiple modality treatment approach (Feighner & Feighner 1974). Any or all of the intervention approaches discussed below may be necessary for an individual child, but treatment must be individualised and based on a comprehensive assessment of each child and his family. The notion that there is one hyperkinetic child who requires only one treatment—stimulant drugs—is a scientific myth (Fish 1971).

Pharmacotherapy

Drug treatment is the easiest, least time-consuming, and most frequently used intervention technique in the management of the hyperkinetic child. Several critical reviews of the voluminous literature on this subject are available (Fish 1968; 1971; Millichap & Fowler 1967; Conners 1972; 1970; Freeman 1966; Klein & Gittelman-Klein 1975b; Werry & Sprague 1972) (see also Chapter 38).

The CNS stimulants, methylphenidate and dextroamphetamine, are currently the drugs of choice in the treatment of hyperactive children. Improvement in behaviour can be expected in two-thirds to three-quarters of children treated with these stimulants, while worsening can be expected in 5 to 10 per cent (O'Malley & Eisenberg 1973; Millichap 1973; Cantwell 1975b).

The therapeutic properties and side effects of the two medications are very similar. They both seem to act by potentiating norepinephrine and dopamine at central synapses (Ferris *et al* 1972; Schildkraut & Kety 1967). Methylphenidate must be given at least twice a day to ensure an effective dose throughout the school day, but dextroamphetamine in the long-acting Spansule need be given only once a day. The initial dosage should be the smallest available with a gradual increase either until clinical improvement is noted or until side effects occur which necessitate discontinuation of the drug. Dosage on a body weight basis provides only *rough* guidelines. For example, Wender (1971) has advocated a high dose of 4·6 mg per kilogram of bodyweight of methylphenidate. However, Sprague and his colleagues showed that teacher ratings show an increased improvement in behaviour ratings up to doses of 0·70 and 1·00 mg per kilogram of methylphenidate and even this dosage is double the dosage at which the peak enhancement of cognitive performance occurs (Sprague & Sleator 1973). There are large individual differences in blood levels of medication for comparable doses of the same drug in children of the same weight. Moreover, one drug may have a therapeutic effect for a particular child only at a particular blood level. Children considered 'nonresponders' to medication often simply have not been given an effective dose (Conners 1972; Wender 1971).

The total amount of bodily activity may actually be increased by the stimulants. The crucial change is an increase in *directed* or controlled motor activity (Witt *et al* (1970); Millichap & Boldrey 1967). Small improvements may occur in tests of general intelligence, visual motor perception and learning (Knights & Hinton 1969; Epstein *et al* 1968; Werry *et al* 1970; Conners *et al* 1967). Some investigators (Breitmeyer 1969) have suggested that children do not retain material they learn while on medication after the medication is stopped, but findings from Sprague's laboratory (Sprague 1972; Sprague & Werry 1971) have failed to substantiate this. Most hyperactive children who respond to one stimulant will respond to the other, but certain hyperactive children respond to only one (Conners 1971; Winsberg *et al* 1974). Anorexia, insomnia, headache, stomach ache, nausea, tearfulness and pallor are common side effects with both stimulants, but anorexia and insomnia seem more frequent and more severe with dextroamphetamine. While stimulants are not thought to produce euphoria in children, systematic evidence is lacking. Long-term use of stimulants is known to produce depression in adults but this is only rarely mentioned with hyperactive children (Ounsted 1955). However, the author has seen depressive episodes in several children on methylphenidate or amphetamine. The stimulant had to be stopped or reduced in dosage and imipramine prescribed.

Hyperactive children on medication rarely become drug abusers (Freedman 1971; Beck *et al* 1975). Suppression of weight may sometimes occur with prolonged use of dextroamphetamine or methylphenidate (height also with dextroamphetamine) (Safer & Allen 1973; Safer *et al* 1972). There is a return to previous growth patterns when the children are taken off the drug (Safer & Allen 1973; Safer *et al* 1972; Schain & Reynard 1975) but all children on medication should be charted on standard growth curves.

When weight loss becomes a significant problem it may be effective to get the child to eat a large meal prior to his morning medication and/or in the evening when the drug effects have generally worn off. Break offs in medication at weekends and during the summer may also help. Appetite stimulants may be tried but their value remains uncertain. Clinical experience suggests that most side effects of medication usually subside with time (Eisenberg 1972; Beck *et al* 1975) but long-term studies are sorely needed.

Little is known about the predictors or mechanisms of drug response. The presence of 'organic factors' has been claimed to predict a good response (Pincus & Glaser 1966; Zrull *et al* 1966; Epstein *et al* 1968; Conrad & Insel 1967; Satterfield 1973a) but the findings have not always been consistent (Burks 1964; Werry 1968a). Barcai (1971) found that, compared with non-responders, responders to amphetamine showed an earlier finger twitch and also more excess body movements, poor language ability, lack of ability to abstract and use imagination constructively, lack of adjustment to the values of society, and lack of planning ability.

Satterfield (1973b) found that drug response was unrelated to family background while Conrad and Insel (1967) found that children whose parents were rated as 'grossly deviant' or 'socially incompetent' were less likely to respond positively to medication, even in the face of other factors which tended to predict a good response. Other authors (Knobel 1962; Kraft 1968) have noted that the attitude of the family to the child's taking medication is likely to affect treatment response. However, few studies have attempted to look at family variables in a systematic way.

In a series of studies, Satterfield and his associates (Satterfield *et al* 1974) found nine predictors of response to methylphenidate: low skin conductance level, high amplitude EEG, high energy in the low frequency band of the EEG, large amplitude evoked cortical response, slow recovery of the evoked response, an abnormal EEG, four or more soft signs on neurological examination, more behavioural abnormalities reported by the teacher, and age (older children had a better response). Six of these predictors were electrophysiological measures, consistent with the hypothesis that the pathophysiology of the majority of children with the hyperactive child syndrome is low CNS arousal level. According to this hypothesis, the low arousal leads to insufficient cortical inhibitory control over both sensory input and motor functions. The stimulants then act by stimulating the mid-brain reticular activating system (Killam 1968) resulting in a net increase of cortical inhibitory control over both sensory and motor functions. This increased control over motor functions enables the hyperkinetic child to reduce nongoal directed, inappropriate motor behaviour. The increased inhibitory control over sensory input should enable the child to inhibit nonmeaningful stimuli in order to selectively attend in a learning situation.

That stimulant medication does result in increased cortical inhibitory control over sensory functions is suggested not only by improvement in behaviour, but also from electrophysiological studies. Satterfield *et al* (1974) found a decrease in evoked response to nonmeaningful auditory stimuli in those hyperkinetic children who responded positively to methylphenidate treatment. Several studies have reported increased habituation of peripheral responsivity to stimuli following administration of stimulant medication to hyperkinetic children. Conners found dextroamphetamine enhanced the rate of habituation of finger blood volume response to auditory stimuli (Conners 1971). Similar results have been reported for heart rate and galvanic skin response following methylphenidate (Conners 1971). Also consistent with the hypothesis of increased inhibitory function are Laufer's findings of an increased photometrazol threshold (Laufer *et al* 1957) and Shetty's finding of an increased amount of alpha rhythm (Shetty 1971) following administration of dextroamphetamine to hyperkinetic children.

Other stimulants have also been tried. Preliminary results with magnesium pemoline (Cylert), a weak, long-acting CNS stimulant, indicate that it decreases hyperactivity and produces improvement on the Performance Scale of the WISC (Conners *et al* 1972; Millichap 1973). Deanol (Deaner) is another central nervous system stimulant but it is of little or no value in the treatment of hyperactive children (Conners 1973b). Coffee (with caffeine the presumed active ingredient) has been reported to be as effective as methylphenidate in one study (Schnackenberg 1973), but studies using caffeine tablets have failed to substantiate the finding (Garfinkel *et al* 1975; Arnold 1974). The side effects of these central nervous system stimulants are similar to those of methylphenidate and dextroamphetamine.

The tricyclic antidepressant imipramine (Tofranil), in a dosage of 50 to 175 mg per day, has been found to be effective with 45 to 85 per cent of hyperactive children (Huessy & Wright 1970; Winsberg *et al* 1972; Waizer *et al* 1974; Rapoport *et al* 1974). Huessy and Wright gave 50 mg in a single bedtime dose and found a therapeutic effect evident the *next day* (unlike the 2- to 3-week delay with the antidepressant effect). However, there is some indication that toxicity from imipramine is increased by a single dose at night time (Winsberg *et al*, in press). Imipramine may prove to be of considerable value in the treatment of hyperactive children but it is not yet approved by the FDA for use with children under the age of 12, except for enuresis, and there are recent reports of electrocardiograph abnormalities in children treated with imipramine (Winsberg *et al* 1975).

Sedatives such as phenobarbital are usually contraindicated for hyperactive children (Conners 1972).

Most studies of antipsychotic and antianxiety agents are poorly controlled and the findings are contradictory (Freeman 1970; Sprague & Werry 1971). However, it appears that the major tranquillisers may produce deleterious effects on learning and cognitive functioning (Hartlage 1965; Conners 1971).

Thioridazine (Melleril) seems to be the most effective of the phenothiazines used with hyperactive children, although it has been used primarily in those who are also mentally retarded or brain damaged. By and large the phenothiazines, when used alone, are not as effective and are potentially more toxic than the stimulant medications (Conners 1972).

Although the antihistamine diphenhydramine (Benadryl) has been suggested, its efficacy has yet to be demonstrated (Fish 1975). Anticonvulsants are useful in the treatment of children with fits but there is no evidence of their value in the absence of seizures even if the EEG is abnormal. Drugs should be used to treat illnesses, not abnormal laboratory findings (Cantwell 1975b).

Lithium carbonate has been tried with varying success by several investigators (Whitehead & Clark 1970; Greenhill *et al* 1973), but it is not as effective as the stimulants in treatment of the usual hyperactive child. In the extremely rare case of mania presenting with hyperactivity in a prepubertal child, lithium carbonate may be the treatment of choice.

More controlled studies are needed but in general no drugs have been found to be as effective as the stimulants (Millichap & Fowler 1967). The clinician who is faced with a child who has not responded or who has responded negatively to a therapeutic dose of the stimulants may want to try one of the above medications. However, he has little other than his clinical intuition to guide him.

Individual psychotherapy with the child

As with the other psychiatric disorders of childhood (Levitt 1957; 1963; Rachman 1971), evidence for the efficacy of individual psychotherapy with children with the hyperkinetic syndrome is lacking (Cytryn *et al* 1960). However, psychotherapy using active techniques, such as those developed by Gardner (1973), is indicated for the secondary emotional symptoms of depression, low self-esteem and poor peer relationships. At the very least, the physician should help the hyperkinetic child understand the nature of his difficulties and how medication (and other therapeutic interventions) are intended to help the child help himself. The role and action of the medication in his life then can make more sense to the hyperkinetic child and he will hopefully see the medication as one of his tools, not something forced on him by his parents, his teachers, or his doctor (Kehne 1974; Wender 1971).

Behaviour modification

Until recently, studies of hyperkinetic children using operant conditioning techniques have been limited to single cases (Patterson *et al* 1965; Ward 1966) or to very small numbers of children (Doubros & Daniels 1966; Sprague 1973). Jacob *et al* (1973) have recently reported a 3-month study of 8 hyperkinetic children treated in ordinary classroom settings using a programme involving daily evaluations of problem behaviours by each child's teacher. A daily reward system was instituted in which the parents gave preselected reinforcers to the child at home if the child achieved certain predetermined goals in school. Each teacher gave reinforcers in the classroom and sent home a note each day the criterion reward was fulfilled. Significant improvement occurred in all children as judged by a variety of rating and observational measures. Although there was no direct comparison made with drug treatment, the changes obtained on the Conners' Teacher Rating Scale (Conners 1969) compared favourably with changes on the same scale obtained by treatment with stimulant medication in other studies.

In a direct comparison of behavioural and drug treatment Christensen and Sprague (1973) compared 6 children receiving placebo and behaviour modification with 6 children receiving methylphenidate and behaviour modification, using seat activity and daily quizzes as outcome measures. The drug-plus-behaviour-modification group had significantly lower seat activity than the placebo plus behaviour modification group, but there were no significant differences between the groups on the number of correct answers on the daily quizzes. In a similar study, Christensen (1973) found a number of significant differences between groups on a variety of measures including: Conners' Teacher Rating Scale, the Werry–Quay observational measures, productivity and accuracy of academic materials, and seat activity. The behaviour modification procedures alone accounted for most of the significant improvements over baseline recordings. Methylphenidate was not found to be consistently superior to behaviour modification alone on any measure. This latter study however was conducted with institutionalised, mentally retarded, hyperkinetic children and the results may not be generalisable to other children with the syndrome. Other authors have suggested that behaviour modification alone is usually not sufficient to manage the average hyperactive child, although it is most valuable as a mechanism of establishing healthy relationships between the child, parents, sibs and teachers (Katz *et al* 1975). The results of behaviour therapy are promising but further research is necessary.

Surgery

There are reports of amygdalotomies (Narabayashi *et al* 1963) and stereotactic hypothalamotomy (Balasubramaniam *et al* 1970) have been used to treat the hyperkinetic syndrome, even in very young children. Seventy-five per cent improvement with little in the way of side effects has been reported. However, this would appear to be a drastic therapeutic intervention reserved only for very severe, intractable cases.

Educational management

Each year a child spends about 1400 hours out of 8760 in school (McCarthy 1973). Thus, it is important that there be consistency of expectations and methods of behavioural reinforcement between the home and the school. Most hyperkinetic children can tolerate, and will need to remain in, a regular classroom. Simple classroom measures such as placing the child close to the teacher and away from distractions, and giving one-to-one attention through the use of teachers' aides may be helpful. For those children with significant learning problems, remedial education based on a thorough assessment is necessary. However, there is little hard evidence to support the efficacy of most special education programmes for any type of child (Dunn 1968; Haywood 1966). Well-controlled studies of special education programmes for hyperkinetic children are few in number and disappointing in results. Conrad *et al* (1971) randomly assigned 68 hyperkinetic children matched for intelligence and degree of hyperactivity to one of four experimental groups: placebo/no tutoring; placebo/tutoring; dextroamphetamine/no tutoring; and dextroamphetamine/tutoring. Tutoring alone produced little benefit while those who received both tutoring and dextroamphetamine showed improvement in behaviour and on a number of psychological tests. However, the dextroamphetamine-only group showed the most improvement. Most disappointing was the fact that only 3 of the 68 children made enough progress in the year of the study to no longer need remedial help. Successful approaches for training individual hyperkinetic children have been described (Palkes *et al* 1968; Santostefano & Stayton 1967; Meichenbaum & Goodman 1971), but long-term follow-up studies are lacking and the availability of such individualised special training in the public school system is limited.

Family involvement

Successful management of the hyperkinetic syndrome required involvement of the entire family. The author has found the use of parent groups to be an effective treatment modality, in the absence of severe psychopathology in the parents. Parents are taught the nature and phenomenology of the syndrome, the basics of behaviour modification, and the principles of structuring the child's environment so that there are regular daily routines and firm limits on his behaviour. The importance of avoiding overstimulation, excessive fatigue and situations known to cause difficulty, are emphasised. Videotape playback of parent–child interaction and of maladaptive behaviours with explicit instructions to the parents on how to deal with them has been found to be helpful (Feighner & Feighner 1974). The use of brothers and sisters to modify behaviour of their hyperkinetic siblings is a promising new technique (Brown & Guiliani 1972). The presence of psychopathology in the parents may require individual treatment of the parent and/or a more dynamically oriented family therapy approach, particularly if the hyperkinetic child has been the 'family scapegoat'.

The author believes that whatever therapeutic modalities are used the key to successful management of the hyperkinetic child is early intervention. Preventing the development of such symptoms as antisocial behaviour, depression, poor self-esteem and learning disabilities is likely to be more successful than treatment of these conditions after they have developed (Cantwell 1974).

DIRECTIONS FOR FUTURE RESEARCH

The hyperactive child syndrome merits serious consideration because of its high prevalence in child guidance clinic populations and its likely role as a precursor of serious psychosocial pathology in adulthood. A great deal of the past research has been limited to studies of drug treatment but other new areas of investigation are important.

It is particularly necessary to determine whether there are meaningful subgroups of the hyperkinetic syndrome which differ in aetiology, prognosis and response to treatment. The work of the Washington University Psychiatry Department in using family and follow-up studies to define psychiatric disorders in adults offers an excellent example to follow in this regard (Woodruff *et al* 1974). It is also important to determine how often hyperkinetic children recover completely as well as the links with particular types of adult problems. What are the factors within the child, within his family or within his social milieu that predict which hyperactive child will develop into a healthy adult and which child in later life will manifest social and psychiatric pathology? What treatment modalities influence the later life development of the hyperactive child and how do they do so?

These questions can only be answered by careful, long-term anterospective studies of large groups of hyperactive children, viewed from several different theoretical vantage points, at several different points in time. For hyperactive children, their families and society, the rewards from such investigative efforts should be great.

REFERENCES

ANDERSON W. (1963) The hyperkinetic child: a neurological appraisal. *Neurology* **13**, 968–973

ARNOLD L. (1974) Personal communication

ARNOLD L., KIRILCUK V., CORSON S. & CORSON E. (1973) Levoamphetamine and dextroamphetamine: Differential effect on aggression and hyperkinesis in children and dogs. *Amer. J. Psychiat.* **130**, 165–170

BAKWIN H. (1949) Cerebral damage and behavior disorders in children. *J. Pediatrics* **34**, 371–382

BAKWIN H. & BAKWIN R. (1967) *Clinical Management of Behavior Disorders in Children*, 3rd edn. Philadelphia: W.B. Saunders

BALASUBRAMANIAM V., KANAKA T. & RAMAMURTHI B. (1970) Surgical treatment of hyperkinetic and behavior disorders. *Internat. Surgery* **54**, 18–23

BARCAI A. (1971) Predicting the response of children with learning disabilities and behavior problems to dextroamphetamine sulfate: the clinical interview and the finger twitch test. *Pediatrics* **47**, 73–80

BECK L., LANGFORD W., MACKAY M. & SUM G. (1975) Childhood chemotherapy and later drug abuse and growth curve: a follow-up study of 30 adolescents. *Amer. J. Psychiat.* **132**, 436–438

BELL R. (1968) Adaptation of small wrist watches for mechanical recording of activity in infants and children. *J. Exp. Child Psychol.* **6**, 302–305

BENDER L. (1956) *Psychopathology of Children with Organic Brain Disorders*. Springfield, Illinois: Charles C Thomas

BRADLEY C. (1955) Organic factors in the psychopathology of childhood. *In* Hoch P. & Zubin J. (eds.) *Psychopathology of Childhood*. New York: Grune & Stratton

BREITMEYER J. (1969) Effects of thioridazine and methylphenidate on learning retention in retardates. Unpublished master's thesis, University of Illinois

BROWN N. & GUILIANI B. (1972) Siblings as behavior modifiers. Paper presented at 6th annual meeting, Association for the Advancement of Behavior Therapy.

BURKS H. (1964) Effects of amphetamine therapy on hyperkinetic children. *Arch. Gen. Psychiat.* **11**, 604–609

BURKS H. (1960) The hyperkinetic child. *Except. Child.* **27**, 18–26

CALLOWAY E. (1973) Personal communication

CAMPBELL S. (1969) Cognitive styles in normal and hyperkinetic children. Unpublished doctoral dissertation, McGill University.

CAMPBELL S., DOUGLAS V. & MORGENSTERN G. (1971) Cognitive styles in hyperactive children and the effect of methylphenidate. *J. Child Psychol. Psychiat.* **12**, 55–67

CANTWELL D. (1976) Genetic factors in the hyperkinetic syndrome. *J. Amer. Acad. Child Psychiat.* **15**, 214–223

CANTWELL D. (1975a) Genetic studies of hyperactive children: Psychiatric illness in biologic and adopting parents. *In* Fieve R., Rosenthal D. & Brill H. (eds.) *Genetic Research in Psychiatry.* Baltimore: Johns Hopkins University Press

CANTWELL D. (1975b) A critical review of therapeutic modalities with hyperactive children. *In* Cantwell D. (ed.) *The Hyperactive Child: Diagnosis, Management and Current Research.* New York: Spectrum Publications

CANTWELL D. (1974) Early intervention with hyperactive children. *J. Operational Psychiat.* **5,** 56–67

CANTWELL D. (1972) Psychiatric illness in the families of hyperactive children. *Arch. Gen. Psychiat.* **27,** 414–417

CANTWELL D. & SATTERFIELD J. Educational retardation in hyperactive children. (In preparation)

CHESS S. (1960) Diagnosis and treatment of the hyperactive child. *N.Y. State J. Med.* **60,** 2379–2385

CHRISTENSEN D. (1973) The combined effects of methylphenidate (Ritalin) and a classroom behavior modification program in reducing the hyperkinetic behavior of institutionalized mental retardates. Unpublished doctoral dissertation, University of Illinois

CHRISTENSEN D. & SPRAGUE R. (1973) Reduction of hyperactive behavior by conditioning procedures alone and combined with methylphenidate (Ritalin). *Behav. Res. Ther.* **11,** 331–334

CLEMENTS S. (1966) *Minimal Brain Dysfunction in Children.* NINDB Monograph No. 3. Washington, DC: US Public Health Service

COLEMAN M. (1971) Serotonin concentrations in whole blood of hyperactive children. *J. Pediatrics* **78,** 985–990

CONNERS C. (1973a) Psychological assessment of children with minimal brain dysfunction. *Ann. N.Y. Acad. Sci.* **205,** 283–302

CONNERS C. (1973b) Deanol and behavior disorders in children: A critical review of the literature and recommended future studies for determining efficacy. *Psychopharmacology Bulletin.* Washington, DC: Department of Health, Education, and Welfare

CONNERS C. (1972) Pharmacotherapy of psychopathology in children. *In* Quay H.C. & Werry J.S. (eds.) *Psychopathological Disorders of Childhood.* New York: Wiley

CONNERS C. (1971) Recent drug studies with hyperkinetic children. *J. Learn. Dis.* **4,** 476–483

CONNERS C. (1970) The use of stimulant drugs in enhancing performance learning. *In* Smith W.L. (ed.) *Drugs and Cerebral Function.* Springfield, Illinois: Charles C Thomas

CONNERS C. (1969) A teacher rating scale for use in drug studies with children. *Amer. J. Psychiat.* **126,** 884–888

CONNERS C. (1967) The syndrome of minimal brain dysfunction: Psychological aspects. *Pediatr. Clin. North Am.* **14,** 749–766

CONNERS C., TAYLOR E., MEO G., KURTZ M. & FOURNIER M. (1972) Magnesium pemoline and dextroamphetamine: A controlled study in children with minimal brain dysfunction. *Psychopharmacologia* **26,** 321–336

CONNERS C., EISENBERG L. & BARCAI A. (1967) Effect of dextroamphetamine on children. *Arch. Gen. Psychiat.* **17,** 478–485

CONRAD W. & INSEL J. (1967) Anticipating the response to amphetamine therapy in the treatment of hyperkinetic children. *Pediatrics* **40,** 96–99

CONRAD W., DWORKIN E., SHAI A. & TOBIESSEN J. (1971) Effects of amphetamine therapy and prescriptive tutoring on the behavior and achievement of lower class hyperactive children. *J. Learn. Dis.* **4,** 509–517

COTT A. (1969) Treating schizophrenic children. *Schizophrenia* **1,** 44–60

CRUICKSHANK W., BENTZEN F., RATZENBURG F. & TANNHAUSER M. (1961) *A Teaching Method for Brain-Injured and Hyperactive Children: a Demonstration-Pilot Study.* Syracuse, New York: Syracuse University Press

CYTRYN L., GILBERT A. & EISENBERG L. (1960) The effectiveness of tranquilizing drugs plus supportive psychotherapy in treating behavior disorders of children: a double-blind study of eighty outpatients. *Amer. J. Orthopsychiat.* **30,** 113–128

DAVIS K., SPRAGUE R. & WERRY J.S. (1969) Stereotyped behavior and activity level in severe retardates: the effect of drugs. *Amer. J. Ment. Def.* **73,** 721–727

DE LA PENA A. (1973) The habitually aggressive individual. Progress report to the National Institute of Mental Health

DE HIRSCH K. (1973) Early language development and minimal brain dysfunction. *Ann. N.Y. Acad. Sci.* **205,** 158–163

DENHOFF E. (1973) The natural life history of children with minimal brain dysfunction. *Ann. N.Y. Acad. Sci.* **205,** 188–205

DOUBROS S. & DANIELS G. (1966) An experimental approach to the reduction of over-active behavior. *Behav. Res. Ther.* **4,** 251–258

DOUGLAS V. (1972) Stop, look and listen: The problem of sustained attention and impulse control in hyperactive and normal children. *Canad. J. Behav. Sci.* **4,** 259–282

DUNN L. (1968) Special education for the mildly retarded—is much of it justifiable? *Excep. Child.* **35,** 5–22

EEG-OLOFSSON O. (1970) The development of the electroencephalogram in normal children and adolescents from the age of 1 through 21 years. *Acta Paediat. Scand.* Suppl. 208

EISENBERG L. (1972). The hyperkinetic child and stimulant drugs. *N. Engl. J. Med.* **287,** 249–250

EISENBERG L. (1966) The management of the hyperkinetic child. *Develop. Med. Child Neurol.* **8,** 593–598

ELLIS N. & PRYER R. (1959) Quantification of gross bodily activity in children with severe neuropathology. *Amer. J. Ment. Def.* **63,** 1034–1037

EPSTEIN L., LASAGNA L., CONNERS C. & RODRIGUEZ A. (1968) Correlation of dextroamphetamine excretion and drug response in hyperkinetic children. *J. Nerv. Ment. Dis.* **146,** 136–146

FEIGHNER A. & FEIGHNER J. (1974) Multimodality treatment of the hyperkinetic child. *Amer. J. Psychiat.* **131,** 459–463

FEINGOLD B. (1973) Food additives and child development. *Hosp. Practice* **8,** 11–12; 17–19

FERRIS R., TANG F. & MAXWELL R. (1972) A comparison of the capacities of isomers of amphetamine deoxypipradrol and methylphenidate to inhibit the uptake of tritiated catecholamines into rat cerebral cortex slices, synaptosomal preparations of rat cerebral cortex, hypothalamus and striatum and into adrenergic nerves of rabbit aorta. *J. Pharmacol. Exper. Ther.* **181,** 407–416

FISH B. (1975) Drug treatment of the hyperactive child. *In* Cantwell D. (ed.) *The Hyperactive Child: Diagnosis, Management and Current Research.* New York: Spectrum Publications

FISH B. (1971) The 'one child, one drug' myth of stimulants in hyperkinesis: Importance of diagnostic categories in evaluating treatment. *Arch. Gen. Psychiat.* **25,** 193–203

FISH B. (1968) Methodology in child psychopharmacology. *In* Efron D. (ed.) *Psychopharmacology, Review of Progress, 1957–1967.* Washington, DC: Public Health Service Publication No. 1836

FOSHEE J. (1958) Studies in activity level. I: Simple and complex task performance in defectives. *Amer. J. Ment. Def.* **62,** 882–886

FREEDMAN D. (1971) Report on the conference on the use of stimulant drugs in the treatment of behaviorally disturbed young school children. *Psychopharmocol. Bull.* **7,** 23–29

FREEMAN R. (1966) Drug effects on learning in children: a selective review of the past thirty years. *J. Spec. Educ.* **1,** 17–44

FREEMAN R. (1970) Psychopharmacology and the retarded child. *In* Menolascino F. (ed.) *Psychiatric Approaches to Mental Retardation.* New York: Basic Books

GARDNER R. (1973) Psychotherapy of the psychogenic problems secondary to minimal brain dysfunction. *Internat. J. Child Psychother.* **2,** 224–256

GARFINKEL B., WEBSTER C. & SLOMAN L. (1975) Methylphenidate and caffeine in the treatment of children with minimal brain dysfunction. *Amer. J. Psychiat.* **132,** 723–728

GESELL A. & AMATRUDA C. (1949) *Developmental Diagnosis.* 2nd edn. New York: Hoeber

GOODWIN F. & BUNNEY W. (1973) A psychobiological approach to affective illness. *Psychiat. Annals* **3,** 19–56

GREENHILL L., RIEDER R., WENDER P., BUCHSBAUM M. & ZAHN T. (1973) Lithium carbonate in the treatment of hyperactive children. *Arch Gen. Psychiat.* **28,** 636–640

HARTLAGE L. (1965) Effects of chlorpromazine on learning. *Psychol. Bull.* **64,** 235–245

HAYWOOD H. (1966) Perceptual handicap: Fact or artifact? *Child Study* **28,** 2–14

HERRON R. & RAMSDEN R. (1967) Continuous monitoring of overt human body movement by radio telemetry: A brief review. *Percept Mot. Skills* **24,** 1303–1308

HOFFER A. (1972) Treatment of hyperkinetic children with nicotinamide and pyridoxine. *Canad. Med. Assoc. J.* **107,** 111–112

HOFFER A. (1971) Vitamin B_3 dependent child. *Schizophrenia* **3,** 107–113

HOFFMANN H. (1845) *Der Struwwelpeter: Oder lustige Geschichten und drollige Bilder.* Leipzig: Insel Verlag

HUESSY H. (1967) Study of the prevalence and therapy of the choreatiform syndrome or hyperkinesis in rural Vermont. *Acta Paedopsychiat.* **34,** 130–135

HUESSY H. & WRIGHT A. (1970) The use of imipramine in children's behavior disorders. *Acta Paedopsychiat.* **37,** 194–199

HUTT C., JACKSON P. & LEVEL M. (1966) Behavioural parameters and drug effects: A study of a hyperkinetic epileptic child. *Epilepsia* (Amst.) **7,** 250–259

INGRAM T. (1956) A characteristic form of overactive behaviour in brain damaged children. *J. Ment. Sci.* **102,** 550–558

JACOB R., O'LEARY K. & PRICE G. (1973) Behavioral treatment of hyperactive children: An alternative to medication. Unpublished paper

JONES H., MACFARLANE J. & EICHORN D. (1960) A progress report on growth studies at the University of California. *Vita Humana* **3,** 17–31

KATZ S., SARAF K., GITTELMAN-KLEIN R. & KLEIN D. (1975) Clinical pharmacological management of hyperkinetic children. *Internat. J. Ment. Health* **4**, 157–181

KEHNE C. (1974) Social control of the hyperactive child via medication: At what cost to personality development: Some psychological implications and clinical interventions. Read before annual meeting, Orthopsychiatric Association

KENNARD M. (1960) Value of equivocal signs in neurologic diagnosis. *Neurology* **10**, 753–764

KEOGH B. (1971) Hyperactivity and learning disorders: Review and speculation. *Except. Child* **38**, 101–109

KILLAM E. (1968) Pharmacology of the reticular formation. *In* Efron D. (ed.) *Psychopharmacology, a Review of Progress 1957–1967*. Washington, DC: Public Health Service Publication no. 1836

KLEIN D. & GITTELMAN-KLEIN R. (1975a) Problems in the diagnosis of minimal brain dysfunction and the hyperkinetic syndrome. *Internat. J. Ment. Health* **4**, 45–60

KLEIN D. & GITTELMAN-KLEIN R. (1975b) *Progress in Psychiatric Drug Treatment*. New York: Bruner Mazel

KNIGHTS R. (1974) Psychometric assessment of stimulant-induced behavior change. *In* Conners C. (ed.) *Clinical Use of Stimulant Drugs in Children*. Holland: Excerpta Medica

KNIGHTS R. & HINTON G. (1969) The effects of methylphenidate (Ritalin) on the motor skills and behavior of children with learning problems. *J. Nerv. Ment. Dis.* **148**, 643–653

KNOBEL M. (1962) Psychopharmacology for the hyperkinetic child—dynamic considerations. *Arch. Gen. Psychiat.* **6**, 198–202

KNOPP W., ARNOLD L. & ANDRAS R. (1972) Electronic pupilography: predicting amphetamine benefit in hyperkinesis. Read at the 125th Annual Meeting of the American Psychiatric Association, Dallas, Texas

KRAFT I. (1968) The use of psychoactive drugs in the outpatient treatment of psychiatric disorders of children. *Amer. J. Psychiat.* **124**, 1401–1407

LAUFER M. (1971) Long-term management of some follow-up findings on the use of drugs with minimal brain dysfunction. *J. Learn. Dis.* **4**, 518–522

LAUFER M. & DENHOFF E. (1957) Hyperkinetic behavior syndrome in children. *J. Pediatrics* **50**, 463–474

LAUFER M., DENHOFF E. & SOLOMONS G. (1957) Hyperkinetic impulse disorder in children's behavior problems. *Psychosom. Med.* **19**, 38–49

LEE D. & HUTT C. (1964) A play-room designed for filming children: a note. *J. Child Psychol. Psychiat.* **5**, 263–265

LEVITT E. (1963) Psychotherapy with children: a further evaluation. *Behav. Res. Ther.* **1**, 45–51

LEVITT E. (1957) The results of psychotherapy with children: an evaluation. *J. Consult. Psychol.* **21**, 189–196

LOPEZ R. (1965) Hyperactivity in twins. *Canad. Psychiat. Assoc. J.* **10**, 421–426

MALMQUIST C. (1971) Depression in childhood and adolescence, II. *N. Engl. J. Med.* **284**, 955–961

McCARTHY J. (1973) Education: The base of the triangle. *Ann. N.Y. Acad. Sci.* **205**, 362–367

McCORD W. & McCORD J. (1960) *Origins of Alcoholism*. Stanford, California: Stanford University Press

McFARLAND J., PEACOCK L. & WATSON J. (1966) Mental retardation and activity level in rats and children. *Amer. J. Ment. Def.*, **71**, 376–380

MEICHENBAUM D. & GOODMAN J. (1971) Training impulsive children to talk to themselves: A means of developing self-control. *J. Abn. Psychol.* **77**, 115–126

MENDELSON W., JOHNSON N. & STEWART M. (1971) Hyperactive children as teenagers: a follow-up study. *J. Nerv. Ment. Dis.* **153**, 273–279

MENKES M., ROWE J. & MENKES J. (1967) A twenty-five-year follow-up study on the hyperkinetic child with minimal brain dysfunction. *Pediatrics* **39**, 393–399

MILLICHAP J. (1973) Drugs in management of minimal brain dysfunction. *Ann. N.Y. Acad. Sci.* **205**, 321–334

MILLICHAP J. & BOLDREY E. (1967) Studies in hyperkinetic behavior. II: Laboratory and clinical evaluations of drug treatment. *Neurology* **17**, 467–471; 519

MILLICHAP J. & FOWLER G. (1967) Treatment of minimal brain dysfunction syndromes. *Pediatr. Clin. North Am.* **14**, 767–777

MINDE K., WEISS G. & MENDELSON N. (1972). A five-year follow-up study of 91 hyperactive school children. *J. Am. Acad. Child Psychiat.* **11**, 595–610

MINDE K., LEWIN D., WEISS G., LAVIGUEUR H., DOUGLAS V. & SYKES E. (1971) The hyperactive child in elementary school: a 5-year, controlled follow-up. *Except. Child.* **38**, 215–221

MORRISON J. & STEWART M. (1974) Bilateral inheritance as evidence for polygenicity in the hyperactive child syndrome. *J. Nerv. Ment. Dis.* **158**, 226–228

MORRISON J. & STEWART M. (1973) The psychiatric status of the legal families of adopted hyperactive children. *Arch. Gen. Psychiat.* **28**, 888–891

MORRISON J. & STEWART M. (1971) A family study of the hyperactive child syndrome. *Biol. Psychiat.* **3**, 189–195

NARABAYASHI H., NAGAO T., SAITO Y., YOSHIDA M. & NAGAHATA M. (1963) Stereotaxic amygdalotomy for behavior disorders. *Arch. Neurol.* **9**, 1–16

O'MALLEY J. & EISENBERG L. (1973) The hyperkinetic syndrome. *Semin. Psychiat.* **5**, 95–103

OMENN G. (1973) Genetic issues in the syndrome of minimal brain dysfunction. *Semin. Psychiat.* **5**, 5–17

OUNSTED C. (1955) The hyperkinetic syndrome in epileptic children. *Lancet* **ii**, 269, 303–311

PALKES H. & STEWART M. (1972) Intellectual ability and performance of hyperactive children. *Amer. J. Orthopsychiat.* **42**, 35–39

PALKES H., STEWART M. & KAHANA B. (1968) Porteus maze performance of hyperactive boys after training in self-directed verbal commands. *Child Dev.* **39**, 817–826

PATTERSON G., JONES R., WHITTIER J. & WRIGHT M. (1965) A behaviour modification technique for the hyperactive child. *Behav. Res. Ther.* **2**, 217–226

PETERSEN I., EEG-OLOFSSON O. & SELLDEN U. (1968) Paroxysmal activity in EEG of normal children. *In* Kellaway P. & Petersen I. (eds.) *Clinical Electroencephalography of Children.* New York: Grune & Stratton

PINCUS J. & GLASER G. (1966) The syndrome of 'minimal brain damage' in childhood. *N. Engl. J. Med.* **275**, 27–35

POND D. (1961) Psychiatric aspects of epileptic and brain-damaged children. Lectures I & II. *Brit. Med. J.* **2**, 1377–1382; 1454–1459

PRECHTL H. & STEMMER C. (1962) The choreiform syndrome in children. *Develop. Med. Child Neurol.* **4**, 119–127

QUAY H.C. (1972) Patterns of aggression, withdrawal, and immaturity. *In* Quay H.C. & Werry J.S. (eds.) *Psychopathological Disorders of Childhood*. New York: Wiley

QUINN P. & RAPOPORT J. (1975) One-year follow-up of hyperactive boys treated with imipramine or methylphenidate. *Amer. J. Psychiat.* **132**, 241–245

QUITKIN F. & KLEIN D. (1969) Two behavioral syndromes in young adults related to possible minimal brain dysfunction. *J. Psychiatr. Res.* **7**, 131–142

RACHMAN S. (1971) *The Effects of Psychotherapy*. Oxford: Pergamon

RAPOPORT J., QUINN P. & LAMPRECHT F. (1974) Minor physical anomalies and plasma dopamine-beta-hydroxylase activity in hyperactive boys. *Amer. J. Psychiat.* **131**, 386–390

RAPOPORT J., LOTT I., ALEXANDER D. & ABRAMSON A. (1970) Urinary noradrenaline and playroom behaviour in hyperactive boys. *Lancet* **ii**, 1141

REITAN R. & BOLL T. (1973) Neuropsychological correlates of minimal brain dysfunction. *Ann. N.Y. Acad. Sci.* **205**, 65–88

RIMLAND B. (1973) High-dosage levels of certain vitamins in the treatment of children with severe mental disorders. *In* Hawkins D. & Pauling L. (eds.) *Orthomolecular Psychiatry*. San Francisco: Freeman

RUTTER M. (1972) Relationships between child and adult psychiatric disorders. *Acta Psychiat. Scand.* **48**, 3–21

RUTTER M. (1968) Lésion cérébrale organique, hyperkinésie et retard mental. *La Psychiatrie de L'Enfant* **11**, 475–492

RUTTER M., SHAFFER D. & SHEPHERD M. (1975) *A Multiaxial Classification of Child Psychiatric Disorders*. Geneva: WHO

RUTTER M., GRAHAM P. & YULE W. (1970a) *A Neuropsychiatric Study in Childhood*. Philadelphia: Lippincott

RUTTER M., TIZARD J. & WHITMORE K. (1970b) *Education, Health and Behaviour: Psychological and Medical Study of Childhood Development*. New York: Wiley

RUTTER M., LEVBOVICI S., EISENBERG L., SNEZNEVSKIJ A.V., SADOUN R., BROOKE E. & LIN T-Y. (1969) A tri-axial classification of mental disorders in childhood. *J. Child Psychol. Psychiat.* **10**, 41–61

SAFER D. (1973) A familial factor in minimal brain dysfunction. *Behav. Genet.* **3**, 175–86

SAFER D. & ALLEN R. (1973) Factors influencing the suppressant effect of two stimulant drugs on the growth of hyperactive children. *Pediatrics* **51**, 660–667

SAFER D., ALLEN R. & BARR E. (1972) Depression of growth in hyperactive children on stimulant drugs. *N. Engl. J. Med.* **287**, 217–220

SANTOSTEFANO S. & STAYTON S. (1967) Training the preschool retarded child in focusing attention: a program for parents. *Amer. J. Orthopsychiat.* **37**, 732–743

SATTERFIELD J. (1973a) EEG issues in children with minimal brain dysfunction. *Semin. Psychiat.* **5**, 35–46

SATTERFIELD J. (1973b) Personal communication

SATTERFIELD J. & CANTWELL D. (1975) Psychopharmacology in the prevention of antisocial and delinquent behavior. *Internat. J. Ment. Health* **4**, 227–237

SATTERFIELD J., CANTWELL D. & SATTERFIELD B. (1974) Pathophysiology of the hyperactive child syndrome. *Arch. Gen. Psychiat.* **31**, 839–844

SATTERFIELD J., CANTWELL D., LESSER L. & PODOSIN R. (1972) Physiological studies of the hyperkinetic child: I. *Amer. J. Psychiat.* **128**, 1418–1424

SCHAIN R. (1972) *Neurology of Childhood Learning Disorders*. Baltimore: Williams & Wilkins

SCHAIN R. & REYNARD C. (1975) Observations on effects of a central stimulant drug (methylphenidate) in children with hyperactive behavior. *Pediatrics* **55**, 709–716

SCHILDKRAUT J. & KETY S. (1967) Biogenic amines and emotion. *Science* **156**, 21–30

SCHNACKENBERG R. (1973) Caffeine as a substitute for Schedule II stimulants in hyperkinetic children. *Amer. J. Psychiat.* **130**, 796–798

SCHULMAN J. & REISMAN J. (1959) An objective measure of hyperactivity. *Amer. J. Ment. Def.* **64**, 455–456

SHELLEY E. & RIESTER A. (1972) Syndrome of minimal brain damage in young adults. *Dis. Nerv. Syst.* **33**, 335–338

SHETTY T. (1971) Alpha rhythms in the hyperkinetic child. *Nature* **234**, 476

SILVER A. (1952) Postural and righting responses in children. *J. Pediatrics* **41**, 493–498

SNYDER S., TAYLOR K., COYLE J. & MEYERHOFF J. (1970) The role of brain dopamine in behavioral regulation and the actions of psychotropic drugs. *Amer. J. Psychiat.* **127**, 199–207

SPRAGUE R. (1973) Minimal brain dysfunction from a behavioral viewpoint. *Ann. N.Y. Acad. Sci.* **205**, 349–361

SPRAGUE R. (1972) Psychopharmacology and learning disabilities. *J. Operational Psychiat.* **3**, 56–67

SPRAGUE R. & SLEATOR E. (1973) Effects of psychopharmacologic agents on learning disorders. *Pediatr. Clin. North Am.* **20**, 719–735

SPRAGUE R. & TOPPE L. (1966) Relationship between activity level and delay of reinforcement in the retarded. *J. Exper. Child Psychol.* **3**, 390–397

SPRAGUE R. & WERRY J.S. (1971) Methodology of psychopharmacological studies with the retarded. *In* Ellis N. (ed.) *International Review of Research in Mental Retardation*, vol. 5. New York: Academic Press

STEWART M., PITTS F., CRAIG A. & DIERUF W. (1966) The hyperactive child syndrome. *Amer. J. Orthopsychiat.* **36**, 861–867

STRAUSS A. & LEHTINEN L. (1947) *Psychopathology and Education of the Brain-Injured Child.* New York: Grune & Stratton

SYKES D., DOUGLAS V. & MORGENSTERN G. (1972) The effect of methylphenidate (Ritalin) on sustained attention in hyperactive children. *Psychopharmacologia* **25**, 262–274

SYKES D., DOUGLAS V., WEISS G. & MINDE K. (1971) Attention in hyperactive children and the effect of methylphenidate (Ritalin). *J. Child Psychol. Psychiat.* **12**, 129–139

TARJAN G., TIZARD J., RUTTER M., BEGAB M., BROOKE E.M., DE LA CRUZ F., LIN T.-Y., MONTENEGRO H., STROTZKA H. & SARTORIUS N. (1972) Classification and mental retardation: Issues arising in the Fifth WHO seminar on psychiatric diagnosis, classification, and statistics. *Amer. J. Psychiat.* **128**, 11; 34–45 (Suppl)

THOMAS A., CHESS S. & BIRCH H.C. (1968) *Temperament and Behavior Disorders in Children.* New York: University Press

THORNDIKE R. (1963) *The concepts of over- and under-achievement.* New York: Bureau of Publications, Teachers College, Columbia University

WAIZER J., HOFFMAN S.P., POLIZOS P. & ENGELHARDT D. (1974) Outpatient treatment of hyperactive school children with imipramine. *Amer. J. Psychiat.* **131**, 587–591

WALDROP M. & HALVERSON C. (1971) Minor physical anomalies and hyperactive behavior in young children. *In* Hellmuth J. (ed.) *The Exceptional Infant.* Vol. 2. New York: Brunner-Mazel

WARD M. (1966) Experimental modification of 'hyperactive' behavior. Unpublished BS thesis, University of Illinois

WARREN R., KARDUCK W., BUSSARATID S., STEWART M. & SLY W. (1971) The hyperactive child syndrome: Normal chromosome findings. *Arch. Gen. Psychiat.* **24**, 161–162

WEISS G., KRUGER E., DANIELSEN U. & ELMAN M. (1975) Effect of long-term treatment of hyperactive children with methylphenidate. *Canad. Med. Assoc. J.* **112**, 159–165

WEISS G., MINDE K., WERRY J., DOUGLAS V. & NEMETH E. (1971) Studies on the hyperactive child. VIII: Five-year follow-up. *Arch. Gen. Psychiat.* **24**, 409–414

WENDER P. (1971) *Minimal Brain Dysfunction in Children.* New York: Wiley-Interscience

WENDER P. (1969) Platelet serotonin level in children with 'minimal brain dysfunction'. *Lancet* ii, 1012

WENDER P., EPSTEIN R., KOPIN I. & GORDON E. (1971) Urinary monoamine metabolites in children with minimal brain dysfunction. *Amer. J. Psychiat.* **127**, 1411–1415

WERKMAN S. (1970) Brain dysfunction in adolescence. IV: Implications of the research. *Amer. J. Orthopsychiat.* **40**, 336–337

WERRY J. (1972) Organic factors in childhood psychopathology. *In* Quay H.C. & Werry J.S. (eds.) *Psychopathological Disorders of Childhood.* New York: Wiley

WERRY J. (1968a) Developmental hyperactivity. *Pediatr. Clin. North Am.* **15**, 581–599

WERRY J. (1968b) Studies on the hyperactive child. IV: An empirical analysis of the minimal brain dysfunction syndrome. *Arch. Gen. Psychiat.* **19**, 9–16

WERRY J. & SPRAGUE R. (1972) Psychopharmacology. *In* Wortis J. (ed.) *Mental Retardation, An Annual Review*, vol. IV. New York: Grune & Stratton

WERRY J., MINDE K., GUZMAN A., WEISS G., DOGAN K. & HOY E. (1972) Studies on the hyperactive child. VII: Neurological status compared with neurotic and normal children. *Amer. J. Orthopsychiat.* **42**, 441–450

WERRY J. (1970) Some clinical and laboratory studies of psychotropic drugs in children: An overview. *In* Smith W. (ed.) *Drugs and Cerebral Function.* Springfield, Illinois: Charles C Thomas

WHITEHEAD P. & CLARK L. (1970) Effect of lithium carbonate, placebo, and thioridazine on hyperactive children. *Amer. J. Psychiat.* **127**, 824–825

WILLERMAN L. (1973) Activity level and hyperactivity in twins. *Child Dev.* **44**, 288–293

WINSBERG B., YEPES L. & BIALER I. Psychopharmacological management of children with hyperactive/aggressive/inattentive behavior disorders: a guide for the pediatrician. *Clin. Pediatr.* (in press)

WINSBERG B., GOLDSTEIN S., YEPES L. & PEREL J. (1975) Imipramine and electrocardiographic abnormalities in hyperactive children. *Amer. J. Psychiat.* **132**, 542–545

WINSBERG B., PRESS M., BIALER I. & KUPIETZ S. (1974) Dextroamphetamine and methylphenidate in the treatment of hyperactive/aggressive children. *Pediatrics* **53**, 236–241

WINSBERG B., BIALER I., KUPIETZ S. & TOBIAS J. (1972) Effects of imipramine and dextroamphetamine on behavior of neuropsychiatrically impaired children. *Amer. J. Psychiat.* **128**, 1425–1431

WITT P., ELLIS M. & SPRAGUE R. (1970) Methylphenidate and free range activity in hyperactive children. Unpublished paper written in support of NIMH grant no. MH 189–9, Children's Research Center, University of Illinois, Urbana

WOODRUFF R., GOODWIN D. & GUZE S. (1974) *Psychiatric Diagnosis.* New York: Oxford University Press

YULE W. (1967) Predicting reading ages on Neale's analysis of reading ability. *Brit. J. Educ. Psychol.* **37**, 252–255

ZRULL P., PATCH D. & LEHTINEN P. (1966) Hyperkinetic children who respond to *d*-amphetamine. Scientific proceedings summary, American Psychiatric Association (Atlantic City, NJ)

CHAPTER 23

Reading difficulties

M. RUTTER AND W. YULE

Severe reading difficulties are common, persistent and handicapping; they are also frequently associated with behavioural and psychiatriatic problems (Rutter & Yule 1973; Rutter 1974). This association has often been observed in clinic attenders but it is not an artefact of referral practices as the finding has been confirmed in several epidemiological studies of the total population (Douglas 1964; Douglas *et al* 1967; Malmquist 1958; Morris 1966; Clark 1970; Rutter, Tizard & Whitmore 1970; Davie *et al* 1972; Varlaam 1974). It is important, therefore, for all professionals concerned with the care of children with psychiatric problems to understand the nature and treatment of reading difficulties and to appreciate the meaning of the association between reading failure and psychiatric disorder. This chapter outlines what is known on these issues but for a fuller account of the detailed research findings the reader is referred to the several extensive recent reviews of the subject (e.g. Vernon 1971; Rutter & Yule 1973).

FACTORS ASSOCIATED WITH READING ATTAINMENT

Reading is a complex skill which involves a number of rather different components. It is a perceptual task in that the reader must be able to make quite fine perceptual discriminations involving closure (e.g. between O and C), line to curve transformations (as between U and V) and rotational transformations (e.g. b and d, or M and W). Although the precise skills which underlie these discriminations remain uncertain (Bryant 1974), the perceptual capacities required for reading follow a regular developmental course (Gibson 1965). Sequencing abilities are also needed in that it is essential to recognise that 'dog' is not the same as 'god', nor does 'man hit cat' have the same meaning as 'cat hit man'. Processes of translating information from one sensory modality to another are also involved. Thus, writing to dictation requires auditory input to be translated into visual symbols and reading aloud from Braille means that tactile impressions are being used to provide a verbal output. However, most of all, reading is a linguistic skill which requires the understanding of a code of visual symbols used to convey meaning. A child who can read mechanically but who does not comprehend what he has read has not yet mastered what reading is all about. Reading, as much as speech, is essentially a language code utilised for communication between people.

Learning to read is also, of course, a specific example of a learning task. As such, success is based in part on general cognitive skills. Thus, reading attainment correlates about +0·6 with IQ (Yule *et al* 1974; Weinberg *et al* 1974). However, as with other forms of learning, learning to read also requires motivation and task involvement. Learning strategies, too, may improve or impede the learning process. How quickly a child acquires reading skills will be determined by the learning opportunities open to him. These will be influenced by his family and sociocultural circumstances. Finally, in so far as reading is a taught skill, the quantity and quality of instruction in reading will also be important. Children who lack schooling are impaired in their cognitive development and reading skills also vary with the quality of education provided (Rutter & Madge 1976).

Because reading is a highly complex activity which utilises a great number of skills (Maliphant *et al* 1974), it has not proved easy to determine the relative importance of each skill in either reading competence or reading difficulties. One way of examining this question is to determine the frequency of reading difficulties in children with different sorts of specific handicap. Thus, the importance of speech and language skills was shown by the Edinburgh follow-up of children with speech delay (Mason 1967; Ingram 1970). Two years after starting school a third of the speech retarded children were backward in reading and spelling compared with some one in twenty of the controls. The reading difficulties occurred both in children with a true delay in spoken language and also in those with just an articulation defect.

In contrast, visuo-spatial skills appear rather less important. Robinson and Schwartz (1973) followed up 41 children identified as having defects in visual perception and/or visuomotor coordination at age 5 to 6 years. Three years later the children showed no more reading difficulties than did a matched control group without visuo-spatial difficulties. The same result comes from a consideration of people with Turner's syndrome (Money 1973). Although they characteristically have severe visuo-spatial difficulties, this is not accompanied by any problems in reading (Alexander & Money 1965). A variety of other studies have also shown that visuo-perceptual difficulties, although associated to some extent with reading difficulties in younger children, are not particularly important correlates of severe and persisting reading difficulties (see Rutter & Yule 1973). At first sight this seems surprising as reading so obviously requires perceptual discriminations. Several possible explanations may be suggested. First, the level of visual discrimination required in reading may be below that usually found in older children with visuo-spatial defects. That is, although they are perceptually impaired compared with their peers they still have sufficient skills in discrimination to learn to read. If this were so, it would be expected that visuo-spatial defects should be more important causes of reading impairment in very young children. There is limited evidence that this may be so (Rutter & Yule 1973; Satz *et al* 1971).

Secondly, it is apparent that good readers do not discriminate each individual word when reading. Rather, they scan the text for key words placing more reliance on context and meaning than on examination of sentences word by word by means of a sequential perception of each visual stimulus (Hochberg 1970; Maliphant *et al* 1974; Willows 1974).

There is an association between patterns of eye movement and reading skills (see Rutter & Yule 1973; also Heiman & Ross 1974) but the evidence suggests that it is not a simple cause and effect relationship. Except rarely, an impaired control of eye movements does not interfere substantially with reading. Presumably, the degree of eye movement control needed for reading is not great.

In an epidemiologically based sample of backward readers with an IQ of 80 or more, Birch and Belmont (1964) found that poor readers did less well than controls on a task requiring the matching of an auditory tap pattern to a visual dot pattern. They suggested that a defect in cross-modal intersensory integration might be one important factor contributing to reading disability. It was further shown that skills in audio-visual integration were correlated with reading ability in the normal population (Birch & Belmont 1965; Kahn & Birch 1968). These findings have been broadly confirmed in a variety of other studies (see review by Rutter & Yule 1973) but there is considerable doubt as to whether cross-modal sensory transfer is the crucial element.

Most of the studies did not differentiate *within* sensory modality perceptual discriminations from *across* modality discriminations, nor did they differentiate temporal-spatial integration from cross-modal integration (Bryant 1975). When appropriate controls are introduced (see e.g. Blank & Bridger 1966; Blank *et al* 1968; Bryden 1972) the results suggest that poor reading is associated with a variety of difficulties in perceptual linking (possibly due to a difficulty in verbal coding), but that the poor reading is *not* specifically associated with either cross-modal transfer or temporo-spatial coordination.

Several studies have indicated that poor readers often have difficulties in the perception of temporal or spatial order sequences (Bakker 1967; 1972; Doehring 1968; Hayes 1975). However, children can be taught to some extent to improve their sequencing (Cashdan 1970; Hayes 1975). Also the sequencing deficit in poor readers is most marked when the test stimuli approximate closely to letters and words. It appears that the sequencing skills vary according to the ease or difficulty with which the stimuli can be labelled (Hayes 1975), suggesting again that poor reading is often related to language difficulties.

It is commonly supposed that left-handedness, left-eyedness or mixed laterality are important causes or correlates of reading difficulties. However, all epidemiologically based studies have shown this to be a mistaken notion and it may be concluded that reading difficulties are not associated with any particular pattern of handedness, eyedness or footedness (Belmont & Birch 1965; Malmquist 1958; Clark 1970; Rutter, Tizard & Whitmore 1970; Douglas *et al* 1967; Helveston *et al* 1970). On the other hand, *confusion* between right and left is associated with reading difficulties (Rutter, Tizard & Whitmore 1970). Of course, left-handed children may well need extra help with writing and teachers should be aware of the modified techniques available for such children (Clark 1959).

The importance of general intelligence in learning to read to shown by Butler's (1971) finding (see also Rutter *et al* 1976b), that an IQ score at age 5 years predicted reading at age 7 years better than a psychological battery designed to identify children with specific disabilities. Similarly, Bax and Whitmore (1973) found that a high frequency of neurodevelopmental difficulties at the time of school entry was associated with a much increased risk of both reading and behavioural difficulties. The relative importance of different types of neurodevelopmental abnormality was not examined.

Numerous studies have shown that children with cerebral palsy show a high rate of reading problems (Rutter, Graham & Yule 1970). Seidel *et al* (1975) have recently demonstrated that this is so even in cerebral palsied children of normal intelligence. Brain damage incurred at an early stage of development markedly impedes the acquisition of reading skills even when IQ is normal. Chronic physical handicaps which do not involve brain pathology have much less impact on scholastic attainment, although there is some effect (Rutter, Tizard & Whitmore 1970; Rutter & Yule 1973).

Follow-up studies of children of low birth weight have shown that a disproportionate number are intellectually backward (Birch & Gussow 1970), but the association with reading difficulties appears less strong (Barker & Edwards 1967; Davie *et al* 1972). Overall, the findings suggest a weak, but possibly meaningful association between low birth weight and reading difficulties (Rutter & Yule 1973).

Although EEG abnormalities are probably somewhat increased in frequency in children with reading difficulties (perhaps especially so in those with poor attainment in other subjects as well, Ingram *et al* 1970), most reading retarded children have a normal EEG and electroencephalographic abnormalities provide a very poor guide to a child's reading skills (Rutter & Yule 1973). On the other hand, preliminary findings using computer analysis of the EEG have shown that poor readers have greater power spectra than good readers in the eye open condition (Maxwell *et al* 1974). This, together with the factor analytic findings (Maxwell 1972) which showed higher loadings on a general factor and a missing verbal factor in poor readers, has been used to argue for less efficient brain functioning in poor readers (Maxwell *et al* 1974). The observation has no direct clinical relevance at the moment but should be productive of further research into the links between cognitive functioning and physiological brain activity.

Temperamental attributes have been found to be quite strongly associated with reading difficulties. Epidemiological enquiries in Britain (Rutter, Tizard & Whitmore 1970) and Scandinavia (Malmquist 1958) have shown that children with reading difficulties are much more likely than other children to show poor concentration even on tasks not involving reading. De Hirsch *et al* (1966) found that the characteristics of 'hyperactive, distractive, impulsive and disinhibited' were associated with poor reading in their predictive study; Kagan (1965) found that 6-year-old children who were impulsive and quick to jump to conclusions read less well than reflective, more deliberate children; and Feshbach *et al* (1973) noted that teacher rating of children's behaviour in their first year at school were the strongest predictors of reading skills 1 year later. These traits are to some extent modifiable, and studies of training suggest that the learning of reading is impaired in impulsive children not so much by their overly rapid responses, as by their poor learning strategies (Egeland 1974).

Many investigations have shown that low socioeconomic status and large family size tend to be associated with both low verbal intelligence and poor reading attainment (Rutter & Madge 1976). In fact, apart from IQ, social class and birth order are much the strongest correlates of reading attainment (Davie *et al* 1972). A detailed consideration of the evidence suggests that the associations reflect both genetic and environmental influences (Rutter & Madge 1976).

It is clear that a very wide range of factors are associated with reading difficulties. However, although the research findings provide valuable information on the causes and correlates of reading difficulty, they are of limited help to the clinician because most of the investigations have been based on the implicit assumption that all reading difficulties, and indeed all learning disabilities, are of the same kind (Applebee 1971). There is now evidence that they are not.

CLASSIFICATION

In considering differential diagnosis in a child presenting with low academic achievement, three basic distinctions have to be made (Rutter 1974). First a failure to acquire educational skills must be differentiated from a later loss of these skills or a later failure to make scholastic progress. Second, there must be a differentiation according to the type of scholastic skill involved (reading or arithmetic, etc.). Third, a distinction must be made between *general* backwardness (i.e. low achievement in relation to the average for that age, but without taking IQ into account) and *specific* retardation (i.e. achievement which is low after taking both age and IQ into account).

Later educational failure

Although systematic comparative research is lacking, children who fall behind in their school work after having mastered the basic scholastic skills almost certainly have a quite different set of problems to the children who have failed to learn to read or to do number work from the very outset (Pearson 1952). Later educational failure usually concerns a wide range of subjects rather than just one specific skill and in most cases the problem concerns a lack of *utilisation* of skills rather than a lack of general or specific cognitive *capacity*.

However, it should not necessarily be assumed that there is anything the matter with a child whose school progress is less good later than it had been earlier. Intellectual development tends to be uneven and it is a common occurrence for normal children to go up or down 10 to 20 points in IQ during the course of their school career (Rutter & Madge 1976). Similarly, scholastic attainment commonly shows troughs, peaks and plateaux. Furthermore, learning tasks change in both complexity and type as education progresses. Because a child learned his multiplication tables easily it does not necessarily follow that he will master differential calculus with the same facility.

The investigation of later educational failure should always include an assessment of general intelligence as well as a history of school progress. Sometimes the problem is simply that a child of limited abilities who coped earlier, runs into difficulties as the work becomes harder, so that he is being expected to do more than he is able to. It is also necessary to find out about the teaching methods. Although frequent changes of school do not usually impair school progress (Rutter & Madge 1976), changes may lead to difficulties if the new teacher assumes knowledge the child does not have or if the methods employed are very different to those to which the child is used. Of course, too, a child's school progress may be impaired by generally bad teaching or poor schooling so that it is wise to enquire if other children in the same class are also having difficulties.

Learning difficulties may arise during the later years of schooling from a variety of causes (Rutter 1974). However, once low intelligence and problems in teaching are ruled out, motivational reasons stand out as particularly important. The rising absenteeism from school during the secondary school stage reflects the increasing proportion of children who fail to see any rewards in schooling and who opt out of the educational process. Many of these adolescents have had scholastic difficulties for many years and have just had enough of failure. However, others were successful scholars in their earlier schooldays. The reasons why they lose interest are varied but poorly documented. A child's interest and involvement in learning will be increased by his identification with the person (either teacher or parent) associated with the learning process, so that he seeks to please him by his learning success. Conversely, a bad relationship may interfere with learning and it is always useful to find out about how the child gets on with his teachers and with his parents. More specifically, a child may work less well because his attention is deflected onto other things (Pearson 1952). This may occur, for example, with worries about difficulties at home, with sexual preoccupations, with daydreams, or with obsessional ruminations. However, evidence is lacking on how often this happens.

Children may also show underachievement because of a positive avoidance of learning (either in general or with respect to a specific subject). Most obviously this is evident in those adolescents whose work falls off as part of a rebellion against adult values. Some intelligent children come to reject education as something which is not worth working for and their educational attainments may suffer accordingly. In other cases, learning comes to be associated in the child's mind with pain or unpleasant feeling. This situation may arise where a parent or teacher keeps punishing a child for not learning properly (Pearson 1952). Eventually, the child may come, by generalisation, to associate learning with punishment and so avoid it. The same phenomenon may result if the child's peer culture regards schoolwork as 'cissy' and to be despised. If the child is teased and tormented as a 'swot' by his friends when he does his schoolwork well, he may learn that scholastic success is to be avoided (Rutter 1974).

Alternatively, it has been argued that schoolwork may be avoided because learning has become involved in a neurotic conflict. In these cases, learning is inhibited because of its symbolic associations. Thus, it has been suggested that reading may come to have a sexual connotation so that reading is associated with sexual 'looking' (Jarvis 1958). The only study to test this hypothesis gave equivocal findings (Walters *et al* 1961) and it remains unknown how commonly underachievement is due to this or any other type of neurotic conflict. Unfortunately, most reports are based on uncontrolled studies of clinic populations (Miller & Westman 1964; Silverman *et al* 1959; Sperry *et al* 1958) or on highly speculative psychoanalytic interpretations (Anthony 1961).

Underachievement may also arise because of general impairment of a child's psychological functions. This most commonly happens in association with depressive disorders in adolescence but it also occurs in a more serious fashion with schizophrenia beginning in this age period (Offord & Cross 1969). Most psychiatric disorders are not accompanied by any fall off in either IQ or reading attainment (and there is no straightforward relation between anxiety and underachievement, Rutter 1974). Thus in the Isle of Wight studies (Rutter *et al* 1976b) whether psychiatric disorder continued or ceased between the ages of 10 and 15 years was unassociated with changes in test score. Psychiatric disorder arising for the first time in adolescence is also not associated with reading retardation (Rutter *et al* 1976a). However, school-work may suffer either when there is a serious generalised psychiatric disorder or when the disorder specifically involves anxieties on conflicts over learning.

Rarely, educational failure may arise as a result of an acquired neurological condition. Although this is not a frequent occurrence, the fact that it occurs makes it necessary to undertake a screening neurological examination in all cases of learning disorder.

Type of scholastic skill involved

The second distinction in differential diagnosis involves classification according to the scholastic skill involved. Most attention in published reports has been paid to reading and spelling, two skills which are very closely associated. Most children with marked reading difficulties also have severe problems in spelling. Nevertheless, although the two skills are closely linked they do not involve identical processes. Because the phonic decoding rules in reading are not quite the same as the encoding rules in spelling, both need to be taught as part of any remedial programme. There has also been a concern with mathematical disabilities (e.g. Cohn 1961; Slade & Russell 1971) and to a lesser extent with other subjects. Surprisingly little attention has been paid to the similarities and differences between underachievement in different subjects. The very limited available evidence suggests that arithmetical difficulties are more associated with visuo-spatial and parietal lobe functions (Slade & Russell 1971; Money 1973) in contrast to the greater link between reading skills and linguistic functions (Rutter & Yule 1973). However, this cannot be regarded as more than a hypothesis worth testing in view of the absence of systematic studies of any large groups of children with arithmetical disabilities.

Nevertheless, for practical as well as theoretical reasons, it is important that assessment clearly delineates the specific subjects in which the child is having difficulties. This requires that reading comprehension is assessed as well as mechanical reading accuracy, as some children master the latter without understanding more than a fraction of what they read. A test such as the Neale Analysis of Reading Ability (1958) is well devised for this purpose. It is also important to test spelling as many children overcome their reading problems only to remain atrocious spellers. The testing of mathematical skills is less satisfactory in view of the wide disparity between the various current teaching methods. The arithmetic subtest of the WISC gives some indication of skills in this area but no really adequate test of mathematics is available, partly due to the major changes in recent years in the teaching of mathematics.

General reading backwardness or specific reading retardation

The third basic distinction is between *general* backwardness and *specific* retardation. Although this distinction can be applied to any area of school-work it has been systematically studied only with respect to reading. General reading backwardness refers to reading which is poor in relation to the average attainment for that age regardless of intelligence. Specific reading retardation is a term used to describe a specific disability in reading—specific that is to say in the sense that reading difficulties are not explicable in terms of the child's general intelligence (Rutter, Tizard & Whitmore 1970). It follows from these definitions that reading backward children will tend to be of well below average intelligence whereas children with specific reading retardation will have a mean IQ which is roughly average for the general population.

In the past there has been some scepticism about the validity of this distinction and certainly the differentiation can only be justified if it can be shown to have practical value (Davis & Cashdan 1963). Recent epidemiological studies in London and on the Isle of Wight have provided that evidence (Rutter & Yule 1975).

The syndrome of specific reading retardation is defined in terms of a discrepancy between attainment as predicted on the basis of age and IQ and actual attainment as observed (see below for a discussion of measurement). On statistical grounds alone there are bound to be some children with extreme degrees of underachievement in reading, so that specific reading retardation could merely represent the lower end of a normal continuum with nothing else remarkable about the children. In fact, this is *not* the case (Yule *et al*

1974). Five population studies have all shown that extreme degrees of specific reading retardation occur much more often than expected on statistical grounds. Children with the disorder form a 'hump' at the bottom of the normal curve.

Other evidence from the same studies indicates that the syndrome is medically as well as statistically valid in that there are important differences between children with specific reading retardation and those with general reading backwardness (Rutter & Yule 1975). The main differences found were as follows: (a) children with specific reading retardation were much more likely to be boys (ratio of about 3 or 4 to 1) whereas the sex distribution for general reading backwardness was nearly equal; (b) overt neurological disorder was much more frequent in the generally backward group; (c) children with general reading backwardness tended to have a wide range of developmental difficulties including motor and praxic abnormalities, whereas specific reading retardation was strongly associated only with speech and language impairment; and (d) more of the generally backward children came from socially disadvantaged homes.

These differences imply that the two types of reading disability have a somewhat different origin. Findings from the same investigation showed that they also carry different educational implications (Yule 1973). As might be expected from their superior general intelligence, the children with specific reading retardation made *more* progress in mathematics between the ages of 10 and 14 years. However, in spite of their better IQ level, they made significantly less progress in both reading and spelling.

The results of a study by Ingram and his colleagues (1970) also suggest the validity of a distinction between specific reading retardation and backwardness in most school subjects. They found that children with a specific reading disability were *less* likely to have neurological or EEG abnormalities but *more* likely to show primitive spelling errors of audiophonic origin.

It may be concluded that the designation of specific reading retardation not only picks out a statistically distinctive category within the broader group of poor readers but also the diagnosis carries with it important clinical and educational implications.

'Dyslexia'

There have been numerous attempts to provide an even finer subclassification of reading difficulties by the identification of a so-called 'dyslexic' group with 'pure' difficulties of constitutional origin which share a common aetiology and a common need for a specific form of treatment. The attempts to define 'dyslexia' have so far left a great deal to be desired (Reid 1969; Rutter 1969;

Rutter & Yule 1975), and the efforts to separate out a dyslexic core from within the broader group of children with specific reading retardation have failed. Neither in a population study (Rutter 1969) nor an investigation of a highly selected clinic sample (Naidoo 1972) was it possible to demonstrate separate subclusters with specific developmental anomalies. Moreover, the evidence clearly indicates that it is common for specific reading retardation to have *multiple* causes (Rutter & Yule 1973). The suggested signs of dyslexia do not constitute a pathognomonic pattern and environmental influences frequently interact with biological factors to give rise to specific reading retardation (Rutter & Yule 1975).

Nevertheless, to some extent the arguments over finer diagnostic subgroups are rather unreal. With a few minor exceptions, the features said to characterise dyslexia are just those which empirical findings show to be associated with specific reading retardation (see below). In both cases the reading difficulties are severe, specific and persistent and in both there is a very strong association with serious and often bizarre spelling errors which frequently involve audiophonic decoding and which tend to persist into adult life (Boder 1971; Critchley 1970; Ingram *et al* 1970; Rutter & Yule 1973; Miles 1974). There is a strong connection with developmental impairment of various specific cognitive functions, especially those involving speech and language and there is good evidence for an important biological component which not infrequently includes genetic factors. There are only two respects, although both important respects, in which the concept of dyslexia seems to be mistaken. The first is the supposition that it is a distinct unitary condition, which is a view running against the evidence. The second is that the presence of a biological condition means that environmental influences are unimportant. Quite the converse is true. Children with a biological impairment tend to be *more* vulnerable to environmental adversities, and reading difficulties are often the outcome of an interaction between constitutional deficits and environmental hazards.

MEASUREMENT OF UNDERACHIEVEMENT

Before discussing specific reading retardation it is necessary first to consider the measurement of underachievement of reading. Obviously, underachievement is not something that is simply present or absent. It is a matter of degree. Very few children will perform *exactly* at the level expected on the basis of their chronological age and IQ. Most will have achievements somewhat below or above expectation and it is mainly when achievements are much below expectation that there has to be concern. The questions then are: what should be the expected level of attainment for any child? And how do you decide what is a lot below that?

The traditional approach has been to use some form of achievement ratio (such as reading age divided by mental age) or discrepancy between mental age and achievement age. Unfortunately, this attractive and commonsense approach is invalid and seriously misleading because it assumes that IQ and reading run exactly in parallel (which they do not) and because it fails to take account of the 'regression effect'. The use of statistics such as the achievement ratio will *over*estimate the number of highly intelligent and *under*estimate the number of less intelligent children with specific reading retardation. The theoretical basis for this artefact is well explained in Thorndike (1963) and the empirical data that the artefact occurs in practice as well as in theory are provided in Yule *et al* (1974).

The appropriate procedure—and the only one that avoids this problem—is the use of some kind of regression equation in which achievement is predicted on the basis of the observed correlations between educational attainment, age and IQ in the general population (Yule 1967; Rutter, Tizard & Whitmore 1970; Berger *et al* 1975; Silberberg *et al* 1969). This approach enables both the calculation of the degree of a child's underachievement in reading and also an estimate of the expected frequency of different degrees of underachievement. However, considerations of frequency are not enough to decide when a child has a clinically significant degree of specific reading retardation. Prognosis is also important. There must be most concern over the child who, without help, is unlikely to 'catch-up' with his contemporaries. So far as reading is concerned, follow-up studies (Yule 1973; Rutter & Yule 1975) show that there is a very poor outlook for children whose reading is well below average in absolute terms and whose achievement is more than two standard errors of prediction below expectation (this cut-off point picks up between 3 and 10 per cent of the general population).

However, while this cut-off point provides a useful guide there are both statistical snares to avoid and other considerations to take into account. First, in obtaining an IQ score for the prediction equation, it is necessary to use a test which does not require the child to read. In practice this means that group tests are inappropriate. Second, although a formula derived from a normal general population sample may be safely applied to other groups (Berger *et al* 1975), it is not valid to extend the equation to age groups other than those on which it was based. This is because the age component in the regression equation will be much influenced by the age spread in the population tested. Thirdly, there is uncertainty about the clinical significance of reading levels which are in the average range but which, because of very high IQ, still reflect severe underachievement. Fourth, although the syndrome is called specific *reading* retardation it is important to recognise that the *spelling* disability is often more severe. Many children who were severely retarded in reading but who have now more or less made up lost ground remain severely impaired in their spelling (and often slow in their writing). This means that spelling must always be tested. Fifth, there are many children with severe reading problems whose attainments are nevertheless better than two standard errors below prediction. In short, this provides a minimal estimate of the number of children with specific reading retardation.

Other educational considerations must also be taken into account when planning remedial treatment. The *rate* of the child's current progress in learning to read is relevant in addition to the *level* of his current achievements. The underachieving child is more likely to suffer from his disability in schools where educational failure results in segregation and opprobrium. Also the extent to which he is at an educational disadvantage will depend on the attainments of other children in his class, the degree of streaming and the extent to which teaching is individualised rather than group based.

SPECIFIC READING RETARDATION*

Specific reading retardation, even in its severe form, is a common problem. On the Isle of Wight it occurred in some 4 per cent of 10-year-olds (Rutter, Tizard & Whitmore 1970) and in Inner London it was twice as common (Berger *et al* 1975). It occurs in children from all types of social background but it is much more prevalent in boys than in girls. The children often have some difficulty with other school subjects (partly because teaching frequently requires the child to read what is printed in books or written on the blackboard), but the difficulties in reading are much more severe than those in other lessons. The one exception is spelling which is often even more severely impaired than reading. Claims have been made that the spelling difficulties are of a specific type but the evidence so far is inconclusive (see Rutter & Yule 1973). *If* there is a characteristic spelling difficulty it is probably of the type which involves phonic confusion (e.g. 'awlake' for 'awake' or 'bun' for 'but') rather than visuo-spatial errors (e.g. confusion of b, d, p) or phonetically correct misspellings (e.g. 'laf' for 'laugh' or 'hows' for 'house') (Boder 1971; Ingram *et al* 1970). The matter requires further study.

Although there is no diagnostic pattern of intellectual performance, there is a well-established tendency for retarded readers to have a lower verbal than performance score on the Wechsler intelligence scales. This finding is in keeping with the extensive evidence that speech and language difficulties are strongly associated with reading retardation. A characteristic story is that the child has been delayed learning to speak, then shows great difficulties learning

* Full references to the research which constitutes the basis for the statements made in this section can be found in Rutter and Yule (1973).

to read and later only severe spelling difficulties persist. Often there is also a family history of speech delay. The association with speech delay and continuing impairment in verbal skills is basic and probably reflects causal influences which affect both written and spoken language. However, it should be noted that reading retardation is also associated with defects in pronunciation even when there is no detectable impairment in spoken language skills.

Other developmental delays are also significantly associated with reading retardation. The most important of these concern verbal coding and sequencing. The children may find it hard to remember the order of months and are likely to have difficulty with any kind of task that involves putting things into an order or sequence, or which requires the learning of a code or a series of links or connections. This problem is probably related, at least in part, to language deficits.

Another common difficulty involves the child's confusion between right and left. Reading retardation is frequently associated with very poorly coordinated writing and may also be connected with a wide range of other developmental deficits including clumsiness, poor motor control and difficulties in differentiating shapes. Nevertheless, although important in individual children (Gubbay *et al* 1965) these are less common factors than speech, language and sequencing problems. It should be added that although most reading retarded children show some form of developmental impairment, some show none at all—at least as detected by currently available methods of assessment. It is important also to recognise that most of these developmental disabilities lessen or disappear as the children grow older so that they are less likely to be detectable in the secondary school child with reading retardation even though he may have shown them when at primary school.

At least in some children, these various developmental delays seem to be due to biological factors involving brain function, and it has been suggested that specific reading retardation may sometimes be due to a relative failure in the normal growth and maturation of certain specific functions of the cerebral cortex (Satz & Sparrow 1970). The chief evidence in support comes from the improvement with age, the link with developmental impairment and the possible association with delayed bone maturation (Frisk *et al* 1967; Rutter, Tizard & Whitmore 1970). Ordinarily some parts of the brain mature more rapidly than others (Marshall 1968) and it would only be an extension of this observation to postulate that *ab*normal delays might also involve certain specific brain functions. It is a plausible hypothesis but it is quite unknown whether, in fact, anything of this kind occurs.

The great majority of children with specific reading retardation show no overt neurological disorder. On the other hand, children with cerebral palsy or epilepsy do have a rate of specific reading retardation well above that in the general population (Rutter, Graham & Yule 1970). Organic brain damage is an important factor in the genesis of reading difficulties in a few individual children, but it is relevant in only a small minority of cases.

All studies have shown that reading difficulties frequently run in families. In part this undoubtedly reflects hereditary influences although it remains uncertain how far reading *skills* are inherited and how far a *condition* of reading retardation is transmitted genetically. In some cases the family history may indicate social transmission, as well as biological inheritance. For example, parents who themselves read badly may inculcate in the child a negative attitude towards reading, may be unable to instruct the children how to read, may provide inadequate verbal or other stimulation and may not establish a milieu in which books are available and libraries are visited.

That this kind of social transmission does indeed play some part is suggested by the association between specific reading retardation and large family size, and by the finding that a family history of reading difficulties is much more common in children from large families (Rutter 1969). Children with many brothers and sisters (three or four or more) tend to have both impaired verbal intelligence and poorer reading attainments. It has been suggested that verbal development is affected by the extent to which children, when learning to talk, come into contact with other preschool children whose vocabulary and elementary grammar offer little verbal stimulation, rather than with adults whose language is richer and more varied (Nisbet 1953). On the other hand it may be the clarity and meaningfulness of stimuli, rather than the complexity or amount of stimulation, which are most important. The often greater amount of conflicting cross-talk when a large family is gathered together may make it more difficult for the young child to make sense of what is being said.

As already noted, several studies have indicated that reading retarded children lack concentration (even on tasks other than reading), are restless, distractible, impulsive and quick to jump to conclusions. As these characteristics are evident in a wide range of situations and (in a few studies) have been observed at the time of starting schooling it seems likely that in many cases they are not a response to reading failure but rather a contributory cause of the reading difficulties.

The importance of wider social influences and of school factors has been clearly shown in the Isle of Wight–Inner London comparative study (Berger *et al* 1975; Rutter *et al* 1976b) which showed that specific reading retardation was twice as common in Inner London. Moreover, the rate of reading difficulties varied considerably from school to school in London, specific retardation being commoner in schools with high rates of teacher turnover, pupil turnover, or a high proportion of children eligible for free school meals. Curiously, large class size is, if anything, associated with better reading attainments. Specific teaching skills are also likely to be important. A pilot study on the Isle of Wight suggested that the in-service training of junior-school teachers may increase children's progress in reading (Rutter, Tizard & Whitmore 1970), the effect on specific reading retardation as such was not examined. On the whole, the precise method of teaching reading is not very important, but an emphasis on phonic methods at the start seems to lead to fewer serious reading problems (Chall 1967).

In summary (Rutter & Yule 1973), it appears that specific reading retardation commonly arises on the basis of a developmental impairment (often involving speech, language or sequencing functions) which may be due to genetic factors, a relative failure in cerebral maturation, brain damage, a lack of suitable environmental stimulation or to a combination of these factors. The developmental impairment is often associated with adverse temperamental features, and these factors interact with family features, social circumstances, and school influences to give rise to reading difficulties. The pattern of factors and their mode of interaction varies from child to child and requires individual assessment.

In the Isle of Wight studies (Rutter *et al* 1976b), retarded readers of average intelligence were unlikely to be reading newspapers or books at age 15 years, most were even further behind in their reading than they had been at age 10 years and most expected to leave school at the earliest opportunity to take a job without further training. Little is known about prognosis into adult life (Herjanic & Penick 1972).

ASSOCIATION BETWEEN READING DIFFICULTIES AND PSYCHIATRIC DISORDER

It has long been known that psychiatric disorder and delinquency are both frequently accompanied by severe reading difficulties (Rutter & Yule 1973). Also, as noted in the introduction to this chapter, the association noted in clinic or Court attender samples has been amply confirmed in numerous epidemiological studies of the general population. For example, in the Isle of Wight studies (Rutter, Tizard & Whitmore 1970) a quarter of the children with specific reading retardation showed antisocial behaviour—a rate several times that in the population at large. Conversely, a third of the children with a disorder of conduct were reading-retarded compared with only 4 per cent in the general population. The association is not just with delinquency; reading retardation was as common among antisocial and aggressive children who were *not* overtly delinquent as any of those who had appeared in Court.

On the other hand, it is noteworthy that epidemiological studies (Clark 1970; Rutter, Tizard & Whitmore 1970) have found that, although there is some association between reading difficulties and emotional disturbance, much the stronger association is with disorders of conduct.

Obviously the key question concerns the nature of the association. Does reading failure lead to antisocial problems?; do conduct disorders predispose to reading difficulties?; are both due to some common third set of factors; or is the association an artefact of overlap between different forms of causal influences? No firm answer is yet available but there is some relevant evidence. Various methods have been used to tackle the problem (Rutter & Yule 1973) but the most fruitful approach has been to determine whether children with *both* specific reading retardation *and* antisocial disorder have more in common with purely antisocial children or with purely reading retarded children. This technique was used in the Isle of Wight studies by Rutter, Tizard and Whitmore (1970) and in London by Sturge (1972) and Varlaam (1974). Both Rutter *et al* (1970) and Varlaam (1974) found that antisocial retarded readers were most closely similar to 'pure' retarded readers and rather *un*like 'pure' antisocial children. Thus, in the Isle of Wight enquiry antisocial disorder in retarded readers was *not* associated with broken homes but was associated with large family size, a family history of reading difficulties, speech delay, poor right–left differentiation and very poor concentration. Similarly in London, children with *both* reading and behaviour difficulties tended to come from a large sibship, from an unstimulating environment or from a West Indian family. Those were the characteristics associated with reading difficulties and *not* those associated with behavioural difficulties (unless these coexisted with reading problems). The findings suggested that in some cases antisocial disorder arose as a result of educational failure. Because reading is such an essential skill at school, reading failure may be a potent source of discouragement, loss of self-esteem and antagonism which may contribute to the development of delinquent activity. With status and satisfaction denied him through schoolwork, the reading retarded child may rebel and seek satisfaction in activities running counter to everything for which the school stands. If this suggestion proves to be correct, correct teaching at the appropriate time might help to prevent the development of some forms of conduct disorder.

Sturge's findings (1972) were partially in keeping with those of Rutter *et al* (1970) and Varlaam (1974). However, her analysis was complicated by the fact that there was a less clear demarcation between the factors leading to reading retardation and those leading to antisocial behaviour. This fact suggested that the association between reading difficulties and conduct disturbance might be due in part to an underlying association between background factors—a reflection of the truism that a depriving environment tends to be depriving in many respects.

It is also likely that there are features in the child which predispose to both forms of handicap (i.e. reading retardation and antisocial disorder). For example, the temperamental features leading to behavioural difficulties (see Chapter 1) probably overlap with those which predispose to difficulties in learning to read. Speech delay probably increases the risk for psychiatric disorder (Rutter & Martin 1972) and it is known to be strongly associated with the development of reading retardation (see above). Furthermore, it is known that organic brain dysfunction predisposes to both reading retardation and psychiatric disorder (Rutter, Graham & Yule 1970), and insofar as brain damage is a factor in the causation of some cases of specific reading retardation this, too, would lead to an association with antisocial disorder.

No evidence suggests that conduct disorders lead to specific reading retardation, although obviously delinquent activities and truancy are likely to interfere with scholastic performance in later childhood and adolescence.

TREATMENT

Much has been written about methods of teaching children with reading difficulties but an evaluation of different techniques is lacking and very little is known about the merits and demerits of each approach (see Rutter & Yule 1973). Most attention has been focussed on various types of perceptual training, on the rationale that if perceptual defects underlie reading problems then alleviation of the perceptual difficulties should improve reading. The whole basis of the approach is shaky in view of the findings on perceptual abnormalities and reading (see above) but more important is the evidence that it does not work (Hammill & Wiederholt 1973). Perceptual training generally does improve scores on tests of perception but the effects on reading are no better than more conventional direct teaching of reading itself (see Rutter & Yule 1973; also Belmont & Birch 1974). It has also often been assumed that children with different perceptual handicaps should be taught through different sensory channels, but again the results of the one study designed to test this hypothesis were negative (Bateman 1969). Data are in any case lacking on whether it is better to teach a child through his strengths or his weaknesses.

It should be said that the effects of most forms of treatment have been modest at best. Remedial help on a small group basis leads to come short-term gains but unless help is continued the improvement tends to be short lived (Carroll 1972; Cashdan & Pumfrey 1969; Cashdan *et al* 1971; Collins 1961; Curr & Gourlay 1953; Sampson 1975; Silberberg *et al* 1973). Individual teaching at the secondary school stage does only little better (Rutter,

Tizard & Whitmore 1970) but perhaps this is rather late in the day. On the other hand Belmont and Birch (1974) have argued that age 7 years is too early to provide remedial help. Again evidence is lacking on whether it is better to concentrate on giving specialised teaching early before the child becomes too discouraged by repeated failure, or rather whether it is preferable to leave remedial teaching until later when the developmental impairments associated with reading are likely to be less—an important question but one which lacks an answer.

A further issue concerns the value of counselling and psychotherapy in the treatment of children with reading difficulties. Once more the evidence is scanty and the findings contradictory (e.g. Elliott & Pumfrey 1972; Gates & Bond 1936; Margolin *et al* 1955; Schiffman 1962; Lawrence 1971; Barcai *et al* 1973; McCollum & Anderson 1974). There is no reason to suppose that, except rarely, specific reading retardation is basically due to a neurotic problem. On the other hand, the factors that lead to the perpetuation of a disorder are not necessarily the same as those which *caused* it in the first instance. However their difficulties arose, children with severe reading failure are usually discouraged, demoralised, lacking in confidence and generally unhappy about their situation. If counselling can help with these problems it may well benefit reading.

Structured teaching techniques have also been used with poor readers. Programmed learning (Winsberg 1969) and operant techniques (Staats 1970) have been shown to be successful in the short-term with both individual children and small groups. However, as with other techniques, the value and limitations over longer periods have yet to be adequately assessed.

Even so, there is a growing awareness of the need to motivate children who have experienced years of frustrating failure with reading. This is where the direct motivating effects of operant approaches come into their own. The provision of appropriate reinforcement given immediately and contingently has been shown to accelerate the learning of reading skills (Bushell *et al* 1968; Clark & Walberg 1968; Lahey & Drabman 1974). Feedback of results (Smith *et al* 1969), the use of rewards, and allowing children to plan their own programme of contingencies (Lovitt & Curtis 1969) can all increase motivation. The use of these techniques together with systematic phonic teaching shows promise in helping poor readers (Cohen 1973; Hayes 1975).

In the absence of good empirical evidence on how best to treat specific reading retardation, there has to be reliance on general principles. An approach on the following lines is suggested (Rutter 1975). The children show varying patterns of disability and varying effects of environmental influences. In planning treatment it is obviously important to ameliorate adverse influences in the home or school. It is also necessary to adapt teaching methods to the child's particular disabilities. Probably it is desirable to utilise the child's assets in the first instance in order to put a premium on success and so gain the child's confidence. However, it will usually be necessary to provide special teaching to cope with his particular deficits and difficulties. Some kind of individualised approach in which the child is seen on his own or in a very small group will generally be required. There is no one best teaching method but the most effective techniques seem to show certain common features. First, the teacher much gain the child's interest and give him confidence in his ability to succeed. As well as personal teaching qualities, a variety of 'gimmicks' may help in this connection. Second, the teacher must accurately appreciate just what the child knows and does not know. Third, the teaching programme should be broken down into a series of very small steps, both to make learning easier and to make it immediately apparent to the child that he is progressing. Fourth, the structuring of the programme should be such that it ensures early success. Reading retarded children will have had many years of failure and discouragement and it is of the first importance that they learn that they can succeed. Fifth, both the teacher and pupil must have accurate feedback to ensure that they can recognise achievements and also identify areas of difficulty. Sixth, there must be systematic rewards for progress and accomplishments. These may consist of the child seeing his gains on a chart with stars or other markers for reaching various levels, of praise and encouragement specifically given by parents and teachers for each piece of successful work, or sometimes of material rewards. However this is organised, it is essential to change the usual emphasis on failure to emphasis on success.

Skilled remedial teaching will almost always be necessary. Unfortunately the existing facilities for this are woefully inadequate and many children who need help fail to receive it (Sampson 1975). However, particularly with some of the older children with reading retardation, the main problem may have come to be the lack of confidence, the sense of failure and the misery consequent upon years of being faced with their own lack of accomplishments. In these cases, counselling or psychotherapeutic techniques may come to be the most important elements in treatment. Usually this will need to be accompanied by specialised teaching but sometimes the youngster may have learned more than he realised and, once his confidence and self-esteem have been restored, he may come to use the skills he was not aware of and so progress on his own.

REFERENCES

ALEXANDER D. & MONEY J. (1965) Reading ability, object constancy, and Turner's syndrome. *Percept. Mot. Skills* **20**, 981–984

ANTHONY E.J. (1961) Learning difficulties in childhood. *J. Amer. Psychoanal. Assoc.* **9**, 124–134

APPLEBEE A.N. (1971) Research in reading retardation: two critical problems. *J. Child. Psychol. Psychiat.* **12**, 91–113

BAKKER D.J. (1967) Temporal order, meaningfulness, and reading ability. *Percept. Mot. Skills* **24**, 1027–2030

BAKKER D.J. (1972) *Temporal Order in Disturbed Reading.* Rotterdam: University Press

BARCAI A., UMBARGER C., PIERCE T.W. & CHAMBERLAIN P. (1973) A comparison of three group approaches to under-achieving children. *Amer. J. Orthopsychiat.* **43**, 133–141

BARKER D.J.P. & EDWARDS J.H. (1967) Obstetric complications and school performance. *Brit. Med. J.* **3**, 695–699

BATEMAN B. (1969) Reading, a controversial view: research and rationale. *In* Tarnopol L. (ed.) *Learning disabilities: Introduction to educational and medical management.* Springfield, Illinois: Charles C Thomas

BAX M. & WHITMORE K. (1973) Neurodevelopmental screening in the school-entrant medical examination. *Lancet* **ii**, 368–370

BELMONT L. & BIRCH H.G. (1965) Lateral dominance, lateral awareness and reading disability. *Child Dev.* **36**, 57–71

BELMONT L. & BIRCH H.G. (1974) The effect of supplemental intervention on children with low reading-readiness scores. *J. Spec. Educ.* **8**, 81–89

BERGER M., YULE W. & RUTTER M. (1975) Attainment and adjustment in two geographical areas. II: the prevalence of specific reading retardation. *Brit. J. Psychiat.* **126**, 510–519

BIRCH H.G. & BELMONT L. (1964) Auditory-visual integration in normal and retarded readers. *Amer. J. Orthopsychiat.* **34**, 852–861

BIRCH H.G. & BELMONT L. (1965) Auditory-visual integration, intelligence and reading ability in school children. *Percept. Mot. Skills* **20**, 295–305

BIRCH H.G. & GUSSOW J.D. (1970) *Disadvantaged Children: Health, Nutrition and School Failure.* New York: Harcourt Brace Jovanovitch

BLANK M. & BRIDGER W.H. (1966) Deficiencies in verbal labeling in retarded readers. *Amer. J. Orthopsychiat.* **36**, 840–847

BLANK M., WEIDER S. & BRIDGER W.H. (1968) Verbal deficiencies in abstract thinking in early reading retardation. *Amer. J. Orthopsychiat.* **38**, 823–834

BODER E. (1971) Developmental dyslexia: prevailing diagnostic concepts and a new diagnostic approach. *In* Myklebust H.R. (ed.) *Progress in Learning Disabilities*, vol. II. New York: Grune & Stratton

BRYANT P.E. (1975) Cross-model development and reading. *In* Duane D.D. & Rawson M.B. (eds.) *Reading, Perception and Language.* Baltimore. York Press

BRYDEN M.P. (1972) Auditory-visual and sequential-spatial matching in relation to reading ability. *Child Dev.* **43**, 824–832

BUSHELL D., WROBEL P.A. & MICHAELIS M.L. (1968) Applying 'group' contingencies to classroom study behaviour of preschool children. *J. Appl. Behav. Anal.* **1**, 55–61

BUTLER S. (1971) Predicting reading failure in the infant school. PhD Thesis, University of London

CARROLL H.C.M. (1972) The remedial teaching of reading: an evaluation. *Remed. Educ.* **7,** 10–15

CASHDAN A. (1970) Backward readers—research on auditory-visual integration. *In* Gardner N.K. (ed.) *Reading Skills: Theory and Practice.* London: Ward Lock Educational

CASHDAN A. & PUMFREY P.D. (1969) Some effects of the remedial teaching of reading. *Educ. Res.* **11,** 138–142

CASHDAN A., PUMFREY P.D. & LUNZER E.A. (1971) Children receiving remedial teaching of reading. *Educ. Res.* **13,** 98–105

CHALL J.S. (1967) *Learning to Read: The Great Debate.* New York: McGraw-Hill

CLARK C.A. & WALBERG·H.J. (1968) The influence of massive rewards on reading achievement in potential urban school dropouts. *Amer. Educ. Res. J.* **5,** 305–310

CLARK M.M. (1959) *Teaching Left-Handed Children.* London: University of London Press

CLARK M.M. (1970) *Reading Difficulties in School.* Harmondsworth: Penguin

COHN R. (1961) Dyscalculia. *Arch. Neurol.* **4,** 301–307

COHEN R. (1973) A preliminary investigation into a method of remedial reading teaching involving a token reinforcement system. MPhil Thesis, University of London

COLLINS J.E. (1961) *The Effects of Remedial Education.* Edinburgh: Oliver & Boyd

CRITCHLEY M. (1970) *The Dyslexic Child.* Springfield, Illinois: Charles C Thomas

CURR W. & GOURLAY N. (1953) An experimental evaluation of remedial education. *Brit. J. Psychol.* **23,** 45–55

DAVIE R., BUTLER N. & GOLDSTEIN H. (1972) *From Birth to Seven: a Report of the National Child Development Study.* London: Longman

DAVIS R.S. & CASHDAN A. (1963) Specific dyslexia. *Brit. J. Educ. Psychol.* **33,** 80–82

DE HIRSCH K., JANSKY J.J. & LANGFORD W.S. (1966) *Predicting Reading Failure.* New York: Harper

DOEHRING D.G. (1968) *Patterns of Impairment in Specific Reading Disability: A Neuropsychological Investigation.* Bloomington: Indiana University Press

DOUGLAS J.W.B. (1964) *The Home and the School.* London: MacGibbon & Kee

DOUGLAS J.W.B., ROSS J.M. & COOPER J.E. (1967) The relationship between handedness, attainment and adjustment in a national sample of school children. *Educ. Res.* **9,** 223–233

DOUGLAS J.W.B., ROSS J.M. & SIMPSON H.R. (1968) *All Our Future.* London: Peter Davies

EGELAND B. (1974) Training impulsive children in the use of more efficient scanning techniques. *Child Dev.* **45,** 165–171

ELLIOTT C.D. & PUMFREY P.D. (1972) The effects of non-directive play therapy on some maladjusted boys. *Educ. Res.* **14,** 157–161

FESHBACH S., ADELMAN H. & FULLER W.W. (1973) Early identification of children with high risk of reading failure. Paper presented at the American Educational Research Association Meeting, February, 1973, New Orleans

FRISK M., HOLMSTROM G. & WASZ-HOCKERT O. (1967) Writing difficulties and the problem of dyslexia among secondary school students. *Sosiaalilaaketieteelinen Aikakauslehti,* **1,** 333–343

GATES A.I. & BOND G.L. (1936) Failure in reading and social maladjustment. *Nat. Educ. Assn. J.* **25**, 205–206

GIBSON E.J. (1965) Learning to read. *Science* **148**, 1066–1072

GUBBAY S.S., ELLIS E., WALTON J.N. & COURT S.D.M. (1965) Clumsy children. A study of apraxic and agnosic defects in 21 children. *Brain* **88**, 295–312

HAMMILL D.D. & WIEDERHOLT J.L. (1973) Review of the Frostig Visual Perception Test and the related training program. *In* Mann L. & Sabatino D. (eds.) *The First Review of Special Education.* Philadelphia: Buttonwood Farms

HAYES C.J.A. (1975) Two types of reading failure: the role of temporal order perception and operant remediation. PhD Thesis, University of London

HEIMAN J.R. & ROSS A.O. (1974) Saccadic eye movements and reading difficulties. *J. Abnorm. Child Psychol.* **2**, 53–62

HELVESTON E.M., BILLIPS W.C. & WEBER J.C. (1970) Controlling eye-dominant hemisphere relationship as a factor in reading ability. *Amer. J. Ophthalmol.* **70**, 96–100

HERJANIC B. & PENICK E.C. (1972) Adult outcome of disabled child readers. *J. Spec. Educ.* **6**, 397–410

HOCHBERG J. (1970) Attention and perception in reading. *In* Young F.A. & Lindsley D.B. (eds.) *Early Experience and Visual Information Processing in Perceptual and Reading Disorders.* Washington, DC: National Academy of Sciences

INGRAM T.T.S. (1970) The nature of dyslexia. *In* Young F.A. & Lindsley D.B. (eds.) *Early Experience and Visual Information Processing in Perceptual and Reading Disorders.* Washington, DC: National Academy of Sciences

INGRAM T.T.S., MASON A.W. & BLACKBURN I. (1970) A retrospective study of 82 children with reading disability. *Develop. Med. Child Neurol.* **12**, 271–281

JARVIS V. (1958) Clinical observations on the visual problem in reading disability. *Psychoanal. Study Child* **13**, 451–470

KAGAN J. (1965) Reflection-impulsivity and reading ability in primary grade children. *Child Dev.* **36**, 609–628

KAHN D. & BIRCH H.G. (1968) Development of auditory-visual integration and reading achievement. *Percept. Mot. Skills* **27**, 459–468

LAHEY B.B. & DRABMAN R.S. (1974) Facilitation of the acquisition and retention of sight-word vocabulary through token reinforcement. *J. Appl. Behav. Anal.* **7**, 307–312

LAWRENCE D. (1971) The effects of counselling on retarded readers. *Educ. Res.* **13**, 119–124

LOVITT T.C. & CURTISS K.A. (1969) Academic response rate as a function of teacher- and self-imposed contingencies. *J. Appl. Behav. Anal.* **2**, 49–53

MALIPHANT R., SUPRAMANIAM S. & SARAGA E. (1974) Acquiring skill in reading: a review of experimental research. *J. Child Psychol. Psychiat.* **15**, 175–185

MALMQUIST E. (1958) *Factors Related to Reading Disabilities in the First Grade of Elementary School.* Stockholm: Almquist

MARGOLIN J.B., ROMAN M. & HARARI C. (1955) Reading disability in the delinquent child: a microcosm of psychosocial pathology. *Amer. J. Orthopsychiat.* **25**, 25–35

MARSHALL W.A. (1968) *Development of the Brain.* Edinburgh: Oliver & Boyd

MASON A.W. (1967) Specific (developmental) dyslexia. *Develop. Med. Child Neurol.* **9**, 183–190

MAXWELL A.E. (1972) The W.P.P.S.I.: a marked discrepancy in the correlations of the subtests for good and poor readers. *Brit. J. Math. Stat. Psychol.* **25**, 283–291

MAXWELL A.E., FENWICK P.B.C., FENTON G.W. & DOLLIMORE J. (1974) Reading ability and brain function: a simple statistical model. *Psychol. Med.* **4**, 274–280

McCOLLUM P.S. & ANDERSON R.P. (1974) Group counselling with reading disabled children. *J. Counsel. Psychol.* **21**, 150–155

MILES T.R. (1974) *The Dyslexic Child.* London: Priory Press

MILLER D.R. & WESTMAN J.C. (1964) Reading disability as a condition of family stability. *Family Process* **3**, 66–76

MONEY J. (1973) Turner's syndrome and parietal lobe functions. *Cortex* **9**, 387–393

MORRIS J.M. (1966) *Standards and Progress in Reading.* Slough: NFER

NAIDOO S. (1972) *Specific Dyslexia.* London: Pitman

NEALE M.D. (1958) *Analysis of Reading Ability Manual.* London: Macmillan

NISBET J.D. (1953) Family environment and intelligence. *Eugenics Rev.* **45**, 31–40

OFFORD D.R. & CROSS L.A. (1969) Behavioral antecedents of adult schizophrenia: a review. *Arch. Gen. Psychiat.* **21**, 267–283

PEARSON G.H.J. (1952) A survey of learning difficulties in children. *Psychoanal. Study Child.* **7**, 322–386

REID J.F. (1969) Dyslexia: a problem in communication. *Educ. Res.* **10**, 126–133

ROBINSON M.W. & SCHWARTZ L.B. (1973) Visuo-motor skills and reading ability: a longitudinal study. *Develop. Med. Child Neurol.* **15**, 281–286

RUTTER M. (1969) The concept of 'dyslexia'. *In* Wolff P. & MacKeith R.C. (eds.) *Planning for Better Learning. Clinics in Develop. Med.* no. **33**, London: SIMP/Heinemann

RUTTER M. (1974) Emotional disorder and educational under-achievement. *Arch. Dis. Child.* **49**, 249–256

RUTTER M. (1975) *Helping Troubled Children.* Harmondsworth: Penguin

RUTTER M. & MADGE N. (1976) *Cycles of Disadvantage: a Review of Research.* London: Heinemann Educational (in press)

RUTTER M. & MARTIN J.A.M. (eds.) (1972) *The Child with Delayed Speech. Clinics in Develop. Med.* no. 43. London: SIMP/Heinemann

RUTTER M. & YULE W. (1973) Specific reading retardation. *In* Mann L. & Sabatino D. (eds.) *The First Review of Special Education.* Philadelphia: Buttonwood Farms

RUTTER M. & YULE W. (1975) The concept of specific reading retardation. *J. Child Psychol. Psychiat.* **16**, 181–197

RUTTER M. GRAHAM P. & YULE W. (1970) *Neuropsychiatric Study in Childhood. Clinics in Develop. Med.* nos. 35/36. London: SIMP/Heinemann

RUTTER M., TIZARD J. & WHITMORE K. (eds.) (1970) *Education, Health and Behaviour.* London: Longman

RUTTER M., GRAHAM P., CHADWICK O. & YULE W. (1976a) Adolescent turmoil—fact or fiction? *J. Child Psychol. Psychiat.* **17**, 35–56

RUTTER M., TIZARD J., YULE W., GRAHAM P. & WHITMORE K. (1976b) Research Report Isle of Wight Studies (1964–1974). *Psychol. Med.* **6**, 313–332

SAMPSON O.C. (1975) *Remedial Education.* London: Routledge & Kegan Paul

SATZ P. & SPARROW S. (1970) Specific developmental dyslexia: a theoretical reformulation. *In* Bakker D.J. & Satz P. (eds.) *Specific Reading Disability: Advances in Theory and Method.* Rotterdam: University of Rotterdam Press

SATZ P., RARDIN D. & ROSS J. (1971) An evaluation of a theory of specific developmental dyslexia. *Child Dev.* **42**, 2009–2021

SCHIFFMAN G. (1962) Dyslexia as an educational phenomenon: its recognition and treatment. *In* Money J. (ed.) *Reading Disability: Progress and Research Needs in Dyslexia.* Baltimore: Johns Hopkins Press

SEIDEL U.P., CHADWICK O. & RUTTER M. (1975) Psychological disorders in crippled children: a comparative study of children with and without brain damage. *Develop. Med. Child Neurol.* **17,** 563–573

SILBERBERG N.E., IVERSEN I.A. & GOINS J.T. (1973) Which remedial reading method works best? *J. Learn. Dis.* **6,** 547–556

SILBERBERG N.E., IVERSEN I.A. & SILBERBERG M.C. (1969) A model for classifying children according to reading level. *J. Learn. Dis.* **2,** 634–643

SILVERMAN J.S., FITE M.W. & MOSHER M.M. (1959) Learning problems. Clinical findings in reading disability children—special cases of intellectual inhibition. *Amer. J. Orthopsychiat.* **29,** 298–314

SLADE P.D. & RUSSELL G.F.M. (1971) Developmental dyscalculia: a brief report on four cases. *Psychol. Med.* **1,** 292–298

SMITH D.E., BRETHOWER D. & CABOT R. (1969) Increasing task behavior in a language arts program by providing reinforcement. *J. Exper. Child Psychol.* **8,** 45–62

SPERRY B., STAVER N., REINER B.S. & ULRICH D. (1958) Renunciation and denial in learning difficulties. *Amer. J. Orthopsychiat.* **28,** 98–111

STAATS A.W. (1970) *Learning, Language and Cognition.* London: Holt Rinehart

STURGE C. (1972) Reading Retardation and Antisocial Behaviour. MPhil Thesis, University of London

THORNDIKE R.L. (1963) *The Concepts of Over- and Under-Achievement.* New York: Bureau of Publications, Teachers College, Columbia University

VARLAAM A. (1974) Educational attainment and behaviour at school. *Greater London Council Intelligence Quart.* no. **29,** 29–37

VERNON M.D. (1971) *Reading and its Difficulties.* London: Cambridge University Press

WALTERS R.H., VAN LOAN M. & CROFTS I. (1961) A study of reading disability. *J. Consult. Psychol.* **25,** 277–283

WEINBERG W.A., DIETZ S.G., PENICK E.C. & MCALISTER W.H. (1974) Intelligence, reading achievement, physical size and social class. *J. Paediatrics* **85,** 482–489

WINSBERG B.G. (1969) Programmed learning, teaching machines and dyslexia. *Amer. J. Orthopsychiat.* **39,** 418–427

WILLOWS D.M. (1974) Reading between the lines: selective attention in good and poor readers. *Child Dev.* **45,** 408–415

YULE W. (1967) Predicting reading ages on Neale's analysis of reading ability. *Brit. J. Educ. Psychol.* **37,** 252–255

YULE W. (1973) Differential prognosis of reading backwardness and specific reading retardation. *Brit. J. Educ. Psychol.* **43,** 244–248

YULE W., RUTTER M., BERGER M. & THOMPSON J. (1974) Over- and under-achievement in reading: distribution in the general population. *Brit. J. Educ. Psychol.* **44,** 1–12

CHAPTER 24

Enuresis

D. SHAFFER

Nocturnal enuresis—usually defined as the involuntary passage of urine during sleep in the absence of any identifiable physical abnormality—is often classified as a psychogenic disorder. The evidence supporting this notion is, at best, debatable and will be dealt with later. But, regardless of aetiology, enuretic children are frequently referred to psychiatrists for treatment. The rate of psychiatric disturbance is higher in enuretics than in nonenuretics and when an enuretic child is treated successfully, behaviour, mood and social adjustment may change for the better. It is, therefore, quite proper that child psychiatrists should acquire a knowledge of the prevalence and natural history of the condition and its association with other pathological states, as well as a mastery of the techniques of treatment.

PREVALENCE AND NATURAL HISTORY

The prevalence of bedwetting has been studied in many populations and widely varying rates have been noted, not only between different countries but also between different communities in the same country (de Jonge 1973). However, a close examination of these studies suggests that these differences are as likely to reflect sampling bias, varying techniques for obtaining information and the adoption of different frequency criteria as genuine community distinctions.

Table 24.1 details prevalence data obtained by Rutter *et al* (1973) during studies carried out on representative samples of children living on the Isle of Wight. It can be seen from this table that prevalence—especially in younger children—varies considerably with the frequency of wetting. Whereas 15 per cent of 7-year-old boys are wet less often than once a week, only 7 per cent wet more frequently than this. This is clinically important because cases referred for treatment are more likely to come from the latter group.

There is an increase in the prevalence of enuresis between the ages of 5 and 7 because of the addition of *secondary* or *'onset'* enuretics to the bedwetting population. Longitudinal studies (Oppel *et al* 1968; Miller *et al* 1960; Miller 1973) have shown that relapse after a period of dryness is most likely to occur at the age of 5 or 6, that it is uncommon after the age of 11 and occurs more often in boys. In their longitudinal study of 859 children born in Baltimore, Oppel *et al* (1968) found that as many as 25 per cent of children who achieve continence for at least 6 months will start to wet again and both Miller *et al* (1960) and Oppel *et al* (1968) have found that more than half of 7 to 12-year-old enuretics have previously had at least 6 months of continence. The findings from longitudinal studies of this sort contrast markedly with clinic based or cross-sectional population studies which tend to report a much lower rate of secondary enuresis. These differences may be due to the parents' defective recall of relatively short periods of earlier dryness.

Table 24.1   Prevalence of enuresis by age, sex and frequency of wetting

Age (years)	Total population	% wet less often than 1/week		% wet at least 1/week		Sex ratio
		Boys	*Girls*	*Boys*	*Girls*	
5	395	(B 13·4%	G 13·9%)			1·00
7	359	15·2%	12·2%	6·7%	3·3%	1·41
9/10	1814	6·1%	3·5%	2·9%	2·2%	1·61
14	1913	1·9%	1·2%	1·1%	0·5%	1·77

Rutter *et al* (1973) *Enuresis and Behavioural Deviance: Some Epidemiological Considerations*, Chapter 17. *In* Kolvin I., MacKeith R. and Meadow S.R. (eds), *Bladder Control and Enuresis*, Clinics in Dev. Med. nos. 48/49. London: Heinemann.

Girls are quicker to acquire urinary continence at night than boys. In the Baltimore study 45 per cent of 2 to 3-year-old girls but only 32 per cent of boys were dry at night. The differences then become less marked and between the age of 4 and 6 wetting is as common in girls as it is in boys. After the age of 7 the ratio of boy to girl wetters increases until by the mid-teens boys are twice as likely to be wet as girls (Rutter *et al* 1973; Oppel *et al* 1968; Douglas 1973; Miller 1973). This greater number of boys is a consequence both of their increased susceptibility to relapse after earlier dryness and to their slower rate of spontaneous cure.

Drawing from data obtained in their Newcastle study, Miller and his colleagues (1960) suggest that final continence in children who have remained enuretic into middle childhood is preceded by a period when wetting takes place less and less often, finally occurring only when the child is unwell or during cold weather, and that wetting very rarely stops suddenly.

The untreated prognosis for various categories of bedwetters can be estimated from Miller's (1960) study. Of 5-year-old children who were only wetting intermittently 74 per cent had become dry by the age of 9 compared to 56 per cent of the children who were wetting every night. The prognosis was worse for secondary enuretics, only 46 per cent becoming dry during the same period, but was good for children who wet both by day and night, 87 per cent of these having become dry by the age of 9.

Finally, the prognosis for older girl enuretics was better than for boys. Of girls wet at age 11 60 per cent had become dry by 13, compared to only 36 per cent of boys. Sex differences were not significant at an earlier age and were less marked in older teenagers.

AETIOLOGY

It is very seldom that the cause of bedwetting can be identified in any individual child. A small number of children with an associated urinary infection will cease to wet the bed when treated with an appropriate antibiotic and a small number of disturbed children will stop wetting after some change that betters their circumstances. But even in these cases the mechanisms which link the apparent cause to night time wetting remain obscure.

A number of associations have been noted and these have led to theories implicating such factors as genitourinary abnormality or malfunction, deep sleep, coercive or early toilet training, the experience of stressful life events during a critical phase of development and adverse psychosocial or psychological states. The evidence with respect to these theories is reviewed. However, this has been an unsatisfactory area of research endeavour because of distorted samples and uncontrolled observations.

Genetic factors

Enuresis commonly runs in families. Approximately 70 per cent of all enuretics have a first degree relative who is, or has been, afflicted with the same condition (Bakwin 1961). Twin studies (Hallgren 1960; Bakwin 1973) show that concordance for enuresis is signficantly greater in uniovular than in binovular twins. Bakwin (1961) reported on 338 same-sexed twins and found a concordance rate of 68 per cent in monozygotic as opposed to 36 per cent in dizygotic pairs. There have been no studies on twins reared separately although Kaffman (1962) has investigated children reared apart from their parents on a kibbutz. He found a significantly greater prevalence of wetting histories amongst the relatives of enuretic children than amongst nonenuretic controls.

Wetting is more common in negroes than in whites (Oppel *et al* 1968;

Dodge *et al* 1970) and in oriental immigrants to Israel than in immigrants of European descent (Thaustein & Halevi 1962). But these differences may reflect social disadvantage rather than genetic difference.

Enuresis as a disorder of the genito-urinary tract

A number of findings suggest that enuresis may be related to abnormalities in the anatomy or function of the urinary bladder. These include a significant association between enuresis and urinary tract infection, the consistent finding that enuretics pass smaller volumes of urine during micturition than nonenuretics, studies suggesting that the anatomical development of the pelvic floor is delayed in children who wet the bed and that their bladders are more 'irritable' and the fact that wetting can be suppressed, seemingly through the peripheral effects of the tricyclic antidepressants.

Association with urinary infection

Savage *et al* (1969) screened all 5-year-old girls entering school for the first time in the city of Dundee. Approximately 1 per cent of these girls had undiagnosed urinary infections. Amongst the infected girls 55 per cent wet the bed at least once a week and a further 30 per cent were wet less often. The prevalence of enuresis in this group of girls with urinary infections was, therefore, 5 times greater than what would be anticipated in an unselected population. These findings have since been replicated in other epidemiological surveys (Meadow *et al* 1969; Dodge *et al* 1970) and in a review of a clinic population (Jones *et al* 1972). Similarly Shaffer *et al* (1968) using careful screening methods found that 5 per cent of a population of enuretics seen at a school treatment clinic had urinary infections which is 5 times the rate in the general population (Kunin *et al* 1962). Girl enuretics are more likely to have an associated infection. Dodge *et al* (1970) found a linear relationship between the frequency of enuresis and the prevalence of infection, 1 in 10 of girls who were wet every night having an infected urine. Jones *et al* (1972) reported that 25 per cent of a group of enuretic girls with associated pyelonephritis stopped wetting after their infection had been treated. However, this was an uncontrolled report and the response rate may be no different to that of any other nonspecific intervention.

The association between wetting and infection is important clinically. Enuretic girls are a high risk group in whom a full bacteriological examination is mandatory. The reason for the association is unclear. On the other hand, bedwetting may result from genitourinary abnormalities of the sort which lead to or result from urinary infection. Alternatively, bedwetting may facilitate ascending per urethral invasion of the bladder by potentially pathogenic organisms and thus itself lead to urinary tract infection. This might explain why even with antibiotic treatment bacteriuria is more likely to persist in girls who continue to wet than in girls who are dry at night (Dodge *et al* 1970).

Urinary tract obstruction

A recent editorial in a leading journal of urology (Mahony & Laferte 1973) put forward the view that enuresis is usually due to subclinical bladder neck or urethral obstruction. Mahony (1971) reported that 96 per cent of boy enuretics and 97 per cent of girl enuretics referred to his clinic had an obstructive lesion, most commonly anterior urethral valves or meatal stenosis alone or in combination with bladder neck obstruction. It is of interest that despite an allegedly significant obstruction fewer than 1 per cent of the boys in Mahony's series had evidence of urinary infection. Mahony postulated that the bladder neck is 'weakened' by the distal obstruction which also results in hypertrophy and irritability of the detrusor muscle and that these factors, coupled with deep sleep (see below) predispose the obstructed child to enuresis. Surgical intervention is advocated. According to Smith (1969), in a sharply critical review, surgery is widely undertaken in the treatment of enuresis, to relieve alleged obstruction.

However, the criteria most commonly used to diagnose outflow obstruction in the absence of gross pathology are the subject of controversy. Visualisation at cystoscopy of apparent detrusor hypertrophy is a sign with low reliability (Cendron & Lepinard 1972) and is present in only a small minority of cases in which outflow obstruction can be satisfactorily verified (Smith 1969). Avoiding pressure of more than 40 mm Hg is used as a criterion of obstruction yet norms have been obtained in only a very few children (Cooper 1968) and opening pressures greater than this have been recorded in children with no urinary pathology (Gleason & Latimer 1962; Pompeius 1971). Diagnosis of urethral obstruction by the use of calibrated bougies has been shown to have little discriminative value (Manley & French 1970) and the significance of urethral irregularities on cystourethrography has not been established by control studies. Furthermore, none of the studies which advocate the treatment of urethral dilation or bladder neck repair satisfactorily document the results of treatment.

The evidence linking marginal urinary outflow tract obstruction and enuresis is unconvincing and provides no justification for potentially hazardous surgical intervention.

Bladder size and function

Troup and Hodgson (1971) measured bladder capacities at 40 mm Hg in groups of anaesthetised enuretic children and in normal controls and could find no difference between the two under these conditions. However, they measured the number and volume of micturitions passed during a 48-hour period by the same children using special napkins to ensure measurement of urine voided during sleep. It was found that the enuretic children passed urine more often and that, on average, the maximum volume of urine passed by them was smaller than that passed by the control group or by the enuretic children when anaesthetised. Consistent with these findings is the study by Starfield (1967) who recorded the maximum volume passed during a single micturition after a fluid load by a large group of enuretics, their nonenuretic siblings and normal controls. She found that on average the maximum volume passed by the enuretics was significantly less than that passed by either control group. Both studies report considerable overlap between enuretic and nonenuretic individuals of the same age.

Pompeius (1971) has used modern cystometric techniques to investigate 63 enuretics seen in a urological clinic. The group is clearly atypical of the enuretic population as a whole in that 45 per cent had a urinary tract infection and 17 per cent had obstructive lesions, but the study is helpful in that it categorises findings according to the clinical state of the children. In the group with neither infection nor obstruction micturition occurred when the bladder contained a smaller volume than expected in 30 per cent, bladder filling was associated with a feeling of urgency in 21 per cent and an undue rise in intravesical pressure in 21 per cent of subjects. In 12 per cent the micturition contractions were of a greater magnitude than expected. The significance of these findings is difficult to interpret because the observations were uncontrolled and normative data has been derived either by extrapolation from studies on adults or else was obtained by using different techniques. However, this is a problem which is inherent in this area of research. Accurate measurement techniques require catheterisation which is unpleasant, and children cannot volunteer for such research.

From these studies it would seem that the bladders of a significant proportion of enuretic children, whilst not structurally different, do in many cases function differently, in that the urge to micturate is felt when the bladder is holding relatively small amounts of urine. The pathophysiology of this reduced 'functional bladder capacity' remains uninvestigated. Presumably it could arise either through an increased sensitivity of vesical receptors or through a defect in the inhibition process. Furthermore, it is not possible to say whether these differences are causal to bedwetting or are a consequence of it. It may be that the large volume of urine accumulated during the overnight period habituates the individual to a larger bladder capacity and that when overnight volumes are reduced because of incontinence this does not take place. It seems unlikely that a small functional bladder capacity is in itself sufficient cause for enuresis. Overlap in capacity between enuretics and nonenuretics of the same age has been noted in all studies and some enuretics with small bladder capacities have dry as well as wet nights.

This problem could be resolved by noting the effect of treatment on functional capacity. Attempts to do this (Hagglund 1965; Zaleski *et al* 1973) have been methodologically defective and do not add to our understanding of the relationship.

Developmental changes in the bladder neck

On the basis of a large number of lateral cystograms done on both enuretic and nonenuretic children, Hutch (1972) has described a series of anatomical changes which take place at the base of the bladder during the first 6 years of life. These changes are alleged to increase the efficacy of the internal sphincter. Hutch (1972) and his group have identified an arrangement of muscular fibres which surround the vesicourethral junction which they have named the 'base plate'. When the base plate is flattened in the resting position the internal sphincter functions most efficiently to prevent the leakage of urine under conditions of high intravesical pressure. In his series Hutch (1972) found that before the age of 36 months all children have a rounded base plate. Between the ages of 4 and 6 years, 74 per cent of the nonenuretics but only 31 per cent of enuretics in his series had a flattened base plate. Between the ages of 10 and 14, 97 per cent of the nonenuretics had a flattened plate, compared to only 52 per cent of the enuretics. Hutch points out that urinary continence at night is acquired in a great many children before the base plate assumes a mature position and so these developmental differences cannot be the sole cause of night-time wetting.

Circadian rhythms of urine output

Hellbregge (1960) has shown that the normal circadian rhythms of water excretion—during which urine output at night falls to only one-third of that during the day—is absent during the first year of life, infants and young children excreting urine at a constant rate. Lewis *et al* (1970) have published two detailed case reports of enuretic children with immature circadian rhythms, and hypothesised that nocturnal polyuria might have been causal in these cases. However, Vulliamy (1956) had earlier studied a small group of hospitalised boy enuretics and controls comparing their day and night urine output. He found no differences between the groups, a few children in each having nocturnal polyuria. Further studies are needed to show the frequency and clinical correlates of absent rhythms in children in more natural surroundings for it is reasonable to suppose that such an abnormality could delay night time continence in some children.

Enuresis as a disorder arising from disturbance in early life

Toilet training

A number of practices are subsumed under the heading of 'toilet training'. Training may take place at night, when it usually consists of waking the child from sleep and then placing it on a pot. It may take place during the day when the child is placed on a pot at set intervals. The process may be carried out in a warm and relaxed fashion with the child being read to or played with, praise or reward being offered for an appropriate elimination and with no negative responses being given if the child chooses not to remain on the pot or fails to perform. At the other extreme it may be a coercive process with the child being punished or being forced to remain on the pot until elimination takes place.

Most children become dry at night without being lifted (MacKeith 1973). Roberts & Schoellkopf (1951) studied a large number of 2½-year-olds in Rochester, USA, and found that less than half had ever been trained at night. These findings were confirmed in a retrospective study in Sweden by Klackenburg (1955). Not surprisingly the Rochester study showed that it was the children who were still wet at night who were most likely to be lifted. In analysing their data the authors conclude that the process of potting did not increase the likelihood of a dry night. If children can become dry at night in the absence of night-time training and remain incontinent in spite of it, the area would not seem a very fruitful one for further enquiry. Nevertheless, it is always possible that day-time training might generalise to provide the basis for night-time continence. This seems unlikely, for in the Rochester study it was shown that a high proportion of children became dry at night before they had stopped wetting themselves during the day.

Brazelton (1962) reports that he advocated the postponement of toilet training until after the age of 2 in a private paediatric practice of 1170 children. He further claimed that by the age of 5 only 1·8 per cent of these children were wetting the bed, which is, of course, far fewer than would be expected. However, this study gave only very scanty data, it implied a 100 per cent follow-up and no attempt was made to see whether the parents had adhered to the advice given. On the other hand Despert (1944) found that training was started later in enuretic children than in children who had become dry. Lovibond (1964), Klackenburg (1955), and Sears *et al* (1957) found no association between the age at which toilet training was started and subsequent bedwetting although the value of these studies is weakened by their reliance on retrospective enquiry.

Both Sears *et al* (1957) and Bostock and Shackleton (1951) found that a higher proportion of mothers of enuretic children recalled using coercive toilet training methods than controls. However, neither of these studies is entirely satisfactory: the criteria for coerciveness are vague, the data were not collected or rated in a blind fashion and were, of course, retrospective.

In summary, studies on the impact of early or coercive training techniques are difficult to conduct and it is not surprising that results are contradictory. However, on balance it seems reasonable to conclude that whereas early training is probably an unrelated factor, the consequences of coercive training are not known.

Stressful life events in early childhood

Douglas (1973) has examined the relationship between certain stressful life events and subsequent enuresis is a longitudinal study of 4500 children.

The events examined were: (1) family break-up through death or divorce; (2) temporary separation from mother for at least one month; (3) birth of a younger sibling; (4) moving home; (5) admission to hospital; (6) accident; and (7) surgical operation. A child who had experienced four or more of such events between the ages of 3 and 4 was twice as likely to be enuretic as a child who had experienced none. The impact of family break-up during the first 6 years of life was studied in greater detail. Loss of a father had no detectable effect. Loss of a mother, especially when this was followed by institutional care or care by foster parents was, however, strongly related to later bedwetting. There was no detectable association between temporary separation from mother unless the separation had resulted from the child being hospitalised. Children admitted to hospital at any time during their first 4 years of life were significantly more likely to be enuretic. The sex of the child and the age at the time of first admission within that period were not important factors, but there was a relationship to the number of admissions.

These findings can be interpreted in different ways. On the one hand it is possible that a stressful event could have a direct effect on the 'learning' of urinary continence at a critical period of development. On the other hand, studies (Heisel *et al* 1973; Schaffer & Schaffer 1968) have shown that the experience of such stressful life events as hospitalisation or going into care are not isolated phenomena but are commonly associated with ongoing disadvantage or repeated stress. The events recorded in Douglas' study may only be indirect 'markers' of a total life situation, and not be of crucial significance in themselves.

Enuresis as a disorder of sleep or CNS function

Depth of sleep

Parents of enuretic children often report that their children sleep deeply and are difficult to rouse. Graham (1973) in a critical review of this subject has pointed out that parents have less cause to wake their nonenuretic children and that their judgements are unlikely to have been made on the basis of direct objective comparison. Boyd (1960) investigated this problem in 100 hospitalised enuretic children and nonenuretic controls. In a blind design an investigator called the child by name when asleep and then shook the child by the shoulder. Enuretics took an average of only 16 seconds to respond whereas the controls took an average of 20·5 seconds, although the difference was not significant.

Ritvo et al (1969) and Evans (1971) have studied the sleep correlates of enuretic events. Wetting takes place most often during stage III or IV sleep and rarely, if ever, takes place during REM sleep. Ritvo et al (1969) found that a given subject could and would wet at all stages of sleep and that there was no consistent pattern for any individual. In neither study was there evidence that the quality of sleep was in any way abnormal. Modification of sleep patterns does not appear to affect the frequency of enuresis. For example, imipramine suppresses enuresis but also reduces the amount of REM sleep in which enuresis is least likely to occur. By contrast phenobarbitone has no antienuretic action (Wallace & Forsyth 1969) and yet is a potent inhibitor of stage IV sleep (Kales et al 1970) the phase during which bedwetting usually takes place.

EEG abnormalities and epilepsy

Petersen and Eeg-Olofsson (1970); Eeg-Olofsson et al (1971) and Eeg-Olofsson (1971) have assessed the prevalence of paroxysmal phenomena and so-called immaturities in the EEGs of a large number of 1 to 15-year-old children. In the design of their study they rigorously defined the normality of their subjects excluding all children with a history of obstetric perinatal or postnatal abnormality, any incident involving a loss of consciousness, a history of paroxysmal headache or abdominal pain, any previous head injury, any family history of epilepsy and any abnormality of intellectual or physical development. They also excluded children who had soiled themselves or wet the bed after the age of 4. In this supernormal population they found an incidence of paroxysmal phenomena at rest of 2·7 per cent, during photic stimulation of 9·1 per cent, and when drowsy of 8·7 per cent. They found an incidence of paroxysmal 14 and 16 cps activity of over 16 per cent. This study is described in some detail because it offers a baseline against which the significance of EEG abnormalities in other clinical groups can be gauged. Studies such as those by Takayusu *et al* (1963); Campbell and Young (1966) and Turton and Spear (1953) all of which report a high rate of paroxysmal phenomena in the EEGs of enuretics tell us little for there is no attempt to control for other factors which might independently influence the rate of abnormality and indeed include subjects with frank epilepsy. In a more informative study Poussaint *et al* (1967) examined a series of enuretic children excluding retarded children and those who had had fits or other identifiable organic abnormalities. They found an incidecne of EEG abnormalities approximating that found in the Scandinavian studies mentioned above. They conclude that there is no foundation to the view that enuresis is an 'epileptic equivalent'. There is furthermore no evidence that bedwetting is any more common in epileptics than in normal children. In their study on the Isle of Wight, Rutter *et al* (1970a) showed that enuresis was in fact less common amongst psychiatrically disturbed epileptic children than amongst children with a psychiatric disorder without epilepsy. The rates in psychiatrically normal children was the same in those with or without epilepsy.

Enuresis as a psychiatric or psychosocial disorder

Parents often assume that bedwetting is a sign of 'nervousness'. The medical literature, too, abounds with references to enuresis as a psychiatric condition. If this really is the case then one should be able to demonstrate an association between bedwetting and psychiatric disorder. Such an association has been convincingly demonstrated by Rutter *et al* (1973). In their survey of the child population of the Isle of Wight they were able to compare the prevalence of psychiatric disorder in enuretics and nonenuretics. Psychiatric disorder was assessed in a number of different ways and it was found that the rate of deviance was significantly greater in enuretics than in children who were dry even when the most conservative method of assessment—analysis of teacher questionnaires—was used (see Table 24.2). Disturbance was most common in girls but was no more common in older enuretics than in younger ones. However, it should be noted that only a minority of enuretics of either sex were rated as psychiatrically deviant and so these findings, whilst confirming an association, give no support to the notion that enuresis is invariably a sign of psychiatric disorder. In the Isle of Wight study the disturbed enuretic children did not show any characteristic type of psychiatric syndrome and this finding is consistent with an earlier study on a clinic population (Lickorish 1960). It had been widely held that enuresis was associated with tics, temper tantrums and nailbiting. However, neither the Isle of Wight nor the Baltimore study (Oppel *et al* 1968) found this to be so, these 'habits' occurring with the same frequency in enuretics and nonenuretics.

Table 24.2   Enuresis and behavioural deviance (teacher's scale)

	Boys			Girls		
Age (years)	*Wet* % *Deviant*	*Dry* % *Deviant*	*Deviance ratio*	*Wet* %*Deviant*	*Dry* % *Deviant*	*Deviance ratio*
5	15·4	8·7	(1·8)	17·9	3·8	(4·7)
7	15·4	17·4	(0·9)	39·3	11·3	(3·5)**
9/10	17·9	10·1	(1·8)*	14·3	5·7	(2·5)**
14	13·8	5·4	(2·6)	25·0	3·9	(6·4)**

*p < 0·05
**p < 0·01

Rutter *et al* (1973) *Enuresis and Behavioural Deviance: Some Epidemiological Considerations*, Chapter 17. *In* Kolvin I., MacKeith R. and Meadow S.R. (eds) *Bladder Control and Enuresis*, Clinics in Dev. Med. nos. 48/49. London: Heinemann.

Certain personality traits in enuretics have been studied and there is some evidence that as a group they are more retiring, less confident and more acquiescent than nonenuretics (Lovibond 1964; Stein & Susser 1965; McHale 1967). Assessment of such subtle personality and behaviour differences is more difficult and less reliable than the assessment of handicapping psychiatric disorder, but consistency, as always, adds weight to these findings.

It is often thought that children with secondary enuresis are especially likely to be psychiatrically disturbed. Whilst it is true that the onset of secondary enuresis often follows a stressful event (Werry & Cohrssen 1965) studies comparing the rate of disorder in the two groups of bedwetters have failed to find any difference in the rate of disturbance (Rutter *et al* 1973; Novick 1966). However, an interesting finding emerged from the Isle of Wight study when the rate of disturbance in different categories of 5-year-olds was compared. The 5-year-old children were re-examined 2 years later and so it was possible to identify those children who although dry at 5 had become enuretic by the age of 7. At the age of 5 these children were significantly more disturbed than other nonenuretics, thus confirming Hallgren's (1956) earlier observation that children with secondary enuresis were often thought to be 'nervous' before the onset of enuresis.

Both Hallgren (1956) and Rutter *et al* (1973) found that psychiatric disturbance was more common in children who wet during the day as well as at night. However, no association was found with the frequency of wetting.

Having established that there is an association between bedwetting and psychiatric disorder it becomes a matter of some interest to explore whether the link is causal, reactive or coincidental. Many psychiatrists hold that enuresis is a direct manifestation of an underlying emotional disturbance or conflict and some of the more common hypotheses are that: (1) wetting is an immature form of self-gratification; (2) wetting is a manifestation of anxiety, mediated by a direct autonomic effect on bladder function; and (3) the act of wetting is an expression of hostility in a child who has difficulty in showing aggression in more direct ways.

Achenbach and Lewis (1971) set out to examine generalisations such as these. In a blind fashion, they studied the edited case-notes of 3 matched groups of boys referred to a psychiatric clinic for the treatment of enuresis, encopresis and learning disorders. Drawing their hypotheses from the literature they predicted that the enuretic boy would be (a) characteristically passive; (b) more ready to 'relinquish the care of his body' than others of his age; and (c) more likely to express aggression indirectly. Scores on the first two of these predicted dimensions were actually lower in the enuretic group than in the controls and although enuretics were rated as more indirectly aggressive' the difference was not significant.

The relationship between anxiety and enuresis is complex and probably operates in different ways in different children. On the one hand there are many children who are usually dry but who can be predicted to be wet before the start of a new school term or after a row or reprimand. On the other hand there are children who become dry between the time that they know they will be receiving treatment and the time that it is prescribed. These children may admit to having felt worried about what the treatment might involve. Children who are dry when they sleep with relatives or in unfamiliar circumstances may also admit to anxiety about wetting, their dryness being bought at the expense of fitful sleep. Finally, specifically anxiolytic drugs are ineffective in controlling the condition (Blackwell & Currah 1973).

A different approach to the hypothesis that enuresis is a manifestation of disturbance is to examine whether nonsymptomatic psychiatric treatment can reduce or cure enuresis. It is commonly found that alteration of the child's psychosocial environment, e.g. admission to sick bay, increased attention, going away on holiday, may reduce the frequency of wetting in some children and this has been noted in carefully documented studies (Molling *et al* 1962;

Stein & Susser 1965). It could be that such changes improve mood or behaviour and that this, in turn, reduces wetting frequency. On the other hand, these changes are also likely to alter the contingencies of wetting, in that it is more likely to be noted or commented upon and this may be the effective mechanism. Controlled studies have shown that psychotherapy by itself is ineffective in reducing enuresis (DeLeon & Mandell 1966; Werry & Cohrssen 1965) and although the tricyclic antidepressants have a potent antienuretic effect (see below) the speed with which they act make it unlikely that this is being mediated through changes in mood or mental state. Finally, one might expect that if wetting was a direct manifestation of psychiatric disorder then purely symptomatic therapies such as the bell and pad would be less effective in disturbed than in nondisturbed enuretics and this has not been found to be the case (Behrle *et al* 1956; Young & Morgan 1973).

Depressed mood may, however, have a role in producing enuresis. Weinberg *et al* (1973) have noted that in a group of depressed enuretic children there were fluctuations in the frequency of their bedwetting in contrast to more continuous bedwetting found in disturbed nondepressed enuretic children, the first group being wet when depressed and dry when not. The data were anecdotal and retrospective but they suggest that enuresis may be affectively triggered in some children.

An alternative explanation might be that bedwetting itself—a distressing and, in some cases, stigmatising condition—results in psychiatric disorders.

There is some evidence from treatment studies to support this notion. Behrle *et al* (1956); Lovibond (1964) and Baker (1969) have all shown that enuretics successfully treated with the 'bell and pad' become more assertive, independent and happy and that they gain in self-confidence. These changes could not be attributed to a nonspecific effect of treatment intervention as they were less marked when treatment was unsuccessful. However, only Behrle's study included clinically maladjusted children. Although these children gained in self-confidence, it is not clear whether there was a more general change in their level of adjustment.

A finding from the Isle of Wight study suggests that, once established, enuresis and psychiatric disorder are in some way linked to each other. Children who were both wet and disturbed at the age of 10 were re-examined at the age of 14. Of those who had stopped wetting 59 per cent were no longer psychiatrically disturbed whereas only 29 per cent of those who had continued to wet had lost their psychiatric disturbance. Of course, these findings could be explained either by the development of continence resulting in psychiatric improvement or by psychiatric improvement resulting in continence. But they are important in suggesting some dynamic relationship between the two conditions.

The existence of such a dynamic relationship, once both conditions are established, does not preclude that both wetting and disturbance arose initially as a result of common factors operating independently through quite different mechanisms. For example, there are several factors which are common to the histories of both enuretic and disturbed children. A number of studies have shown that social disadvantage and low social class is associated with enuresis—especially in older girls (Rutter *et al* 1973; Stein *et al* 1965; Miller *et al* 1960; Miller 1973; Douglas 1973). Enuresis occurs more commonly in families where there are extremes of poverty, repeated disruptions of maternal care, a reliance on welfare support, inadequate nutrition and clothing, parental delinquency, large crowded families, etc. Umphress *et al* (1970) found that parents of bedwetters were less concerned over home-making, wage-earning, or the mental and physical health of their children. Oppel *et al* (1968) found that poor marital adjustment was significantly more common amongst the parents of girl enuretics than amongst either non-enuretics or amongst boy enuretics. Most of these factors are also known to be associated with psychiatric disorder in childhood (Rutter *et al* 1970b). It may be that families such as these experience more stressful life events at a critical and specific phase of development (see above) or that there are certain characteristic rearing practices or pattern of expectations which are conducive to the persistence of wetting, but that there are other quite separate aspects of their lives which lead to psychiatric disturbance. Or, interaction might operate in a more fundamental way. Hallgren (1957) found that the mothers of enuretic children who had themselves wet the bed as children were more likely to have had difficulties in marital adjustment than mothers who had not been enuretic as children. It is possible that in these cases the parent is not only passing on a genetic predisposition to bedwetting but also brings with her qualities which lead to an unsatisfactory home life, which, in turn, increase the likelihood of disturbance in her children. Biological factors might act in the same way. For example, Hallgren (1957) and Kolvin (1974) have found a relationship between wetting and a delay in early speech development; Miller (1973) found that enuretics were shorter than nonenuretics and Douglas (1973) has reported an association between bedwetting persisting into the mid-teens and delayed puberty. All these factors are known, in turn, to be associated with psychiatric disturbance. There have been no studies to examine whether biological or developmental abnormalities are more characteristic of disturbed than of nondisturbed enuretics but such a finding would provide yet another example of how the association between psychiatric disorder and bedwetting was, in turn, linked to some other common factor.

Although the association between bedwetting and psychiatric disturbance in a minority of enuretics is well established, its nature remains obscure. There are a number of factors which are common in the histories of both bed-wetters and disturbed children and it is possible that these factors predispose to both wetting and disturbance by quite separate mechanisms. There is no good evidence to support the notion that enuresis is a symbolic act, but both clinical observation and treatment studies suggest that there is a dynamic relationship between the behaviour and mood of the child and his wetting. This dynamic relationship probably operates in different directions in different children. In some, depressed mood or environmental stress diminish the child's ability to be continent at night, in other cases the act of bedwetting undermines confidence and affects social functioning. It should be emphasised that there is no evidence that wetting is either 'necessary' or beneficial to the disturbed child and there is a great deal of evidence that treatment of enuresis is helpful. The coexistence of disturbance and enuresis is, therefore, an indication rather than a contraindication to initiate effective symptomatic-treatment.

TREATMENT OF BEDWETTING

Comparatively few bedwetters receive treatment. In 1960 Miller *et al* found that fewer than 30 per cent of 11-year-old enuretics had ever been assessed or treated for their complaint. In view of the satisfactory way with which the condition responds to treatment it must be assumed that the high prevalence rates reported in more recent studies reflect a similar situation. There has been no research done on why parents do not seek treatment for their children, although clinical experience suggests that many families accept bed-wetting as an unavoidable part of growing-up.

An unknown proportion of children stop wetting as soon as a clinic appointment is made for them. Others stop wetting the night after they have seen the doctor for the first time and before any treatment has been started, yet others stop wetting as soon as a bell and pad is fitted to their bed. The bell never rings to waken them and so conditioning cannot have taken place. We know little about these responses to 'non-specific intervention'. We do not know if the children who respond in this way are themselves distinctive nor do we know whether the quality or duration of cure is satisfactory. However, responses of this sort often anger the parents of the newly dry child, confirming them in their beliefs that the child could have stopped wetting before, had he so wished.

Night lifting and fluid restriction before bed

These commonsense measures are frequently adopted by the parents of younger children who are still wetting the bed. Roberts and Schoellkopf (1951) investigated these practices intensively in a community study and concluded that they did little to increase the chances of a dry night. The only controlled study into lifting and fluid restriction in older children was that carried out by Hagglund (1965) on a group of psychiatric inpatients. He found that although there was an initial reduction in the frequency of wetting, the response was shortlived, and after 3 months the group treated in this way were wetting as often as a no-treatment control group.

Theoretical arguments against fluid restriction and lifting have been advanced by workers who believe that a small functional bladder capacity is aetiologically significant. Hagglund (1965) found that the bladder capacities of children treated with fluid restriction showed a significantly smaller increase in capacity than the no-treatment control group over a 3-month period and this provides some evidence to support this view. On the other hand, it is well to remember that the effects of lifting and restriction have only been critically examined in this single study and it may be that these practices are more effective in the majority of bedwetters who are never referred for specialist treatment. Indeed a positive response to lifting may be one of the reasons why professional advice is not sought.

Day-time training

In 1948 Smith suggested that enuretic children could be treated by training them to defer micturition during the day. More recently the results of such treatment have been described in a systematic and controlled fashion. Paschalis *et al* (1972) describes a controlled treatment trial in which a group of children with nocturnal enuresis were given token rewards for deferring day-time micturition. The children and their parents were instructed to delay micturition in increments of 2–3 minutes each day after feeling the urge to void. The treatment was continued for 20 days by which time the children were deferring micturition for 45 minutes on each occasion. During this period half of the children became dry at night, none of the controls acquiring continence. The token was awarded just before use of the toilet. The authors feel that the timing was important, and that awarding the token after micturition would have the effects of reinforcing voiding behaviour rather than the deferment of voiding. A similar approach has been described in a small number of cases by Stedman (1972) and by Miller (1973).

This treatment requires skilled supervision and further studies are needed to define its usefulness. Theoretically it might be possible to shorten the duration of treatment by increasing the number of stimuli available for reinforcement, i.e. by giving the child an artificial fluid load. A similar approach was used successfully in the treatment of day time incontinence (Foxx & Azrin 1973).

Surgical treatment

The rationale for the surgical treatment of enuresis has been outlined above. It is worth noting that not a single treatment study has been published in which results have been demonstrated in more than anecdotal form. The usual forms of surgical intervention are urethral dilation, meatotomy or bladder neck repair. The hazards of the latter are now well documented (Smith 1969) and include urinary incontinence, recurrent epidydimitis and aspermia. It is now incumbent on urologists recommending such treatment to demonstrate both the safety and the efficacy of their interventions in an acceptable form.

Drug treatment

A very large number of drugs have been used in the treatment of enuresis. Blackwell and Currah (1973) have written a critical and comprehensive review of this very active area of research.

Three principal classes of drugs have been used in the treatment of wetting.

Amphetamines

The rationale for using amphetamines is that they reduce the depth of sleep, but there is no evidence that enuretics sleep more heavily than nonenuretic children (see above). Only one double study has been carried out (McConaghy 1969) and this found amphetamines to be no more effective than placebo and to be markedly inferior to either the bell and pad apparatus or to imipramine. On the other hand amphetamines may hasten the response to conditioning treatment (see below).

Anticholinergic drugs

Such anticholinergic drugs as belladonna and propantheline have all been used extensively in the treatment of bedwetting. The rationale behind their use is that they inhibit detrusor contractions and in medical practice their use may be associated with urinary retention. However, a number of double blind controlled studies have now been carried out none of which have shown any significant antienuretic effect (Wallace & Forsyth 1969).

Tricyclic antidepressants

The efficacy of imipramine in suppressing bedwetting was first reported by MacLean in 1960. Sophisticated studies have followed (Shaffer *et al* 1968) as a result of which much clinically useful information has been accumulated.

Comparative studies between imipramine, amitryptyline and nortrypty-line show that all have an antienuretic effect and there is little evidence favouring the choice of one over any other (Blackwell & Currah 1973).

Provided that the dose of the drug is tailored to the child's weight or surface area (Shaffer *et al* 1968), increasing the dosage level seems to have little effect. Indeed, Maxwell and Seldrup (1971) have actually found that the antienuretic effect of imipramine is less at high dose levels. Children weighing less than 66 lb (30 kg) should receive a single dose of 25 mg, children over this weight a dose of either 35 or 50 mg. The timing of administration has been studied by Alderton (1970) who found no significant difference in the effects of medication given in mid-afternoon or in the evening.

All of the studies have shown that the maximal effect can be seen within one week of starting treatment. Imipramine will reduce wetting frequency in about 85 per cent of bedwetters and will suppress wetting completely in about 30 per cent. Relapse after withdrawal of medication may be immediate or delayed, but within 3 months of stopping treatment nearly all children treated with imipramine will be wetting again at or near their previous wetting frequency. The technique of stopping the drug—gradual or abrupt withdrawal—does not seem in influence the relapse rate. The effect of very prolonged treatment has not been studied. However, variations in duration with periods of less than 6 months do not influence outcome.

Side effects from the tricyclic compounds used in therapeutic doses are uncommon. The most frequent include dizziness, headache and constipation. Some hyperactive children may show a worsening of their restlessness and distractibility. The tricyclic drugs should not be prescribed for children under the age of 4 years. Goel and Shanks (1974) have reported a number of cases of acute tricyclic poisoning in this age group, although poisoning was most common in the untreated younger siblings of the enuretic children, who had taken the drugs accidentally. The toxic dose lies between 10–20 mg/ kg and the minimum lethal dose is approximately 30 mg/kg. Manifestations of toxicity include cardiac irregularities, convulsions, hallucinations, retention of urine and ataxia. Death, when it occurs, is usually due to a cardiac arrhythmia.

The discovery of a group of drugs which can effectively control bedwetting is important, not only for therapeutic reasons, but because a knowledge of the way in which these drugs work could eventually lead to a better understanding of the underlying pathology.

Imipramine has an effect on sleep patterns, reducing the quantity of REM sleep. However, other drugs such as the amphetamines have a similar or even more powerful REM suppressant activity and yet have no antienuretic effect. Furthermore, as enuresis takes place least frequently during the REM phase of sleep (see above) there seems no obvious reason why this action should be therapeutic. There is a contrast between the rapidity with which tricyclic drugs control enuresis and the slowness of their antidepressant activity. This is sometimes used as an argument against the effects of the drug being mediated through changes in mental state. However, Werry *et al* (1975) have demonstrated nonspecific psychotropic effects of more rapid onset in enuretics being treated with the tricyclics. It is therefore probably inappropriate to draw conclusions solely from a comparison between the latencies of treatment response in adult depressives and childhood enuretics. Nevertheless, a primarily psychotropic effect seems unlikely for other reasons, such as the marked effect on bladder function which can be demonstrated after the administration of the drug to anaesthetised animals.

How are these bladder responses mediated? It has been most frequently proposed that the effects are through the drug's marked cholinolytic activity. However, even more powerful cholinolytic drugs such as propantheline are ineffective in enuresis and a study by Petersen *et al* (1973) has shown that N-aminoimipramine, a drug similar to imipramine but with much reduced cholinolytic activity, nevertheless has a potent antienuretic action. Imipramine also acts to both potentiate and block noradrenaline at the synaptic junction. However, a study by Shaffer (1976) has shown that a pure alpha-adrenolytic agent is ineffective in the management of the condition. The cholinolytic and local anaesthetic actions of imipramine have also been studied more directly in a series of animal experiments (Stephenson *et al* 1976). Bladder responsiveness to filling was reduced by imipramine but this effect did not appear to have been brought about by activity at a peripheral sensory or autonomic level. Although the precise site of action remains to be identified, it therefore seems likely that the effects of the drug are largely central.

Treatment involving night waking

Pfaundler (1904) devised an alarm system to alert nurses after their patients had wet the bed. He noted that when this was done the children soon ceased to wet. Despite this early report of a successful treatment for enuresis the method was not generally applied for another 30 years when Mowrer and Mowrer (1938) described a similar device. The Mowrer apparatus, with some technical refinements, has continued in use and constitutes the most effective form of therapy now available. The device usually consists of an auditory signal linked to two electrodes in the form of perforated metal or foil sheets upon which the child sleeps. The sheets are separated by an ordinary cotton sheet. When the child passes urine, contact is made between the two electrodes.

A number of theories have been advanced to explain the efficacy of the alarm system. In the Classical Conditioning paradigm, bladder distension or the micturition contraction is assumed to be the Indifferent Stimulus. Treatment introduces an Unconditioned Stimulus (the auditory signal) in proximity to the IS which then acquires the properties of a Conditioned Stimulus leading to a Conditioned Response (waking). Support for a Conditioning model is provided by the findings that: (a) when the introduction of the UCS is delayed treatment is ineffective; and (b) extinction of the CR after initial cure can be inhibited by intermittent reinforcement (Finley *et al* 1973) and by overlearning (Young & Morgan 1972) (see below).

However, it seems likely that other learning processes are also involved. The 'gadget effect' whereby the child becomes dry when the apparatus is placed on the bed but not switched on (DeLeon & Mandell 1966) suggests that avoidance learning may be important. Crosby (1950) put forward the view that the apparatus worked primarily through punishment training. He devised an instrument which applied an electric shock to the legs of the child after micturition. In fact, this instrument has proved no more effective than the Mowrer device and is understandably less acceptable to parents (Lovibond 1964). Turner (1973) has pointed out that the use of the bell and pad focusses the family's attention on the wetting habits of the child and that dry nights are more liable to be noted and rewarded by praise. He suggests that social learning is an important component in the bell's efficacy.

Cure with the bell and pad varies in different studies from 60 per cent to 100 per cent. 'Cure', defined as 14 nights of continuous dryness, is usually reached during the second month of treatment (Kolvin *et al* 1972). Responses may be hastened by the simultaneous use of a stimulant drug such as methylamphetamine (Young & Turner 1965) but this also increases the likelihood of relapse. Young and Morgan (1973) have examined the characteristics associated with a delayed response to treatment. Significant factors are maternal anxiety, disturbed home background and a failure of the child to waken with the alarm. Age of the child and initial wetting frequency were not significantly related to delay. Another major problem with this form of treatment is the high proportion of families who discontinue treatment before cure. In discussing this problem, Turner (1973) has suggested that the elements in treatment most likely to lead to drop-out are: failure to understand or to follow the instructions; failure of the apparatus to wake the child and irritation at false alarms.

Relapse after initial cure is a major therapeutic problem. Turner (1973) summarising results from studies in which follow-up was maintained for at least a year computed that the average relapse rate within a year of completing treatment was 35 per cent. Young and Morgan (1973) found that relapses were more likely in older children but failed to find other factors associated with the phenomenon. Two techniques appear to reduce the relapse rate. (a) *Intermittent reinforcement*—this may involve the use of special apparatus designed to waken the patient after only a proportion of micturitions (Finley *et al* 1973). Such apparatus is not readily available and the treatment requires a great deal of parental cooperation. Lovibond (1964) has suggested that by using ordinary apparatus during 3 or 4 days in each week similar results may be obtained. It should be noted that when the approach is used initial cure may be delayed. (b) *Overlearning*—Young and Morgan (1972) have found that if children are given a fluid load of 2 pints after having reached dryness criterion, the relapse rate is reduced from 35 per cent to 11 per cent. This approach has the advantage of not delaying the initial 'cure'.

As mentioned above, the bell and pad offers the opportunity of a cure to the great majority of bedwetters. However, its successful use requires that the therapist be acquainted with practical problems that are likely to arise during treatment and that he be available for a fairly intensive level of support and guidance during the early stages of the treatment process.

PRACTICAL GUIDE TO ASSESSMENT AND TREATMENT

Assessment

Assessment of the enuretic child should include:

(a) Enquiring into symptoms suggestive of associated urinary tract infection, such as frequency, urgency and dysuria, unexplained vomiting or fevers. Urine should be examined microscopically and bacteriologically. Simple chemical examination for the presence or absence of albumen is of no value in detecting urinary infection.

(b) Systematic enquiry into other conditions which are known to be associated with wetting, such as encopresis and educational and behavioural difficulties.

(c) Enquiries into factors which might influence the choice of treatment such as:

Sleeping and housing arrangements.

Parental attitudes towards the enuretic child. Where there is a good deal of hostility, resentment or indifference it may be difficult to enlist the parents' cooperation and patience without which symptomatic treatment is unlikely to work.

Parental attitudes towards different types of treatment. Some parents view the bell and pad as a punitive device and will be reluctant to use it without explanation and support. Others will have equally strong feelings about the use of drugs.

(d) Enquiries into ways in which the symptom might be self-reinforcing. For example, some children regularly go into their parents' bed at night after they have wet. This may be a source of gratification to either parent or child which they will be reluctant to give up.

Treatment

(1) Treatment should be preceded by a period of *observation*. During this period it may be found that the child is only wet very infrequently, or the child may, in fact, stop altogether. Observation can be carried out by using a simple star chart. The child sticks in a star whenever he has a dry night. If this is displayed for the rest of the family to see, the social rewards for being dry may themselves have a therapeutic effect. During this period of baseline observation—which should last for at least 2 weeks—various simple interventions, such as lifting or fluid restriction can be assessed.

(2) Although day-time training seems to be a promising form of treatment we do not yet know enough about its applicability nor do we yet know for how long children treated in this way remain dry. Every effort, therefore, should be made to treat the child with the *bell and pad*. This is a safe, relatively brief form of treatment and is more likely to result in a permanent cure than any other method.

Ideally instruction on how to fit the bell and pad on the patient's bed should be given at home with both parents and child being present. If this is not possible then a clear demonstration on a clinic couch made up for this purpose should be given. Initial follow-up should take place a few days after the bell and pad have been supplied in order to deal with any difficulties that the patient or parents might experience.

Many children are not woken by the alarm and parents should be warned of this possibility before treatment is started. Sleeping arrangements may need to be altered so that the parent can hear the bell and waken the child after it has sounded. Booster alarms of differing volumes and tones are available and are often helpful. Some children will turn the bell off before going to bed and parents should be advised to place it as far from the child's bed as possible so that it is out of reach. They should also check that the switch is still on before they retire to bed.

Once the bell has rung the child should get up, turn off the alarm, and empty his bladder into a chamber pot. He should then be encouraged to assist the parents in removing the wet sheets and replacing them with dry ones. The bell is switched back on and the child will in almost all cases return to sleep without delay. If a second micturition should occur during sleep it is reasonable to advise parents not to reset the alarm a third time.

False alarms are a source of irritation to the family and may be due to contact between the clips or metal sheets through movement or else through a worn intervening sheet. Both the top sheet and intervening sheet should be sufficiently large as to be able to be tucked in under the mattress, thus securing the metal sheets in position. Dische (1973) in her excellent review of the practical aspects of treatment with the bell and pad, has pointed out that another cause of false alarms may be inadequate laundering of the intervening sheet. Urinary electrolytes deposited in the soiled sheet may facilitate conduction by perspiration.

After the child has been dry for two continuous weeks the parent should be told that the chances of relapse can be reduced by continuing with the bell and pad for a further 2 weeks, during which time the child is encouraged to drink up to 2 pints of fluid at night before retiring. In a very few cases this will result in a complete breakdown of continence and the procedure should then be abandoned, however, in most cases continence at night is maintained despite this stress.

Drug treatment

The bell and pad method can result in a permanent cure in a high proportion of cases and is therefore the treatment of choice. Nevertheless, there are a number of situations in which treatment with imipramine or other tricyclic drugs might seem appropriate. Examples of such situations would be: (a) when it is important to obtain an immediate short-term effect as when a child is first seen just before going away on holiday; (b) in a situation in which the wetting has become the focus of aggressive and hostile behaviour on the part of parents or siblings. A rapidly effective treatment may serve to reduce the stresses in the family until such a time as the bell and pad can be used; (c) when conditions for the use of the buzzer are likely to improve in the near future. For example, a family living in overcrowded conditions but anticipating rehousing, or a family living in a cold or draughty house presenting for treatment in the winter months. Treatment with the bell and pad will be more acceptable in warmer weather; (d) when the bell and pad is not practicable. This should be a conclusion based on actual experience rather than anticipation. Some apparently disorganised and inadequate families seem able to use the bell and pad successfully under the most appalling circumstances even for example when the enuretic child is sharing the bed with a sibling; and (e) after failure of conditioning treatment.

DAY-TIME WETTING

DeJonge (1973) has reviewed the prevalence of diurnal enuresis from a number of different studies. Approximately 2 per cent of 5-year-olds are wet during the day at least once a week and about 8 per cent are wet at least monthly. The condition becomes progressively less common with age and Oppel *et al* (1968) found that only 1 per cent of 12-year-olds had had at least one wet day per month. All studies show that, unlike nocturnal enuresis, daytime wetting is commoner in girls than in boys.

Most children who wet during the day also wet when asleep. Blomfield and Douglas (1956) studied the association between day-and night-time wetting in 5–7-year-olds. Of the boys 80 per cent and of the girls 60 per cent who wet during the day were also wet at night. The proportion of nocturnal enuretics who also wet during the day varies with age. Data from Hallgren's (1956) study of Swedish school children showed that at the age of 5 years, 16 per cent of boys and 30 per cent of girl nocturnal enuretics also wet during the day, whereas at 7 years only 8 per cent of boys and 16 per cent of the girl enuretics wet during the day.

Combined day and night wetting is associated with a higher rate of psychiatric disturbance (Rutter *et al* 1973) than is simple nocturnal enuresis. Bedwetters who have an associated urinary tract infection are also more likely to wet during the day. Comparing rates from the studies of Savage *et al* (1969) and Hallgren (1956), both dealing with 5-year-old girls, the rate of combined day and night wetting was 4 times greater when the enuretic child had an associated urinary infection than in the population of enuretics as a whole.

Management of day-time wetting

It is especially important that the urine of children who wet during the day be examined bacteriologically to exclude the presence of an occult urinary infection.

In some cases day-time wetting is situation specific. The patient is a young, timid child who has started to wet only since starting school, wets only at school and never during weekends or holidays. In these children school anxiety may be the most important factor, the child being reluctant to use the school lavatories or leave the classroom during lessons. In such cases a suggestion to the teacher that she tactfully encourage the child to use the toilet at regular intervals may be all that is needed.

More systematic approaches to treatment include 'habit training' and operant reinforcement of appropriate elimination. Habit training requires the child to go regularly and frequently to the toilet at predetermined times. This approach has been widely used amongst retarded adults and children and the results of various treatment studies are reviewed by Rentfrow and Rentfrow (1969).

Rather than relying on prescheduled toileting, Azrin and Foxx (1971) and Foxx and Azrin (1973) have given their treatment subjects an increased fluid intake and have reinforced appropriate toileting when the urge to pass urine was felt spontaneously by their subjects. By increasing fluid intake the number of responses available for reinforcement has been increased and good results with very young and retarded children have been obtained after short but extremely intensive treatment sessions.

CONCLUSIONS

Why do children wet the bed?

This chapter has reviewed many of the factors known to be associated with bedwetting. These include biological associations such as an increased rate of urinary infection, apparent abnormalities in the rate of development of the structures at the base of the bladder, a low threshold of responsiveness of the bladder and a genetic predisposition. There are also a number of associations of a social or environmental nature. Enuretic children are more likely to come from large or broken or impoverished or unhappy families. Their parents may be less caring and are more likely to have allowed or been forced to allow their children to be separated from them during early childhood. Enuresis occurs more often in children living in institutions and it may respond to psychosocial changes and interventions which have in common the effect of increasing the attention that is paid to the child and possibly to his bedwetting.

A social motivational model would seem to bring together many of these apparently disparate associations. Enuresis can then be viewed as a socially unacceptable response that has persisted either because the social reinforcement or social inhibitory influences have not acted at an optimal level, or because biological deviance renders the force of these influences inadequate. Azrin *et al* (1973) have pointed out that social reactions to the act of bedwetting are delayed because the event takes place at night and the child does not wake after the event. In some cases the effectiveness of even these delayed responses in still further reduced by the unsatisfactory nature of the child's environment. In other cases the appropriate social response is hindered by abnormal bladder function. The bell and pad is effective because it focusses the family's attention on the symptom in a consistent fashion and because it reduces the delay between the act of wetting and the social response. The tricyclics and day-time training are presumably effective because they facilitate the child's appropriate inhibitory response.

Irrespective of the cause of bedwetting it is important that practitioners appreciate that this common symptom can be treated successfully in nearly all cases, that there are no contraindications to treatment, and that treatment, as well as bringing practical relief to the family will often benefit the child socially and emotionally.

REFERENCES

ACHENBACH T. & LEWIS M. (1971) A proposed model for clinical research and its application to encopresis and enuresis. *J. Am. Acad. Child Psychiat.* **10,** 535–554

ALDERTON H.R. (1970) Imipramine in childhood enuresis. *Canad. Med. Assoc. J.,* **102,** 1179–1180

AZRIN N.H. & FOXX R.M. (1971) A rapid method of toilet training the institutionalised retarded. *J. Appl. Behav. Analysis* **4,** 89–99

AZRIN N.H., SNEED T.J. & FOXX R.M. (1973) Dry bed: A rapid method of eliminating bed-wetting (enuresis) of the retarded. *Behav. Res. Ther.* **11,** 427–434

BAKER B.L. (1969) Symptom treatment and symptom substitution in enuresis. *J. Abnorm. Psychol.* **74,** 42–49

BAKWIN H. (1961) Enuresis in Children. *J. Pediatrics* **58,** 806–819

BAKWIN H. (1973) The genetics of bed-wetting. *In* Kolvin I., MacKeith R. & Meadow S.R. (eds.) *Bladder Control and Enuresis.* Clinics in Dev. Med. nos. 48/49. London: SIMP/Heinemann

BEHRLE F.C., ELKIN M.H. & LAYBOURNE P.C. (1956) Evaluation of a conditioning device in the treatment of nocturnal enuresis. *Pediatrics* **17,** 849–855

BLACKWELL B. & CURRAH J. (1973) The psychopharmacology of nocturnal enuresis.

In Kolvin I., MacKeith R. & Meadow S.R. (eds.) *Bladder Control and Enuresis.* Clinics in Dev. Med. nos. 48/49. London: SIMP/Heinemann

BLOMFIELD J.M. & DOUGLAS J.W.B. (1956) Bedwetting—prevalence among children aged 4–7 years. *Lancet* **i,** 850–852

BOSTOCK J. & SHACKLETON M.G. (1951) Enuresis and toilet training. *Med. J. Aust.* **2,** 110–113

BOYD M.M. (1960) The depth of sleep in enuretic school children and in non-enuretic controls. *J. Psychosom. Res.* **4,** 274–281

BRAZELTON T.B. (1962) A child-oriented approach to toilet training. *Pediatrics* **29,** 121–128

CAMPBELL E.W. & YOUNG J.D. (1966) Enuresis and its relationship to electroencephalographic disturbances. *J. Urol.* **96,** 947–949

CENDRON J. & LEPINARD V. (1972) Maladie du Col Vesical chez l'enfant. *Urol. Int.* **27,** 355–360

COOPER D.G.W. (1968) Bladder studies in children with neurogenic incontinence with comments on the place of pelvic floor stimulation. *Brit. J. Urol.* **40,** 157–174

CROSBY N.D. (1950) Essential enuresis. Treatment based on physiological concepts. *Med. J. Aust.* **2,** 533–543

DE JONGE G.A. (1973) Epidemiology of enuresis: A survey of the literature. *In* Kolvin I., MacKeith R. & Meadow S.R. (eds.) *Bladder Control and Enuresis.* Clinics in Dev. Med. nos. 48/49. London: SIMP/Heinemann

DE LEON J. & MANDELL W. (1966) A comparison of conditioning and psychotherapy in the treatment of functional enuresis. *J. Clin. Psychol.* **22,** 326–330

DESPERT J.L. (1944) Urinary control and enuresis. *Psychosom. Med.* **6,** 294–307

DISCHE S. (1973) Treatment of enuresis with an enuresis alarm. *In* Kolvin I., MacKeith R. & Meadow S.R. (eds.) *Bladder Control and Enuresis.* Clinics in Dev. Med. nos. 48/49. London: SIMP/Heinemann

DODGE W.F., WEST E.F., BRIDGFORTH M.S. & TRAVIS L.B. (1970) Nocturnal enuresis in 6–10 year-old children. *Amer. J. Dis. Child* **120,** 32–35

DOUGLAS J.W.B. (1973) Early disturbing events and later enuresis. *In* Kolvin I., MacKeith R. & Meadow S.R. (eds.) *Bladder Control and Enuresis.* Clinics in Dev. Med. nos. 48/49. London: SIMP/Heinemann

EEG-OLOFSSON O. (1971) The development of the electroencephalogram in normal children from the age of 1 through 15 years—positive spike phenomena 14 and 6 Hz. *Neuropädiatrie* **2,** 405–427

EEG-OLOFSSON O., PETERSEN I. & SELLDEN U. (1971) The development of the electroencephalogram in normal children from the age of 1 through 15 years: paroxysmal activity. *Neuropädiatrie* **2,** 375–404

EVANS J.I. (1971) Sleep of enuretics. *Brit. Med. J.* **3,** 110

FINLEY W.W., BESSERMAN R.L., BENNETT L.F., CLAPP R.K. & FINLEP P. (1973) The effect of continuous, intermittent and placebo reinforcement on the effectiveness of the conditioning treatment for enuresis nocturna. *Behav. Res. Ther.* **11,** 289–297

FOXX R.M. & AZRIN N.H. (1973) Dry pants. A rapid method of toilet training children. *Behav. Res. Ther.* **11,** 435–442

GLEASON D.M. & LATIMER J.K. (1962) The pressure flow study: a method for measuring bladder neck resistance. *J. Urol.* **87,** 844–852

GOEL K.M. & SHANKS R.A. (1974) Amitryptyline and imipramine poisoning in children. *Brit. Med. J.* **1,** 261–263

GRAHAM P.J. (1973) Depth of sleep and enuresis: a critical review. *In* Kolvin I., Mac-Keith R. & Meadow S.R. (eds.) *Bladder Control and Enuresis*. Clinics in Dev. Med. nos. 48/49. London: SIMP/Heinemann

HAGGLUND T.B. (1965) Enuretic children treated with fluid restriction or forced drinking. A clinical and cystometric study. *Ann. Paediat. Fenn.* **11**, 84–90

HALLGREN B. (1956) Enuresis. II: A study with reference to certain physical, mental and social factors possibly associated with enuresis. *Acta Psych. Neuro. Scand.* **31**, 405–436

HALLGREN B. (1957) Enuresis: A clinical and genetic study. *Acta Psychiat. Neuro. Scand.*, Suppl. 114

HALLGREN B. (1960) Nocturnal enuresis in twins. *Acta Psych. Neuro. Scand.* **35**, 73–90

HEISEL J.S., REAM S., RAITZ T., RAPPAPORT M. & CODDINGTON R.D. (1973) The significance of life-events as contributory events in the diseases of children. *J. Pediatrics* **83**, 119–123

HELLBREGGE T. (1960) The development of circadian rhythm in infants. *Cold Spring Harbour Symp. Quart. Biol.* **25**, 311–323

HUTCH J.A. (1972) *Anatomy and Physiology of the Bladder, Trigone and Urethra*. New York: Appleton-Century-Crofts

JONES B., GERRARD J.W., SHOKEIR M.K. & HOUSTON C.S. (1972) Recurrent urinary infection in girls: relation to enuresis. *Canad. Med. Assoc. J.* **106**, 127–130

KAFFMAN M. (1962) Enuresis amongst kibbutz children. *J. Med. Assoc. Israel* **63**, 251–253

KALES A., TAN T-L., PRESTON T.A. & ALLEN C. (1970) Stage 4 Sleep. Studies of hypnotic, tranquillizing and anti-depressant drugs. *Psychophysiology* **7**, 342–343

KLACKENBURG G. (1955) Primary enuresis: when is a child dry at night? *Acta Paed. Scand.* **44**, 513–518

KOLVIN I., TAUNCH J., CURRAH J., GARSIDE R.F., NOLAN J. & SHAW W.B. (1972) Enuresis: A descriptive analysis and a controlled trial. *Develop. Med. Child Neurol.* **14**, 715–726

KOLVIN I. (1974) Personal communications.

KUNIN C.M., ZACHA E. & PAQUIN A.J. Jnr. (1962) Urinary tract infections in school children. I: Prevalence of bacteriuria and associated urologic findings. *New Engl. J. Med.* **266**, 1287–1296

LEWIS H.E., LOBBAN M.C. & TREDRE B.E. (1970) Daily rhythms of renal excretion in a child with nocturnal enuresis. *J. Physiol.* **210**, 42P–43P

LICKORISH J.R. (1964) One hundred enuretics. *J. Psychosom. Res.* **7**, 263–267

LOVIBOND S.H. (1964) *Conditioning and Enuresis*. Oxford: Pergamon

MACKEITH R. (1973) The causes of nocturnal enuresis. *In* Kolvin I., MacKeith R. & Meadow S.R. (eds.) *Bladder Control and Enuresis*. Clinics in Dev. Med. nos. 48/49, 173–180. London: SIMP/Heinemann

MACLEAN R.E. (1960) Imipramine hydrochloride and enuresis. *Amer. J. Psychiat.* **117**, 551

McCONAGHY N. (1969) A controlled trial of imipramine, amphetamine, pad and bell, conditioning and random awakening in the treatment of nocturnal enuresis. *Med. J. Aust.* **2**, 237–239

McHALE A. (1967) An investigation of personality attributes of stammering, enuretic and school phobic children. *Brit. J. Educ. Psychol.* **37**, 400–403

MAHONY D.T. (1971) Studies of enuresis. I: Incidence of obstructive lesions and patho-physiology of enuresis. *J. Urol.* **106**, 951–958

MAHONY D.T. & LAFERTE R.O. (1973) Editorial: Enuresis. A plea for objectivity and sensitivity. *J. Urol.* **109**, 531–532

MANLEY C.B. & FRENCH R.S. (1970) Urinary tract infection in girls: Prevalence of spina bifida occulta. *J. Urol.* **103**, 348–352

MAXWELL C. & SELDRUP J. (1971) Imipramine in the treatment of childhood enuresis. *The Practitioner* **207**, 809–814

MEADOW S.R., WHITE R.H.R. & JOHNSTON N.M. (1969) Prevalence of symptomless urinary tract disease in Birmingham school children. I: Pyuria and bacteriuria. *Brit. Med. J.* **3**, 81–84

MILLER F.J.W., COURT S.D.M., WALTON W.S. & KNOX E.G. (1960) *Growing Up in Newcastle-upon-Tyne.* London: Oxford University Press

MILLER P.M. (1973) An experimental analysis of retention control training in the treatment of nocturnal enuresis in two institutionalised adolescents. *Behav. Ther.* **4**, 288–294

MOLLING P.A., LOCKNER A.W., SAULS R.J. & EISENBERG L. (1962) Committed delin-quent boys. *Arch. Gen Psychiat.* **7**, 70–76

MOWRER O.H. & MOWRER W.M. (1938) Enuresis: a method for its study and treatment. *Amer. J. Orthopsychiat.* **8**, 436–459

NOVICK J. (1966) Symptomatic treatment of acquired and persistent enuresis. *J. Abnorm. Psychol.* **71**, 363–368

OPPEL W.C., HARPER P.A. & RIDER R.V. (1968) Social, psychological and neurological factors associated with nocturnal enuresis. *Pediatrics* **42**, 627–641

PASCHALIS A.P., KIMMEL H.D. & KIMMEL E. (1972) Further study of diurnal in-strumental conditioning in the treatment of enuresis nocturna. *J. Behav. Res. Exp. Psychiat.* **3**, 253–256

PETERSEN K.E., ANDERSON O.O. & HANSEN T. (1973) Mode of action and relative value of imipramine and similar drugs in the treatment of nocturnal enuresis. *Eur. J. Clin. Pharmacol.* **7**, 187–194

PETERSEN I. & EEG-OLOFSSON O. (1971) The development of the electroencephalogram in normal children from the age of 1 through 15 years. Non-paroxysmal activity. *Neuropädiatrie* **2**, 247–304

PFAUNDLER M. (1904) Demonstration eines Apparetes zur selbstätigen Signalisieurung stattgehabter Bettnässung. *Verhandlungen der hesellschuft Kinde. heilkd.* **21**, 219–220

POMPEIUS R. (1971) Cystometry in paediatric enuresis. *Scand. J. Urol, Nephrol.* **5**, 222–228

POUSSAINT A.F., KOEGLER R.R. & RIEHL J.L. (1967) Enuresis, epilepsy and the EEG. *Amer. J. Psychiat.* **123**, 1294–1295

RENTFROW R.K. & RENTFROW D.K. (1969) Studies related to toilet training of the men-tally retarded. *Amer. J. Occup. Ther.* **23**, 425–430

RITVO E.R., ORNITZ E.M., GOTTLIEB F., POUSSAINT A.F., MARON B.J., DITMAN K.S. & BLINN K.A. (1969) Arousal and non-arousal enuretic events. *Amer. J. Psychiat.* **126**, 77–84

ROBERTS K.E. & SCHOELLKOPF J.A. (1951) Eating, sleeping and elimination practices of a group of 2½ year old children; elimination practices: bladder. *Amer. J. Dis. Child.* **82**, 144–152

ROBINS L.N. (1966) *Deviant Children Grown Up.* Baltimore: Williams & Wilkins

RUTTER M., GRAHAM P. & YULE W. (1970a) *A Neuropsychiatric Study in Childhood.* Clinics in Dev. Med. nos. 35/36. London: SIMP/Heinemann

RUTTER M., TIZARD J. & WHITMORE K. (eds.) (1970b) *Education, Health and Behaviour.* London: Longman

RUTTER M., YULE W. & GRAHAM P. (1973) Enuresis and behavioural deviance: some epidemiological considerations. *In* Kolvin I., MacKeith R. & Meadow S.R. (eds.) *Bladder Control and Enuresis.* Clinics in Dev. Med. nos. 48/49. London: SIMP/Heinemann

SAVAGE D.C.L., WILSON M.I., ROSS E.M. & FEE W.M. (1969) Asymptomatic bacteriuria in girl entrants to Dundee primary schools. *Brit. Med. J.* **3,** 75–80

SCHAFFER H.R. & SCHAFFER E.B. (1968) *Child Care and the Family.* Occasional papers on social administrations no. 25. London: Bell

SEARS R.R., MACCOBY E.M. & LEVIN H. (1957) *Patterns of Child Rearing.* Evanston, Illinois: Row, Peterson

SHAFFER D. (1976) Unpublished data

SHAFFER D., COSTELLO A.J. & HILL I.D. (1968) Control of enuresis with imipramine. *Arch. Dis. Childh.* **43,** 665–671

SMITH D.R. (1969) Critique of the concept of vesical neck obstruction in children. *J. Amer. Med. Assoc.* **207,** 1686–1692

SMITH S. (1948) *The Psychological Origin and Treatment of Enuresis.* Seattle: University of Washington Press

STARFIELD S.B. (1967) Functional bladder capacity in enuretic and non-enuretic children. *J. Paediat.* **70,** 777–781

STEDMAN J.M. (1972) The extension of the Kimmel treatment method for enuresis to an adolescent: a case report. *J. Behav. Ther. Exp. Psychiat.* **3,** 307–309

STEIN Z.A. & SUSSER M.W. (1965) Socio-medical study of enuresis among delinquent boys. *Brit. J. Prev. Soc. Med.* **19,** 174–181

STEIN Z.A., SUSSER M.W. & WILSON A.E. (1965) Families of enuretic children. I: Family type and age. II: Family culture, structure and organisation. *Develop. Med. Child Neurol.* **7,** 658–676

STEPHENSON J., SHAFFER D. & THOMAS V. (1976) Unpublished data

TAKAYASU H., SATO S., HIROKAWA L. & SHIBUYA M. (1963) Electroencephalogram findings in 140 enuretic patients. *Urol. Int.* **15,** 171–190

THAUSTEIN J. & HALEVI H.S. (1962) Enuresis amongst school entrants in the changing population of Israel. *Brit. J. Prev. Soc. Med.* **16,** 40–45

TROUP C.W. & HODGSON N.B. (1971) Nocturnal functional bladder capacity in enuretic children. *J. Urol.* **105,** 129–132

TURNER R.K. (1973) Conditioning treatment of nocturnal enuresis: present status. *In* Kolvin I., MacKeith R. & Meadow S.R. (eds.) *Bladder Control and Enuresis.* Clinics in Dev. Med. nos. 48/49. London: SIMP/Heinemann

TURTON E.C. & SPEAR A.B. (1953) EEG findings in 100 cases of severe enuresis. *Arch. Dis. Child.* **28,** 316–320

UMPHRESS A., MURPHY E., NICKOLS J. & HAMMAR S. (1970) Adolescent enuresis. A social study of family interaction. *Arch. Gen. Psychiat.* **22,** 237–244

VULLIAMY D. (1956) The day and night output of urine in enuresis. *Arch. Dis. Child.* **31,** 439–443

WALLACE I.R. & FORSYTHE W.I. (1969) The treatment of enuresis. A controlled clinical trial of propantheline, propantheline-and-phenobarbitone, and a placebo. *Brit. J. Clin. Pract.* **23,** 207–210

WEINBERG W., RUTMAN J., SULLIVAN L., PENICK E. & DIETZ S. (1973) Depression in children referred to an educational diagnostic centre: Diagnosis and treatment. *J. Paed.* **83,** 1065–1072

WERRY J.S. & COHRSSEN J. (1965) Enuresis: An etiologic and therapeutic study. *J. Pediatrics* **67,** 423–431

WERRY J.S., DOWRICK P.W., LAMPEN E.L. & VAMOS M.J. (1975) Imipramine in enuresis—psychological and physiological effects. *J. Child Psychol. Psychiat.* **16,** 289–299

YOUNG G.C. & MORGAN R.T.T. (1972) Overlearning in the conditioning treatment of enuresis. *Behav. Res. Ther.* **10,** 147–151

YOUNG G.C. & MORGAN R.T.T. (1973) Rapidity of response to the treatment of enuresis. *Develop. Med. Child Neurol.* **15,** 488–496

YOUNG G.C. & TURNER R.K. (1965) C.N.S. stimulant drugs and conditioning treatment of nocturnal enuresis. *Behav. Res. Ther.* **3,** 93–101

ZALESKI A., GERRARD J.W. & SHOKEIR M.H.K. (1973) Nocturnal enuresis: The importance of a small bladder capacity. *In* Kolvin I., MacKeith R. & Meadow S.R. (eds.) *Bladder Control and Enuresis.* Clinics in Dev. Med. nos. 48/49. London: SIMP/Heinemann

CHAPTER 25

Faecal soiling

L. HERSOV

The descriptive term 'faecal soiling' is used to describe disorders of bowel function and control occurring in children over a certain age in the absence of any physical abnormality or disease. It avoids arguments about the use and definition of terms such as 'encopresis' and 'psychogenic megacolon'. The age at which faecal incontinence is considered abnormal varies and some authors have set the age limit at 2 years (Berg & Jones 1964; Bakwin & Bakwin 1953) assuming that most children have achieved bowel control by then. In fact, there is much variation in the age at which control is achieved by children in different cultures (Whiting & Child 1953; Anthony 1957) and probably within our own culture, depending on parental expectation (Brazelton 1962). Stein and Susser (1967) studying the development of bladder and bowel control in 671 British preschool children concluded that seasonal variation, depth of sleep, family size, birth-rank, maternal age, occupational class and economic status could not be shown to influence achievement of control. This was achieved by more than half of the children in the age-group of 18–24 months and almost all of the children aged $2\frac{1}{2}$ years had achieved this both by day and night. At 42–48 months nearly 100 per cent of the sample had achieved control. Quay and Werry (1972) suggest that these findings and those of Bellman (1966) point to 4 years as a more realistic minimum age for judging abnormality of bowel control.

EPIDEMIOLOGY

Bellman (1966) studied the prevalence of encopresis among 7-year-olds in their first year at school using a parent questionnaire with 8863 children. Responses showed that bowel control was firmly established in the majority during the child's fourth year. There was a decreasing frequency of encopresis until 16 years of age when the numbers were practically zero. Among children between 7 to 8 years of age the frequency was 1·5 per cent with boys (2·3 per cent) predominating over girls (0·7 per cent) in a ratio of 3·4 to 1. More recently Rutter, Tizard and Whitmore (1970) found the prevalence of at least once-a-month soiling among 10–12 year olds on the Isle of Wight to be 1·3 per cent for boys and 0·3 per cent for girls. Davie *et al* (1972) using retrospective reports found soiling by day after 5 years of age in slightly over 1 per cent of children in their Cohort Study and this occurred three times more commonly in boys than girls. This higher rate in boys is also a constant finding in clinical studies of encopretic children attending paediatric and psychiatric clinics (Anthony 1957; Davidson *et al* 1963; Berg & Jones 1964; Bellman 1966; Olatawura 1973). Rutter *et al* (1970) also found a highly significant association between enuresis and encopresis confirming similar findings by Hallgren (1956), Davidson *et al* (1963), Bellman (1966) and Stein and Susser (1967).

PHYSIOLOGY AND PSYCHOLOGY OF BOWEL CONTROL

Normal faecal continence has been described by Gaston (1948) as the ability to retain faeces until delivery is convenient. This ability results from the interplay of several factors. First, there is the rectal response to distension by faecal material and the acute sensitivity of the upper anal canal to contact (Duthie & Gairns 1960). Rectal sensation is difficult to define and children are often unable to respond to questions about whether they have a feeling of rectal fullness or can sense the passage of a stool. In normal people distension of the lower rectum with a balloon produces pelvic floor discomfort and an associated sense of urgency (Parks 1975).

Second, the motor element of the external sphincter and the puborectoanalis sling of the levator ani make up the striated sphincter together with the smooth muscle of the internal sphincter (Nixon 1973). These two types of muscles serve different functions. The striated sphincter is able to contract strongly to prevent the passage of a stool at an inconvenient time when it is forced down by a rectal contraction wave. This sphincter can only function for up to 30 seconds or so, long enough to contain the rectal contraction wave till it passes. The internal sphincter can maintain persistent tonic activity so preventing leakage of stool between periods of rectal activity by maintaining closure of the resting anal wall. Both sphincter activities complement each other in conditions of normal continence, but clinical experience (Nixon 1975) suggests that the external sphincter is of much less importance than the puborectoanalis sling and the internal sphincter.

Third, rectal motility to accommodate faeces is important as well as the mechanical support of muscles anchoring the anus, which allow the muscles to act at a mechanical advantage. The resilience of the wall of the anal canal plays some part in maintaining the resting tone of the normal anal canal which is cleverly constructed to allow a weak muscle to resist a strong force. The mobility of the anal mucosa causes it to pucker into folds as the canal is narrowed so plugging the anal canal and exerting a strong obstructive action (Nixon 1973).

However, bowel control is a very complex function including involuntary peristaltic waves of contraction of the colon, the physiological mechanisms of sphincter function described above, and the voluntary initiation and delay of defaecation under different conditions and in terms of different social and cultural demands. Voluntary defaecation is a total neuromuscular response, not a simple localised reaction and it involves maturational factors, interacting with social learning. The development of patterns of bowel behaviour fluctuates as the child matures and the acquisition of bowel control must be understood in terms of growth, maturity and personality differences rather than just in habit formation and learning (Gesell, Ilg & Ames 1974).

By 40 weeks the infant is able to sit and reacts adaptively to toilet training but by 1 year 'successes' are less frequent and resistance again appears. At 15 months the child can stand upright and the irregularities and resistances lessen for he now likes to go to the toilet and some children instinctively assume the squat pattern. The developmental task is to achieve a working balance between contraction and relaxation and at first each comes under voluntary control separately. By 18 months, speech is developing and the articulate child who is able to say a word for 'toilet' can relate this to his bowel movement and so increase his voluntary control. He will remain trained with few accidents unlike a second type of child who has the same amount of 'training' but is slow in 'learning'. He is not so apt with words and does not seize on the essentials of the toilet situation in terms of process and product. He may even smear stools and does not relate the act of toilet going to the social situation or even to his mother and may pass his stools when alone, standing in his playpen.

Gesell *et al* (1974) point out that some 2-year-olds are often trainable if left to their own devices after their pants have been taken off. By the age of 3 years there is increased ability to withhold and postpone and the child accepts and even asks for help. Bowel function has become a private affair by the age of 4 years with insistence on a closed toilet door coexisting with curiosity as to how bowel function occurs in others. The child is interested in the size, shape, colour and consistency of his stools, outspoken in his comments and pleased with his prowess and productiveness.

Training goes reasonably well in most children and by 3 or 4 years of age can be taken for granted, but some children appear to make no progress whatever toward having bowel movements while on the toilet. This can lead to disappointments and emotional tensions in parents particularly where children engage in frequent stool-smearing as well. Parents may try to deal with this with punitive measures of varying severity sometimes leading to habitual 'holding back' of stools, chronic constipation, rectal inertia and 'overflow incontinence' (Nixon 1961). The call to stool is diminished in the presence of an enlarged rectum and the absence of the stretch required to produce the sensation of fullness.

Regularity of the bowels was almost the first rule of health in Victorian times and the first subject asked about by a doctor in cases of illness. The process of bowel training was left to folk wisdom and oral tradition and the subject was omitted entirely in otherwise comprehensive manuals of child care (Robertson 1976).

Toilet training is a major topic of interest to modern writers on the subject of child-care and advice to mothers appears frequently in various magazine articles. The pendulum has swung from a rather casual approach in the 1950s to a more structured advice in the 1960s and it is likely that conflicting advice may often be given to a mother depending on whether she listens to her own mother, her neighbours, the health visitor or the doctor in the maternity and child welfare clinic. Caldwell (1964) in a survey of trends in the time of starting toilet training concludes that this has been gradually postponed over the past 30 years or so. Caldwell (1964) also comments that it is a universal training situation, i.e. learning not to soil within the immediate living area is expected of infants in every human social group that has been observed. This is not confined to humans for piglets learn to excrete in a corner of the pen away from the lying area and it appears that those piglets reared without their mothers have a random pattern of elimination and are continually dirty (Laird 1973).

Studies on the reaction of the child to bowel training (Huschka 1942; Sears, Maccoby & Levin 1957) indicate that this varies in accordance with both age of beginning training and the severity of training procedures. The greatest degree of upset is associated with severe training carried out by a cold and undemonstrative mother (Caldwell 1964).

Huschka (1942) using clinical case histories, found an association between training began before 8 months of age and completed by 18 months and emotional disturbance in the children. Prugh (1953–54) found a higher incidence of constipation and faecal incontinence in boys (and to a lesser extent girls) who had been trained early and coercively according to Huschka's (1942) criteria. Both studies are open to criticism on the grounds of unreliability of parents accounts of past toilet training.

Anthony (1957) set out to investigate the alleged causal relationships between bowel training, bowel functioning and the presence of certain subsequent negative attitudes in the children. The initial focus on the act of soil-

ing and the precipitating affect proved fruitless as abnormal toilet functioning had by then become an automatic and stereotyped activity. The abnormal
training methods of mothers of soiling children then became the main subject
for investigation. Anthony (1957) draws attention to the 'potting couple', a
situation between mother and child which has a system of stimulus cues for
communication. Under normal conditions, the mother responds promptly
to the child's physiological cues and her own communications in return make
the child aware of his own cues so that he is able to achieve eventual autonomy in bowel function. However, there were some mothers in the study who
missed stimulus cues so that their child's learning became deficient, and
others who misinterpreted cues and responded inappropriately without
regularly reinforcing the appropriate behaviour.

There are difficulties in the hypothesis that abnormal training methods
lead to bowel dysfunction. Not all children who are coercively trained develop
faecal soiling, and not all children who have bowel dysfunction experience
abnormal training. Finally primitive children with deviant training according
to our standards do not appear prone to bowel dysfunction. Anthony suggests
that the degree of coercion is but one factor within the context of the total
mother–child situation and may have different effects depending on the
mother's motivation and degree of general responsiveness to the child's needs.

Anthony (1957) used an ingenious experimental method to study the connections between methods of toilet training and encopresis (defined as the
regular passage of a formed motion of normal consistency into clothes, bedclothes or any receptacle not intended for the purpose). Seventy-six clinic
children aged 4–15 years of age were studied and at least 3 types of soiling
were identified: (a) continuous—children who do not appear to have ever
been continent and whose soiling is part of a general messiness and a lack of
concern for cleanliness; (b) discontinuous—children with faecal soiling in
contrast to the orderly tenor and cleanliness of their everyday life. They
usually have normal stools with a few showing episodic retention; and
(c) retentive—children with stubborn constipation later giving way to soiling.
Statistically significant associations were found between continuous soiling
and neglectful training and between coercive training and the discontinuous
and the retentive group.

Anthony's (1957) paper contains a mass of clinical observations and vivid
descriptions of parental attitudes, family interactions and children's behaviour. It is often difficult to separate the statistically significant findings from
the rest of the detail and therefore to discern the frequency of the differentiating factors between the 3 groups for the descriptions are composite rather
than discrete.

CLASSIFICATION

There have been many schemes of classification in the literature on soiling (Anthony 1957; Pinkerton 1958; Coekin & Gairdner 1960; Easson 1960; Davidson *et al* 1963; Woodmansey 1967). These have emphasised variables such as constitutional factors in bowel function, psychodynamic factors in the child, deviant parent–child relationships and expectations with regard to bowel training.

The different findings in these clinical studies and the conclusions drawn from them are very likely to be artefacts of the different clinical populations seen by paediatricians and psychiatrists. Paediatricians are more likely to see younger children from socially disadvantaged homes whose soiling is due to faulty training (Berg & Jones 1964), or cases of retention with overflow (Mac-Carthy 1976; Jolly 1976). They are less likely to see the older child whose pattern of faecal soiling is more fixed and often associated with gross personal psychopathology and family problems which make treatment difficult, for these are usually referred to the psychiatrist. The classification put forward in this chapter is based on the description of the soiling behaviour which is used to identify the psychological mechanisms leading to the soiling. From this a rational treatment plan can be derived.

It is necessary to distinguish between faecal soiling: (a) where it is known that there is adequate bowel control in the sense that the child can control the physiological process of defaecation but deposits his normal faeces in inappropriate places; (b) cases where there is a true failure to gain bowel control as shown by the fact that the child is either unaware that he is soiling, or while being aware, is unable to control his bowels; and (c) cases in which the soiling is due to excessively fluid faeces, this may be a result of diarrhoea due to physical disease or anxiety or may arise from constipation leading to retention with overflow.

In the first group where bowel control has been adequately established, stools are normal, but control may break down temporarily in circumstances of psychological stress (for example, the birth of a sibling, admission to hospital, starting at school or a traumatic separation from parents). Usually control is regained when stress is relieved provided the situation is well managed and the home environment is stable. In other circumstances of psychological stress arising from parental dysharmony, family instability and punitive management the child may respond by depositing his faeces in unlikely places, often, it appears, to cause maximum irritation to his family; there may also be smearing of faeces and other evidence of psychiatric disorder including anti-social behaviour. At the same time the children often show massive denial of soiling and covert aggressiveness in their dealing with other family members.

In the second group with failure to learn bowel control, the stools are normal in consistency and appearance, but deposited randomly in clothes often both at school and at home. A few children may suffer from severe mental retardation or neurological disorders such as cerebral palsy or spina bifida which impair the capacity to learn bowel control. Others who are of normal intelligence and without major physical handicap are usually younger than average, also suffer from enuresis, are behind at school, socially aggressive and come from socially disadvantaged families where parents may be limited in personality and intellect (Anthony 1957; Easson 1960; Berg & Jones 1964; Rutter 1975). The reasons for failure to gain control may lie in faulty or inconsistent training or in stresses interfering with the acquisition of control during the toddler training period.

In the third group the stools are abnormal in appearance and consistency, such as occurs in gastrointestinal disease and ulcerative colitis. Diarrhoea can also occur in states of severe anxiety under stress or when a child has to confront a situation which is greatly feared. In other children who pass small amounts of foul watery stools, examination may reveal faecal masses in a palpable colon, a normal anal reflex but a rectum packed with hard faeces so that retention with overflow is present. There may be a history of an episode of painful defaecation possibly due to an anal fissure with holding back of stools and eventual constipation and impaction. In other cases there is a history of a constant struggle between parent and child over bowel training and use of the lavatory, associated with reluctance to open bowels and faecal retention in the mother's presence or near a pot or toilet (Garrard & Richmond 1952; Anthony 1957; Pinkerton 1958; Call *et al* 1963; Woodmansey 1967).

Faecal soiling unlike enuresis occurs most commonly during the day but occasionally the child may pass formed stools in the bedclothes. A rarer form of soiling at night is due to anal masturbation where bedclothes are stained but formed stools are only rarely passed. Children will usually deny behaving in this way but inspection of fingernails will often show faecal material and so give a clue to the anal masturbation.

ASSOCIATED FACTORS

Social class

The influence of social class is not looked at in most of the reported studies. Stein and Susser (1967) found that the occupational class of parents did not influence the attainment of sphincter control in preschool children and Rutter *et al* (1970) found no significant association between encopresis and social class in the Isle of Wight study. Anthony (1957) stated that children who soiled continuously from infancy were commonly found in families from the lower social classes. However, Olatawura (1973) also found 26 cases of 'discontinuous' encopresis as defined by Anthony (1957) among 32 encopretic children coming from low socioeconomic status families so that the differentiation by social class is not a reliable index.

Constitutional factors

Coekin and Gairdner (1960) analysed 69 cases of soiling and found 44 in which they maintained soiling could be very simply accounted for on a mechanical basis with primary constipation. A history of constipation in the first 6 months of life was present in 12 (27 per cent) of these 44 cases. They gave case histories to support their contention of a congenital basis for constipation in these children and argue that in the remaining 7 per cent of cases a congenital factor provided a predisposition to later constipation and soiling, triggered off by apparently trivial incidents. This view of constipation and soiling as a congenital condition finds little support apart from Davidson *et al* (1963) who write of a predisposition to constipation and formed stools rendering the child more amenable to toilet training and consequent early control over defaecation.

Psychogenic factors in the child

Coekin and Gairdner (1960) also judged psychogenic factors to play an important or predominant part in a smaller group of cases and feel the term encopresis is more appropriately applied to these. There was less evidence of constipation and only a few showed faecal masses in the abdomen so that in the majority the stool passed was of normal consistency but was studiously deposited in the wrong place. They remarked, too, that nearly all the children showed obvious signs of emotional disorder and many came from 'unsatisfactory' homes.

Mother–child relationships

The psychogenic aspects of soiling have been very fully described in the early literature with the emphasis on the quality of toilet training carried out by mothers and the nature of the mother–child relationship and maternal personality. Pinkerton (1958) found that 57 per cent of 30 cases of encopresis had suffered primary coercive training with the majority showing evidence of tension between mother and child which had been described by Anthony

(1957) as 'the battle of the bowel'. Pinkerton (1958) assumed that the children responded to the rigid perfectionistic parents' demands with retention of stools and later soiling. Bell and Levine (1954) also espouse the notion of coercive training but Prugh (1954) concludes that although early training may indeed be coercive, the mother's personality and the character of the mother–child relationship are more important. Anthony (1957) suggests that coercive training is only one factor within the context of the total mother–child relationship. Easson (1960) invokes maternal ambivalence towards the child's needs for autonomy and independence as a factor in soiling and regards it and constipation as signs of family pathology. Kessler (1960) mentions the existence of pregnancy wishes with retention of stools as the symbolic expression of these wishes. Bellman (1966) described mothers of encopretic children as anxious, unreliable, emotional, overprotective and indulgent while also reacting to soiling in boys by anger punishment and beating. Such mothers used coercive training methods to a greater extent and had higher expectations of early bowel control than the parents of the control group. Although the study compares the findings in an experimental and control group the measures of parental attitudes and behaviour were of doubtful validity and reliability.

Family pathology

Later papers on supposed family factors (Bemporad *et al* 1971; Hoag *et al* 1971) have not given convincing data of any particular pattern of family structure and function which can be clearly differentiated from that found in other types of childhood psychiatric disorder, although Wolters (1974) found a high frequency of family dysharmony and marital problems.

Developmental factors in the child

Slow language development and poor coordination had also been noted (Bemporad *et al* 1971) while Olatawura (1973) recorded low intelligence, neurological impairment and associated neurotic and developmental disorder among his group of 'discontinuous' encopretics. McTaggart and Scott (1959) described enuresis, stubbornness and negativism, immature speech, hyperactivity, temper tantrums, withdrawal, school phobia, feeding problems, transvestism and fire-setting as associated factors among 10 out of 12 children with encopresis. It is difficult to decide from the above data whether such behaviour is primary or secondary to the encopresis, although Bellman (1966) inclines to the view that those factors observed among the children in her sample were probably aetiological rather than secondary to encopresis.

There is also confusion in the literature over the significance of soiling as an indicator of psychiatric disorder. Some authors regard it as evidence of serious general disturbance in psychological function, others as a developmental disorder in itself with persistent soiling leading to secondary disturbances of affect, interpersonal behaviour and relationships. In younger children successful treatment of the soiling apparently results in the concomitant disappearance of the associated symptoms and improvement in disturbed parent–child relationships. In older children, however, both the soiling and the associated difficulties have proved more difficult to alter for the better.

MANAGEMENT

Management of the individual case depends on assessment of the type of faecal soiling and the mechanisms responsible for its occurrence (see section on classification).

In the pattern of soiling seen mainly in younger children when the child has failed to gain bowel control some form of bowel training is needed as well as attention to the wider social and psychological problems which are usually found in the families of these children. Various procedures can be used such as simple 'star charts' recording success in using the toilet regularly, or more complex schemes of material and social reinforcement contingent on normal defaecation in the toilet (Gelber & Meyer 1965; Lai & Lindsley 1968; Pedrini & Pedrini 1970; Conger 1970; Edelman 1971; Neale 1963; Sluckin 1975).

In those cases where soiling is due to secondary overflow of loose motions from partial blockage of the bowel, examination will reveal the reasons for this in the form of palpable faecal masses on abdominal examination as well as a packed rectum on digital examination. This clinical picture can arise in different ways. A young child may experience pain on defaecation due to the passage of large hard faeces or a lesion such as an anal fissure. He comes to fear going to the lavatory, holds back his faeces and becomes constipated. In severe cases there is a diminution in the normal call to stool (Nixon 1975) so that the previously existing regular pattern is now disrupted and increasing faecal impaction occurs. A second mechanism leading to retention comes into play when there is struggle between parent and child over toilet training. A parent using strict coercive methods and punishment may encounter a child striving for autonomy who refuses to open his bowels on demand. This response may increase punitive attempts to make the child conform, leading to negativism and fearfulness in the child and finally severe constipation, bowel distension and overflow of fluid faeces.

In both instances the first line of treatment is to clear the blockage of faeces in the bowel for this will remove pain and fear especially in the younger child and prevent gross impaction of faeces in the pelvis which may cause retention of urine (MacCarthy 1976). Bowel washouts are considered appropriate in severe cases (Nixon 1973), but this approach is criticised by Berg and Jones (1964) and Jolly (1976) on the grounds that it merely produces temporary emptying of the bowels without dealing with the basic psychological mechanisms of retention. For this reason many clinicians favour enemas initially, either a phosphate enema or the use of microenemata containing sodium alkylsulphoacetate (Micralax). Then the child is put on to a regular bowel training programme using senna laxatives (Senokot) usually with a stool softener, such as dioctyl sodium sulphosuccinate (Dioctyl-Medo), or lactulose (Duphalac) to ensure the passage of soft painless stools. Any painful anal conditions should be treated, but it is often more important to try to alter the struggle between parent and child over toilet training along with other faulty patterns of interaction. Sometimes methods of bowel training using systematic reinforcement have been effective without parent participation (Neale 1963; Young & Goldsmith 1972) but there are many advantages in involving parents in the retraining programme. Tensions may exist in the family so that the soiling child is liable to be scapegoated for general uncleanliness and negative behaviour, and some form of parental counselling is usually required to ensure that treatment is carried out systematically and not given up if immediate success is not achieved.

Those children who have apparently achieved bowel control and then begin soiling as part of a more general psychiatric disorder often prove difficult to treat because of abnormal emotional and behavioural traits in the child and deviant parental and family attitudes toward the developing child's emotional and social needs. Such children may need a combination of different forms of treatment aimed in the first instance at relieving constipation followed by a system of simple rewards for regular toilet use (Neale 1963). More often the child suffers much shame guilt and anxiety and his family shows obsessional traits and overconcern about cleanliness requiring some form of psychotherapy to deal with these attitudes and other problems of family interaction. A bowel training programme may be difficult to carry out while family tensions are high but can be introduced effectively at a later stage if the soiling is continuing as a habit.

Young and Goldsmith (1972) describe an interesting combination of individual psychotherapy, milieu therapy and behaviour modification in the treatment of a 9-year-old boy attending a day-treatment centre. Encopresis began aged 7 years during a visit to a relative and this was associated with enuresis, anxiety, uncleanliness, petty stealing and compulsive collecting. Two years of individual psychotherapy and parental case-work and environmental manipulation had little effect on the course of the encopresis which flared up in stress situations of separations, the rejection by peers, fear of a teacher and crisis situations at home. A behaviour modification programme was set up in which the boy chose his own reinforcers and took part in buying them. With improvement in soiling this formerly meek, submissive and passive boy displayed violent physical attacks on his peers, disruptive classroom behaviour and aggressive acting-out in therapy sessions. A similar behaviour pattern is reported by Balson (1973) in a treatment programme of an 8-year-old boy using an extinction schedule for soiling and behaviour rehearsal with the parents helping them reinforce appropriate behaviour by expressing verbal attention in new ways while avoiding reinforcing soiling behaviour. Both case-reports discuss the issue of symptom substitution and conclude that the aggressive behaviour was probably primary, so that successful treatment of the secondary (defensive) soiling led to its reemergence. Young and Goldsmith (1972) also point out that the parents did not participate at all in the treatment programme beyond providing clean underwear but that the change in behaviour did generalise to the child's total living situation, although it was entirely carried out in the day-centre.

Results of treatment

Bellman (1966) in a follow-up of 186 children with encopresis seen at two psychiatric clinics found a steady decline of the symptoms from age of 6 in boys and 8 in girls until it disappeared in all by 16 years, except for relapses in two cases at 17 and 19 years respectively. There are no controlled trials of treatment so that the relative effectiveness of different types of treatment is most difficult to judge. Coekin and Gairdner (1960) and Davidson *et al* (1963) claim a high success rate (80 per cent–90 per cent) in soiling with constipation using laxatives and enemas. Good results with psychotherapy are claimed by McTaggart and Scott (1959) with 10 out of 12 children either cured or improved, while Pinkerton (1958) recorded success in 21 or 30 cases using three techniques of eliciting fantasy, free drawing and expression of aggression. Berg and Jones (1964) claim freedom from symptoms for a minimum of 6 months in 33 out of 38 cases (87 per cent) with severe constipation using a combination of oral laxatives and simple psychological treatment. The results were also good (8 out of 10 cases) in those with training problems without constipation.

CONCLUSIONS

The evidence to date suggests a multifactorial aetiology for faecal soiling in which physiological predisposition to a particular pattern of bowel function may play a part, together with the age at which bowel training is begun and the methods of training used by parents. Parent–child relationships, family structure and function and environmental stresses are also influential, possibly more so in those cases of soiling which are part of a general psychiatric disorder. It is clear that no single treatment will suffice for the varieties of soiling encountered in clinical practice. A programme embodying several methods of treatment, including counselling, psychotherapy and behaviour modification in various combinations as well as the use of laxatives and softeners is best set up in terms of the type of faecal soiling and the mechanisms responsible. These methods will be effective in the majority of children treated as outpatients but in some difficult problems the resources of a day-hospital or an inpatient unit may be required.

REFERENCES

ANTHONY E.J. (1957) An experimental approach to the psychopathology of childhood: encopresis. *Brit. J. Med. Psychol.* **30,** 146–175

BAKWIN H. & BAKWIN R. (1953) *Clinical Management of Behaviour Disorders in Children.* Philadelphia: W.B. Saunders

BALSON P.M. (1973) Case study: Encopresis. A case with symptom substitution. *Behav. Ther.* **4,** 134–136

BELL A.I. & LEVINE M.I. (1954) The psychological aspects of paediatric practice. I: Causes and treatment of chronic constipation. *Pediatrics* **14,** 259–266

BELLMAN M. (1966) Studies on encopresis. *Acta Paediat. Scand.* Suppl. 170

BEMPORAD J.L., PFEIFER C.M., GIBB L., CORTNER R.H. & BLOOM W. (1971) Characteristics of encopretic patients and their families. *J. Amer. Acad. Child. Psychiat.* **10,** 272–292

BERG I. & JONES K.V. (1964) Functional faecal incontinence in children. *Arch. Dis. Child.* **39,** 465–472

BRAZELTON T.B. (1962) A child-oriented approach to toilet training. *Pediatrics* **29,** 121–128

CALDWELL B.M. (1964) 'The effects of infant care'. *In* Hoffman M.L. & Hoffman L.W. (eds.) *Review of Child Development Research,* vol. 1. New York: Russell Sage Foundation

CALL J.D., CHRISTIANSON M., PENROSE F.R. & BACKLAR M. (1963) Psychogenic megacolon in three pre-school boys. A study of aetiology through collaborative treatment of child and parents. *Amer. J. Orthopsychiat.* **33,** 923–928

COEKIN M. & GAIRDNER D. (1960) Faecal incontinence in children. *Brit. Med. J.* **2,** 1175–1180

CONGER J.C. (1970) The treatment of encopresis by the management of social consequences. *Behav. Ther.* **1,** 386–390

DAVIDSON M., KUGLER M. & BAUER C. (1963) Diagnosis and management in children with severe and protracted constipation and obstipation. *J. Pediatrics* **62,** 261–275

DAVIE R., BUTLER N. & GOLDSTEIN H. (1972) *From Birth to Seven.* London: Longman

DUTHIE H.L. & GAIRNS F.W. (1960) Sensory nerve endings and sensation in the anal region of man. *Brit. J. Surg.* **47**, 585–595

EASSON W.M. (1960) Encopresis—psychogenic soiling. *Canad. Med. Assoc. J.* **82**, 624–628

EDELMAN R.I. (1971) Operant conditioning treatment of Encopresis. *J. Behav. Ther. Exper. Psychiat.* **2**, 71–73

GARRARD S.D. & RICHMOND J.B. (1952) Psychogenic megacolon manifested by faecal soiling. *Pediatrics* **10**, 474–481

GASTON E.A. (1948) The physiology of fecal continence. *Surg. Gynecol. Obstet.* **87**, 280–290

GELBER H. & MEYER V. (1965) Behaviour therapy and encopresis: the complexities involved in treatment. *Behav. Res. Ther.* **2**, 227–231

GESELL A., ILG F.L. & AMES L.B. (1974) *Infant and Child in the Culture of Today*, (revised edn.) New York: Harper & Row

HALLGREN B. (1956) Enuresis. I: a study with reference to the morbidity risk and symptomatology. *Acta Psychiat. Scand.* **31**, 379–403

HOAG J.M., NORRISS N.G., HIMENO E.T. & JACOBS J. (1971) The encopretic child and his family. *J. Amer. Acad. Child Psychiat.* **10**, 242–256

HUSCHKA M. (1942) The child's response to coerceive bowel training. *Psychosom. Med.* **4**, 301–308

JOLLY H. (1976) A paediatrician's views on the management of encopresis. *Proc. roy. Soc. Med.* **69**, 21–22

KESSLER J.W. (1960) *Psychopathology of Childhood.* New Jersey: Prentice-Hall

LAI H. & LINDSLEY O.R. (1968) Therapy of chronic constipation in a young child by arranging social contingencies. *Behav. Res. Ther.* **6**, 484–485

LAIRD R. (1973) The excretory habits of piglets. *In* Kolvin I., MacKeith R. & Meadow S.R. (eds.) *Bladder Control and Enuresis.* Clinics in Develop. Med. nos. 48/49. London: SIMP/Heinemann

MACCARTHY D. (1976) Encopresis. *Proc. roy. Soc. Med.*, **69**, 19–20

MCTAGGART A. & SCOTT M. (1959) A review of twelve cases of encopresis. *J. Pediatrics* **54**, 762–768

NEALE D.H. (1963) Behaviour therapy and encopresis in children. *Behav. Res. Ther.* **1**, 139–149

NIXON H. (1961) *In* Discussion on megacolon and megarectum. *Proc. roy. Soc. Med.* **54**, 1037

NIXON H. (1973) Sphincter cripples. *Proc. roy. Soc. Med.* **66**, 575–578

NIXON H. (1975) The diagnosis and management of faecal incontinence in children. *Arch. Chirurg. Neerlandicum* **27**, 171–177

OLATAWURA M. (1973) Encopresis: A review of thirty-two cases. *Acta Paediat. Scand.* **62**, 358–364

PARKS A. (1975) Anorectal incontinence. *Proc. roy. Soc. Med.* **68**, 21–30

PEDRINI B. & PEDRINI D.T. (1970) Reinforcement procedures in control of encopresis. A case study. *Psychol. Rep.* **28**, 937–938

PINKERTON P. (1958) Psychogenic megacolon in children: The implications of bowel negativism. *Archiv. Dis. Childh.* **33**, 371–380

PRUGH D.G. (1954) Childhood experience and colonic disorder. *Ann. N.Y. Acad. Sci.* **58**, 355–376

QUAY H.C. & WERRY J.S. (1972) *Psychopathological Disorders in Childhood*. New York: Wiley

ROBERTSON P. (1976) Home as a nest: Middle class childhood in nineteenth-century Europe. *In* de Mause L. (ed.) *The History of Childhood*. London: Souvenir Press

RUTTER M., TIZARD J. & WHITMORE K. (eds.) (1970) *Education, Health and Behaviour*. London: Longman

RUTTER M. (1975) *Helping Troubled Children*. Harmondsworth: Penguin

SEARS R.R., MACCOBY E.E. & LEVIN H. (1957) *Patterns of Child Rearing*. Evanston, Illinois: Row Peterson

SLUCKIN A. (1975) Encopresis: a behavioural approach described. *Social Work Today* **5**, 643–646

STEIN Z. & SUSSER M. (1967) Social factors in the development of sphincter control. *Develop. Med. Child Neurol.* **9**, 692–706

WHITING J.W. & CHILD I.L. (1953) *Child Training and Personality*. New Haven: Yale University Press

WOLTERS W.H.G. (1974) Kinderin mit Encopresis, een psychosomatische benadering. Utrecht: Elinkivijk BV

WOODMANSEY A.C. (1967) Emotion and the motions: an inquiry into the causes and prevention of functional disorders of defecation. *Brit. J. Med. Psychol.* **40**, 207–223

YOUNG I. & GOLDSMITH A. (1972) Treatment of encopresis in a day treatment program. *Psychother. Theory Res. Pract.* **9**, 231–235

CHAPTER 26

Drug taking

H. BLUMBERG

The literature on the nonmedical use of drugs is by now a very large one, with contributions from many disciplines, including psychiatry, psychology, sociology, anthropology, education, and psychopharmacology. The main concerns have been: (a) to estimate prevalence; (b) to understand the aetiology, process, and results of using drugs; and (c) to understand how such knowledge speaks to the practical business of helping those in need.

PREVALENCE

Drug taking is nearly universal if one includes all cases of substances being intentionally used in a *nonmedical, non-nutritional context for psychological, physical, and/or social effect*. The relative benefits and difficulties from drug use cannot all be easily sorted out. 'Excess' (or 'dependence') cannot be partitioned by any single fine line: one of the few characteristics that, in general, probably does hold across drugs and large samples of people is that frequency of use is *not* biomodal (as would be the case if a distinct group of people used a drug in large quantities), but rather the distribution of use (and potential use) forms a smooth curve, and increasingly large usages show progressively smaller numbers of people (Smart & Fejer 1971). One can invoke semi-arbitrary points to define probable effects, e.g. 100 ml daily intake of absolute alcohol is associated with pathologies such as liver cirrhosis (cited by Smart & Fejer 1971). The probability that 'trying a drug will be followed by frequent use' varies a great deal from one population to another, and the particular drug(s) for which this is likely also varies across populations. A much needed review of the literature on psychosocial correlates of adolescent drug use has been prepared by Braucht et al (1973).

The widespread use of a drug need not be cause for concern, but a summary of prevalence rates is helpful in providing some perspective as regards drug use. Having some idea of the numbers of people involved serves as part of the necessary background for sensible discussion and policies.

628

The results of over 50 pre-1970 American surveys, mostly of undergraduates and secondary school students, have been summarised in tabular form by Berg (1970; additional studies of relevance are cited in works by Advena 1972; Blumberg 1975; Pearlman 1969).

If one excludes studies with exceptionally low response rates or unrepresentative samples, the approximate ranges, among high school students, for rates of drug use ('ever tried') were: marijuana, 9 per cent (1967 females in San Mateo County, California) to 42 per cent (1969 males, same county); LSD, 2 to 7 per cent (but more recent studies tend to show higher rates); barbiturates, 3 to 15 per cent (as tabulated for only a few studies); opiates, 1 to 4 per cent. Corresponding figures for undergraduates: marijuana, 23 to 59 per cent (lower in one or two studies); LSD mostly 4 to 5 per cent; amphetamines (only a few samples), 7 to 26 per cent; barbiturates, 1 to 12 per cent; opiate-type drugs, 1 to 4 per cent.

It seems clear that prevalences can increase markedly in a relatively short time (e.g. see Fejer *et al* 1972; San Mateo County 1972) and that there is no single pattern of correlates with drug use.

At the time of these studies, users in most secondary schools still constituted a minority group who (more often than nonusers in some samples) were regarded as troublemakers at school and were given lower grades; whereas users in some colleges and universities were close to becoming a majority and were doing comparatively well in their studies.

As regards use at the undergraduate level, Gergen *et al* (1972) carried out a survey of 5050 people in a clustered random sample of all American college students. Prevalences (use ever) were as follows: alcohol 59 per cent, marijuana 37 per cent, hallucinogens 12 per cent, stimulants and depressants 8 per cent, heroin and/or cocaine 2 per cent. In a survey of 9000 students at seven selected British universities and colleges, cannabis prevalences ranged from about 10 per cent to about 39 per cent (Hawks *et al* 1971; Kosviner *et al* 1974).

CROSS-NATIONAL CONTRASTS

Examination of the results of recent studies in over a dozen countries suggests that the diversity of patterns (of prevalence and correlates) across nations is commensurate with the diversity among various British, Canadian, and American samples (Blumberg 1975). The tendency to treat drug use as a criminal act rather than as a 'medical problem' or simply a social phenomenon persists in many countries.

Student attitudes toward use of drugs have been found by Gordon (1972) to be similarly favourable in six different Westernised nations, though less positive in Finland and Sweden than in Canada, Denmark, the Netherlands, and the United States. As an example of a cross-cultural effect, Sargent (1971) has demonstrated that attitudinal differences between cultural groups within the Australian undergraduate population can be manifest in behaviour such as relative likelihood of drinking patterns—abstinent (Chinese), ritual (Jewish), convivial (Japanese), and utilitarian (abstention or heavy drinking, among Australian-born).

Almost dramatic evidence of the degree to which patterns of drug use can be culture-specific is to be found in Westermeyer's (1971) account of the use of opium and alcohol by the Meo of Laos, a tribal group of Asian mountaineers. Opium is freely available, smoked by about 10 per cent of the group, and generally neither leads to addiction nor interferes with ability to work.

DETERMINANTS AND CORRELATES

Social factors

Like much other behaviour, the use of any drug invariably follows from *both* social and personal factors. If a given drug ritual has been taken up by most people in a particular social network (e.g., the use of marijuana or alcohol by students in a particular class), then personal factors are largely irrelevant to initiation. Social factors predominate—usually called 'peer influence' but including any inputs from the social/communications network. In other words, one of the reasons why people may start to use a drug is that their friends do so and have favourable attitudes towards use. Special processes do not have to be invoked to account for 'social influences in drug taking' (much less for the taking of any particular drug or drugs), for a very large social-psychological literature documents conformity to social norms (see Blumberg 1976) in such diverse matters as subjects agreeing with people's 'estimates' of the lengths of lines and passersby joining a crowd that is looking up at a building. The relevant literature is a bit weak in the systematic explanation of how these influences operate, but people are probably 'ready to learn' to model others' behaviour from an early age and such modelling is positively rewarded in many social situations, especially when the source person is held in high regard (cf. Mettlin 1973). Certain general principles have been documented: conformity is more likely if the 'correct' response is ambiguous, if the group agreeing with the behaviour is large, if the group is unanimous, and if there are negative sanctions (expressed displeasure or other penalties from others) for violating the behavioural norm. Termination of use can be part of the initial innovation (e.g. conformity to a norm to 'try a drug a few times') and/or can be a separate innovation (a wave of termination following a wave of use).

Personal factors

To the extent that a particular drug ritual comes to apply only to some of the people in a social network, individual factors will be relevant. These have to do with personal background and development, motivation, learning, and personality.

Background and development

Some of the relevant studies, by no means all, have found significant relationships between family background and various forms of drug use. The most frequent significant correlations are with parents' drug use, socioeconomic status (generally positive with use of cannabis and LSD), and absence of one or both parents in childhood (cf. Streit & Oliver 1972). Although a minority group (e.g. upper class or parent-absent) may in some cases be *overrepresented*, they typically still form a minority of the sample of drug users in question.

Motivation

People may use drugs in order to satisfy a variety of common (not mutually exclusive) needs (cf. Blumberg *et al* 1974a) among them, needs for (a) affiliation, (b) curiosity, sensation (Farley & Dionne 1972; Moran 1970; Zuckerman *et al* 1970) and what Weil (1972b) describes as a universal drive to experience altered states of consciousness, (c) recreation, and (d) anxiety reduction and general drive reduction (Baum 1970; Buies 1971). Continued heavy use of a drug may be associated with the maintenance of a particular physiological and/or psychological equilibrium—as has most clearly been documented in the case of tobacco (see DeLong 1972a; Dunn 1973; Evans 1969; Holden 1968, and recent issues of *Psychopharmacology Abstracts* and *Psychopharmacology Bulletin*).

Learning

Regardless of the particular needs in question any behaviour is likely to be repeated if it is rewarding (i.e. directly or indirectly drive-reducing) or if its cessation is punishing. Both operant and classical conditioning (cf. Gilbert

& Keehn 1973) provide a framework for understanding the baseline properties, if not the richer context, of drug use among young people.

Computer simulations and studies based on nonhuman populations are
useful in framing potentially valid paradigms. For instance, according to one
series of studies, mice [but not rats] that have received LSD or cannabis show
significant reductions in the frequency of aggressive postures; and various
animals receiving LSD or cannabis became more likely to aggregate with one
another (Siegel 1971).

Personality and psychiatric factors

There is not a large amount of consistency in tests employed or in significant
findings, either within or across drugs. In a number of cases—if one had to
make generalisations—drug users would be expected to be low on authoritarianism, low on aggression (higher for alcohol-only, court or. prison
samples), high on extraversion, and high on anxiety (especially for clinic and
psychiatric samples). Using approximately matched groups of females, Baldinger *et al* (1972) found that college marijuana smokers were in essence less
authoritarian than: college nondrug users, noncollege nondrug users, and
noncollege heroin users.

If one simply lists some of the correlates with drug use found recently
by different researchers in various populations, the results are quite contradictory. Clearly, personality correlates (if any) with drug use depend to
a large extent on the specific population and the particular measures chosen
by a given investigator.

Interrelation of factors

As a start in sorting out the various correlates of drug use, let us consider
one recent analysis of data based on a particular drug and population (cannabis among British university students). As with most processes of role
learning and diffusion of innovation, the use of any drug requires several
steps—exposure, decision to try, first use, later use. (This is like the persuasion process in the information-processing paradigm for attitude change—
see McGuire 1972 for the steps and measuring operations.)

One might have imagined that background and social variables (such as
socioeconomic status, and the 'number of people gone out with') would operate more at the level of *exposure* (how many times have you been 'present
when someone was using' a particular drug?) whereas motivation and personality variables would operate more at the level of *yielding* (considering
only those who have been exposed: 'Have you ever used' the drug?), and
some of the attitudinal variables might change in tandem with use.

However, what was in fact found in analysing the cannabis data (collected in the survey by Hawks *et al* 1971; Kosviner *et al* 1974) was that most of the variables which predicted use were significantly operative for *both* exposure *and* yielding. Findings were replicated on a separate sample. The list of such items included secondary school truancy, nonscience course, no religion nor main political party, heavier alcohol and tobacco use, number of people gone out with, 'less purpose', and various consonant attitude items about drug use and Western society. Were these items themselves significantly intercorrelated or did they operate independently? Nearly all of the variables that were associated with cannabis use were directly or indirectly linked together, but the two samples yielded different patterns as to which variables were directly linked to which other variables. In other words, even for this particular drug and culture, there is no demonstrated orderly process of cause and effect for either exposure or yielding, but rather there is a (varying) network of variables which are simultaneously integrated with both exposure and yielding.

SPECIFIC DRUGS AND DRUG CLASSES

In this section are described the main concluions of various recent studies and reviews. The amount and content of research have varied for different drugs.

Cannabis

Several investigators have provided carefully detailed reports regarding marijuana use. According to Grinspoon (1969)—whose review emphasises historical, clinical, medical and psychological factors—evidence suggests that marijuana is not addictive and that physiological effects, if any, are slight (cf. Snyder 1971; Paton & Crown 1972).

Tart (1970) has compiled an extensive description of the sensations of marijuana intoxication, divided into the following categories: visual (e.g. 'If I try to visualise something, I see it in my mind's eye more sharply'), auditory (e.g. 'I can hear more subtle changes in sounds'), taste, smell, space-time perception, perception of the body, physical movement, interpersonal relations (e.g. 'I empathise tremendously with others'), sexual, thought processes, memory functioning, emotions, self-control, sense of identity, and sleep.

Some social contexts of marijuana use have been described and analysed by Goode (1969), who also considers the question of progression to opiates. Some studies, based on special populations such as adolescents in New York City with criminal convictions, 'have largely upheld' the hypothesis of progression among some users; 'others have found the existence or absence of the relationship almost entirely contingent on neighbourhood, style of use and 'type' of user, and the existence of a subculture of illicit drug use; still other studies have found that heroin use among marijuana users is virtually absent' (Goode 1969, pp. 48–49).

Messer concludes that marijuana use is especially interesting not as a dependent variable, but for its predictive value for a number of variables some of which comprise a 'normative system which has taken on the proportions of a social movement . . . to . . . a radically redefined world view' (Messer 1969, pp. 96–97).

Hallucinogens

In his extensive review of the experimental and impressionistic literature dealing with the use of LSD and other hallucinogens, Buckman (1971) describes prevalence and reasons for use, characteristics of users, the nature of the LSD experience (with emphasis on transcendental aspects), possible dangers, and reactions of society. In the conclusions to his paper, Buckman states, 'The real dangers of informal taking of LSD certainly do exist, but they are related to the personality of the user and the lack of preparation and support before, during, and after the session' (Buckman 1971, p. 173; cf. Abruzzi 1974).

Amphetamines and barbiturates

Despite the fact that they are so widely used by adult populations relatively little research has dealt specifically with young people's use of amphetamines and barbiturates (see Brook *et al* 1974). McGrath (1970) has presented a profile of adolescent pill users who appeared before an American juvenile court. An interview/questionnaire study of 218 young amphetamine users in metropolitan Toronto (volunteers) did not reveal any single prototype or profile of the user or his culture (Levine *et al* 1972). Carey and Mandel (1968) have described the San Francisco 'speed scene', emphasising the need to take into account not only drug effects but also the social and legal setting of use.

Overdose is a particular hazard associated with the use of barbiturates (oral or injected), although the probability of overdose is low on any one occasion. The problem arises especially because tolerance develops to the psychoactive effects (one needs progressively more for the same effect) while the fatal dose remains relatively constant. (At the very least anyone who insists on using barbiturates should be warned about this property.)

Tolerance to amphetamines develops rapidly. Heavy use, which may be associated with general difficulties in functioning, is apt to be only temporary. Cocaine has effects similar to those of amphetamines (but toxic amounts may be more likely to be taken) (DeLong 1972a).

Opiate-type drugs

With some exceptions, the frequent self-injection of opiate-type drugs is uncommon among overall populations of people under 20 years of age (Bransby *et al* 1973; DuPont 1971; Hager *et al* 1971; Hawks 1971; Klein & Philips 1968; Ramer *et al* 1972; Rathod 1972; see also, DeFleur *et al* 1969; Glaser *et al* 1971; Kramer 1972; Rosenberg 1968; Sells 1967; Stimson & Ogborne 1970).

In many locales increases in prevalence rates have been found to be temporary (e.g. see Harris 1973). A main concern is that addiction, method of administration, and the social-legal context can act together to cause serious difficulties for users. Rates of mortality and of physical complications (overdose, abscesses, hepatitis) can be high, partly (among some users) because of unhygienic injection procedures, impurities, uncertainty about potency, and the use of barbiturates especially when opiates are unavailable. Evidence that a person's regular use of heroin need not persist indefinitely and that use depends partly on environmental context is provided by a study of American servicemen returning from Vietnam (Robins 1973; see Chapter 27). Of various alternative treatments, voluntary programmes providing methadone (mainly injectable in Britain, mainly oral in America) appear to be having the greatest overall success (DeLong 1972b).

In Britain, as of 1975, there are still relatively few regular users of opiate-type drugs—probably no more than a few thousand people. They form a broad cross-section of the population except that they still tend to be urban (especially from London) males of about 18 to 28 years of age. Almost half are employed full time. Rates of illegal activities are high but (a) 'serious' (e.g., violent) crimes are infrequent and (b) the rates for this population are no higher after drug use than they were prior to drug use (in spite of increased police surveillance) (Blumberg 1973; Blumberg *et al* 1974a; 1975).

Tobacco

Not surprisingly, some studies have shown a range of factors significantly related to the use of tobacco, while others have shown hardly any.

In a stratified random sample consisting of 5601 English and Welsh schoolboys, 10 to 15 years of age, the four main differentiators of nonsmoking-*vs.*-smoking were: number of friends who smoke, anticipation of adulthood, parents' permissiveness towards smoking, and whether put off by the danger of lung cancer (Bynner 1969 and additional relevant material cited by Russell 1971a). The effects of peer group on smoking among schoolchildren have been documented in several countries (see e.g., Hill 1971; Levitt & Edwards 1970).

In a sample of first-year students at the University of Texas not only was use related to sex (higher for males), but also smokers scored significantly lower in cognitive ability, high school and college grades, two self-report health indices, self-esteem, and work motivation, and higher in social confidence and acceptance of ambiguity (Veldman & Bown 1969).

According to Nesbitt's (1972) research, and other studies cited by him, it appears that smokers—as children before they ever started to smoke—are rated by themselves and others as being high on 'emotionality'; however, after they begin to smoke they rate themselves relatively low (with those who smoke the most feeling least emotional) although others still find them to be emotional. One of the factors in the amount habitually smoked may be a sort of 'self-titration' of emotionality reduction.

There have been many educational campaigns regarding tobacco; the long-range effects on prevalence remain to be seen.

In Britain, preventive propaganda in schools has been largely ineffective; however, no coordinated large-scale nationwide antismoking efforts (with adequate provision for evaluation) have yet been attempted (Russell 1971b).

Alcohol

Since about 1970, research interest in the use of alcohol among young people has been relatively diminished compared with that for cannabis and other substances.

In a number of studies the main predictors of use among young people are the familiar ones of sex (higher for males) (e.g. Forslund & Gustafson 1970) and use by parents and peers (e.g. Eisenthal & Udin 1972; Forslund & Gustafson 1970; Riester & Zucker 1968).

Among the personality dimensions positively associated with alcohol consumption in at least one sample are lower expectation of achievement- and affection-need satisfaction (Jessor et al 1968), higher social maturity and impulse expression (Strassburger & Strassburger 1965), low self-esteem (Williams 1965), incongruence between 'manifest' and 'latent' masculinity (Parker 1969), and extraversion, adventurous/pleasure-seeking, tough-mindedness (Orford et al 1974). Some of the effects reported in American studies are incidental to the drinking itself, namely the common incidence of false (age) identification cards, illicit drinking establishments, and the need to conceal the truth from one's parents (Bruyn 1966; Mandell *et al* 1962). One direct effect of drinking: increased blood-alcohol level is associated with direct impairment of sensory-motor ability relevant to driving an automobile in contrast with the much milder effects of cannabis (allowing for the difficulty of equating doses, Binder 1971).

A paradoxical finding in some studies is that Jews are more likely to drink but have a much lower rate of social complications due to drinking than other groups (e.g. than individuals having loose affiliation with an abstinence-oriented religion). A possible explanation, of potential broad general interest, has to do with the presence of norms which guide use (even including general or individual occasions when moderate excess is approved) and render uncontrolled drinking less likely (studies cited by Braucht *et al* 1973).

As regards the effects of alcohol: as male undergraduates at a cocktail party drank more, action predominated over thought, and aggressive and self-centred themes increased (Williams 1968). The more one drinks, and the earlier the age at which one first drinks heavily, the more one might be expected to become an alcoholic later on (potential problems may be related as much to personality or social traits as to the drinking *per se*). Most teenagers handle alcohol in an orderly manner (Maddox 1966).

When data from questionnaire items about drinking habits (among male college students) were subjected to factor analysis, the two main factors were related to quantity/frequency (of drinking) and evaluation (degree to which use was for positive reasons or occasions) (Park 1967, cf. Orford *et al* 1974). Park cites a number of studies which show that, not surprisingly, 'problem drinking' is related to the quantity/frequency dimension. It would be interesting to know whether it is related to any of the other dimensions as well.

Glue sniffing and related behaviour can produce euphoria, but repeated use appears to be correlated with damage to the central nervous system (Gellman 1968; Langdell 1969; Weil 1972a).

DIFFICULTIES, SERVICES, SOURCES

Difficulties in drawing conclusions from available research

Because the literature on drug taking is not very well integrated, and many studies have methodological and theoretical shortcomings, it seems worth spelling out in some detail those characteristics of drug taking which have made it difficult to draw firm general conclusions (cf. Zinberg & DeLong 1974).

Many investigators unwittingly project their own biasses into the conclusions they draw. Even behaviour that appears to be directly related to some forms of drug taking is often associated only circumstantially.

Drug initiation is subject to the general process of 'diffusion of innovation' (see Katz *et al* 1963). That is, patterns of use tend to spread via the social network, so that if a particular drug ritual were to spread from a *randomly* chosen point (e.g. an American urban ghetto or an English new town), significant correlations could be generated between the use of that drug and a host of demographic, personality, attitude and behavioural dimensions. A significant correlation merely shows statistical association, i.e. that the people in a particular sample who have higher scores on one variable (such as amount used of a particular drug) also have higher scores on a specified other variable.

Notions of whether a particular finding (such as 'euphoria' or 'intermittent unemployment') is good or bad are themselves subject to diffusion among researchers. Moreover, as Clark and Funkhouser (1970) and others have pointed out, psychiatrists and law enforcement personnel are apt to draw conclusions based on unrepresentative samples of drug takers. Sometimes one must read even a well-written article (e.g. Carney *et al* 1972) quite carefully to realise that the 'young drug abusers' with poor school records (usually prior to drug use) and unsatisfactory work histories are in fact a sample of hospital in- and outpatients, many of them court referrals.

Moreover, the effects of psychoactive drugs are notoriously subject to setting. Expectations and attitudes (even if they began as fortuitous correlates) can be transmitted through the social network along with patterns of use. Arousal which is physically caused by a drug can be felt as pleasurable or anxiety-provoking depending upon the user's expectations and knowledge of how to deal with the sensations (Becker 1967; Schacter 1964, but cf. Paton & Crown 1972). Thus even if there were no initial differences between populations of users and nonusers, they could become different, and the differences could vary in the degree to which they were drug-intrinsic. The deleterious effects of alcohol and nicotine are probably close to the 'drug-intrinsic' end of the spectrum—unlike most of the correlations between the use of various drugs and social class or personality or attitude. These latter correlations are found to be significant only in some populations, though are nevertheless worthy of consideration.

As a further note of caution, even 'hard data' are subject to interpretation. For instance, published figures which seemed to show a positive link, in one sample of opiate users, between the start of drug use and amount of criminal activity, in fact demonstrated what was either a negative association or else no link at all (Blumberg 1973).

Difficulties for users

One can separate three kinds of difficulty—external, psychological, and physical—although they are not fully distinct from one another. The first has to do with social and legal difficulties which are not physically related to the drugs themselves. Here distinctions such as those between hard and soft drugs become operative. The user of tobacco and alcohol (and perhaps the user of amphetamine pills and barbiturates), even if rather young, may experience little or no social or legal difficulties. In smoking cannabis (and, to some extent, in using hallucinogens) one's every use may be labelled 'abuse' in some contexts and a large portion of the adult population may disapprove, but, increasingly, someone who is caught by the police is apt to receive a fine or probation rather than a prison sentence (see e.g. Carruthers 1972).

In most Western countries a rather strong stigma may be attached to the use of opiate-type drugs and to any self-injection in a nonmedical context. In England about half of the users who receive their drugs by prescription are employed full time and lead what the general population might regard as 'reasonably normal lives'. Even so, police surveillance is still considerable and clinic prescriptions outside London are often difficult to obtain (Blumberg *et al* 1974a, b).

A second concern has to do with 'dependence' or psychological difficulties accompanying drug use. In practice there may be no sharp line between habit (a learned psychological effect) and physical addiction. Many regular users of heroin in America may spend a great deal of time trying to satisfy a craving even when the heroin is so adulterated that the actual amount used is insufficient for its absence to produce any marked withdrawal symptoms (Steinberg 1969).

For the third concern, direct physical damage, there seems to be no significant correlation between the harm done by a drug and typical public and legal implications as to how 'dangerous' that drug is. The most clearly substantiated deleterious effects are for tobacco and alcohol, perhaps because they are so widely used and heavily researched.

Services

Because of the multiplicity of factors involved in drug taking, one approach to follow if someone should seek advice because of the use of drugs is to try to work supportively with the person in learning the *specific needs of the individual situation* and then to explore as broad an array as possible of alternatives that the person might feel would meet these needs. Such an approach does not preclude the possibility that some of the alternatives might be standardised, e.g. a particular drug prescription or referral to a likely place for meeting legal/employment/accommodation needs. The events that led up to a person's 'present needs' should always be considered, if only to suggest *whether* dealing with these antecedents is relevant to meeting the present needs. Direct help—or referral to a wide variety of social, medical, and legal services—is provided by a large number of free clinics and alternative information services (e.g. for England see *Alternative England and Wales* 1975; *Church of England Council for Social Aid* 1971; *Consumer's Guide to Drug Treatment Facilities* 1973, and for America see Hoover 1972; Minkowski *et al* 1972; Ramer *et al* 1972). In his review of drug treatment facilities, McCarthy (1972) emphasises that little can be accomplished without a client's willing it.

CONCLUSIONS

Drug taking has no one 'cause', and even one person taking a particular drug in a given context is likely to do so for a number of reasons. Even to speak of 'causes' of drug taking is misleading; it is more accurate to think of arrays of interrelated behaviours (including drug taking) which continually influence one another.

Use is invariably related to both social and personal factors. No 'special principles' need be involved, as a wide variety of behaviours are known to spread via the social network.

Amongst the factors that may make some individuals more likely than others to try drugs (or to try a particular drug) are: family background (e.g. parents' drug use), motivation (to satisfy needs for affiliation, altered states of consciousness, recreation, and/or reduction of curiosity or anxiety), learning, and a variety of personality dimensions. Physical addiction cannot account for initial use of a drug and is not necessarily the major reason for continued use even of opiates, barbiturates, or tobacco.

A variety of drug-specific considerations are described, but even most of these are probably relevant only to patterns of use in particular sets of cultures. The legal sanctions against the use of drugs appear to be inconsistent with the likelihood of a drug being used to the point of causing physical damage.

One could argue that the social consequences of drug use are at least as dependent on other people's reactions as on the use and user themselves; drug 'problems' seem especially to be created when users are treated with intolerance.

A strong need remains for (a) the integration of findings regarding the potential effects of different drug-using behaviours in a variety of social contexts and (b) the open communication of such material in a way which is at one objective, sympathetic to people's needs, and open to refinement and change.

REFERENCES

ABRUZZI W. (1974) 5000 bad trips. *Contemporary Drug Problems* **3**, 345–372

ADVENA J.C. (1972) *Drug Abuse Bibliography for 1971.* Troy, New York: Whiston

Alternative England and Wales (1975) London: Nicholas Saunders

BALDINGER R., CAPEL W.C., GOLDSMITH B.M. & STEWART G.T. (1972) Pot smokers, junkies, and squares: a comparative study of female values. *Int. J. Addict.* **7**, 153–166

BAUM M. (1970) Effect of alcohol on the acquisition and resistance-to-extinction of avoidance responses in rats. *Psychol. Rep.* **26**, 759–765

BECKER H.S. (1967) History, culture and subjective experience: an exploration of the social bases of drug-induced experiences. *J. Health Soc. Behav.* **8**, 163–176

BERG D.F. (1970) The non-medical use of dangerous drugs in the United States: a comprehensive view. *Int. J. Addict.* **5**, 777–834

BINDER A. (1971) An experimental approach to driver evaluation using alcohol drinkers and marihuana smokers. *Accident Analysis and Prevention* **3**, 237–256

BLUMBERG H.H. (1973) Violence among attenders at a London drug clinic. *Brit. J. Psychiat.* **122**, 619

BLUMBERG H.H. (1975) Surveys of drug use among young people. *Int. J. Addict.* **10**, 699–719

BLUMBERG H.H. (1976) Group processes. *In* Eysenck H. & Wilson G. (eds.) *A Textbook of Human Psychology.* Lancaster, Lancashire: MTP

BLUMBERG H.H., COHEN S.D., DRONFIELD B.E., MORDECAI E.A., ROBERTS J.C. & HAWKS D. (1974a) British opiate users. I: People approaching London drug treatment centres. *Int. J. Addict.* **9**, 1–23

BLUMBERG H.H., COHEN S.D., DRONFIELD B.E., MORDECAI E.A., ROBERTS J.C. & HAWKS D. (1974b) British opiate users. II: Differences between those given an opiate script and those not given one. *Int. J. Addict.* **9**, 205–220

BLUMBERG H.H., COHEN S.D., DRONFIELD B.E., MORDECAI E.A., ROBERTS J.C. & HAWKS D. (1975) Opiate use in London. *J. Amer. Med. Assoc.* **232**, 1131–1132

BRANSBY E.R., CURLEY G. & KOTULANSKA M. (1973) A study of patients notified by hospitals as addicted to drugs: second report. *Health Trends* **5**, 17–20

BRAUCHT G.N., BRAKARSH D., FOLLINGSTAD D. & BERRY K.L. (1973) Deviant drug use in adolescence: a review of psychosocial correlates. *Psychol. Bull.* **79**, 92–106

BROOK R., KAPLUN J. & WHITEHEAD P.C. (1974) Personality characteristics of adolescent amphetamine users as measured by the MMPI. *Brit. J. Addict.* **69**, 61–66

BRUYN H.B. (1966) Alcohol and college youth. *Ann. N.Y. Acad. Sci.* **133**, 866–872

BUCKMAN J. (1971) Social and medical aspects of illicit use of LSD. *Int. J. Soc. Psychiat.* **17**, 163–176

BUIES R. (1971) Aspects psycho-dynamiques de l'usage non medical des drogues à l'adolescence. *Laval Med.* **42**, 81–83. *Drug Dependence* **1**, abstract 182

BYNNER J.M. (1969) *The Young Smoker*. London: HMSO

CAREY J.T. & MANDEL J. (1968) A San Francisco Bay area 'speed' scene. *J. Health Soc. Behav.* **9**, 164–174

CARNEY P.A., TIMMS M.W.H. & STEVENSON R.D. (1972) The social and psychological background of young drug abusers in Dublin. *Brit. J. Addict.* **67**, 199–207

CARRUTHERS J. (1972) Canadian courts more lenient toward drug offenders in 1971. *Journal (Toronto)* **11**, 9. *Drug Dependence* **1**, abstract 600

CHURCH OF ENGLAND COUNCIL FOR SOCIAL AID (1971) *Drug Aid*. London

CLARK W.H. & FUNKHOUSER G.R. (1970) Physicians and researchers disagree on psychedelic drugs. *Psychology Today* **3** (11), 48–50, 70–73

CONSUMER'S GUIDE TO DRUG TREATMENT FACILITIES (1973) *Drugs and Society* **3** (3), 5–19

DeFLEUR L.B., BALL J.C. & SNARR R.W. (1969) The long-term social correlates of opiate addiction. *Social Problems* **17**, 225–234

DeLONG J.V. (1972a) The Drugs and their Effects. *In Dealing with Drug Abuse*. A report to the Ford Foundation. London: Macmillan

DeLONG J.V. (1972b) Treatment and Rehabilitation. *In Dealing with Drug Abuse*. A report to the Ford Foundation. London: Macmillan

DUNN W.L. (ed.) (1973) *Smoking Behavior: Motives and Incentives*. Washington, DC: Winston

DuPONT R.L. (1971) Profile of a heroin-addiction epidemic. *N. Engl. J. Med.* **285**, 320–324

EISENTHAL S. & UDIN H. (1972) Psychological factors associated with drug and alcohol usage among Neighbourhood Youth Corps enrollees. *Dev. Psychol.* **7**, 119–123

EVANS W.O. (1969) Alternate conceptual frameworks involved in considering drug taking. *In* Wittenborn J.R. *et al* (eds) *Drugs and Youth*. Springfield, Illinois: Charles C. Thomas

FARLEY F.H. & DIONNE M.T. (1972) Value orientations of sensation-seekers. *Percept. Mot. Skills* **34**, 509–510

FEJER D., SMART R.G. & WHITEHEAD P.C. (1972) Changes in the patterns of drug use in two Canadian cities: Toronto and Halifax. *Int. J. Addict.* **7**, 467–479

FORSLUND M.A. & GUSTAFSON T.J. (1970) Influence of peers and parents and sex differences in drinking by high-school students. *Quart. J. Studies Alcohol* **31**, 868–875

GELLMAN V. (1968) Glue-sniffing among Winnipeg school children. *Canad. Med. Assoc. J.* **98**, 411–413

GERGEN M.K., GERGEN K.J. & MORSE S.T. (1972) Correlates of marijuana use among college students. *J. appl. soc. Psychol.* **2**, 1–16

GILBERT R.M. & KEEHN J.D. (eds) (1972) *Schedule Effects: Drugs, Drinking, and Aggression*. Toronto: University of Toronto Press

GLASER D., LANDER B. & ABBOTT W. (1971) Opiate addicted and non-addicted siblings in a slum area. *Social Problems* **18**, 510–521

GOODE E. (1969) Multiple drug use among marijuana smokers. *Social Problems* **17**, 48–64

GORDON L.V. (1972) Value correlates of student attitudes on social issues: a multination study. *J. appl. soc. Psychol.* **56**, 305–311

GRINSPOON L. (1969) Marihuana. *Sci. Am.* **221**, 17–25

HAGER D.L., VENER A.M. & STEWART C.S. (1971) Patterns of adolescent drug use in Middle America. *J. Counsel. Psychol.* **18**, 292–297

HARRIS T.G. (1973) 'As far as heroin is concerned, the worst is over.' *Psychology Today* **7** (3, August), 68—79; 85

HAWKS D.V. (1971) The dimensions of drug dependence in the United Kingdom. *Int. J. Addict.* **6**, 135–160

HAWKS D.V., KOSVINER A. & WEBB M.G.T. (1971) Cannabis use by tertiary students. Paper discussed at the Second International Institute on the Prevention and Treatment of Drug Dependence, Baden, Austria

HILL D. (1971) Peer group conformity in adolescent smoking and its relationship to affiliation and autonomy needs. *Aust. J. Psychol.* **23**, 189–199

HOLDEN H.M. (1968) Drug taking among young people. *Medical Digest (London)* **13**, 580–588

HOOVER J.P. (1972) College drug scene as it is. *N.Y. State J. Med.* **72**, 1866–1872

JESSOR R., CORMAN R.S. & GROSSMAN P.H. (1968) Expectations of need, satisfaction and drinking patterns of college students. *Quart. J. Stud. Alcohol* **29**, 101–116

KATZ E., LEVIN M.L. & HAMILTON H. (1963) Traditions of research on the diffusion of innovation. *Amer. Sociol. Rev.* **28**, 237–252

KLEIN J. & PHILIPS D.L. (1968) From hard to soft drugs: temporal and substantive changes in drug usage among gangs in a working-class community. *J. Health Soc. Behav.* **9**, 139–145

KOSVINER A., HAWKS D. & WEBB M.G.T. (1974) Cannabis use amongst British university students. I. Prevalence rates. *Brit. J. Addict.* **69**, 35–60

KRAMER J.P. (1972) The adolescent addict: the progression of youth through the drug culture. *Clin. Pediat.* **11**, 382–385

LANGDELL J. (1969) Psychological aspects of glue-sniffing by juveniles. *In* Szurek S.A. & Berlin I.N. (ed.) *The Antisocial Child: His Family and His Community*. Palo Alto, California: Science & Behavior

LEVINE S.V., LLOYD D.D. & LONGDON W.H. (1972) The speed user: social and psychological factors in amphetamine abuse. *Canad. Psychiat. Assoc. J.* **17**, 229–241

LEVITT E.E. & EDWARDS J.A. (1970) A multivariate study of correlative factors in youthful cigarette smoking. *Dev. Psychol.* **2**, 5–11

MCCARTHY M. (1972) The youthful drug abuser: some considerations for treatment. *Md. State Med. J.* **21**, 63–69

MCGRATH J.H. (1970) Adolescent pill users. *Int. J. Addict.* **5**, 173–182

MCGUIRE W.J. (1972) Attitude change: the information-processing paradigm. *In* McClintock C.F. (ed.) *Experimental Social Psychology*. New York: Holt, Rinehart & Winston

MADDOX G.L. (1966) Teenagers and alcohol: recent research. *Ann. N.Y. Acad. Sci.* **133**, 856–865

MANDELL W., COOPER A., SILBERSTEIN R.M., NOVICK J. & KOLOSKI E. (1962) *Youthful Drinking New York State 1962*. Staten Island, New York: Wakoff Research Center

MESSER M. (1969) The predictive value of marijuana use: A note to researchers of student culture. *Sociol. Educ.* **42**, 91–97

METTLIN C. (1973) Smoking as behavior: applying a social psychological theory. *J. Health Soc. Behav.* **14**, 144–152

MINKOWSKI W.L., WEISS R.C. & HEIDBREDER G.A. (1972) A view of the drug problem: a rational approach to youthful drug use and abuse. *Clin. Pediat.* **11**, 376–381

MORAN E. (1970) Gambling as a form of dependence. *Brit. J. Addict.* **64**, 419–428

NESBITT P.D. (1972) Chronic smoking and emotionality. *J. appl. soc. Psychol.* **2**, 187–196

ORFORD J., WALLER S. & PETO J. (1974) Drinking behaviour and attitudes and their correlates among university students in England. *Quart. J. Stud. Alcoh.* **35**, 1316–1374

PARK P. (1967) Dimensions of drinking among male college students. *Social Prob.* **14**, 473–482

PARKER F.B. (1969) Self-role strain and drinking disposition at a prealcoholic age level. *J. Soc. Psychol.* **78**, 55–61

PATON W.D.M. & CROWN J. (eds.) (1972) *Cannabis and its Derivatives: Pharmacology and Experimental Psychology.* London: Oxford University Press

PEARLMAN S. (1969) Drugs on the campus—an annotated guide to the literature. *Int. J. Addict.* **4**, 249–300

RAMER B.S., SMITH D.E. & GAY G.R. (1972) Adolescent heroin abuse in San Francisco. *Int. J. Addict.* **7**, 461–465

RATHOD N.H. (1972) The use of heroin and methadone by injection in a New Town: progress report. *Brit. J. Addict.* **67**, 113–121

RIESTER A.E. & ZUCKER R.A. (1968) Adolescent social structure and drinking behaviour. *Personnel and Guidance J.* **47**, 304–312

ROBINS L.N. (1973) *A Follow-up of Vietnam Drug Users.* Washington, DC: Special Action Office (for Drug Abuse Prevention) Monograph, Series A, Number 1

ROSENBERG C.M. (1968) Young drug addicts: addiction and its consequences. *Med. J. Aust.* **1**, 1031–1033

RUSSELL M.A.H. (1971a) Cigarette smoking: natural history of a dependence disorder. *Brit. J. Med. Psychol.* **44**, 1–16

RUSSELL M.A.H. (1971b) Smoking in Britain: strategy for future emancipation. *Brit. J. Addict.* **66**, 157–166

SAN MATEO COUNTY (1972) *Preliminary Report—1972; Alcoholic Beverages, Amphetamines, Barbiturates, Heroin, LSD, Marijuana, Tobacco: Levels of Use Reported by Junior and Senior High School Students; Trends shown in Five Annual Surveys.* San Mateo, California: Department of Public Health and Welfare

SARGENT M.J. (1971) A cross-cultural study of attitudes and behaviour towards alcohol and drugs. *Brit. J. Sociol.* **22**, 83–96

SCHACTER S. (1964) The interaction of cognitive and physiological determinants in emotional state. *In* Berkowitz L. (ed.) *Advances in Experimental Social Psychology.* New York: Academic Press

SELLS H.F. (1967) *A Bibliography on Drug Dependence.* Fort Worth, Texas: Texas Christian University Press

SIEGEL R.K. (1971) Towards a psychology of psychedelics and population behaviour. *J. Psychedelic Drugs* **3**, 67–71

SMART R.G. and FEJER D. (1971) Recent trends in illicit drug use among adolescents. *Canad. Ment. Health* Suppl. 68

SNYDER S.H. (1971) Work with marijuana. I: Effects. *Psychology Today* **4**, 37–38, 40, 64–65

STEINBERG H. (ed.) (1969) *The Scientific Basis of Drug Dependence.* London: Churchill

STIMSON G.V. & OGBORNE A.C. (1970) A survey of a representative sample of addicts prescribed heroin at London clinics. *Bull. Narcotics* **22**, 13–22

STRASSBURGER F. & STRASSBURGER Z. (1965) Measurement of attitudes toward alcohol and their relation to personality variables. *J. Consult. Psychol.* **29**, 440–445

STREIT F. & OLIVER H.G. (1972) The child's perception of his family and its relation to drug use. *Drug Forum* **1**, 283–289

TART C.T. (1970) Marijuana intoxication: common experiences. *Nature* **226**, 701–704

VELDMAN D.J. & BOWN O.H. (1969) Personality and performance characteristics associated with cigarette smoking among college freshmen. *J. Cons. Clin. Psychol.* **33**, 109–119

WEIL A. (1972a) Altered states of consciousness. *In Dealing with Drug Abuse.* A report to the Ford Foundation. London: Macmillan

WEIL A. (1972b) *The Natural Mind: a New Way of Looking at Drugs and the Higher Consciousness.* Boston: Houghton Mifflin

WESTERMEYER J. (1971) Use of alcohol and opium by the Meo of Laos. *Amer. J. Psychiat.* **127**, 1019–1023

WILLIAMS A.F. (1965) Self-concepts of college problem drinkers. I: A comparison with alcoholics. *Quart. J. Studies Alcohol* **26**, 586–594

WILLIAMS A.F. (1968) Psychological needs and social drinking among college students. *Quart. J. Studies Alcohol* **29**, 355–363

ZINBERG N.E. & DeLONG J.V. (1974) Research and the drug issue. *Contemporary Drug Prob.* **3**, 71–100

ZUCKERMAN M., NEARY R.S. & BRUSTMAN B.A. (1970) Sensation-seeking scale correlates in experience (smoking, drugs, alcohol, 'hallucinations', and sex) and preference for complexity (designs). *Proceedings of the Annual Convention of the American Psychological Association* **5**, 317–318

The author wishes to express his appreciation to Iain Crow, Griffith Edwards, David Hawks, Will Pollard, Colin Roberts and Michael Russell whose helpful comments on reading and earlier draft of this chapter are gratefully acknowledged. This work was supported in part by funds from the Medical Research Council and the Department of Health and Social Security.

CHAPTER 27

Clinical aspects of drug misuse

P. CONNELL

In the early 1960s young people showed an increasing interest in drugs and put forward various reasons to explain this such as; to keep awake, to be able to communicate with others (particularly the opposite sex) and for 'kicks'. Initially, amphetamines were the preferred drugs and others such as heroin were regarded as dangerous; to use them would be 'mad'. Clinical reports at that time foreshadowed the danger of a move towards injectable drugs such as heroin and the development of methamphetamine and polydrug use (Connell 1964; 1965; Scott & Willcox 1965).

The rapid growth in numbers of heroin-dependent persons and the appearance of heroin-dependent adolescents led to the setting up of special clinics for the treatment of drug addiction. The increasing use of cannabis and other drugs in schools and centres of higher learning also led to various enactments and regulations designed to bring the drug situation under greater control.

Drug misuse among the under 14s in the UK is comparatively rare and addiction to drugs under the age of 16 even rarer. Home Office statistics now show a fall in the numbers of young addicts compulsorily notified. Nevertheless, there are many problems of drug misuse which are relevant to children and adolescents. Because there are few published data on this age group, this chapter will deal mainly with older groups and with populations attending the special clinics, hospital casualty departments or treated in special institutions.

DEFINITIONS

Throughout the years attention has focussed on the problems of definition of drug addiction, habituation, tolerance and dependence. The World Health Organisation has given special attention to these matters through its Expert Committee on Drug Dependence (WHO 1950; 1957; 1964; 1965; 1969). The label 'drug dependence' was preferred and types were defined according to

646

the drug used (WHO 1964). More recently, the following definitions were adopted (WHO 1969):

Drug   Any substance that, when taken into the living organism, may modify one or more of its functions.

Drug abuse   Persistent or sporadic excessive drug use inconsistent with or unrelated to acceptable medical practice.

Drug dependence   A state, psychic, and sometimes also physical, resulting from the interaction between a living organism and a drug characterised by behavioural and other responses that always includes a compulsion to take the drug on a continuous or periodic basis in order to experience its psychic effects, sometimes to avoid the discomfort of abstinence.

Physical Dependence Capacity (PDC)   The ability of a drug to act as a substitute for another upon which an organism has been made physically dependent, i.e. to suppress abstinence phenomena which would otherwise develop after abrupt withdrawal of the original dependence-producing drug.

Some authorities prefer the word misuse rather than abuse since the latter is rather moralistic and censorious. Misuse is used here since, in considering childhood and adolescence, attention must be given to the family as well as to the individual. The family is important in the clinical evaluation of drug taking in children and parents, unwittingly, may misuse drugs of potential danger by giving them for *bona fide* reasons to their children. For instance, parents may give their own sleeping tablets to an adolescent who complains of insomnia, or slimming tablets to a plump adolescent, or patent cough mixtures or stomach medicines (chlorodyne or linctus codeine etc.) which may have an effect in easing psychological problems but may then lead to interest in such drugs and also dependence.

DIAGNOSIS OF DRUG TAKING

The particular problems facing the clinician in relation to the diagnosis of drug taking, when the patient does not admit to taking drugs or when he/ she does not admit to taking more than one drug, can be summarised:

1   Drugs, and particularly drugs of dependence, can be and often are used to ameliorate symptoms of nervous and mental disorder and emotional disturbance.

2   Some drugs may themselves produce symptoms of nervous and mental disorder as simple side effects or as complications due to excessive dosage.

3   Having regard to the illegal aspects of drug taking it is often impossible to obtain a truthful account, and in particular the dose used.

4   Where drugs are being peddled illegally, it is not possible to be sure that the drug is the one it is claimed to be and it may be contaminated by impurities or mixed with other substances.

5   The development of polydrug use makes diagnosis particularly difficult since classical symptoms of the use of one drug may be masked by another.

Examination of the mental state

The examination of the mental state of an adolescent who is thought to be taking drugs is, in general, similar to that of any adolescent referred for psychiatric evaluation. However, it is wise to carry out the general evaluation without reference to drugs so leaving this exploration to the end. General data which might lead to suspicion of drug taking may thus be obtained which can be used in tackling the drug question later. Direct questions such as 'are you taking drugs?' or 'are you taking amphetamines?' are less likely to produce a positive response than questions such as 'when did you first smoke pot?' or 'how old were you when you first tried pills?'

Many adolescents referred because they may be taking drugs are uncooperative and may also display adolescent rebelliousness, antisocial attitudes and hostility to adults. It is, therefore, particularly important to avoid a censorious or critical approach and to build up empathy slowly in the interview by demonstrating a knowledge of, and sympathy with, the problems adolescents face and an understanding of their feelings.

It is also most important to obtain independent information from another informant, preferably a parent, sibling or guardian, who has known the patient for some time and can therefore give a historical account of changes in behaviour, attitudes, and life style.

Of course, many changes in behaviour or in life style (including the visiting of places where drugs are taken) may be normal in adolescence.

A parent or teacher may couch their suspicions in terms of a definite claim that the adolescent is taking drugs, but such claims should not be assumed as fact. Many adolescents who are 'dropping out' of their cultural milieu but not taking drugs may appear like the popular stereotype of a 'druggie'.

Unless there are clear symptoms and signs of drug overdose in the present examination or past history, it will usually be impossible to detect drug taking by examination of the mental state of a patient who does not admit drug taking. Chronic use of drugs of dependence, in which tolerance to the drug develops, is compatible with a normal mental state on high regular doses of the drug.

Physical examination

Laymen and some medical men believe that drug taking can be diagnosed by physical examination and that signs of toxicity will be present and can be demonstrated by physical examination. However, knowledge about the phenomena of tolerance and drug dependence is lacking, for the latter is a relatively recent phenomenon in adolescents in the United Kingdom.

When a drug is being taken by a hypodermic syringe it is common to find injection marks over accessible veins in the antecubital fossa, the backs of hands and wrists, the ankles and legs. There may be signs of local infections, or thromboses, past or present, along the line of veins which, in time, may become obliterated.

There are many complications, both local and systemic, of injection of substances by dirty syringes. The injection of barbiturates manufactured for oral use, is a common cause of local painful abscesses which may be sterile. Some patients begin by subcutaneous or intramuscular injection (skin popping); here the injection marks will not be found concentrated over the sites of veins.

Users of opioids (a term which includes opiates and synthetic drugs with similar actions) will have constricted pupils which do not react normally to light or darkness. Tolerance does not develop to this effect. This sign is present, of course, whether the user is taking the drug orally, by the nasal route (snorting) or by injection.

Large amounts of amphetamine can be ingested regularly without the appearance of diagnostic physical signs (Connell 1958). The symptoms of CNS stimulation, such as tachycardia, tremor, anxiety, restlessness and dilated pupils, are not diagnostic of amphetamine use, since they are common in patients referred to doctors and may be merely those of anxiety consequent upon the examination, or due to the existence of an actual anxiety state which requires medical treatment (Connell 1968). Use of cannabis can lead to a reddening of the eyes and a desire to eat sweet substances.

Chronic use of barbiturates, tranquillisers, amphetamines and other drugs of misuse does not lead to diagnostic symptoms or signs unless they are side effects or a result of a much larger than normal dose in which case toxic symptoms such as blurred speech, ataxia, drowsiness, disorientation, may occur with some drugs. A psychosis indistinguishable from paranoid schizophrenia may occur with amphetamine misuse (Connell 1958, see also Chapter 31).

LSD (lysergic acid diethylamide) can produce disorders of perception, particularly visual perception, and synaesthesiae (a merging of different perceptions) can occur. Misinterpretations, paranoid ideas, delusions and hallucinations can also occur along with severe anxiety states and agitation. Such adverse reactions are generally regarded as 'bad trips' and can cause continued distress.

Laboratory aids to diagnosis

The development of chromatography, especially thin-layer chromatography and gas-liquid chromatography, has introduced a new factor in the detection of drug taking. It is, however, important to understand the meaning of such tests and their advantages and limitations. A comprehensive evaluation of the use of special tests in drug detection including more complex procedures, is available (WHO 1974).

Urine is the biological fluid usually tested because of convenience, for some drugs of dependence cannot yet be easily detected in blood or plasma. Supervised voiding of urine is advisable since many drug users are manipulative and have evolved methods to avoid detection such as bringing a bottle of someone else's urine with which they fill the hospital receptacle, or secreting a bottle of someone else's urine under clothing which leads by tube to the underside of the penis.

The reliability of urine testing and in particular thin-layer chromatography, depends on a number of factors, not least the close working cooperation with the clinical pathology services so that the laboratory staff can become interested and involved in the clinical situation. In this way a 95 per cent or even higher reliability is obtained by the use of appropriate tests. Conversely, the least reliable results are likely to arise from large central or distant laboratories which do large numbers of tests on a routine basis. Here the reliability may be as low as 45 per cent. The banking of specimens for repeat testing is important (Angelis De 1972, 1973; May 1972; Montalvo *et al* 1972; Lewis *et al* 1972).

All that can be inferred from an apparently reliable positive test is that, at the time the urine was voided, the individual had the drug in his/her body. It gives no information as to:

1   The size of the dose taken.
2   Whether the individual is dependent on the drug and taking it continuously or merely a sporadic user or taking the drug was for the first and only time.

The danger of accepting one positive result as evidence of dependence has been pointed out in the UK where some sporadic users have been converted into continuous users in a treatment centre (Gardner & Connell 1971).

Certain drugs, notably LSD and cannabis, cannot yet be detected in urine though much research endeavour is being expended to fill this gap (WHO 1974).

Diagnosis of dependence (addiction)

The diagnosis of drug dependence rests on establishing the fact that the individual is taking the drug continuously and will suffer psychologically, and with some drugs, physically, if there is a sudden cessation of drug use.

Bearing in mind the unreliability of data obtained from patients and their relatives, a reasonable diagnostic criterion would be the finding of three positive urines over a period of 10 days to 2 weeks before making a diagnosis of drug dependence (Gardner & Connell 1970). However, clear independent evidence of the compulsion to obtain the drug by whatever means is also an important finding.

Summary of diagnostic points

In view of the difficulties in demonstrating conclusively the presence of drug taking or drug dependence certain possible indicators have been proposed (Connell 1974).

1   Admission that a person is taking drugs.
2   Disturbed behaviour, such as sleepiness, inability to sleep, slurred speech, extreme restlessness, staggering gait, inability to communicate clearly, abnormal mental symptoms (hallucinations, delusions) which are known to be symptoms possibly due to the effects of drugs.
3   Reports from others (school friends, parents, teachers) of such behaviour and actual or suspected taking of drugs.
4   The discovery of injection marks.
5   The discovery of pills or suspicious substances in the possession of the person (including syringes).
6   Reports of an increase in spending money which cannot be accounted for by the price of the items for which the money is requested and claims that money or goods have been lost on several occasions.
7   The disappearance, from the family drug cupboard, of parents' pills; particularly sleeping tablets, appetite suppressants and tranquillisers.

CLINICAL FEATURES

The appendix to this chapter contains a summary of the findings from recent British studies of drug-dependent individuals who have come to the notice of psychiatrists. The studies vary in sophistication and coverage and are not readily comparable. However, it is clear that the patients constitute a heterogeneous group of individuals about whom few generalisations are possible.

In most clinic samples of opioid addicts young adult and older adolescents form the bulk of the population, but drug taking usually began rather earlier in the teenage period. In many cases this started with cannabis or amphetamine, and then after a while hallucinogens, before opioids were used. Males usually outnumber females in a ratio of about 4 to 1. Many come from discordant, disrupted or otherwise unsatisfactory homes, although some have had an unexceptionable upbringing. There is little consistency in social background. Many, perhaps most, have unstable personalities and often there is a history of antisocial behaviour before drug taking commenced. It is difficult to disentangle which factors are causal, but any treatment plans must take into account the findings that drug dependent patients seen by psychiatrists often have a disturbed family background, prior antisocial behaviour and personality problems.

Of course, psychiatric patients who are dependent on opioids are not representative of the much larger number of young people who occasionally experiment with cannabis or amphetamine, or even take them regularly (see Chapter 31). The factors that lead people to take drugs in the first instance are not necessarily the same as those which cause them to proceed to 'hard' drugs. The factors that predispose to drug dependence and those that are associated with psychiatric referral may be different yet again. Much has still to be learned about the process leading to socially handicapping drug dependence.

TREATMENT

Treatment of drug misuse and drug dependence is complex and multifactorial. There is a high mortality among opioid users (James 1967; Bewley *et al* 1968; Gardner 1970; Chapple *et al* 1972) and among users of barbiturates. Overdoses and complications of injection are common (Wright & Turner 1971). Withdrawal symptoms or claims that withdrawal symptoms are present, by opioid users, present difficulties in management to casualty departments as well as special treatment units. Withdrawal fits in those taking large and regular amounts of barbiturates and some tranquillisers can cause concern.

Although, traditionally, treatment and rehabilitation are usually dealt with separately, treatment of drug dependence (apart from the simple matter of withdrawal from the drug if the patient so wishes) merges inextricably with rehabilitation.

There is much discussion, often heated, about methods of treatment and rehabilitation but there is an absence of data which clearly demonstrates the relationship of a particular treatment regime to outcome. Treatment involves multifactorial aspects which are themselves difficult to quantify and record, and scientific evaluation requires a long-term follow-up of some 90 per cent of those treated. The lack of data is not difficult to understand. The drug dependent individual is less likely than most to stick to long-term contact and evaluation and the rights of the individual to drop out of follow-up systems has to be respected. At the Maudsley Hospital Drug Dependence Unit it is unusual to be able to follow up more than 70 per cent of a drug dependent population over 3 years.

The key factor is the level of motivation for treatment and this varies greatly. What appears to be strong motivation at outpatient interview may decline overnight or even earlier, and then after admission to hospital appear weak or absent.

The treatment of drug dependence can conveniently be subdivided as follows:

1   Maintenance of the drug of dependence.
2   Treatment of acute intoxications and other drug misuse emergencies.
3   Withdrawal of drug of dependence from the chronic user.
4   Treatment of the early abstinent phase.
5   Long-term treatment and rehabilitation.

Treatment of acute intoxications will usually be dealt with by the family doctor or casualty department and is outside the scope of this chapter, as are complications of unsterile injections such as hepatitis, carditis, septicaemia, pulmonary complications, local abscesses, phlebitis.

Examination of 107 opioid users (Gardner & Connell 1970) attending a special drug dependence clinic, suggested that even if three consecutive urines were positive for opioids great caution should be used in prescribing heroin or methadone on a maintenance basis for adolescent opioid users. Maintenance on other drugs such as amphetamines and barbiturates is rarely indicated, if at all.

Withdrawal of drugs from a dependent person is usually best carried out in hospital—preferably in a special hospital unit—though there is no problem in withdrawing someone who is very strongly motivated (a very rare occurrence) as an outpatient.

Opioids

Heroin, morphine, methadone and other opioids should be withdrawn slowly over the course of several days according to the chronic dose taken. This is in order to prevent the opiate withdrawal syndrome which includes yawning, perspiration, lachrymation and rhinorrhoea, followed by mydriasis, goose-flesh, tremors and muscle twitches, hot and cold flushes, aching bones and muscles, anorexia and later agitation, restlessness, diarrhoea, depression. The syndrome can be very distressing and painful (Blachly 1966). Since it is often difficult or impossible to establish the actual dose taken, a system which allows flexibility of dosage for the first 36 hours or so is advisable. Heroin-dependent patients are usually withdrawn under cover of reducing doses of methadone but other drugs such as chlormethiazole edisylate (Heminevrin) have been used. The latter is itself a drug which has been mis-used by patients who have received it as part of withdrawal treatment and have later become dependent on it. Withdrawal, as long as the patient stays for the withdrawal, is a simple procedure in expert hands and withdrawal symptoms can be kept to the minimum and even eliminated. Since with-drawal need seldom last more than 10–14 days it would seem that undue attention has been given to the replacement drug used. Methadone with-drawal is relatively easy to manage, for it does substitute for heroin or mor-phine and can be taken orally, and as the patient can be kept comfortable, this is the drug of choice.

Barbiturates

Barbiturates should never be withdrawn abruptly from a dependent patient since withdrawal fits (sometimes leading to status epilepticus) and a with-drawal psychosis (similar to delirium tremens) can occur (see Blachly 1966).

Hypnotics and tranquillisers

Chlordiazepoxide (Librium), diazepam (Valium) and other drugs of these classes should be withdrawn slowly since experience has shown that with-drawal fits can occur and that this complication may be more likely in the present days of multiple drug use.

Amphetamines and amphetamine barbiturate mixtures

Although, theoretically, there is no reason why amphetamines cannot be withdrawn abruptly there is a need to watch carefully for withdrawal depres-sion which can be so intense that there is a risk of suicide. Withdrawal in hospital is usually necessary. If the depression is marked or continues for a week or more, some authorities would treat the patient with antidepressants.

The overactivity and disturbed behaviour of amphetamine psychosis, if severe, can be treated effectively with phenothiazines.

Amphetamine-barbiturate mixtures (Drinamyl) cause no trouble, apart from depression, if withdrawn abruptly, but as many patients are taking barbiturates in addition to that contained in the pill, a barbiturate withdrawal regime may be advisable.

Treatment of the early abstinent phase

Withdrawal from the drug of dependence is relatively easy but this is only a small part of the total treatment plan. In the early abstinent phase, craving, insecurity feelings, and mood swings are common since it takes some weeks for the psychophysiology of the body to return to normality. At this time, support, and exploration of the basic problems leading to drug dependence, should be carried out. The presence of neurotic fears or other psychiatric or social problems may indicate special treatment needs.

Long-term treatment and rehabilitation

Rehabilitation back to the community, in full occupation and off drugs, is clearly the ideal goal. Unfortunately, many drug-dependent patients find this goal impossible to achieve often because of craving for drugs or lack of motivation. A more realistic method has been to maintain heroin addicts on oral methadone and about 100 000 or more such patients are currently being maintained in this way in the USA.

Other systems which have achieved prominence include self-help communities, such as Phoenix House, Daytop, Synanon and various offshoots, in which a drug-free environment is created and a hierarchical system of progression through the community is arranged which has its basis in encounter groups and the disciplining of members by the group.

Whatever the system used in rehabilitation, it must be remembered that although many common problems exist in the drug-dependent populations, each member has a different constellation of personality characteristics and problems. The question is not what is the best method of treating drug-dependent persons but which of the available methods is suitable for each individual patient. Many, for instance, could not take part in methadone maintenance and many could not tolerate the self-help community discipline.

NEONATAL ADDICTION

The existence of opioid-dependent pregnant women has drawn attention to the problems of the fetus and the neonate in relation to opioid dependency. The opiate withdrawal syndrome in neonates has been well known in the USA for many years.

Women chronically dependent on opioids often have amenorrhoea and the pregnancy may not be noticed for several months. Attendance at antenatal clinics may be irregular or infrequent. There is an above average incidence of maternal syphilis, toxaemia, breech presentation, premature rupture of membranes and prolapsed cord or limbs at delivery, and these factors contribute to a high fetal wastage which may reach 24 per cent (Perlmutter 1967). The infant is often born at home, in the ambulance, or in other adverse conditions and labour is often premature and delivery precipitous (Kahn *et al* 1969; Stone *et al* 1971).

Although the onset of symptoms is said to range from before birth (in which violent fetal kicking may be noticed when the addict is overdue for a dose of drug), in most cases the symptoms appear between the first and third days after delivery though occasionally a week later (Rosenthal *et al* 1965). There are symptoms of withdrawal (tremors, shrill cry, irritability, vomiting, diarrhoea, feeding problems, fever, yawning and sneezing); and symptoms of narcosis (cyanosis, depressed Moro reflex) and respiratory difficulty which could be due to narcosis or withdrawal. Although it is said that withdrawal symptoms are only detectable if the mother has been taking 10–15 mg of heroin (or equivalent dose of other opioids) the unreliability of drug histories precludes the use of these data in planning treatment.

Kahn (1974) notes that coarse tremors are the hallmark of the withdrawal syndrome and are bilateral and sufficiently coarse to shake the whole extremity. They are quite distinct from the fine tremors seen in hypoglycaemia. Extreme irritability and a shrill high-pitched cry are also common.

Treatment of neonatal dependence

Treatment depends not only on the individual problems presented by a particular patient but also on the individual preferences, beliefs and policies of physicians and paediatricians. The disorganised life style of mothers is a potent factor which makes assessments of morbidity difficult. Mortality is claimed to be high in untreated neonates. As gastrointestinal disturbances are frequent it is often necessary to correct fluid and electrolyte imbalance in addition to the use of drug withdrawal therapy.

Reddy (1974) suggests the following regimen for different replacement drugs:

Initial drug dosages

Drug use	Range of dosage
Paregoric	3–10 drops every 4 hours
Phenobarbitone	5–10 mg/kg per day
Chlorpromazine	1–2·5 mg/kg per day
Valium	1–2 mg every 8 hours

Kahn (1974) suggests the following regimes:

Medication for heroin withdrawal manifestations in infancy (ORAL)

Group 1 (narcotic replacement which abolishes most or all the heroin withdrawal symptoms in adequate dosage—the objective being to keep
the patient mildly symptomatic on decreasing doses until completely
withdrawn. It being usually possible to discontinue the drug after
some weeks or months).

Camphorated Opium Tincture USP (Paregoric)

5–10 drops every 4 hours.

Methadone

First day: 0·25 mg every 4 hours

Thereafter: 1·125 mg every 4 hours

Group 2 (drugs which counteract at best only one or two of the many withdrawal symptoms but which are, for practical purposes not habit
forming. Phenobarbital, for instance, reducing the irritability of
afflicted infants, reduced periods of wakefulness and may prevent
withdrawal seizures but has no effect on other symptoms, including
myoclonic jerks).

Phenobarbitone

8·0 mg/kg/24 hours, divided into 3–4 doses.

Chlorpromazine

2·8 mg/kg/24 hours, divided into 3–4 doses.

A narcotic replacement such as Paregoric or Methadone, which suppresses withdrawal symptoms in toto, and which is based upon a gradual
withdrawal over 10–21 days, is scentifically preferable to other methods. One
must bear in mind, however, that mild symptoms which could be considered
as theoretically relevant to narcotic withdrawal are more likely, after 10–15
days, to be due to other factors and that continuing with narcotic medication

longer than 21 days (having gradually lowered the dose) is rarely, if ever, necessary.

SPECIAL ASPECTS OF THE TREATMENT OF ADOLESCENT DRUG MISUSE AND DEPENDENCE

The discussion on treatment so far has been of a general nature although relevant to adolescents, particularly the older adolescent, does not touch on any special difficulties in the treatment of the younger age groups.

A general discussion of addiction in adolescence (Connell 1974) noted the following features of adolescence which made adolescents a vulnerable group in terms of drug dependence.

1 Adolescence is the period of life during which many individuals develop mood swings and depressive reactions or even depressive illness.

2 It is a period during which sensitivities increase and social sensitivities in particular create problems which require solution if the person is to mature.

3 It is a period during which loneliness, boredom, and the striving for independence and identity definition is a basic challenge.

It must be clearly stated that of the adolescent population as a whole the vast majority exposed to drugs either do not use them or use them experimentally and then give them up.

Within this age range one can, perhaps, define groups which are particularly vulnerable to adolescent emotional disturbance and also to drug dependence. By far the largest group are those who reach puberty already emotionally disturbed and, in particular, suffering from marked emotional immaturity, with few resources to deal with the challenges and problems of adolescence. (This concept has been supported by a controlled study of adolescents in the USA using the MMPI, Brook *et al* 1974.) A second group, much smaller and perhaps not so clearly defined, except on theoretical grounds are those who, although emotionally mature for their age may develop marked mood swings and depression, perhaps on the basis of a genetic factor, and who treat their depression with drugs and become dependent on them.

It is the author's view that medical practitioners should never prescribe drugs of dependence to adolescents, particularly barbiturates or amphetamines, and that they should resist pressures from such individuals for drugs. It is very rare for an adolescent to require night sedation especially, for insomnia alone, and very common for adolescent drug users to use insomnia as a complaint for which they expect, and unfortunately often receive, sedatives from doctors.

Although adolescents are seen at most special drug-dependence clinics

there is only one in Britain which caters exclusively for children and adolescents up to 18 years of age. The early experience of this unit was reported
and some findings are of interest (Boyd *et al* 1971). Under stress and
without drugs, neurotic features and depression became more pronounced.
Inpatient stay usually lasted many months, and in some cases readmission
was necessary. It was impossible to gain cooperation from many of the
parents. Problems of a new pioneering project such as inexperience of staff
and the lack of any previous therapeutic model were mentioned and it was
noted that the combination of firmness and patience and consistent staff team-
work are not easily achieved in this setting, which lies outside the established
pattern of psychiatry.

In a general discussion (Boyd 1972) it was stressed that if the drug taking
was not an expression of serious psychological disturbance the general practitioner had an important role in helping the family to motivate the adolescent
in the right direction. It was also observed that 'many general practitioners
today are often out of touch with young people, unaware of their difficulties
and vulnerability, and ill-equipped in training and experience to provide the
appropriate form of assistance'.

As in the treatment of psychiatric disorder in general, in this age group,
it is as important for the therapist and his team to avoid being identified as
an authoritarian group siding with the parents and preaching the harmfulness
of drugs at an opinionated didactic level, as it is to give factual and accurate
data. Unfortunately, all too few professional workers actually know the data
or how to evaluate the relevance of the many articles and papers appearing
on drug misuse. These data help the patient to make an individual choice
without telling him what to do.

CONCLUSIONS

The lack of precise knowledge of clinical aspects of drug abuse has been
stressed and the need therefore to deal with each adolescent as an individual
within a family unit using traditional psychiatric methods, is clear. Drug misuse can be seen as a possible complication of preexisting, or recent psychiatric
disturbance, which produces secondary complications such as dependence,
physical illness, infringement of laws, etc.

Psychiatric treatment alone holds no definitive answer to the problem of
personality disorders of the type which often exist in drug misusers. Other
approaches, such as self-help communities, have therefore been mentioned.
Unduly optimistic claims by psychiatrists do no service to the patient or to
the profession.

This chapter has not dealt with prevention or education. Emphasis has been laid on the importance of psychiatrists imparting factual knowledge, rather than belief systems, to patients and their families, and the avoidance of an authoritarian approach in discussions concerning the effects of drugs. It is recognised that many professionals working in child and adolescent psychiatry have little opportunity of obtaining scientific knowledge (including the knowledge that there are little or no precise data on many points, including the harmfulness of some drugs).

If drug misuse and drug dependence continue to be a problem in the UK there appears to be a strong case for educational seminars aimed at the needs of those working in the field of child and adolescent psychiatry.

APPENDIX

Studies of patients in the hospital service and some other institutions

It would have been preferable to review studies of patients in terms of special aspects, such as family background; psychiatric diagnosis; or factors specific to childhood and adolescence. However, most of the available studies in the UK do not focus on such specific areas and are not easily comparable. Accordingly, a broad sketch is given of recently described clinical populations, in which there are details relevant to the practice of child and adolescent psychiatry.

London (Hospital Services)

Bransby (1971) designed a study to include every patient notified by hospitals as addicted to heroin, methadone or cocaine. A questionnaire was completed using data obtained at first attendance. Out of a total of 2580 patients, questionnaires were completed for 2187 covering the period up to February 1970. This group represented about two-thirds of all addicts notified by all sources (including prisons, GPs, etc.).

Of attenders 82 per cent were male and 18 per cent female, with four-fifths born in England and one-tenth in other parts of the UK or the Irish Republic. The social class distribution of the fathers of English born male patients was much the same as the national distribution. The fathers of female patients, however, showed a higher representation of professional and intermediate occupations and a lower representation of partly skilled and unskilled occupations.

Of the English-born patients about 5 per cent had attended child-guidance clinics and about 25 per cent were on probation. Many had taken amphetamines, amphetamine–barbiturate mixtures, hallucinogens and cannabis in the past. Forty per cent males and 28 per cent females reported that they were still working and 86 per cent claimed to be working full time.

A second report (Bransby *et al* 1973) referred to 666 patients notified between 1 March 1970 and 31 December 1971. The same questionnaire was used with the addition of questions on living arrangements and broken homes. Similar results were found. One-third of patients came from a broken home as compared with an estimated national average of about one-tenth. A higher proportion of patients had used methadone (possibly due to a switch to methadone by many treatment centres) and 50 per cent said that they had used these drugs at least 2 years before coming to hospital. Amphetamine and cannabis were most frequently used at early stages and the wider use of barbiturates and synthetic hallucinogens began a few years later.

Stimson and Ogborne (1970) using an interview schedule with a representative sample of addicts prescribed heroin at London clinics, reported upon 111 subjects (86·7 per cent of the sample selected) who were interviewed between March and November 1969. The mean age was 25 years with a range from 17–32 years. Forty per cent were under 21 years of age. Those currently in full time employment (40 per cent of the total), compared with others, had worked for a greater proportion of the time since they began using heroin and fewer reported having lost a job through use of heroin. Forty-three per cent reported that they had been convicted for an offence under one of the drug acts and 51 per cent reported a conviction for a nondrug offence before their first use of heroin. Thirty-six per cent reported a nondrug offence since using heroin. Separation from both parents for a year or more prior to the age of 16 was reported in 22 per cent and a further 25 per cent had been separated from one parent only. Twenty-eight per cent reported no trouble at school and 13 per cent reported that they were known as 'troublemakers' at school. Thirty-six per cent had, at some time, been given hospital treatment for physical complications associated with drug use; the most frequent complication being abscesses.

Blumberg *et al* (1974a, b) describe a long-term (5 years) prospective study of opiate users attending treatment centres in Greater London during 1971 (see Chapter 23). The findings are similar to and support Bransby (1971). The sample comprised 307 eligible subjects (injectors) and 210 were interviewed; (a response of 90 per cent). The sex ratio was approximately 4 : 1 in favour of males and the median age was 21·7 years, with 26 per cent in the late teenage years. Younger subjects were more extroverted. Educational backgrounds were similar to British norms; employment record showed 39 per cent in full time employment; 4 per cent part time; 50 per cent unemployed; 7 per cent housewives, students or miscellaneous. Personality profiles were low in authoritarianism, and 'normal' on anxiety and extroversion. The incidence of parental death appeared to be no higher than in samples of psychiatric patients or normal controls. The parents of 20 per cent were alive and living apart. About 33 per cent had been separated from one or both parents for more than a year before the age of 15. Just under 74 per cent had been brought up by their natural parents and on average they had between two and three siblings. Of the 180 subjects with siblings, 55 had at least one sibling who had been convicted. At least 50 per cent of the total sample had first injected an opiate 3 years or more prior to approaching a clinic.

Gardner and Connell (1970; 1971) reported on the 107 opioid users attending a special drug-dependence clinic between 25 March 1968 and 28 February 1969 using a questionnaire given to 83 per cent of all new cases. (This questionnaire was designed by the authors with the help of members of the Addiction Research Unit of the Institute of Psychiatry and used, and later modified, for the purposes of the studies reported by Bransby (1971).) Seventy-seven per cent attenders were born in the UK; 3·7 per cent were born in the Republic of Ireland and there were 11 Canadians (10·3 per cent all over age 29 who had lived in England for a mean duration of 6·6 years). Patients of all 'other' nationalities were over 26 years. Fifty-four (50 per cent) were aged between 16 and 22. Heroin users aged 35 years or over were overrepresented in the series as compared with Home Office (1968) figures. The ratio of male to female was 4 : 1 and the sexes were similar with respect to age distribution and patterns of drug misuse.

There was no signficant correlation between age at first attendance and social class, nor between sex and social class unlike the earlier findings (Bransby 1971; Bransby *et al* 1973). A background of behaviour disorder and adolescent problems was not uncommon. Twelve per cent had a history of attendance at child guidance clinics and 2 patients had attended schools for maladjusted boys. Suicidal attempts or gestures had occurred in 20·6 per cent. Some of these were related to depression following the withdrawal of CNS stimulants. A number of patients showed paranoid symptoms due to the direct psychotoxic effects of these drugs (cocaine or amphetamine). The mean onset of drug misuse was 18 years with a range of 13 to 59 years. All but five individuals had started before the age of 25 years. Fifty-eight subjects had first used an opioid between the ages of 14 and 19. The progression from sporadic to daily misuse was within a year in 59 cases and there was a change to methadone.

Gardner and Connell (1972) described 104 amphetamine and other nonopioid drug users attending a special drug dependence clinic between March 1968 and February 1969 who were given a special questionnaire on first attendance. Nearly one-third gave a history of starting amphetamine misuse while at school (13 per cent) or within a year of leaving school (16 per cent). Amphetamine psychosis had occurred in 35 per cent and was a more frequent complication of intravenous than of oral abuse. Although maintenance therapy was considered most unlikely to be effective, about one-quarter of the younger patients had obtained prescriptions from general practitioners after starting their drug abuse illicitly.

Forty-seven patients were between 14 and 19 years of age in a ratio of 4 males to 1 female. A background of behaviour disorders and adolescent problems before, as well as after, starting misuse of drugs was not uncommon. Five patients gave a history of depressive illness which had been treated with ECT and two were suffering from a paranoid psychosis unconnected with drug taking. Twenty-one (20 per cent) had made a suicidal attempt or gesture and 36 (23 per cent) had experienced paranoid symptoms from the use of amphetamines. Three clinical groupings were defined: the older tablet users; the young tablet users; and the intravenous users. It was considered that those taking large doses of amphetamines tended to be more restless, agitated and verbally aggressive than others.

A study of 64 amphetamine addicts (1964–67) examined retrospectively in relation to theories of causation of drug addiction (Connell & Thorn 1971) found that 88 per cent were aged 15–25 years at first attendance. No significant socioeconomic factor emerged. Diagnostic labels included inadequate personality, immature personality, adolescent emotional disturbance, delinquency and drug addiction. Only one was diagnosed as schizophrenic but depression was noted in those suffering from personality disorders. Fifty-eight per cent had been referred for psychiatric advice before attending the Maudsley Hospital outpatient department because of drug dependence. Forty per cent reported a family background in which one or more parents had a psychiatric history which involved outpatient or inpatient treatment. Seventy-five per cent gave a forensic history when first seen of which 39 per cent was not related to drug taking. Nonspecific factors common to many forms of 'maladjustment' were demonstrated in the sample, without any specific factor responsible for drug dependence.

Boyd *et al* (1971) report on the treatment and follow-up of adolescent heroin addicts in the only unit (opened in April 1968) specifically designed to deal with drug dependent persons under the age of 18 years. Home Office figures for 1968 showed that about 27 per cent of addicts were teenagers. Of 130 patients referred 52 were not accepted for treatment for reasons of age, failure to attend, or because they were not really addicted. Social class III families predominated and there was a history of severe emotional disturbance in one or other parent in 24 cases, in 6 of which one parent was absent through death. In a further 17 cases one or both parents were absent from the family. Five adolescents began using nonopioid drugs at the age of 11 and the youngest using heroin was 13 years of age with 6 at age 14, and 24 at age 15. Although no overtly psychotic patients presented and the term psychopath was not considered appropriate, many neurotic features were evident in the patients, 'especially obsessive-compulsive patterns and depressive moods'. 'A form of chronic depression expressed as apathy and boredom seemed to underlie most cases. The youngsters tended to be highly suspicious, especially of adults in authority but, paradoxically were also dependent on and demanding of the adults.' Many were emotionally immature and had failed in their social and educational environments. They showed low tolerance to anxiety and frustration, often responding to these by aggression and destructive outbursts or by illicit drug taking. It was considered that youngsters in the unit had profound personal problems, of which their drug taking was both a symptom and a deviant attempt at resolution.

Hicks (1969) described the clinical and social features of the first 57 patients referred to a general hospital drug addiction treatment centre: 43 per cent were 16–19 years of age; 82 per cent were single; 64 per cent were in social class V; and 14 per cent had never worked. Unlike the experience of Merry (1967), other psychiatric patients in the unit complained vociferously about the behaviour of the addicts.

Connell (1970) stressed that most people dependent on drugs have an unstable personality, and often there were antisocial features before drug taking began. Nevertheless, 'normal' people are not immune from drug dependence, especially at times of stress or emotional disturbance.

A retrospective study of the case-notes of all patients treated during the first 17 months of a treatment unit for drug addicts set up in the East End of London (Crawley 1971) covered the period from 1 March 1968 to 31 July 1969 and included only those who attended on five or more separate occasions after initial registration as an addict. The report covered 134 patients. All were addicted to 'hard' drugs used intravenously. Twenty-three patients were aged 15–17 years and 70 aged 18–20 years. Three main points emerged from the study. First, problems ranged from the young adolescent barely addicted to drugs but showing considerable disturbance in the process of maturation, to the hardened heroin addict of 20 years of age. Second, there was the degree of the clinic's work so that relatively little work was undertaken with patients' families with some form of structural breakdown, and third, the ways in which the policy of not delineating catchment areas for the special treatment centres affected the orientation of the clinic's work so that relatively little work was undertaken with patient's families even though 62 per cent of the patients were living at home at the time of referral and were mainly adolescents.

A study of outpatients with narcotic addiction (Oppenheim *et al* 1973) noted that, from the beginning, treatment had to take into account the individual personality problems which were invariably present. During the first 3 years of the clinic's practice (it opened in February 1968) 643 patients attended requesting drugs. 260 came only for the initial interview with the nurse and failed to keep any subsequent appointment. A total of 185 patients received long-term treatment and of these 17 had died. At the Charing Cross Clinic a community orientated approach was adopted. Two groups were studied: a follow-up group of the first 40 patients who came off drugs and a control group of 40 patients, chosen by taking the next patient registering after each individual follow-up patient, and still attending the clinic at the time of the study. The follow-up sample was similar to that reported by Bransby (1971) and 18 per cent were female. It appeared that girls were much more disturbed and more difficult to treat than boys. The age at first attendance of the control group was 24 years and 21 years in the follow-up group. It seemed that patients were unlikely to have been seriously drug dependent at the age of 16–18 years. In both groups 50 per cent had had some form of further education. Home backgrounds showed little difference between the two groups. More than half the patients in both groups had shown some degree of antisocial behaviour prior to their drug involvement. Less than 30 per cent admitted to inpatient units did well. The importance of a continuing relationship with the patient was stressed.

London delinquency services and special studies of delinquency

A report on youngsters on entry to two London remand homes, using urine tests for amphetamine to differentiate a urine-positive and urine-negative population, showed no difference between the two groups with regard to types of offence which had led to admission; average numbers of previous offences; seriousness of offence; ethnic groupings; average number of siblings or family backgrounds. The drug taking was thought to be incidental to the delinquency though 'probably having similar roots in opportunity and predisposition' (Scott & Willcox 1965).

Of 188 offenders attending courts in Middlesex who had been convicted of drug offences, only 20 were 17 years of age or under, although two-thirds were under 25 (Report on a Drug Survey 1967, 1969).

A description (Garvey 1970), of a year's experience at the Kilburn Square Drug Abuse Centre, set up by the Probation Service, noted that of a total of 63 cases, 57 (79 per cent) had been taking amphetamines. All took oral amphetamines but only 6 were not using parenteral methedrine. Fourteen were between the ages of 14 and 17 years. Delinquency/criminality traits, aggressiveness, and social inadequacies were common.

A follow-up study of girls in a London remand home during 1966–68 (Noble & Barnes 1971) showed that 21 per cent of those taking nonnarcotic drugs on admission, but only 1 per cent of nondrug-taking control admissions, had used narcotics by June 1970. Narcotic use on admission and progression to narcotic use were associated with frequent drug taking of other kinds and marked involvement in a drug milieu. Adolescents who used illicit drugs and had a history of court appearances for any reason were particularly vulnerable to subsequent narcotic usage and other forms of serious drug abuse. Urine tests were carried out where possible and of about 1000 girls, 194 had used nonnarcotic drugs and 33 had also used narcotics. Most girls came from homes which were materially adequate and had parents who worked in skilled or semiskilled jobs. The families tended to be large and were characterised by disruption, parental separation, poor discipline and hostility and only a minority of the girls were still living with both parents. The progressors and narcotic groups tended to have a higher incidence of psychiatric morbidity with long-standing personal abnormalities. The incidence of recent depressive symptomatology and suicidal attempts among the narcotic groups was particularly high. The overall incidence of family morbidity was higher than that shown in a similar study of drug-taking delinquent boys (Noble 1970). Compulsory admission to psychiatric hospitals led to a majority absconding or discharging themselves against medical advice (Noble *et al* 1972).

D'Orban (1970), a psychiatrist in Holloway Prison, reported on 66 of all female heroin addicts admitted during January 1967 to June 1968—most of them remanded in custody for psychiatric reports; the mean age was 20 years and the women tended to come from opposite ends of the social class spectrum: 53 per cent were of no fixed abode, 63 per cent had a history of a broken home before the age of 15, nearly half showed homosexual orientation with all but one being multiple drug users, and nearly two-thirds had a history of court appearances before addiction. They showed more severe psychiatric abnormality than male heroin addicts with evidence of severe personality disturbance predating their addiction. Seventeen per cent had a history of psychiatric inpatient treatment before addiction, and some had attended outpatient and child guidance clinics or had been given psychiatric help at approved school. Fifty per cent had a history of admission to psychiatric hospitals since addiction and 30 per cent had had more than one admission, 16 per cent were illegitimate children (more than three times the expectation from the general population). The usual hospital diagnosis was personality disorder usually precipitated by a suicidal gesture, or by a transient amphetamine psychosis.

Gordon (1973) examined patterns of delinquency in 60 consecutive male patients attending a London drug clinic in 1970 (Maudsley Hospital), who had commenced their drug use before the age of 21 years.

Urine tests for the presence of drugs were carried out in all cases. The mean age of the sample was 22 years and the mean age of first drug use was 16 years. Social class showed a normal distribution, 41 per cent had lost a parent for at least 1 year before the age of 16 and 58 per cent of predrug offenders had experienced parental loss compared with 26 per cent of postdrug offenders—a significant difference. Paternal loss exceeded maternal loss in all groups and was significantly more frequent in predrug offenders than postdrug offenders. Of the subjects 56 per cent who had experienced parental loss had been separated from a parent before the age of 6. The most frequent causes were temporary separation and care by authorities. Sixty per cent gave a history of truancy and 40 per cent of recurrent theft in childhood. The incidence of these antisocial traits did not differ significantly between subgroups. Twenty per cent had attended a psychiatric clinic, or child guidance clinic, and 13 per cent had been inpatients in a psychiatric hospital. In terms of diagnosis 55 per cent were diagnosed as drug dependent only, 33·3 per cent as personality disorders, 5 per cent as neurotic and 1·7 per cent as schizophrenic. This pattern of classification did not differ significantly between subgroups. Gordon concluded that treatment plans should take into account the antisocial nature of the individuals who became drug dependent rather than adopt a permissive approach to therapy.

Dundee

Ballinger (1972) reported on 378 patients admitted to a psychiatric service in Dundee in 1970 who received continuous psychotropic medication for 4 weeks. A quarter were regarded as drug dependent but opiates and amphetamines did not appear in the list of drugs used and very few gave a history of illicit drug taking. Only 21 patients were aged 10–19 and only one of these was considered drug dependent.

East Midlands

A clinical study of 139 patients (mean age 23 years) referred to an addiction unit in the East Midlands during 1969 and 1970 (Ritson *et al* 1973), showed that problems of drug abuse in the East Midlands differed from those described in metropolitan areas, in that the problem of notified opiate addiction was small, although over half the sample had had at least one experience with opiates. There was a low incidence of physical disability due to drug abuse compared with London clinics. Dependence on the drug subculture rather than on any particular drug was stressed. Social pressures appeared more important in the genesis of drug abuse than did mental distress. No social class was disproportionately represented and all were British by birth. Seventy-three patients were aged 15–20 years and none was under 15 years of age. About one-quarter gave a history of self-poisoning with attendant thoughts of suicide, though these data require cautious interpretation since some may have been accidental overdoses. There had been an increase in delinquency since the onset of drug misuse. Over half were unemployed at first contact with the clinic, and an unstable work record was common. Twenty-one per cent of the sample reported excessive drinking by at least one member of their nuclear family, usually the father. Twelve patients reported drug abuse by at least one member of their nuclear family; in six cases by mother and in six cases by siblings. This was a higher incidence than that among nuclear families of alcoholic patients referred to the unit during the same period. Oral amphetamines were the principal drug abused in 56 cases.

Edinburgh

A total of 252 consecutive admissions of drug abuse patients admitted to the regional poisoning treatment centre, Edinburgh, during 1971–72 included 146 males and 43 females and showed a mean age of 20 years (Forrest & Tarala 1973). Seventy-two per cent of admissions occurred between 6 p.m. and 8 a.m. and Saturday was the most common day for admission. Barbiturates were the drugs most commonly abused, followed by LSD and methaqualone (Mandrax). Of these 65 per cent had previously abused drugs, 60 per cent were in social class IV or V. Psychiatric and social support was required in only a small minority of patients. Opiates were involved in 6 per cent of cases (16 patients) of which 13 were intravenous users. Of those with psychiatric illness 26 per cent were suffering from personality disorders and five patients were depressed; 30 per cent had received psychiatric treatment in the past. Seventeen patients were regarded as alcoholics and a further 24 had taken alcohol excessively. A diagnosis of drug addiction was made in 35 patients (19 per cent).

Woodside (1973) studied the first 100 referrals (during a period of 3 years) to a drug addiction treatment centre established at the Royal Edinburgh Hospital in April 1968. From the date of opening all heroin addicts in the area were referred to the centre for investigation and treatment.

Thirty-one per cent were aged 15–19 years and 51 per cent between 20 and 24 years; 41 per cent had a broken home in childhood.

Almost half the group had a disturbed family background and as children 'they grew up in poverty in loveless homes, characterised by parental "arguments", drunken quarrels and scenes of violence'. Education had ceased at 15 for 57 per cent and for the majority schooldays had been endured rather than enjoyed. Work records were poor; sexual lives were often promiscuous and amoral, and 49 patients had a known criminal record. Multiple drug use was the pattern. Compared with reports from other treatment centres—particularly London—few of those seen in Edinburgh conformed to the stereotype of a 'real' heroin addict. None was extremely ill or on the point of death and withdrawal symptoms were the exception. Two categories were defined: those who gave a credible history of continued use of opiates (45 per cent) and those who experimented with any and every drug available. Of the former group, contact with London was thought to be of 'noxious significance'.

Glasgow

McKay *et al* (1973) noted that male medical students smoked and drank more than females. Bennie (1970) described 90 drug addicts attending a Glasgow hospital between 1961–68. Isolation from parents, mobility of abode and a tendency to form a subculture were all noted.

Hertfordshire

A study was made of 50 patients in a New Town Area who took heroin (Anumonye & McClure 1970) and who were seen at the addiction clinic, or in the wards of a general hospital in Hertfordshire between April and September 1968. Four patients were 15–16 years of age; 7 patients 17–18 years; 23 patients 19–20 years. The findings differed from those of other studies in the southern suburbs of London (Alarcón & Rathod 1968; Kosviner *et al* 1968; Dixon 1968). For instance, the subjects lived predominantly with their parents and were not displaced drifters. All the patients would be placed in classes IV and V of the Registrar General's Classification (1966). Drug abuse was associated with chance friendship patterns. Academic pressures and parental expectations were high in this new industrial town. Permanent separation from one, or both parents, before the age of 16 was present in 13 cases, and in 28 families there was severe marital disharmony. Neurotic traits in childhood were noted in 18 cases; timidity in 12; anxiety proneness in 8; schizoid tendencies in 4 and aggressiveness in 3. Many other drugs other than heroin had been used. All the drug abusers were considered to have some personality disorder assessed as mild (14 cases), moderate (29 cases) and severe (7 cases). Formal psychiatric diagnoses were psychoses (mainly amphetamine-induced) 26 cases; neuroses 13 cases and no illness 11 cases.

Special studies

A controlled study of 'psychoticism' in four groups of drug users (Teasdale *et al* 1971) which included as experimental groups a provincial heroin group; an inpatient injector group; and an inpatient oral user group, and a control group, suggested a higher P score than the control group.

The findings should not be taken as suggesting the assumption of a unique 'addictive personality' in that there was ample evidence that drug-users, even on the same drug, are a heterogenous population in which a number of 'types' can be recognised. Three of the drug-using groups were also significantly higher in 'neuroticism' scores and this finding was a more consistent feature of drug-users than deviation on 'extraversion'.

A study of young male heroin dependent patients in relation to intellectual assessment (Kaldegg 1973a, b) examines three groups of patients differentiated by years of admission to hospital (1963–64; 1965–67; 1969–70). No patient was under 18 years of age. The majority were of above average IQ and it was inferred from variation on individual performances on the subtests of the WAIS that they were underfunctioning and their potential level was higher.

Other studies also suggested that the intellectual level of drug-dependent persons was above average (Mott 1972; Halstead & Neal 1968) whereas some studies have concluded that there is no difference between drug addicts and the general population in relation to intelligence (Rosenberg 1969; Gerrard & Kornetsky 1955).

A study of young male heroin-dependent patients (Kaldegg 1973a), b) in relation to attitudes to members of the family, using a sentence completion test, examined 97 subjects separated into 3 groups. Group 1 comprised 52 patients under psychiatric treatment for heroin dependence with a mean age of 24 years. Group 2 comprised 24 psychoneurotic patients who had never used heroin and who were under psychiatric treatment and had a mean age of 24 years. Group 3 comprised 21 men of no known psychiatric illness or drug use of mean age 26. No significant differences between the heroin group and the controls were found. The heroin users were found to be nearer to controls than the psychiatric patients nonheroin users.

Vietnam veterans

Although the studies so far refer to the problem of drug abuse and drug dependence in the UK it is appropriate to mention one of the most important recent researches in this field. Robins *et al* (1974) studied drug use by US Army enlisted men in Vietnam, who were followed up on their return home. This classic, methodologically excellent, study has thrown light upon the use of drugs of dependence in a total population who, under the stress of war, were subjects to pressures affecting their general behaviour which led many of them to take drugs.

Robins *et al* (1974) sought 943 men who had returned to the USA from Vietnam in September 1971, in order to carry out interviews and collect urine specimens. A total of 900 were personally interviewed and urine specimens collected from 876. Almost half tried heroin or opium while in Vietnam and one-fifth developed physical or psychological dependence. In the 8–12-month period after their return, about 10 per cent had some experience with opiates but less than 1 per cent had shown signs of opiate dependence. Among those who were 'drug positive' three-quarters felt they had been addicted to narcotics in Vietnam. One-third had some further experience with opiates but only 7 per cent showed signs of dependence. Rather than giving up drugs altogether many had shifted from heroin to amphetamines or barbiturates. Almost none expressed a desire for treatment. Preservice use of drugs and the extent of use in Vietnam were strongest predictors of continued use after Vietnam. The authors conclude that, contrary to conventional belief, the occasional use of narcotics without becoming addicted appears possible even for men who had been previously dependent on narcotics.

This conclusion is an important counter to the conventional view that once a person regularly misuses a drug of dependence he will be dependent on that drug for the rest of his life. It also lends support to the clinical and theoretical view that stability of personality prior to drug use may be a protective factor against the development of severe and long lasting drug dependence.

COMMENTS ON THE REVIEW OF UK LITERATURE

The review has attempted to cover the majority of papers in which adolescents were included in the clinical material. In particular it gives a starting point for considering the question of delinquency and drug use. Studies of drug users in the general population and studies of patient groups in which the adolescent representation was very small or absent have not been included (cf. Alarcón & Rathod 1968; Alarcón 1969; Arroyave *et al* 1973; Fish *et al* 1974; Rathod *et al* 1967; Rathod 1972; Willis 1971; Glatt 1962; 1965; Bewley 1968).

No attempt has been made to undertake a comprehensive analysis of the papers reviewed. Indeed, the lack of comparability of populations, the general rather than specific nature of the subject matter, and the differences in recording data are some of the factors which would make such an analysis unproductive. The presentation of the review in terms of geographical location demonstrates the differences between the populations attending Scottish centres and those attending London centres (Bennie 1970; Ballinger 1972; McKay *et al* 1973). This is mainly due to the fact that London has been the first and remains the main centre for abuse and dependence on drugs such as heroin and methadone so that special treatment clinics were set up to deal solely with the heroin problem. Little attention was given to dependence on drugs other than opioids (only two or three centres in London included dependence on drugs other than opioids in their clinical practice) so that there was little attention given (and little time available) to deal with problems of amphetamine misuse, barbiturate misuse etc. in the early days. By contrast, the small problem of opioid misuse in Scotland meant that the total field of other drug misuse could be dealt with.

Most of the studies were retrospective and without controls, and often no attempt was made to use questionnaires to collect standard data. Even when a questionnaire was used (Gardner & Connell 1971) a later study (Gordon 1973) demonstrated a higher incidence of delinquent behaviour, as shown by court appearances, than the first questionnaire had revealed. This demonstrates the unreliability of some data obtained from drug dependent patients at initial enquiry. The Department of Health Studies (Bransby 1971; Bransby *et al* 1973) concluded that it was of satisfactory reliability in relation to the data they were collecting. A criticism is that much of the data from the clinics were obtained only later by research workers' examination of case-notes.

It is of interest that later studies confirm an earlier clinical view from the late 1960s (Connell 1970) that the majority of persons who become dependent on drugs had unstable personalities and showed antisocial behaviour before taking drugs.

Whether disturbed family background, prior antisocial behaviour, depression or neurotic traits are *aetiologically* significant in the development of drug misuse and drug dependence remains uncertain, but it is inescapable that the kind of patients attending hospital for help or admitted to special institutions through the courts, do show such features in their backgrounds and in their present status. Any process of management or treatment must, perforce, take them into account.

REFERENCES

ALARCÓN R. DE & RATHOD N.H. (1968) Prevalence and early detection of heroin abuse. *Brit. med. J.* **2,** 549–554

ALARCÓN R. DE (1969) The spread of heroin abuse in a community. *Bull. Narcotics* **21,** 17–22

ANGELIS DE G.G. (1972) Testing for drugs. I: Advantages and disadvantages. *Int. J. Addict.* **7,** 365–385

ANGELIS DE G.G. (1973) Testing for drugs. II: Techniques and issues. *Int. J. Addict.* **8,** 997–1014

ANUMONYE A. & McCLURE J.L. (1970) Adolescent drug abuse in a North London suburb. *Brit. J. Addict.* **65,** 25–3

ARROYAVE F., LITTLE D., LETEMENDIA F. & ALARCÓN R. DE (1973) Misuse of heroin and methadone in the city of Oxford. *Brit. J. Addict.* **68,** 129–135

BALLINGER B.R. (1972) Drug dependence in psychiatric admissions. *Brit. J. Addict.* **67,** 215–220

BENNIE E.H. (1970) A study of drug addiction at the Eastern District Hospital, Glasgow. *Brit. J. Addict.* **65,** 341–346

BEWLEY T.H., BEN-ARIE O. & JAMES I.P. (1968) Morbidity and mortality from heroin dependence. I: Survey of heroin addicts known to Home Office. *Brit. med. J.* **1,** 725–726

BEWLEY T.H. (1968) Recent changes in the incidence in all types of drug dependence in Great Britain. *Proc. roy. Soc. Med.* **61,** 175–177

BLACHLY P.H. (1966) Management of the opiate abstinence syndrome. *Amer. J. Psychiat.* **122,** 742–744

BLUMBERG H.H., COHEN S.D., DRONFIELD B.E., MORDECAI E.A., ROBERTS J.C. & HAWKS D. (1974a) British opiate users. I: People approaching London drug treatment centres. *Int. J. Addict.* **9,** 1–23

BLUMBERG H.H., COHEN S.D., DRONFIELD B.E., MORDECAI E.A., ROBERTS J.C. & HAWKS D. (1974b) British opiate users. 2: Differences between those given an opiate script and those not given one. *Int. J. Addict.* **9,** 205–220

BOYD P. (1972) Adolescents—drug abuse and addiction. *Brit. med. J.* **4,** 540–543

BOYD P., LAYLAND W.R. & CRICKMAY J.R. (1971) Treatment and follow-up of adolescents addicted to heroin. *Brit. med. J.* **4,** 604–605

BROOK R., KAPLUN J. & WHITEHEAD P.C. (1974) Personality characteristics of adolescent amphetamine users measured by the MMPI. *Brit. J. Addict.* **69,** 61–66

BRANSBY E.R. (1971) A study of patients notified by hospitals as addicted to drugs: first report. *Health Trends* **3,** 75–78

BRANSBY E.R., CURLEY G. & KOTULANSKA M. (1973) A study of patients notified by hospitals as addicted to drugs: second report. *Health Trends,* **5,** 17–20

CHAPPLE P.A.L., SOMEKH D.E. & TAYLOR M.E. (1972) Follow-up of cases of opiate addiction from the time of notification to the Home Office. *Brit. med. J.* **2,** 680–683

CONNELL P.H. (1958) *Amphetamine Psychosis.* Institute of Psychiatry. Maudsley Monograph no. 5. London: Chapman & Hall

CONNELL P.H. (1964) The present position with regard to misuse of amphetamine–barbiturate mixtures. *Brit. J. Addict.* **60,** 9–27

CONNELL P.H. (1965) Adolescent drug taking. *Proc. roy. Soc. Med.* **58,** 409–412

CONNELL P.H. (1968) The use and abuse of amphetamines. *The Practitioner,* **200,** 234–243

CONNELL P.H. (1970) Clinical aspects of drug addiction. *J. Roy. Coll. Physicians Lond.* **4,** 254–263

CONNELL P.H. (1974) Addiction in adolescence—some comments about its diagnosis, treatment, and vulnerable groups. *Community Health* **6**, 29–31

CONNELL P.H. & THORN W.A.J. (1971) 64 amphetamine addicts (1963–67) examined retrospectively in relation to theories of causation of drug addiction. *In Proc. of the Vth World Con. of Psychiatry, Mexico.* Amsterdam: Excerpta Medica

CRAWLEY J.A. (1971) A case-note study of 134 out-patient drug addicts over a 17 month period. *Brit. J. Addict.* **66**, 209–218

DIXON A. (1968) Drug addiction: some aspects of treatment. *Occup. Ther.* **31**, 32–35

D'ORBAN P.T. (1970) Heroin dependence and delinquency in women—a study of heroin addicts in Holloway prison. *Brit. J. Addict.* **65**, 67–78

FISH F., WELLS B.W.P., BINDEMAN S., BUNNEY J.E. & JORDAN N.M. (1974) Prevalence of drug misuse among young people in Glasgow 1970–72. *Brit. J. Addict.* **69**, 343–355

FORREST J.A.H. & TARALA R.A. (1973) Abuse of drugs 'for kicks': a review of 252 admissions. *Brit. med. J.* **4**, 136–139

GARDNER R. (1970) Deaths in United Kingdom opioid users 1965–69. *Lancet* **ii**, 650–653

GARDNER R. & CONNELL P.H. (1970). One year's experience in a drug-dependence clinic. *Lancet* **ii**, 455–459

GARDNER R. & CONNELL P.H. (1971) Opioid users attending a special drug dependence clinic 1968/1969. *Bull. Narcotics*, **23**, 9–15

GARDNER R. & CONNELL P.H. (1972) Amphetamine and other non-opioid drug users attending a special drug dependence clinic. *Brit. med. J.* **2**, 322–326

GARVEY B.M. (1970) The Kilburn Square drug abuse centre. *Brit. J. Addict.* **64**, 383–394

GERARD D.L. & KORNETSKY C. (1955) Adolescent opiate addiction: a study of control and addiction subjects. *Psychiat. Quart.* **29**, 457–486

GLATT M.M. (1962) The abuse of barbiturates in the United Kingdom. *Bull. Narcotics* **14**, 19–38

GLATT M.M. (1965) Reflection on heroin and cocaine addiction. *Lancet* **ii**, 171–172

GORDON A.M. (1973) Patterns of delinquency in drug addiction. *Brit. J. Psychiat.* **122**, 205–210

HALSTEAD H. & NEAL C.D. (1968) Intelligence and personality of drug addicts: a pilot study. *Brit. J. Addict.* **63**, 237–240

HICKS R.C. (1969) The management of heroin addiction at a general hospital drug addiction treatment centre. *Brit. J. Addict.* **64**, 235–243

JAMES I.P. (1967) Suicide and mortality amongst heroin addicts in Britain. *Brit. J. Addict.* **62**, 389–391

KAHN E.J., NEUMANN L.L. & POLK G.A. (1969) The course of the heroin withdrawal syndrome in newborn infants treated with phenobarbital or chlorpromazine. *J. Pediatrics.* **75**, 495–500.

KAHN E.J. (1974) The heroin withdrawal syndrome of newborn infants. *In* Bourne P.G. (ed.) *A Treatment Manual for Acute Drug Abuse Emergencies.* National Clearing House for Drug Abuse Information. Rockville, Maryland: National Institute on Drug Abuse

KALDEGG A. (1973a) A study of young male heroin dependent patients. Part I: Intellectual assessment. *Brit. J. Addict.* **68**, 251–256

KALDEGG A. (1973b) A study of young male heroin dependent patients. Part II: Attitudes to father, mother and family as revealed in a sentence completion test. *Brit. J. Addict.* **68**, 257–263

KOSVINER A., MITCHESON M.C., MYERS K., OGBORNE A., STIMSON G.V., ZACUNE J. & EDWARDS G. (1968) Heroin use in a provincial town. *Lancet* **i**, 1189–1192

LEWIS V.S., PETERSEN D.M., GEIS G. & POLLACK S. (1972) Ethical and social-psychological aspects of urinalysis to detect heroin use. *Brit. J. Addict.* **67**, 303–307

McKAY A.J., HAWTHORNE V.M. & McCARTNEY H.N. (1973) Drug taking among medical students at Glasgow university. *Brit. med. J.* **1**, 540–543

MAY L. (1972) Total analysis of an illicit or 'street' narcotic sample by thin-layer chromatography. *Bull. Narcotics* **24**, 35–36

MERRY J. (1967) Out-patient treatment of heroin addiction. *Lancet* **i**, 205–206

MONTALVO J.G. Jr., SCRIGNAR C.B., ALDERETTE E., HARPER B. & EYER D. (1972) Flushing, pale-coloured urines and false negatives—urinalysis of narcotic addicts. *Int. J. Addict.* **7**, 355–364

MOTT J. (1972) The psychological basis of drug dependence: the intellectual and personality characteristics of opiate users. *Brit. J. Addict.* **67**, 89–99

NOBLE P.J. (1970) Drug-taking in delinquent boys. *Brit. med. J.* **1**, 102–105

NOBLE P.J. & BARNES G. Gorell (1971) Drug taking in adolescent girls: factors associated with the progression to narcotic use. *Brit. med. J.* **2**, 620–623

NOBLE P.J., HART T. & NATION R. (1972) Correlates and outcome of illicit drug use by adolescent girls. *Brit. J. Psychiat.* **120**, 497–504

OPPENHEIM G.B., WRIGHT J.E., BUCHANAN J. & BIGGS L. (1973) Out-patient treatment of narcotic addiction. Who benefits? *Brit. J. Addict.* **68**, 37–44

PERLMUTTER J.F. (1967) Drug addiction in pregnant women. *Amer. J. Obstet. Gynecol.* **99**, 569–572

RATHOD N.H., ALARCÓN R. DE & THOMSON I.G. (1967) Signs of heroin usage detected by drug users and their parents. *Lancet* **ii**, 1411–1414

RATHOD N.H. (1972) The use of heroin and methadone by injection in a New Town: A progress report. *Brit. J. Addict.* **67**, 113–121

REDDY A.M. (1974) The management of the narcotic withdrawal syndrome in the neonate. *In* Bourne P.G. (ed.) *A Treatment Manual for Acute Drug Abuse Emergencies*. National Clearing House for Drug Abuse Information, Rockeville, Maryland: National Institute on Drug Abuse

REPORT ON A DRUG SURVEY, 1967 (1969) *Brit. J. Addict.* **64**, 257–271

RITSON E.B., TOLLER P. & HARDING F. (1973) Drug abuse in the East Midlands. A study of 139 patients referred to an addiction unit. *Brit. J. Addict.* **68**, 65–71

ROBINS L.N., DAVIS D.H. & GOODWIN D.W. (1974) Drug use by U.S. Army enlisted men in Vietnam: a follow-up on their return home. *Amer. J. Epidemiol.* **99**, 235–249

ROSENBERG C.M. (1969) Young drug addicts; background and personality. *J. Nerv. Ment. Dis.* **148**, 65–73

ROSENTHAL T., PATRICK S.W. & KRUG D.C. (1965) The development of narcotics addiction among the newborn. *In* Harms E. (ed.) *Drug Addiction in Youth*. Monographs on Child Psychiatry (3), 5–18. International Series

SCOTT P.D. & WILLCOX D.R.C. (1965) Delinquency and the amphetamines. *Brit. J. Psychiat.* **111**, 865–875

STIMSON G.V. & OGBORNE A.C. (1970) A survey of a representative sample of addicts prescribed heroin at London clinics. *Bull. Narcotics* **22**, 13–22

STONE M.L., SALERNO L.J., GREEN M. & ZELSON C. (1971) Narcotic addiction in pregnancy. *Amer. J. Obstet. Gynecol.* **109**, 716–723

TEASDALE J.D., SEGRAVES R.T. & ZACUNE J. (1971) 'Psychoticism' in drug-users. *Brit. J. soc. clin. Psychol.* **10**, 160–171

WILLIS J. (1971) Delinquency and drug dependence in the United Kingdom and the United States. *Brit. J. Addict.* **66**, 235–248

WOODSIDE M. (1973) The first 100 referrals to a Scottish drug addiction treatment centre. *Brit. J. Addict.* **68**, 231–241

WORLD HEALTH ORGANIZATION (1950) *Report of Expert Committee on Addiction-producing Drugs*. Wld. Hlth. Org. techn. Rep. Ser., no. 21, 6. Geneva: WHO

WORLD HEALTH ORGANIZATION (1957) *Report of Expert Committee on Addiction-producing Drugs*. Wld. Hlth. Org. techn. Rep. Ser., no. 166. Geneva: WHO

WORLD HEALTH ORGANIZATION (1964) *Thirteenth Report of Expert Committee on Addiction-producing Drugs*. Wld. Hlth. Org. techn. Rep. Ser., no. 273. Geneva: WHO

WORLD HEALTH ORGANIZATION (1965) *Fourteenth Report of Expert Committee on Dependence-producing Drugs*. Wld. Hlth. Org. techn. Rep. Ser., no. 312. Geneva: WHO

WORLD HEALTH ORGANIZATION (1969) *Sixteenth Report of the Expert Committee on Drugs Dependence*. Wld. Hlth. Org. techn. Rep. Ser., no. 407. Geneva: WHO

WORLD HEALTH ORGANIZATION (1974) *Detection of Dependence-producing Drugs in Body Fluids*. Wld. Hlth. Org. techn. Rep. Ser., no. 556, Geneva: WHO

WRIGHT D.J. & TURNER A.G. (1971) An analysis of the effects of drug abuse as seen and treated in a casualty department. *Brit. J. Addict.* **66**, 77–80

CHAPTER 28

Tics and Tourette's syndrome

J. CORBETT

Tics are an infrequent cause of referral to psychiatric clinics for children, accounting for only between 5–7 per cent of cases (Zausmer 1954; Torup 1962). However, they are important in terms of the theoretical issues they raise and the problems they pose in treatment. Perhaps because of the unusual appearance of the symptoms and their obvious outward manifestations they have given rise to a large literature which has been the subject of several recent reviews (Kellman 1965; Fernando 1967; Corbett *et al* 1969; Shapiro 1973).

DEFINITION

The word 'ticque' was originally used in veterinary medicine to describe the movements made by horses when restrained but it did not enter the medical literature until the middle of the last century. Meige (1905) described the tic as a 'coordinated purposive act, provoked in the first instance by some external cause or idea; repetition leads to its becoming habitual and finally to its involuntary reproduction without cause and for no purpose. At the same time its form, intensity and frequency are exaggerated and it assumes the character of a convulsive movement; inopportune and excessive. Its execution is often preceded by an irresistible impulse and its suppression with malaise. The effect of distraction or of volitional activity is to diminish its activity while in sleep it disappears'. Although biologically purposeful (protective, defensive or offensive), the tic serves no apparently useful purpose since its object is nonexistent (Zausmer 1954).

Perhaps the most useful clinical definition is Kanner's (1957) that 'tics or habit spasms are quick, sudden and frequently repeated movements of circumscribed groups of muscles serving no apparent purpose'. The term habit spasm is not satisfactory as spasms, unlike tics, are essentially uncoordinated, variable and incapable of voluntary imitation. Other forms of stereotyped behaviour which are frequently seen in disturbed, retarded or psychotic children tend to occur in specific situations and do not have the same

674

convulsive or sudden nature. Manneristic or other habitual motor activities comprise more complex and variable movements, involving the combined or successive activity of at least two parts of the body as in hair-pulling and finger-sucking. They often include manipulation of objects in the environment, and unlike tics are usually capable of voluntary interruption.

NATURE OF TIC MOVEMENTS

Tics appear in all parts of the body, involving many different groups of muscles but particularly those which are usually coordinated in purposive acts, blinking, throat-clearing, head-shaking, shoulder-shrugging and flexion of the arms and legs.

Wilder and Silberman (1927) analysed the frequency of tics involving different muscle groups in 370 cases and found a descending order of frequency from the upper part of the face to the feet, so that eye blinking tics were most common, followed by tics of the lower part of the face, neck and shoulders, the least frequent being tics of the lower extremities. This has been confirmed in more recent studies (Corbett *et al* 1969).

This motor pattern is very similar to that seen in the startle reflex described in detail by Landis and Hunt (1939). This reflex which emerges at the age of 4 or 5 months, is of a flexion type and is similarly produced almost universally by a sudden powerful stimulus such as a rifle shot or other loud noise. There is blinking of the eyes, followed after a very short latent period by a charactcristic facial expression, head movements forwards, raising and drawing forward of the shoulders, abduction of the upper arms and flexion of the elbows passing down to the lower limbs.

High speed photography and videotape recording shows that, as in the case of multiple tics, the average latent period between the eye blink and upper limb movements is of the order of 100 milliseconds, the whole movement being complete within half a second. As in the pattern of tic movements the eye blink is almost invariably present followed in descending order of frequency by movements of the lower part of the body; although these may be more marked on one side or another and there is some evidence that other neurophysiological accompaniments of the startle reaction, such as the galvanic skin response may occur in the case of tics (Corbett 1976). These similarities between tics and the startle response may perhaps serve best to explain the original nature of the tic movements, while, as discussed later, a learning theory hypothesis may account for their perpetuation.

Frequency of tics in the general population

Tics are more frequent in younger children and are rarely noted for the first time in adolescence or adult life. One of the main difficulties of assessing their frequency concerns their differentiation from other repetitive movements of childhood. Thus Boncour (1910) reported that 23 per cent of 2 to 3-year-old children had tics, but these were not defined. MacFarlane *et al* (1954), who clearly distinguished tics from other habits, found that 4 per cent of children showed tics. The peak frequency of 10–11 per cent was reached at 6–7 years. Pringle *et al* (1967), in the National Child Development Study, found that by the age of 7, only 5 per cent of children had a history of tics. It is clear that many children suffer from tics as a transient phenomenon without presenting for treatment.

However, vocal tics may be more persistent. These are often preceded by multiple body tics which during adolescence become associated with vocal tics, initially in the form of grunting or throat clearing noises. Later a few develop into recognisable swear words (coprolalia) which are occasionally associated with obscene gestures (copropraxia). The association of vocal with multiple body tics comprise the syndrome first described by Gilles de la Tourette (1885) and given his name. Sufferers from this fully fledged picture of the tic syndrome naturally tend to be more socially incapacitated than those with simple tics and thus to present more regularly for treatment. However, the rarity of this condition is suggested by the fact that only a little over 100 cases have been described in the literature. Tourette's syndrome is more frequently associated with symptoms of severe emotional disturbance and tends to persist into adult life, but apart from these characteristics it does not differ from other features of the tic syndrome Corbett (1971), and the following account of the aetiology and clinical picture applies to both situations unless stated otherwise.

Age of onset

Most clinic studies show that the average age of onset of tics is 7 years and that they rarely appear before the age of 4 or for the first time after late adolescence. Mahler *et al* (1945) suggests that although the tic syndrome does not 'crystallise' before the sixth or seventh year of life, in most patients there have been previous behavioural symptoms, either in the form of hyperkinesis, dyskinesia or impulsiveness with increased muscle tension and overreactiveness. Overactive behaviour predating the tics has also been reported in other cases (Tobin & Reinhardt 1961; Walsh 1962; Rapoport 1959; Eisenberg *et al* 1959). These symptoms may indicate an underlying temperamental vulnerability to the development of tics.

Sex incidence

Most studies have shown a preponderance of boys, although the sex ratio has varied from 2:1 (Zausmer 1954) to 3·7:1 (Mahler *et al* 1945).

PRECIPITATING FACTORS

Both emotional and physical factors have been noted as possible precipitants but specific emotional causes are found in only a minority of cases. The stresses reported have been quite varied; seeing a pet dog run over, sexual assault (Corbett *et al* 1969); serious home conflicts, serious frights and acute physical conditions (Torup 1962). In many cases no acute factors are evident, although chronic stress is present in a larger proportion. Fernando (1967) found precipitating factors in a third of 65 Tourette's cases in the literature. Tonsillitis or tonsillectomy was the commonest but others included an attack by a dog (Creak & Guttmann 1935), birth of a sibling (Eisenberg *et al* 1959; Dunlap 1945), parental separation (Stevens 1964) and parental illness (Faux 1966). However, in view of the fact that the evidence is retrospective and without controls, little weight can be attached to the findings.

Local upper respiratory tract infection has been invoked by Selling (1929) and Brown (1957) but tics occur at an age period when such infections are particularly common. Nevertheless, it is wise in the case of sniffing and throat clearing tics to exclude local irritants of this type, with X-rays of the paranasal sinus where indicated. Refraction to exclude visual defects leading to blepharospasm (Brescia 1938) may also be justified. Both Straus (1927) and Creak and Guttmann (1935) noted the occurrence of tics following Sydenham's chorea. In the latter series of 14 patients, 6 had a previous history of acute chorea, but this has not been reported in more recent studies at a time when rheumatic fever is much less common.

The importance of movement restraint, which had been long recognised as a cause of tic-like movements in animals, was investigated by Levy (1944) and Bergmann (1945). Following observation of children whose movements were restrained either by physical handicap or orthopaedic immobilisation it was concluded that tics did not result, although in some situations of restraint or deprivation stereotypies such as head banging or rocking were more common.

Organic brain damage

Pasamanick and Kawi (1956) found significantly more complications of pregnancy in a group of tiqueurs than in a similar number of controls, who were matched for race, sex and maternal age but not for other social factors. However, only 21 out of 83 tiqueurs compared with 10 controls showed perinatal difficulties. Shapiro *et al* (1973) found abnormalities on psychological testing in three-quarters of 34 adults with Tourette's syndrome, in terms of a Wechsler Scale verbal-performance discrepancy of 19 or more and findings suggestive of brain damage on the Rorschach and Bender Gestalt tests. A history of hyperactivity and clumsiness and perseveration, confabulation or disturbed cognition on clinical examination were found in half; a similar frequency to that found by Mahler *et al* (1945) and Lucas *et al* (1967). Shapiro and his colleagues also found that half of the patients had abnormalities on neurological examination and EEG. Unfortunately, in the absence of a comparably studied control group, it is difficult to know what significance to attach to these minor signs of non-specific brain dysfunction.

EEG findings

Abnormalities of a nonspecific kind have been found in some cases in most studies (Field *et al* 1966; Ungher *et al* 1962) but it is not known whether they are more common than in other psychiatric disorders.

Intelligence

Most studies have shown tiqueurs to be of average (Corbett *et al* 1969) or somewhat above average intelligence (Wilson 1927; Mahler *et al* 1945; Zausmer 1954). Moreover although stereotypies are more common in mentally retarded children, tics are not (Corbett 1973). In the Maudsley study (Corbett *et al* 1969) tiqueurs did not differ from matched controls in terms of level of intelligence, verbal-performance discrepancies on the WISC or reading skills. However, tiqueurs were superior on the coding subtest, which seems to be dependent on motor speed. Crown (1953) also found adult tiqueurs to be better than controls on tests of motor skill. The findings are possibly in keeping with the hypothesis that tics are a form of learned motor behaviour (see below).

Neuropathological studies

Balthasar (1956) reported residual changes of previous meningitis and an immature cell pattern in the corpus striatum in an adult with Tourette's syndrome who died accidentally. However, very few postmortem studies have been undertaken.

The evidence for an organic basis for tics is conflicting. Although organic factors may play an important part in some cases of Tourette's syndrome persisting into adult life, there is little indication of a specific neurological lesion in the majority of cases.

Family history

Twenty per cent of parents and 5 per cent of siblings had suffered from tics in Zausmer's (1954) study while Torup (1962) found 30–40 per cent of first and second degree relatives to be affected. The latter study suggested that where close relatives had tics persisting into adult life the prognosis for the children was worse.

Zausmer (1954) described most parents as anxious, restrictive and rigid and suggested that a disturbed mother–child relationship was a major source of stress. One third of parents were said to have some form of psychoneurosis and over half were pathologically anxious. However, no diagnostic criteria were given and no controls were studied. On the other hand, Corbett *et al* (1969) found that 31 per cent of tiqueurs had a parent who had received psychiatric care. This was higher than the 19 per cent in the parents of children attending the same hospital for other psychiatric problems and much higher than the 6 per cent found in the parents of children attending a dental clinic (Rutter 1966). Over half the psychiatrically disturbed parents of the tiqueurs consisted of mothers with affective illness. While, clearly, tics may be responsible for generating anxiety in the family, it does seem that parental psychiatric disturbance may well be an important primary factor in the aetiology of tics, possibly by reinforcing anxiety in the child.

OTHER SYMPTOMS OF EMOTIONAL DISTURBANCE

Most studies of children with tics and Tourette's syndrome report a high frequency of associated emotional disturbance. In 171 children with tics in the Maudsley study (Corbett *et al* 1969) only half (89) had presented with tics as the major complaint, while in the remainder tics were noted incidentally on examination or were reported in the course of obtaining an account of a wide variety of additional symptoms. When symptoms in tiqueurs were compared with those in children with other psychiatric (but nonpsychotic) disorders attending the hospital it was found that there was a marked similarity between the two groups.

Over 30 per cent of children in both groups showed sleep disorders, tension habits, tempers, aggression, disobedience, anxiety and disturbed relationships in the family and at school. Five symptoms (gratification habits, speech disorders, encopresis, obsessional and hypochondriacal symptoms) occurred significantly more frequently in the children with tics while four others (tempers and aggression, truancy, fighting and depression) occurred significantly more frequently in the control group. This is in keeping with the suggestion that tiqueurs are not characterised by the overt expression of affect (e.g. aggression of depression) and that tics may be an alternative mode of affective response. As MacDonald (1963) has pointed out, tics occur at a time when 'children are struggling with the problem of ego control' and may have difficulty in the controlled expression of affect.

Even in children referred to paediatric clinics, tics are usually associated with other symptoms of emotional disturbance. For example, Torup (1962) found restlessness and sensitivity to be common features, while 'additional nervous symptoms' were found in the majority of her cases. Meige (1905) also emphasised the frequent presence of obsessional features.

On the basis of isolated case studies, psychoanalysts have suggested that tics are symbolic of repressed desires and conflicts (such as masturbation or aversion from the primal scene), or that they represent identification with the behaviour of animals or younger children (Fenichel 1945; Mahler *et al* 1945; Kulovesi 1929; Gerard 1946). The multiplicity of explanations leaves some doubt as to their validity. As with other disorders, the symptom may in due course become incorporated into the psychopathology of the individual child, but it seems unlikely that the movements themselves have a symbolic function.

It appears more probable that the coprolalic utterances of Tourette's syndrome may be explained in terms of the subject's response to his tics, which in turn subsequently shapes the tics along a feedback mechanism (MacDonald 1963). The recent description of Tourette's syndrome in different cultures in which the coprolalia is determined more by the sexual content of the words than by their sound would seem in keeping with such a hypothesis (Singer 1963; Chakraborty 1968).

Maturational delay

There are various indications that tics may be associated with delays in biological maturation. In the first place, as already noted, the motor pattern in tics is very similar to the startle response which is most obvious in infants and children. Secondly, tics usually develop in early childhood and are often seen as transient phenomena in young children. Thirdly, tics are commonly associated with speech disorders, encopresis and habits like thumb-sucking which are features of immaturity. Fourthly, like most delays in development, tics are much commoner in boys.

Of course, tics differ from speech delay and similar disorders in the respect that tics are not a universal and normal phenomena at any age. However, a parallel may be drawn with stuttering (Andrews & Harris 1965). Like tics, stuttering is not an inevitable aspect of development. However, stuttering is common as a transient feature in young children, it usually develops first in early childhood, and it is commoner in children who are delayed in their speech acquisition. It may be that with both stuttering and tics, a biological immaturity predisposes to the occurrence of the symptom, but that many other factors involving learning and temperamental vulnerability are important in its continuation.

PROGNOSIS

At first, tics tend to be transient, lasting just for a few days or weeks. However, in some children there is a spread downwards of tic movements with the disorder becoming more persistent and handicapping around the age of 10 years when referral is most common. In Tourette's syndrome, vocal utterances in the form of barking noises or grunts also come on at about this age. Only later in adolescence do recognisable words develop, although occasionally these may be present from the start or as the only symptom of the condition. The prognosis in the first reported cases of the fully developed syndrome was thought to be poor, with the majority of cases requiring long-term hospitalisation or even developing schizophrenia (Tourette 1885).

Recently reported studies however suggest a more favourable outcome. In 73 patients in the Maudsley series (Corbett *et al* 1969) who presented with tics as the major complaint, and who were followed up from 1 to 18 years after the original attendance, none showed clear-cut deterioration while only 6 per cent were unchanged. Over half had improved to some degree and two-fifths had completely recovered.

Improvement most often took place in late adolescence. The chance of complete disappearance of the tics was directly related to their severity. Thus, in Tourette's syndrome, multiple tics are more likely to persist into adult life.

The most rapid improvement also seemed to occur in those cases where the first onset of tics was between the ages of 6 and 8 years rather than in either the younger or older age groups.

In spite of the improvement of the tics in the majority of cases, symptoms of psychiatric disturbance and particularly anxiety and neurotic disorders tended to persist. This tendency was related more to the original symptoms of emotional disturbance than to the severity of the tics themselves.

In cases where the tics did improve, this tended to occur in an ascending order with eye blinking and facial tics being the last to disappear.

TREATMENT

General management

Because tics are often associated with more widespread psychiatric problems and with family stresses of various kinds, a full psychiatric and psychosocial appraisal is indicated. Neurological examination is also required and physical assessment should be undertaken to exclude possible local irritants.

Most simple tics occurring in the absence of severe emotional disturbance respond to simple explanation of the mechanisms. Preferably, this should take place over several interviews with the child and parents in which family tensions and other difficulties can also be discussed. The tic may be explained as an expression of anxiety which is likely to be perpetuated by overcorrection or excessive restriction. The family should be encouraged to disregard the tics as far as possible. Associated emotional disturbance and difficulties in the family relationships should be dealt with appropriately in individual or family group psychotherapy.

In more severe or persistent tics, and particularly in the case of Tourette's syndrome, the condition is usually sufficiently handicapping to restrict the child's life and to be embarrassing at school. Symptomatic treatment may be required together with more extensive environmental manipulation. In some cases admission to hospital away from a possibly tense and reinforcing family situation may be beneficial.

Psychotherapy

There have been numerous individual reports of the use of psychotherapy, usually based on psychoanalytic techniques. Most have stressed the importance of treating the child rather than the tic (Nelson 1950) and often treatment has been lengthy (Fenichel 1945; Rosenheim 1948; Durkin 1949; Kurland 1965).

In the Maudsley series (Corbett *et al* 1969), those who received psychotherapy had the same outcome as those who did not. Zausmer (1954) found no difference in outcome according to the duration of psychotherapy. However, as neither study was a controlled trial of treatment, and as the more severe cases tended to receive prolonged psychotherapy, no conclusions are warranted from the negative findings.

In adults with Tourette's syndrome, abreactive techniques using CO_2 and sodium pentothal have been used by Michael (1957) and MacDonald (1963) with marked improvement in both cases, but such energetic measures have not been reported in younger patients.

Symptomatic treatment

Behaviour therapy

Dunlap (1945) claimed that undesirable habits (including tics) could be eliminated by making the subject repeat them voluntarily and deliberately. He gave few details of his procedure and no experimental demonstration of its validity, merely asserting that the tics disappeared rapidly.

Behaviour therapy, using massed practice in this way, was first used systematically by Yates (1958) and Gwynne Jones (1960) who obtained temporary relief in a woman with multiple tics. They hypothesised that the tic is a conditioned avoidance response, evoked initially by stress, and reinforced by the reduction of anxiety. The treatment was based on Hull's (1943) theory which suggests that the extinction of learned responses can be produced by the building up of conditioned inhibition, through the practice of negative habits.

Eysenck and Rachman (1964) state that the essence of such treatment is that repeated voluntary evocation of the tics produces an inhibition effect which eventually exhausts the movements. Yates (1958) found experimentally that prolonged massed practice, followed by lengthy rest periods, was most successful. Rafi (1962) and Walton (1961) have claimed similar success using negative practice, while Clarke (1966) used this technique successfully in Tourette's syndrome (with massed practice of the coprolalic utterances).

Barrett (1962) used an operant technique in which music was played contingently upon nonperformance of the tics, and white noise was used aversively when tics occurred. Partial success was claimed. More recently, failures have been reported for both negative practice (Feldman & Werry 1966; Sand & Carlson 1973) and aversive techniques (Stevens & Blachly 1966). However, in both cases where negative practice was used, the periods of treatment were shorter than in the previous successful studies. The effects of behaviour therapy in reducing the frequency of tics throws light on the way in which tics may become a learned habit, but further research is required before they can be regarded as routine treatments. One problem in the use of massed practice is that tics are frequently multiple and often difficult to practice. However, it seems possible from the work on the startle response, described earlier, that the eye-blink may act as a trigger to tics lower down in the face and body. The writer's clinical experience indicates that successful treatment of the eyeblink by massed practice may be effective in extinguishing multiple tics. Accordingly when there is an eyeblink tic it may be worthwhile to instruct the child in massed practice which may be carried out at home over 5-minute periods several times a day over a period of 2 to 3 weeks.

Drug treatment

Most tranquillisers and sedatives have been used in the treatment of tics and chlorpromazine (Lucas 1964) and diazepam (Connell *et al* 1967) seem to be particularly effective through the reduction of anxiety in selected patients. Haloperidol was first used in Tourette's syndrome and has since been the subject of over 20 reports, notably by Seignot (1961), Shapiro and Shapiro (1968) and Bixby (1970). However, Ford and Gottlieb (1969), in one of the few controlled trials, has cast doubts on its efficacy. The use of haloperidol has since been successfully extended to the treatment of simple tics (Connell *et al* 1967). It seems to have a more specific effect that can be accounted for by mere reduction of anxiety, but possibly the benefits are associated with its dystonic side effects and dopamine blocking action.

With simple tics a dose of 0·5 mg t.d.s. may suffice. In more severe cases with multiple tics 1·5 mg t.d.s. or more may be required, and a daily dosage as high as 20 mg daily has been used (Craven 1969) in one case of Tourette's syndrome. With doses larger than 2 mg a day concurrent administration of an antiparkinsonian agent such as orphenadrine (disipal) 50 mg t.d.s. or benzotropine methonsulphate (cogentin) 2 mg t.d.s. may be required. For the more severely affected patient the drug regime should preferably be established in hospital where accompanying psychiatric disorders can be treated.

Although haloperidol and other tranquillisers often effectively suppress tics, their side effects may offset the benefits. The sedative and depressant effects of these drugs may be troublesome, but the tendency to cause akathisia and motor restlessness (to which tiqueurs seem particularly sensitive) is even more so. Akathisia does not respond to antiparkinsonian drugs but it may be helped by the concomitant administrations of a small dose of amytal (30 mg t.d.s.).

Haloperidol, in small doses, may be a useful adjunct to psychological treatments in mild cases of tics. In Tourette's syndrome the handicapping nature of the symptoms may warrant higher dosage.

CONCLUSION

Tics may be seen as a distortion of an underlying physiological process, which in the vulnerable child becomes a learned habit. This may be more likely to occur in the biologically immature child, and such learning is facilitated by emotional stress.

However, the symptoms themselves come to acquire reinforcing properties, so that symptomatic treatment combined with general psychotherapeutic strategies, is usually justified in the case of persistent tics.

At a later stage, particularly in the case of Tourette's syndrome, the tics may become firmly incorporated into the psychopathology of the child and his family. In these cases a full range of available treatments may be needed. If the child can be helped through this difficult stage with a minimising of psychosocial handicaps, an eventually favourable outcome is likely in the great majority of cases.

REFERENCES

ANDREWS G. & HARRIS M. (1965) *The Syndrome of Stuttering.* Clinics in Dev. Med. no. 17. London: SIMP/Heinemann

BALTHASAR K. (1956) Uber des anatomische substrät der generalisierten Tic Krankheit (Maladie des tics, Gilles de la Tourette): Entwicklungscemmung des corpus striatum. *Arch. Psychiat. Nervenkr.* **195,** 531–549

BARRETT B.H. (1962) Reduction in rate of multiple tics by free operant conditioning methods. *J. Nerv. Ment. Dis.* **135,** 187–195

BERGMAN T. (1945) Observations on children's reactions to motor restraint. *Nerv. Child.* **4,** 318–328

BIXBY E.W. (1970) Haloperidol for the Gilles de la Tourette's syndrome. *J. Amer. Med. Ass.* **114,** 345–349

BONCOUR G.P. (1910) Les tics chez l'ecolier et leur interpretation. *Progrès Med.* **26,** 445–453

BRESCIA M.A. (1938) Tics in childhood. *Arch. Pediat.* **55,** 703–709.

BROWN E.C. (1957) Tics (habit spasms) secondary to chronic sinusitis. *Arch. Pediat.* **74,** 39–46

CHAKRABORTY A. (1968) Gilles de la Tourette syndrome. *Brit. J. Psychiat.* **114,** 125

CLARKE D.F. (1966) Behaviour therapy of Gilles de la Tourette's syndrome. *Brit. J. Psychiat.* **112,** 771–778

CONNELL P.H., CORBETT J.A., HORNE D.J. & MATTHEWS A.M. (1967) Drug treatment of adolescent ticqueurs: a double-blind study of diazepam and haloperidol. *Brit. J. Psychiat.* **113,** 375–381

CORBETT J.A. (1976) The nature of tics and Gilles de la Tourette's syndrome. *In* Abuzzahab F. & Anderson F. (eds) *Gilles de la Tourette's Syndrome*, Vol. I. Minnesota: Mason.

CORBETT J.A., MATHEWS A.M., CONNELL P.H. & SHAPIRO D.A. (1969) Tics and Gilles de la Tourette's syndrome: A follow-up study and critical review. *Brit. J. Psychiat.* **115,** 1229–1241

CORBETT J.A. (1971) The nature of tics and Gilles de la Tourette's syndrome. *J. Psychosom. Res.* **15,** 403–409

CORBETT J.A. (1973) The neuropsychiatric handicaps of mentally retarded children. Paper delivered to Second Conference of European Paediatric Neurologists, Oxford

CRAVEN E.M. (1969) Gilles de la Tourette's syndrome treated with haloperidol. *J. Amer. Med. Ass.* **210,** 134–135

CREAK M. & GUTTMANN E. (1935) Chorea, tics and compulsive utterances. *J. Ment. Sci.* **81,** 834–839

CROWN S. (1953) An experimental inquiry into some aspects of the motor behaviour and personality in tiqueurs. *J. Ment. Sci.* **99,** 84–91

DUNLAP K. (1945) *Habits; their Making and Unmaking.* New York: Liverright

DURKIN H. (1949) Psychotherapy with a ticqueur. *Quart. J. Child. Dev.* **1,** 50–60

EISENBERG L., ASCHER E.A. & KANNER L. (1959) A clinical study of Gilles de la Tourette's disease (maladie des tics) in children. *Amer. J. Psychiat.* **115,** 715–726

EYSENCK H. & RACHMAN S. (1964) The application of learning theory to child psychiatry. *In* Howells J. (ed.) *Modern Perspectives in Child Psychiatry.* Edinburgh: Oliver & Boyd

FAUX E.J. (1966) Gilles de la Tourette Syndrome. *Arch. Gen. Psychiat.* **14,** 139–142

FELDMAN R.B. & WERRY J.S. (1966) An unsuccessful attempt to treat a tiqueur by massed practice. *Behav. Res. Ther.* **4,** 111–117

FENICHEL O. (1945) Uber organlibidinoese Begleiterscheinungen der Triebabwehr. *Int. Zeitschr. f. Psa.* **14,** 45–64

FERNANDO S.J.M. (1967) Gilles de la Tourette's syndrome. A report on four cases and a review of published case reports. *Brit. J. Psychiat.* **113,** 607–617

FIELD J.R., CORBIN K.B., GOLDSTEIN N.P. & KLASS D.W. (1966). Gilles de la Tourette's syndrome. *Neurology* **16,** 453–462

FORD C.U. & GOTTLIEB F. (1969) An objective evaluation of haloperidol in Gilles de la Tourette's syndrome. *Dis. Nerv. Sys.* **30,** 328–332

GERARD M.W. (1946) The psychogenic tic in ego development. *Psychoanal. Study Child.* **2,** 133–162. New York: International Universities Press

HULL C.L. (1943) *Principles of Behavior.* New York: Appleton-Century-Crofts

JONES H.G. (1960) Continuation of Yates' treatment of a tiqueur. *In* Eysenck H.J. (ed.) *Behaviour Therapy and the Neuroses.* Oxford: Pergamon

KANNER L. (1957) *Child Psychiatry.* Springfield, Illinois: Charles C Thomas

KELLMAN D.H. (1965) Tics: a critical evaluation of the literature. Dissertation for Dip. Psychol., University of London

KULOVESI Y. (1929) Origin of tic. *Int. Zeitschr. Psa.* **15,** 82–95

KURLAND M.L. (1965) Gilles de la Tourette's syndrome: the psychotherapy of two cases. *Comp. Psychiat.* **6,** 298–305

LANDIS C. & HUNT W.A. (1939) *The Startle Pattern.* New York: Farrar & Rinehart

LEVY D.M. (1944) On the problems of movement restraint. *Amer. J. Orthopsychiat.* **14,** 644–671

LUCAS A.R. (1964) Gilles de la Tourette's disease in children. Treatment with phenthiazine drugs. *Amer. J. Psychiat.* **121,** 606–608

LUCAS A.R., KAUFFMAN P.E. & MORRIS E.M. (1967) Gilles de la Tourette's disease. A clinical study of 15 cases. *J. Amer. Acad. Child Psychiat.* **6,** 700–722

MACDONALD I.J. (1963) A case of Gilles de la Tourette's syndrome with some aetiological observations. *Brit. J. Psychiat.* **109,** 206–210

MACFARLANE J.W., HONZIK M.O. & ALLEN L. (1954) *Behaviour Problems in Normal Children.* Berkeley: University of California Publications in Child Development

MAHLER M., LUKE J. & DALTROFF W. (1945) Clinical and follow-up study of the tic syndrome in children. *Amer. J. Orthopsychiat.* **15,** 631–647

MEIGE L.D.H. (1905) *Tics* Monographies Clinicques No. 42. Paris: Masson

MICHAEL R.P. (1957) Treatment of a case of compulsive swearing. *Brit. Med. J.* **1,** 1506–1508

NELSON W.E. (1950) *Textbook of Paediatrics,* 6th edn. Philadelphia: Mitchel

PASAMANICK B. & KAWI A. (1956) A study of the association of prenatal and paranatal factors with the development of tics in children. *J. Paediatrics.* **48,** 596–601

PRINGLE M.L.KELLMER, BUTLER N.R. & DAVIE R. (1967) *11,000 Seven Year Olds.* Nat. Bureau for Co-operation in Child Care. London: Longman

RAFI A.A. (1962) Learning theory and the treatment of tics. *J. Psychosom. Res.* **6,** 71–76

RAPOPORT J. (1959) Maladie des tics in children. *Amer. J. Psychiat.* **116,** 177–178

ROSENHEIM F. (1948) Animal identifications in a tiqueur. *Amer. J. Orthopsychiat.* **18,** 529–535

RUTTER M. (1966) *Children of Sick Parents: An Environmental and Psychiatric Study.* Institute of Psychiatry Maudsley Monograph no. 16. London: Oxford University Press.

SAND R.L. & CARLSON C. (1973) Failure to establish control over tics in the Gilles de la Tourette syndrome with behaviour therapy techniques. *Brit. J. Psychiat.* **122,** 665–670

SEIGNOT M.J.N. (1961) A case of Gilles de la Tourette cured by R.1625. *Ann. med-psychol.* **119,** 587–590

SELLING L. (1929) The role of infection in the etiology of tics. *Arch. Neurol. Psychiat.* **22,** 1163–1171

SHAPIRO A.K. & SHAPIRO E. (1968) Treatment of Gilles de la Tourette's syndrome with haloperidol. *Brit. J. Psychiat.* **114,** 345–350

SHAPIRO A.K., SHAPIRO E., WAYNE H. & CLARKIN J. (1973) Organic factors in Gilles de la Tourette's Syndrome. *Brit. J. Psychiat.* **122,** 659–664

SINGER K. (1963) Gilles de la Tourette's disease. *Amer. J. Psychiat.* **120,** 80–81

STEVENS H. (1964) The syndrome of Gilles de la Tourette and its treatment: report of a case. *Med. Ann. D.C.* **33,** 277–279

STEVENS J.R. & BLACHLY P. (1966) Successful treatment of the Maladie des Tics. Gilles de la Tourette's syndrome. *Amer. J. Dis. Child.* **122,** 541–545

STRAUS E. (1927) Untersuchunger über die postchoreatischen Motilatstorungen ins besondere die Beziehungen der Chorea minor zum Tic Morats. f. *Psychiat. u. Neurol.* **66,** 261–268

TOBIN W.G. & REINHARDT J.B. (1961) Tic de Gilles de la Tourette. *Amer. J. Dis. Child.* **101,** 778–783

TORUP E. (1962) A follow up study of children with tics. *Acta Paediat.* **51,** 261–268

TOURETTE G. de la (1885) Etude sur une affection nerveuse caracterisée par l'incoordination motrice, accompagne d'echolalic et de coprolalic. *Arch. Neurol.* **9,** 17–42; 158–200

UNGHER J., CIUREA E. & VOLANSCHI D. (1962) EEG analysis of motor neurosis in children (infantile tics). *Electroenceph. Clin. Neurophysiol.* **14,** 147–152

WALSH P.J.F. (1962) Compulsive shouting and Gilles de la Tourette's Disease. *Brit. J. Clin. Prac.* **16,** 651–655

WALTON D. (1961) Experimental psychology and the treatment of a tiqueur. *J. Child Psychol. Psychiat.* **2,** 148–155

WILDER J. & SILBERMAN J. (1927) *Beitrage zum Ticproblem.* Berlin: Kalger

WILSON S.A.K. (1927) The tics and allied conditions. *J. Neurol. Psychopath.* **8,** 93–109

YATES A.J. (1958) The application of learning theory to the treatment of tics. *J. Abnorm. Soc. Psychol.* **56,** 175–182

ZAUSMER R.C.M. (1954) Treatment of tics in childhood. *Arch. Dis. Child.* **29,** 537–542

CHAPTER 29

Speech delay

M. RUTTER

The child who is slow to talk poses a common problem of considerable importance to child psychiatrists. Above 1 per cent of children are seriously retarded in their production of spoken language and approximately 1 child in 20 is speaking so poorly when he starts school that he is unable to make himself understood by strangers (Morley 1965). Many of these children are referred to psychiatric clinics because of a concern about possible mental retardation; because a psychiatric condition such as infantile autism is suspected; because it is thought that psychosocial adversity may have impeded language development; or because speech delay has become associated with secondary emotional or behavioural disturbance. The parents of children with speech delay frequently complain that doctors gave them no help when their children were younger, but just said 'he will grow out of it', advice which was not only unhelpful but which, in their case, proved to be wrong.

This state of affairs arises in part because there is a wide range of normal variation. Many essentially normal children are very slow to start speaking, but they catch up later and *do* 'grow out of it'. Accordingly, the problem is how to determine which children will and which will not grow out of it, which children will turn out to be normal youngsters and which will be found to have a continuing handicap. It is sometimes suggested that the safest policy is to just wait and see, as time will resolve the dilemma. However, there are four good reasons why this is not an acceptable solution (Rutter 1974). First, the doctor may miss remediable conditions which require treatment (Ingram 1972). Second, there are ill effects which may ensue from language retardation and for which preventive action is required (Rutter 1972). Third, parental anxiety will not allow a prolonged delay in diagnostic assessment. Fourth, regardless of the diagnosis, parents need to be helped to know what to do. Even if the child with speech delay is thought to be basically normal, parents need to know how to talk to the child and how far to press him to speak.

If the need for early diagnosis is accepted, the next issue is whether it

688

is possible, and if it is, how early in life a reliable diagnosis may be made. Firm knowledge on this point is lacking, as it is only in recent years that speech delay has been subjected to much extensive research. However, it is probable that in most (but certainly not all) cases, a reasonably confident assessment should be possible by age 2 years. Two-thirds of children say their first words by 12 months and approximately the same proportion begin to use phrases by 24 months (Morley 1965). This means that many normal children are not speaking much more than the odd word by their second birthday. As a consequence, if a diagnosis is to be made it cannot rely on the qualities of the child's speech. Instead, reference must be made to features such as the characteristics of his babble, the nature of his play, his social responsiveness, his response to sounds and his understanding of language. This chapter will consider these issues in terms of the clinical assessment of children presenting with speech delay, with special reference to the commoner causes of speech delay which are of psychiatric concern.

NORMAL DEVELOPMENT OF SPEECH AND LANGUAGE

A knowledge of the biology and psychology of normal development constitutes an essential basis from which to assess children who show deviant or retarded development. At birth, the human brain is about a quarter of its adult weight but by the third birthday it has attained some four-fifths of its final mass (Marshall 1968). It not only increases in weight after birth but also neural structures grow considerably, there is increasing myelination, and the net of intercommunicating nerve fibres extends and becomes more complex. These microscopic changes are parallelled by alterations in the chemical composition of the brain.

It is important that different parts of the brain mature at different rates. Thus, the motor area advances more quickly than the sensory area and the auditory association areas lag somewhat behind the visual. Whereas the study of brain structure indicates where the brain *might* be functional, it cannot indicate whether the brain is in fact functioning. Nevertheless, these findings suggest that the infant's understanding of what he hears takes longer to develop than his appreciation of what he sees. If the normal disparity in rates of development between different parts of the cortex were greater in some children than others, this might offer some clue as to why some children are so much behind in one aspect of development (such as speech) in spite of a normal rate of development in others.

The neonatal brain is particularly susceptible to injury by virtue of its immaturity and rapid rate of growth. However, so far as language is concerned, this vulnerability is to a great extent compensated for by the great plasticity of the immature brain. Accordingly, the effects of unilateral lesions in early childhood tend to be transient because the normal hemisphere takes up the functions which would normally be performed by that which was damaged. This means that a persisting language impairment very rarely follows unilateral lesions (such as caused by a cerebral abscess or head injury) in the first few years of life. This is markedly different from the situation in adulthood (Lenneberg 1967; Rutter, Graham & Yule 1970).

During the first few months of life there is a marked development in the baby's ability to make fine auditory discriminations (Friedlander 1970). At 20 weeks babies can discriminate between phonemes as similar as 'p' and 't', 'b' and 'g', or 'i' and 'a'. By their first birthday, before they can speak, babies will not only discriminate but will respond to language differences which concern who is speaking, the intonation used, the vocabulary, and the amount of repetitiveness in what is said. It is not possible to be sure how much the infant *understands* (as distinct from differentiates) what is said to him. However, it is clear that toddlers and young children show an extraordinary interest in language and will often understand words or phrases said to them well before they can produce the words themselves. Language comprehension normally precedes language production (Fraser *et al* 1963; Lovell & Dixon, 1967) and the process of developing an understanding of language begins in infancy well before speech emerges.

Vocalisations develop greatly during the first year (McCarthy 1954; Murphy 1964; Ervin-Tripp 1966; Rebelsky *et al* 1967). The young child's understanding of gesture is developing at the same time and frequently he can respond to and wave 'bye bye' before he can say it. For a brief period before speech emerges, gesture may be used to communicate. This tendency is much more marked in twins and triplets or when speech is retarded, but will not occur if the neural structures underlying the relevant linguistic and cognitive functions are not intact. The way language develops is dependent not only on language competence but also on the child's general level of cognition and social maturity.

The first meaningful words normally appear about 12 months of age but there is considerable variation, so that in some 5 per cent of children this occurs by 8 months and in another 5 per cent it does not occur until after 18 months (Morley 1965). At the same time as the first words are being spoken, the child is also likely to be using long 'sentence-like' patterns of sounds with complex inflections and intonations. Murphy (1964) noted how children may string words together with a litanical quality. Words may be used to attract attention, to play with sounds, or to accompany actions, as well as to communicate.

At the beginning of the second year, after a gap of a month or so following the first meaningful word, there is a gradual increase in vocabulary which markedly accelerates from about 18 months, so that by 2 years of age the average child will understand several hundred words and will regularly use some 200 (see Rutter & Bax 1972). However, as with nearly all aspects of speech development, there is very wide individual variation and a few normal children may use only 12 or so words by their second birthday. The great majority of the first words learned are nouns and the main speech activity is naming objects or (a bit later) pictures in a book. A child's first words are little more than reflex responses to an object but particularly during the latter half of the second year, he develops a flexibility in the use of words which indicates the beginnings of true language. The child may learn to use familiar words for objects never seen before or he may start using words to ask for some object which he wants but which is not present (Lewis 1951). Even during this early stage of single word utterances, words are used in different ways to convey a variety of meanings (Lenneberg 1967). After words have first appeared but before phrases are used, there is an intermediate stage when words may be linked in a fixed way, such as 'go-now' or 'get-down', as if they were single words and without the child realising that he is using a combination of words.

Following the use of nouns, verbs increase in frequency, as do adjectives and adverbs. By the second birthday the proportion of nouns used is falling as a function of the greater use of other parts of speech. Pronouns generally appear just before 2 years and prepositions just after, but conjunctions are rare before 30 months (McCarthy 1930). A child's first sentences are tele-grammatic, containing only the key words and none of the connecting words. The latter are introduced during the second year but the use of different tenses takes longer. The present tense is used first, the future tense becomes common after the third birthday, and the past tense follows shortly after. When children are first learning to speak they frequently go through a stage when they often echo the last few words of whatever is said to them, but in normal children this echolalia (which seems to be a function of poor under-standing, Fay & Butler 1971) generally does not persist beyond 30 months (Fay 1971).

During the second year children's understanding of language markedly increases so that they are able not only to respond to single words but are able to understand and follow simple instructions, to perform common actions, to get up or to sit down, or to fetch something which is in sight. The child is all the time listening to the speech around him, understanding more and more of adult conversation, as well as gaining information and following straightforward instructions. He is taught nursery rhymes and his enjoy-ment of their rhythm and simple language helps to reinforce basic speech patterns. Oft repeated stories, too, add their share to the building up of language skills.

Those aspects of play which reflect language also develop in striking fashion (Sheridan 1969). Early in the second year infants begin to use common objects in a way that indicates an understanding of their use and function. Some months later the child will extend functional play to involve dolls and large toys, and by his second birthday he may be expected to use miniature toys in similar fashion. The first half of the second year is also the time when imitative gestural games, such as 'peek-a-boo', 'bye bye', and 'pat-a-cake', are prominent features of the child's activity. The linguistic functions of imitation are unclear but these activities have a communicative purpose and are usually impaired in cases of severe global language retardation.

During the preschool years following the child's second birthday there is a tremendous upsurge in the child's competence in all aspects of speech and language. Vocabulary increases from some 200 words to several thousand, and the length of the average utterance rises by about 1 word per year, from just less than 2 words at 2 years to just less than 5 words at 5 years (McCarthy 1954). The way words are used also changes. Exclamatory remarks decrease and questions increase. At 2 years most questions are of the 'what?' variety, by 3 years 'where?' and 'who?' queries are becoming more prominent and 4 is the age of asking 'why?' (Watts 1947). While questions are frequently used to seek information, it is obvious that many times questions are asked to which the child already knows the answers. It seems that he is mainly concerned to hear how the adult formulates a reply. Perhaps he is seeking information about language rather than about any object or event.

At the same time as vocabulary and utterance length are increased, sentences are becoming more functionally and structurally complete, and more often complex or compound (about 6 to 7 per cent by the time of starting school). To begin with children tend to refer to themselves by name but soon personal pronouns are accurately used. Whereas most of the main principles of grammar have been learned by age 5 years, considerable linguistic development continues to take place after the child starts school (Chomsky 1969; Kessel 1970). The child's understanding of the complexity of language increases in relation to his ability to make abstractions. Language cannot be considered as independent of general cognitive development.

This whole process is a real learning of 'language', not just a copying of a fixed number of phrases (McNeill 1970). This is evident from the rapid rise in word combinations (from 14 to over 2500 over a period of 6 months in one child studied), by the fact that children use word combinations that they could never have heard, and from the observation that the combinations follow certain rules. Exactly how words are learnt is not known but it is evident that the process involves meaning and understanding rather than mere reflex associative learning (Morton 1971). Furthermore, children learn language *rules* rather than specific grammatical constructions (Brown 1973; Brown & Bellugi 1964).

Numerous studies have shown that girls are slightly more advanced than boys in language development (McCarthy 1954; Rebelsky *et al* 1967), a difference that parallels the greater maturity of girls in all aspects of physical development (Rutter 1970). However, the sex difference in rate of language development is quite small and is largely confined to the later stages of development. Indeed, what is striking is that the sex difference is so small within the normal range in view of the fact that marked *delays* in development are so much commoner in boys than in girls (Ingram 1959, 1969). Curiously, the early use and understanding of words provides a much better prediction of verbal skills in middle childhood in girls than is the case in boys (Moore 1967).

Environmental influences on language development

Although we remain largely ignorant concerning the processes of language development, we do know something of the environmental factors which affect the growth of language (Rutter & Mittler 1972). These have implications for treatment.

Several studies have shown that both verbal enrichment and social reinforcement can substantially increase the amount of an infant's vocalisation and babble (Irwin 1960; Weisberg 1963; Todd & Palmer 1968; Routh 1969). However, for verbal enrichment to have any value it must have meaning and/or reinforcing properties. Mere increase in vocal noise is not enough.

Surprisingly little is known about *how* family interactions influence children's language development. Brown and Hanlon (1970) studied parental approval and disapproval in relation to children's utterances. Only three families were studied, so that generalisations are not yet warranted, but it seems that reinforcement may be important with respect to phonetic and semantic development but not to syntactic development. Cazden (Cazden 1966; Brown *et al* 1969), in a study of 2 to 3-year-old children attending a day centre, found that children's progress in language was greater when there was an emphasis on conversational interchange with adults than when play activities on their own were provided. Interestingly it appeared that a rich, varied and informative verbal interchange *without* direct modification of the child's own utterance provided the best stimulus for syntactical development.

Many studies have shown that prolonged institutional care frequently has a profoundly depressing effect on language development (Haywood 1967; Tizard 1970). The effects are demonstrable even in infancy and persist throughout childhood, accompanied by a similar depression of verbal intelligence. However, recent studies have shown that the language retardation is a function of poor quality care rather than institutional upbringing as such. Children reared in institutions where there is adequate conversation experiences and appropriate staff–child interaction show normal language competence (Tizard *et al* 1972).

Although there are few consistent associations between family size and early speech development (Rebelsky *et al* 1967), there are strong associations with later verbal intelligence. Several large scale studies have shown that children in large families have lower scores on tests of vocabulary and verbal IQ than do children with only one or two brothers or sisters (Nisbet 1953; Douglas 1964; Douglas *et al* 1968). The same association applies to reading ability which requires skills in written language (Rutter & Yule 1973). It seems probable that the association between family size and language skills is a function of family conditions in early childhood. In large families there is probably less intensive interaction and less communication between parents and children. Also, the presence of many children tends to lead to a tumultuous clamour with people speaking over one another. Accordingly, the lack of *clarity* of the language environment in large families may also be important.

Twins and triplets generally start speaking several months later than singletons (Day 1932; Howard 1946). Characteristically, children of multiple births make more use of gesture and mime to communicate than do other children, and quite often they have a jargon which is intelligible only to their cotwins (Zazzo 1960). The (usually slight) retardation in spoken language persists through the preschool years and in middle childhood the language deficit is still evident in a slightly lower verbal intelligence scores compared with singletons. The effect is a consequence of the pattern of upbringing of twins, as shown by the finding that there is no verbal impairment in the case of twins whose cotwin was stillborn or who died in early infancy (Record *et al* 1970). It should be added, however, that the delay in onset of speech in twins is not usually great enough for the children to be referred for failure to speak.

It might be thought the lack of spoken language in the environment of the hearing child brought up by deaf parents would be likely to have a profoundly depressing influence on linguistic development, but Critchley (1967) has shown that this is not necessarily so. Apparently the parental use of gesture and sign provides an important stimulus to communication and oral stimuli may be provided by others.

Bilingualism is not a cause of failure to develop speech and whether the possession of two languages rather than one constitutes an advantage or disadvantage depends on the social context, on the abilities of the child, on the extent to which he is truly bilingual, and on whether he is taught mainly in his preferred language (Smith 1935a, b; 1949, 1957). Truly bilingual children of good intelligence may even have linguistic and cognitive advantages (Peal & Lambert 1962) but the intellectually dull child may have difficulties coping with two languages. Children who have to learn a second language in situations where there are social barriers and prejudice involved in the differences between two language cultures are also likely to be at a disadvantage (Darcy 1953; Soffietti 1955).

COMMON CAUSES OF SPEECH DELAY

Much the most frequent disorder associated with speech delay is mental retardation (Ingram 1969). However, it is also the commonest *mistaken* diagnosis. That is, many children who are slow to speak are wrongly thought to be mentally retarded when in fact they are of normal intelligence. This arises through a lack of care in assessing children's development as a whole and also because many IQ tests rely heavily on verbal skills. Accordingly, although mental retardation is a common 'cause' of speech delay, great care is needed in making that diagnosis.

Deafness, cerebral palsy, and developmental disorders are the next commonest conditions associated with mild to moderate delays in the acquisition of speech (MacKeith & Rutter 1972). The deaf child fails to speak through the lack of sensory input and the cerebral palsied child may be slow to talk either through brain dysfunction or sometimes through peripheral effects on the speech apparatus. Sex chromosome anomalies have been reported in children with severe language delay associated with other physical disorders (Garvey & Mutton 1973).

The developmental disorders are an important group of conditions in which there is a specific delay in the emergence of a biologically impaired function. In this case the impaired functions concern speech and language, but other functions (such as motor coordination or reading) may be delayed in the same way (Ingram 1959; 1969). All types of developmental disorder are very much commoner in boys. At least in its severer forms it is not just a variation of normal because development may follow a slightly unusual course. In most cases development ultimately 'catches up' but many children are left with subtle handicaps (see below).

Sociocultural privation is an important cause of the milder type of speech delay, although obviously its frequency in clinical practice will depend on the community served. Language requires appropriate environmental stimulation in order to develop normally and without it language development will be retarded.

Infantile autism is a less common cause of mild to moderate speech delay but it is a very important cause for severe and persistent delay.

Lastly, differential diagnosis must consider elective mutism, a condition in which, because of emotional disturbance, children speak in some situations but not in others. Strictly speaking it is not a cause of initial speech delay but it has to be considered as a possibility in the consideration of possible reasons for a young child failing to speak. While there are a variety of other conditions which sometimes lead to speech delay (Ingram 1972), these are the main common conditions which have to be borne in mind.

Intellectual retardation

Children with severe mental subnormality are nearly always markedly delayed in their language development. Those with an IQ below 20 rarely use spoken language as a form of communication even when they reach adulthood. Among children with mild intellectual retardation, language delay is also common. Articulation defects, too, occur in about 1 in 2 children with any degree of mental subnormality (Spreen 1965; Jordan 1967). The strength of the association between IQ and language development is shown by the consistently positive correlations between the two, both in the normal range of intelligence and in the subnormal range (Spreen 1965; Matthews 1959; Moore 1967). Nevertheless, there are sufficient mentally subnormal individuals with fair language competence to make it clear that there is far from a one-to-one relationship between IQ and language. Also, some children with mild intellectual retardation have a language handicap out of all proportion to their intellectual level (Morley 1965). Thus, the diagnosis of mental subnormality should not be taken as a sufficient explanation for language delay. It is necessary to investigate fully in order to determine whether the language difficulties are due to organic brain disease, deafness, psychosocial deprivation, or other factors.

The extent to which language development in intellectually retarded children is deviant as well as delayed is uncertain. However, in Down's syndrome, one of the few conditions systematically studied, language development follows much the same pattern as in normal children with two marked exceptions: (a) that in Down's syndrome language ceases to develop at a time when behavioural development is still continuing (Lenneberg *et al* 1964; Cornwell and Birch, 1969); and (b) that the development of articulation is out of step with and lags behind language development (Lenneberg *et al*

1964). Less is known about the process of language development in children with other types of mental retardation but it seems that echolalia is sometimes a more prolonged and more pronounced feature than it is in normal children (Stengel 1964; Morley 1965).

Psychosocial retardation

Psychosocial adversity is a common cause of poor speech but it is a less common cause of a marked delay in speech development. Although the literature includes frequent references to psychosocial retardation of language, there is a surprising paucity of studies into the condition and its prevalence is not known. Nevertheless, psychosocial deprivation may lead to a delay in the onset of speech and in some circumstances it may even impair preverbal vocalisation and babble (Brodbeck & Irwin 1946; Provence & Lipton 1967). When speech develops there is usually a global impairment of both spoken language and word-sound production. Gesture is not much used in most cases. On the other hand, the comprehension of language is not usually retarded to the same extent (Provence & Lipton 1962; Klaus & Gray 1968). Speech is delayed but it probably follows a normal pattern of development. There are infantile consonant substitutions and omissions, poor vocabulary and immature grammar, as is usually seen in normal children just beginning to speak. One feature which makes psychosocial retardation of language different from many other language disorders is that it possibly occurs about as often in girls as in boys (Gerber & Hertel 1969), although this point requires further study.

Poor quality instituional upbringing is the best documented cause of deprivation leading to language retardation, but poor circumstances in the home leading to speech delay are probably much more common. Prince (1968) has described psychosocial language retardation in West Indian children. Unsatisfactory child-minding arrangements in which a large number of children are left to their own devices in the care of one adult seem particularly likely to lead to language impairment.

The quality of language itself offers few clues to the diagnosis of psychosocial retardation of language, except that this would be a doubtful diagnosis if language *comprehension* were markedly impaired. The behaviour and social responses of deprived children follow no pathognomonic pattern but either extreme of social apathy or indiscriminately affectionate and demanding behaviour are fairly common. Diagnosis depends largely on the demonstration of environmental circumstances sufficiently severe to have caused language retardation. Differential diagnosis is complicated, however, by the fact that the children most vulnerable to deprivation are those already handicapped in intellect, personality or language. This is illustrated, for example, by the adverse effect of an institution environment on the language development of children with severe mental retardation (Lyle 1960).

Deafness

Mild hearing loss is a relatively common condition affecting some 3 to 4 per cent of children (Anderson 1967). The number requiring hearing aids is perhaps a twentieth of that, about 2 per 1000 (Rutter, Tizard & Whitmore 1970), and the number with severe hearing loss even less. Barton *et al* (1962) found that 0·7 per 1000 children attended schools for the deaf. Nearly all of these had a serious language deficiency and the rate of marked language retardation due to deafness is probably in the order of 1 per 1000.

The quality of babble is of diagnostic importance with respect to the profoundly deaf. The vocalisations of the deaf child are normal up to about 6 months (Lenneberg 1964a, b; Murphy 1964). Between 6 and 9 months there may be subtle changes in the amount of babble and in the range of sounds produced at any one time. By 9 months there will be a loss of vocal quality, the consonants begin to disappear, the vowels become diphthongs, and eventually only gutterals and primitive noises remain. This deterioration of vocalisation is a most useful guide to diagnosis.

The detailed opinion of the parents should always be sought on the child's hearing, as they have countless opportunities to observe hearing responses. The deaf infant may not startle when there are loud noises, such as by the door banging. The deaf child is likely to fail to look up when an aeroplane flies overhead, fail to turn round when the radio is switched on or off when he is not looking, and he will not run to the door when the doorbell rings. In the clinic the child's responses to sound should be carefully observed when interesting and meaningful noises of low intensity are made to one side and out of his sight (not in the mid-line). The rustling of cellophane paper, the gentle stroking of the rim of a china cup with a metal teaspoon, and the whirr of a friction car may be suitable stimuli. Because of the difficulty of excluding partial hearing loss on the basis of clinical assessment in a noisy clinic, all children with speech delay should have a proper assessment of hearing loss by someone experienced in testing children. Over the age of $3\frac{1}{2}$ years free field audiometry may be used, in conjunction with conditioning techniques if necessary (see Martin 1972). Distracting techniques are needed for younger children and testing may prove very difficult when the child also shows behavioural disturbance (as may be the case with mentally retarded or autistic children). Whenever there is the slightest doubt, hearing assessment should be repeated and, if necessary, followed by special techniques such as EEG audiometry or an electrocochleagram (Beagley & Kellogg 1969).

Developmental disorders of speech/language

Among physically healthy children of normal intelligence slightly less than 1 per 1000 have a marked language delay such that they are still markedly handicapped by the time they enter school (Ingram 1963; Rutter, Tizard & Whitmore 1970; Herbert & Wedell 1970). A much larger proportion of children (probably about 5 per cent) have a marked articulation defect in their speech but are not seriously impaired in their use of language. Specific developmental speech/language disorder is the term given to this group of conditions which range in severity from simple uncomplicated articulation defects, through delays in expressive language, to the rare (and severe) disorders of language comprehension (Ingram 1959; 1969). These developmental disorders are two or three times as common in boys as in girls and often there is a family history of slow speech development or difficulties in learning to read.

Most of the children with a developmental language disorder have a normal understanding of language. However, *transient* comprehension problems are present in perhaps a quarter to a sixth (Ingram 1959). Persistent receptive difficulties are much rarer still (Morley 1965) and probably occur in less than one child per 10 000. This rare form of severe receptive developmental language disorder, unlike the milder form, is equally common in boys and girls and is often accompanied by a partial high tone hearing impairment (Rutter *et al* 1971).

There is some uncertainty about how far language disorder in these children is deviant as well as delayed. In milder cases development is probably substantially normal in course although it is delayed in timing. However, in the more severe cases there may be some differences in the pattern of development (Menyuk 1964; 1969; 1974; Morehead & Ingram 1973). Language may not be used as creatively as normal and sometimes skills in grammar and competence in the meaning of words, which usually develop in parallel (see Herriott 1970), may be out of step.

The diagnosis of a developmental speech/language disorder is indicated by a delay in development which is out of keeping with the child's general level of intelligence, which is not associated with a gross hearing loss or any overt neurological condition, and which is associated with a normal social usage of the language available to the child.

Childhood autism

This condition is described in Chapter 30.

Elective mutism

Elective mutism is a term coined by Tramer (1934) to describe children who are silent with all but a small group of intimates. It is a condition in which the children are able to talk but do not or cannot in certain circumstances or to certain people. It occurs with approximately the same frequency in boys and girls, and generally develops about age 3 to 5 years after a period of normal speech development (Salfield 1950; Mora *et al* 1962; Reed 1963; Pustrom & Speers 1964; Elson *et al* 1965). The mutism then comes to attention after the child starts school. The usual pattern is that the child speaks normally, fluently and freely at home but never at school. The crucial point in diagnosis is the establishment that there is no abnormality in language comprehension or production but rather a motivational disorder with respect to speaking. Because of the initial difficulty in getting the child to talk at the clinic, this issue may have to be decided on the basis of the parental account and the confirmation by formal testing that language comprehension is normal.

Neurological examination shows no abnormality, hearing is normal, and there is no family history of mutism. Intelligence is usually within the normal range and there is no verbal deficit on cognitive tasks. Developmental milestones are generally within normal limits. When the children do speak, their sentence structure, vocabulary, and articulation are normal. The children vary in personality but most show temperamental features which are abnormal in some respect. Some are apathetic, morose, unprepossessing and withdrawn, while others are timid, tense, anxious and fearful. Relationships with other children are often poor. In some cases mutism is the only symptom but in most instances there are other indications of emotional disorder. Usually there is an abnormally strong tie between the child and his mother, who is frequently anxious, dominating and overprotective. The children are often very dependent on their parents but frequently, too, the dependency is accompanied by ambivalence and hostility.

Much of the psychiatric literature suggests that elective mutism is usually a 'pure' emotional disorder. However, this is probably misleading and a more representative series of cases (Wright 1968) showed that in about a fifth of the children the mutism develops as a reaction to an underlying speech or language handicap. In some cases this is the main cause of the child being reluctant to speak (Smayling 1959). While an abnormally dependent relationship is the main pathogenic factor in most cases, some children avoid speech because of the teasing and mockery they receive on account of mispronunciations or other speech defect.

Depending on the particular psychogenic mechanism which is operating, psychotherapy, social relearning, or reciprocal inhibition may be used in treatment. However, in many cases the most effective approach is a combination of measures to reduce social anxiety (e.g. desensitisation) and systematic encouragement or reinforcement of speaking in social situations (Straughan *et al* 1965; Reid *et al* 1967; Griffith *et al* 1975). The ultimate prognosis is good but in more resistant chronic cases treatment may need to extend over several years (Reed 1963; Elson *et al* 1965; Wright 1968).

CLINICAL ASSESSMENT

In making a differential diagnosis between the main conditions discussed above, much can be learned by simple clinical observation and history taking. Specialised investigations may be required for the final diagnosis but ordinary clinical study can usually take one a long way towards the answer.

Table 29.1   Scheme for assessment of speech and language

---

1   Imitation
2   'Inner language'
3   Comprehension of language
    a   'hearing behaviour' (hearing; listening and attention; understanding of spoken language)
    b   understanding of gesture
    c   understanding of written language
4   Vocalisation and babble
5   Language production
    a   mode used (spoken language, gesture, etc.)
    b   syntactical complexity
    c   semantic complexity
    d   abnormal qualities to spoken language
    e   social situations in which communication occurs
    f   amount of communication
6   Word-sound production
7   Phonation
8   Rhythm of speech
9   Other aspects of development
    a   cognition
    b   socialisation and interpersonal relationships

Table 29.1 notes the main elements to be considered (see Rutter 1972). In this connection it should be noted that speech and language are not synonymous. Language is a symbolic code for the generation of novel messages and its essence lies in its productivity. Spoken language is its commonest form but there are also other language modalities such as the written word, Braille, gesture and sign. Speech involves the use of spoken language but also it involves word-sound production and in order to avoid confusion with spoken language, speech will be used here only to refer to articulation skills.

Imitation, 'inner language' and language comprehension

Imitation bears a complex relationship to language but there should always be concern if a nonspeaking child is not imitating normally, as shown by his waving goodbye, or by his active participation in baby games such as 'peek-a-boo' or 'pat-a-cake'. Autism is the language disorder most consistently associated with seriously impaired imitative skills.

'Inner language' refers to a child's ability to use a symbolic code in his thought processes. It can be indirectly assessed by the child's ability to make meaningful use of objects such as toy cars, a miniature hairbrush, or a toy telephone (Sheridan 1969). A 2-year-old child should be able to use these for their intended purpose rather than just spin the car wheels or feel the brush bristles. More complex 'inner language' is reflected slightly later in the child's use of imaginative or pretend play, as shown by make-believe tea parties or by playing schools, mothers and fathers, or cowboys and Indians. In older children drawing is also associated with similar functions. Inner language is most seriously impaired in infantile autism (Bartak *et al* 1975) and also occasionally it may be affected in the most severe receptive developmental language disorders and in severe mental retardation.

Language comprehension is very important in both differential diagnosis and prognosis. A lack of understanding indicates a poorer outlook for development. Hearing may be assessed in terms of the child's response to sound in the absence of visual cues (see above). Attention and listening should be observed in connection with sounds which it is known the child can hear. Normal functioning is indicated by the child's looking at the person who speaks to him, by his watching faces, and by his looking up when called. Understanding of language should be assessed by the child's ability to follow instructions given *without* visual contextual or gestural cues. In very young children it is understanding of spoken language which is most important in differential diagnosis but in middle childhood understanding of gesture and of written language are also important.

Table 29.2 summarises the characteristics of language comprehension as used in differential diagnosis with some of the main disorders associated with speech delay. The deaf child cannot hear, shows no response to sounds, and no understanding of sounds but he does watch faces and he does understand gestures. The mentally retarded child hears normally but he is rather inattentive, he shows only limited understanding of what is said to him. The autistic child hears but is *very* inattentive, shows poor understanding and does not

Table 29.2 Comprehension in differential diagnosis

	'Inner language'	Hearing	Attention to sounds	Watch- ing face	Under- standing spoken language	Under- standing gesture
Severe deafness	+	–	–	+	–	+
High frequency loss	+	low freq. only	+	+	limited	+
Mental retarda- tion	limited	+	±	+	limited	±
Autism	–	+	–	No	poor	±
Elective mutism	+	+	+	+	+	+
Psychosocial retardation of language	+	+	+	+	+	+

watch faces or come when called. The socially deprived child, the elective mute and children with an expressive developmental language disorder are usually normal on all these counts.

Vocalisation and babble

In the past there has been a tendency to ignore vocalisation and babble in clinical assessment but recent work has indicated that much can be learned from their study. By history and observation the clinician should note the amount, range, type and rhythm of the child's vocal productions. As noted above, in the deaf child babble characteristically diminishes and becomes distorted in quality after 6 to 9 months of age. In both infantile autism and receptive developmental language disorders babble is frequently reduced in amount, lacks complexity and may be abnormal in its features (Bartak *et al* 1975; Ricks 1975; Ricks & Wing 1975). The quality of vocalisations may also be distorted in the dysarthria associated with cerebral palsy or other neurological disorders.

If the 2-year-old child is producing sentence-like patterns of sound with complex inflexions and speech cadences, if there is well developed imitative behaviour and if there is normal comprehension of language, a serious language disorder is unlikely although it does not necessarily follow that the child is normal. However if *any* of these features are abnormal, it would be most *un*wise to follow a 'wait and see' policy.

Language production

Even if the child is not speaking, he may still be capable of communication. Thus, the child with deafness or a developmental language disorder (and to a lesser extent the mentally retarded child) will use gesture and mime to indicate his needs from the age of about 3 or 4 years. The autistic child characteristically does not use gesture although he usually does pull people's arms and, less often, he may point with his hand.

If the child is speaking, it is necessary to achieve some measure of his language skills both with regard to grammar (syntax) and the use of words (semantics). A useful guide to the state of language production is afforded by the child's average length of utterance, as observed or as reported by the parents. With respect to language abnormalities, echolalia is the most important. Normal children tend to repeat what is said to them up to about 30

Table 29.3 Language production in differential diagnosis

	Use of gesture	Social conversation	Echolalia	Word-sound production
Deafness	+ + +	+ +	—	defective
Mental retardation	+	+	+ +	poor
Autism	—	—	+ + +	variable
Developmental language disorder	+ +	+ +	±	variable/poor
Elective mutism	—	dependent on situation	—	normal

months of age, but after that age it should definitely be regarded as abnormal. The presence of echolalia roughly reflects the child's lack of understanding of language (Fay 1971; Fay & Butler 1971) and it is most often observed in autism and in mental retardation.

Both the social context in which communication occurs and the amount of communication are important, especially with respect to the diagnosis of autism and elective mutism. The autistic child speaks little even when speech is developed and he tends not to use speech for social communication. He does not 'chat' in the way that a normal toddler does. The elective mute talks normally in some situations but not at all in others.

Word-sound production, or articulation, may be abnormal for several different reasons and the quality of speech may be a useful guide to diagnosis. In the developmental language disorders, mental retardation and autism, speech is often immature with infantile pronunciations but it is less often abnormal in other respects. Articulation will be distorted if there is defective sensory input and the speech of both the deaf child and of the youngster with a high-tone hearing defect has quite distinctive qualities. Motor incoordination, as in dysarthria, will also lead to a characteristic type of articulation defect.

Phonation and rhythm are generally less useful diagnostic features but whispering is a common accompaniment to elective mutism and various oddities of voice production are occasionally found in autistic children who may also have an abnormality of rhythm resulting in a malcoordination in speaking and breathing.

Cognition, emotions and socialisation

As well as assessing speech and language it is important to make some evaluation of other aspects of the child's development. By the age of 3 or 4 years a good rough estimate of the child's intellectual level can be obtained from his play, both as reported by the parents and as seen at the clinic. Normal intelligence will be shown by the child's curiosity and interest in the environment, by his constructional skills, by the system and logic he shows in his manipulation of objects and in his finding out how a new toy works, as well as in the complexity of his play, the extent to which he is able to look after himself and the degree to which he can help about the house.

Social and emotional development may be gauged by whether the child cuddles and comes to his parents for comfort when tired or upset, by his attachment to parents, by normal separation anxiety, by his showing a full and appropriate range of emotions and by his interactions and friendships with other children.

The mentally retarded child will be delayed in these aspects of development just as he is in speech and language; the elective mute may be socially anxious and inhibited but will be otherwise normal or near normal; the autistic child on the other hand will be seriously deficient in all his social responses.

Medical examination and study of parent–child interaction

The possibility that speech delay may be associated with a mild cerebral palsy emphasises the importance of a careful neurological examination. In this connection it is essential to watch the child's gait and manipulation of objects as well as examining reflexes and the like (see Chapter 12).

With respect to the possibility of psychosocial deprivation it is important to note how much the parents play and talk with the child, what toys are available and the quality of the child-minding arrangements when the parents are out. A careful history and an observation of the quality of parent–child interaction in the clinic are both necessary in this connection—a home visit will also add valuable information.

Psychological testing

Psychological assessment of both general cognition and language ability is essential whenever a child has a marked speech delay.

In the 2 to 5 year age period the most generally useful test of cognition for language impaired children is the Merrill-Palmer Scale (Stutsman 1948). The test has the advantage of being interesting to most young children, of requiring the minimum of spoken instructions, of having a wide range of items requiring no speech from the child—all important characteristics for this group of children (Lockyer & Rutter 1969). A further feature is that it has a procedure for dealing with items refused rather than failed; a common occurrence in behaviourally disturbed children whose cooperation is difficult to obtain. The Arthur adaptation of the Leiter International Performance Scale (Leiter & Arthur 1955) requires no spoken instructions or responses and is particularly appropriate for deaf children or children with receptive language difficulties. The test has no time limit which is an asset when testing young children not used to working against the clock. For school-age children the Wechsler scales are the most generally useful. There are versions for the age range 4–6½ years (Wechsler 1955) and for 5–16 years (Wechsler 1967). Both versions provide a differentiation between 'verbal' and 'performance' IQs.

When it proves impractical to assess the child in a test situation it is still possible to obtain some estimate of his level of development through the Vineland Social Maturity Scale (Doll 1947). This involves systematically asking the parent about the child's accomplishments in various areas such as dressing, feeding and communication. In younger children scores correlate moderately highly with IQ (Pringle 1966) and so yield a crude estimate of intellectual level. Mecham (1958) has used a similar approach in deriving a scale for language development.

The cognitive assessment of young children with language delay is described more fully by Berger and Yule (1972) and the concepts involved in psychological testing are outlined in Chapter 13.

The Reynell Developmental Language Scales (Reynell 1969) provides the best general measures of language level. It is particularly useful in its clear distinction between receptive and expressive skills. Normative data are available between the ages of 6 months and 6 years. The Peabody Picture Vocabulary Test (Dunn 1959) also provides a simple measure of vocabulary recognition which is a rather different aspect of language to that which is assessed by the Reynell scales. A wide variety of other tests are also available (see Mittler 1972) and these may be useful when more detailed measures of other aspects of speech and language (such as auditory discrimination of articulation) are required.

SECONDARY PROBLEMS ASSOCIATED WITH SPEECH AND LANGUAGE DELAY

A serious delay in speech or language is often associated with a variety of other problems in development (Rutter 1972). There has been much discussion on the connections between language and thinking. Although the mechanisms involved remain obscure (Herriott 1970) it seems that language is an aid to many, but not all, forms of learning. Deaf children perform as well as hearing children on puzzle-type tasks but are slightly below normal on tests involving concepts (Lenneberg 1967; Furth 1964; 1966). However, it seems that their poor performance is partly due to their lack of experience rather than their lack of ability. Spoken language is important not so much in its own right but rather because its use greatly enlarges a person's experiences and hence his opportunities for learning.

As already noted there is an association between complexity of language and the amount of symbolic play. It has been suggested (Sheridan 1969) but not yet demonstrated, that treatment which encourages the development of imitation and of imaginative play activities may aid language development.

Children who are delayed in talking are likely also to be delayed in reading, because both reflect language impairment. Ingram and his colleagues found that most speech retarded youngsters had some difficulties in learning to read when they entered ordinary primary schools (Ingram 1963; Mason 1967). Children with more severe handicaps at special schools have also been found to have pronounced reading difficulties (Canning & Davies-Eysenck 1966; Griffiths 1969). Children who have difficulties in articulation but not in language also often have difficulties in learning to read (Crookes & Green 1963) possibly because of associated problems in perception. Preliminary findings suggest that their educational difficulties are usually less persistent and widespread than those of children with language retardation.

Communicative skills are very important in social relationships and the child with speech delay is somewhat more likely than other children to become shy, easily frustrated, socially isolated and to have difficulties in group play (see Rutter 1972). The reasons for these various secondary social and emotional problems (which affect only some speech delayed children) are many and various. Some of the more important are the effects of associated brain dysfunction (when this is present); the effects of teasing and rejection by other children arising from the child's speech difficulties; the lack of social integration and the effect of this on the child's self-image; the effect of poor communication on social relationships; the effects of educational difficulties.

TREATMENT

Obviously the treatment required for a child with speech delay depends in part on the underlying condition. However there are certain general principles which apply to the steps taken to aid language development in any child who is slow to talk. First the main aim must always be for language skills which are used for social communication and the development of ideas. This requires that the child has an understanding of language, that he uses language spontaneously and that he applies it in a social context. The mere acquisition of words is not enough and the correct pronunciation of words is of secondary importance.

Secondly, imaginative play, imitation and the understanding of language are important parts of language development. Receptive language training may aid expressive language skills (Pothier *et al* 1974) and the fostering of imitation and creative play may also provide the child with skills which facilitate language development. Thirdly, social interaction is the main medium for learning both language and social skills. It is for this reason, amongst others, that almost all approaches to language training are now increasingly involving parents in the treatment programme. While the child will often also have individual treatment, much attention is given to helping the parents know best how to aid the development of communication by the way they respond to the child at home. In this connection the intensity and quality of parent–child interaction are probably more important than the absolute amount of time spent together per day. It is not necessary, and may be harmful, to urge parents to spend more time with the child. What is important is that there is an uninterrupted 30 minutes or so a day, when they can do things together. Fourthly, the content and interest of what is said to the child are crucial. Communications must be meaningful to him if they are to be of value. Constant background noise does not aid development.

Fifthly, it is necessary to remember the distinction between the 'objective' and the 'effective' environment (Rutter & Sussenwein 1971). The advice to 'keep talking to him' is not helpful. If the language environment provided for the child is to be beneficial it must impinge on him and it must be meaningful. Thus, for example, the child with limited language comprehension may make better progress when he is spoken to in short rather than long sentences (Browning 1974). Similarly, for the deaf child, signs and gesture will have more meaning than speech which he cannot hear. It is perhaps for this reason that Meadow (1968) found that deaf children reared by deaf parents made better progress on the whole than deaf children reared by hearing parents. Sixthly, if for some reason the child cannot acquire speech he should be taught other means of communication. Sign language (Fenn & Rowe 1975) and the use of symbols (Deich & Hodges, 1975) may both be useful in this connection. It used to be thought that if you used gesture to a deaf or otherwise speech delayed child it would inhibit speech development. In fact the reverse is probably nearer the truth. *Any* meaningful communication with the child should aid speech development.

The particular means used to aid any of the aspects of language development are many and varied and numerous programmes have been devised. Many utilise operant techniques to a greater or lesser extent and although much of the operant research is open to methodological criticism there is now reasonable evidence that operant training techniques can be successfully used to aid the development of speech and language (Yule & Berger 1972; Yule *et al* 1975; Garcia & De Haven 1974). Behavioural programmes using parents as primary language therapists have appeared effective (MacDonald *et al* 1974). In addition, preliminary studies have also suggested the benefits of more broadly used intervention programmes which have placed the emphasis on language comprehension (Cooper *et al* 1974).

Children with more severe language disorders are likely to need specialised teaching in either a separate class or a special school. This may be of benefit, not only in aiding language development, but also in fostering normal social and emotional development in children whose social relationships are greatly impeded by the severity of their language handicap (Ministry of Education 1963; Griffiths 1969). Of course, it is also important that speech delayed children learn to mix with normally speaking children and learn to adjust to the ordinary social environment. The timing and manner of transition to ordinary school need to be carefully planned to ensure that the child copes successfully. A few children need special education throughout their schooling.

PROGNOSIS AND OUTCOME

Clearly the prognosis for the children with speech delay depends on the underlying condition. Prognosis is worst for children with severe mental retardation, severe deafness or infantile autism (particularly where this is accompanied by intellectual retardation). Less is known about the course of development for children with uncomplicated speech or language problems such as those shown by children with a developmental disorder. However such data as are available (Ingram 1963; Mason 1967; Griffiths 1969; Garvey & Gordan 1973; Sheridan 1973; Renfrew & Geary 1973) provide some guidance. The great majority of children acquire normal spoken language eventually but the majority of children have educational difficulties which persist into secondary school. Prognosis is less good for those children who have low intelligence, who have difficulties with imitation, who have poor auditory discrimination and who show an impairment in language comprehension. However, even among a group of normally intelligent children who gained no useful speech and who were educated throughout at a residential school specialising in severe language problems, it was found that most made a fair social adjustment and were able to hold a steady job (Moor House School 1969). Whether the results would be equally good for children who had not received such skilled education remains uncertain. Much has still to be learned about the psychological difficulties of language retarded children. Although, in part, they may be intrinsic, in larger part they appear secondary to the way in which these children are dealt with by society. Potentially, therefore, they are preventable. It is important not only to aid the language development of children with speech delay but also to do everything possible to ensure that secondary emotional, behavioural and educational handicaps do not develop.

REFERENCES

ANDERSON U.M. (1967) The incidence and significance of high-frequency deafness in children. *Amer. J. Dis. Child.* **113**, 560–565

BARTAK L., RUTTER M. & COX A. (1975) A comparative study of infantile autism and specific developmental receptive language disorder. I: The children. *Brit. J. Psychiat.* **126**, 127–145

BARTON M.E., COURT S.D. & WALKER W. (1962) Causes of severe deafness in schoolchildren in Northumberland and Durham. *Brit. Med. J.* **1**, 351–355

BEAGLEY H.A. & KELLOGG S.E. (1969) A comparison of evoked response and subjective auditory thresholds. *Int. Audiol.* **8**, 345

BERGER M. & YULE W. (1972) Cognitive assessment in young children with language delay. *In* Rutter M. & Martin J.A.M. (eds.) *The Child with Delayed Speech*. Clinics in Dev. Med. no. 43. London: SIMP/Heinemann

BRODBECK A.J. & IRWIN O.C. (1946) The speech behavior of infants without families. *Child Dev.* **17**, 145–156

BROWN R. (1973) *A First Language: The Early Stages*. Cambridge, Massachusetts: Harvard University Press

BROWN R. & BELLUGI U. (1964) Three processes in the child's acquisition of syntax. *Harvard Educ. Rev.* **34**, 133–151

BROWN R., CAZDEN C. & BELLUGI-KLIMA U. (1969) The child's grammar from I to III. *In* Hill J.P. (ed.) *Minnesota Symposia on Child Psychology*, vol. 2. Minneapolis: University of Minnesota Press

BROWN R. & HANLON C. (1970) Derivational complexity and order of acquisition in child speech. *In* Hayes J.R. (ed.) *Cognition and the Development of Language.* New York: Wiley

BROWNING E.R. (1974) The effectiveness of long and short verbal commands in inducing correct responses in three schizophrenic children. *J. Autism Child. Schiz.* **4,** 293–300

CANNING A. & DAVIES-EYSENCK M. (1966) An attempt at analysis of developmental disorders of language and articulation. *De Therapia Vocis et Loquelae,* **1,** 35–39

CAZDEN C. (1966) Subcultural differences in child language: an interdisciplinary review. *Merrill–Palmer Quart.* **12,** 185–219

CHOMSKY C. (1969) The acquisition of syntax in children from 5 to 10. *In* Chomsky N. (ed.) *Aspects of the Theory of Syntax.* Cambridge, Massachusetts: MIT Press

COOPER J., MOODLEY M. & REYNELL J. (1974) Intervention programmes for pre-school children and delayed language development: a preliminary report. *Brit. J. Dis. Commun.* **9,** 81–91

CORNWELL A.C. & BIRCH H.G. (1969) Psychological and social development in home-reared children with Down's syndrome (mongolism). *Amer. J. ment. Defic.* **74,** 341–350

CRITCHLEY E. (1967) Language development of hearing children in a deaf environment. *Develop. Med. Child Neurol.* **9,** 274–280

CROOKES T.G. & GREEN M.C.L. (1963) Some characteristics of children with two types of speech disorder. *Brit. J. educ. Psychol.* **33,** 31–40

DARCY N.T. (1953) A review of the literature on the effects of bilingualism upon the measurement of intelligence. *J. genet. Psychol.* **82,** 21–57

DAY E.J. (1932) The development of language in twins. II: The development of twins—their resemblances and differences. *Child Dev.* **3,** 298–316

DEICH R.F. & HODGES P.M. (1975) Learning from Sarah. *Hum. Behav.* **4,** 40–42

DOLL E.A. (1947) *The Vineland Social Maturity Scale, Manual of Directions.* Minneapolis: Educational Tests Bureau

DOUGLAS J.W.B. (1964) *The Home and the School.* London: MacGibbon & Kee

DOUGLAS J.W.B., ROSS J.M. & SIMPSON H.R. (1968) *All our Future.* London: Peter Davies

DUNN L. (1959) *The Peabody Picture Vocabulary Test.* Minneapolis: American Guidance Service

ELSON A., PEARSON C., JONES C.D. & SCHUMACHER E. (1965) Follow-up study of childhood elective mutism. *Arch. gen. Psychiat.* **13,** 182–187

ERVIN-TRIPP S. (1966) Language development. *In* Hoffman L.W. & Hoffman M.L. (eds.) *Review of Child Development Research,* vol. 2. New York: Russell Sage Foundation

FAY W.H. (1971) On normal an autistic pronouns. *J. Speech Hear. Dis.* **36,** 242–249

FAY W.H. & BUTLER B.V. (1971) Echo-reaction as an approach to semantic resolution. *J. Speech Hear. Dis.* **14,** 645–651

FENN G. & ROWE J.A. (1975) An experiment in manual communication. *Brit. J. Dis. Commun.* **10,** 3–16

FRASER C., BELLUGI U. & BROWN R. (1963) Control of grammar in imitation, comprehension and production. *J. verbal Learn.* **2,** 121–135

FRIEDLANDER B.Z. (1970) Receptive language development in infancy: issues and problems. *Merrill–Palmer Quart.* **16**, 7–51

FURTH H.G. (1964) Research with the deaf: implications for language and cognition. *Psychol. Bull.* **62**, 145–164

FURTH H.G. (1966) *Thinking without Language.* New York: Free Press

GARCIA E.E. & DeHAVEN E.D. (1974) Use of operant techniques in the establishment and generalization of language: a review and analysis. *Amer. J. Ment. Defic.* **79**, 169–178

GARVEY M. & GORDAN N. (1973) A follow-up study of children with disorders of speech development. *Brit. J. Dis. Commun.* **8**, 17–28

GARVEY M. & MUTTON D.E. (1973) Sex chromosome aberrations and speech development. *Arch. Dis. Child.* **48**, 937–941

GERBER S.E. & HERTEL C.G. (1969) Language deficiency of disadvantaged children. *J. speech Res.* **12**, 270–280

GRIFFITHS C.P.S. (1969) A follow-up study of children with disorders of speech. *Brit. J. Dis. Commun.* **4**, 46–56

GRIFFITH E.E., SCHNELLE J.F., McNEES M.P., BISSINGER C. & HUFF T.M. (1975) Elective mutism in a first grader: the remediation of a complex behavioral problem. *J. Abnorm. Child Psychol.* **3**, 127–134

HAYWOOD H.C. (1967) Experimental factors in intellectual development: the concept of dynamic intelligence. *In* Zubin J. & Jervis G.A. (eds.) *The Psychopathology of Mental Development.* New York: Grune & Stratton

HERBERT G.W. & WEDELL K. (1970) Communication handicaps of children with specific language deficiency. Paper read at the Annual Conference of the British Psychological Society, Southampton, April 1970

HERRIOTT P. (1970) *An Introduction to the Psychology of Language.* London: Methuen

HOWARD R.W. (1946) The language development of a group of triplets. *J. genet. Psychol.* **69**, 181–188

INGRAM T.T.S. (1959) Specific developmental disorders of speech in childhood. *Brain* **82**, 450–467

INGRAM T.T.S. (1963) Delayed development of speech with special reference to dyslexia. *Proc. roy. Soc. Med.* **56**, 199–203

INGRAM T.T.S. (1969) Developmental disorders of speech. *In* Vinken P.J. & Bruin W. (eds.) *Handbook of Clinical Neurology,* vol. 4. Amsterdam: North-Holland

INGRAM T.T.S. (1972) The classification of speech and language disorders in young children. *In* Rutter M. & Martin J.A.M. (eds.) *The Child with Delayed Speech.* Clinics in Dev. Med. no. 43. London: SIMP/Heinemann

IRWIN O.C. (1960) Infant speech: effect of systematic reading of stories. *J. Speech Hear. Res.* **3**, 187–190

JORDAN T.E. (1967) Language and mental retardation: a review of the literature. *In* Schiefelbusch R.L., Copeland R.H. & Smith J.O. (eds.) *Language and Mental Retardation: Empirical and Conceptual Considerations.* New York: Holt, Rinehart & Winston

KESSEL F.S. (1970) The role of syntax in children's comprehension from ages six to twelve. *Monogr. Soc. Res. Child Develop.* **35**, no. 6 (Serial no. 139)

KLAUS R.A. & GRAY S.W. (1968) The early training project for disadvantaged children: a report after five years. *Monogr. Soc. Res. Child Develop.* no. 120

LEITER R.G. & ARTHUR G. (1955) *Leiter International Performance Scale.* New York: C. H. Stoelting

LENNEBERG E.H. (1964a) Language disorders in childhood. *Harvard Educ. Rev.* **34,** 152–177

LENNEBERG E.H. (1964b) Speech as a motor skill with special reference to nonaphasic disorders. *Monogr. Soc. Res. Child Develop.* **29,** 115–127

LENNEBERG E.H. (1967) *Biological Foundations of Language,* New York: Wiley

LENNEBERG E.H., NICHOLS I.A. & ROSENBERGER E.T. (1964) Primitive stages of language development in mongolism. *Proc. Ass. Res. Nerv. Ment. Dis.* **42,** 119–137

LEWIS M.M. (1951) *Infant Speech.* London: Routledge

LOCKYER L. & RUTTER M. (1969) A five to fifteen year follow-up study of infantile psychosis. III: Psychological aspects. *Brit. J. Psychiat.* **115,** 865–882

LOVELL K. & DIXON E.M. (1967) The growth of the control of grammar in imitation, comprehension, and production. *J. Child Psychol. Psychiat.* **8,** 31–39

LYLE J.G. (1960) The effect of an institutional environment upon the verbal development of imbecile children. II: Speech and Language. *J. Ment. Defic. Res.* **4,** 1–13

McCARTHY D. (1930) *The Language Development of the Preschool Child,* Institute of Child Welfare Monograph Series, no. 4. Minneapolis: University of Minnesota Press

McCARTHY D. (1954) Language Development of the Preschool Child. *In* Carmichael L. (ed.) *Manual of Child Psychology,* 2nd edn. London: Chapman & Hall

MacDONALD J.D., BLOTT J.P., GORDON K., SPREGEL B. & HARTMANN M. (1974) An experimental parent assisted treatment program for preschool language delayed children. *J. Speech Hear. Dis.* **39,** 395–415

MacKEITH R.C. & RUTTER M. (1972) A note on the prevalence of speech and language disorders. *In* Rutter M. & Martin J.A.M. (eds.) *The Child With Delayed Speech.* Clinics in Dev. Med. no. 43. London: SIMP/Heinemann

McNEILL D. (1970) The development of language. *In* Mussen P.H. (ed.) *Carmichael's Manual of Child Psychology,* 3rd edn., vol. 1. New York: Wiley

MARSHALL W.A. (1968) *Development of the Brain.* Edinburgh: Oliver & Boyd

MARTIN J.A.M. (1972) Hearing loss and hearing behaviour. *In* Rutter M. & Martin J.A.M. (eds) *The Child With Delayed Speech.* Clinics in Dev. Med. no. 43. London: SIMP/Heinemann

MASON A.W. (1967) Specific (developmental) dyslexia. *Develop. Med. Child. Neurol.* **9,** 183–190

MATTHEWS J. (1959) Speech problems of the mentally retarded. *In* Travis L.E. (ed.) *Handbook of Speech Pathology.* London: Peter Owen.

MEADOW K.P. (1968) Toward a developmental understanding of deafness. *J. Rehab. Deaf* **2,** 1–18

MECHAM M. (1958) *Verbal Language Development Scale.* Minneapolis: Educational Test Bureau

MENYUK P. (1964) Comparison of grammar of children with functional deviant and normal speech. *J. Speech Hear. Res.* **7,** 109–121

MENYUK P. (1969) *Sentences Children Use.* Cambridge, Massachusetts: MIT Press

MENYUK P. (1971) *The Acquisition and Development of Language.* Englewood Cliffs, NJ: Prentice-Hall

MENYUK P. (1974) The bases of language acquisition: some questions. *J. Autism Child. Schiz.* **4**, 325–345

MINISTRY OF EDUCATION (1963) *Report on a Survey of Deaf Children who have been Transferred from Special Schools or Units to Ordinary Schools.* London: HMSO

MITTLER P. (1972) Psychological assessment of language abilities. *In* Rutter M. & Martin J.A.M. (eds) *The Child with Delayed Speech.* Clinics in Dev. Med. no. 43. London: SIMP/Heinemann

MOOR HOUSE SCHOOL (1969) *A Report on a Follow-up in 1969 of Ten Receptive Aphasic Ex-Pupils of Moor House School.* Moor House School.

MOORE T. (1967) Language and intelligence: a longitudinal study of the first eight years. Part I: Patterns of development in boys and girls. *Hum. Dev.* **10**, 88–106

MORA G., DeVAULT S. & SCHOPLER E. (1962) Dynamics and psychotherapy of identical twins with elective mutism. *J. Child Psychol. Psychiat.* **3**, 41–52

MOREHEAD D.M. & INGRAM D. (1973) The development of base syntax in normal and linguistically deviant children. *J. Speech Hear. Res.* **16**, 330–352

MORLEY M.E. (1965) *The Development and Disorders of Speech in Childhood*, 2nd edn. Edinburgh: E. & S. Livingstone

MORTON J. (1971) Psycholinguistics. *Brit. Med. Bull.* **27**, 195–199

MURPHY K. (1964) Development of normal vocalisation and speech. *In* Renfrew C. & Murphy K. (eds) *The Child Who Does Not Talk.* Clinics in Dev. Med. no. 13. London: SIMP/Heinemann

NISBET J. (1953) Family environment and intelligence. *Eugen. Rev.* **45**, 31–40

PEAL E. & LAMBERT W.E. (1962) The relationship of bilingualism to intelligence. *Psychol. Monogr.* **76** (27)

POTHIER P., MORRISON D. & GORMAN F. (1974) Effects of receptive language training on receptive and expressive language development. *J. Abnorm. Child Psychol.* **2**, 153–164

PRINCE G.S. (1968) Mental health problems in preschool West Indian children. *Matern. Child Care* **3**, 483–486

PRINGLE M.L. KELLMER (1966) *Social Learning and its Measurement.* London: Longman

PROVENCE S. & LIPTON R.C. (1962) *Infants in Institutions.* New York: International Universities Press

PUSTROM E. & SPEERS R.W. (1964) Elective mutism in children. *J. Amer. Acad. Child Psychiat.* **3**, 287–297

REBELSKY F.G., STARR R.H. & LURIA Z. (1967) Language development: the first four years. *In* Brackbill Y. (ed.) *Infancy and Early Childhood.* New York: Free Press

RECORD R., McKEOWN T. & EDWARDS J.H. (1970) An investigation of the difference in measured intelligence between twins and single births. *Ann. Hum. Genet.* **34**, 11–20

REED G.F. (1963) Elective mutism in children: a reappraisal. *J. Child Psychol. Psychiat.* **4**, 99–107

REID J.B., HAWKINS N., KEUTZER C., McNEAL S.A., PHELPS R.E., REID K.M. & MEES H.L. (1967) A marathon behaviour modification of a selectively mute child. *J. Child Psychol. Psychiat.* **8**, 27–30

RENFREW C.E. & GEARY L. (1973) Prediction of persisting speech defect. *Brit. J. Dis. Commun.* **8**, 37–41

REYNELL J.K. (1969) *The Reynell Developmental Language Scales.* Slough: NFER

RICKS D.M. (1975) Vocal communication in pre-verbal normal and autistic children.

In O'Connor N. (ed.) *Language, Cognitive Deficits and Retardation*. London: Butterworths

RICKS D. & WING L. (1975) Language, communication, and the use of symbols in normal and autistic children. *J. Autism Child. Schiz.* **5**, 191–222

ROUTH D.K. (1969) Conditioning of social response differentiation in infants. *Develop. Psychol.* **1**, 219–226

RUTTER M. (1970) Psychological development—predictions from infancy. *J. Child Psychol. Psychiat.* **11**, 49–62

RUTTER M. (1972) Clinical assessment of language disorders in the young child. *In* Rutter M. & Martin J.A.M. (eds) *The Child with Delayed Speech*. Clinics in Dev. Med. no. 43. London: SIMP/Heinemann

RUTTER M. (1974) The child who is slow to talk. *Update* (March), 777–786

RUTTER M. & BAX M. (1972) Normal development of speech and language. *In* Rutter M. & Martin J.A.M. (eds) *The Child with Delayed Speech*. Clinics in Dev. Med. no. 43. London: SIMP/Heinemann

RUTTER M., BARTAK L. & NEWMAN S. (1971) Autism—a central disorder of cognition and language? *In* Rutter M. (ed.) *Infantile Autism: Concepts, Characteristics and Treatment*. Edinburgh: Churchill-Livingstone

RUTTER M., GRAHAM P. & YULE W. (1970) *A Neuropsychiatric Study in Childhood*. Clinics in Dev. Med. no. 35/36. London: SIMP/Heinemann

RUTTER M. & MARTIN J.A.M. (1972) (eds.) *The Child with Delayed Speech*. Clin. Devel. Med. no. 43. London: SIMP/Heinemann

RUTTER M. & MITTLER P. (1972) Environmental influences on language development. *In* Rutter M. & Martin J.A.M. (eds) *The Child with Delayed Speech*. Clinics in Dev. Med. no. 43. London: SIMP/Heinemann

RUTTER M. & SUSSENWEIN F. (1971) A developmental and behavioral approach to the treatment of preschool autistic children. *J. Autism Child. Schiz.* **1**, 376–397

RUTTER M., TIZARD J. & WHITMORE K. (eds) (1970) *Education, Health and Behaviour*. London: Longman

RUTTER M. & YULE W. (1973) Specific reading retardation. *In* Mann L. & Sabatino D. (eds.) *The First Review of Special Education*. Philadelphia: Buttonwood Farms

SALFIELD D.J. (1950) Observations on elective mutism in children. *J. Ment. Sci.* **96**, 1024–1032

SHERIDAN M. (1969) Playthings in the development of language. *Health Trends*, **1**, 7–10

SHERIDAN M.D. (1973) Children of seven years with marked speech defects. *Brit. J. Dis. Commun.* **8**, 9–16

SMAYLING L.M. (1959) Analysis of six cases of voluntary mutism. *J. Speech Hear. Dis.* **24**, 55–58

SMITH M.E. (1935a) A study of some factors influencing the development of the sentence in preschool children. *J. Genet. Psychol.* **46**, 182–212

SMITH M.E. (1935b) A study of the speech of eight bilingual children of the same family. *Child Dev.* **6**, 19–25

SMITH M.E. (1949) Measurement of vocabularies of young bilingual children in both of the languages used. *J. Genet. Psychol.* **74**, 305–310

SMITH M.E. (1957) Word variety as a measure of bilingualism in preschool children. *J. Genet. Psychol.* **90**, 143–150

SOFFIETTI J.P. (1955) Bilingualism and biculturalism. *J. Educ. Psychol.* **46**, 222–227

SPREEN O. (1965) Language functions in mental retardation: a review. 1: Language development, types of retardation, and intelligence level. *Amer. J. Ment. Def.* **69**, 482–494

STENGEL E. (1964) Speech disorders and mental disorders. *In* de Reuck A.V. & O'Connor N. (eds.) *Disorders of Language*, Ciba Foundation Symposium. London: Churchill

STRAUGHAN J.H., POTTER W.K. & HAMILTON S.H. (1965) The behavioural treatment of an elective mute. *J. Child Psychol. Psychiat.* **6**, 125–130

STUTSMAN R. (1948) *Merrill-Palmer Scale of Mental Tests.* New York: Harcourt, Brace and World

TIZARD B., COOPERMAN O., JOSEPH A. & TIZARD J. (1972) Environmental effects on language development: a study of young children in long-stay residential nurseries. *Child Dev.* **43**, 337–358

TIZARD J. (1970) The role of social institutions in the causation, prevention and alleviation of mental retardation. *In* Haywood H.C. (ed.) *Social-Cultural Aspects of Mental Retardation.* New York: Appleton-Century-Crofts

TODD G.A. & PALMER B. (1968) Social reinforcement of infant babbling. *Child Dev.* **39**, 591–596

TRAMER M. (1934) Electiver Mutismus bei Kindern. *Z. Kinderpsychiat.* **1**, 30–35

WATTS A.F. (1947) *Language and Mental Development of Children.* London: Harrap

WEISBERG P. (1963) Social and nonsocial conditioning of infant vocalizations. *Child Dev.* **34**, 377–388

WECHSLER D. (1955) *Wechsler Adult Intelligence Scale.* New York: Psychological Corporation

WECHSLER D. (1967) *Wechsler Pre-School and Primary Scale of Intelligence.* New York: Psychological Corporation

WRIGHT H.L. (1968) A clinical study of children who refuse to talk in school. *J. Amer. Acad. Child Psychiat.* **7**, 603–617

YULE W. & BERGER M. (1972) Behaviour modification principles and speech delay. *In* Rutter M. & Martin J.A.M. (eds) *The Child with Delayed Speech.* Clinics in Dev. Med. no. 43. London: SIMP/Heinemann

YULE W., BERGER M. & HOWLIN P. (1975) Language deficit and behaviour modification. *In* O'Connor N. (ed.) *Language, Cognitive Deficits and Retardation.* London: Butterworths

ZAZZO R. (1960) *Les Jumeaux: le Couple et la Personne.* Paris: PUF

CHAPTER 30

Infantile autism and other child psychoses

M. RUTTER

HISTORICAL BACKGROUND

Isolated cases of young children with severe mental disorders, which might be termed psychotic, were reported from as early as the beginning of the nineteenth century (Bender 1969), but Maudsley (1867) was the first psychiatrist to pay serious attention to child psychoses and it was not until very much later that these conditions became generally recognised. During the first half of this century, a number of supposedly different psychotic syndromes were described. In 1906, De Sanctis reported psychoses in prepubertal children and coined the term 'dementia precocissima'. Two years later, under the heading of dementia infantilis, Heller (1930) described a picture of severe regression in young children which was accompanied by stereotypies, restlessness and loss of speech. In the mid-30s, Potter, (1933) proposed a set of criteria for schizophrenia as it occurred in childhood, and in 1943, Kanner provided a particularly clear and incisive account of a syndrome which he called 'infantile autism'. The following year Asperger (1944) gave a somewhat similar description of a disorder designated 'autistic psychopathy'. About the same time, Bender (1947) wrote about 'childhood schizophrenia' in referring to a very broad and ill-defined group of severe disorders of childhood. Shortly after that the concepts of 'symbiotic psychosis' (Mahler & Gosliner 1955) and the 'atypical child' (Rank 1955) came into the literature. Since then an immense literature on child psychoses has amassed and a host of classifications has been proposed (see Laufer & Gair 1969; Hingtgen & Bryson 1972; Ornitz 1973; Churchill *et al* 1971; Rutter 1971a; Miller 1974; Wing 1976).

CLASSIFICATION OF CHILD PSYCHOSES

For a long time most writers tended to group all the psychoses of childhood together, usually under the term schizophrenia of childhood (Creak 1961), and the diagnostic concepts of child psychosis could only be described as chaotic. However, in recent years the situation has changed radically and there is a general (but not quite universal) recognition that the generic term 'childhood schizophrenia' covers a number of quite different syndromes which should be differentiated (Rutter 1972; 1976; Eisenberg 1972; Kolvin 1974; Makita 1974).

Schizophrenia

First, it is clear that schizophrenia as described in adults can begin in childhood (Kolvin 1971; Vrono 1974). It does so most often during the preadolescent or adolescent period (see Chapter 31) but the onset may be as early as 7 years and, rarely, even before that. The symptomatology is generally similar to that seen in adults. Kolvin *et al* (1971a) found that a disorder of thought association was present in three-fifths of children with a psychosis beginning in later childhood, the same proportion showed thought blocking, and a similar percentage exhibited delusions (most often of persecution). Over 80 per cent had auditory hallucinations and nearly half of these had bodily or visual hallucinations as well. However, no child had bodily or visual hallucinations without there also being auditory hallucinations. Disturbances of mood were usual, and especially in the early stages, perplexity was highly characteristic. Nevertheless, blunting of affect was present in nearly two-thirds of the cases. Mannerisms and grimacing were common and ambitendency was observed in three-fifths of the children. Most were of normal intelligence but there was a downward shift in that the mean IQ was 86. Obvious psychological precipitating factors were present in nearly half the cases. One in ten of the parents was themselves schizophrenic. The main difference from adult schizophrenia was the preponderance of boys among the schizophrenic children.

Childhood precursors of adult schizophrenia

Not only do schizophrenic psychoses occur in later childhood and adolescence, but also there is good evidence that individuals who do not develop overt schizophrenia until adult life frequently show abnormalities of a non-psychotic type in childhood (Offord & Cross 1969; Rutter 1972). It seems that schizophrenia is more likely to develop in individuals of somewhat below average intelligence, with poor academic attainment at school, who were rather socially isolated, showed oddities of personality and had impaired relationships with peers. Most commonly, they have shown a mixture of introverted and extroverted characteristics. When they had an overt psychiatric disorder in childhood, it has not followed any distinctive pattern; there may have been neurotic or antisocial problems, most often the disorders have shown features of both. It is apparent from this account that there is nothing particularly distinctive about the child psychiatric disorders which precede the onset of schizophrenia. It would be a great advance to identify a syndrome which could be diagnosed as 'preschizophrenia' but, despite claims to the contrary (Lebovici 1974), so far this has not proved possible. Nevertheless, what is sure is that among the mixture of children attending child psychiatric clinics some will have disorders which are a forerunner of schizophrenia in adult life. Unfortunately, we have no means at the moment of telling which children these are.

Disintegrative psychosis

A third group of conditions is best described under the term disintegrative or regressive psychoses, although they roughly fit Heller's account of dementia infantilis (Heller 1930). In these conditions, development usually appears normal or near normal on all counts up to the age of 3 or 4 years at which time there is a profound regression and behavioural disintegration. Often there is a premonitory period of vague illness and the child then becomes restive, irritable, anxious and overactive. Over the course of a few months there is an impoverishment and then a loss of speech and language. Comprehension of language deteriorates and intelligence often declines, although an intelligent facial expression is usually retained. There is a loss of social skills, impairment of interpersonal relationships, a general loss of interest in objects, and development of stereotypies and mannerisms.

Sometimes these psychoses come on after measles encephalitis or some other clear-cut organic illness which damages the brain. More often there are no clinical signs of neurological damage, although the subsequent course and postmortem studies often later reveal some kind of organic cortical degeneration, such as that associated with the lipoidoses or leucodystrophies (Kanner 1957; Malamud 1959; Ross 1959; Creak 1963b; Corbett *et al* 1976). The prognosis is very poor, with the children usually remaining without speech and severely mentally handicapped. In many cases a plateau is reached but the course obviously depends on the underlying pathology, and in the case of many lipoidoses and leucodystrophies there is a progressive deterioration leading to death. It will be appreciated that neither the aetiology nor the clinical picture in this group of psychoses is uniform. Nevertheless, the patterns of symptomatology differ in crucial respects from both schizophrenia and autism. It seems highly desirable for this reason, as well as on the high proportion of cases with clear-cut evidence of gross structural brain pathology (sometimes of a progressive kind) to differentiate the disintegrative psychoses from the other psychoses beginning in childhood.

Infantile autism

Infantile (or childhood) autism was first systematically described by Kanner (1943) in terms of a severe disorder of development which began in infancy and which had a number of highly characteristic features. These included an inability to develop relationships with people, a delay in speech acquisition, the noncommunicative use of speech after it develops, delayed echolalia, pronominal reversal, repetitive and stereotyped play activities, an obsessive insistence on the maintenance of sameness, a lack of imagination, a good rote memory, and a normal physical appearance. Kanner's observations were confirmed by other workers all over the world (Despert 1951; Van Krevelen 1952; Bosch 1953; Bakwin 1954) and the syndrome came to be generally accepted (see Rutter 1974; Wing 1976). It is discussed more fully below.

There is now extensive evidence that autism differs in many crucial respects from schizophrenia. The key studies in this connexion are those by Kolvin and his colleagues (Kolvin 1971). They found that children with infantile psychoses and those with psychoses beginning in later childhood differed significantly in terms of social class, family history of schizophrenia, evidence of cerebral dysfunction, symptom patterns and level of intelligence. Like Makita (1966) and Vrono (1974) they also found that the age of onset of psychoses followed a markedly bipolar distribution with one peak in infancy and one in adolescence. The course of autism and of schizophrenia also differ; an episodic course with remissions and relapses is more characteristic of schizophrenia than autism (Rutter 1968), and follow-up studies have indicated that autistic individuals rarely develop delusions or hallucinations when they reach adulthood (Rutter 1970). The evidence leaves no alternative but to conclude that there are so many differences between autism and schizophrenia that they should be regarded as separate conditions (Rutter 1972; 1974). This has been disputed (Bender 1971; Miller 1974) but the contrary 'evidence' relies on reports which fail to make systematic comparisons by age of onset (e.g. Bomberg *et al* 1973; Ornitz 1971) and/or which use concepts of schizophrenia that are so wide as to be virtually meaningless (Bender 1947; 1960).

Taxonomic techniques have been used to determine whether further subdivisions are possible within the group of infantile psychoses (Prior & Macmillan 1973; Prior *et al* 1975a, b). It has been found that the best differentiation (in numerical taxonomy terms) was between, on the one hand, children whose disorders began during the first 2 years and were characterised by impaired social development, language abnormalities and stereotyped play, and on the other, children with disorders that usually began later and which showed a more varied symptomatology. Within the first group, there were differences in terms of the number of symptoms suggestive of 'insistence or sameness' but this distinction seemed less important than that between the infantile psychoses (autism) and other psychotic conditions beginning later in childhood.

Autistic psychopathy

Autistic psychopathy (Asperger 1944) is a syndrome which resembles autism in many respects, but it is thought to be a personality trait not evident until the third year of life or later and with a good social prognosis (Van Krevelen & Kuipers 1962; Van Krevelen 1971). Intelligence is unimpaired but coordination and visuo-spatial perception are poor, there are gross social impairments and obsessive preoccupations or circumscribed interest patterns (Mnukhin & Isaev 1975; Isaev & Kagan 1974). Such cases undoubtedly exist but it remains uncertain whether the syndrome is distinct from autism.

Manic-depressive psychosis

Emotional disorders in which depression is one manifestation are common in adolescence and later childhood (see Chapter 17), but manic-depressive psychosis (see Chapter 31) is quite rare in prepubertal children. When it occurs it constitutes a clinical picture quite different from the other child psychoses and for this reason it will not be discussed further here.

Other psychoses in childhood

In addition to the relatively distinct syndromes already described there are a number of other less well defined psychotic* conditions which arise in childhood. First, there are a number of cases in which disorders otherwise similar to infantile autism develop after the age of 30 months (the age cut-off usually taken for autism, see below). Whether they constitute examples of autism of unusually late onset or whether they represent a different type of disorder remains uncertain. Second, there are rare cases in which severe disorders, apparently involving a loss of reality sense, arise about the age of 3 or 4 years but in which there is not the profound regression characteristic of disintegrative psychosis. Thirdly, there is a larger number of nonspecific disorders of

---

* It should be appreciated that the term 'psychosis' has no precise meaning. It is used here in the usual sense to refer to severe conditions in which there is a lack of insight or reality sense, behaviour which differs qualitatively as well as quantitatively from normal, and marked social handicap.

psychotic intensity which do not exactly fit the criteria for autism, schizo-phrenia or disintegrative psychosis. Often these arise in children with severe mental retardation and/or organic brain disease, in whom stereotypies, pica, disorders of mobility and perception, and social impairment are frequently prominent in the symptomatology. In other cases, severe anxiety, obsessive manifestations, impulsive behaviour and disturbed personal identity are more characteristic. Bender (1960) has used the term 'pseudoneurotic' type to de-scribe this variety. The severity of their disturbance suggests the adjective 'psychotic' but it is uncertain how much these conditions have in common with any of the other varieties of child psychosis. The heterogeneous group of 'other' child psychoses is an unsatisfactory one but it is necessary to dif-ferentiate them in order that the better defined syndromes of autism, schizo-phrenia, disintegrative psychosis and manic-depressive psychosis may be kept distinct.

As autism is the 'psychosis' most characteristic of childhood, the rest of this chapter will be concerned with its characteristics, nature and treatment.

INFANTILE AUTISM

Prevalence

Two epidemiological studies (Lotter 1966; 1967; Brask 1967) have produced broadly similar findings for the prevalence of autism. About four children in every 10 000 show the picture of child psychosis and probably about half these have the specific syndrome of autism.

Definition

Since Kanner first described the syndrome of infantile autism it has become clear that autistic children show a wide range of symptomatology. Some of their problems (for example temper tantrums and sleep disturbance) are ones which may be found in many normal children and others (for example stereo-typies), although rarely shown by normal children, are quite common in other psychiatric conditions, particularly when there is associated mental retarda-tion. On the other hand, by calling autism a syndrome, Kanner implied that not only were there certain behaviours which tended to group together but also that these behaviours differed from those found in other psychiatric conditions. Accordingly, research was needed to find out which symptoms were both *universal* and *specific*—that is, those which were present in all or nearly all autistic children and also which were relatively infrequent in child-ren which did not have the syndrome. A differentiation had to be made between behaviours which *could* occur in autism (but which also occurred in other conditions) and those behaviours which were specially characteristic of autism. In doing this, it was obviously important to control for age, sex, IQ and presence of psychiatric disorder in order to ensure that any differences found were not merely a reflection of the fact that children's behaviour varies according to these nonspecific features (Rutter, Tizard & Whitmore 1970; Rutter 1971b).

Diagnostic criteria and symptomatology

Studies which compared autistic children with children exhibiting other psychiatric conditions showed that three broad groups of symptoms were found in all (or almost all) children diagnosed as suffering from infantile autism or psychosis *and* were also much less frequent in children with other psychiatric disorders (Rutter 1966; Rutter & Lockyer 1967). These symptom groups were: (1) a particular kind of profound and general failure to develop social relationships; (2) a form of language retardation which involved impaired comprehension, echolalia and pronominal reversal; and (3) various ritualistic or compulsive phenomena (i.e. 'an insistence on sameness').* In addition, stereotyped, repetitive movements (especially hand and finger mannerisms), a short attention span, self-injury and delayed bowel control were also more common in autistic children, but these symptoms did not occur in all cases.

A further diagnostic criterion which has emerged from research is an onset before the age of 30 months. The disorders originally described by Kanner all began in early infancy but later observations by Eisenberg and Kanner (1956) as well as by other investigators (Rutter *et al* 1967; Lotter 1966) showed that a clinical picture indistinguishable from autism could arise after apparently normal development in the first 1 to 2 years. Whether development has been truly normal in these children is hard to judge in that they have rarely advanced as far as conversational speech and imaginative play, although some of them have acquired some limited speech and have not appeared to show any marked social impairment. As a result of these observations, it is now generally accepted that autism can occur with an onset up to, but not later than, 30 months. However, in some four-fifths of cases, development has clearly been abnormal from the outset.

---

* The assessment of these symptoms must take into account both the child's mental age and the specific features of social impairment and language retardation shown by autistic children.

IQ

Originally, Kanner (1943) had thought that autistic children were really of normal intelligence and that their poor functioning on IQ tests was simply a secondary consequence of their autistic failure to make relationships. The children's often good rote memory, their serious facial expression and the lack of physical stigmata were in keeping with this view, which many other writers followed. However, subsequent research has shown Kanner's view to be mistaken (almost the only respect in which his original description has not stood the test of time—a most remarkable achievement). The evidence on autistic children's intelligence can be summarised as follows: First, numerous studies have shown that some three-quarters of autistic children have IQ scores in the retarded range (see Rutter & Lockyer 1967; Lotter 1967; DeMyer *et al* 1974). Second, IQ scores in autistic children have been found to have the same properties that they show in other children—namely there is moderate stability of scores throughout middle childhood and adolescence and IQ scores provide a reasonable predictor of later educational attainment (Lockyer & Rutter 1969; Bartak & Rutter 1971; 1973; Gittelman & Birch 1967; DeMyer *et al* 1974; Rutter & Bartak 1973; Mittler *et al* 1966). Third, the low IQ scores are not a function of poor motivation. Hingtgen and Churchill (1969; 1971) showed that even when motivation was greatly increased through operant techniques, intellectual performance still remained well below normal and long-term follow-up studies have shown that IQ level tends to remain much the same* in spite of major improvements in autism (Lockyer & Rutter 1969). Fourth, both short-term (Alpern 1967; Alpern & Kimberlin 1970) and long-term studies (Lockyer & Rutter 1969) have shown that autistic children who fail to score on IQ tests do so because they are severely retarded rather than because of an unwillingness to attempt the task.

It may be concluded that autistic children with low IQs are just as retarded as anyone else with a low IQ and the score means much the same thing; autism and mental retardation frequently coexist. This finding has very important implications for both diagnosis and research. In the first place, it means that mental age must be taken into account in assessing behaviour. If the 4-year-old child has a mental age of 6 months, obviously he cannot be expected to show friendship patterns and communicative speech. To regard these as 'autistic' is to totally ignore developmental considerations. Lack of social responsiveness and impaired language can only be taken as

---

* However, several studies have shown a slight tendency for IQs to fall in severely retarded autistic children and to rise in those of normal intelligence.

indicators of autism if the impairment is out of keeping with the child's mental age and if it shows the special features characteristic of autism rather than normal development (see below). In the second place, studies which set out to compare autistic and nonautistic children must control for mental age as well as for chronological age. Unfortunately, a large number of otherwise sound pieces of research are virtually uninterpretable because they have failed to do this (Hingtgen & Bryson 1972).

However, it must be emphasised that autism and mental retardation are far from synonymous. Autistic children differ from nonautistic retarded children in their pattern of scores on IQ tests as well as in their behaviour, prognosis and family background (Rutter *et al* 1967; Rutter & Lockyer 1967; Lockyer & Rutter 1969; 1970; Wolf *et al* 1972). In addition, experimental studies (see Hermelin & O'Connor 1970) have demonstrated a host of ways in which autistic children differ from matched groups of retarded children. Autistic children make less use of meaning in their memory processes, are impaired in their use of concepts, and are generally limited in their powers of coding and categorising. Other investigators, too, have found autism to be associated with specific cognitive deficits (Gillies 1965; Tubbs 1966; Schopler 1966). The findings all indicate that, unlike mentally retarded children, autistic children have a particular cognitive deficit which involves language and central coding processes.

As already noted, about a quarter of autistic children have a normal intellectual level on nonverbal tests. The question arises then as to whether autism in association with mental retardation is a different condition from that occurring in children of normal intelligence (Bartak & Rutter 1976a). Certainly there are differences between the groups. In the first place, the prognosis is both worse and different for retarded autistic children (Rutter 1970). They are much less likely to gain speech and far fewer acquire skills in the 3 Rs. Similarly, half those with normal intelligence go on to higher education or acquire regular paid employment whereas scarcely any autistic children with an IQ below 70 do so. Moreover, a third of mentally retarded autistic youngsters develop epileptic fits whereas this is much rarer in those of normal intelligence. Second, several studies have shown that the pattern of cognitive deficit is somewhat different in very low IQ children (Hermelin & O'Connor 1970). In general, the mentally retarded children show a wider cognitive deficit which involves general difficulties in sequencing and feature extraction, whereas in the normally intelligent autistic children the defects mainly affect verbal and coding skills. Third, there are also some differences in symptomatology (Bartak & Rutter 1976). Although low IQ and high IQ autistic children are closely similar in terms of the main phenomena specifically associated with autism, the mentally retarded autistic children show a more severe disorder of social development and are more likely to exhibit deviant social responses (such as smelling people), sterotypies and self-injury.

It is not clear from these findings whether the differences represent different ends of the same continuum, or rather a qualitative distinction. However, the differences in outcome according to IQ are so marked that obviously it is essential to obtain an accurate assessment of intelligence in every case.

Impaired social relationships

Several studies (e.g. Wolf & Chess 1964; Hutt & Vaizey 1966; Sorosky *et al* 1968; Wing 1969; Churchill & Bryson 1972; Bartak *et al* 1975) have shown that autistic children's social development has a number of rather distinctive features. First, there is a lack of attachment behaviour and a relative failure of bonding which is most marked in the first 5 years. Unlike the normal toddler, autistic children tend not to follow their parents about the house and they do not run to greet them when the parents return after having been out, such as for shopping or work. They tend not to go to their parents for comfort when they are hurt or upset, and almost always they do not develop the bedtime kiss and cuddle routine followed by so many normal children. They tend not to discriminate between people, so that they will approach a stranger almost as readily as their parents. However, they do *not* usually physically withdraw from people and may enjoy a tickle or a rough and tumble. In the first year, quite often they do not take up an anticipatory posture or put up their arms to be picked up in a way that normal children do. On the other hand, especially in the more intelligent autistic children, social abnormalities may not be obvious until well into the second year of life. Of course, a failure in bonding is also seen in conditions other than autism (see Chapter 3). But it should be noted that the style of social interaction is different in these conditions. Thus children reared in poor quality institutions with multiple caretakers tend to be indiscriminate in their relationships with people and often do not develop personal bonds. On the other hand, quite unlike autistic children, they do show marked attachment behaviour and are often clinging and attention seeking (Tizard & Rees 1975).

Lack of eye-to-eye gaze is usually said to be particularly characteristic of autistic children. However, clinical observation suggests that it is not so much the amount of eye-to-eye gaze (which may be normal) but rather the way eye-to-eye gaze is used which is characteristic (this observation has yet to be confirmed by systematic studies). The normal child, like the normal adult, uses eye-to-eye gaze in a highly discriminating fashion, looking up at people's faces when he wants to gain their attention, when he wants to be picked up, when he is being aggressive towards them or when he is being spoken to. What is striking about the autistic child is that he does not use eye-to-eye gaze in these ways. It should be noted that this pattern of eye-to-eye gaze is also different from that of the very shy or very anxious child whose gaze avoidance is characteristically highly specific to intense social interaction.

After age 5 years or thereabouts, many of the social impairments may no longer be evident (at least, not to the same degree), but serious social difficulties continue. This is most evident in (1) a lack of cooperative group play with other children; (2) a failure to make personal friendships; and (3) a lack of empathy and a failure to perceive other people's feelings and responses. The last abnormality often results in the child saying or doing socially inappropriate things.

As autistic children grow older they may well become affectionate and friendly with their parents but it is striking that their family relationships improve long before their peer relationships do. Among those autistic individuals who make most progress there is often a desire for friendships in later adolescence. But a gaucheness of approach, a lack of response to other people's interests and emotions, and especially a lack of appreciation of other people's feelings usually prevent the development of friendships. Autistic adolescents and adults generally have ordinary sexual feeings, but their lack of social skills means that it is rare for a sexual relationship to develop, and exceedingly rare for marriage to take place.

Language and prelanguage skills

Not only are autistic children usually markedly delayed in their acquisition of speech, but also their pattern of language development and their usage of language is strikingly different, both from normal children and from children with other language disorders (see Rutter 1965; 1966; Ricks 1975; Ricks & Wing 1975; Bartak *et al* 1975). First of all there are serious impairments in a variety of skills which are often thought to underlie or precede language. For example, autistic children usually fail to show much social imitation. They do not wave 'bye-bye', they do not participate in imitative games like pat-a-cake and they are less likely than other children to copy or follow their parent's activity (in terms of cleaning, hoovering, mowing the lawn, household repairs, etc.). They are delayed in their meaningful use of objects so that when they are very young they may spin the wheels of a toy car or put the car in their mouth rather than use it in the intended way. They are also much delayed in their appropriate use of miniature objects (such as a toy brush or tea-set) and, most of all, they lack imaginative or make-believe play. Thus, they are unlikely to engage in pretend games, such as mothers and fathers, schools, tea-parties or cowboys and Indians.

Sometimes an autistic child does have some make-believe actions in which he engages but, if so, these tend to be stereotyped and repetitive rather than imaginative, creative and ever-changing like the pretend play of normal children.

Frequently, but not always, patterns of babble are also impaired or abnormal (Ricks 1975; Bartak *et al* 1975). This tends to be especially the case towards the end of the second year when normal children (if they are not speaking) are engaging in a rich, varied pattern of babble with the cadences of speech. While this occurs in some autistic children, it is decidedly unusual.

Almost always autistic children are impaired in their understanding of the spoken language. Whereas they may follow simple instructions if given in a familiar social context or with the aid of gesture they usually do not follow instructions which lack these cues or which involve the combination of two or more ideas (e.g. 'Please fetch my book which is on the table by my bed'). Equally characteristically, autistic children lack gesture and mime. They tend to make their needs known by taking the adult by the wrist (not usually by the grasped hand). Often they do not point (and, if they do, it is usually with the hand rather than with the extended index finger) and rarely is it accompanied by mime, demonstration or symbolic gesture.

About half autistic children, especially those who are also mentally retarded, never gain useful speech. However, in those who do learn to speak there are a variety of characteristic abnormalities. First, immediate echolalia and the delayed repetition of stereotyped phrases is usual for quite a long period after speech first develops. Characteristically, this is accompanied by I–You pronominal reversal (e.g. 'You want biscuit' meaning 'I want a biscuit'). This phenomenon is closely associated with echolalia (Bartak & Rutter 1974) and seems to be a function of the echoing tendency (Rutter 1968). Second, speech tends not to be used in the usual way for social communication. Thus, the autistic child tends to talk much less than the normal child of a comparable level of language development. Although the normal toddler may well be silent in the presence of a stranger, he is likely to chatter nonstop as he follows his mother about the house—autistic children rarely do this. Indeed they strikingly lack the ordinary to-and-fro chatter with the reciprocal interaction which is so characteristic of normal conversation. What they say is less often related to what they have heard—they give the impression of talking *to* someone rather than *with* someone. Also they are usually very poor in talking about anything outside the immediate situation so that they do not, for example, tell their parents what they have done at school during the day. While speech is still developing autistic children show much the same kinds of immaturities of grammar that are found in any child with limited speech. There may also be some difficulties in articulation but in neither of these respects is the speech of the autistic child characteristic. However, often the autistic child's use of words is somewhat unusual, with curious metaphors and odd ways of putting things (Kanner 1946; Rutter 1965).

In later childhood and adolescence many of the autistic children of normal intelligence achieve an average level of language competence. However, abnormalities in language usage and speech delivery often remain. A monotonous, flat delivery with little lability, change of emphasis or emotional expression is characteristic. In some cases speech is staccato and lacking in cadence and inflexion. Frequently, there is a formality of language and a lack of ease in the use of words, leading to a pedantic mode of expression. Until quite late in adolescence, and sometimes always, autistic children tend to converse mainly by a series of obsessive questions related to the particular preoccupation of that time. Difficulties with abstract concepts and with sequences of ideas (such as are needed to follow the plot of a play) continue in some degree in most cases.

'Insistence on sameness'

The term 'insistence on sameness' is not a very satisfactory one, in that it involves inferences. However, since Kanner's original description it has been widely used to cover a variety of stereotyped behaviours and routines. Characteristically, in early childhood, there are rigid and limited play patterns which lack both variety and imagination. Thus, the children may endlessly line up toys, or make patterns of household implements, or collect curious objects such as tins, or stones of a special shape. Secondly, there may be intense attachments to these objects, so that the children *have* to carry round with them a piece of grit in the fold between the thumb and the index finger, or they *have* to have a particular belt at all times. Usually, these attachments persist in spite of extreme distortions in the size or shape of the object, so that the function of the object is irrelevant to the attachment (Marchant *et al* 1974). The attachment is to a specific object and children protest if it is removed. However, if the object is not eventually returned to the child, attachment to a new object frequently takes place. Thirdly, especially in middle childhood and later, many autistic children have unusual preoccupations which they follow to the exclusion of other activities. Typically, these involve things like bus routes, train timetables, colours, numbers and patterns. Sometimes, the preoccupation takes the form of repeatedly asking stereotyped questions to which specific answers must be given. Fourthly, ritualistic and compulsive phenomena are very common. In early and middle childhood these usually take the form of rigid routines but in adolescence it is not infrequent for them to develop into frankly obsessional symptoms, with touching compulsions and the like. Fifthly, there is sometimes a marked resistance to changes in the environment so that the child becomes extremely distressed if furniture in the house is moved or if the ornaments are changed.

The course of development of these behaviours as the children grow older is much less predictable than with social relationships and language. On the whole autistic children tend to become more adaptable and malleable as they grow older but there are marked exceptions to this. There is however a tendency for ritualistic and compulsive phenomena to become more complex and more obviously obsessive.

Other behaviours

Many autistic children, when young, have quite marked feeding difficulties. Extreme food fads are especially characteristic so that, for example, children may insist on eating nothing but Marmite sandwiches.

Stereotyped, repetitive movements, especially hand and finger mannerisms (often twisting, flicking movements carried out near the face at the periphery of vision) are present in many autistic children but are more frequent in those who are also mentally retarded (Bartak & Rutter 1976). Whole body movements or spinning the self or other objects are also often present. Many of the mentally retarded autistic children tend to injure themselves by biting their wrists or banging their heads. Less often, this also occurs in those of normal intelligence. Other problems may include marked overactivity (often developing into underactivity in adolescence), short attention span, lack of initiative, extreme fears, tantrums and aggression.

Cognitive deficits

It is now well established that autistic children have a specific cognitive deficit which involves language impairment (Rutter 1974). As already noted, many autistic children are also mentally retarded. However, in many cases, the intellectual retardation is not global. Usually, autistic children show a marked variability in cognitive function such that they score relatively well on tests of visuo-spatial functions or short-term memory but poorly on any tests which involve sequencing or language skill. This is not just a question of low scores on tests requiring a verbal response as autistic children also perform poorly on tests which require no speech but in which the task involves abstraction, coding or sequencing. Moreover, the pattern of language deficit in autism is a distinctive one. Tubbs (1966) found that autistic children were particularly poor in their understanding of the meaning of the spoken word, in their use of gesture and in the transfer from one sensory modality to another. Hermelin, O'Connor and Frith have investigated linguistic skills by means of memory tasks (Hermelin & O'Connor 1970). Normal children remember meaningful phrases much better than random collections of words but this does not occur to the same extent with autistic children. Similarly, normal children given a set of mixed up words to remember tend to group them together in some meaningful way, whereas this occurs in autistic children only to a minor extent. Autistic children are impaired in their usage of both the semantic and syntactical aspects of language. On the other hand, their use of phonological elements of speech is generally normal.

Other experiments (Hermelin & O'Connor 1970) were undertaken by the same group of investigators to find out if this disability extended to the use of visual as well as verbal stimuli. A set of perceptual-motor tasks was chosen to represent nonverbal analogues of various linguistic operations. It was found that the autistic children without speech were handicapped on these tasks but that the speaking autistic children were not. The results suggest that the pattern of cognitive deficit might vary according to the level of cognitive skills. This conclusion was supported by a later experiment of Frith's (1970a) which showed that autistic children with a low memory-span suffered from an inability to recall sequences of words even when the sequence had no language content. However, this was not found with the autistic children who showed a higher memory-span.

On the other hand, studies of pattern perception and spontaneous pattern-making (Frith 1970b; 1971; 1972; Hermelin & Frith 1971) have shown that autistic children of all levels of intelligence have considerable difficulties in dealing with sequences, in appreciating rules and, generally, in feature extraction. They lack flexibility and originality and tend to impose rigid stereotyped rules, more or less regardless of situation. Other investigations have suggested that autistic children have difficulties in responding to multisensory input and that in this situation, they tend to respond to just one aspect of the complex stimulus, virtually ignoring other aspects (Lovaas *et al* 1971, Schreibman & Lovaas 1973; Koegel & Wilhelm 1973). However, it has been found that autistic children's performance is much influenced by the nature of the task (O'Connor & Hermelin 1972; 1973; Hermelin 1976). They can use kinesthetic cues flexibly and efficiently and they can deal with visuo-spatial sequences. On the other hand, they generally have considerable difficulty in processing temporal sequences if they are at all complex.

The main conclusion from the studies is that autistic children perform particularly poorly on tasks which require either language or temporal sequencing skills—skills which tend to be interconnected (Rutter & Yule 1973; Rutter 1974). Because of this and because language retardation is an essential part of autism, several writers have suggested that autism might arise on the basis of a language deficit and that autism might be related to the developmental receptive language disorders (Rutter 1968; Churchill 1972). In order to examine this question Rutter, Bartak and their colleagues (Rutter *et al* 1971; Bartak *et al* 1975; Bartak, Rutter & Cox 1976) compared autistic children with children showing a receptive developmental language disorder. Many similarities were found but also there were several important differences.

Language comprehension was more seriously impaired in autistic children who also showed more echoing and pronominal reversal. Autistic children had a greater impairment in the use and understanding of gesture, less imaginative play, and less use of language skills for social communication. Autistic children had scores on the digit span (reflecting short-term memory) which were considerably higher than their scores on other verbal subtests, whereas this was not true for the dysphasic children. The one area in which the dysphasic children were more impaired was in articulation skills. The extent of differences in pattern of language between the autistic and dysphasic children was so great that there was almost no overlap on a discriminant functions analysis. The findings show that the cognitive deficit in autistic children was deeper and wider but also to some extent different from that found in dysphasic children.

In fact, language is a complex skill which is based on multiple cognitive processes and which operates in a social context (Hockett 1960). Accordingly, rather than ask whether autism is explicable in terms of a language deficit, it is more meaningful to ask 'which specific cognitive functions have to be defective in order for the behavioural syndrome of autism to develop?'. No precise answer to that question is possible as yet, but it is clear that the cognitive deficit involves skills relevant to the use and understanding of all language modalities, to the central coding of information, and to temporal sequencing. Defects in visual perception seem less important (see Rutter 1974). It remains uncertain how far this cognitive deficit serves to cause the social and behavioural abnormalities of autism. However, experimental studies have suggested that cognitive failure leads to increased stereotypies and impaired social responsiveness (Churchill 1971; Koegel & Covert 1972).

Family background

In his initial papers Kanner (1943; 1949) commented that the parents of autistic children tended to be highly intelligent, rather obsessive individuals who
lacked real warmth. Later writers have suggested that autism might be a response to these personality characteristics, to deviant parent–child interaction
or to severe early stresses of various kinds (see Cox *et al* 1975 for references).
The evidence regarding these hypotheses is far from satisfactory. Findings
held to support a psychogenic viewpoint have come from projective tests and
selected family observations but similar techniques have also produced
largely negative findings (see Cox *et al* 1975). Clinical questionnaire and interview studies have also failed to confirm any of the stereotypes concerning
deviant parental characteristics or parent–child interaction (see for example
Creak & Ini 1960; Pitfield & Oppenheim 1964; Kolvin *et al* 1971b; DeMyer
et al 1972; Cox *et al* 1975). There are several reasons why the findings have
sometimes been contradictory. First, many of the studies have been based
on heterogeneous and poorly defined groups of children, only some of whom
are autistic. Second, the studies with positive findings have usually lacked
adequate controls. It is relevant that using adequate measures, properly
defined groups and appropriate controls have almost all shown the parents
of autistic children to be an unexceptionable group. Research findings so far
run entirely counter to the notion that autism is due to any kind of family
stress or disorder.

However, there are three family characteristics where the findings have
been sufficiently contradictory for conclusions to be uncertain. First, almost
all studies have shown that the parents of autistic children include a disproportionate number of middle class individuals of above average intelligence.
On the other hand, the meaning of this observation is unclear. However,
there is one large study with negative findings (Ritvo *et al* 1971). The
difference is only relative (autism is found in all social groups), and the meaning of the difference is quite obscure. Second, Schopler and Loftin (1969a)
found that the parents of autistic children showed more 'thought disorder'
than did the parents of normal children. A further study suggested that this
was an artefact of circumscribed test anxiety (Schopler & Loftin 1969b). Netley *et al* (1975) also showed that a higher proportion of mothers of autistic
children showed thought disorder (as measured on a different test to that
employed by Schopler and Loftin). However, data were obtained on only
a small proportion of families and a replication study by Lennox *et al* (1976)
failed to show any excess of thought disorder in either mothers or fathers
of autistic children using either test. Third, Goldfarb and his colleagues
(Meyers & Goldfarb 1961; Goldfarb *et al* 1966; Goldfarb *et al* 1973) have

observed various abnormalities in the communication styles of the mothers of a loosely diagnosed group of 'schizophrenic' children. Cantwell (1976) has attempted to replicate these studies with a well defined group of autistic children, with results that are entirely negative. On the whole, it seems likely that the parents of autistic children are not characterised either by thought disorder or impaired communication, but that they do show some tendency to be middle class. However, further studies of other samples are required before firm conclusions can be drawn, and at the moment the family findings throw no light on the aetiology of autism.

Biological basis

Although it is generally accepted that some type of cognitive deficit probably plays a crucial part in the genesis of autism, little is known about the biological basis of the deficit. The development of epileptic fits in adolescence, together with other evidence, strongly suggests some kind of organic brain dysfunction, at least in retarded autistic children. However, the nature of this dysfunction remains a matter for speculation (Rutter 1967; Hingtgen & Bryson 1972; Ornitz 1973; Wing 1976). A very recent pneumoencephalographic study (Hauser *et al* 1975) has shown enlargement of the left temporal horn in many cases of autism. If this finding can be confirmed, it would suggest pathology of the medial temporal lobe. Growth retardation has been found in psychotic children but it remains uncertain how far this finding applies specifically to the autistic and also how far the retardation is in any way different to that found in many retarded children. A variety of EEG studies (see Creak & Pampiglione 1969; Small 1975) suggest that autistic children have a rate of EEG abnormalities which are above that found in the general population. However, the type of abnormality does not seem to be specific and it is uncertain whether the rate of abnormality is any higher than that found in other psychiatric disorders. Moreover, the studies do not differentiate between autistic children who do and those who do not have other evidence of neurological abnormality. There have been numerous attempts to discover neurochemical and metabolic defects in autistic children (see reviews by Rutter 1967; Sankar 1969; Hingtgen & Bryson 1972; Ornitz 1973). Some studies have produced unreplicated positive findings, but most have been negative. Perinatal complications may be marginally more frequent in the histories of autistic children as compared with controls, but the difference is not a great one (Rutter 1967; Ornitz 1973).

Cytogenetic investigations have so far proved negative. Twin study findings are rather inconclusive, but many of the earlier reports are methodologically unsatisfactory (Rutter 1967) and there has been only one adequately controlled investigation of a relatively large series (Folstein & Rutter 1976). This showed that concordance for infantile autism was fairly low in both monozygotic (4/11) and dizygotic (0/10) pairs. However, concordance for autism, cognitive impairment or language delay was present in 9 out of 11 monozygotic pairs but only 1 out of 10 dizygotic pairs. Discordance was usually associated with definite or suggestive evidence of organic brain dysfunction in the affected twin. The findings suggest that autism may arise on the basis of a combination of genetic predisposition and biological impairment.

The pattern of REM sleep in autistic children is similar to that found in young infants; also, autistic children tend to suppress vestibular nystagmus under conditions of visual fixation (Ornitz 1971; 1973). The significance of these findings remains uncertain. It should be noted that the results are based on a rather wide definition of autism, and on comparisons which failed to take into account mental age level. Two studies (McCulloch & Williams 1971; Hutt *et al* 1975) have noted an increased variability in heart rate in autistic children. However, this variability is greatest during stereotypies and is least during task performance.

Autism may be particularly common in children with 'hypsarrhythmia' (Taft & Cohen 1971) and in congenital rubella children with mental retardation and sensory defect (Chess *et al* 1971), but a heterogeneous mixture of other conditions has also been associated with autism.

Type of disorder

In short, although there is good reason to suppose that infantile autism may well arise on the basis of some type of organic brain disorder, very little is known about what type of brain disorder it might be. It has been suggested that the locus of abnormality may be in the reticular system, in the midbrain, in the association areas or in the left hemisphere. However, so far there are no good grounds for placing the lesion in any one particular area of the brain. Moreover, the plasticity of function in the infant's brain (Rutter, Graham & Yule 1970) makes it almost certain that a central or a bilateral lesion would be required to produce the deficits found in autism. The existence of language impairment does little to help localise the lesion because the deficit is not just an impairment of speech, and furthermore it is not known whether the disorder is of language as such or whether the language disability stems from a more widespread cognitive deficit affecting skills needed for language.

Also, it is premature to make assumptions about the type of condition autism will turn out to be. Much medical research has been planned on the basis that autism will turn out to be a single medical condition with one main cause. However, it seems more likely that it will turn out to be a behavioural syndrome without a single cause but with a common biological causation (as in the case of cerebral palsy). If this is the case, of course, the syndrome may include several different but distinct conditions (as occurs with mental retardation). A third, but less likely possibility, is that autism may be the end-product of a wide and heterogeneous range of factors both biological and psychosocial. The alternative of a nonspecific syndrome of biological impairment seems the most likely, but it is too early to regard the matter as settled (Rutter 1974; 1976).

Treatment

As a result of the growing appreciation that autistic children were not schizo-phrenic or emotionally withdrawn but rather had a specific cognitive deficit which might have given rise to other symptoms, methods of treatment have undergone a radical change during the last decade. Individual psychotherapy designed to give insight has not proved effective (Rutter 1967) and has been used less and less. Instead, there has been increasing focus on the measures needed to aid more normal social and linguistic development in spite of cognitive deficits, and on the steps required to avoid the development of secondary handicaps (Rutter & Sussenwein 1971). Because of this shift of focus, there has been more attention to ways of treating the preschool child (Clancy & McBride 1969; Clancy *et al* 1969; Rutter & Sussenwein 1971), and to working directly with the autistic child's parents, helping them to cope better with the problems faced at home (Schopler & Reichler 1971; Berger *et al* 1973; Howlin *et al* 1973). Similarly, as it has become clear that autism is a disorder of development rather than a basically normal child's withdrawal into psy-chosis, greater emphasis has been placed on relating treatment to the child's developmental level and on using behavioural modification techniques in a developmental context.

Furthermore, the problems of the autistic child, unlike those of other children, cannot be considered in isolation from his family. The stresses created by an autistic child can be considerable and case-work techniques need to be used in conjunction with behavioural methods (Howlin *et al* 1973). Nearly all autistic children need skilled specialised education—as this has become generally accepted there has been a very considerable growth in the number of special units and special classes for autistic children. With all treatment approaches, unless special steps are taken, improvements in beha-viour tend to be specific to the situation where they have been treated (Rutter & Bartak 1973). This is one of the reasons why long-term follow-up studies have shown that behaviour changes as a result of inpatient hospital treatment are of little social benefit unless parents and schools are included in the treatment programme (Lovaas *et al* 1973). Accordingly, it is important in treatment to plan the approach specifically to ensure that problems in each setting are dealt with and that steps are taken to encourage generalisation of behaviour change (Wulbert *et al* 1974).

There have been few controlled studies of the use of drugs and physical treatments with autistic children (Campbell 1973; 1975; Corbett 1976). No drug has been found to have a specific effect in autism and, at most, drugs have a contributory role in treatment. However, they may be helpful in controlling the sleep disturbance which occurs in many young autistic children and the major tranquillisers may sometimes be valuable in aiding behavioural control.

Numerous single case studies have shown that behavioural techniques can be effective in modifying many of the maladaptive behaviours shown by autistic children (Gelfand & Hartmann 1968; Yule & Berger 1972; Howlin *et al* 1973) and one study (Ney *et al* 1971) suggested that operant conditioning was more effective than play therapy. However, less is known about the long-term social benefits. Lovaas *et al* (1973) found that the long-term gains associated with behavioural methods in an institutional setting were quite limited but the findings of a recent comparative study using appropriately matched groups indicates that a home-based approach which utilises a combination of behavioural treatments and counselling in a developmental context may be more effective (Hemsley *et al* 1976). Much has still to be learned about the specific techniques which are most effective. However, in aiding social development it seems that attention is needed to the factors which facilitate attachment in normal children (Rutter & Sussenwein 1971). Means must be found not only to involve the child in social interaction but also to make it rewarding and interesting to him. What works with ordinary children may not be effective with autistic children. Thus, merely smiling at the children may not facilitate social interaction (Richer & Richards 1975). In language training it is essential to increase the child's understanding of language as well as his use of words. Extending his range of play and increasing imitation may often be helpful in this connexion. It seems that some autistic children cannot be taught a useful degree of spoken language even after prolonged intensive speech training. In these cases, it may be worthwhile developing gesture both to facilitate the child's understanding (Webster *et al* 1973) and also his communicative skills (Fenn & Rowe 1975). Operant techniques, desensitisation and graded change may all be useful in the reduction of deviant disruptive behaviour (Howlin *et al* 1973; Marchant *et al* 1974).

Bartak and Rutter (Bartak & Rutter 1973; Rutter & Bartak 1973) made a systematic comparison of the progress made by autistic children in three different educational settings. It was found that the best results were obtained by the unit which used extensive specific teaching in an organised and structured programme with an emphasis on using techniques appropriate to the children's cognitive handicaps. Least progress was made by the children in a permissive environment where regressive techniques were used. The progress made in all units was limited but many of the children made worthwhile social and educational gains. Nevertheless, the degree of progress was related to the child's IQ level and none of the children with an IQ below 50 gained useful skills in the 3 Rs. Other studies (Schopler *et al* 1971) have also demonstrated the advantages of a structured environment and of using short sentences appropriate to the child's level of verbal comprehension (Browning 1974). However, although autistic children appear to benefit from an organised and systematic approach to teaching, this does not mean either rigidity or harshness. Furthermore, it is most important to pay attention to autistic children's understanding of what they have learnt (Rutter & Bartak 1973).

Prognosis and follow-up into adult life

There have been four main studies in which well diagnosed autistic children have been followed into adolescence or adult life (Creak 1963a, b; Eisenberg 1957; Kanner 1971; Lotter 1974a, b; Rutter *et al* 1967; Rutter 1970), as well as a number of shorter follow-ups (De Myer *et al* 1973; also see Rutter 1970) and follow-up studies of less homogeneous groups (see Rutter 1970, also Goldfarb 1970; 1975). The findings are in good agreement in showing that about 60 per cent of autistic children remain severely handicapped and totally unable to lead an independent life; and that about one in six make a good social adjustment, holding a job and getting along in society. However, even those with a good adjustment generally have continuing difficulties in relationships and some oddities of behaviour. About a quarter have an intermediate outcome, with some degree of independence and only minor problems in behaviour but still a need for supervision and an inability to hold a job. A detailed description of the characteristics of those with the best adjustment has been provided by Kanner *et al* (1972). As already noted, a substantial minority of autistic children develop epileptic fits during adolescence (28 per cent did so in the Maudsley study, Rutter 1970). The likelihood of fits developing is however strongly related to IQ. Fits are distinctly infrequent in those of normal intelligence. About a third of retarded autistic children develop fits and the proportion is even higher in those who are severely retarded.

The most important prognostic factor is the child's IQ. Of those with an IQ below 50 almost all have a very poor outcome. Conversely, of those with a nonverbal IQ of 70 or more, about half show a good adjustment in adolescence and adult life. It should be noted however that a substantial proportion of intelligent autistic children do not do well in spite of their good intelligence. Within this group the severity of language impairment is a further important prognostic factor. A good outcome is *less* likely if language comprehension was severely impaired in the preschool years, or if the child had not gained useful speech by age 5. The severity of the overall behavioural disturbance in early childhood is also of some prognostic significance and probably the complexity and variety of play patterns is particularly so (autistic children without constructive play seem to do particularly badly). Good schooling, of the kind appropriate for autistic children, improves the outcome and Lotter's study (1974a, b) also suggests that children from harmonious, middle class homes do better than those from disrupted or socially disadvantaged families.

Childhood autism remains a severe condition from which very few children recover completely. However, treatment can serve to reduce the level of handicap and sometimes, especially in those who do not have the additional problem of mental retardation, to aid development to the stage of social adjustment and the holding of a regular job.

REFERENCES

ALPERN G.D. (1967) Measurement of 'untestable' autisitic children. *J. Abnorm. Psychol.* **72**, 478–486

ALPERN G.D. & KIMBERLIN C.C. (1970) Short intelligence test ranging from infancy levels through childhood levels for use with the retarded. *Amer. J. Ment. Defic.* **75**, 65–71

ASPERGER H. (1944) Die 'Autistischen Psychopathen' Kindesalter. *Arch. Psychiatr. Nervenkr.* **117**, 76–136

BAKWIN H. (1954) Early infantile autism. *J. Pediatrics.* **45**, 492–497

BARTAK L. & RUTTER M. (1971) Educational treatment of autistic children. *In* Rutter M. (ed.) *Infantile Autism: Concepts, Characteristics and Treatment.* London: Churchill-Livingstone

BARTAK L. & RUTTER M. (1973) Special educational treatment of autistic children: a comparative study. I: Design of study and characteristics of units. *J. Child Psychol. Psychiat.* **14**, 161–179

BARTAK L. & RUTTER M. (1974) Use of personal pronouns by autistic children. *J. Autism Child. Schiz.* **4**, 217–222

BARTAK L. & RUTTER M. (1976) Differences between mentally retarded and normally intelligent autistic children. *J. Autism Child. Schiz.* **6**, 109–120

BARTAK L., RUTTER M. & COX A. (1976) A comparative study of infantile autism and specific developmental receptive language disorder. III: Discriminant functions analysis. (In preparation)

BARTAK L., RUTTER M. & COX A. (1975) A comparative study of infantile autism and specific developmental receptive language disorder. I: The children. *Brit. J. Psychiat.* **126**, 127–145

BENDER L. (1947) Childhood schizophrenia. Clinical study of one hundred schizophrenic children. *Amer. J. Orthopsychiat.* **17**, 40–56

BENDER L. (1960) Treatment in early schizophrenia. *Progr. Psychother.* **5**, 177–184

BENDER L. (1969) The nature of childhood psychosis. *In* Howells J.G. (ed.) *Modern Perspectives in International Child Psychiatry.* Edinburgh: Oliver & Boyd

BENDER L. (1971) Alpha and omega of childhood schizophrenia. *J. Autism Child. Schiz.* **1**, 115–118

BERGER M., HOWLIN P.A., MARCHANT R.L., HERSOV L.A., RUTTER M.L. & YULE W. (1973) Instructing parents in the use of behaviour modification techniques as part of a home-based approach to the treatment of autistic children. *Behaviour Modification Newsletter*, Issue **5**, 15–27

BOMBERG D., SZUREK S.A. & ETEMAD J.G. (1973) A statistical study of a group of psychotic children. *In* Szurek S.A. & Berlin I.N. (eds.) *Clinical Studies in Childhood Psychoses.* London: Butterworths

BOSCH G. (1953) Über primären Autismus im Kindesalter. Cited by Bosch G. (1970) *Infantile Autism: A clinical and phenomenological-anthropological investigation taking language as the guide.* New York: Springer-Verlag

BRASK B.H. (1967) The need for hospital beds for psychotic children: an analysis based on a prevalence investigation in the County of Ärthus. *Ugeskrift for Laeger* **129**, 1559–1570

BROWNING E.R. (1974) The effectiveness of long and short verbal commands in inducing correct responses in three schizophrenic children. *J. Autism Child. Schiz.* **4**, 293–300

CAMPBELL M. (1973) Biological interventions in psychoses of childhood. *J. Autism Child. Schiz.* **3**, 347–373

CAMPBELL M. (1975) Pharmacotherapy in early infantile autism. *Biol. Psychiat.* **10**, 399–423

CANTWELL D., RUTTER M. & BAKER L. (1976) Family factors in infantile autism. Paper read at the International Symposium on 'Autism: reappraisal of concepts and treatment'. St. Gallen, 12–15 July 1976

CHESS S., KORN S.J. & FERNANDEZ P.B. (1971) *Psychiatric Disorders of Children with Congenital Rubella.* New York: Brunner/Mazel

CHURCHILL D.W. (1971) Effects of success and failure in psychotic children. *Arch. Gen. Psychiat.* **25**, 208–214

CHURCHILL D.W. (1972) The relation of infantile autism and early childhood schizophrenia to developmental language disorders of childhood. *J. Autism Child. Schiz.* **2**, 182–197

CHURCHILL D.W. & BRYSON C.Q. (1972) Looking and approach behaviour of psychotic and normal children as a function of adult attention or preoccupation. *Compr. Psychiat.* **13**, 171–177

CHURCHILL D.W., ALPERN G.D. & DEMYER M.K. (eds.) (1971) *Infantile Autism: Proceedings of the Indiana University Colloquium.* Springfield, Illinois: Charles C. Thomas

CLANCY H. & MCBRIDE G. (1969) The autistic process and its treatment. *J. Child Psychol. Psychiat.* **10**, 233–244

CLANCY H., ENTSCH M. & RENDLE-SHORT J. (1969) Infantile autism: the correction of feeding abnormalities. *Develop. Med. Child Neurol.* **11**, 569–578

CORBETT J. (1976) Medical management. *In* Wing L. (ed.) *Early Childhood Autism: Clinical Educational and Social Aspects.* 2nd edn. Oxford: Pergamon

CORBETT J., HARRIS R. & TRIMBLE M. (1976) Psychiatric aspects of the neurodegenerative disorders: Dementia and disintegrative psychosis in children. Paper read at the Brit. Paed. Neurol. Assoc., Durham, Jan. 1976

COX A., RUTTER M., NEWMAN S. & BARTAK L. (1975) A comparative study of infantile autism and specific developmental receptive language disorder. II: Parental characteristics. *Brit. J. Psychiat.* **126**, 146–159

CREAK M. (Chairman) (1961) Schizophrenia syndrome in childhood: progress report of a working party. *Cerebral Palsy Bull.* **3**, 501–504

CREAK M. (1963a) Childhood psychosis: a review of 100 cases. *Brit. J. Psychiat.* **109**, 84–89

CREAK M. (1963b) Schizophrenia in early childhood. *Acta Paedopsychiat.* **30**, 42–47

CREAK M. & INI S. (1960) Families of psychotic children. *J. Child Psychol. Psychiat.* **1**, 156–175

CREAK M. & PAMPIGLIONE G. (1969) Clinical and EEG studies on a group of 35 psychotic children. *Develop. Med. Child Neurol.* **11**, 218–227

DeMYER M.K., ALPERN G.D., BARTON S., DeMYER W., CHURCHILL D.W., HINGTGEN J.N., BRYSON C.Q., PONTIUS W. & KIMBERLIN C. (1972) Imitation in autistic, early schizophrenic and non-psychotic subnormal children. *J. Autism Child. Schiz.* **2**, 264–287

DeMYER M.K., BARTON S., DeMYER W., NORTON J.A., ALLEN J. & STEELE R. (1973) Prognosis in autism: a follow-up study. *J. Autism Child. Schiz.* **3**, 199–246

DeMYER M.K., BARTON S., ALPERN G.D., KIMBERLIN C., ALLEN J., YANG E. & STEELE R. (1974) The measured intelligence of autistic children. *J. Autism Child. Schiz.* **4**, 42–60

DE SANCTIS S. (1906) On some varieties of dementia praecox. *Rivista Sperimentale di Freniatria* **32**, 141–165. Translated and reprinted in Howells J.G. (ed.) *Modern Perspectives in International Child Psychiatry.* Edinburgh: Oliver & Boyd

DESPERT J.L. (1951) Some considerations relating to the genesis of autistic behavior in children. *Amer. J. Orthopsychiat.* **21**, 335–347

EISENBERG L. (1957) The course of childhood schizophrenia. *Arch. Neurol. Psychiat.* **78**, 69–83

EISENBERG L. (1972) The classification of childhood psychosis reconsidered. *J. Autism Child. Schiz.* **2**, 338–342

EISENBERG L. & KANNER L. (1956) Early infantile autism, 1943–1955. *Amer. J. Orthopsychiat.* **26**, 556–566

FENN G. & ROWE J.A. (1975) An experiment in manual communication *Brit. J. Dis. Commun.* **10**, 3–16

FOLSTEIN S. & RUTTER M. (1976) Infantile autism: a genetic study of 21 twin pairs. Paper read at the International Symposium on 'Autism: a Reappraisal of Concepts and Treatment.' St. Gallen, Switzerland

FRITH U. (1970a) Studies in pattern detection in normal and autistic children. I: Immediate recall of auditory sequences. *J. Abnorm. Psychol.* **76**, 413–420

FRITH U. (1970b) Studies in pattern detection in normal and autistic children. II: Reproduction and production of colour sequences. *J. exp. Child Psychol.* **10**, 120–135

FRITH U. (1971) Spontaneous patterns produced by autistic, normal and subnormal children. *In* Rutter M. (ed.) *Infantile Autism: Concepts, Characteristics and Treatment*. London: Churchill-Livingstone

FRITH U. (1972) Cognitive mechanisms in autism: experiments with color and tone sequence production. *J. Autism Child. Schiz.* **2**, 160–173

GELFAND D.M. & HARTMANN D.P. (1968) Behavior therapy with children: a review and evaluation of research methodology. *Psychol. Bull.* **69**, 204–215

GILLIES S.M. (1965) Some abilities of psychotic children and subnormal controls. *J. Ment. Def. Res.* **9**, 89–101

GITTELMAN M. & BIRCH H.G. (1967) Childhood schizophrenia: intellect, neurologic status, perinatal risk, prognosis and family pathology. *Arch. Gen. Psychiat.* **17**, 16–25

GOLDFARB W. (1970) A follow-up investigation of schizophrenic children treated in residence. Psychosocial process. *Issues in Child Mental Health*, **1**, 9–63

GOLDFARB W. (1975) *Growth and Change of Schizophrenic Children—a Longitudinal Study*. Washington, D.C.: Winston

GOLDFARB W., GOLDFARB N. & POLLACK R.C. (1966) Treatment of childhood schizophrenia. *Arch. Gen. Psychiat.* **14**, 119–128

GOLDFARB W., YUDKOVITZ E. & GOLDFARB N. (1973) Verbal symbols to designate objects: an experimental study of communication in mothers of schizophrenic children. *J. Autism Child. Schiz.* **3**, 281–298

HAUSER S.L., DeLONG G.R. & ROSMAN N.P. (1975) Pneumographic findings in the infantile autism syndrome: a correlation with temporal lobe disease. *Brain* **98**, 667–688

HELLER T. (1930) About dementia infantilis. Reprinted in Howells J.G. (ed.) *Modern Perspectives in International Child Psychiatry*. Edinburgh: Oliver & Boyd

HEMSLEY R., HOWLIN P., BERGER M., HERSOV L., HOLBROOK D., RUTTER M. & YULE W. (1976) Treating autistic children in a family context. Paper read at the International Symposium on Autism: reappraisal of concepts and treatment. St. Gallen, 12–15 July 1976

HERMELIN B. (1976) Coding and the sense modalities. *In* Wing L. (ed.) *Early Childhood Autism: Clinical, Educational and Social Aspects* (2nd edn). Oxford: Pergamon

HERMELIN B. & FRITH U. (1971) Psychological studies of childhood autism: Can autistic children make sense of what they see and hear? *J. Spec. Ed.* **5**, 107–117

HERMELIN B. & O'CONNOR N. (1970) *Psychological Experiments with Autistic Children*. Oxford: Pergamon

HINGTGEN J.N. & BRYSON C.Q. (1972) Recent developments in the study of early childhood psychoses: Infantile autism, childhood schizophrenia and related disorders. *Schiz. Bull.* **5**, 8–53

HINGTGEN J.N. & CHURCHILL D.W. (1969) Identification of perceptual limitations in mute autistic children. *Arch. gen. Psychiat.* **21**, 68–71

HINGTGEN J.N. & CHURCHILL D.W. (1971) Differential effects of behavior modification in four mute autistic boys. *In* Churchill D.W., Alpern C.D. & DeMyer M. (eds) *Infantile Autism*. Springfield, Illinois: Charles C. Thomas

HOCKETT C.F. (1960) The origin of speech. *Sci. Amer.* **203**, 89–96

HOWLIN P.A., MARCHANT R., RUTTER M., BERGER M., HERSOV L. & YULE W. (1973) A home-based approach to the treatment of autistic children. *J. Autism Child. Schiz.* **3**, 308–336

HUTT C., FORREST S.J. & RICHER J. (1975) Cardiac arrhythmia and behaviour in autistic children. *Acta psychiat. Scand.* **51**, 361–372

HUTT C. & VAIZEY M.J. (1966) Differential effects of group density on social behaviour. *Nature*, Lond. **209**, 1371–1372

ISAEV D.N. & KAGAN V.E. (1974) Autistic syndromes in children and adolescents. *Acta Paedopsychiat.* **40**, 182–190

KANNER L. (1943) Autistic disturbances of affective contact. *Nerv. Child.* **2**, 217–250

KANNER L. (1946) Irrelevant and metaphorical language in early infantile autism. *Amer. J. Psychiat.* **1c3**, 242–246

KANNER L. (1949) Problems of nosology and psychodynamics of early childhood autism. *Amer. J. Orthopsychiat.* **19**, 416–426

KANNER L. (1957) *Child Psychiatry*, 3rd edn. Oxford: Blackwell Scientific Publications

KANNER L. (1971) Follow-up study of eleven autistic children originally reported in 1943. *J. Autism Child. Schiz.* **1**, 119–145

KANNER L., RODRIGUEZ A. & ASHENDEN B. (1972) How far can autistic children go in matters of social adaptation? *J. Autism Child. Schiz.* **2**, 9–33

KOEGEL R.L. & COVERT A. (1972) The relationship of self-stimulation to learning in autistic children. *J. App. Behav. Anal.* **5**, 381–387

KOEGEL R.L. & WILHELM H. (1973) Selective responding to the components of multiple visual cues by autistic children. *J. Exp. Child Psychol.* **15**, 442–453

KOLVIN I. (1971) Psychoses in childhood—a comparative study. *In* Rutter M. (ed.) *Infantile Autism: Concepts, Characteristics and Treatment.* London: Churchill-Livingstone

KOLVIN I. (1974) Research into childhood psychoses: A cross-cultural comparison and commentary. *Int. J. Ment. Health* **2**, 194–212

KOLVIN I., OUNSTED C., HUMPHREY M. & McNAY A. (1971a) Studies in the childhood psychoses. II: The phenomenology of childhood psychoses. *Brit. J. Psychiat.* **118**, 385–395

KOLVIN I., GARSIDE R.F. & KIDD J.S.H. (1971b) Studies in the childhood psychoses. IV: Parental personality and attitude and childhood psychoses. *Brit. J. Psychiat.* **118**, 403–406

LAUFER M.W. & GAIR D.S. (1969) Childhood schizophrenia. *In* Bellak L. and Loeb L. (eds) *The Schizophrenic Syndrome.* New York: Grune & Stratton

LEBOVICI S. (1974) Vrono's study on childhood and adolescent schizophrenia. *Int. J. Ment. Health* **2**, 117–125

LENNOX C., CALLIAS M. & RUTTER M. (1976) Parental thought disorder and infantile autism. Paper read at International Symposium on 'Autism: a reappraisal of concepts and treatment'. St. Gallen, 12–15 July 1976

LOCKYER L. & RUTTER M. (1969) A five to fifteen year follow-up study of infantile psychosis. III: Psychological aspects. *Brit. J. Psychiat.* **115**, 865–882

LOCKYER L. & RUTTER M. (1970) A five to fifteen year follow-up study of infantile psychosis. IV: Patterns of cognitive ability. *Brit. J. Soc. Clin. Psychol.* **9**, 152–163

LOTTER V. (1966) Epidemiology of autistic conditions in young children. I: Prevalence. *Soc. Psychiat.* **1**, 124–137

LOTTER V. (1967) Epidemiology of autistic conditions in young children. II: Some characteristics of the parents and children. *Soc. Psychiat.* **1**, 163–173

LOTTER V. (1974a) Social adjustment and placement of autistic children in Middlesex: a follow-up study. *J. Autism Child. Schiz.* **4,** 11–32

LOTTER V. (1974b) Factors related to outcome in autistic children. *J. Autism Child. Schiz.* **4,** 263–277

LOVAAS O.I., KOEGEL R., SIMMONS J.Q. & LONG J.S. (1973) Some generalizations and follow-up measures on autistic children in behavior therapy. *J. App. Behav. Anal.* **6,** 131–166

LOVAAS O.I., SCHREIBMAN L., KOEGEL R. & REHM R. (1971) Selective responding by autistic children to multiple sensory input. *J. Abnorm. Psychol.* **77,** 211–222

MACCULLOCH M.J. & WILLIAMS C. (1971) On the nature of infantile autism. *Acta Psychiat. Scand.* **47,** 295–314

MAHLER M.S. & GOSLINER B.J. (1955) On symbiotic child psychosis: genetic, dynamic and restitutive aspects. *Psychoanal. Stud. Child* **10,** 195–212

MAKITA K. (1966) Operant conditioning for investigating speech sound discrimination in aphasic children. *J. Speech Hear. Dis.* **9,** 519–528

MAKITA K. (1974) What is this thing called childhood schizophrenia? *Int. J. Ment. Health,* **2,** 179–193

MALAMUD N. (1959) Heller's disease and childhood schizophrenia. *Amer. J. Psychiat.* **116,** 215–218

MARCHANT R., HOWLIN P., YULE W. & RUTTER M. (1974) Graded change in the treatment of the behaviour of autistic children. *J. Child Psychol. Psychiat.* **15,** 221–227

MAUDSLEY H. (1867) *The Physiology and Pathology of the Mind.* London: Macmillan

MILLER R.T. (1974) Childhood schizophrenia: a review of selected literature. *Int. J. Ment. Health* **3,** 3–46

MITTLER P., GILLIES S. & JUKES E. (1966) Prognosis in psychotic children. Report of follow-up study. *J. Ment. Def. Res.* **10,** 73–83

MNUKHIN S.S. & ISAEV D.N. (1975) On the organic nature of some forms of schizoid or autistic psychopathy. *J. Autism Child. Schiz.* **5,** 99–108

MEYERS D.I. & GOLDFARB W. (1961) Studies of perplexity in mothers of schizophrenic children. *Amer. J. Orthopsychiat.* **31,** 551–564

NETLEY C., LOCKYER L. & GREENBAUM G.H.C. (1975) Parental characteristics in relation to diagnosis and neurological status in childhood psychosis. *Brit. J. Psychiat.* **127,** 440–444

NEY P.G., PALVESKY A.E. & MARKELY J. (1971) Relative effectiveness of operant conditioning and play therapy in childhood schizophrenia. *J. Autism Child. Schiz.* **1,** 337–349

O'CONNOR N. & HERMELIN B. (1972) Seeing and hearing and space and time. *Perception Psychophysics* **11,** 46–48

O'CONNOR N. & HERMELIN B. (1973) The spatial or temporal organisation of short-term memory. *Quart. J. exp. Psychol.* **25,** 335–343

OFFORD D.R. & CROSS L.A. (1969) Behavioral antecedents of adult schizophrenia. *Arch. gen. Psychiat.* **21,** 267–283

ORNITZ E.M. (1971) Childhood autism: a disorder of sensorimotor integration. *In* Rutter M. (ed.) *Infantile Autism: Concepts, Characteristics and Treatment.* London: Churchill-Livingstone

ORNITZ E.M. (1973) Childhood autism—a review of the clinical and experimental literature. *Calif. Med.* **118,** 21–47

PITFIELD M. & OPPENHEIM A.N. (1964) Child rearing attitudes of mothers of psychotic children. *J. Child Psychol. Psychiat.* **5,** 51–57

POTTER H.W. (1933) Schizophrenia in children. *Amer. J. Psychiat.* **89,** 1253–1270

PRIOR M. & MACMILLAN M.B. (1973) Maintenance of sameness in children with Kanner's syndrome. *J. Autism Child Schiz.* **3,** 154–167

PRIOR M. & MACMILLAN L.M.B. (1973) Maintenance of sameness in children with Kanner's syndrome. *J. Autism Child Schiz.* **3,** 154–167

PRIOR M., PERRY D. & GAJZAGO C. (1975b) Kanner's syndrome of early-onset psychosis: a taxonomic analysis of 142 cases. *J. Autism Child. Schiz.* **5,** 71–80

RANK B. (1955) Intensive study and treatment of preschool children who show marked personality deviations, or 'atypical development', and their parents. *In* Caplan G. (ed.) *Emotional Problems of Early Childhood.* New York: Basic Books

RICHER J. & RICHARDS B. (1975) Reacting to autistic children: the danger of trying too hard. *Brit. J. Psychiat.* **127,** 526–529

RICKS D.M. (1975) Vocal communication in pre-verbal normal and autistic children. *In* O'Connor N. (ed.) *Language, Cognitive Deficits and Retardation.* London: Butterworths

RICKS D.M. & WING L. (1975) Language, communication, and the use of symbols in normal and autistic children. *J. Autism Child. Schiz.* **5,** 191–221

RITVO E.R., CANTWELL D., JOHNSON E., CLEMENTS M., BENBROOK F., SLAGLE S., KELLY P. & RITZ M. (1971) Social class factors in autism. *J. Aut. Child. Schiz.* **1,** 297–310

ROSS I.S. (1959) Presentation of a clinical case: an autistic child. Pediat. Conf., The Babies Hosp. Unit, United Hosp. Newark, NJ 2, no. 2

RUTTER M. (1965) Speech disorders in a series of autistic children. *In* Franklin A.W. (ed.) *Children with Communication Problems.* London: Pitman

RUTTER M. (1966) Behavioural and cognitive characteristics of a series of psychotic children. *In* Wing J. (ed.) *Early Childhood Autism.* London: Pergamon

RUTTER M. (1967) Psychotic disorders in early childhood. *In* Coppen A. & Walk A. (eds.) *Recent Developments in Schizophrenia.* London: RMPA

RUTTER M. (1968) Concepts of autism: A review of research. *J. Child Psychol. Psychiat.* **9,** 1–25

RUTTER M. (1970) Autistic children: infancy to adulthood. *Semin. Psychiat.* **2,** 435–450

RUTTER M. (1971a) The description and classification of infantile autism. *In* Churchill D.W., Alpern G.D. & DeMyer M.K. (eds.) *Infantile Autism.* Springfield, Illinois: Charles C. Thomas

RUTTER M. (1971b) Psychiatry. *In* Wortis J. (ed.) *Mental Retardation: an Annual Review*, Vol. 3. New York: Grune & Stratton

RUTTER M. (1972) Childhood schizophrenia reconsidered. *J. Autism Child. Schiz.* **2,** 315–337

RUTTER M. (1974) The development of infantile autism. *Psychol. Med.* **4,** 147–163

RUTTER M. (1976) Definition of childhood autism. Paper read at NIH Workshop on Neurobiological Basis of Autism. 26–27 Feb. 1976 (in press)

RUTTER M. & BARTAK L. (1973) Special education treatment of autistic children: A comparative study. II: Follow-up findings and implications for services. *J. Child Psychol. Psychiat.* **14,** 241–270

RUTTER M., BARTAK L. & NEWMAN S. (1971) Autism—a central disorder of cognition and language? *In* Rutter M. (ed.) *Infantile Autism: Concepts, Characteristics and Treatment.* London: Churchill-Livingstone

RUTTER M., GRAHAM P. & YULE W. (1970) *A Neuropsychiatric Study in Childhood.* Clinics in Dev. Med. nos. 35/36. London: SIMP/Heinemann

RUTTER M., GREENFELD D. & LOCKYER L. (1967) A five to fifteen year follow-up study of infantile psychosis. II: Social and behavioural outcome. *Brit. J. Psychiat.* **113,** 1183–1199

RUTTER M. & LOCKYER L. (1967) A five to fifteen year follow-up study of infantile psychosis. I: Description of sample. *Brit. J. Psychiat.* **113,** 1169–1182

RUTTER M. & SUSSENWEIN F. (1971) A developmental and behavioural approach to the treatment of pre-school autistic children. *J. Autism Child. Schiz.* **1,** 376–397

RUTTER M., TIZARD J. & WHITMORE K. (1970) (eds.) *Education, Health and Behaviour.* London: Longman

RUTTER M. & YULE W. (1973) Specific reading retardation. *In* Mann L. & Sabatino D. (eds) *The First Review of Special Education.* Philadelphia: Buttonwood Farms

SANKAR D.V.S. (ed.) (1969) *Schizophrenia: Current Concepts and Research.* Hicksville, New York: PTD

SCHOPLER E. (1966) Visual versus tactual receptor preference in normal and schizophrenic children. *J. Abnorm. Psychol.* **71,** 108–114

SCHOPLER E., BREHM S.S., KINSBOURNE M. & REICHLER R.J. (1971) Effect of treatment structure on development in autistic children. *Arch. Gen. Psychiat.* **24,** 415–421

SCHOPLER E. & LOFTIN J. (1969a) Thought disorders in parents of psychotic children: a function of test anxiety. *Arch. gen. Psychiat.* **20,** 174–181

SCHOPLER E. & LOFTIN J. (1969b) Thinking disorders in parents of young psychotic children. *J. Abnorm. Psychol.* **74,** 281–287

SCHOPLER E. & REICHLER R.J. (1971) Developmental therapy by parents with their own autistic child. *In* Rutter M. (ed.) *Infantile Autism: Concepts, Characteristics and Treatment.* London: Churchill-Livingstone

SCHREIBMAN L. & LOVAAS O.I. (1973) Overselective response to social stimuli by autistic children. *J. Abnorm. Child Psychol.* **1,** 152–168

SMALL J.G. (1975) EEG and neurophysiological studies of early infantile autism. *Biol. Psych.* **10,** 385–397

SOROSKY A.D., ORNITZ E.M., BROWN M.B. & RITVO E.R. (1968) Systematic observations of autistic behavior. *Arch. gen. Psychiat.* **18,** 439–449

TAFT L.T. & COHEN H.J. (1971) Hypsarrhythmia and infantile autism: a clinical report. *J. Autism Child. Schiz.* **1,** 327–336

TIZARD B. & REES J. (1975) The effect of early institutional rearing on the behaviour problems and affectional relationships of four year old children. *J. Child Psychol. Psychiat.* **16,** 61–73

TUBBS V.K. (1966) Types of linguistic disability in psychotic children. *J. Ment. Def. Res.* **10,** 230–240

VAN KREVELEN D.A. (1952) Early infantile autism. *Acta Paedopsychiat.* **19,** 81–97

VAN KREVELEN D.A. (1971) Early infantile autism and autistic psychopathy. *J. Autism Child. Schiz.* **1,** 82–86

VAN KREVELEN D.A. & KUIPERS C. (1962) The psychopathology of autistic psychopathy. *Acta Paedopsychiat.* **29,** 22–32

VRONO M. (1974) Schizophrenia in childhood and adolescence. *Int. J. Ment. Health* **2,** 7–116

WEBSTER C.D., MCPHERSON H., SLOMAN L., EVANS M.A. & KUCHAR E. (1973) Communicating with an autistic boy by gestures. *J. Autism Child. Schiz.* **3,** 337–346

WING L. (1969) The handicaps of autistic children—a comparative study. *J. Child Psychol. Psychiat.* **10,** 1–40

WING L. (ed.) (1976) *Early Childhood Autism: Clinical, Educational and Social Aspects,* 2nd edn. Oxford: Pergamon

WOLFF S. & CHESS S. (1964) A behavioral study of schizophrenic children. *Acta Psychiat. Scand.* **40,** 438–466

WOLF E.G., WENAR C. & RUTTENBERG B.A. (1972) A comparison of personality variables in autistic and mentally retarded children. *J. Autism Child. Schiz.* **2,** 92–108

WULBERT M., BARACH R., PERRY M., STRAUGHAN J., SULZBACHER S., TURNER K. & WILTZ N. (1974) The generalization of newly acquired behaviors by parents and child across three different settings: A study of an autistic child. *J. Abnorm. Child Psychol.* **2,** 87–98

YULE W. & BERGER M. (1972) Behaviour modification principles and speech delay. *In* Rutter M. & Martin J.A.M. (eds.) *The Child with Delayed Speech.* Clin. Devel. Med. no. 43. London: SIMP/Heinemann

CHAPTER 31

Psychotic disorders in adolescence

D. STEINBERG

Psychosis is an imprecise term usually used to refer to mental disorders in which there is a serious disorganisation of thinking, or a gross abnormality of mood, together with a marked schism between the patient's understanding of his experiences and other people's perception of them. Behaviour which is qualitatively different from normal is present and often there is a difficulty in empathising with the patient. These features are most obvious in schizophrenia (Schneider 1925; Jaspers 1963). However because the designation of psychosis tends to be associated with incomprehensible behaviour, it is suspected more often than it is present. Among adolescents referred to psychiatrists, many appear troubled, incoherent, difficult to understand and hard to help, with rapport impeded by pre-existing differences in behaviour and attitudes as well as by the results of psychiatric disorder. Few of them suffer from psychotic illnesses but diagnosis may present many problems.

PREVALENCE OF PSYCHOSES IN ADOLESCENCE

Epidemiological studies (see Chapter 17) show that psychiatric disorders in young people are quite common, and that the rate is probably slightly higher in adolescence than in earlier childhood. Not all teenagers with psychiatric disorder necessarily require treatment by psychiatrists. Nevertheless, the epidemiological findings confirm the everyday experience of psychiatrists dealing with young people in a variety of settings that a large number of adolescents are referred to psychiatric services for very varied reasons (Steinberg *et al*, in preparation).

The general population surveys indicate that psychoses are quite rare in the mid-teens. Of course, psychotic conditions are more frequent among those adolescents referred to psychiatric outpatient clinics, but even in this group psychoses are relatively uncommon. Thus, Evans and Acton (1972) diagnosed psychosis in only 1 per cent of 239 new outpatients aged 12–19

748

years in Edinburgh; a further 1 per cent received the diagnosis of organic brain syndrome. Similarly, Steinberg *et al* (in preparation) found that only 5 per cent of 500 referrals in the 11 to 18 year age group had definite or probable psychotic conditions. Three-fifths of this small group had schizophrenia, and the remainder showed a severe, bizarre but transient disturbance in the context of emotional (and sometimes intellectual) problems, together with serious social and family stress. No child showed a classical manic-depressive illness.

For obvious reasons, psychoses are more often found in inpatients. Framrose (1975) found that 9 per cent of 70 adolescent inpatients were psychotic, and Bruggen *et al* (1973) reported 20 per cent in the first 50 patients referred for admission to an adolescent inpatient unit. Six had schizophrenia and four showed an affective psychosis or psychotic excitement. Among 187 patients aged 11–19 years treated at the Bethlem Royal Hospital inpatient adolescent unit, only 25 (less than 14 per cent) were psychotic (Warren 1965a). Thus, it appears that psychiatric disorder is common in adolescence but psychosis is comparatively rare.

AUTISM

Childhood autism is fully discussed in Chapter 30, and only the special problems posed by adolescence are considered here. All studies confirm the major handicaps which continue to be experienced by the great majority of autistic children through adolescence (Eisenberg 1956; Rutter 1970). Two-thirds remain seriously socially handicapped and about half are in long-term institutional care. A further problem is the appearance of epileptic fits about the time of adolescence in a sixth to a quarter of autistic children—especially in those who are also mentally retarded. The fits are usually major in type but as they tend to occur infrequently, anticonvulsant medication is not necessarily indicated (Corbett 1976).

Hyperkinesis is common in young autistic children, but during adolescence it is often replaced by marked underactivity and lack of initiative and drive (Rutter, Greenfeld & Lockyer 1967) which serves to add to teenage difficulties. While aggression does not usually increase in frequency, assertiveness and disruptive behaviour may sometimes increase in intensity with the hormonal changes of puberty. The fact that the autistic child is approaching adult stature makes this behaviour much more difficult to deal with. It is sometimes associated with marked anxiety and tension and in these circumstances the phenothiazines can be very helpful (more so than in younger autistic children). The rebelliousness and attempts at independence of normal adolescence seem to occur rather later in autistic young people (Corbett 1976), which can lead to additional problems.

The autistic adolescent's sexual behaviour is marked by naïvete, childish sexual curiosity, and a lack of appreciation of the mutual social signalling that normally modifies and regulates the expression of sexual feelings. A failure to understand other people's responses and a lack of awareness of social cues and conventions, together with a normal rise in sexual drive may lead to socially embarrassing behaviour such as masturbation in public, self-exposure, or sexual touching of other people. However, promiscuity is not a problem, although occasionally there is a risk of seduction. Parents need to be helped to lay down certain rules of conduct, expressed in simple terms and repeated until the individual has learned the social conventions. The problem does not lie in abnormal sexual drive, but rather in the difficulties that stem from social naïvete and a lack of empathy at a time when autistic adolescents are often both becoming more interested in social contact and experiencing sexual feelings for the first time. Only rarely are drugs to reduce sexual drive appropriate. However, Corbett (1976) mentions that hormones are sometimes useful to regulate menstruation in the case of severely handicapped autistic girls who have difficulties in coping with menstrual periods, or who are disturbed by dysmenorrhoea or premenstrual fluid retention.

Dewey and Everard (1974) have reviewed the difficulties experienced by 50 adolescents with relatively mild autism. Social problems often stemmed from a lack of social perception, from continuing problems in comprehension, from socially inappropriate fixed interest patterns and from a tendency to make irrelevant and inappropriate remarks. These young people need emotional support, understanding and education to help them cope with life's demands. Perceptive and sympathetic training in social skills together with 'feedback' to help them appreciate the effect on other people of what they say and do may be helpful.

Most of the disturbances associated with adolescence in autistic children need a broadly educational and behavioural approach, together with counselling for parents and supportive psychotherapy for some of the more intelligent and socially aware adolescents. Drugs, especially the major tranquillisers, also play a part in treatment. However, with some of the more severe disturbances of behaviour seen in autistic adolescents, inpatient psychiatric care may be needed. This poses problems in that they do not readily fit into most psychiatric units for adolescents, and hospitals for the severely retarded may not always be appropriate.

AFFECTIVE PSYCHOSIS

Feelings of depression are common in adolescence (Warren 1965a; Easson 1969; Rutter *et al* 1976) but psychotic depression, including manic-depressive psychosis, is rare (Hall 1952; Warren 1965a, b). These disorders are almost unknown before puberty (Anthony & Scott 1960; Rutter 1972), but they increase in frequency as adulthood approaches. This is parallelled by a similar increase in the rate of suicide and attempted suicide during adolescence (Connel 1971; Shaffer 1974).

Although characteristic adult-type symptomatology may occur, depressive disorders in childhood and adolescence present problems of classification and diagnosis (see Chapter 17 and 18) quite as great as those which surround depressive conditions in adults (Kendell 1968; Lewis 1971). Frommer (1972) considered that adult-type 'endogenous' depressive signs were particularly likely to be associated with suicidal feelings, but Connell (1971) emphasised the need for a wider appraisal. The manifestations of disorders in adolescence are not always the same as those in adult life. In Shaffer's (1974) account of 30 children aged 12–14 who had committed suicide, only a very small proportion had showed such symptoms and signs as hypochondriasis, self-denigration, ideas of reference and morbid preoccupations, whereas 22 had shown antisocial behaviour.

There have been comparatively few reports of frank manic-depressive psychosis in adolescence (Olsen 1961; Anthony & Scott 1960; Berg *et al* 1974). In Warren's (1965a, b) series of 187 adolescents treated as inpatients, five were diagnosed as suffering from manic-depressive conditions and two showed a mixed schizoaffective state.

Sands (1956) commented on the rarity of a truly cyclothymic picture among his inpatient adolescents, finding manic attacks more common than depressive periods. In 6 years, two boys and two girls out of a total of 180 had classical manic attacks, with euphoria, flight of ideas, mischievousness and aggressive behaviour.

The question arises as to whether some episodic disorders of behaviour without adult type depressive symptomatology are in fact early manifestations of manic-depressive illness (Anthony & Scott 1960; Frommer 1972). Follow-up studies are limited but those which have been undertaken have failed to demonstrate any connection between childhood behaviour problems and manic-depressive illness in adult life (Robins 1966; Huffman & Wenig 1954; Dahl 1971). Campbell (1952) reported that 3 of his 18 cases of adolescent manic-depressive disorder had cyclothymic symptoms before puberty and 15 first showed these features between 12 and 16 years. He suggested that the children showed a characteristic premorbid personality in that they were extraverted, sensitive, tense, easily frightened, worried about the future and anxious for group approval. The change of mood was the first overt evidence of disorder and it seemed that the earlier this occurred the stronger was the family history of affective psychosis. Campbell noted that cyclothymic children had great difficulty adjusting in a family with a manic-depressive parent. Strain and responsibility in adolescence seemed to precipitate the onset of manic-depressive illness. Campbell's interesting clinical observations warrant further testing.

Lithium salts have become well established in the treatment and prevention of manic-depressive illness in adults (Granville-Grossman 1971; Schou 1968; Crammer *et al* 1974) and there has been a recent report of its use in nonaffective disorders where other treatment has failed (Van Putten & Sanders 1975). Annell (1969a, b) has described the successful use of lithium with children but controlled trials are lacking. Lena and O'Brien (1975) have described how the disturbed behaviour of a 9-year-old child improved when his serum lithium reached the therapeutic range (0·07–1·3 mmol/1). Schou (1971) has pointed out that children tolerate and require large doses of lithium because of their high renal clearance of this drug, and this was borne out in the case of the 14-year-old girl treated by Berg and his colleagues (1974). More evidence is required before there can be an adequate assessment of the value of lithium in the treatment of adolescent disorders. However, it appears to be of use in properly selected cases.

Frommer (1972) has reviewed the use of drugs in affective disorders in children (see also Chapter 38). Adequate studies of drug treatment of children are very few but there are indications that antidepressants are of value and they have a definite place in treatment. Because of the need for dietary restrictions, tricyclics are generally to be preferred to the monoamine oxidase inhibitors. Adolescents vary considerably in their response to medication and generalisations about dosage may be misleading; on the whole, it is wisest to start with a small dose increasing up to adult levels in the absence of side effects. If there is no response to an antidepressant within 4 to 6 weeks, the drug should be changed or discontinued. Chlordiazepoxide, diazepam and the hypnotics should be avoided wherever possible.

Not much is known of how to predict adolescents' responses to drugs in the treatment of affective disorders. Schildkraut (1974) has reported a number of clinical and biochemical methods of predicting adult responses to lithium and to antidepressive drugs. A start has also been made correlating the excretion of urinary MHPG (3 methoxy 4 hydroxyphenyl ethyl glycol) with affective disturbance in children and adolescents (Cytryn & McKnew 1974).

Very little has been written on the use of electroconvulsive therapy in adolescents (Toolan 1971). It is very rarely indicated, but it should be considered when a *severe* and handicapping affective disorder fails to respond to an adequate dose of antidepressants together with appropriate psycho-therapeutic measures and environmental modification. However, it should only be used if the affective disorder shows the characteristics associated in adults with a good response to ECT. A failure to respond to treatment is not a sufficient indication on its own.

PSYCHOSES ASSOCIATED WITH NEUROLOGICAL DISORDER

Adolescents presenting with psychotic states should always receive a careful physical examination, as psychoses occasionally arise on the basis of organic brain disease. Rivinus *et al* (1975) described 12 children, seen over the course of 1 year at a paediatric neurological clinic, in which neurological disease presented in the form of a psychiatric disorder. Two of the 12 had been diagnosed as psychotic. The group was characterised by *deteriorating* school performance, visual loss and postural disturbance—symptoms which are unusual in psychiatric disorder and which should alert the physician to the need for repeated neurological examination and diagnostic re-evaluation. Continuing psychotherapy for an adolescent and his or her family is not incompatible with the repetition, if necessary, of physical investigations. If these are needed they should be brought into the therapeutic discussion along with other realities that are being faced. Also, of course, the emergence of a physical illness does not mean that the family have any less need of help with their emotional problems.

The possible presence of neurodegenerative disorder should be kept in mind. Corbett *et al* (1976) have described two cases of adolescents in whom prolonged behaviour disorder in the setting of disturbed family psychopathology was followed by psychotic symptoms and signs and later by dementia and overt neurological disease. One boy had bizarre thoughts, auditory hallucinations and believed that voices from the television were ordering him to kill his mother. Such neurodegenerative conditions are rare, and diagnosis does not, at present, lead to effective treatment of the disease process itself. Nevertheless it is important to recognise such disorders when they occur, not least for the sake of the family as a whole.

Although children with neuroepileptic disorders have a much increased risk of psychiatric disorder (see Chapter 8), there is no established specific association with psychoses in adolescence. However, temporal lobe epilepsy seems to be linked with the development of schizophrenia some years later (Slater *et al* 1963), and Taylor (1971) has observed that psychosis in such cases is particularly likely in the case of epilepsy beginning at puberty; he suggested that this is related to the emotional changes taking place at that time.

Abnormal and puzzling mental states are occasionally due to previously unrecognised centrencephalic epilepsy, and these may respond well to anti-convulsants (Neidermeyer & Khalifeh 1965; Stores 1971). However, the drugs prescribed for epilepsy can also produce psychotic states which may be confused with schizophrenia. These have been reported with primidone, phenytoin, carbamazepine, and sulthiame (Stores 1975). In these cases estimating drug blood levels may be more useful than trying to obtain an accurate picture of recent drug ingestion from a confused young person and his parents.

DRUG PSYCHOSES

Although significant drug abuse may be more often feared or suspected than actually present, the misuse of drugs of dependence is well recognised among adolescents. Moreover, the taking of some drugs can cause psychotic states (see also Chapter 27).

Connell (1958) described paranoid psychotic states occurring in 42 people who had been taking between 50 and 325 mg of amphetamine per day. Ideas of reference and delusions of persecution were prominent, and the conviction that the individual was being pursued by a gang was particularly common. Although many of the subjects had personality problems, drug intoxication was the direct cause of the psychosis. These stimulant drug psychoses usually subside in a matter of weeks or a few months, and prolongation of symptoms suggests either continuing drug usage or schizophrenia. No physical signs are diagnostic of amphetamine intoxication, and when this is suspected the patient's urine should be tested. Normally, amphetamine is excreted in 2 days but it may be detectable for 10. It is excreted quickly in an acid urine, so that urine testing will be only briefly positive in a disturbed, anorexic, acidotic patient. Conversely, the consumption of sodium bicarbonate will delay the excretion of amphetamine, prolong its effect and confuse test results (Buckell, personal communication).

Mood changes and social deterioration, but not particularly psychosis, occur with the abuse of morphine derivatives. Lysergic acid diethylamide (LSD) and related drugs are well known for their psychotogenic and hallucinogenic effects. The effects, like the drug itself, come and go within hours, but in some people lasting personality changes, including persisting psychoses, have been reported (Sedman & Kenna 1965). The clinical picture includes marked autonomic changes (including pyrexia and dilatation of the pupils), visual hyperaesthesia, illusions and, occasionally, hallucinations, accompanied by excitement, elation or despair. The phenomenology is difficult to separate from aspects of the individual's personality, and the social setting in which the drug is taken. 'Flashbacks', brief re-experiences of aspects of the 'trip', may be reported long after the original drug has been metabolised, and are difficult to explain. They may represent a variety of phenomena, including brief anxiety attacks and possibly emotionally laden perceptions that have in some way been learned. The identification of LSD excretion by clinical testing is not yet a practical possibility.

Psychotic reactions to cannabis use have been reported (Kolansky & Moore 1971; Spencer 1971) but the evidence remains inconclusive (Rathod 1975). Until recently there has been no clinically practical method for the detection in blood or urine of cannabis and its derivatives, but a radioimmunoassay technique has recently been reported by Teale and his colleagues (1974).

SCHIZOPHRENIA

Schizophrenia has been associated with adolescence since its early classical descriptions (Kraepelin 1899; Bleuler 1911), and most of what is known concerning schizophrenia arising in adult life applies equally to similar disorders arising during the teenage period. However, the literature is difficult to interpret because of diverging concepts of schizophrenia. Kraepelin, who was particularly influential in Europe, laid strong emphasis on symptoms such as hallucinations, thought disorder, delusions and emotional blunting. Bleuler, on the other hand, whose influence was greater in the USA, saw many of these as secondary symptoms and pointed to what he saw as the primary abnormalities: disturbance of associations, thought disorder, changes in emotional reactions, tendency to prefer fantasy to reality, and autistic seclusion. His attempt to understand the basic psychological processes underlying schizophrenia has been consonant with developments in psychoanalysis and ego psychology. One result has been a single comprehensive frame of reference, loosely co-extensive with ego psychology, which is widely used for the descriptions of normal development, neurotic development, and psychotic or near psychotic states (e.g. Sullivan 1953; Freud 1958; Laing 1960; Erikson 1965).

The 'borderline state', a term applied diagnostically to a large and heterogeneous collection of adult and adolescent disorders, is a useful example of this tendency. It has a most extensive literature (e.g. Schmideberg 1959; Kernberg 1967; Masterson 1972; 1973), with extremely muddled beginnings. The isolated unhappy adolescent who has major difficulties in coping with thoughts, feelings and external realities; who resorts to narcissistic magical fantasy and bizarre acting-out; who experiences serious difficulties in becoming independent of his or her mother (who allegedly shares such problems), is perhaps the stereotype of the 'borderline adolescent'. 'Borderline', in this terminology, refers to the risk that such people are said to run of slipping into transient psychotic states when under severe stress. Some clarification has been achieved with the fairly wide agreement that the borderline state is neither incipient nor early schizophrenia (Knight 1954; Masterson 1973); management is largely described in terms of individual psychotherapy and such social measures as removal from the home. What seems to be consistently described in the language of ego psychology is a problem of personality development. While much of the literature is of considerable value from the point of view of understanding development, the border-line state remains an unsatisfactory and usually inappropriate diagnostic category.

Unfortunately, Bleuler's valiant attempt to specify the fundamental disorders of schizophrenia fell short of its aims in that the symptoms were so insusceptible of definition that the boundaries of the condition could be made to vary too widely by those making the diagnosis (WHO 1973). One result has been the well documented transatlantic differences in diagnosis, with schizophrenia much more widely diagnosed in the USA (Cooper *et al* 1972). This is a difference in diagnostic concepts and practice rather than in the prevalence of schizophrenia. When a standardised approach is followed, such as the 'present state examination' developed by Wing *et al* (1967), it has proved possible in countries throughout the world to identify a diagnostically concordant group of psychiatric patients with clinical features such as auditory hallucinations, ideas of reference, delusions of persecution and thought disorder (WHO 1973).

Diagnosis of schizophrenia in adolescence

Schneider (1959) outlined a number of 'first rank' symptoms of schizophrenia: hearing own thoughts spoken aloud; hearing voices talking to each other; voices that comment on the behaviour of the patient; feelings of influences on bodily functions; interference with thoughts; thought stealing; communication of own thoughts to others; and feelings of being influenced from the outside with regard to emotions, drives and volition. Schneider did not suppose that these symptoms were primary or fundamental in Bleuler's sense; rather the symptoms were chosen on pragmatic grounds as being found clinically to be most nearly pathognomonic of schizophrenia. Findings from the International Pilot Study of Schizophrenia have broadly confirmed the usefulness of these symptoms in differentiating schizophrenia from other conditions (Carpenter *et al* 1974) but slight modifications appear advantageous (WHO 1973). The results show that the most useful discriminatory symptoms are delusions of control; thought insertion, broadcast or with-drawal; auditory hallucinations in the third person; and nonaffectively based auditory hallucinations addressing the patient. If these symptoms are present, and certain other conditions are fulfilled (particularly no disturbance of consciousness, no memory loss, no history of excessive alcohol intake, and no probability of subcultural beliefs mimicking the symptoms, the diagnosis of schizophrenia is clear and unambiguous.

The problem arises with individuals who do not show these symptoms but yet who have disorders similar in many other respects to schizophrenia. Genetic studies suggest that some of these conditions may be schizophrenic in type even though they lack the pathognomonic symptoms. Thus, the non-psychotic co-twins in monozygotic pairs discordant for schizophrenia often show various abnormalities of personality and behaviour (see Gottesman & Shields 1966; Rosenthal & Kety 1968). Furthermore, the first degree relatives of schizophrenic patients are characterised by a wide variety of conditions (Heston 1966). These findings do not unequivocably demonstrate that these heterogeneous schizoid disorders are truly schizophrenic because schizo-phrenics often marry nonschizophrenic individuals with other psychiatric problems. Nevertheless, the observations do suggest that a rigidly applied narrow concept of schizophrenia could be misleading.

The real difficulty with this broader view of schizophrenia is the failure to find any diagnostic criteria which could reliably identify schizophrenic dis-orders in the absence of the key discriminating symptoms (WHO 1973). In the absence of these it seems desirable to continue to place reliance on first-rank symptoms, whilst bearing in mind that some disorders not fulfilling the diagnostic criteria may eventually turn out to be schizophrenic.

Diagnostic problems particularly arise in the case of acute psychoses with marked affective features, and in the very different case of insidious deteriora-tion of personality. Kasanin (1933) coined the term 'schizo-affective psychosis' for disorders 'characterised by a very sudden onset in a setting of marked emotional turmoil with a distortion of the outside world'. He noted that in most cases the psychosis lasted only a few weeks or months and was followed by a good recovery. Langfeldt (1939) used the term 'schizophreniform states' for rather similar acute conditions often arising in connection with mental stress. Kety's recent study (1974) seems to confirm Langfeldt's view that these acute psychoses may differ genetically from the chronic conditions. On the other hand, a few of these schizoaffective disturbances are followed by chronic deterioration.

Diagnosis is also difficult in the case of young people who show a progres-sive and gradual deterioration of personality with social withdrawal, emotional blunting, and a handicapping decline in social performance.

Occasional brief, mild psychotic episodes may ultimately make clear the diagnosis of schizophrenia but these do not always occur and recourse is needed to the admittedly vague diagnosis of 'simple schizophrenia'.

On the whole, however, the phenomenology of schizophrenia arising in adolescence is essentially similar to that found in adults with the exception that systematised paranoid delusions are less common in the youngest age groups. High levels of anxiety, incoherent speech, bizarre actions such as grimacing or stereotyped movements, maintenance of emotional distance (as with a limited facial expression), intense preoccupation with inner thoughts, poor emotional control with apparently inappropriate outbursts of rage, poor social judgement and diminishing academic and social performance have been described as characteristic accompaniments of schizophrenia in adolescence (Spivack & Spotts 1967; Weiner 1970; Sands 1956). Eggers (1973) found that schizophrenia beginning in childhood or early adolescence is often preceded by a prodromal phase of some weeks in which depression, weeping, excitement and sometimes suicidal feelings are prominent. In comparing psychotic (mostly schizophrenic) with nonpsychotic adolescents, Warren (1949) reported that psychotic adolescents tended to be preoccupied with idiosyncratic matters rather than the more usual concerns about such matters as sexuality, independence and self-confidence as seen in the nonpsychotic youngsters. However, thought content alone is not enough for a diagnosis of schizophrenia, however bizarre and disturbing it may be (Fish 1956). Normal adolescents may often express unusual ideas in their remarks, their essays and their diary entries. There is a rather uncertain line between creative and exploratory experimentation, and abnormal, disturbing thoughts indicative of psychopathology. Furthermore, in assessing incongruous or inappropriate thoughts or behaviour, it is important to make comparisons with the current adolescent culture and not with adult expectations. Styles of hair, clothing and interpersonal behaviour alter with the generations and what is considered deviant in one era may be the height of conformity in the next.

Aetiological factors

There is now overwhelming evidence that genetic influences play a substantial part in the origin of the schizophrenic disorders (Kety *et al* 1968; Heston & Denny 1968; Rosenthal *et al* 1971; Kety 1974). However, uncertainty remains on the mode of transmission and on precisely what is inherited (Shields & Gottesman 1973). Furthermore, there is still no clear link between the genetic component and the various theories of the nature of schizophrenia in terms of higher levels of biological organisation.

During recent years there have been many attempts to identify the bio-logical and psychological precursors of schizophrenia by the prospective study of the offspring of schizophrenic women—a particularly high risk group (see review by Garmezy 1974a, b). Mednick and Schulsinger and their col-leagues in Denmark (Mednick *et al* 1974; Schulsinger & Mednick 1975) found that the high risk children had a distinctive psychophysiological re-sponse to stress, as shown by an unusually marked autonomic reaction fol-lowed by rapid recovery and slow habituation. Schizophrenia was most likely to develop if this hyperlabile hypersensitive autonomic functioning was associated with disturbed cognitive associations, an excess of perinatal complications and early stressful separation experiences. The findings are im-portant and provocative but, so far, attempts at replication have produced results which provide at most only partial support for the Danish study (see Garmezy 1974a, b). On the other hand, research with adult schizophrenics suggests that they may be overaroused and hypersensitive to their environ-ment (Venables 1968). Further research is needed to determine how far the heterogeneity in findings are a consequence of differences in research tech-niques or in the composition of the samples studied.

There is abundant evidence from both retrospective and prospective studies that individuals who develop schizophrenia in adolescence and adult life have often shown behavioural abnormalities of a nonpsychotic type in later childhood prior to the onset of psychosis (Offord & Cross 1969; Rutter 1972; Garmezy 1974a, b). Schizophrenia is more likely to develop in socially isolated children with oddities of personality and a mixture of emotional dis-turbance and disorders of conduct. Unfortunately, this is far too general a pattern for it to be of much value for either prediction or an understanding of the precursors of schizophrenia. However, it is notable that in most studies of adolescents with schizophrenia a sizeable proportion initially received other diagnoses with disorders of conduct, mood and interpersonal relation-ships particularly prominent (Sands 1956; Symonds & Herman 1957; Mas-terson 1967; Warren 1965a, b).

Several theories have been put forward suggesting that schizophrenia arises as a result of abnormal patterns of family interaction involving 'double-bind' or contradictory messages in parent–child communication (Bateson *et al* 1956); marital schism and stress with parental irrationality and distortions of reality (Lidz 1958); family mystification and excessive control (Laing 1960); 'pseudo-mutuality' (Wynne *et al* 1958) or other abnormal patterns of communication (see review by Hirsch & Leff 1975). Much of the research is open to serious methodological criticism and very little has directly tested the specific hypotheses put forward. It seems that the parents of schizo-phrenics show more conflict and disharmony than the parents of normals and possibly more than the parents of individuals with other forms of psychiatric disorder. Also, there is evidence that mothers of schizophrenics tend to show both personality abnormalities and overintrusive and overprotective behaviour toward their schizophrenic child. However, it remains uncertain how far any of these family features are genetic in origin or are responses to an abnormal child, rather than environmental influences which cause schizophrenia in the children. There is no satisfactory evidence for the atypical parental dominance patterns thought by Lidz to predispose to the development of schizophrenia.

The most striking findings with respect to abnormalities of family communication are those from the studies of Wynne and Singer (Wynne & Singer 1963; Wynne 1968). Rorschach responses were used to assess communication defects and deviances, by employing a specially devised set of scoring criteria. It was found that such defects and deviances (disruptions, vagueness, irrelevance, lack of closure, etc.) were very much more common in the parents of schizophrenics than in the parents of neurotics, with almost no overlap between the groups. However, Hirsch and Leff (1975) in a particularly careful and thorough replication of this work were unable to confirm these findings. They found that the fathers of schizophrenics talked more than the fathers of neurotics; also there were minor, but statistically significant, differences in communication deviance in the same direction as found by Wynne and Singer. However, these were a function of the greater verbosity of the parents of schizophrenics and when this was taken into account the difference between groups disappeared. The results are incompatible with Wynne and Singer's 'transactional' hypothesis of the genesis of schizophrenia. The marked discrepancy between the findings of the two studies remains to be explained but it may be a function of transatlantic differences in the diagnosis of schizophrenia (see above). If this is the case, it would imply that abnormalities of family communication may be important in the genesis of 'borderline' disorders which lack the first-rank symptoms of schizophrenia.

Whether or not there are specific patterns of parent–child interaction which precede and cause schizophrenia is quite uncertain. However, there is good evidence that psychosocial factors play a part in the precipitation of schizophrenia and in its course once the disorder has started. Brown and Birley (Brown & Birley 1968; Birley & Brown 1970) have shown convincingly that the onset of florid symptoms is often preceded during the previous 3 weeks by a significant change in the patient's social environment. The time relationships suggest that the environmental stress precipitated the psychosis, but did *not* cause it in an individual who would not have had it otherwise. Brown and his colleagues (Brown *et al* 1962; Brown, Birley & Wing 1972) have also shown that overinvolvement with a relative who expresses a lot of critical feeling is associated with symptomatic relapse during the 9 months after the patient's discharge from hospital. Both a limitation of face-to-face contact with the intrusive, critical, overinvolving relatives and the regular taking of appropriate medication had a protective effect.

Kohn (1972) has argued that the association between low social class and schizophrenia reflects a causal connection. However, the evidence strongly suggests that this is not the case. Rather, schizophrenia results in a downward social drift (Dunham 1964; Goldberg & Morrison 1963; Wardle 1963).

Course and prognosis

Weiner (1970) concluded, on the basis of data from Warren (1965a, b), Carter (1942) and Masterson (1956), that the course of schizophrenia arising in adolescence followed a bimodal distribution. On the whole, there was a tendency either to early substantial recovery or to continuing incapacity frequently resulting in prolonged hospital care. Annesley (1961) and Pollock (1960) found that the best outcome was associated with relatively high intelligence, a normal EEG and a late onset. Vaillant (1962; 1964) and Stephens *et al* (1967), studying adults, found that a relatively good prognosis was associated with an acute onset, marked affective symptoms, the presence of confusion in the acute episode, and the presence of clear-cut precipitating factors. A family history of affective disorder seems a good prognostic feature (Vaillant 1964), whereas a large number of relatives with schizophrenia indicates a poor prognosis (McCabe *et al* 1971). King and Pittman (1971) in a follow-up study of 65 adolescents with schizophrenia, also found that a family history of affective illness predicted remission whereas a long duration of symptoms prior to admission was associated with a poor prognosis.

Eggers (1973) made a 20-year follow-up of 57 children with schizophrenia which had begun before 14 years of age. Eleven children had recovered completely and altogether about half had improved. The worst prognosis was in those with an onset before 10 years and in the children with previously abnormal personality characteristics. Above average intelligence and a secure, friendly and outgoing personality were associated with a good prognosis. However, a family history of schizophrenia, a disturbed family atmosphere and the type of symptoms were all unrelated to outcome.

The florid symptoms (such as delusions and hallucinations) which are of the greatest value in diagnosis, are of little value in prognosis (Jansson 1968; Strauss & Carpenter 1972; Vaillant 1964). Rather it is the so-called 'negative' symptoms such as blunting of affect (Astrup & Noreik 1966) and persistently disturbed interpersonal relationships (Phillips 1966; Strauss & Carpenter 1974) which point to a poor outcome—possibly because they are in turn linked with a long duration and an insidious onset.

Treatment

Knowledge of the factors which contribute to the onset or recurrence of schizophrenia (see above) suggest ways in which adolescents with schizophrenia should be treated. One of the most important factors is tailoring management to the particular needs of the individual patient.

Schizophrenia appears to be a complex disorder of psychological development based on an interaction between an unfavourable psychosocial environment and a genetically determined vulnerability. There is the possibility of preventive work in relation to perinatal complications and social hazards, and further research on family interaction and communication may eventually result in findings making it possible to give precise and practical advice to parents and others involved with vulnerable children. For the moment, management should be planned to ensure that the schizophrenic adolescent has controlled contact with overconcerned, intrusive and critical relatives. Carefully planned family interviews can be useful to explore ways of improving the family situation and to help family members to understand the adolescent's needs. However, heated, chaotic family meetings should be avoided, particularly with outpatients.

It is always essential to avoid unwittingly contributing to parental guilt. Parents of disturbed children will have faced many difficulties with their offspring and often feel distressed and angry—feelings sometimes directed onto the therapists. It is necessary to accept these feelings calmly and uncritically, responding to bitterness sensibly and constructively. Parents particularly need support when issues such as the chronicity of the illness or the need for long-term residential care have to be considered. Perplexed parents with mixed feelings are particularly vulnerable to inconsistent and muddled advice on medication or on how best to respond to their disturbed child. The clinician should be clear in what he says to the parents and should ensure that others concerned with the adolescent are equally clear about what is intended. Often several family discussions will be necessary because anxieties and ambivalence may impede understanding.

Psychotherapy with the schizophrenic adolescent should be of the friendly, supportive, noninterpretive sort. Usually, but not always, it is best on an individual basis. Both group activities and individual treatment can usefully include help with social skills and also gentle 'feedback' to the patient about the effects of his behaviour on others.

There is no doubt about the value of phenothiazine medication in schizophrenia (Leff & Wing 1971; Cawley 1967), although it is not invariably helpful (Leff 1975). Drugs like haloperidol or the phenothiazines should be used in order to contain anxiety and arousal without causing sedation. Brown *et al* (1972) found that the protective value of drugs was most apparent in those patients living with relatives who expressed high negative emotion at the time of admission. The extent to which these observations (on adults) apply to adolescents is not known, but drug treatment in schizophrenia, as with other conditions (Tyrer & Steinberg 1975) should be seen as a method by which psychotherapeutic, educational and social measures can be given the best chance of working; but because the adolescent has to learn new coping methods, it should be remembered that tranquillisers such as the phenothiazines can also interfere with the learning process (Eisenberg & Connors 1971; McAndrew *et al* 1972).

Chlorpromazine is the most generally useful drug when there is overactivity and high arousal but trifluoperazine may be preferable when there is apathy and inertia. Haloperidol is a useful alternative to the phenothiazines. A small dose should be used to start, building up to adult levels, and orphenadrine should be given in addition to prevent dystonic reactions.

Very occasionally a seriously disturbed adolescent may need enforced medication. This can cause great distress all round and some would feel this to be incompatible with a psychotherapeutic approach. However, an honest and open discussion with patient, family and staff on the reasons for medication together with an explanation that it is the only way to contain the situation and continue treatment (if that is the case) is infinitely preferable to an avoidance of the issue, pretending that it is 'only for the patient's own good', or, even worse, abandoning attempts at treatment.

Reference has already been made to difficulties in diagnosis. It is not necessary to await a firm diagnosis of schizophrenia before using phenothiazines or similar drugs. A boy or girl showing high levels of anxiety, with distress, incoherence, odd behaviour and similar signs in his or her efforts to cope with intrusive relatives or other social problems, may be helped by such medication if psychotherapeutic and social measures are inadequate. As always, the minimum necessary dose should be prescribed.

GENERAL ASPECTS OF MANAGEMENT: SOME CONCLUSIONS

Puzzlement, ambivalence and feelings of helplessness are common reactions in those involved in the referral of seriously disturbed adolescents. In trying to come to terms with their anxiety and despair, people may conclude that the young person is 'beyond reach', has 'lost control' and 'can only be helped by hospital admission'. This may or may not be the case, but it is necessary to recognise that a great deal of agitation and distress often surrounds referral to an adolescent unit, and can complicate diagnosis.

An understanding of these feelings and an assessment of the situation which generated them is as essential to the diagnostic formulation as an evaluation of the adolescent's mental state. If useful decisions are to be made and practical advice given, the clinician must appreciate the teenager's socio-cultural background, the feelings and attitudes at home and at school, as well as the attitudes, expectations and capacities of others involved with the ado-lescent. Plans for future care should be initiated from the beginning. The family, as well as other professionals (future teachers for example, or the com-munity social workers concerned with the adolescent), should be involved in discussions about the nature of the problem and the implications for future needs and care.

When it is evident after acute hospital admission that chronic handicap is likely, it may sometimes be necessary to consider long-term psychiatric hospital care. However, this should only be considered after exploring the possibilities of care at home with the family, in a special school, in a Children's Home, or at a hostel, *in conjunction with appropriate psychiatric support*. Such support should be planned, explicit and practical, and in terms of a sharing of skill and experience with those providing future care. Thus, adolescent unit nurses may have predischarge meetings with residential child-care workers. Similarly, the unit's school staff can liaise with teachers at the school which the adolescent is to attend. This is time consuming, but a practical and comprehensive follow-up, arranged at a personal level with those to be involved in the future helps to relieve anxiety and to prevent crises. It enables education, training and social development to proceed in as near normal a setting as the child's handicaps permit.

Many adolescent inpatient units cover a wide geographical area, and so may be able to take this direct approach with only a proportion of patients. However, even with families living at a distance, it is the unit team's responsi-bility to mobilise appropriate local advice and support by contact with com-munity agencies. This task may severely stretch their capacity for consultative work and diplomacy.

The number of adolescents needing *long-term* hospitalisation is small but cumulative, and too few units are available. While these long-term treatment units should retain community links, it is most appropriate for them to oper-ate on a regional basis. Units offering short- to medium-term treatment should be geographically much closer to the areas they serve and should be able to cater comprehensively for adolescents with neurotic or psychotic dis-orders. However, adolescents with mental handicap, especially if it is severe, do not readily fit into such general psychiatric adolescent units.

Some psychiatrists are reluctant to combine psychotherapeutic and phar-macological approaches, or to link an approach based on psychodynamic prin-ciples with techniques derived from other conceptual frameworks. However, any psychotherapeutic method which includes honest and open discussion between clinical colleagues, adolescent and family, and aims at clarification rather than mystification, should be quite compatible with the introduction of, for example, medication or social skills training if this is needed. It no more implies the much-maligned 'sick role' than does, for example, individual psychotherapy. There is no doubt that it is more comfortable for a psychiatric team to adhere fairly closely to a particular ethos or line of diagnosis and treatment, but our understanding of psychiatric disorder, so far, makes this inappropriate. In the case of psychotic disorders, the evidence points to multi-factorial causation involving a continuing and complex interaction between the developing nervous system and a changing environment. This requires the use of developmental, biological and social models of disorder (Eisenberg 1973) and a correspondingly broad-based approach to assessment and management.

REFERENCES

ANNELL A.L. (1969a) Manic-depressive illness in children and effect of treatment with lithium carbonate. *Acta paedopsychiat.* **36**, 292–301

ANNELL A.L. (1969b) Lithium in the treatment of children and adolescents. *Acta Psychiat. Scand.* Suppl. **207**, 19–30

ANNESLEY P.T. (1961) Psychiatric illness in adolescence: presentation and prognosis. *J. Ment. Sci.* **107**, 268–278

ANTHONY E.J. & SCOTT P.D. (1960) Manic-depressive psychosis in childhood. *J. Child Psychol. Psychiat.* **1**, 53–72

ASTRUP C. & NOREIK K. (1966) *Functional Psychoses: Diagnostic and Prognostic Models.* Springfield, Illinois: Charles C. Thomas

BATESON G., JACKSON D.D., HALEY J. & WEAKLAND J.H. (1956) Towards a theory of schizophrenia. *Behav. Sci.* **1**, 251–264

BERG I., HULLIN R., ALLSOPP M., O'BRIEN P. & MACDONALD R. (1974) Bipolar manic-depressive psychosis in early adolescence: a case report. *Brit. J. Psychiat.* **125**, 416–417

BIRLEY J.L.T. & BROWN G.W. (1970) Crises and life changes preceding the onset or relapse of acute schizophrenia: clinical aspects. *Brit. J. Psychiat.* **116**, 327–333

BLEULER E. (1911) *Dementia praecox or the Group of Schizophrenias.* Vienna. (Trans. J. Zinkin 1950.) New York: International Universities Press

BROWN G.W. & BIRLEY J.L.T. (1968) Crisis and life changes and the onset of schizophrenia. *J. Health Soc. Behav.* **9**, 203–214

BROWN G.W., BIRLEY J.L.T. & WING J.K. (1972) Influence of family life on the course of schizophrenic disorders: a replication. *Brit. J. Psychiat.* **121**, 241–258

BROWN G.W., MONCK E.M., CARSTAIRS G.M. & WING J.K. (1962) Influence of family life on the course of schizophrenic illness. *Brit. J. prev. soc. Med.* **16**, 55–68

BRUGGEN P., BYNG-HALL J. & PITT-AIKENS T. (1973) The reason for admission as a focus of work for an adolescent unit. *Brit. J. Psychiat.* **122**, 319–329

BUCKELL H.M.B. (1976) Personal communication.

CAMPBELL J.D. (1952) Manic-depressive psychosis in children: report of eighteen cases. *J. Nerv. ment. Dis.* **116**, 424–439

CARPENTER W.T., STRAUSS J.S. & BARTKO J.J. (1974) The diagnosis and understanding of schizophrenia. I. Use of signs and symptoms for the identification of schizophrenic patients. *Schiz. Bull.* no. **11**, 37–49

CARTER A.B. (1942) Prognostic factors of adolescent psychoses. *J. Ment. Sci.* **88**, 31–81

CAWLEY R.H. (1967) The present status of physical methods of treatment of schizophrenia. *In* Coppen A. & Walk A. (eds.) *Recent Developments in Schizophrenia.* Ashford: Headley Brothers

CONNELL P.H. (1958) *Amphetamine Psychosis.* Institute of Psychiatry Maudsley Monograph no. 5. London: Chapman & Hall

CONNELL P.H. (1971) Suicidal attempts in childhood and adolescence. *In* Howells J.G. (ed.) *Modern Perspectives in Child Psychiatry.* New York: Brunner-Mazel

COOPER J.E., KENDELL R.E., GURLAND B.J., SHARPE L., COPELAND J.R.M. & SIMON R. (1972) *Psychiatric Diagnosis in New York and London.* Institute of Psychiatry, Maudsley Monograph no. 20. London: Oxford University Press

CORBETT J.A. (1976) Medical management. *In* Wing L. (ed.) *Early Childhood Autism. Clinical Educational and Social Aspects,* 2nd edn. Oxford: Pergamon

CORBETT J.A., HARRIS R. & TRIMBLE M. (1976) Dementia and disintegrative psychosis in children. Paper given at meeting of British Association of paediatric neurologists, Durham

CRAMMER J.L., CRANE G. & ROSSER R.M. (1974) Blood levels and management of lithium treatment. *Brit. Med. J.* **3**, 650–654

CYTRYN L. & McKNEW D.H. (1974) Biochemical correlates of affective disorders in children. *Arch. gen. Psychiat.* **31**, 659–661

DAHL V. (1971) A follow-up study of child psychiatric clientele with special regard to manic-depressive psychosis. *In* Annell A.L. (ed.) *Depressive States in Childhood and Adolescence.* Proc. 4th UEP Congr., Stockholm, 1971. Stockholm: Almquist & Wiksell

DEWEY M.A. & EVERARD M.P. (1974) The near-normal autistic adolescent. *J. Autism Child. Schiz.* **4**, 348–356

DUNHAM H.W. (1964) Social class and schizophrenia. *Amer. J. Orthopsychiat.* **34**, 634–642

EASSON W.M. (1969) *The Severely Disturbed Adolescent.* New York: International Universities Press

EGGERS CH. (1973) *Verlaufsweisen Kindlicher und Präpuberaler Schizophrenien.* Berlin: Springer-Verlag

EISENBERG L. (1956) The autistic child in adolescence. *Amer. J. Psychiat.* **112**, 607–612

EISENBERG L. (1973) The future of psychiatry, *Lancet,* **ii**, 1371–1375

EISENBERG L. & CONNERS C.K. (1971) Psychopharmacology in childhood. *In* Kagan J. & Eisenberg L. (eds.) *Behavioural Science in Paediatric Medicine.* Philadelphia: W.B. Saunders

ERIKSON E.H. (1965) *Childhood and Society.* London: Hogarth Press

EVANS J. & ACTON W.P. (1972) A psychiatric service for the disturbed adolescent. *Brit. J. Psychiat.* **120**, 429–432

FISH F.J. (1956) *Schizophrenia.* Bristol: John Wright

FRAMROSE R. (1975) The first seventy admissions to an adolescent unit in Edinburgh: general characteristics and treatment outcome. *Brit. J. Psychiat.* **126,** 380–389

FREUD A. (1958) Adolescence. *Psychoanal. Study Child.* **13,** 255–278

FROMMER E. (1972) *Diagnosis and Treatment in Clinical Child Psychiatry.* London: Heinemann

GARMEZY N. (1974a) Children at risk: the search for antecedents of schizophrenia. Part I, conceptual models and research methods. *Schizophrenia Bull.* **8,** 14–90

GARMEZY N. (1974b) Children at risk: the search for antecedents of schizophrenia. Part II, ongoing research programs, issues and intervention. *Schizophrenia Bull.* **9,** 55–125

GOLDBERG E.M. & MORRISON S.L. (1963) Schizophrenia and social class. *Brit. J. Psychiat.* **109,** 785–802

GOTTESMAN I.I. & SHIELDS J. (1966) Schizophrenia in twins: sixteen years' consecutive admissions to a psychiatric clinic. *Brit. J. Psychiat.* **112,** 809–818

GRANVILLE-GROSSMAN K. (1971) (ed.) *Recent Advances in Clinical Psychiatry.* London: Churchill

HALL M.B. (1952) Our present knowledge about manic-depressive states in childhood. *Nervous Child* **9,** 319–325

HESTON L.L. (1966) Psychiatric disorders in foster home reared children of schizophrenic mothers. *Brit. J. Psychiat.* **112,** 819–825

HESTON L.L. & DENNY D. (1968) Interactions between early life experience and biological factors in schizophrenia. *In* Rosenthal D. & Kety S.S. (eds.) *The Transmission of Schizophrenia.* Oxford: Pergamon

HIRSCH S.R. & LEFF J.P. (1975) *Abnormalities in Parents of Schizophrenics.* Institute of Psychiatry Maudsley Monograph no. 22. London: Oxford University Press

HUFFMAN P.W. & WENIG P.W. (1954) Prodromal behaviour patterns in mental illness, quoted by Robins L.N. (1971). Follow-up studies investigating childhood disorders. *In* Hare E.H. & Wing J.K. (eds.) *Psychiatric Epidemiology.* London: Oxford University Press

JANSSON B. (1968) The prognostic significance of various types of hallucinations in young people. *Acta Psychiat. Scand.* **44,** 401–409

JASPERS K. (1963) *General Psychopathology.* Translated from 7th edn. (1913) by Hoenig J. & Hamilton M.W. London: Manchester University Press

KASANIN J. (1933) The acute schizo-affective psychoses. *Amer. J. Psychiat.* **13,** 97–126

KENDELL R.E. (1968) The problem of classification. *In* Coppen A. & Walk A. (eds.) *Recent Developments in Affective Disorders.* Ashford: Headley Brothers

KERNBERG O. (1967) Borderline personality organisation. *J. Amer. Psychoanal. Assoc.* **15,** 641–685

KETY S.S. (1974) From rationalisation to reason. *Amer. J. Psychiat.* **131,** 957–963

KETY S.S., ROSENTHAL D., WENDER P.H. & SCHULSINGER F. (1968). The types and prevalence of mental illness in the biological and adoptive families of adopted schizophrenics. *In* Rosenthal D. & Kety S.S. (eds.) *The Transmission of Schizophrenia.* Oxford: Pergamon

KING L.J. & PITTMANN G.D. (1971) A follow-up of 65 adolescent schizophrenic patients. *Dis. Nerv. Syst.* **32,** 328–334

KNIGHT R.R. (1954) Borderline states. *In Psychoanalytic Psychiatry and Psychology.* Austin Riggs Center. New York: International Universities Press

Kohn M.L. (1972) Class, family and schizophrenia: a reformulation. *Social Forces* **50**, 295–304

Kolansky H. & Moore W.T. (1971) Effects of marijuana on adolescents and young adults. *J. Amer. Med. Assoc.* **216**, 486–492

Kraepelin E. (1919) *Dementia Praecox and Paraphrenia*. Trans. Barclay, R.M. Edinburgh: Livingstone

Laing R.D. (1960) *The Divided Self*. London: Tavistock Publications

Langfeldt G. (1939) *The Schizophreniform States*. Copenhagen: Munksgaard

Leff J.P. (1975) The maintenance of schizophrenic patients in the community. *In* Lader M.H. (ed.) *Studies of Schizophrenia*. Ashford: Headley Brothers

Leff J.P. & Wing J.K. (1971) Trial of maintenance therapy in schizophrenia. *Brit. med. J.* **3**, 599–604

Lena B. & O'Brien E.M.D. (1975) Success with lithium in a disturbed child. *Lancet* (correspondence) **ii**, 1307–1308

Lewis A. (1971) 'Endogenous' and 'exogenous': a useful dichotomy? *Psychol. Med.* **1**, 191–196

Lidz T. (1958) Schizophrenia and the family. *Psychiatry* **21**, 21–27

McAndrew J.B., Case Q. & Treffert D.A. (1972) Effects of prolonged phenothiazine intake on psychotic and other hospitalized children. *J. Autism Child. Schiz.* **2**, 75–91

McCabe M.S., Fowler R.C., Cadoret R.J. & Winokur G. (1971) Familial differences in schizophrenia with good and poor prognosis. *Psychol. Med.* **1**, 326–332

Masterson J.F. (1956) Prognosis in adolescent disorders: schizophrenia. *J. nerv. ment. Dis.* **124**, 219–232

Masterson J.F. (1967) *The Psychiatric Dilemma of Adolescence*. Boston: Little, Brown

Masterson J.F. (1972) *Treatment of the Borderline Adolescent: a Developmental Approach*. New York: Wiley-Interscience

Masterson J.F. (1973) The borderline adolescent. *In* Feinstein S.C. & Giovacchini P. (eds) *Adolescent Psychiatry. II Developmental and Clinical Studies*. New York: Basic Books

Mednick S.A., Schulsinger F., Higgins J. & Bell B. (1974) *Genetics, Environment and Psychopathology*. New York: American Elsevier

Niedermeyer E. & Khalifeh R.K. (1965) Petit mal status ('spike wave stupor')—an electroclinical appraisal. *Epilepsia* **6**, 250–262

Offord D.R. & Cross L.A. (1969) Behavioral antecedents of adult schizophrenia. *Arch. gen. Psychiat.* **21**, 267–283

Olsen T. (1961) Follow-up study of manic-depressive patients whose first attack occurred before the age of 19. *Acta Psychiat. Scand.* **37**, Suppl. 162

Phillips L. (1966) Social competence, the process-reactive distinction, and the nature of mental disorder. *In* Hoch P.H. & Zubin J. (eds) *Psychopathology of Schizophrenia*. New York: Grune & Stratton

Pollack M. (1960) Comparison of childhood, adolescent and adult schizophrenics. *Arch. Gen. Psychiat.* **2**, 652–660

Rathod N.H. (1975) Cannabis psychosis. *In* Connell P.H. & Dorn N. (eds) *Cannabis and Man*. Edinburgh: Churchill-Livingstone

Rivinus T.M., Jamison D.L. & Graham P.J. (1975) Childhood organic neurological disease presenting as psychiatric disorder. *Arch. Dis. Child.* **50**, 115–119

Robins L.N. (1966) *Deviant Children Grown Up*. Baltimore: Williams & Wilkins

ROSENTHAL D. & KETY S.S. (eds.) (1968) *The Transmission of Schizophrenia*. Oxford: Pergamon

ROSENTHAL D., WENDER P.H., KETY S.S., WELNER J. & SCHULSINGER F. (1971) The adopted-away offspring of schizophrenics. *Amer. J. Psychiat.* **128**, 307–311

RUTTER M. (1970) Autistic children: infancy to adulthood. *Semin. Psychiat.* **2**, 435–450

RUTTER M. (1972) Relationships between child and adult psychiatric disorders. *Acta Psychiat. Scand.* **48**, 3–21

RUTTER M., GRAHAM P., CHADWICK O. & YULE W. (1976) Adolescent turmoil: fact or fiction? *J. Child Psychol. Psychiat.* **17**, 35–56

RUTTER M., GREENFELD D. & LOCKYER L. (1967) A five to fifteen year follow-up study of infantile psychosis: II. Social and Behavioural Outcome. *Brit. J. Psychiat.* **113**, 1183–1199

SANDS D.E. (1956) The psychoses of adolescence. *J. Ment. Sci.* **102**, 308–316

SEDMAN G. & KENNA J.C. (1965) The use of L.S.D. 25 as a diagnostic aid in doubtful cases of schizophrenia. *Brit. J. Psychiat.* **111**, 96–100

SCHILDKRAUT J.J. (1974) Current states of biological and psychopathological criteria for classifying the depressive disorders and predicting responses to treatment. *Psychopharmacol. Bull.* **10**, 5–25

SCHMIDEBERG M. (1959) The borderline patient. *In* Arieti S. (ed.) *American Handbook of Psychiatry*, vol. 1. New York: Basic Books

SCHNEIDER K. (1925) quoted *in* Slater E. & Roth M. (eds.) *Clinical Psychiatry*, 1969. London: Baillière, Tindall & Cassell

SCHNEIDER K. (1959) *Clinical Psychopathology*, English translation of 1950 edition. New York: Grune & Stratton

SCHOU M. (1968) Lithium in psychiatric therapy and prophylaxis, *J. Psychiat. Res.* **6**, 67–95

SCHOU M. (1971) quoted *in* Lena B. & O'Brien E.M.D. *Lancet* **ii**, 1307–1308

SCHULSINGER F. & MEDNICK S.A. (1975) Nature–nurture aspects of schizophrenia. *In* Lader M.H. (ed.) *Studies of Schizophrenia*. Ashford: Headley Brothers

SHIELDS J. & GOTTESMAN I.I. (1973) Genetic studies of schizophrenia as signposts to biochemistry. *Biochem. Soc.* Special Publication **1**, 165–174

SHAFFER D. (1974) Suicide in childhood and early adolescence. *J. Child Psychol. Psychiat.* **15**, 275–291

SLATER E., BEARD A.W. & GLITHERO E. (1963) The schizophrenia-like psychoses of epilepsy. *Brit. J. Psychiat.* **109**, 95–150

SPENCER D.J. (1971) Cannabis-induced psychosis. *Int. J. Addict.* **6**, 323–326

SPIVACK G. & SPOTTS J. (1967) Adolescent symptomatology. *Amer. J. Ment. Def.* **72**, 74–95

STEINBERG D., GALHENAGE D.P.C., BERNARD F. & ROBINSON S.C. Two years' referrals to a regional adolescent unit (in preparation).

STEPHENS J.H., ASTRUP C. & MANGRUM J.C. (1966) Prognostic factors in recovered and deteriorated schizophrenics. *Amer. J. Psychiat.* **122**, 1116–1121

STORES G. (1971) Cognitive function in epilepsy. *Brit. J. Hosp. Med.* **6**, 207–214

STORES G. (1975) Behavioural effects of anti-epileptic drugs. *Develop. Med. Child Neurol.* **17**, 647–658

STRAUSS J.S. & CARPENTER W.T. (1972) The prediction of outcome in schizophrenia. I: Characteristics of outcome. *Arch. gen. Psychiat.* **27**, 739–746

STRAUSS J.S. & CARPENTER W.T. (1974) The prediction of outcome in schizophrenia. II: Relationships between predictor and outcome variables. *Arch. gen. Psychiat.* **31**, 37–42

SULLIVAN H.S. (1953) *Conceptions of modern psychiatry.* New York: Norton

SYMONDS A. & HERMAN M. (1957) The patterns of schizophrenia in adolescence. *Psychiat. Quart.* **31**, 521–530

TAYLOR D.C. (1971) Ontogenesis of chronic epileptic psychoses: a reanalysis. *Psychol. Med.* **1**, 247–253

TEALE J.D., FORMAN E.J., KING L.J. & MARKS V. (1974) Radioimmunoassay of cannabinoids in blood and urine. *Lancet* **ii**, 553–555

TOOLAN J.T. (1971) Depression in adolescents. *In* Howells J.G. (ed.) *Modern Perspectives in Adolescent Psychiatry.* Edinburgh: Oliver & Boyd

TYRER P.J. & STEINBERG D. (1975) Symptomatic treatment of agoraphobia and social phobias: a follow-up study. *Brit. J. Psychiat.* **127**, 163–168

VAILLANT G.E. (1962) The prediction of recovery in schizophrenia. *J. nerv. ment. Dis.* **135**, 534–543

VAILLANT G.E. (1964) Prospective prediction of schizophrenic remission. *Arch. Gen. Psychiat.* **11**, 509–518

VAN PUTTEN T. & SANDERS D.G. (1975) Lithium in treatment failures. *J. nerv. ment. Dis.* **161**, 255–264

VENABLES P.H. (1968) Experimental psychological studies of chronic schizophrenia. *In* Shepherd M. & Davies D.L. (eds.) *Studies in Psychiatry.* London: Oxford University Press

WARDLE C.J. (1962) Social factors in the major functional psychoses. *In* Welford A.T., Argyle M., Glass D.V. & Morris J.N. (eds.) *Society: Problems and Methods of Study.* London: Routledge & Kegan Paul

WARREN W. (1949) Abnormal behaviour and mental breakdown in adolescence. *J. Ment. Sci.* **95**, 589–624

WARREN W. (1965a) A study of adolescent psychiatric in-patients and the outcome six or more years later. I: Clinical histories and hospital findings. *J. Child Psychol. Psychiat.* **6**, 1–17

WARREN W. (1965b) A study of adolescent psychiatric in-patients and the outcome six or more years later. II: The follow-up study. *J. Child Psychol. Psychiat.* **6**, 141–160

WEINER I.B. (1970) *Psychological Disturbances in Adolescence.* New York: Wiley

WING J.K., BIRLEY J.L.T., COOPER J.E., GRAHAM P. & ISAACS A.D. (1967) Reliability of a procedure for measuring and classifying 'Present Psychiatric State'. *Brit. J. Psychiat.* **113**, 499–515

WORLD HEALTH ORGANIZATION (1973) *The International Pilot Study of Schizophrenia,* Vol. 1. Geneva: WHO

WYNNE L.C. (1968) Methodological and conceptual issues in the study of schizophrenics and their families. *In* Rosenthal D. & Kety S.S. (eds.) *The Transmission of Schizophrenia.* Oxford: Pergamon

WYNNE L.C., RYCKOFF I., DAY J. & HIRSCH S. (1958) Pseudo-mutuality in the family relations of schizophrenics. *Psychiatry* **21**, 205–220

WYNNE L.C. & SINGER M.T. (1963) Thought disorder and family relations of schizophrenics. *Arch. Gen. Psychiat.* **9**, 191–206

CHAPTER 32

Psychosomatic relationships

P. GRAHAM

Twenty years ago Aubrey Lewis (1954) suggested that the term 'psychosomatic' reflected 'only a rather muddled phase of specialised ignorance', and that the need for a special psychosomatic division of medicine would be less evident, when, amongst other things 'all doctors appreciate fully the psychiatric as well as the physical aspects of illness'. Such a golden age cannot yet be said to have arrived. Yet there is now much greater acceptance of his view that any separation of disease entities into those that are 'psychosomatic' and those that are not, is arbitrary and potentially misleading. The term is best reserved to describe an area of interest where a variety of methods may be used to study the evidence for interrelationships between psychological states and physical changes.

Even this modest definition leaves many conceptual problems unsolved and many questions of terminology unanswered. Most workers in this field would however probably accept David Graham's suggestion (1972) that it is illogical to divide events up into those that are physiological and those that are psychological. The same event may be described in psychological language or in terms of physiological change. Anger, for example, is usually defined in psychological language, but could equally well be described in terms of bodily change. This 'double aspect' or 'double language' approach goes some way to resolve difficulties in conceptualising causal mechanisms between psychological and physical events. There are logical problems, for example, in ascribing the cause of an ulcer to anxiety, but such problems may be partly avoided if the phenomena of anxiety are described in physiological as well as in psychological terms.

It is also important to attempt precision in defining 'psychogenesis'. The term is used in two ways (Graham 1972). It may be used to describe a situation where one state of the organism, e.g. excitement, produces another state, e.g. ulcerative colitis, but it is also used to describe situations where an environmental stimulus, e.g. a restrictive upbringing, is thought to be producing a physical change, e.g. asthma. The lack of evidence for psychogenicity in one respect does not neceesarily mean that it would be lacking in the other. Similarly the term 'stress' sometimes leads to confusion as it also is used in two ways (Lader 1970); to define an external painful or threatening stimulus, and to describe the behaviour of the organism ('stress reaction') in response to such a stimulus.

In childhood, there are certain special problems of definition. The possible significance of psychophysical interaction must be considered for example in relation to the maturation of the organism. The loss of a significant family figure before the age of 6 months cannot be appreciated by an infant in the same way as a similar loss occurring in the third year of life when the child is capable of discriminating between persons and has developed strong attachments. This is not to say that the life of an infant before 6 months will be unaffected by such a loss—merely that the mechanisms whereby physical and emotional changes are produced are likely to be different from those in the older child.

A further complication in considering psychophysical relationships in the maturing organism is the possibility that stress may not be producing physical pathology, but may nevertheless be influencing the rate of progress of normal physical development. Influences on growth and physical habit formation (including bowel and bladder control) form very much part of the area of study of the clinician interested in psychosomatic interaction in the child.

This chapter considers some of the questions which have been raised in the study of psychosomatic relationships, but no attempt has been made to provide a complete coverage of the literature. Most emphasis is given to recent work and, because asthma is a common and well researched condition it forms the basis for much of the discussion.

STRESSFUL EVENTS AND PHYSICAL CHANGE IN CHILDHOOD

It is assumed in some quarters that the symbolic value of an environmental stress is of considerably greater importance than its objective value. Unfortunately, the symbolic nature of stress is difficult to quantify, and recent attempts to evaluate stress have not considered symbolic value. Meyer and Haggerty (1962) investigated signs of streptococcal illness and family life events over the course of a year in 100 people. It was found that Group A β-haemolytic streptococcal infection was more likely to occur after, rather than before, a period of acute family stress. The level of chronic family stress also predicted whether the antistreptolysin O titre increased following the acquisition of streptococci in the throat. Heisel *et al* (1973) investigated the more general significance of life events as contributory factors in diseases of children. Initially, they asked 243 people to rate a variety of hypothetical events in terms of their potentially traumatic effect in comparison to the birth of a sib. They then obtained biographies of 3500 healthy children in order to obtain standardised information on the frequency with which these events occurred to children in the general population. Finally, they obtained the frequency with which stressful life experiences had occurred in five groups of sick children—general paediatric cases, general surgical cases, haemophiliacs, psychiatric patients and sufferers from rheumatoid arthritis. All of these groups, apart from the haemophiliac children, had significantly raised rates of stressful life events occurring in the year before investigation. Even with the haemophiliacs those with high rates of bleeding had higher life event rates than those who had bled less. Stein (1971) compared potentially disturbing early life events in a group of 38 young diabetics with those of a similar number of patients suffering from congenital conditions. It was found that the diabetic patients had had a distinctly higher rate of earlier traumatic events to contend with—for example 69 per cent had suffered parental loss or severe family disturbance compared with only 19 per cent of the controls.

What these studies (and there are numerous others) have in common, is an attempt to link nonspecific events in a child's life to the development of physical disorders of different types. The methodological problems in this approach have been well summarised by Brown *et al* (1973) in their discussion of precipitating events in relation to schizophrenia and depressive illness.

They point out the need to establish a causal link between life events and the condition under study. In order to do this it is necessary to show that the life events occurred in excess in the period before the onset of the condition, and more frequently than they occurred at other times. It is also, of course, important to be sure that the life events could not have been secondary to the early undetected development of the condition itself. Sometimes, in childhood at least, this can be a matter of great difficulty.

Specificity of symptoms in childhood

The concept of vulnerability, or particular predisposition to develop psychiatric disorder, is discussed in Chapter 1 in relation to temperamental characteristics and in Chapter 8 in relation to neurological disease and epilepsy. Other work suggests that inherited constitutional patterns of autonomic functioning may be identifiable in childhood. Lacey and his coworkers (Lacey 1950; Lacey & Lacey 1958; Lacey & Van Lehn 1952) suggested that:

i Individuals exhibited characteristic and persistent somatic responses to stress, e.g. some responded by increased sweat gland activity, some by increased heart rate and some by an increase in blood pressure.

ii This pattern of response was not just limited to single situations, but generalised to other situations.

Lacey and Van Lehn (1952) investigated 110 children aged 6–18 years and found that they responded to various stresses with a patterned autonomic reaction which was much more variable for some children than for others. This work has apparently not been extended to groups of children with psychiatric disorder, and it would be particularly interesting to know if children suffering, for example, from anxiety symptoms could be identified as showing characteristic patterns of autonomic response to stress. As our knowledge of psychopharmacology increases, it is not inconceivable that it may be possible in time to prescribe specific medication for unpleasant anxiety symptoms reflecting a particular type of severe autonomic dysfunction.

Other work on specificity of symptomatology in childhood is rather limited. It seems reasonable to suppose that children who, for physiological reasons, have been particularly late to develop bladder control, might more readily regress to become enuretic, but there is little evidence on this point (see Chapter 24). Similarly, there is no evidence that secondary encopresis occurs frequently amongst children late to gain bowel continence (see Chapter 25), although it has been suggested that children with early treated rectal anomalies do respond to stress with overflow soiling later in life (Nixon 1975).

Psychological factors affecting physical growth

Obesity

It is generally agreed that childhood obesity is multifactorially determined by various genetic and environmental factors (Mayer 1966; Crisp 1970; Werry 1972). Genetic factors have been shown to be important in Shields twin study (1962). Both food intake and calorie expenditure through physical activity are obviously of major environmental importance.

Familial patterns of obesity do not necessarily imply the operation of genetic factors. Overeating and underactivity may occur in families as a pattern of behaviour induced by sociocultural mechanisms. A little girl who models herself upon her sluggish and gluttonous mother stands a good chance of developing obesity regardless of her genotype. Quaade (1955) in an epidemiological study of Danish schoolchildren suggested that some mothers of obese children have placed undue emphasis on the value of food, and regarded themselves as unsatisfactory mothers unless all they provided was eaten.

These factors alone could account for the fact that Quaade found obesity to be nearly three times as common in the children of obese mothers compared to the children of mothers of normal weight.

Studies of the general emotional and behavioural adjustment of obese children do not reveal these to be a highly deviant group (e.g. Sallade 1973). A minority of fat children overeat as a comforting habit which compounds their problems, but once a child is fat, that child will remain overweight even on an ordinary diet. It has been suggested that the development of an excessive number of fat cells can occur in the first year of life and lead to a likelihood of obesity occurring later on (Brook 1972). If this were so, this would have important implications for early feeding practices and for the relevance of early mother–child relationships in the aetiology of obesity. The methodology of this type of research is however not well worked out, and no firm conclusions can be drawn from published studies about the relevance of psychological factors. Further research in progress may clarify these issues.

In the meantime it may be important to note that a series of studies carried out by Richardson (1970) suggests that obese children are likely to be more stigmatised and less liked by their peers than children with other types of physical deformity or handicap. Richardson asked children to choose which child they liked best when they were shown pictures of boys and girls with a wide variety of disability, including facial deformity and limb amputations. Obese children were selected on average last by children of different ages (Richardson 1970) and from a variety of different social backgrounds (Richardson *et al* 1961).

Anorexia nervosa

Although Crisp (1965) claimed that anorexia nervosa occurs only rarely in the prepubertal period, there are several studies of young children with this condition (Lesser *et al* 1960; Blitzer *et al* 1961; Warren 1968). Crisp's diagnostic criteria appear the most useful. He suggests that the onset of the condition is characterised by 'apparently elective restriction of food intake, a wish not to eat ... usually based on an apparent belief by the patients that they were plump, leading to a conscious desire to lose weight'. There are a number of associated characteristics, including abnormal or unusual premorbid personality traits (hysterical, obsessional or schizoid) and current concern over developing sexuality and physical maturation. Such characteristics appear to be as common in prepubertal children developing the condition as in adolescents and young adults. Clearly, by definition, amenorrhoea cannot be a feature of the condition in the prepubertal girls, but there is no recorded case of a child achieving menarche whilst in the acute phase of the condition.

Young girls are affected much more frequently than young boys, although Falstein *et al* (1956) were able to describe four prepubertal males with the condition aged between 10 and 12 years.

King (1963) draws a helpful distinction between primary and secondary anorexia in adults, the latter occurring particularly in depressive illness but also in schizophrenia. In childhood the same distinction is useful, although the possible range of differential diagnosis is perhaps rather broader and less well defined. Refusal to eat can occur in a variety of behaviour and emotional disorders. A girl with a conduct disorder can go on conscious 'hunger strike' in order to achieve her aim in a family battle over control. A child with an anxiety state can develop a fear of swallowing resulting in refusal to eat food except perhaps in fluid or semi-solid form. Many children, even with mild school refusal, go without breakfast on Mondays to Fridays in term-time. Some children, particularly girls, with abdominal pain or feelings of abdominal fullness which have developed on a hysterical basis, may refuse food because it appears to exacerbate the symptom. As in adulthood, the unusual case of childhood depression may show marked anorexia. In none of these situations would it be reasonable to diagnose anorexia nervosa on Crisp's criteria. However, there may be a continuum of anorexic behaviour in which only the most extreme form should be described as anorexia nervosa (Fries 1974). Some type of anorexia occurring in other childhood psychiatric disorders may be precursors of the full-blown condition.

The psychopathology of the illness is less well worked out in childhood than in adult life. But family conflict seems to be more often overt, and unusual internalised fantasies appear less prominent in younger patients. Certainly, fantasies of oral impregnation, said to be common in adult women, seem to be rare in the young child. However, treatment usually follows similar lines. Children who are losing weight should be admitted to hospital in order to establish control over the situation. Graded rewards, in the shape of increased activity and the promise of discharge, work best in the context of a trusting relationship with a specified member of the medical or nursing staff. Chlorpromazine is usually used as an adjuvant and probably promotes more rapid increase in weight than would occur otherwise. With this regime, a return to a reasonable weight can usually, though not always, be assured, but there is much less optimism about long-term results in terms of personality changes and social adjustment. Liebman *et al* (1974) have recently described a rather different approach using family therapy. Superior results are claimed but it is too early to know whether this claim has substance.

The value of long-term psychotherapy, and the whole question of prognosis is reviewed by Tolstrup (1975). Warren (1968) described the outcome in a series of 20 girls aged from $10\frac{1}{2}$ years to $15\frac{3}{4}$ years many of whom had been followed up for several years. Two had died, 13 out of the 20 (65 per cent) had recovered and the remainder still suffered significantly disabling symptoms. This experience seems fairly typical of others who have followed up a smaller number of young patients.

Failure to thrive

Children who fall below the third percentile in height and weight may be suffering from a variety of conditions, but in most no single cause can be identified (Raiti 1969). Genetic factors are probably important, and charts are available so that children can be assessed in relation to others of similar parental height (Tanner *et al* 1970). However, high correlations between parental and child height do not necessarily imply a genetic mechanism. Mothers themselves reared in poor institutions may attain short stature because of inadequate diet, and then find difficulty in providing adequate nourishment for their own children.

Bentovim (1970) has reviewed a hospital population of children with feeding problems including finicky appetites, and he discusses the various distortions of parent–child relationship of which these problems may be a reflexion. Although inadequate nutrition is generally regarded as responsible for failure to thrive, and psychological factors as important only insofar as they may militate against the child ingesting enough food, it has been suggested that some children may fail to grow for psychological reasons despite plentiful food intake. This syndrome of 'deprivation dwarfism' described by Powell *et al* (1967) has been reviewed by Rutter (1972) who concludes that the evidence for psychological aetiology is slender. Chimpanzees reared in grossly isolated conditions but with adequate food intake put on weight normally (Davenport *et al* 1966). Three stunted infants whose mothers claimed they were on a normal diet were observed at home by Whitten *et al* (1969). The infants did eat normally, but they also started to grow and put on weight, and it was reasonably assumed by the authors that the mothers' previous account of food intake was inaccurate. It is likely that the main importance of psychological factors in failure to thrive lies in distorted relationships resulting in nutritional privation.

Dorner and Elton (1973) have reviewed personality development and family situation of children of very short stature referred to a clinic for consideration of treatment with human growth hormone. Such children are under considerable stress for they are frequently taken to be much younger than their years and, not surprisingly, their behavioural reactions often lead them into difficulties at school or failure to develop their intellectual potential.

Influence of family relationships on body functions

Just as the most potent influences for healthy psychological development of children lie in the families in which they are brought up, so the stresses to which children are most vulnerable from the point of view of their physical functioning, lie within the family. Distortions of family relationships occur in a variety of ways, some of which may be more important in the development of bodily symptomatology than others. Severe marital disharmony with relative rejection of the child by one or both parents is more likely to produce a delinquent pattern of behaviour, though its possible importance in the aetiology of faecal soiling is also discussed in Chapter 25. Persistent abdominal pain occurring as a symptom in school refusal, and arising often as a result of the mother rewarding a bodily complaint by paying undue anxious attention is discussed in Chapter 19. Most interest, however, has centred around the importance of parental, especially maternal, influences in the precipitation of asthmatic attacks.

It is generally agreed that childhood asthma arises 'primarily as an inborn lesion causing hyperreactivity in the bronchi' (Pinkerton and Weaver 1970). Narrowing of the bronchi can occur as a result of exposure to allergens such as the house mite, pollen and various dusts, as well as in response to infection. The importance of parental influence has been demonstrated by a variety of research findings, although the mechanism by which they operate remains uncertain. Purcell and Weiss (1970) investigated 22 asthmatic children who were looked after in their own homes by parent substitutes, thus being exposed to the same physical allergens, but separated from their parents. The authors were able to predict with remarkable success which children would improve in their asthma in response to this drastic environmental manipulation. Making the same point in a different and perhaps less convincing way, Long *et al* (1958) separated asthmatic children from their parents by admitting them to hospital. The asthma improved, and did not recur when dust from the patient's own home was pumped into his room in the hospital. Clearly, an allergic response to house dust was not in itself sufficient explanation for the development of attacks. The frequent success of residential placement in ameliorating the frequency and severity of asthmatic attacks provides clinical evidence for the importance of familial factors in provoking attacks.

As mentioned above the mechanism whereby parental proximity evokes asthma remains obscure. Purcell and Weiss (1970) suggest four possible mechanisms. Autonomic activity associated with emotional arousal can initiate airways obstruction—for example vagal stimulation may lead to bronchospasm. Certain emotional states (perhaps more likely to occur in the presence of parents) are associated with respiratory behaviour such as laughing and crying, and these can lead to airways obstruction. Emotional states are associated with raised endogenous adrenal steroid output, and this in itself could alter the course of chronic asthma. Finally, it is possible that CNS processes may affect immunological phenomena and thus produce tissue change. It is probable that children are vulnerable to develop asthmatic attacks in response to stress not so much because of the specifically asthmatogenic nature of certain types of stress, but because of specific vulnerability in the child.

Nevertheless, attempts continue to be made to identify specifically asthmatogenic stimuli in the family. Little and Cohen (1951) showed that, in an experimental situation, the mothers of asthmatic children set higher goals for their children than mothers of nonasthmatic controls. Epstein (1964), in an investigation of 100 asthmatic boys aged between 7 and 12 years, showed that differences existed in their ease of response to a verbal operant conditioning technique depending on how 'approval-motivated' they were. Owen and Williams (1961) compared 20 asthmatic children with 20 controls in terms of respiratory changes observed on hearing their mothers' voices on a tape recorder. The asthmatic children were seen to show more respiratory change.

Whatever the importance of parental influences psychologically induced on the precipitation of individual attacks, it is unlikely that the long-term course of asthma is affected by emotional factors. McLean and Ching (1973) followed 45 asthmatic children over 10 years and showed that although their behavioural adjustment followed closely upon the degree of family disturbance, the course of the asthma was independent of the degree of family disturbance.

Further data relating psychological status to the development and maintenance of asthma are provided by McNichol *et al* (1973). The emphasis on asthma in this section reflects the fact that most work on the relationship between physical disorders and family relationships has been carried out on this condition, but studies in relationship to other conditions in childhood have been carried out and are reviewed, for example, by Prugh and Jordan (1969) in relation to ulcerative colitis, by Apley and Hale (1973) in relation to nonorganic abdominal pain and by Millar (1969) in relation to peptic ulcers in childhood.

Psychological effects of hospitalisation

Although children have suffered severely from the psychological effects of hospitalisation ever since the practice of separating them from their families for admission to hospital began (and on a widespread scale, this occurred in the second half of the nineteenth century), the psychological study of such suffering did not begin until the 1940s, public concern was not raised until the 1950s and the first reflection of a change in public policy in this matter in the UK did not occur until the end of that decade (Ministry of Health 1959). Probably, a combination of factors was involved. Before the 1940s children were likely to be admitted only for serious illnesses for many of which no effective treatment was available. Naturally, in this situation, concern for survival overrode concern for psychological well-being. With the advent of antibiotics children's beds became much more freely available, so that children were probably admitted with less serious conditions. Antibiotics also reduced the concern that the free introduction of parents would raise the risk of crossinfection. War-time evacuation with wholesale separation of children from their families as a matter of social policy raised questions about separation which the young science of child psychology was eager to take up in a more general way.

Edelston (1943) was one of the first both to describe emotional reactions to hospitalisation and to postulate various mechanisms which might underlie them. He described the behaviour of hospitalised children as following a characteristic course. Initially, there is a good deal of emotional upset, which is followed by a settling-down period. On return home there is a 'stage of awkwardness' or negativism which Edelston explained as a testing-out period. Bowlby (1961) and Robertson (1958) elaborated considerably on these descriptions in terms of successive stages of 'protest', 'despair' and 'detachment'. In some ways these later elaborations are rather less satisfactory than Edelston's more general formulation, for they suggest that the first stage is entirely taken up with angry communication and the second with self-absorbed emotional pain, whereas in fact there is much more of a mixture of reactions throughout, as observation of Robertson's own films confirms.

The further question has been raised whether a fairly brief hospitalisation could have lasting effects on personality development. The work of Bowlby *et al* (1956) suggests even a prolonged admission does not usually have lasting ill-effects but National Survey data (Douglas 1975) indicates that recurrent hospital admissions are associated with disorders of conduct as long as 10 years afterwards (see also Chapter 3).

Since the first description of distress produced by hospitalisation appeared, the main interest in this field has been directed to three main areas—the factors modifying distress, the mechanisms involved and the development of techniques to reduce distress. The first of these is reviewed by Vernon *et al* (1965), the second by Rutter (1972).

Factors modifying distress

The age of the child is most important. Illingworth and Holt (1955) studied children aged 1 to 14 years, and found decreasing effects with increasing age in all measures studied. Less is known on the effects of admission below 1 year of age although Schaffer and Callender's (1959) study included infants. On the basis of their data, it is often stated (Rutter 1972) that 'under the age of about 6 months there is usually *no* distress associated with admission to hospital'. Although, obviously it is more difficult for infants to communicate their distress, there is no doubt that infant behaviour *changes* with admission without the mother. It would be surprising if a break in continuity of the mother–child relationship did not have at least some short-term adverse effects. There is need for more research on the effects of hospital admission in infancy in view of the increasing number of very early admissions for treatment of congenital conditions.

The *preparation* of the child for hospitalisation may have an important modifying effect, although studies using control groups have come up with conflicting results as to its effectiveness. Preparations could include advance trial brief separations (Swift 1959), a visit to the ward prior to admission, the explanation of procedures before they are applied, honest admission of the likelihood of pain (e.g. before a venepuncture) where this is unavoidable, the use of special procedures such as puppetry to enable the child to obtain a feeling of control over his situation, the allocation of nurses to individual child patients to enable the child to form a special trusting relationship, and the general application of a child-centred rather than an institution-centred or staff-centred approach.

The importance of *visiting* to reduce the distress produced by separation has already been mentioned. Its feasibility has been well demonstrated (MacCarthy *et al* 1962). Frequency of visiting, presence of the mother at induction of anaesthesia, advantages of rooming in over daily visiting etc., have all been discussed by various authors and the evidence is well summarised by Vernon *et al* (1965).

Other factors which Vernon *et al* (1965) review include the amount of sensorimotor restriction imposed on the child whilst in hospital, e.g. if his legs are immobilised in a traction apparatus and he is relatively isolated in a cubicle. Parent–child relationships and parental attitude to the hospitalisation are obvious further modifying factors. The child's own personality has been studied by Shaffer (1966) who showed that active infants showed smaller decrements in developmental quotients than inactive ones hospitalised for similar periods.

Previous experience of hospitalisation and the nature of the disability from which the child is suffering must also be considered. However, little evidence is available on these issues. The nature of the condition for which the child is admitted is likely to be of indirect importance. For example Howarth (1972) found that, amongst a group of children suffering from leukaemia, the amount of distress suffered seemed to be related as much to the medical procedures involved (venepunctures, sternal marrow punctures, transfusions etc.) as to anything else.

Mechanisms underlying production of adverse effects

These have been thoroughly described by Rutter (1972) in relation to the concept of 'maternal deprivation'. As well as bond disruption because of the separation, he considers the possible importance of the entry into a strange environment, the existence of an already disturbed mother–child relationship, deprivation of care by substitute caretakers and separation from significant figures in the child's life other than the mother.

Over the past 20 years a very considerable volume of research has been conducted in this area, and practice in relation to visiting and the general standard of patient care on children's wards has improved enormously. Nevertheless, a number of aspects of the subject have been little studied and would repay investigation. Effects on the mental health of parents when their children go into hospital and the effect on children when one or other parent is hospitalised are little known. The importance of visiting mother in general hospitals and in mental hospitals is sometimes mentioned but has been little researched. A further area of possible research is an examination of possible *beneficial* effects of hospitalisation on the child—increasing independence and self-help skills etc. Finally, there is still a good deal of uncertainty about the nature of the 'settling-in' response which so many hospitalised young children show after a few days or even hours in hospital. It would be helpful to know whether it is possible to distinguish a realistic adaptation to the situation from a withdrawal reaction with more ominous indication for future adjustment.

Physical disorder and its impact on education

Although the effect on educational achievement of brief physical illness may be fairly trivial, chronic physical handicap of whatever kind is likely to alter the child's capacity and opportunities to learn in a variety of ways. The subject has been reviewed by Rutter, Tizard and Whitmore (1970) in relation to physical handicap generally, and by Rutter, Graham and Yule (1970) specifically in relation to neurological and epileptic disorders.

The Isle of Wight studies showed that school absence was more frequent in children with chronic physical handicaps than in the general population. Children with brain disorders differed somewhat from the others in their pattern of educational disability (see Chapter 8). Of children without brain damage, only asthmatics differed in their mean level of intelligence. The fact that the verbal ability of asthmatic children was significantly higher than that of the control group is probably just a reflexion of the fact that this particular group were of higher social class than controls. By contrast, specific reading disability was significantly commoner in physically-handicapped children than controls and this was so for all groups including the asthmatics. There was a definite relationship between absence from school and specific reading retardation within the physically-handicapped group, and it is likely that the educational backwardness of these children was at least in part produced by missed schooling.

The question of asthmatic children's intelligence remains one of controversy. Recently, Mitchell and Dawson (1973) described a total population study of Aberdeen schoolchildren aged 7 years. The IQ of the asthmatic children, who formed 4·8 per cent of the total population, was 102 compared with 95 for the general population. This highly significant finding is the more striking in that the severely asthmatic children studied tended to come from semi-skilled and unskilled manual class families. The parents of asthmatic children were found to have rather rigid, orthodox and overprotective personalities. How all these variables—slightly higher intelligence, average school achievement and perfectionist parental attitudes—are linked together is a matter of controversy, and probably varied a good deal from child to child and from family to family. It seems possible that a common pattern of linkage is that the asthma is originally determined by organic factors, but induces a sense of insecurity in the parents to which they react by developing overprotective and anxious responses. This promotes general intellectual development, but school absence due to physical illness prevents the child from achieving the expected educational level. In many cases the asthma eventually improves or clears up completely, and the allergic child is then able to fulfil his intellectual potential more effectively.

The need for special schoooling for children with physical handicaps arises for a variety of reasons. Some handicaps, such as blindness and deafness are rare, and the education of these children requires specialised teachers working in specially equipped centres. For other physical conditions, such as asthma, removal from home to a special boarding school sometimes produces a considerable improvement in the symptom, even though nursing and medical care within the school may remain necessary because of the child's continuing vulnerability to attacks. The desirability of segregated schooling for the physically handicapped has recently been questioned more forcefully than hitherto. Anderson (1971) discusses some of the arguments against it, and describes attempts at greater integration of the physically handicapped into ordinary schools. One of the difficulties in segregated schooling arises at the time of school-leaving when the handicapped child may have to re-enter the world in a relatively unprotected way. Tuckey *et al* (1973) describe a survey of physically-handicapped school leavers and make suggestions for improving the present situation.

Implications of psychosomatic studies for clinical management

There is an infinite variety of relationships between body and mind. Some authors, such as Pinkerton & Weaver (1970) and Schmale *et al* (1970), have made heroic attempts to achieve a theoretical synthesis of all aspects of these relationships, but it may be more profitable at this stage of our knowledge to use the positive findings of studies relatively limited in their scope without necessarily trying to encompass them beforehand into a grand scheme. Purcell and Weiss (1970) have described very successfully how this might be achieved in bronchial asthma, and there is a great need for workers in the clinical field to draw together findings from organic and psychological work in other conditions and point to ways in which clinical management can combine information from both sources.

In some conditions, such as asthma and perhaps obesity and failure to thrive, the appropriate starting point for a discussion of clinical management would be the organic disease with which the child presents. In others, a discussion of management would focus initially on an entirely different aspect of the problem. For example, in the 'battered baby syndrome' it is the phenomenon of maltreatment which is the starting point rather than the bruises, burns, haemorrhages, fractures or poisoning with which the child may present.

For the paediatrician, perhaps the most important implication of recent work in the area is the need to focus on the possibility of significant psychophysical interaction regardless of the conditions from which the child is suffering. The most organic sounding orthopaedic complaint may have significant psychopathology in its aetiology, and, of course all physical conditions have a psychological impact on the affected child and his family. There is also a need to re-examine the view that some conditions always have important psychological factors in their aetiology. Asthma and obesity are two conditions where this has been alleged to be the case, but there is ample evidence that both these can arise without significant antecedent psychopathology.

For the child psychiatrist there is the important implication that psychiatric work with physically-handicapped children should involve more than the diagnosis and treatment of the overtly disturbed physically-handicapped child. Reducing the stress of hospitalisation, working with the medical social worker to alleviate the distress of the family with a dying child, helping the paediatrician to remain aware of the need for continuous assessment of psychological adjustment as well as of physical state—these are but a few of the tasks which recent work has suggested are likely to be of frequent importance. For both paediatricians and child psychiatrists the clinical relevance of work in the psychosomatic area in childhood lies mainly in its pinpointing the need for close collaboration between them, not least so that the child psychiatrist can retain a biological viewpoint which is essential to the understanding of the nonorganic conditions with which he is faced.

REFERENCES

ANDERSON E.M. (1971) *Making Ordinary Schools Special.* London: College of Special Education

APLEY J. & HALE B. (1973) Children with recurrent abdominal pain. How do they grow up? *Brit. Med. J.* **iii**, 7–9

BENTOVIM A. (1970) The clinical approach to feeding disorders of childhood. *J. Psychosom. Res.* **14**, 267–276

BOWLBY J. (1961) Childhood mourning and its implications for psychiatry. *Amer. J. Psychiat.* **118**, 481–498

BLITZER J.A., ROLLINS N. & BLACKWELL A. (1961) Children who starve themselves. *Psychosom. Med.* **23**, 369–381

BOWLBY J., AINSWORTH M.D., BOSTON M. & ROSENBLUTH D. (1956) The effects of mother–child separation: a follow-up study. *Brit. J. Med. Psychol.* **29**, 211–247

BROOK C. (1972) Evidence for a sensitive period in adipose-cell replication in man. *Lancet* **ii**, 624–627

BROWN G.W., SKLAIR F., HARRIS T.O. & BIRLEY J.L.T. (1973) Life events and psychiatric disorders. Part I: some methodological issues. *Psychol. Med.* **3**, 74–87

CRISP A.H. (1965) Clinical and therapeutic aspects of anorexia nervosa. *J. Psychosom. Res.* **9**, 67–78

CRISP A.H. (1970) Psychological aspects of some disorders of weight. *In* Hill O. (ed.) *Modern Trends in Psychosomatic Medicine*—No. 2. London: Butterworths

DAVENPORT R.K., MENZEL E.W. & ROGERS C.M. (1966) Effects of severe isolation on 'normal' juvenile chimpanzees: health, weight gain, and stereotyped behaviors. *Arch. Gen. Psychiat.* **14**, 134–138

DORNER S. & ELTON A. (1973) The social and educational problems of short stature children. *Spec. Education* **62**, 12–16

DOUGLAS J.W.B. (1975) Early hospital admissions and later disturbances of behaviour and learning. *Develop. Med. Child Neurol.* **17**, 456–480

EDELSTON H. (1943) Separation anxiety in young children. *Genet. Psychol. Monogr.* **28**, 1–95

EPSTEIN R. (1964) Need for approval and the conditioning of verbal hostility in asthmatic children. *J. Abnorm. Soc. Psychol.* **69**, 105–109

FALSTEIN E.I., FEINSTEIN E.C. & JUDAS I. (1956) Anorexia nervosa in the male child. *Amer. J. Orthopsychiat.* **26**, 751–772

FRIES H. (1974) Secondary amenorrhea, self-induced weight reduction and anorexia nervosa. *Acta Psych. Scand.* Suppl. 248

GRAHAM D.T. (1972) Psychosomatic medicine. *In* Greenfield N.S. & Sternbach R.A. (eds) *Handbook of Psychophysiology.* New York: Holt, Rinehart & Winston

HEISEL J.S., REAM S., RAITZ R., RAPPAPORT S. & CODDINGTON R.D. (1973) The significance of life events as contributory factors in the diseases of children. III: A study of pediatric patients. *J. Pediatrics.* **83**, 119–123

HOWARTH R. (1972) The psychiatry of terminal illness in children. *Proc. Roy. Soc. Med.* **65**, 1039–1040

ILLINGWORTH R.S. & HOLT K.S. (1955) Children in hospital: some observations on their reactions with special reference to daily visiting. *Lancet* **ii**, 1257–1262

KING A. (1963) Primary and secondary anorexia nervosa syndromes. *Brit. J. Psychiat.* **109**, 470–479

LACEY J.I. (1950) Individual differences in somatic response patterns. *J. Comp. Physiol. Psychol.* **43**, 338–350

LACEY J.I. & LACEY B.C. (1958) Verification and extension of the principle of autonomic response-stereotypy. *Amer. J. Psychol.* **71**, 50–73

LACEY J.I. & VAN LEHN R. (1952) Differential emphasis in somatic response to stress. *Psychosom. Med.* **14**, 71–81

LADER M. (1970) Psychosomatic and psychophysiological aspects of anxiety. *In* Hill O. (ed.) *Modern Trends in Psychosomatic Medicine.* No. 2. London: Butterworths

LESSER L.I., ASHENDEN B.J., DEBUSKEY M. & EISENBERG L. (1960) Anorexia nervosa in children. *Amer. J. Orthopsychiat.* **30**, 572–580

LEWIS A.J. (1954) Aspetti psicosomatici della medicina clinica. *Recenti Prog. Med.* **16**, 434–453

LIEBMAN R., MINUCHIN S. BAKER L. (1974) An integrated treatment program for anorexia nervosa. *Amer. J. Psychiat.* **131**, 432–436

LITTLE S.W. & COHEN C.D. (1951) Goal-setting behaviour of asthmatic children and of their mothers for them. *J. Personality* **19**, 377–389

LONG R.T., LAMONT J.H., WHIPPLE B., BANDLER L., BLOM G.E., BURGIN L. & JESSNER L. (1958) A psychosomatic study of allergic and emotional factors in children with asthma. *Amer. J. Psychiat.* **114**, 890–899

MACCARTHY D., LINDSAY M. & MORRIS I. (1962) Children in hospital with mothers. *Lancet* **i**, 603–608

MCLEAN J.A. & CHING A.Y.T. (1973) Follow-up study of relationships between family situation and bronchial asthma in children. *J. Amer. Acad. Child Psychiat.* **12**, 142–161

MCNICHOL K.N., WILLIAMS H.E., ALLAN J. & MCANDREW I. (1973) Spectrum of asthma in children. III: Psychological and Social Components. *Brit. Med. J.* **4**, 16–20

MAYER J. (1966) Some aspects of the problem of regulation of food intake and obesity. *N. Engl. J. Med.* **274**, 610–616

MEYER R.J. & HAGGERTY R.J. (1962) Streptococcal infections in families. *Pediatrics* **29**, 539–549

MILLAR T.P. (1969) Peptic ulcers in children. *In* Howells J.G. (ed.) *Modern Perspectives in International Child Psychiatry.* Edinburgh: Oliver & Boyd

MINISTRY OF HEALTH (1959) *The Welfare of Children in Hospital.* London: HMSO

MITCHELL R.G. & DAWSON B. (1973) Educational and social characteristics of children with asthma. *Arch. Dis. Child.* **48**, 467–471

NIXON H. (1975) The diagnosis and management of faecal incontinence in children. *Archiv. Chirurg. Nierland.* **27**, 171–177

OWEN F. & WILLIAMS G. (1961) Patterns of respiratory disturbances in asthmatic children evoked by the stimulus of the mother's voice. *Amer. J. Dis. Child.* **102**, 759–60

PINKERTON P. & WEAVER C.M. (1970) Childhood asthma. *In* Hill O. (ed.) *Modern Trends in Psychosomatic Medicine.* No. 2. London: Butterworths

POWELL G.F., BRASEL J.A. & BLIZZARD R.M. (1967) Emotional deprivation and growth retardation simulating idiopathic hypopituitarism. I: Clinical evaluation of the syndrome. *N. Engl. J. Med.* **276**, 1271–1278

PRUGH D.G. & JORDAN K. (1969) The management of ulcerative colitis in childhood. *In* Howells J.G. (ed.) *Modern Perspectives in International Child Psychiatry.* Edinburgh: Oliver & Boyd

PURCELL K. & WEISS J. (1970) Asthma. *In* Costello C. (ed.) *Symptoms of Psychopathology.* New York: Wiley

QUAADE F. (1955) *Obese children: Anthropology and Environment.* Copenhagen: Danish Service Press

RAITI S. (1969) The short child: clinical evaluation and management. *Brit. J. Hosp. Med.* **2**, 1640–1643

RICHARDSON S.A. (1970) Age and sex differences in values toward physical handicaps. *J. Health Soc. Behav.* **11**, 207–214

RICHARDSON S.A., GOODMAN N., HASTORF A.H. & DORNBUSCH S.M. (1961) Cultural uniformity in reaction to physical disabilities. *Amer. Soc. Rev.* **26**, 241–247

ROBERTSON J. (1958) *Young Children in Hospital.* London: Tavistock Publications

RUTTER M. (1972) *Maternal Deprivation Reassessed.* Harmondsworth: Penguin

RUTTER M., GRAHAM P. & YULE W. (1970) *A Neuropsychiatric Study in Childhood.* Clin. Dev. Med. nos. 35/36. London: SIMP/Heinemann

RUTTER M., TIZARD J. & WHITMORE K. (eds.) (1970) *Education, Health and Behaviour.* London: Longman

SALLADE J. (1973) A comparison of the psychological adjustment of obese vs. non-obese children. *J. Psychosom. Res.* **17**, 89–96

SCHAFFER H.R. (1966) Activity level as a constitutional determinant of infantile reaction to deprivation. *Child Dev.* **37**, 596–602

SCHAFFER H.R. & CALLENDER W.M. (1959) Psychological effects of hospitalisation in infancy. *Pediatrics* **24**, 528–539

SCHMALE A.H., MEYEROWITZ S. & TINLING D.C. (1970) Current concepts of psychosomatic medicine. *In* Hill O. (ed.) *Modern Trends in Psychosomatic Medicine.* No. 2. London: Butterworths

SHIELDS J. (1962) *Monozygotic Twins Brought Up Apart and Brought Up Together.* London: Oxford University Press

STEIN S.P. (1971) Emotional factors in juvenile diabetes mellitus: a study of early life experiences of adolescent diabetics. *Amer. J. Psychiat.* **128**, 700–704

SWIFT A. (1959) Symposium on children in hospital: preparation and aftercare. *Roy. Soc. Hlth. J.* **79**, 561–564

TANNER J.M., GOLDSTEIN H. & WHITEHOUSE R.H. (1970) Standards for children's height at ages 2 to 9 years allowing for height of parents. *Arch. Dis. Childh.* **45**, 755–762

TOLSTRUP K. (1975) Treatment of anorexia nervosa in children. *J. Child Psychol. Psychiat.* **16**, 75–78

TUCKEY L., PARFIT J. & TUCKEY B. (1973) *Handicapped School Leavers.* Slough: NFER

VERNON D.T.A., FOLEY J.M., SIPOWICZ R.R. & SCHULMAN J.L. (1965) *The Psychological Responses of Children to Hospitalization and Illness.* Springfield, Illinois: Charles C Thomas

WARREN W. (1968) A study of anorexia nervosa in young girls. *J. Child Psychol. Psychiat.* **9**, 27–40

WERRY J.S. (1972) Psychosomatic disorders. *In* Quay H.C. & Werry J.S. (eds) *Psychopathological Disorders of Childhood.* New York: Wiley

WHITTEN C.F., PETTIT M.G. & FISCHHOFF J. (1969) Evidence that growth failure from maternal deprivation is secondary to undereating. *J. Amer. Med. Assoc.* **209**, 1675–1682

YARROW L.J. (1961) Maternal deprivation: towards an empirical and conceptual re-evaluation. *Psychol. Bull.* **58**, 459–490

CHAPTER 33

Atypical psychosexual development

R. GREEN

TYPICAL PSYCHOSEXUAL DEVELOPMENT

By the age of 3 or 4 years most children know whether they are a girl or a boy (Gesell 1940; Rabban 1950). However, the fact that a child recognises its own sex does not mean that it comprehends the full concept of sex differences. As their awareness of sexual identity grows children develop a peer group preference for those of their own sex. This appears earlier and more consistently in boys than girls (Hartup & Zook 1960; Hetherington 1967; Kohlberg 1967). Sex differences in attitudes, choice of games and other activities become evident and gradually increase up to 8 or 9 years (Kagan 1964; Kohlberg 1967).

Core morphological identity, gender-role behaviour and direction of sexual interest (sexual object choice) are different aspects of psychosexual development which may be determined by different forces (see Rutter 1971). The following sections deal with varying influences which come to bear on atypical psychosexual development.

SEXUAL IDENTITY

Anatomical and physiological sex takes five forms—chromosomal sex, gonadal sex, hormonal sex, internal reproductive structures and external genital morphology (Money, Hampson & Hampson 1955). Normally, these are the same (male or female) for any individual but there are a number of medical conditions in which they are at variance. When at variance, they have been used to investigate possible biological factors in the determination of sexual identity (Hampson & Hampson 1961; Money & Ehrhardt 1973). The striking finding from these studies is that the most important influence on sexual identity is whether the child is regarded by the parents as a boy or girl and brought up as such. The bulk of the evidence indicates that a child unambigously raised as a female will consider itself female, and a child unambiguously raised as a male will consider itself male, even though the sex chromosomes, gonads, hormones and physical appearance may point in the opposite direction. While body appearance has a bearing on the development of sexual identity, the sex of assignment and rearing appear more important. Thus, Lev-Ran (1974) studied 24 people in which the appearance of the external genitalia was markedly anomalous in relation to the sex assigned at birth and the sex of rearing. The findings stressed the apparent immutability of sexual identity even in the face of gross bodily contradictions. For example, one case was a 5-year-old boy whose phallus measured 1·5 cm. In spite of this he evolved a male identity and behaved in a typically masculine fashion. Another was an adult female with a phallus measuring 7 cm erect who presented with the complaint that this structure interfered with heterosexual intercourse. She had no question that she was female and she behaved in a feminine manner. Another 22-year-old woman with congenital adrenal hyperplasia had also been reared as female in spite of the fact that she had an erect phallus of 9 cm, no breast development, excessive body hair and a low voice. When adult, she was told that she was male, disbelieved the doctors, demanded clitoridectomy and refused sex reassignment. After developing female secondary sex characteristics following cortisone treatment, she wrote: 'It is simply unbelievable, this spring is the first real spring in my life, as if I was born anew!'

Inevitably, the evidence from these studies derives from atypical populations and some writers have suggested that this may influence the findings. Because the individuals had atypical hormone levels and were biologically ambiguous they may have been more susceptible than normal to psychological 'imprinting' (Diamond 1965). There are a few reports of isolated cases where members assigned to one sex felt that they belonged to the opposite sex, and at puberty developed cross-sex anatomical changes, in effect confirming their earliest gender wishes (Dewhurst & Gordon 1963; Baker & Stoller 1968). These, and accounts of successful late changes in gender role, suggest that biological factors may play some part in determining sexual identity (Dewhurst & Gordon 1963; Berg *et al* 1963).

The above cases appear, however, to be the exception rather than the rule. Twin studies demonstrate the proponderant effect of sex assignment and rearing. Thus, Money and Ehrhardt (1973) reported a pair of monozygotic male twins in which one child was being reared as a male and the other as a female. The reason for this happening was that one twin suffered severe penile sloughing as a consequence of circumcision trauma at about age 6 months. At a year and a half the decision was made to reassign the penisless co-twin as female. It is too early to know the final outcome but at 9 years the children were evolving different psychosexual patterns, appearing as a typical boy–girl pair. This case is of particular interest because genetically and hormonally (prenatally) the twins were similar.

Two pairs of monozygotic twins given the same sex assignment but discordant for gender-role behaviour have also been reported (Green & Stoller 1971). One was a pair of 10-year-old boys in which one was typically masculine and the other was behaviourally feminine and held fantasies of becoming a girl. The other twin pair consisted of 25-year-old females, one of whom was unremarkably feminine and the other wanted androgens and surgery in order to live as a man. In both cases different socialisation patterns were reported for the cotwins; patterns which were consistent with subsequent sexual identity in terms of existing theories of psychosexual development.

Sex differences in behaviour and attitudes

In Western culture, there are numerous attitudes and behaviours which are regarded as typically masculine or typically feminine. Many of these appear to be culturally determined (see Maccoby & Jacklin 1975) but two, aggressivity and rough-and-tumble play, seem to be biologically determined, in part. Primate research, human and nonhuman, points to the influence of prenatal androgens on these characteristics. Female rhesus monkeys whose mothers received testosterone during gestation are 'tomboyish' (Young, Goy & Phoenix 1964). Preadolescent human females exposed to elevated levels of androgen (those with the adrenogenital syndrome or those whose mothers received synthetic progesterone agents during gestation) appear more interested in athletics, rough-and-tumble play, wearing boys' clothes; and less interested in doll-play and raising children (Ehrhardt, Epstein & Money 1968; Ehrhardt & Baker 1974). Males (both pre- and postpubertal) whose mothers received oestrogens during pregnancy (along with lesser amounts of progesterone) have been reported as less aggressive and less athletic (Yalom, Green & Fisk 1973).

Hormonal influences may predispose individuals to more 'masculine' or more 'feminine' behaviour. These biological predispositions are likely in turn to influence the relationships the child has with his parents and with other children (see also Chapter 1). The resulting sex-linked behaviours and attitudes will be a result of this interaction between the biological substrate and socialisation practices. The latter are discussed more fully in relation to children with atypical sexual development (see below).

Other gender-related behaviours may also be hormone-influenced. Maternalism (and its equivalent in doll-play) is currently under the scrutiny of neuroendocrinologists. Previously thought to be a purely sex-typed social-learning phenomenon, present rethinking considers it neurally programmed in part. Male and female nonhuman primates show differences in their attention to newborns of their species. Females attend to them more and more often hold them in a ventral–ventral position (Lancaster 1971). Some nonhuman primates (the female rhesus) do not even require exposure to adult maternal role models for their greater infant interest to emerge. Monkeys raised on surrogate mothers (terry cloth figures) show the same sex difference (Chamove, Harlow & Mitchell 1967). And, the female preadolescents noted above, exposed *in utero* to masculinising hormones, show a significantly diminished interest in both doll-play and the wish to bear children.

CROSS-CULTURAL ASPECTS

Many societies include subgroups of young males and females whose dress and activities are more typical of the children of the opposite sex. Cross-gender behaviour is typically reported to begin during the earliest years and to remain as a lifelong behavioural feature. Cultures, other than our own, have generally accommodated to such behaviour, sometimes affording these children high priority status.

Among the Cocopa Indians of North America, males called 'e L ha' reportedly showed feminine character 'from babyhood'. As children they purportedly talked like girls, sought the company of girls and performed activities in women's style. Females known as 'warhemeh' sought a male peer group, constructed bows and arrows, and later fought in battles (Gifford 1933). The Yuma Indians identify young boys who during later childhood will be 'transformed into women'. Among the Mohave Indians a prestigious role was afforded the Shaman. These are priest-doctors who used magic. When boys, Shamans 'refuse to play with boys' toys or to wear boys' clothes. They pull back their penis between their legs and then display themselves to women saying "I too am a woman, I am just like you are!" ' Similarly, girls are described who rejected dolls, copied boys' behaviour and refused to don girls' attire (Devereux 1937; Green 1974).

Other cultures have practised similar customs. In Madagascar, among the Sakalavas, boys who were delicate and girlish in appearance were raised as girls. And, on the Aleutians, very handsome boys would also be brought up as girls, having their beard plucked at puberty (Westermarck 1917). Of especial interest in these accounts is the early onset of a lifelong cross-gender identity. What is lacking is how they got that way.

Female childhood cross-gender behaviour

Many preadolescent females show varying degrees of culturally masculine behaviour. However, female childhood cross-gender behaviour has not been well studied. Tomboyishness is much more common than is boyhood femininity and to a considerably greater degree the parental statement 'She'll outgrow it' is a valid prediction.

Research with adult females who request sex-change procedures indicate that some preadolescent tomboys do not outgrow their masculine orientation. How can this subgroup be discriminated from the larger population of masculine-behaving young girls whose teenage behaviour will be feminine? We have insufficient data in this regard. A few preadolescent females who insist on wearing boys' clothes, refuse to play with girls, insist on sports, trucks and guns, and say they want to be boys, have been evaluated. They appear to have a stronger degree of masculine identity than most tomboys and their behaviour begins to approximate that retrospectively described by adolescent and adult females who request sex change. However, this research is only in a pilot phase. A few case histories of such girls have been reported (Green 1974), but their significance must await the passage of time.

STUDIES OF FEMININE BOYS

Rationale and background

Sexual identity consists first of the self-concept of being male or female, secondly of sex-linked behaviours and attitudes, and thirdly of genital sexual orientation (towards males, females or both). The most atypical expression of all these components is found in transsexualism, in which persons identify with people of the opposite sex, show the sex-typed behaviour characteristic of the opposite sex, and are sexually attracted to persons of the same anatomic sex. They request contrasexed hormones and genital surgery so that they may live as persons of the other sex and have full civic status as members of that sex.

Methodological pitfalls await the investigator who wishes to fully understand the aetiology of atypical sexual identity by studying adult transsexuals. Reflections on early childhood experiences and behaviour are distorted by the passage of time, and other people (notably parents) are rarely available for corroboration of the transsexuals' remembered events or behaviour. These are better investigated by direct study of families with children in whom an atypical sexual identity is emerging. Toward this goal we constructed a composite picture of children whose behaviour was similar to that retrospectively recalled by adults requesting sex-change.

While both adult males and females request sex-change procedures, we focussed on boys' behaviour which seemed similar to that of adult males wanting to live as women. The reasons were several. First, more males than females eventually request sex change or show other aspects of atypical sexual identity (transvestism or homosexuality). Second, although the adult ratio favours atypical males, more girls show behaviour recalled by females requesting sex change (tomboyism). Thus, compared with tomboyism, feminine behaviour in boys is more likely to represent an enduring atypical identity. Third, feminine behaviour in boys is socially frowned upon, causing the boy and parents considerable distress. Tomboyism is not. Thus parents are more likely to bring the atypical boy for evaluation.

In the first study phase, adult transsexuals were interviewed. Twenty-five adult males requesting sex change gave retrospective reports that, in childhood, they had had atypical preferences for toys, clothing and playmates and ambiguity over whether they felt like boys or girls. Fifty-seven per cent had preferred girl playmates and only 3 per cent clearly preferred boys. Sixty-seven per cent preferred girls' toys and 48 per cent preferred girls' clothes. Nearly half did not recall unambiguously seeing themselves as boys. Next, a sample of boys with similar behaviour was collected. Sixty-five families with such children referred from a wide variety of agencies have been evaluated. The boys' age range is 4 to 10 years with about half between 4 and 7. They are anatomically normal (not intersexed) and come from a varied social background. Four families are black and five are Mexican-American.

Study procedure

Prior to the initial interview, the family was sent a simple behavioural item check list (The Cross-Gender Index) on which the parent notes whether cross-dressing, doll-playing, cosmetic use, female role-playing, feminine gestures, assertions of wanting to be a girl and the labelling of the boy as 'sissy' by peers occurs frequently, occasionally or not at all. If cross-gender behaviour is present at least frequently across most parameters, parents are seen together and singly for tape recorded interviews of 3 to 5 hours. Information is sought on the boy's feminine and masculine behaviour and parental attitudes towards each; the boy's appearance and behaviour as an infant and during the first 5 years of life; the availability of mother and father to the child during the first 5 years with comparative data on siblings; the parents' own childhood and relationship with their parents; parental psychosexual development; and the current marital relationship. Concurrently, the child was involved in a variety of testing procedures. These included the Draw-A-Person Test, the It-Scale for Children, the Family Doll Preference Test, the Parent and Activity Preference Test, the Playroom Toy Preference Test, and the Quick Test.

The Draw-a-Person Test requires that the child draw a person (Machover

1948); no clue is given as to whether a male or female should be drawn. The It-Scale presents the child with a card depicting a neuter stick figure (It). 'It' then selects, from a series of cards, masculine or feminine toys, articles, activities, clothes and playmates (Brown 1956). In the Family Doll Preference Test the child verbally composes a 10-minute story utilising doll representations of grandparents, parents, children of both sexes and an infant. The extent of time spent utilising each doll figure is recorded (Green 1974). The Parent and Activity Preference Test presents the child with 28 sets of two-card picture sequences which constitute the first two pictures in what will be a three-card sequence. One card depicts an adult male engaged in either a masculine, a feminine or a gender-neutral activity. The other depicts an adult female. Representative activities include car repair, dusting and reading. The third card is selected by the child from two options. One shows a child of the same sex as the subject having joined the male in his activity; the other shows the child having joined a female (Green 1974). The Playroom Toy Preference Test permits the child free access to a variety of culturally masculine and feminine toys. The time spent with each toy is recorded by an observer in the adjacent room via a one-way mirror (Green 1974). The Quick Test is a brief measure of intelligence (Ammons & Ammons 1962). The child is also interviewed regarding his understanding of why his parents brought him to the Clinic, his ideas about being a boy or a girl, his activity and role preferences, the reasons for them, and his understanding of anatomic sex differences and the possibility of becoming a girl.

Fifty families with a feminine boy were matched with a contrast family in which the same-aged (within 6 months) boy displayed culturally typical masculine behaviour. The families were matched for marital intactness, race, father's educational level and the child's sibling order (age and sex). Contrast families were obtained from newspaper advertisements offering payment for participation in a 'pleasant psychological study'. The identical procedures were carried out with the contrast family.

Feminine boys' behaviour

For all boys, cross-dressing began prior to their sixth birthday and for two-thirds it had started by the fourth. Articles worn included high-heeled shoes, dresses, jewelry and cosmetics. When genuine articles of feminine attire were unavailable, a variety of materials were utilised to improvise costumes. Large towels and adult-size T-shirts were simulated dresses and small towels or hooded jackets were used to simulate long hair. Cross-dressing was not an occasional activity. To the question: 'How often does your son cross-dress?', the typical mother's reply was 'As often as you let him'.

Playmate preference was for girls. 'Boys play too rough' was the typical reason given for avoiding male age mates. When playing house or mother–father games, 'mother' was the usual role taken. Since playmates were girls (who also wanted to be mother) the boys might role-play sister or teacher. 'I don't know what a daddy does' was one boys' reason for refusing to play daddy. 'Barbie' doll is the favourite toy. Hours at a time might be spent costuming and recostuming Barbie to the exclusion of all other play. Some parents attempted to divert their boys' attention to a male-type doll ('Ken'—Barbie's counterpart), however, they were unsuccessful. Feminine gestures and mannerisms were prominent, leading to the label 'sissy'.

The following quotes illustrate the boys' behaviour (see Green, 1974 for further details).

Onset of the atypical behaviour Mother A: 'It started out as he liked to play with high heels ... He always wanted my high heels' (at about 2, $2\frac{1}{2}$).

Mother B: At 2 years ... 'He liked to put things on his hair. Dish towels, anything that looked like hair. He would tie them with rubber bands ... As far as his feminine actions and everything, he's been like this since he was a very small child.'

Doll Play Dr.: 'What are his favourite toys?'

Father: 'Barbie ... Anything feminine. He's got two GI Joes, and he doesn't play with them.'

Mother: 'It's kind of embarrassing when he says. "I don't want to (play with those children) because they don't have any dolls." '

Pictures drawn Mother: (He draws) 'Girls. Only girls. Practically refuses to draw pictures of boys. ... He says "I don't know how to draw a boy ... I can't do it! I can't do it!" '

Attention to mother's clothes Mother: (He'll say) 'Oh, Mommy, can I pick out what I want you to wear?' or ... 'Comb your hair *this* way.'

Peer group teasing Mother: 'I told him, "Go out and play with the boys" ... And when he tries ... they tease him and make fun of him and they don't want to play with him.'

Reasons for wanting to be a girl Boy (age 5): 'Cause you dress up in makeup—cause you dress in girls' dresses, which I like the best ... Girls, they don't have to have a penis ... they can have babies. ... I wish I was a girl.'

Mother's attitude   Mother: 'He has put on my bathrobe, my nightgown ...
I've caught him in a slip ... a half slip that looks like a skirt ... I thought
it was a little normal stage.'

    Dr.: 'When did he begin?'

    Mother: 'When he was 4. I probably thought it was cute.'

Psychological testing

Feminine boys had scores which were similar to same-aged girls but different
from same-aged boys. Unlike typical boys, they were more likely to draw
a female first on the Draw-a-Person Test (see Green, Fuller & Rutley 1972).
On the It-Scale their toy and activity preferences were decidedly feminine
with scores in the normal range for girls (Green, Fuller & Rutley 1972). On
the Family Doll Preference Test their fantasy play, like that of typical girls,
utilised female family members more than male family members and also
often included the infant doll. The control group boys utilised the male figures
more and spent relatively little time with the infant (Green & Fuller 1973).
In the Parent and Activity Preference Test, feminine boys (and girls) more
often completed the picture sequence with the child having joined the adult
female in a feminine activity. The control boys more often selected the card
with the child and the adult male engaged in a masculine activity (Green
1974). In the experimental playroom, compared with the control boys, the
feminine boys and girls spent significantly more time engaged in doll play and
less engaged in truck play (Green 1974). Thus, in a variety of testing situations, the feminine boys behaved more like girls than boys of the same age.
Their identity, role and activity preference appeared to be feminine.

Aetiology

Systematic comparisons between the families of feminine and masculine boys
are needed to determine which factors or combination of factors (if any) are
critical for boys' atypical psychosexual development. However, the following
items seem to play a part:

1   Innate features which make rough-and-tumble, physically aggressive activities less appealing than sedentary behaviour.

2   Unusual physical beauty which influences adults to react to him as though
he were a girl.

3   Family encouragement (or absence of discouragement) for distinctly
feminine behaviour during the preschool years.

4   Being cross-dressed and otherwise treated as a girl by a parent or other
key figure during the preschool years.

5 Lack of psychological separation from the mother. This may result from excessive holding of a cuddly baby and from lack of other channels for the mother's affectionate, loving feelings (Stoller 1968).

6 Maternal overprotection of a young boy, with inhibition of rough-and-tumble play and male-peer-group interaction.

7 Unavailability of male playmates during the first years of socialisation, coupled with accessibility of female companions, resulting in the development of feminine social skills.

8 Absence of an older male figure who is invested with positive attributes and who may serve as an identity model during the boy's first years; and/or gross rejection by the father.

The development of boyhood femininity seems to follow a sequence of interactions. A mother considers her infant son to be unusually attractive and finds him very responsive to being held. She is able to devote considerable time to the boy and directs more attention toward him than toward any of her other children. During his early exploratory play, the boy finds mother's accessories—cosmetics, jewelry and shoes—attractive and begins to play with them. This play is considered cute, funny or least of no significance relative to later behaviour. The father interacts with the boy significantly less than the mother and may prefer another sibling. He, too, ignores the feminine behaviour. As the child moves out into peer group socialisation, either girls are primarily available or the available boys are considered by the boy and mother as too rough. An innate low level of aggressivity or low level disposition to rough-and-tumble play may make the companionship and socialisation experiences of females more agreeable. The son's activities and interests are more in tune with mother than father and lead to increased closeness with mother and distancing from father. With the start of school, the boy's greater comfort in culturally feminine activity sets him farther apart from other boys and results in his being labelled 'sissy'. The mother continues to be supportive or at least not discouraging of cross-dressing, doll-play and female role-playing. The father sees his son as rejecting his adult male role and withdraws further from the boy's life. During mid-grade school years, peer group teasing on account of the boy's preference for girl companions and activities, coupled with teacher or neighbour complaints of the boy's continuing feminine behaviour, causes the mother to reconsider its significance. She may then seek professional consultation, perhaps over her husband's objection that 'All boys go through that'.

A few interview excerpts illustrate some of these factors (see Green 1974 for further details).

Parental indifferent attitude   Mother: 'It never occurred to me to bring him anywhere.'

Dr.: 'How do you feel about his doll playing?'

Mother: 'There's nothing wrong with it.'

Father: 'I just thought it was something natural ... I figured it was just a fad.'

Overprotection by mother   'He was a very delicate baby. He didn't belong out there with the other boys. He belonged inside with me.'

Excessive attention by mother   Mother: 'I think he was made a lot over.'

Father: (The other kids), 'they got about 25 per cent of what he had. When he was a baby, there was your mother, and a sister or two ... as soon as he cried, he was picked up. But when we had the other two ... they cried, they cried.'

Father rejection   Mother: 'He wasn't as close to his father as the other brother ... his father was more proud of the oldest boy and his interest in sports ... they talked on the same level.'

Being cross-dressed by others   Mother: 'When it first started he was a year and a half and these two little girls took him and they dressed him up completely ... he started to play with dolls then.'

Father: 'Everyone thought it was cute.'

No male playmates   Mother: 'There were no boys on the street. ... From $2\frac{1}{2}$ to 4, he only had girl companions.'

Or, they may be unsuitable:

Mother: (there were boys) ... 'but he wouldn't play with them ... If they hit him he would cry and run upstairs ... He always found a girl friend to play with.'

Treatment

Questions have been raised as to the ethics of intervention into the lives of children with atypical psychosexual behaviour. Is there a basis for expecting or desiring that a child should manifest gender-role behaviour which is conventional for his culture? If he wants to wear a dress instead of pants or play with dolls rather than trucks, so what? Such idealism is challenged by the social milieu in which the child lives coupled with the milieu which will probably accompany adulthood. The very feminine boy is teased, bullied and ostracised. In spite of all that is written, read and said about a 'unisexed' movement, with a blurring of sex roles, that ethic has barely (if at all) filtered down to children. Today's feminine boy is being subjected to a degree of stigma comparable with that experienced by the 'sissy' of a generation ago. Those who come to us are unhappy in consequence of peer group pressure. While privately we might wish to immediately eradicate sexism within our culture, such a goal remains out of reach. More basis exists for optimism in promoting change in the individual child.

What of the change to be promoted? Are the boys to be forged into aggressive, athletically driven males devoid of aesthetics and sensitivity?—hardly. An alternative is available. These boys' gender role orientation is skewed so greatly as to preclude options for what the culture encompasses under 'boyish' behaviour. They cannot effectively integrate into a male peer group because they lack the required confidence and social skills. They may, however, with assistance, be able to experience comfort in playing with boys *and* girls, not just girls. Though they may see no positive feature in being a boy and maturing into a man, are they to be reassured that with modern endocrine and surgical technology they should just be patient and in a decade will 'change sex'? What of the fact that males who undergo such procedures do not become normal females but harbour a flaw in their female sexual identity—the inescapable biographical fact that they were born with male genitalia?

The primary goals of intervention for those boys unhappy over their current behaviour is to increase their comfort in being anatomically male, to enable them to perform some behaviours appropriate for boys of their age and to promote a positive anticipation of an adult male role.

We have initiated several strategies to reach these goals. First, we have utilised an adult male as therapist. By the nature of his authority, and comfort in being male, it is hoped that the boy's identification with this person will be effected. If he does not already know, then the boy is told the anatomical and physiological differences between boys and girls, men and women. The irreversibility of these differences is stressed, with the philosophy that it makes more sense to learn to be satisfied with what you are than strive for something impossible.

When feminine gestures and mannerisms label him sissy, the boy is alerted to the way he walks, talks or uses his hands, which results in teasing.

An attempt is made to find a male peer group which will not reject the feminine boy, thus permitting him to develop comfort in a wider range of social situations than previously experienced. This may necessitate the parents scouting for other boys in the school or neighbourhood, who are themselves not overly aggressive or rough-and-tumble, and invite them home to provide a new milieu for their son. Boys who reject the 'traditional' roles of the young male, with the priority role given sports and aggressivity, may rebound to the 'only' alternative—a female milieu. However, a third world exists—one which will cause them less social discomfort.

An attempt is made to promote a closer father son relationship where one of alienation exists. Activities may be found which are mutually agreeable to both father and son which will enhance the quality of their interaction, and hopefully promote a more positive male identification. These boys' fathers need to know that their sons are not innately aggressive, rough-and-tumble boys and are not suited to athletics. Their sons should not be thrust into Little League or another highly competitive activity which will alienate them further from the male peer group. A different kind of father son group experience, such as 'Indian Guides' may prove compatible. Boys and fathers share activities within the competence of the boy and which can be fun for the father. The boys' aesthetic interests are met by handicrafts, outdoor camping and cooking. Sports are not featured.

Typically, fathers of feminine boys are alienated from their sons. This may result from the boy having rejected the father's activities and from the father withdrawing to focus affection on another sibling. Because of their sons' feminine orientation, fathers may see themselves as having failed to provide male identification. Or, fathers may be overly demanding of masculinity in their sons, causing the boys to withdraw and the fathers to react to the withdrawal by anger and rejection. Some fathers' image of ideal masculinity may be so far from the capacity of the boy that an *identification gap* ensues. The special nature of his son's interests and the special effort needed to promote comfortable interaction should be discussed with the father (see Green 1974, for detailed strategies).

Parental reinforcement for the boy's femininity can be interrupted. Prior to referral, the typical parental response has been positive or neutral. No consistent pattern of discouragement has been practised. The boys may have been shown off to other adults while cross-dressed, posed while cross-dressed for pictures for the family album and laughed at in an accepting way. Or, more subtle forces may have operated. Parents may have discouraged male peer group contact because boisterous play is less tolerable than quieter doll-play with girls. A boy manifesting feminine behaviour which does not elicit parental disapproval may see his parents as supportive of that behaviour. Whatever the style of encouragement, overt or covert, the parents can be sensitised to the manners by which they are promoting behaviour which is causing conflict for their son.

Father's image and life-role may provide additional negative input to the boys' anticipation of male adulthood. A father denigrated by his wife and lamenting his job does not provide a compellingly positive image for current identification or future behaviour. Many children lack a clear idea of what their father does away from home during the workday, a vacuum which can be filled by imagery from a trip to place of employment and positive input from father's coworkers. In families in which marital role-division is decidedly skewed, with mother the sole decision-maker and provider of sustenance to the child, an equalisation of influence can be encouraged.

Boyhood femininity—meaning and treatment

It is not only the retrospective reports of transsexuals which suggest that gender role behaviour in boyhood portends atypical adult sexuality. One-half of a sample of 500 transvestites recalled the onset of cross-dressing as being prepubertal (Prince & Bentler 1972). For these males it endured and took on a fetishistic component. Reports by many adult male homosexuals also suggest that certain behaviours, culturally labelled feminine or non-masculine, more frequently constitute their childhood. Bieber and colleagues (1962) described 200 homosexuals and heterosexuals in psychoanalytic treatment. Thirty-three per cent of the homosexuals recalled preferring girls as playmates versus 10 per cent of the heterosexual sample. Less than 20 per cent of the homosexuals participated in competitive group games compared to 65 per cent of the heterosexuals. Saghir and Robins (1973) reported that two-thirds of 72 homosexual males (one-fourth of whom had been in or were in psychotherapy) described themselves as having been 'girl-like' during childhood versus only 3 per cent of the heterosexual control group. Three-fourths of those who were 'girl-like' recalled having had no male buddies, having avoided boys' games and having played predominantly with girls. All of them were called sissy and teased.

There are three follow-up studies of boys whose femininity was directly documented during boyhood. They lend the strongest support to the thesis that atypical gender role behaviour during boyhood is positively correlated with adult atypical sexuality. Green and Money have reevaluated five young adult males interviewed with their family about 15 years previously. Their boyhood behaviour had included statements of wanting to be a girl, dressing in girls' clothes, considerable doll-play, and gestures and mannerisms more typical of girls. Currently all of these men appear to be primarily homosexually oriented. A second study, also a follow-up evaluation of six males previously feminine during boyhood, found three to be homosexually oriented and one possibly transsexual (Zuger 1966). Lebovitz (1972) found that of 16 previously feminine boys, three were transsexual, two were homosexual and one was transvestic. Thus 15 of 27 atypical children are now atypical adults.

What if the feminine boy is pretransvestic—not pretranssexual? Are there social consequences during adolescence and adulthood which derive from the compulsion or need to wear women's clothing for sexual arousal? Apart from the illegality of cross-dressing in some areas (which may cease to be so), will not the transvestic male experience greater difficulty in finding a compatible dating or marital partner? Will not intrafamilial conflict result from the question of cross-dressing in the presence of the couple's children?

What if the feminine boy is prehomosexual, without subsequent desire to change sex or cross-dress? Will the results of the current efforts by the homophile movement (gay liberation groups) be successful in changing laws and public opinion so as to render the adult homosexual's life comparable to that of the heterosexual? Can we expect a style of behaviour, which is illegal in 75 per cent of the USA (and much of the remainder of the world), considered a sin by most organised religions and a social threat by so many people, to be comfortably embraced in time for today's prehomosexual boy? While laws may become equitable and religions more tolerant, if extrapolation from other societal biases is valid (such as religious and racial prejudice) how much basis is there for optimism with homosexuality? Two males engaging in anal intercourse may well remain anathema, or at the least offensive to most people, for at least a generation.

What can be expected from behavioural intervention during preadolescence? If the very feminine boy is pretranssexual, pretransvestic or prehomosexual, at what ages will intervention yield an effect? And, on which components of sexual identity?

Most of the adult transsexuals interviewed in our research were not treated during childhood. Their parents had considered their behaviour to be a 'passing phase' and not until adolescence or adulthood was professional help sought (Green 1974; Stoller 1968). Both basic identity (female) and gender-role behaviour (feminine) remained atypical. Sexual partner orientation became directed toward same-sexed persons. Most transvestites who have completed biographical questionnaires report not having been treated during childhood or adulthood (Prince & Bentler 1972). Most adult male homosexuals were also not treated (nor recognised as atypical) during childhood. A few feminine boys seen by Green and Money some 15 years ago in a pilot study were 'treated' only so far as inculcating the idea that they could not become girls. Their parents were advised to discourage feminine behaviour. At follow-up their basic identity was male, their gender-role behaviour masculine and their sexual orientation homosexual. On the basis of these reports and additional research we can speculate as to which aspect(s) of sexual identity are influenced by intervention during childhood.

Age at referral is a first consideration. Basic sexual identity is incorporated during the first 3 years. While it continues to be overlaid during the next 2 to 3 years (and to a lesser degree beyond) much has been affected by the time the atypical male is first seen (usually 7 or 8). With a younger child, both basic sex identity and the child's satisfaction with it, may be more fluid. However, clues revealing an enduring atypical identity are less clear at earlier ages, and most parents do not recognise them even if present.

In the case of children whose identity includes both male and female components, perhaps sufficient comfort with typical gender role behaviour may be introduced to preclude the transsexual's relentless quest for genital-altering surgery. Grossly feminine male children, through further identification with a male therapist and training in sex-typed physical behaviours, may come to appear more masculine. Social feedback from the peer group in the face of these new behaviours may in turn alter the boy's self-concept. Perhaps basic sexual identity may then change, granting a greater degree of comfort with anatomical maleness. The long-term effect may be that the person will not need to resort to years of hormonal and surgical intervention to make (as far as is technically feasible) the body fit the mind. If so, anyone who has interviewed a large number of transsexual adults should agree that much distress and many life hurdles will have been avoided.

Socialisation experiences in adolescence as well as childhood may influence sexuality. Many adult homosexuals report estrangement from their male peer group during preadolescence and early teenage. Whether this alienation led to wanting love from that group during later years, and/or was a reflection of an early identification with another peer group which *also* later seeks males (the female peer group), is speculative. Beyond this speculation, gross femininity in a male during early adolescence does pose extraordinary hurdles to developing heterosexual relationships and may augment opportunities for homosexual ones. Within the teenage social hierarchy, the grossly feminine male will probably hold a lower heterosocial ranking and be a less attractive partner for heterosexual dating. His femininity may also render him a more attractive partner for a homosexual male interested in feminine males, and further render him more vulnerable to homosexual assaults by sadistic 'heterosexual' males.

Study of the period of adolescence and its effect on adult sexuality remains a largely unharvested field. Initial postpubertal experiences may leave an enduring imprint. Self-image, in terms of desirability–undesirability, rapidly consolidates. The temporal association of fantasy, external experience and sexual pleasure provides new and varied linkages. The transient nature of many adolescent behaviours is widely acknowledged; this includes certain sexual behaviours. The incidence of fetishistic cross-dressing during adolescence which later disappears is unknown. By contrast, most early adolescent same-sexed genital experience is known to not endure as an exclusively homo-sexual preference (Kinsey, Pomeroy & Martin 1948). However, some adult homosexuals do assert they were conditioned into a homosexual life style by adolescent genital experiences. Whether this sexual pattern emerged pri-marily as a result of conditioning on a neutral behavioural substrate, or rein-forced a uniquely receptive substrate is not thoroughly researched. Finally, the picture for transsexualism is no clearer. There is one report of an ado-lescent patient who appeared transsexual but who was behaviourally reoriented to a male identity and heterosexual orientation (Barlow, Reynolds & Agras 1973). However, other adolescent transsexuals have persisted in their cross-sexed identity and at least one has undergone sex-reassignment surgery (Newman 1970).

Thus, modification of atypical psychosexual behaviour in preadolescent males may reduce social alienation during childhood, increase the oppor-tunity for heterosexual experiences (if desired) during adolescence and adult-hood, and preclude the quest for transsexual surgery.

REFERENCES

AMMONS R. & AMMONS C. (1962) The Quick test. *Psych. Rep. Monogr.* Supp. I–VII, 111–161

BAKER H. & STOLLER R. (1968) Sexual psychopathology in the hypogonadal male. *Arch. Gen. Psychiat.* **18,** 631–634

BARLOW D., REYNOLDS E. & AGRAS W. (1973) Gender identity change in a transsexual. *Arch. Gen. Psychiat.* **28,** 569–576

BERG I., NIXON H.H. & MACMAHON R. (1963) Change of assigned sex at puberty. *Lancet* **ii,** 1216–1217

BIEBER I. *et al* (1962) *Homosexuality: a Psychoanalytic Study of Male Homosexuals.* New York: Basic Books

BROWN D. (1956) Sex role preference in young children. *Psychol. Monogr.* **70,** no. 14 (whole no. 421)

CHAMOVE A., HARLOW H. & MITCHELL G. (1967) Sex differences in the infant-directed behavior of preadolescent Rhesus monkeys. *Child Dev.* **38,** 329–335

DEVEREUX G. (1937) Institutionalized homosexuality among the Mohave Indians. *Human Biol.* **9,** 508–527

DEWHURST C.J. & GORDON R.R. (1963) Change of sex. *Lancet* **ii,** 1213–1216

DIAMOND M. (1965) A critical evaluation of the ontogeny of human sexual behaviour. *Quart. Rev. Biol.* **40,** 147–175

EHRHARDT A. & BAKER S. (1974) Fetal androgens, human central nervous system dif-ferentiation and behavior sex differences. *In* Friedman R., Richart R. & Wiele R.L.V. (eds) *Sex Differences in Behavior.* New York: Wiley

EHRHARDT A., EPSTEIN R. & MONEY J. (1968) Fetal androgens and female gender identity in the early-treated adrenogenital syndrome. *Johns Hopkins Med. J.* **122,** 160–167

GESELL A. (1940) *The First Five Years of Life*. London: Methuen

GIFFORD E. (1933) University of California Publications in American Archaeology and Ethnology, vol. 31. University of California Press

GREEN R. (1974) *Sexual Identity Conflict in Children and Adults*. New York: Basic Books

GREEN R., FULLER M. & RUTLEY B. (1972) It-scale for children and draw-a-person test. Thirty feminine vs. 25 masculine boys. *J. Person. Assess.* **36,** 349–352

GREEN R. & FULLER M. (1973) Family doll play and female identity in preadolescent males. *Amer. J. Orthopsychiat.* **43,** 123–127

GREEN R. & STOLLER R. (1971) Two monozygotic (identical) twin pairs discordant for gender identity. *Arch. Sex Behav.* **1,** 321–327

HAMPSON J.L. & HAMPSON J.G. (1961) The ontogenesis of sexual behaviour in man. *In* Young W.C. & Corner G.W. (eds.) *Sex and Internal Secretions*, vol. II, 3rd edn. Baltimore: Williams & Wilkins

HARTUP W.W. & ZOOK E.A. (1960) Sex-role preferences in three and four year old children. *J. Cons. Psychol.* **24,** 420–426

HETHERINGTON E.M. (1967) The effects of familial variables on sex typing, on parent–child similarity and on imitation in children. *In* Hill J.P. (ed.) *Minnesota Symposia on Child Psychology*, vol. 1. Minneapolis: University of Minnesota Press

KAGAN (1964) Acquisition and significance of sex typing and sex-role identity. *In* Hoffman M.L. & Hoffman L.W. *Review of Child Development Research*, vol. I. New York: Russell Sage Foundation

KINSEY A., POMEROY W. & MARTIN C. (1948) *Sexual Behavior in the Human Male*. Philadelphia: W.B. Saunders

KOHLBERG L. (1967) A cognitive-developmental analysis of children's sex role concepts and attitudes. *In* Maccoby E.E. (ed.) *The Development of Sex Differences*. London: Tavistock Publications

LANCASTER J. (1971) Play mothering. *Folia Primat.* **15,** 161–182

LEBOVITZ P. (1972) Feminine behaviour in boys: Aspects of its outcome. *Amer. J. Psychiat.* **128,** 1283–1289

LEV-RAN A. (1974) Gender role differentiation in hermaphrodites. *Arch. Sex Behav.* **3,** 391–424

MACCOBY E.E. & JACKLIN C.N. (1975) *The Psychology of Sex Differences*. London: Oxford University Press

MACHOVER K. (1948) *Personality Projection in the Drawing of the Human Figure*. Springfield, Illinois: Charles C. Thomas

MONEY J. & EHRHARDT A. (1973) *Man and Woman, Boy and Girl*. Baltimore: The Johns Hopkins University Press

MONEY J., HAMPSON J.G. & HAMPSON J.L. (1955) An examination of some basic sexual concepts: evidence of human hermaphroditism. *Bull. Johns Hopkins Hosp.* **97,** 301–319

NEWMAN L. (1970) Transsexualism in adolescence. *Arch. Gen. Psychiat.* **23,** 112–121

PRINCE V. & BENTLER P. (1972) Survey of 504 cases of transvestism. *Psychol. Rep.* **31,** 903–917

RABBAN M. (1950) Sex-role identification in young children in two diverse social groups. *Genet. Psychol. Mon.* **42,** 81–158

RUTTER M. (1971) Normal psychosexual development. *J. Child Psychol. Psychiat.* **11,** 259–283

SAGHIR M. & ROBINS E. (1973) *Male and Female Homosexuality*. Baltimore: Williams & Wilkins

STOLLER R. J. (1968) *Sex and Gender: On the Development of Masculinity and Femininity*. New York: Science House

WESTERMARCK E. (1917) *The Origin and Development of the Moral Ideas*, vol. II. London: Macmillan

YALOM I., GREEN R. & FISK N. (1973) Prenatal exposure to female hormones: effect on psychosexual development in boys. *Arch. Gen. Psychiat.* **28,** 554–561

YOUNG W., GOY R. & PHOENIX C. (1964) Hormones and sexual behavior. *Science* **143,** 212–218

ZUGER B. (1966) Effeminate behavior present in boys from early childhood. I: The clinical syndrome and follow-up studies. *J. Pediatrics.* **69,** 1098–1107

CHAPTER 34

Mental retardation— medical aspects

B. KIRMAN

THE SCOPE OF THE PROBLEM

Mental retardation is not an entity. As the term implies, it is a relative concept. For some purposes an individual may be seen as mentally retarded, for others, not. He may attend a school for the educationally subnormal but then make a satisfactory social adjustment and cease to be a statistic. If the sole criterion of intelligence is taken many will be judged retarded. Patients who are occupying beds in hospitals for the mentally retarded are clearly labelled as being mentally subnormal or severely subnormal. Those living in their own homes are more difficult to enumerate. The position varies geographically and historically. The recent Census of Mentally Handicapped Patients in Hospital in England and Wales (Department of Health and Social Security, 1972) gives figures for the mentally handicapped in hospital per 100 000 population varying from 24 in Tynemouth to 294 for Lincoln. This 12-fold difference is remarkable in such a small and, at first glance, culturally and economically homogeneous country as England and Wales. Internationally, the differences are very much greater. Penrose (1963) quotes figures for about 1935 ranging from 146 for Denmark and 1 per 100 000 for Japan. The position in Japan has changed markedly since that time but in 'developing' countries which are beset by many other problems there is limited interest in or special provision for mental handicap.

Historically also, there have been remarkable changes. The numbers of the mentally handicapped in hospital in England and Wales rose from some 6000 in 1916 to some 64 000 between 1960 and 1970 when the numbers levelled off, partly as a result of a change in policy and partly because the hospitals were overcrowded. Dramatic changes are also to be seen in provision of school places for the educationally subnormal. From 1950 to 1969 the numbers rose from 15 000 to 53 000 in England and Wales. Similar considerations apply to training centres, provision of places in which rose from 12 000 in 1956 to 42 000 in 1968, though the demand was far from being fully met. These changes have been shown in graphic form and discussed in more detail elsewhere (Kirman 1976).

CLINICAL NEEDS

It will be evident, if only from the considerations mentioned above, that mental retardation is not entirely, or indeed primarily, a medical problem. Some cases are due to structural abnormality in the brain (Crome & Stern 1972). This is broadly true of all those with a major degree of intellectual retardation which may for practical purposes be defined as functioning with a mental age of less than half the average. There are exceptions to this general rule but at this point it should be noted that there is no single major cause for the majority of such abnormalities and, indeed, the cause is unknown in a majority of such patients, even when exhaustive investigation has been undertaken (Angeli 1971; Angeli & Kirman 1971). The only group of any size which emerges from such surveys is that of Down's syndrome which accounted for 16 per cent of our sample of children in hospital with a marked degree of mental retardation. There is evidence that such children now have a better chance of survival and Carter (1958) found a 4-fold increase in children with Down's syndrome surviving to the age of 10 years between 1929 and 1958. Similar considerations probably apply to other children with a comparable level of retardation. Nonetheless, Tizard (1964) found no evidence of any overall increase in the prevalence of the severer degrees of mental handicap since the time of Lewis' survey (1929).

It is clear that the great fluctuations mentioned above in provision for the mentally handicapped have little to do with the incidence of clinical entities and problems. They relate rather to the availability of resources for this type of social and educational need which tends to take last place in a hierarchy of demands. The problem of mental retardation arises in a developed society as better educational facilities become available and as greater demands in the way of technical education are made of the employee. Medical involvement is incidental to and peripheral to these major factors.

This is, however, not to belittle the role of the medical practitioner in this field. On the contrary there is need for much greater medical awareness and involvement in the problem. Ireland (1877) had some difficulty in persuading the managers at Larbert that a doctor was necessary and a negative attitude to mental handicap is still encountered within and outside the profession. This stems from lack of knowledge and failure to appreciate the value of medical work in this area. It is not possible to list all of the ways in which the medical profession may be involved. For a century the asylum or hospital doctor has had the care of an increasing number of people labelled as idiots or severely subnormal or mentally handicapped. At one time he attended to all their needs. He is now designated a psychiatrist and has the assistance of his colleagues in the somatic specialities. He is part of a multidisciplinary team with social workers, psychologists and others if he is fortunate. He is expected under the new regime to provide an area and community based service, together with the school medical officer and specialist in community medicine, hopefully, in close liaison with the general practitioner (Department of Health & Social Security 1971).

There can be no area of medical work which is not related to mental handicap. The more severely mentally handicapped child living at home is likely to visit his doctor more often because of proneness to respiratory and other incidental infections. He is likely to be the subject of advice from the family doctor to the parents and may need to be referred to appropriate specialists. The medical adviser may also be interested in procuring necessary aids or housing or other facilities for such a child or may be interested in the type of education provided. He is likely to be asked for advice on specific problems such as enuresis, temper tantrums, hyperactivity, head-banging, self-destructiveness or more general difficulty in management. Problems which parents may take in their stride with a normal chiild because they are shortlived persist for months and years with the more severely handicapped and may place undue strain on the mother and other members of the family.

The general practitioner is also likely to be involved with the mentally retarded because of multiplicity of handicap. The retarded child may also suffer from a heart lesion as in Down's syndrome or have a squint, or perhaps a cleft palate. About 10 per cent of children operated for spina bifida suffer from 'severe subnormality' (Abbas 1971; Spain 1969; 1970). There is a considerable overlap between mental handicap on the one hand and epilepsy or cerebral palsy on the other so that about one-third of our hospital population of children with severer degrees of mental handicap have epilepsy and about one-third have cerebral palsy (Donoghue *et al* 1970). The family doctor with an intimate knowledge of his practice will be aware of the much larger proportion of his patients who are of limited intelligence as distinct from those who have a major degree of mental handicap. As a rough working basis the latter group will comprise some 0·4 per cent of the child population at age 7 whilst the mildly retarded, i.e. those below IQ 70 and above IQ 50 on a standard test make up to a total of 2·2 per cent.

It should be emphasised that these figures are a very rough guide only. On the one hand the incidence of severe handicap in infancy is higher than the 7-year-old figure since there is heavy mortality in this group. Half of children with Down's syndrome fail to reach the age of 5 years (Collmann & Stoller 1963a, b). The mortality for similarly handicapping conditions is comparably raised (Forssman & Akesson 1970; Richards & Sylvester 1969). On the other hand, especially with mild mental handicap, intelligence is only one facet of the personality and social competence. In this connexion the triaxial classification recommended by Rutter *et al* (1969) is applicable to mental retardation. This approach considers clinical problems and behavioural problems as well as intellectual development, mentioning social difficulties as a fourth axis. The mildly retarded youngster may have little referral to his doctor if he is emotionally stable, has no superadded clinical difficulty such as epilepsy, and if he has a good home and a well knit adequate family with sufficient resources. The practitioner who knows the families in his care well will, however, know that among his patients are some who need special handling because of limited intelligence; perhaps they need very simple explanations, they may be unable to read instructions on the medicine bottle, they may be unable to understand advice in the same way as their more intelligent brothers and sisters; they are more likely to be brought to the surgery with their parents even when they are adolescent. They are very likely to be over-protected by their parents at this stage and the general practitioner may help in overcoming this difficulty.

The research worker, the geneticist, the community physician, the obstetrician and the paediatrician are among those who want to know much more about mental handicap so that it can be prevented or its incidence reduced. Whilst the perennial discussion as to the role of nature and nurture continues undiminished, this argument becomes increasingly academic in the face of much evidence to show that improvements are possible, principally by modification of the environment, though also by such measures as genetic counselling, family planning, amniocentesis and selective termination of pregnancy when this is wished. As Peel (Butler & Alberman 1968) points out in his introduction to the second report of the British Perinatal Mortality survey: 'More and more importance today is being attached to the possible environmental influences operative during pregnancy and labour upon the later growth and development of the child.' Further reports of the National Child Development Study convert the possibility into a certainty, leaving no room for doubt that if the less advantaged children could be brought up to the level of the most advantaged in respect of maternal health, environment during and about the time of delivery and in early life, there would be a marked reduction in the problem of mental handicap (Pringle *et al* 1966; Davie *et al* 1972). From the genetic angle there is a steadily increasing gain of knowledge in areas of disturbed metabolism, as an example of which may be quoted recent work in the mucopolysaccharidoses which has led to tentative attempts at treatment, and to the possibility of real therapy at an early date (Fratantoni *et al* 1969; Benson *et al* 1970). An interesting example of the interaction of genetic anomaly and environment was noted in the survey by Angeli and Kirman (1971) mentioned above in the course of which a mother of seven markedly retarded and microcephalic children herself proved to be a sufferer from phenylketonuria. In regard to genetic counselling Carter (Berg 1971) reported on a follow-up of 400 cases who had attended for genetic advice; of this group 142 parents had a child with severe mental handicap. Of these, 34 couples were again given a high risk of recurrence. This study showed that genetic advice given was on the whole reliable and that parents tended to take the advice. It should, however, be emphasised that cases of mental handicap in which aetiology can reliably be established are in a minority and that of these only a small number can be shown to be due to a single major genetic factor. This is not to say that useful practical and psychotherapeutic advice cannot be given to parents. This consideration alone makes adequate clinical examination of all cases of mental handicap imperative (Kirman 1971).

CLASSIFICATION

There is insufficient knowledge of the nature of mental handicap to permit of any very satisfactory classification. The American system (Heber 1959) is a pragmatic approach which is an improvement on previous efforts. It uses similar categories to those employed by Penrose (1938) in his classical Colchester survey and a useful analysis of a hospital series on this basis has been carried out by Roboz and Pitt (1968; 1969; 1970; 1971). To be useful a classification should be adapted for the purpose for which it is intended. The international classification of mental handicap involves the concept of different levels of intelligence or mental age which is of obvious value to the educationist and may be employed by the physician when giving advice to the parent on prognosis and handling; though due caution and great knowledge of the subject is necessary, especially in considering the young child (under 5 years, or those with multiple handicap). Definition by intelligence quotient is not included in the current Mental Health Act but is to be preferred to vague estimates based on subjective impressions or 'do it yourself' tests (Carr & Stephen 1964; Table 34.1).

In our latest hospital survey quoted above we were concerned with the genetic risk and wished particularly to find out what the risk of a subsequent sib being affected was, when no precise aetiological diagnosis could be made. For this purpose we needed three or at the most four groups of cases, those due to genetic causes, those of environmental origin and those, the cause of which was not known. This scheme is an ideal one and not wholly practical in the present state of development. So often the necessary data are not available, though records of pregnancy and perinatal events are now much more adequate. A necessary fourth category is that which includes conditions thought to be due to multiple factors such as hydrocephalus with spina bifida. The use of any such system involves many arbitrary decisions as to whether environmental or genetic factors are thought to be of major importance in determining the handicap.

Most classifications are much more complicated than this and involve a variety of categories other than the aetiological. Both Penrose and Roboz and Pitt employed a category which took into account neurological impairment other than mental handicap itself. This is, of course, relevant to the question of care, since if there is a neurological condition, such as athetosis or hemiplegia, there are different care needs and job prospects than if the patient is able-bodied. Kushlick's approach is more informative in this respect and will commend itself to those who have to look after hospital populations, or

Table 34.1   Degree of mental handicap

Contemporary term	Intelligence quotient	Old statutory term	Current statutory term	Other
Mild retardation	50–70	Feeble-minded	Subnormal	Educationally subnormal (children) Moron
Moderate retardation	35–49 ⎰	Imbecile ⎱	Severely subnormal	
Severe retardation	20–34 ⎰			
Profound retardation	0–19	Idiot ⎰		

hostel cases or are dealing as school medical officers with children attending schools for the educationally subnormal (including those schools which were designated as training centres prior to the implementation of the 1970 Education Act). Kushlick graded patients as to whether they were ambulant, clean, dry and as to the amount of help they needed in feeding, washing, dressing etc. (Kushlick 1970; Stephen 1970). This approach was used in the recent census (Department of Health and Social Security 1972) and yielded a large amount of very valuable information as to the degree of dependence of patients at present occupying hospital beds for the mentally handicapped.

The problem about most methods of classification is that they involve categorisation of different types of phenomena. On the one hand we have classification by intellectual level, which is very useful but tells us little about aetiology. Classification by degree of incapacity is also valuable but does not cover the clinical aspect. Some clinical categories, such as phenylketonuria, are precise, though even here more sophisticated knowledge recognises multiple alleles at the one locus, one of which may be associated with benign hyperphenylalaninaemia and combinations of which may produce very complex genetic situations (Woolf *et al* 1968; Woolf 1970). Other categories are morphological and dependent on a subjective impression since the individual components of the '*Gestalt*' are difficult to measure. To some extent these are capable of being objectified and Donoghue among others has attempted to do this for Down's syndrome (Donoghue, 1975; Hilliard & Kirman 1965). It is now possible to check this particular morphological concept against laboratory criteria, i.e. the karyotype, which demonstrate that the notion conceived by Down (1866) of a clinical entity was fully justified. Another such concept which has been validated by laboratory tests is that of gargoylism (McKusick 1969). Contemporary classification of this group of disorders depends on the chemical characteristics of the inclusion and on the output of excess metabolites in the urine; but is now extending, as in other metabolic disorders causing mental handicap, such as galactosaemia, to identification of the faulty enzyme.

Metabolic disorders such as the mucopolysaccharidoses, however, have another means of identification in that they conform to a classical pattern of transmission, being autosomally inherited in the case of the Hurler and Sanfilippo syndromes or sex-linked in the case of the Hunter syndrome. In some cases the diagnosis is self-evident from the family pattern as with the woman who recently consulted the author on account of an affected son by two different partners. This circumstance together with the characteristic morphology made the diagnosis of Hunter's syndrome self-evident though it is possible to confirm it both by classical chemical techniques and the new cross matching procedure (Ferrante *et al* 1971). Classification based on a single feature may be unjustified and may distract attention from multiplicity of causation. This applies to microcephaly, cataract and to ichthyosis. Microcephaly is very commonly associated with severer degrees of mental retardation and it is customary to speak of 'true microcephaly' as an entity. No support for this view was found in an extensive study (Brandon *et al* 1959) and it should be recognised that microcephaly is the common end product of many different processes which may be environmental or genetic in nature. Similar considerations apply to cataract, the association of which with mental handicap does not define a syndrome. There are, however, some families in which such a genetic entity can be established by its mode of transmission (Sjögren 1935). In the same way the association of ichthyosis with mental handicap is not sufficient to identify a syndrome since there are several which produce this combination (Wells & Kerr 1965; 1966).

There is a qualitative change in clinical findings on moving to the left down the somewhat skewed but near Gaussian curve of distribution of human intelligence. The mildly retarded look like dull normal people whereas the more severely handicapped seem conspicuously different. The continuum can be seen better if developmental concepts such as those of Piaget are employed; and even the profoundly retarded show a similar sequence of developmental stages to the normal (Woodward 1959). The obvious difference in appearance and quality of ability between the more severely handicapped and the simple-minded has led to the notion that the mildly retarded are part of 'normal variation', or to be seen as part of a 'subcultural' group (Lewis 1933), whilst the majority of the more severely mentally retarded, who are responsible for the skewness of the curve of distribution of intelligence, are seen as being pathological. This type of classification oversimplifies the problem and merely restates it in statistical terms. It does not clarify our understanding of what causes normal variation and what causes pathology. There is in reality a large overlap between these two concepts. Much of normal variation is due to adverse factors producing varying degrees of pathology and interacting with variation in genetic potential. The difference is that there is to be found more gross pathology and more evidence of major causal factors, be these genetic or environmental, among the more severely handicapped. This applies to major gross chromosomal errors, point mutations, meningitis, perinatal anoxia, lead poisoning and hundreds of other agents which damage the brain. It is self-evident that all of these adverse factors can act in lesser degree, depressing cerebral function to a milder extent.

CLINICAL EXAMINATION

It is always desirable to attempt an aetiological diagnosis of mental handicap despite the fact that the best efforts may be unsuccessful. A detailed history is essential. The author recently saw a profoundly retarded child where measles vaccine encephalitis was thought to be the causal factor. However, it was noted that the parents were first cousins. The initial diagnosis may be correct but the less likely possibility of one of the leucoencephalopathies (formerly known as Schilder's disease) must be excluded. The occupation of the parents must be noted in as precise a manner as possible, i.e. the actual job and the degree of responsibility. An effort should also be made to assess the schooling and educational level of the parents. This has a 2-fold purpose; mildly handicapped parents may have mildly handicapped children, though the tendency is to revert towards the mean. The intelligence of the parents and their educational level will also have a bearing on their attitude to the handicap in their child. Details should also be obtained about the grandparents, both from the genetic angle and because of the present role which they may play in helping the parents to cope with the handicapped member of the family. A note should be made of the number of sibs of either parent and such details of their children as can be obtained with a special note of any who might be thought to be retarded, epileptic or otherwise handicapped. Permission should be obtained if possible to follow any such leads by writing to the hospital or the doctor concerned with the affected relative. Similar considerations are particularly relevant in the case of sibs and a careful note should be made of abortions and miscarriages. In some cases autopsy reports may be available on deceased sibs. A note of the name and date of birth of each sib should be made as this will help in assessment of the total family situation and provide a basis for counselling, as well as providing a framework for genetic advice.

The obstetric history

A careful history of the pregnancy should be sought and in this connexion a note should be made of the date of the marriage. The health of the mother during the pregnancy, any vaginal bleeding, intercurrent illness, toxaemia or other complications should be noted. The amount and source of obstetric care should be recorded as also details of the place of birth, birth weight, length of labour, complications of delivery and neonatal history. This information is well worth taking in detail from the mother and can be taken down with advantage by a skilled social worker with experience in the field during her visit to the home. Letters should subsequently be written to the obstetrician in charge of the case or to the paediatrician concerned, or to any hospital in which investigation has been undertaken. Only in this way can a complete history be obtained, though it should be remembered that information provided by the mother as to early development is usually roughly accurate (Donoghue & Shakespeare 1967).

Early development

In some cases of mental handicap the diagnosis can be made before birth, for example, by amniocentesis, which provides cells of fetal origin for culture and for study of the karyotype and of enzymes (Nadler 1968; 1969; Nadler & Gerbie 1970; Navon & Padeh 1971). It seems just possible that future improvements in techniques of fetoscopy may permit prenatal detection of conditions such as spina bifida which may lead to mental handicap. However, these procedures are not without risk and should not be undertaken lightly. It seems likely that only a small minority of cases will be diagnosed by these methods which are used where there is a special risk. For example, the rare Lesch-Nyhan syndrome (Nyhan 1968) a form of congenital hyperuricaemia, can be diagnosed in the early stages of pregnancy by means of aminocentesis in time to permit of termination if this is required. Since this condition is sex-linked the simple establishment of female sex of the fetus will permit reassurance of the mother, whilst in the male assay of the relevant enzyme will decide the issue. Attention will, however, only be directed to the possibility of this type of anomaly by the previous occurrence of a case in the family. Another category of mother who will come for this type of examination is the woman over 40 years of age at the time of her pregnancy. The measure may also be legitimately resorted to when there is excessive maternal anxiety as to the outcome of the pregnancy even though there are no strict biological grounds for this.

The neonate

Careful examination of the newborn should raise the question of mental handicap in a minority of cases. Those at risk will include babies with a poor Apgar score, great delay in establishing respiration, gross hypoglycaemia, hypernatraemia, hyperbilirubinaemia and similar anomalies. The twin, especially the second twin is at special risk (Berg & Kirman 1960).

Time of recognition

It is self-evident that different modes of presentation of mental handicap are more likely to be encountered at different ages (Kirman 1958). Grosser malformations become apparent at or soon after birth. In another group failure to thrive will invoke the whole range of screening procedures for metabolic anomaly. Cerebral palsy will be apparent at an early stage and may manifest with failure of spontaneous movement of the limbs of one or both sides as in crying, alterations of tone, more usually increased but, especially at an early stage, sometimes decreased with excessive floppiness, failure to assume the horizontal position on ventral suspension, poor response to traction on the arms. Absence of the placing reaction may be particularly suggestive of severe defect of cerebral function (Zappella *et al* 1964; Foley *et al* 1964). The forms of neurological handicap associated with severe mental handicap are analysed by Foley (Kirman & Bicknell 1975). Spastic quadriplegia is the commonest form, but hemiplegia also occurs in a minority. Athetosis is not apparent in the newborn infant but gradually declares itself as movement patterns become more developed.

A minor but important group of children with mental handicap are those whose condition is due to new pathology acquired in infancy. These include those due to meningitis or encephalitis, to encephalopathy resulting from dehydration, trauma, carbon monoxide poisoning or lead poisoning. The 'battered baby' may suffer severe and irreversible damage to the brain. Lead becomes a problem when the child is old enough to indulge pica or an undifferentiated appetite (Bicknell 1967; Bicknell *et al* 1968). Most acquired brain pathology results in a static brain lesion but the child with lead poisoning may show progressive deterioration or improvement with treatment. There is a small group of progressive lesions of late onset which includes the neurolipidoses and the leucoencephalopathies. An important differential diagnosis of these conditions is subacute encephalitis due to the measles virus. This is to be distinguished from the sequelae to acute measles or measles vaccine encephalitis which is not progressive. Apart from serological clues the electroencephalogram may be helpful in making the distinction (Cobb 1966; 1968; Scollo Lavizzari 1968).

EPILEPSY

Like cerebral palsy, epilepsy is a frequent concomitant of mental handicap. It is more common in the severely than in the mildly mentally handicapped and more common in the profoundly retarded than in those above this level (Kirman 1956; 1957). Fits tend to become less frequent with increasing age. The type of fit also changes with age. Epilepsy may first draw attention to mental handicap. In infants the typical major attack is often modified; there may be salaam spasms, minor but long continued and diffuse jerking movements without full loss of consciousness; brief absences which may or may not be interpreted as classical petit mal. There is no essential difference between epilepsy occurring in the mentally handicapped and in those of better levels of intelligence. In fact the care of the mentally retarded affords a useful opportunity of studying epileptic phenomena and their treatment. Febrile convulsions are not essentially different from other epileptic attacks and should always lead to careful observation and assessment, though in many cases they are the only convulsive episode in the life of an otherwise normal individual.

The prognosis in infantile spasms is bad, especially when these are associated with hypsarrythmia (Friedman & Pampiglione 1971). These authors studied 105 children whose EEG records fulfilled their criteria for hypsarrthymia in the first year of life; some 7 to 13 years later, 25 per cent were dead and of the survivors 77 per cent were classed as subnormal, two-thirds severely subnormal in intelligence. It is usual to treat infantile spasms with steroids which often produce short-term benefit but there is no good evidence that the ultimate prognosis is affected.

TUBEROUS SCLEROSIS

This syndrome is worthy of special mention since it is not rare, occurring perhaps in 1 : 50 000 of the population (Pampiglione *et al* 1968) but this may be an underestimate since cases not associated with mental handicap are less likely to be detected. The condition usually remains undiagnosed until the pathognomonic rash of adenoma sebaceum (Figure 34.1) becomes obvious at some 3 to 4 years, though it may be suspected earlier on the basis of white naevi or of hypsarrythmia (Bundey & Evans 1959).

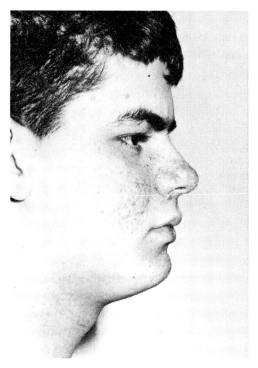

Figure 34.1   The typical rash (adenoma sebaceum) in tuberous sclerosis may not be obvious until about 4 years of age.

Unclassified encephalopathy   Even among the more severely mentally handicapped unclassified cases constitute the majority. In them, in the absence of fits or cerebral palsy, the defect may not be very apparent early and realisation of the retardation by parents and medical attendant may be much delayed. Much will depend on the experience and expectation of the parents and their opportunities for comparison with other children or on involvement of grandparents. Many parents worry unnecessarily but there are others who fail to notice gross defect. Regular clinic attendance provides some safeguard, with increasing professional awareness of mental handicap. Routine screening is impracticable except for such specific entities as phenylketonuria by the Guthrie test from heelprick and, at a later stage, for deafness by routine assessment of hearing. In every case, however, where there is any doubt as to progress, full investigations should be undertaken.

Investigations   These will include full clinical and neurological examination. Many children with severe retardation look normal anatomically, though

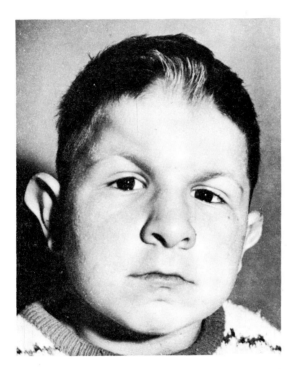

Figure 34.2   Rubinstein–Taybi syndrome with characteristic facies.

most are of reduced height for their age (Rundle 1970). Others have an odd look about them which may or may not amount to a recognisable syndrome (Figures 34.2 and 34.3). Many syndromes such as that of Franceschetti or Treacher-Collins are ill defined and may merge into one another. This applies to the Pierre Robin syndrome of which the most conspicuous component is micrognathia, but many persons of normal intelligence have a very small lower jaw. Similar problems apply to concepts such as oxycephaly or turricephaly. Walter Scott was considered to have an unusually tall head whilst Anatole France had a very small one. The Cornelia de Lange syndrome (Amsterdam dwarf) (Figure 34.4) is distinguished among other things by fusion of the eyebrows (synophris) (Berg *et al* 1970) and it may be that the clinician would be reluctant to make this diagnosis unless there was fusion of the eyebrows. Since judgements are usually formed in such matters on the relationships between features, rather than on the individual attribute, and on angles e.g. the slope of the eyes or inclination of the pinnae, measurement is difficult but can be applied to some aspects. Thus, the head circumference should always be noted and compared with norms such as those established by Westropp and Barber (1956) for age and sex. The author has arbitrarily

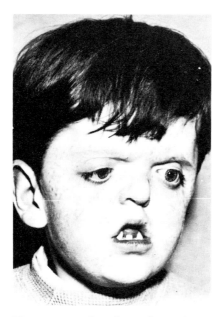

Figure 34.3 Apert's syndrome (acrocephalo-syndactyly).

accepted three standard deviations below such a norm as a definition of microcephaly. Dermatoglyphics may be helpful in some cases but they seldom define a syndrome. The atd angle is reliably large in most cases of Down's syndrome but for diagnostic purposes, in this as in other chromosome anomalies, direct investigation of the karyotype is more profitable. The study of hand and foot prints is time consuming and depends on a high level of expertise, being more in the nature of a research tool (Holt 1961).

The number of laboratory and special investigations which may be applied to a child with severe retardation is now considerable. Many of these tend to become routine, as resources and expertise increase. Some are, however, undesirable and the author would, for example, not recommend cerebral biopsy since information so gained is limited, unreliable and other methods, such as diagnostic appendicectomy, may provide the evidence required. Air studies should only be carried out if there is a specific indication, as in hydrocephalus. Full details of diagnostic tests are to be found in Crome and Stern (1972). A rough scheme is set out in Table 34.2

The ascertainment of mild retardation will almost always depend on psychological assessment and attention will first be directed to the problem by delay in achievements, e.g. as in dressing. In many cases it is only when school attendance has begun that a mild degree of retardation is appreciated.

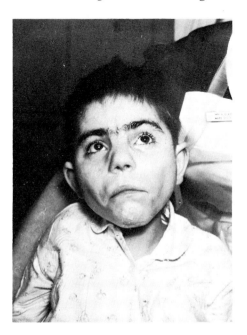

Figure 34.4 Cornelia de Lange syndrome showing synophris.

In a minority of cases a physical basis for the delay will be found. Some untreated cases of phenylketonuria have only a mild degree of retardation, this also applies to tuberous sclerosis, the Sturge Weber syndrome, to a minority of cases of Down's syndrome and a majority of some other chromosome errors such as Klinefelter's syndrome and Turner's syndrome. Mild retardation is perhaps commoner than the severer degrees with hypertelorism and acrocephalosyndactyly.

Some other medical problems   A major psychological problem with families of the mentally handicapped may stem from medical attitudes to care. In general the best rule seems to be to provide all the medical care which would ordinarily be available to the normal child. If this is accompanied by a kindly,

Table 34.2   Some special investigations in mental handicap

Time	Tests	Indication
Prenatal (12th–16th week)	Amniocentesis	(a) Age of mother ($>$40) (b) Previously affected child (e.g. maternal D/G translocation or hyperuricaemia in sib)
	Investigation of maternal serology	(a) rubella (b) ? syphilis, toxoplasmosis, cytomegalic disease, herpes genitalis (c) rhesus negativity (d) metabolic error in mother (e.g. maternal phenylketonuria)
Perinatal	Coomb's test (cord blood) serum bilirubin.	Rhesus negativity
	Galactose-1-phosphate uridyl transferase in erythrocytes (cord blood)	Previous galactosaemic child
Neonatal	Guthrie or modified Scriver (amino acid chromatography)	Routine on all babies
When retardation first noticed	Blood and urine chromatography. Spot tests for phenylketonuria, maple syrup urine disease, histidinaemia, homocystinuria.	All retarded babies
	Toluidine blue test on urine. Inclusion bodies in lymphocytes.	Suspicion of mucopolysaccharidosis.
	Protein bound iodine.	Any suggestion of hypothyroidism.
	Child's serology for evidence of intrauterine infection: rubella, toxoplasmosis, cytomegalic disease. Buccal smear.	All retarded babies.
	Chromosome studies on lymphocytes and/or fibroblast culture.	Dysplastic children and others if facility available.
	Blood lead	Pica, uncontrolled appetite or mouthing. Poor housing.
	EEG	Any epileptic feature, episodic behaviour disorder or doubt as to organic basis for retardation.

Table 34.2—*continued.*

Evoked potentials	Deafness and delayed speech development.
Appendicular biopsy	Genetic counselling—suspicion of neurometabolic disorder.
Specific enzyme studies	Family history or suspicion (e.g. in metachromatic leucodystrophy).

These investigations have a poor yield of positive results but such a programme is obligatory since treatment is sometimes possible, e.g. phenylketonuria and it is necessary for informal genetic counselling. In our hospital survey (Angeli 1971) 16 per cent of our series comprised patients with Down's syndrome and 5 per cent other genetic entities.

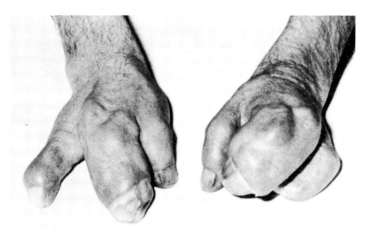

Figure 34.5 Hand in Apert's syndrome (acrocephalo-syndactyly): useful digits following plastic surgery.

interested and helpful attitude the parents will not feel that they or their child are rejected or unwanted. The more severely retarded are prone to respiratory difficulties arising in the main from inhalation of food or difficulty in clearing the air passages. These are mitigated by careful feeding and by frequent postural changes such as are likely to occur in normal home care of the baby. Infection may, however, supervene and require antibiotics.

Difficulty in feeding of the cerebral palsied child seems sometimes to be combined with imperfect absorption so that iron deficiency anaemia is not uncommon in the severely handicapped. Especially in patients on long term anticonvulsants, there may be a shortage of folic acid and of vitamin D, requiring supplements (Hawkins & Meynell 1958; Dent *et al* 1970). Associated physical abnormalities may require treatment (Figures 34·5 and 34.6). In some cases as in Down's syndrome this may be of the cardiac anomalies and the main aim of treatment is related to an extension of the span of life. In other cases as with rubella cataract surgical intervention may relieve the degree of psychological handicap and permit better social adaptation. It is evident that this consideration applies to correction of refractive errors and provision of suitable hearing aids.

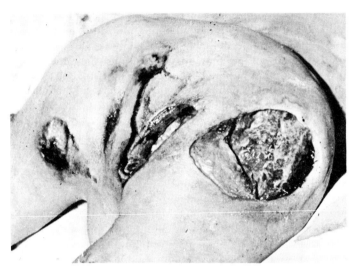

Figure 34.6 Congenital insensitivity to pain. A small proportion of children with mental handicap are totally dependent and require careful nursing to avoid bedsores. In the case illustrated absence of pain sense complicated treatment.

The lower the level of intelligence the greater is the likelihood of associated anomalies. Something like one-third of a resident hospital population of the more severely handicapped (IQ 50) will have epilepsy and a similar proportion cerebral palsy. In a recent survey of our hospital series (Donoghue *et al* 1970) of 285 children 101 had, or had had, epilepsy (36 per cent) whilst 130 (46 per cent) had cerebral palsy. Nine per cent had hydrocephalus. Twenty-five per cent of the group had a squint, and blindness or partial sight was found in 20 per cent, nystagmus in 11 per cent and other eye defects in 14 per cent.

The hold on life of the severely mentally handicapped is always precarious. Their existence may be terminated by such complications as status epilepticus or renal failure in tuberous sclerosis, more often by inhalation. There is no call for heroic treatment which is not normally available, but all accepted and routine methods of succour should be applied in the interests of the patient, the family, the medical and nursing attendants and of society generally. Whilst the aim of medical science is to reduce the total of mental handicap the care of those who are with us is an important criterion of civilised behaviour.

REFERENCES

ABBAS K.A. (1971) Personal communication

ANGELI E. (1971) *Genetic Prognosis in Mental Handicap*. MD Thesis. University of Athens

ANGELI E. & KIRMAN B.H. (1971) Genetic counselling. *Proc. 2nd Congr. internat. Ass. sci. Study ment. Defic., Warsaw, 1970*. Warsaw: Polish Medical Publishers

BENSON P.F., BOWSER-RILEY F. & GIANNELLI F. (1970) Beta-galactosidases in fibroblasts: Hurler and Sanfilippo syndromes. *New Engl. J. Med.* **283**, 999–1000

BERG J.M. (1971) (ed.) *Genetic Counselling in Relation to Mental Retardation*. Oxford: Pergamon

BERG J.M. & KIRMAN B.H. (1960) The mentally defective twin. *Brit. med. J.* **1**, 1911–1917

BERG J.M., McCREARY B.D., RIDLER M.A.C. & SMITH G.F. (1970) *The de Lange Syndrome*. Oxford: Pergamon

BICKNELL J. (1967) Selective pica and lead poisoning in a severely subnormal child. *J. ment. defic. Res.* **11**, 278–281

BICKNELL J., CLAYTON B.E. & DELVES H.T. (1968) Lead in mentally retarded children. *J. ment. defic. Res.* **12**, 282–293

BRANDON M.W.G., KIRMAN B.H. & WILLIAMS C.E. (1959) Microcephaly. *J. ment. Sci.* **105**, 721–747

BUNDEY S. & EVANS K. (1959) Tuberous sclerosis: a genetic study. *J. Neurol. Neurosurg. Psychiat.* **32**, 591–603

BUTLER N.R. & ALBERMAN E.D. (1968) *Perinatal Problems; the Second Report of the 1958 British Perinatal Morbidity Survey*. Edinburgh: Livingstone

CARR J. & STEPHEN E. (1964) Paediatricians and developmental tests. *Develop. Med. Child Neurol.* **6**, 614–620

CARTER C.O. (1958) A life-table for mongols with the causes of death. *J. ment. defic. Res.* **2**, 64–74

COBB W. (1966) The periodic events of sub-acute sclerosing leucoencephalitis. *Electroenceph. clin. Neurophysiol.* **21**, 278–294

COBB W. (1968) Depth recording in sub-acute sclerosing leucoencephalitis. *In* Kellaway P. & Petersen I. (eds) *Clinical Electroencephalography of Children*. New York: Grune & Stratton

COLLMANN R.D. & STOLLER A. (1963a) A life table for mongols in Victoria, Australia. *J. ment. defic. Res.* **7**, 53–59

COLLMANN R.D. & STOLLER A. (1963b) Data on mongolism in Victoria, Australia, prevalence and life expectation. *J. ment. defic. Res.* **7**, 60–68

CROME L. & STERN J. (1972) *Pathology of Mental Retardation*. 2nd edn. Edinburgh: Churchill-Livingstone

DAVIE R., BUTLER N. & GOLDSTEIN H. (1972) *From Birth to Seven: a Report of the National Child Development Study.* London: Longman

DENT C.E., RICHENS A., ROWE D.J.F. & STAMP T.C.B. (1970) Osteomalacia with long-term anticonvulsant therapy in epilepsy. *Brit. med. J.* **4**, 69–72

DEPARTMENT OF HEALTH AND SOCIAL SECURITY (1971) *Better Services for the Mentally Handicapped.* London: HMSO

DEPARTMENT OF HEALTH AND SOCIAL SECURITY (1972) *Census of Mentally Handicapped Patients in Hospital in England and Wales at the End of 1970.* London: HMSO

DONOGHUE E.C. (1975) Unpublished data.

DONOGHUE E.C., ABBAS K.A. & GAL E. (1970) The medical assessment of mentally retarded children in hospital. *Brit. J. Psychiat.* **117**, 531–532

DONOGHUE E.C., KIRMAN B.H., BULLMORE G.H.L., LABAN D. & ABBAS K.A. (1970) Some factors affecting age of walking in a mentally retarded population. *Develop. Med. Child Neurol.* **12**, 781–792

DONOGHUE E.C. & SHAKESPEARE R.A. (1967) The reliability of paediatric case history milestones. *Develop. Med. Child Neurol.* **9**, 64–69

DOWN J.L. (1866) Observations on an ethnic classification of idiots. *Clin. Lectures and Reports, London Hospital* **3**, 259–292

FERRANTE N., NICHOLS B.L., DONNELLY P.V., NERI G., HRGOVCIC R. & BERGLUND R.K. (1971) Induced degradation of glycosaminoglycans in Hurler's and Hunter's syndrome by plasma infusion. *Proc. nat. Acad. Sci. (Wash.)* **68**, 303–307

FOLEY J., COOKSON M. & ZAPPELLA M. (1964) The placing and supporting reactions in cerebral palsy. *J. ment. defic. Res.* **8**, 17–24

FORSSMANN H. & AKESSON H.O. (1970) Mortality of the mentally deficient: a study of 12 903 institutionalised subjects. *J. ment. defic. Res.* **14**, 276–294

FRATANTONI J.C., NEUFELD E.F., UHLENDORF B.W. & JACOBSON C.B. (1969) Intra-uterine diagnosis of the Hurler and Hunter syndromes. *New Engl. J. Med.* **280**, 686–688

FRIEDMAN E. & PAMPIGLIONE G. (1971) Prognostic implications of electroencephalographic findings of hypsarrythmia in first year of life. *Brit. med. J.* **4**, 323–325

HAWKINS C.F. & MEYNELL M.J. (1958) Macrocytosis and macrocytic anaemia caused by anticonvulsant drugs. *Quart. J. Med.* **27**, 45–63

HEBER R. (1959) *A Manual on Terminology and Classification in Mental Retardation.* Pineville: The American Association of Mental Deficiency

HILLIARD L.T. & KIRMAN B.H. (1965) (2nd edn) *Mental Deficiency.* London: Churchill

HOLT S.B. (1961) Quantitative genetics of finger-print patterns. *Brit. med. Bull.* **17**, 247–250

IRELAND W.W. (1877) *On Idiocy and Imbecility.* London: Churchill

KIRMAN B.H. (1956) Epilepsy and cerebral palsy. *Arch. Dis. Childh.* **31**, 1–7

KIRMAN B.H. (1957) Epilepsy and mental deficiency. *Congr. nat. Sci. méd. Commun. des Invités étrangers.* Bucharest

KIRMAN B.H. (1958) Early disturbance of behaviour in relation to mental defect. *Brit. med. J.* **2**, 1215–1219

KIRMAN B.H. (1971) Genetic counselling of parents of mentally retarded children. *In* Berg J.M. (ed.) *Genetic Counselling in Relation to Mental Retardation.* Oxford: Pergamon

KIRMAN B.H. (1976) *The Mentally Handicapped Child.* Amsterdam: Elsevier

KIRMAN B.H. & BICKNELL J. (1975) *Mental Handicap.* Edinburgh: Churchill-Livingstone

KUSHLICK A. (1970) Residential care for the mentally subnormal. *Roy. Soc. Hlth. J.* **90,** 255–261

LEWIS E.O. (1929) Report on an investigation into the incidence of mental deficiency in six areas, 1925–1927. *In Report of the Mental Deficiency Committee,* Part IV. London: HMSO

LEWIS E.O. (1933) Types of mental deficiency and their social significance. *J. ment. Sci.* **79,** 298–304

McKUSICK V.A. (1969) The nosology of the mucopolysaccharidoses. *Amer. J. Med.* **47,** 730–747

NADLER H.L. (1968) Antenatal detection of hereditary disorders. *Pediatrics* **42,** 912–918

NADLER H.L. (1969) Prenatal detection of genetic defects. *J. Pediatrics* **74,** 132–143

NADLER H.L. & GERBIE A.B. (1970) Role of amniocentesis in the intrauterine detection of genetic disorders. *New Engl. J. Med.* **282,** 596–599

NAVON R. & PADEH B. (1971) Prenatal diagnosis of Tay–Sachs genotypes. *Brit. med. J.* **4,** 17–20

NYHAN W.L. (1968) A genetic disorder of uric acid metabolism and cerebral function. *Proc. 1st Congr. internat. Ass. sci. Study ment. Defic., Montpellier, 1967.* Reigate: Michael Jackson Publishing

PAMPIGLIONE G., EVANS P.R., HARRIS R. & MOYNAHAN E.J. (1968) Aspetti electroclinici della sclerosi tuberosa. *Conferenze de Aggioramento Della Societa Italiana Di Elettroencefalografia e Neurofisiologia.* Napoli

PENROSE'S COLCHESTER SURVEY (1938) *A Clinical and Genetic Study of 1280 Cases of Mental Defect.* London: IRMMH. Re-issue 1975

PENROSE L.S. (1963) *The Biology of Mental Defect,* 3rd edn. London: Sidgwick & Jackson

PRINGLE M.L. KELLMER, BUTLER N.R. & DAVIE R. (1966) *11,000 Seven-Year-Olds.* London: Longman

RICHARDS B.W. & SYLVESTER P.E. (1969) Mortality trends in mental deficiency institutions. *J. ment. defic. Res.* **13,** 276–292

ROBOZ P. & PITT D. (1968) Studies on 782 cases of mental deficiency. Parts I and II. *Aust. paediat. J.* **4,** 79–95, 260–270

ROBOZ P. & PITT D. (1969) Studies on 782 cases of mental deficiency. Parts III and IV. *Aust. paediat. J.* **5,** 38–53, 137–148

ROBOZ P. & PITT D. (1970) Studies on 782 cases of mental deficiency. Part V. *Aust. paediat. J.* **6,** 185–191

ROBOZ P. & PITT D. (1971) Studies on 782 cases of mental deficiency. Part VI. *Aust. paediat. J.* **7,** 12–19

RUNDLE A.T. (1970) Anthropometry: a ten-year survey of growth and sexual maturation. *In* Richards B.W. (ed.) *Mental Subnormality: Modern Trends in Research.* London: Pitman

RUTTER M., LEBOVICI S., EISENBERG L., SNEZNEVSKIJ A.V., SADOUN R., BROOKE E. & LIN T.-Y. (1969) A tri-axial classification of mental disorder in childhood. *J. Child. Psychol. Psychiat.* **10,** 41–61

SCOLLO-LAVIZZARI G. (1968) Continuous EEG and EMG recordings during night sleep in a case of subacute sclerosing leucoencephalitis. *Electroenceph. clin. Neurophysiol.* **25,** 170–174

SJÖGREN T. (1935) Klinische und vererbungsmedizinische Untersuchungen über Oligophrenie mit kongenitaler Katarakt. *Z. ges. Neurol. Psychiat.* **152**, 263–292

SPAIN B. (1969) Estimation of the future school population of spina bifida children within London. *Quart. Bull. Res. and Intelligence Unit of the Greater London Council* **7**, 18

SPAIN B. (1970) Spina bifida survey. *Quart. Bull. Res and Intelligence Unit of the Greater London Council* **12**, 5–12

STEPHEN E. (ed.) (1970) *Residential Care for the Mentally Retarded.* Oxford: Pergamon

TIZARD J. (1964) *Community Services for the Mentally Handicapped.* London: Oxford University Press

WELLS R.S. & KERR C.B. (1965) Genetic classification of ichthyosis. *Arch. Derm.* **92**, 1–6

WELLS R.S. & KERR C.B. (1966) Clinical features of autosomal dominant and sex-linked ichthyosis in an English population. *Brit. med. J.* **i**, 947–950

WESTROPP C.K. & BARBER C.R. (1956) Growth of the skull in young children. I: Standards of head circumference. *J. Neurol Psychiat.* **19**, 52–54

WOODWARD M. (1959) The behaviour of idiots interpreted by Piaget's theory of sensori-motor development. *Brit. J. educ. Psychol.* **29**, 60–71

WOOLF L.I. (1970) Phenylketonuria and phenylalaninaemia. *In* Wortis J. (ed.) *Mental Retardation: an Annual Review*, vol. 2. New York: Grune & Stratton

WOOLF L.I., GOODWIN B.L., CRANSTON W.I., WADE D.N., WOOLF F., HUDSON F.P. & McBEAR M.S. (1968) A third allele at the phenylalanine hydroxylase locus in mild phenylketonuria (hyperphenylalaninaemia). *Lancet* **i**, 114–117

ZAPPELLA M., FOLEY J. & COOKSON M. (1964) The placing and supporting reactions in children with mental retardation. *J. ment. defic. Res.* **8**, 1–16

CHAPTER 35

Mental retardation—
psychiatric aspects

J. CORBETT

Over the past few years there has been a reappraisal of the role of the child psychiatrist in the care of mentally-handicapped children. This has arisen from three main sources. Firstly there has been an increasing dissatisfaction with the traditional demarcation between the role of the psychiatrist responsible for the general assessment and care of the mentally handicapped in institutions, largely separated from the community, and the child psychiatrist involved with the community services for children of normal ability—a demarcation which has led to critical comment from other workers in the field (Tizard 1966).

Secondly, with an increasing awareness of the ill effects of some aspects of institutional care on the handicapped child, together with a progressive difficulty in providing an optimal level of care in such institutions, there has been a move towards the provision of community services (DHSS 1971) in which the child psychiatrist will be increasingly involved.

Finally, there is greater interest in the similarities and differences between the psychiatric handicaps of retarded children and those of normal ability and this chapter will be concerned with reviewing our present state of knowledge of these psychiatric disorders and their treatment.

Mental subnormality and mental deficiency are administrative concepts with legal implications used to describe people who need the type of care or control provided by specialists in mental deficiency (Burt 1921). From a scientific point of view this can lead to confusion when any attempt is made to examine associations between mental disorder and mental retardation. When used in this way there is a tendency to include individuals as subnormal on account of their social handicap or social inadequacy which may be a result of emotional or behavioural disturbance. It was shown, for example, that a considerable proportion of people in mental deficiency hospitals were, in fact, of normal intelligence (Castell & Mittler 1965; O'Connor & Tizard 1954) and this was even true, although to a lesser extent in the case of children (Mittler & Woodward 1966). When investigating populations of this sort it is merely tautological to examine associations between mental handicap and psychiatric disorder as they are often synonymous.

The pitfalls associated with the use of social inadequacy as the sole criterion of mental defect have been discussed in detail by Clarke (1965), Lewis (1960), Wootton (1959), Rutter (1971) and others. They are particularly evident when comparisons are made between the numbers of individuals ascertained as mentally ill or subnormal in different cultures or within the same culture at different times. Thus, the statistics may vary considerably depending on the availability of employment and education, public attitudes to handicap and the facilities which are available for care and treatment.

It is for these reasons that, in examining the association between mental disorder and mental retardation, the use of the psychometric concept of intellectual retardation is more appropriate (Rutter 1971); the term 'mental handicap' being reserved for those individuals who because of additional social, psychiatric or physical handicaps associated with intellectual deficit require special services or treatment.

There are important problems in the use of standardised tests to measure intelligence (Tarjan *et al* 1972) but for all practical purposes in this country intellectual retardation may be considered to be equivalent to an IQ score at least two standard deviations below the mean; in other words, an IQ of 70 on a test with a mean of 100 and a standard deviation of 15. This means that 2·5–3 per cent of children fall into this category. Most of these are mildly retarded, with an IQ between 50 and 70 and their backwardness usually becomes apparent for the first time when they start school at the age of 5 or later at the age of 7 when they are seen to be making poor school progress. They are particularly difficult to detect before school age (Kirk 1952) and it is in this group that social factors are probably as important as biological factors (Birch *et al* 1970). Severe intellectual retardation (IQ less than 50) is much less common; the prevalence being between 3 and 4 per 1000 and nearly all of these children have organic brain disease.

THE RATE OF PSYCHIATRIC DISORDERS IN RETARDED CHILDREN

It has long been recognised that retarded children have a high rate of psychiatric disorder, but there have been surprisingly few systematic studies of the extent and nature of this association (Chazan 1964). Burt (1937) found that a third of the backward children he investigated had emotional difficulties and surveys of individuals of all ages in institutions for the retarded have shown high rates of mental disorder (Craft 1959; O'Connor 1951; Penrose 1938).

In studying mildly retarded children attending ESN schools, Chazan (1964) found that the rate of maladjustment was twice that in a control group of children attending normal school, but as not all mildly retarded children attend special schools, it is not possible to draw any firm conclusions from this study. Similarly, when the parents of severely retarded children in Tizard and Grad's (1961) epidemiological study were questioned about behaviour problems 43 per cent reported problems such as underactivity, overactivity or uncontrolled behaviour and the proportions were similar for children living in hospital, although little detail is given about the nature of the disturbance.

In a comprehensive epidemiological study of 9, 10 and 11-year-old schoolchildren living in the Isle of Wight (Rutter *et al* 1970a, b) it was found that 2·51 per cent were intellectually retarded, that is, they had a score 2 SD below the mean on the group screening tests and the short form of the WISC. Severe mental retardation ascertained during a further neurological survey of 5- to 15-year-old children on the island showed a prevalence of 3·1 per 1000. When behavioural questionnaires were completed by the parents and teachers 30 per cent of the retarded children were rated as disturbed by the parents and 42 per cent by the teachers which are three and four times respectively the rates found in a randomly selected control group.

In the severely retarded group, psychiatric disorder was assessed on the basis of standardised interviews with the parents and on psychiatric examination of the children it was found that 50 per cent of children with severe retardation showed psychiatric disorder compared with 7 per cent in the general population.

Although the rates of psychiatric disorder and behavioural disturbance were much raised in retarded children, there was little that was distinctive about the type of the disorder. The distribution of disorders found in this study was much the same as in children of average IQ and, at least in the mildly retarded group, the rates of neurosis, antisocial conditions, personality deviations and developmental disorders were all appreciably higher than in the general population. The same applied to individual items of behaviour and almost all types of deviance were considerably more frequent in retarded children. As might be expected, the association with low IQ was particularly marked in the case of poor concentration but items such as fighting, misery, unpopularity and stuttering were also appreciably commoner in children of low intelligence.

It is important to note that this association applied across the whole IQ range and not just at the retarded end; that is, deviant behaviour is more frequent in children of average ability than in those of superior intelligence just as it is more frequent in retarded children than in those of normal intelligence. Thus misery was reported in 3 per cent of the most intelligent boys and 6 per cent, 11 per cent and 20 per cent for successive IQ groups going from the highest to the lowest. The association between low IQ and both behavioural deviance and psychiatric disorder is therefore strong and clinically important. Although these epidemiological studies support the findings of hospital and clinic studies in showing that psychiatric disorders in mentally retarded children are as heterogeneous as in any other group of children, this particularly holds for the mildly retarded group. In spite of this there are certain disorders (namely psychosis and the hyperkinetic syndrome) and certain items of deviant behaviour (particularly stereotyped movements) which are more common in the retarded, particularly in the more severely handicapped, than amongst children of normal intelligence.

This was confirmed in an epidemiological study of severely retarded children aged 0–15 in an area of South East London (Corbett *et al* 1975). In this study there were 140 children with an IQ below 50 in a population of 175 000. Using similar standardised interviews with the parents and examination of the child it was found that 43 per cent of the children showed behaviour disturbance and this was somewhat higher in the 29 per cent of children who were admitted to long-term residential care from this area. In these severely retarded children childhood psychosis was present in 13 per cent of children, hyperkinetic disorders in 12 per cent and severe stereotypies in 5 per cent while neurotic and conduct disorders occurred in 3 per cent and 9 per cent of the children respectively. Thus, while the disorders in mildly retarded children are fairly similar to those in children of normal intelligence the distribution of disorders in severely retarded children is considerably different.

MECHANISM INVOLVED IN THE ASSOCIATION WITH PSYCHIATRIC DISORDERS

The very heterogeneity of psychiatric disorders makes it most unlikely that a single mechanism will be found to account for the association with intellectual retardation. Nevertheless, it is necessary to consider the relative importance of the possible mechanisms involved as treatment plans will have to take these into account.

First, it is necessary to get the direction of the association right. Although emotional disturbance may occasionally impair intellectual performance, that is not the explanation of the association. Low IQ generally antedates the psychiatric disorder so that the retardation or factors associated with it must lead to psychiatric disorder rather than the other way round.

This is confirmed by the results of longitudinal studies such as the British National Survey (Douglas *et al* 1968) where, in a representative sample of children who were followed from birth to maturity, it was shown clearly that low IQ in early childhood is associated with both neurotic symptomatology and delinquency as shown in adolescence.

Virtually all children with an IQ below 50 have demonstrable organic brain disease (Crome 1960) and this is also true for a substantial minority (25–50 per cent) of mildly retarded children (Rutter *et al* 1970b; Stein & Susser 1960). There is good evidence that children with organic brain dysfunction have a greatly increased susceptibility to psychiatric disorder (Rutter *et al* 1970a) and it may well be that brain damage in intellectually retarded children is in part responsible for their high rate of psychiatric disorder. In these children malfunction of the brain seems more important than loss of function. This is strikingly seen in the behavioural improvement which follows hemispherectomy in children with infantile hemiplegia associated with the behaviour disorder and epilepsy (Griffith & Davidson 1966; White 1961; Wilson 1970) when the child is often better off psychiatrically with only one hemisphere than with two, one of which is producing active electrical disturbance. Similarly, behavioural abnormalities are more frequent in children with fits and with other types of active brain disturbance (Eyman *et al* 1970; Anastasi 1968; Davis *et al* 1969). Often the behaviourally disruptive effects stem less from the brain lesion itself than from the effect of the lesion upon the remaining intact nervous system (Kennedy & Ramirez 1964).

On the other hand, it is evident that this cannot be the only factor because the rate of psychiatric disorder is high even in intellectually retarded children who have no evidence of brain damage and in severely retarded children there is some evidence that active brain dysfunction, for example seizures, are less strongly associated with behaviour disturbance than in children of more normal intelligence (Corbett *et al* 1975).

There is considerable evidence that social factors, for example social rejection, play an important part in causing emotional disturbance in retarded children. Children with a wide range of physical and mental handicaps tend to be less often chosen as friends compared with nonhandicapped children (Baldwin 1958; Soldwedel & Terril 1957). The relationship between such social rejection and psychological development is complex, and while rejection may adversely affect a child's emotional disturbance, children may equally be rejected just because of their undesirable behavioural characteristics (Jacobs & Pierce 1968). Temperamental features, such as poor adaptability to new situations, a high intensity of emotional response and a marked irregularity of physiological functioning, have been shown to be important in the genesis of behavioural disorders in children of normal intelligence (Rutter 1964; Thomas *et al* 1968; Graham & George 1972). It is likely that some of these temperamental characteristics which render a child more susceptible to behaviour disturbance are more common in retarded children and that they probably play some part in the causation of psychiatric disorder. For example there is some suggestion that very poor concentration, which is more common in retarded children, is a trait particularly irritating to parents and one that tends to have a poor prognosis (Tizard 1962).

Intellectually retarded children may be adversely influenced by the same kinds of family and social pathologies that are associated with disorder in children of average ability (Rutter 1970; Wolff 1970). Thus parental instability, unsatisfactory discipline and family discord may all lead to behaviour disturbance. It may be that retarded children are in some instances more vulnerable to such social factors and even that, in some instances, the presence of a handicapped child in the family may lead to disturbance in other members of the family, although the evidence on this is conflicting. Some studies have shown that the rate of broken homes in the families of retarded children does not differ from that in the general population, and similarly that there are no marked differences in the rate of parental neurosis (Erickson 1969; Rutter *et al* 1970a), or in the rate of behavioural disturbance amongst the siblings of retarded children compared with the normal population (Caldwell & Guze 1960; Wolfensberger 1968; Carr 1975). Where differences have been found there is some suggestion that they are associated with other stress factors in the family, for example increased maternal age, larger family size and lower social class, as in studies of siblings of children with Down's syndrome (Gath 1973; Carr 1974).

It is, however, likely that overall family pathology is less important in the genesis of psychiatric disorder among severely retarded children than among other children because of the importance of other factors. In the mildly retarded where social factors are more important in causing the retardation, it is economic factors, lack of education and other opportunities and a cycle of deprivation which recurs in one generation after another that causes first the retardation and subsequently the behaviour disturbance, and these influences are more important than specific intrafamilial factors (Heber & Garber 1971).

Many retarded children are cared for in institutions for prolonged periods and emotional and behavioural disorders in these children may stem in part from the ill-effects of poor quality institutional care (Rutter 1972). Such adverse affects are far from an invariable consequence and depend to a very large extent on the quality of care provided. Children may spend long periods in institutions during early childhood and yet develop normally provided that the environment is sufficiently stimulating and there is the opportunity to develop lasting relationships with other people. Nowadays when fewer children with less severe handicaps are admitted to institutional care, it is likely that much more of the behaviour disturbance which is seen in children in residential care is the cause, rather than the result, of such substitute care.

Certain sorts of behaviour disturbance, for example overactivity, are seen more often in younger children (Lapouse & Monk 1964) and it may be that intellectually retarded children show no more than the normal amount of deviant behaviour expected of a younger child. Overall this is unlikely to be an important factor, as intellectual retardation is associated with an increase in most types of deviant behaviour whereas age differences are only found in a few (Cullen & Boundy 1966; Cummings 1944).

Such immaturity may account to some extent for the increased frequency of hyperkinetic behaviour disorders and poor concentration among more severely retarded children.

More specific delays in development such as language handicaps which are particularly frequent in retarded children may have an important effect in causing behaviour disturbance. For example, the child may have insufficient comprehension of language to mediate his behaviour in social interaction with others and having less contact with other children and adults also has less opportunity to learn from others. It is also likely that severe disturbances in language development play an important part in the increased frequency of autism in severely retarded children. Particularly in the mildly retarded child educational retardation may contribute to the maladjustment by impairing school learning. Educational failure may then lead the child to react against school values. Denied status and satisfaction through school work, he may rebel and seek satisfaction in activities contrary to school rules and so become involved in disruptive behaviour. This is particularly seen both in mildly and severely retarded children when unrealistic expectations of both parents and teachers lead to a child being maintained in a school situation with which he cannot cope. There may be considerable improvement when, following careful psychological and psychiatric assessment, he receives special educational help more appropriate to his needs.

There is, thus, a complex interaction between intellectual retardation and psychiatric disorder and only limited evidence on the relative importance of different mechanisms (Rutter 1971). However, it seems that in the severely retarded child organic brain dysfunction and deviant temperamental attributes are the two most important factors. These also play a part in the mildly retarded child, but the adverse social consequence of educational failure, social rejection, general immaturity and language retardation are equally important. Institutional care and the side effects of drugs, for example, anticonvulsants, may be contributory factors and, as in any child, family and social pathology may be important.

PREVENTION OF PSYCHIATRIC DISORDERS

Although there have been few studies specifically directed towards the prevention of psychiatric disorders in the retarded, there is increasing evidence concerned with the possibility of preventing retardation itself, and in view of the associations discussed above, this has clear implications for the prevention of these secondary handicaps.

It has been estimated that perhaps 20 per cent of mildly retarded children suffer from various pathological conditions similar to those seen in more severely retarded children (Clarke 1969). Of these, perhaps the prevention of Down's syndrome utilising amniocentesis (Nadler & Gerbil 1970; Stein, Susser & Guterman 1973), of rubella by prophylactic immunisation of susceptible girls prior to school leaving (Cooper 1968), kernicterus by prevention and early treatment (Liley 1968), and perinatal brain injury by early detection of fetal distress, placental insufficiency and special care within the immediate postnatal period (Rhodes 1973), hold out most hope of substantial reduction of this figure within the foreseeable future.

About 40 per cent of mild mental retardation is the result of polygenic inheritance and these children would thus form the lower end of the normal distribution curve of intelligence were this not skewed by the addition of pathological conditions. In a further 40 per cent such polygenic inheritance is combined with severe environmental deprivation and it is in this group that there is much controversy about the possible beneficial effects of early intervention in preventing the retardation.

Early studies such as those of Skeels (1966) and Skodak (1968) have shown that young children removed from institutions where they are subject to severe deprivation to more satisfactory residential environments are capable of making considerable gains in IQ scores over short periods, while control subjects remaining in impoverished environmental circumstances show a corresponding decrease. These differences persist into adult life and are reflected in the occupational status and adjustment of the subjects. Similar differences have been reported in isolated case studies of children removed from conditions of extreme isolation and adversity (Mason 1942; Davis 1947; Koluchová 1972, 1976) although where this deprivation has been associated with brain damage or a specific behaviour syndrome, such as autism (Itard 1962) these effects have been less marked. Many attempts to enrich the environment of culturally deprived children (as in the Headstart programmes reviewed by Bereiter and Engelmann (1966) and Bronfenbrenner (1975)) have unfortunately foundered because of the short duration and unsystematic nature of the techniques used and lack of subsequent reinforcement.

Some of these difficulties have been overcome in more recent studies, admittedly of smaller numbers of deprived children, and most strikingly in the study of Heber and Garber (1971). This study avoided one of the major difficulties of early intervention programmes which is that of identifying pre-school mildly retarded children (Kirk 1952). In an epidemiological study in a deprived area of Milwaukee it was found that a maternal IQ of less than 80 correlated most highly with retardation in children. This was taken as the index for intervention which was undertaken from the age of 3 months in a specific and structured fashion involving the prevention of language handicaps and the acquisition of specific educational skills. At the age of $4\frac{1}{2}$ there was a 27·4 point increment in IQ in the experimental group compared with a matched control group.

The Milwaukee study has been criticised on methodological grounds both in terms of biasses in selection of groups (Page 1972) and on the more basic grounds of the design of the experiment (Throne 1975). These criticisms and, more importantly, the flattening out of the early striking gains after children ceased to be exposed to the experimental interventions (Heber & Garber 1975) should be noted. However, the experimental children continue to show intellectual functioning well superior to the controls and the project remains a milestone in the history of mental retardation research. It is difficult to know which aspects of the intervention were most influential but the findings have led to a renewal of concern and interest in the topic of early intervention (Caldwell *et al* 1975).

Other studies confirm that early intervention and enrichment directed in such a specific way may make a valuable contribution to the prevention of subcultural retardation and as it is known that there is a greatly increased frequency of the psychiatric disturbance in children living in deprived areas of large cities (Rutter 1973) it may be postulated that such intervention would also be effective in reducing the frequency of psychiatric disorder in children retarded for this reason.

TREATMENT IN MILDLY RETARDED CHILDREN

Because psychiatric disorders in this group take many forms and have many causes, being frequently determined by multiple aetiological factors, the assessment and treatment of such disorders requires the same skills and many of the techniques used in children of normal intelligence. There have been few systematic attempts to evaluate the role of special education for these children in separate schools, or in special units in schools for children of normal ability. However, careful psychological assessment is crucial to ensure that the child is not placed in a situation with which he is unable to cope and to enable parents to adjust their expectations of the child's educational progress, avoiding the experience of successive educational failure in an inappropriate situation.

With mildly retarded children the team approach to psychiatric assessment is particularly appropriate and the complete range of psychiatric treatments have a place. Although a deeper understanding of the nature of the child's handicaps is the main requirement, drug treatment as used in children of normal IQ and individual psychotherapy may be most appropriate. In the case of the latter, less demands may have to be placed on the child for verbal interaction and the use of play techniques, appropriate to younger children of a similar developmental level, may be most valuable. As in the case of prevention, social factors frequently play an important part, and in families where the parents and other siblings are similarly handicapped much may be achieved with practical help and advice to the parents on child and family management. In this connection, the day-care and family rehabilitation units which have been experimented with by some Social Services Departments and voluntary agencies may be particularly appropriate.

SYNDROMES HAVING A SPECIFIC ASSOCIATION WITH INTELLECTUAL RETARDATION

Although most psychiatric disorders in mildly retarded children take the same form as those in children of average IQ, as has been discussed before, infantile autism, disintegrative psychosis, the hyperkinetic syndrome and stereotyped behaviour are much more common, particularly amongst the severely retarded.

Autism

Autism (see Chapter 30) is frequently associated with mental retardation. About 40 per cent of autistic children have an IQ below 50; 30 per cent have an IQ in the 50–69 range and 20 per cent have an IQ of 70 or more (Rutter & Lockyer 1967; Lotter 1967). In addition to those showing the full syndrome of autism, many severely retarded children show some features of the condition (Wing 1975). Stereotypies, mannerisms, and defects in language comprehension and symbolic usage (which are out of proportion to IQ) are the most common.

Recent reports suggest that autistic symptoms are particularly frequent in certain syndromes associated with severe mental retardation. For example, Chess et al (1971), in a study of 243 preschool children with rubella embryopathy, found that 10 showed the full syndrome of autism while another 8 showed a partial syndrome. However, it is uncertain whether the association with autism was a result of rubella virus *per se* or rather with the deafness and severe retardation which resulted from the infection. Although there are clearly difficulties in the diagnosis of autism when there are such gross sensory handicaps, the autistic features seemed to be more than just a response to blindness and deafness. Possibly, rubella may cause a central impairment of coding of language which predisposes to autism. However, stereotyped and repetitive behaviour is particularly frequent in rubella embryopathy and this should not lead to a diagnosis of autism.

Another condition particularly associated with autism is the syndrome of infantile spasms associated with hypsarrythmia on the EEG (Knobloch *et al* 1956; Kolvin *et al* 1971; Taft & Cohen 1971; Corbett *et al* 1975). The seizures usually commence during the first year of life and take the form of characteristic salaam attacks. It is doubtful whether this clinical picture is itself the result of one single aetiology, as such spasms have been noted with a number of organic conditions associated with severe mental retardation and brain damage. Many of these children are very severely retarded indeed, but show typical lack of social responses, absence of useful language, resistance to change and stereotypies.

There is sometimes a difficulty in differentiating autism of later onset from disintegrative psychosis (see Chapter 30). The term disintegrative psychoses is confined to rarer disorders in which development appears normal up to the age of 3 or 4 years, when, usually following a period of vague illness, there is loss of speech and social skills, general regression and a decline in intelligence often associated with the development of stereotyped manner-isms. Such a picture is seen in a number of other syndromes associated with severe retardation including encephalitis, particularly subacute sclerosing panencephalitis. This is associated with a measles-like infection, dementia usually occurring around the age of 7 following some years after the original infection with measles. A similar picture is seen in some forms of lipoid storage disease (Malamud 1959; Creak 1963) and it seems likely that the con-dition originally described by Heller (1930) in which there is profound regres-sion associated with behavioural disintegration will increasingly be found to be caused by such rare biochemical and other degenerative neurological con-ditions.

Hyperkinetic syndrome

The diagnosis of the hyperkinetic syndrome also presents difficulties in men-tally retarded children. Many severely retarded children are very overactive, impulsive and distractible, with a short attention span. This clinical picture is particularly common in young children with severe language disorders; the overactivity becomes less marked in adolescence. It seems likely that the behaviour may be a response to impairments in language and play skills and so different from the syndrome of hyperkinesis found in children of normal intelligence (see Chapter 22).

The hyperkinetic syndrome in mentally retarded children is particularly associated with epilepsy, which occurs in nearly half (Corbett *et al* 1975). This is a higher proportion than in young autistic retarded children, who often develop seizures but not usually until adolescence or early adult life (Lockyer & Rutter 1969).

Stereotypies

Stereotyped repetitive movements, such as body rocking, are primitive self-stimulating activities that occur when individuals cannot respond to the environment in an effective way, either because of their own incapacities or because of the poverty of the environment. Thus, they are most frequent in severely retarded individuals with limited mobility and poor social skills. Stereotypies tend to increase in barren unstimulating environment such as the back wards of poor long-stay institutions and to decrease when playthings are available or where there is ample opportunity for personal interaction (Kaufman 1967; Berkson & Mason 1963; Klaber & Butterfield 1968).

The handicaps of the individual are also important with respect to the exhibition of stereotyped behaviours; they are more common in blind retarded subjects than in those who can see, and more frequent in nonambulant than mobile children (Guess 1966). Overall, however, stereotyped behaviours are very frequent indeed in severely retarded children and in one recent epidemiological study, occurred in 40 per cent of those under the age of 16 (Corbett *et al* 1975).

Pica

Pica (the ingestion of inedible substances) occurs in children of all levels of intelligence, but it is a symptom that is certainly more common among the retarded, and Kanner (1957) noted that half the children referred to him with pica were severely retarded. Blind children have been shown to be particularly prone to discriminative pica compensating for their other sensory handicaps by mouthing objects. In these and other retarded children several workers have reported high rates of lead intoxication (Bicknell 1972; Gibson *et al* 1967). It is important to make this diagnosis because of the possibility of preventing any increase in the degree of retardation.

SYNDROMES WITH PARTICULAR BEHAVIOURAL AND PERSONALITY CHARACTERISTICS

Children with Down's syndrome have been held to be friendly, amiable and easy-going individuals, rarely given to aggression and destructive behaviour. Although systematic epidemiological studies have given only limited support to this stereotype, and there have been some negative findings (Blacketer-Simmonds 1953), most behaviour rating studies have shown mongols to be less hyperactive, aggressive and destructive than other mentally retarded persons (Domino *et al* 1964; Moore *et al* 1968; Johnson & Abelson 1969). Most of the differences have been quite small and more severely retarded institutionalised children with Down's syndrome show an increased incidence of hyperactivity and aggressiveness over those in the community. In general, it may be said that mongols do not appear to have a characteristic personality pattern. However, they less often exhibit conduct disorders than other retarded children and are slightly more likely to be more cheerful and friendly in behaviour, although withdrawn, introverted, behaviour is not uncommon (Rollin 1946). Similarly, children with phenylketonuria in institutions tend to be more hyperactive and aggressive than others (Johnson 1969). The differences are relatively small, although there is some evidence that the behaviours may be altered by a low phenylalanine diet (Bentovim 1968; Bruhl *et al* 1964).

Other metabolic disorders associated with mental retardation have not been subject to systematic study, although there is now a large literature demonstrating a definite relationship between sex chromosome abnormalities and personality.

Hydrocephalic children have been said to be verbose; their speech being superficial and lacking in content or appropriateness to the situation (Hadenius *et al* 1962; Hagberg 1962; Ingram & Naughton 1962), but other studies such as that of Fleming (1968) have shown that there is only very limited substance to this stereotype.

PREVENTION OF PSYCHIATRIC DISORDERS IN SEVERELY RETARDED CHILDREN

Studies of the possible prevention of psychiatric disorders among severely retarded children are more sparse than for the mildly retarded.

Some evidence has begun to emerge that very early intervention can go some way towards preventing such problems. Studies such as those of Bricker and Bricker (1971) and Hayden and Haring (1974) suggest that significant gains in ability, with a decrease in behavioural problems can be achieved through very early intervention with young children with Down's syndrome attending a day centre. The findings suggest that they make better progress than children with this syndrome cared for at home from a younger age (Carr 1974). The most interesting features of such intervention programmes has been the training of parents as therapists for their children, either using non-specific stimulation techniques (Brinkworth 1973) or more specifically behavioural techniques (Berkowitz & Graziano 1972; Callias & Jenkins 1973). These experiments provide parents with specific skills in managing children which may do much to offset feelings of guilt and rejection, and thus be more appropriate than the more traditional forms of counselling.

Mentally handicapped children show an increased vulnerability to all sorts of environmental hazards such as those involved in stressful separation from parents at an early age and in institutionalisation. It has been shown that mentally handicapped children matched for intelligence and other variables show an increase in language development if cared for at home rather than in hospital (Lyle 1959). As shown in the Brooklands experiment, if children do have to be in residential care, they make better progress in small units run on family lines than in the large understaffed wards of mental subnormality hospitals (Tizard 1960). Again, the major difference was in their language development and behavioural handicaps. Experimental studies of substitute care (Kushlick 1972) have confirmed that community care for mentally handicapped children utilising small hostels serving a population of approximately 100 000 is feasible. Apart from staff training, the main essential in such units may be an adequate number of staff, at least equivalent to those found in psychiatric units and children's homes for the nonretarded child.

TREATMENT IN SEVERELY RETARDED CHILDREN

Whether hostels or children's homes can cope in the long term with the full range of severe behavioural disorders seen in the mentally retarded is yet to be fully evaluated. It is likely that hospital units of a similar size with a wider range of facilities may be necessary for short and medium-stay treatment in some children. Such units will have many of the characteristics of in-patient psychiatric units for children of normal intelligence. The general regime of such a unit, and the educational facilities provided, will be of paramount importance in alleviating behaviour disturbance. A full range of psychiatric treatments, including drug treatment, behaviour therapy and psychotherapy should be utilised, although these need to be modified to take into account the child's language and other specific handicaps.

The number of such psychiatric units needed for a particular community will depend on several factors including the adequacy of other substitute residential care and educational facilities, their level of tolerance to behaviour disturbance in the children and the presence of outpatient and peripatetic psychological and psychiatric services. With optimal provision of such services it seems likely that these units will be required on a regional or subregional basis. They may serve a population of perhaps 500 000 and provide supportive services for say five hostels each serving 100 000 people (Corbett & Wing 1972).

Such units should be closely associated with teaching hospitals and undertake both staff training and research into the evaluation of treatment methods. Ideally both day and residential treatment and assessment facilities should be provided with outpatients psychiatric clinics and consultative services to hostels and special schools and to the regional and district Handicapped Assessment Centres.

Community services for mentally handicapped children

Adequate residential provision for severely retarded children will be one of the most important components of any comprehensive community service and will be required for between one-fifth and one-quarter of all children with an IQ under 50 (Kushlick 1972). This will mainly take the form of hostels for approximately 20 children, smaller children's homes or foster homes. These should be in the community and be able to provide both short and long-term care in a flexible way which will provide additional support for parents wishing to have their child at home part of the time or in the long term. If adequate residential provision of this sort is available only a minimum number of children (between 5 to 10) for a population of 100 000 will require long-term residential care in special paediatric or psychiatric units because of severe additional physical or behaviour handicaps (Corbett & Wing 1972; Corbett 1976). Adequate residential provision will only form part of a comprehensive community service and a number of other resources will be required if the residential care needs are to be reduced to a minimum and additional psychiatric handicaps alleviated.

Firstly preventative and early assessment facilities will be needed. At a primary core level screening for handicaps will take place in 'Wellbaby' and paediatric clinics and through general practitioners and health visitors. When significant handicap has been detected, referral to clinics with more specialised facilities will be required. These should be based in assessment centres in which multidisciplinary teams comprising child psychiatrists, psychologists, paediatricians and other specialists can provide ongoing assessment and treatment.

The preschool retarded child will usually live at home but adequate day-care is needed in special units, day nurseries, playgroups and nursery schools. In these, all but the most profoundly handicapped children may have contact with and learn from normal children by modelling or imitation.

Coordination with social work services at this age will be mainly carried out by the health visitor with the psychologist providing early practical training to enhance the development of skills and prevent behavioural handicaps (see above).

All children of school age will require appropriate education in schools for the mildly or severely educationally subnormal whether the child lives at home or is in residential care. Special provision, including pychiatric and psychological consultation, will be needed in such schools for those with behavioural disorders including psychosis and perceptual handicaps. Social Services Departments provide family case-work, supportive counselling and residential care for retarded persons throughout their life. They also play a key role in coordinating the child's overall care.

Behaviour modification

All the forms of psychotherapy which are used in child psychiatric practice are applicable to the treatment of emotional disorders in severely retarded children. However, particular difficulties arise because of their impaired language development. This means that the verbal interaction on which most conventional forms of psychotherapy are based, is often severely restricted. In this case behaviour therapy based particularly on the use of operant techniques Skinner (1961) is especially applicable (see Chapter 39). Treatment is based on the concept that the major handicap of severely retarded children is their slow learning of new skills and their propensity to learn deviant behaviours.

In the example of self-induced vomiting in a retarded child living in an institution described by Wolff *et al* (1965) a functional analysis showed that the child's vomiting was having the systematic effect of inducing increased attention from her adult caretaker. The girl was returned to her dormitory from the classroom after each episode of vomiting. It was hypothesised that the attention derived from this action reinforced the vomiting. At the same time, she was being deprived of the opportunity to develop other positive behaviours in the classroom situation. Treatment consisted of keeping her in the classroom even though vomiting occurred and an attempt was made to build up other desirable behaviours using tangible and social rewards. With such a programme the vomiting and associated behavioural disorders, including screaming, tearing of clothes and destructiveness declined to zero over a period of 30 days.

The rewards or reinforcers used with mentally retarded children may take the form of attention, affection, or praise and approval (social rewards) or they may be tangible (such as food). For children who can eventually understand the concept, tokens may be used. These may be accumulated to purchase back-up reinforcers, (for example toys or preferred activities such as outings). If edible or other tangible rewards are used they are always paired with social reinforcement to form a bridge towards the eventual exclusive use of social rewards. For any individual child the particular reward will depend entirely on what the child will respond to. Sometimes considerable ingenuity may be required in the search for something new and effective. Recent research indicates that some severely handicapped children will respond to novel and unusual visual stimuli and sounds better than to food and social rewards (Callias *et al* 1973; Ohwaki *et al* 1973; Campbell 1973).

The essence of such operant treatment with retarded children is that the reinforcement must be given immediately and consistently following the desired response. Once the response has been learned, however, intermittent positive reinforcement may be more effective than rewarding each individual response. Another essential feature of this approach is the detailed analysis of the child's behaviour and the construction of a learning programme which is broken down into small steps so that more complex forms of behaviour can be taught in easy stages and the behaviour thus shaped by reinforcing these steps one at a time.

A good example of behaviour shaping involving many of these features has been described by Azrin and Foxx (1971) who reported success in toilet training institutionalised retarded patients. They point out that self-initiated toileting for the severely mentally handicapped person is a complex sequence of social behaviours, involving indication of the need to use the toilet, undressing and so on. Using a transistorised alarm in the patient's pants and in the toilet to ensure immediacy of reinforcement the toileting behaviour was broken down into a sequence of small steps which were successively reinforced or shaped. For example, a patient may have been unable to completely pull down his trousers but was initially prompted (giving an indication and minimal help) and reinforced for successful completion of the action. The prompts were then gradually faded out or removed as the behavioural sequence was successfully acquired. This project included many of the features of successful behaviour modification programmes used for other problems and demonstrates clearly how staff caring for handicapped children can be trained to use such a programme initiated experimentally by a psychologist.

Of course, behaviour modification utilises techniques employed by many good teachers or parents. It also provides a clear theoretical framework for the management of severe behaviour problems and lack of social and educational skills in handicapped people who are very slow to learn and for whom repeated unsystematic attempts at teaching have failed. Recently, there has been considerable interest in the training of parents in the use of behaviour modification techniques (Schopler & Reichler 1971; Cunningham & Jeffrie 1971; Berkowitz & Graziano 1972; Callias & Jenkins 1973; O'Dell 1974). The use of parents as therapists with severely retarded children has many advantages in that the techniques can be introduced early in the child's life in a preventative fashion. Parents are able to provide the one-to-one relationship which is frequently a prerequisite of such treatment particularly in the early stages. Also they provide a consistency which is difficult to replace in any educational or substitute care situation. Moreover, the learning of practical skills in the management of behaviour problems and development of new skills do much to offset the feelings of guilt and hopelessness which the parents of severely retarded children experience during the child's early years.

An essential prerequisite of all behaviour modification programmes is a very detailed assessment of the child's developmental progress so that attempts are only made to reinforce the next developmental stage which the child might realistically be expected to acquire.

Behaviour modification programmes have been used to develop a wide range of social, language and educational skills in the retarded (Larsen & Bricker 1968; Gardner 1971; Yule, Berger & Howlin 1975). Language handicaps are among the core defects in severe mentally handicapped children and a lack of communicative skills underlies many of the behaviour problems seen in the retarded. Speech may be developed by initial building up of the child's attention by systematic reinforcement of on-task behaviours followed by the training of eye contact, motor imitation, mouth movements, imitation of sounds, and eventually the use of words (Lovaas 1966; Jenkins 1973). Hyperactive behaviour, which is often a problem in the severely retarded nonspeaking child, diminishes with such training when the environment is adequately structured (Bricker & Bricker 1970).

Evaluation of such programmes is limited by the lack of adequate published data on the children and by an undue emphasis on executive speech rather than on communication skills (Yule & Berger 1972). Training the child to respond to simple gestural commands may be particularly appropriate in the very severely retarded, while more complex gestural language may be taught to the intelligent deaf child and to those autistic children who can imitate gesture (Corbett 1972).

When emphasis is placed, on increasing positive skills and activities, the extinction of problem behaviours by withdrawal of reinforcement contingent on their occurrence becomes less of a concern. A second way of decreasing undesirable behaviours is to reinforce alternative responses, preferably ones which are incompatible with the response to be decreased. Punishment techniques may also be used. These may be primary, using stimuli which are noxious or unpleasant to the individual, or secondary, when stimuli acquire punishing characteristics through being paired with primary punishers. Used in this precise and consistent fashion the term punishment may be applied to techniques involving the withdrawal reinforcement or time-out. This may mean, for example, simple withdrawal of attention from the child who is having a temper tantrum and immediate positive reinforcement on cessation of the tantrum. In certain rare circumstances in severely retarded children where the deviant behaviour is life threatening (as with severe self-mutilating behaviour), a punishment by the use of electric shock may be justified (Callias *et al* 1973; Gardner 1969; Corbett 1975).

Drug treatment

The use of drugs in the treatment of behaviour disorders in the retarded has been reviewed by Freeman (1970) and by Sprague and Werry (1971). Although drug treatment is used very frequently in severely retarded patients in institutional care (Lipman 1970), there is a paucity of well controlled drug trials and a virtual absence of outpatient studies. Few studies have used adequate double blind procedures and samples of patients have tended to be heterogenous and ill described. Behaviour rating scales have often been invalid or inadequately tested for reliability and few studies have used objective measures or appropriate statistical analysis. Most knowledge on psychopharmacology has resulted from the study of nonretarded children (see Chapter 38) but the general principles of drug treatment probably remain the same in the severely retarded population.

There are few adequate comparative studies of phenothiazine treatment in children, although the evidence suggests that promazine is less effective than chloropromazine or thioridazine. The latter has been reported to be particularly effective in controlling stereotyped behaviour (Davis *et al* 1969) but other drugs have been less studied. Chlorpromazine appears most effective in reducing psychomotor restlessness and disorganised and psychotic behaviour.

The piperazine subgroup (trifluoperazine) and (perphenazine) are reputed to be less sedative while the butyrophenone derivative, haloperidol, is now well established in the treatment of the disturbed retarded child. Its preparation as an odourless, colourless concentrate is an advantage for young disturbed patients. The major tranquillisers all have similar side effects including anticholinergic effects, such as dryness of the mouth, constipation and blurring of vision and extrapyramidal effects such as Parkinsonism and dys-kinesia. These extrapyramidal effects can be reversed by antiparkinsonian drugs such as orphenadrine. The phenothiazines are said to be contraindi-cated in patients with epilepsy, but there is little evidence to support this. Haloperidol may have markedly beneficial effects in epileptic patients with behaviour disorders. This is a major consideration as nearly a third of severely retarded children have a life long history of epilepsy (Corbett *et al* 1975). Akathisia (motor restlessness), blood dyscrasias, skin reactions and jaundice may occur and as with the other side effects there may be a considerable degree of individual sensitivity.

Of the minor tranquillisers, chlordiazepoxide and diazepam are effective in anxiety states and phobic reactions, but there is little evidence to support their efficacy in other disorders in the retarded (apart from the parenteral use of diazepam in status epilepticus).

The use of barbiturates is generally contraindicated in retarded children as they often cause an increase in motor restlessness and disturbed behaviour. Stimulants such as amphetamine or dexamphetamine have been used for many years in the treatment of hyperkinetic disorders, but there are few studies of their use with the retarded. They are best given in the early part of the day to prevent sleeplessness at night. Methylphenidate lacks the adrenergic affects of amphetamines and may alleviate the drowsiness caused by other drugs, but itself causes similar side effects of insomnia and anorexia. Beclamide, a drug previously used as an anticonvulsant has been reported to have a delayed effect in controlling behaviour disorders in the retarded, and while adequate studies of its efficacy are not available it certainly has the merit of being virtually free from side effects.

The indications for the use of antidepressants in the retarded are similar to those in other patients, but again, there are few studies to justify claims for their effectiveness in children.

Guidelines have been suggested by Freeman (1970) for the use of drugs in the mentally handicapped. Parenteral chlorpromazine or paraldehyde may be given for emergency treatment to control acutely disturbed behaviour while the agitated hyperactive or psychotic child should be tried first on chlor-promazine, pericyazine or thioridazine and if these are unsuccessful then full doses of haloperidol may be given. Trifluoperazine or perphenazine may be used in the withdrawn underactive child, while in the hyperactive nonpsy-chotic child amphetamine of methylphenidate may be tried. Diazepam or chlordiazepoxide are used when there are phobic anxiety symptoms while in established depression and nocturnal enuresis imipramine may be given. Finally, for night sedation, barbiturates should be avoided while chloral-hydrate, promethazine or nitrazepam are preferred.

Conclusion

Because of their importance with severely retarded children, particular attention has been paid to behavioural and drug treatment. However, the role of the child psychiatrist is in no way restricted by the narrow constraints of such clinical treatment. Because of his experience of community services and of working in a multidisciplinary setting, he will have a special role to play in coordinating the facilities for treatment and care of the mentally handicapped. Working as a member of the team in a handicapped assessment centre, together with the paediatrician and workers from many other disciplines, he will need to have a detailed knowledge of the underlying biological causes of mental retardation, the assessment of secondary physical handicaps, epilepsy and perceptual difficulties and of other aspects of developmental assessment. He will also need to be aware of the role of others in the assessment and care team and be able to counsel staff on the wide range of settings, including special schools and hostels. Of particular importance will be the counselling of families with a mentally handicapped child. Particular knowledge will be required of the stresses experienced by families and others caring for handicapped children.

Systematic scientific evidence about the nature of psychiatric problems in children with mental retardation is grossly inadequate so far. Handicaps are frequently multiple and complex. Their assessment and treatment provide as special and exciting a challenge to both the clinician and research worker as any other aspect of child psychiatry. It is likely that many of the lessons still to be learnt in this field will lead to greater understanding of psychiatric problems in less handicapped children.

Grateful thanks are due to Dr Janet Carr for helpful advice and criticism on this chapter.

REFERENCES

ANASTASI A. (1968) *Psychological Testing*, 3rd edn. New York: Macmillan

AZRIN N.H. & FOXX R.M. (1971) A rapid method of toilet training the institutionalized retarded. *J. Appl. Behav. Anal.* **4,** 89–96

BALDWIN W.K. (1958) The social position of the educable mentally retarded child in the regular grades in the public schools. *Except. Child.* **25,** 106–112

BENTOVIM A. (1968) Controlled observations of phenylketonuric children on and during withdrawal from low phenylalanine diet. *Arch. Dis. Child.* **43,** 745–746

BEREITER C. & ENGELMANN S. (1966) *Teaching Disadvantaged Children in the Preschool.* Englewood Cliffs, NJ: Prentice-Hall

BERKOWITZ B.P. & GRAZIANO A.M. (1972) Training parents as behavior therapists: a review. *Behav. Res. Ther.* **10,** 297–317

BERKSON G. & MASON W.A. (1963) Stereotyped movements of mental defectives: 111 situation effects. *Amer. J. Ment. Defic.* **68**, 409–412

BICKNELL J. (1972) *Lead Poisoning and Mental Retardation.* Institute for Research into Mental Retardation Symposium, London

BIRCH H.G., RICHARDSON S.A., BAIRD D. Sir, HOROBIN G. & ILLSLEY R. (1970) *Mental Subnormality in the Community, a Clinical and Epidemiological Study.* Baltimore: Williams & Wilkins

BLACKETER-SIMMONDS D.A. (1953). An investigation into the supposed differences existing between mongols and other mentally defective subjects, with regard to certain psychological traits. *J. Ment. Sci.* **90**, 702–719

BRICKER W.A. & BRICKER D.D. (1970) A program of language training for the severely language handicapped child. *Except. Child.* **37**, 101–111

BRICKER D.D. & BRICKER W.A. (1971) *Toddler Research & Intervention Project.* Year 1. IMRID Behav. Science Monograph no. 20. Nashville, Tennessee

BRINKWORTH R. (1973) Personal communication

BRONFENBRENNER U. (1975) Is early intervention effective. *In* Friedlander B.Z., Sterritt G.M. & Kirk G.E. (eds.) *Exceptional Infant*, vol. III: *Assessment and Intervention.* New York: Brunner/Mazel

BRUHL H.H., ARNESEN J.F. & BRUHL M.G. (1964) Effects of low-phenylalanine diet on older phenylketonuria patients (long range controlled study). *Amer. J. Ment. Defic.* **69**, 225–235

BURT C. (1921) *Mental and Scholastic Tests.* London: King

BURT C. (1937) *The Backward Child.* London: London University Press

CALDWELL B.M., BRADLEY R.H. & ELARDO R. (1975) Early stimulation. *In* Wortis E.J. (ed.) *Mental Retardation and Developmental Disabilities*, vol. VII. An annual review. New York: Brunner/Mazel

CALDWELL B.M. & GUZE S.B. (1960) A study of the adjustment of parents and siblings of institutionalized and non-institutionalized retarded children. *Amer. J. Ment. Defic.* **64**, 845–861

CALLIAS M., CARR J., CORBETT J.A. & JENKINS J. (1973) Use of behaviour modification techniques in a community service for mentally handicapped children. *Proc. roy. Soc. Med.* **66**, 1140–1142

CALLIAS M. & JENKINS J. (1973) Personal communication

CAMPBELL H.J. (1973) *The Pleasure Areas: A New Theory of Behaviour.* London: Eyre Methuen

CARR J. (1974) The effect of the severely subnormal on their families. *In* Clarke A.M. & Clarke A.B.D. (eds) *Mental Deficiency: the Changing Outlook.* London: Methuen

CARR J. (1975) *Young Children with Down's Syndrome.* London: Butterworth

CASTELL J. & MITTLER P. (1965) Intelligence of patients in mental subnormality hospitals. A survey of admissions in 1961. *Brit. J. Psychiat.* **111**, 219–225

CHAZAN M. (1964) The incidence and nature of maladjustment among children in schools for the educationally subnormal. *Brit. J. Educ. Psychol.* **34**, 292–304

CHESS S., KORN S.J. & FERNANDEZ P.B. (1971) *Psychiatric Disorders of Children with Congenital Rubella.* New York: Brunner/Mazel

CLARKE A.D.B. (1969) *Recent Advances in the Study of Subnormality.* 2nd edn. London: NAMH

CLARKE A.M. (1965) Criteria and classification of mental deficiency. *In* Clarke

A.M. & Clarke A.B.D. (eds.) *Mental Deficiency: the Changing Outlook*. London: Methuen

COOPER L.Z. (1968) Rubella: a preventable cause of birth defects. *In* Bergman D. (ed.) *Birth Defects*. New York: National Foundation

CORBETT J.A. (1972) Services for the mentally retarded. *In* Wing J.K. & Hailey A. (eds) *Evaluating a Community Psychiatric Service. The Camberwell Register 1964–71*. London: Oxford University Press

CORBETT J.A. (1975) Aversion in the treatment of self-injurious behaviour. *J. Ment. Defic. Res.* **19**, 79–95

CORBETT J.A. (1976) Community care for severely mentally retarded children. *In* Proceedings of Vth European Congress of Paedopsychiatrists, Vienna, 1975 (in press)

CORBETT J.A. & WING L. (1972) A Plan for a comprehensive service for the mentally retarded, *In* Wing J.K. & Hailey A.M. (eds) *Evaluating a Community Psychiatric Service. The Camberwell Register 1964–71*. London: Oxford University Press.

CORBETT J.A., HARRIS E. & ROBINSON R. (1975) Epilepsy. *In* Wortis J. (ed.) *Mental Retardation and Developmental Disabilities*, vol. VII: *An annual review*. New York: Brunner/Mazel

CRAFT M. (1959) Mental Disorder in the Defective: a Psychiatric Survey Among Inpatients. *Amer. J. Ment. Defic.* **63**, 829–834

CREAK E.M. (1963) Childhood psychosis: a review of 100 cases. *Brit. J. Psychiat.* **109**, 84–89

CROME L. (1960) The brain and mental retardation. *Brit. Med. J.* i, 897–904

CULLEN K.J. & BOUNDY C.A.P. (1966) Factors relating to behaviour disorders in children. *Aust. Paed. J.* **2**, 70–80

CUMMINGS J.D. (1944) The incidence of emotional symptoms in schoolchildren. *Brit. J. Educ. Psychol.* **14**, 151–161

CUNNINGHAM C. & JEFFRIE D. (1971) *Working with Parents: Developing a Workshop for Parents of Young Mentally Handicapped Children:* Manchester: National Society for Mentally Handicapped Children (North West Region)

DAVIS K. (1947) Final note on a case of extreme isolation. *Amer. J. Sociol.* **52**, 432–437

DAVIS K.V., SPRAGUE R.L. & WERRY J.S. (1969) Stereotyped behavior and activity level in severe retardates: The effects of drugs. *Amer. J. Ment. Defic.* **73**, 721–727

DEPARTMENT OF HEALTH AND SOCIAL SECURITY (1971) *Better Services for the Mentally Handicapped*. Cmnd no. 4683. London: HMSO

DOMINO G., GOLDSCHMID M. & KAPLAN M. (1964) Personality traits of institutionalized mongoloid girls. *Amer. J. Ment. Defic.* **68**, 498–502

DOUGLAS J.W.B., ROSS J.M. & SIMPSON H.R. (1968) *All Our Future*. London: Peter Davies

ERICKSON M.T. (1969) MMPI profiles of parents of young retarded children. *Amer. J. Ment. Defic.* **73**, 728–732

EYMAN R.K., MOORE B.C., CAPES L. & ZACHOFSKY T. (1970) Maladaptive behavior of institutionalised retardates with seizures. *Amer. J. Ment. Defic.* **74**, 651–659

FLEMING C.P. (1968) *The Verbal Behaviour of Hydrocephalic Children*. Develop. Med. Child Neurol., Supp. 15. London: Heinemann

FREEMAN R.D. (1970) Psychopharmacology and the Retarded Child. *In* Menalascino F. (ed.) *Psychiatric Approaches to Mental Retardation*. New York: Basic Books

GARDNER W.I. (1971) *Behaviour Modification in Mental Retardation*. London: University of London Press

GARDNER W.I. (1969) Use of punishment procedures with the severely retarded. A review. *Amer. J. Ment. Defic.* **74**, 86–103

GATH A. (1973) Schoolage siblings of mongol children. *Brit. J. Psychiat.* **123**, 161–167

GIBSON S.L.M., LAM C.N., McCRAE W.M. & GOLDBERG A. (1967) Blood lead levels in normal and mentally deficient children. *Arch. Dis. Child.* **42**, 573–578

GRAHAM P. & GEORGE S. (1972) Children's response to parental illness: individual differences. *J. psychosom. Res.* **16**, 251–255

GRIFFITH H. & DAVIDSON M. (1906) Long-term changes in intellect and behaviour after hemispherectomy. *J. Neurol. Neurosurg. Psychiat.* **29**, 571–576

GUESS D. (1966) The influence of visual and ambulation restrictions on stereotyped behavior. *Amer. J. Ment. Defic.* **70**, 542–547

HADENIUS A.M., HAGBERG B., HYTTNES-BEUSCH K. & SJÖGREN I. (1962) The natural prognosis of infantile hydrocephalus. *Acta Paediat.* **51**, 117–118

HAGBERG B. (1962) The sequelae of spontaneously arrested infantile hydrocephalus. *Devel. Med. Child. Neurol.* **4**, 583–587

HAYDEN A. & HARING N. (1974) Early intervention for high risk infants and young children. Programmes for Down's syndrome children at the University of Washington. Mimeographed manuscript

HEBER R. & GARBER H. (1971) An experiment in prevention of cultural-familial mental retardation. *In* Primrose D.A. (ed.) *Proc. Second Cong. Intern. Assoc. Scientif. Stud. Ment. Defic.* Warsaw: Polish Medical Publishers

HEBER R. & GARBER H. (1975) The Milwaukee project: A study of the use of family intervention to prevent cultural family retardation. *In* Friedlander B.Z., Garritt G.M. & Kirk G.E. (eds) *Exceptional Infant*, vol. III. New York: Brunner/Mazel

HELLER T. (1930) About Dementia Infantilis. *Zeitschrift fuer Kinderforschung*. Berlin: Julius Springer Verlag. *Trans.* Hulse W.C., *In* Howells J.G. (ed.) *Modern Perspectives in International Child Psychiatry* (1969) Edinburgh: Oliver & Boyd

INGRAM T.T.S. & NAUGHTON J.A. (1962) Paediatric and psychological aspects of cerebral palsy associated with hydrocephalus. *Develop. Med. Child Neurol.* **4**, 287–292

ITARD J.M.G. (1962) *The Wild Boy and Aveyron*. New York: Appleton-Century Crofts

JACOBS J.F. & PIERCE M.L. (1968) The social position of retardates with brain damage and associated characteristics. *Except. Child* **34**, 677–681

JENKINS J. (1973) Programme for language training with severely mentally retarded children. Unpublished manual

JOHNSON R.C. (1969) Behavior characteristics of phenylketonurics and matched controls. *Amer. J. Ment. Defic.* **74**, 17–19

JOHNSON R.C. & ABELSON R.B. (1969) The behavioral competence of mongoloid and non-mongoloid retardates. *Amer. J. Ment. Defic.* **73**, 856–857

KANNER L. (1957) *Child Psychiatry*. Springfield, Illinois: Charles C. Thomas

KAUFMAN M.E. & LEVITT H. (1965) A study of three stereotyped behaviors in institutionalized mental defectives. *Amer. J. Ment. Defic.* **69**, 467–473

KAUFMAN M.E. (1967) The effects of institutionalization on development of stereotyped and social behaviors in mental defectives. *Amer. J. Ment. Defic.* **71**, 581–585

KENNEDY C. & RAMIREZ L.S. (1964) Brain damage as a cause of behaviour disturbance in children. *In* Birch H.G. (ed.) *Brain Damage in Children: the Biological and Social Aspects.* Baltimore: Williams & Wilkins

KIRK S.A. (1952) Experiments in the early training of the mentally retarded. *Amer. J. Ment. Defic.* **56,** 692–700

KLABER M.M. & BUTTERFIELD E.C. (1968) Stereotyped rocking: a measure of institution and ward effectiveness. *Amer. J. Ment. Defic.* **73,** 13–20

KNOBLOCH H., RIDER R., HARPER P. & PASAMANIK B. (1956) Neuropsychiatric sequelae of prematurity. *J. Amer. Med. Assoc.* **161,** 581–585

KOLUCHOVÁ J. (1972) Severe deprivation in twins: a case study. *J. Child Psychol. Psychiat.* **13,** 107–114

KOLUCHOVÁ J. (1976) The further development of twins after severe and prolonged deprivation: a second report. *J. Child. Psychol. Psychiat.* **17,** 181–188

KOLVIN I., OUNSTED C. & ROTH M. (1971) Studies in the childhood psychoses: Cerebral dysfunction and childhood psychoses. *Brit. J.Phychiat.* **118,** 407–414

KUSHLICK A. (1972) The need for residential care of the mentally handicapped. *Brit. J. Hosp. Med.* **8,** 161–167

LAPOUSE R. & MONK M.A. (1964) Behavior deviations in a representative sample of children: variation by sex, age, race, social class and family size. *Amer. J. Orthopsychiat.* **34,** 436–446

LARSEN L.A. & BRICKER W.A. (1968) *A Manual for Parents and Teachers of Severely and Moderately Retarded Children,* vol. 5, no. 22. London: Institute for Mental Retardation & Inst. Development

LEWIS A.J. (1960) The study of defect. *Amer. J. Psychiat.* **117,** 289–304

LILEY A.W. (1968) Diagnosis of erythroblastosis in the fetus. *Adv. Paediat.* **15,** 29–63

LIPMAN R.S. (1970) The use of psychopharmacological agents in residential facilities for the retarded. *In* Menolascino F. (ed.) *Psychiatric Approaches to Mental Retardation.* New York: Basic Books

LOCKYER L. & RUTTER M. (1969) A five to fifteen year follow-up study of infantile psychosis. III: Psychological aspects. *Brit. J. Psychiat.* **115,** 865–882

LOTTER V. (1967) Epidemiology of autistic conditions in young children. II: Some characteristics of the parents and children. *Soc. Psychiat.* **1,** 163–173

LOVAAS O.I. (1966) A programme for the establishment of speech in psychotic children. *In* Wing J.K. (ed.) *Early Infantile Autism: Clinical, Educational and Social Aspects.* Oxford: Pergamon

LYLE J.G. (1959) The effect of an institution environment on the verbal development of imbecile children. I: Verbal intelligence. *J. Ment. Def. Res.* **3,** 122–128

MALAMUD N. (1959) Heller's Disease and childhood schizophrenia. *Amer. J. Psychiat.* **116,** 215–218

MASON M. (1942) Learning to speak after years of silence. *J. Speech Hear. Dis.* **7,** 245–304

MITTLER P. & WOODWARD M. (1966) The education of children in hospitals for the subnormal: a survey of admissions. *Develop. Med. Child. Neurol.* **8,** 16–25

MOORE B.C., THULINE H.C. & CAPES L.V. (1968) Mongoloid and non-mongoloid retardates: A behavioural comparison. *Amer. J. Ment. Defic.* **73,** 433–436

NADLER H.L. & GERBIL A.B. (1970) The role of amniocentesis in the intrauterine detection of genetic disorders. *Obstet. Gynal. Survey* **25,** 762–766

O'CONNOR N. (1951) Neuroticism and emotional instability in high grade male defectives. *J. Neurol. Neurosurg. Psychiat.* **14,** 226–230

O'CONNOR N. & TIZARD J. (1954) A survey of patients in twelve mental deficiency institutions. *Brit. Med. J.* **1**, 16–18

O'DELL S. (1974) Training parents in behaviour modification: a review. *Psychol. Bull.* **81**, 418–433

OHWAKI S., BRAHLE J. & STAYTON S.E. (1973) Preference for vibratory and visual stimulation in mentally retarded children. *Amer. J. Ment. Defic.* **77**, 733–736

PAGE E.B. (1972) Miracle in Milwaukee: raising the IQ. *Educ. Res.* **1**, 8–16

PENROSE L.S. (1938) *A Clinical and Genetic Study of 1280 Cases of Mental Defect.* London. Medical Research Council. Special Report

RHODES P. (1973) Obstetric prevention of mental retardation. *Brit. Med. J.* **1**, 399–402

ROLLIN H.R. (1946) Personality in mongolism with special reference to the incidence of catatonic psychosis. *Amer. J. Ment. Defic.* **51**, 219–237

RUTTER M. (1964) Intelligence and childhood psychiatric disorder. *Brit. J. Soc. Clin. Psychol.* **3**, 120–129

RUTTER M. & LOCKYER L. (1967) A five to fifteen year follow-up study of infantile psychosis. 1: description of the sample. *Brit. J. Psychiat.* **113**, 1169–1182

RUTTER M. (1970) Autism: concepts and consequences. *Spec. Educ.* **59**, 20–23

RUTTER M., GRAHAM P. & YULE W. (1970a) *A Neuropsychiatric Study in Childhood.* Clinics in Dev. Med. nos. 35/36. London: SIMP/Heinemann

RUTTER M., TIZARD J. & WHITMORE K. (1970b) (eds.) *Education, Health and Behaviour.* London: Longman

RUTTER·M. (1971) Psychiatry. *In* Wortis J. (ed.) *Mental Retardation*, vol. III: An annual review. New York: Grune & Stratton

RUTTER M. (1972) *Maternal Deprivation Reassessed.* Harmondsworth: Penguin

RUTTER M. (1973) Why are London children so disturbed? *Proc. roy. Soc. Med.* **66**, 1221–1225

SCHOPLER E. & REICHLER R.J. (1971) Parents as cotherapists in the treatment of psychotic children. *J. Autism Child Schiz.* **1**, 87–102

SKEELS H.M. (1966) Adult status of children with contrasting early life experiences: a follow up study. *Monogr. Soc. Res. Child Develop.* **31**, 3. No. 105

SKINNER B.F. (1961) *Cumulative Record.* New York: Macmillan

SKODAK M. (1968) Adult status of individuals who experienced early intervention. *In* Richards B.W. (ed.) *Proc. First Congr. Internat. Assoc. Sci. Study Ment. Defic.* Reigate: Michael Jackson

SOLDWEDEL B. & TERRIL I. (1957) Physically handicapped and non-handicapped children in the same elementary school. *Except. Child.* **23**, 371–383

SPRAGUE R.L. & WERRY J.S. (1971) Methodology of pharmacological studies with the retarded. *In* Ellis N.R. (ed.) *International Review of Research in Mental Retardation*, vol. 5. New York: Academic Press

STEIN Z. & SUSSER M. (1960) Families of dull children. *J. Ment. Sci.* **106**, 1296–1319

STEIN Z., SUSSER M. & GUTERMAN A.V. (1973) Screening programme for the prevention of Down's Syndrome. *Lancet* **i**, 305–310

TAFT L.T. & COHEN H.J. (1971) Hypsarrhythmia and infantile autism: A clinical report. *J. Autism Child Schiz.* **1**, 327–336

TARJAN M.D., TIZARD J., RUTTER M., BEGAB M., BROOKE E.M., DE LA CRUZ F., LIN T.-Y., MONTENEGRO H., STROTZKA H. & SARTORIUS N. (1972) Classification and mental retardation. Issues arising in the Fifth WHO Seminar on Psychiatric Diagnosis, Classification & Statistics. *Amer. J. Psychiat.* **128**, 34–45. (Suppl.)

THOMAS A., CHESS S. & BIRCH H.G. (1968) *Temperament and Behaviour Disorders in Children.* New York: University Press

THRONE J.M. (1975) The replicability fetish and the Milwaukee project. *Ment. Ret.* **13,** 14–17

TIZARD B. (1962) The personality of epileptics: a discussion of the evidence. *Psychol. Bull.* **59,** 196–210

TIZARD J. (1960) Residental care of mentally handicapped children. *Brit. Med. J.* **i,** 1041–1046

TIZARD J. (1966) Mental subnormality and child psychiatry. *J. Child Psychol. Psychiat.* **7,** 1–15

TIZARD J. & GRAD J.C. (1961) *The Mentally Handicapped and Their Families: a Social Survey.* London: Oxford University Press

WHITE H.H. (1961) Cerebral hemispherectomy in the treatment of infantile hemiplegia. *Confin. Neurol.* **21,** 1–50

WILSON P.J.E. (1970) Cerebral hemispherectomy for infantile hemiplegia. A Report of 50 cases. *Brain* **93,** 147–180

WING L. (1975) A study of language impairment in the severely retarded. *In* O'Connor N. (ed.) *Language, Cognitive deficits and Retardation.* London: Butterworths

WOLF M.M., BIRNBRAUER J.S., WILLIAMS T. & LAWLER J. (1965) A note on apparent extinction of the vomiting behaviour of a retarded child. *In* Ullman L.P., Krasner L. (eds) *Case Studies in Behavior Modification.* New York: Holt, Rinehart & Winston

WOLFENSBERGER W. (1968) Vocational preparation and occupation: *In* Baumeister A.A. (ed.) *Mental Retardation Appraisal, Rehabilitation and Education.* London: University of London Press

WOLFF S. (1970) Behaviour and pathology of parents of disturbed children. *In* Anthony E.J. & Koupernik C. (eds) *The Child in His Family.* New York: Wiley

WOOTTON B. (1959) *Social Science and Social Pathology.* London: Allen & Unwin

YULE W. & BERGER M. (1972) Behaviour modification principles and speech delay. *In* Rutter M. & Martin J.A.M. (eds) *The Child with Delayed Speech.* Clin. in Devel. Med. no. 43. London: SIMP/Heinemann

YULE W., BERGER M. & HOWLIN P. (1975) Language deficit and behaviour modification. *In* O'Connor N. (ed.) *Language, Cognitive Deficits and Retardation.* London: Butterworth

PART V

Approaches to treatment

CHAPTER 36

Treatment of delinquents

T. GIBBENS

The treatment of a delinquent should be taken to include everything that happens to him as a result of detection or arrest. Although we are mainly concerned with the part which psychiatrists should or can play in this process, the forensic psychiatrist at least should be familiar with the wider criminological aspects of the problem. Expertise may include special techniques, but it must incorporate a knowledge of the range of facilities available, and especially of how the crime-control system works so that the delinquent can be guided with as little damage and as much profit as possible through the maze of official reaction.

The last 10 or 15 years have seen the end of what might be called the era of psychiatric dominance in delinquency studies. Hitherto more and better psychiatric assessment and treatment was thought to hold the key to delinquency control; social scientists were ready collaborators. More recently criminal sociology has emerged, no longer in collaboration with but often in sharp opposition to psychiatric and psychological ideas of causation and treatment. Psychiatrists find themselves accused of exaggerating the pathological aspects of delinquency and in the process unwittingly contributing to the deviance of the delinquent not only in his own eyes but those of society (Taylor *et al* 1973).

This trend has been supported to some extent by much more accurate studies of the distribution of delinquent behaviour, either by self-report or by victim studies—asking the public how often they have offended or how often they have been the victims of offences, compared with official figures. Among a 3 per cent sample of the Stockholm school population 57 per cent admitted at least one serious offence and of these 93 per cent were not caught. Between them these boys claimed they had committed 1430 serious offences but the culprit was known to the police in only 41 of them. The proportion of crimes for which an offender was apprehended was thus only 2·9 per cent (Elmhorn 1965). In Oslo 56 per cent of young men entering the army admitted shoplifting and a similar proportion admitted smashing street lamps or other public property (Christie *et al* 1965). In London Belson (1968) found that between a third and a half of 1400 boys admitted theft in a variety of situations. In their detailed study of London boys from 8 until they were

17 West and Farrington (1973) found 20·4 per cent (11·4 per cent once, and 9 per cent more than once) had been found guilty in court; a proportion similar to that of Power (1965) who noted a 24 per cent delinquency rate in another working class area of London. From Douglas' national survey of children Wadsworth (1972) calculated a figure of 13·7 per cent for London. West and Farrington (1973) compared these court appearances with self-report studied by the boys at 15 and 17. Minor offenders were almost universal but serious offences included housebreaking 9·3 per cent, planned housebreaking 7·1 per cent, shopbreaking 12·7 per cent. West and Farrington's study however does to some extent answer the sociological criticism that arrests are largely a matter of chance or of police or class prejudice. They found that when the 80 most serious self-reporting delinquents were compared with the 84 convicted delinquents, half of the self-reported delinquents were among those already convicted. Furthermore, the five background factors which most distinguished the delinquents from the nondelinquents (low family income, large family size, parental criminality, low intelligence and poor parental behaviour) were in general also present in the most serious undetected delinquents.

The most influential of the sociologists' theories deals with 'labelling'. Crudely expressed, this states that all or nearly all boys are delinquent in some degree, that one of the most powerful factors in creating a recidivist delinquent career is arrest and conviction, and the attachment of a label of 'delinquent' which alters the attitudes of teachers and parents as well as the boy's self-image, persuades him that he is a black sheep. His social contacts undergo a subtle or obvious change. Treatment tends to consist in isolating him in 'reeducational' institutions which concentrate those with similar outlook, with a secret social system dominated usually by the most antisocial and antiauthoritarian amongst the inmates.

Psychiatrists as well as magistrates have always been aware of the strength of such views, but nothing can undermine the view of the Gluecks (1950) that delinquency is a biopsychosocial phenomenon, like all other behaviour; differences of view can only be those of emphasis. But aspects of labelling have clearly had a considerable influence upon modern penal policy expressed in the Children's Act of 1969, which aimed at removing the emphasis upon the delinquent act itself, reducing the number of juveniles charged or brought to court, encouraged the spread of the juvenile liaison system of cautions by the police, and placed an emphasis upon treatment in the community rather than in institutions.

Labelling theory is easy to state but validation by research is difficult and has rarely been attempted. It should follow, for example, that it is better for a delinquent not to be detected or arrested and that severe punishment for first or early offenders should be noticeably unproductive. Gold and Williams (1969) studied two groups of boys who self-reported four serious offences; half had been arrested for the last offence and half never arrested. True to the hypothesis, those not arrested had subsequently fewer convictions than those dealt with by the courts. On the other hand among a group of boys given severe punishment for first offences, Thornberry (1971) found that coloured lower class boys were usually not convicted later, but white middle class boys were very frequently reconvicted after this experience. A study by McEachern (1968) to assess the relative effectiveness of different dispositions and supervision practices in the probation system sometimes supported labelling theory and sometimes not. The problem is discussed by Mahoney (1974).

PREVENTION

One of the important functions of the child psychiatrist is to help in preventing juvenile delinquency. Proof of the effectiveness of such intervention is lacking owing to the great difficulty of designing research but this is not likely to deter the psychiatrist when dealing with evident problems. A thorough physical, mental, psychological, educational, and social assessment in the early stages of behaviour disorder, well described many years ago by Edelston (1952), will point to defects in development, some more remediable than others. It may be just as important to soothe the anxieties or punitive reactions of parents as to diagnose serious handicaps and defects which will require concentrated care. Treatment will often merge into extended diagnosis, leading for example to the conclusion that further deterioration is inevitable unless the child is provided with special education, wider contact with members of the extended family, or even removal from home. Conversely, perhaps more important, recommendations to be allowed to persist in treatment in spite of reconviction for minor offences may protect the child from excessive and automatic severity which will not be constructive—a policy now well understood by the child welfare authorities, the magistrates, and incorporated to some extent in the Children and Young Persons Act of 1959.

An abiding interest has been to devise methods by which preventive action could be concentrated where it is most needed, since social and welfare programmes will always fall short of what is necessary. The Gluecks (1959) spent many years elaborating methods of predicting future delinquency and maintained that their Social Prediction table* predicted with 80–90 per cent

* Based upon 5 Social Factors: Discipline by Father, Supervision by Mother, Affection of Father, Affection of Mother, Cohesiveness of Family. There are also predictions for 4 Factors and 3 Factors.

accuracy those who would be become delinquent. Their data however were prepared retrospectively from the situation of confirmed delinquents. It is generally accepted that their method overpredicts delinquency and West and Farrington (1973) showed that accuracy becomes much less marked if the ratio of delinquents to nondelinquents is reduced from 50 : 50, as in their study, to the actually observed population of 30 : 70 or 25 : 75. However, there have now been two genuinely predictive studies, in which schoolchildren were studied before they became delinquent and then followed up. In the first of these studies by the New York Youth Board (Craig & Glick 1963; 1964) the Glueck scales predicted that 30 per cent would become delinquent. But they lent support to this result by saying that the school teachers thought it was accurate.

West and Farrington (1973) studied some 400 children in a working class London area at age 8 and followed them till 18; that is, the data were truly predictive, based on the information collected before they became delinquent. They showed that social factors, teachers' ratings and ratings by school fellows could all significantly predict later delinquency. Stott (Stott 1963; Stott & Wilson 1968) showed that his Bristol Social Adjustment Guide scores (which uses teachers' ratings) distinguished boys on probation from a control group in the same school, differentiated to some extent between boys who succeeded and those who failed on probation, and identified many of the delinquents who were reconvicted as young adults. The Bristol Guides are possibly less successful in identifying future delinquency in an initially nondelinquent population.

West and Farrington (1973) also referred to the capacity of children to predict delinquency among their school companions, a method used by Skaberne (1965) among Yugoslav children. West and Farrington asked 353 children of 10 to rate the characteristics of their contemporaries (who had a subsequent delinquency of 19·3 per cent). Among the top and bottom quarters, 38 per cent of those 'most daring', 35·5 per cent of those rated 'most troublesome', 37·5 per cent of those 'least honest' (which the boy took to mean stealing rather than untruthfulness) were subsequently proved delinquent compared with about 6 per cent of each of the best quarters. An interesting commentary on the yearning of most children to be free from the pangs of conscience is perhaps suggested by the fact that the quarter rated as 'most like I am' or 'most what I would like to be' showed no discrimination between future delinquents and nondelinquents. Nothing, it is said, has such power to undermine morale as to contemplation of someone breaking the rules and also appearing not to care that he does so.

West and Farrington tried to find combinations of their own most significant social predictors (criminal parents, low family income, large family size, poor parental behaviour, low intelligence) with teacher ratings (troublesome, truant, ill-disciplined, unkempt appearance, lazy, were their most significant assessments) and peer ratings (most daring, least popular, most troublesome, least honest, least clever) but no method of general combination established a greater than 50 per cent chance of delinquency as compared with some 15 per cent for those excluded.

TREATMENT

The role of the child psychiatrist in contributing to the treatment of this 'submerged tenth' is ill-defined. Many will never come his way or indeed that of most 'caring' agencies. There is no doubt that his role is essentially collaborative, contributing where he can to advise on family limitation, psychiatric treatment of parents or siblings, whose problems seem to cause a scapegoating effect upon the child, the identification of handicaps and defects before they are overlaid or hardly recognisable beneath environmentally induced distortions. There is much discussion of the need for 'community psychiatry', in which the psychiatrist will more often leave his clinic (and the school-teacher his school) to collaborate more closely with services providing care. There is also more concentration upon the need to consider the tension within the family as a whole. As the 'intermediate' treatment provided in the CYP Act 1969, and community service projects develop, there will be more opportunity to guide the delinquent into activities which enhance his self-confidence and self-respect.

West and Farrington (1973) present a gloomy picture of the subgroup of children who seemed destined to develop severe character disorders but whose parents evade or resist help because of suspicious antiauthoritarian attitudes, dullness, poverty and overwork. The psychiatrist, however, has to resist the view sometimes implied by social workers that their cases are either easy, complicated, or psychiatric (excessively complicated), and that psychiatry has a special competence with almost insoluble problems. Psychiatric advice, collaboration, short and long-term treatment is applicable to some cases throughout the range of severity of delinquent potential.

Individual psychotherapy is probably most effective in the early stages of the behaviour disorder when it is confined to the home or has not caused too large a public reaction, and among those who either have psychiatric symptoms or show a 'neurotic' causation in the sense that they are anxious, in conflict, well verbalised and prepared to see that there is a problem in themselves as well as the outside world. The home background is likely to be sufficiently stable to permit regular attendance. For many others the customary public attitude to the doctor–patient relationship gives the psychiatrist a great advantage; parents feel that their problems can be kept at a confidential level; there is an expectation of experienced help without moral condemnation; parents accept that confidential details of marital and family discord are relevant to the doctor's work, and will consider advice which they would resent from others.

Quite apart from personal psychotherapeutic skill, medical consultation can open doors to a further range of services, e.g. admission to a school for the educationally maladjusted. Asuni (1960) compared a series of children in a maladjusted school and in an approved school; two-thirds of the approved schoolboys were predominantly delinquent and had minimal disturbance or maladjustment in other respects; and two-thirds of the maladjusted were nondelinquent, with multiple neurotic symptoms, school difficulties etc. But a third of each population had a similar background and symptomatology, and experience of both child guidance clinics and courts. The maladjusted came from smaller families and had less family criminality. Better educated parents are more likely to seek medical and social help for their problem children and there can be little doubt that diversion in this way is a powerful factor in preventing future delinquency.

Methods of psychotherapy tend to be modified in two respects. Delinquents arrive with a label of blame attached to them for wrong-doing. They are likely to be suspicious, cautious and reserved. The various aids to self-expression—play therapy for the youngest, drawing, TAT or Symonds Adolescent Fantasy Cards for somewhat older boys, and group discussion or psychodrama for the younger adolescent may be needed. Secondly treatment for the great majority will demand collaboration not only with parents but child care officers, psychologists, schoolteachers and employers, and occasionally the police.

There are long-term cases, unfortunately not very infrequent, in which treatment does not appear to progress although the situation is held in balance without deterioration. When treatment is broken off there is a rapid relapse. One effect of a durable treatment relationship is to keep alive in the offender a sense of having a problem. As the recidivist matures, unresolved delinquent impulses tend to become self-accepted or 'ego-syntonic'—the road to professionalised crime; though there are a few who can find a means of direct expression of tendencies in an eccentric but noncriminal form (e.g. the voyeur who settled happily as a prostitute's runner in a brothel). Any process which delays self-acceptance of delinquency is worthwhile, for time is always on the therapist's side. A very small proportion of the juvenile delinquent population becomes persistently criminal in adult life, though as Lee Robins (1966) has shown they may cause much difficulty to themselves and others in other respects. There is a marked contrast with the main problems of medicine and psychiatry, which increasingly concern irremediable problems in late adult life.

Within institutions for delinquents, the role of the visiting psychiatrist has been described by Cameron (1960) and Connell (1965) as essentially supportive to the staff, increasing their confidence and understanding, becoming manifestly valuable to them in helping to deal with particular crises. He would also be of value (as in the remand home in dealing with local authorities) in being able to make a relatively independent analysis of critical situations, which may involve discordant policies and professional tensions and loyalties.

Those who have concerned themselves with the individual psychotherapy of delinquents of less mature characteristics in or out of institutions have tended to evolve a more confronting approach (Schmideberg 1960; 1965). The most direct statement of this policy is in Glasser's 'Reality Therapy' (1965). The aim is to confront the patient without moralising with the consequences of his behaviour and 'become so involved with the patient that the patient begins to face reality and see that his behaviour is unrealistic'. 'Our job is to help the patient himself to fulfil his needs right now', without reference to the past. The major skill is 'the building of a strong emotional relationship quickly between two relative strangers'. This method is probably effective in the hands of those who have extensive psychotherapeutic training and experience; in the hands of others it easily deteriorates into mere exhortation.

The principles of the therapeutic community have also been applied to juvenile delinquents. Clark (1965) has reviewed their application in mental hospitals and Morrison (1967) their relevance to the treatment of delinquents. The main features (Rapaport 1960) consists of democratisation, free communication and sharing of amenities; a more permissive tolerance of acting-out than would be accepted elsewhere so that behavioural tendencies emerge freely; and 'reality confrontation'—free discussion in both small and institutional groups of the sources of tension and individuals' contribution to it. These principles are applied with varying thoroughness in different institutions, depending largely on the range of inmate or patient which has to be accepted. Full application requires careful selection, and either freedom to abscond or be transferred, since many find such methods confusing and too stressful. In the field of institutional treatment the pioneers have often been schoolmasters; Aichorn, Homer Lane, Neill, Lyward and Wills, who exercised a strong personal influence on small institutions and made much use of critical moments in daily life. Miller's (1964) Northways hostel for ex-Borstal boys, and the boys' wing at Grendon prison have special interest.

Behavioural psychotherapy

Aspects of learning theory have of course always been used in the 're-education' and training of delinquents, but more recently the strict application of operant conditioning methods have been used either based on reinforcement of desired behaviour or the avoidance of undesirable behaviour. In either case the plan chosen must be clearly understood and applied. In the CASE Two project (contingencies applicable to special education) in the National School for boys a group of delinquents were placed in attractive private rooms with good meals. Subsequently they had to earn points to maintain this situation; if not, they were regarded as 'relief students' and provided only with simple meals later than the others etc. When successful, further points earned could be exchanged for buying magazines, extra snacks and articles ordered from mail catalogues, etc. Most of these systems operate a 'token' economy, tokens being immediately earned to be exchanged later for the more conspicuous primary awards. Such systems are at their most effective when there is a clear-cut objective and readily identifiable stages of learning. They have achieved notable success for example in the educational system, but for less easily distinguished types of good or bad behaviour they may be difficult to operate clearly. Behavioural treatment requires a great deal of personal attention and critics have suggested that this may be the primary influence.

At the Youth Centre Project at O.H. Close and Carl Holten's schools Jesness (1963) has attempted to contrast the effects of two residential schools with different regimes to which delinquents aged 15–17 were randomly allocated. The Carl Holten School was devoted to behaviour modification by a token economy system which was applied to general behaviour ('convenience behaviour'), educational progress and 'critical behaviour'—the sort of response which had most often got the boy into trouble. The regime at O.H. Close's school was that of 'transactional analysis' in which through group counselling meetings the boys were invited to consider the consequences of behaviour patterns characteristic of them and encouraged to make 'contracts' to modify them either in general or in relation to individuals. Preliminary reports show that success rates for both systems have been about the same but better than those obtained from the previous regime.

Research into treatment

One of the earliest studies of effectiveness was made by Weeks (1958) in the Highfields' Project. Boys of 16 to 17 liable to be sent to a closed Borstal-type institution were allowed to volunteer as a condition of probation to go to Highfields, a small well-staffed institution where they received a form of group treatment (guided group interaction) for 5 evenings a week for about 4 months instead of the 12 months residence usual in Annandale. The results showed that the Highfields' boys were slightly less often reconvicted in the 12 months following release. All the improvement however was attributed to the marked effect on the coloured boys. Coloured boys never formed more than a fifth of intake and the authors make the point that it did not follow that the same effect would have been produced if the whole population had been coloured. Nevertheless the study suggested that for a certain stratum of delinquent 4 months of relaxed treatment and discussion of their problems achieved as much as 12 months of institutional training, and at one third of the cost.

The Grants (1959) published an account of the differential treatment of naval disciplinary detainees, which first raised the issue of the effect of different types of staff upon different types of offender. They produced slight but suggestive evidence that when 'mature' offenders were managed by 'mature' disciplinary staff, rehabilitation was successful. This advantage was however lost if such prisoners were managed by immature staff and mature staff had little impact on immature prisoners.

This theme of differential treatment was taken up in the large scale PICO (Pilot Intensive Counselling Organization) project (Adams 1961). Some 400 institutionalised delinquents aged 17 to 23 with rather bad criminal records were divided (it turned out to be about 50 : 50) into 'amenables' and 'non-amenables', after excluding grossly subnormal cases etc. Amenables were characterised as 'bright, verbal, anxious' with 'awareness of problems', 'insight', 'desire to change', 'acceptance of treatment'. They and a control group of nonamenables had 9 months of once or twice weekly individual counselling and also occasional group sessions. Two further groups of amenables and nonamenables were left to follow the standard regime. After 30 months of postrelease follow-up, the results (by some dozen criteria of parole reports, months in subsequent custody etc.) showed much greater success rate for treated amenables (most marked in the first 12 months but always maintaining a difference). Control nonamenables and amenables behaved in exactly the same way, but there was interesting if somewhat inconclusive evidence that treated nonamenables did *worse* than all the others.

It has long been supposed that the reason for the oft-repeated failure to demonstrate differences in results of quite different treatments (e.g. detention centres as opposed to Borstal) might be that there has been inadequate selection, the 'best' (usually thought of as psychotherapeutic) treatment being effective for some but showing no overall effect because it might actually make unsuitable persons worse by producing confusion, overstress, resentment.

The differential treatment of juveniles of 14 to 18 was also studied by

Empey and Rabow (1961) in the Provo experiment in which boys who might have been put on probation or sent to a custodial institution were randomly allocated to an intermediate system involving an intensive programme of group meetings, with planned school or work schedules. The study was highly original in securing the cooperation of magistrates in allowing, in marginal cases, a random allocation to the different resources, and it encountered considerable problems in maintaining the schedule. During a 4-year follow-up the experimental programme was not markedly more successful than probation but those who would otherwise have been subjected to custodial treatment performed rather better than comparable cases given institutional treatment.

In a later project, the Silver Lake experiment Empey and Lubeck (1971) contrasted the consequences of sending juveniles to a traditional training school for delinquents (Boys Republic) or to Silver Lake, a hostel from which delinquents could go out to school while receiving group counselling or guided group interaction. Significant differences in the rate of arrests following the first year after release were not established.

The largest and most sophisticated ongoing study of these problems has been the Community Treatment Project of the California Youth Authority, undertaken between 1961 to 1973 by Professor Marguerite Warren, and still in operation in a modified form. Unfortunately the main results are available only in duplicated documents. Attempts to summarise the results (Palmer 1971; 1974) are not particularly comprehensive. The aim was to test the theory that juveniles committed to the Youth Authority (aged 13–19, average 15; normally receiving 8 to 10 months custodial treatment followed by 2 to 3 years of parole) could be just as effectively (and more humanely and cheaply) treated in the community to which they would have to return ultimately, provided that supervision was very close and many community resources were mobilised. Secondly, since delinquents varied so widely it would be necessary to use some diagnostic typology, both to test the outcome of comparable cases and to see if the policy could be applied successfully to all types. Thirdly, a study was made of the effects of 'matching' the type of supervising officer to the type of delinquent.

After excluding a (rather large) minority of 35 per cent of boys whose immediate release would cause public or police protest because of the nature of the offence (armed robbery, forcible rape etc.), the remainder were matched for age, race, socioeconomic situation and above all, diagnostic categorisation. Representatives of each group were then randomly allocated either to a control group which underwent the standard institutional training, or an experimental group which was immediately returned to the community under intensive supervision by officers with a case-load of never more than twelve. Moreover for each 'type' released a different programme of needs was evolved and provided—hostels, foster homes, day-attendance centres, educational, vocational guidance, in addition to intensive supervision. After the scheme had been applied (1961–64) with success in the two medium-sized cities of Sacramento and Stockton with boys who were 58 per cent Caucasian, 18 per cent Negro, it was extended to the large conurbation of San Francisco (25 per cent Caucasian, 65 per cent Negro), where a day-attendance centre for 'guided group interaction' was also established.

Table 36.1

			Boys %	Later usage %	
Level 2	**1**	Asocial Aggressive (Aa)	1		
	2	Asocial Passive (Ap)	5		
Level 3	**3**	Immature Conformist (Cfm)	14	Passive Conformist	14
	4	Cultural Conformist (Cfc)	9		
	5	Manipulator (Mp)	12	Power Oriented	21
Level 4	**6**	Neurotic (Acting out) (Na)	25		
	7	Neurotic (Anxious) (Nx)	28	Neurotic	53
	8	Situational Emotional Reactive (Se)	2	All	
	9	Cultural Identifier (Ci)	4	Rare types	12

An essential part of the scheme was the diagnostic typology (Table 36.1, Warren (1966)).* This was a development of the views of Sullivan, Grant and Grant (1959) on 'the development of interpersonal maturity'. Criminal behaviour can be usefully regarded as essentially egocentric behaviour of an unacceptable kind, whether transitory or persistent; at least this aspect is probably more closely related to the prognosis than others. Marguerite Warren's (1966) 'Interpersonal Maturity Level Classification', the study manual of personality diagnosis, has great interest quite apart from its use

---

* Types are difficult to summarise briefly but level 3 describes the offender who interacts primarily in terms of oversimplified rules and formulas rather than from more complex internalised values. Understands few of the feelings and motives of others. Tends to assume that peers and adults operate mainly on a rule-oriented or intimidation/manipulation ('power') basis. The passive conformist is a passive unhappy youth, who tends to feel inadequate and lacking in social 'know-how' complying usually with other adults or peers to seem to have 'power' at the moment. The Cfc thinks of himself as delinquent and tough responding readily to delinquent peers. The Mp manipulates and undermines the power of authority figures and usurps the power. Typically he does not want

in the research, each type being discussed in relation to how he perceives the world, how he responds to it and how others perceive him, as well as the supposed best method of treatment. The 'I level' diagnosis was made at first from taped interviews but later by a personality test (Jesness Inventory 1962) covering the crucial questions. This Inventory has also been used in England (Davies 1967; Mott 1969). With regard to the parole officers it was presumed for example that those most effective with 'neurotic' (level 4) delinquents would be those with 'a great degree of interest in working with youths' feelings about themself and others in reference to guilt, hostility, aggression and rejection'; those dealing best with the immature (level 3 cases) would be 'more likely to focus upon issues relating to external control and limit setting, maintain a greater degree of social distance, and be more likely to be forward, direct and outspoken'.

There are few measures of outcome which can be given without more detailed comment than can be provided here but for the whole period the reconviction rate for boys after a 2-year follow-up was 42 per cent for experimentals and 64 per cent for controls. Expressed in other terms and considering subtypes, 39 per cent of boys responded better to treatment in the community than in institutions, 10 per cent did better in institutions; 27 per cent did equally well in both and 24 per cent equally badly in both.

With the passage of 14 years the research problems have become increasingly complex, particularly with regard to the criterion of 'success' in relation to later relapses. They showed, for example, that the immature conformist tended to respond to supervision very well but relapsed when it was ended. Similarly in a 15-year follow-up of Borstal boys Gibbens and Prince (1965) showed that the independent somewhat aggressive youth with initiative often resented supervision and improved when it stopped; while the passive inadequate responded well, only to fail later.

The latest phase of the CTP has concentrated on the 25–30 per cent who did not respond to treatment at liberty or cannot be set at liberty because of public reaction. Controlled study is being made to see if a relatively short period of custody (2–3 months) in close contact with officers who will supervise them later, will be better than long periods of custody. It will also be seen (Table 36.1) that a recurring problem with diagnostic categories is that some groups are much smaller than others and are difficult to manipulate statistically. Later analyses condensed the types into the three principal ones, ignoring rare varieties.

---

to conform to peers or adults. The latter two groups were for some purposes condensed as 'power-oriented'. Level 4 'neurotic' refers to those with internalised standards of what they judge their own and other's behaviour, recognise interpersonal interactions, have ability to understand some underlying reasons for behaviour etc.

English research has been concerned with similar problems but with the exception of Miller's (1964) study of the effects of group therapy in a hostel for homeless ex-Borstal boys and Craft's (1966) comparison of hospital regimes, they have not tended to be 'action' studies. Craft studied the results of randomly allocating young, dull, deprived and delinquent youths committed to hospital usually as psychopaths to either a ward with a 'community therapy' regime with much discussion and self-determination, or to a ward run on more traditional 'paternalistic' principles with plenty of advice, persuasion and direction. The experiment suggested that for this type of confused and immature boy (level 3) the paternalistic regime was more effective. Similar studies are in progress at Grendon prison boys' wing.

The enormous expense of mounting 'demonstration' projects on any scale has obliged English researchers to take advantage of new procedures planned by the authorities. It is nowadays appreciated that new methods should be accompanied by 'built in' evaluation but perhaps not sufficiently that if the research worker is involved at the earliest planning stage he may be able to suggest ways of setting up the procedure (e.g. in one place but not at all in another) which will greatly assist evaluation.

The psychologists of the Borstal service (1970) had a rather rare opportunity to allocate at random to one of three 'open' Borstals with rather different regimes from a pool of suitable cases. One institution focussed on group counselling methods, one applied 'case-work' principles, and a third was a more traditional training regime. One object was to study the mechanisms and usefulness of detailed allocation. It was found that a few relatively simple facts about the offender could be shown to predict in about 85 per cent of cases whether a boy would be sent to a closed or open institution. The three institutions showed some persistent variations in success rates but although predictors of success or failure made on the basis of the past or present behaviour made before allocation remained fairly accurate, predictions based upon knowledge of the particular institution and whether the regime would especially suit the individual case proved actually less accurate.

The most recent and detailed English study of delinquents (Bottoms & McClintock 1973) took advantage of the initiation of a new type of regime in a Borstal designed to make it more sensitive to individual needs. A group of boys discharged under the old regime in 1962 was contrasted with a group discharged under the new regime in 1966. On the basic criteria of the rate of reconviction within 18 months, there was, in fact, no difference between the two regimes of treatment. Although this was disappointing there were many other research results of great interest, e.g. the validity of staff estimates of future behaviour, which has a bearing upon the accuracy of recommendations to courts.

A series of important studies of probation treatment has been carried out for the Home Office Research Unit by Folkard (1966) and his colleagues. He paid attention to one of the principal problems—that a highly personal and sophisticated system of diagnostic labels may have educational value but cannot be applied equally by a large number of officers throughout the country. A group of probation officers were asked to agree about a variety of types of supervision which they provided on which all their colleagues would probably agree. They considered two aspects—support and control, alone or together. Each however might be individual (face to face) or 'situational' (e.g. focussed upon home visits, advice to family, employers etc.). There was also 'nominal' situational or individual supervision, making in all eight varieties or combinations of supervision. Each officer thereafter classified a series of his cases according to his view of what their needs were and later the success rates were followed up. Although success rates never fell below 35 per cent (in cases thought to need 'situational' control) the highest success rates of 85 per cent and 86 per cent respectively were in the groups classified as needing only 'situational nominal' and 'individual nominal' supervision without apparently either support or control. These constituted almost exactly a half of all cases. One might tentatively conclude that in these cases a fine or conditional discharge would have been equally effective as implied by the judgements or diagnoses of the officers. It is planned to test this hypothesis; in the meantime this sort of research is of practical importance in showing where scarce resources should be most concentrated.

Success rates among the different types of supervision were also related to differences in probation officers, according to sex, age, training, years of service, and previous work.

There are of course many other classifications or diagnostic systems, some of which have been used in research and treatment. Warren (1969; 1973) has shown that there is now a considerable consensus about types in spite of the rather varied and obscure nomenclature. Scott's (1960) typology of ill-trained, well-trained to wrong standards, reparative and maladaptive is well known. Quay (1964) has recently made use of his categories of inadequate–immature, neurotic–conflictive, unsocialised aggressive, psychopathic un-socialised, and subcultural, in random allocations to different regimes in the Kentucky Youth Centre.

Legal provisions

The treatment of juvenile offenders is prescribed mainly by the Children and Young Persons Act (CYPA) of 1969, which makes further strides in implementing the policy of 'blurring the distinction between those who commit offences and those who are in trouble for some other reason . . . criminal behaviour in children (10–13) and young persons (14–17) is seen less as a problem in itself, to be treated in isolation, than as one of several factors in the child's personality, history and background, the existence of any of which might point to a lack of care or control requiring social intervention'.

The Act is a far-sighted measure which provides a blueprint for the future. It provides that no child under 10 can be guilty of any offence. After that a child may be subject to criminal or care proceedings. The Act makes provision to raise the minimum age for criminal proceedings to 14; in 1970 the government declared its intention to raise it in time to 12. The Act has already come into force in various stages (e.g. 'remand homes' and 'approved schools' under the former system were in most cases amalgamated under a comprehensive system of community homes in April 1973—4 years later). The Act provides the power eventually to withdraw the power to send offenders to attendance centres and detention centres and the power to commit (and transfer) to a Borstal sentence first to 16 and then to 17. In 1973 the government indicated its intention not to withdraw the present powers until it is possible to gauge the adequacy of the new provisions being established.

Section 1 of the Act makes comprehensive provision relating to care proceedings for those under 17. For an order to be made the juvenile court must be satisfied that any of a number of conditions is met* one of which in the case of a child or young person over the age of 10, is that an offence has been committed; the court *must also* be of opinion that the child or young person is 'in need of care or control which he is unlikely to receive unless an order under the section is made'. Care proceedings, when an offence is alleged, may be initiated by the local authority or the police if they reasonably believe that there are grounds for making an order under Section 1.

The following orders are available to the court in both care and criminal proceedings.

Care order   A care order commits the child or young person to the care of the local authority in whose area he appears to the court to live. The order places the local authority in loco parentis, with a prior right to the custody of the child and additional power to restrict his liberty if necessary; a person who has attained the age of 18 may still be subject to this latter power while the care order remains in force. The local authority may board the child out with foster parents; maintain him in a community home or a home provided

* (a) His progress is prevented or neglected or health impaired or neglected, avoidably, or he is ill-treated; (b) is a member of the same household as above and it is probable he will also suffer; (c) is exposed to moral danger; (d) beyond control; (e) not receiving efficient full-time education.

under Section 64 of the Act (which empowers the Secretary of State to provide homes for the accommodation of children who are in the care of local authorities and are in need of particular facilities and services which are ... unlikely to be readily available in community homes—for example, those who need long-term psychiatric treatment or who because of their behaviour present special problems of management. Three such homes are planned to serve the whole country and one is already in existence). The authority has power to allow a child in its care to be under the charge and control of a parent, guardian, relative or friend, e.g. to provide a trial period at home or elsewhere, while the child remains legally in local authority care. A care order, unless it is changed or extended ceases to have effect when the child attains the age of 18 years or, if he has already attained the age of 16 when the order is made, when he attains the age of 19. The local authority has the duty to review the case of every child in care not less than every 6 months and, if the child has been committed to care by a care order, to consider whether to make an application for the discharge of the order. A Juvenile Court has power to discharge a care order on an application by the local authority, the child or the parent or guardian on the child's behalf. A Juvenile Court also has power, on the application of the local authority, to extend to the nineteenth birthday a care order which would otherwise expire at 18. This may be done only if the child is accommodated in a community home or a home provided under Section 64 of the Act and it appears to the court that, by reason of his mental condition or behaviour, it is in his interests or the public interests for him to remain there after he attains the age of 18. With the consent of the Secretary of State for Social Services a local authority may bring before a Juvenile Court a person who has attained the age of 15 who is subject to a care order and who is accommodated in a community home. The court may order removal to Borstal if satisfied that the person's behaviour is such that it would be detrimental to the persons accommodated in any community home for him to be accommodated there.

Supervision order   A supervision order places a juvenile under the supervision of the local authority or a probation officer; it lasts for 3 years or for a shorter time specified by the court and, except where the order is made in criminal proceedings, may not expire later than the supervised person's eighteenth birthday. The court may designate as supervisor either a local authority or for a child aged 12 under certain circumstances, a probation officer. The supervisor has a duty to advise, assist and befriend the supervised person. A supervision order may include:

a   a requirement to reside with an individual or a relative;

b   a requirement to submit to treatment for a mental condition similar to the requirement which may be included in a probation order;
c   in due course, a requirement to comply with the directions, given by a supervisor to live in a specified place or to report to a specified person at a time and place arranged in relation to particular activities. This requirement relates to what is commonly called 'intermediate treatment'.

An order requiring the child's parent or guardian to enter into recognisance to take proper care of him or exercise proper control of him.

A hospital order or guardianship order.

Payment of compensation provided an offence has been proved, to a maximum of £100.

Various additional orders are available to the courts in criminal proceedings, e.g. (1) binding over, (2) absolute or conditional discharge, (3) fines of not more than £50, (4) attendance centre order if the offender is a boy and a centre is available to the court. There are 60 junior attendance centres (for boys aged 10–17) situated mainly in the larger centres of population. (5) Detention centre order if the offender is a boy aged 14 or over a centre is available to the court. (6) Borstal training if the offender is 15 or over and is either convicted by the Crown Court or committed there for sentence. (7) In the case of grave crimes (those carrying a maximum prison sentence of 14 years for an adult) detention under Section 53 of the CYP Act of 1933 in a place approved by the Secretary of State; these last two can be ordered only by the Crown Court.

The CYP Act of 1969 abolished the power to commit to an approved school, to place an offender under the age of 17 on probation and to make a *fit person order*. The Act provides for approved schools and remand homes to become part of a comprehensive system of community homes available to all children in care. England and Wales have been divided into twelve areas for the purpose of planning the community homes system and the local authorities in each area have formed a children's regional planning committee to plan the system in conjunction with the voluntary bodies concerned.

The children's regional planning committees are also responsible for drawing up schemes of 'intermediate treatment' for juveniles under supervision, which must be either of a category approved by the Secretary of State or individually approved by him. 'Intermediate treatment' is the term used to describe new forms of treatment for children under supervision to be made available to juvenile courts and supervisors under Part 1 of the CYP Act. The provisions are intermediate between the previous two alternatives of removing a child from his home or relying on supportive social work with the child and his family in the community. (Examples of activities mentioned include sailing, canoeing, climbing, handicrafts, canal reclamation, various other forms of community service activity, and attendance at evening classes.) The child may either spend up to 90 days (single period) in a residential treatment centre or attend a nonresidential centre within reach of his home for up to 30 days in any one year. Schemes are on a regional basis and will consist of a wide variety of recreational, education and other socially valuable activities which, while allowing the child to remain in his home, will bring him into contact with a new environment, interests and experience in company with other children in his community. Intermediate treatment is now available to a number of courts and it is hoped that they will gradually be extended.

These provisions for juveniles have been coordinated with proposals for the future treatment of young adult offenders of 17–21 considered by the Advisory Council on the Penal System in its report of October 1974. The details do not concern us here, but broadly it is proposed that the distinction for this age group between prison, Borstal and detention centre training should be abolished. These would be replaced by a generic 'custody and control' order for offences punishable in the case of an adult by imprisonment. The court would determine the length of the order without restriction other than the statutory maximum for the offence, which would be the same as the statutory maximum prison sentence, but a court should not, in the pursuit of a 'treatment' objective, make a longer order than the sentence of imprisonment it would pass on an adult who had committed the same offence and had similar antecedents.

The maximum length of a custody and control order that a court should be able to impose should be 6 months, with power to commit to the Crown Court if considered necessary. The minimum length for all courts should be 3 months. Offenders should be released at any time after the minimum period on the recommendation of a licence advisory committee attached to each institution (or group of institutions) or, in orders of over 3 years, the Parole Board. On release the youth would be under the supervision of a probation officer for the remainder of his sentence, or at least 6 months. For the first 2 months after release the Governor of the institution should have the right to recall on any reasonable grounds without appeal; thereafter the offender would only be recalled for a clear breach of the conditions of release and with right of appeal. The supervisor could alternatively bring the offender before a magistrates' court, who could order a noncustodial penalty, or exceptionally a return to custody.

In order to encourage the more frequent use of noncustodial measures, there should be a new and stronger noncustodial sentence—a supervision and control order (in addition to the existing probation order). The supervisor should have available a wide range of potential requirements to be invoked as and when he considers their use desirable, with or without the offender's consent. For a breach the offender could be brought before a magistrates' court and the supervisor should have power if he has grounds for believing that the offender is contemplating a breach or commission of an offence, to apply to a magistrate for the offender's detention for up to 72 hours, usually in the nearest young adult establishment. The recommendations have not yet been accepted.

REFERENCES

ADAMS S. (1961) Interaction between individual interview therapy and treatment amenability in Youth Authority Wards. Sacramento: California Board of Corrections

ASUNI T. (1960) Examination of the administrative categories of maladjusted and delinquent children receiving residential treatment. MD thesis, University of Dublin.

BELSON W.A. (1968) The extent of stealing by London boys and some of its origins. *Adv. Sci.* **25**, 171–184

BOTTOMS A.E. & McCLINTOCK F.H. (1973) *Criminals Coming of Age.* London: Heinemann

CAMERON K. (1960) The role of the psychiatrist in an approved school. *J. Child Psychol. Psychiat.* **1**, 306–312

CHRISTIE N., ANDENEAS J. & SKIRBECK S. (1965) A study of self-reported crime. *In* Christiansen K.O. (ed.) *Scandinavian Studies in Criminology* **1**, 86–116. London: Tavistock

CLARK D.H. (1965) The therapeutic community—concept, practice and future. *Brit. J. Psychiat.* **111**, 947–954

CONNELL P.H. (1965) Views on psychiatry and approved schools. *Brit. J. Criminol.* **5**, 150–167

CRAFT M.J. (ed.)(1966) *Psychopathic Disorders and their Assessment.* Oxford: Pergamon

CRAIG M. & GLICK S. (1963) Ten years experience with the Glueck Prediction Table. *Criminal Delinquency* **9**, 249–261

CRAIG M. & GLICK S. (1964) *A Manual of Procedures for Application of the Glueck Prediction Table.* New York: New York City Youth Board

CHILDREN AND YOUNG PERSONS ACT (1969)

DAVIES M. (1967) *The Use of the Jesness Inventory on a Sample of British Probationers.* Home Office Research Unit Study, no. 12. London: HMSO

DOUGLAS J.W.B. (1966) Delinquency and social class. *Brit. J. Criminol.* **6**, 294–302

EDELSTON H. (1952) *The Earliest Stages of Delinquency.* Edinburgh: Livingstone

ELMHORN K. (1965) A study of self-reported delinquency among school children in Stockholm. *In* Christiansen K.O. (ed.) *Scandinavian Studies in Criminology* **1**, 117–146. London: Tavistock

EMPEY L.T. & LUBECK S.G. (1971) *The Silverlake Experiment.* Chicago: Aldine

EMPEY L.T. & RABOW J. (1961) The Provo experiment in delinquency rehabilitation. *Amer. Sociol. Rev.* **26**, 679–696

EMPEY L.T. & LUBECK S.G. (1971) *The Silverlake Experiment.* Chicago: Aldine

FOLKARD S. (1966) *Probation Research: a Preliminary Report.* Home Office Research Unit Report, no. 7. London: HMSO

GIBBENS T.C.N. & PRINCE J. (1965) *The Results of Borstal Training.* Sociological Review Monograph no. 9: Sociological Studies in the British Penal System: Keele, Staffs: University of Keele

GLASSER W. (1965) *Reality Therapy: a New Approach to Psychiatry.* New York: Harper & Row

GLUECK S. & GLUECK E. (1950) *Unraveling Juvenile Delinquency.* New York: Commonwealth Fund

GLUECK S. & GLUECK E. (1959) *Predicting Delinquency and Crime.* Cambridge, Massachusetts: Harvard University Press

GOLD M. & WILLIAMS J.R. (1969) National study of the aftermath of apprehension. *Prospectus* **3**, 3–12

GRANT J.D. & GRANT M.Q. (1959) A group dynamic approach to the treatment of nonconformists in the Navy. *Ann. Am. Acad. Pol. Soc. Sci.* **322**, 127–135

JESNESS C.F. (1962) *The Jesness Inventory: Development and Validation.* Sacramento: California Youth Authority Research Report no. 29.

JESNESS C.F. (1963) *Redevelopment and Revalidation of the Jesness Inventory.* Sacramento: California Youth Authority Research Report no. 35

MAHONEY A.R. (1974) Youths in the juvenile justice system: some questions about empirical support for labelling them. University of Denver Juvenile Justice Standards Project (Minneapolis)

McEACHERN A.W. (1968) The juvenile probation system. *Amer. Behav. Scientist* **11**, 1–43

MILLER D. (1964) *Growth to Freedom: the Psychosocial Treatment of Delinquent Youth.* London: Tavistock

MORRISON R.L. (1967) The idea of therapeutic communities. *In New Thinking About Institutional Care.* (pamphlet). London: Association of Social Workers

MOTT J. (1969) *The Jesness Inventory: Application to Approved School Boys.* London: HMSO

PALMER T. (1971) California Community Treatment Program for delinquent adolescents. *J. Res. Crime Delinquency* **8**, 74–92

PALMER T. (1974) *The Community Treatment Project in perspective 1961–1973.* Community Treatment Project Series, 1973, 1. Reprinted from Youth Authority Quarterly, **26**, 3. Sacramento, California

POWER M.J. (1965) An attempt to identify at first appearance before the courts those at risk of becoming persistent juvenile offenders. *Proc. roy. Soc. Med.* **58**, 704–705

PSYCHOLOGISTS (Borstal Service) (1970) *A Borstal Typology Study.* London: Office of Chief Psychologist, Prison Department, Home Office

QUAY H.C. (1964) Personality dimensions in delinquent males as inferred from the factor analysis of behaviour ratings. *J. Res. Crime Delinquency* **1**, 33–37

RAPAPORT R.M. (1960) *Community as Doctor.* London: Tavistock

ROBINS L.N. (1966) *Deviant Children Grown Up.* Baltimore: Williams & Wilkins

SKABERNE B., BLEJEC H., SKALAR V. & VODOPIVEC K. (1965) Criminal prevention and elementary schoolchildren. *Revija za Kriminalistiks in Kriminologio* **16**. 8–14

SCHMIDEBERG M. (1960) Making the patient aware. *Crime and Delinquency* **6,** 255–261

SCHMIDEBERG M. (1965) Reality therapy with offenders. *Brit. J. Criminol.* **5,** 168–182

SCOTT P.D. (1960) Assessing the offender for the courts. III: The role of the psychiatrist. *Brit. J. Criminol. 1,* 116–129

STOTT D.H. (1963) *The Social Adjustment of Children; Manual to the Bristol Social Adjustment Guides,* 2nd ed. London: University of London Press

STOTT D.H. & WILSON D.M. (1968) The prediction of early adult criminality from school age behaviour. *Int. J. Soc. Psychiat.* **14,** 5–8

SULLIVAN C., GRANT M.Q. & GRANT J.D. (1957) The development of interpersonal maturity: applications to delinquency. *Psychiatry* **20,** 373–385

TAYLOR I., WALTON P. & YOUNG J. (1973) *The New Criminology.* London: Routledge

THORNBERRY T.P. (1971) Effect of legal dispositions on subsequent criminal behaviour. PhD dissertation, University of Pennsylvania

WADSWORTH M.E.J. (1972) Personal communication. See West (1973)

WARREN M.Q. (1966) *Interpersonal Maturity Level Classification: Juvenile.* Mimeographed. Sacramento: California Youth Authority

WARREN M.Q. (1969) The case for differential treatment of delinquents. *Ann. Amer. Acad, Pol. Soc. Sci.* Philadelphia **381,** 47–59

WARREN M.Q. (1973) *Correctional Treatment in Community Settings.* Madrid: International Congress of Criminology

WEEKS H.A. (1958) *Youthful Offenders at Highfields.* Ann Arbor, Michigan: University of Michigan Press

WEST D.J. & FARRINGTON D.P. (1973) *Who Becomes Delinquent?* London: Heinemann

CHAPTER 37

Inpatient units and day-hospitals

L. HERSOV & A. BENTOVIM

Inpatient psychiatric units for children were first set up in the USA to care for those large numbers of children with behaviour disorders following the epidemic of encephalitis lethargica at the close of World War I (Chess 1969). The units were planned to 'contain' children's problems by care and management. As other units were opened they came to provide for children with all types of emotional disturbance who could not be treated as outpatients. There was a transition from a mainly custodial function to a use of the inpatient setting as a therapeutic agent in itself. Many older established units found the change difficult and retained 'custodial' and 'correctional' methods rather than adopting therapeutic approaches (Robinson 1957).

The treatment procedures in these newer units were naturally derived from the outpatient practice of the time, i.e. the clinical team approach of psychiatrist, psychologist and psychiatric social worker using mainly psychotherapy and case-work. They included the additional features of an individual treatment programme for each child, the constructive use of group interaction, and the integrated help of other professional disciplines. The modern inpatient units usually also include the disciplines of nursing, special education, paediatrics, occupational therapy and sometimes child psychotherapy. More specialised units may employ child care workers, speech and language therapists and recreational therapists depending on the age of the children, and the range of disorders which require assessment and treatment.

The newer ideas of inpatient placement for assessment and treatment rather than merely 'containment', required dimensions of knowledge over and above that of the child's individual psychopathology (Sonis 1967). In order to use the environment to bring about therapeutic change, many issues must be carefully considered. These include the attitudes of staff toward parents (Christ & Wagoner 1966); the parents' role in treatment; the therapeutic amosphere in the unit; the overall daily routine; the structure and content of each child's daily treatment programme; the expectations and opportunities provided by a group living situation; and especially the place and objectives of individual dynamic or behavioural psychotherapy.

AIMS OF INPATIENT TREATMENT

Earlier views of inpatient treatment as a benign neutral setting to offset the adverse family influences which get in the way of psychotherapy have been rightly superseded by a broader approach. This includes both treatment skills developed from clinical experience and practice in managing deviant children of all types in groups, together with individual treatment based on psychodynamic understanding and the principles of learning. The bedrock of inpatient hospital treatment is to provide physical care, meet children's personal and social needs, and give the opportunity for satisfying interpersonal experience along with appropriate education. The reliance on time as the healing agent is not enough; there must also be a therapeutic attitude to make use of the many opportunities which all disciplines have to help a child and his family overcome personal and social problems. The primary aim of inpatient treatment is to reunite the child and his family and the goal is to return the child to normal life in his school and community. In the majority of cases admission to hospital is one phase in the overall treatment plan which will have often included outpatient treatment before admission and will usually include further work with the child, family and school after discharge, either in a day-unit or as outpatients.

The modern approach favours the linking of general hospital and community services with hospital units which accept responsibility for meeting the psychiatric needs of a community including children and their families. In this framework, the inpatient psychiatric unit for children is in a functional working relationship with the outpatient services and other child guidance clinics and community agencies concerned with children in need. The aim is to provide help for children with a variety of psychiatric disorders by providing the *appropriate* treatment for each problem and not the *same* treatment for all problems. In this sense the hospital inpatient unit provides a *specialised* treatment service within a range of services.

CHARACTERISTICS OF INPATIENT UNITS

What are the characteristics of hospital inpatient units and how do they differ from other residential treatment units? Nonhospital educational units for disturbed children have existed in Great Britain for many years, providing an appropriate environment for emotional and social development (Laslett 1975). Since the late 1930s there has also been a tradition of residential treatment for neurotic and delinquent children on the model of 'planned environment therapy' (Righton 1975). Robinson (1957) defined an inpatient unit as a psychiatric treatment service in a medical institution or unit. Its function is the diagnosis and treatment *in residence* of children with psychiatric disorders. It provides a 24-hour service and in most instances a 7-day-a-week service for children whose family situation or severity of disturbance make such a service *the treatment of choice* in contrast to outpatient or other forms of treatment. In such units the decisions about admission, plan of treatment and discharge based on the diagnostic and therapeutic findings are made ultimately by the psychiatric staff in discussion and consultation with other professional disciplines in the unit. The psychiatrist, whether as a consultant or director, carries the final medical, and corresponding legal, responsibility for the diagnosis and management of the patients in his care regardless of the way in which aspects of the daily work are delegated to others.

Inpatient units vary a great deal in the size, type and configuration of the actual building, its site, whether isolated or in proximity to other facilities, whether a separate villa type building or a total or part floor in a medical tower block. There are differences in the amount of space for sleeping and for play or other creative activities. A school is usually part of the unit but there is great variation in the number, type and quality of other staff. Units vary in the catchment area served, in the social characteristics of the community from which it draws its patients, and in the amount of training and research which is undertaken. The philosophy of each unit is influenced by the outlook and personalities of the senior staff and by their beliefs about the aetiology, psychopathology, and treatment of psychiatric disorders in childhood.

USES AND ABUSES OF INPATIENT TREATMENT

An inpatient unit can only solve some, but not all, of the problems of a psychiatrically ill child and his family when the child has not responded to other efforts at treatment. Much effort, dedication and resourcefulness must go into a comprehensive inpatient treatment plan for a child and his family but this may not be enough to overcome the handicaps of parental personality disorder and the distorting effects of severe deprivation on the child's development. Too often parents are given an unrealistic picture of what to expect from inpatient admission in order to 'sell' this form of treatment. Experience shows that it is much better to spell out the objectives and limitations of any treatment plan and to let the parents and child look over the unit before admission, so that all have as clear a picture as possible of the layout and facilities, the routine, the visiting arrangements, etc., but above all of what is demanded of them by the plan of treatment.

Inpatient treatment can be of use in a whole range of psychiatric disorders in childhood and adolescence. These include cases of child abuse in preschool children where the hospital has the role of a place of safety for the child while the parents are inolved in a treatment programme aimed at improving parent–child interaction and helping parents over their difficulties. More commonly, children with developmental delay, hyperkinetic disorders, emotional disturbance, conduct disorders or psychosis are admitted. Some children suffer from various forms of brain damage but most will have a psychiatric disorder whose form, persistence and severity constitute a severe handicap. Suicidal and acutely psychotic children may need to be admitted as emergencies. A short stay in hospital for some children in a crisis of acute family tension allows the family to regroup its resources and enter into a definite treatment plan on an outpatient basis.

In general, inpatient admission is the treatment of choice in children:

a   Where thought and behaviour are so severely irrational and bizarre that outpatient treatment is impossible, or where the child may be a danger to himself or to others.

b   Where socially unacceptable behaviour arises from a degree of psychiatric disorder which is unaffected by ordinary social measures or outpatient treatment.

c   Where a complex psychiatric problem requires skilled observation, assessment and treatment which must be continuous and of an intensity not possible on an outpatient basis.

d   Where the family interaction is so distorted that life at home leads to a continuing or progressive interference with the child's development and progress. In this situation the child may need a controlled therapeutic environment to provide healthier life experiences and relationships.

Experience has shown that inpatient treatment has dangers where the disturbed child has become the family scapegoat, or target of parental hostility. When the child is admitted, often as a result of great pressure from referral agencies or the parents themselves, he may become permanently extruded from the family unless powerful efforts are made to keep child and family in psychological touch. Admission under these circumstances can easily create strong feelings of rejection in the child and a sense of failure in the parents which are both very difficult to overcome.

Nakhla *et al* (1969) have described the rationale and advantages of taking a total family into hospital where the hospital setting and facilities permit this method of treatment. They argue that doing so alters the family's view of the identified patient as the 'sick' one, which would otherwise be strengthened were he alone admitted to hospital. Keeping the family intact in this way also avoids potentially damaging separations from family members and gets over the difficulty which arises when admission of one member would be intolerable for the patient and the family. Where the admission of a whole family is not possible, it is most important that the affectionate support and interest of parents and family is assured from the outset so that children can return home regularly during treatment and permanently on discharge.

It is utterly inappropriate to use an inpatient unit merely as a prelude to boarding school placement unless the time is specifically used to deal with particular difficulties and so ensure the success of later school placement. At times, however, careful appraisal of the child and family's responses to hospital admission (Gair & Salomon 1962) and the child's own needs for help in developing emotional and social independence lead to a decision that admission to a special boarding school would continue the improvement gained in hospital.

THERAPEUTIC MILIEU AND ORGANISATION

In the treatment of adults the terms *therapeutic community* and *therapeutic milieu* are sometimes used interchangeably. There are differences of opinion over the practical usefulness of a self-governing community of disturbed children and adolescents and in practice the staff of most inpatient units shape and control the setting for the group of children as a whole while attempting to meet the treatment needs of the individual child.

We mean by therapeutic milieu those aspects of inpatient ward structure, organisation and setting which can help to reduce the emotional and behavioural disorders of children. We assume that deviant behaviour is largely due to faulty or maladaptive social learning which interferes with a child's capacity to relate to other children and adults, to apply himself in a school setting to control impulsive and aggressive feelings and behaviour and to conform to the standards of a social group. Deviant behaviour is also the overt accompaniment of anxiety, depression and loss of self-esteem arising from internal conflict, experiences of loss and rejection, and distorted family relationships. A therapeutic milieu is a structured environment which provides a variety of human relationships, satisfying emotional interactions, opportunities for new learning and experiences, mastery of new situations and the development of personal and social competence. It should aim to meet emotional needs for respect, appreciation, approval and praise, to reduce anxiety, guilt and psychological conflict and strengthen impaired ego functions where possible.

Within the milieu a variety of treatments can be planned and integrated for the individual child and his family, but the clinical team should define tentative goals of treatment before admission to hospital. We have found that a preadmission home visit is most helpful for the clinical team to meet the child and his family in their own setting. This reduces psychological distance between home and hospital, allows the team to make an appraisal of the patient and his whole family. The nurse in the team makes contact with the child on home ground through favourite toys and pets and talks about life in hospital. The same clinical team welcomes the family to hospital and the same nurse supports the child during the introductory phase on the basis of the trust and confidence which was established at the home visit.

Once in hospital the tentative treatment plan made prior to admission is repeatedly looked at and modified in the light of more detailed daily observation, psychological testing and the results of special investigations which reflect the capacity of child and family for different types of therapeutic intervention. Medication is prescribed where appropriate and long-term plans for future schooling are drawn up.

Specific aspects of milieu therapy

Once the child enters hospital the specific objectives of treatment must be clearly defined for all those working with the child and family. This task may be completed early on the basis of the initial assessment. More often, a period of 2–3 weeks is needed to assess the child and family's response to admission, to amplify the history and to observe how the child functions. Attention is paid to the child's peer group relationships, his communication and inter-action with adults, his handicaps and areas of competence, the factors which reinforce or modify his behaviour, and to the way the child talks about his fears, worries and concerns.

Further assessment of educational problems may be needed, leading to a specific programme of remedial teaching. Response to drugs can be monitored by daily observation of seizure pattern and behaviour in cases of intractable epilepsy, so arriving at the right dose of the appropriate medica-tion. One-way viewing screens and videotape recordings are helpful in observing parent–child or family interaction.

In certain disorders, particularly in young children, an objective of treatment may be to modify parent–child interaction when inappropriate or inconsistent handling appears to be producing and maintaining behavioural disturbance. Family interaction can be observed by the clinical team, or parents can observe the child and therapist together. Parents can watch video-tape recordings of their own interaction with their children and discuss this with the therapists. Treatment programmes can then aim to modify faulty interaction and improve behaviour, using techniques of shaping and model-ling as well as guidance on how to deal with any new behaviour problems. It may be necessary to help parents with mixed or hostile feelings about their child and his behaviour. Expectations may be unreal, as in the case of brain damaged children, and interviews focussed on these issues can help parents toward a more tolerant understanding of the many difficulties these children have. Parenting skills can be taught to immature young mothers and fathers in cases of actual or suspected child abuse.

The social group on a ward can greatly assist children who have difficulties with social relationships or are lacking in social skills because of handicaps such as developmental dysphasia. Others may have withdrawn from social relationships as part of a depressive illness or have missed social experiences as a result of long-standing school absence. Social skills training programmes can be established for children with severe social incompetence whereas others will gain confidence and skills by taking part in planned group activities which focus on gaining mastery in a particular skill or game previously feared or avoided (such as swimming, model-making or acting).

The daily programme for an individual child can be structured to overcome a particular difficulty. For example, a graded programme of activities in occupational therapy can be used to overcome poor muscular coordination in a brain damaged child or training in the use of gesture or sign language may be employed in children with severe language disorders. Very short periods of 'time out' from pleasurable activities can be used as needed throughout the day to help children with impulsive disruptiveness or temper tantrums to learn self-control. This will usually be done in conjunction with the family to provide a continuity of approach and ensure generalisation of improved behaviour to situations at home as well as in hospital. Behaviour contracts may sometimes be set up with parents and children using principles of social learning (Patterson 1971).

An effective system of communication is necessary for any treatment plan so that all the professional disciplines involved are clear about the objectives, the methods of achieving these within the ward milieu, the family's place in treatment, and any changes of plan that are needed (Hersov 1974). The nature of the work on inpatient units makes demands on the professional staff's personal stability, resourcefulness, patience and tolerance (Bettelheim 1966) as well as requiring a high degree of trained skills in nursing care and the various forms of social and behavioural treatment. Brown *et al* (1974) have discussed these issues in detail in relation to training programmes for child psychiatric nurses engaged in residential care of disturbed children.

ROLE OF INDIVIDUAL TREATMENT

The place of individual psychotherapy in the treatment of psychiatrically disturbed children in hospital has altered in keeping with the changes in the structure and function of therapeutic environments. Noshpitz (1962) has described how the earlier 'holding' role of residential institutions has evolved over time into two lines of approach to treatment within the areas of ego support and ego interpretation. Treatment tactics now involve the whole staff of the unit not only the child's individual therapist. Noshpitz (1962) also remarks that providing ego support is a complex task requiring highly trained staff capable of understanding the theory of ego functions and able to work specifically on strengthening these. Other experienced workers (Greenwood 1955; Redl 1959; Shaw & Lucas 1970) have found that effective therapeutic interaction is possible using different methods and professional staff other than psychiatrists or psychotherapists alone.

The goals of psychotherapeutic treatment in an inpatient unit may not necessarily be the resolution of unconscious conflicts and the modification of basic character structure. Instead the objective may be to help the child tolerate emotional stress and develop stronger and more effective defences against anxiety, without attempting to deal with the unconscious causes of conflict. There needs to be a focus on the here-and-now conflicts in real life in order for the child to reach effective solutions and mastery of the situation. The emphasis is on the child's behaviour on the ward and on his expressed concerns in relation to adults and other children. The 'Life Space Interview' (Redl 1959) is an example in dealing with immediate crisis situations. In both the ward and individual treatment setting the patient is offered a chance of a new kind of human relationship rather than the distorted and anxiety-ridden one he may have with his parents. In this sense, psychotherapy is re-educative and supportive rather than uncovering. 'No insight, no emotional discharge, no recollection can be as reassuring as accomplishment in an actual life situation in which the individual has failed (Alexander & French 1946, p. 40).

Behaviour modification techniques are now well established as useful methods of treatment in a variety of psychiatric problems. Systematic desensitisation of specific phobias, the use of implosion, or the reduction of obsessional rituals by reinforcement of normal behaviour are some of the methods used in neurotic disorders. Token economy programmes to alter aggressive impulsive behaviour can be most effective, and speech and language training with autistic children has proved successful. Parents and even entire families are increasingly involved in treatment programmes aimed at helping parents develop skills in dealing with specific behavioural problems at home, so complementing the individual treatment of the child in hospital (see Chapter 39).

PLACE OF SCHOOLING

Academic failure is a potent cause of psychiatric disorder in children (Rutter, Tizard & Whitmore 1970). In addition the children often have unsatisfactory peer relationships so accentuating the sense of chronic failure leading to social withdrawal and a further turning away from intellectual work. Often the only satisfaction is through attention-seeking behaviour in the classroom or antisocial disorder outside. The special school in an inpatient unit gives the child another chance to experience a feeling of competence and mastery in a learning situation through individual attention and remedial help with subjects in which they are retarded. The situation is much freer than in a conventional school but the emphasis is always on a steady progression of work with gains in skill and confidence. A teacher may become the key person in the therapeutic programme and this relationship can be most beneficial if handled with understanding.

MOTHER–CHILD AND FAMILY UNITS IN HOSPITAL

Main (1958) has described how he was influenced by the work of James Spence in Newcastle-upon-Tyne in deciding to admit neurotically ill mothers in need of treatment to hospital with their children. Eventually, this became the practice at the Cassel Hospital, but like all departures from a conventional pattern of treatment, it required time for staff attitudes to change and for the growth of new methods of providing care and treatment for total families. Once in hospital, the suspected emotional disturbance in both parents and child became obvious even though the mother may have originally been the designated patient. Treatment procedures on psychodynamic and psycho-therapeutic lines were then developed to help alter mothers' attitudes and ways of handling their children while at the same time providing treatment for the children as well (Folkart 1967).

More recently Lynch *et al* (1975) and Ounsted *et al* (1974) have described a hospital unit designed and staffed for the management of disorders of parent–child relationships. Alongside the main hospital building is a unit with communal domestic facilities but separate bedrooms for 3 mothers. Children may sleep in the same room as their mothers or in the main building where mothers can also be admitted. The mother and child unit is mainly concerned with the younger age group. The range of disorders among the children fell into four main categories (a) children at risk from physical abuse (about half of all admissions), (b) behaviour disorders, (c) developmental delay, (d) seizure disorders. Observation of disturbed family relationships was made easier in this setting but often still took time. Many of the mothers showed psychiatric disorder and some had physical complaints or 'minor health problems'.

This method of treatment is still evolving and the results have yet to be evaluated. However, Lynch and Ounsted believe that units of this kind can serve a useful purpose in meeting crises in which baby battering has already occurred or appears imminent. It provides a resource for hard-pressed Social Service Departments to deal with families and an opportunity for joint hospital and community collaborative work with families.

Another advantage of having mothers and children together in hospital is that treatment programmes can be set up specifically to modify those distorted behaviour patterns which have grown up between parent and child over the years. One-way screens and videotapes allow parents to observe their own family interactions as well as the interactions between children and staff, and so help them arrive at a more effective way of managing behaviour based on discussion, shaping and modelling.

DAY-HOSPITAL UNITS AND TREATMENT

With the greater sophistication of inpatient management, the gap increased between the range of strategies available in this setting and help which could be given in the outpatient clinic. To remedy this fault, Connell (1961) developed a Day-Hospital Unit for children. Through partial hospitalisation the severely disturbed child could benefit from being in a carefully planned therapeutic environment on a daily basis, and yet remain with his family for some of the time. This has proved a helpful, flexible model of intervention with widespread applications.

Aims and objects

If inpatient treatment aims to reunite the disturbed child and his family, with the goal of returning him to normal life in his school and community, day-patient treatment has a similar goal. The difference is that the day unit shares the physical care and nurturance of the child with the parent, and provides a variable amount of time away from the family during the day (for between 1 and 5 days a week, rather than for 24 hours a day and up to 7 days a week).

Like the inpatient unit, the day-centre or hospital should be seen as fulfilling part of the psychiatric needs of the community (Bentovim & Lansdown 1973). It needs to have a functional relationship with other child and family psychiatric services, and yet provide a specialised treatment service to children and families with a wide range of psychiatric problems. It is specifically designed for those children who do not require a treatment setting where complete 24-hour care has to be provided, yet need more than outpatient treatment combined with the network of ordinary and special educational settings and child care services available in the community.

With the rapid development of day-services for children it is important to distinguish between psychiatric day-hospitals or centres, day-care and day-schools for disturbed or 'maladjusted' children. All facilities stress the need for a therapeutic environment for the children attending them. However, 'day-care centres' should be thought of as providing day-to-day nurturant care in the absence of parents (Dingman 1964; 1969) with the therapeutic element introduced to prevent disturbance and deprivation. The day-school for disturbed or 'maladjusted' children is basically an educational provision for children with established psychiatric problems. Although such schools have similar services and facilities to the psychiatric day-centre (Gritzka 1970), the essential difference is that psychiatric staff offer guidance and *consultation to* schools, but supervise and take *responsibility* for treatment of children and families in the psychiatric day-centre (Laufer, Laffey & Davidson 1974). Like the inpatient unit, it is a medical setting, which relies on the joint participation of a wide variety of nonmedical personnel in a multidisciplinary team.

Differences

Relieved of the responsibility of providing 24-hour care, the variation in day-centre settings and configuration can be even wider than in inpatient care. They can be an integral part of an inpatient unit or a separate entity; in a converted house or purpose-built premises; cater for between 4 and 40 children with or without parents and siblings; provide participation for specific diagnostic social or age groups; or for the whole age and diagnostic range. Children and families can attend daily or for varying numbers of days a week, for months or several years. Centres can be part of a child psychiatric, paediatric or adult psychiatric day hospital; can serve a wide catchment area or be within pram-pushing distance.

Without the need for total care, staff in continuous contact with children can come from a wide range of disciplines. Registered or Enrolled Nurses can form the core but others can be drawn from among nursery nurses, teachers, social workers, group workers, occupational therapists, child care workers, play specialists, in various combinations.

The common factor to all models of care is the joint endeavour of the staff to provide a therapeutic milieu, and the philosophy employed to reach this end is dictated in part by the specific site, general setting, population, and problems to be met, and in part by the outlook and beliefs and personality of the senior staff.

Uses and abuses

Originally, day-treatment was seen as a provision for those children whose problems required more than outpatient setting, and yet who were not so disturbed as to require inpatient treatment, so that similar indications to those for inpatient treatment were put forward; irrationality and bizarreness of thought and behaviour, socially unacceptable behaviour, complexity of problems, and distortion of family relationships.

However, the argument has been advanced (Devlin 1962) that, not only can such problems of lesser intensity be dealt with in day-centres (Chazin 1969), but also that it may be optimal treatment for all such problems, even the more severe. The main advantage is that complete separation from the family does not occur, lessening the danger of mutual rejection and scapegoating. To achieve similar results to inpatient treatment the major additional factor is the ability and motivation of the family to cooperate in the treatment, whether for the child or themselves. It also presumes a certain stability in the home (La Viètes *et al* 1965). Although it would appear that children who are in danger of physical harm (whether from abuse or from their own impulses, suicidal or anorexic) require inpatient management, Atkins (1962) has claimed equal success with more severely disturbed children using either inpatient or day-hospital treatment.

Where day-centres and inpatient units coexist, flexibility of case-management is possible for more severely disturbed children. The day-centre can be used to determine whether a particular child requires a controlled therapeutic environment, whether residential or day special school. It can also be particularly useful in the reuniting phase of treatment for the child who has been an inpatient, and who needs further help before completing rejoining his family and re-entering life in the community (Marshall & Stewart 1969).

A day-centre setting seems most useful for certain sorts of problems. It provides a base for the child refusing school, and for the shared care with schools of children whose behaviour can only just be contained. Specialised day-centres for psychotic or autistic children have been developed (Fenichel *et al* 1960), utilising specific treatment techniques involving parents (Schopler & Reichler 1971) and operant conditioning approaches. The day-centre also appears to have a specific role in the assessment and treatment of disturbance in the preschool child. Separation as a result of hospital admission may well be contraindicated in this age group, and a setting allowing for work with with both parents and children seems essential. Bentovim and Boston (1973) have described the day-centre treatment of a wide range of severe management problems, mother–infant problems, developmental speech and language disordered children, developmental behavioural problems, hyperkinetic behaviour and psychotic disorders in this age group.

When inpatient treatment is necessary in this age group, usually because of anticipated or actual abuse, admission to a family unit of parent and child may be preferable (Ounsted *et al* 1974). Family units for a variety of problems have been set up (Folkart 1967) and a brief period of inpatient treatment for a family in crisis can be a helpful prelude to a longer period of day-centre or outpatient care in a variety of conditions.

Like inpatient units, there can be abuse of day-hospital facilities by families, schools and social agencies demanding action which may affect therapeutic on-going relationships in these situations, and prevent reintegration after treatment. However, it has been observed (D'Amato 1969) that when day-hospitalisation is available, the demand for residential inpatient facilities does lessen.

Therapeutic milieu and organisation

The therapeutic milieu and the methods used in many day-hospitals is similar to that created in inpatient units. The organisation provides a variety of human relationships, satisfactory interactions and emotional experiences, and attempts to meet emotional needs to improve psychological functioning. Specific treatments for the individual child or families also need to be meshed within the milieu by careful preplanning, and review of progress by the whole team involved with case and centre.

A number of specific areas in day-hospital functioning need to be considered. The intake of child and family is extremely important considering the relevance of parental attitudes and motivation to successful outcome. We find several preliminary meetings with the family help to overcome the crisis attending commencing day-centre attendance, particularly when parents are expected to attend regularly. For parents to define themselves (rather than the child) as being in need of help, work has to do be done on resistances. Introductions to the day-centre workers and to other children and parents can help to overcome stranger anxieties and the panic felt in groups. This is particularly relevant when the first aim is to ensure the child or parents' attendance the next day. An individual day-centre worker or psychiatric team member needs to be assigned to help take up the anxieties engendered in crossing the boundary, the remaining 'within the circle', and further individual or family work may be necessary to reinforce attendance (c.f. the 'second day packing' phenomenon described by Ounsted *et al* 1974).

Where the day-centre's focus is on joint work with parent and the pre-school child, such issues are vital, since the parent is not a patient in his or her own right, yet needs to be open to the therapeutic milieu if there is to be modification in family relationships (Bentovim 1973). We have found parent groups which discuss the shared problems of coping with disturbed children helpful. A therapeutic community attitude of sharing responsibility and decision-making for the centre and its organisation with parents may also help them find a role and a status which does not foster unhelpful regression.

When working with groups of parents and preschool children a development sequence of behaviour is noted which parallels the children's and parents' relationships to the centre and its workers (Bentovim 1974). This commences with dependency and reliance, and evolves through rivalry, splitting into positive and negative attitudes to the workers, before being able to integrate and model themselves on the caring staff. Following this they are then able to relate appropriately and meet the needs of their disturbed or handicapped young children.

Unless families are severely deprived and disorganised, it is not likely that very young children and their parents will attend for more than 1 or 2 days weekly, although the children themselves may need additional days attending, particularly if specific (speech) language or behavioural programming is necessary. A number of models of intervention with young children and parents have been described depending on whether the groups are treated separately (Frommer 1967) or conjointly (Bentovim & Boston 1973). A variety of individual, group, marital and family modalities are fitted in to the day's programme in a regular predictable way.

There are two basic ways of creating a therapeutic milieu for the older child in a day-hospital setting. One uses a school model, separate from the inpatient unit, and relies on specially trained teachers and assistants to provide the setting. Parents are usually at the periphery as older children have experienced separation in school and would not expect parents to be present except for specific events. Groups are generally small to encourage socialisation and the daily programme (Godwin *et al* 1966) is set in collaboration with the psychiatric team, incorporating education (including remedial teaching) and social recreational activities to encourage competence, as well as individual and family therapeutic work when appropriate.

The other common model is that in which the day-patient has an integral place in a joint day and inpatient unit. This gives considerable flexibility of treatment for a specific child, but can present problems for the staff member in his approach to the child who is in his care for 24 hours a day, compared with the child in his charge for a limited period only. In this setting the day-patient is likely to meet a wider variety of staff, and to have schooling separately. Unless the day-patients represent a reasonable number of children, their needs can be swamped by the insistent demands of inpatients, and a specific time is often necessary to consider their needs.

Regular meetings are required to maintain a therapeutic milieu. As well as attending to the on-going needs of specific patients and their families, projections onto the staff by specific groups of children and parents need to be kept in mind. Failure to observe such group phenomena in the staff can create opposition to attempts to foster specific treatment programmes. Although the psychiatrist has medical and legal responsibility, and the senior staff create the treatment philosophy, all staff need to provide mutual support and be involved and share in decision making about intake, about changes in treatment planning, and how to achieve a therapeutic milieu (Vaughan & Davis 1963).

Specific aspects of milieu therapy

Once a child has begun regular attendance at the day-hospital or centre with or without his parents or siblings, a specific programme must soon start. After an initial period of observation, a process of putting together earlier information and current assessment is pursued, as with a child in the inpatient setting. Specific solutions and strategies for particular problems need to be devised, so that these activities can be fitted in to the daily pattern. For instance, a child with a separation problem needs a relationship with a particular worker or nurse so that he can find adequate comfort to tolerate a parent's brief absence. The worker must also make a sufficiently good relationship with the parents to enable them to leave with a feeling of trust. Once initial separation is achieved, then the child should be incorporated into the rest of the group to gain increasing confidence in social relationships. At the same time individual, or group work with the parents should help to uncover the precipitating and perpetuating factors in the family which have led to separation problems.

An excessively shy or fearful child also needs a small group which will not overwhelm him but rather draw him in to shared games, play and music and movement. A regular, predictable timetable is necessary with structured and unstructured periods of play to develop creativity and control. Individual and group activities will help a child play through particular anxieties and help in socialisation and sharing. Stories and music aid language skills. Regular snacks and meal-times can help children who have feeding problems. Orderly, predictable attendance of staff, other children or families is essential to provide the expected human environment; introductions and terminations should be thought out and well prepared. Holidays and breaks in attendance both of children and staff must be talked about and worked through. The setting of timetable, people and activities acts as a holding or adaptive framework to encourage intellectual and social growth; the situation both shapes and is in turn shaped, by those it contains.

Aggressive overactive children need a firm predictable setting and a milieu prepared to use 'time-out from reinforcement' techniques or periods of specific work devoted to lengthening attention and concentration. To increase tolerance of frustration and reduce violent responses, the reward for impulsiveness has to be lessened, and social reward and attention must be given for self-control. Families need help to model themselves on methods which replace punitiveness by firmness. Parents have to be taken into partnership during individual activities with children so that they can be supported to persist in attempts to interact and play with an unresponsive, self-stimulating handicapped or autistic child, or continue with a speech programme initiated by a clinical psychologist or speech therapist.

The help of other older children in the group can be enlisted to help a child who feels forced to perpetuate a battle with authority. At times social pressures from peers can be more powerful than the staff's in helping a child to attend to a teacher with whom he has had a previous conflict. The peer culture can also work against the therapeutic programme; for instance, a child who is having individual work may use the fact that other children are not to strengthen his resistance during a phase of hostile feelings. Or else, those children who are envious of individual attention may undermine his trust. A parent may feel left out if another child is having a programme carried out for a problem area she identifies as similar to her own child's. One worker may be compared unfavourably with another. Workers may themselves collude and overidealise or criticise one child or family and thus provide excess care or otherwise extrude them without being aware of the motivation. A reasonable degree of identification between workers, parents and children is essential to create a satisfactory therapeutic milieu. Detachment and lack of involvement are unhelpful and can be experienced as rejection. Maintaining a balance between concern, caring and overinvolvement without awareness is not easy, but this is essential to meet the individual and group needs.

PROBLEMS ASSOCIATED WITH DAY-CENTRES AND HOSPITALS

There are many advantages to flexible day-patient treatment, with the variety of treatment strategies available and the therapeutic power of the group to create a favourable milieu (Gold & Reisman 1970). However, problems can arise in the parent–child preschool setting. Frommer (1967) has pointed to the high incidence of psychiatric disorders in parents of children attending day-centres; this means that their needs can dominate the centre's resources, to the detriment of the children's needs. There is a definite boundary between the adult day-hospital which caters for children and the children's day-hospital which caters for parents. Confusion and mistaken admissions can drive away other families and children who could be helped in one or other setting.

Similarly the structure of the group of children for intake has to be carefully considered. Groups seem to function best with a good mixture of children and problems. Too many aggressive children or children with severe language problems can distort the group and prove antitherapeutic, unless centres are particularly organised for these problems. Paradoxically, a small group of 2 to 3 older children can be more difficult to control because of the sibling rivalry felt towards the worker or teacher, so that size of groupings needs to be considered and kept under review.

There are also problems for staff working in day-centres and inpatient units. Staff in continuous contact with highly disturbed children experience feelings of despair, inadequacy, terror and rage at times. They need a setting to share such feelings, without criticism and understanding. Problems such as closeness to, and identification with certain children, and feelings of rivalry and tension with parents need to be aired. A sequence of messianic hope, despair and a final realistic appraisal of what can be achieved with children and families needs to be traversed (Stroh 1968) by all workers entering the field.

When workers from different fields as nursing, teaching, social work, and occupational therapy come together they can pool their resources and teach each other in evolving skills. However, constant contact with problem behaviour may make the staff feel deprived of skills with blurred roles and the fear that they will lose their professional base. The senior staff, day and inpatient workers need to work together to lessen anxieties or loss of self and ability, so that the major aim of providing a therapeutic milieu can be realised with the minimum damage to those creating it. Helping the staff's personal growth and maturation helps the children and families in turn.

Outcome of treatment in inpatient and day-hospital units

There are real problems involved in the study of the effects of treatment which have been well discussed by Robins and O'Neal (1969) and by Barker (1974). A control group is needed to compare complaints, symptoms and diagnosis. The selection of a particular treatment is influenced by many factors, such as the beliefs or convictions of the clinicians involved and the ways in which the child and his family receive and respond to the offer of treatment (Schuham *et al* 1964). In a therapeutic milieu there are many potentially helpful influences acting on the child and family and it is difficult to tease out the relative effectiveness of each.

There are very few studies of the outcome of inpatient treatment, reflecting the difficulties involved in carrying these out, and certainly none in which there has been a controlled comparison between a treated and an untreated group. As it is usually the more severely ill children who are offered inpatient treatment there are also problems in obtaining a suitably matched comparison group. The published results of follow-up studies cannot easily be compared, as they refer to different clinical populations in different hospital settings using different methods of assessment such as interviews, questionnaires, telephone conversations and the like. In general it appears that children with neurotic disorders do better than those with psychotic or organic disorders (Levy 1969; Treffert 1969; Warren 1965; Barker 1974). However, all studies tend to show that the goal of reuniting a child with his family without the need for further treatment is reached in only a small proportion of cases, usually with neurotic children. The majority still require further special help in other hospital units or residential and day-schools for maladjusted children (Capes, Gould & Townsend 1971). In Barker's (1974) words 'Inpatient care was thus often a passport to further help rather than a complete treatment in itself' (p. 307).

The evaluation of day-hospital treatment is beset by similar problems. Children referred are often amongst the most difficult, so that comparable control groups, or random allocation of treatment modalities is difficult to put into operation. Devlin (1962) reported on randomly assigned children who were suitable for inpatient treatment to a day-hospital. He noted that although all children did make gains, parental attitudes were more important in relation to the children who were withdrawn from treatment or subsequently admitted to the inpatient unit.

Follow-up studies (Gold & Reisman 1970), although showing a two-thirds improvement rate, also indicate the necessity for longer term special educational facilities or continuing treatment when children have required day-hospitalisation. Young children have a rather better outcome, and our own experience indicates a favourable outcome for children with emotional disturbances who are anxious, fearful and have separation problems. Children with conduct problems, psychotic disorders or severe speech and language disturbances do less well. However, as with inpatient care, day-patient attendance also helps toward a confident assessment of long-term needs, both for education and management. D'Amato (1969) also noted that in a 2-year period demand for inpatient treatment diminished by 16 per cent whilst day-hospital places nearly tripled in number. The aim of day-hospitalisation to return a child to normal life in the community does seem to be reached, even though he may often need some special educational setting to help do so.

CONCLUSION

Hospital treatment of psychiatric disorders in children has evolved steadily since its beginnings where the objectives were 'containment' to its present sophisticated use of 'milieu therapy' embodying psychodynamic and behavioural techniques of management. The advent of family units, mother–child units and day-hospital units has increased the range of problems that can be treated and opened the way to direct work with children in their families.

REFERENCES

ALEXANDER F. & FRENCH T. (1946) *Psychoanalytic Therapy*. New York: Norton

ATKINS T. (1962) *Criteria for the Differential Use of Treatment Settings for Children with Emotional Disorders*. New York: Child Welfare League of America

BARKER P. (1974) 'The results of in-patient care.' *In* Barker P. (ed.) *The Residential Psychiatric Treatment of Children*. London: Crosby Lockwood Staples

BENTOVIM A. & LANSDOWN R. (1973) Day hospitals and centres for disturbed children in the London area. *Brit. Med. J.* **4,** 536–538

BENTOVIM A. (1973) Disturbed and under five. *Spec. Educ.* **62,** 31–36

BENTOVIM A. & BOSTON M. (1973) A day centre for disturbed young children and their parents. *J. Child Psychother.* **3,** 46–60

BENTOVIM A. (1974) Group processes in a Parent–Child centre. *Group Analysis*, **7,** 50–57

BETTELHEIM B. (1966) Training the Child-Care Worker in a Residential Center. *Amer. J. Orthopsychiat.* **36,** 694–705

BROWN S., KOLVIN I., SCOTT D.McI. & TWEDDLE E.G. (1974) The child psychiatric nurse: training for residential care. *In* Barker P. (ed.) *The Residential Psychiatric Treatment of Children*. London: Crosby Lockwood Staples

CAPES M., GOULD E. & TOWNSEND M. (1971) *Stress in Youth*. London: Oxford University Press

CHAZIN R.M. (1969) Day treatment of emotionally disturbed children. *Child Welfare* **48,** 212–218

CHESS S. (1969) *An Introduction to Child Psychiatry*, 2nd edn. New York: Grune & Stratton

CHRIST A.E. & WAGONER N.N. (1966) Iatrogenic factors in child residential treatment. *In* Masserman J.H. (ed.) *Current Psychiatric Therapies*. New York: Grune & Stratton

CONNELL P.H. (1961) The day hospital approach in child psychiatry. *J. Ment. Sci.* **107,** 969–977

D'AMATO G. (1969) *Residential Treatment for Child Mental Health*. Springfield, Illinois: Charles C. Thomas

DEVLIN M. (1962) Criteria for a day treatment type of setting. *In Criteria for the Differential Use of Treatment Setting for Children with Emotional Disorders*. New York: Child Welfare League of America

DINGMAN P.R. (1964) Day hospitals for children. *In* Epps R.L. & Hanes L.D. (eds.) *Day Care of Psychiatric Patients*. Springfield, Illinois: Charles C. Thomas

DINGMAN P.R. (1969) Day programs for children: a note on terminology. *Mental Hygiene* **53**, 646–647

FENICHEL C., FREEDMAN A.M. & KLAPPER Z. (1960) A day school for schizophrenic children. *Amer. J. Orthopsychiat.* **30**, 130–143

FOLKART L. (1967) Some problems of treating children in the in-patient setting. *J. Child Psychother.* **2**, 46–55

FROMMER E. (1967) A day hospital for children under five. *Lancet* i, 377–379

GAIR D.S. & SALOMON A.D. (1962) Diagnostic aspects of psychiatric hospitalization of children. *Amer. J. Orthopsychiat.* **32**, 445–460

GODWIN M.P., CONNOR M.E., ATKINS S. & MULDOON J.F. (1966) The role of the educational program in a psychotherapeutic day-care center for children and teenagers. *Amer. J. Orthopsychiat.* **36**, 345–346

GOLD J. & REISMAN J. (1970) An outcome study of a day treatment unit school in a community mental health center. *Amer. J. Orthopsychiat.* **40**, 286–287

GREENWOOD E.D. (1955) The role of psychotherapy in residential treatment. *Amer. J. Orthopsychiat.* **25**, 692–698

GRITZKA K. (1970) An inter-disciplinary approach in day treatment of emotionally disturbed children. *Child Welfare* **49**, 468–472

HERSOV L.A. (1974) Neurotic disorders with special reference to school refusal. *In* Barker P. (ed.) *The Residential Psychiatric Treatment of Children.* London: Crosby Lockwood Staples

LASLETT R. (1975) Aspects of change in the education of maladjusted children. *J. Assoc. Work Malad. Child.* **3**, 13–19

LAUFER M.W., LAFFEY J.J. & DAVIDSON R.E. (1974) Residential treatment for children and its derivatives. *In* Caplan G. (ed.) *American Handbook of Psychiatry*, vol. II, 2nd edn. New York: Basic Books

LA VIÈTES R., COHEN R., REENS R. & RONALL R. (1965) Day treatment center and school: seven years' experience. *Amer. J. Orthopsychiat.* **35**, 160–169

LEVY E.Z. (1969) Long-term follow up of former inpatients at the Children's Hospital of the Menninger Clinic. *Amer. J. Psychiat.* **125**, 1633–1639

LYNCH M., STEINBERG D. & OUNSTED C. (1975) Family unit in a children's psychiatric hospital. *Brit. Med. J.* ii, 127–129

MAIN F.T. (1958) Mothers with children in a psychiatric hospital. *Lancet* ii, 845–847

MARSHALL K. & STEWART M.F. (1969) Day treatment as a complementary adjunct to residential treatment. *Child Welfare* **48**, 40–44

NAKHLA F., FOLKART L. & WEBSTER J. (1969) Treatment of families as in-patients. *Family Process* **8**, 79–96

NOSHPITZ J.D. (1962) Notes on the theory of residential treatment. *J. Amer. Acad. Child Psychiat.* **1**, 284–296

OUNSTED C., OPPENHEIMER R. & LINDSAY J. (1974) Aspects of bonding failure: the psychopathology and psychotherapeutic treatment of families of battered children. *Develop. Med. Child. Neurol.* **16**, 447–456

PATTERSON G.R. (1971) *Families.* Champaign, Illinois: Research Press

REDL F. (1959) The Life Space Interview. I. Strategy and techniques of the life space interview. *Amer. J. Orthopsychiat.* **29**, 1–18

RIGHTON P. (1975) Planned environmental therapy: a reappraisal. *J. Assoc. Work. Malad. Child.* **3**, 3–12

ROBINS L.M. & O'NEAL P.L. (1969) The strategy of follow-up studies with special reference to children. *In* Howells J.G. (ed.) *Modern Perspectives in International Child Psychiatry.* Edinburgh: Oliver & Boyd

ROBINSON J.F. (ed.) (1957) *Psychiatric In-patient Treatment of Children.* Washington: American Psychiatric Association

RUTTER M., TIZARD J. & WHITMORE K. (eds) (1970) *Education, Health and Behaviour.* London: Longman

SCHOPLER E. & REICHLER R.J. (1971) Parents as cotherapists in treatment of psychotic children. *J. Autism Child. Schiz.* **1,** 87–102

SCHUHAM A.I., COE R.M. & RAE-GRANT N.I. (1964) Some social-psychological variables influencing parental acceptance of residential treatment for their emotionally disturbed children. *J. Child Psychol. Psychiat.* **5,** 251–261

SHAW C.R. & LUCAS A.R. (1970) *The Psychiatric Disorders of Childhood,* 2nd edn. New York: Appleton-Century-Crofts

SONIS M. (1967) Residential treatment. *In* Freedman A.M. & Kaplan H.L. (eds) *Comprehensive Textbook of Psychiatry.* Baltimore: Williams & Wilkins

STROH G. (1968) The function of in-service training in the management of disturbed children. *J. Child Psychol. Psychiat.* **9,** 189–201

TREFFERT D.D. (1969) Child-adolescent unit in a psychiatric hospital. *Arch. Gen. Psychiat.* **21,** 745–752

VAUGHAN W.T. & DAVIS F.E. (1963) Day hospital programming in a psychiatric hospital for children. *Amer. J. Orthopsychiat.* **33,** 542–544

WARREN W. (1965) A study of adolescent psychiatric in-patients and the outcome six or more years later. II. The follow-up study. *J. Child Psychol. Psychiat.* **6,** 141–160

CHAPTER 38

Drug treatment

D. SHAFFER

Few issues in contemporary psychiatric practice give rise to such controversy as the use of psychoactive drugs for the treatment of disturbed children. It is held by some that drugs dull natural exuberance or creativity or that they silence the child's just protest without dealing with the cause of that protest. More reasoned anxieties are that reliance upon pharmacotherapy reduces the therapist's incentive to use other treatment methods such as counselling, psychotherapy or educational assistance; that prolonged administration in childhood might interfere with learning processes and with physical and intellectual growth or may lead to the development of dependence or addiction.

Drug treatment may or may not do all or any of these things but it is clearly important that both the usefulness and hazards of drugs intended for use in childhood be evaluated with care.

Inappropriate drugs should be avoided and adverse effects need to be identified and where possible minimised by modification of the therapeutic regime. However, the evaluation of drug treatment in a child psychiatric population is not easy and the difficulties are reflected by the generally poor quality of research, the bulk of which is uncontrolled, anecdotal or without appropriate statistical treatment. Some areas of difficulty peculiar to child psychiatry are detailed below.

Normative studies

These are useful in identifying the effect of drugs on cognitive and somatic functions. However, children cannot be expected to give their informed consent to volunteer for such experiments, and some may doubt whether parents can do so on their behalf.

Diagnostic homogeneity

In adult studies, the need to examine drug effects in diagnostically homogeneous groups has become widely recognised, but this is less the case with children. In part this is a reflection of disagreement amongst child psychiatrists on a meaningful classification system. As a result, children may be grouped together under an uncontentious label such as 'behaviour disorder' or categorised by the presence or absence of an index behaviour such as 'hyperactivity' which may fail to distinguish meaningfully between conditions with quite different aetiology and natural history. Yet unless the nature of the disorder that is being treated can be described in a reliable and discriminating way, it is not possible to generalise from any results that the study might produce.

Controls

The psychiatrist interested in assessing the effects of a drug may choose to match the treatment group with an alternative or control group, or else may decide to use each patient as its own control in a 'cross-over' design. Both of these methods present difficulties. If children are to be assigned to different treatment conditions it is especially important that the groups be matched for diagnosis. The importance of this can be illustrated by Cytryn *et al's* (1960) study in which it was found that 71 per cent of children with predominantly neurotic symptoms responded to placebo, although only 10 per cent of children with antisocial behaviour did so. Studies where diagnostic differences are ignored and subjects are randomly assigned to different treatment groups may thereby result in quite misleading findings.

Matching may be required for other factors which will influence treatment response. For example, in one report it was found that adherence to a treatment regime was related to social class (Eisenberg 1962). Older children with school refusal are said to carry a worse prognosis than younger ones (Coolidge *et al* 1960). No doubt there are other variables which influence treatment response and about which we are currently ignorant. All of these factors make the formation of truly comparable alternate treatment groups most difficult and necessitate large groups and access to a generous clinical pool from which subjects may be drawn.

A cross-over design has the advantage of reducing the number of subjects that are needed to ensure comparability, and also takes account of the unknown variables which may influence therapeutic response. However, the design is not appropriate to conditions in which initial improvement may, itself, lead to further change. For example, in school refusal a rapid return to school increases the likelihood of persisting school attendance and hence this condition is unsuited to cross-over study. More obscure time and sequence effects have been noted in other conditions and these need to be looked for and taken into account in assessing results. Attention also needs to be paid to the intervals between different treatment conditions. It seems likely that drug effects may persist for some while after administration has ceased, and also that in some cases withdrawal symptoms may cause an actual deterioration in the child (Molling *et al* 1962). These effects are inadequately documented and yet information is clearly needed for the design of cross-over trials with an adequate 'wash-out' period. Finally, cross-over studies are often lengthy, and in general the longer the clinical trial the higher the drop-out rate.

There are some advantages in studying the effect of drugs amongst children living in an institutional setting. There is likely to be less day-to-day variation of routine, it is easier to ensure that drugs are taken and it may be possible to obtain ratings of behaviour change from a number of professional workers of different descriptions. However, institutional studies create problems of their own, especially as far as obtaining appropriate controls is concerned.

A carefully documented example of this is provided by Molling *et al's* (1962) study. Tranquillisers or placebo were given to randomly selected groups of delinquent boys in a given 'cottage' within a large penal institution. Boys from another cottage were used as no treatment controls. The investigation found no difference between the active drug and placebo groups, both sets of children in that cottage showing a marked improvement. However, the control boys from the other cottage actually deteriorated during the course of the study. The authors attributed the positive improvement in the treatment cottage to the increased interest and optimism engendered by the study, and similarly the deterioration in the control group to the feelings of exclusion by the boys not involved in treatment.

Standardisation of dosage

The rate of absorption, metabolism and clearance of a drug will vary with the child's size. For this reason drug trials in childhood ought to adopt a reference point against which the dose can be standardised. Surface area is the most satisfactory standard (Butler & Ritchie 1960) and this can easily be calculated if the child's height and weight are known.

Because of the large variability between different individuals in their sensitivity to a given drug it is common practice to increase the dose until either a therapeutic effect is obtained or unwanted effects develop. This procedure may be necessary in the early stages of research on an untried drug.

However, it may make it difficult to assess the frequency of unwanted effects and may obscure paradoxical effects in which a large dose is less effective than a smaller one (Maxwell & Seldrup 1971).

As unwanted effects are usually dose-related it is clearly desirable that the smallest effective dose be identified. This is only possible by comparing standardised doses. A good example of this approach is given in Werry and Sprague's (1973) study of methylphenidate. By contrasting the effects of different dose levels they were able to show that side effects increased significantly when a dose of more than 0·03 mg/kg was used, and also that there was little or no therapeutic advantage at higher dose levels.

The construction of a satisfactory drug trial is therefore no easy task. On the other hand the nature of the most common child psychiatric disorders lend themselves more easily to objective evaluation than do psychiatric disorders in the adult population. Reliable and meaningful assessment of behaviour change can be made with the use of appropriate rating scales by both teachers and parents. A number of such scales, especially designed for use in psychopharmacological research, have been published by the US National Institute for Mental Health (Conners 1973) and these are appropriate not only for large scale clinical trials but also for the evaluation of the individual case.

STIMULANT DRUGS

The effects on behaviour and cognitive function of the sympathomimetic amines, *d*-amphetamine and methylphenidate, have been studied in greater detail than any other group of psychoactive drugs. Much of the work has been carried out in North America and detailed reviews have been prepared by Sprague and Sleator (1973), Conners (1972b), Sykes *et al* (1972) and Sroufe (1975).

Most studies have been concerned with children who showed conduct disorders or behaviour difficulties in the classroom. Behaviour changes in natural settings and cognitive and motor performance in the laboratory have both been evaluated.

Behaviour changes

Classroom behaviour is often strikingly improved in those children who respond to stimulants; they become less disruptive and easier to manage, more attentive and less distractable. Teachers often rate them less active although this may be a situation specific response. Measurements of total daily behaviour suggests that there may actually be an increase in gross motor activity during treatment (Millichap & Boldrey 1967). A feature of several different studies has been that whilst improvement has been noted at school it has been less apparent at home. Possible reasons for this are discussed below.

The effect of these drugs on children with neurotic disorders has not been examined so extensively. However Winsberg *et al* (1974) noted that ratings of anxiety in a group of hyperactive and aggressive children showed little change during treatment.

Cognitive and motor changes

Effects of the stimulants noted in the laboratory tests include a reduction in reaction time and better performance on tests of fine motor coordination (Knights & Hinton 1969) and more reflection and less impulsivity on such tests as the Porteus Maze.

The effect on attentiveness is complicated. Sykes *et al* (1972) have carried out a series of investigations into the effects of methylphenidate on hyperactive children who did poorly on a test which required them to respond to infrequent stimuli presented at a predetermined rate (experimenter paced), but better on a task which allowed the child to control the rate of presentation (self-paced). The main effect of treatment was to improve performance on experimenter paced tasks. It is difficult to know whether such artificial laboratory experiments are indicating the mechanisms through which these drugs influence behaviours in the real life situation. However, they may explain why stimulants seem to assist concentration in a structured, task-oriented classroom setting and why parents or teachers in an unstructured setting are less likely to note improvement (Schleifer *et al* 1975). Fears have been expressed that this effect on concentration might reduce normal exploratory or socially oriented behaviour but experimental studies suggest that this is not so (Ellis *et al* 1974).

However, intelligence tests are largely insensitive to the changes brought about by stimulants and no consistent or characteristic patterns of improvement are seen during treatment (Werry 1970). Werry (1970) has summarised the effects of stimulants on test performance; tests requiring vigilance, response speed, short-term memory, resistance to fatigue and an ability to ignore distracting stimuli are those most likely to improve. However, drug treatment does not boost IQ or allow the child to do better on tasks which require a higher level of cerebral organisation, only improving performance when the difficulty level is appropriate to the child's abilities.

Stimulants and conditioning treatment

The use of drugs as adjuncts to other forms of treatment has not been extensively studied. Young and Turner (1965) found that enuretics responded more rapidly to the bell and pad when being treated simultaneously with methylamphetamine. However, they found that the relapse rate after treatment was significantly higher than when treatment had been by conditioning alone. Christensen and Sprague (1973) have experimentally treated a group of overactive children with a conditioning procedure used concurrently with the administration of methylphenidate or placebo. There was a greater reduction in restlessness when the active drug was used, but the persistence of this effect was not studied.

Persistence and generalisation of effects

Overton (1970) has suggested that learning which takes place under the influence of drugs or alcohol is 'state dependent' i.e. does not persist when the drug has been removed. Aman and Sprague (1974) have looked at this problem experimentally in a small group of children. They found no difference in retention of material learned after an acute administration of methylphenidate as compared to material learned after receiving placebo.

Most studies carried out on the amphetamines have been of short duration and there have been few systematic investigations into whether improvement persists either after drug withdrawal or even during prolonged treatment. Studies by Klein and Gittelman-Klein (1973) and Conrad *et al* (1971) suggest that initial improvement on cognitive measures may not be maintained even when treatment is continued. Sleator *et al* (1974) reported on a small group of conduct disturbed children who had shown a good response during 2 years of treatment with methylphenidate. At the end of this period placebo was substituted for active drug. Sixty per cent of the children deteriorated but the remainder showed no change, and in these children drugs were discontinued without adverse effect. It was not possible to predict which of the children would need more prolonged treatment. Therefore transfer to placebo should be regularly attempted as part of an on-going treatment assessment. Little is known about the impact of treatment on long-term adjustment. Mendelson *et al* (1971) and Weiss *et al* (1975) have done long-term follow-ups on children who had been labelled hyperkinetic. A number of children in these studies had previously been treated with stimulants and the results of follow-up suggest that drug treatment had done little to improve the outcome.

Sedation or stimulation

The ways in which the amphetamine-like drugs bring about improvements in behaviour remain obscure. Wender (1971) has suggested that children who respond to these drugs are characteristically underaroused and that this state is corrected by the drug's *stimulant* effects. However, the evidence that 'hyperactive' children are underaroused is inconsistent and contradictory (Satterfield & Dawson 1971; Montagu 1975) and the notion that amphetamines increase 'arousal' has not been borne out by experiment (Montagu & Swarbrick 1975). It is widely held that the amphetamine-like drugs have a 'paradoxical' *sedative* effect on children, and a stimulant effect on adults. However, amphetamines increase vigilance and attention in both children and adults (Weiss & Laties 1962) and insomnia is a troublesome side effect at all ages, although drowsiness may be noted in the period immediately after administration (Montagu & Swarbrick 1975).

Predicting a favourable response

Most studies have shown that a proportion of children treated with stimulants do not respond favourably and that children who do respond vary in their patterns of improvement. These variations are probably due to the heterogeneity of the samples chosen for study. To overcome this problem Conners (1972a, b) has attempted to predict a favourable response by categorising a large number of children on the basis of their initial performance on a comprehensive test battery. In these studies, children who showed least improvement were those with a behaviour disturbance only and without deficits on tests of intelligence, perception and attention and without evidence of EEG or neurological abnormality. Disturbed children with such deficits and abnormalities were more likely to respond to treatment. These observations are in broad agreement with those made by Satterfield (1973) and Steinberg *et al* (1971) who found more responders amongst hyperactive children with abnormal EEGs and 'soft' neurological signs, and in a number of animal studies in which the drugs were found to have a greater effect on motor activity of rats after induction of a cerebral lesion (Adler 1970).

Which stimulant?

Both intergroup comparisons and cross-over studies suggest that *d*-amphetamine and methylphenidate (Conners 1972b; Winsberg *et al* 1974) are equally effective and that children who respond to one drug are likely to respond to the other, relatively few responding to only one. The effects of the related drug magnesium pemoline have been studied (Conners *et al* 1972), but it seems to hold few advantages and treatment needs to be continued for longer before a therapeutic effect is noted. Schnackenburg, in an open study (1973), suggested that caffeine might be a safe and effective alternative to the other stimulant drugs, but a more systematic double blind study comparing a lower dose of caffeine (average dose 160 mg t.d.s.), decaffeinated coffee, methyl-phenidate and placebo (Garfinkel *et al* 1975) found methylphenidate to be the most effective treatment. The issue remains to some extent unresolved because of the difference in dose levels.

The choice, therefore, lies between methylphenidate and *d*-amphetamine, and rests on the comparative safety and freedom from unwanted effects of the two drugs. A study of the growth effects of the two drugs (Safer *et al* 1975) suggests that when the dose of methylphenidate is held below a critical level (see below) long-term effects on growth are minimised, whereas high doses of methylphenidate and even low doses of *d*-amphetamine interfere with growth rate over prolonged periods of treatment. If only on the basis of these findings, methylphenidate would seem to be the drug of choice.

Dosage and side-effects

Werry and Sprague (1973) have used a variable dose technique to assess the optimal dose of methylphenidate. They found no therapeutic advantage in using a dose greater than 0·3 mg/kg/day and also noted that the frequency and severity of side effects was markedly increased when the dose was greater than 1 mg/kg/day. This dose is well below that recommended by some practi-tioners (Wender 1973). Methylphenidate is active for 4–5 hours and is custo-marily given either as a single morning dose or else as a divided dose in the morning and at mid-day. The most common side effects are insomnia and anorexia. Some children become excitable but more commonly irritable, oversensitive and depressed during treatment. It has been suggested that depressive reactions are especially likely in children with epilepsy or struc-tural brain damage (Ounsted 1955). Reversible psychotic episodes have been reported with therapeutic doses of both methylphenidate and *d*-amphetamine (Lucas & Weiss 1971). There have also been reports of dyskinetic states with tremor and orofacial tics.

Toxic overdose with the sympathomimetic amines produces cardiovascular and CNS abnormalities and may lead to death. CNS signs include restless-ness, tremor, ataxia, confusion, hallucinations and hyperpyrexia. Cardiovas-cular signs include arrhythmias and hypertension. Death is usually associated with hyperpyrexia or intracranial haemorrhage. Chlorpromazine should be given to control the hyperpyrexia, and a rapidly acting alpha blocking drug, such as phenoxybenzamine or phentolamine to control the hypertension.

Growth retardation in children on long-term stimulant treatment was first reported by Safer *et al* in 1972. More detailed studies (Safer *et al* 1975) suggest that children on *d*-amphetamine or high doses of methylphenidate may lose up to 20 percentile points of height over a 3-year period of treatment. However, no growth changes were noted when the dose of methylphenidate was less than 20 mg daily and when the drug was administered intermittently and not given during summer holidays. Safer and Allen (1973) did, however, note a compensatory acceleration of growth when treatment was discontinued. Interference with growth has been attributed to a reduction in caloric intake but there is also evidence that amphetamine interferes with the release of Human Growth Hormone (Rees *et al* 1970). Regardless of the reason for growth failure it is clearly important to maintain percentile-related growth charts for children being treated with stimulants over any period of time.

Summary

Stimulant drugs should be considered for use with children who present with a behaviour disturbance, especially when the clinical picture is dominated by poor attention, overactivity and disruptiveness in class, and when clinical and psychometric examination reveals the presence of neurological 'soft' signs, EEG abnormalities or deficits in cognitive function. However, use in frankly brain-damaged children should be approached with care because of the risk of adverse psychiatric sequelae. The drug of choice is methylphenidate which should be used at a dose of 0·3 mg/kg/day, the total daily dose not exceeding 20 mg/day. Treatment effects can usefully be monitored by classroom observations made by a teacher and these may be more sensitive than parental observations. It is important that height and weight changes be monitored on a growth chart.

MAJOR TRANQUILLISERS

These include the phenothiazines and butyrophenones.

Use in conduct disturbance

A number of well controlled and carefully evaluated studies have shown that children with severe conduct disturbance may benefit from treatment with the major tranquillisers (Garfield *et al* 1962; Alderton & Hoddinott 1964;

Werry *et al* 1966; Barker & Frazer 1968; Alexandris & Lundell 1968). Children who respond to these drugs show less aggressive and oppositional behaviour, become more manageable, concentrate better and have fewer fights and arguments with other children. Tranquillisers may reduce gross motor activity, but seem to have little effect on restless and fidgety activity. Little is known about the sort of child who will do well on these drugs but neither the presence or absence of family psychopathology nor of organic indicators appear to discriminate between responders and nonresponders. Similarly, little is known about the persistence of favourable change or the effects of withdrawal. However, Molling *et al* (1962) noted that children's behaviour deteriorated after withdrawal of treatment with perphenazine. Garfield *et al* (1962) similarly found that neurotic children became more anxious after treatment with chlorpramazine had been discontinued than they had been before the start of the treatment.

The usefulness of these drugs is generally limited by the high incidence of significant side effects at therapeutic dose levels, Werry *et al* (1976) have conducted a comparative cross-over study using a high and low dose of haloperidol (0·05 and 0·025 mg/kg respectively) and methylphenidate on a group of conduct disordered children. They noted a high rate of unwanted effects with the larger dose of haloperidol on both behaviour and cognitive function. However, the lower dose resulted in improvements in behaviour, memory and learning which were comparable to those found with methylphenidate. Clearly, the effects of low doses of haloperidol deserve further investigation.

Use in emotional disturbance

Eisenberg *et al* (1961) found no difference between placebo, psychotherapy and perphenazine in the treatment of children with neurotic disorders, the children responding well to all types of treatment.

Garfield *et al* (1962) treating a number of emotionally disturbed children found that they became less aggressive during treatment, but at the same time they appeared to have become increasingly depressed.

Use in movement and habit disorders

The major tranquillisers have been shown to reduce the frequency of stereotypies (Davis *et al* 1969) and self-destructive behaviour (Fish 1973) in severely subnormal and autistic children. Connell *et al* (1967) have shown that haloperidol reduces the frequency and severity of tics and vocalisations in ticqueurs of normal intelligence.

Effect on cognition and perceptual-motor function

Normative studies on human adults and on animals show that the major tranquillisers slow down reaction time, interfere with sustained attentiveness and reduce the speed and accuracy of fine motor movements. The drugs also interfere with conditioning processes (Hartlage 1965). There have been no normative studies on children but Helper *et al* (1963) found that children being treated with chlorpromazine did less well on a paired associate learning test, although once learned, retention was normal. McAndrew *et al* (1972) noted that when phenothiazines were withdrawn from a small number of children after long-term treatment their performance on the Stanford Achievement Battery showed a rapid improvement. In the individual patient, therefore, it is important to determine whether benefit, in terms of improved concentration and less disruptive social behaviour, outweighs any simultaneous impairment in cognitive function.

A similar approach needs to be adopted in children being treated in institutions. A survey in the United States (Lipman 1970) revealed that very large doses of tranquillisers are often given to institutionalised subnormal or autistic children. In this setting there is clearly a danger of reducing still further the already limited stimulus properties of the environment. This risk needs to be balanced against any enhancement of social opportunities that may result from an improvement in the child's behaviour and attentiveness.

Unwanted effects

The most common unwanted effects of the major tranquillisers are drowsiness, dystonic states, sialorrhoea, nausea and vomiting and excessive weight gain. Corneal opacities are a hazard after prolonged treatment with large doses of promazine or chlorpromazine. Photosensitivity states occur in some individuals and there may be an increase in seizure frequency in brain damaged or epileptic children receiving the drugs. Lucas and Pasley (1969) found that half of a group of children receiving therapeutic doses of haloperidol experienced drowsiness, a quarter had slurred speech and a similar proportion sialorrhoea.

Dystonic symptoms occur most commonly during or after discontinuation of treatment with fluphenazine, trifluperazine and haloperidol and much less frequently during and after treatment with thioridazine. Dystonias developing during treatment will usually respond to antiparkinsonian drugs. However, a syndrome marked by the appearance of ataxia and choreiform movements a few days after tranquillisers are discontinued has been described (McAndrew *et al* 1972; Polizos *et al* 1973). This remits rapidly with the reintroduction of phenothiazines but is unresponsive to antiparkinsonian drugs. This condition—which occurs most commonly after prolonged treatment with large doses—will usually remit spontaneously within 3–12 months after the drugs are withdrawn. It is clinically dissimilar to the syndrome of tardive dyskinesia as seen in adults, in that the extremities are more often involved and the head and mouth less so.

Although thioridazine is less likely than other drugs in this group produce dystonic side effects, inordinate weight gain is a frequent feature of treatment. McAndrew *et al* (1972) reported that a group of children receiving doses varying between 25 and 400 mg of thioridazine daily, gained on average 18 percentile points in weight during the first 3 months of treatment. Weight gain is however reversible when the drug is discontinued.

The effect on skeletal growth of this group of drugs has not yet been studied. However, it is known that both the phenothiazines and the tricyclic antidepressants, reduce circulating Growth Hormone levels and interfere with the Growth Hormone response to insulin-induced hypoglycaemia (Sherman *et al* 1971). There is therefore some theoretical basis for fearing that growth in height might be affected by such drugs. The heart rate of children receiving chlorpromazine is increased (Garfield *et al* 1962), a finding which may reflect a raised circulating Prolactin level, or alpha blockade. However, Aman and Werry (1975) have found no effect on heart rate of haloperidol, when used at doses of 0·035 mg/kg or less.

Dosage

Young children may be less sensitive to haloperidol and the phenothiazines so that any single dose/unit body weight formula may result in too small a dose being given to young children or too large a dose being given to older children. A safer method is to calculate an optimal adult dose and to tailor the child's dose to that on the basis of relative surface areas, as advocated by Catzel (1966).

MINOR TRANQUILLISERS AND ANTICONVULSANTS

Short-lived anxiety states or mild emotional disorder commonly occur in childhood. They have a good prognosis and psychoactive drugs are rarely indicated for their treatment. More persistent phobic or anxiety states or more severe emotional disorders are often distressing or handicapping but the usefulness of drugs in their treatment is poorly documented.

The benzodiazepine tranquillisers, diazepam and chlordiazepoxide, are widely used in the management of anxiety states in adults and are undoubtedly employed by both family doctors and psychiatrists for disorders in childhood as well. However, the few published investigations suggest that these drugs may be not only ineffective in childhood but also may produce unwanted behaviour changes, especially in younger children. Zrull *et al* (1964) found that the behaviour of a group of 6–12-year-old hyperactive children was worse on diazepam than on placebo. Lucas and Pasley (1969) treated a group of children with emotional disorders with between 5 and 20 mg of diazepam daily. The treatment failed to relieve apparent anxiety or tension in any of the prepubertal children and in some cases there was actually an increase both in anxiety and in disturbed conduct. These findings are of interest and generally lend support to studies by Dimascio (1973) and Salzman *et al* (1974) which have shown that certain adults—especially those with a history of aggressive, destructive or impulsive behaviour—show an increase in hostility, aggression and irritability whilst being treated with diazepam.

The other group of sedating drugs, at one time widely used in child psychiatry, is the barbiturates. However, the use of phenobarbitone in child psychiatry seems to have followed the familiar pattern of overenthusiastic and uncritical advocacy leading to equally enthusiastic and uncritical rejection. It is now commonly held that the drug, rather than sedating, may actually increase activity and difficult behaviour in disturbed children. This may be so but it has not been adequately demonstrated.

One of the few studies to examine the effects of phenobarbitone on behaviour is that by Frommer (1967) who used the drug as a control medication in a study designed to examine the effects of the antidepressant phenelzine. There was no placebo condition and only global assessments of behaviour change were noted but it is of interest that 2 weeks after starting on phenobarbitone, 11 children with anxiety symptoms were noted to have improved as compared with 2 who were worse. Because of its design this study is far from satisfactory. However, on the face of it the effects of phenobarbitone were certainly no worse and may be better than those described in the benzodiazepine studies above.

The effect of the barbiturates on cognitive functioning in childhood is also an area which requires further research. Hutt *et al* (1968) in a study on adult volunteers found that therapeutic levels of phenobarbitone impaired verbal learning and vigilance performance. However, the comparability of that situation to that of children receiving long-term treatment is difficult to assess and it may be that some adaptation takes place with continued treatment. Wapner *et al* (1962) found no change in Stanford–Binet or Maze learning test scores in a group of 8–12-year-old children before and after being placed on phenobarbitone but the test retest interval was short and the tests used may have been insensitive to short-term changes. Unwanted effects will of course be related to dosage and at blood levels greater than 60 μg/ml there is inevitably clinical evidence of confusion and intellectual deterioration. Reynolds and Travers (1974) have noted changes amongst adults in psychomotor and intellectual performance with levels as low as 16 μg/ml.

Phenobarbitone is often thought to be an inappropriate anticonvulsant in childhood because of its alleged adverse effects on behaviour and cognition. It should be made clear that the behavioural and cognitive effects of the common anticonvulsants remain largely unexplored, and, whilst in any individual child undesirable effects may be noted, there is simply not enough information available at this stage to allow predictions to be made about the behavioural hazard of one anticonvulsant as opposed to any other (Stores 1975).

It has been claimed that phenytoin has a beneficial effect on behaviour problems in both epileptic and nonepileptic children. However, this has been looked at systematically by Conners *et al* (1971) who found the drug to have no psychotropic value. Furthermore, the drug may impair both concentration and fine motor coordination (Idestrom *et al* 1972) and may lead to apparently irreversible changes (Logan & Freeman 1969). The relationship between serum level and unwanted effects has not been noted in children, but in adults these effects are uncommon at dose levels below 15 μg/ml (Haerer & Grace 1969).

Other anticonvulsants, and in particular sulthiame (Ospolot), carbamazepine (Tegretal) and beclamide (Nydrane) have been promoted as having a beneficial effect on disturbed children. Al-Kaisi and McGuire (1974) have studied the effect of sulthiame at a dose of up to 15 mg/kg on groups of young disturbed mentally retarded patients in an institution. Ratings on nurses' behaviour scales were contrasted before and after 4 months of treatment with either sulthiame or placebo. Improvement was noted in hyperactivity and aggressiveness. Although this study suggests that these very difficult patients were improved on the drug, the characteristics of the two treatment groups are not compared and it is not possible to say whether these patients did better on sulthiame than on better established tranquillisers, nor were effects on cognition assessed. Nevertheless, this appears to be a promising tranquilliser, at least for very disturbed institutionalised patients.

The effect of carbamazepine are less well documented. Dalby (1971) reported improvement in psychiatric state in a large group of patients with temporal lobe epilepsy. However, it is not clear whether improvement was a direct result of drug treatment or occurred indirectly as a result of better seizure control.

Claims that beclamide is of value in behaviour disorders rest on an inadequately described study by Price and Spencer (1967) which has not been replicated to date.

Antidepressants

In 1967 Frommer described a study in which a significantly greater improvement was noted in children with phobic disorders and mood disturbance during treatment with a combination of phenelzine and chlordiazepoxide than during treatment with phenobarbitone. The study presents numerous methodological problems, not least because of the use of polypharmacy and the absence of a placebo control. Eisenberg *et al* (1961) had earlier demonstrated that the placebo response rate in children with predominantly emotional symptoms is considerable and it is therefore especially important to include a placebo condition when assessing the treatment of this sort of child). However, subsequent work has tended to confirm Frommer's early conclusions that antidepressants may be of value in the treatment of emotional disturbance in childhood. Gittleman-Klein and Klein (1971) randomly assigned school phobic children to a group that received treatment with imipramine and a group receiving placebo. Both groups received other supportive treatment. After 6 weeks of treatment more than four-fifths of the active treatment group were attending school—almost twice as many as in the control group. The doses used were in the order of 100–200 mg per day, i.e. comparable to those that would be given to an adult. There was a lessening of observed depression, phobic behaviours and somatic symptoms in the imipramine group and it was thought that the drug might have acted through a reduction in separation anxiety. Weinberg *et al* (1973) found that a group of children with a positive family history of depression presenting with a recent change in mood, and a fall off in academic achievement, were significantly more likely to recover when treated with imipramine than a similar group of patients who were not so treated. This last study contains major methodological defects. However, there does seem to be sufficient evidence from the studies to warrant a trial of therapy with an antidepressant drug in children who present with a phobic disorder, mood change and somatic symptomatology. The effects of these drugs may not be seen for several weeks and such a trial should therefore not be abandoned prematurely.

There is some evidence that imipramine is also of value in the management of behaviour disturbances in childhood. At a dose level of 150 mg daily Winsberg *et al* (1972) found a significantly reduced rate of aggressive and overactive behaviour in 69 per cent of a group of 41 disturbed children. Rapoport *et al* (1974) compared methylphenidate, imipramine and placebo during a 6-week trial on 72 children with a hyperactive behaviour disorder. Although imipramine was more effective than placebo, it produced significantly less improvment than methylphenidate and was not very well tolerated. The mean dose of imipramine was 80 mg/day and significant weight loss was noted during the course of the study. The children were advised to remain on medication during follow-up and a year later Quinn and Rapoport (1975) found that (a) twice as many of the children on imipramine had discontinued treatment; (b) there was no difference in behaviour at home between children who had discontinued treatment and either of the active drug groups who had continued with treatment; (c) that both persistent groups did better than those who had discontinued on a classroom behaviour rating scale; and (d) both drug groups lost a significant number of weight percentile points. On the basis of these studies it would seem as if the stimulant drugs—in doses of less than 20 mg/day—are to be preferred to imipramine and that long-term treatment with either class of drug should be monitored by checks on height and weight.

Imipramine and the other tricyclic drugs are also of value in the suppression of enuresis (Shaffer *et al* 1968). Most enuretics will wet less often when receiving the drug although most will relapse once the drug has been discontinued. It seems unlikely that the tricyclics suppress enuresis through their antidepressant action as in most cases a therapeutic response occurs almost immediately after treatment is instituted.

The drug lithium carbonate, which is used to stabilise and reduce relapses in adults with bipolar affective psychoses, is also known to reduce combative behaviour in animals (Weischer 1969). These two actions have led to the application of the drug in childhood and uncontrolled anecdotal accounts have been published suggesting that it may be useful (Annell 1969).

Hypnotics

Transient sleep disorders, in particular, reluctance on the part of the child to go to bed or fall asleep unless the parent can be present at the same time, are common in childhood. This may lead to a self-reinforcing situation which may fatigue both child and parent. Whilst often a sign of a more fundamental disturbance in the family, it may be helpful and necessary to focus on treatment of the sleep disorder. In such cases a brief period of treatment with a hypnotic may be required.

The hypnotics most commonly used are the antihistamines such as diphenhydramine or promethazine, or chloral hydrate and its derivatives. Either chloral hydrate or its more palatable formulation triclofos will usually induce sleep in 20–50 minutes when given at a dose level of 70 mg/kg. It has been claimed that triclofos is less likely to cause gastric irritation and is more palatable than chloral hydrate (Millichap 1972). Cardiac arrythmias are an important feature of chloral overdose state. Some degree of arrhythmia, however, seems to be relatively common and Silver and Stein (1971) reported the development of sinus arrythmia or wandering pacemakers in 5 out of 12 children receiving therapeutic doses of chloral hydrate for sedation before routine electoenchephalography.

Antihistamine drugs such as diphenhydamine commonly induce sleepiness at dose levels of 2–4 mg/kg body weight. Although side effects include nasal stuffiness and gastrointestinal upset, it is clinical experience that some children respond to the drug by becoming overexcited and active. Overdose may cause convulsions and a confusional state. Although widely used, hypnotics have not yet been subject to any systematic investigation in childhood.

CONCLUSIONS

On the basis of careful research findings it is apparent that psychopharmacological agents do have a useful part to play in the management of certain conduct disorders (especially those associated with defects of attention and perceptual and cognitive functioning), of very gross behaviour difficulties in retarded and psychotic children, of stereotypies and of tics. The value of drugs, in particular the tricyclic antidepressants, in the treatment of emotional disorders of childhood is much less certain. Research is still at a very preliminary stage and requires replication and expansion, but the prospects seem hopeful. Practitioners need to bear in mind the hazards—in particular to growth and learning—of treating children, especially when such treatment is maintained over a long period of time.

REFERENCES

ADLER M.W. (1970) Drug response following brain damage. *In* Smith W.L. (ed.) *Drugs and Cerebral Function*. Springfield, Illinois: Charles C. Thomas

ALDERTON H.R. & HODDINOTT B.A. (1964) A controlled study of the use of thioridazine in the treatment of hyperactive and aggressive children in a children's psychiatric hospital. *Can. Psychiat. Assoc. J.* **9**, 239–247

ALEXANDRIS A. & LUNDELL F.W. (1968) Effects of thioridazine, amphetamine and placebo on the hyperkinetic syndrome and cognitive area in mentally deficient children. *Canad. Med. Assoc. J.* **98**, 92–96

AL-KAISI A.H. & McGUIRE R.J. (1974) The effect of sulthiame on disturbed behaviour in mentally subnormal patients. *Brit. J. Psychiat.* **124**, 45–49

AMAN M.G. & SPRAGUE R.L. (1974) The state-dependent effects of methylphenidate and dextroamphetamine. *J. Nerv. Ment. Dis.* **158**, 268–279

AMAN M.G. & WERRY J.S. (1975) The effects of methylphenidate and haloperidol on the heart rate and blood pressure of hyperactive children, with special reference to time of action. *Psychopharmacologia* **43**, 163–168

ANNELL A.L. (1969) Lithium in the treatment of children and adolescents. *Acta Psychiat. Scand. Suppl.* **207**, 19–30

BARKER P. & FRAZER I.A. (1968) A controlled trial of haloperidol in children. *Brit. J. Psychiat.* **114**, 855–857

BUTLER A.M. & RITCHIE R.H. (1960) Simplification and improvement in estimating drug dosage and fluid and dietary allowances for patients of varying sizes. *N. Engl. J. Med.* **262**, 903–908

CATZEL P. (1966) *The Paediatric Prescriber.* Oxford: Blackwell Scientific

CHRISTENSEN D.E. & SPRAGUE R.L. (1973) Reduction of hyperactive behavior by conditioning procedures alone and combined with methylphenidate (Ritalin). *Behav. Res. Ther.* **11**, 331–334

CONNELL P.M., CORBETT J.A., HORNE D.J. & MATTHEWS A.M. (1967) Drug treatment of adolescent ticqueurs: a double blind study of diazepam and haloperidol. *Brit. J. Psychiat.* **113**, 375–381

CONNERS C.K. (1972a) Stimulant drugs and cortical responses in learning and behavior disorders in children. *In* Smith W.L. (ed.) *Drugs, Development and Cerebral Function.* Springfield, Illinois: Charles C. Thomas

CONNERS C.K. (1972b) Symposium: Behavior modification by drugs. II: Psychological effects of stimulant drugs in children with minimal brain dysfunction. *Pediatrics* **49**, 702–708

CONNERS C.K. (1973) Rating scales for use in drug studies with children. *Psychopharm. Bull.* Special supplement to vol. 9. *Pharmacotherapy in children*, 24–84

CONNERS C.K., KRAMER R., ROTHSCHILD G., SCHWARTZ L. & STONE A. (1971) Treatment of young delinquent boys with diphenylhydantoin sodium and methylphenidate: a controlled comparison. *Arch. gen. Psychiat.* **24**, 156–160

CONNERS C.K., TAYLOR E., MEO G., KURTZ M.A. & FOURNIER M. (1972) Magnesium pemoline and dextroamphetamine: a controlled study in children with minimal brain dysfunction. *Psychopharmacologia* **26**, 321–336

CONRAD W.G., DWORKIN E.S., SHAI A. & TOBIESSEN J. (1971) Effects of amphetamine therapy and prescriptive tutoring on the behavior and achievement of lower class hyperactive children. *J. Learn. Dis.* **4**, 509–517

COOLIDGE J.C., WILLER M.C., TESSMAN E. & WALDFOGEL S. (1960) School phobia in adolescence. *Amer. J. Orthopsychiat.* **30**, 599–607

CYTRYN L., GILBERT M.S.W. & EISENBERG L. (1960) The effectiveness of tranquilising drugs plus supportive psychotherapy in treating behavior disorders of children: a double blind study of 80 outpatients. *Amer. J. Orthopsychiat.* **30**, 113–129

DALBY M.A. (1971) Antiepileptic and psychotropic effect of carbamazepine (Tegretol) in the treatment of psychomotor epilepsy. *Epilepsia* **12**, 325–334

DAVIS K.V., SPRAGUE R.L. & WERRY J.S. (1969) Stereotyped behavior and activity level in severe retardates: The effect of drugs. *Amer. J. Ment. Def.* **73**, 721–727 727

DIMASCIO A. (1973) The effect of benzodiazepines on aggression: reduced or increased. *In* Garratini S., Mussini E. & Randall L.O. (eds.) *The Benzodiazepines.* New York: Raven Press

EISENBERG L. (1962) If not now, when? *Amer. J. Orthopsychiat.* **32**, 781–793

EISENBERG L., GILBERT A., CYTRYN L. & MOLLING P.A. (1961) The effectiveness of psychotherapy alone and in conjunction with perphenazine or placebo in the treatment of neurotic and hyperkinetic children. *Amer. J. Psychiat.* **117**, 1088–1093

ELLIS M., WITT P.A., REYNOLDS R. & SPRAGUE R.L. (1974) Methylphenidate and the activity of hyperactives in the informal setting. *Child Dev.* **45**, 217–220

FISH B. (1973) Summary report of the children's psychopharmacology unit of New York University Medical Center. *Psychopharm. Bull.* Special Supplement to vol. 9. *Pharmacotherapy in children*, 13–18

FROMMER E.A. (1967) Treatment of childhood depression with anti-depressant drugs. *Brit. med. J.* **1**, 729–732

GARFIELD S.L., HELPER M.M., WILIOTT R.C. & MUFFLY R. (1962) Effects of chlorpromazine on behaviour in emotionally disturbed children. *J. Nerv. Ment. Dis.* **135**, 147–154

GARFINKEL B.D., WEBSTER C. & SLOMAN L. (1975) Methylphenidate and caffeine in the treatment of children with minimal brain dysfunction. *Amer. J. Psychiat.* **132**, 723–728

GITTELMAN-KLEIN R. & KLEIN D.F. (1971) Controlled imipramine treatment school phobia. *Arch. gen. Psychiat.* **25**, 204–207

HAERER A.F. & GRACE J.B. (1969) Studies of anticonvulsant levels in epileptics. *Acta Neurol. Scand.* **45**, 18–31

HARTLAGE L. (1965) Effects of chlorpromazine on learning. *Psychol. Bull.* **64**, 235–245

HELPER M.M., WILCOTT R.C. & GARFIELD S.L. (1963) Effects of chlorpromazine on learning and related processes in emotionally disturbed children. *J. Consult. Psychol.* **27**, 1–9

HUTT S.J., JACKSON P.M., BELSHAM A. & HIGGINS G. (1968) Perceptual motor behaviour in relation to blood phenobarbitone levels. *Develop. Med. Child. Neurol.* **10**, 626–632

IDESTROM G.M., SCHALLING D., CARLQUIST V. & SHOQUIST F. (1972) Acute effects of Diphenylhydantoin in relation to plasma levels. Behaviour and psychophysiological studies. *Psychol. Med.* **2**, 111–120

KLEIN D.F. & GITTELMAN-KLEIN R. (1973) Comparative drug effects in hyperkinetic children. *Psychopharm. Bull.* Special supplement to vol. 9. *Pharmacotherapy of children*, 20–21

KNIGHTS R. & HINTON G. (1969) The effects of methylphenidate (Ritalin) on the motor skills and behavior of children with learning problems. *J. Nerv. Ment. Dis.* **148**, 643–653

LIPMAN R.S. (1970) The use of psychopharmacological agents in residual facilities for the retarded. *In* Menolascino F.J. (ed.) *Psychiatric Approaches to Mental Retardation.* New York: Basic Books

LOGAN W.J. & FREEMAN J.M. (1969) Pseudodegenerative disease due to diphenylhydantoin intoxication. *Arch. Neurol.* **21**, 631–637

LUCAS A.R. & PASLEY F.C. (1969) Psychoactive drugs in the treatment of emotionally disturbed children: Haloperidol and diazepam. *Compr. Psychiat.* **10**, 376–386

LUCAS A.R. & WEISS M. (1971) Methylphenidate hallucinosis. *J. Amer. Med. Assoc.* **217**, 1079–1081

McANDREW J.B., CASE Q. & TREFFERT D.A. (1972) Effect of prolonged phenothiazine intake on psychotic and other hospitalised children. *J. Autism Child. Schiz.* **2**, 75–91

MAXWELL C. & SELDRUP J. (1971) Imipramine in the treatment of childhood enuresis. *The Practitioner* **207**, 809–814

MENDELSON W., JOHNSON N. & STEWART M.A. (1971) Hyperactive children as teenagers: a follow-up study. *J. Nerv. Ment. Dis.* **153**, 273–279

MILLICHAP J.G. (1972) Electro-encephalographic evaluation of triclofos sodium sedation in children. *Amer. J. Dis. Child.* **124**, 526–527

MILLICHAP J.G. & BOLDREY E.E. (1967) Studies in hyperkinetic behavior. II: Laboratory and clinical evaluations of drug treatment. *Neurology* **17**, 467–471

MOLLING P.A., LOCKER A.W., SAULS R.J. & EISENBERG L. (1962) Committed delinquent boys. The impact of perphenazine and of a placebo. *Arch. gen. Psychiat.* **7**, 70–76

MONTAGU J.D. (1975) The hyperkinetic child: a behavioural, electrodermal and E.E.G. investigation. *Develop. Med. Child Neurol.* **17**, 299–305

MONTAGU J.D. & SWARBRICK L. (1975) Effect of amphetamines in hyperkinetic children: Stimulant or sedative? A pilot study *Develop. Med. Child Neurol.* **17**, 293–298

OUNSTED C. (1955) The hyperkinetic syndrome in epileptic children. *Lancet* **ii**, 303–311

OVERTON D.A. (1970) Discriminative control of behavior by drug states. *In* Cheistad G.T., Thompson T. & Pickens R. (eds.) *Stimulus Properties of Drugs.* New York: Appleton

POLIZOS P., ENGELHARDT D.M., HOFFMAN S.P. & WAIZER J. (1973) Neurological consequences of psychotropic drug withdrawal in schizophrenic children. *J. Autism Child. Schiz.* **3**, 247–253

PRICE S.A. & SPENCER D.A. (1967) A trial of beclamide (Nydrane) in mentally subnormal patients with disorders of behaviour. *J. Ment. Subnorm.* **13**, 75–77

QUINN P.O. & RAPOPORT J. (1975) One year follow-up of hyperactive boys treated with imipramine or methylphenidate. *Amer. J. Psychiat.* **132**, 241–245

RAPOPORT J., QUINN P.O., BRADBARD G., RIDDLE K.D. & BROOKS E. (1974) Imipramine and methylphenidate treatment of hyperactive boys. *Arch. gen. Psychiat.* **30**, 789–793

REES L., BUTLER P.W.P., GOSLING C. & BESSER G. (1970) Adrenergic blockade and the corticosteroid and growth hormone responses to methylamphetamine. *Nature* **228**, 565–566

REYNOLDS E.H. & TRAVERS R.D. (1974) Serum anticonvulsant concentrations in epileptic patients with mental symptoms. *Brit. J. Psychiat.* **124**, 440–445

SAFER D.J. & ALLEN R.P. (1973) Factors influencing the suppressant effect of two stimulant drugs on the growth of hyperactive children. *Pediatrics* **51**, 660–667

SAFER D.J., ALLEN R.P. & BARR E. (1972) Depression of growth in hyperactive children on stimulant drugs. *N. Engl. J. Med.* **287**, 217–220

SAFER D.J., ALLEN R.P. & BARR E. (1975) Growth rebound after termination of stimulant drugs. *J. Paediatrics* **86**, 113–116

SALZMAN C., KOCHANSKY G.E., SHADER R.I., PORRINO L.J., HARMATZ J.S. & SWETT C.P. (1974) Chlordiazepoxide induced hostility in a small group setting. *Arch. gen. Psychiat.* **31**, 401–405

SATTERFIELD J.H. (1973) E.E.G. issues in children with minimal brain dysfunction. *Semin. Psychiat.* **5**, 35–47

SATTERFIELD J.H. & DAWSON M.E. (1971) Electrodermal correlates of hyperactivity in children. *Psychophysiology* **8**, 191–197

SCHLEIFER M., WEISS G., COHEN N., ELMAN M., CVEJIC H. & KRUGER E. (1975) Hyperactivity in preschoolers and the effect of methylphenidate. *Amer. J. Orthopsychiat.* **45**, 38–50

SCHNACKENBURG R.G. (1973) Caffeine as a substitute for schedule II stimulants in hyperkinetic children. *Amer. J. Psychiat.* **130**, 796–798

SHAFFER D., COSTELLO A.J. & HILL J.D. (1968) Control of enuresis with imipramine. *Arch. Dis. Child.* **43**, 665–671

SHERMAN L., KIM S., BENJAMIN F. & KOLODNY H. (1971) Effects of chlorpromazine on serum growth hormone concentration in man. *N. Engl. J. Med.* **284**, 72–74

SILVER W. & STIER M. (1971) Cardiac arrythmias from chloral hydrate. *Pediatrics* **48**, 332–333

SLEATOR E.K., VON NEUMANN A. & SPRAGUE R.L. (1974) Hyperactive children. A continuous long-term placebo controlled follow up. *J. Amer. Med. Assoc.* **229**, 316–317

SPRAGUE R.L. & SLEATOR E.K. (1973) Effects of psychopharmacologic agents on learning disorders. *Pediatr. Clins. North Am.* **20**, 719–735

SROUFE L.A. (1975) Drug treatment of children with behaviour problems. *In* Horowitz F.D. (ed.) *Review of Child Development Research.* Chicago: University of Chicago Press

STEINBERG G.C., TROSHINSKY C. & STEINBERG H.A. (1971) Dextroamphetamine responsive behavior disorder in school children. *Amer. J. Psychiat.* **128**, 174–179

STORES G. (1975) Behavioural effects of anti-epileptic drugs. *Develop. Med. Child. Neurol.* **17**, 647–658

SYKES D.H., DOUGLAS V.I. & MORGERNSTERN G. (1972) The effect of methylphenidate (Ritalin) on sustained attention in hyperactive children. *Psychopharmacologia* **25**, 262–274

WAPNER I., THURSTON D.L. & HOLLOWACH J. (1962) Phenobarbital: Its effects on learning in epileptic children. *J. Amer. Med. Assoc.* **182**, 937

WEINBERG W.A., RUTMAN J., SULLIVAN L., PENICK E.C. & DIETZ S.G. (1973) Depression in children referred to an educational diagnostic centre: Diagnosis and treatment. *J. Pediatrics* **83**, 1065–1072

WEISCHER M. (1969) On the anti-aggressive behavior of lithium. *Psychopharmacologia* **15**, 245–254

WEISS B. & LATIES V.G. (1962) Enhancement of human performance by caffeine and the amphetamines. *Pharmacol. Rev.* **14**, 1–36

WEISS G., KRUGER E., DANIELSON U. & ELMAN M. (1975) Effect of long term treatment of hyperactive children with methylphenidate. *Canad. Med. Assoc. J.* **112**, 159–165

WENDER P. (1971) *Minimal Brain Dysfunction in Children.* New York: Wiley

WENDER P. (1973) *The Hyperactive Child.* New York: Crown

WERRY J.S. (1970) Some clinical and laboratory studies of psychotropic drugs in children—an overview. *In* Smith W.L. (ed.) *Drugs and Cerebral Function.* Springfield, Illinois: Charles C Thomas

WERRY J.S., AMAN M.G. & LAMPEN E. (1976) Haloperidol and methylphenidate in hyperactive children. *Acta Paedopsychiat.* **42**, 26–40

WERRY J.S. & SPRAGUE R.L. (1973) Methylphenidate in children, effects of dosage. Mimeographed paper. University of Illinois, Urbana-Champaign: DPRGMH 46–92

WERRY J. S., WEISS G., DOUGLAS V. & MARTIN J. (1966) Studies on the hyperactive child. III: The effect of chlorpromazine upon behaviour and learning ability. *J. Amer. Acad. Child Psychiat.* **5**, 292–312

WINSBERG B., BIALER I., KUPIETZ S. & TOBIAS J. (1972) Effects of imipramine and dextroamphetamine on behavior of neuro-psychiatrically impaired children. *Amer. J. Psychiat.* **128**, 1425–1431

WINSBERG B., PRESS M., BIALER I. & KUPIETZ S. (1974) Dextroamphetamine and methylphenidate in the treatment of hyperactive/aggressive children. *Pediatrics* **53**, 236–241

YOUNG G. & TURNER R.K. (1965) C.N.S. stimulant drugs and conditioning treatment of nocturnal enuresis. *Behav. Res. Ther.* **3**, 93–101

ZRULL J.P., WESTMAN J.C., ARTHUR B. & RICE D.L. (1964) A comparison of diazepam, *d*-amphetamine and placebo in the treatment of the hyperkinetic syndrome in children. *Amer. J. Psychiat.* **120**, 590–591

CHAPTER 39

Behavioural approaches

W. YULE

It has become customary to discuss behavioural approaches to the alleviation of human problems as if they were concerned solely with the application of learning theory to treatment. Whilst the two areas are intimately linked (in part because the same professionals are often involved in both areas), behavioural approaches relate to many areas of knowledge about human development and behaviour other than learning theory alone. What distinguishes behavioural approaches to treatment from other approaches (and in particular from approaches based on psychoanalytic theory) is their commitment to a scientific approach to problem solving, in Popper's sense of science (see Popper 1972; also, Magee 1973).

This chapter describes in some detail the basic problem-solving approach and discusses the rapidly expanding principles and techniques of behaviour modification as applied to children's disorders. The review concentrates on substantive issues rather than describing the techniques in a do-it-yourself cookbook manner. Particular attention is paid to the advances in training parents, teachers and others in the use of behavioural techniques, and to the advances in application to problem areas such as subnormality and antisocial behaviour which have proved resistant to more traditional therapies. Finally, an attempt is made to evaluate the limitations of behavioural approaches and their efficacy within these limits, and to consider current problems and future developments.

Behavioural approach as a problem-solving strategy

Clinical psychology in Britain has developed as an applied science. Yates (1970), in his critical review of behaviour therapy, considers the appled-scientific role as crucial in the development of behavioural treatments. The applied psychologist looks at a problem and then relates his observations to his knowledge of general psychology and, in the present instance, of child development. He attempts to apply this knowledge so as both to understand the problem better and to effect some change for the better. The differences between this approach and a traditional, experimental one is that the individual patient is the focus of study rather than a large group of patients. The difference between this approach and other therapeutic approaches lies in the crucial emphasis placed on evaluating changes in the individual patient and in demonstrating that these changes were the direct result of the intervention procedures.

In Britain, intensive investigation of individual patients, coupled with an understanding of the phenomena of classical conditioning, led to the refinement of desensitisation techniques in the treatment of phobias in both adults and children. In America, the application of findings from studies of operant conditioning in the laboratory to problem behaviour in real life settings led to the use of a sophisticated research methodology for investigating and treating individual cases. Both developments underlie behavioural approaches to the treatment of children's disorders.

There are four distinct steps in the behavioural approach:
1   Defining the problem objectively
2   Setting up hypotheses to account for the observation
3   Testing these hypotheses
4   Evaluating the outcome.

Defining the problem objectively

When a parent brings a child to the clinic and complains that he is aggressive, this conveys something to the therapist but not enough to formulate any therapeutic problem. The task of the interviewer is to obtain as much *relevant* information as possible, and in particular he has to translate the parental 'trait' description into an objective, behavioural account of the problem (Mischel 1968; Holland 1970).

One parent may call a child aggressive if he hits his sister; another may use the label 'jealousy'. Breaking toys, pulling the cat's tail, swearing, smearing faeces—all these, and many more besides, might be considered 'aggressive'. It is important, then, to obtain precise behavioural referrants for the complaint. Not only *what* happens, but also the frequency and severity of occurrence as well as the circumstances surrounding the act. What happened immediately before the aggressive behaviour; what happened immediately afterwards? Are there things which seem to reduce or increase the problem? Detailed answers to these questions form the beginning of an objective definition of the problems.

Notice that one obtains the usual background information on the patient—early developmental, social and educational data, history of the current complaint—but that the questioning concentrates much more on the present than on the past. This is because treatment will focus on manipulating factors which exist in the present, and it is important to have a good understanding of what these are.

Setting up hypotheses

In setting up hypotheses, one is not merely interested in seeking to describe how the problem arose (it is unlikely that one can even be certain of this by any retrospective enquiry) but, more importantly, one is seeking to make predictions that if a particular intervention is made then the child's behaviour will improve. It is important to emphasise that while such an approach may be viewed as ahistorical (in the sense of not being concerned with events in the past), it most certainly is not acontextual. The therapist is very much concerned with the circumstances surrounding the child's behaviour and he attempts to understand the problem in the context of the child's present social situation both at home and at school, with peers and with adults.

The hypotheses can arise from the congruence of the interview data with any theory or finding in child development. Thus, presented with a 4-year-old showing severe temper tantrums and also a marked delay in both language comprehension and expression despite normal nonverbal intelligence, then one testable hypothesis would be that if the parents speak in simpler sentences, the child will have less of a problem. A second hypothesis would be that improving his language development would improve his behaviour. These hypotheses are readily testable (and can be falsified) by obtaining good measures of parental speech, child's language attainment, and frequency and duration of tantrums.

Even before any therapeutic intervention, it is possible to examine the relationship between the child's behaviour and the circumstances surrounding its occurrence. The aim of such an investigation is to establish what, if anything, is functionally related to the occurrence of the behaviour. Put more formally, the therapist undertakes *a functional analysis* of behaviour, leading to an identification of the 'sufficient and necessary conditions for a particular response to occur and persist' (Evans 1971). In practice, this may involve systematically varying the environment and observing the effects on the child's behaviour, the aim being to specify the environmental conditions which affect the behaviour to be modified.

More usually, a functional analysis of the presenting problem or problems will be more broadly based (Gelfand & Hartmann 1975). Hypotheses concerning the relationship between the problem behaviour and the effective social environment will be developed both on the basis of careful interview with the parents (Holland 1970; Wahler & Cormier 1970) and from a knowledge of similar cases in the past. Kanfer and Saslow (1969) suggest a fairly comprehensive scheme for arriving at a functional analysis of the problem. They suggest that five components of the situation are borne in mind—stimulus events present when the problem shows, the actual response made by the child (the problem), the contingent relationship (if any) between response and reinforcement, the consequences of the behaviour which may be reinforcing, and the biological condition of the patient.

Bearing these five components in mind, the therapist would then try to identify behavioural excesses and deficits which are seen as the problem. However, unlike traditional therapeutic approaches, the focus is not only on pathology. In addition, the therapist actively seeks to identify other behavioural strengths and assets which may later be harnessed in therapy. Kanfer and Saslow (1969) provide a fuller account of the whole process.

Having identified a clearly defined set of problem behaviours, the next step is to gather *baseline* data on the frequency of occurrence, severity or direction of the problem. Exactly which measure is taken will depend on the problem under consideration, and how the data are to be gathered. Not infrequently, the behaviour therapist will visit the child at home or in the classroom to see at first hand what the problem is. Then, he will suggest an appropriate way of sampling the problem and getting reliable and valid measures during treatment.

Testing the hypotheses

As seen above, once hunches, clinical experience, knowledge of the literature and the like are brought together, testable hypotheses can emerge. It is important that the hypotheses are tested systematically, since every child is an individual and even the most 'standard' treatment will interact with the child in a unique manner. In order to understand fully how to help the child, the effects of intervention must be monitored closely.

Careful monitoring implies good measurement, and this is one of the keys to behavioural treatments. By translating the presenting problem into aspects of the child's existence which can be measured, one gets a richer understanding of his individual adjustment. Moreover, small changes can be more readily perceived, and treatment can be quickly altered or intensified depending on the direction of change. This constant feedback of data permitting the rational alteration of treatment is another of the crucial characteristics of behavioural approaches. If one cannot show a change in the desired direction within a few sessions, then back to the drawing board!

Historically, most of the intervention techniques employed have stemmed from learning theory formulations of child development. These have certainly been extremely fruitful, as will be demonstrated later. However, there is no necessary connection between this applied science model and learning theory.

Evaluating the outcome

Evaluation involves more than good measurement of crucial behaviour. One needs to demonstrate not only that a change in the predicted direction occurred, but also that that change was causally related to the intervention. The problem which faced therapists for years was that they could never be sure that success was due to what they had done rather than to some extraneous, chance event. Now, with the explosion of literature on behaviour modification, there is a variety of research designs for use with the single case, all of which can demonstrate the connection between treatment and outcome (Wolf & Risley 1971; Hall 1971; Leitenberg 1973; Kazdin 1973). These are discussed in more detail below.

Unequivocal conclusions are hard to come by in treatment research. We are fully aware that it is easier to formulate a theoretical ideal for treatment than to achieve this in practice. Nevertheless, in our present state of knowledge, on-going evaluation should form an integral part of any treatment procedure. It is only in so doing that premature and extravagant claims can be avoided (Levitt 1971; Tizard 1973). This is particularly important if we are to avoid producing unwarranted optimism in already troubled parents.

PRINCIPLES AND TECHNIQUES OF BEHAVIOUR MODIFICATION

The guiding principles of behaviour modification principles are that (a) behaviour is responsive to particular stimulus configurations, and (b) behaviour may be modified by its consequences. When one talks here of behaviour being affected by the environment, one is not talking merely of physical attributes such as space, temperature and colour of furnishings, but also of the social environment—the parents and other people, and how they behave towards the child.

Respondent behaviour—phobias

The well-known principles of classical conditioning (e.g. Yates 1970) account for the development of many abnormal respondent behaviours. Thus, Watson and Rayner (1920) are credited with first demonstrating that a young child *learned* to fear an object, in their case a white rat, by pairing a loud noise with approaches to the rat. After only seven pairings, the child showed marked fear to the rat, although he had played happily with the rat before these traumatic events. Equally importantly, it was noted that this fear generalised to other furry objects sharing similar stimulus properties.

If a fear can be learned, then can it also be unlearned? In a famous demonstration study, Mary Cover Jones (1924a, b) showed that there were a number of techniques which could eliminate these acquired fears. She anticipated by 35 years, the techniques of desensitisation, graded reintroduction and modelling which were placed on firmer theoretical footing later by Wolpe (1958), Bandura (1969) and others.

Thus it comes about that *desensitisation* is at present the treatment of choice for most childhood (and adult) phobias (Marks 1969; Rachman 1974). In a phobia, a fear response is elicited by circumscribed sets of stimuli. In assessing the child's disorder for treatment, the therapist elicits the exact circumstances which give rise to fear reactions. This is done both by interview and by reality testing, e.g. measuring how closely the child can approach the feared object. The therapist then constructs a hierarchy of objects and situations of which the child is afraid.

Desensitisation involves a graded approach to the feared object whilst the subject is relaxed. The aim is to reciprocally inhibit the feared response by keeping the child relaxed. In adults, this can be done by training the patient in Jacobsonian relaxation techniques, and then, in the security of the clinic, asking them to imagine being in the feared situations. With children, although no definitive studies have been undertaken, it is generally recognised that desensitisation in imagination and relaxation training are more problematical. This means that desensitisation is usually undertaken in vivo—in real life setting—and alternative means are used to relax the child.

Relaxation is accomplished by having a trusted adult (often the parent) talking to the child, or by having him eating a favourite food, or by playing with peers. Then the lowest item on the hierarchy is presented at a distance. Slowly, this item is brought closer, pausing if the child indicates signs of distress. Gradually, more feared items are presented in turn.

This simple technique has been used successfully to treat a wide variety of children's phobias—of cars (Lazarus 1960), bathwater (Bentler 1962), snakes (Ritter 1968), buses and dogs (Obler & Terwilliger 1970), examination fears (Kondas 1967), and fear of the dark (Lazarus & Abramovitz 1962). In addition, similar techniques have been used to combat separation anxiety in young children (Montenegro 1968). The crucial thing in reducing fear and anxiety in all these cases was the gradual reintroduction of the child to the feared situation.

Desensitisation is not always successful. In one case of a noise phobia in a 10-year-old boy, all fears except those aroused by bursting balloons were successfully eliminated by desensitisation (Yule, Sacks & Hersov 1974). The remaining fear was successfully treated by 'flooding' in two sessions. Flooding (sometimes called 'implosion') involves bringing the patient into contact with the most feared item on the hierarchy, and keeping him in contact until the induced fear has been extinguished. This technique has been widely used with adult patients (Marks 1972), but no other published case exists of its use with children. However, this single case and others treated in our department suggest that where desensitisation has not worked, an alternative behavioural treatment is available.

Phobias have also been successfully treated by *modelling* (Rachman 1972) (see later). The phobic child is allowed to watch nonphobic children playing happily with, say, dogs (Meyer & Chesser 1970). As he shows less fear, so he is encouraged to participate in the play of the other children and the phobic object (Bandura, Grusec & Menlove 1967). Modelling is being used more extensively as a way of speeding up desensitisation techniques. The combined techniques appear to be extremely powerful as a recent pilot study of treating fears of dentists confirms (White & Davis 1974).

School phobia (see Chapter 19) has also been tackled from a behavioural viewpoint (Patterson 1965; Hersen 1971; Garvey & Hegrenes 1966; Lazarus, Davison & Polefka 1965). However since it is not always clear from these reports whether the child was phobic, refusing school or being withheld by the parents, it is equally unclear which techniques are most suited to which problem. All approaches agree in emphasising the importance of getting the child back to school as quickly as possible, in part to avoid the social and educational complications that prolonged absence may bring. However, as Miller, Barrett and Hampe (1974) emphasise, the confrontation with the phobic stimulus requires sensitive handling. Both the child and the school need to be well prepared. Occasionally, return to school may be temporarily postponed until other, more pressing problems have been dealt with. It will be noted that in treating phobias, little attention is given to aetiology and past history. The present is the focus of treatment.

Operant behaviour

The problems presented by children are usually qualitatively different from those presented by adults. As Eysenck and Rachman (1965) put it: 'Most often the aim in therapy with adults is to break down a behaviour pattern, whereas in treating children the therapist usually has to build up an adequate behaviour pattern.' Thus, whilst desensitisation and modelling are used in the alleviation of phobias and anxiety states, most interest in treating children's disorders has centred around the application of operant conditioning (Rachman 1962; Risley & Baer 1973).

At its simplest, the guiding principle of behaviour modification procedures based on operant principles is that much behaviour can be modified by its consequences. Behaviour which is followed by pleasant consequences will tend to increase in frequency, whereas behaviour which culminates in unpleasant consequences will tend to decrease. To the extent that the consequences can be controlled by parents, teachers, nurses or therapists, then those consequences can be given or withheld systematically contingent on the child's behaviour. Providing there exists a functional relationship between the behaviour and its consequences, the behaviour will then change in the desired direction. The science of behaviour modification enables one to identify environmental events which are functionally related to the child's behaviour; the art lies in the systematic ways in which individualised treatment programmes are devised.

The principles of operant conditioning are well documented elsewhere (Ferster & Perrott 1968), and are clearly described in relation to modifying children's behaviour in a number of publications (Risley & Baer 1973; Hall 1971; Krumboltz & Krumboltz 1972; Patterson & Gullion 1968; Larsen & Bricker 1968). Here, some of the more important principles and techniques are outlined.

Reinforcement

'Any event or stimulus consequence that increases the strength or probability of the behaviour it follows is called a reinforcer' (Hall 1971). For example, if a child sits down to constructive schoolwork more readily after such behaviour has been warmly praised by his class teacher, then teacher praise is a positive reinforcer for that child. It would be a reasonable (and testable) hypothesis to suppose that if the teacher then gave her praise to that pupil contingent on some other behaviour which she wanted to increase, then that new behaviour should appear with greater frequency.

A number of points must be emphasised regarding reinforcement. Firstly, note that a reinforcer is defined primarily in terms of its *effects* on the behaviour of interest. At times, the term is sloppily equated with 'reward'. The point to note is that at all times one looks to the data to see whether adult attention, extra time playing, more pocket money, ice-cream or whatever is actually achieving the desired increase in the child's behaviour. Some children find teacher's attention to be an unwelcome event, in which case the supposed reward will actually reduce the frequency of the desired behaviour and act as a punishment. The golden rule is always to pay attention to the effects of the contingent stimulus on the behaviour of the individual child. Don't assume that you know what is reinforcing for that child; let the observations tell you.

Secondly, it should be noted that the *timing* of the reinforcement is crucial. *When* reinforcement is given is as important as *what* is given. Reinforcement must immediately follow the desired behaviour, at least in the early stages of building up the desired behaviour. Whilst a child's noisy, disruptive behaviour immediately impinges on the parent or teacher (and all too often earns an immediate reprimand), it is much more difficult to 'catch the child being good'. Observations of teacher–child and parent–child interaction all too often reveal that the child does occasionally behave in the way that is desired, but that the adult in charge either ignores its occurrence deliberately (the thank-God-he's-quiet, let's-leave-him-alone syndrome) or simply fails to notice that the child is behaving appropriately. One of the tasks in training therapists, then, is to sensitise them to the child's good behaviour and to teach them to reinforce it immediately.

Thirdly, the discussion so far has emphasised the application of *social reinforcement*. Children and adults respond to smiles, nods, hugs, verbal praise and other essentially human social behaviour. However, very young children, severely subnormal and autistic children may not initially find social attention from adults in the least bit rewarding. In those cases, one has first to use so-called primary reinforcers—food, drink and the like—in order to get treatment moving. However, it is another golden rule that whenever a primary reinforcer has to be used, it should be coupled with clear social stimulation from the therapist. The aim of this pairing is to make the therapist's social responses become secondary reinforcing stimuli for the child (Yule & Berger 1972).

Extinction

If a piece of behaviour is being maintained by some particular reinforcement, and then that reinforcement is withdrawn, the behaviour in question will decrease in frequency. For example, if every time a 4-year-old has a mild temper tantrum, his parents immediately rush to him and pick him up, then the parents' concerned behaviour may be inadvertently maintaining the child's tantrum behaviour. If this is so, and if then the parents institute a regime of deliberately ignoring the tantrums, then these tantrums will diminish in frequency, severity and duration.

This technique has been successfully used in treating bed-time tantrums (Williams 1959) and classroom misbehaviour (Hall, Lund & Jackson 1968). However, extinction on its own is a problematic technique to use. In the first place, it depends on withdrawing *all reinforcement* and, of course, in real life the attention of brothers and sisters, or the remarks passed by classmates may also be maintaining the behaviour. Secondly, when reinforcers are first withdrawn, the child characteristically *increases* the rate of undesired behaviour. After all, if a mild tantrum always got attention in the past, it is not unreasonable to expect that a severe one will now have the same effect. Parents and teachers have to beware of losing their resolve and reinforcing the child for an even more deviant behaviour. Thirdly, as implied above, the process of extinction is a slow one. Teachers cannot ignore a child who is going to throw a hard toy at an innocent classmate. Other techniques must usually be used in conjunction with extinction. Nevertheless, it is important to attempt to withdraw positive reinforcement for unacceptable behaviours.

Schedules of reinforcement

So far in this discussion, reinforcement has been described as if it were given immediately following every occurrence of the desired behaviour. Whilst this is necessary in initial stages, later it is more effective if only a proportion of the child's responses are reinforced. Paradoxically, behaviour which is reinforced intermittently is more resistant to extinction. In other words, if parents 'give in' only occasionally to a child's unreasonable demands, it will be more difficult to extinguish that behaviour than if it were reinforced every time. Risley and Baer (1973) provide a fuller discussion of these points.

Shaping

Operant techniques are very useful in maintaining or strengthening behaviours which exist in the child's repertoire. However, what must be done to build up new behaviours from scratch? Clearly, this is a more difficult process, but the same principles apply. Thus, a hyperactive boy may never sit still throughout a complete 40-minute reading lesson. If this is the goal of the treatment, the class teacher will never be in a position to reinforce the child if she insists on his attaining the goal immediately. However, if she catches him sitting reasonably quietly for even one minute, she should immediately reinforce that behaviour. Gradually, she should *reinforce successive approximations* to the goal behaviour. This process of step-by-step reinforcing successive approximations is more commonly called *shaping* new behaviour.

Shaping is widely used in training all manner of desirable behaviour from self-help skills (Larsen & Bricker 1968) to speech and language (Yule & Berger 1972). Risley and Baer (1973) claim that ' ... this technique is so consistently successful as to suggest that some sequence of shaping can always be found which will produce the behaviour change planned, if effective re-inforcement is available.'

It would appear that shaping is the crucial feature in the art of behaviour modification. There is some evidence to suggest that most parents are relatively effective in spontaneously reinforcing endpoint behaviour, but that without training they are not so well able to analyse the goal behaviour into successive small steps (Filler, Bricker & Smith 1973). The analysis of target behaviours into a sequence of discrete steps is crucial in all behaviour modification.

Prompting and fading

Some children's repertoire of behaviour is so limited that even greater structuring of the learning environment is needed. In particular, more supports are required by children presenting with severe mental subnormality. Even when a simple task, such as, say, putting on a pullover has been broken in to a sequence of ten or more simpler steps, something extra is needed to get the child started. This 'something extra' can take take the form of verbal or physical prompts. Thus, the child can be helped to put his arms and head into the pullover, and then the therapist says '. . . and pull it down'. Instead of waiting for the child to do this on his own, the therapist or cotherapist (its usually best to have two people) actually moves the child's hands through the actions. On completion, the child is immediately reinforced, even though it is all done for him. Over the succeeding trials, the cotherapist gradually *fades-out* the physical prompts until the child is responding to the command alone. Once this step has been achieved reliably, another step is added on.

In the preceding example, some readers will have noticed that the training started with the last step first. This was not accidental. Experience has shown that combining successive steps in reverse order—so-called *'backward chaining of responses'*—is more effective in teaching subnormal children these complex, self-help skills (Gardner 1971).

On a practical point, such learning can be further accelerated by the skillful use of training 'equipment'. For example, instead of trying to teach the child to put on his own pullover, use an adult's sweater. Physically it is easier to get the child's arms in, even though the end result may look comical. Again, this is an example of structuring the environment so as to maximise the probability of the child experiencing success, and then altering the environmental conditions in a gradual and systematic manner so that that success can be maintained.

Imitation

Clearly, not all of a child's rich repertoire of behaviour is learned in the slow, painstaking, step-by-step procedures outlined above. No parent would take his teenage son into the car for the first time and then shape up his car-driving repertoire in a stepwise fashion, praising the skilled aspects and ignoring the bumps. Rather, the father will instruct his son, and in particular he will show him what to do. The human child's capacity for learning vicariously i.e. learning by imitating another's actions, or by modelling, is well recognised. Bandura (1969) lays great emphasis on modelling or imitation as a powerful mechanism of behavioural change (see also Chapter 9).

It has been established that children will more readily imitate an action which they have seen reinforced; are more likely to imitate a prestigious figure; and are more likely to imitate children of the same sex. This has been used therapeutically in the treatment of socially withdrawn nursery children (O'Connor 1969). After observing television recordings of appropriate social interactions, the previously withdrawn children become indistinguishable from their well-socialised peers. O'Connor's study has recently been replicated by Evers and Schwarz (1973). The same film was used within a controlled study with preschool children. Significant reductions in isolate play were achieved.

Bandura (1969) makes the important point that whilst children may *learn* new behaviours by imitation, they may not *perform* them until later. He argues that modelling procedures are useful in instituting novel responses. Once established by modelling, new responses can then be strengthened by positive reinforcement.

Some experimenters argue that imitation can be understood in an operant conditioning paradigm (Gewirtz 1969; Risley & Baer 1973). Such theoretical niceties need not concern us here, except to point out the valuable studies which have shown that imitation skills can be taught to children who do not spontaneously imitate (Metz 1965; Lovaas *et al* 1967; Bricker & Bricker 1970).

Token reinforcement

One of the realistic aims of operant training is to develop the child's behaviour to a point at which the ordinary, everyday, intermittent social responses will maintain the new behaviour. Whilst the use of appropriate schedules of reinforcement help in attaining this goal, another means of extending the period of time which elapses between the occurrence of a particular behaviour and its reinforcement is the use of *token reinforcement*. Particularly where children do not respond well to adult praise, and where—as in a classroom situation—it would be impracticable to use primary reinforcers, then the child can be reinforced by giving him a token contingent on the occurrence of the desired behaviour. This token can be anything from a plastic disc to a gold star to a tick on a piece of paper. At the end of a specified time period or after accumulating a pre-arranged number of tokens, the tokens are exchanged for 'back-up reinforcers'—small toys, edibles, privileges such as visits to the zoo, getting out of school early—in fact, anything at all which is reinforcing.

Token reinforcement has been successfully used both in school settings (Axelrod 1970; O'Leary & Becker 1967; Altman & Linton 1971), and in hospital inpatient units (Browning & Stover 1971) and in the child's own home (Christopherson *et al* 1972; Patterson 1973). Of particular interest to clinicians is Allen *et al*'s (1975) use of tokens to improve social skills in 9 and 10-year-old children. Reductions in isolate play and improvements in sociometric status were recorded. One development involves the use of '*contingency contracting*'. Here, the therapist chairs a meeting between the child and his parents. All parties give their view of the problems and a contract is drawn up whereby each party modifies his or her behaviour in one area contingent on the other party also altering. The agreement is typed out and signed by all parties, and can only be renegotiated in the presence of the therapist. By making explicit what the parents require of the child and vice versa, many problem behaviours of late childhood and early adolescence have been successfully resolved (Tharp & Wetzel 1969; Homme *et al* 1970).

Summary

There exists a body of knowledge and a set of techniques (Table 39.1) which can be applied to help manage a very wide range of childhood problems. These include everyday management difficulties in normal children; training self-help skills such as feeding, washing, dressing and toileting to mentally retarded children; training speech and language development in subnormal and autistic children; working with aggressive children and other delinquent children both in their own homes and in institutional settings. Examples of application in all these areas are included in the references. The techniques can be readily taught and are effective when applied consistently and systematically. How effective they are is discussed below.

Some distinguishing features of behavioural approaches

In summary, behavioural approaches involve an emphasis on dealing with observable behaviour, although this behaviour need not be directly observ-

Table 39.1   Thirteen principles for modifying children's behaviour

To strengthen new behaviour
   1 Positive reinforcement

To develop new behaviour
   2 Successive approximations (shaping)
   3 Modelling (imitation)
   4 Cueing or prompting
   5 Discrimination

To maintain new behaviour
   6 Substitution
   7 Intermittent reinforcement

To stop inappropriate behaviour
   8 Satiation
   9 Extinction
  10 Incompatible alternative
  11 Negative reinforcement

To modify 'emotional' behaviour
  12 Avoidance—aversive conditioning
  13 Fear reduction—desensitization

Adapted from Krumboltz, J.D. and Krumboltz, B.H. (1972) *Changing Children's Behavior*. New Jersey: Prentice-Hall.

able by the patient. Recent advances in biofeedback techniques have shown that behavioural principles can effect changes in internal bodily symptoms (e.g. Birk 1973). However, the concern with observation and measurement is directly related to a deliberate attempt to evaluate the efficacy of intervention. A whole new technology of evaluation is associated with developments in this field (Leitenberg 1973; Kazdin 1973).

Behavioural approaches stem directly from the application of the findings of experimental, general and child psychology to the problems of children and families. At present, no other therapeutic approach has such an intimate link with such a large body of fundamental research. In part, this applied psychology approach is connected with the renunciation of a 'medical model' or an 'illness' model of childhood behavioural and emotional disorders (Yates 1970). In most cases, the presenting problem behaviour *is* the problem. There is no need to view it as 'symptomatic' of something else. Instead of seeking *explanations* as to aetiology, behavioural therapists focus on *treating* the problems in the present. As was seen above, the distinction is drawn between conditions which give rise to a behaviour pattern, and those which maintain it. Frequently, treatment is aimed at altering the latter.

Finally, another characteristic which distinguishes behavioural approaches—or rather those who use them—is their concern with tackling difficult, nonglamorous, socially relevant problems. In the field of children's disorders, this is shown in work with the mentally retarded (Larsen & Bricker 1968; Gardner 1971; Bricker & Bricker 1973), with delinquents and so-called 'predelinquents' (Phillips *et al* 1973; Tharp & Wetzel 1969; Patterson 1973a, b), with autistic children (Lovaas *et al* 1973; Howlin *et al* 1973) and with problem behaviours in the home (Patterson 1973a, b; Christopherson 1973) and, equally importantly, in the classroom and school settings (Hall 1971; Berger 1972). It should be emphasised that not only are socially relevant behaviours tackled, but a deliberate attempt is made to train other people— be they parents, teachers, nurses or others—to act as cotherapists. Behaviour therapists recognise that the old model of restricting the numbers who can be treated by keeping the therapeutic skills in the hands of a few highly trained people is not a practical way of delivering services to the many children who need help (Rutter, Tizard & Whitmore 1970).

Training cotherapists

One way of helping a larger number of patients is to train suitable adults to act as cotherapists. Usually, the most suitable people to train for such a role are the child's parents and teachers.

Tharp and Wetzel (1969) argued that responsible adults should and could be trained to carry out behavioural treatments. There now exist a large number of manuals which are a useful starting point for training nonpsychologists to act as cotherapists (Patterson & Gullion 1968; Patterson 1971; Becker 1971; Hall 1971; Krumboltz & Krumboltz 1972; Peine & Howarth 1975). The texts written by Larsen and Bricker (1968) and Baldwin, Fredericks and Brodsky (1973) are particularly useful for parents of mildly and severely mentally handicapped children.

Most of these texts emphasise the desirability of training the cotherapists in the *principles* underlying the techniques rather than just instructing them how to deal with the immediate problems. This is so that parents, say, can deal effectively with future problems without having resource to further professional help.

Many of the issues involved in training parents are covered in recent reviews (Berkowitz & Graziano 1972; Johnson & Katz 1973; O'Dell 1974). Elsewhere, these issues have been examined together with the problems met in clinical practice, and areas requiring empirical research have been delineated (Yule 1975).

In brief, the issues involved in training parents as cotherapists revolve round the following areas:

1   What should be the nature and extent of the parents' responsibility for

the treatment? Whilst the ideal may be to turn some parents into sophisticated, independent therapists, it is already clear that many parents have difficulty in generalising the techniques taught. They can become excellent cotherapists, but, particularly with chronically handicapped children, they require extended contact with professional therapists over lengthy periods.

2   Which methods of training parents are most efficient? Merely giving manuals can occasionally be useful, but most therapists adopt a training model which involves a mixture of didactic teaching of principles, together with practical workshops in applying these principles to particular problems. At present, there is a concensus that the more didactic approach is less appropriate for parents with limited formal education, but there is little formal research in this area (Patterson, Shaw & Ebner 1969; Salzinger *et al* 1970; Gardner 1973). Increasingly, there is a trend towards training parents in groups, but again this has rarely been adequately evaluated.

3   There are many practical problems involved in training parents. For example, when only one child is identified as the patient, should all the children in the family be included in any formal programme of treatment? Christopherson *et al* (1972) advocate placing all children on their token economy system, but there is little evidence that this is always necessary.

4   One cannot ignore the feelings of inadequacy and guilt that parents may have. Too simple a behavioural approach, if it reinforces the idea that the parents' behaviour caused the child's problem behaviour, will only make matters worse. By focussing on the conditions which are maintaining the problem behaviour, one bypasses some of the pit-falls. However, it is possible to deal with such expressed difficulties within a broad behavioural framework as has been shown in an on-going study with the parents of autistic children (Howlin *et al* 1973).

From a review of published studies in which parents and teachers have been involved as cotherapists, it is clear that such an approach to service-delivery can be very effective. However, as O'Dell (1974) points out, the technology is, at present, being applied more quickly than the empirical basis would justify. Therefore, the next decade should witness the consolidation of research in training cotherapists, and should result in vastly improved ways of treating children and families with behavioural techniques.

Treatment of antisocial disorders

Among the most exciting applications of behavioural techniques have been the rigorous and imaginative programmes of Patterson and of Wolf and Phillips in treating antisocial and aggressive behaviour in the home and in an institution respectively. Given that antisocial behaviour is generally held to have poor prognosis and to be difficult to treat (Robins 1966; Rutter 1965), any therapy which claims to reduce the incidence of such behaviour merits close study.

For the past 10 years, Patterson and his colleagues in Oregon have been developing both a social learning theory of aggression and a treatment approach for parents of aggressive children to apply in their own homes (Patterson, Littman & Bricker 1967; Patterson & Reid 1970; Patterson 1974). The key to the programme has been the development of a complex, reliable and valid system of observing and coding interactions between aggressive children and family members within the home setting (Patterson *et al* 1969). Through reading Patterson's programmed manuals (Patterson & Gullion 1968; Patterson 1971) and in individual and group sessions, parents are taught to define, pinpoint and measure the deviant and prosocial behaviour they wish to alter in their own children. They are helped to construct and execute appropriate modification programmes in their own homes. The results are evaluated in a number of ways—through the direct observation procedure, as well as through the data the parents collect and changes in parent rating scales.

Patterson has now conducted a number of studies of the efficacy of this treatment package with consecutive referrals. One of the most recently completed series (Patterson 1973b) involved 27 consecutive referrals from community agencies. Merely reading the manuals appeared to have a modest effect on the rates of undesirable behaviour. Following 8 weeks of treatment, there was an average reduction of 60 per cent in the rates of occurrence of target behaviours. Three-quarters of the children showed significant drops in the frequency of undesirable behaviour. In only six cases (22 per cent) were there increases in the observed rates of target behaviours. Similar findings are reported on other measures within this study.

Two studies used subgroups of these 27 families, and compared the results with either no treatment controls (Wiltz 1969) or families given a placebo 'treatment' (Walter & Gilmore 1973). Results showed differences between the groups, in that parents enrolled in the programme produced significantly greater reductions in problem behaviour in their children. When the control parents were then enrolled in the treatment condition they also were successful in bringing their children's behaviour under control. Thus, it appears that Patterson's package is instrumental in bringing about change, but it is not yet clear which are the necessary and most potent elements in that treatment package (Ferber, Keeley & Shemberg 1974).

As a byproduct of this research programme, it has emerged that children who are not only aggressive, but who also steal, are more difficult to treat. Using as criterion of success in treatment a 33 per cent reduction in the rate of deviant behaviour, Reid and Hendricks (1973) looked more closely at the previously mentioned 27 families. They found that 6 of 14 stealers compared with 9 of 11 nonstealers were classified as successes (data were missing on two cases). It was found that the stealers exhibited less overall deviant behaviour, and that they came from families which exhibited much lower rates of positive, friendly behaviours. Clearly, the wealth of data gathered in studies such as these are invaluable in leading both to a better understanding of the dynamics of families of aggressive children and to effective methods for treating the problems in the natural environment.

Other investigators have worked with delinquents and their families using behavioural interventions. Alexander and Parsons (1973) compared the use of short-term family behavioural treatment (N=46) with client-centred family groups (N=19), eclectic psychodynamic family treatment (N=11) and no treatment control (N=10). In the county in which they worked, the general recidivism rate for delinquents was 51 per cent. In their study, the recidivism rates in the 6- to 18-month posttreatment period were respectively 26 per cent (behavioural), 47 per cent (client-centred), 73 per cent (psychodynamic) and 50 per cent (control). The authors concluded that a focus on families *per se* is not sufficient to modify family interaction patterns or to reduce rates of delinquency. Behavioural methods offer something more, but just what that something is has not been clearly identified.

Another model for helping young delinquents has been developed by Wolf, Phillips and their colleagues at Achievement Place in Kansas; a family-style small-group home for up to ten delinquent boys aged 12 to 16 years. In addition to their delinquency, most of the youths are 3 to 4 years behind academically. The home is run as a sophisticated token economy wherein points are earned for appropriate prosocial behaviour, and lost for antisocial behaviour. The house is run by a couple who are professional 'teaching-parents', well versed in behavioural approaches. Whilst at Achievement Place, the boys continue to attend the same schools as they did before conviction. They continue contact with their natural families, and as they improve so they spend longer time at home and the token economy is faded out.

The treatment programme is educational in intent and skill-oriented in practice. It aims to teach the young delinquents the rules of everyday living and to train them in any skills in which they are not proficient. For example, adolescents often are not skilled in resolving conflicts with their parents and other authority figures. They can be taught simple negotiating skills as a means to more positive family interactions (Kifer *et al* 1974).

The token economy developed at Achievement Place has been described in a number of publications (Fixsen, Phillips & Wolf 1973; Phillips 1968;

Phillips *et al* 1971). The results of the first 6 years of the programme have been presented (Phillips *et al* 1973) and compare very favourably with place-ment in a traditional reformatory or on probation. Equally important were the academic gains which were maintained in the Achievement Place boys. The emphasis on this, and on other behavioural programmes (Cohen & Filipczack 1971; Stumphauzer 1973) on giving training in relevant social skills to young delinquents stands in marked contrast to the more traditional custodial and punitive regimes.

Applications in mental retardation

The field of mental retardation has been revolutionised since psychologists demonstrated the unrealised potential of mentally retarded individuals. This change has been accelerated since behaviour modification techniques have become widely and systematically applied. Remarkable advances in toilet training, training in self-help skills, and language development have been well documented in a number of reviews (e.g. Gardner 1971; Kiernan & Wood-ford 1975; Yule & Berger 1975; see also Chapter 35).

Current problems and future developments

Sufficient examples of behavioural approaches to the treatment of children's disorders have been given to indicate that this is one of the fastest growing therapeutic areas. Even so, few people would want to claim that behavioural treatments are, at present, a panacea for all problems. Because of the empirical bias of behaviour therapists, the next few years should witness a clearer demarcation of those situations and problems in which behavioural approaches will be the treatment of first choice. At present, problem areas requiring clarification are becoming more evident.

The first major problem area is that of *generalisation*. It is clear that child-ren's behaviour is very often situation specific. A child will often behave one way at school, and quite differently at home; he will behave docilely when father is at home, but be beyond mother's control when she is on her own. Such specificity is a fact of life all too often ignored by professionals giving treatment in the artificial clinic setting.

Many of the early single case studies using behaviour modification demonstrated that hitherto unexpected changes could not only be brought about, but could be brought about very quickly. However, many therapists soon found that changes which occurred in the clinic did not automatically transfer to real-life settings. This is well illustrated in Lovaas's follow-up study of autistic children treated in his hospital setting. Changes only generalised to the home setting and were maintained at follow-up where the parents had been actively involved in the treatment programme (Lovaas *et al* 1973). As Patterson and Brodsky (1966) pointed out, generalisation of treatment effects should never be assumed. It must be actively worked for. Treatment programmes must include systematic means of ensuring that generalisation will occur. This means that more treatment will take place in the natural environment, and that more of the 'therapists' will be people with whom the child normally interacts.

The second major, but related, problem is that of *maintenance* of therapeutic change. Whilst many well controlled single case studies have demonstrated beyond reasonable doubt that major behavioural changes have been effected directly as a result of behavioural treatment, there are few long-term follow-up studies demonstrating that these gains are maintained. Many more are needed.

For example, token economies are widely used both within institutions and within individuals. Kazdin and Bootzin (1972) conclude that in some institutional settings, therapeutic gains are only maintained while the token economy is operating. This being so, it may be appropriate to regard them as prosthetic devices which improve the quality of life within the institution. In noninstitutional settings, however, the problem of fading out the token system without losing the desirable gains becomes acute. Some therapists have adopted a more cognitive stance, and the literature on 'self-control' is growing rapidly (Cautela 1969; Thoresen & Mahoney 1974). Only more empirical research will demonstrate the place of such cognitive variables in maintaining behavioural change.

Currently, much of the literature in behavioural treatment relies on sophisticated single case studies to demonstrate that observed changes are due to the form of treatment employed. Recent reviews of this methodology have begun to discuss both its enormous strengths and unsuspected weaknesses (Mathews 1975; Yule & Hemsley 1976).

It has become clear that there is a complex interaction between the behaviour to be changed, the measures of outcome to be taken, and the appropriate single case research design required to demonstrate change. Doubtless, this methodology will continue to develop and be applied to monitoring other forms of treatment (Yule & Hemsley 1976), but there is still a need for good group studies to demonstrate the comparative value of behavioural approaches and other therapeutic methods.

In the early days of behaviour therapy, critics often derided the treatments as being 'merely symptomatic', and confidently expected substitution of other problems. Such confidence has been eroded across the years. However, one side effect of such naive criticism has been that behaviour therapists have adopted a much broader set of criterion measures to monitor outcome (Patterson 1973b; Howlin *et al* 1973). Such moves are to be welcomed.

Within the confines of a short chapter, it is not possible to summarise all the studies relevant to an understanding of behavioural approaches to treatment. Instead, this chapter has attempted to indicate the general problem-solving approach common to such therapies as well as to describe the major principles and current areas of application. As more therapists become well trained in these approaches, so the range of problems tackled will widen while, simultaneously, the limitations will become clear. It is inherent in a problem-solving approach that when limitations are observed, they will be viewed as obstacles to be overcome rather than as necessary limits to be docilely accepted. Thus, behavioural philosophy brings a much needed optimism to the field of treating children's disorders.

REFERENCES

ALEXANDER J.F. & PARSONS B.V. (1973) Short-term behavioral intervention with delinquent families: impact on family process and recidivism. *J. Abnorm. Psychol.* **81,** 219–225

ALLEN R.P., SAFER D.J., HEATON R., WARD A. & BARRELL M. (1975) Behavior therapy for socially ineffective children, *J. Amer. Acad. Child Psychiat.* **14,** 500–509

ALTMAN K.I. & LINTON T.E. (1971) Operant conditioning in the classroom setting: a review of the research. *J. Educ. Res.* **64,** 277–286

AXELROD S. (1970) Token reinforcement programs in special classes. *Except. Child.* **37,** 371–379

BALDWIN V.L., FREDERICKS H.D.B. & BRODSKY G. (1973) *Isn't it Time he Outgrew This? or A Training Program for Parents of Retarded Children.* Springfield, Illinois: Charles C. Thomas

BANDURA A. (1969) *Principles of Behavior Modification.* New York: Holt, Rinehart & Winston

BANDURA A., GRUSEC J.E. & MENLOVE F.L. (1967) Vicarious extinction of avoidance behavior. *J. Pers. soc. Psychol.* **5,** 16–23

BECKER W.C. (1971) *Parents are Teachers: a Child Management Program.* Champaign, Illinois: Research Press

BENTLER P.M. (1962) An infant's phobia treated with reciprocal inhibition therapy. *J. Child Psychol. Psychiat.* **3,** 185–189

BERGER M. (1972) Modifying behaviour at school. *Spec. Educ.* **61,** 18–21

BERKOWITZ B.P. & GRAZIANO A.M. (1972) Training parents as behavior therapists: a review. *Behav. Res. Ther.* **10,** 297–317

BIRK L. (ed.) (1973) *Biofeedback: Behavioral medicine.* New York: Grune & Stratton

BRICKER W.A. & BRICKER D.D. (1970) A program of language training for the severely language handicapped child. *Except. Child.* **37,** 101–111

BRICKER W.A. & BRICKER D.D. (1973) Behavior modification programs. *In* Mittler P. (ed.) *Assessment for Learning in the Mentally Handicapped.* Edinburgh: Churchill-Livingstone

BROWNING R.M. & STOVER D.O. (1971) *Behavior modification in child treatment.* Chicago: Aldine-Atherton

CAUTELA J.R. (1969) Behavior therapy and self-control: Techniques and implications. *In* Franks C.M. (ed.) *Behavior Therapy: Appraisal and Status.* New York: McGraw-Hill

CHRISTOPHERSON E.R. (1973) Behavior modification in the family. In Hymovich D.P. and Barnard M.U. (eds.) *Family Health Care.* New York: McGraw-Hill

CHRISTOPHERSON E.R., ARNOLD C.M., HILL D.W. & QUILITCH H.R. (1972) The home point system: Token reinforcement procedures for application by parents of children with behavior problems. *J. Appl. Behav. Anal.* **5,** 485–497

COHEN H.L. & FILIPCZACK J. (1971) *A New Learning Environment.* San Francisco: Jossey-Bass

EVANS I.M. (1971) Theoretical and experimental aspects of the behaviour modification approach to autistic children. *In* Rutter M. (ed.) *Infantile Autism: Concepts, Characteristics and Treatment.* Edinburgh: Churchill-Livingstone

EVERS W.L. & SCHWARZ J.C. (1973) Modifying social withdrawal in pre-schoolers: the effects of filmed modelling and teacher praise. *J. Abnorm. Child Psychol.* **1,** 248–256

EYSENCK H.J. & RACHMAN S. (1965) *The Causes and Cures of Neurosis.* London: Routledge & Kegan Paul

FERBER H., KEELEY S.M. & SHEMBERG K.M. (1974) Training parents in behavior modification: Outcome of and problems encountered in a program after Patterson's work. *Behav. Ther.* **5,** 415–419

FERSTER C.E. & PERROTT M.C. (1968) *Behavior Principles.* New York: Appleton-Century-Crofts

FILLER J., BRICKER W. & SMITH R. (1973) Modification of maternal teaching style: the effects of task arrangement on the match-to-sample performance of delayed children. *In* Bricker D.D. & Bricker W.A. (eds.) *Infant, Toddler and Preschool Research and Intervention Projects,* Report—Year III IMRID. Nashville, Tennessee: George Peabody College for Teachers

FIXSEN D.L., PHILLIPS E.L. & WOLF M.M. (1973) Achievement place: experiments in self-government with predelinquents. *J. Appl. Behav. Anal.* **6,** 31–47

GARDNER J.M. (1973) Training the trainees: A review of research on teaching behavior modification. *In* Rubin R.D., Brady J.P. & Henderson J.D. (eds.) *Advances in Behavior Therapy:* vol. 4. London: Academic Press

GARDNER W.I. (1971) *Behaviour Modification in Mental Retardation.* London: University of London Press

GARVEY W.P. & HEGRENES J.R. (1966) Desensitization techniques in the treatment of school phobia. *Amer. J. Orthopsychiat.* **36,** 147–152

GELFAND D.M. & HARTMANN D.P. (1975) *Child Behaviour Analysis and Therapy.* Oxford: Pergamon

GEWIRTZ J.L. (1969) Mechanisms of social learning: Some roles of stimulation and behaviour in early human development. *In* Goslin D.A. (ed.) *Handbook of Socialization Theory and Research.* Chicago: Rand McNally

HALL R.V. (1971) *Managing Behaviour,* Parts I, II and III. Lawrence, Kansas: H & H Enterprises

HALL R.V., LUND D. & JACKSON D. (1968) Effects of teacher attention on study behaviour. *J. Appl. Behav. Anal.* **1,** 1–12

HERSEN M. (1971) The behavioral treatment of school phobia. *J. Nerv. Ment. Dis.* **153,** 99–107

HOLLAND C.J. (1970) An interview guide for behavioural counselling with parents. *Behav. Ther.* **1,** 70–79

HOMME L., CSANYI A.P., GONZALES M.A. & RECHS J.R. (1970) *How to use Contingency Contracting in the Classroom.* Champaign, Illinois: Research Press

HOWLIN P., MARCHANT R., RUTTER M., BERGER M., HERSOV L. & YULE W. (1973) A home-based approach to the treatment of autistic children. *J. Autism Child. Schiz.* **3,** 308–336

JOHNSON C.A. & KATZ R.C. (1973) Using parents as change agents for their children: a review. *J. Child Psychol. Psychiat.* **14,** 181–200

JONES M.C. (1924a) The elimination of children's fears. *J. Exper. Psychol.* **7,** 383–390

JONES M.C. (1924b) A laboratory study of fear: the case of Peter. *Pedagog. Semin.* **31,** 308–315

KANFER F.H. & SASLOW G. (1969) Behavioral diagnosis. Chapter 12 *in* Franks C.M. (ed.) *Behavior Therapy: Appraisal and Status.* New York: McGraw-Hill

KAZDIN A.E. (1973) Methodological and assessment considerations in evaluating reinforcement programs in applied settings. *J. Appl. Behav. Anal.* **6,** 517–531

KAZDIN A.E. & BOOTZIN R.R. (1972) The token economy: An evaluation review. *J. Appl. Behav. Anal.* **5,** 343–372

KIERNAN C.C. & WOODFORD F.P. (eds.) (1975) *Behaviour Modification with the Severely Retarded.* Amsterdam: Assoc. Scientific Publishers

KIFER R.E., LEWIS M.A., GREEN D.R. & PHILLIPS E.L. (1974) Training predelinquent youths and their parents to negotiate conflict situations. *J. Appl. Behav. Anal.* **7,** 357–364

KONDAŠ O. (1967) Reduction of examination anxiety and 'stage fright' by group desensitization and relaxation. *Behav. Res. Ther.* **5,** 275–281

KRUMBOLTZ J.D. & KRUMBOLTZ H.B. (1972) *Changing Children's Behavior.* New Jersey: Prentice-Hall

LARSEN L.A. & BRICKER W.A. (1968) A manual for parents and teachers of severely and moderately retarded children. *IMRID Papers*, vol. V, no. 22. Nashville: George Peabody College for Teachers

LAZARUS A. (1960) The elimination of children's phobias by deconditioning. *In* Eysenck H.J. (ed.) *Behaviour Therapy and the Neuroses.* Oxford: Pergamon

LAZARUS A. & ABRAMOVITZ A. (1962) The use of 'emotive imagery' in the treatment of children's phobias. *J. Ment. Sci.* **108,** 191–195

LAZARUS A., DAVISON G. & POLEFKA D. (1965) Classical and operant factors in the treatment of school phobia. *J. Abnorm. Psychol.* **70,** 225–229

LEITENBERG H. (1973) The use of single-case methodology in psychotherapy research. *J. Abnorm. Psychol.* **82,** 87–101

LEVITT E.E. (1971) Research on psychotherapy with children. *In* Bergin A.E. & Garfield S.L. (eds.) *Handbook of Psychotherapy and Behavior Change: an Empirical Analysis.* New York: Wiley

LOVAAS O.I., FREITAS L., NELSON K. & WHALEN C. (1967) The establishment of imitation and its use for the development of complex behaviour in schizophrenic children. *Behav. Res. Ther.* **5,** 171–181

LOVAAS O.I., KOEGEL R., SIMMONS J.Q. & LONG J.S. (1973) Some generalization and follow-up measures on autistic children in behaviour therapy. *J. Appl. Behav. Anal.* **6**, 131–166

MAGEE B. (1973) *Popper.* Harmondsworth: Penguin

MARKS I.M. (1969) *Fears and Phobias.* London: Heinemann

MARKS I.M. (1972) Perspectives in flooding. *Semin. Psychiat.* **4**, 129–138

MATHEWS A. (1975) Research design and clinical practice in behaviour therapy. *B.A.B.P. Bull.* **3** (3), 43–46

METZ J.R. (1965) Conditioning generalized imitation in autistic children. *J. exp. Child Psychol.* **2**, 389–399

MEYER V. & CHESSER E.S. (1970) *Behaviour Therapy in Clinical Psychiatry.* Harmondsworth: Penguin

MILLER L.C., BARRETT C.L. & HAMPE E. (1974) Phobias of childhood in a prescientific era. *In* Davids A. (ed.) *Child Personality and Psychopathology: Current Topics*, vol. I. New York: Wiley

MISCHEL W. (1968) *Personality and Assessment.* New York: Wiley

MONTENEGRO H. (1968) Severe separation anxiety in two preschool children: successfully treated by reciprocal inhibition. *J. Child. Psychol. Psychiat.* **9**, 93–103

OBLER M. & TERWILLIGER R.F. (1970) Pilot study of the effectiveness of systematic desensitization with neurologically impaired children with phobic disorders. *J. Cons. Clin. Psychol.* **34**, 314–318

O'CONNOR R.D. (1969) Modification of social withdrawal through symbolic modelling. *J. Appl. Behav. Anal.* **2**, 15–22

O'DELL S. (1974) Training parents in behaviour modification: A review. *Psychol. Bull.* **81**, 418–433

O'LEARY K.D. & BECKER W.C. (1967) Behavioral modification of an adjustment class: a token reinforcement program. *Except. Child.* **33**, 637–642

PATTERSON G.R. (1965) A learning theory approach to the treatment of the school phobic child. *In* Ullman L.P. & Krasner L. (eds.) *Case Studies in Behavior Modification.* New York: Holt, Rinehart & Winston

PATTERSON G.R. (1971) *Families: Applications of Social Learning to Family Life.* Champaign, Illinois: Research Press

PATTERSON G.R. (1973a) Reprogramming the families of aggressive boys. *In* Thoresen C.E. (ed.) *Behavior Modification in Education.* Chicago: National Society for the Study of Education

PATTERSON G.R. (1973b) Multiple evaluations of a parent training program. *In* Thompson T. & Dockens W.S. (eds.) *Proceedings of the International Symposium on Behavior Modification.* New York: Appleton-Century-Crofts

PATTERSON G.R. (1974) Interventions for boys with conduct problems: Multiple settings, treatments, and criteria. *J. Cons. Clin. Psychol.* **42**, 471–481

PATTERSON G.R. & BRODSKY G. (1966) A behaviour modification programme for a child with multiple problem behaviour. *J. Child Psychol. Psychiat.* **7**, 277–295

PATTERSON G.R. & GULLION M.E. (1968) *Living with Children: New Methods for Parents and Teachers.* Champaign, Illinois: Research Press

PATTERSON G.R., LITTMAN R.A. & BRICKER W. (1967) Assertive behavior in children: a step toward a theory of aggression. *Monogr. Soc. Res. Child Dev.* **32**, no. 5 (Serial No. 113)

PATTERSON G.R., RAY R.S., SHAW D.A. & COBB J.A. (1969) A manual for coding of family interactions. Unpublished manuscript, Oregon Research Institute

PATTERSON G.R. & REID J.B. (1970) Reciprocity and coercion: Two facets of social systems. *In* Neuringer C. & Michael J.L. (eds.) *Behavior Modification in Clinical Psychology.* New York: Appleton-Century-Crofts

PATTERSON G.R., SHAW D.A. & EBNER M. (1969) Teachers, peers and parents as agents of change in the classroom. *In* Benson F.A.M. (ed.) *Modifying Deviant Social Behaviors in Various Classroom Settings.* Eugene, Oregon: University of Oregon Press

PEINE H.A. & HOWARTH R. (1975) *Children and Parents: Everyday Problems of Behaviour.* Harmondsworth: Penguin

PHILLIPS E.L. (1968) Achievement place: token reinforcement in a home-style rehabilitation setting for pre-delinquent boys. *J. Appl. Behav. Anal.* **1,** 213–223

PHILLIPS E.L., PHILLIPS E.A., FIXSEN D.L. & WOLF M.M. (1971) Achievement place: modification of the behaviours of pre-delinquent boys within a token economy. *J. Appl. Behav.* **4,** 45–59

PHILLIPS E.L., PHILLIPS E.A., FIXSEN D.L. & WOLF M.M. (1973) Achievement place: behavior shaping works for delinquents. *Psychol. Today,* June 1973, 75–79

POPPER K. (1972) *The Logic of Scientific Discovery,* 3rd edn. London: Hutchinson

RACHMAN S. (1962) Learning theory and child psychology: therapeutic possibilities. *J. Child Psychol. Psychiat.* **3,** 149–163

RACHMAN S. (1972) Clinical applications of observational learning, imitation and modeling. *Behav. Ther.* **3,** 379–397

RACHMAN S. (1974) *The Meanings of Fear.* Harmondsworth: Penguin

REID J.B. & HENDRIKS A.F.C.J. (1973) A preliminary analysis of the effectiveness of direct home intervention for treatment of predelinquent boys who steal. *In* Clark I.W. & Hamerlynck L.A. (eds.) *Critical issues in research and practice: Proceedings of the Fourth Banff International Conference in Behavior Modification.* Champaign, Illinois: Research Press

RISLEY T.R. & BAER D.M. (1973) Operant behavior modification: the deliberate development of behavior. *In* Caldwell B.M. & Ricciuti H.N. (eds). *Review of Child Development Research* vol. 3: *Child Development and Social Policy.* Chicago: University of Chicago Press

RITTER B. (1968) The group desensitization of children's snake phobias using vicarious and contact desensitization procedures. *Behav. Res. Ther.* **6,** 1–6

ROBINS L.N. (1966) *Deviant Children Grown Up.* Baltimore: Williams & Wilkins

RUTTER M. (1965) Classification and categorization in child psychiatry. *J. Child Psychol. Psychiat.* **6,** 71–83

RUTTER M., TIZARD J. & WHITMORE K. (eds.) (1970) *Education, Health and Behaviour.* London: Longman

SALZINGER K., FELDMAN R. & PORTNOY S. (1970) Training parents of brain injured children in the use of operant conditioning procedures. *Behav. Ther.* **1,** 4–32

STUMPHAUZER J.S. (ed.) (1973) *Behavior therapy with delinquents.* Springfield, Illinois: Charles C. Thomas

THARP R.G. & WETZEL R.J. (1969) *Behavior Modification in the Natural Environment.* London: Academic Press

THORESEN C.E. & MAHONEY M.J. (1974) *Behavioral Self-control.* New York: Holt, Rinehart & Winston

TIZARD J. (1973) Maladjusted children and the child guidance service. *London Educ. Rev.* **2,** 22–37

WAHLER R.G. & CORMIER W.H. (1970) The ecological interview: A first step in out-patient child behavior therapy. *J. Behav. Ther. Exper. Psychiat.* **1**, 279–289

WALTER H.I. & GILMORE S.K. (1973) Placebo versus social learning effects in parent training procedures designed to alter the behavior of aggressive boys. *Behav. Ther.* **4**, 361–377

WATSON J.B. & RAYNER R. (1920) Conditioned emotional reactions. *J. exper. Psychol.* **3**, 1–14

WHITE W.C. & DAVIS M.T. (1974) Vicarious extinction of phobic behaviour in early childhood. *J. Abnorm. Child Psychol.* **2**, 25–32

WILLIAMS C.D. (1959) The elimination of tantrum behaviors by extinction procedures. *J. Abnorm. Soc. Psychol.* **59**, 269

WILTZ N.A. (1969) Modification of behaviors of deviant boys through parent participation in a group technique. PhD Thesis, University of Oregon. Cited by Patterson, 1973b

WOLF M.M. & RISLEY T.R. (1971) Reinforcement: applied research. *In* Glaser R. (ed.) *The Nature of Reinforcement*. London: Academic Press

WOLPE J. (1958) *Psychotherapy of Reciprocal Inhibition*. Stanford: Stanford University Press

YATES A.J. (1970) *Behavior Therapy*. New York: Wiley

YULE W. (1975) Teaching psychological principles to non-psychologists. 2: Training parents in child management. *J. Ass. Educ. Psychol.* **10**, (3), 5–16

YULE W. & BERGER M. (1972) Behavior modification principles and speech delay. *In* Rutter M. & Martin J.A.M. (eds.) *The Child with Delayed Speech*. Clinics in Develop. Med. no. 43. London: SIMP/Heinemann

YULE W. & BERGER M. (1975) Communication, language and behaviour modification. *In* Kiernan C.C. & Woodford F.P. (eds.) *Behaviour Modification with the Severely Retarded*. Amsterdam: Assoc. Scientific Publishers

YULE W. & HEMSLEY D. (1976) Single case methodology in medical psychology. *In* Rachman S. (ed.) *Advances in Medical Psychology*. Oxford: Pergaman

YULE W., SACKS B. & HERSOV L. (1974) Successful flooding treatment of a noise phobia in an eleven-year-old. *J. Behav. Ther. Exp. Psychiat.* **5**, 209–211

CHAPTER 40

Dynamic treatments

C. DARE

Ellenberger (1970) subtitles his volume *The Discovery of the Unconscious*, as *The history and evolution of dynamic psychiatry*. He gives no definition of what is meant by the phrase 'dynamic psychiatry', but he describes the subject as originating in primitive healing, magnetism and hypnosis and surveys the 'great dynamic psychiatric systems, notably those of Janet, Adler and Jung'. Presumably these systems share with their postulated origins, notions of human motivation stemming from powerful unconscious forces.

More explicitly, Boring (1950) defines dynamic psychology as 'the psychology of motivation', of which 'the principal source . . . is, of course, Freud'. Freud himself described psychoanalytic thinking as including a 'dynamic point of view'. This referred specifically neither to the importance of unconscious aspects of mental functioning (which was subsumed under the 'topographical point of view') nor to the operation of forceful mental energies (the 'economic point of view') but to yet a third aspect—the effects of conflicts between differing processes in the mental apparatus (Freud 1915). As Hartmann (1959) put it: 'The consideration of mental processes from (the) angles of synergistic or antagonistic motivating forces is what has been known . . . as the dynamic aspect of psychoanalysis' (p. 326).

In broad terms, dynamic treatment methods will be understood, for the purposes of this chapter, as being those therapies which are based on the assumptions of psychoanalytic psychology (Sandler, Dare & Holder 1972a). These assumptions can be summarised as follows: that it is possible to postulate a psychological system in which normal and abnormal mental functioning are conceptualised as determined by conflicts between opposing would-be-adaptational and largely unconscious processes within a mental apparatus. In this context, 'unconscious' implies a forceful exclusion of an idea, memory, or thought from consciousness and not merely a lack of immediate conscious awareness of a mental content.

Dynamic psychology and psychiatry are largely concerned with acquired, environmental determinants of personality structure and of mental disorder. However, even in the early years of psychoanalysis there was no denial of the importance of innate, constitutional factors (cf. Freud 1896; 1913; 1916/17) but such factors have not been subject to much psychoanalytical investigation. Nevertheless, the investigation of Fries and Woolf (1953) and of Escalona (1969) into constitutional differences between newborn infants are notable evidence of psychoanalytical interest in congenital differences as manifested in infantile behaviour.

The early history of Freud's views on the origin of neurosis suggest a change from an environmentalist viewpoint (the traumatic, seduction theory) to a viewpoint putting more stress on constitutional determinants (neurosis resulting from the vicissitudes of innate, somatically derived instinctual drives). In this aspect of the development of psychoanalytic theory, later formulations rarely entirely supplanted former views (see Sandler, Dare & Holder 1972b, 1973).

The great strength of psychoanalytic psychology of the personality lies in its postulation of the mental apparatus as a developing structure ('the genetic point of view'). This developmental basis (initially a psychosexual model) means that most dynamic psychologies present an outline of the normal course of childhood, and relate adult personality to an intimate inter-action between the experienced events of childhood and the innately deter-mined maturational sequence. However, it is quite apparent that, different dynamic psychologies are based on different developmental schemata. This can be seen in the differences in the central concerns of the developmental phases as described by, for example, A. Freud (1966), Segal (1973), Erikson (1964) and Fordham (1969).

The great importance that dynamic psychology gives to the retrospective understanding of the adult in terms of childhood processes may account for the greater influence such psychology has had on child psychiatry than on adult psychiatry in Great Britain. This, too, accounts for the ready application of such psychologies to the search for effective therapies in child psychiatry. For, of course, psychoanalysis refers not only to a psychology but also to a specific treatment method, the process of which can be defined with reason-able precision (Sandler, Dare & Holder 1973). Although the specific treatment method of psychoanalysis has been widely applied to children for half a century since the first full-length studies appeared (A. Freud 1926/27; Klein 1932), many other treatment methods can be called psychoanalyti-cal and hence deserve the term dynamic.

This chapter mainly concentrates on two topics. The first and principal one is psychoanalytic psychotherapy with children. The second topic, which is more briefly discussed, concerns psychoanalytic approaches to the treatment and management of pathology in the relationship between children and parents.

These two topics specifically exclude the important application of psychoanalysis to the treatment of children and adolescents in various residential and group settings such as Aichhorn's work with delinquents (1925) and the Hampstead Nursery Projects with infants (Burlingham & Freud 1942; 1944). The application of psychoanalytic thinking to treatment of children as inpatients is extensive (e.g. Bettelheim 1950; Redl 1966; Easson 1969; Noshpitz 1962) and the use of psychodynamic concepts and methods in the therapeutic work in residential establishments for children is also an increasing field (e.g. Szurek 1947; Ekstein, Wallerstein & Mandelbaum 1959; Montalvo & Pavlin 1966; Borowitz 1970). Psychoanalytic principles have been widely applied in community mental health programmes with children (Caplan 1961; Brockbank 1971) and infants (Chandler, Lourie & Peters 1968; Provence 1972).

Even with these exclusions and without a detailed discussion of formal psychoanalysis of children, the topic of dynamic psychotherapies is huge. Two very important topics can only be mentioned in passing. First, neither the status of these psychotherapies as scientific activities nor the question of the testing of their efficacy* are discussed. Instead, the chapter focusses on a description of the techniques.

Second, there is the difficult problem of what constitutes the subject matter of psychoanalysis, taken here to encompass a person's subjective experiences of himself. Such a field must be approached by observations of the verbal and nonverbal behaviours of the person, but these behaviours are not the same as the inner experiences that they partially reveal. Psychoanalysis can be considered to have a dual nature. On the one hand, there is Freud's vigorous and oft repeated statements claiming that the subject is a branch of science, akin to the physical sciences. On the other hand, other psychoanalysts adopt an existentialist stance, arguing that psychoanalysis is an attempt to express the subjective experiences of being human. Yankelovich and Barrett (1971) have put it: 'Thus, psychoanalysis has one foot firmly planted in scientific materialism and the other equally firmly in existentialism, which is at violent odds with the former and indeed was largely conceived in opposition to it. A vigorous adherence to both philosophies would tear psychoanalysis apart.' Hartmann (1927) has stated 'Psychoanalysis is, therefore, an inductive science of the connections between complex mental structures. Its propositions are obtained empirically and have to be verified empirically. The inductive basis of its knowledge is slim compared to that of the physical sciences, and its accessibility to experimental verification is fraught with difficulties. But where such experiments have been performed, the results have supported analytic theories.' Rycroft (1966) expressed the contrary view that

* Some discussion relevant to the evaluation of psychotherapy is included in Chapter 41 on psychiatric social work.

Freud's achievement was not to explain phenomena but to 'understand it and give it meaning, and the procedure he engaged in was not the scientific one of elucidating causes but the semantic one of making sense of it' (p. 14).

This confusion as to the philosophical basis of psychodynamic theory and the actual nature of its subject matter, together account for the methodological problems of defining and elucidating the nature and outcome of dynamically oriented psychotherapy. Psychodynamic therapists are on the whole either indifferent or averse to empirical 'objective' investigation of the efficacy or even the process of their treatments. This is not simply due to the lack of scientific training in their background, or to their lack of acquaintance with such evaluation techniques. Moreover this state of affairs is not only due to the complexity of the topic, the difficulty of establishing proper controls, or the problem of establishing criteria for change and cure (although these are wide difficulties). In part the problem arises because psychoanalytic therapists evaluate their work in terms of its significance as a human encounter for themselves and their patients. In this respect, scientific evaluations of psychotherapy would be equivalent to an objective assessment of prospective marital partners to enable them to decide whether to marry.

This chapter will concentrate on descriptions of technique and on the setting of child psychotherapies.

Psychodynamic psychotherapy with children

The first child case reported by Freud (1909) gave an account of treatment of a 5-year-old boy carried out by his father under Freud's supervision. A number of psychoanalysts attempted the direct psychoanalytic treatment of children or adolescents in the first 20 years of this century, but Hug-Hellmuth (1921) is generally given credit as the first analyst to suggest procedures adapted to children. However, Melanie Klein (1932) and Anna Freud (1926/27) gave impetus to the whole topic and are still the major influences behind two divergent schools in child psychoanalysis (see A. Freud 1972a). Anna Freud has her major international influence in the USA whilst still directing the Hampstead Child-Therapy Course and Clinic in London. Melanie Klein never herself established an institutional basis for her teaching, although the child psychotherapy course at the Tavistock Clinic, London, is the main formal training centre run by her close followers. The Kleinian school outside of the UK, is most influential in South America (especially the Argentine) and in France. Other centres, notably in the USA, have developed the psychoanalytic treatment of children. The most important works on psychotherapy with children concentrate on full psychoanalysis.

Apart from the works of the founding mothers mentioned above, there are two handbooks of Child Psychoanalysis. One edited by Pearson (1968) emanates from the Institute of the Philadelphia Association for Psychoanalysis and is in the school of A. Freud. The other edited by Wolman (1972) is a compendium of a wide range of view points of the theoretical background and technical procedures in the application of various forms of psychodynamic systems to the treatment of children.

PSYCHOANALYTIC TREATMENT OF CHILDREN

Elsewhere, Dare (1975) has classified the range of interventions that can be deployed in establishing a treatment relationship with children and in helping children to change in that relationship. In order to manage a condensation of a large body of psychoanalytic thought, the elements of the treatment process are categorised in this chapter as interventions and for each intervention the psychodynamic theory which is implicit is noted.

Settings for psychotherapy

Psychotherapy based on psychodynamic psychology is not concerned with applying specific technical measures to eliminate or enhance particular behaviours. The therapist seeks to ensure that as many as possible of his interactions with the patient enhance the significance of the encounter for the child. For this reason the setting has to be considered with care. The whole manner in which the interaction between the child and the therapist is managed and conducted communicates to the child a view of himself. If the encounter is important enough to the child, the child will make that view part of himself. That is, he will change a little. The fact that the therapist sets aside a sufficient length of time at sufficiently frequent intervals for the child, lets the child know that the psychotherapist sets some importance by their meetings. That process is enhanced if the therapist is reasonably strict about the timing of the interviews, starting on time and keeping to the scheduled time period.

Children of an age to tell the time can be observed to know if their time has been cut short, or that they have been seen late, and to draw conclusions about their importance in the eyes of the therapist. Similarly, if the privacy of the treatment time is preserved from interruption by other people coming to the room or by the telephone, the child understands that the therapist is trying to give his wholehearted attention to the meeting.

The psychotherapy situation has a very special nature. For the child, the adult (the psychotherapist) is solely concerned with a sustained listening and looking at the child to discover the meaning of what the child is saying and experiencing. A moment's reflection shows that this is an unusual situation. Most interactions between adults and children are brief, instrumental or instructional transactions (such as teaching, disciplining, checking or showing affection), or the interaction is concerned with some joint activity—playing, nurturing and the like. Many children may never have had an adult who pays exclusive (benign) attention to them for a period of 45–60 minutes (the normal length of a psychoanalytic psychotherapy session).

Regularity, reliability and punctuality convey to the child that the psychotherapist is endowing the treatment with some importance, but it is also necessary to provide means by which the child can feel sufficiently comfortable in the treatment setting for him to communicate unselfconsciously. This means that the therapist has also to be able to feel reasonably relaxed and unpressured by the setting.

A medium for communication other than private conversation is made available to enable the child to reveal his feelings and thoughts. This provision constitutes the specifics of the setting of child psychotherapy. Children under the age of 12–14 years are not expected to be able to speak about themselves by direct conversation. Even a verbally gifted child, eager to talk to a friendly adult, will not be able to tell his passing thoughts in the manner expected of the adult patient in psychoanalytic psychotherapy. When anxiety-provoking or hostile thoughts predominate and resistances to treatment arise, exhortation and silence by the therapist do not evoke talk in children but result in uncomfortable silence. (In other words, children are found not to tell of their 'free associations' in conformity to Freud's 'fundamental role of psychoanalysis'.) It was this psychoanalytic observation that led Melanie Klein (1932) to invent the technique of the analysis of the child's spontaneous play. Child psychotherapists of all schools provide the sort of natural media of expression that children use for symbolic and expressive play so that the setting includes toys, artistic and modelling materials that are appropriate to the age of the child being treated.

A distinction should be made between the use of toy and play in three different situations. The first is the playroom or waiting-room provision of toys, that enable the child to feel that he is in a place meant for children. The second is the playgroup or recreational setting where play materials are freely available on the grounds that play is part of the normal activity in childhood and should be encouraged, particularly for socially disadvantaged or physically ill children under the special circumstances of being in hospital or coming from a home without play facilities. The third situation is that of psychotherapy where play and creative material, selected as appropriate for a particular child, are provided for him specifically to facilitate communication with the therapist. A doll's house, furniture, wire dolls, soldiers and fort and assorted toys, lying around a psychiatrist's room and available to every child coming for a diagnostic or treatment interview, do not constitute a setting for child psychotherapy.

The practice of the Kleinian school of child psychotherapy at the Tavistock Clinic is that each child who attends the psychotherapist should have his own particular play materials that are available only to him, so that their state and preservation is entirely the responsibility of that one child.

Establishment of the therapeutic alliance

Dynamic psychology has as its subject matter the person's subjective experience of themselves, and dynamic psychotherapies, therefore, are concerned with an exploration of the person's subjective experience in a personal relationship with the therapist. The general setting is designed to facilitate the development of a helping relationship. The provision of toys and play materials implies that the child will come to understand that these materials are present so that the therapist may learn more about the structure and content of the child's emotional world. The setting can be structured to communicate to the child the nature of the therapeutic work. This constitutes part of the work of establishing an alliance with the child. This alliance has come to be known in psychoanalytic writings as the treatment alliance (see Sandler, Dare & Holder 1973). Initially, Freud (1912; 1913b) thought that the work of the analysis was carried through the patient's resistance by the positive regard and respect the patient had for the physician ('nonerotic transferences'). Later Sterba (1934; 1940) described the situation as one in which an observing, self-appraising aspect of the personality ('the observing ego') could motivate the patient to engage in the therapeutic work despite the discomfort entailed by discovery of unwelcome or disturbing aspects of the self. Before this time A. Freud (1926/27) was advocating that, in child analysis, the child had first to become attached to the analyst by the deliberate utilisation of an introductory phase. In this the analyst seeks to ally himself with 'his (the child patient's) conscious ego against a split-off part of his nature' so that the analyst offers himself 'as a partner against his (the child's) surroundings' and may hence creep into a confidence which was not to be won directly. Over time, the work of developing and maintaining an alliance with the child has come to be an integral aspect of treatment, which is carried on throughout the therapy by drawing the child's attention to the nature of the work being undertaken and commenting on the forces within the child working against the treatment process.

In this process, as in all aspects of the treatment relationship with the child, the psychotherapist has to be constantly searching for a vocabulary which is appropriate to the child's knowledge of words. This need is sometimes denied by child psychoanalysts who use a highly complicated, specialised language. If the limitations of the expressed vocabulary of the child is drawn to their attention they say that the 'child's unconscious will understand'. Although it is possible that the child will understand more than he can express, and that nonverbal cues in posture, tone of voice and manner, will help his understanding, it seems more reasonable to make all efforts to use only words the child knows, or which he can be expected to learn from their usage in therapy.

Anna Freud pointed out (1972a) that it was Bornstein who enabled the elimination of the introductory nonanalytic period by 'the ingenious use of defense interpretation for creating a treatment alliance with the child patient'.

Interpretative work of child psychotherapy

The characteristic activity of the psychodynamic psychotherapist is interpretation but, 'because the psychoanalytic technique is predominantly a *verbal* one, and because the psychoanalytic training has become so specialised, it is perhaps natural that a certain mystique has become attached to the analyst's interpretations' (Sandler, Dare & Holder 1973, p. 104). This mystique seems to be especially liable to develop in work with children when there are uncertainties about the extent of the child's understanding and when, as so often occurs in child psychotherapy, responses to any intervention are monitored more by the subsequent nature of the play or creations and by the meaning of these as understood by the therapist, than by the child's verbal responses. Some workers (for example Zulliger 1953; Elkisch 1968; Woltmann 1955) have explored what are essentially nonverbal techniques of child psychotherapy. There are no published works known to this author on nonverbal 'interpretative' techniques in child psychotherapy although it seems clear that a great deal is conveyed to the child by the setting and by nonverbal means. These may supplement or actually constitute that which, if verbalised, would fulfil the criteria of interpretation.

Interpretation is a word that has been given a wide range of meanings within psychoanalysis but here it will be used '... to include within it all comments and other verbal interventions which have the aim of immediately making the patient aware of some aspects of his psychological functioning of which he was not previously conscious' (Sandler, Dare & Holder 1973). This use of the concept of interpretation goes alongside a view that '... therapeutic change as a consequence of analysis depends, to a large degree, on the provision of a structured and organized conceptual and effective framework within which the patient can effectively place himself and his subjective experience of himself and others' (Sandler, Dare & Holder 1973). An important theme of this chapter is that, for a child, it is likely that the changing view of himself that psychotherapy provides is as much dependent on the nonverbal aspects of the treatment as by the verbal interpretations. Unfortunately it is extremely difficult to be as clear about the meaning and intent of nonverbal expressions, as it is for verbal interventions. Verbal interpretations are addressed to any aspect of what the therapist understands the child to be experiencing, and which he regards as being unclear, confusing or unknown to the child. This understanding by the therapist may be based on his own emotional reactions to the child, his observations, or his knowledge of the child's development and current life situation.

An interpretation may consist simply of the therapist expressing his awareness of the child's feelings of the moment, for example at having to be seen in the psychiatric clinic. At all times the therapist seeks by his comments, including his interpretations, to show the child that he, the therapist, knows that the child is responding to the immediate present. Further interpretations make connections between the current state of affairs, the here-and-now situation in the therapy room, and other aspects of the child's life. The interpretations are directed two ways. First, there are comments that link the child's feelings and thought content (as revealed in play, drawings, words and so on) to other current life events. For example, the therapist may link the immediate state of the child's self-experience to his current developmentally determined preoccupations or to his reactions to family events or relationships. Second, the therapist's interpretations are addressed to his understanding of the way current experience is determined by the past experiences of the child. Interpretations thus attempt to help the child become aware of the comprehensibility of his inner experience in terms of his own history and of his own current world. One rationale for the use of interpretation is, of course, based on the notion of insight. 'Insight' consists of a state of affairs in which the child becomes aware, not only of the possibility that what he feels makes sense in terms of his current and past life experiences, but also that making sense of his life will enable him to manage the conflicts that he experiences in a less self-damaging and painful way. The connotation of increasing the child's mastery of his inner turmoil and external predicament by interpretation has only recently received emphasis in child psychotherapy.

Establishment of a common language with the child

Verbal psychotherapeutic interventions can only be effective in the way intended by the therapist if the child understands the words used by the therapist in more-or-less the same way as the therapist understands them himself. However, the nonverbal message conveyed by the therapist's words may be effective in furthering the development of the relationship between the child and the adult and may therefore enhance the treatment situation without the child really understanding what is being said. Nevertheless, part of what goes on in psychotherapy must include the development of a vocabulary shared by the two partners in the process. This process is especially important in work with young children and can be thought of as essential if the child is to be able to benefit from the treatment's verbal interventions. It can also be understood that the child's learning of a vocabulary to understand his experience may itself contribute to his ability to master both his inner and his outer conflicts. At a simple level young children show some relief when an affect they are experiencing is named with a word that they recognise. The didactic learning aspect of child psychoanalysis was emphasised in A. Freud's earlier works (1926/27), but it remains true that learning is considered part of the psychoanalytic treatment process (Strupp 1968). In the course of psychotherapy, the child learns an understanding (a 'model') of himself that places his experience of himself in an historically and contemporaneously comprehensible context. It must be made clear that this is by no means exclusively, or even principally, a cognitive process. Nonetheless the verbal aspects of the acquisition of a knowledge of the self that renders the self and its inner turmoil bearable and manageable is strongly dependent on a firm verbal basis.

Transference and reconstruction in child psychoanalysis

Finch and Cain (1968) comment that: 'Perhaps the most studied attention regarding technique (in child psychoanalysis) has been given to the question of whether children are capable of developing a full transference neurosis and the related questions of the degree to which the child analyst serves as a new, real object vs. a transference figure for the child, and whether the child's object-related attitudes and images are extended, externalised or fully transferred to the analyst.' (p. 447). The controversy around the importance of transference in child psychoanalysis concerns the time in the child's life when the crucial events determining the core of the child's difficulties occurred. Melanie Klein (1932) considered that vitally important processes in the first year of life (the 'paranoid–schizoid position' and the 'depressive position') determined subsequent development to a very important extent. Thus Segal (1973) says 'In describing the paranoid–schizoid position, I tried to show how successful negotiation of the anxieties experienced in the early months of the infant's development leads to a gradual organisation of his universe.' (p. 67.) She says of the depressive position: 'If the infant has been able to establish a good internal object relatively securely in the depressive position, situations of depressive anxiety will not lead to illness, but to fruitful working through, leading to further enrichment and creativity.' (p. 68.) In placing great importance on the early months of life, Melanie Klein understood that in the psychoanalysis of even young children, the psychotherapist was attempting to help the child master the impingements of the past (largely in the form of fantasies) on the present. Klein (1932) believed, therefore, that the psychoanalyst must attempt to discern, in the unfolding relationship between therapist and patient, evidence of the fantasies derived from experiences of the first year of life of the child. Her view was that the infant underwent the experiences of the two positions in relation to its view of its mother and would repeat something of those times anew, in relation to the therapist. The core of the child's disturbance was thus thought by Klein to become re-expressed in relationship to the therapist and a transference neurosis could be said to develop.

Most psychoanalytic models of child development maintain that crucial developments occur throughout childhood and adolescence in the relationship between the child and its parents, the wider family and society. Hence, an analysis of the past, as it occurs in a transference neurosis, could not be particularly comprehensive. Moreover, the on-going role of the parents in the child's life limits the extent to which the analyst can ever become the central reference point for the child's problems in the way an adult patient's difficulties may centre on his analyst.

All schools of dynamic child psychotherapy emphasise a technique whereby the understanding of the relationship between the psychotherapist and the child is explored. Most psychotherapists accept that there will be elements of distortions in the child's perception of the relationship, and some of those distortions will derive from preceding child–parent situations. That is, transferences will occur. Psychotherapists, however, differ in the extent to which the relationship between the therapist and child is explored mainly because it is an ever present example of what the child does to those close to him, and also in the extent to which the relationship is explored mainly for purposes of a transference analysis.

Similarly, therapists vary in the extent they help the child construct a history of himself in relation to the present predicaments, or, alternatively, keep the focus of interest mainly on the present and future interpersonal life situation of the child.

We believe that often it may be extremely useful to help a child understand the influence of his past life on his present life problems. The interpretation of transference material may be extremely useful in some cases, whereas in other cases it may be unhelpful or irrelevant.

AIMS OF CHILD PSYCHOTHERAPY*

Psychodynamic views on child development (see Chapter 11) provide the theoretical framework for psychotherapy. It is clear that the dynamic approach, with its emphasis on the origins of disturbance as an outcome of mental conflicts of largely unconscious origins, does not concern itself principally with the elimination of target symptoms or with the production of a socially conforming child. Segal (1972) summarises Kleinian views succinctly: ... 'essentially the aim of psychoanalysis is the same whatever the age of the patient: it is always to get in touch with his psychic realities. The analysis of defenses and of object relations in fantasy and reality should help him to differentiate between external and internal realities, and to foster the process of psychic growth.' (p. 414.)

Anna Freud shows less belief in the efficacy of psychoanalytic therapeutic interventions and correspondingly has more cautious expectation of the nature of aims of treatment (1972b). 'Children are in urgent need of analytic therapy when normal progressive development is arrested or has been slowed up significantly, whether the reason for this is symptom formation, or excessive defense activity, or undefended anxiety, or massive regression, etc. From this follows that they should be considered cured as soon as the developmental forces have been set free again and are ready to take over ... in practice it is not at all easy to determine when precisely this welcome change in the child's personality is taking place and what exactly in his structure it is operating.' (p. 14.)

Although there are marked divergencies between the two main schools of child psychotherapy about the nature and extent of treatment possibilities, these two quotations show the shared understanding that therapy consists of the freeing of a child from defensive inhibition and the attempt to facilitate future development.

Dynamic psychotherapy in children should take place in the context of an assessment of the child that includes a detailed account of the child's developmental state at the beginning of treatment. Thus, treatment is seen as attempting to bring the child's actual developmental state to its age appropriate level. Each dynamic psychology will emphasise different aspects of the developmental assessment which will in turn decide the language in which aims at outcome are expressed.

Smirnoff (1971) expresses his view that 'Even if the ultimate aim of treatment is viewed in terms of 'adjustment', this is not to be understood in the sense of 'social conformity' but rather that the patient should be free

* Brody (1964) has discussed this topic and related aims to techniques in child psychotherapy.

to find his own way of life and to speak and act in his own name.' (p. 177.) Such an idealised, generalised notion is impractical as a guide to treatment. Instead a criterion such as freedom from outstanding conflicts (as revealed in the child's play, drawing, dreams and conversation) must be used, in conjunction with an assessment of the child's ability to enjoy and manage experiences for peer relationships and skills development that his school life provides. Clearly, preschool, latency and adolescent age groups are engaged in different life and developmental tasks. A child's ability to engage in these tasks must be assessed in the evaluation of progress in psychotherapy.

DYNAMIC APPROACHES TO THE FAMILY SETTING OF THE CHILD

As mentioned above, Freud (1909) reported the treatment of 5-year-old Hans by the boy's father. This is one approach to the role of parents in the psychoanalytical psychotherapy of children.

All approaches to the psychoanalytic understanding and treatment of children acknowledge the importance of the child's relationship with his parents for the origins, course and management of the disturbance. Thus, Klein (1932) says of the parents: 'The child is dependent on them and so they are included in the field of the analysis; yet it is not they who are being analysed ... The relationship of the parents to their child's analyst entails difficulties of a peculiar kind, since it touches closely upon their own complexes ... (These) give rise to a more or less ambivalent attitude in the parents ... and this is not removed by the fact of their having conscious insight into their child's need for analytic treatment.' (p. 75.) Klein mentions that she had sometimes taken both mother and child into analytic treatment herself, which is another approach to the management of the parent–child context of the psychotherapy with children. All psychodynamic theories recognise the importance of the parents' own personalities in determining their offsprings' personality and difficulties. Dynamic child psychotherapists have to evolve techniques which take account of the past, present and future role of the parental figures in relation to the child (in ways that are appropriate to his age and background).

Such techniques constitute a very large part of the practice of child psychiatry and this chapter describes briefly four strategies used to manage the family context of a child's disturbance.

Psychotherapeutic treatment of the child with minimal family contact

In working with adolescent children, especially at the age of 16 years and above, it can be perfectly straightforward to treat the child like an adult in psychotherapy, particularly if the adolescent has referred himself (as is encouraged by walk-in clinics). Even in such a circumstance most therapists would discuss with the patient whether or not the parents should be seen on one occasion by himself or a colleague.

The younger the patient the less it is possible to treat him like an adult and the more the parents' commitment to the treatment will determine the attendance and possible usefulness of the treatment. Most child therapists have experienced subtle or overt sabotage of treatments by the parents, even when the initiative for the first contact came from apparently cooperative and helpful parents.

Parent guidance approach

The phrase 'parent guidance' is one used by Anna Freud (e.g. 1972a, b) for an instructional contact between an analytically trained worker and parents. The parent is informed of the worker's understanding of the child's developmental stage. The needs and anxieties of that stage are explained in the context of the details that the parent brings of the day-to-day happenings of the child's life. This process is clearly very similar to counselling as carried out in many child treatment settings. The ingredients of instruction and explanation about the treatment method could be expected to accompany any other form of work with the parents of children in treatments.

Parent and child treated equally as 'patients'

In response to the recognition that a detailed connection is frequently apparent between the child's disturbance and the nature of the parent's psychopathology as revealed in coincidental psychotherapeutic intervention (cf. Burlingham 1935; Johnson 1969), it became logical to consider treating child and parent (predominantly the mother) as an equally involved duo. Sperling (1950; 1951; 1954) in New York, reported treatments of children and their mothers in fully psychoanalytic therapies. The Hampstead Clinic have published a number of simultaneous analyses of children and their mothers, carried out by different child psychotherapists who were both supervised by the same psychoanalyst. In order to enhance the research usefulness of the simultaneous analysis, the two therapists in the duo do not communicate to each other directly, so that parallels in psychological structure as interpreted from the analytic material, are not unduly open to the possibility of the therapists influencing each other's understanding of their respective patients (cf. Burlingham 1955; Hellman 1960). The technique as a treatment of wider application than full psychoanalysis has not been widely applied. Of course many mothers attending child psychiatric clinics commonly feel and verbalise the belief that they are being seen as 'the patient', but it is rare that the treatment of the parents, as practised in casework, framework, actually amounts to a simultaneous and symmetrical dynamic psychotherapy. Johnson (1969) discussed the interwoven psychopathology of the parents and children in child psychiatric work and attempted to treat the pair symmetrically. Bonnard (1949) similarly pioneered appreciation of the interrelationship of parent–child psychopathology and attempted treatments acknowledging this.

Most contemporary dynamic child psychiatric and child guidance work with parents tends to treat the family situation by using a case-work approach to the mother's problems. Essentially this consists of a mixture of parent guidance and a gradual process of trying to move the mother towards seeing her own implication in the child's disturbance (arising at least in part from her own psychological make-up). The move to include fathers in this has grown and nowadays most British clinics assess the father for his suitability and need for dynamically orientated case-work. This has also led to interventions whereby the parents of the child patient are seen together for psychodynamically orientated marital case-work whilst the child is seen in individual psychotherapy.

Family therapy

The extent to which whole family treatments can be described as 'dynamic' is contentious, for the process of treating a whole family together in conjoint therapy is bound to be different to that which goes on in individual therapies. Hence if the notion of psychodynamic treatments is thought to apply to a *treatment* method based on classical psychoanalysis, then very few whole family therapies are derived from the dynamic schools. If on the other hand the phrase 'dynamic' applies to the way the family is understood to work (i.e. that 'dynamic' principles of unconsciously determined, conflictually interacting mechanisms are utilised as a conceptual tool for the basis of the treatment), then whole family psychodynamic psychotherapy undoubtedly exists.

Skynner (1969) has reviewed the growth of family therapy. Dare (1975) has suggested that there are elements in the treatment concepts imbuing psychoanalytic therapy that do lead to parallels in whole family therapies. The establishment of a treatment alliance, the development of a common language, takes place between therapist and family and the whole group can work together to establish a coherent 'model' of the origin and sources of the family distress. This much can occur in many family therapies. There is little in the literature so far on the use of the transference concept in whole family therapy. It seems that the transference concept is most useful in whole family work in its application to the distortion of the marital relationship by the intrusion of childhood parenting needs from the parents' past.

Freud's initial formulations of neuroses as originating in family events— secret seductions and so forth—was followed by formulations of neurosis as the product of family turmoil: the oedipus complex. It does not seem illogical that psychodynamic therapies should eventually be evolved that take the family occurrences as the location of interest of the therapist.

SUMMARY

Thus chapter gives an account of psychodynamic psychotherapy with children as applied in current practice. These therapies are undergoing continual modification and have yet to be evaluated. The strategic changes in dynamic therapy which reflect parents' importance in the genesis and continuation of children's disorders is one example of the modifications which are taking place.

REFERENCES

AICHORN A. (1925) *Wayward Youth*. transl. 1935. New York: Viking Press

BEETTELHEIM B. (1950) *Love is Not Enough*. New York: Free Press

BONNARD A. (1949) Reprinted in Lorand S. & Schneer H.I. (eds.) *Adolescents*. New York: Hoeber 1961

BORING E.G. (1950) *A History of Experimental Psychology*. New York: Appleton-Century-Crofts

BOROWITZ G.H. (1970) The therapeutic utilisation of emotions and attitudes evoked in the caretakers of disturbed children. *Brit. J. med. Psychol.* **43**, 129–139

BROCKBANK R. (1971) The contribution of psychoanalytic theory to community mental health. *Brit. J. med. Psychol.* **44**, 319–328

BURLINGHAM D.T. (1935) Child analysis and the mother. Reprinted in *Psychoanalytic Studies of the Sighted and the Blind*. New York: International Universities Press 1972

BURLINGHAM D.T. (1955) Simultaneous analysis of mother and child. Reprinted in *Psychoanalytic Studies of the Sighted and the Blind*. New York: International Universities Press 1972

BURLINGHAM D.T. (1972) *Psychoanalytic Studies of the Sighted and the Blind*. New York: International Universities Press

BURLINGHAM D.T. & FREUD A. (1942) *Young Children in Wartime*. London: Allen & Unwin

BURLINGHAM D.T. & FREUD A. (1944) *Infants without Families*. London: Allen & Unwin

CAPLAN G. (1961) *An Approach to Community Mental Health*. London: Tavistock

CHANDLER C.A., LOURIE R.S. & PETERS A.D. (1968) *In* Dittman L.L. (ed.) *Early Child Care: the New Perspective.* New York: Atherton Press

DARE C. (1975) A classification of interventions in child and conjoint family therapy. *Psychother. Psychosom.* **25,** 116–125

EASSON W.E. (1969) *The Severely Disturbed Adolescent.* New York: International Universities Press

EKSTEIN R., WALLERSTEIN J. & MANDELBAUM A. (1959) Countertransference in the residential treatment of children. *Psychoanal. Study Child.* **14,** 186–218

ELKISCH P. (1968) Nonverbal, extraverbal, and autistic verbal communication in the treatment of a childhood tiqueur. *Psychoanal. Study Child.* **23,** 423–437

ELLENBERGER H.F. (1970) *The Discovery of the Unconscious.* London: Allen Lane

ERIKSON E.H. (1964) *Childhood and Society.* New York: Norton

ESCALONA S.K. (1969) *The Roots of Individuality.* London: Tavistock

FINCH S.M. & CAIN A.C. (1968) Psychoanalysis of children: problems of etiology and treatment. *In* Marmor J. (ed.) *Modern Psychoanalysis.* New York: Basic Books

FORDHAM M. (1969) *Children as Individuals.* London: Hodder & Stoughton

FREUD A. (1926/1927) Introduction to the technique of child analysis. Reprinted in *The Psychoanalytical Treatment of Children.* London: Imago 1946

FREUD A. (1966) *Normality and Pathology in Childhood.* London: Hogarth Press

FREUD A. (1972a) A short history of child analysis. *In Problems of Psychoanalytic Technique and Therapy 1966–70.* London: Hogarth Press

FREUD A. (1972b) Problems of termination in child analysis. *In Problems of Psychoanalytic Technique and Therapy 1966–70.* London: Hogarth Press

FREUD S. (1896) Heredity and the aetiology of the neuroses. *Standard Edition* **3.** London: Hogarth Press

FREUD S. (1909) Analysis of a phobia in a five-year-old child. *Standard Edition* **10.** London: Hogarth Press

FREUD S. (1912) The dynamics of transference. *Standard Edition* **12.** London: Hogarth Press

FREUD S. (1913a) The disposition to obsessional neurosis. *Standard Edition* **12.** London: Hogarth Press

FREUD S. (1913b) On beginning the treatment. *Standard Edition* **12.** London: Hogarth Press

FREUD S. (1915) The unconscious. *Standard Edition* **12.** London: Hogarth Press

FREUD S. (1916/17) *Introductory Lectures on Psychoanalysis. Standard Edition* **15–16.** London: Hogarth Press

FRIES M.E. & WOOLF P.J. (1953) Some hypotheses on the role of the congenital activity type in personality development. *Psychoanal. Study Child.* **8,** 48–62

HARTMANN H. (1927) Understanding and explanation. Reprinted in *Essays on Ego Psychology.* London: Hogarth Press

HARTMANN H. (1959) Psychoanalysis as a scientific theory. Reprinted in *Essays on Ego Psychology.* London: Hogarth Press 1964

HELLMAN I. (1960) Simultaneous analysis of a mother and child. *Psychoanal. Study Child.* **15,** 359–377

HUG-HELLMUTH H. VON (1921) Zur Technik der Kinderanalyse. *Int. Zeitschrift Psychoanal.* **7,** 179–197

JOHNSON A.M. (1969) *Experience, Affect and Behaviour.* Chicago: University of Chicago Press

KLEIN M. (1932) *The Psycho-analysis of Children.* London: Hogarth Press

MONTALVO B. & PAVLIN S. (1966) Faulty staff communications in a residential treatment center. *Amer. J. Orthopsychiat.* **36**, 706–711

NOSHPITZ J.D. (1962) Notes on the theory of residential treatment. *J. Amer. Acad. Child Psych.* **1**, 284–296

PEARSON H. (1968) *A Handbook of Child Psycho-analysis.* New York: Basic Books

PROVENCE S. (1972) Psychoanalysis and the treatment of psychological disorders of infancy. *In* Wolman B.B. (ed.) *Handbook of Child Psychoanalysis.* New York: van Nostrand Rheinhold

REDL F. (1966) *When We Deal with Children.* New York: Free Press

RYCROFT C. (ed.) (1966) *Psychoanalysis Observed.* Harmondsworth: Penguin

SANDLER J., DARE C. & HOLDER A. (1972a) Frames of reference in psychoanalytic psychology. III: A note on the basic assumptions. *Brit. J. med. Psychol.* **45**, 143–147

SANDLER J., DARE C. & HOLDER A. (1972b) Frames of reference in psychoanalytic psychology. I. Introduction. *Brit. J. med. Psychol.* **45**, 127–131

SANDLER J., DARE C. & HOLDER A. (1973) *The Patient and the Analyst.* London: Allen & Unwin

SEGAL H. (1972) Melanie Klein's technique of child analysis. *In* Wolman B.B. (ed.) *Handbook of Child Psychoanalysis.* New York: van Nostrand Rheinhold

SEGAL H. (1973) *Introduction to the Work of Melanie Klein.* London: Hogarth

SKYNNER A. (1969) A group-analytic approach to conjoint family therapy. *J. Child Psychol. Psychiat.* **10.** 81–106

SMIRNOFF V. (1971) *The Scope of Child Analysis.* London: Routledge & Kegan Paul

SPERLING M. (1950) Children's interpretation and reaction to the unconscious of their mothers. *Int. J. Psycho-Anal.* **31**, 36–41

SPERLING M. (1951) The neurotic child and his mother: a psychoanalytic study. *Amer. J. Orthopsychiat.* **21**, 351–362

SPERLING M. (1954) Reactive schizophrenia in children. *Amer. J. Orthopsychiat.* **24**, 506–512

STERBA R. (1934) The fate of the ego in analytic therapy. *Int. J. Psycho-Anal.* **15**, 117–126

STERBA R. (1940) The dynamics of the dissolution of the transference resistance. *Psychoanal. Rev.* **11**, 166–174

STRUPP H. (1968) Psychoanalytic therapy of the individual. *In* Marmor J. (ed.) *Modern Psychoanalysis.* New York: Basic Books

SZUREK S.A. (1947) Dynamics of staff interaction in hospital psychiatric treatment of children. *Amer. J. Orthopsychiat.* **17**, 652–664

WOLMAN B.B. (ed.) (1972) *Handbook of Child Psychoanalysis.* New York: van Nostrand Rheinhold

WOLTMANN A. (1955) Therapeutic play techniques: concepts of play therapy technique. *Amer. J. Orthopsychiat.* **25**, 771–783

YANKELOVICH D. & BARRETT W. (1971) *Ego and Instinct.* New York: Vintage Books

ZULLIGER H. (1953) Child psychotherapy without interpretation of unconscious content: a theoretical exposition of pure play: the use of a child's talisman as a psychotherapeutic agent. Translated by Ekstein R. & Wallerstein J. *Bull. Menninger Clin.* **17**, 180–188

CHAPTER 41

Psychiatric social work

F. SUSSENWEIN

Initially, social work was mainly concerned with the practical day-to-day needs of the poor, the deviant and the disadvantaged (Goldstein 1975). During the nineteenth century social workers employed a meagre set of skills and techniques applicable to the limited goals of determining people's eligibility for basic commodities and services and then providing them. However, around the turn of the century social workers became more concerned with people suffering from emotional and interpersonal difficulties, and an interest in mental hospital aftercare in the United States led to specialisation in psychiatric social work. In 1906 the first aftercare social worker was appointed and soon a need for specialised training was recognised by a scheme of apprenticeship at the Boston Psychopathic Hospital and subsequently, in 1918, by a training in psychiatric social work at Smith College. The development of psychiatric social work owed much to Healy and Bronner's recognition of the importance of the interplay between social disadvantage and personal problems in the genesis of delinquency and hence the need for an interdisciplinary approach to treatment. In the early 1920s several demonstration child guidance clinics were established in the USA by the Commonwealth Fund. A 'team' of psychiatrist, psychologist and social worker formed the nucleus of each clinic which aimed to serve community needs (Kanner 1959). As a result of the interest of Mrs. Jo Strachey, a British magistrate, similar clinics were established in England. Five British social workers received training at the New York School of Social Work and soon after in 1929 the London School of Economics started its mental health course, the first course within a British university with the acknowledged aim of giving professional training in psychiatric social work (Timms 1964).

Social workers came to be concerned with the importance of children's interpersonal relationships at home and at school as factors in the development of psychiatric disorder. The existing notions and concepts of social welfare practice no longer fitted this new type of work. The emergence of Freudian psychology rescued social work from this dilemma and psychoanalytic theory came to be the cornerstone of psychiatric social work (Goldstein 1975). Case-work came into its own as a method substantiated by a borrowed theory.

As time passed, social workers increasingly sought to justify their work by the development of an all-encompassing theory which could be based on psychoanalytic or other theories and yet have something which was distinctive to social work (Hollis 1964; Smalley 1967). Heavy reliance came to be placed on 'the relationship' (Ferard & Hunnybun 1962) and on the importance of gaining 'insight' (Salzberger-Wittenberg 1970). Views of this kind had earlier come under devastating attack from Barbara Wootton (1959), who pointed to the vagueness of many of the concepts, the lack of empirical support for the theories, the lack of evidence for the efficacy of the practice and the failure to respond to continuing social inequality and deprivation. Further attempts to provide a coherent theoretical base led to a proliferation of theories (reviewed in Roberts & Nee 1970) which could well be regarded as conceptual chaos.

It is necessary to recognise the validity of many of the criticisms which have been made of this unsatisfactory state of affairs but it is also necessary to appreciate that there have been major changes in the theory and practice of psychiatric social workers as a result of the recognition by social workers themselves that a reliance on intrapsychic mechanisms and on the healing power of the relationship was an insufficient basis for social work.

It has become only too apparent that social disadvantage and social discrimination are still very evident in Western society (see Rutter & Madge 1976). As a result, social workers have come to see that their professional work must be concerned with the removal of social injustice as much as with people's adaptation to existing conditions (Lees 1972; Jones 1975). However, this does not mean a return to nineteenth century social welfare. First, there is an acceptance that social workers must take a professional as well as a personal responsibility for the improvement of social conditions in addition to personal life circumstances. This has had its main application in social workers' involvement in community development projects of various kinds (Perlman 1971; Cheetham & Hill 1973; Lees & McGrath 1974; Edward & Batley 1974). Second, it has become clear that there is no simple one-to-one relationship between social disadvantage and psychiatric disorder. Improved housing and improved economic status are worthwhile in their own right but they will not necessarily lead to alleviation of psychiatric disorder which is found in all segments of society. This does not deny the reality of personal stresses and of social disadvantage as factors in the causation of psychiatric disorder (see Rutter & Madge 1976; also Chapters 3 and 5). However, it is a recognition that social disadvantage does not inevitably lead to personal or family malfunction. A knowledge of the processes involved in social interaction and of the mode of operation of social forces is essential to the development of effective remedies for the family difficulties which stem from social stresses and social privation (Leonard 1966; Pincus & Minahan 1973; Middleman & Goldberg 1974). It is that which constitutes social workers' special contribution to child psychiatric practice.

PRINCIPLES OF SOCIAL WORK

There is no one model or theory which can encompass psychiatric social work (Goldstein 1975). However, the central characteristic which differentiates it from psychology or psychiatry is the emphasis on the *social context* of behaviour. The focus of social work practice is on the interactions between people and on the relevance of formal and informal support systems, that is both community organisations and personal relationships within and outside the family (Pincus & Minahan 1973). Individual problems are not primarily viewed as personal pathology but rather as a manifestation of social disturbance (Middleman & Goldberg 1974). Of course, personal variables and personal illness may play a crucial role in the causation of psychiatric disorder (see Chapters 1 and 8). It is essential that social workers understand the nature of these personal influences and recognise their importance in making plans for treatment. But the special contribution of the social worker lies in understanding how individual responses (whether to personal attributes, illness or external stresses) are influenced by the social situation.

The same applies to child development. Children change and grow as a result of physical maturation and a variety of personal influences. However, development is also greatly influenced by the child's interactions with other people in a social and community framework. These interactions not only shape development but also influence how he responds to later stresses and difficulties.

The scientific basis for social work practice remains fragmented and incomplete but the main sources lie in sociology, social and developmental psychology, social administration and social anthropology. Before any kind of therapy can begin, the social worker, in collaboration with colleagues, must make an accurate *social diagnosis* (Richmond 1917; Sainsbury 1970). This does not mean diagnosis in the sense of identifying illness but rather an appraisal of the nature of the problem, the factors which led to its development and those which now lead to its perpetuation; together with an assessment of personal, family and social resources and the possible means of alleviation of the difficulties. Necessarily the process involves the accumulation of facts, their interpretation and weighting in the light of research knowledge and personal experience, and the development of a formulation of the problem and intervention hypotheses which may constitute the basis for treatment and for its evaluation. The process is on-going and should be part of treatment. It has much in common with child psychiatric diagnosis (see Rutter 1975; and Chapter 12) and like it relies heavily on skilled interviewing techniques requiring a reciprocity in which the therapist shares plans and perceptions with the client. The main difference is to be found in the special focus on interpersonal interaction and on social functioning in terms of 'coping behaviour in relation to life tasks and environmental demands' (Bartlett & Saunders 1970).

Of course, these approaches are not and cannot be context-free. The current emphasis in Britain on generic training has been useful in bringing the profession together as a whole and in developing the assessment and therapeutic skills specific to social work. However, in applying these skills in practice it is essential that the social worker have particular knowledge relevant to the field in which he or she is working. This requires specialised training after generic courses; unfortunately not as yet adequately available. Thus, for work in the field of child psychiatric disorders, the social worker must have a good understanding of normal and abnormal child development, of the nature of psychiatric problems in childhood, of the factors which influence psychological development, of the variety of therapeutic methods available to influence child and family behaviour, and a special knowledge of community services and resources available to children and their families.

INTERVENTION STRATEGIES

Social work includes a large repertoire of interventive strategies which differ in both technique and setting. They differ from psychotherapy in that they are not primarily concerned with intrapsychic conflict and intrapsychic mechanisms. They differ from behaviour therapy in that they are not primarily concerned with altering individual items of personal behaviour. Of course they utilise concepts and methods which are common to both, but what is distinctive about social work is its concern with influencing interpersonal interaction as a means of aiding social functioning. This may involve casework with individuals, conjoint therapy with married couples or families, group counselling or efforts to influence change in social conditions affecting large population groups (Bartlett & Saunders 1970; Haines 1975). The last of these involves social workers in professional action which goes beyond help to individual clients. However, it differs from political activity in that its concern is with the use of professional skills with respect to social interaction and social influences to assist community work in mobilising resources and in finding solutions to local problems.

The particular intervention approaches involved in psychiatric social work have been considered by many writers over the years (see for example Richmond 1922; Hollis 1949; Brown 1964; Reid & Epstein 1972; Haines 1975), without any one classification receiving general acceptance. Many of the earlier writers laid most emphasis on the two techniques of psychological support and of providing insight into unconscious thought processes (Hollis 1958), paralleling the traditional subdivision of psychotherapy into supportive and insight giving (Alexander and French 1946). However, in recent years there has been much greater appreciation of the need for a focussed task-centred approach (Reid & Epstein 1972) in which there is a greater concern for a more active and directive approach to environmental and behavioural change (Jehu *et al* 1972). While there is considerable overlap between the approaches and while most therapeutic interactions involve more than one strategy, it may be convenient to consider interventions under the general headings of provision of advice and material aid, use of the interview interaction, modification of behaviour, and environmental manipulation.

This chapter is concerned with social work practice in relation to child psychiatric services where the families have sought help. It does not deal with the rather different situations where the social worker may have statutory duties.

Provision of advice and material aid

The upbringing of normal children does not require the parent to follow a set of rules. However, special knowledge may well be advisable when dealing with children who present unusual difficulties. For example, children vary markedly in their temperamental make-up and some temperamental characteristics are much more likely to predispose to difficulties than are others (see Chapter 1). Chess, Thomas and their colleagues have indicated the usefulness of parent counselling in these circumstances (Thomas *et al* 1968; Chess *et al* 1965). For example, they note the parental anxieties which surround the child who withdraws from new situations and from fresh social encounters. This withdrawal may reflect deep-seated insecurity or it may be an expression of temperament in a child who is 'slow to warm up'. If a careful analysis of the child's social behaviour suggests the latter, parents may be helped by advice on how to help the child adapt to new situations by a patient gradual introduction rather than by a search for some hidden fear or insecurity.

Children with a chronic physical illness (Rutter, Tizard & Whitmore 1970), or even more so those with brain damage (see Chapter 8) have an increased risk of psychiatric disorder. While the risk is much increased the psychiatric problems do not stem directly from the chronic illness or the brain pathology (Rutter 1976). Parents need to be helped to understand how the child's difficulties stem from factors such as cognitive impairment, effect on self-esteem, attitudes to the handicap, stigmatising reactions from other people, and from overprotective or rejecting responses in the family or at school. Normal parents often find it quite difficult to know how to respond to a handicapped child and they need information and guidance on this. If the social worker is to provide this it is necessary that he or she have a good working knowledge of the various handicaps that are likely to be encountered, and of the developmental needs that stem from the natures of these handicaps.

The latter issue is well illustrated by the problems of autistic children (Rutter & Sussenwein 1971), whose social unresponsiveness and language impairment make them peculiarly unrewarding children unless their particular needs are understood. Specific guidance on how to aid social involvement and language development is required and there is a need for skilled and experienced counselling to help parents work out constructive and acceptable ways of coping with the difficulties presented by their autistic child. However, it is not enough to provide information. The guidance must be given with a sensitivity to the feelings of the parents and to the meanings they attach to the child's behaviour. The special considerations involved in the counselling of parents of mentally retarded children have been well discussed by Wolfensberger (1967) and Carr (1974).

Some of the distress associated with admission to hospital may stem from parents' ignorance about normal children's reactions to this experience. Parents may feel that it is better not to visit because children cry when they are visited, and they may find their children's aggression and anger hard to tolerate at a time when they themselves are anxious and uncertain. Following discharge from hospital many children are whiney and clinging and this may be irritating to a parent who will not necessarily realise that this is a normal reaction in young and sensitive children following a distressing hospital admission. It has been found that interviews with a psychiatric social worker may do much to aid parental understanding and thereby to reduce children's emotional upsets following discharge (Woodward & Jackson 1961).

Practical help of various kinds also has an important place. Parents of handicapped children need to be made aware of the various allowances to which they are entitled; holiday provision of several kinds is available for handicapped children; social workers can help parents obtain special clothing or equipment required for the handicapped; and families can be assisted to obtain aid with housing when this is appropriate. With enuretic children it may be possible to tap financial resources to obtain an extra bed or to arrange laundry assistance (Dische 1973). These needs may also arise with families where children have a quite different set of problems. The social worker needs to be alert and prepared to act when poverty, housing difficulties and other kinds of material deprivation impede family functioning. One of the social worker's tasks is to know about the range of benefits, allowances and other sources of material or financial help which may be made available. The social worker also has an important role in advising parents on the merits and demerits of various forms of short-term and long-term residential care and to arrange for such care as necessary. Parents should be informed of the relevant parents groups (National Society for Autistic Children, Association for All Speech Impaired Children, etc.) and of the books written specifically for the parents of handicapped children. These books vary in topic, quality and orientation but among those which may be useful are those by Lorna Wing (1970) and Howarth and Peine (1975).

Use of the interview interaction

Haines (1975) has described the 'enabling' roles of the interview under the headings of release of feelings, clarification, encouragement, and promotion of self-understanding. To these might be added the role of relationships in providing a secure base and in providing social and emotional learning experiences.

It is common for people to wish to ventilate their feelings and emotions to a good empathetic listener and this frequently takes place in the social work interview. This may well be very beneficial but the widespread notion that catharsis always serves to reduce emotional disturbance is probably false (Mallick & McCandless 1966; Holmes 1966). The truth is more complicated. Animal experiments suggest that the most damage is done by stressful situations from which the animals cannot escape and in which they get no feedback as to whether their attempts to escape from the situation are effective (Weiss 1972). This suggests that the 'bottling up of emotions' is harmful if, as is usually the case, this is associated with feelings of impotence and an inability to do anything about the situation. Expression of these negative emotions may increase or decrease the feelings of distress according to whether or not their ventilation does anything to aid the resolution of the difficulties.

Suppression of negative feelings is harmful in so far as it causes people to brood on their problems rather than to take steps to remedy them. The therapeutic release of feelings is probably beneficial mainly because it enables people to face up to what is really happening and to recognise their own emotional reactions. Bringing tensions into the open is the first step to finding a constructive and rational solution. The skill lies in utilising the catharsis for this purpose. Merely expressing strong emotions will rarely be beneficial on its own.

Clarification involves the use of discussion to enable people to think more clearly about their situation, to appreciate the links between different aspects of their problem, and to consider the advantage and disadvantages of alternative courses of action. The approach is task-centred and the aim is to give people the means to develop their own solutions to their problems. Of course, the ways to do this are many and varied and include both psychodynamic and behavioural approaches. The social worker may appropriately take a quite active role in this process, helping the family to select short-term and long-term objectives, pointing out the consequences of various actions, noting how other people might respond and generally aiding the family in exploring ways of meeting their problems. However, the purpose is to increase the family's own capacity to cope and it will very rarely be helpful for the social worker to impose views and solutions. Also, problem-solving is not just an intellectual exercise designed to produce a logical solution. It is necessary for the social worker to appreciate the emotions and feelings involved in any particular course of action. It may be better for parents to ignore disruptive behaviour when its purpose is to gain parental attention but they are unlikely to accept this solution if their dominant (but unexpressed) feeling is that disruptive behaviour 'deserves' punishment. Similarly, it may be advantageous for parents to press their school-refusing child to attend school but this course may be resisted if the parental anxieties or their need to have the child dependent go unrecognised. In short, clarification involves making links between emotions and behaviour, between the reactions of different people, and between behaviours and their social consequences.

Parents of children with psychiatric problems often have their own difficulties whether in terms of a deprived upbringing, a mental disorder, or a stressful life situation. As a consequence, they are often discouraged individuals lacking in self-esteem and self-confidence. The same frequently applies to the children themselves and whether the social worker is treating the child or the parents, there is often the need to restore self-respect and self-confidence. An important part of the therapeutic interaction is providing a relationship and setting where this can occur. This does not mean giving false reassurance nor does it involve denial of difficulties or approval of harmful acts. What is involved is a real care and concern for the client as a person, a recognition of his strengths and assets and confidence in his ability to cope. Of course, this is not enough in itself but it may be an essential ingredient if the person is to make use of his therapeutic experience.

The relationship with a social worker may also serve as a secure base which provides a sense of trust and stability enabling the client to have the confidence to deal with difficulties he has been unable to tackle hitherto. It is more than just encouragement in that it involves a feeling of being of consequence to someone else, of personal worth and of emotional commitment. For young children the presence of a parent serves to bring security and comfort so that strange situations are no longer frightening when the parent is there (Bowlby 1971; 1975; Rutter 1975). Personal bonds and attachments continue to serve that function in adult life, although obviously their nature alters with maturity. Adults, like children, become distressed and insecure if they lose these bonds (through separation, death, rejection or loss of friendships). Of course, the professional relationship a child or adult has with a social worker cannot be a substitute for personal loves or friendships. But, in some ways, it may provide elements which serve the same ends to a sufficient degree for the individual to go on to form the new relationships which he has lacked.

In addition, professional relationships may serve as learning experiences. The development of good social relationships requires social skills which have to be learned during the course of development (Argyle 1967). When individuals lack these skills or have learned maladaptive social behaviour, it may sometimes be necessary to teach the appropriate skills in explicit fashion (see below). However, quite often the learning can take place in the context of a relationship, partly by modelling the behaviour of the therapist and partly by learning from the therapist's responses. This may be done in a one-to-one situation, in a family context, or in a group counselling situation. Although it is possible to apply what is learned in one relationship to another of a different kind, peer relationships are so different from those experienced in individual therapy that a group is to be preferred if the relationship difficulties mainly involve peers.

To some degree, people tend to bring to the therapeutic relationship feelings experienced in other relationships. Thus, the client may project on to the social worker his feelings towards his parents or towards authority figures through the process of 'transference'. If these feelings can be recognised and understood for what they are, the client may be helped to appreciate his difficulties in the transferred relationship and hence be in a better position to deal with his difficulties. In receiving these 'transference' feelings, social workers should be aware that there can be an unconscious impact on their own emotional equilibrium; they need the sensitivity to accept this and to attempt to understand not only what the 'transference' means to the client but also how this affects their own responses to their clients.

The promotion of insight or self-understanding is the aspect of case-work which owes most to psychoanalysis. This involves an appreciation of why the client acts in the way he does; of how his attitudes and inner feelings govern his behaviour; of how his current responses to situations have been shaped by what has happened in the past, and of how his reactions to people or situations may be biassed by their symbolic meaning for him. This does not mean the acceptance of a particular theoretical explanation and it should be recognised that insight does not necessarily lead to changes in behaviour nor do changes in behaviour necessarily require insight. Nevertheless, it is often helpful for people to have some appreciation of why they act in the way they do so that they may be in a stronger position to know how best to bring about the changes they desire. In essence this is merely an extension of the process of clarification, but it differs in that it may also make use of 'interpretations' in which the therapist makes overt to the patient his inferences regarding the unconscious meaning or significance of some aspect of what the patient has said or done (Greenson 1967; Sandler *et al* 1971). However, it would be unduly restricting to view insight only in unconscious terms and, as discussed below, interpretations can have other uses.

Modification of behaviour

The strategies discussed so far all involve the bringing about of change but the emphasis is on indirect means of influence. However, the social worker will frequently want to use more direct techniques. Before doing so he must understand the meaning and function of his client's behaviour, and this requires an analysis of the various factors in the person and his environment which either increase or decrease the likelihood of the behaviour occurring (Rutter 1975). Apparently similar behaviours may have quite different meanings and serve different functions and these must be taken into account when planning treatment (Freud 1966). Particular attention needs to be paid to prior circumstances, precipitants and contingencies (Rutter 1975).

By prior circumstances is meant the more long-lasting conditions which play a part in determining behaviour. Thus, a child may develop tantrums because of the difficulties stemming from his mother's depression and irritability; another may do so because a lack of language impairs his ability to deal with frustration. By precipitants is meant the happenings which immediately precede the problem behaviours and seem to trigger them off. Thus, the presence of a dog may precipitate a panic in a child with a dog phobia or the giving of his mother's attention to a baby sister may provoke disruptive behaviour in a child troubled by sibling jealousy. By contingencies is meant what immediately *follows* the behaviour in question in circumstances where the behaviour seems to bring about a certain result in reliable fashion. This may be apparent when a child learns that the one sure way to get parental attention is to complain of headache or have a tantrum. Any plan to modify behaviour must be based on a proper understanding of mechanisms of this and other kinds.

A large number of techniques are available to modify behaviour. Some of these have been specifically developed by psychologists using a learning theory framework (see Chapter 39), but many have their roots in methods used by social workers and psychiatrists for a long time. Thus, David Levy (1943), the American psychoanalyst, described how overprotective mothers were taught by 'advice and demonstration' to ignore their children's attention-seeking behaviour, to replace nagging by direct and explicit commands, and to provide a consistent pattern of discipline with immediate reprimand or punishment for disruptive behaviours. The main contribution of behaviourist psychologists has not been to develop new methods of treatment (although this has been done to some extent), but rather to bring a systematic approach to the use of old methods. These advances need to be incorporated into social work practice (Jehu *et al* 1972). However, that they cannot be considered in isolation. The methods form part of a wider therapeutic repertoire of approaches to be employed in the context of an empathetic relationship.

While the specific behavioural techniques are many, the general approaches fall into a smaller number of broad groups. First, there are those based on so-called 'operant' principles, which simply mean that activities which bring immediate pleasure and reward are likely to recur whereas those which do not are less likely to do so. In this connection two points require emphasis. First, interest and approval from a loved or respected person are among the most powerful rewards and these are readily available to both parents in dealing with their children and therapists in dealing with their clients. Second, to be effective the responses must be immediate. Just as punishments given long after the misdeed tend to be rather ineffective so also delayed praise is of limited value. Operant techniques have a wide application but have been shown to be particularly valuable in teaching handicapped children social and language skills and in controlling any form of disruptive behaviour which serves to gain attention.

Second, there are the methods based on graded change, meaning that behaviour is most readily altered by means of a series of very small steps. This approach has been used with effect in the treatment of fears, rituals and abnormal attachments to objects. Frequently these first two approaches can be fruitfully combined. Often the best teaching involves proceeding step-by-step in such a way that each step leads to success and is met with encouragement and approval.

Third, modelling has an important place in aiding behavioural change; people learn from watching others. This has been utilised in the treatment of fears (children may overcome their fears by seeing other people being unafraid and relaxed in the situation they fear—whether it be the presence of dogs or the dentist's chair) and may be particularly valuable in helping people who are socially ineffective.

Fourth, if people are to alter how they behave it is necessary for them to appreciate what is going wrong. The interview technique of confrontation in which the social worker faces the client with the consequences of his behaviour is one way to provide this sort of feedback. Videotape recording and one-way screens have also been used in this connection with social difficulties and with problems in parent–child interaction. Modelling, demonstration and specific instruction can then be used to help people improve their social functioning.

The importance of both feedback and rewards has become particularly apparent in marital and family counselling. Family members frequently get at loggerheads with rising tension and hostility but without any clear recognition by anyone just what it is that each wants changed. In this situation it is sometimes helpful to get the family or married couple to list the things they most want the others to do or not to do; and then to draw up a contract which specifies what is expected of each person. It sounds a mechanical procedure but, if well planned, it may provide recognition of the many ways in which people behave well and it may allow a break in what is otherwise a vicious circle. Once people are beginning to get some overt encouragement in the family, there is a beginning of a way out of the family difficulties.

Although specific behavioural techniques may not usually constitute the main therapeutic approach in social case-work, the factors influencing behavioural changes are always operative and it is important for social workers to appreciate how these may best be mobilised for improved functioning whatever the therapeutic approach being employed. Whether intended or not, the way in which the social worker shows interest or lack of interest, approval of disapproval in what the client says or does will inevitably shape his behaviour. Also, of course, the whole process of discussion of problems will serve to induce behaviour change (or lead to persistence of behaviour). One psychotherapeutic technique which requires special mention is that of the challenging interpretation in which the interpretative prediction is intended to have a self-falsifying effect. Taylor (1969) has described how these may often be used effectively once a strong therapeutic relationship has been formed.

Environmental change

Because environmental influences play a most important part in the genesis and prolongation of child psychiatric disorders (see Chapters 3 and 4), case-work is usually likely to contain some element of environmental change. Sometimes this will concern family interactions, in which case the strategy overlaps considerably with those already discussed, and in others, influences outside the home.

Levy (1943) emphasised the importance of environmental manipulations and of education in his classical study of 'maternal overprotection'. Although dynamic factors played an important role in the development of maternal overprotective behaviour, psychotherapy proved to be the least effective of the treatments tried, possibly because both mother and child were gaining satisfaction from the maladaptive overprotective relationship with the result that there was little incentive for change. In summarising what was done in the treatment of these abnormally intense and restricting relationships, Levy concludes: 'In evaluating the therapeutic processes, first to be noted is the importance of using methods of separating mother and child and making possible every opportunity for social contacts outside the family for them, second, the increase of the father's prestige in the family has been neglected. The modification in cases where it was used is very revealing. Third, the most convincing proof to the mother that her methods were wrong were the demonstrations in the home showing definitely that the child responded to other forms of management.'

The goal of treatment in these cases was to develop greater independence within the mother–child relationship. Attempts were made to widen the scope of the mother's interests outside the home; to socialise the relationship between husband and wife by encouraging joint activities which they could both enjoy; to encourage the father to do more with the child; to engage the child in activities away from his mother (by going to camps, joining in group activities with peers, and going on outings with the social worker); and suggestions and demonstrations in the handling of specific situations with the child (how to encourage self-help, how to ignore attention-seeking behaviour, etc.) were given in the home.

Obviously in other cases different goals will be required but the model set by Levy (1943) on how to tackle problems in parent–child interaction is a good one. The lessons of including fathers in what is done and of using practical demonstrations are particularly important.

Environmental interventions outside the home include working with fellow professionals (youth leaders, probation officers, school counsellors, teachers, etc.), with volunteer workers of various kinds, and with friends and neighbours of the client. Often, too, it may be necessary to mobilise community resources (home help, meals-on-wheels, day-centre attendance, holiday provision, etc.) to help individuals. In addition, because psychiatric clinics are there to serve particular communities, it is important for social workers to play a role in community development helping local people to develop solutions to their own problems (e.g. the need for adventure playgrounds, playgroups, day care facilities, community support for the ill or the isolated, etc.).

DIFFERENT SETTINGS

Up to this point, the discussion has been concerned with therapeutic techniques rather than with the settings in which they are employed. Traditionally, the usual pattern was for social workers in child psychiatric clinics mainly to undertake individual case-work with mothers at the clinic. As is implicit in what has already been said, that is no longer the case today. While that approach is certainly often appropriate, it is frequently necessary to involve fathers in treatment so that both parents will need to be seen either separately or together. Also, of course, the social worker may well be involved in therapy with the children or adolescents rather than the parents. Obviously modifications in technique and approach are needed according to who is being seen but the same general principles apply. The social worker, like other professionals, needs to adopt the therapeutic role appropriate to each family's needs. Also, in many cases the social worker will need to see people in their own homes rather than at a clinic. For various reasons it may be more effectively therapeutic to provide help in the situation where the family difficulties actually arise rather than to talk about them somewhere else.

There are major differences in emphasis when the social worker is involved in seeing groups rather than individuals. This is so whether the 'group' is a married couple, a family with children, a group of parents, or a group of children or adolescents. The difference lies in the fact that the prime agent in therapy concerns the *interaction* between the people in the group rather than just the individual–therapist interaction. Because social interaction is so much a concern of social workers it is particularly appropriate that they be involved in therapeutic activities of this kind. The indications and contraindications for family therapy have not yet been adequately defined. However, it has been suggested (Rutter 1975) that the chief indications are (1) the main problem lies in family communication or interaction; (2) this problem is a major factor in the disorder which led the family to seek help; (3) there are substantial emotional ties between family members; and (4) there should be some wish or need for the family to remain together. The main emphasis in therapy is on the family interaction as shown by patterns of dominance, the kinds of communication, the type of feedback given to other family members, and patterns of isolation or scapegoating. The family is viewed as a miniature social system in which the therapist's task is to understand the forces acting within the system as they lead to unhappiness and maladaptive behaviour and to alter the forces accordingly. The therapist may comment on the exclusion or victimisation of certain family members, or point out the effect of conflicting messages. Skynner (1969) has emphasised the importance of re-establishing adequate family communication and developing effective patterns of dominance. Role playing and behavioural rehearsal may be used to bring about improved patterns of interaction. A behavioural analysis of family problems (Liberman 1970) may also consist in working out a plan of action for the family to follow between therapy sessions.

Group counselling is probably most indicated when children's main problems concern interactions with other youngsters. By focussing on the nature of group interactions and communication, the therapist can help children deal better with problems of isolation, rejection, teasing and the like. Parent groups may be particularly useful when the children have chronic handicapping conditions (Rutter 1975). Parents may derive support and comfort from talking with others in a similar predicament; guided group discussion can help develop ways of coping with common problems (tantrums, sleep difficulties, feeding problems etc.); and the group situation may allow people to come to terms with mixed emotions engendered by having a handicapped child. Sometimes, too, groups where parents and preschool children meet together in a nursery or day-hospital setting may be valuable in helping parents learn by example and discussion how to play and talk with children, how to enjoy them, and how to cope with the many common difficulties that they present.

Quite apart from working directly with clients, whether individually or in groups, the social worker has an important consultative role, in which the aim is to help other people deal better with children in their own way and in their own setting. Often this will concern children who are not in therapy but who require care because they are in a Children's Home, a hospital ward or a school. The strategies in these circumstances require modification because of the different requirements and expectations.

For disadvantaged families, the infant school may well be a suitable meeting ground. Parents often lack appreciation of how they can aid their children's development, and teachers face difficulties in the lack of cultures between home and school. Social workers while maintaining a clinic base, can help resolve some of these difficulties through community work in schools which sets out to solve problems in a way which enhances the competence and self-respect of parents, teachers and children (Gorell-Barnes 1975).

EVALUATION

Social workers have been concerned to determine the effectiveness of their therapeutic endeavours for the last half-century. As long ago as 1931, Richard Clarke Cabot in his presidential address to the National Conference on Social Work laid strong emphasis on the need for systematic evaluation (Mullen *et al* 1972). Unfortunately, until relatively recently, the few attempts to evaluate the effectiveness of social work produced results which gave little guide on how to improve clinical practice.

One of the first controlled evaluations was the Cambridge–Somerville Youth Study (Powers & Witmer 1951) devised by Cabot. Six hundred and fifty 11-year-old boys from a high delinquency area were divided, by random assignment, into treatment and control groups. The aim of the project was to provide close intimate friendship with a counsellor, as a means of preventing delinquency. Unfortunately, for a variety of reasons (including the Second World War) there was a high turnover of counsellors and boys were seen much less frequently than intended. Systematic follow-up showed equal delinquency rates in the two groups and no evidence was found for any benefit from the counselling. The fact that both the counsellors and the boys felt that the treatment had been helpful emphasises that the views of those involved in therapy are not a good guide to the effectiveness of what has been done.

The failure of the Cambridge–Somerville study could have been due in part to the lack of consistent relationships due to turnover of staff. However, this seems unlikely as several subsequent attempts to prevent delinquency by similar means have also proved largely unsuccessful (Tait & Hodges 1962; Craig & Furst 1965; Meyer *et al* 1965). It must be concluded that traditional counselling of children and adolescents is an ineffective way of preventing delinquency. Whether the results would have been equally poor if the social workers had paid more attention to helping the families rather than the youngsters, if there had been more explicit focus on dealing with actual problems and if more material help had been provided must remain unknown.

More recently, there have been several attempts to use mental health programmes in schools as a means of preventing problem behaviour and delinquency. Gildea *et al* (1967) found that neither films, discussions nor group therapy in schools made any difference to problem behaviour. Kellam *et al* (1975) compared children's progress in six schools which offered group meetings for teachers, parents and children with that in six control schools. Inevitably there were a variety of difficulties in delivering the kind of mental health programme intended and parent participation was less than optimal. Follow-up showed that the experimental children had made some cognitive gains but there were no appreciable psychiatric benefits from the intervention.

These results are discouraging and provide no evidence for the value of individual or group counselling as a means of preventing either psychiatric problems or delinquency. On the other hand, Rose and Marshall's (1974) study of counselling and school social work in Blackburn, England, provides convincing evidence that school counselling can be effective. The delinquency rates of boys in experimental and control secondary schools were similar during their first year, but by the end of the fourth year the delinquency rate in experimental schools was down 30 per cent. In trying to draw lessons from this study it is necessary to determine the ways in which what was done differed from that in the other studies. While none of the studies made any detailed study of therapeutic process, several differences are apparent.

In all the projects there was an attempt to engage the school and community as a whole in what was being provided. However, only in the Blackburn project were the counsellors appointed to the schools on a permanent basis with services available at all times. Furthermore, in the Rose and Marshall study, the main emphasis was on providing focussed help for individual children referred for current problems, rather than on making available a preventive service for all children. Although the majority of children were referred by teachers, a substantial proportion came on their own initiative or were referred by parents. Whether these were the crucial differences leading to success cannot be determined from the data, nor is it known how far the benefits stem from the individual help given or from changes in the school as a whole. However, it may be concluded that for counselling to be effective it must be given to individuals who themselves appreciate the need because of a current crisis or current problems. Other methods of prevention may be effective but the counselling of healthy individuals who do not perceive themselves as needing help is probably a waste of time.

There have been several American studies of case-work with multiproblem or poor families (see reviews by Mullen *et al* 1972, and by Goldberg 1973), most of which showed little benefit. However, their goals and methods tended to lack direction and little help was provided in connection with the many material difficulties faced by the families. On the other hand, as social workers frequently provide treatment for parents with psychiatric problems, the results are of some relevance to the field of child psychiatry. Two recent, rather different, British studies both indicate that social work can be effective when well undertaken. Cooper *et al* (1974) examined the therapeutic value of attaching a social worker to a general practice group to help patients with chronic neurotic problems. Compared with similar patients in practices without a social worker, the experimental group showed greater improvement in both psychiatric symptoms and social adjustment one year later.

Shaw (1974) carried out a study in which prisoners were randomly allocated to either an experimental or control group. The experimental group had 1 hour weekly case-work sessions with a welfare officer during the last 6 months of their sentence, whereas the control group were seen only when they requested interviews. Reconvictions after discharge were significantly lower in the experimental group but the differences were apparent only after

8 months. Interestingly, the introverted men responded best to case-work (introverts in the experimental group were *least* likely to be reconvicted and in the control group they were *most* likely).

This last finding is in keeping with the results of the California treatment programmes for delinquents which suggest that different personalities need different therapeutic approaches (Palmer 1971; Warren 1969). It seems that anxious youths with feelings of guilt and anxiety do better with permissive therapists who encourage introspection and exploration of feelings. In contrast, the tough delinquent conforming to subcultural norms or the manipulative antiauthority nonconformist may respond better to more direct formal therapists who focus less on feelings and more on issues related to external controls and the setting of limits. The findings are not conclusive and require replication (Quay 1975) but the indication is that the type of therapy needs to be carefully tailored to individual needs (Rutter 1975).

That conclusion, of course, highlights the need for studies to examine *which* aspect of therapy is effective for which disorders in which sort of individual. Case-work and counselling include so many different elements that a finding that, in general, they are better, or are not better, than no treatment (or some other form of treatment) is not much help to the practising social worker. One of the few investigations to contrast different varieties of case-work in the important and well-planned study by Reid and Shyne (1969). They studied 120 families presenting difficulties in marital or parent–child relationships and compared planned short-term case-work (up to 8 interviews within a 3-month period) with an open-ended approach involving up to a hundred interviews over an 18-month span. Results were assessed in terms of systematic measures of various aspects of personal and family functioning. They showed a significantly higher proportion of favourable outcomes for the short-term case-work group. Examination of what actually happened in therapy suggested that the greater benefits of the brief approach lay in its better definition of goals and its better treatment focus. The findings are particularly impressive because the advantages of the brief focussed approach still held at the end of the follow-up period, and because the same therapists applied both approaches. Regardless of their personal preferences, all six case-workers did better with the planned short-term treatment.

Less is known about other dimensions of case-work. There have been several rather unsatisfactory studies of counselling as a method of helping the parents of retarded children (reviewed by Wolfensberger 1967). The results are inconclusive and the methods of counselling utilised were rather different from those favoured today. During recent years many workers have been concerned to train parents of handicapped or disturbed children in the use of appropriate behaviour modification techniques (see reviews by Patterson 1972; O'Dell 1974; Johnson & Katz 1973). The methods have been shown to be effective in modifying particular problem behaviours of individual children but little is known on either the persistence of the benefits or how far the methods increase parental coping skills for any new problems that emerge. The same applies to the use of behavioural techniques in improving teacher–child interaction in the classroom (Becker 1972). There is sufficient good evidence that these methods are effective when applied in the ordinary classroom or family situation for such skills to be included in the therapeutic repertoire of every social worker (Jehu *et al* 1972). However, research is needed to compare the methods with other case-work approaches, and to determine how far behavioural methods can improve family functioning in a way which enables them to cope better with fresh difficulties as they arise.

Marital and conjoint family therapy has been used increasingly by social workers. There are isolated studies which demonstrate the benefits of these approaches (Azrin *et al* 1973; Alexander & Parsons 1973; Langsley *et al* 1969) but reliable data on their efficacy are largely lacking (Gurman 1973; Wells *et al* 1972). Studies are particularly needed to compare the relative advantages and disadvantages of different types of marital or family therapy (Crowe 1973).

There have been several systematic controlled evaluations of group counselling or group psychotherapy. The results have been variable but mainly positive, the benefits being most marked at follow-up rather than immediately after treatment (Robins 1973). Thus Persons (1967) found that one year later, delinquent boys who had participated in 40 group and 20 individual therapy interviews while in a penal institution, had a better community adjustment and a lower rate of recidivism than a matched control group who had not received this treatment. However, very little is known about the content of group treatment and there are no data to indicate what type of counselling or psychotherapy is most effective, other than the fact that the one study of group methods using confrontation techniques actually led to a *worse* outcome than in the control group (California Youth Authority, cited by Robins 1973).

Quite apart from evidence on the broad techniques applied in case-work, there is a need for knowledge on the advantages and disadvantages of particular interview strategies. Most of this type of research has been undertaken in the field of psychotherapy but the findings are obviously relevant to casework. There is extensive evidence that in all types of treatment (drugs as well as psychotherapy) the therapist's interest, enthusiasm and optimism are important factors leading to improvement. With respect to counselling, the importance of therapist variables has been most extensively explored by

Truax and his colleagues (1967). Their findings suggest that the most effective therapists are those who are sensitive to their clients' feelings and able to communicate their understanding in appropriate language; and who provide a trusting and open relationship in which they are warm and accepting. Conversely, therapists who were not warm, empathetic and open seemed actually to make people worse! The outcome measures in their research leave a lot to be desired and none of the studies concern children. Nevertheless the research clearly demonstrates important differences between therapists and suggests that these differences probably influence the course and effects of counselling (Shapiro 1969), as well as the ways in which the social worker is viewed by his clients (Sainsbury 1975).

The findings emphasise the importance of the therapist–client relationship, but it should not be assumed that the same type of relationship suits all people (see the California studies above). Moreover, it would be wrong to conclude that *merely* forming a good relationship is enough in itself. Much of the benefits of case-work stem from what is done with the relationship. Supposedly 'nondirective' techniques in fact can have a strong directive effect as a result of the timing of warmth and interest in relationship to what the client says during interviews (Truax 1966; 1968). It is important for therapists to recognise that they will necessarily influence how their clients behave and to use this influence in a thoughtful and constructive way.

Studies of case-work (using tape-recorded interviews) have shown that most of the time is spent in exploration, description and ventilation, with very little on either the discussion of intrapsychic factors or on giving advice (Reid 1967; Hollis 1968). However, Mayer and Timms (1970) found that clients tend to be puzzled by passive exploratory techniques which pay little attention to their definition of their problems and their current needs. There is now a good deal of evidence to indicate that most people prefer their therapists to be reasonably active and directive (Bierman 1969). This may be particularly the case with unsophisticated clients at the beginning of therapy (Heilbron 1971). More important, the Reid and Shyne study (1969) clearly showed that short-term active intervention using focussed techniques to promote behavioural change is more effective than long-term unfocussed, open-ended, more passive therapy. The findings do *not* mean that social workers should decide their clients' lives for them, but they do mean that passivity and a failure to guide clients in how they can learn to best cope with their difficulties is likely to be unhelpful and unappreciated.

CONCLUSIONS

The studies of case-work are too fragmentary and inconclusive for anyone to be at all certain about the relative value of different approaches. However, there is enough to indicate that case-work and counselling can be effective methods of treatment. The shortcomings of much of the ineffective case-work probably stem from a failure to define goals and values and a general diffuseness and vagueness about the therapeutic techniques employed. The traditional emphasis on the development of a relationship has been shown to be important but, equally, effective treatment depends on the discriminating use of the therapeutic interaction to provide a flexible but focussed approach to personal and family problems. A wide range of techniques may be utilised for this purpose. These should include behavioural as well as insight-oriented methods; conjoint family and group therapy as well as personal counselling; material aid as well as case-work; community involvement as well as individual therapy; and above all by an emphasis on all means to enable families to increase their coping mechanisms and to have an environment which allows them to function optimally.

I would like to express my appreciation to Professor Michael Rutter for his assistance with the section on evaluation.

REFERENCES

ALEXANDER F. & FRENCH T. (1946) *Psychoanalytic Therapy*. New York: Ronald Press

ALEXANDER J.F. & PARSONS B.V. (1973) Short-term behavioral intervention with delinquent families: impact on family process and recidivism. *J. Abnorm. Psychol.* **81,** 219–225

ARGYLE M. (1967) *The Psychology of Interpersonal Behaviour*. Harmondsworth: Penguin

AZRIN N.H., NASHER B.J. & JONES R. (1973) Reciprocity counseling: a rapid learning-based procedure for marital counseling. *Behav. Res. Ther.* **11,** 365–382

BARTLETT H. & SAUNDERS B.N. (1970) *The Common Base of Social Work Practice*. New York: Nat. Assoc. Soc. Workers

BATLEY R. & EDWARD J. (1974) The urban programme: a report on some programme funded projects. *Brit. J. Social Work* **4,** 305–332

BECKER W.C. (1972) Application of behavior principles in typical classrooms. *In* Thoresen C.E. (ed.) *Behavior Modification in Education*. Chicago: National Society for the Study of Education

BIERMAN R. (1969) Dimensions of interpersonal facilitation in psychotherapy and child development. *Psychol. Bull.* **72,** 338–352

BOWLBY J. (1971) *Attachment and Loss*. vol. 1: *Attachment*. Harmondsworth: Penguin

BOWLBY J. (1975) *Attachment and Loss*. vol. 2: *Separation, Anxiety and Anger*. Harmondsworth: Penguin

BROWN M.A.G. (1964) *A Review of Casework Methods*. Suppl. to Case Conference, Feb. 1964

CARR J. (1974) The effect of the severely subnormal on their families. *In* Clarke A.M. & Clarke A.D.B. (eds.) *Mental Deficiency: the Changing Outlook*, 3rd edn. London: Methuen

CHEETHAM J. & HILL M. (1973) Community work: social realities and ethical dilemmas. *Brit. J. Social Work* **3**, 331–348

CHESS S., THOMAS A. & BIRCH H. (1965) *Your Child is a Person*. New York: Viking Press

COOPER B., HARWIN B.G., DEPLA C. & SHEPHERD M. (1974) An experiment in community mental health care. *Lancet* **ii,** 1356–1358

CRAIG M.M. & FURST P.W. (1965) What happens after treatment. *Social Service Review* **39**, 165–171

CROWE M.J. (1973) Conjoint marital therapy: advice or interpretation? *J. Psychosom. Res.* **17,** 309–315

DISCHE S. (1973) Treatment of enuresis with an enuresis alarm. *In* Kolvin I., MacKeith R.C. & Meadow S.R. (eds.) *Bladder Control and Enuresis*. Clinics in Dev. Med., nos. 48/49. London: SIMP/Heinemann

FERARD M. & HUNNYBUN N. (1962) *The Caseworker's Use of Relationships, Mind-Medicine, Monograph* no. 7. London: Tavistock

FREUD A. (1966) *Normality and Pathology in Childhood*. London: Hogarth Press

GILDEA MC-L., GLIDEWELL J.C. & KANTOR M.B. (1967) The St. Louis school mental health project: history and evaluation. *In* Cowen E.L., Gardner E.A. & Zax M. (eds.) *Emergent Approaches to Mental Health Problems*. New York: Appleton

GOLDBERG E.M. (1973) Services for the family. *In* Wing J.K. & Häfner H. (eds.) *Roots of Evaluation: The Epidemiological Basis for Planning Psychiatric Services*. London: Oxford University Press

GOLDSTEIN H. (1975) A unitary approach: its rationale and structure. *In* Ainsworth F. & Hunter J. (eds.) *A Unitary Approach to Social Work Practice—Implications for Education and Organisation*. Dundee: University of Dundee School of Social Administration

GORELL-BARNES G. (1975) Seen but not heard. *Social Work Today* **5**, 606–609; 646–648; 689–693

GREENSON R.R. (1967) *The Technique and Practice of Psychoanalysis*, vol. 1. New York: International Universities Press

GURMAN A.S. (1973) The effects and effectiveness of marital therapy: a review of outcome research. *Family Process* **12,** 145–170

HAINES J. (1975) *Skills and Methods in Social Work*. London: Constable

HEILBRUN A.B. (1971) Female preference for therapist initial interview style as a function of 'client' and therapist social role variables. *J. Counsel. Psychol.* **18,** 285–291

HOLLIS F. (1949) The techniques of casework. *J. Soc. Casework* **30,** 235–244

HOLLIS F. (1958) Personality diagnosis in casework. *In* Parad H. (ed.) *Ego Psychology and Dynamic Casework*. New York: Family Service Assoc. America

HOLLIS F. (1964) *Casework: A Psychosocial Therapy*. New York: Random House

HOLLIS F. (1968) A profile of early interviews in marital counselling. *J. Soc. Casework* **49,** 35–43

HOLMES D.S. (1966) Effect of overt aggression on level of physiological arousal. *J. Pers. soc. Psychol.* **4,** 189–194

HOWARTH R. & PEINE H.A. (1975) *Children and Parents: Everyday Problems of Behaviour*. Harmondsworth: Penguin

JEHU D., HARDIKER P., YELLOLY M. & SHAW M. (1972) *Behaviour Modification in Social Work*. New York: Wiley-Interscience

JOHNSON C.A. & KATZ R.C. (1973) Using parents as change agents for their children: a review. *J. Child. Psychol. Psychiat.* **14,** 181–200

JONES H. (ed.) (1975) *Towards a New Social Work.* London: Routledge & Kegan Paul

KANNER L. (1959) Trends in child psychiatry. *J. Ment. Sci.,* **105,** 581–593

KELLAM S.G., BRANCH J.D., AGRAWAL K.C. & ENSMINGER M.E. (1975) *Mental Health and Going to School: the Woodlawn Program of Assessment, Early Intervention and Evaluation.* Chicago: University of Chicago Press

LANGSLEY D.G., FLOMENHAFT K. & MACHOTKA P. (1969) Follow-up evaluation of family crisis therapy. *Amer. J. Orthopsychiat.* **39,** 753–759

LEES R. (1972) *Politics and Social Work.* London: Routledge & Kegan Paul

LEES R. & McGRATH M. (1974) Community work with immigrants. *Brit. J. Social Work.* **4,** 175–186

LEONARD P. (1966) *Sociology in Social Work.* London: Routledge & Kegan Paul

LEVY D.M. (1943) *Maternal Overprotection.* New York: Columbia University Press

LIBERMAN R. (1970) Behavioral approaches to family and couple therapy. *Amer. J. Orthopsychiat.* **40,** 106–118

MAYER J.E. & TIMMS N. (1970) *The Client Speaks: Working Class Impressions of Casework.* London: Routledge & Kegan Paul

MALLICK S.K. & McCANDLESS B.R. (1966) A study of catharsis of aggression. *J. Pers. soc. Psychol.* **4,** 591–596

MEYER H.J., BORGATTA E.F. & JONES W.C. (1965) *Girls at Vocational High: an Experiment in Social Work Intervention.* New York: Russell Sage Foundation

MIDDLEMAN R.R. & GOLDBERG G. (1974) *Social Service Delivery: a Structural Approach to Social Work Practice.* New York: Columbia University Press

MULLEN E.J., DUMPSON J.R. *et al* (1972) *Evaluation of Social Intervention.* London: Jossey-Bass

O'DELL S. (1974) Training parents in behavior modification: a review. *Psychol. Bull.* **81,** 418–433

PALMER T.B. (1971) California's community treatment program for delinquent adolescents. *J. Res. Crime Delinq.* **8,** 74–92

PATTERSON G.A. (1972) Reprogramming the families of aggressive boys. *In* Thoresen C.E. (ed.) *Behavior Modification in Education.* Chicago: National Society for the Study of Education

PERLMAN H.H. (1971) *Perspectives on Social Casework.* Philadelphia: Temple University Press

PERSONS R.W. (1967) Relationship between psychotherapy with institutionalized boys and subsequent community adjustment. *J. Consult. Psychol.* **31,** 137–141

PINCUS A. & MINAHAN A. (1973) *Social Work Practice: Model and Method.* Itasen, Illinois: Peacock

POWERS E. & WITMER H. (1951) *An Experiment in the Prevention of Delinquency:* The Cambridge–Somerville Youth Study. New York: Columbia University Press

QUAY H.C. (1975) Classification in the treatment of delinquency and antisocial behavior. *In* Jobbs N. (ed.) *Issues in the Classification of Children,* vol. 1. London: Jossey-Bass

REID W.J. (1967) Characteristics of casework intervention. *Welfare in Review* **5,** 11–19

REID W.J. & EPSTEIN L. (1972) *Task-centered Casework.* New York: Columbia University Press

REID W.J. & SHYNE A.W. (1969) *Brief and Extended Casework*. New York: Columbia University Press

RICHMOND M. (1917) *Social Diagnosis*. New York: Russell Sage Foundation

RICHMOND M. (1922) *What is Social Casework?* New York: Russell Sage Foundation

ROBINS L.N. (1973) Evaluation of psychiatric services for children in the United States. *In* Wing J.K. & Häfner H. (eds.) *Roots of Evaluation: the Epidemiological Basis for Planning Psychiatric Services*. London: Oxford University Press.

ROBERTS R.W. & NEE R.H. (eds.) (1970) *Theories of Social Casework*. Chicago: University of Chicago Press

ROSE G. & MARSHALL T.F. (1974) *Counselling and School Social Work*. London: Wiley

RUTTER M. (1975) *Helping Troubled Children*. Harmondsworth: Penguin

RUTTER M. & MADGE N. (1976) *Cycles of Disadvantage: a Review of Research*. London: Heinemann

RUTTER M. (1976) Brain damage syndromes in childhood: concepts and findings. *J. Child Psychol. Psychiat.* (in press)

RUTTER M. & SUSSENWEIN F. (1971) A developmental and behavioral approach to the treatment of preschool autistic children. *J. Autism Child Schiz.* **1**, 376–397

RUTTER M., TIZARD J. & WHITMORE K. (eds.) (1970) *Education, Health and Behaviour*. London: Longman

SAINSBURY E.E. (1970) *Social Diagnosis in Casework*. London: Routledge & Kegan Paul

SAINSBURY E.E. (1975) *Social Work with Families*. London: Routledge & Kegan Paul

SALZBERGER-WITTENBERG S.I. (1970) *Psychoanalytic Insight and Relationships: a Kleinian Approach*. London: Routledge & Kegan Paul

SANDLER J., DARE C. & HOLDER A. (1971) Basic psychoanalytic concepts. X: Interpretations and other interventions. *Brit. J. Psychiat.* **118**, 53–59

SHAPIRO D.A. (1969) Empathy, warmth and genuineness in psychotherapy. *Brit. J. clin. soc. Psychol.* **18**, 350–361

SHAW M. (1974) *Social Work in Prison*. London: HMSO

SKYNNER A.C.R. (1969) A group-analytic approach to conjoint family therapy. *J. Child Psychol. Psychiat.* **10**, 81–106

SMALLEY R. (1967) *Theory for Social Work Practice*. New York: Columbia University Press

TAIT C.D. & HODGES E.F. (1962) *Delinquents, Their Families and the Community*. Springfield, Illinois: Charles C. Thomas

TAYLOR F.K. (1969) Prokaletic measures derived from psychoanalytic technique. *Brit. J. Psychiat.* **115**, 407–419

THOMAS A., CHESS S. & BIRCH H.G. (1968) *Temperament and Behavior Disorders in Children*. New York: University Press

TIMMS N. (1964) *Psychiatric Social Work in Great Britain (1939–1962)*. London: Routledge & Kegan Paul

TRUAX C.B. (1966) Reinforcement and non-reinforcement in Rogerian psychotherapy. *J. Abnorm. Psychol.* **71**, 1–9

TRUAX C.B. (1968) Therapist interpersonal reinforcement of client self-exploration and therapeutic outcome in group psychotherapy. *J. Psychol.* **15**, 225–231

TRUAX C.B. & CARKHUFF R.R. (1967) *Towards Effective Counseling and Psychotherapy: Training and Practice*. Chicago: Aldine

WARREN M.Q. (1969) The case for differential treatment of delinquents. *Ann. Amer. Acad. Pol. Soc. Sci.* **381,** 47–59

WEISS J.M. (1972) Influence of psychological variables on stress-induced pathology. *In* Porter R. & Knight J. (eds.) *Physiology, Emotion and Psychosomatic Illness.* Ciba Foundation Symposium 8. Amsterdam: Associated Scientific Publications

WELLS R.A., DILKES T.C. & TRIVELLI N. (1972) The results of family therapy: a critical review of the literature. *Family Process* **11,** 189–207

WING L. (1970) *Children apart—autistic children and their families.* London: BMA and NAMH Family Doctor Booklet

WOLFENSBERGER W. (1967) Counselling the parents of the retarded. *In* Baumeister A.A. (ed.) *Mental Retardation: Appraisal, Education and Rehabilitation.* London: University of London Press

WOODWARD J. & JACKSON D. (1961) Emotional reactions in burned children and their mothers. *Brit. J. Plastic Surgery* **13,** 316–324

WOOTTON B. (1959) *Social Science and Social Pathology.* London: Allen & Unwin

Index

Abortion, in teenage pregnancy 146–147
  postoperative feelings 147–148
  refused, and the unwanted child 392
Acrocephalosyndactyly 820, 823
Adaptability, response to experience 15–16
Adenoma sebaceum in tuberous sclerosis 818
Adolescence
  autism 727, 729, 749–750
  development, normal 407–416
    emotions 412
    friendships 412
    parent–adolescent relationships 414–416
    personality development 413
    physical changes 407–408
    psychological correlates of physical changes 408–410
    psychosexual development 411–412
    social changes 410
  disorders 407–427
  drug-taking see Drug-taking
  drug misuse, special aspects 658–659
    see also Drug misuse
  EEG findings in behaviour disorders 341–343
  idealism and rebellion 414
  interviewing 291–292, 294
  peer group influences 415
  personality development 413–414
  Piaget's theories 242 et seq.
  pregnancy see Pregnancy in adolescence
  psychiatric disorders, aetiology 422
    classification 422–423
  course 420–422
    manic-depressive psychosis 420
    pattern 417–418
      changes 418–420
    prevalence 416–417
    prognosis 420–422
    schizophrenia 420
    school refusal 419–420
    sex ratio 419
    treatment 422–423
  psychotherapeutic approach 961–962
  psychotic disorders 748–770
  secular trends 416
  unemployment 410
  see also Maturity
Adopted children, delinquency, and parent's criminality 31–32, 33–35, 515
  psychiatric disorders in 150–158
    biological and social factors related to pregnancy 154–155
    experience prior to placement 155
    personality attitudes and expectations of adoptive parents 155–158
    statistics 150–154
Adoption 136–159
  and adolescent girls 144–148
  alcoholism 37
  assessment of children 140–140
    acceptance of 'imperfect' child 142–143
    medical 140–141
    mental defect 141–142
    parental psychiatric disorders 143–144
    physical disorders 143
    predictability of development 148–150

Adoption (*contd*)
  attitudes 137
  and bonding 65
  children with special needs 137–138
  coloured children 137–138
  criminality 31–32, 33–35, 515
    crossfostering 34
  and environment 36
  heredity factors 36
  information about biological
    parents 157
  matching parents and child 149–150
  polygenic influences 22–46
  psychopathy 35–36
  residential care children 138
  statistics 136–139
  telling the child 156–157
  trends 136–139
Adoptive parents, characteristics
    139–140
Adult neurosis, and childhood
    emotional disorder,
    relationship 449
Affective psychoses in adolescents
    751–753
  drug treatment 752
Age distribution
  aggressive behaviour 497
  psychiatric disorders 368
Age scores in psychological testing
    309
Aggressive behaviour
  age distribution 497
    sex distribution 497
    social class 497–499
  antecedents 496–503
  behavioural approaches 938–941
  and catharsis 94–95
  classification 363
  and frustration 93–94
  imitation 97–98
  interpretation 95–96
  in marijuana smokers 632
  mass media 501–503
  in normal children 491–492
  and overprotection 78
  parental dominance 499
  with psychiatric disturbances 490–491
  punishment 96–97
  response 96–97

sex differences 4–5
sibship size 499
twin studies 29–30
and XYY syndrome 170
Aggressive behaviour disorders
  and brain damage 494–495
  and delinquency 494, 518
    sex ratio 492
  and emotional disturbance 493
  marital discord 499–500
  nondelinquent 487–506
    incidence 488–489
    outcome and treatment 503–506
    specific associated disorders
      492–503
  in psychotic and borderline
    psychotic states 495–496
  and school failure 493–494
  social processes within schools 501
  family composition 499
Agoraphobia 435, 436
Alarm system in enuresis 601–602,
    603–604
Alcohol
  drug use 629–630
    among young people 636–637
    culture-specific 630
Alcoholism, adoption studies 37
Amitriptyline, in enuresis 599–600
Amniocentesis, prenatal diagnosis of
    chromosome anomalies 179–180
Amphetamine
  barbiturate mixtures, misuse 660
    withdrawal treatment 654–655
  causing paranoid psychotic state
    754
  contraindication in adolescence 658
  effects 904, 906, 907, 908, 909
  in enuresis 598
  misuse 660 *et seq.*
    general factors 634–635
    physical signs 649
    prevalence 629
    tolerance 634
    withdrawal treatment 654–655
  in mental retardation disturbances
    848
  side effects 907
  see also Stimulant drugs
Amsterdam dwarf 820, 821
Amygdalotomy in hyperkinetic
    syndrome 544

Amytal, in tics and Tourette's
        syndrome   684
Anaesthesia, in electroencephalography
        335
Aneuploidy, definition   163
Animals, fear, infants   48
Anorexia nervosa
    prognosis   370
    psychological factors   775–777
Anticholinergic drugs in enuresis
        598–599
Antidepressant drugs
    in affective psychosis   752
    in psychiatric disorders   915–916
    dosage   915
Antisocial behaviour, behavioural
        approaches   938–941
    and broken home   59–62
    in hyperkinetic syndrome   526–527
    and marital discord   59–62
    and reading difficulties   572
    following separation   55–56
Anxiety
    in emotional disorders   431–433
    and enuresis   593
    existential theory   432
    morbid and normal, difference
        432–433
    objective or neurotic   432
    in obsessional disorders   443, 444
    overconcern
        of parents to dangers   493
    prone children   433
    in school refusal   459, 460
    separation, and school refusal   463–
        464
Anxiety states
    at adolescence   418
    in emotional disorders   433–435
    precipitation   434
    tranquillisers   912–913
    treatment   434–435
Apert's syndrome   820, 823
Appearance, and behaviour   10
Articulation   704
Asphyxia, neonatal
    relation to behaviour   193
    relation to intelligence   193
Assertive behaviour   500–501
Assessment
    and psychological testing, distinction
        between   306–308
    target   321–322

Asthma
    and family background   778–779
    IQ of children   783
Attachments
    in early life   48–51
        multiple   49–50
    to inanimate objects   50
    in institution-reared children   50–
        51
Attainment
    and family size   86–87
    and ordinal position   87
Attention, diagnostic testing   317
Attentional deficit disorder   530
    see also Hyperkinetic syndrome
Audiovisual integration in reading
        558
Auditory discriminations in early life
        690
Authoritarianism, in marijuana
        smokers   632
Autism, infantile   720–739
    adolescence   420, 727, 729
        management   750
        sexual behaviour   750
        social behaviour   750
    age of onset   723
    association with mental
        retardation   725, 838–839
    association with brain
        damage   198–199
    biological basis   734–735
    and brain damage   366
    cognitive deficits   730–732
    definition   722–723
    diagnostic criteria   723
    differentiation from disintegrative
        psychosis   839
    distinction from schizophrenia
        720
    family background   733
    feeding difficulties   730
    follow-up into adult life   738–
        739
    and 'hypsarrhythmia'   735
    insistence on sameness   729–730
    IQ   724-726
        importance in prognosis   738–
            739
        and progress   738
    language, comprehension   703
        and prelanguage skill   727–729,
            730–732

Autism, infantile, language (*contd*)
   production   704
   prevalence   722
   prognosis   738–739
   psychological testing   326
   rapid eye movements   352
   and reading difficulties   367
   and speech   704
   and speech delay   696
   repetitive movements   730
   and rules, lack of appreciation
      731
   and sequence patterns   731, 732
   and social relationships   726–727
   symptomatology   723
   treatment   736–738
   treatment at day-hospital   891
   type of disorder   735–736
   visual stimuli, reaction   731, 735
Autistic
   maliciousness   495
   psychopathy   721
Autonomic nervous system and
   delinquency   516
Autosomal trisomy G, and
   mongolism   175–179

Babies, difficult, and psychiatric
   disorder   392
Barbiturates
   and behaviour   913
   contraindication in adolescence   658
   in mental retardation
      disturbances   848
   misuse general factors   634–735
      mortality   652
      physical signs   649
      prevalence   629
      withdrawal treatment   654
   overdose   634
Battered baby and mental handicap
   817
Beclamide, in mental retardation
   disturbances   848, 914
Bedwetting treatment   596–605
   assessment   601–603
   bell and pad   601–602, 603–604
   day-time training   597–598
   drug   598–600
      assessment   604–605

   fluid restriction   597
   night lifting   597
   spontaneous cure   596
   surgery   598
   see also Enuresis
Behaviour
   abnormal, and learning theories
      227–30
   changes and stimulant drugs   904–
      905
   classification, clustering
      technique   364
   clinging after separation   52, 54,
      56
   see also Hospital admission
   contingencies   278, 279
   deviance, and psychosocial
      disadvantage, head
      injuries   199–201
   differences, early infancy   3–4
      sex-related   4–5
      vulnerability   16
      see also Temperament
   disorders, and dwellings   396–397
      EEG findings   338–343
      see also Electroencephalography,
         behaviour disorders
      preschool, *see* Preschool disorders
      prognosis   398
      and sex chromosome
         abnormalities   165–167
      XYY syndrome   169–170
      see also Behaviour problems
   genetic factors   22–23
   and neonatal asphyxia   193
   parental, *see* Parental behaviour
   polygenic influences   22–46
   phobias, respondent   927–929
      desensitisation   928–929
      modelling   928, 929
   precipitants   278, 279
   prior circumstances   278
   problems, in preschool children
      387–388, 389–390
      treatment at day-hospital   891
   rating, and lead levels   196–197
   relation to learning   229–230
   school influence   122–123
   surgical improvement of appearance
      10
   towards brain-damaged children
      203–204
Behavioural approaches   923–948

Behavioural approaches (*contd*)
  antisocial disorders 938–941
  current problems and future
    developments 941–943
  defining the problem
    objectively 924–925
  disorders treated 937
  distinguishing features 935–943
  evaluating the outcome 927
  in mental retardation 844–847,
    941
  modification in hyperkinetic
    children 543
  modification in mental
    retardation 844–847
  modification principles 927–943
  modification techniques 927–943
    in inpatient units 887
    thirteen principles 936
  operant 929–935
    extinction 931–932
    imitation 934
    mental retardation
      disturbances 844–847
    prompting and fading 933
    psychiatric social work 977
    reinforcement 930–931
    shaping 932–933
  setting up hypotheses 925–926
  techniques in autism 736–737
  testing the hypotheses 926–927
  training cotherapists 937–938
  treating rather than
    explaining 936
Behaviour therapy
  in aggressive behaviour disorders
    505–506
  in mental retardation 844–847
  in obsessional disorders 444
  in preschool disorders 400–401
  in school refusal 466–470
  in tics and Tourette's syndrome
    683
Bell and pad in enuresis 601–602,
  603–604
Benadryl *see* Diphenhydramine
Benzodiazapine drugs, in anxiety
  states 435
Bereavement
  and depression 445
  effect 58–59
  parental, 393
    effect on emotional stability 402

Bilingualism, and speech
  development 695
Birth of sib, causing stress 57
Bladder
  neck, developmental changes in
    enuresis 587
  size and function in enuresis 586–
    587
Blindness and mental retardation 840
Body
  function, and family relationships
    778–779
  rocking and mental retardation 840
Bonding
  in early life 48–51
  lack of 65–66
Bowel
  control, physiology and psychology
    614–617
  see also Faecal soiling
  training 615–617
    faulty 617, 618
Boys without fathers 63–64
Boyhood femininity, meaning and
    treatment 801–804
  see also Feminine boys
Brain damage *see* Brain injury
Brain disorder, type, in autism 735
Brain dysfunction and hyperkinetic
    syndrome 524–525
Brain function, and reading
    retardation 569
Brain injury 185–215
  and aggressive behaviour 494–495
  and autism 366
  and behavioural differences 6
  detection 204–207
    EEG 206
    psychometry 206–207
    'soft' signs 204–206
  and disintegrative psychosis 366
  and hyperkinetic syndrome 366,
    524
  and intelligence 373
  likelihood of psychiatric disorder
    185–187
  in mental retardation 833
  minimal 190–197
    behaviour 193
    CNS infection 194
    educational difficulties 193–194
    head injury 194–195
    intelligence 193

Brain injury, minimal (*contd*)
  metabolic upset   196–197
  perinatal illness   192–196
  pregnancy complications   191–
    193
pathognomonic syndromes   197–
  199
  hyperkinetic syndrome   197–
    198
    infantile autism   198–199
    'rage' syndrome   199
  prognosis   209–210
  and psychiatric classification   366–
    367
  psychiatric complications, factors
    modifying   187–190
    age   187–188
    brain damage severity   190
      type   189–190
    locus   188–189
    mechanisms   199–204
      intellectual and educational
        handicap   201–202
      social and family disadvantage
        199–201
      social stigma and handicap
        201
      temperament   202–203
      transactional effects   203–204
  and psychological testing   317
  treatment   207–209
    anticonvulsant drugs   208
    counselling   207–208
    psychotropic drugs   208–209
    surgery   209
Brain, organic changes
  and chromosome abnormalities   166
  in triple-X sex chromosome
    constitution   174
  Turner's syndrome   173
Broken home
  and antisocial behaviour   59–62
  and delinquency   59–62
  and teenage pregnancy   92
  West Indian children   126
    see also Family background:
      Marital discord: Parent–child
      relationship

Cambridge–Somerville study   59, 982
Cannabis
  see Marijuana

Carbamazepine, effect on mental
  retardation   914
Care order, Children and Young
  Persons Act 1969   873–874
Castration anxiety   75–76
Catastrophic rage syndrome, and brain
  injury   199
Catecholamines in hyperkinetic
  syndrome   532, 533
Catharsis   94–95
Central nervous system
  abnormalities and drug toxicity
    908
  arousal in hyperkinetic children
    532
  and enuresis   590–591
  infection and psychiatric disorder
    194
Cerebral palsy
  and reading retardation   569
  recognition   816–817
  and speech delay   695
Cerebral tumours, psychiatric features,
  EEG findings   345
Characteristics, individual, in
  preschool children   391–394
Child abuse
  inpatient unit treatment   882–883
  see also Battered baby
Child psychology, relation to 'adult'
  psychology   219–220
Child-rearing patterns   74–87
  catharsis   94–95
  childhood experiences and parental
    behaviour   92–93
  discipline   80–82
  dominance   83–85
  family communication   83–85
  family size   86–87
  frustration   93–94
  identification and conscience   98–
    99
  imitation   97–98
  infant care   77
  interpretations and perceptions   95–
    96
  moral development   93–99
  ordinal position   87
  overprotection   77–80
  parental constraint   77–80
  parental deviance   87–91
  psychosexual development   74–76
  response to aggression   96–97

Childhood experiences
  adverse, and adult behaviour 92–93
  and parental behaviour 92–93
Children and Young Persons Act 1969
  care order 873–874
  legal provisions 872–877
  supervision order 874–877
    custody and control 876
Chloral hydrate, in mental retardation
    disturbances 848
  in sleep disorder 916
Chlordiazepoxide (Librium)
  in anxiety states 912
  in mental retardation disturbances
    848
  misuse, withdrawal treatment 654
Chlormethiazole edisylate
    (Heminevrin), in drug
    dependence treatment 654
Chlorpromazine
  in anorexia nervosa 776
  in mental retardation disturbances
    847, 848
  in neonatal drug addiction
    treatment 657
  in schizophrenia 763
  in tics and Tourette's syndrome
    684
  in sympathomimetic amines
    overdose 908–909
Chromosome(s)
  and aggressiveness 5
  anomalies 163–184
    autosomal 163, 175
    Cri-du-chat syndrome 178–179
    deletion, definition 164
    Edward's syndrome 177–178
    Klinefelter's syndrome 167
    mongolism 175–179
    prenatal diagnosis 179–180
    sex chromosome 163
      and mental and behavioural
        disorders 165–167
      organic brain changes 166
    and speech delay 695
    terminology 163
    triple-X sex chromosome
      constitution 173–175
    Turner's syndrome 171–173
    XYY syndrome 168–171
      in hyperkinetic children 532–533
Circadian rhythms of urine output and
    enuresis 587–588

City life stresses 118–121
  anonymity 119
  community 119
  high-rise flats 119
  homelessness 120–121
  rehousing 120
Classification, of psychiatric disorders
    359–383
  adaptation/adjustment reaction 372
  adolescent disorders 422–423
  adult adjustment 375
  adult disorders found in childhood
    371, 372
  aetiological basis 359
  age and sex distribution 368
  approach 376–378
  biological factors 366–367
  brain damage 366–367
    and intelligence 373
  clinical syndromes 362–372
  cognitive correlates 367–368
  conduct disorders 372
  criteria 360–361
  emotional disorders 372
  employment and adult adjustment
    375
  enuresis and encopresis 372
  family characteristics 364–366
  family history 374
  fertility 374
  hyperkinetic syndrome 372, 529–
    530
  intellectual level 373–375
  labelling 376–378
  long-term course 369–370
  mental retardation 811–814
  mixed disorders 372
  mortality 374
  multiaxial framework 361–362
    five axes 362
  principles 359–360
  psychiatric correlates and IQ 374
  psychoses 372
  psychosocial situations 362
  reliability 375–376
  schizophrenia 372
  scholastic attainment 374–375
  social class distribution 374
  specific development delays 362,
    372–373
  subcategories 371
  symptom clusters and multivariate
    techniques 362–364

Classification of psychiatric disorders
      (*contd*)
   theoretical concepts   360
   treatment response   369
   variables   362
Clinging behaviour following
      separation   52, 54, 56
Clumsiness
   assessment in diagnostic
      appraisal   296
   prognosis for adulthood   370
Coffee in hyperkinetic syndrome   541
Cogentin (Benztropine mesylate) in tics
      and Tourette's syndrome   684
Cognitive
   changes and stimulant drugs   905
   disabilities in hyperkinetic
      children   527
   learning theories   225–226
Communication, family
   and disturbed children   83–85
   and psychiatric social work   980–981
   see also headings under Family
Community
   centres, in stress and emergency
      400
   factors and emotional disorder
      119–120
   services for mentally handicapped
      843
Compendium tests, use in diagnostic
      testing   318
Competence, and response to
      experience   15–16
Competition, in school, effects   123–
      124
Compulsive behaviour   441–444
   see also Obsessive–compulsive
      behaviour
Compulsions *see* Compulsive
      behaviour
Conception, extramarital, and
      childhood experiences   92, 93
Conditionability, and learning   228
Conditioning
   forms in learning   224–225
   treatment, use of stimulants   906
Conduct disorders
   at adolescence   418
   classification   372
   family background   84–85
   and family size   86–87
   inpatient unit admission   883

and institutional rearing   65, 66
   nondelinquent   487–509
   see also Aggressive behaviour
   leading to delinquency   504
   outcome   503–504
   prevalence   496
   treatment   504–506
   prognosis for adulthood   369–370
   and reading difficulties   367, 572
   and reading retardation   125
   use of tranquillisers   909–910
   West Indian children   125, 216
Conduct disturbance variable,
      classification   363
Congenital anomalies
   and behavioural differences   5–6
   parental behaviour   11–12
   and psychiatric illness   14
Conner's Teacher Rating Scale in
      hyperkinetic syndrome   543
Conservation experiment, Piaget's
      theories   249–252
Constipation and faecal soiling   620
Constitutional factor in crime   516
Constraint, parental   77–80
Cornelia de Lange syndrome   819
Council housing and behavioural
      disorders   396–397
Counselling, and hospital admissions
      52, 54
   see also Genetic counselling
Cri-du-chat syndrome   178–179
Criminal records and delinquency
      512–513
   self-reports of crime   512–513
Criminality
   adoption studies   31–32, 33–35, 515
   parental and delinquency   87–88,
      514–515
   twin studies   30–32
Cultural factors in preschool
      disorders   397
Cyclothymic symptoms and adolescent
      manic-depressive disorders
      751

Dark, fear, infants   48
Day-hospital units   889–896
   aims and objects   889–890
   differences   890
   problems   895–896

Day-hospital units (*contd*)
  siting 890
  staffing 890
  therapeutic milieu and organisation
      892–895
    specific aspects 894–895
    treatment outcome 896–897
    uses and abuses 891–892
Day nurseries, provision 399
Daytime wetting, treatment 605–607
  management 606
Deaf children
  effects of hearing or deaf parents
      14–15
  and deaf parents, progress in
      speech 694, 709
  language production 704
  severe, language comprehension
      703
  and speech delay 695, 698
Deaf parents
  and deaf children, progress in
      speech 709
  effect on speech development in
      children 694
Deanol in hyperkinetic syndrome 541
Delinquents
  aggression 492, 518
  definition 512
  deviant personality 514, 517–518
  EEG findings in 342–343
  labelling 512, 860–861
  social background and conviction
      513
  treatment 859–879
    behavioural approaches 940
    diagnostic typology 868–870
    differential 867–868
    group therapy 871
    legal provisions 872–877
    probation 872
    psychiatrist's attitudes 859–861
    psychotherapy, behavioural 866
      individual 863
    recent trends 859–861
    reconviction 870, 864, 867, 868,
      871
    research 866–872
    therapeutic community 865
    visiting psychiatrist's role 865
Delinquency 510–513
  and aggressive behaviour disorders
      492

  early 492
  sex ratio 492
  area distribution 510–511
  autonomic nervous system
      responses 516
  contracultures 114–115
  criminal records 511
  differential association 113–114
    causing spread of crime 113
  and drug misuse 664–665
  in economically favoured
      backgrounds 521
  family background 514–515
  female 517
  follow-up to adulthood 510
  genetic factors 515–516
  geographical areas 109–110
  group behaviour 519
  hereditary influences 88
  labelling 114, 512, 860–861
  male 514
  modelling 88
  multiple occupancy dwellings 118
  nonpathological approach 511
  opportunitistic offences 519
  and parental criminality 87–88,
      514–515
  and predelinquency 514
  prediction 861–863
    by school companions 862
  prevalence 510
  prevention 861–863
  and reading difficulties 571
  recidivist 112, 870, 864, 867, 868,
      871
  risk-taking 519
  school origins 520–521
  school variations 121–124
  self-reported 512–513
  social class 510, 511, 519, 521
  social learning 517
  social status 110–111
  sociocultural theories 111–115
  as subculture 519, 521
    normal pattern of behaviour 112
  and subnormality 513
    before the courts 514
  twin studies 29–32
  West Indian children 126
Delirium tremens and barbiturate
      withdrawal 654
Depressants, misuse, prevalence
      629

Depression
  in adolescence   418, 751–753
    treatment with drugs   752–753
  and enuresis   594
  female vulnerability   419
  in hyperkinetic children   528–529
  masked   446–447
  in mothers of young children   394–
    395
  relation to stress   57–58
  and school refusal   464–466
  with and without psychiatric
    disorder   446–447
Depressive disorders   444–448
  characteristics   446
  criteria   444–445
  prevalence   445–446
  treatment   448–449
Depressive equivalents   446–447
Depressive syndromes   447–449
  discriminant functions analysis
    447–448
  symptoms   447–448
Development
  emotional   47–51
  Piaget's theories   240–242
  process, and diagnostic appraisal
    273
  psychosexual   74–76
    see also Psychosexual development
  social, early fears and
    responses   47–51
Developmental disorders
  inpatient unit admission   883
  prognosis for adulthood   370
  and speech delay   695
  of speech/language   699, 704
Developmental factors in preschool
    disorders   390–391
Developmental language disorder,
    language production   699, 704
Dextroamphetamine, in hyperkinetic
    syndrome   538–542
  in mental retardation disturbance
    848
Diagnosis
  in emotional disorders   429–431
  reliability and classification   375–
    376
Diagnostic appraisal   271–279
  developmental process   273
  epidemiology and follow-up   274–
    277

problem-solving approach   277–279
  reasons for referral   271–273
  parental backgrounds   272
  understanding behaviour   278–279
Diagnostic testing, expectancy tables
    319–320
  use of psychological tests   317–320
  regression procedures   318–319
Diazepam (Valium)
  in anxiety states   912–913
  in mental retardation disturbances
    848
  misuse, withdrawal treatment   654
  in neonatal drug addiction treatment
    657
  in tics and Tourette's syndrome
    684
Differences
  behaviour, sex-related   4–5
  individual, early infancy   3–4
  temperamental, early infancy   3–4
    see also Temperament
Differential treatment of
    delinquents   867–868
Diphenhydramine (Benadryl), in
    hyperkinetic syndrome   542
  in sleep disorder   916, 917
Discipline   80–82
  balance of rewards and punishment
    82
  behaviours most affected   82
  efficiency of techniques   81
  and family size   86
  inconsistency   82
  quality of parent–child relationship
    80–81
  school   124
  timing of responses   81
  understanding of rules   81–82
  and West Indian families   128
Disintegrative psychosis
  and brain damage   366
  differentiation from autism   839
Distractability in hyperkinetic
    syndrome   525
Distress, following separation   52–
    57
    see also Hospital admission:
    Separation
Disturbed children, family
    background   84–85
Dominance patterns in the family
    83–85

Dominance patterns in the family (*contd*)
  relation to psychiatric disorder   84
Down's syndrome   175–179, 821
  autosomal trisomy G   175–176
  mental handicap   177
  and mental retardation   808, 809,
    841
  mosaicism   176
  physical features   176–177
  and speech delay   696
  translocations   176
  see also Edward's syndrome: Cri-du-
    chat syndrome
Drinamyl misuse withdrawal
    treatment   655
Drug abuse, definition   647
  see also Drug misuse; Drug taking;
    Drugs of dependence
Drug addiction
  habituation, tolerance, definitions
    646–647
  neonatal   656–658
    morbidity and mortality   656
    treatment of dependence   656–
     658
  patients' studies   660–662
  psychiatric disorders   662 *et seq.*
Drug dependence
  definition   646–647
  diagnosis   651
  patients' surveys   660–669
  treatment   655–652
  adolescents, special aspects   658
Drug misuse, clinical aspects   646–673
  clinical features   651–652
  definitions   646–647
  and delinquency   664–665
  patients' studies   660–669
  rehabilitation   655
  treatment   652–655
    early abstinent phase   655
    long-term   655
    special aspects of adolescents
     658–659
  see also Drug-taking
Drug psychoses   754–755
Drug taking   628–645
  alcohol, general factors   636–637
  amphetamines, general factors
    634–635
  background   631
  barbiturates, general factors   634–
    635

cannabis, review   633–634
cross-national contrasts   629–630
determinants and correlates   630–
  633
development   631
diagnosis   647–651
  of dependence   651
  laboratory aids   650
difficulties, in drawing conclusions
  637–638
  for users   639
EEG findings   346
effects   638
glue sniffing   637
hallucinogens, general factors   634–
  635
initiation   638
learning   631–632
LSD, general factors   634
marijuana, review   633–634
mental state, examination   648
motivation   631
opiate-type drugs, general factors
  635
personality factors   631
  and psychiatric factors   632–633
  interrelation   632–633
physical examination   649–650
prevalence   628–629
psychiatric factors   632–633
recent history   646
services   639–640
social factors   630–631
specific drugs   633–637
tobacco, general factors   635–636
Drug treatment   901–922
  in affective psychoses   752
  anticonvulsants   912–915
  controls   902–903
  diagnostic homogeneity   902
  mental retardation disturbances
    847–848
  normative studies   901
  in preschool disorders   401
  in schizophrenia   762–763
  standardisation of dosage   903–904
  stimulants   904–909
    behaviour changes   904–905
    choice   907–908
    cognitive and motor changes
     906–907
    conditioning treatment   906
    dosage and side effects   908–909

1004   *Index*

Drug treatment (*contd*)
  stimulants (*contd*)
    growth retardation 909
    persistence and generalisation of
      effects 906
    predicting a favourable response
      907
    sedation or stimulation 907
    toxic overdose 908–909
  tranquillisers 909–917
  tranquillisers, major 909–912
    cognition and perceptual-motor
      function 911
    in conduct disturbance disorders
      909–910
    dosage 912
    in emotional disturbances 910
    movement and habit disorders
      910–911
    unwanted effects 911–912
  tranquillisers, minor 912–915
Drugs
  of dependence, contraindication in
    adolescence 658
  physical dependence capacity (PDC)
    definition 647
Dwarf, Amsterdam 820, 821
Dwarfism, psychological factors 777
Dynamic treatments 949–966
  definition 949–950
  see also Psychotherapy,
    psychodynamic
Dysdiadochokinesis, and brain injury
  205
Dysgraphaesthesia, and brain injury
  205
Dyslexia 565–566
  definition 565
  diagnostic subgroups 566
  EEG findings 353
  polygenic influences 39–40

Echolalia 704
Education
  difficulties, and perinatal morbidity
    193–194
  failure, later in childhood 561–563
  handicap, in brain injury 201–202
  higher, and dependence on parents
    410
  management in hyperkinetic
    syndrome 544

see also Intelligence quotient:
    Scholastic: School:
Edward's syndrome 177–178
  mental subnormality 178
Elective mutism *see* Mutism, elective
Electroconvulsive therapy in
    adolescence 753
  in depressive disorders 449
  in drug addiction disorders 662
Electroencephalography 334–358
  anaesthesia 335
  in autistic children 734
  behaviour disorders 338–343
    adolescents 341–343
    severe 334–335
    hyperkinetic 339, 531, 532
    spike discharges 340–341
    with or without neurological
      impairment 338–339
  in brain injury 206
  in delinquents 342–343
  emotional disorders 344
  in enuresis 590–591
  epilepsy 347–349
  in hyperkinetic children 339, 531–
    532
  in Kinefelter's syndrome 167
  in mental retardation 350
  in normal children 335–338
    paroxysmal abnormalities 336–
      338, 341
  organic illnesses presenting with
    psychiatric features 345–347
  in psychiatric illness 338–350
  psychoses of childhood 344–345
  psychosomatic disorders 344
  in reading difficulties 559–560
  sleep recordings 351
  special procedures 350–353
  technique 334–338
  in tics and Tourette's syndrome
    678
  in triple-X sex chromosome
    constitution 175
  in Turner's syndrome 173
Emotion, and interview 284
  and speech delay 705
  see also Distress
Emotional disorders 428–454
  at adolescence 412–413
  and aggressive behaviour disorders
    493
  anxiety states 433–435

Emotional disorders (*contd*)
  childhood and adult neurosis,
    relationship 449
  depressive 444–449
  diagnosis 429–431
  clinical-descriptive/psychoanalytical
    approaches 429–430
  EEG 344
  fear and anxiety 431–433
  hyperkinetic syndrome 528–529
  hysteria 437–441
  see also Hysteria
  inpatient unit admission 883
  obsessional 441–444
  phobic states 435–437
  prognosis for adulthood 369–370
  and reading difficulties 572
  with or without psychiatric
    disorder 428, 429
  in tics and Tourette's syndrome
    679–681
  treatment, response 369
  variable, classification 363
Empathy, and interview 284–285
Encephalopathy, and mental
    retardation 816–817
Encopresis *see* Faecal soiling
Enuresis 581–612
  aetiology 583–584
  and anxiety 593
  assessment 602–603
  and behavioural deviance 591–593
  and bladder neck developmental
    changes 587
  bladder size and function 586–587
  and central nervous system function
    590–591
  circadian rhythms of urine output
    587–588
  and depression 594
  and early life disturbances 588–589
  and encopresis, in psychiatric
    classification 363, 364, 372
  EEG findings 352, 590–591
  and epilepsy 590–591
  ethnic factors 583–584
  genetic factors 583–584, 595
  as genitourinary tract disorder
    584–588
  natural history 581–583
  nonsymptomatic treatment 593–
    594
  polygenic influences 40

prevalence 581–583
prognosis 583
as psychiatric disorder, causal,
    reactive, or coincidental 593–
    596
  or psychosocial disorder 591–596
  statistics 594–595
rapid eye movements 590
  effect of imipramine 600
relapse, age 582
sex ratio 582
  and urinary infection 584
as sleep disorder 590–591
and social class 595
and stressful life events 57, 589–
    590
and toilet training 588–589
treatment 596–607
  bedwetting 596–605
    alarm system 601–602, 603–
      604
    assessment 601–603
    bell and pad 601–602, 603–
      604
    day-time training 597
    drug 598
      assessment 604–605
    fluid restriction 597
    night lifting 597
    nonspecific intervention 596
    spontaneous cure 596
    surgical 598
  daytime 605–607
and urinary infection 584
  girls 584–585
and urinary tract obstruction 585
Environmental factors
  and adoption 36
  in preschool disorders 396–397
Epilepsy
  and autism 734
  fits at adolescence 420
  centrencephalic, unrecognised, in
    psychotic disorders 754
  EEC findings 347–349
    drug intoxication 349–350
  and enuresis 590–591
  and Klinefelter's syndrome 166
  and mental handicap 817
  and reading difficulties 569
  psychomotor type, EEG findings
    347–348
  social stigma 201

Epilepsy (*contd*)
   in triple-X sex chromosome
      constitution   174
Experimental psychology
   and child development   223–224
   and personality
      characteristics   230–235
      biological theory   231–235
      learning theory approach   233–
      235
Extraversion, degree,and learning
      ability   228
Eye movements, and reading   558

Facial expression at interview   288,
   293
Faecal soiling   613–627
   abnormal stools   619
   anal masturbation   619
   bowel control, physiology and
      psychology   614–617
   classification   618–619
      failure to learn control   619
      temporary   618
   constipation   620
   constitutional factors   620
   developmental factors, child   621–
      622
   epidemiology   613–614
   family pathology   621
   impaction   619, 622–623
   laxative   623, 624
   management   622–624
      results   624
   mother–child relationships   620–
      621
   night-time   619
   as psychiatric disorder   622
   psychogenic factors, child   620
   psychotherapy   623–624
   punishment   621, 622
   sex ratio   613–614
   social class   619–620
   toilet training   615–617
Failure to thrive, psychological
      factors   777
Family
   admission to inpatient unit   883–
      884
   adversity, and psychiatric disorder
      117
   attitudes, to day-hospitals   892–893

   to inpatient unit admissions
      883–884, 885
background and asthma   778–779
   in autistic children   733–734
   and delinquency   514–515
   and drug-taking   631
   and enuresis   589–590, 595
   and faecal soiling   621
   in hyperkinetic syndrome   534–
      535
   and mental retardation   374
   in obesity   774–775
   in schizophrenia   759–760
   in school refusal   457
   in tics and Tourette's syndrome
      679
characteristics, and classification
      364–366
communication   83–85
   and psychiatric social work   980–
      981
composition, and aggressive
      behaviour   499
   see also Family size
disadvantage and brain injury   199–
      201
discord, and adolescent psychiatric
      disorders   419
   in psychiatric classification   365
doctor, involvement in diagnostic
      appraisal   297
factors in preschool disorders   394–
      396
immigrant   *see* Immigrant families
interaction and body functions
      778–779
   discord and quarrelling   59–62
   in inpatient units   885–886
   at interview   289–290
   in school refusal   470–472, 477–
      478
involvement in hyperkinetic
      syndrome   544–545
large, and reading difficulties   570
patterns of dominance   83–85
relationships   *see* Family
      interaction; Broken homes;
      Marital discord
size, and aggressive behaviour   499
   intelligence level and attainment
      86–87
   and language development   694
   West Indian   127

Family (*contd*)
  therapy, in psychotherapy   963–964
  units in hospital   888–889
Father's role
  and feminine boy   797, 800
  in school refusal   471, 472
Fears
  in early life   47–51
  imaginary   48
  role in emotional disorders   431–
    433
Feeding difficulties in autism   730
Feminine boys   792–804
  aetiology   796–798
  age referral   802–803
  behaviour   794–796
    parents' accounts   794–796, 798,
      800, 801
  and later homosexuality   801–802
  procedure for study   793–794
  psychological testing   796
  rationale and background   792–793
  testing procedures   793–794
  treatment   798–801
Femininity, boyhood, meaning and
    treatment   801–804
  see also Feminine boys
Fertility, and mental retardation   374
Fetal distress, relation to preschool
    disorders   391
Finger-sucking, in early infancy   4
Flats
  and depressive illness   396–397
  high-rise, stresses   119
Fluphenazine, side effects   911
Fostering, and behavioural
    disturbances   37, 38
Franceschetti syndrome   819
Friendships, at adolescence,
    importance   412
Frostig Test   320–321
Frustration and aggression   93–94

Gangs, adolescent   520
Genetic counselling in mental
    retardation   811
Genetic factors
  adoption studies   33–38
  and delinquency   88, 515–516
  in enuresis   583–584, 595
  in hyperkinetic syndrome   534
  in mental retardation   374

in obesity   774
in schizophrenia   757, 758–759
in temperament differences   5–6
twin studies   22–32, 38
Genitourinary tract disorder, and
    enuresis   584–588
Geographical areas
  and delinquency   109–110
  and psychiatric disorders   115–117
Girls
  masculine-behaving, and sexual
    identity   791–792, 793
  without mothers   63
Glue sniffing   637
Group
  behaviour in delinquency   519
  counselling in psychiatric social
    work   981, 985
  therapy of delinquents   871
Growth
  hormone levels, and tranquilliser
    dosage   912
  physical, psychological factors
    774–777
  retardation and stimulant drugs
    909

Haemophilia, and stress   773
Hallucinations in schizophrenia   718,
    756–757, 761
Hallucinogens
  misuse   660, 661
    general factors   634
    prevalence   629
  see also LSD
Haloperidol
  in conduct disturbance   910
  in mental retardation
    disturbances   847, 848
  in schizophrenia   762, 763
  side effects   911, 912
  in tics and Tourette's
    syndrome   684
Handicap, and emotional
    disturbance   402
Handicapped children, psychological
    testing   326
  see also Physical handicaps
Handwashing ritual   441
Head
  injury, relation to psychiatric
    disorder   194–195

Head, injury (*contd*)
  locus and psychiatric
    disorders 188
Heminevrin *see* Chlormethiazole
  edisylate
Heredity and adoption 36
Heritability of traits 24–25
Heroin
  addiction, maintenance on
    methadone 655
  misuse 661, 662, 663, 665, 667,
    669
    prevalence 629
  in neonatal drug addiction
    treatment 657
  withdrawal treatment 653–654
Highfields' Project 866
High-rise flats
  and depressive illness 396–397
  stresses 119
Hindu families 128
Home visits for interviews 290
Homelessness, and psychiatric
    disorders 120
Homosexual behaviour and
    Klinefelter's syndrome
    165
Homosexuality and boyhood
    feminity 801–802
  see also Feminine boys
Hormone influences on sex
    differences 789, 790
Hospital admission, clinging behaviour
    after reunion 52, 54, 56
  distress following 52–57
    causes 52–53
    counselling 52, 54, 781
    daily visiting 52, 781
    effect of good care 54
    modification 780–782
    parent's stay, effect 52
  long-term effects 56
  mechanism producing adverse
    effects 782
  mother–child and family units
    888–889
  preparation of child 52, 54, 781
  previous experience 781
  psychological factors 779–784
  recurrent 56
  visiting 52, 781
  see also Inpatient psychiatric units;
    Day-hospitals

Hostility towards child, and
    overprotection 80
House moving and behavioural
    disorders 397
Households, overcrowded, and
    delinquency 118
Housing
  estates, and delinquency 109
  high density, stresses 118–119
  immigrant families 127
Hullian learning approach theory
    228
Hyperactive children, EEG findings
    352
Hyperactivity
  and hyperkinetic syndrome 525
  syndrome 198
Hyperkinetic syndrome 524–555
  at adolescence 420, 749–750
  aetiology 529–530
  antisocial behaviour 526–527
  behaviour modification 543
  biochemical studies 532–533
  and brain damage 197–198, 366
  chromosomal studies 532–533
  classification 529–530
    difficulties 371, 529–530
  clinical picture 525–529
  cognitive disabilities 527–528
  definition 524
  depression 528–529
  distractability 525–526
  educational management 544
  EEG studies 339
  epidemiology 530
  familial-genetic factors 534, 535
  family involvement 544–545
  future research 545–546
  hyperactivity 525
  impulsivity 526
  inpatient unit admission 883
  and intellectual retardation 839–
    840
  laboratory studies 531–534
  learning disabilities 527–528
    management 544
  maturational changes 529
  metabolic studies 532–533
  natural history 535–538
  neurological findings 530–531
  pharmacotherapy 538–542
  physical findings 530–531
  prognosis 535–538

Hyperkinetic syndrome (*contd*)
  and psychiatric classification 363, 366
  psychometric studies 533–534
  psychotherapy, individual 542
  and reading difficulties 367–368
  surgery 544
  terminology 524–525
  treatment 538–542
    at day-hospital 891
    drug 537–538, 538–539
Hypnotics
  in sleep problems 916
  withdrawal treatment 654
Hypoparathyroidism, EEG findings 345
Hypsarrythmia
  and autism 735, 839
  in epilepsy 817
Hysteria 437–441
  abnormal illness behaviour 439
  conversion 437, 438, 440
  epidemic 440–441
  management 440
  prevalence 437–438
  psychological mechanism 439
  sick role 439, 440

Idealism at adolescence 414
Identification and moral development 98–99
Illegitimacy
  and delinquency 62
  and perinatal morbidity 192–193
  progress when not adopted 137, 152
  statistics 145
Illinois Test of Psycholinguistic Abilities 321
Immigrant families 124–128
  behaviour difficulties 125
  housing problems 127
  low scholastic attainments 127
  preschool and adolescent children, psychiatric disorders 126
Imipramine
  in behaviour disturbances 915–916
  in enuresis 599–600, 916
  in hyperkinetic syndrome 537, 541
Imitation, in speech and language 702
Impulsions, young boys 441–442

Impulsive aggressive children, and overprotection 78
Impulsivity
  diagnostic testing 317
  in hyperkinetic syndrome 526
  testing 313
Inborn errors of metabolism, EEG findings 345
Individual characteristics, in preschool children 391–394
Infancy, early, individual differences 3–4
Infant care 77
Information, eliciting, at interview 280–283
Inner city life, stresses 118–121
Inner language and speech assessment 702
Inpatient psychiatric units 842, 880–889
  admission, reasons for 883
  characteristics 881–882
  clinical team 880
  problems 895–896
  schooling 887–888
  therapeutic milieu and organisation 884–886
    specific aspects 885–886
  treatment aims 881
    individual 886–887
    outcome 896–897
    uses and abuses 882–884
Insistence on sameness in autism 729–730
Institutional reared children 66–67
  attachment behaviour 50–51
  and bonding 65
  and language development 694
  and mental retardation 834
  and social attitudes 365
  see also Residential
Intellectual retardation
  associated syndromes 838–840
  and autism 838–839
  and hyperkinetic syndrome 839–840
  in speech delay 696–697
Intelligence
  and CNS infection 194
  in early maturing adolescents 408
  level, and family size 86–87
  and 'heritability' 24–25
  and neonatal asphyxia 193

Intelligence (*contd*)
    tics and Tourette's syndrome   678
Intelligence quotient (IQ)
    asthmatic children   783
    autism   724–726
        importance in prognosis   738–739
        and progress   738
    in brain injury   205
    and deviant behaviours   367–368
    in hyperkinetic children   527–528
    and infantile autism   367
    in mental retardation   830–831
    and psychiatric classification   373–375
    and psychiatric disorders   494
    and reading ability   559
    and reading difficulties   564–565
    in schizophrenia   718
    and speech delay   696–697, 706
    validity   314
Intelligence tests   309, 310, 311
    see also Psychological tests and
        testing: and specific names
Interpersonal Maturity Level
        Classification   869
Interviewing
    children and adolescents   291–297
        neurological screening   295–296
        play   294–295
        reliability and validity   293
    parents   279–291
        assessing disorder   291
        assessing family life and
            relationships   287–289
        combining techniques   287
        conjoint interviews   289–291
        eliciting emotions and feelings
            284
        eliciting information   280–283
        establishing therapeutic
            relationship   286–287
        family interaction   289–291
        retrospective recall   283–284
    problem-solving approach   277–279
    school relationships   296–297
Invariance of quantities, Piaget's
        theories   249–252
    interpretations   250–251
IQ   *see* Intelligence quotient
Irritability, early infancy   4
Isle of Wight survey
    aggressive behaviour disturbances
        493

brain damage and IQ   201
    and psychiatric disorder   495
    depression, adolescence   419
depressive disorders   445
emotions at adolescence   413
and enuresis   591, 592
    and psychiatric disorder   594
hyperactivity   197
hyperkinetic syndrome   530
hysteria   438
obsessional disorders   442
parent–adolescent relationships   415
physical handicaps and absenteeism
        782
psychiatric disorders, adolescence,
        pattern and changes   417–418
    and broken homes, and family
        adversity   59, 117, 200
    epidemiology   116
    prevalence   417
puberty   409
reading difficulties   564
    and physical handicap   14
reading retardation   568
school failure   494
school refusal   460
social class and psychiatric
        disorder   498

Junior Eysenck Personality Inventory
        321
Juvenile Courts   874
    see also Children and Young Persons
        Act 1969

Ketamine hydrochloride, in EEG
        study   335
Klinefelter's syndrome   821
    association with epilepsy   166
    EEG changes   167
    homosexual behaviour   165
    psychiatric disorder   167–168
    stature   166

Labelling
    of delinquents   860–861
    in psychiatry   376–378
Language
    assessment   701
    in diagnostic appraisal   296

Language (*contd*)
  comprehension, in speech
    assessment 702
  delay, secondary problems 707–708
    see also Speech delay
  development, in autism 727–729,
    730–732
    bilingualism 695
    and deaf parents 694
    normal 689–695
      environmental influences 693–
      695
  developmental disorders 699,704
    treatment at day-hospital 891
  difficulties, Illinois Test of
    Psycholinguistic Abilities 321
  handicap in mental retardation 835
  'inner', and speech assessment 702
  production and speech delay 704–
    705
Lead
  levels, relation to psychiatric
    disorder 196–197
  poisoning, EEG findings 345, 346
    in mental retardation 817, 840
Learning
  ability, and degree of extraversion
    228
  difficulties, and brain injury 201–
    202
  disabilities in hyperkinetic syndrome
    527–528
  in drug-taking 631–632
  positive avoidance 562
  to read 557–560
Learning theories 219–238
  and abnormal behaviour 227–230
  and behaviour therapy in school
    refusal 466–470
    characteristics of approach 224–
    226
  cognitive 225–226
  conditioning 224–225
  experimental psychology and child
    development 223–224
  models of man and behaviour 220–
    223
  and personality differences 230–
    235
    see also Personality differences
  psychology and child psychology
    219–220
  social 226–227

stimulus-response 225
traditional 223
Left-eyedness in reading 558
Left-handedness, and reading 558
Legal provisions of Children and
  Young Persons Act 1969 872–
  877
Leiter International Performance Scale
  in speech delay 706
Leucoencephalopathies in mental
  retardation 814
Librium *see* Chlordiazepoxide
Lincoln–Oseretsky test in hyperkinetic
  children 534
Lithium carbonate
  in affective psychosis 916
  in hyperkinetic syndrome 542
  in manic-depressive illness 752
LSD *see* Lysergic acid diethylamide
Lysergic acid diethylamide
  misuse 666
    causing persistent psychoses
    754–755
    general factors 634
    physical signs 649–650
    prevalence 629

Magnesium pemoline
  effects 908
  in hyperkinetic syndrome 541
Mandrax *see* Methaqualone
Manic-depressive psychosis 721
  in adolescence 420, 751
Marijuana
  misuse 660, 661
    prevalence 629
    psychotic reactions 755
  review 633–634
  progression to opiates 633
Marital
  background in nondelinquent
    conduct disorders 491–492
  discord, and aggressive
    behaviour 499–500
    effect on separation 55
    and mental disorder 90, 91
    prolonged, effect on child 61
    relation to antisocial behaviour
    59–62
    relation to delinquency 59–62
    and school refusal 457
    unhappy unbroken homes 60

Marital (*contd*)
  relationships, effect on child 395
    eliciting at interview 288–289
Mass media, and aggressive behaviour
    501–503
Matching Familiar Figures Test 313
Maternal
  anxiety in school refusal 471, 477
  factors, in enuresis 595
    in obesity 774–775
  see also Mother–child relationships
Maternalism 790–791
Maturational delay in tics and
    Tourette's syndrome 680–681
Maturity, intelligence and personality
    factors 408–409
  sex differences 407–408
Measles, and EEG pattern 336
Mechanistic/organismic behaviour
    theories 221–223
Melleril *see* Thioridazine
Memory, diagnostic testing 317
Menarche, consequences and
    psychological implications
    409–410
Mental disorder, parental, effect on
    children 89–91, 465, 471
Mental retardation
  and attitude to play 294
  and autism 725
  classification 811–814
  clinical examination 814–817
  clinical needs 808–811
  community services 843–844
  degree of handicap 812
  and Down's syndrome 841
  early development 815–816
  EEG findings 350
  epilepsy 817
  family history 374
  and intellectual retardation 833,
    834, 835
  IQ 830–831
  language comprehension 703
  language production 704
  medical aspects 807–828
  and metabolic disorders 813, 841
  mild, and prevention of psychiatric
    disorders 836–837
    treatment 837–838
  and mortality 374
  neonatal examination 816
  obstetric history 815

pain, congenital insensitivity 824
pica 840
prevalence 807
psychiatric aspects 829–855
psychiatric disorders, behaviour
    modification programmes
    844–847
  mechanism involved in the
    association 832–835
  prevention 836–837
  rate 830–832
  treatment, behaviour modification
    techniques 844–847
  drugs 847–848
    side effects 848
psychiatrist's role 829
severe, prevention of psychiatric
    disorders 841–848
  treatment 842–843
social factors 833–834
special investigations 822–823
and speech delay 695
statistical changes 807–808
stereotypes 840
time of recognition 816–817
treatment, behavioural approaches
    941
tuberous sclerosis 818–823
Merrill–Palmer Scale in speech
    delay 706
Metabolic disorders
  and mental retardation 813, 841
  relation to psychiatric disorder
    196–197
Methadone
  in heroin addiction 655
  misuse 660, 669
  withdrawal treatment 653–654
Methaqualone, misuse 666
Methohexitone, in EEG study 335
3 Methoxy 4 hydroxyphenyl ethyl
    glycol, in affective psychoses
    752
Methylphenidate
  effects 904, 906, 907, 908, 910
  in hyperkinetic syndrome 537,
    538–542, 543
  in mental retardation disturbances
    848
Mirror movements in diagnostic
    appraisal 296
Models, psychological 220–223
  mechanistic 221

Models (*contd*)
  organismic 221–223
Mongolism *see* Down's syndrome
Monoamine
  metabolism in hyperkinetic
    syndrome 532–533
  oxidase inhibitors in depressive
    disorders 449
Mood changes 444
Moral development 93–99
Morphine, withdrawal treatment
  653–654
Mortality and mental retardation 374
Mosaicism, definition 163
Moslem families 218
Mother–child relationships
  in faecal soiling 620–621
  effect on later behaviour 402
Mother–child units in hospital 888–
  889
  see also headings under Family;
    Maternal; Parent–child
    relationship
Mothers, working, effect on children
  64, 65
Motor coordination
  diagnostic testing 317
  and stimulant drugs 905
Movement, sudden, infant's reaction
  48
  see also Repetitive movements
Moving home, causing stress 57
Mowrer apparatus 601
Muscle tension, early infancy 4
Mutism, elective
  language comprehension 703
  language production 704
  in speech delay 700–701

Names, peculiar, and psychiatric
  disorder 10
Neale Analysis of Reading Ability
  323, 563
Neonatal period, Piaget's
  theories 241, 243–246
  see also Drug addiction, neonatal
Neuroepileptic child, prevalence of
  psychiatric disorder 186
Neurological
  disorders and disintegrative
    psychosis 719
  associated with psychoses 753

examination in brain injury 204–
  207
findings in hyperkinetic children
  531
screening, in psychiatric diagnostic
  appraisal 295
Neurophysiological studies in
  hyperkinetic children 531–532
Neuropsychological tests in diagnostic
  appraisal 296
Nightmares 48
Nipple withdrawal, effects in early
  infancy 4
Nitrazepam, in mental retardation
  disturbances 848
Noise, sudden, infant's reaction 48
Nondelinquent disturbances of
  conduct *see* Conduct
    disorders, nondelinquent
Nortryptyline in enuresis 599
Nursery schools, provision 399–400

Obesity, psychological factors 774–
  775
Objects, permanence, Piaget's
  theory 239–254
  interpretations 244–245
  see also Piaget's theories
Obsessional disorders 441–444
  incidence 442
  outcome 443–444
  psychological mechanisms 443
  treatment 443–444
Obsessional thoughts, in depression
  442, 444
Obsessions *see* Obsessional disorders
Obsessive–compulsive behaviour
  441–444
  at adolescence 418
  diagnosis from schizophrenia 442
Obstetric complications *see* Perinatal;
  Pregnancy
Oedipus complex 75–76
  adolescence 76
One-parent families 62–64
  and behavioural disorders 395
  and delinquency 62–64
Operant approach 929–935
  extinction 931–932
  imitation 934
  in mental retardation disturbances
    844–847

Operant approach (*contd*)
  prompting and fading 933
  psychiatric social work 977
  reading difficulties
  reinforcement 930–931
    schedules 932
    token 934–935
  school refusal 468
  shaping 932–933
Opiate-type drugs, general factors
    635
  self-injection 635
  misuse, prevalence 629
Opioids
  misuse 661, 665, 666, 668
    mortality 652
    physical signs 649
  withdrawal treatment 653–654
Opium misuse culture-specific 630
Ordinal position, attainment and
    emotional disorder 87
Organic illnesses presenting with
    psychiatric features 345–347
Orphenadrine in tics and Tourette's
    syndrome 684
Overactivity in mental
    retardation 835
Overcrowding, immigrant
    families 127
Overprotection, parental 77–80
  comparison with control group
    78–79
  emotional disturbances 80
  father's role 79
  hostility towards child 80
  mother's own childhood 79
  need for dependency 80
  pregnancy problems 79

Pacification, reaction, early infancy 4
Pain, congenital insensitivity in mental
    retardation 824
Paraldehyde, in mental retardation
    disturbances 848
Paregoric in neonatal drug addiction
    treatment 657
Parent
  attitude, towards brain-damaged
    children 203–204
    to feminine boys 794–796, 798,
      800, 801

  to obsessional disorders 442, 443
  background and aggressive
    behaviour 491–492, 499
  behaviour influence of child
    11–13
    response to children's
      characteristics 12–14
  constraint 77–80
  criminality 31–32, 33–35, 87–88
    and delinquency 514–515
      adopted children 515
    and deaf children 14–15
  deviance 87–91
    criminality 87–88
    mental disorder 89–91
  dominance in aggressive
    behaviour 499
  intelligence and mental
    retardation 814
  interviewing *see* Interviewing
    parents
  involvement, in behaviour therapy
    505–506, 846, 937–938
    in hyperkinetic syndrome 544–
      545
    in psychotherapy 962
    see also Psychotherapy
  mental disorder 89–91
    and school refusal 465–471
    see also Parental psychiatric
      disorder
  overprotection 77–80
  and preschool children, adaptability
    387
  psychiatric disorder, and in children
    365, 394
    and day-hospital management of
      children 895–896, 888–889
  training in behaviour modification
    techniques 505–506, 846, 937–
      938
Parent–adolescent relationships 414–
    416
Parent–child relationships
  in autism 726–727
  and discipline 80–81
  interfering factors 392–394
  in schizophrenia 759–761
  in school refusal 465, 467, 470–
    472, 477–478
  in speech delay 705–706
  and temperamental differences 11–
    13

Parent–child treated equally in
    psychotherapy 962–963
Parenting, deficient 393
Peabody Picture Vocabulary Test
    317
    in speech delay 706
Perinatal
    complications in autism 734
    difficulties, relation to preschool
        disorders 391
        and behaviour differences 6
    morbidity, and brain injury 192–
        196
Perphenazine
    in emotional disturbance 910
    in mental retardation disturbances
        847, 848
Personality
    characteristics of delinquents 514,
        517–518
    defects in XYY syndrome 170
    development at adolescence 413–414
    differences, biological 231–235
        neonatal behaviour 232–234
        situational determination 231–
            232
        twin studies 234–235
        learning theory approach 233–
            235
    features in Turner's syndrome 172
    in drug-takers 632
    variation, twin studies 25–26
    see also Temperament
Peterson–Quay neuroticism scale, in
    hyperkinetic children 537
Phenobarbitone
    effect of barbiturates 913–914
    contraindicated in hyperkinetic
        syndrome 541
    in neonatal drug addiction
        treatment 657
Phenothiazines, in anxiety states 435
    in hyperkinetic syndrome 537
    in mental retardation disturbances
        847, 848
    in schizophrenia 762, 763
    side effects 912
Phenylketonuria 821
Phenytoin, effect on epileptic
    behaviour 914
Phobia(s), behaviour 927–929
    desensitisation 436–437, 928–929
    modelling 928, 929

school, behavioural technique 929
Phobic states
    desensitisation 436–437
    in emotional disorders 435–437
    management 436–437
Physical
    dependence, capacity of drugs,
        definition 647
Physical handicap
    effect on education 782
    special schooling 783–784
Piaget's theories
    approach 240
    causes and alternatives 239–254
    development 240–241
    developmental changes 241–253
        causal question 252–253
        concrete operations period 242
        conservation experiment 249–
            252
        transitive inferences 246–249
    formal operations period 242
    sensori-motor period 241, 243–
        246
    permanence of objects 243–246
        interpretations 244–245
    range 239–240
Pica and mental retardation 840
Pierre Robin syndrome 819
Pilot Intensive Counselling
    Organisation 867
Piperazine drugs in mental retardation
    disturbances 847
Placebo treatment, 906, 910, 912, 913,
    915
Play
    and clinical assessment 294–295
    facilities, preschool child 396
    fantasy, interpretation 295
Playgroups
    therapeutic NSPCC 399
    variation in provision 399
Poisoning
    lead, or carbon monoxide, and
        mental handicap 817, 840
    EEG findings 345, 346
Polygenic influences
    specific disorders 39–42
        dyslexia 39–40
        enuresis 40
        stuttering 41
    twin and adoption studies 22–38
Prediction of delinquency 862

Predisposition to psychiatric
    disorder   773–774
Pregnancy
  in adolescent and adoption   144–
    148
    complications   145–146
    and childhood experiences   92–93
    incidence   412
    termination   145, 146–147
      post-operative feelings   147–
      148
      psychosocial aspects   146
  complications, and brain injury
    191–192
Prenatal diagnosis, chromosome
    anomalies   179–180
Preschool children disorders   387–406
  behavioural   389–390
  cultural influences   397
  developmental factors   390–391
  environmental factors   396–397
  family factors   394–396
  identifying problems   387–388
  individual characteristics   391–394
  individual symptoms   388
  and parent–infant relationships
    392–394
  and parental psychiatric illness   394
  prevention   401–403
  prognosis   398
  screening   401
  services   398–400
  significant disorder   388–390
  social influences   397
  therapeutic measures   400–401
  treatment at day-hospital   891
Privacy, lack, and emotional disorder
    118
Probation treatment, delinquents   872
Promazine in mental retardation
    disturbances   847
Promethazine
  in mental retardation disturbances
    848
  in sleep disorder   916
Provo experiment   868
Psychiatric classification   *see*
    Classification
Psychiatric disorders
  in adopted children   150–158
  see also Adoption, psychiatric
    disorders
  area differences   115–117

  assessing, at parental interview   291
  brain injury   185–215
    see also Brain injury
  diagnostic appraisal   271–279
  diagnostic formulation   277–279
  epidemiology   274–277
  non-recognition   272
  sex prevalence   188
  situation specificity   276–277
  social status   116–117
  and transient isolated problems
    274–275
Psychiatric features in organic
    illnesses   345–347
Psychiatric social work   967–991
  different settings   980–981
  evaluation   981–986
    Cambridge–Somerville Youth
      Study   982
    mental health programmes in
      schools   982–983
    multiproblem families   983
    prisons   983–984
  marital and conjoint family
      therapy   985
    case-work   984–986
    therapist–client relationship   986
  family communication   980–981
  group counselling   981, 985
  intervention strategies   970–979
  justification and recognition   967–
    969
  principles   969–970
  provision of advice and material
    aid   971–973
  scientific basis   969
  use of interview interaction   973–978
    clarification   974
    confrontation   978
    environmental change   978–979
    graded change   977
    insight   975–976
    modelling   977
    modification of behaviour   976–
      978
    operant principles   977
    parents' reactions   974
    professional relationships   975
Psychiatric units   *see also* Inpatient
    psychiatric units
Psychoanalysis   951–952
  see also Psychotherapy   psycho-
    dynamic

Psychoanalytic approach to diagnosis
  in emotional disorders 429–
  430
Psychoanalytic theories 255–268
  attitudes towards 257–258
  contemporary thought 255–256
  of development 258–265
    Erikson's views 262–263
    Freud, Anna 259–260, 265
    Freud, Sigmund 255, 258–259,
      265
    Klein 261–262, 266
    Mahler 256, 263–264, 265
    Winnicott 264–265
  modifications 256
  origin 255
Psychoanalytic treatment of children
  953–959
  setting for psychotherapy 953–955
  establishing common language
    957–958
  establishment of therapeutic
    alliance 955–956
  interpretative work 956
  transference and reconstruction
    958–959
Psychogenesis, definition 771
Psychology, child, relation to 'adult'
  psychology 219–220
  experimental, and child
    development 223–224
Psychological factors
  in anorexia nervosa 776–777
  in failure to thrive 777
  in hospitalisation 779–784
  in obesity 774–775
Psychological mechanisms, obsessional
  disorders 443
Psychological tests and testing 306–
  333
  and assessment, distinction between
    306–308
  for children 316–317
  in clinical practice 323–328
    floor and ceiling effects 323–325
    interactions 324
    physical setting 324
    scoring 324
    special problems in children
      325–328
    test format 323
    variation 323–325
  diagnostic testing 317–320

expectancy tables 319–320
  of feminine boys 796
  length 323
  nature 308–310
  norm- and criterion-referenced tests
    310
  prescriptive teaching 320–321
  regression procedures 318–319
  reliability 313–314, 315
  scoring 308–310
  selection 311–316
    availability 312–313
    clarity 311–312
  single cases 328
  and speech delay 706–707
  standardised and non-standardised
    310–311
  suitability 313–316
  target assessment 321–322
  terminology 307
  the untestable child 327
  validity 314–316
Psychometry in brain injury 206–207
  in hyperkinetic syndrome 533–534
Psychopathy, adoption studies 35–36
Psychosexual behaviour, atypical,
    treatment 798–801
  see also Feminine boys; Sexual
    Identity
Psychosexual development 74–76
  at adolescence 411–412
  anal phase 75
  atypical 788–806
  castration anxiety 75–76
  Oedipus complex 75–76
  oral phase 74
  phallic stage 75
  see also Sexual development
Psychosis(es)
  in adolescence 748–770
    prevalence 748–749
  affective See Affective phychoses
  amphetamine 662
  associated with neurological disorder
    753–754
  child, classification 372, 717–739
    disintegrative 719–723
    EEG findings 344–345
    inpatient unit admission 883
  drug 754–755
  manic-depressive see Manic-
    depressive psychosis
  non-specific disorders 721–722

Psychosis(es) (*contd*)
and schizophrenia in adolescents
757–758
treatment at day-hospital 891
withdrawal, and barbiturate misuse
treatment 654
Psychosocial retardation
language comprehension 703
in speech delay 697–698
Psychosomatic disorders,
EEG findings 344
specificity of symptoms 773–774
Psychosomatic relationships 771–787
definition 771
effect of stress and change 772–
785
implications for clinical management
784–785
Psychotherapy
in adolescence 961–962
behavioural, in delinquency 866
borderline, and aggressive
behaviour 495–496
in emotional disturbance 910
individual, in delinquent treatment
863
in hyperkinetic syndrome 542
in inpatient units 886–887
in obsessional disorders 444
psychodynamic, aims 960–961
psychodynamic, with children
952–960
child with minimal family contact
961–962
common language 957–958
establishment of therapeutic
alliance 955–956
family setting 961–964
family therapy 963–964
interpretative work 956–957
parent–child treated equally
962–963
parent guidance approach 962
setting 953
transference and reconstruction
958–959
in schizophrenia 762
in tics and Tourette's syndrome 682
Psychotic states
aggressive behaviour 495–496
anorexia nervosa 776–777
Puberty
normal development 407–408

sex differences 407–408
sexuality 411–412
see also Maturity
Puerperal psychosis, and child care
and disorder 392–393
Punishment
of aggression 96–97
disciplinary 82
and faecal soiling 621, 622
first offence, severe, results 861
techniques in mental retardation
847
see also Discipline

Quadriplegia, spastic, recognition 816
Quantities, invariance, Piaget's
theories 249–252
interpretations 250–251

Rapid eye movement
in autism 735
in psychiatric disorders 352
Reactions
in early life 47–51
distress, following separation 51–
55
Reading
attainment, skills required 556–560
audiovisual integration 558
eye movements 558
and IQ 559, 564–565
learning 557–560
left-handedness and left-eyedness
558
sensory modality perceptions 558
and speech retardation 557
tests, Neale Analysis of Reading
Ability 323
Schonell Graded Word 323
and visual perception 557
Reading difficulties 556–580
avoidance of learning 562
classification 560–566
dyslexia 565–566
general reading backwardness
564–565
later educational failure 561–563
scholastic skill involved 563–564
cognitive correlates 367–368
EEG 559–560
general, or specific retardation
564–565

Reading (*contd*)
  and hyperkinetic syndrome 367–368
  and large families 570
  and left-handedness 558
  measurement of underachievement 566–568
  personality 570
  and psychiatric disorders 571–573
  and psychological functions 562–563
  and speech delay 707
  temperamental attributes 560
  treatment 573–575
    counselling 574
    individual 573–574
    operant approach 574–575
    psychotherapy 574
    remedial 573–574, 575
  see also Reading retardation, specific
Reading retardation, specific 564–565, 568–571
  and brain function 569
  and conduct disorders 125
  diagnosis 318–319
  individual test, case report 329
  and low verbal performance 568–569
  right and left confusion 569
  school factors 570–571
  and verbal coding and sequencing difficulties 569
Referral to clinic, reasons 271–273
  dynamics 272–273
  parental background 272
Reflection–impulsivity 313
Rehousing, causing stress 120
Rejection, and social appearance 10
Reliability
  of diagnostic interview 293
  of psychological tests 313–314, 315
    interrater 314
    retest 314, 315
    and test length 323
Repetitive movements
  in autism 730
  and mental retardation 840
Residential
  care, effect 393
  nursery, distress following admission 52–57
  see also Institutional-reared children

Retardation, psychosocial *see* Psychosocial retardation
Rewards and tokens *see* Operant approach
Reynell Developmental Language Scales 706
Rheumatic disease, relation to psychiatric disorder 194
Risk-taking in delinquency 519
Rituals
  mild 441
  obsessional 441–443
  see also Sameness
Rubella embryopathy and autism 838–839
Rubinstein–Taybi syndrome 819

Sameness, insistence, in autism 729–730
Schizoaffective psychosis 757
Schizophrenia
  adult, childhood precursors 718–719
  biological and psychological precursors 758–759
  classification 372
  diagnosis from obsessive–compulsive neurosis 442
  distinction from autism 720
  early onset 718
  'preschizophrenia' 719
Schizophrenia in adolescence 755–763
  aetiological factors 758–761
  'borderline state' 755–756
  course 761
  diagnosis 756–758
  family background 759–760
  hospitalisation 764–765
  management 763–765
  prevalence 420
  prognosis 761
  and psychotic states 757–758
  symptoms 756–757
  treatment 762–763
    drug 762–763
    psychotherapy 762
Schizophreniform states 757
Scholastic
  attainment, and classification 374–375
  skill involved in reading 563–564
  see also Education

Schonell Graded Word Reading
    Test 323
School
    and antisocial conduct 501
    and changes of attitudes 122
    competition 123–124
    and delinquency 520–521
        streaming 123, 521
    discipline 124
    influence on behaviour 122–123
    in inpatient units 887–888
    phobia 437
        see also School refusal
    relationships and diagnostic
        appraisal 296–297
    significance 461–462
    streaming 123, 521
    teacher–pupil turnover, high rates,
        effects 122–123, 125
    teaching styles 123–124
    variations, and delinquency 121–
        124
School refusal 455–486
    in adolescents 419–420
    aetiology 462–464
    and aggressive behaviour disorders
        493–494
    behaviour therapy 466–470
    clinical picture 458–460, 478–479
    concept 455–457
    definition 456
    and depression 464–466
    differential diagnosis 462
    family background 470–472, 477–
        478
    follow-up to adulthood 475–476
    incidence 460
    learning theory 466–470
    and leaving home 466–468
    operant approach 468
    parental involvement 465, 467,
        468, 470–472, 477–478
    and psychiatric disorder 475
    psychological mechanisms 462–464
    and reading difficulties 561–562
    reciprocal inhibition 468
    referral to psychiatric clinic 476–
        477
    separation anxiety 463–464
    somatic disguise 459
    treatment 472–476, 479–480
        assessment 476–479
        behaviour therapy 466–470

    at day-hospital 891
    early return 474, 479
    residential 473, 475, 479–480
    and truancy, distinction 456, 457–
        458
    types I and II 469–470
Scoring
    in diagnostic tests 318
    in psychological tests 308–310, 324
Screening for at risk children 401
Seizures, EEG findings 348
Sensory input, multiple or complex,
        and diagnostic appraisal 296
Separation
    acclimatisation 54–55
    distress reaction following 51–55
        clinging behaviour after reunion
            52, 54, 56
        detachment 52
    for hospital admission 52–57
        see also Hospital admission
    long-term disorders following 55–
        57
    from unhappy home 55, 56
Serotonin values in hyperkinetic
        children 532
Sex
    behavioural differences, early
        infancy 4–5
    and attitudes 790–791
    vulnerability 16
    development, and interest, at
        puberty 411–412
    distribution, aggressive behaviour
        497
    psychiatric disorders 368
Sexual identity
    cross-cultural aspects 791–792
    cross-gender behaviour 791
        female childhood 791–792
    determination 788–790
    rationale and background 792–793
Sikh families 128
Silver Lake experiment 868
Situation specificity, in psychiatric
        disorders 276–277
Situationism, and personality
        differences 231–232
Sleep
    depth, and enuresis 590
    disorders and enuresis 590
    disturbance in autism 735, 737
    problems, use of hypnotics 916–917

Sleep (*contd*)
  recordings, EEG 351
Slum areas, and delinquency 109,
    116, 118
Smiling, phases, infant 48
Smoking, in school and college
    students, general factors 635–
    636
Social class
  and adherence to treatment 902
  aggressive behaviour 497–499
  and autism 733
  and delinquency 510, 511, 519,
    521
  and enuresis 595
  and faecal soiling 619–620
  maternal attitudes 498
  and mental retardation 374
  and psychiatric disorders 116–117
  in schizophrenia 760
Social factors
  and brain injury 199–201
  in drug taking 630–631, 660–669
  in mental retardation 833
  in preschool disorders 397
  in speech delay 695
Social relationships
  in autism 726–727
  among children 500–501
Social-learning theory 226–227
  and delinquency 517
Socialisation and feminine boys 803
'Soft' signs 204–206
  in diagnostic appraisal 296
  and EEG findings, behaviour
    disorders 339
  in hyperkinetic children 531
Spasms, infantile, and autism
    839
Speech
  assessment 701
    in diagnostic appraisal 296
  in autism 728–729
Speech delay 688–716
  assessment 701–708
  babble 703
  causes 695–701
  cognition 705
  deafness 698
  elective mutism 700–701
  emotions 705
  intellectual retardation 696–
    697

language production 704–705
  normal variation 688–689
  parent–child interaction 705–706
  prognosis and outcome 709–710
  psychosocial retardation 697–698
  psychological testing 706–707
  socialisation 705
  secondary problems 707–708
  treatment 708–709
    at day-hospital 891
Speech development, and bilingualism
    695
  disorders 699
  normal 689–695
  and reading 557
Spelling difficulties, individual test,
    case report 329
Stature
  abnormal, and chromosome
    anomalies 166
  in Turner's syndrome 172
  in XYY syndrome 170
Status epilepticus, and barbiturate
    withdrawal 654
Step-parent–child relationship 63
Stereotaxic hypothalamotomy in
    hyperkinetic syndrome 544
Stereotypes
  and mental retardation 840
  use of tranquillisers 910
Stigma, social 201
Stimulant drugs 904–909
  behaviour changes 904–905
  choice 907–908
  cognitive and motor changes 906–
    907
  conditioning treatment 906
  dosage and side effects 908–909
  growth retardation 909
  in hyperkinetic syndrome 537–538,
    538–539
  misuse 629
  persistence and generalisation of
    effects 906
  predicting a favourable response
    907
  sedation or stimulation 907
  toxic overdose 908–909
Strange objects, infant reaction 47
Strangers, infant's reaction to 47
Streaming in schools and delinquency
    521
  effects 123

Streptococcal infection, and stress
 772–773
Stresses
 in childhood 57–58
 see also Bereavement; Separation;
  Broken homes; Marital discord
  and other specific headings
 and depression 57–58
 and family illness 772–773
 in infancy 4
 inner city life 118–121
 maternal, and behavioural
  differences 6
Sturge Weber syndrome 821
Stuttering
 polygenic influences 41
 in tics and Tourette's syndrome
  680
Suicide and adolescent psychosis 751
 and depression 445, 447, 448
 and drug addiction 662, 666
 and drug withdrawal treatment
  654
 rate, area differences 115–116
Sulthiame, effect on mentally
  disturbed children 914
Supervision order, Children and
  Young Persons Act 1969 874–
  877
 intermediate treatment 875–876
 custory and control 876
Sympathomimetic amines, toxic
  overdose 908
Symptom clusters, classification 362–
  364

Tantrums, school, use of target
  assessment 322
Target assessment 321–322
Teachers, effect on behaviour 123–
  124
Teaching methods and later
  educational failure 562–563
Teenagers see Adolescence
Television violence and aggressive
  behaviour 501–503
Temperament
 and brain injury 202–203
 and reading difficulties 560
 see also Personality
Temperament, individual differences,
  early infancy 3–4

competence 15–16
 association with disorder 7–10
 effective environment 14–15
 influence on development 11–13
 origins 5–6
 persistence 6–7
 range of experience 13–14
 temperamental adversity index 7–
  16
 vulnerability 16
Temperamental adversity index
 and disorders and circumstances
  7–11
 and development 11–16
Testing, psychological see
  Psychological tests and testing
Thioridazine
 in hyperkinetic syndrome 542
 in mental retardation disturbances
  847
 side effects 911, 912
Thoughts, obsessional, in depression
  442
Tics 674–687
 age of onset 676
 definition 674–675
 EEG findings 678
 emotional disturbance 679–681
 family history 679
 frequency 676
 intelligence 678
 maturational delay 680–681
 movements, nature 675
 neuropathological syndrome 678
 organic brain damage 677–678
 precipitating factors 677
 prognosis 681
 sex incidence 677
 tranquillisers, use of 910
 treatment 682–684
  drug 684
  psychotherapy 682
  symptomatic 683
Ticques see Tics
Tofranil see Imipramine
Toilet training
 and enuresis 588–589
 and faecal soiling 615–617, 618
 in mentally handicapped
  children 845
Tokens and rewards see Operant
  approach
Tomboyishness 4, 792, 793

Tourette's syndrome 674–687
  see also Tics
  EEG findings 678
  emotional disturbance 679–681
  family history 679
  frequency 676
  intelligence 678
  maturational delay 680–681
  neuropathological studies 678
  organic brain damage 677–678
  precipitating factors 677
  prognosis 681
  sex incidence 677
  treatment 682–684
    drug 684
    psychotherapy 682
    symptomatic 683
Toxicity of drugs 909
Tranquillisers
  in hyperkinetic syndrome 542
  major 909–912
    in cognition and motor function
      disorders 911
    in conduct disturbance disorders
      909–910
    dosage 912
    in emotional disturbances 910
    movement and habit disorders
      910–911
    unwanted effects 911–912
  minor 912–915
  misuse, physical signs 649
  in psychiatric disturbances of mental
    retardation 847
  withdrawal treatment 654
Transactional effects, brain injury
  203
Transformation, rotational, in
  reading 556
Transitive inferences, Piaget's
  theories 246–249
Translocation, definition 164
Transsexualism, 793, 792
  see also Feminine boys: Sexual identity
Treacher-Collins syndrome 819
Triclofos, in sleep disorder 916
Tricyclic antidepressants in enuresis
  599–600
  side effects 599
  see also specific names
Trifluoperazine
  in mental retardation disturbances
    847, 848

in schizophrenia 763
  side effects 911
Triplets, language development 694
Triple-X sex chromosome constitution
  brain changes 174
  epilepsy 174
  incidence 173–174
  mental disorder 173–175
Trisomy
  autosomal trisomy G, and
    mongolism 175–179
  definition 163
Truancy
  causes 457–458
  and delinquency 458
  and school refusal 456, 457, 458
Tuberous sclerosis
  investigations 819–821
  mental retardation 818–823
  unclassified encephalopathy 818–
    819
Turner's syndrome 821
  brain changes 173
  EEG changes 173
  psychological features 171–173
  and reading 557
  stature 166
Twins
  language development 694
  personality variation 25–26
  polygenic influences 22–46
    intelligence and 'heritability' 24–
      25
  sexual identity 789–790
  studies of abnormal behaviour 26–
    32
    in autism 734–735
    concordance for difficulties 31–
      32
    concordance expression 28–30
    diagnostic groups 29–32
    genetic factors 27–28
      influence of disorder 29–30
    reared apart 28
    in schizophrenia 757
Typology, diagnostic, in delinquency
  treatment 868–870

Unemployment in adolescents 410
Urinary
  infection, and enuresis 584–585
  tract obstruction, and enuresis 585

Urine
    circadian rhythms, and
        enuresis 587–588
    examination in suspected drug
        misuse 650

Validity
    of diagnostic interview 293–294
    of psychological tests 314–316
Valium *see* Diazepam
Vietnam veterans, survey of drug
    abuse 668
Vineland Social Maturity Scale in
    speech delay 706
Violence and television 501–503
Visual perception, and reading 557
Visuomotor disabilities in diagnostic
    appraisal 296
Vocalisations, use of tranquillisers
    910
Vomiting self-induced in mental
    retardation, management 844
Vulnerability, sex-related, and
    temperament 5

Wechsler Intelligence Scale for
    Children
    achievement of hyperkinetic
        children 527

in autism 315
    scoring 319
    and speech delay 706
West Indian
    children and adoption 137–138
        delinquency 126
        psychiatric disorders 125
    families 124–128
        discipline 128
        importance of play 128
        quality of relationships 128
        size 127
    see also Immigrant families
Withdrawal symptoms, and drug-
    taking 652–653
    see also specific disorders and
        drugs
Working mothers, effect on
    children 64, 65
Writing difficulties, individual test,
    case report 329

XYY syndrome
    aggression 170
    behavioural disorders 169–170
    psychiatric disorders 168–171
    stature 170